Managing Tourism Firms

Economics and Management of Tourism

Series Editors: Larry Dwyer
Qantas Professor of Travel and Tourism Economics
University of New South Wales, Australia
Peter Forsyth
Professor of Economics
Monash University, Australia

Wherever possible, the articles in these volumes have been reproduced as originally published using facsimile reproduction, inclusive of footnotes and pagination to facilitate ease of reference.

For a list of all Edward Elgar published titles visit our site on the World Wide Web at
www.e-elgar.com

Managing Tourism Firms

Edited by

Clive L. Morley

Professor of Quantitative Analysis
RMIT University, Australia

ECONOMICS AND MANAGEMENT OF TOURISM

An Elgar Reference Collection
Cheltenham, UK • Northampton, MA, USA

Published by
Edward Elgar Publishing Limited
Glensanda House
Montpellier Parade
Cheltenham
Glos GL50 1UA
UK

Edward Elgar Publishing, Inc.
William Pratt House
9 Dewey Court
Northampton
Massachusetts 01060
USA

A catalogue record for this book is available from the British Library.

ISBN: 978 1 84542 375 9

Printed and bound in Great Britain by MPG Books Ltd, Bodmin, Cornwall.

Contents

Acknowledgements

The editor and publishers wish to thank the authors and the following publishers who have kindly given permission for the use of copyright material.

Cognizant Communication Corporation for article: Andreas H. Zins (1999), 'Explaining and Predicting Willingness to Pay in Tourism: A Methodological Framework and Empirical Illustration', *Tourism Analysis*, **4**, 19–27.

James Cook University for article: Mike Peters and Klaus Weiermair (2000), 'Tourist Attractions and Attracted Tourists: How to Satisfy Today's "Fickle" Tourist Clientele?', *Journal of Tourism Studies*, **11** (1), May, 22–9.

Elsevier for articles: H. Anthea Rogers (1995), 'Pricing Practices in Tourist Attractions: An Investigation into How Pricing Decisions are Made in the UK', *Tourism Management*, **16** (3), 217–24; Jan G. Laarman and Hans M. Gregersen (1996), 'Pricing Policy in Nature-based Tourism', *Tourism Management*, **17** (4), 247–54; Steven Tufts and Simon Milne (1999), 'Museums: A Supply-Side Perspective', *Annals of Tourism Research*, **26** (3), 613–31; Brian Garrod and Alan Fyall (2000), 'Managing Heritage Tourism', *Annals of Tourism Research*, **27** (3), 682–708; Diego Medina-Muñoz and Juan Manuel García-Falcón (2000), 'Successful Relationships Between Hotels and Agencies', *Annals of Tourism Research*, **27** (3), 737–62; Terry Lam, Hanqin Zhang and Tom Baum (2001), 'An Investigation of Employees' Job Satisfaction: The Case of Hotels in Hong Kong', *Tourism Management*, **22**, 157–65; Soyoung Kim and Mary A. Littrell (2001), 'Souvenir Buying Intentions for Self versus Others', *Annals of Tourism Research*, **28** (3), 638–57; Soo Cheong Jang, Alastair M. Morrison and Joseph T. O'Leary (2002), 'Benefit Segmentation of Japanese Pleasure Travelers to the USA and Canada: Selecting Target Markets Based on the Profitability and Risk of Individual Market Segments', *Tourism Management*, **23**, 367–78; Suchada Chareanpunsirikul and Roy C. Wood (2002), 'Mintzberg, Managers and Methodology: Some Observations from a Study of Hotel General Managers', *Tourism Management*, **23**, 551–6; Karl W. Wöber (2003), 'Information Supply in Tourism Management by Marketing Decision Support Systems', *Tourism Management*, **24**, 241–55; James Wong and Rob Law (2003), 'Difference in Shopping Satisfaction Levels: A Study of Tourists in Hong Kong', *Tourism Management*, **24**, 401–10; Michael Riley and Edith Szivas (2003), 'Pay Determination: A Socioeconomic Framework', *Annals of Tourism Research*, **30** (2), 446–64; Christine A. Hope (2004), 'The Impact of National Culture on the Transfer of "Best Practice Operations Management" in Hotels in St. Lucia', *Tourism Management*, **25**, 45–59; Woo Gon Kim and Dong Jin Kim (2004), 'Factors Affecting Online Hotel Reservation Intention Between Online and Non-online Customers', *International Journal of Hospitality Management*, **23**, 381–95; Brent W. Ritchie (2004), 'Chaos, Crises and Disasters: A Strategic Approach to Crisis Management in the Tourism

Industry', *Tourism Management*, **25**, 669–83; Joanne Connell (2005), 'Managing Gardens for Visitors in Great Britain: A Story of Continuity and Change', *Tourism Management*, **26**, 185–201; Donald Getz and Tage Petersen (2005), 'Growth and Profit-oriented Entrepreneurship Among Family Business Owners in the Tourism and Hospitality Industry', *International Journal of Hospitality Management*, **24**, 219–42; Sunny Ham, Woo Gon Kim and Seungwhan Jeong (2005), 'Effect of Information Technology on Performance in Upscale Hotels', *International Journal of Hospitality Management*, **24**, 281–94; Chris Guilding, Jan Warnken, Allan Ardill and Liz Fredline (2005), 'An Agency Theory Perspective on the Owner/Manager Relationship in Tourism-based Condominiums', *Tourism Management*, **26**, 409–20; Carlos Pestana Barros (2005), 'Measuring Efficiency in the Hotel Sector', *Annals of Tourism Research*, **32** (2), 456–77; Tim Lockyer (2005), 'The Perceived Importance of Price as One Hotel Selection Dimension', *Tourism Management*, **26**, 529–37; Hong-bumm Kim and Woo Gon Kim (2005), 'The Relationship Between Brand Equity and Firms' Performance in Luxury Hotels and Chain Restaurants', *Tourism Management*, **26**, 549–60.

Emerald Group Publishing Ltd for article: Michael A. Callow and Dawn B. Lerman (2003), 'Consumer Evaluations of Price Discounts in Foreign Currencies', *Journal of Product and Brand Management*, **12** (5), 307–21.

Haworth Press, Inc. for article: Leif E. Hem, Nina M. Iversen and Herbjørn Nysveen (2002), 'Effects of Ad Photos Portraying Risky Vacation Situations on Intention to Visit a Tourist Destination: Moderating Effects of Age, Gender and Nationality', *Journal of Travel and Tourism Marketing*, **13** (4), 1–26.

IP Publishing Ltd for article: Zvi Schwartz (1997), 'The Economics of Tipping: Tips, Profits and the Market's Demand–Supply Equilibrium', *Tourism Economics*, **3** (3), 265–79.

Michael Lynn for his own article: (2001), 'Restaurant Tipping and Service Quality: A Tenuous Relationship', *Cornell Hotel and Restaurant Administration Quarterly*, **42** (1), 14–20.

Multilingual Matters Ltd for article: Peter M. Burns (1993), 'Sustaining Tourism Employment', *Journal of Sustainable Tourism*, **1** (2), 81–96.

Sage Publications, Inc. for articles: Zvi Schwartz and Stephen Hiemstra (1997), 'Improving the Accuracy of Hotel Reservations Forecasting: Curves Similarity Approach', *Journal of Travel Research*, **36** (1), Summer, 3–14; David Bowen (2002), 'Research Through Participant Observation in Tourism: A Creative Solution to the Measurement of Consumer Satisfaction/ Dissatisfaction (CS/D) among Tourists', *Journal of Travel Research*, **41**, August, 4–14; Arch G. Woodside and Chris Dubelaar (2002), 'A General Theory of Tourism Consumption Systems: A Conceptual Framework and an Empirical Exploration', *Journal of Travel Research*, **41**, November, 120–32; Seong-Seop Kim and John L. Crompton (2002), 'The Influence of Selected Behavioral and Economic Variables on Perceptions of Admission Price Levels', *Journal of Travel Research*, **41**, November, 144–52; Yvette Reisinger and Lindsay W. Turner (2002), 'Cultural Differences Between Asian Tourist Markets and Australian Hosts, Part 1', *Journal of Travel Research*, **40**, February, 295–315; Kenneth F. Hyde and Rob Lawson

(2003), 'The Nature of Independent Travel', *Journal of Travel Research*, **42**, August, 13–23; Sara Dolničar (2004), 'Beyond "Commonsense Segmentation": A Systematics of Segmentation Approaches in Tourism', *Journal of Travel Research*, **42**, February, 244–50.

John Wiley and Sons Ltd for articles: Sandra Watson and Martin McCracken (2002), 'No Attraction in Strategic Thinking: Perceptions on Current and Future Skills Needs for Visitor Attraction Managers', *International Journal of Tourism Research*, **4**, 367–78; Nigel Evans and Sarah Elphick (2005), 'Models of Crisis Management: An Evaluation of their Value for Strategic Planning in the International Travel Industry', *International Journal of Tourism Research*, **7**, 135–50; Nigel Hemmington, David Bowen, Evgenia Wickens and Alexandros Paraskevas (2005), 'Satisfying the Basics: Reflections from a Consumer Perspective of Attractions Management at the Millennium Dome, London', *International Journal of Tourism Research*, **7**, 1–10.

Every effort has been made to trace all the copyright holders but if any have been inadvertently overlooked the publishers will be pleased to make the necessary arrangement at the first opportunity.

In addition the publishers wish to thank the Marshall Library of Economics, University of Cambridge, UK and the Library at the University of Warwick, UK for their assistance in obtaining these articles.

Introduction

Clive L. Morley

The intent of this volume is to showcase leading published research into the problems and issues to do with managing tourism firms. Management is often defined as getting things done with and through other people (e.g. Chin, 2002). It has to do with setting and achieving goals through planning, organising, staffing, leading and controlling. A key aspect of a manager's job is decision-making. Management may be variously seen as an art, a science and/or a practice. In this book, the focus is on the practice of management as applied in the tourism industry, to which theory, arts and sciences can all make a contribution.

There are vital aspects that distinguish managing a company in the tourism business from managing companies in other industries (as shown below). This is primarily because the customers of tourism companies, namely the tourists, are different in key respects from other consumers. From this foundation it follows that the companies servicing them will need to respond and react to their customers in ways that recognise these differences, and to do this well they have to be different to other types of companies. Therefore, the management of tourism companies is different. There are also special aspects of the goals and motivations of tourism industry managers, and in the business environment of tourism, that differentiate, in some ways, what tourism company managers do from business managers more generally.

The quality and usefulness of the research presented in the papers here are evidence that the current state of knowledge contains contributions of interest and value as guides to effective action in managing tourism firms.

Tourists are Different

Tourists are, in general terms, people away from home in pursuit of pleasure from leisure (this is not a formal definition, but it captures the essence: for discussion of definitions of 'tourists' and the 'tourism industry' see Morley, 1990; Wilson, 1997, and the debates referenced therein). An important aspect is that tourists usually are spending money earned elsewhere. If they have travelled internationally, they are a form of export, but one where the consumer moves to the product or service rather than the much more usual other way around.

In many tourist destinations certain times of the year are more amenable to pleasure and leisure pursuits, for obvious reasons, so tourism flows are usually highly seasonable. This is reinforced by tourists' own holiday time-frames.

There are a number of ways that tourists differ from other consumers, which are directly and vitally important to the management of the firms whose services they use. These differences include:

- the services they utilise and pay for, such as a concern for a room and/or bed to sleep in;

- the leisure mind-set they bring to their consumption;
- the information needs and imbalances resulting from being away from home;
- the differences in their normal behaviour and thought patterns due to being away from home and work;
- the (perhaps subjective) loss of power or heightened uncertainty they feel in dealing in a strange culture;
- the desire for novelty and new experiences;
- the high place of leisure in any needs hierarchy.

Tourism Firms

The designation 'tourism firm' raises definitional issues. For the purposes of this collection, a tourism firm is considered to be a company or other commercial enterprise which derives a major part of its revenue directly from tourists. This is consistent with most definitions of 'tourism' and the 'tourism industry', which also use demand side based definitions, founded on tourists. Tourism firms thus include those hotels, shops and restaurants that cater to a large degree to tourists and serve large numbers of tourists, tourist attractions where an admission fee is charged, and travel agents. The key terms 'large degree', 'large numbers' and 'major part' are not defined quantitatively here, but can be taken to be such that the firm's managers identify tourists as an important market to them, with implications for the management of the firm.

Tourism firms have characteristics that tend to differentiate them from other firms, even service providers, more generally. Key amongst these characteristics are:

- a predominance, in some areas of the industry, of small and medium enterprises (SMEs) (Page, 2003, p. 264; Getz and Carlsen, 2005; Getz and Petersen, 2005, Chapter 3 in this volume);
- an emphasis on lifestyle and location motivations over profit and return for many owner-managers (Getz and Carlsen, 2005; Getz and Petersen, 2005; Chapter 3 in this volume);
- at the other end, some large, major international travel, accommodation and attractions companies (e.g. Accor, Sheraton and other hotel chains, Disney and Club Med);
- the importance, in some sectors, of invested capital indivisibility and fixed capacity (in the short term) leading to large fixed costs of operations (Sinclair and Stabler, 1997, pp. 87–8);
- strong seasonality of demand;
- an inability to inventory many services (due to the perishability of services such as a hotel stay, transport seat, attraction visit);
- the need to overcome distance, and sometimes language, barriers to information flows.

Tourism is a business with a great deal of customer involvement, concerned with some fundamental human concerns ranging from accommodation and food, through transport to pleasure. The structure of the tourism industry and markets are 'complex and may consist of different sub-sectors characterized by alternative competitive structures', ranging from the oligopolistic to strongly competitive (Sinclair and Stabler, 1997, p. 84), interacting and interrelated.

Tourism Management

Given the characteristics of tourists and tourism companies outlined above, whilst tourism management may have much in common with the management of business generally, it has some particular concerns and emphases.

Tourism marketing is shaped through tourism being in major respects a service rather than product, delivering intangible experiences to the customer, and which experiences are difficult to assess, measure, visualise and evaluate for quality. The services and experiences are diverse, transient and seasonal. The customer is initially in a different location to the service provider, so the marketing function of linking potential customers to the supplier is made problematic by distance, and by cultural and possibly language differences. For similar reasons, understanding the customers and market research are more difficult than usual. Pressing marketing issues for tourism firms are (Oh, Kim and Shin, 2004):

- understanding consumer behaviour, shifting preferences and needs, changes in demographic characteristics;
- customer satisfaction, the factors that affect it and customer loyalty management;
- the use of the Internet, for information provision, marketing and sales;
- customer safety and security issues, with disaster recovery and effects, driven by terrorism concerns (September 11, the Bali bombings, etc.);
- branding, its importance and how to build and sustain brands in tourism;
- the effects of ageing source populations.

Operations also have their particularities. The inability to inventory services and experiences (a hotel room or bus seat not used one day cannot be stored and sold the next day) has important implications for operations, as well as for pricing and marketing. Many tourism businesses are both labour intensive and highly seasonal in their need for staff, leading to reliance on seasonal and casual staff for vital customer contact roles. Important decisions often have to be made quickly and on the spot, requiring a high degree of delegation of responsibility to relatively low-level, front-line staff.

Problems in human resource management specific to tourism, arising from these and other characteristics of tourism, have been listed by Page (2003, p. 258) as:

- demographic issues related to the shrinking pool of potential employees and the resultant shortages;
- the tourism industry's image as an employer;
- cultural and traditional perceptions of the tourism industry;
- rewards and compensation for working in the sector;
- education and training;
- skill shortages at the senior and technical levels;
- linking human resource concerns with service and product quality;

- poor manpower planning;
- a remedial rather than proactive approach to human resource issues.

Information needs and the transmission of information are major issues in tourism. These are being drastically affected by the growth of Internet usage. As more companies and information suppliers and brokers provide greater information via the Internet, a virtuous circle of positive feedback is being built up: more potential customers using the Internet prompts more tourism firms to make more information and services available through the Internet, stimulating greater use by potential tourists, etc. The Internet has become a vital channel for tourism marketing, including greater pricing transparency and more detailed information (e.g. pictures of hotel rooms), services such as bookings and other interactions with customers.

Pricing has been an area of management particularly challenged by growth in the use of the Internet. Not only are there demands on the firm to continually update Internet information and the facilitation of price comparison shopping, but many firms (such as hotels) have experienced some loss of control over their own pricing due to the rise of middle-men services. These services utilise their own economies of scale and scope to become key determiners of the actual price, via a combination of the discounts they can force firms to allow them and their own added fee for service (O'Connor and Murphy, 2004, p. 474). Hotels can become dependent on these intermediaries, the effect of which is to drive down prices and hence profits (Carroll and Siguaw, 2003; Enz, 2003).

There are necessarily managerial implications for operators in these circumstances. Particular issues identified in the literature are:

1. *strategy*, as in all industries, special characteristics (internal and external) ensure strategising in tourism has its own peculiarities, including issues such as disaster recovery, that are important but can be neglected in day-to-day operations management;
2. *marketing*, the unique characteristics of the service and customers make segmentation and differentiation important, but needing to be on different bases to those used in other industries;
3. *information technology*, as a means to overcome information flow deficiencies and for marketing;
4. *pricing*, in the face of demand seasonality, the intangible nature of the supply and inability to inventory, the need to cover fixed costs, strong information asymmetries and sometimes volatile and even fickle demand; a subsidiary matter in pricing is the ability, in some aspects, for the consumer to partly determine the price actually paid, through the widespread use of tipping for service;
5. *managing staff*, due to tourism's high customer contact and content, seasonality and reliance on many casual staff, special motivations and service requirements.

Research Literature on Key Issues

Strategy

Research on strategy in tourism is, with a few exceptions, mainly that of descriptive case studies. There has not yet developed much in the way of a tourism-specific strategy literature.

Olsen (2004) reviews recent literature on strategic management in the hospitality sector of tourism. This paper has some conceptual flaws: for example, it deliberately, but wrongly, confounds the resource-based view of the firm with the implementation dimension of strategy, on the basis that implementation involves the allocation of resources (Olsen, 2004, p. 418). But the review does demonstrate that, in hospitality, strategic analysis is predominantly the use of concepts and knowledge from the strategic domain generally, with very few (if any) specifically hospitality strategic concepts or ideas and no contribution back from hospitality to strategy more generally, nor (until recently) much testing of strategic concepts empirically for their applicability. For example, to sustain competitive advantage, Dubé and Renaghan (1999) recommend knowing well your basis for competitive advantage, aligning internal processes to the strategy, focus, some innovation, financial strength and clear strategic positioning. Maister (2001) provides evidence that quality and customer service are the keys to improved financial performance. Such findings are in line with strategy textbook prescriptions and are unsurprising. Okumus (2002) makes some relevant and interesting points on these matters also.

The same points, by extension and observation, would be true of strategy in tourism more widely (Olsen, 2004, concurs), with the clear exception of the airline industry, wherein distinctive strategy contributions are apparent in topics such as global alliances (see e.g. Morley, 2003), strategic groups versus innovative strategy (e.g. Southwestern Airlines versus many established US carriers) and operational strategies and efficiencies (hub-and-spoke versus point-to-point networks).

It is therefore to be expected that the recommendations coming from the tourism and hospitality literatures on strategy differ little from the generic ideas in strategic management more widely. This may be indicative of the general power and applicability of established strategic concepts and techniques, but the lack of ideas from tourism influencing strategy more generally does suggest a possible gap, perhaps indicative of a lack of depth of strategic analysis and thinking in tourism. Some special aspects of the tourism business, such as the pronounced importance of seasonality and the leisure mind-set of consumers, appear to offer potential for valuable research into strategic management.

Marketing

A large proportion of academic articles on tourism marketing are segmentation studies (Oh, Kim and Shin, 2004, estimate over 20 per cent in a recent literature review). Many of these are to do with destination marketing, and are thus beyond the scope of this volume (see the companion volume by Papatheodorou, 2006). Most of the others are attraction or firm specific (or, as Oh et al., 2004, p. 433 put it, 'fragmentary and local'). They contribute little of general value. There are methodological concerns with many of the segmentation studies, to do with over-analysis of data (data mining, in the negative sense), the *post hoc* nature of segmentation devoid of theoretical foundations, and lack of out-of-sample testing or validation. A feature of much of the published literature in tourism segmentation is a surplus of studies demonstrating the application of analytic techniques in a particular case, but resulting in little general insight, relevance or theory development. The emphasis on techniques of data analysis, over theory and knowledge accumulation, is a serious weakness in the tourism marketing literature generally (see Oh *et al.*, 2004, pp. 440–41).

IT and the Internet

The Internet provides a new channel for reaching customers, and perhaps addressing some of the marketing problems tourism faces. Many tourism companies still have a way to go towards making best practice use of information technology and its opportunities, for example, in the use of email to respond to customers (Mattila and Mount, 2003; Murphy and Tan, 2003). There are (obviously enough) national, demographic and other cultural differences in the propensity to use and trust the Internet for gathering information, booking and paying by tourists (Money and Crotts, 2003; Gursoy and Umbreit, 2004). Unfortunately, as noted in discussing other areas of importance in managing tourism firms, much of the research into Internet issues is methodologically poor, for example, relying on unrepresentative samples, being merely descriptive, case specific and generally weak on theory (O'Connor and Murphy, 2004, p. 481).

Human Resource Management

For tourism firms, the management of employees is a very important matter, as the industry is highly people intensive in the supply of its services. Recent research in tourism human resource management (HRM) has focused on issues in employee resourcing (such as retention of staff, workforce flexibility and induction), employee relations (such as remuneration, including tipping, motivating staff, fostering a quality service ethos, empowerment and the role of unions) and employee development (such as learning, training and development of staff and career prospects) (Lucas and Deery, 2004). There are also more general HRM issues, such as culture, change and performance, which need to take into account the features of the tourism industry.

As with the tourism strategy literature, most of the tourism HRM literature is concerned with applying, or analysing the application of, more general HRM concepts and theories in the tourism arena (Lucas and Deery, 2004). There is very little specifically tourism HRM theory, with the partial exception of the tipping issue, despite the opportunities for tourism concerns to provide a lead on issues such as seasonal and casual staffing and the encouragement of quality service practices.

Scope and Selection Criteria

Tourism firms, for present purposes, exclude international, national, regional and local government and industry bodies (associations, marketing arms, etc.) as not deriving significant revenue directly from tourists. The scope does cover:

- *hospitality providers*: restaurants and hotels ranging from international chains to small bed and breakfast suppliers, hostels and cafés;
- *facilitators*: convention organisers, travel agencies and tour operators;

- *attractions*: casinos, natural, historical, cultural and recreational attractions, entertainment venues, festivals and events;
- *transport operators*: rail, bus and ferry, hire cars and cruise ships.

Airlines are a special case, as there is a very large, sophisticated specialist literature devoted to airline management (to be found in journals such as the *Journal of Air Transport Management*, *International Journal of Transport Management*, *Transport Reviews* and *Transportation Research*). This specialist literature often has little specifically to do with tourists, and has not been reviewed for this collection, to maintain the prime focus on tourism.

The five key management issues identified in the previous section have been used to structure the topics used to organise the papers in this book. An obvious alternative would be to structure along the lines of industry sectors or components (transport, accommodation, restaurants, attractions, etc.). The reasons for not using industry sectors to determine the structure are an attempt to see tourism as an industry, in alignment with the theme of this book series, and that many issues run across such sectors. It has not been possible to totally stick to this plan, as there are some good papers to be included which concentrate on the management of a certain sector (especially some part commonly neglected): these are included in the sixth part of this Introduction on sectoral studies.

The focus is on management issues and matters concerned specifically with tourism, covering general management issues only in so far as they have particular aspects in their application to tourism firms. Not covered herein are the many managerial matters that tourism firms have in common with firms across other industries. For example, the legal issues involved in structuring a firm, preparing a business plan and raising capital investment are important, but not special to tourism firms and not addressed in the papers in this collection. On the other hand, marketing does have many specifically tourism-related issues, due to the small size of many tourism firms, the fact that the marketing needs to target and reach people from, and often in, other regions, or even other countries, and information imbalances between the local operator and the tourist.

The selection has been made from articles published in academic journals, and excluding conference and working papers and book chapters. Journal papers have passed a first round of quality checking in the peer review process, thereby establishing a prima facie minimum level of quality. Tourism journals (including some in hospitality) were concentrated on as the sources of papers, as the collection aims to focus on the particular issues for tourism firm management. The main journals covered in the review and selection process were: *Annals of Tourism Research*, *Journal of Travel Research*, *Tourism Management*, *Tourism Economics*, *Tourism Analysis*, *International Journal of Tourism Research*, *Journal of Hospitality and Tourism Management*, *Journal of Travel and Tourism Marketing*, *Journal of Sustainable Tourism*, *Journal of Tourism Studies*, *Progress in Tourism and Hospitality Research*, *Tourism and Hospitality Research*, *Tourism Review International* (formerly *Pacific Tourism Review*), *Current Issues in Tourism* and *Tourism Culture and Communication*. Some articles from *Cornell Hotel and Restaurant Administration Quarterly* and *International Journal of Hospitality Management* were also reviewed.

The approach adopted has been to favour more recent articles over the less recent, so that a good up-to-date article may be preferred to an older classic article it references. This is particularly the case for heavily time-dependent issues such as the use of IT and the Internet, and staff recruitment. This approach is driven by the desire to maximize the usefulness of the collection to researchers and practitioners.

The relevant literature, and hence this collection, is weighted towards empirical and practice orientated papers. It can be observed that there is not as much emphasis on theory in tourism management as in other areas of tourism studies. Some good theory papers are included, where they were available; where they were not may indicate future research opportunities for theory development.

In reviewing the literature in order to select articles for this collection, numerous marketing segmentation studies, for various cases, were found. Many of these appeared to be grounded in the particular needs and circumstances of a case, or to do not much more than demonstrate the application of a known analysis technique in tourism. Unless they show a clear, wider application, or a very interesting methodology is developed, such studies are not included here, because of their limited use or interest. Similarly for studies of tourists' satisfaction, perceived value, etc. done for particular cases (destinations, resorts or attractions). In general, case studies were not favoured, unless they offered significantly more beyond the case application. Articles to do with management of tourist destinations or in developing countries have been left to the companion volumes in this series.

These selection criteria are quite similar to those of Papatheodorou (2006) in a companion volume, adopted for much the same reasons. The main difference has been to consider articles dating as recently as practicable, so as not to lose important and very recent contributions to some rapidly developing topics. In the end, a subjective, but hopefully informed, quality assessment has been necessary to reduce the list to a manageable size.

Overview of Papers in the Collection

Part I: Strategy

Watson and McCracken (2002; Chapter 8) find that tourism companies put emphasis on managers with the necessary skills to handle immediate, operational matters and people management abilities. Whilst the need for attractions to have adaptable, flexible, future-oriented managers is acknowledged, there is little evidence of strategic thinking actually being valued as a managerial competency.

In a fragmented industry like tourism, the total customer experience involves many companies servicing aspects of the whole (accommodation, travel, food, attractions, souvenirs, etc.). Strategically, relationships and alliances between tourism companies offering complementary services is an important concern for management. Medina-Muñoz and García-Falcón (2000; Chapter 5) aim to identify those factors that will ensure successful relationships between hotels and travel agencies.

Forecasting demand at the firm level has not received much attention. But Schwartz and Hiemstra (1997; Chapter 7) demonstrate how the shape of the booking curve gives information to improve forecasts (by analogy with airline reservations forecasting) and that a forecasting method based on choosing a most similar curve from past experience appears to perform better than time-series methods.

High-impact crises and disasters are a particular problem. Ritchie (2004; Chapter 6) advocates a strategic approach to crisis management in tourism. Tourism managers and researchers need to learn from other disciplines to improve the planning for and management of crisis situations, and build up the knowledge to guide management action which can limit the impacts of disasters. A start on this is made by Evans and Elphick (2005; Chapter 2), who also detail the case of a tour operator reacting to the '9/11' crisis.

Growth and return on investment are commonly the bottom-line strategic goals of business enterprises. But many tourism businesses are family owned and run, with lifestyle and autonomy motivations at the forefront, as Getz and Petersen (2005; Chapter 3) show. But they also find and profile a smaller group for whom the more usual business goals are paramount. Away from family owned and run businesses, the agency problem of aligning owners' and managers' interests is explored by Guilding, Warnken, Ardill and Fredline (2005; Chapter 4) in regard to condominiums located in major tourism regions.

Data Envelopment Analysis provides a valuable set of tools for assessing the relative efficiency of companies amongst a set of peers, in terms of multiple inputs and outputs. Barros (2005; Chapter 1) demonstrates the use of the technique in a hotel chain and the derivation of management implications.

Part II: Marketing

Understanding tourists – their attitudes and behaviours, decision drivers and spending patterns – is a vital issue for marketing tourism. Viewing tourist behaviour as a consumption system leads to greater understanding of the thoughts and actions of tourists, before, during and after travel, argue Woodside and Dubelaar (2002; Chapter 17). Their theory of tourist consumption systems shows the complexities that unfold during a tour and the multiple decisions and actions involved, with implications for marketing and market segmentation. The segmentation study of Japanese tourists to North America by Soo Cheong Jang, Morrison and O'Leary (2002; Chapter 16) illustrates the use of profitability and risk measures to choose target markets. Dolničar (2004; Chapter 10) provides an interesting critique of segmentation studies in tourism, with some useful points for practitioners. Also on tools for marketing analysis, Bowen (2002; Chapter 9) espouses the advantages of observation over the commonly used customer service questionnaires (the latter are superficial, inflexible and not effective in understanding processes, nor in considering changes).

Changes in tourists' behaviour and attitudes, driven by a growing desire for a 'dream holiday' escape from the ordinary, require changes in the design, operation and marketing of attractions, argue Peters and Weiermair (2000; Chapter 14). The many marketing implications of cultural differences between international tourists and their hosts and service providers are well brought out by Reisinger and Turner (2002; Chapter 15). Hyde and Lawson (2003; Chapter 12) investigate the nature of the growing independent travel sector of tourism, the extent of planning conducted by such tourists and the implications for management. How marketing can easily misfire is illustrated by Hem, Iversen and Nysveen (2002; Chapter 11), who show the need to carefully consider the use of photographs of visitors in dangerous settings, for getting attention in such ways can impact negatively on intentions to visit.

Brand equity can be a major asset for tourism companies. Kim and Kim (2005; Chapter 13) show that, for luxury hotels and chain restaurants, brand equity has a significant positive impact on sales revenue. Brand loyalty, awareness and perceived quality are important components of brand equity for hotel revenue, although only in the case of the latter two for restaurants.

Part III: The Internet and IT

The differences between Internet-using customers and those not using the Internet has been a concern of researchers, with potentially useful results for managers. In particular, the practice of making hotel bookings online is growing rapidly. Kim and Kim (2004; Chapter 19) analyse differences between hotel customers who booked via the Internet and those who did not. The factors that influence their propensity to book online vary with past online buying experience, and convenience, ease of information search, ease of the transaction and safety were as important as price in booking.

Efficient and effective information management is becoming increasingly important, driven by Internet technology and the information needs in dynamic markets. Wöber (2003; Chapter 20) assesses implementation experiences with an online marketing decision support system and the information needs of tourism management. The effect of IT use on the performance of hotels is a vital consideration, as examined by Ham, Kim and Jeong (2005; Chapter 18). Front-office applications and restaurant and banquet management systems positively impacted on performance, but guest-related interface applications did not.

Part IV: Pricing

The price of tourism services is a key factor in the relationship between the tourist consumer and the service provider. Approaching the matter from the consumer side, Kim and Crompton (2002; Chapter 22) show how perceptions of attraction prices are influenced by a number of economic variables, whilst Lockyer (2005; Chapter 24) looks at the importance of price perceptions in choosing accommodation, and argues that previous research and pricing methods neglect the complexity of the choice process and consumers' use of 'trigger points'. Methodologically, Zins (1999; Chapter 28) makes the case that conjoint analysis is better than willingness to pay questions and attitudinal surveys in explaining and predicting tourists' willingness to pay (a point supported by Wong and Lam, 2001).

The impact of an unfamiliar currency on purchasing is an issue for international tourism, investigated in regard to attitudes towards price reductions by Callow and Lerman (2003; Chapter 21). They find that price reduction strategies can be ineffective when customers are unfamiliar with the currency, especially if it is in very different sized units to the home currency.

From the managerial perspective, Laarman and Gregersen (1996; Chapter 23) review pricing by nature-based attractions and argue that it is a powerful, but under-utilised, tool for greater efficiency, fairness and environmentally sustainable management. Rogers (1995; Chapter 26) is also critical of the under-utilisation of pricing, in managing attractions, characterising pricing practice as 'overly cautious and conservative' (Rogers, 1995, p. 217) and recommending more active management and experimentation.

Schwartz (1997; Chapter 27) tackles the issue of tipping in an interesting theoretical consideration from an economics perspective, also drawing out the managerial implications.

Lynn (2001; Chapter 25) reviews published and unpublished studies on the relationship between service quality and restaurant tips, finding only a tenuous relationship, so that it is not good management practice to judge waiters' performance by the size of their tips.

Part V: Managing Staff

The question has been raised as to the applicability of typologies and other concepts from management generally to tourism management. Chareanpunsirikul and Wood (2002; Chapter 30) investigated what a group of hotel general managers actually do in their work in terms of Mintzberg's ten managerial roles. They found that the work did have much in common with the more general model, especially sharing the characteristics of being varied and fragmentary, with frequent interruptions.

The international scope of the industry means companies at times wish to import good ideas and practices from one country to another. Hope (2004; Chapter 31) looks at evidence from fieldwork that national culture can be a barrier to the introduction of managerial and operational approaches from another cultural context. That is, 'best practice' may not be the same everywhere, but depend on the context, especially in implementation. Methods can be imported, but to achieve success it is important that it is well managed, and to tailor training and communication to the employees' culture.

In an older, but still valuable, review of relevant issues arising from the special characteristics of employment in tourism, Burns (1993; Chapter 29) offers a critique of a general lack of concern amongst tourism employers with developing their employees, observing instead a tendency to de-skill them. Not surprisingly, then, high employee turnover is a major concern for many tourism company managers. Lam, Zhang and Baum (2001; Chapter 32) suggest that, at least in the context of Hong Kong hotels, training and development programmes and a total quality management approach may help improve employee job satisfaction, and hence reduce turnover.

Pay rates in tourism are relatively low, with narrow differentials. To understand how pay levels are determined in tourism, Riley and Szivas (2003; Chapter 33) develop a valuable and interesting theoretical framework. Features are the attractiveness of the industry to employees, an industry culture of low pay and the need for flexibility of labour supply. Basic managerial assumptions, maintained by industry norms, and strong downwards pressures on wages are key aspects of the framework.

Part VI: Sectoral Studies

Some of the less regarded aspects of tourism (outside of major tourism sectors like travel agents, hotels, transport and attractions in general) can be neglected, although these smaller sectors can be interesting and significant parts of the industry. A number of important and useful studies have concentrated on a particular sector or aspect of the tourism industry and the management issues peculiar to it.

Tufts and Milne (1999; Chapter 38) describe the means being adopted by museums in response to competitive pressures arising, in part, from their involvement in tourism, including changes in revenue sources, technologies used, labour practices and the use of networks. Garrod and Fyall (2000; Chapter 35) investigate the fundamental mission of built heritage management, factors affecting the charging for admission, the roles of self-funding and public agencies in conserving such attractions, and the roles of these issues in strategies for sustainability. Connell (2005; Chapter 34) looks at issues in managing gardens for visitors, including an historical perspective on these attractions.

Shopping is an important activity of many tourists. Kim and Littrell (2001; Chapter 37) examine influences on tourists buying souvenirs, especially the differences between buying for themselves as against buying gifts for friends. Wong and Law (2003; Chapter 39) analyse tourists' expectations and satisfaction with shopping in Hong Kong.

Reflection on failures can provide as valuable learning experiences as analysis of successes. Hemmington, Bowen, Wickens and Paraskevas (2005; Chapter 36) reflect on what can be learnt for attractions management from the case of the Millennium Dome in London.

References

Carroll, B. and Siguaw, J. (2003), 'The evolution of electronic distribution: effects on hotels and intermediaries', *Cornell Hotel and Restaurant Administration Quarterly*, **44**(4), 38–50.

Chin, T. (ed.) (2002), *1001 Management Terms Explained*. Kuala Lumpur: Malaysian Institute of Management.

Dubé, L. and Renaghan, L.M. (1999), 'Sustaining competitive advantage: lodging industry best practice', *Cornell Hotel and Restaurant Administration Quarterly*, **40**(6), 27–33.

Enz, C. (2003), 'Hotel pricing in a networked world', *Cornell Hotel and Restaurant Administration Quarterly*, **44**(1), 4–5.

Getz, D. and Carlsen, J. (2005), 'Family business in tourism: state of the art', *Annals of Tourism Research*, **32**(1), 237–58.

Gursoy, D. and Umbreit, W.T. (2004), 'Tourist information search behaviour: cross-cultural comparisons of European Union member states', *International Journal of Hospitality Management*, **23**(1), 55–70.

Lucas, R. and Deery, M. (2004), 'Significant developments and emerging issues in human resource management', *International Journal of Hospitality Management*, **23**, 459–72.

Maister, D.H. (2001), 'The path to performance: what managers must do to create a high achievement culture', *Cornell Hotel and Restaurant Administration Quarterly*, **42**(6), 90–96.

Mattila, A.S. and Mount, D.J. (2003), 'The role of call centres in mollifying disgruntled guests', *Cornell Hotel and Restaurant Administration Quarterly*, **43**(4), 75–80.

Money, R.B. and Crotts, J.C. (2003), 'The effect of uncertainty avoidance on information search, planning and purchases of international travel vacations', *Tourism Management*, **24**(2), 191–202.

Morley, C.L. (1990), 'What is tourism? Definitions, concepts and characteristics', *Journal of Tourism Studies*, **1**(1), 3–8.

Morley, C.L. (2003), 'Impacts of international airline alliances on tourism', *Tourism Economics*, **9**(1), 31–52.

Murphy, J. and Tan, I. (2003) 'Journey to nowhere? E-mail customer service by travel agents in Singapore', *Tourism Management*, **24**(5), 543–50.

O'Connor, P. and Murphy, J. (2004), 'Research on information technology in the hospitality industry', *International Journal of Hospitality Management*, **23**, 473–84.

Ohm H., Kim, B.-Y., and Shin, J.-H. (2004), 'Hospitality and tourism marketing: recent developments in research and future developments', *International Journal of Hospitality Management*, **23**, 425–47.

Okumus, F. (2002), 'Can hospitality researchers contribute to the strategic management literature?' *International Journal of Hospitality Management*, **21**, 105–10.

Olsen, M.D. (2004), 'Literature in strategic management in the hospitality industry', *International Journal of Hospitality Management*, **23**, 411–24.

Page, S.J. (2003), *Tourism Management: Managing for Change*. Oxford: Butterworth Heinemann.

Papatheodorou, A. (2006), *Managing Tourist Destinations*. Cheltenham: Edward Elgar.

Sinclair, M.T. and Stabler, M. (1997), *The Economics of Tourism.* London and New York: Routledge.

Wilson, K.G. (1997), 'Market/industry confusion in tourism economic analyses', *Annals of Tourism Research*, **25**(4), 803–17.

Wong, K.K.F. and Lam, C.-Y. (2001), 'Predicting hotel choice decisions and segmenting hotel consumers: a comparative assessment of a recent consumer based approach', *Journal of Travel and Tourism Marketing*, **11**(1), 17–33.

Part I
Strategy

[1]

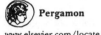

Pergamon

www.elsevier.com/locate/atoures

Annals of Tourism Research, Vol. 32, No. 2, pp. 456–477, 2005
© 2005 Elsevier Ltd. All rights reserved.
Printed in Great Britain
0160-7383/$30.00

doi:10.1016/j.annals.2004.07.011

MEASURING EFFICIENCY IN THE HOTEL SECTOR

Carlos Pestana Barros
Technical University of Lisbon, Portugal

Abstract: This study discusses, by means of data envelopment analysis, the efficiency of individual hotels belonging to the Portuguese state-owned chain, Pousadas de Portugal, which is managed by the enterprise, ENATUR. The use of this technique for the analysis of intrachain comparative hotel efficiency can be of value in examining the competitiveness of the chain as a whole. By identifying the efficient hotels in a sample, the slacks in inputs and outputs of the inefficient hotels and the peer group of efficient hotels, the data envelopment analysis stands out as one of the most promising techniques to aid the improvement of efficiency. Managerial implications arising from this study are also considered. **Keywords:** hotel efficiency, DEA, Portugal. © 2005 Elsevier Ltd. All rights reserved.

Résumé: Le mesurage du bon fonctionnement dans le secteur hôtelier. Cette étude discute, par moyen d'une analyse d'enveloppement de données, le bon fonctionnement de plusieurs hôtels individuels qui appartiennent à la même chaîne étatisée portugaise Pousadas de Portugal, qui est gérée par l'entreprise ENATUR. L'utilisation de cette technique pour l'analyse du rendement comparative des hôtels d'une même chaîne peut être utile pour l'évaluation de la compétitivité de la chaîne entière. En identifiant les hôtels efficaces dans un échantillon, les ralentissements dans les intrants et les rendements des hôtels inefficaces et les hôtels efficaces similaires, l'analyse d'enveloppement de données se distingue comme une des techniques les plus prometteuses pour promouvoir l'amélioration du fonctionnement. On examine aussi les implications pour la gestion qui proviennent de cette étude. **Mots-clés:** bon fonctionnement des hôtels, AED, Portugal. © 2005 Elsevier Ltd. All rights reserved.

INTRODUCTION

The competitiveness of a country derives from the performance of its enterprises. At the national level, it is reflected in the performance of the economy, while at the operational level, it is viewed in terms of the size of the market share secured by an enterprise (Begg 1999; Porter 1998, Krugman 1996). In both cases, the importance of performance is highlighted. Performance at company level, which is what motivates the present study, is measured either by productivity or efficiency. However, while identifying that efficiency is a key determinant of competitiveness, it should also be acknowledged that it is, by itself, an insufficient determinant. Competitiveness often has more to do with

C.P. Barros is Auxiliary Professor of Economics at Instituto Superior de Economia e Gestao, Technical University of Lisbon (Rua Miguel Lupi, 20.1249-078 Lisbon, Portugal. Email <www.cbarros@iseg.utl.pt>). One of his principal research interests is tourism, with a focus on the performance of the hotel sector and demand analysis. He has published articles in a number of leading academic journals.

"pursuing the correct strategy" (its effectiveness in terms of its contribution to the Government's stated goals). Operational efficiency is, on the other hand, a management objective, since it relates to earnings and profits and thus is a vital factor in competitive markets such as tourism.

Productivity is defined as the ratio of outputs over inputs, which renders it a different concept from efficiency, being measured and defined in different metrics. This ratio yields a relative measurement of performance that may be applied to any factor of production. The ratio can be calculated for a single input and output or by aggregating multiple inputs and outputs. It is, however, more usually applied to a single production factor, because of the aggregation problem posed when combining different factors. Since it is a relative measurement, there is the need to look to external benchmarks to interpret the productivity ratio. Moreover, there are many alternative productivity ratios, and choosing from among them is somewhat arbitrary. All of these measurement limitations are overcome by the efficiency concept.

Economic efficiency relates to the concept of the production possibility frontier (Anderson, Lewis and Parker 1999). A production function is widely used to define the relationship between inputs and outputs by depicting graphically the maximum output obtainable from the given inputs consumed. Thus, it reflects the current status of technology available to the industry. As the economic efficiency is a relative measurement with reference to the production function, a benchmark is included in its definition, meaning the production frontier. This being the case, an external benchmark is not required. The technical efficiency of a hotel is a comparative measure of how well it actually processes inputs to achieve its outputs, as compared to its maximum potential for doing so, as represented by its production possibility frontier. A hotel can be technically inefficient if it operates below the frontier.

The methodology applied in this article addresses the above issues in developing a framework for effective hotel evaluation and rationalization. The article utilizes DEA, or data envelopment analysis, which is a nonparametric, multifactor, productivity analysis tool, that considers multiple input and output measurements in evaluating relative efficiencies. DEA does not require *a priori* assignments of financial performance dimensions utilized in the evaluation process. It allows for the identification of appropriate benchmarks, and, above all, those hotels which are performing poorly.

The efficiency of each of the individual hotels is a key issue of ENATUR's competitiveness, since the global profitability of any enterprise depends on the profitability of its parts. For this reason, intrachain comparative efficiency is of paramount importance. In spite of this, there is a paucity of research into this aspect of hotel management. Recent exceptions are Morey and Dittman (1995) and Anderson, Fish, Xia and Michello (1999).

The motivation for this research stems from four critical issues associated with the management of hotels, in addition to the advantage of applying DEA analysis to intrachain comparative efficiency. First, evaluation techniques developed by ENATUR's Human Resources division for use by the individual hotel managers are presently based only on subjective evaluation. What is often difficult to clarify in an objective manner is the operational efficiency behind the subjective evaluation, since no view or analysis of the operational performance is included. This results from the conceptualization of the instrument to obtain the data, in addition to the fact that for the hotel managers, this report is merely one of many that they are obliged to compile. Furthermore, they are usually unable to observe behavior accurately, resulting either in subjective positive or negative discrimination, or central tendency problems, meaning all employees rated as average (Baker and Riley 1994).

The operational activities are considered by management theory to be a vital component of any strategy to achieve improvements. Thus, this neglect of operational activities is an obvious limitation of an evaluation technique in which the final ranking of hotels is heavily dependent on the assignment of the involuntary, biased, reported performance alone (Anderson, Fish, Xia and Michello 1999). Second, in order for hotels to improve their decisionmaking effectiveness in relation to their production activities by means of operational-process improvement, the effective deployment of scarce or costly resources for operational programs and restructuring of the operational base, there is a need for an objective and comprehensive method which can be consistently and universally applied to all hotels in the chain (Morey and Ditman 1995). Third, the adoption of a "best-practice" approach to hotels requires ongoing monitoring of hotel management procedures and their influence on hotel performance, because the inputs and outputs that contribute to inefficiency are identified by the DEA (Bessent, Bessent, Charnes, Cooper and Thorogood 1983). Fourth, the evaluation techniques used by the central body are usually based heavily on financial reports.

Seeking to overcome the above-mentioned limitation, this study contributes to the methodology used to assess the efficiency of a multi-unit state-owned hotel chain. This approach could, however, equally benefit private-sector hotel chains. In addition, the study highlights some of the challenges in attaining operating efficiency and professionalism in a public-sector operation that is overseen by a political entity. Finally, the study sheds some insight into the interesting approach taken by Portugal to promote its historical and cultural tourism assets.

POUSADAS DE PORTUGAL

According to WTO (1999), Portugal was ranked in 19th place as a destination in 1990 and in 24th place in 1998, accounting for 1.1% of total tourism in 1998 (Financial Times 2002). This value compares with a figure of 6.7% for its neighbor, Spain. At the international level it is in sharp contrast to the importance of the tourism industry at the national level (estimated to be 5% of GDP in 2000). To attempt to

CARLOS PESTANA BARROS   459

account for this increase in arrivals, the study chose to focus on the operational efficiency of one specific category of the Portuguese accommodation market, a nationwide hotel chain known as the Pousadas de Portugal.

The pousadas have various characteristics, which distinguish them from other chains, associations, or forms of accommodation available in the Portuguese market. The primary distinction is that the chain, indeed the particular category of hotel, was created by Portugal and remains a state-owned and run enterprise. It is centrally run by ENATUR, an autonomous company within the Ministry of the Economy. The ENATUR management is appointed from among those public-sector personnel specialized in tourism, on a political basis by the Secretary of State for Tourism, who is accountable to the Minister of the Economy.

The concept behind the pousadas, the first of which opened in 1942, was to provide comfortable, rustic, genuinely Portuguese lodging in locations of outstanding historic or scenic merit, while restoring and preserving country's cultural, historic, and architectural heritage. The cuisine at all of today's 45 pousadas highlights traditional dishes and wines of the regions where they are situated. The pousadas are found outside densely populated areas and are generally located away from Portugal's mass-tourism destinations. Each has its own unique characteristics, ranging from the sober to the luxurious, with a limited number of rooms (ranging from 9 to 41). ENATUR has developed two branches of the pousada chain: the historic and the regional. The former are situated in carefully restored monuments, mainly castles, monasteries, and convents, and adapted to the needs of the modern hotel industry. The latter are purpose-built, the architecture respectfully blending into the local environment, in locations of great natural beauty or historic interest.

To summarize the pousadas' distinction, they are not necessarily on a par with the best or the most comfortable hotels, or with those which offer a complete range of services. However, they possess their own identity, catering for discerning tourists seeking a memorable experience and atmosphere far removed from what is offered by the large international hotel chains (Santos 2004). According to the clientele breakdown for the year 1999, 49% of the guests were Portuguese and 51% no. Among the latter, the strongest representation (17.2%) was from Germany, followed by the United States (15.7%), and the United Kingdom (10.4%).

Committed to the restoration and conservation of the Portuguese heritage, as well as the promotion of tourism, the public enterprise ENATUR is confronted with conflicting objectives. The pousadas are small hotels, with small scale economies, a high level of indebtedness (given the high cost of restoring and modernizing buildings which are sometimes many hundreds of years old). Further, they are dispersed throughout the country (Figure 1), in some cases situated in areas in which there is no other tourism infrastructure. These are characteristics which must be taken into account when analyzing factors affecting the performance of the chain.

　　　　　　HOTEL EFFICIENCY

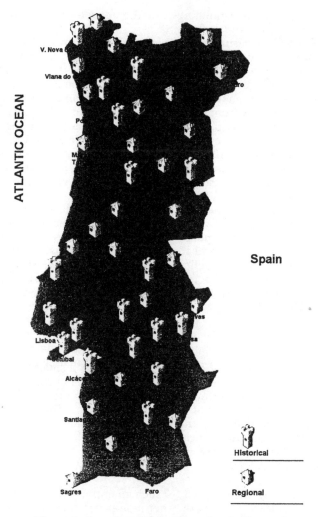

Figure 1. Locations of the Pousadas de Portugal

　　Related to the macroeconomic environment, the pousadas were the result of a government initiative for nonmass tourists in order to alleviate partially the austerity enforced by World War II (Portugal remained neutral). In the 40s, the nascent Portuguese tourism industry was naturally suspended until the war was over. Since the 60s, the industry was developed and expanded into a key sector of the economy, exploiting the wide range of possibilities that Portugal can offer to satisfy the demands and tastes of any type of tourist. Since 1942, ENATUR has contributed to the development of tourism by training managers who were later contracted by the private sector, by attracting tourism to remote regions, for the sake of regional development, and

CARLOS PESTANA BARROS   461

by preserving historical buildings, for the appreciation of Portugal's cultural heritage (Santos 2004).

The role of the government as a provider of tourism services restricts the expansion of the private sector. The planned privatization of ENA-TUR is a sound public policy, insofar as it maintains the historical and architectural heritage, while allowing the chain to be managed from a market-oriented, commercial perspective. This planned privatization reflects the drive away from nationalized industry on which the country embarked some years ago, and owes much to European integration. The latter is based on the European Union's Single Market Program, which was established in 1992 with the aim of facilitating the free movement of goods and services throughout the union. Hence the need to foster economic policies leading to greater internal monetary stability in each member-state and favoring increased growth and the expansion of a strong market block. The Single Market Program is a vital component of the plan of convergence of EU national economies in prices and costs and its emphasis is on competitiveness. The introduction of the euro has removed the possibility of national governments monetarizing their public deficits, while the Maastricht Treaty places restrictions on the deficits in financing public services, including state-owned hotels. These policies oblige EU-member governments to privatize industries.

Hotel Efficiency

The analysis of hotel efficiency is restricted to a small number of studies. Among the earliest, Baker and Riley (1994) propose the use of ratios to analyze the performance of the lodging industry. Wijeysinghe (1993) suggests the use of break-even analysis to discern the effectiveness of tourism management. Brotherton and Mooney (1992) and Donaghy, McMahon and McDowell (1995) apply yield management to analyze the efficiency of hotel management. Table 1 presents the studies on tourism frontier models, which are more in line with the present study.

Eleven studies are clearly brief for such an important tourism issue in the market context, particularly when compared with other field research, such as banking (Berger and Humphrey 1997). Moreover, Anderson's (2003) is more a methodological exposition of the DEA than an applied study. The present work intends to enlarge the economics of tourism in this specific respect and to call the attention of other researchers to this neglected area. It departs from the previous studies in that it uses intrachain cross-section data of ENATUR's hotels.

Theoretical Framework

Following Farrell (1957), Charnes, Cooper and Rhodes (1978) first introduced the data envelopment analysis to describe what is a mathematical programming approach to the construction of production frontiers and the measurement of efficiency of developed frontiers.

462   HOTEL EFFICIENCY

Table 1. Literature Survey of Frontier Models on Tourism

Study	Method	Units	Inputs	Outputs	Prices
Morey and Dittman (1995)	DEA	54 hotels	(1) room division expenditure; (2) energy costs; (3) Salaries; (4) nonsalary expenditure for property; (5) salaries and related expenditure for advertising; (6) nonsalary expenses for advertising; (7) fixed marked expenditure for administrative work.	(1) total revenue; (2) level of service delivered; (3) market share; (4) rate of growth.	–
Bell and Morey (1995)	DEA	31 units of Corporate Travel Departments	(1) actual level of travel expenditure; (2) nominal level of other expenditure; (3) level of environment factors (ease of negotiating discounts, percentage of legs with commuters, flights required); (4) actual level of labor costs.	(1) level of service provided, qualified as excellent and average.	–
Johns, Howcroft, and Drake, L., (1997)	DEA	15 UK hotels over a 12-month period	(1) number of room nights available; (2) total labor hours; (3) total food and beverage costs; (4) total utilities cost.	(1) number of rooms nights sold; (2) total covers served; (3) total beverage revenue.	–
Anderson, Lewis and Parker (1999)	DEA and Stochastic Frontier	31 corporate travel departments	(1) total air expenses; (2) hotel expenses; (3) car expenses; (4) labor expenses; (5) hourly labor; (6) part-time labor; (7) fee expenses; (8) technology costs; (9) building and occupancy expenses.	(1) number of trips.	(1) price of labor, estimated by dividing the labor expenses by the number of trips; (2) price of travel, obtained dividing the travel expenses by the number of trips; (3) price of capital, obtained by dividing the capital expense by the number of trips.

CARLOS PESTANA BARROS   463

Table 1 (*continued*)

Study	Method	Units	Inputs	Outputs	Prices
Anderson, Fish, Xia and Michello (1999)	Stochastic Translog Production Frontier	48 hotels	(1) number of full-time equivalent employees; (2) number of rooms; (3) total gaming-related expenditure; (4) total food and beverage expenses; (5) other expenses.	(1) Total revenue	(1) price of labor proxied by the hotel revenue per full-time equivalent employee; (2) room price proxied by hotel revenue by the product of number of rooms times the occupancy rate and day per-year; (3) Price of gaming, food, beverage and other expenses proxied as the percentage of total revenue.
Anderson, Fok and Scott (2000)	DEA (Technical and Allocative)	48 hotels	(1) full-time equivalent employees; (2) the number of rooms; (3) total gaming-related expenses; (4) total food and leverage expenses; (5) other expenses.	(1) total revenue; (2) other revenue.	(1) wages proxied by the hotel revenue per full-time employee; (2) rooms price proxied by hotel revenue divided by the product of rooms times occupancy rate and day per-year).
Brown, J. R. and Ragsdale, C. T. (2002)	DEA-CCR model and cluster analysis	46 US hotels rated in consumer report	(1) median price; (2) problems (defined in a 4-point scale); (3) service; (4) upkeep; (5) hotels and (6) rooms.	(1) satisfaction value (defined on a 100-point scale); (2) value (defined in a 5-point scale).	–
Reynolds, D. (2003)	DEA CCR and BCC model	38 restaurants	(1) front-of-the-house hours worked per day during lunchtime; (2) front-of-the-hours worked during dinner per day; (3) average wages; Uncontrollable input (4) number of competitors within a two-mile radius; (5) seating capacity.	(1) sales; (2) customer satisfaction.	–

(*continued on next page*)

Table 1 (*continued*)

Study	Method	Units	Inputs	Outputs	Prices
Hwang and Chang (2003)	CCR DEA model; super efficiency model; Malmquist	45 Taiwan hotels	(1) number of full time employees; (2) number of guest rooms; (3) total area of meal department; (4) operating expenses.	(1) room revenue; (2) food and beverage revenue; (3) other revenue.	–
Barros (2004)	Cobb-Douglas Cost Frontier	43 Enatur hotels	(1) sales; (2) nights occupied; (3) a dummy (historical vs. regional).	operational cost	(1) price of labor; (2) price of capital; (3) price of food.
Chiang, Tsai and Wang (2004)	DEA-CCR and BCC model	25 Taipei hotels	(1) Rooms; (2) food; (3) beverages; (4) number of employees; (5) total cost.	(1) yielding index; (2) food; (3) beverage revenue; (4) miscellaneous revenue.	

The latter authors proposed a model (CCR, named after them) that had an input orientation and assumed constant returns-to-scale (CRS). Later studies have considered alternative sets of assumptions. Banker, Charnes and Cooper (1984) first introduced the assumption of variable returns-to-scale (VRS). This model is known in the literature as the BCC model (named after them).

There are five other basic DEA models, less common in the literature: the additive model (Charnes, Cooper, Gollany, Seiford and Stutz 1985), the multiplicative model (Charnes, Cooper, Seiford and Stutz 1982), the cone-ratio DEA model (Charnes, Cooper and Huang 1990), the assurance region DEA model (Thompson, Langemeier, Lee and Thrall 1990; Thompson, Singleton, Thrall and Smith 1986), and the super-efficiency model (Anderson and Peterson 1993). The cone-ratio and the assurance region models include *a priori* information (experts' opinion, opportunity costs, rate of transformation, or rate of substitution) to restrict the results to the single best-performing decisionmaking unit (assurance region DEA model), or linking it with multicriteria analysis (cone-ratio DEA model). Other developments of DEA include the disentangling of technical and allocative efficiency (Anderson, Fok and Scott 2000) and the Malmquist index (Malmquist 1953).

Since the model is well established and extensively applied, only a brief description of the model is outlined (details on model development can be found in Charnes, Cooper, Lewinard Seiford, 1995; Coelli 1996; Coelli, Prasada and Battese 1998; Cooper, Seiford and Tone 2000; Fare, Grosskopf and Lovel 1994; and Thanassoulis 2001). The two scientific methods used to analyze efficiency quantitatively, namely, the econometric frontier and DEA, have their advantages and drawbacks. Unlike the econometric stochastic frontier approach (Anderson et al. 1999), the DEA allows the use of multiple inputs and outputs (Bell and Morey 1995; Morey and Dittman 1995). Moreover, since it is estimated with a nonparametric methodology (DEA), there is no need to impose any functional form on the data, or to make distributional assumptions for the inefficiency term.

Both methods assume that the production function of the fully efficient decision unit is known. In practice, this is not the case and the efficient isoquant must be estimated from the sample data. In these conditions, the frontier is relative to the sample considered in the analysis.

DEA is applied to unit assessment of homogeneous units such as hotels. The unit of assessment is normally referred to as a decisionmaking unit (DMU). It converts inputs into outputs, and the identification of these in an assessment is as difficult as it is crucial. The literature review, the availability of data, and managers' subjective opinions all play a role. Thus, in this study, these three procedures are followed to select the inputs and outputs used.

In the programming method, DEA "floats" a piece-wise linear surface to rest on the top of the observation (Seiford and Thrall 1990). The facets of the hyperplane define the efficiency frontiers, and the degree of inefficiency is quantified and partitioned by a series of metrics that measure various distances from the hyperplane and its facets.

In order to solve the linear-programming problem, the user must specify three characteristics of the model: the input-output orientation system, the returns-to-scale, and the weights of the evaluation system. In relation to the first of these, the choice of input- or output-oriented DEA is based on the market conditions of the DMU. As a general rule of thumb, in competitive markets, the DMUs are output-oriented, since it is assumed that inputs are under the control of the decisionmaking unit, which aims to maximize its output, subject to market demand, outside the control of the DMU. With exogenous inputs, the production function is the natural choice (Khumbhakar 1987). In monopolist markets, the DMUs are input-oriented, because output is endogenous, while input is exogenous and the cost function is the natural choice. The input-orientation system searches for a linear combination of DMUs that maximizes the excess input usage of DMUi, subject to the inequality restraints presented below. With regard to the returns-to-scale, they may be either constant or variable. Both forms (CCR and BCC models) are calculated for comparative purposes. In relation to the weights possibly placed on inputs and outputs in the objective function, these are subject to the inequality constraints. Weights are endogenous defined by the algorithm in the CCR and BCC models used and measure the distance between the DMU and the frontier.

DEA optimizes each observation for the purpose of constructing the production frontier (Figure 2), which consists of a discrete curve formed exclusively by efficient DMUs, those that maximize outputs. The inefficient ones are below the frontier, since they do not maximize output.

A Pareto-efficient or DEA-efficient DMU is defined in cases in which the DMU uses $k \geqslant 1$ inputs to secure $m \geqslant 1$ outputs in either an output orientation or an input orientation.

The general-purpose DEA developed by Charnes, Cooper and Rhodes (1978) considers n DMUs $(j = 1, \ldots, n)$. using k inputs to

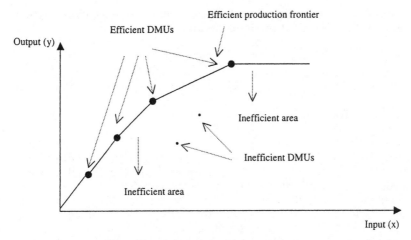

Figure 2. Efficient Production Function

secure m outputs. Let x_{ij}, y_{ij} denote the observed level of the kth input and mth output, respectively, at DMU j.

An efficiency score for the nth DMU can be obtained by maximizing the ratio of total weighted output over total weighted input for all units, subject to the constraint on all such ratios of the other DMUs in the sample being less than, or equal to, one. Mathematically, this can be written as:

$$\max_{u,v} \frac{u'y_i}{v'x_i}$$

$$\text{s.t.} \quad \frac{u'y_j}{v'xj} - 1 \leqslant 0 \tag{1}$$

$$u, v \geqslant 0$$

where u is a vector of output weights and v are the input weights. The system of equation 1 is a fractional programming model for computing technical efficiency and can be solved with nonlinear techniques. One problem with this ratio is that it has an infinite number of solutions. To simplify computation, a transformation of the fractional model allows the system of equation 1 to be formulated as a linear programming problem. The multiplier form of the linear is presented in equation 2:

$$\max_{u,v}(u'v_i)$$

$$\text{s.t.}$$

$$v'x_i = 1 \tag{2}$$

$$u\hat{y}_j - v'x_j \leqslant 0, \quad j = 1, 2, \ldots, N,$$

$$u, v \geqslant 0$$

Using duality, it is possible to derive an equivalent envelopment form which is the DEA CCR reference model.

$$\min_{\theta, \lambda} \theta_i$$

s.t.

$$-y_i + Y\lambda \geqslant 0 \qquad\qquad (3)$$

$$\theta x_i - X\lambda \geqslant 0$$

$$\lambda \geqslant 0$$

where θ is a scalar variable, measuring the level of efficiency and λ is a $N \times 1$ vector of constants. This envelopment form of the DEA model involves fewer constants and is thus the favored form in order to solve the model. The model works as follows. For a given set of feasible θ values, which are the efficient scores, the LHSs of the input- and output-related constraints specify a production point within the production possibility set. The model seeks a production possibility set point which offers at least the output levels of DMU j_0 while using as low a proportion of its input levels as possible. With the superscript * denoting optimal values, the j_0 DMU is DEA-efficient if, and only if, $\theta_0^* = 1$. If $\theta_0^* \leqslant 1$ the j_0 DMU is DEA—inefficient. θ_0^* is a measurement of the radial DEA efficiency of DMU j_0. Note that the linear programming problem must be solved N times, once for each DMU in the sample. A value of θ is then obtained for each DMU.

The model assesses efficiency in a production context. Its dual does this in a value context. By virtue of duality, the primal and dual models yield the same efficiency ratings in respect to DMU j_0. (Charnes, Cooper and Rhodes 1978).

Study Data and Results

To estimate the production frontier, the study uses cross-section data on 43 pousada hotels for the year 2001, which are listed in Table 3. The data was obtained from ENATUR's Financial Control Report and supplemented with additional data available from the company.

In order to choose the inputs of the DMUs, the distinction between controllable and uncontrollable factors must be taken into account. However, only the former were available for this study. The inputs are measured by 7 indicators. Labor is measured by the number of full-time equivalent employees and by the cost of labor. Capital is measured by the number of rooms, the surface area of the pousada in square meters, the book value of the premises, and the operational costs and the external costs. The study measures output by 3 indicators: sales, the number of guests and the aggregated number of nights spent.

The observations and the variables used ensure the DEA convention that the minimum number of DMUs is greater than three times the number of inputs plus output [$48 \geqslant 3(3 + 7)$] (Raab and Lichty 2002). Table 2 presents the characteristics of the variables and verifies

Table 2. Characteristics of the Inputs and Outputs for Year 2001

Variables	Units	Range	Mean	Square Deviation
Outputs				
Sales	Value in Euro	236.211–2.300.592	850.699	491.143
Number of guests	Number	2452–13359	6100	2476,37
Nights spent	Number	3615–18149	9013	3808
Inputs				
Full time workers	Number	11–52	26	9
Cost of labor	Value in Euro	122.200–696.087	342.146	135.476
Rooms	Number	9-51	24	10
Surface area of the hotel	Square meters	344–3904	1613	979
Book value of property	Value in Euro	23.868–7.768.983	1.954.570	2.113.910
Operational costs	Value in Euro	984–426.536	158.874	95.476
External costs	Value in Euro	54.144–387.913	152.303	85.857,85

that the mean hotel has 24 rooms and 26 employees, signifying that the pousadas are small hotels.

The DEA index can be calculated in several ways. An output-oriented, technically efficient DEA index is estimated in this study (Khumbhakar 1987). The output-oriented technical efficiency defines a production frontier and the measurement addresses the question: "By how much can output quantities be proportionally increased without changing the input quantities used?". The variable return-to-scale (VRS) hypothesis was chosen because scale size is controllable by the central management of ENATUR. The CRS scores measure pure technical efficiency only. However, for comparative purposes, This measurement index is also presented. The VRS index is composed of a nonadditive combination of pure technical and scales efficiencies. A ratio of the overall efficiency scores to pure technical efficiency scores provides a scale measurement. The reason for including this ratio to measure scale efficiencies stems from the fact that VRS is due to scale effects, while CRS is due to the absence of the latter. Therefore, a ratio between the two captures the scale effect, when this is present in the data. The relative efficiency of the pousadas is presented below in Table 3.

The rankings are ordered from the most efficient to the least efficient, according to the VRS hypothesis. It is verified that the DEA index is equal to 1 for the majority of the hotels when the overall level of efficiency is assumed (CRS scores), while a large number of pousadas, including all the CRS-efficient pousadas, are only efficient when VRS is assumed, signifying that the dominant source of inefficiency is due to scale economies. The average efficiency score under CRS is equal to 0.909. Including all sources of inefficiency, pousadas could operate, on average, at 90.9% of their current output level and maintain the input value. However, the efficiency score assuming VRS is equal to 0.945. Given the scale of operation, a majority of pousadas are efficient in managing their resources, the mean loss amounting to

CARLOS PESTANA BARROS   469

Table 3. DEA Technical Efficiency Scores for ENATUR Pousadas (2001)

Location	Designation	Technically efficient, Constant Return-to-Scale index (CCR Model)	Technically Efficient, Variable Return-to-Scale index (BCC model)	Technically Efficient Scale index
Évora	Pousada dos Loios	1.000	1.000	1.000
Guimarães	Pousada de Santa Marinha	1.000	1.000	1.000
Óbidos	Pousada do Castelo	1.000	1.000	1.000
Queluz	Pousada de Dona Maria I	1.000	1.000	1.000
Batalha	Pousada do Mestre A. Domingues	1.000	1.000	1.000
Bragança	Pousada de São Bartolomeu	1.000	1.000	1.000
Condeixa	Pousada de Santa Cristina	1.000	1.000	1.000
Gerês	Pousada de São Bento	1.000	1.000	1.000
Guimarães	Pousada de Nossa Senhora da Oliveira	1.000	1.000	1.000
Manteigas	Pousada de São Lourenço	1.000	1.000	1.000
Marvão	Pousadade Santa Maria	1.000	1.000	1.000
Miranda do Douro	Pousada de Santa Catarina	1.000	1.000	1.000
Monsanto	Pousada Monsanto	1.000	1.000	1.000
Murtosa	Pousada Ria	1.000	1.000	1.000
São Brás de Alportel	Pousada de São Brás	1.000	1.000	1.000
Sagres	Pousada do Infante	1.000	1.000	1.000
Santiago do Cacém	Pousada Quinta da Ortiga	1.000	1.000	1.000
Viana do Castelo	Pousada do Monte de Santa Luzia	1.000	1.000	1.000
Santiago do Cacém	Pousada de São Tiago	0.984	1.000	0.984
Póvoa das Quartas	Pousada de Santa Bárbara	0.956	1.000	0.956
Estremoz	Pousada de Santa Isabel	0.897	1.000	0.897
Marão	Pousada de São Gonçalo	0.864	0.997	0.867
Crato	Pousada Flor da Rosa	0.924	0.944	0.978
Caramulo	Pousada de São Jerónimo	0.726	0.990	0.733
Arraiolos	Pousada de Nossa Senhora da Assunção	0.969	0.984	0.985
Amares	Pousada de Santa Marta do Bouro	0.879	0.954	0.921
Palmela	Pousada de Palmela	0.799	0.951	0.840
Alijó	Pousada do Barão de Forrester	0.905	0.937	0.966
Sousel	Pousada de São Miguel	0.919	0.921	0.997
Torrão	Pousada do Vale do Gaio	0.830	0.912	0.910
Serpa	Pousada de São Gens	0.901	0.905	0.995
Alcácer do Sal	Pousada D. Afonso II	0.901	0.902	1.000
Vila Viçosa	Pousada D. João IV	0.824	0.856	0.963
Santa Clara a Velha	Pousada de Santa Clara	0.840	0.849	0.989
Setúbal	Pousada de São Filipe	0.802	0.845	0.948
Alvito	Pousada do Castelo do Alvito	0.835	0.840	0.994
Ourém	Pousada Conde de Ourém	0.827	0.839	0.986
Beja	Pousada de São Francisco	0.817	0.828	0.987
Vila Nova de Cerveira	Pousada D. Diniz	0.774	0.812	0.954
Castelo de Bode	Pousada de São Pedro	0.805	0.806	1.000
Valência do Minho	Pousada de São Teotónio	0.803	0.806	0.996
Elvas	Pousada de Santa Luzia	0.709	0.745	0.952
Almeida	Pousada da Senhora das Neves	0.592	0.599	0.987
Mean		0.909	0.945	0.972

$1 - 0.945 = 5.5\%$. A hotel is output-oriented Pareto-efficient if it is not possible to raise any of its output levels without lowering at least one of its other output levels and/or without increasing at least one of its input levels. The technical output efficiency of a hotel is the inverse of the maximum factor by which its output levels could be jointly expanded while its input levels do not rise.

Managerial Implications

A number of points emerge from the present study. First, the best-practice calculations indicate that many pousadas under the VRS hypothesis (51.1%) operated at a high level of pure technical efficiency in 2001. However, almost half of the pousadas were technically ineffi-cient, with different slacks in different inputs and outputs. Second, all technically efficient constant return-to-scale pousadas are also tech-nically efficient at variable return-to-scale, signifying the dominant source of efficiency is scale. Third, inefficiency is more prevalent among the historic pousadas (66%) than among the regional pousadas (46%). Fourth, the location appears to be an explanatory factor of effi-ciency, with pousadas in, or near, the cities more efficient than those in more remote locations. A rationale for this result is that demand plays a role in organizational efficiency, with the hotels near more populated zones attracting more clients. This higher demand enables greater effi-ciency. Hence, assuming that there are two hotels with the same man-agerial expertise, the one with more demand tends to be more efficient. Fifth, although DEA identifies the inefficient hotels in the sample, it does not reveal the cause of the inefficiency. DEA suggests the slacks for the inefficient hotels and gives to each a reference set (peer group) which allows for specific recommendations to improve efficiency. Adjustments for the inefficient hotels can be identified for outputs and inputs in order for them to join the efficient frontier.

Technical inefficiency is a consequence of one or more factors. One, factors of substructural rigidities associated with the pattern of owner-ship may induce the principal-agent relationship (Jensen and Meckling 1976). The difficulty of controlling those empowered as managers to act on behalf of the owner (the State) is a prevalent issue in public enterprises. The job tenure of the ENATUR managers may encourage the development of principal-agent problems, since the managers are always connected to (and often dependent on) influential friends in the governing political party. Two, structural rigidities associated with the labor market (Ingram and Baum 1997) give rise to the collective-action problem (Olson 1965) in which workers can free-ride on the management's own efforts to improve performance. This situation oc-curs when job tenure is not linked to performance, which is frequently the case in the public sector.

Three, organizational factors associated with X-inefficiency (Leiben-stein 1966) relate to the fact that the production function is not com-pletely specified or known, the contracts for labor are incomplete, and not all inputs are marketed on equal terms to all buyers. Inefficiencies associated with incomplete markets exist everywhere, but are particu-larly prevalent in the public domain. In this situation, the managers may be unable to adopt the correct strategy, since they do not know what it should be. Four, other factors outside the control of the man-agement are the contextual causes of technical inefficiency, such as scale and scope economies, economies of scale (Chung and Kalnins 2000), and location and agglomeration effects. All of these factors may play a role, as multiple causes active in the market interact to con-tribute to the level of technical inefficiency. With the politically-ap-pointed senior management liable to be replaced after every change of the elected government, there is scant tenure in their activity, and the stakeholders may exercise an inadequate control of the management procedures. Against such a background, incentives are absent for management to adopt a resource-based strategy. This dynamic gives rise to a depletion of variable critical resources, such as committed, high-quality managers.

Due to any, some, or all of these factors, ENATUR's pousadas may produce at a level below their potential, the maximum possible output, in the production environment specific to tourism. As an example of adjustment based on slacks, in Table 4 shows, the adjustments proposed for the Pousada do Castelo do Alvito, in central-southern Portugal. It is verified that there are slacks in the aggregated nights spent and this output should be increased for the projected value. In relation to inputs, there are slacks in the surface area, the book value of the property, and the number of employees, signifying that these inputs are used inefficiently by the pousada. There is a margin to decrease those inputs and to increase the outputs with slacks, for the unit to catch up with the frontier.

A peer group for the above-mentioned pousada consists of Sagres, Viana, Bragança, S. Tiago do Cacém, Miranda, and Évora. This peer group of efficient hotels is defined only for the Pousada do Alvito, because their data characteristics render them more similar to the inefficient Alvito. Thus, notably, not all the efficient pousadas are included in the peer group for the inefficient ones, only those defined by DEA as eligible for this purpose (other slacks for the other inefficient hotels are not shown, but are available on request from the author).

DEA does not identify the factors that cause inefficiency and only directs attention to the units where inefficiency exists. Nonetheless, this is valid information, since the inputs and outputs that contribute to this inefficiency are also identified (Bessent et al. 1983). However, concerns have been raised as to the robustness of DEA models on the grounds that since DEA only determines relative efficiency, it cannot identify all of the inefficient units, because all of the units in the sample may in fact be inefficient. Nevertheless, the exercise is still valid, because it ranks the units under analysis according to a benchmark. Even in a completely inefficient sample, some units will be more inefficient

Table 4. DEA Results for the Pousada do Castelo do Alvito

Outputs and Inputs	Original Value	Radial Movement	Slack	Projected Value
Number of guests	5143	977	0	6120
Nights spent	7277	1.383	0	8660
Sales	568.769	108.114	47.105	724.016
Rooms	20	0	0	20
Surface area	1.809	0	−524,97	1.284
Property	2.986.690	0	−1.997.438	989.251
Operational cost	108.376	0	0	108.376
Number of employees	23	0	−1.43	21.57
Cost of labor	270.491	0	0	270.491
External cost	117.967	0	0	117.967

than others and can profit from improving their operational activities. Despite the advantages of DEA, a further qualitative analysis on a case-by-case basis is usually necessary, to determine the true source of their inefficiencies and the appropriate corrective actions to be taken.

The DEA approach has several managerial advantages: the DEA score is a surrogate for the "overall competence and capability" of the pousadas, which cannot be easily and cost-efficiently discerned through the company's audited accounts. Using audits is an expensive, time-consuming means of gathering, analyzing and evaluating. The methodology proposed in this study overcomes some of these difficulties, allowing ENATUR to gather useful data cost-efficiently and swiftly. Further, since multiple dimensions are simultaneously considered in evaluating the overall operational competence of the pousada, it is more robust and comprehensive than any of the typical productivity ratios commonly used in financial analysis.

Another advantage of this approach is in identifying strategically important hotels. The performance-output-based evaluation methods are based on evaluating "point-in-time" data, in that the data are snapshots of the hotel's performance at a particular time. In evaluating hotels from a strategic perspective, it can be argued that evaluations based on inherent competence and capabilities are likely to be more comprehensive. That is, pousadas with high efficiency scores are likely to sustain a high level of capabilities and thus are better candidates for inclusion in an environment in which they are performing as best-practice role models in the organization.

Considering the results, several managerial implications can be proposed. First, the central management of ENATUR must upgrade its follow-up inspection procedure of pousadas' activities, in order to provide more explicitly binding incentives for increasing productive efficiency, while constructing the procedure so as to prevent manipulations by internal parties. Second, the central management must expand the scope of the data obtained in the follow-up inspection to include contextual factors beyond managerial control, since it is not clear if different pousadas have the same operating environment. Socioeconomic and environmental factors can be used as indicators of the quality of customer service provided by each pousada. Third, a benchmark analysis should be carried out, in order to enforce an efficient adjustment of the least-performing pousadas. Fourth, a better analysis of the efficiency of the pousadas for the future of ENATUR, in terms of market strategy, would be welcome. The implications of those locations and dimensions which attract more guests and earn financial profits for the historic pousadas are not matched by efficient procedures at the latter. Consequently, this branch of the pousadas presents a lower proportion of efficiency.

Fifth, the regional pousadas of smaller dimensions and in more remote areas of the country are disadvantaged in terms of their competitiveness. Sixth, better analyses are required to establish the precise significance to ENATUR of each involved element, whether they be suppliers, partners, guests, or employees. Too often, companies assume that as long as they meet their contractual obligations to each of these elements, then everything is fine. In other words, complacency easily sets in. Recalling that ENATUR is a state-owned creation, the world moves on with time and the organization needs to align its interests with those of the stakeholders. For example, it needs to communicate to the employees how and why they personally stand to benefit from the successful growth of the enterprise. Finally, the planned privatization in a competitive environment is felt to be a wise policy, since it is known that privatization coupled with competition tends to improve efficiency (Jones, Tandon and Vogelsang 1990).

Limitations and Extensions of this Study

With reference to the data set, the homogeneity of the pousadas used in the analysis is questionable, since it has compared pousadas with different dimensions, production characteristics, and locations. These may face different restrictions and thus might not be considered directly comparable. However, it can always be claimed that the units are not comparable and the traditional ratio analysis (Vogel 2001) equally could not be carried out. Yet the fact that the pousadas are under a common administration and seem to follow similar strategies gives sufficient justification for analyzing them as a unit.

Since this research is an exploratory study, the intent is not to obtain definitive results for the direct use of the central management. Rather, it calls the attention of ENATUR to the value of benchmarking its pousadas in order to measure their performance (serving as a management tool). Moreover, since the data set is short, the conclusions are limited. In order to generalize, a larger panel data set would be necessary. Reducing the number of observations in DEA variables increases the likelihood that a given observation will be judged relatively efficient (Banker 1993).

A variety of extensions to this study can be undertaken. One, in this analysis, the DEA model allowed for complete weight flexibility. In situations in which some of the measurements are likely to be more important than others, DEA allows for restricting factor weights through linear constraints. These linear constraints represent ranges for relative preferences among factors based on managerial input. Such analysis enables effective incorporation of managerial input into the DEA evaluations. Two, the input and output dimensions considered are context-specific. More comprehensive input and output measurements, (allowing for nondiscretionary factors such as environmental, socioeconomic, and quality inputs and outputs) need to be taken into consideration. The influence of discretionary variables being excluded from the analysis, amounts to an assumption that these factors are constant across the sample.

Three, allocative efficiency can be estimated, as well as the total-productivity Malmquist index, provided that there are more years of observation. Four, nonparametric or parametric free-disposal hull analysis can be used to assess the efficiency scores. However, previous research

474   HOTEL EFFICIENCY

has shown that the DEA scores are inferior in value to econometric scores, but the ranking is preserved (Bauer, Berger, Ferrier and Humphrey 1998). Finally, the hypothesis of the homogeneity of the pousadas under analysis is based on their nature, on the fact that they compete in the same market and that they all have the same stakeholders. However, nondiscretionary factors can render the pousadas nonhomogenous.

CONCLUSION

This article has proposed a simple framework for the evaluation of hotels and the rationalization of their operational activities in the tourism industry. The analysis is based on a DEA model that allows for the incorporation of multiple inputs and outputs in determining relative efficiencies. Benchmarks are provided for improving the operations of poorly-performing hotels. Several interesting and useful managerial insights and implications from the study are discussed. The general conclusion is that the majority of the ENATUR Pousadas de Portugal are efficient, although this leaves a proportion which are inefficient. For the inefficient pousadas, a peer group was identified among the efficient operators, in addition to the slacks that they should adjust in order to reach the efficient frontier. The findings suggest that scale economies and location are major issues in determining a unit's efficiency in Portugal or elsewhere.∎

REFERENCES

Anderson, P., and N. Peterson
    1993   A Procedure for Ranking Efficient Units in Data Envelopment Analysis. Management Science 39:1261–1264.
Anderson, R., M. Fish, Y. Xia, and E. Michello
    1999   Measuring Efficiency in the Hotel Industry: A Stochastic Frontier Approach. International Journal of Hospitality Management 18:45–57.
Anderson, R., D. Lewis, and M. Parker
    1999   Another Look at the Efficiency of Corporate Travel Management Departments. Journal of Travel Research 37:267–272.
Anderson, R., R. Fok, and J. Scott
    2000   Hotel Industry Efficiency: An Advanced Linear Programming Examination. American Business Review 18(1):40–48.
Baker, M., and M. Riley
    1994   New Perspectives on Productivity in Hotels: Some Advances and New Directions. International Journal of Hospitality Management 13:297–311.
Banker, R.
    1993   Maximum Likelihood, Consistency and Data Envelopment Analysis. Management Science 39:1265–1273.
Banker, R., A. Charnes, and W. Cooper
    1984   Some Models for Estimating Technical and Scale Inefficiencies in Data Envelopment Analysis. Management Science 30:1078–1092.
Barros, C.
    2004   A Stochastic Cost Frontier in the Portuguese Hotel Industry. Tourism Economics 10:177–192.

Bauer, P., A. Berger, G. Ferrier, and D. Humphrey
    1998   Consistency Conditions for Regulatory Analysis of Financial Institutions:
        A Comparison of Frontier Efficiency Methods. Journal of Economics and
        Business 50:85–114.
Begg, J.
    1999   Cities and Competitiveness. Urban Studies 36:795–807.
Bell, R., and R. Morey
    1995   Increasing the Efficiency of Corporate Travel Management through
        Macro Benchmarking. Journal of Travel Research 33(3):11–20.
Berger, A., and D. Humphrey
    1997   Efficiency of Financial Institutions: International Survey and Directions
        for Future Research. European Journal of Operational Research 98:175–212.
Bessent, A., E. Bessent, A. Charnes, W. Cooper, and N. Thorogood
    1983   Evaluation of Educational Program Proposals by means of DEA.
        Education and Administrative Quarterly 19(2):82–107.
Brotherton, B., and S. Mooney
    1992   Yield Management Progress and Prospects. International Journal of
        Hospitality Management 11:23–32.
Brown, J., and C. Ragsdale
    2002   The Competitive Market Efficiency of Hotel Brands: An Application of
        Data Envelopment Analysis. Journal of Hospitality and Tourism Research
        26:260–332.
Charnes, A., W. Cooper, A. Lewin, and L. Seiford
    1995   Data Envelopment Analysis: Theory, Methodology and Applications.
        Dordrecht: Kluwer Academic Publishers.
Charnes, A., W. Cooper, and W. Huang
    1990   Polyhedral Cone-Ratio DEA with an Illustrative Application to Large
        Commercial Banks. Journal of Econometrics 46:73–91.
Charnes, A., W. Cooper, B. Gollany, L. Seiford, and J. Stutz
    1985   Foundations of Data Envelopment Analysis for Pareto-koopmans Effi-
        cient Empirical Productions Functions. Journal of Econometrics 30(1/
        2):91–107.
Charnes, A., W. Cooper, L. Seiford, and J. Stutz
    1982   A Multiplicative Model of Efficiency Analysis. Socio-Economic Planning
        Sciences 16:223–224.
Charnes, A., W. Cooper, and E. Rhodes
    1978   Measuring the Efficiency of Decision-making Units. European Journal of
        Operations Research 2:429–444.
Chiang, W., H. Tsai, and L. Wang
    2004   A DEA Evaluation of Taipei Hotels. Annals of Tourism Research
        31:712–715.
Chung, W., and A. Kalnins
    2000   Agglomeration Effects and Performance: A Test of the Texas Lodging
        Industry. Strategic Management Journal 22:969–988.
Coelli, T.
    1996 A Guide to DEAP version 2.1: A Data Envelopment Analysis (Computer)
        Program. Working Study no 8/96, Centre for Efficiency and Productivity
        Analysis. University of New England. Armidale, Australia.
Coelli, T., R. Prasada, and G. Battese
    1998   An Introduction to Efficiency and Productivity Analysis. Dordrecht:
        Kluwer Academic Press.
Cooper, W., L. Seiford, and K. Tone
    2000   Data Envelopment Analysis. Boston: Kluwer.
Donaghy, K., U. McMahon, and D. McDowell
    1995   Yield Management: An Overview. International Journal of Hospitality
        Management 14:1339–1350.
Fare, R., S. Grosskopf, and C. Lovell
    1994   Production Frontiers. Cambridge University Press.
Farrell, M.
    1957   The Measurement of Productive Efficiency. Journal of the Royal
        Statistical Society, Series A 120(3):253–290.

Financial Times
    2002   Financial Times Survey on Portugal (October 21):1.
Hwang, S., and T. Chang
    2003   Using Data Envelopment Analysis to Measure Hotel Managerial Efficiency Change in Taiwan. Tourism Management 24:357–369.
Ingram, P., and J. Baum
    1997   Chain Affiliation and Failure of Manhattan Hotels, 1898–1980. Administration Science Quarterly 42:68–102.
Jensen, M., and W. Meckling
    1976   Theory of the Firm: Managerial Behaviour, Agency Costs and Capital Structure. Journal of Financial Economics 3:305–360.
Johns, N., B. Howcroft, and L. Drake
    1997   The Use of Data Envelopment Analysis to Monitor Hotel Productivity. Progress in Tourism and Hospitality Research 3:119–127.
Jones, L., P. Tandon, and I. Vogelsang
    1990   Selling Public Enterprises: A Cost-Benefit Methodology. Cambridge: MIT Press.
Khumbhakar, S.
    1987   Production Frontiers and Panel Data: An Application to US Class 1 Railroads. Journal of Business and Economics Statistics 5:249–255.
Krugman, P.
    1996   Making Sense of the Competitiveness Debate. Oxford Review of Economics and Policy 12:17–25.
Leibenstein, H.
    1966   Allocative Efficiency vs. "X-efficiency". American Economic Review 56:392–414.
Malmquist, S.
    1953   Index Numbers and Indifference Surfaces. Trabajos de Estadística 4:209–242.
Morey, R., and D. Dittman
    1995   Evaluating a Hotel GM's Performance: A Case Study in Benchmarking. Cornell Hotel Restaurant and Administration Quarterly 36(5):30–35.
Olson, M.
    1965   Logic of Collective Action. Cambridge: Harvard University Press.
Porter, M.
    1998   The Competitive Advantage of Nations. London: Macmillan.
Raab, R., and R. Lichty
    2002   Identifying Sub-areas that Comprise a Greater Metropolitain Area: The Criterion of County Relative Efficiency. Journal of Regional Science 42:579–594.
Reynolds, D.
    2003   Hospitality–Productivity Assessment using Data Envelopment Analysis. Cornell Hotel and Restaurant Administration Quarterly 44(2):130–137.
Santos, C.
    2004   Framing Portugal: Representational dynamics. Annals of Tourism Research 31:122–138.
Seiford, L., and R. Thrall
    1990   Recent Developments in DEA: The Mathematical Programming Approach to Frontier Analysis. Journal of Econometrics 46:7–38.
Thanassoulis, E.
    2001   Introduction to the Theory and Application of Data Envelopment Analysis: A Foundation Text with Integrated Software. Dordrecht: Kluwer Academic Publishers.
Thompson, R., L. Langemeier, C. Lee, and R. Thrall
    1990   The Role of Multiplier Bounds in Efficiency Analysis with Application to Kansas Farming. Journal of Econometrics 46:93–108.
Thompson, R., F. Singleton, R. Thrall, and B. Smith
    1986   Comparative Site Evaluation for Locating a High-Energy Physics Lab in Texas. Interfaces 16(6):35–49.

CARLOS PESTANA BARROS 477

Wijeysinghe, B.
1993 Breakeven Occupancy for Hotel Operation. Management Accounting 712:23–33.
Vogel, H.
2001 Travel Industry Economics: A Guide to Financial Analysis. London: Cambridge University Press.

Submitted 23 November 2003. Resubmitted 9 March 2004. Resubmitted 12 July 2004. Accepted 28 July 2004. Final version 13 October 2004. Refereed anonymously. **Coordinating Editor: Peter U.C. Dieke**

Available online at www.sciencedirect.com

SCIENCE DIRECT®

[2]

INTERNATIONAL JOURNAL OF TOURISM RESEARCH
Int. J. Tourism Res. 7, 135–150 (2005)
Published online in Wiley InterScience (www.interscience.wiley.com). DOI: 10.1002/jtr.527

Models of Crisis Management: an Evaluation of their Value for Strategic Planning in the International Travel Industry

Nigel Evans* and Sarah Elphick
Centre for Travel and Tourism, Newcastle Business School, Northumbria University, Newcastle upon Tyne NE1 8ST, UK

ABSTRACT

Tourism is particularly prone to external shocks, which by their nature are unpredictable and need to be addressed through effective crisis management processes. The paper reviews the literature relating to crisis management in tourism and identifies and briefly critiques several models that have been developed to help managers in their strategic planning for such contingencies. The terrorist attacks of '9/11' are used as an exemplar of the type of external shock that can lead to crisis if travel industry managers fail to take immediate and decisive action. This paper discusses the reactions of leading UK based tour operators to the terrorist attacks and a case study is presented to examine the reaction of a particular company to '9/11' and to review the 'turnaround' strategies used. The crisis management process model is compared and contrasted with the steps actually undertaken at the company. It is evident that there are wider lessons for the travel industry including the need to: integrate crisis management with strategic planning processes, prepare detailed contingency plans, define decisional roles and responsibilities, and to retain a degree of flexibility. Copyright © 2005 John Wiley & Sons, Ltd.

Received 20 January 2004; Revised 10 January 2005; Accepted 22 January 2005

Keywords: crisis management; terrorism; tour operators.

INTRODUCTION

Tourism and the vast travel industry that has grown up to facilitate it are particularly prone to external shocks beyond the control of its managers. Internal corporate shocks such as financial irregularities by contrast are also important to the industry. Arguably, however, these are not distinguishing characteristics of the industry, for as the events of Enron, Arthur Andersen, WorldCom and Parmalat have demonstrated they are prevalent in many industries where management have proved to be too ambitious, fraudulent or incompetent.

The travel industry, although not unique in its vulnerability, is nevertheless highly exposed to risks and prone to crises as the result of external events. Unlike internal events, which can be assessed and controlled by managers, external events are beyond their control and therefore inherently provide a greater degree of risk and uncertainty. Furthermore the inherent characteristics of this service based industry (such as the perishability of the product and the interdependence of elements of the product) make the risks potentially very difficult to manage, because supply often cannot quickly be matched to rapid declines in demand (Evans *et al.*, 2003).

External shocks, such as wars, hurricanes, terrorist attacks, pollution, adverse publicity

*Correspondence to: N. Evans, Centre for Travel and Tourism, Newcastle Business School, Northumbria University, Newcastle upon Tyne NE1 8ST, UK.
E-mail: nigel.evans@unn.ac.uk

and accidents, can have a dramatic and speedy effect upon levels of business in the travel industry. The external shocks can quickly develop into crises and indeed can be and should be viewed as a central concern of competent managers in the industry. Recent events such as the Bali bombing and '9/11' have clearly shown that terrorism in particular poses a major threat to the industry.

By their nature these events are unpredictable in relation to their geographical location, their timing and their scale and hence provide difficulties for industry managers in a number of ways. It is difficult to forecast such events in the first place and to foresee the full implications and the management steps that need to be taken can be complex at a strategic level but also in terms of effective implementation of management actions at an operational level. A brand, which, may have been assiduously developed over many years can be severely damaged or even destroyed by sudden events. For example, The Gulf War led to a severe downturn in travel and tourism in the early 1990s (which extended far beyond the Middle East location of the conflict), and the terrorist attacks in New York and Washington on 11 September 2001 had an immediate effect upon the industry.

Managers, although not being able to plan directly for such events (because they are by definition not capable of being foreseen), nevertheless need to be able to assess the risks that the business is prone to and to have robust and clearly articulated contingency plans in place so that they are able to react quickly and effectively. One approach is to spread the risks so that one upset does not destroy the business entirely. Thus a tour operator specialising in tours to only one country would be at risk if a war or environmental catastrophe were to occur there, but by operating to several countries the risks are spread and the overall risk is reduced. Such spreading of risks, however, is not always possible and may conflict with other commercial imperatives that require specialisation and focus.

In view of the central concern that crises in general, and terrorism in particular, should have for managers in the international travel industry the objectives of this paper are:

(1) to discuss the effects of terrorism on the international travel industry in general and UK tour operators after '9/11' in particular;
(2) to review the current literature relating to crisis management processes and to select a crisis management model to examine in greater detail;
(3) to apply the selected model to a UK based tour operator as an exemplar of how crises are managed;
(4) to derive lessons for the management of crises for the wider international travel industry.

TERRORISM AS A TOURISM CRISIS

This paper focuses on terrorism as a crisis situation for travel managers to deal with. The events of 11 September 2001 will be used as an exemplar of a terrorist attack and the effects of '9/11' on UK tour operators will be discussed.

Acts of terrorism, which have been defined as 'a systematic and persistent strategy practiced by a state or political group against another state or group through a campaign of acts of violence . . . to achieve political, social or religious ends' (Pizam and Smith, 2000) have had a major effect upon tourism destinations since before the end of the Cold War. The effects of terrorism are experienced throughout society and many industries are disrupted by such acts, but the effects upon the tourism sector are particularly profound. Indeed it would be difficult to argue with observers when they suggest that there is probably no industry in the world where a crisis (brought about by an act of terrorism) can have a greater effect than with tourism.

A number of authors, including Ryan (1993), Sonmez (1998), Sonmez *et al.* (1999), Pizam and Mansfeld (1996) and Pizam and Smith (2001), have researched the link between terrorism and tourism and conclude that targeting tourists clearly helps terrorists in achieving their objectives by disrupting the industry and assuring publicity (Sonmez *et al.*, 1999). Owing to the negative publicity by the media a tourist destination can experience a crisis whereby its reputation may be damaged and the operation of tourism-related businesses might experience a severe turndown. The effect of the dis-

                    Int. J. Tourism Res. **7**, 135–150 (2005)

ruption and violence on the industry is a crisis, which needs careful and decisive management (Somnez, 1998).

Tourist habits have been affected by recent events including the Gulf War in 1991 and the attacks in Luxor, Egypt in 1997. During the Gulf War in 1991 the countries in the Middle East and the eastern Mediterranean suffered a severe decline in the number of tourist visits. Cyprus, for example, experienced a fall in visitor numbers from 3.38 million in 1990 to 2.94 million in 1991 (BBC, 2001). More recently the terrorist incident that occurred in Bali in October 2002 killed over 180 people (most of whom were tourists), when a bomb exploded in a nightclub. Here the terrorists gained power as a political weapon through the mass media coverage of the event. Tourists were targeted, which had both short- and long-term effects on Bali's tourism industry. People fled the island; there were inevitable cancellations of bookings and a drastic reduction in new bookings, similar to the reaction of the public during the Gulf War. Furthermore, persistent acts of terrorism can tarnish the image of a destination's safety and attractiveness to such an extent that it may jeopardise its entire tourism industry (Sonmez *et al.*, 1999).

On Tuesday 11 September 2001 ('9/11') three passenger planes were hijacked and flown into major buildings in the USA: the World Trade Center in New York and the Pentagon in Washington. The attacks (and fear of subsequent attacks) brought the world travel industry to a virtual standstill as governments, businesses, airlines and individual travellers took immediate action (Tate, 2002). Airspace over the USA was closed for two days and during that time the airlines lost over $100 million in sales revenue (Goodrich, 2002). In the short term there was a cancellation of bookings, particularly those to America, and people avoided USA airlines. Prior to '9/11' there had been a marked slackening in the growth rate for world travel in line with a deteriorating worldwide economy: the event accelerated the decline with the public being frightened to travel internationally. According to the World Tourism Organisation (WTO) international visitor numbers for 2001 decreased by 0.6% to 692 million (Tate, 2002). In the quarter following '9/11' they were 9%

Table 1. International tourist arrivals in 2001 compared with 2000. Source: Tate (2002), adapted by the authors

Continent	Percentage Change
Africa	(–1.4%)
Americas	(–20%)
East Asia/Pacific	(–4%)
Europe	(–6.5%)
Middle East	(–20%)
South Asia	(–24%)

down with the impact being felt worldwide (Tate, 2002). Table 1 shows, however, that areas with high Muslim populations (South Asia and the Middle East) were particularly badly affected, with the Americas also exhibiting a major downturn.

The 11 September incident had a dramatic effect on the travel industry, with the airline sector being hardest hit; the number of passengers worldwide fell suddenly by 10% (Tate, 2002). In its wake, crisis management plans were rapidly implemented in an attempt to revive the travel industry. New security precautions were introduced at airports with increased surveillance of baggage and more random checks of passengers (Goodrich, 2002). It was not only the airlines that experienced problems, however, the international tour operators based in the UK, as with other tour operators worldwide, saw bookings fall and had to cut costs accordingly.

APPROACH AND METHODOLOGY

This paper discusses the reactions of a number of leading travel companies but focuses particularly on the reactions of the UK outbound tour operating sector to terrorist attacks. The terrorist attacks of 11 September 2001 are used as an exemplar of the type of external shock that can lead to crisis if managers fail to take immediate and decisive action. A case study is presented of a specific company, which is a major subsidiary of one of the leading companies in this sector (and where one of the authors was employed at the time of the crisis). A crisis management model is applied to the company and the case study is used to examine the reaction of the company to the events of '9/11' and to review the 'turnaround' strategies used.

A literature review of the effects of terrorism on tourism and on the crisis management process was carried out, which is presented as a discussion in this paper. A deductive approach is used to inform this research whereby the starting point is the theory of crisis management and models that have been developed, which are contrasted and analysed against the information collected, with a view to accept or refute the theory (Finn *et al.*, 2000).

Qualitative research methods were applied and the approach is grounded in the perspective that no two crises are identical. Information is derived from semi-structured interviews with key company mangers and by observational recall, as one of the authors worked for the company at the time of '9/11' and subsequently. The interviews were carried out by telephone and supplemented by email contacts. The semi-structured interviews allowed the interviewees to expand and talk freely about the subject in question, which may have generated more information than if the questions had been fully structured.

The information derived was analysed and is discussed in this paper in order to assess the reaction of the company and derive wider lessons. The information is then compared with the crisis management process as conceptualised in the form a model from the relevant literature.

The approach enabled some empirical (but limited) findings to be combined with secondary information and allows the paper to illustrate the theory with realities. It is nevertheless accepted that multiple case studies might be valuable for comparisons between the different tour operators or responses to different crises. In focusing on a typical case study there are inherent difficulties in separating what is unique to the company and what is held in common with other UK tour operators. Such multiple case studies, however, are beyond the scope of this paper, and the authors would maintain that a single case nevertheless provides an informative and relevant case from which some lessons can be drawn.

THE EFFECT OF '9/11' ON UK TOUR OPERATORS

Outbound tour operators based in the UK, which number over 1800 (Civil Aviation Authority, 2003), faced a crisis with the terrorist attacks of '9/11' and feared the worst in terms of the need to cut capacity and jobs as a result of falling sales. Although the sector has been characterised by its volatility both in terms of its sales and in terms of returns attributable to share holders (Evans and Stabler, 1995), and tour operators can be viewed as having become increasingly adept at balancing supply with fickle demand levels, the aftermath of '9/11' posed particularly acute problems for managers.

Fears of a business downturn developed into reality with immediate effect and immediate contingency plans had to be put into action. With a downturn of 20–25% in high street trading in the week following '9/11' (Travel Weekly, 2001a), tour operators had no option but to adjust capacity levels for winter 2001–2002 and summer 2002 to reflect a likely decline in bookings to the eastern Mediterranean, North Africa and the USA. Companies had to devote themselves to dealing with passengers already in America and those who were due to travel to the USA. The four largest European tour operators: TUI, MyTravel, First Choice and Thomas Cook had to cut capacity to minimise the chaos they would face in the late booking market (Holmes, 2001).

In the immediate aftermath of the attacks, all four operators cut capacity, made staff redundant and reviewed their marketing strategies as summarised in Table 2. Nevertheless, the UK tourism minister of the time (Kim Howells) accused the tour operators of 'being too quick to throw in the towel in times of trouble' (Gannoway, 2001). Sales fell and operators were taking half the number of bookings they had expected at this time of year for summer 2002 (Huxley, 2001). Analysts predicted that people would still take holidays but would not book until nearer departure time — which would leave operators no time to increase capacity (Huxley and Holmes, 2001). The tour operators were experiencing rapid decline and needed to work together to save the travel industry. The Association of British Travel

Table 2. The Effects of September 11th 2001 on UK Tour Operators. Source: various *Travel Weekly* and *Travel Trade Gazette* editions from 17 September 2001 to 9 September 2002, adapted by the authors

Tour operator	Jobs	Capacity and/ or the brochure	Strategies	Other comments
MyTravel (formerly Airtours)	350 jobs were lost after '9/11' with the chief executive announcing that a further 2000 jobs may be cut, which would include 300–400 in the UK	The group did not cut capacity sufficiently and hoped that there would be only 500000–700000 left to sell but instead there was 1 million	They acted rapidly: cut costs and the number of holidays on sale. They started to promote new global brands and offered up to 55% off holidays for 4 weeks	Shares fell by about one-quarter in the immediate wake of attacks. Currently concentrating on UK core businesses
TUI UK (formerly Thomsons)	400 jobs have been lost which is partly due to the name change to TUI. However, there could be more job losses on the way	Suspended winter 2002–03 brochures until 2002	Have spent to stimulate the market and starting shifting seat only deals to the sun and promoted their new global brands	Retail staff told to clean their own branches
First Choice	500 jobs have been lost with the cuts expecting them to save £20 million a year	Contingency plans to adjust capacity for the winter (by 15%) and next summer (20%). Also cut the aircraft fleet from 32 to 26	They have cut costs and capacity (eastern Mediterranean cut by 40%). They have repeated a tried and tested theory but with less spending	Greece and Turkey sold very well, although Florida suffered. Crisis cost them £10 million
Thomas Cook	1930 jobs were lost which included 60 UK managers. Staff offered unpaid leave, reduced hours or voluntary redundancy. Pay cuts were up to 10% for remaining staff and 15% for senior staff	Slashed summer 2002 capacity between 15 and 20%	Costs and capacity were cut with the plan to cut its role of sales administrators in the smaller shops. They have focused on internal matters	Grounded some charter flights and closed 100 agencies after reporting a 12% fall in bookings

Agents (ABTA) launched a £50000 public relations campaign and worked closely with tour operators in an attempt to boost summer 2002 bookings and regain customer confidence (Travel Weekly, 2001b).

Following the crisis of '9/11' it can be seen that all tour operators took slightly different actions and had different outcomes. MyTravel suffered greatly from '9/11' and did not cut capacity sufficiently, which resulted in 1 million holidays left over in Summer 2002 instead of their prediction of 500000 (Travel Weekly, 2002).

TUI suffered to a certain extent and successfully suspended their winter brochures for 2002 (Robinson, 2001) and concentrated on promoting their new global brands (TTG, 2002). First Choice survived the crisis quite well and calculated the capacity cuts accurately, which saved them £20 million (Dennis,

2001). Thomas Cook made a large number of people redundant and cut capacity between 15 and 20% for summer 2002 (Travel Weekly, 2001b).

CRISIS TYPOLOGIES

A crisis can threaten reputation, lives and the survival of an organisation (Seymour and Moore, 2000). Many definitions of a crisis have been constructed, such as those developed by Heath (1998), Seymour and Moore (2000) and Regester and Larkin (2002). To Heath (1998), for example, a crisis represents 'A serious incident affecting, for example, human safety, the environment and/or product or corporate reputation — and which has either received or been threatened by adverse publicity.'

Examples of crises may include life threatening incidents, product recalls and damage to the environment (Bland, 2000). A service based sector (such as tour operating), however, which trades predominantly in the international arena and relies to a large extent upon customer goodwill accumulated partly as the result of delivering safe and reliable products, is particularly susceptible to the effects of crises such as those that arise from terrorist incidents. Tour operators, although susceptible to financial crises owing to the uncertainty of the industry, are particularly vulnerable to crises where lives may actually be threatened or the perception of such a threat exists.

A number of authors have sought to develop typologies of crises, which can be useful in developing an understanding of crises and developing appropriate managerial responses. Meyers (1986), for example, in a very broadly based interpretation of what constitutes a crises identifies nine types of business crises: crises in public perception, sudden market shifts, product failures, top-management succession; finances, industrial relations, hostile takeovers, adverse international events, and regulation and deregulation.

Coombes (1995) in classifying crisis situations focuses on stakeholders' perceptions of the crisis. Such perceptions are based on whether the cause of the crisis is internal or external and result from intentional or unintentional acts. Using a combination of these internal–external and intentional–unintentional dimensions, Coombes (1995)

specifies that *faux pas*, accidents, terrorism and transgressions represent crisis situations. *Faux pas* refers to unintentional acts (initially considered appropriate by the organisation). Accidents are unintentional events, which occur during organisational operations. A transgression is an event where the organisation knowingly places others at risk. Terrorism is an intentional act by an outside group intended to do direct or indirect harm to the organisation.

Perhaps the most useful typologies for managers, however, focus on the gestation period for crises. Those that are sudden and unexpected are inherently more difficult to manage than those that build up over a period of time. Seymour and Moore (2000), for example, have suggested that crises are of two types: the cobra and the python according to the way in which they develop. Booth (1993) argues that there are three types: gradual, periodic threat and a sudden threat. The types of crisis and the responses to them as suggested by Seymour and Moore (2000) and Booth (1993) are summarised in Table 3.

THE CRISIS MANAGEMENT PROCESS

In broad terms crisis management can be viewed simply (and easily remembered) as involving the '4 Rs' of a four-stage process of: reduction, readiness, response and recovery. Corporate managers, however, are faced with the reality of trying to implement this process and a broad literature has evolved relating to the processes involved in successfully managing crisis situations. Several models and conceptualisations (such as Caplan, 1970, cited in Cassedy, 1991; Arnold, 1980, cited in Booth, 1993; Slatter, 1984, cited in Booth, 1993; Smith 1990; Booth, 1993; Smith and Sipika, 1993; Seymour and Moore, 2000; Clarke and Varma, 2004) have been developed in order to help them. This paper briefly critiques a number of available models presented in Table 4, but focuses on the model of the crisis management process developed by Smith (1990) and further developed by Smith and Sipika, 1993.

A literature has also developed which focuses on the management of crises in travel and hospitality. Thus Glaesser (2004) in his book assesses a wide range of issues, including the influence of the mass media, the effect

Table 3. Crisis typologies. Source: Booth (1993) and Seymour and Moore (2000), adapted by the authors

Seymour and Moore (2000)	Response	Booth (1993)	Response
The 'Cobra' type of crisis is sudden, for example, a disaster, which may come as a shock (e.g. 11 September)	Defensive response with reliance on the known and trusted	Sudden threat or loss to whole organisation	Defensive response with reliance on the known and trusted
The 'Python' type of crisis creeps upon a company gradually, for example, caused by poor management or high costs	Bureaucratic response when crisis is not recognised — negotiated response when crisis recognised	Periodic threat or loss to part or whole of the organisation Gradual threat with an increasing threat to part of the organisation	Negotiated response and recognition of problem Bureaucratic response as the crisis is not recognised

Table 4. Crisis management models. Source: Caplan (1961), Slatter (1984), Arnold (1980), Booth (1993), Clarke and Varma, (2004), Seymour and Moore (2000) and Smith (1990), Adapted by the authors from the sources cited

Model	Approach	Limitations
Caplan's (1970) crisis model	Psychological perspective, whereby the focus is on how the individual copes with a crisis	The model lacks precision and is descriptive. The most important criticism is that it is homeostatic
Slatter's (1984) crisis susceptibility model	Economic approach to crises	It suggests only the factors that are susceptible to a crisis in an organisation. It is not a process, merely a model stating factors which may cause a crisis
Arnold's (1980) model of crisis	Sociological perspective and looks at how communities react to crisis	Only focuses on the sociological view and centres on the individual in relation to a group. The way an individual views the crisis may be different to the organisation
Process model of crisis development (Booth, 1993)	Aims to identify features that appear to be common in many crises	Too general and simple — all crises are unique in terms of the particular causes and effects involved
The crisis life cycle (Seymour and Moore, 2000)	Looks at the obstacles to decision making during a crisis	Too descriptive and general — although can be made to fit any organisation
Clarke and Varma (2004)	Presents a model of risk management as a strategic process	Difficult to put into operation
Model of crisis management (Smith, 1990; Smith and Sipika, 1993)	A process from start to finish of a crisis	May be too general and descriptive

of crises on purchase decisions and brand image and relevant managerial responses, whereas Sharpley (2004) presents an overview and categorisation of tourism crises.

A number of notable contributions have focused particularly on a tourism destination perspective of disasters and emergencies. Faulkner (2001), for example, presents a broad disaster management framework in which disaster management responses are categorised into six sequential steps: precursors, mobilisation, action, recovery, reconstruction and reassessment and review. Faulkner's wide-ranging theoretical discussion draws from previous contributions focusing on destinations, particularly those of Murphy and Bayley (1989), Cassedy (1991), Drabek (1995) and Young and Montgomery (1998). Cassedy (1991) outlines the strategic processes involved in developing successful crisis management responses by destinations, whereas Drabek's (1995) focus is more on the detailed operational steps necessary to deal with emergency situations. The communication aspects of crisis management are emphasised by Young and Montgomery (1998) in the detailed crisis management model they propose.

The responses of particular sectors to crises are also examined in the literature. For example, Alderighi and Cento (2004) and Gillen and Lall (2003) consider the practices of airlines in relation to crises, with Ray (1999) and Henderson (2003) focusing particularly on the lessons to be drawn from the airline industry with respect to their management of strategic communications at times of crisis. With regard to the hospitality sector, Israeli and Reichal (2003) and Chien and Law (2003), for instance consider crisis management practices in relation to Israeli hotel experiences and SARS in Hong Kong, respectively, and Henderson (2002) focuses on the role of national tourism organisations in managing crises. Faulkner (2000) also draws attention to the usefulness of quantitative techniques using linear programming, as discussed by Arbel and Bargur (1980) for circumstances where the parameters of the crisis can be clearly identified, such as in the case of an individual hotel operation.

The academic literature, however, provides few insights into the behaviour of travel intermediaries such as tour operators, which this paper seeks to address.

THE APPLICATION OF A MODEL OF CRISIS MANAGEMENT TO A MEDIUM SIZED UK TOUR OPERATOR

The aims of crisis management according to Heath (1998) are:

(1) to plan and provide for possible crisis events which may occur — the pre-crisis stage;
(2) to reduce or mitigate the impacts of a crisis by improving the response management — the crisis;
(3) to swiftly and effectively determine the damage caused by the crisis — the post-crisis stage.

This paper focuses on the approach developed by Smith (1990) and further developed by Smith and Spipika (1993), and its application to a medium sized UK based tour operator. The model (shown in Figure 1) contains three distinct phases of the crisis management process: crisis of management, operational crisis and crisis of legitimation, and as such provides a process which enables the various stages of crises to be tracked and furthermore allows for learning within the process. The feedback loop represents the passing of the crisis and for lessons to be learned so that the organisation can return to the pre-crisis stage.

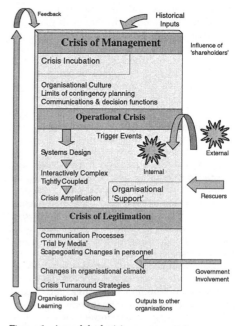

Figure 1. A model of crisis management

The company in question (which is not identified by name for commercial reasons) is a direct-sell tour-operating subsidiary of a major vertically integrated UK travel group with approximately 250000 clients a year travelling mainly to Mediterranean destinations. The company was amongst the first to use the direct-sell approach to the holiday industry and was the also the first to offer fully bookable package holidays on-line in the UK during 1999.

In the first pre-crisis period, organisations need to be aware of the possible scenarios that may take place and successful planning needs to involve a large number of staff in order to experience how to react in a real crisis (Harrison, 2000). In the case of the terrorist attack on 11 September this was a sudden crisis. Even though the crisis was unexpected it is possible to prepare for such an event by developing a crisis management plan. The influences from the management and the shareholders at the company encouraged a policy to be drawn up and reviewed each year. It is clear, however, that many companies are not well prepared for crises. It has been suggested that the reason firms do not plan lies in the myths of planning, in that such plans are viewed as a waste of time if inaccurate, and can lead to a paralysis in relation to making necessary changes and thereby can reduce flexibility. There can also be a general complacency about the crisis management policies found in firms, as they are perceived to be rather comforting when in fact people are unsure how to use it (Bland, 1998).

The company in question had a crisis management policy in place at the time of '9/11', which was derived from the overall policy for the group as a whole and which was updated annually. The policy featured the crisis and incident management structure, notification and activation criteria, information flows and response to the media, response plans and training. The training includes general training, table-top exercises and real time and live exercises with the aim to test the organisation, communications and the teamwork of those concerned and the ability of individual actions. The policy states that, 'it is imperative to have a framework in place to handle all such events swiftly, effectively and at an appropriate level'

and goes on to suggest that the aim of incident and crisis management processes is to 're-establish control of the situation as speedily as possible, and in doing so minimise any actual or potential adverse consequences of the event'.

The policy states communication and decision flows along with clear role descriptions to ensure that the crisis is handled swiftly and effectively at an appropriate level. Training is included as part of the policy to test the organisation, the communication and individual roles, as it increases familiarity and capability among those being trained and makes the organisation aware of potential crisis situations (Heath, 1998). This phase allows organisations to plan and prepare for a crisis. In the case of '9/11', the crisis had not had time to incubate, as it was unexpected. By nature crises are chaotic and every contingency cannot be covered (Bland, 1998) but it is still prudent for a certain amount of preparation to be done in the pre-crisis stage.

Phase 2 is usually recognised as the crisis, with the crash of the planes into the twin towers on 11 September 2001 creating the immediate crisis period at the tour operator. The aim of this phase is to prevent a worsening of the situation — and to be supportive to those involved, particularly when involving loss of life (Smith, 1990). Here, the emphasis will focus on the rescuers, which may include the emergency services as well as the crisis decision units, who attempt to pull the organisation through the crisis. They may not be able to contain the crisis within the organisation and significant control is needed on what strategies should be implemented.

The culture and structure of the rescuers and the communication flows play a large part in how effectively the crisis is managed (Smith and Sipika 1993). The culture of an organisation is often held as being of critical importance to corporate decision-making (Johnson and Scholes, 2002). A lack of communication between the rescuers can result in becoming crisis prone. In reducing the impact of the crisis the human face of management is important as this could determine whether the firm benefits or fails from the crisis (Smith and Sipika 1993). The key activities in this stage focus on the role of crisis management teams, crisis containment, development and control of strategies and the process of communication.

As the first plane crashed into the twin towers the office came to a standstill. The employees were shocked by the unbelievable pictures shown of the terrorist attack on TV — which was almost like something out of a film. They realised that this event may have a significant impact on the company and the travel industry worldwide. As no holidaymakers were in New York it was not a direct crisis and merely a crisis of the travel industry, which would evolve from the event itself. The immediate issue, however, was to look after people who were due to fly out to Florida and those in resorts.

At this point firms may want to decide on a strategy, however, some writers advocate caution at this stage to avoid making rushed decisions, which may turn out be wrong strategically (Bland, 1998). If firms follow the model by Smith (1990) then this will encourage them to wait until the third stage to make the strategic decisions, instead concentrating on the decisive operational details. The case study company decided to take this course of action, play it safe, consistent with the model, and carried on as normal (in the very short term) regarding capacity and advertising.

The model identifies that firms should focus on system design in this stage. The company had the system as represented by its crisis management policy in place, which they followed. This included references to decisional, informational and communicational flows. This system can be viewed as having been effective owing to the structure and the culture of the organisation, as the company encouraged open, informal communication between employees at all levels and during this period staff were kept informed of the situation at all times. During office hours, staff were informed by e-mail or telephone. The duty office at the company is open 24 hours, with staff available in case such an emergency arises. If the crisis amplifies then the firm must take action and use 'turnaround' strategies. In the case of '9/11', the attacks escalated from the first plane crash to the second and then the attack on the Pentagon in Washington.

As the crisis intensifies it enters the final stage of 'crisis of legitimation', which involves

the period of turnaround and recovery (Smith, 1990). Here communication processes are important, with the media hungry for news (Regester and Larkin, 2002). At the company in question the media were not immediately in contact, although they may have been in contact since the crisis (unlike a coach or air crash, for example), as the incident was not specific to the company and the parent company was fully equipped to deal with such enquiries. The media were, however, in contact regarding capacity levels a few months after '9/11'. The stage is important as corporate reputation and morale can be directly affected by the activities of the media (Seymour and Moore, 2000), and although the reputation of the company itself was undamaged by the event the reputation of the travel industry as a whole was damaged with consumer confidence low, which in turn led to a fall in bookings across the entire industry.

The government stepped in to help with ABTA, setting up a campaign to help restore consumer confidence. The tour operators included contributed to this in an attempt to increase sales. The model encourages the organisation to identify external groups such as the government and to communicate and collaborate with them in the time of crisis. This model may not be suitable for all types of crisis, as not all will require government involvement.

The application of Smith's model to the tour operator in question is shown in Figure 2. The model prepares firms to expect a change in organisational climate. In the aftermath of the terrorist attacks the morale was low due to fears over job security and the redundancies that had already occurred. 'Turnaround' strategies are needed in such a crisis to help firms return to their normal state of operation. Although, responsibilities in this case were widely shared in this period, the marketing department played a large part in this stage with cost-cutting exercises being the primary focus. The main actions taken by the department are summarised in Table 5.

After this period the organisation will learn from their mistakes and will return to the pre-crisis stage whereby they produce the contingency plans for the future. The model is an ongoing process, which can be reviewed and improved each time a crisis occurs.

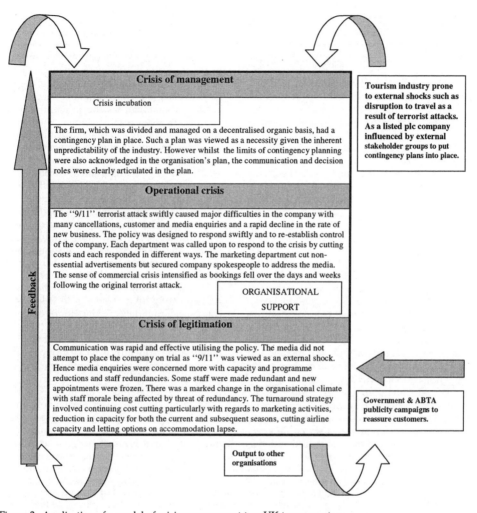

Figure 2. Application of a model of crisis management to a UK tour operator

LESSONS OF CRISIS MANAGEMENT FOR THE TRAVEL INDUSTRY

It is evident from the preceding discussion that the process of in crisis tunaround is 'a complex phenomenon which requires careful pre-planning by management if they are to be effective in dealing with the aftermath of a major crisis' (Smith and Spika, 1993). Fundamentally crisis management can be viewed as a key strategic issue (Clarke and Varma, 1999), which should be addressed by senior management as a central concern. As such crisis management, it can be argued, should be an integral part of the strategic planning processes that companies adopt (since crises represent a challenge to the very survival of organisations in many cases) and not merely a 'bolt-on' extra that is added at some later date. Thus if the view is taken that crises of one sort or another are

Table 5. Marketing department actions in the aftermath of 11 September 2001

Date	Events	Marketing department actions
Immediately after '9/11'	Very few phone calls were received enquiring about future booking	Had to play it safe and assume the worst and costs had to be cut Meetings were held and non-urgent expenditure was cut — the luxuries in the department had to go. Five employees were made redundant from a group of 19 Staff parties and educational trips in the brochure production section were stopped The quality of paper used for the brochure was down graded to save costs The advert tracking research which is completed before and after a campaign had to be stopped, which was due to start on the 12 September Non-essential adverts — at airports and those overseas were cut Prices on selected holidays were decreased considerably Advertising did not stop altogether as they still had to keep selling Press trips were stopped and PR activities were cut for three months Promotional activities such as the brochure and magazine inserts were not cancelled
January 2002	The UK Department of Trade and industry, Foreign Office, ABTA and the Civil Aviation Authority all had their own PR campaigns to help restore customer confidence — the operators could contribute to the activities if they wished Surveys showed that people would still want to go on holiday but may book later or only go for cheap deals Normally 40% of people that are going to on holiday in the summer book in January — but it was estimated in this year that 40% would book but spread out over January and February	Consequently an advertisement campaign was run to the maximum over 8 weeks instead of 4–5 The advertising used was flexible — with press advertisements being the most flexible, which can be added or cut at the last minute. Press inserts were not so flexible although very effective and were distributed over 6 weeks instead of 4. Direct mailing activities were continued as they were perceived as providing value for money Outdoor and TV advertisements were cut
September 2002	Summer 2002 actually sold early, which left very few late deals to be sold Having reduced capacity in 2002 the company expanded for summer 2003 The company returned to normal sales figures and advised people to book early which generally they did	

inevitable, particularly in a volatile sector such as travel with its inherent susceptibility to external shocks, prudently managed companies should consider the potential risks and managerial responses to them at the analysis and formulation phases of the strategic planning process and put into force a strategic response to crises in the implementation phase.

Organisations, however, have to be mindful of the fact that no two crisis situations are identical and that therefore, although managerial responses are planned in advance, such responses need to be flexible to take account of the requirements of the exact circumstances encountered. Thus responding to a crisis in an appropriate way is not merely about developing a series of contingency plans and putting them into practice in the event of a crisis (although such plans are an important aspect). The turnaround process is also concerned in the longer term with issues (explored by Dynes and Aguirre (1979) and Smith and Sipika (1993) such as organisational learning, configuring the structure of the organisation to respond effectively, creating a culture that is responsive and flexible and developing managerial competences as part of the management development process.

In implementing a crisis management strategy of Ray (1999) stresses that a crisis management team or crisis decision unit then needs to be selected with a clear framework for communication flows. The key to a successful crisis management plan is clear and precise communication, both internally and externally, which might be tested or rehearsed, as major problems in the framework need to be identified before a crisis occurs (Harrison, 2000). The whole organisation needs to be aware of the framework or strategy, in case such an event occurs, thus indicating the importance of sharing knowledge. The way in which a firm prepares for a crisis may depend on its culture, as this will directly influence how a firm communicates (Ray, 1999). The culture will dominate the management's actions and will reflect in the attitudes and norms of the organisation (Ray, 1999).

It is to be expected that individuals and groups who have experienced disasters and managerial responses to them are likely to be better equipped to respond to similar situations in the future (Faulkner, 2001), but some evidence points to this rarely occurring in practice (Burling and Hyle, 1997). Such knowledge can be gained only through a thorough and systematic debriefing procedure after the event as a basis for refining the strategy for future management of crisis situations. Consequently by drawing on the knowledge of individuals and groups derived from their experiences of managing in a crisis, the role of organisational learning is stressed. In considering learning approaches in relation to crisis management Richardson (1994) distinguishes between single and double loop learning. Single loop learning concerns learning from the managerial responses themselves in keeping with the accepted framework of existing systems' objectives and roles, whereas double loop learning additionally questions the systems, roles and objectives themselves as well as the response to the crisis to see what lessons might be forthcoming. It is suggested that double loop learning provides a more rigorous and wide-ranging basis for future strategic changes but may in some cases be contrary to the cultural norms of the organisation.

After incorporating the crisis management model developed by Smith (1990) with the steps undertaken by the company being used as a case study regarding the '9/11' crisis there are some generic lessons for the travel industry, which are identified in Table 6.

As the travel industry is unpredictable and many external factors can create a crisis it is almost certain that a crisis of some sort will occur at some point in time. Furthermore given the perishability of the travel product it cannot be stored for future use. Thus, the travel industry needs to be aware of the potential crises and be prepared for a sudden and unexpected crisis. Events such as '9/11' are extremely hard to prepare for, as this was a one off event that cannot be practised. The longer run effects of such a crisis are also difficult to predict and it can be argued that these can be categorised into primary and induced effects.

(1) Primary effects are the fall in sales of holidays in the travel industry owing to consumers being scared to travel and losing confidence in the travel industry.

                                    Int. J. Tourism Res. 7, 135–150 (2005)

Table 6. Lessons and action to be taken by the travel industry. Sources: Smith (1990), Richardson (1994), Smith and Sipika, 1993, Heath (1998) and Regester and Larkin (2002) — Adapted by the authors

Lesson	Action
Prepare Contingency plans	Draw up contingency plans, which may be in the form of a crisis management policy as the travel industry is unpredictable, its product is perishable and unexpected crises may occur at any time
Develop communicational and decisional roles and flow diagrams	This can be incorporated into a crisis management policy with clear role descriptions to ensure that the crisis is handled swiftly and effectively at an appropriate level
Training should be encouraged	Training should be included as part of the policy, as it increases familiarity and capability among those being trained as well as making the organisation aware of potential crisis situations (Heath, 1998). This could be in the form of scenario planning, paper based exercises and live exercises
Do not rush decision making in the immediate aftermath	Firms should not rush strategic decision-making in the immediate aftermath of a crisis and should consider all options before making a choice
Co-operate with the media	Firms must co-operate with the media, as poor management regarding the media could lead to the general public and the media being negative and judgemental about mistakes made in handling the crisis (Heath, 1998). As Regester and Larkin (2002) suggest you must 'tell your own story, to tell it all and to tell it fast'
Identify external groups who may intervene in the time of crisis	Firms should identify groups that may be able to help in the time of crisis such as the government. They must communicate and collaborate with them in times of crisis as well as in the pre-crisis stage
A thorough and systematic debriefing procedure after the event	A debriefing forms a basis for refining the strategy for future management of crisis situations. By drawing on the knowledge of individuals and groups derived from their experiences of managing in a crisis, the role of organisational learning is stressed. Richardson (1994) distinguishes between single and double loop learning
The turnaround process is also concerned with longer term issues	The organisation, to respond effectively to future crises, should be concerned with creating structures which are configured to respond effectively, creating a culture that is responsive and flexible and developing managerial competences as part of the management development process

(2) Induced effects are the downturn of other sectors, thereby causing less people to travel. For example, people may be wary of their spending habits owing to political uncertainty and therefore the retail industry will suffer as a result.

CONCLUSION

This paper explores the crisis management process in relation to the UK tour operating sector and a case study is used to examine the reaction of the company to '9/11' and to review the 'turnaround' strategies used. The crisis management process model is compared and contrasted with the steps actually undertaken at the company in the wake of '9/11'.

It is evident from the analysis that there are lessons to be learned, which could be useful for the travel industry in general, including the need to:

(1) prepare detailed contingency plans;
(2) define decisional and informational roles and responsibilities;
(3) retain a degree of flexibility in order to react swiftly and decisively at an operational level but not to rush into more strategic level decision-making.

Furthermore it is important that lessons are fed-back into the company once the immediate crisis is over, as the crisis management model presented implies, crisis management is a continuous process involving a feedback loop back to the pre-crisis stage once the crisis is over. This enables organisational learning to take place whereby companies are able to improve their performance through learning from mistakes and preparing for the next potential crisis.

No two crises are the same and as companies vary in their scale, complexity and orientations reactions will vary from one company to the next in order to match the reaction to individual circumstances. A schematic model (such as the one developed by Smith (1990) and Smith and Sipika (1993)), however, can provide a useful starting point for managers to assess the risks involved and to identify the roles and responsibilities of the various internal and external stakeholders. It is of course necessary for organisations to adapt the model appropriately to suit their individual circumstances so that companies can be assured that robust and clear crisis management processes are in place. In applying the model, however, although it is a useful device in identifying and categorising issues, it is nevertheless imperative that the limitations of contingency planning are recognised and that flexibility of response is maintained.

REFERENCES

Alderighi M, Cento A. 2004. European airlines conduct after September 11. *Journal of Air Transport Management* **10**: 97–107.

Arbel A, Bargur J. 1980. A planning model for crisis management in the tourism industry. *European Journal of Operational Research* **52**: 77–85.

Arnold W. 1980. *Crisis Communication*. Gorsuch Scarisbrook: Dubuque, Iowa.

BBC. 2001. *What now for Tourism?* Available online at URL: http://www.bbc.co.uk/news (accessed 18 September 2001).

Bland M. 1998. *Communicating Out of a Crisis*. Macmillan Business: London.

Booth S. 1993. *Crisis Management Strategy, Competition and Changes in Modern Enterprises*. Routledge: London.

Burling WK, Hyle A. 1997. Disaster preparedness planning policy and leadership issues. *Disaster Prevention and Management* **64**: 234–244.

Caplan G. 1970. *The Theory and Practice of Mental Health Consultation*.

Cassedy K. 1991. *Crisis Management Planning in The Travel and Tourism Industry: a Study of Three Destinations and a Crisis Planning Manual*. Pacific Asia Travel Association (PATA): San Francisco.

Chien GCL, Law R. 2003. The impact of the Severe Acute Respiratory Syndrome on hotels: a case study of Hong Kong. *International Journal of Hospitality Management* **22**: 327–332.

CAA. 2003. *ATOL Business* 22 July 2003. Civil Aviation Authority: London.

Clarke CJ, Varma S. 2004. Strategic risk management: the new competitive edge. *Long Range Planning* **32**(4): 414–424.

Coombes WT. 1995. The development of guidelines for the selection of the 'appropriate' crisis response strategies. *Management Communication Quarterly* **4**: 447–476.

Dennis J. 2001. Big four axe jobs and move to restructure. *Travel Weekly* **8 October**: 6.

Drabek TE. 1995. Disaster responses within the tourism industry. *International Journal of Mass Emergencies and Disasters* **131**: 7–23.

Dynes RR, Aguirre BE. 1979. Organizational adaptation to crises: mechanisms of coordination and structural change. *Disasters* **31**: 71–74.

Evans N, Stabler MJ. 1995. A future for the package tour operator in the 21st century? *Tourism Economics* **13**: 245–263.

Evans N, Campbell D, Stonehouse G. 2003. *Strategic Management for Travel and Tourism*. Butterworth-Heinemann: Oxford.

Faulkner B. 2001. Towards a framework for tourism disaster management. *Tourism Management* **22**(2): 135–147.

Finn M, Elliot-White M, Walton M. 2000. *Tourism and Leisure Research Methods — Data Collection. Analysis and Interpretation*. Pearson Education: Harlow, Essex.

Gannoway B. 2001. You only have yourselves to blame. *Travel Weekly* **8 October**: 6.

Gillen D, Lal A. 2003. International transmission of shocks in the airline industry. *Journal of Air Transport Management* **9**: 37–49.

Glaesser D. 2004. *Crisis Management in the Tourism Industry*. Butterworth-Heinemann: Oxford.

Goodrich JN. 2002. September 11, 2001 attack on America: a record of the immediate impacts and reactions in the USA travel and tourism industry. *Tourism Management* **23**: 573–580.

Harrison S. 2000. *Public Relations: an Introduction*, 2nd edn. Business Press: London.

Heath R. 1998. *Crisis Management for Managers and Executives*. Financial Times Publishing: London.

Henderson J. 2002. Managing a tourism crisis in South-East Asia: the role of national tourism organisations. *International Journal of Hospitality and Tourism Administration* 31: 85–105.

Henderson J. 2003. Communicating in a crisis: flight SQ006. *Tourism Management* 243: 279–287.

Holmes K. 2001. Operators urged to reduce capacity. *Travel Trade Gazette* 24 **September**: 9.

Huxley L. 2001. Crisis talks follow slump in bookings. *Travel Trade Gazette* 15 **October**: 3.

Huxley L, Holmes K. 2001. Discounting frenzy 'could be avoided'. *Travel Trade Gazette* 15 **October**: 2.

Israeli AA, Reichal A. 2003. Hospitality crisis management practices: the Israeli case. *International Journal of Hospitality Management* 22: 353–372.

Johnson G, Scholes K. 2002. *Exploring Corporate Strategy*, 6th edn. Prentice Hall: London.

Meyers GC. 1986. *When it Hits the Fan: Managing the Nine Crises of Business*. Mentor: New York.

Murphy PE, Bailey R. 1989. Tourism and disaster planning. *Geographical Review* 791: 36–46.

Pizam A, Mansfeld Y (eds). 1996. *Tourism Crime and International Security Issues*. Wiley: Chichester.

Pizam A, Smith G. 2000. Tourism and terrorism: a quantitative analysis of major terrorist acts and their impact on tourism destinations. *Tourism Economics* 62: 123–138.

Ray SJ. 1999. *Strategic Communication in Crisis Management: Lessons from the Airline Industry*. Quorum Books: Westport, CT.

Regester M, Larkin J. 2002. *Risk Issues and Crisis Management: a Casebook of Best Practice*, 2nd edn. Kogan Page: London.

Richardson B. 1994. Crisis management and the management strategy: time to 'loop the loop'. *Disaster Prevention and Management* 33: 59–80.

Robinson F. 2001. Empty shelves compound crisis. *Travel Weekly* 29 **October**: 5.

Ryan C. 1993. Crime, violence, terrorism and tourism: an accidental relationship or intrinsic relationship. *Tourism Management* 143: 173–183.

Seymour M, Moore S. 2000. *Effective Crisis Management: Worldwide Principles and Practice*. Cassell: London.

Sharpley R. 2004. International tourism: the management of crisis. In *The Management of Tourism*, Pender L, Sharpley R (eds). Sage: London.

Slatter S. 1984. *Corporate Recovery*. Penguin: Harmondsworth.

Smith D. 1990. Beyond contingency planning: towards a model of crisis management. *Industrial Crisis Quarterly* 4: 263–275.

Smith D, Sipika C. 1993. Back from the brink — post crisis management. *Long Range Planning* 261: 28–38.

Sonmez S. 1998. Tourism, terrorism and political instability. *Annals of Tourism Research* 252: 416–445.

Sonmez S, Apostolopoulous Y, Tarlow P. 1999. Tourism in crisis: managing the effects of terrorism. *Journal of Travel Research* 381: 13–18.

Tate P. 2002. The impact of '9/11': Caribbean, London and NYC case studies. *Travel and Tourism Analyst* 5(October): 1–25.

Travel Weekly. 2001a. Winter sales down 20% on last year. *Travel Weekly* 24 **September**: 7.

Travel Weekly. 2001b. Ad campaign aims to boost 2002 bookings. *Travel Weekly* 5 **November**.

Travel Weekly. 2002. We blundered admits Wilson. *Travel Weekly* 28 **October**: 7.

TTG. 2002. Independent travel bookings boom. *Travel Trade Gazette* 28 **January**: 5.

Young WB, Montgomery RJ. 1998. Crisis management and its impact on destination marketing: a guide to convention and visitors bureaus. *Journal of Convention and Exhibition Management* 11: 3–18.

[3]

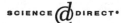

Available online at www.sciencedirect.com

SCIENCE @ DIRECT®

Hospitality Management 24 (2005) 219–242

International Journal of
Hospitality Management

www.elsevier.com/locate/ijhosman

Growth and profit-oriented entrepreneurship among family business owners in the tourism and hospitality industry

Donald Getz[a],*, Tage Petersen[b]

[a]Haskayne School of Business, Faculty of Management, University of Calgary, 2500 University Drive, NW, Calgary, Alberta, Canada
[b]Regional and Tourism Research Centre, Stenbrudsvej 55-3730, Nexo, Bornholm, Denmark

Abstract

Surveys were conducted among family business owners in the tourism and hospitality industry in two resort areas (one in Canada and one in Denmark) with a view to identifying growth and profit-oriented entrepreneurs. Analysis of owners' attitudes and goals reveals the predominance of lifestyle and autonomy orientations, but also profiles those who are more profit and growth oriented. This small sub-group differs somewhat in the two resorts—in both cases profit and growth orientation is significantly higher among those who purchased their business, particularly accommodation establishments and restaurants. Bed and breakfast and arts and craft businesses are clearly associated with lifestyle and autonomy. Theoretical, management and policy implications are discussed.
© 2004 Elsevier Ltd. All rights reserved.

Keywords: Entrepreneurship; Growth and profit orientation; Bornholm; Denmark; Canmore; Canada

1. Introduction

Growth and profit-oriented entrepreneurs are highly valued. From the perspective of economic development and tourism industry competitiveness, a typical goal is to

*Corresponding author. Tel.: +1-403-220-7158; fax: +1-403-282-0095.
E-mail address: don.getz@haskayne.ucalgary.ca (D. Getz).

0278-4319/$ - see front matter © 2004 Elsevier Ltd. All rights reserved.
doi:10.1016/j.ijhm.2004.06.007

attract and cultivate businesses that can compete, grow, and create jobs. In this policy context not all entrepreneurs are equal. For example, the emphasis in regional development in the European Community has shifted towards support for areas "…that demonstrate an understanding of the need to reinforce the local economic environment in order to contribute to job creation" (Leat et al., 2000). There will likely always be an emphasis on growth and job creation in economic development programs, even though this tends to undervalue the majority of tourism-related businesses that remain small.

This research therefore aimed to identify growth and profit-oriented entrepreneurs among a sample of family business owners in two resort settings. It was hypothesized that a segment of owners would; (a) reveal profit and growth-oriented attitudes and goals that clearly separate them from autonomy and lifestyle-oriented respondents and (b) growth and profit-oriented entrepreneurs would display different business characteristics such as type of business. By identifying the growth-oriented group and characteristics of their businesses, tourism and economic development agencies should be able to evaluate the competitive and growth prospects of destinations and formulate programs conducive to attracting and sustaining growth-oriented investors.

The paper begins with a review of pertinent literature concerning growth orientation among entrepreneurs, both generically and specific to tourism and hospitality. Evidence is then presented from two surveys, in Canada and Denmark, that tests four hypotheses on growth versus lifestyle and autonomy orientations among family business owners. Data were obtained on motives and goals for starting or purchasing the business, and on attitudes and goals for the future of the business. Both theoretical and policy-related implications are drawn in the conclusions.

1.1. Growth and profit-oriented entrepreneurship

There does not exist an accepted, universal definition of "entrepreneur" or "entrepreneurship" (Ucbasaran et al., 2001), let alone agreement on the existence of particular sub-types. Therefore it is useful to refer to the eight "themes" of entrepreneurship literature and theory that Gartner (1990) identified from a Delphi survey of experts: personality traits, innovation, creation of organizations, value creation, profit versus not-for-profit organizations, growth, uniqueness, and the owner-manager. Specific ideas on profit and growth-oriented entrepreneurship are found in two particular themes.

The first pertinent theme focuses on the entrepreneur's personality traits, although many authors (e.g., Sexton and Kent, 1981; Gartner, 1988; Brockhaus, 1994; Risker, 1998) have rejected the personality traits approach, concluding that it has failed to identify a set of common traits for entrepreneurs or to differentiate them from managers. Within this theme, Katz (1995) identified "growth entrepreneurs" as those who measure their success by business size and growth, and contrasted these people with "autonomy-seeking" business owners, the kind who want to be their own boss or occupy their own place. Smith (1967) separated craftsmen from "opportunistic" entrepreneurs, with major differentiating factors being the "craftsman's" aversion to

D. Getz, T. Petersen / Hospitality Management 24 (2005) 219–242 221

risk, less growth, and a focus on making a comfortable living. Small business owners are often portrayed as being "craftsmen" or "lifestyle entrepreneurs", and family businesses in particular are frequently assumed to be risk averse because they must place family security ahead of potential growth.

The growth theme is also controversial. Carland et al. (1984) claimed that to be an entrepreneur requires establishment of a business for the principal purpose of profit or growth, plus accompanying strategic management, but what exactly is growth? Growth and "value-adding" are not the same (Katz, 1994). Value can be added to a business through contracting out or by mechanization, without growth in capitalization, scale or output. The kind of growth desired by economic development agencies is normally expressed in terms of wealth (which is linked to profitability) and jobs created. In tourism, growth is also measured by demand (i.e., increasing volumes of tourists) or yield (greater tourist expenditure in the destination).

Ambitions to increase wealth and grow the business are not always present among small or family business owners (Vesper, 1980). Growth is often not easy or feasible, owing to a lack of capital, and might consciously be avoided because of its implications for increased debt, more work, or risk. Smith (1967) argued that among autonomy-oriented owners growth is secondary to achieving a consistent living. Westhead and Cowling (1998) said that some family firms defer investments and job creation, thereby becoming less competitive, in order to minimize tax liability. These authors also referred to a number of studies that have revealed that family firms tend to be smaller in terms of sales and employees. Hoy and Verser (1994, p. 17) said that in family businesses "The growth goals of the founder may be in direct conflict with the desire for wealth accumulation by the family".

Employment growth has been observed to be more prevalent among businesses owned by "habitual" entrepreneurs, especially in rural areas, compared to novice business owners (Ucbasaran et al., 2001). Katz (1994) also noted that growth can be designed into a business by way of its structure, such as through legal incorporation to facilitate capitalization.

The literature, although controversial, does support the notion that some business owners are more growth and profit-oriented. It is also apparent that growth is frequently not desired by, nor achieved, among family business owners. What is uncertain is the prevalence of growth and profit-oriented entrepreneurship in various industries and settings, and how best to identify growth potential.

1.2. Entrepreneurship in the tourism and hospitality literature

There can be little doubt that in many countries small tourism and hospitality businesses predominate, and most are owned by sole proprietors and families (see, for example: Shaw and Williams, 1990; Buhalis and Cooper, 1998; Morrison et al., 1999; Thomas et al., 1999; Getz and Carlsen, 2000). The National Survey of Small Tourism and Hospitality Firms in the UK (cited in Thomas, 1999) found that at least 80% of the firms were independently owned, single outlets, and 80% of respondents were sole or joint owners. Nevertheless, Roberts and Hall (2001, p. 206) observed

222   *D. Getz, T. Petersen / Hospitality Management 24 (2005) 219–242*

that a "…paucity of information on the behavior of small tourism firms means that entrepreneurial activity in the tourism sector is poorly understood."

Shaw and Williams (1998), drawing on their own earlier work in Cornwall, England, as well as other studies of the industry, concluded that many owners were "non-entrepreneurs" or "constrained entrepreneurs". Under-capitalization was a serious constraint resulting in little if any improvement or development of small accommodation businesses, and business failure is frequently observed to be high in this sector. Shaw and Williams also characterized small-scale entrepreneurs in tourism in these ways: having little or no formal qualifications; using mostly family resources and labor; lacking business planning and growth strategies; doing little if any marketing, and possessing non- economic motives. Typically such owners moved to resorts for semi-retirement and other lifestyle reasons. "True entrepreneurship" was associated with non-personal sources of capital and innovative management skills.

Several researchers have identified the prominence of lifestyle motives among tourism and hospitality business owners. Getz and Carlsen (2000), from analyzing a survey of 200 family businesses in tourism and hospitality in Western Australia, determined that the predominant motive for starting or buying the business was that of lifestyle enhancement, including moving to, or remaining in a rural area. Middleton (2001) examined the importance of micro businesses (defined as those employing fewer than ten people) in European tourism. He believed (p.198) they "…comprise a seedbed of entrepreneurial and enterprise 'culture' on which much of the profit and employment prospects of big businesses ultimately depends." They constitute 95% of tourism businesses and generate a third of total tourism revenue (p.199), earn money that tends to stay in the local economy, and are a vital part of new job creation, especially in areas of rural and urban regeneration. They also perform a vital role in stabilizing fragile economic areas, even if few jobs are created. Middleton also noted that many micro-tourism businesses are formed for lifestyle reasons and consequently do not want to grow the business.

A number of researchers have made explicit reference to the weaknesses associated with small and family business ownership in the tourism industry. For example, Dewhurst and Horobin (1998) noted that lifestyle entrepreneurs face long-term survival problems that can negatively impact on the economic health and social fabric of their communities. Harrison and Leitch (1996), based on analysis of small and medium-sized enterprises in Northern Ireland, concluded that individual self-employment in the tourism industry might not make much of a long-term contribution to local development. Russell (1996) examined small Irish tourism businesses and concluded that few owners had identified substantial growth as a key goal, and innovation was not an integral part of most enterprises. In the context of research on the tourism industry in a peripheral part of Sweden, Klenell and Steen (1999) correlated lifestyle and the motive not to grow a business with insolvency. Shaw and Williams (1998) believed that small business owners can be unresponsive to policy initiatives designed to foster economic development or industry competitiveness.

D. Getz, T. Petersen / Hospitality Management 24 (2005) 219–242 223

Drawing on both the generic and tourism-specific literature on entrepreneurship, the following hypotheses were formulated for testing among family business owners in Canada and Denmark:

H1: Lifestyle and autonomy goals predominate.

H2: Lifestyle and autonomy-oriented owners are attracted to specific business types.

H3: Growth and profit-oriented entrepreneurs will be clearly differentiated from lifestyle and autonomy-oriented owners, as measured by a set of attitude statements and future-oriented goals.

H4: Growth and profit-oriented entrepreneurs are attracted to specific business types.

2. Research method

The comparative case study method was selected for this research. No two destinations or resort environments are the same, hence any sample is very limited in terms of statistical inferences or generalizability. Nevertheless there are major advantages in taking this approach. As argued by Stake (2000, p. 24), case studies can be used to test hypotheses, "...particularly to examine a single exception that shows the hypothesis to be false." In this research the hypotheses have been derived from previous research and may be considered to be propositions about the behavior of family businesses and entrepreneurs in the tourism industry. Therefore, disproving the hypotheses is a challenge to the underlying theory or weakens the generalizability of the cases.

Selection of case studies should avoid atypical situations, however this implies foreknowledge of the complete range of tourism environments and a predetermination of what variables in particular are most important—conditions that could not be met. Picking these two resorts in difference countries is not a systematic selection of case studies as recommended by Gomm et al. (2000). However, it does constitute a reasonable test of the hypotheses, given that the resorts are different in many ways. Finding similar motives, goals and behavior in two settings provides support for the emerging theory on entrepreneurship in this industry, while any deviations can be used to generate new research questions or hypotheses.

Research was undertaken in 2001, consisting of almost-identical, self-completion, mail-back questionnaires in Bornholm and Canmore. The Canmore instrument was prepared first, in English, translated by Danish researchers, then back-translated into English by a third party to ensure consistency. The peak tourism season (summer) was deliberately avoided. The sampling frame in both cases was a census of businesses, with owner-managers selected for study. In Canmore the researchers were assisted in this selection by the local economic development agency, as they possess intimate knowledge of the community. In Bornholm the researchers relied on detailed personal knowledge and input from local business owners to determine the sample.

Privately owned accommodation, food and tour services, attractions, recreation facilities, taxi and bus companies, and tourist-oriented manufacturing and retailing (specifically arts and crafts producers) were included, plus antique dealers, gift shops and candy manufacturers. Grocery, clothing, furniture and other stores were excluded even though in resorts a portion of their trade would likely come from non-residents. Consequently, the samples can be said to represent all the major elements of the tourism and hospitality sectors within a resort.

2.1. The questionnaires

Questionnaires were mailed to respondents with a self-addressed, postage-paid return envelope. Follow-up telephone calls were made to encourage a larger response rate. Anonymity was promised, and data have been analyzed and reported in a format that will not permit identification of individual respondents or their businesses. The questionnaire consisted of mostly closed, tick-the-box questions, in the following sequence:

- description of the business, including type, age, origin, ownership, participation of family members,
- open-ended questions on what aspects of the business provided the most satisfaction and were most difficult,
- plans for disposition of the business (e.g., sell or inherit),
- problems facing the business (e.g., highly seasonal demand; quality or quantity of workers),
- the degree of importance that respondents attached to a list of "goals when starting this business" (based on Getz and Carlsen, 2000) using a 5-point Likert scale,
- level of agreement with a list of "statements about this business" (encompassing factual and attitudinal statements, and future-oriented goals) based on Getz and Carlsen (2000), using a 5-point Likert scale,
- problems that might impact on inheritance, if applicable (3 responses were provided for each: not a problem, somewhat of a problem, or a serious problem),
- an open-ended question asking for other reasons why the business might not be passed on within the family,
- the relative importance of family related goals, measured on a 5-point Likert scale (based on Getz and Carlsen, 2000),
- personal information (gender, age, marital status, education, previous business ownership).

In this paper the analysis concentrates on goal statements and the identification of profiles reflecting the growth and profit-oriented, versus autonomy and lifestyle-oriented owners.

D. Getz, T. Petersen / Hospitality Management 24 (2005) 219–242 225

3. Profiles of Canmore and Bornholm

The two selected resorts display a number of contrasts, especially in terms of their physical and economic environments (Canmore with mountains versus Bornholm with the seashore), age (young and growing rapidly versus mature), and seasonality (some all-year demand versus extreme summer peaks). And despite the obvious cultural differences between Canada and Denmark, there are key structural similarities in terms of entrepreneurial, free-market development, a range of accommodations, and domination by small, family businesses. It is, in both settings, a matter of personal choice that dictates the motives for locating there, the nature and type of investment that owners have made, and the degree to which they expand their businesses.

Canmore is a rapidly growing resort town situated just outside the boundary of Banff National Park, a one hour drive west of Calgary, Alberta, Canada. Its very recent transition from coal-mining village to tourist destination is attributable to several major factors: staging of part of the 1988 Winter Olympics in Canmore, which generated publicity and a world-class facility for cross-country skiing; a development freeze within the national park, resulting in spill-over development in Canmore; and mounting demand for second homes in the mountains. Consequently, since 1988, tourism has become the town's major industry. Numerous accommodation, retail, tour and other services have opened there.

Table 1 provides a profile of the respondents, and subsequent references will be made to these data. Canmore's Business Registry, with interpretation by local economic development officials, revealed 1034 businesses of which 61% were considered to be "family owned", that is owned by identifiable persons, not corporations. A total of 198 tourism-related businesses were identified and it was estimated that 78% of these were "family owned" (see Table 2). Almost all the "family owned" businesses are owner-managed with resident owners, although a very small proportion lived outside the community. A total of 100 respondents completed the survey.

A breakdown of accommodation businesses in Canmore reveals that it is heavily weighted to bed and breakfast houses (79 out of 106), and 36 of these B and B owners replied to the questionnaire. All B and B operations were family businesses. In addition there are 27 other accommodation businesses (hotels and motels plus one campground) of which 16 (59%) were believed to be family owned. The survey yielded 9 respondents from these other accommodation types.

The island of Bornholm (in the Baltic Sea) is one of the most renowned destinations in Denmark, having been popular since the late 19th century. It has been described as "...a mature seaside resort with an established tourism infrastructure dominated by small enterprises" (Gyimothy, 2000, p. 56). The climate is temperate and often sunny, but winters are harsh and not attractive for visitors. The main attractions are unspoilt rural and coastal scenery, quaint fishing villages, outdoor recreational activities, historic churches, arts and crafts (especially glass blowing and ceramics), and visiting small museums. Tourist demand is extremely seasonal, being concentrated in July and August.

226 *D. Getz, T. Petersen / Hospitality Management 24 (2005) 219–242*

Table 1
Profiles of the respondents

Profile variables	Categories	Bornholm $N=84$	Canmore $N=100$
Gender	Male	63.3%	45.8%
	Female	36.7	54.2
Marital status	Married	88.8%	87.8%
	Other	11.3	12.2
Age	Under 25	1.3%	0%
	25–34	5.0	10
	35–44	27.5	40
	45–54	31.3	28
	55–64	30.0	15
	65+	5.0	7
Included in the business (respondents were asked to indicate the activities included in their business, yielding multiple answers)	Accommodation	31	45
	Restaurant/Cafe	22	19
	Attraction	5	2
	Art/Craft	21	—
	Recreation	—	3
	Retail	8	20
	Tour Service	4	12
	Other	23	26
Year business started	2000	2.6%	10
	1990s	33.3	67
	1980s	14.1	14
	1970s	12.8	3
	1960s	15.4	1
	1950s	7.7	2
	Older	14.1	0
Years in this business (cumulative percentage)	−1 or less	7.3%	13%
	−5 or less	31.7	65
	−10 or less	53.7	88
	−20 or less	79.3	96.7
	−30 or less	91.5	98.9
	−40 or less	100	100
Purchased or started the business?	Purchased	38.1%	74.5%
	Started Myself	56.3	25.5
	Inherited	2.5	—
	Renting	1.3	—
Ownership (multiple responses permitted)	Husband/Wife	21	50
	Ltd. Company	14	29
	Sole Proprietor	38	26
	Partnership, no family	2	5
	Partnership with family	4	1
	Other	4	2
Family involvement (multiple answers permitted)	Only Me	30	25
	With spouse	41	64

D. Getz, T. Petersen / Hospitality Management 24 (2005) 219–242 227

Table 1 (*continued*)

Profile variables	Categories	Bornholm N=84	Canmore N=100
	Child(ren)	11	12
	Other family	7	5
Paid employees	none	53.0%	62.5%
(non-family, full-time)	1	12.0	6 .3
	2–10	28.9	21.9
	over 10	6.0	9.4
	Range	0–35	0–35
Education	Post-secondary	76.3%	66%
Previous business	Yes	31.2%	43.4%
ownership	No	68.8	56.6

Table 2
Profile of Canmore tourism-related businesses and the survey sample

Type	Total number of businesses	Estimated % family businesses	Questionnaire sample (number and % of type; N = 100)
Construction	269	45	
Wholesale and retail	180	65	19 (all retail)
Personal and other services	130	68	
Accommodation	106	90	45
Professional services	104	66	
Food and beverage	60	80	19
Arts, entertainment and recreation	56	38	2
Real estate, rental, leasing	31	61	
Manufacturing	27	52	
Transportation, warehousing and utilities	25	36	13 (all tour services)
Other	46	Range: 0–73	2
Total	1034	61	100

Bornholm is similar to two other Baltic islands, Aland and Gotland. All three islands possess high levels of local ownership and control, and Twining-Ward and Baum (1998) concluded that all three had entered a period of decline and were suffering from the ill-effects of seasonally low demand. The problems are augmented by a dominance of small, family enterprises "...which in many cases lack the professional training required to secure a high quality of service" (Twining-Ward and Baum, 1998, p. 135).

Table 3

Bornholm: estimated number of businesses and proportion of family businesses

Type of business	Estimated number in study area	Estimated number and proportion of family businesses
Hotels/pensions	61	54 (88.5%)
Holiday centers	5	3 (60)
Hostels	5	5 (100)
Campgrounds	12	11 (92)
Summer house rentals	7	7 (100)
Restaurants/cafes	48	48 (100)
Attractions/recreation	37	35 (94.5)
Arts/crafts	51	51 (100)
Other retail	39	39 (100)
Transport	21	19 (90.5)
Other services	31	30 (97)
Total	317	302 (95.3%)

Table 4

Bornholm: business activities of respondents (multiple answers permitted)

Business activities	Number including each activity
Accommodation	31
Restaurant or cafe	22
Arts and crafts	21
Attraction or recreation	11
Other retail (most arts and crafts include both production and retailing)	8
Tour company	4
Other	23

An estimate was made by local researchers of the total number of tourism and hospitality businesses in the study area, using municipal directories, and the proportion that was family owned (based on detailed local knowledge). As in Canmore, the principal criterion for determining if a business was "family owned" was the presence of resident, owner-managers. Table 3 shows there were 317 identifiable tourism/hospitality businesses in the two Bornholm municipalities covered by the research, of which fully 95.3% were deemed to be family businesses. The main sector of corporate ownership was that of larger accommodation establishments.

The questionnaire sample of 84 owners on Bornholm is not directly comparable to the categories used in Table 3, because each respondent was asked to indicate all the different activities of their business and a small number of them ran multiple businesses or multi-activity businesses (such as hotel plus restaurant). Of the 120 activities listed by respondents (see Table 4), accommodation was the largest category (31), followed by restaurants/cafes (22), and arts and craft producers (21; most of which are combined production and retail operations).

Regarding the industry, Canmore has attracted more chain hotels and restaurants which are larger and typically not family owned or controlled (although owning a franchise counted as a family business in this research). It is unknown if investors in either resort have greater access to capital or other forms of business assistance.

4. Data and analysis

In both samples (see Table 1 again) the respondents were predominantly married (88–89%), but there were more males in the Bornholm group (63% compared to 46%), and they were, on average, older. This reflects the older age of the businesses covered by the sample (i.e., 65% of the Canmore owners had owned their business for 5 years or less, compared to 32% in Bornholm), and in turn the much longer history of tourism development on the island.

Data on business types are not directly comparable, as the industry is somewhat different in these resorts. The largest group in both cases were accommodation operators, but in Canmore there was a high proportion of bed and breakfast owners while the Bornholm sample consisted mostly of operators of small hotels and "pensions" (pensions are sometimes smaller than hotels, but often indistinguishable). The Bornholm sample also contained a group of 21 arts and craft producers/retailers, but there were none of these in the Canmore sample.

Ownership was largely in the hands of married couples and sole proprietors. Quite a few families have formed companies, but partnerships were a small minority. There was a higher proportion of sole proprietors in Bornholm and a higher proportion of married couples as owners in Canmore. Exact percentages are not possible because multiple answers were permitted on the ownership question.

In both samples the businesses were very small, with mostly just the owner(s) being employed. In Bornholm less than half had non-family, full-time, paid employees; only 11 involved children, and 7 others involved other family members beside spouses. Companies (as opposed to other ownership forms) and non-accommodation businesses had more paid, full-time, non-family employees. In Canmore, less than half had employees and only 17 involved children or other family members beside a spouse. Those Canmore businesses owned by companies had more employees, and these were primarily hotels, restaurants, and to a lesser extent tour companies. None of the bed and breakfast establishments had non-family, full-time paid employees.

In Canmore, a relatively new resort, 74.5% of the businesses were started by the respondents, compared to 56.3% in Bornholm. There were no inherited businesses in Canmore, but several existed in Bornholm (i.e., 2.5% of the sample). Previous business ownership was high (31% of respondents in Bornholm and 43% in Canmore), but it is unknown what kinds of businesses these were.

4.1. Testing the hypotheses: motives and goals for starting the business

In order to test hypotheses 1 and 2, mean responses to the start-up goals (see Table 5) were analyzed, and *T*-tests were used to compare responses between the two samples. To

230   D. Getz, T. Petersen / Hospitality Management 24 (2005) 219–242

Table 5
Level of agreement with "goals when starting this business"

Goals when starting this business	Bornholm: means[*] (N = 71−74)	Standard deviations	Canmore: means[*] (N = 92−97)	Standard deviations
1. To be my own boss.	3.99	1.39	4.20	1.16
2. To keep my family together.	2.99	1.69	3.18	1.73
3. To keep this property in the family.	2.29	1.63	2.12	1.49
4. To live in the right environment.	4.03	1.33	4.02	1.27
5. To support my/our leisure interests.	3.16[**]	1.57	3.73[**]	1.40
6. To enjoy a good lifestyle.	3.90	1.37	4.23	1.05
7. To make lots of money.	2.76[**]	1.32	3.18[**]	1.17
8. To gain prestige by operating a business.	2.06	1.39	2.19	1.21
9. To meet interesting people.	3.74	1.16	3.84	1.04
10. To provide a retirement income.	2.72[**]	1.59	3.40[**]	1.53
11. To provide me with a challenge.	4.36[**]	.99	3.75[**]	1.21
12. To permit me to become financially independent.	4.03	1.40	3.95	1.37
13. To supplement my income (from other sources).	2.10	1.47	Not asked	
14. To avoid unemployment.	2.63	1.73	N.A.	
15. To move to Bornholm.	2.83	1.77	N.A.	

[*]Means out of five; 1 = "not at all important" and 5 = "very important".
[**]Significant differences using 2-tailed T-tests; P<.05.

discover the underlying structure of motives and goals, factor analysis with Varimax rotation was conducted.

Table 5 displays mean scores (out of 5, with 1 being "not at all important" and 5 being "very important") and standard deviations pertaining to start-up goals. Note that three additional items were provided to the Bornholm sample. Overall, there was a high degree of congruence between these two samples on their start-up goals. In terms of means, the highest 6 were the same for each sample, although the ranking was different. Several were significantly different (T-test, Sig. <.05) as indicated in the table. "To make lots of money" appealed more to the Canadians, as did "to support my/our leisure interests", and "to provide a retirement income". The goal "to provide me with a challenge" was ranked significantly higher by the Danish owners. None of the three extra items for the Danish sample attracted high means, although "to move to Bornholm" was apparently a motivator for some of the respondents.

Results of the factor analysis are displayed in Table 6. For Bornholm, six factors were derived with a cumulative 72.2% of variance explained. Given the sample size

Table 6
Bornholm start-up goals: rotated factor matrix ($N = 66-74$; loadings of .70 or higher are significant)

Goal statements	F-1 life-style	F-2 chal-lenge	F-3 money matters	F-4 family first	F-5	F-6
To enjoy a good lifestyle.	.88376					
To live in the right environment.	.83252					
To support my/our leisure interests.	.77297					
To provide me with a challenge.		.77177				
To be my own boss.		.70503				
To move to Bornholm.		.67553			.38384	
To make lots of money.			.84841			
To gain prestige by operating a business.			.79378			.31960
To provide a retirement income.			.61859	.52600		
To keep this property in the family.				.83733		
To meet interesting people.		.49632		.60839		
To avoid unemployment.					.78860	
To supplement my income (from other sources).					.60068	-.57988
To keep my family together.				.54514	.55483	
To permit me to become financially independent.						.84555
Percent of variance explained	24.6%	12.2	10.1	9.3	8.2	7.8
Cumulative percentage	24.6%	36.9	47.0	56.2	64.4	72.2

(66–74 respondents for each goal), significant loadings are those of .70 or higher (Hair et al., 1998). Factor 1 (explaining 24.6% of variance) consists of three goals all clearly linked to "lifestyle" considerations, demonstrating the synergistic allure of an island location ("to live in the right environment", "to support my/our leisure interests", and "to enjoy a good lifestyle").

Factor 2 explains 12.25% of variance. It is called "challenge" and encompasses two goals: "to provide me with a challenge" and "to be my own boss". There is definitely a high degree of autonomy-orientation in this grouping. Factor 3 (10.1% of variance) has been called "money matters" based on the goal "to make lots of money". As well, "to gain prestige by operating a business" might be related to the goal of obtaining a higher income. "To provide a retirement income" conceptually links to the money motive. It is important to note that the means for these three items (see Table 5) are all low, likely indicating that money and prestige were a minor set of goals among the Danish owners. There is a possibility, however, that this reflects a cultural bias against overtly stating a profit orientation.

Table 7
Canmore start-up goals: rotated factor matrix ($N = 92–97$; loadings of .60 or higher are significant)

Goal statements	F-1: life-style	F-2: money matters	F-3: family first	F-4: prestige
To enjoy a good lifestyle.	.84976			
To support my/our leisure interests.	.77066			
To be my own boss.	.65299			
To make lots of money.		.82027		
To permit me to become financially independent.		.80559		
To provide a retirement income.		.58998	.45377	
To keep this property in the family.			.74376	
To live in the right environment.	.46626		.61631	−.37406
To keep my family together.			.61277	
To gain prestige by operating a business.		.44694		.70623
To meet interesting people.		−.30344		.66076
To provide me with a challenge.	.30743			.54982
Percent of variance explained	26.9%	13.8	11.4	10.9
Cumulative percentage	26.9%	40.7	52.1	63.0

Factor four (9.3%) is called "family first" and includes one statistically significant goal ("to keep this property in the family") and another that is closely linked: "to keep my family together". The goal "to meet interesting people" also loads here, but not significantly. Factor 5 (8.2%) has only one significant goal: "to avoid unemployment". Factor 6 (7.8%) contains only one significant goal: "to permit me to become financially independent".

Turning to the Canmore sample, a four-factor solution was derived (see Table 7), cumulatively explaining 63% of variance. The sample size (ranging from 92 to 97 on each goal) requires a minimum loading of .60 to be significant (Hair et al., 1998). As with the Danish sample; Factor 1 is labeled "lifestyle" (explaining 26.9% of variance). It contains two of the same goals (lifestyle and leisure) and another goal statement that achieved high means in both samples: "to be my own boss". "To live in the right environment" and "to provide me with a challenge" are also linked to this factor, and all five goals received high means.

Factor 2 (13.8%) is called "money matters" as it contains two significant loadings: "to make lots of money" and "to permit me to become financially independent". Making lots of money was significantly more important to the Canmore owners (means: 3.18 vs. 2.76) whereas financial independence was important in both samples (Bornholm 4.03; Canmore: 3.75). "To provide a retirement income" is loaded here, although not significantly. Given its fairly high mean in the Canmore sample (3.40 vs. 2.72 in Bornholm), it can be concluded that a substantial number had sought retirement in a resort setting.

D. Getz, T. Petersen / Hospitality Management 24 (2005) 219–242 233

Factor 3 (11.4%) has been called "family first" including three significant loadings: "to keep this property in the family" "to live in the right environment", and "to keep my family together". The goal pertaining to property was ranked low (mean: 2.12), whereas living in the right environment was more important (mean: 4.02). Factor 4 (11.4%) is called "prestige", but the two items loading significantly are a strange mix. "To gain prestige by operating a business" achieved a very low mean of 2.19 among the Canmore respondents, whereas "to meet interesting people" was a much higher 3.84. The "challenge" goal loads here as well, but not significantly.

4.1.1. Who are the lifestyle-oriented entrepreneurs?

Analysis confirms hypothesis 1, that lifestyle was the dominant motivational factor in both samples. Autonomy-related goals (especially the highly ranked "to be my own boss" and "to permit me to become financially independent") were also very important. In Canmore, financial independence correlated more closely with making lots of money whereas in Bornholm it stood alone. In some owners' mind-set, being one's own boss might be a lifestyle consideration (as in Canmore) and to others it is more linked to challenge (as in Bornholm). Although "money matters" emerged as a distinct factor in both samples, it was not very important to a majority of respondents.

Within each sample a search was undertaken for the business types and ownership characteristics most associated with lifestyle goals. The procedure began with creation of a new variable called "Lifestyle", consisting of the combined means of the three goals significantly loaded on this factor. Subsequently, the independent Means *T*-test was employed to detect any significant effects on the new variable.

In Bornholm it was determined that sole proprietors and owners of arts and crafts establishments were significantly more lifestyle oriented. Although gender was not a significantly different variable, it is noteworthy that more females than males were sole proprietors, and of the 19 arts and crafts owners, 11 were female. Among Canmore owners, lifestyle start-up goals were predominant among all types of owners and businesses. Hypothesis 2 is thereby partially confirmed, as lifestyle and autonomy-oriented owners were identifiable with ownership and business types in Bornholm.

4.1.2. Attitudes and future-oriented goals

Respondents were asked to indicate their level of agreement with 18 "statements about this business" (see Table 8), using a five-point Likert scale where 1 = "completely disagree" and 5 = "completely agree". The scales were identical in both samples. The items include attitudinal statements that are likely to shape strategy, explicit goals for the future, plus some factual statements about the nature of the business. For purposes of factor analysis, the five factual statements (i.e., 4, 5, 10, 11, 12 in Table 8) were deleted.

Almost everyone in both samples agreed strongly that "it is crucial to keep this business profitable" (means: 4.73 and 4.48) and "I believe in hands-on management" (means: 4.67; 4.43). Canmore respondents displayed a higher level of interest in starting new businesses (means: 1.79 in Bornholm vs. 2.84 in Canmore), but this cannot be viewed as anything more than neutral on the scale of five. Debt avoidance

Table 8
Level of agreement with "statements about this business"

Statements about this business	Bornholm Means*(N = 77−82)	Standard deviations	Canmore means* (N = 96−100)	Standard deviations
1. It is crucial to keep this business profitable.	4.73**	.64	4.48**	.86
2. I want to keep the business growing.	3.54**	1.24	4.10**	1.05
3. Enjoying the job is more important than making lots of money.	3.88	1.08	3.96	1.03
4. In this business customers cannot be separated from personal life.	2.91	1.50	2.95	1.30
5. This business currently meets my performance targets.	3.73	1.13	3.40	1.09
6. It should be run on purely business principles.	3.11	1.42	2.92	1.17
7. I would rather keep the business modest and under control than have it grow too big.	3.99	1.20	3.78	1.27
8. My personal/family interests take priority over running the business.	3.28**	1.26	3.70**	1.05
9. Eventually the business will be sold for the best possible price.	3.46	1.61	3.57	1.31
10. This business is highly seasonal.	4.23	1.32	4.23	1.15
11. I come into daily contact with my customers.	4.46	1.15	4.24	1.08
12. It is hard to separate work and family/personal life in a tourism business.	3.71	1.36	3.69	1.25
13. I enjoy taking risks.	3.81	1.16	3.46	1.24
14. After making this business a success I want to start another.	1.79**	1.21	2.84**	1.46
15. The business is a legacy for my children.	2.01	1.40	1.90	1.17
16. I am always trying something new.	3.53	1.31	3.55	1.17
17. I believe in hands-on management.	4.67**	.80	4.43**	.82
18. It is best to avoid debt as much as possible.	4.65**	.92	4.15**	1.09

*Means out of five; 1 = "not at all important" and 5 = "very important".
**Significant differences using 2-tailed T-tests; $P = <.05$.

D. Getz, T. Petersen / Hospitality Management 24 (2005) 219–242 235

was also highly valued in both samples (4.65 and 4.15). Based on means alone, the best item for differentiating growth-oriented entrepreneurs is the obvious one: "I want to keep the business growing". Canmore respondents were much more growth oriented (chi-square, Sig. .002) with a mean of 3.54 for Bornholm and 4.10 for Canmore.

Table 9 displays the results of factor analysis for Bornholm. The total variance explained by four factors is 55.9%. Given the number of respondents to each statement ($n = 77-82$), loading values of at least .65 are required for significant correlations (Hair et al., 1998). Factor one, "control" explained 19.5% of variance among Bornholm respondents. The three significantly loaded statements relate to control, hands-on management and debt avoidance. All three displayed high means, demonstrating that a majority were autonomy oriented.

Factor 2, "innovation" (l4.5%) includes two significant loadings: "I am always trying something new" and "I enjoy taking risks". The means for these statements were 3.53 and 3.81, much less than those for the "control" items. Given the overall lifestyle and autonomy orientation of the Bornholm sample, it is probable that most innovation occurs within the business, especially in arts and crafts, rather than in the form of new ventures and growth.

Factor 3, "profit" (12.4%) contains 2 significant statements: "eventually the business will be sold for the best possible price" (mean $= 3.46$) and "it is crucial to

Table 9
Bornholm attitudes and future-oriented goals: rotated factor matrix ($N = 73-82$; loadings of .65 or more are significant)

Goals	F-1: control	F-2: Innovation	F-3: profit	F-4: enjoyment
I believe in hands-on management.	.80653			
It is best to avoid debt as much as possible.	.79088			
I would rather keep the business modest and under control than have it grow too big.	.70602			
After making this business a success I want to start another.	−.44847	.40056		
I am always trying something new.		.86106		
I enjoy taking risks.		.78510		
The business is a legacy for my children.		.40762	−.31856	−.40470
Eventually the business will be sold for the best possible price.			.69576	.37440
It is crucial to keep this business profitable.			.68239	
It should be run on purely business principles.			.64402	
I want to keep the business growing.	−.34569		.34864	
Enjoying the job is more important than making lots of money.				.63255
My personal/family interests take priority over running the business.				.61969
Percent of variance explained	19.5%	14.5	12.4	9.4
Cumulative percentage	19.5%	34.0	46.5	55.9

keep this business profitable" (mean = 4.73). Almost everyone valued sustained profitability, but "I want to keep the business growing" and "it should be run on purely business principles" are also loaded on this factor, albeit not significantly. This grouping of goals can therefore be interpreted as defining the profit and growth-oriented entrepreneur, and they were definitely in the minority. The sixth factor for Bornholm is labeled "enjoyment" (9.4%), although neither of the two statements were significantly loaded.

Table 10 displays the results for Canmore, and this four-factor solution explains 55% of variance. With the number of respondents being 96–100, loading values of .60 or higher are considered to be significant. "Profit" is factor 1, explaining 20.8% of variance. Means for the three significant statements in this factor are high ("it is crucial to keep the business profitable", 4.48; "I want to keep the business growing", 4.10; "eventually the business will be sold for the best possible price", 3.57). This factor appears to define the growth and profit-oriented entrepreneur in Canmore in terms of attitudes and future goals.

Factor 2 for Canmore has been called "innovation" (12.7%) because of the two significant loadings ("I am always trying something new", mean = 3.55; and "I enjoy taking risks", mean = 3.46). Factor 3, "enjoyment" (11.1%), contains two significant

Table 10
Canmore attitudes and future-oriented goals: rotated factor matrix ($N = 97-100$); loadings of .60 or higher are significant)

Statements about this business	F-1: profit	F-2: innovation	F-3: enjoyment	F-4: debt avoidance
It is crucial to keep this business profitable.	.73717			
I want to keep the business growing.	.67195			−.37462
Eventually the business will be sold for the best possible price.	.61051			
I believe in hands-on management.	.50974		.32188	
I am always trying something new.		.84016		
I enjoy taking risks.		.80035	−.38376	
The business is a legacy for my children.		.45138		
Enjoying the job is more important than making lots of money.			.69843	
My personal/family interests take priority over running the business.			.64387	
I would rather keep the business modest and under control than have it grow too big.			.54539	.40465
It is best to avoid debt as much as possible.				.75112
After making this business a success I want to start another.				−.66799
It should be run on purely business principles.				.49837
Percentage of variance explained	20.8%	12.7	11.1	10.2
Cumulative percentage	20.8%	33.6	44.7	54.9

D. Getz, T. Petersen / Hospitality Management 24 (2005) 219–242   237

loadings: "enjoying the job is more important than making lots of money" (mean = 3.96), and "my personal/family interests take priority over running the business" (mean = 3.70). Factor 4 contains one significant loading and has been called "debt avoidance" (10.2%). The mean for this item in the Canmore sample was a high 4.15, but significantly lower than in the Bornholm sample.

4.1.3. Who are the growth and profit-oriented entrepreneurs?

In both samples the "profit" factor encompasses the growth-oriented goal. The orientation towards profit and growth is much stronger in Canmore, however. To identify characteristics of the growth-oriented owner and business, the starting point was to create a new variable, called "Profit", derived from the means of the items that formed the "profit" factors (in Canmore these are statements 1, 2, and 9, whereas in Bornholm they are statements 1, 6 and 9). Next, the Independent Means *T*-test was employed to detect any significant effects on the new variable. Results are summarized in Table 11.

For both Bornholm and Canmore, owners who purchased their business were significantly correlated with the "Profit" factor. Purchasers were apparently more inclined to seek out the right opportunity, whereas lifestyle and autonomy-oriented entrepreneurs were more likely to start up a small business. In Canmore, the one type of business significantly correlated with the profit factor was "restaurant and café", whereas bed and breakfast owners were definitely associated with lifestyle and autonomy. In Bornholm, accommodation enterprises were correlated with the profit factor, while arts and crafts owners were definitely lifestyle and autonomy-oriented. In Bornholm, copreneurial owners were more profit and growth oriented than sole proprietors without family involvement in their businesses. In Canmore, owners with children working in their business were significantly correlated with profit and growth.

Previous ownership of a business was not correlated with profit and growth orientation in either sample. The gender of respondents did not matter in Bornholm,

Table 11
Who are the profit and growth-oriented owners?

Variable	Bornholm	Canmore
Started or purchased the business	Purchased	Purchased
Type of business	Accommodation owners (NOT arts and crafts owners)	Restaurant or café owners (NOT bed and breakfast owners)
Ownership	(NOT sole proprietors)	No significant difference
Family involvement	Copreneurs (married couples)	Children work in the business
Gender	No significant difference	Male owners
Age	No significant difference (comparing means for those aged 45+ with younger)	No significant difference (comparing means for those aged 45+ with younger)
Previous Business Ownership	No significant difference	No significant difference

(Significant correlations between the means of goals in the "profit" factor and selected variables using independent means *T*-tests; $P = <.05$).

238   *D. Getz, T. Petersen / Hospitality Management 24 (2005) 219–242*

but in Canmore males were associated with profit and growth. Female respondents in Canmore were mostly in the B and B business, retailing and tour services, while males were more prominent in hotels and restaurants.

Hypothesis 3 is confirmed, as growth and profit-oriented entrepreneurs were clearly differentiated from lifestyle and autonomy-oriented owners in terms of attitudes and future-oriented goals. As well, it was demonstrated that growth and profit-oriented entrepreneurs were more likely to be purchasers and accommodation and restaurant owners, thereby confirming hypothesis 4. However, different cultures and industry composition in these two resort settings resulted in variations. Three variables in particular require further exanimation in this context: gender, copreneurial ownership, and the involvement of children in the business.

5. Discussion and conclusions

5.1. Theoretical implications

General confirmation of the hypotheses lends strength to the underlying propositions: that lifestyle and autonomy goals predominate in the industry, and these owners are attracted to specific business types; that profit and growth-oriented entrepreneurs can be clearly differentiated in terms of goals and attitudes, and that they are also attracted to specific business types. In both cases lifestyle and autonomy goals underlay entrepreneurship, but only for a minority is it also desirable to grow their business.

Having based the hypotheses on previous research findings, and tested them in two resort environments in two countries, some degree of confidence can be expressed in the theoretical generalizability of the propositions. However, conducting similar research a wider range of resort and tourism settings is likely to reveal differences. For example, these two cases in Denmark and Canada suggest that life-cycle stage and seasonality might have an impact on entrepreneurial opportunities and behavior, with the newer, all-season resort of Canmore attracting higher levels of profit orientation. Gender was significant in Canmore in profiling profit and growth-oriented entrepreneurs (they were mostly males), but the data from Bornholm merely suggested that females were more lifestyle oriented. Cultural differences might also be more profound when testing the propositions in different settings.

"Lifestyle and autonomy-oriented" entrepreneurs (i.e., those who rated these goals highest and also did not pursue growth) were easily identified, as they were the majority. Many of them fit the classic "craftsman" label (Smith, 1967), especially the arts and crafts producers/retailers of Bornholm and the bed and breakfast owners in Canmore. In these businesses there were many more females than males. While bed and breakfast businesses in Canmore created no jobs for non-owners, and none for children, a few arts and craft firms in Bornholm did achieve growth. Accordingly, it is generally not possible to predict growth by reference only to the type of business.

"Autonomy", being the desire for self-employment and control, accompanied both the lifestyle and profit/growth oriented entrepreneurs. Almost all respondents

D. Getz, T. Petersen / Hospitality Management 24 (2005) 219–242 239

wanted business profitability and preferred hands-on management, so these were not good differentiating factors.

The "growth entrepreneurs" identified by Katz (1995) exist as a minority among owners of family businesses in the tourism and hospitality industry. In the Danish and Canadian samples they exhibited significantly different goals and attitudes from lifestyle and autonomy-oriented owners, including the explicit goal to keep growing their business. Many of these growth-oriented entrepreneurs were purchasers, and they tended to acquire certain types of businesses (i.e., accommodations and restaurants) which undoubtedly were perceived to present better opportunities for profit and growth. Bed and breakfast owners (found only in Canmore) and arts/craft producers and retailers (found only in Bornholm) were definitely not growth oriented as a group, yet a few exceptions were revealed.

In Canmore it was also found that owners with children working in the business were more growth oriented, while in Bornholm it was discovered that copreneurial owners (couples owning and operating the business together) were more growth oriented than sole proprietors. In both samples those involving children or other family members (besides the spouse) were a small minority. Some of them were definitely profit and growth oriented and had created jobs for others. Many micro and small businesses in tourism and hospitality do not have the potential for involvement of children, nor of being inherited. It seems probable that only the larger ones, in particular hotels, restaurants, attractions and tour services, can involve children.

What has not been determined in this research is whether the growth-oriented entrepreneur seeks out larger businesses in order to involve children, or if involvement comes later. Earlier family business researchers found that family owned firms tend to be smaller, and that professionally managed businesses tend to be more aggressively growth-oriented (Daily and Dollinger, 1992). Providing opportunities for children was not revealed to be a motivating factor for very many enterprise founders (Ambrose, 1983). Ambrose also determined that long-established businesses have a greater chance of being inherited, and that to encourage succession children have to become involved in the business as early as possible, in responsible positions. The limited evidence therefore gives rise to a new hypothesis: that profit and growth-oriented entrepreneurs are not primarily motivated by considerations of possible future inheritance, but that growth facilitates getting children involved and thereby increases the likelihood of eventual inheritance.

5.1.1. Research needs

Testing the new hypotheses, as stated above, is one important research need. If it can be demonstrated that the involvement of children is pre-determined not by the founders' family oriented goals but by their growth orientation and ability to grow the business, it forces some re-consideration of basic family business theory. It has generally been assumed that families set up businesses, or perpetuate them, for the sake of children.

Also revealed in this research were differences between males and females that should be explored in greater depth, both in terms of their goals (more males were observed to be profit and growth-oriented) and the types of businesses they operated (more females in arts, crafts, and micro-sized accommodations). It is quite possible that cultural factors rather than motives and abilities shape some of these important gender differences, given the evidence provided in the family business and tourism literature on gender (e.g., Dumas, 1992; Kinnaird and Hall, 1994; Apostolopoulos et al., 2001). There are undoubtedly biases acting against female entrepreneurs, but what combination of incentives and assistance can overcome the barriers?

5.2. Policy and management implications

The prevailing economic development climate in many countries leads to the strategy of cultivating an entrepreneurial environment, and that requires the channeling of resources toward those who can and want to create jobs. A focus on growth-oriented entrepreneurs will also pay off for policy makers and planners interested in maximizing tourism competitiveness, as the profit and growth-oriented owner might be more likely to innovate with products and marketing initiatives rather than value-adding within a given business type and size.

This is not to conclude that expansionist goals are always appropriate, or should be pursued on their own, especially in rural and remote tourism destinations where growth in the number and improvement in the quality of micro and small businesses might be more feasible and appropriate. Nevertheless, indiscriminate support for small and family businesses in this industry is unwarranted when job-creation is the goal. As well, directing assistance to purchase businesses might be more useful for employment generation than assistance to new ventures, as many growth-oriented entrepreneurs seek out opportunities to grow an established firm. Cultivating the purely autonomy and lifestyle-oriented owner will not produce many jobs, nor necessarily lead to industry competitiveness and community stability.

Research should be conducted on "constrained entrepreneurship" in tourism and hospitality, looking at the influences of culture, gender, sole versus copreneurial ownership, and economic conditions including development policies and the resort life cycle. It might be the case that many more investors and business founders in this industry can be induced or assisted in growing their business, but the exact barriers at work and the best ways of facilitating this process are not understood. For example, will children brought into a family business be more or less entrepreneurial than parents, and if they are entrepreneurial will they want to take over the existing business as opposed to going their own ways? And given that female owners face different obstacles, will they respond better to different forms of assistance or incentive?

For the family business owner there are several management implications linked to policy. To acquire resources and other support from tourism and economic development agencies, growth-oriented entrepreneurs should focus on their potential to improve competitiveness and create employment. There might be value for them in lobbying to secure assistance for business acquisitions, not just start-ups, and in establishment of both informal networks and formal alliances among owners with similar goals.

D. Getz, T. Petersen / Hospitality Management 24 (2005) 219–242 241

Specific to family business growth and profitability, the research demonstrates that there is an entrepreneurial mindset associated with this orientation, distinct from lifestyle and autonomy-seekers. Owners should examine their own and their family's motives and goals carefully as the starting point for business strategy.

Acknowledgements

The authors are grateful for support from the Family Business Research Endowment, University of Calgary, and from the Regional and Tourism Research Centre of Bornholm.

References

Ambrose, D., 1983. Transfer of the family-owned business. Journal of Small Business Management 21 (1), 49–56.

Apostolopoulos, Y., Sonmez, S., Timothy (Eds.), 2001, Women as Producers and Consumers of Tourism in Developing Regions. Westport Connecticut, Praeger.

Brockhaus, R., 1994. Entrepreneurship and family business: comparisons, critique, and lessons. Entrepreneurship Theory and Practice Fall, 25–38.

Buhalis, D., Cooper, C., 1998. Competition or cooperation? Small and medium sized tourism enterprises at the destination. In: Laws, F., Faulkner, B., Moscardo, G. (Eds.), Embracing and Managing Change in Tourism. Routledge, London, pp. 324–346.

Carland, J., Hoy, W., Boulton, F., Carland, J.C., 1984. Differentiating entrepreneurs from small business owners: a conceptualisation. Academy Of Management Review 9 (2), 354–359.

Daily, C., Dollinger, M., 1992. An empirical examination of ownership structure in family and professionally managed firms. Family Business Review 5 (2), 117–136.

Dewhurst, P., Horobin, H., 1998. Small business owners. In: Thomas, R. (Ed.), The Management of Small Tourism and Hospitality Firms. Cassell, London, pp. 19–38.

Dumas, C., 1992. Integrating the daughter into family business management. Entrepreneurship Theory and Practice 16 (4), 41–55.

Gartner, W., 1988. "Who is the entrepreneur?" is the wrong question. American Journal of Small Business 12, 11–32.

Gartner, W., 1990. What are we talking about when we talk about entrepreneurship? Journal of Business Venturing 5 (1), 15–28.

Getz, D., Carlsen, J., 2000. Characteristics and goals of family and owner-operated businesses in the rural tourism and hospitality sectors. Tourism Management 21, 547–560.

Gomm, R., Hammersley, M., Foster, P., 2000. Case study and generalization. In: Gomm, R., Hammersley, M., Foster, P. (Eds.), Case Study Method: Key Issues Key Texts. Sage, London, pp. 99–115.

Gyimothy, S., 2000. The quality of visitor experience. a case study in peripheral areas of Europe. Research Centre of Bornholm, Report 17/2000.

Harrison, R., Leitch, C., 1996. Whatever you hit call the target An alternative approach to small business policy. In: Danson, M. (Ed.), Small Firm Formation and Regional Economic Development. Routledge, London.

Hair, J., Anderson, R., Tatham, R., Black, W., 1998. Multivariate Data Analysis, 5th ed. Prentice-Hall, Upper Saddle River NJ.

Hoy, F., Verser, T., 1994. Emerging business, emerging field: entrepreneurship and the family firm. Entrepreneurship Theory and Practice 19 (1), 9–23.

242   *D. Getz, T. Petersen / Hospitality Management 24 (2005) 219–242*

Katz, J., 1994. Modelling entrepreneurial career progressions; concepts and considerations. Entrepreneurship Theory and Practice 19 (2), 23–29.

Katz, J., 1995. Which track are you on? Inc. 17, 27–28.

Kinnaird, V., Hall, D. (Eds.), 1994, Tourism A Gender Analysis. Wiley, Chichester.

Klenell, P., Steen, M., 1999. I am in charge—small business problems and insolvency in Jamtland (translated from Swedish). Cited in Public Support for Tourism SMEs in Peripheral Areas: The Arjeplog Project, Northern Sweden, P. Nilsson, T. Petersen, and S. Wanhill (n.d.). Centre for Regional and Tourism Research of Bornholm, Denmark.

Leat, P., Williams, F., Brannigan, J., 2000. Rural competitiveness through quality and imagery across lagging regions of the European Union. In: Proceedings of the Conference on European Rural Policy at the Crossroads. The Arkleton Centre, University of Aberdeen.

Middleton, V., 2001. The importance of micro-businesses in European tourism. In: Roberts, L., Hall, D. (Eds.), Rural Tourism and Recreation: Principles to Practice. CABI, Wallingford, Oxon, pp. 197–201.

Morrison, A., Rimmington, M., Williams, C., 1999. Entrepreneurship in the Hospitality Tourism and Leisure Industries. Butterworth Heinemann, Oxford.

Risker, D., 1998. Toward an innovation typology of entrepreneurs. Journal of Small Business and Entrepreneurship 15 (2), 27–41.

Roberts, L., Hall, D., 2001. Rural Tourism and Recreation: Principles to Practice. CABI, Wallingford, Oxon.

Russell, B., 1996. Innovation in small Irish tourism businesses. In: Thomas, R., Shacklock, R. (Eds.), Spring Symposium Proceedings of International Association of Hotel Management Schools. Leeds Metropolitan University, pp. 116–120.

Sexton, D., Kent, C., 1981. Female executives versus female entrepreneurs. In: Vesper, K. (Ed.), Frontiers of Entrepreneurship Research: The Proceedings of the 1981 Babson, Conference on Entrepreneurship. Babson College, Wellesley MA, pp. 40–45.

Shaw, G., Williams, A., 1990. Economic development, and the role of entrepreneurial activity. In: Cooper, C. (Ed.), Progress in Tourism, Recreation and Hospitality Management, vol. 2. Belhaven Press, London, pp. 67–81.

Shaw, G., Williams, A., 1998. Entrepreneurship, small business, culture and tourism development. In: Ioannides, D., Debbage, K. (Eds.), The Economic Geography of the Tourist Industry: A Supply Side Analysis. Routledge, London, pp. 235–255.

Smith, R., 1967. The Entrepreneur and the Firm. Bureau of Business and Economic Research, MSU, East Lansing, MI.

Stake, R., 2000. The case study method in social inquiry. In: Gomm, R., Hammersley, M., Foster, P. (Eds.), Case Study Method: Key Issues and Key Texts. Sage, London, pp. 20–26.

Thomas, R., Friel, M., Jameson, S., 1999. Small business management. In: Thomas, R. (Ed.), The management of Small Tourism and Hospitality Firms. Cassell, London.

Thomas, R. (Ed.), 1999, The Management of Small Tourism and Hospitality Firms. Cassell, London.

Twining-Ward, L., Baum, T., 1998. Dilemmas facing mature island destinations: cases from the Baltic. Progress in Tourism and Hospitality Research 4, 131–140.

Ucbasaran, D., Westhead, P., Wright, M., 2001. The focus of entrepreneurial research: contextual and process issues. Entrepreneurship Theory and Practice, Summer, 57–80.

Vesper, K., 1980. New Venture Strategies. Prentice-Hall, Englewood Cliffs, NJ.

Westhead, P., Cowling, M., 1998. Family firm research: The need for a methodolological rethink. Entrepreneurship Theory and Practice, Fall, 31–56.

Donald Getz is a Professor in the Haskayne School of Business at the University of Calgary, Canada. He has special interests in tourism planning, event management, wine tourism, small family businesses and entrepreneurship.

Tage Petersen is a researcher at the Centre for Regional and tourism Research on the island of Bornholm, Denmark. He is a doctoral candidate at the University of Roskilde, Denmark, and his dissertation concerns entrepreneurship in tourism.

[4]

Available online at www.sciencedirect.com

SCIENCE @ DIRECT®

Tourism Management 26 (2005) 409–420

ELSEVIER

TOURISM
MANAGEMENT

www.elsevier.com/locate/tourman

An agency theory perspective on the owner/manager relationship in tourism-based condominiums

Chris Guilding[a,*], Jan Warnken[b], Allan Ardill[c], Liz Fredline[d]

[a] Service Industry Research Centre and School of Accounting & Finance, Griffith University—Gold Coast Campus, Queensland, Australia
[b] School of Environmental & Applied Sciences, Griffith University—Gold Coast Campus, Queensland, Australia
[c] School of Law, Griffith University—Gold Coast Campus, Queensland, Australia
[d] Service Industry Research Centre and School of Tourism & Hospitality Management, Griffith University—Gold Coast Campus, Queensland, Australia

Received 19 May 2003; accepted 4 November 2003

Abstract

This paper draws on field study data to provide an examination of the condominium owner/manager relationship in the Australian tourism context. Although there has been considerable growth in tourism accommodation owned through strata-title, no research examining the somewhat idiosyncratic relationship between unit owners and resident managers has been found in the literature. The peculiar nature of the relationship underlines its significance as a context in which to apply the agency theoretical model. As Australian condominium resident unit managers provide letting and caretaker services for condominium unit owners, it appears that the relationship can be justifiably viewed as a principal-agent exchange (Mills, P.K., J. Business Res. 20 (1990) 31).

The study specifically focuses on strata title condominiums located in major tourism regions. This sub-sector of the condominium management industry was chosen for study because it exhibits several key attributes distinguishing it from the non-tourist-based condominium sector. For example, two different parties represent the principal (resident owners and investor owners), also a significant proportion of a resident manager's work relates to the management of short-term holiday unit letting. In light of the particular agency relationship dynamics arising in large tourist-based condominium governance, several suggestions concerning the legal environment of the industry are provided.
© 2004 Elsevier Ltd. All rights reserved.

Keywords: Tourism; Condominium; Agency theory

1. Introduction

This study is concerned with the governance of condominium complexes (sometimes referred to as "strata-titled" complexes). In Australia and New Zealand, the typical condominium complex comprises multiple dwelling units in a shared community title scheme whereby there are as many private owners of units as there are lots within a scheme. These complexes can assume a variety of physical forms. They can be designed as detached villas, duplexes or townhouses; as low rise (typically 2–3 storeys) apartment complexes comprising usually around 6–12 units;[1] or as high-rise apartment complexes generally comprising eight or more storeys and comprising many units (can be up to 500 or more units).

In Australia, there are 35,000 holiday apartments in condominium complexes with more than 15 apartments in the holiday letting pool (Australian Bureau of Statistics, 2002). If we impute an average value of AUS $250,000 per unit, this represents an overall investment of AUS $8.75 billion in the tourism accommodation sector. Due to Australian income tax provisions that provide a tax deduction for expenditure related to investment properties, most units are owned by individuals. In the 2001/2002 financial year, this investment generated AUS $932 million in rental income (i.e., about one-fifth of total accommodation sector earnings).

The majority of financial institutions that finance condominium complex developments require 25–50% of the apartments to be sold off the plan (i.e. prior to building commencement), before releasing the capital

*Corresponding author. School of Accounting and Finance, Griffith University—Gold Coast Campus, PMB 50 Gold Coast Mail Centre, Queensland 9726, Australia. Tel.: +61-7-5594-8790; fax: +61-7-5594-8068.

E-mail address: c.guilding@griffith.edu.au (C. Guilding).

[1] Some of these low-storey complexes can comprise as many as 100 units, however.

0261-5177/$ - see front matter © 2004 Elsevier Ltd. All rights reserved.
doi:10.1016/j.tourman.2003.11.021

required to complete the major building works. Without investor owners who plan to use their apartments for holiday lettings, the number of potential buyers would be substantially lower and initial 'off the plan' sales would take much longer to reach the required quota. Furthermore, holiday apartments are often purchased as a means to diversify investment portfolios for retirement funds. Appropriate governance of condominium complexes is therefore not only a tourism management issue, it also carries more general socio-economic implications.

The last quarter of a century has seen major growth in the provision of tourist accommodation in condominium complexes. While one tends to think first of hotels when conceiving of tourist accommodation, this is becoming an out-dated notion as condominiums now represent the primary form of accommodation in many tourist resorts such as Australia's Gold Coast (Warnken, 2002; Warnken, Russell, & Faulkner, 2003). In light of this condominium tourist accommodation growth, relative to the volume of research conducted into hotel management, there is a startling paucity of research concerned with condominium management. The study reported herein was conducted in light of this apparent gap in the literature.

The study draws on the agency theory framework to provide insights into the idiosyncratic nature of condominium governance and also the conflicts that can arise between a condominium complex's unit owners and its resident manager. This appraisal is conducted in the context of condominiums located in tourist regions. In tourist region condominiums there are two main types of unit owner: resident owners and investor owners that sub-let their units to short-term stay holiday-makers. Tourist region condominiums also carry the additional dynamic of a broadened resident manager responsibility due to the provision of a short-term letting management service.

The validity of drawing on the agency theory framework in connection with condominium operations becomes evident when comparing the nature of a hotel's operational and logistical operations with those of a tourist-based condominium. Data for this study has been collected from parties involved with large condominiums located, in the main, close to Australia's Gold Coast. This area represents an archetypal tourist centre with a high density of high-rise buildings located adjacent to a commercially developed beach-front. For some time it has been widely acknowledged to represent Australia's premier tourist destination (Russell & Faulkner, 1999). Condominiums in tourist regions can be compared to hotels due to the provision of a reservation management and room cleaning service. From an operational perspective, the primary difference between a tourist-based condominium and a hotel is the fact that condominiums generally provide no or minimal food and beverage services other than self-catering

facilities.[2] A hotel represents a commercial setting where the conventional owner/manager relationship that has been the primary subject of agency research can be readily applied. Similarly, the conventional workings of a condominium complex signifies an agency relationship where the wealth-seeking objectives of unit owners have to be reconciled with the wealth-seeking objectives of a resident manager. As will be noted below, however, the governance arrangement typically implemented in Australian condominiums departs radically from the generally applied owner/manager governance structure evident in most Western commercial organisations.

The remainder of the paper is organised as follows. The next section overviews the agency theory model and the nature of research conducted within the agency theory tradition. Following this, the particular nature of agency relationships apparent in the context of condominium management are outlined. The qualitative data collection research methods applied and also findings made in connection with the specific issues arising in this relationship are then presented. The paper concludes with a summary of the main findings, a discussion of the practical implications arising from the study and an outline of some research initiatives that can build on the study reported herein.

2. Agency theory

Agency theory concerns exchanges where one party, the principal (typically represented by the owner(s) of a business), delegates work to a second party, the agent (typically represented by a manager or some other employee of the business owned by the principal). It attempts to draw out contractual problems that can arise as a result of agents acting opportunistically when their interests depart from those of the principal (Berle & Means, 1967; Jensen & Meckling, 1976). These problems are exacerbated where information asymmetry favouring the agent exists.[3]

Agency theory has been a popular conceptual framework for researchers interested in conflicts of interest, incentive problems and also mechanisms for managing incentive problems (Eisenhardt, 1989; Mills, 1990;

---

[2] A particular aspect of the provision of a short-term stay condominium unit may in fact give rise to more complex labour management implications than is the case for hotel guest management. As condominiums provide self-catering facilities, it is to be expected that in many cases the time taken to clean a unit following a guest's departure will be greater than the time taken to clean a hotel room following a hotel guests departure. The provision of self-catering facilities also carries implications for maintenance and control of self-catering infrastructure.

[3] Information asymmetry arises when one party has access to information that the second party cannot access.

C. Guilding et al. / Tourism Management 26 (2005) 409–420 411

Bohren, 1998; Lambert, 2001).[4] Identification of an organisational setting where there is a potential for conflicting interests between one or more parties is a fundamental precept of agency theory modelling. Lambert (2001) notes four typical reasons for agent–principal conflict arising. These are: (i) there is a potential for effort aversion by the agent (e.g., a manager may well experience a desire to not apply an optimal effort when completing his/her work), (ii) the agent can use his work situation as an opportunity to divert resources towards his own personal benefit, (iii) there can be differential time horizons i.e., while an owner may see their involvement in the agency relationship in the context of 10 or more years, the agent might have little concern with the long-term implications of his actions as he does not expect to be in the relationship over the long-term, (iv) there may be different attitudes to risk held by the principal and the agent.

Two streams of research drawing on agency theory can be identified. Jensen (1983) refers to these as the positivist and the principal–agent streams. Research conducted within the positivist tradition has tended to identify and describe principal–agent relationships where conflicting interests are evident and to comment on governance mechanisms implemented to police the self-interested agent. Eisenhardt (1989) sees several key studies falling within this research tradition. These include Jensen and Meckling's (1976) work concerned with corporate ownership structures, Fama and Jensen's (1983) focus on the board of directors' role and senior executive opportunism, and studies concerned with somewhat controversial practices such as golden parachutes and corporate raiding (e.g., Jensen, 1984; Jensen & Roeback, 1983). Principal–agent researchers are more concerned with the development of a general agency model. Studies characteristic of this second research tradition tend to be based on theoretical deduction and mathematical proof. As this study concerns the application of agency theory to a particular organisational context, it relates most closely to the positivist agency research tradition.[5]

Agency theorists refer to two costs that a principal can incurr when attempting to manage an agent who has the benefit of asymmetric information: (1) costs of monitoring and (2) costs of metering (Williamson, 1985; Sharma, 1997). Monitoring costs are incurred when the principal attempts to monitor an agent's behaviour. If an agent is observed to be acting in ways that conflict with the spirit of the relationship (ways that are

detrimental to the interests of the principal), the principal can impose sanctions on the agent. If it is costly to monitor the agent's actions, a principal may choose to focus on metering the outcomes of the agent's actions. For example, a widely-used outcome based contract is evident when workers are reimbursed on a piece-rate basis. A key distinction between the behaviour monitoring approach and the outcome metering approach is that the latter results in risk being transferred from principals to agents. When outputs are measured, the agent is exposed to the risk of uncontrollable factors (e.g., random machine breakdown, faulty raw materials, changing competitive environment), affecting the appraised performance. It is a fundamental tenet of agency theory that the costs of monitoring and metering incurred by the principal should not outweigh the principal's derived benefit from appraising the agent's performance. Despite actions that a principal can take to influence the performance of an agent, research has shown the degree to which principals can be at the mercy of agents (Bazerman, Neale, Valley, Zajac, & Kim, 1992; Kesner, Shapiro, & Sharma, 1994).

The agency model has been applied in a range of transactional settings concerned with a variety of issues (e.g., vertical integration (Walker & Weber, 1984), executive compensation (Baker, Jensen, & Murphy, 1988), tender offers (Cotter & Zenner, 1994)). It has also been used in a variety of disciplinary contexts (e.g., accounting (Demski & Feltham, 1978), marketing (Basu, Lal, Srinivasan, & Staelin, 1985; Bergen, Dutta, & Walker Jr, 1992) and organisational behaviour (Eisenhardt, 1988)). As the relationships that researchers have appraised from an agency perspective are broad, following the lead of Sharma (1997), the particular agency issues of interest in this study will be appraised in the context of the owner–manager agency relationship which has dominated agency research (Eisenhardt, 1989; Walsh & Seward, 1990).

3. The ownership/management structure of queensland condominiums

Agency theory would appear to represent a particularly pertinent framework to draw upon when considering incentive issues arising in the context of condominium management. Eisenhardt notes:

> (T)he domain of agency theory is relationships that mirror the basic agency structure of a principal and an agent who are engaged in co-operative behavior, but have differing goals and attitudes toward risk (1989, p. 59).

It would certainly appear that the nature of the condominium owner/manager relationship is one exemplifying two parties engaged in a scenario representing

---

[4] See Kakabadse and Kakabadse (2001); La Porta, Lopez-de-Silanes. and Shleifer (1999); Letza and Smallman (2001); Stoney and Winstanley (2001) and Zingales (2000) for some recent critiques of this literature.

[5] Unlike most studies in this research tradition, however, this study does not focus on the shareholder/manager relationship in a corporation.

412   *C. Guilding et al. / Tourism Management 26 (2005) 409–420*

a highly co-operative venture. In addition to the factors normally present in the archetypal principal/agent relationship of the corporate world, two further factors highlighting a heightened need for co-operation are present in the condominium unit-owner/manager relationship. Firstly, with respect to condominium resident owners, the additional dynamic of proximity of domicile between the principal and agent is also evident. This is because in Australia, the manager usually owns and resides in the designated resident manager unit within the condominium complex. This signifies that the condominium owner/manager relationship moves well beyond the confines of a working relationship restricted to normal business hours. Secondly, the financial implications at stake for both the principal and agent would appear to be heightened in most condominium owner–manager relationships. In the vast majority of corporate owner/manager relationships most owners have a relatively small proportion of personal wealth at stake in any particular corporate enterprise due to the common investment strategy of investment portfolio diversification. Also, most employees make no financial investment in their job (although loss of job may well carry fundamentally significant financial implications for many employees). Compare this with the owner/manager situation in a condominium complex. Purchase of a condominium unit represents a significant investment that in many cases will constitute the bulk of an individual's personal wealth, particularly where the investor intends to occupy the purchased apartment. Also, in Australia, condominium managers buy the rights to manage a building as well as title to the resident manager's unit. This model was developed in an attempt to increase the resident manager's general interest in the building thereby improving his/her overall motivation to act effectively as caretaker. Some recent sales of condominium resident manager rights in large Australian complexes have commanded prices in excess of a million dollars. As a result, it is evident that the financial stakes of the two parties involved in a condominium owner/manager relationship are considerably greater than is the case in the context of the conventional corporate owner/manager relationship.

The nature of the unit-owner/resident manager relationship is depicted in Fig. 1. Mediating the relationship between owners and the resident manager is a body corporate committee that is elected by the unit owners. The role of the body corporate committee parallels the role of a board of directors in a corporation as it serves the interest of the principal (i.e., the owners) in managing the agents (i.e., managers in a corporation and the resident manager in a condominium). Fig. 1 highlights the two distinct unit owner categories mentioned earlier: resident owners and investor owners. This distinction between unit owner types is significant,

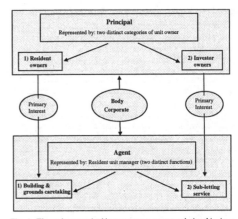

Fig. 1. The unit owner/resident manager agency relationship in a tourist-based condominium.

and its practical implications will be elaborated upon in the paper's "findings" section.

One distinguishing facet of the interest of resident owners and investor owners is evident from Fig. 1. An investor owner can be expected to be primarily interested in the resident manager's sub-letting performance. A resident owner, however, gains no financial advantage from the success of the resident manager's sub-letting performance. Many resident owners might actually desire that the condominium complex has a low occupancy level and therefore derive satisfaction from a resident manager proving to be ineffective with respect to sub-letting activities. The resident owner can be expected to be more narrowly interested in the resident manager's performance with respect to efficiently and effectively completing his caretaking responsibilities (i.e., maintenance and cleaning of the condominium building and grounds).

The body corporate committee's activities include overseeing a resident unit manager's performance, setting and administering an operational budget and setting and raising levies for a sinking fund established for the purpose of periodic major building maintenance expenditure.

As already noted, in most parts of Australia the resident unit manager buys the rights to manage the building. Management right holders in a tourism complex usually derive most of their return in the form of sub-letting commissions for renting units assigned to the holiday letting pool. In theory, sub-letting rights can be withdrawn by individual investor owners at any time and transferred to an outside real estate agent at short notice. Further, should the resident unit manager's performance with respect to his building caretaking performance be deemed unsatisfactory, a simple voting

C. Guilding et al. / Tourism Management 26 (2005) 409–420 413

majority of unit owners can elect to terminate his building service contract.

4. Research method

The empirical data collection method employed comprised two distinct phases. Initially, the research team hosted a panel discussion of parties interested in condominium ownership and management. The purpose of this initial data collection phase was to strengthen the research team's appreciation of ownership, governance and operational management issues arising in large condominium complexes located in tourist regions. The discussion took place in the context of a two and a half hour working lunch hosted in a Gold Coast hotel seminar room. Panel discussants were informed of the research team's interest in condominium development and management in tourist regions. To provide greatest scope for the invited panelists to influence the research team's agenda, the meeting was conducted in a relatively unstructured manner with all participants being encouraged to raise issues they felt pertinent to an academic inquiry of the industry. The panel comprised the following interested parties:

- A representative of the Queensland Resident Accommodation Managers Association.
- A representative of the Body Corporate Managers Institute of Queensland.
- Real estate agents with a specialism in the sale of condominium strata title units.
- A representative of the hotel/tourism accommodation management industry.

The second stage of empirical data collection involved a slightly more focussed interview approach. Two group interview sessions were held with three representatives of the Queensland Unit Owners Association. In addition, two interviews were held with a freelance consultant who provides specialist advice in connection with condominium management and ownership (this individual has more than 20 years of experience in the industry). All these interviews were audio-taped and ran in total for more than 10 h. This research approach was taken as some of the issues addressed appeared relatively sensitive. In the course of conducting the interviews, considerable rapport developed between members of the research team and the interviewees. It is believed this rapport has facilitated greater appreciation of some of the key issues confronting the industry as the interviewees became noticeably more candid as the interviews progressed. Despite this, on a couple of occasions the interviewees requested that the tape recorder be turned off for portions of the meetings. It should also be noted that the research team's apprecia-

tion of key issues in the condominium unit owner/manager agency relationship has been further informed by numerous casual conversations conducted with past and present condominium unit owners and other parties involved in condominiums (e.g., property developers and sub-contractors providing condominium maintenance services).[6]

5. Results and discussion

In this section, observations pertinent to providing insights into the particular nature of the condominium unit owner/resident manager relationship are presented. Initially, the ways in which the condominium unit owner/resident manager relationship departs from the archetypal corporate owner/manager agency relationship are described. Following this, Lambert's (2001) four-point classification of typical factors accounting for principal/agent conflict is drawn upon to provide a framework facilitating further appreciation of the problematical nature of the condominium unit owner/manager relationship. Following the lead provided by several interviewees, when talking of "Resident Unit Managers" the acronym "RUM" will be used.

5.1. The idiosyncratic nature of the condominium unit owner/resident manager agency relationship

In conventional agency theory modelling the principal/agent relationship is conceived in terms of two parties where each party comprises a set of relatively homogeneous agents with uniform self-maximising interests. As already discussed and highlighted in Fig. 1, this does not appear to be the case in tourism-based condominium management, as the principal is represented by two distinct groups with substantially different interests in regard to the role of the RUM. This view of principals as a heterogeneous group with competing interests highlights a significant departure from the conventional agency model. Despite this departure, in Australian legislation pertaining to condominium management there appears to be limited acknowledgement of the potential for conflict between resident and investor owners.

---

[6] Given the nature of the subject matter under study, judgement had to be exercised with respect to which parties would yield the most substantial insights into the owner/resident unit manager relationship. The approach that was taken involved initially casting a wide data collection net in terms of parties represented, in order to secure representation of a range of perspectives. As discussions proceeded, it was then determined that more focussed and narrower representation should be sought in repeated interviews in order that trust could develop between the interviewers and interviewees. Owners had greater representation in the interviews conducted than RUMs because much of the agency framework concerns how the principal can secure stronger control over the agent.

414   *C. Guilding et al. / Tourism Management 26 (2005) 409–420*

The different perspectives of the two owner types appear to have a major bearing on the relationship between a RUM and an individual owner. Because both the investor owners and the RUM derive a substantial portion of their investment returns from letting out apartments to holiday makers, their goals appear to be relatively well-aligned. The goals of the RUM and resident owners can be characterised more by divergency than convergency, however. In some cases this goal incongruity can result in resident owners sensing an antagonistic manner from the RUM. This antagonism appears to result from RUM's earning no letting agency income from the resident owner units. One interviewee commented:

> We've got friends who own a unit and we go up there a bit and the first time we walked in the manager there was really nice to us. Then he realised where we were going and now he treats us like dirt because he's getting no money. Our friends don't rent their unit out. They're not on the rent file so he's not interested and honestly its terrible.

Such behaviour, particularly if extended to tourists using apartments hired out by an outside (i.e. real estate) agent, could provide a serious impediment to word-of-mouth promotion which is one of the most critical marketing instruments in the tourism sector.

Berle and Means (1967) distinction between active and passive roles of the principal appears pertinent to a consideration of the differing interests of resident and investor owners. With respect to the execution of the RUM's caretaker role, resident owners are likely to be the much more active party. This is because the cost of monitoring the performance of the caretaker role will be much less for the resident owner. Due to proximity of domicile, a resident owner will be readily able to see the nature and outcome of the RUM's caretaking effort. Further, as the resident owner's quality of life will be directly affected by the standard of the RUM's caretaking service provided, it is to be expected that resident owners will have a greater propensity to complain should the caretaking performance fall below what is deemed acceptable. Investor owners can also suffer from a decline in a RUM's caretaking performance due to the adverse implications for sub-letting occupancy levels. This link between sub-letting performance and caretaking performance is unlikely to be apparent to most investor owners due to the range of parameters affecting occupancy levels, e.g., a general decline or stagnation in a region's visitor numbers. As a result, relative to resident owners, investor owners are more passively engaged with the aesthetic impact of a RUM's caretaking performance. As already noted, investor owners will directly experience the results of a RUM's poor sub-letting efforts and (where these are

clearly evident) are often forced to actively find a solution to this problem. By comparison, resident owners are likely to remain passive in regard to issues that have no, or even positive, effects on their personal welfare.

This inconsistency of the interests of resident and investor owners raises the potential of a power struggle in terms of representation on the body corporate committee. As indicated earlier, members of the sub-letting pool of owners can, by a simple voting majority, serve a nine months notice to terminate the RUM's sub-letting contract under current Queensland legislation. As, in most large tourism condominium complexes, income earned from sub-letting constitutes the vast bulk of the RUM's total income, termination of the sub-letting contract signifies a greatly diminished incentive for the RUM to remain in the building and continue to undertake caretaker duties. If, however, the RUM elects to remain in the building and continue to undertake caretaking services, a somewhat unworkable situation arises with respect to the sub-letting function. This is because the RUM's property ownership includes the office space dedicated to the sub-letting management function. If this scenario arises, it can be difficult for investor owners to arrange effective management of the sub-letting function. As a result, if the RUM appears likely to resist leaving the building following a termination of sub-letting rights, the investor owners may be reluctant to invoke their right to terminate a sub-letting contract and try to attract long-term tenants or sell their apartment and move their investment outside the tourism industry. Both scenarios signify a withdrawal of resources from the tourism industry.

A second idiosyncratic aspect of the condominium owner/resident manager agency relationship concerns the degree to which investor owners can be seen to be in direct competition with one another. In the tourism condominium context, revenue from investment (i.e. rent collected from holiday lettings) is not pooled across all relevant apartments but awarded by the RUM, the agent, to the individual owner who owns the particular apartment that has been sublet. This particular dynamic lies in stark contrast to most other corporate ownership structures where returns on investment are awarded as a percentage of the business's overall earnings, weighted in accordance with the number of shares held by the investor. This direct involvement of the agent, the RUM, in the allocation of returns earned opens up the possibility of collusion between a particular investor owner and the RUM, i.e. one individual principal and the agent. An investor owner might be motivated to offer a RUM inducements in order to increase the occupancy rate of his or her unit. While comments made by interviewees suggest this potential is significant, two factors may curtail a RUM's propensity

C. Guilding et al. / Tourism Management 26 (2005) 409–420 415

to unevenly allocate rental bookings across the sub-letting pool:

(a) As a result of a poor sub-letting performance, an investor owner might sell their unit and the purchaser of the unit might withdraw it from the letting pool.

(b) As a result of poor sub-letting performance, an investor owner might withdraw his unit from the letting pool. The incidence of this outcome is likely to be limited by the fact that the investor owner would have to either move into the unit, or personally manage its letting.

More importantly though, the influence wielded by the RUM in the allocation of investor returns provides him/her with considerable power that can be exploited to secure proxy votes from interstate owner investors. As noted earlier, in Queensland a RUM becomes owner of a unit (typically on the ground floor) under a conventional management rights agreement. Ownership of a unit confers the right to attend and vote at unit owners' meetings. Many investor owners live far from the unit they own, however, and it is therefore not easy for them to attend owners' meetings. In many aspects of the day-to-day management of holiday units, the RUM is the first point of contact for the owner investor and therefore frequently becomes a key source of information. As it is in the interests of investor owners to maintain a positive relationship with a RUM (as their primary point of contact and key arbiter in the allocation of returns), it is common for investor owners to assign their proxy voting rights over to the RUM. The propensity of RUMs to control considerable investor owner voting rights at owner meetings underlines a fundamentally significant factor that can contribute to a schism between resident and investor owners. It also highlights a fundamental breakdown in accountability. The RUM is accountable to the body corporate committee as the elected representatives of the owners, yet the RUM can have considerable influence with respect to who is elected to the body corporate committee, and ultimately how the entire building is operated. Practically all interviewees concurred that assignment of proxies to RUMs is not uncommon and that it can contribute to a gradual deterioration of the building due to a loss of RUM accountability.

5.2. Potential for effort aversion by the RUM (moral hazard)

Moral hazard can arise when owners and the RUM have different interests and the owners cannot determine whether the RUM has acted appropriately. On several occasions representatives referred to owner apathy. As no recompense is earned for services provided as a member of a body corporate committee, many owners may feel reluctant to becoming involved in closely monitoring the caretaking performance of a RUM. From field data collected, it appears many owners feel considerable reluctance to initiate any sanctioning of a RUM. When referring to this reluctance one interviewee commented:

> Owners go weak at the knees when it comes to admonishing a resident manager.

The propensity for owner apathy appears to be greatest in large buildings where owners might well feel that the amount of personal benefit they can derive from an improved RUM service is insufficient to justify exertion of personal effort. For a given increase in a RUM's effort, a unit owner in a 100 unit complex would only derive 1% of the benefit resulting from the greater RUM effort. In a 20 unit complex, however, a unit owner would derive 5% of the benefit resulting from an improved RUM performance. Smaller complexes would also appear to have a greater potential to develop an "esprit de corps" amongst the owners, as opposed to a "number in the crowd" culture that can be expected to develop in a large condominium complex with a diffuse ownership. Unit owner apathy was an issue repeatedly referred to in the interviews. The following quotes typify comments made:

> We've got our AGM coming up in a week or so and one of the owners rang me and said 'I see there's two quotes here. How can we be sure that the work needs to be carried out?'. I said that I can assure you we wouldn't be carrying out $30,000 worth of work on a building that didn't need to be carried out. All you need do is go up there and have a look at the building and you'll see what it needs. I said how long since you've been there? He lives here in Brisbane. Its only 1 hour and 10 minutes to the Sunshine Coast and they never go there.

> Some of the unit owners aren't even interested in having a look at a budget.... We are lucky to get a quorum. Last year we had to ring someone and get them to fax their proxy so that we could have a quorum for our AGM. We've got 30 units.... We only need to have eight people.

> We've got a situation here where there's one or two resident owners who know about this crap. The rest of them are ignorant and apathetic members of the mushroom club who are part of the diffuse ownership of the building. You can't get them to collaboratively agree on anything.

The potential for a sub-standard performance with respect to the RUM's sub-letting activities would appear to be constrained by the commission received by the RUM for sub-letting revenue earned. If, however, a RUM's sub-letting performance is widely perceived to be deficient, each investor owner may feel disinclined to discuss the matter with the RUM. This is because a complaint might damage the investor owner's relationship with the RUM and result in a decline in the investor owner's share of the sub-letting pool's occupancy levels.

One of the interviewees traced a problem of loosely drafted RUM contracts to a financial incentive for condominium complex developers. In addition to selling off the units, the developer also sells off the RUM management rights. Obviously a potential buyer of management rights is willing to pay more if the contractual rights are drafted in a manner that provides a degree of autonomy and protection to the RUM. With respect to developers he commented:

> He creates the caretaking letting agent contracts, which are done on extremely favourable terms. They are weak, wishy-washy contracts, non-performance based. You could drive a truck through the things and it wouldn't matter. You'd never catch the guy out and sue him for negligence, or breach of duties, or whatever.

For a developer considering designing a condominium's management rights contract in a manner that caters to the interest of the RUM, it appears that the upside in additional revenue from selling the management rights at an inflated price is greater than the downside of reduced unit marketability. This may be because many purchasers of new units do not carefully consider the particular resident management contract applying to their complex.

In addition to moral hazard, the agency theory literature also refers to adverse selection, which concerns an agent's ability to mis-represent their ability prior to securing a job. As no approval of owners is required prior to a RUM purchasing condominium management rights, this particular facet of the agency model does not appear pertinent to the condominium management context.

5.3. Agent's diversion of resources in a self-interested manner

Moral hazard problems arise when one party in an agency relationship takes an action that is damaging to the second party. The action is motivated by the first party's self-interest and the fact that the second party has insufficient information to detect the action. A widely-acknowledged form of moral hazard that might well be significant in condominium management concerns the possibility of a RUM accepting a payment from a building service sub-contractor in return for granting a particular building service sub-contract. The frequency with which this type of "back-hander" activity was referred to in connection with RUMs suggests it is not an isolated occurrence. It should be

noted, however, that the owner of a small electrical servicing business commented on a particular factor constraining the incidence of sub-contracting "back-handers". He felt that many RUMs were loathe to receive back-handers because if the contract with the sub-contractor has to be terminated due to poor-quality service, the sub-contractor may well inform the owners of the RUM's unscrupulous behaviour.

A second example of moral hazard concerns the possibility of a RUM not recording a short-term rental of a unit and failing to make the appropriate reimbursement to the unit's owner. Alternatively, a RUM may report the sub-letting of a unit, but at a rate that is below the actual amount charged to the sub-letting tenant.

A third example of moral hazard concerns the possibility of a RUM over-stating the cost of maintaining or housekeeping a room following the departure of a sub-letting guest and keeping the difference between the cost recorded to the unit owner and the actual cost remitted to the sub-contractor providing the service. One owner had a specific complaint about the amount charged by a RUM following a family holiday in his own unit:

> It cost us $183 to clean our unit and to change the sheets on the three beds. We took blow-up beds for the extra kids and visitors, our own linen for the extra beds, our own towels etc. I can assure that the (gives his name) family are not untidy and we left the unit quite clean and ready for the benches to be cleaned and the floors to be cleaned. We had everything put away in the kitchen. $183 to clean—now that's a scam. That's where the resident managers in holiday letting can make real dough.

5.4. Differential owner/RUM time horizons

If a RUM is planning to sell his management rights in the short-term, principal–agent time horizon asymmetry will result. This is because the RUM can be expected to have a shorter time perspective on his condominium involvement than the time horizon held by most unit owners. When taking a short-term perspective on his condominium involvement, the RUM can be expected to become particularly focussed on taking actions that will increase the marketability of the condominium's management rights. As the value of management rights are primarily determined by the sub-letting commission received by the RUM, it would seem likely that the RUM would become highly focussed on increasing sub-letting occupancy as well as accommodation rates charged. This potential highlights a further example of goal incongruency between the RUM and resident unit owners. Efforts to increase sub-letting occupancy levels may well come at the expense of a RUM's attendance to

C. Guilding et al. / Tourism Management 26 (2005) 409–420 417

his caretaking responsibilites. This is because the RUM will become increasingly less concerned by the ability of owners to sanction him or any negative relationships that might result from a poor caretaking performance due to his planned termination of involvement with the condominium in the short-term. As it has already been noted that resident owners are most interested in a RUM's caretaking performance, the scenario of a RUM with a short time perspective on his condominium involvement represents a further particular example of a RUM's interests not being well-aligned to the interests of resident owners.

The case of an owner planning to sell their unit does not appear to raise as great a potential for owner–manager mis-alignment of interests.[7] Nevertheless, the particular scenario of a condominium complex suffering from poor physical maintenance due to inadequate sinking fund levies raised from owners appears worthy of consideration. In this scenario, there may be a high propensity for a downward spiraling effect with respect to building maintenance. An increasing proportion of owners can be expected to want to sell their units as they become aware of the decline in the building's physical condition and the inadequacy of the condominium's accumulated sinking fund to rectify the deterioration (i.e., an increasing proportion will assume a short-term perspective on the condominium). Somewhat ironically, this increased tendency for a short-term perspective will be occurring at a time that long-term oriented actions are required to reverse the building's physical decline. The potential for a downward spiral effect being invoked becomes evident when it is recognised that owners seeking to sell their units will strongly resist any proposed increase in the sinking fund levy as this will adversely affect the marketability of their units. An increasing proportion of owners resisting an increase in sinking fund levies will accelerate a building's deterioration which will result in still further owners seeking to sell their units. The possibility of this downward spiral scenario arising underlines the importance of maintaining an accumulated sinking fund at a level that avoids the need for significant short-term increases in a condominium's sinking fund levies.

5.5. Differential in owner/RUM attitudes to risk

A major dimension of agency theory research concerns a principal/agent differential in attitude to risk. Agents are generally viewed as more adverse to risk due to the fact that they cannot diversify their employment. A principal (shareholder), can achieve a diversi-

fied portfolio of investments, however, and is therefore seen to be more risk neutral. A parallel to the company equity owner/company manager differential in attitudes to risk would appear to be presented in a muted form in the context of the condominium owner/manager agency relationship.

It was noted earlier that when a principal appraises an agent's performance by metering outcomes rather than monitoring behaviour, risk associated with satisfactory completion of the task in question is assigned to the agent. Investor owners can be seen to be heavily reliant on the metering outcomes dimension of control as many will reside at a distance from the condominium that precludes the possibility of monitoring a RUM's behaviour. As the investor owner's use of outcome controls signifies heightened risk assumed by the RUM, with respect to a RUM's sub-letting activities, a degree of risk congruency between the RUM and investor owners is apparent. Some monitoring of a RUM's behaviour can be conducted by resident owners due to the proximity of their domicile to the RUM's place of work. Care taken in conducting property maintenance work and also the nature of a RUM's interactions with a building's residents (both owners and sub-letting tenants) represent particular facets of a RUM's behaviour that will be readily observable for resident owners. As some RUM's can be expected to resent this relatively intrusive form of control, this dimension of a resident owner's control might well place a further strain on the resident owner/RUM relationship. Despite this, it appears likely that the majority of resident owners will base their views of a RUM's performance on the degree to which the building is maintained in a clean and well-ordered manner at a reasonable cost (i.e., outcome metering).

Similar to the company manager situation, the RUM's position represents a job that cannot be diversified. Further, by buying condominium management rights, the resident manager can be seen as exposed to significant down-side vulnerability should the condominium's letting performance decline relative to the conventional employee situation where no "job purchase" is made. For this reason, the RUM can be seen to have more at stake than an employee in a more conventional principal/agent relationship. Nevertheless, due to the absolute size of the investment required to become the owner of a condominium unit, the vast majority of condominium owners will not be able to achieve the same degree of investment diversification as that attainable by most shareholders of corporations.

Despite the parallels that can be drawn between the risk differential evident in the shareholder/manager corporate relationship and the condominium owner/RUM relationship, it appears that the scope for a RUM's attitude to risk affecting a condominium's management is relatively small. Once built, the nature

---

[7] When planning to sell a unit, an investor owner would experience a heightened incentive to offer inducements to the RUM to increase the unit's sub-letting occupancy rate as this will have a positive impact on the unit's value as an investment property.

418   *C. Guilding et al. / Tourism Management 26 (2005) 409–420*

of a condominium's business is highly defined. Unlike corporations, it cannot move in and out of business activities with differing risk profiles. Apart from fairly isolated decision-making issues such as whether to employ a provocative advertising campaign that is designed to garner "shock attention", there appears little that a RUM can do to that would have a fundamental impact on a condominium's risk profile. Consistent with this view, no empirical observations highlighting management issues resulting from a differential in owner/RUM attitude to risk have been noted.

6. Conclusion and discussion

When considered in the context of the tourism literature, two relatively novel dimensions are evident in this study. Firstly, despite the considerable growth in tourism accommodation provided by condominiums, no prior academic enquiry focussed on the use of condominiums for tourism has been found in the literature. Secondly, there appears to be a lack of studies focusing on the agency theory perspective on tourism business.

With respect to the study's agency perspective, the only tourism-related empirical study that has been found to draw on the agency model is Guilding's (2003) investigation of capital budgeting issues arising in hotels. Application of agency theory in the tourism management context appears particularly overdue as 20 years have now elapsed since Jensen commented of the agency model: "the foundations are being put into place for a revolution in the science of organizations" (1983, p. 319). Subsequent to Jensen's commentary, Ross (1987) described agency theory as the central approach to the theory of managerial behaviour.

This examination of the condominium unit owner/ resident manager relationship provides a useful extension to the agency theory literature in several ways. Although the relationship exhibits many characteristics of the traditional business owner/manager relationship widely noted in prior agency theory studies, several key differentiating attributes arise when tourist-based condominiums are considered. These attributes include:

(1) The principal (i.e., owners), do not comprise a homogeneous group with the same interests, but two distinct groups (resident owners and investor owners) with divergent interests. This is contrary to mainstream agency modelling which holds the basic presumption that owners have homogeneous interests.

(2) Income generated from investment in holiday apartments is not pooled and then allocated based on proportionate owner interests held in the building. The resident manager, through his/her sub-letting role, determines the allocation of invest-

ment returns. This highlights the extent to which investor owner relationships can be characterised as occurring in a competitive context. As the backdrop of most agency modelling is the corporate world in which owners reap the benefits of their investment in proportion to their relative share of investment in a company, the potential for the RUM to mediate in the allocation of returns to unit owners represents a significant idiosyncratic aspect of the scenario reviewed in this study.

(3) There appears to be considerable potential for agent moral hazard due to the incentive for developers to formulate condominium management rights contracts that favour the interest of the agent (manager) and a self-motivated disincentive for individual investor owners to take any actions that might adversely affect their relationship with a manager. These perspectives should be considered in the context of Bohren's (1998) view that agency model theorists have unduly overstated the presumption that agents and principals are indifferent to honesty, and have insufficiently recognised the potential of contracted agents to exhibit altruism. Sharma (1997) recognises the potential of professionals to have "pride in the craft and a calling to serve the public" (p. 775–776). The potential of some RUMs to feel a calling to serve the tourist is not a far-fetched notion, yet it is an emotion that is inconsistent with the agent model framework.

In light of the issues raised in this study, the following recommendations appear worthy of consideration.

(1) One significant problem uncovered in the study appears to be the possibility of the RUM sub-letting units but not reporting the accommodation sale to the owner and therefore fraudulently retaining the accommodation rental received. A provision that could be implemented to lessen the potential of this activity occurring could be to recommend that in large tourist-based condominium complexes, investor owners hire an auditing agent to conduct periodic random reviews of the units occupied on a particular night. To facilitate this control, the RUM would have to be required to maintain an up-to-date register of unit reservations and this register should be recorded in a form that enables real-time access by any investor owner. Such a system of control would also carry the added advantage of unit owners being able to check the occupancy levels of their unit with the occupancy levels of other units in the letting pool.

(2) Inequitable allocation of sub-letting occupancy might be a significant factor restraining investment in tourism infrastructure. If an investor owner feels that a RUM is not managing the allocation of

C. Guilding et al. / Tourism Management 26 (2005) 409–420 419

sub-letting equitably through the sub-letting pool, they will experience a reduced incentive to up-grade their unit. The main financial incentive for refurbishing an investment unit is the increased revenue generated due to the unit's improved standing relative to other units in the sub-letting pool. As a consequence, if an investor has a concern as to whether refurbishment will result in sufficient increased revenue, the likelihood of refurbishment occurring will be diminished. If this is a widespread phenomenon, the quality of accommodation provided to tourists will suffer. Because of this, so long as investor owners meet certain standards with respect to the quality of their unit's refurbishment and presentation, they should be entitled to an equitable proportion of the sub-letting occupancy sold by resident managers. A review of whether sub-letting has been distributed equitably across the letting pool should be facilitated by the resident manager making available a record of all sub-lettings made in the complex to any interested owner.

(3) Differences in the interests of resident owners and investment owners that have been highlighted in this paper may be sufficient to warrant legislation for the development of new strata title management modules restricted to particular owner types. For example, investment owner complexes could be distinguished from resident owner complexes. Such an innovation would circumvent governance problems resulting from conflicting interests of the two distinct owner categories. This distinction would facilitate local government zoning areas for investor owner complexes or owner occupied complexes. Development of particular condominiums solely focused on the provision of tourist accommodation may facilitate the design of common-use tourism focused facilities and also enable a tourism focused building to gain economies of scale in its sub-letting promotional and operating activities.[8]

(4) Due to the divide that can result between investor and resident owners when a RUM controls the body corporate proxy voting rights of many investor owners, RUM's should not be entitled to attend or vote at body corporate owners' meetings. Such an amendment would rectify a fundamental

---

[8] Certain shortcomings of this proposal should also be noted. Firstly, as it is unlikely that legislation of this type would be retrospective, a proliferation of building types could result, i.e., resident, tourism, and mixed (resident and investor owners would continue to own units in buildings developed prior to the legislative change). Further, some investor owners might like to retain the option of becoming a resident owner in the future. As this model signifies a loss of owner flexibility, a negative impact on property values would result. In light of this, such a proposed module is likely to meet with stiff resistance from property development lobby groups.

loss of RUM accountability which results from RUMs' enjoying considerable influence on who represents owners on the body corporate committee. A potential shortcoming of this suggestion relates to the problem of owner apathy. Without the RUM as a proxy option, many owners may find it difficult to identify a willing proxy, and achieving a quorum might prove increasingly problematical.

A potentially fruitful strategy for the interested researcher seeking research topics that build on this exploratory enquiry into condominium management would be to review published studies in hospitality journals and to consider the extent to which condominiums might constitute a novel context in which to revisit the hospitality issues addressed. In light of the relative novelty of this study's research domain, one can conceive of a host of related avenues of original academic enquiry. A useful corollary study that has the potential to supplement our understanding of the issues reported herein could involve conducting interviews with a larger sample of resident unit managers. Resident unit managers could be presented with scenarios that underline some of the inherent conflicts between investor owners and resident owners as well as conflicts between resident owners and resident unit managers and asked about the incidence of such problems and how they might be best managed. Also, it was noted during the conduct of this study that the price setting of short-term stays in condominiums presents novel issues that are absent in hotel accommodation price setting. For instance, what is the nature of owner influence with respect to the pricing of short-term lettings when a unit is placed in the holiday letting pool? Also, to what extent do variations of the quality of refurbishment in units result in short-term letting price differentials? Another novel area of research enquiry could focus on issues surrounding the setting and collection of condominium sinking fund (long-term property maintenance) owner contributions.

References

Australian Bureau of Statistics (2002). *Tourist accommodation.* Series 8635, March Quarter 2002. Canberra: AGPS.

Baker, G. P., Jensen, M. C., & Murphy, K. J. (1988). Compensation and incentives: Practice vs. theory. *Journal of Finance, 43*(3), 593–616.

Basu, A., Lal, R., Srinivasan, V., & Staelin, R. (1985). Sales-force compensation plans: An agency theoretic perspective. *Marketing Science, 4,* 267–291.

Bazerman, M. H., Neale, M. A., Valley, K. L., Zajac, E. J., & Kim, Y. M. (1992). The effects of agents and mediators on negotiation outcomes. *Organizational Behavior and Human Decision Processes, 53,* 55–73.

Bergen, M., Dutta, S., & Walker Jr, O. C. (1992). Agency relationships in marketing: A review of the implications and applications of agency and related topics. *Journal of Marketing, 58*, 1–24.

Berle, A. A., & Means, G. C. (1967). *The modern corporation and private property*. New York: Harcourt, Brace & World.

Bohren, O. (1998). The agent's ethics in the principle–agent model. *Journal of Business Ethics, 17*(7), 745–755.

Cotter, J. F., & Zenner, M. (1994). How managerial wealth affects the tender offer process. *Journal of Financial Economics, 35*, 63–97.

Demski, J., & Feltham, G. (1978). Economic incentives in budgetary control systems. *Accounting Review, 53*, 336–359.

Eisenhardt, K. M. (1988). Agency and institutional explanations of compensation in retail sales. *Academy of Management Journal, 31*, 488–511.

Eisenhardt, K. M. (1989). Agency theory: An assessment and review. *Academy of Management Review, 14*(1), 57–74.

Fama, E., & Jensen, M. (1983). Separation of ownership and control. *Journal of Law and Economics, 26*, 301–325.

Guilding, C. (2003). Hotel owner/operator structures: Implications for capital budgeting process. *Management Accounting Research, 14*(3), 179–199.

Jensen, M. (1983). Organization theory and methodology. *Accounting Review, 56*, 319–338.

Jensen, M. (1984). Takeovers: Folklore and science. *Harvard Business Review, 62*(6), 109–121.

Jensen, M., & Meckling, W. (1976). Theory of the firm: Managerial behavior, agency costs and ownership structure. *Journal of Financial Economics, 3*, 305–360.

Jensen, M., & Roeback, R. (1983). The market for corporate control: Empirical evidence. *Journal of Financial Economics, 11*, 5–50.

Kakabadse, A., & Kakabadse, N. (2001). *The geopolitics of governance*. Hampshire: Palgrave.

Kesner, I. F., Shapiro, D. L., & Sharma, A. (1994). Brokering mergers: An agency theory perspective on the role of representatives. *Academy of Management Journal, 27*(3), 703–721.

Lambert, R. A. (2001). Contracting theory and accounting. *Journal of Accounting and Economics, December*, 3–87.

La Porta, R., Lopez-de-Silanes, F., Shleifer, A. (1999). Corporate ownership around the world. *The Journal of Finance LIV* (2), 471–517.

Letza, S., & Smallman, C. (2001). In pure water there is a pleasure begrudged by none: On ownership, accountability and control in a privatised utility. *Critical Perspectives on Accounting, 12*(1), 65–85.

Mills, P. K. (1990). On the quality of services in encounters: An agency perspective. *Journal of Business Research, 20*, 31–41.

Ross, S. A. (1987). The interrelations of finance and economics: Theoretical perspectives. *American Economic Review, 77*, 29–34.

Russell, R., & Faulkner, B. (1999). Movers and shakers: Chaos makers in tourism development. *Tourism Management, 20*(4), 411–423.

Sharma, A. (1997). Professional as agent: Knowledge asymmetry in agency exchange. *The Academy of Management Review, 22*(3), 758–798.

Stoney, C., & Winstanley, D. (2001). Stakeholding: Confusion or utopia? Mapping the conceptual terrain. *Journal of Management Studies, 38*(5), 603–626.

Walker, G., & Weber, D. (1984). A transaction cost approach to make or buy decisions. *Administrative Science Quarterly, 29*, 373–391.

Walsh, J. P., & Seward, J. K. (1990). On the efficiency of internal and external corporate control mechanisms. *Academy of Management Review, 15*(3), 421–458.

Warnken, J. (2002). Tourism infrastructure audit—Gold Coast. *Project 2.2 of the Gold Coast Visioning Project CRC Research Report Series*. Co-operative Research Centre for Sustainable Tourism, Griffith University Gold Coast.

Warnken, J., Russell, R., & Faulkner, B. (2003). Condominium developments in maturing destinations: Potentials and problems for long-term sustainability. *Tourism Management, 24*(2), 155–168.

Williamson, O. E. (1985). *The economic institutions of capitalism*. New York: Free Press.

Zingales, L. (2000). In search of new foundations. *The Journal of Finance, LV*(4), 1623–1653.

[5]

Pergamon

www.elsevier.com/locate/atoures

Annals of Tourism Research, Vol. 27, No. 3, pp. 737–762, 2000
© 2000 Elsevier Science Ltd. All rights reserved
Printed in Great Britain
0160-7383/00/$20.00

PII: S0160-7383(99)00104-8

SUCCESSFUL RELATIONSHIPS BETWEEN HOTELS AND AGENCIES

Diego Medina-Muñoz
Juan Manuel García-Falcón
University of Las Palmas de Gran Canaria, Spain

Abstract: The establishment of cooperative relationships with other organizations is becoming increasingly crucial for tourism organizations. Indeed, interorganizational relationships are becoming a key research paradigm in the hospitality literature. However, there has been little empirical research dealing with this topic in the hospitality industry. Furthermore, while some studies may have been carried out with a view to reevaluating individual hotels' relationships with travel agents, the empirical research of this study is the first aiming to identify the determinants of successful relationships between hotels and travel agencies, the most cost-effective way for a hotel to extend its sales and marketing efforts. **Keywords:** interorganizational relationships, strategic alliances, collaboration, cooperation, hotels, travel agencies. © 2000 Elsevier Science Ltd. All rights reserved.

Résumé: Le succès des rapports entre hôtels et agences de voyages. La création de rapports de collaboration avec d'autres organisations devient de plus en plus importante pour les organismes touristiques. En effet, les rapports inter-organisationnels sont en train de devenir un paradigme clé de recherche dans la littérature hôtelière. Cependant, il n'y a pas eu beaucoup de recherches empiriques concernant ce sujet dans le secteur hôtelier. En outre, même si certaines études ont été réalisées dans le but de réévaluer les rapports entre les hôtels individuels et les agents de voyage, la recherche empirique de cette étude est la première qui essaie d'identifier les déterminants du succès des rapports entre les hôtels et les agences de voyage, ceci étant le moyen le plus rentable pour qu'un hôtel puisse augmenter ses efforts de vente et de marketing. **Mots-clés:** rapports inter-organisationnelles, alliances stratégiques, collaboration, hôtels, agences de voyage. © 2000 Elsevier Science Ltd. All rights reserved.

INTRODUCTION

All tourism organizations have relationships with other entities such as suppliers, distributors, competitors, public organizations, governments, and other firms carrying out complementary activities. Some relationships are relatively trivial, whereas others are of the utmost importance to the parties involved. For this reason, the establishment of cooperative relationships with other organizations

Diego Medina-Muñoz is Professor of Strategic Management and Hospitality Management, (Facultad de Empresariales, Universidad de Las Palmas de G.C., Saulo Torón 4, Las Palmas de Gran Canaria 35017, Spain. Email ⟨drmedina@empresariales.ulpgc.es⟩). His current research interests include interorganizational relationships, strategic management for hospitality, and sustainable tourism development. **Juan Manuel García-Falcón** is Professor of Strategic Management and Head of the Department of Management at the same university. He has authored numerous papers on strategic groups, organizational culture, management information systems, and strategic planning in universities.

is increasingly regarded as a crucial factor for organizational performance and survival (Child and Faulkner 1998). Indeed, interorganizational relationships (IRs) management is becoming a central research paradigm in literature covering hospitality and tourism management. On the whole, it is argued that, when used under the appropriate circumstances and environmental conditions, IRs will be successful (Harrigan 1985, 1988). However, a large percentage of these relationships do not succeed even when their creation seemed to be appropiate. Given this inconsistency, determining and understanding the factors associated with successful evolution of IRs is a valuable research objective and one which this study addresses.

Within this context, hotels and travel agencies have not established an entirely satisfactory business relationship. Despite the fact that travel agencies book more than 95% of cruises, about 90% of airline tickets, and 50% of car rentals, only 20–25% of all hotel rooms are reserved through agencies (Angelo and Vladimir 1994; Schulz 1994). Hoteliers are, however, seeking ways to increase revenues by working with travel agencies to expand sales in a cost-effective fashion. At the same time, they are turning to hotel bookings to bolster their revenues as airline commissions are decreasing. Generally speaking, new technologies, particularly the Internet, are forcing them to change their traditional modes of operation. For example, traditional retail agencies will greatly reduce their bookings unless they become virtual operations (Hotel and Motel Management 1995). According to Poon (1998), the role of travel agencies is expected to grow in importance for three reasons: they are very close to the industry's consumers and often play a key role in determining the type of services sought: though travel agents are not necessary to computerized reservations systems (CRSs), they are key players in the spreading of new technologies, including reservation; there are tremendous opportunities for CRSs to flexibly package holidays.

To address the ways in which hotels and travel agents could establish satisfactory business relationships, the literature on successful evolution of IRs was reviewed. Dimensions were identified that had a theoretical reason, to be considered as contributors to the success of relationships—interorganizational trust, commitment towards the relationship, interorganizational communication (coordination, communication quality, information exchange, participation), conflict resolution, and interorganizational dependence. The result, a comprehensive theoretical model of the characteristics of IR success, was then tested examining the relationship between hotels and travel agents, two organizations which have not as yet established an entirely satisfactory alliance (Angelo and Vladimir 1994; Koss 1992). The findings of such practical fieldwork should provide hotel operators and potential investors with important information with which to make strategic decisions. For instance, the findings should be useful in deciding whether or not the creating or continuing of a relationship is strategically advantageous, as well as in improving the success of ongoing relationships with travel agents.

SUCCESSFUL EVOLUTION OF RELATIONSHIPS

Generally speaking, IR success refers to the overall evaluation of the relationship. It can thus be defined as the generation of satisfaction by the parties involved in it as a result of the achievement of performance expectations. However, there are two distinct approaches to the concept of *IR success*. One approach (Anderson 1990; Van de Ven and Ferry 1980) associates the term *IR success* with participants' overall satisfaction with the relationship. Satisfaction refers, in this case, to an organization's positive experience as regards its partners' ability to obey rules and fulfil performance expectations (Anderson and Narus 1990; Biong 1993). A second approach (Johnston and Lawrence 1988; Narus and Anderson 1987), defines *IR success* as a quantitative measure of the mutual benefit that participants reap from the relationship. Specifically, an IR is considered to be successful according to how fully its objectives have been satisfied.

With regard to factors contributing to the success of IRs, two main streams of research can be identified in existing literature, depending upon whether or not the relationship is already built. Several models have been proposed for a successful IR creation (Devlin and Bleackley 1988; Lynch 1993; Pekar and Allio 1994). An overview of such models leads to five factors: one, the participation in an IR, compared with the other alternatives (such as internal development and going to the open market for a particular transaction), should be suitable for the focal organization; two, a particular organization should be careful in choosing potential partners; three, an operative plan for the IR should be established; four, potential partners should negotiate about overall IR conditions; and, five, participants should choose an appropriate structure and legal status for this relationship.

Once the system is created, another set of factors seems to determine the successful evolution of any IR, which is the object of this study. First, Anderson and Narus (1990) presented a model which includes efforts to resolve interorganizational conflicts, coordination measures, the influence of a given partner firm over the rest of the partners, influence over a partner firm, and assessment of the results from the relationship in comparison with expectations based on present and past experience with similar relationships. These factors are influenced, according to the same source, by partners' trust in the IR, interorganizational communication, and relative dependence.

More recently, Bucklin and Sengupta (1993) developed a model for organizing successful co-marketing alliances, which is comprised of the presence of a power balance, the extent of interorganizational conflict in the relationship, how beneficial the relationship is, partner compatibility and prior history of business relations, and other variables such as the age of the IR and turbulence in the environment. Furthermore, Morgan and Hunt (1994) claim that successful

IRs require participant commitment towards the IR and mutual trust. They also found that interorganizational communication contributes to trust and commitment. Finally, Mohr and Spekman (1994) developed a more precise model which sets out those IR characteristics which make them successful. Specifically, they suggest three sets of behavioral characteristics as success determining factors: attributes of the IR (commitment, trust, coordination, and interdepence), communication behaviors (communication quality, information exchange, and participation in decision making), and techniques utilized to resolve conflicts.

A comprehensive examination of the models presented previously, together with other studies related to determining factors for the successful evolution of IRs (Biong 1993; Devlin and Bleackley 1988; Dwyer, Schurr and Oh 1987; Ganesan 1994; Gyenes 1991; Shamdasani and Sheth 1995; Wray, Palmer and Bejou 1994), leads to identify several factors as contributors to successful IR evolution: interorganizational trust, commitment towards the IR relationship, interorganizational communication, interorganizational conflicts, and participants power and dependence. Each of these factors is explored in depth before stating the hypotheses.

Interorganizational Trust. Trust reflects the extent to which IR negotiations are fair and commitments are satisfied (Anderson and Narus 1990), as well as the belief that participants will fulfil their commitments (Anderson and Weitz 1989). As a result, interorganizational trust exists during the creation of the relationship and should be enough to ensure a correct negotiating procedure. Once the IR is established, this climate of confidence should be maintained and increased in order to guarantee a lasting and successful relationship (Barney and Hansen 1994; Ganesan 1994; Mohr and Spekman 1994; Morgan and Hunt 1994; Williamson 1985).

Trust as a determinant of successful IR evolution has received special attention by the resource based and transaction cost theory. Under a resource based perspective, intangible resources such as reputation and trustworthiness are scarce, complex, and difficult to market and imitate, thereby being contributors to performance differences among organizations (Rao 1994). Bearing in mind that trust decreases the probability that participants in an IR behave in an opportunistic way, the transaction cost theory would conclude that trust minimizes the transaction costs inherent in any relationship and, as a result, makes the arrangement more attractive. Furthermore, Williamson (1985) claims that trusting relationships are able to confront stressful situations much better and are also more flexible.

In accordance with these congruence predictions, a positive causal relationship between trust and the successful evolution of IRs can be foreseen. In addition, trust seems to be especially important in relationships between hotels and travel agents, to the extent that successful systems can be identified by their participants trusting each other and meeting their commitments (Emmer, Tauck,

Wilkinson and Moore 1993; Knight 1994; Schulz 1994). Thus, the following hypothesis can be made:

H1: Relationships between hotel companies and travel agents with the highest levels of interorganizational trust are expected to be the most successful.

Commitment Towards the Relationship. Generally speaking, an organization's commitment towards an IR may be defined as its desire to make an effort to maintain the relationship, which is perceived as being sufficiently worthwhile (Anderson and Weitz 1992; Morgan and Hunt 1994). Essentially, commitment implies sacrifice on the part of the partners and IR durability, in the sense that committed partners show a long-term orientation, including a desire to make sacrifices in the short term with a view to obtaining benefits in the long term (Dwyer et al 1987). By doing so, they believe that the relationship will be stable and will last long enough to provide them with long-term benefits.

In this context, theorists consider that commitment is central to the successful IR evolution. In fact, it is seen as crucial to achieving efficiency which, in turn, generates benefits for participants in a relationship (Anderson and Weitz 1992; Dwyer et al 1987; Ganesan 1994; Mohr and Spekman 1994; Morgan and Hunt 1994; Provan and Gassenheimer 1994). For example, transaction cost theory suggests that there are potential costs associated with opportunistic behavior by IR partners, which might be limited if participants showed commitment to the relationship (Williamson 1985). Also, in the relationship between hotels and travel agents, committed hotels seem to show relatively more reservations through travel agents (Schulz 1994). Therefore, the following prediction about the relationship between hotels and travel agents can be stated:

H2: Relationships between hotel companies and travel agents with the highest levels of partners' commitment are expected to be the most successful.

Interorganizational Communication. Communication, which is broadly defined by Anderson and Narus (1990:44) as "the formal as well as informal sharing of meaningful and timely information between firms", is another factor referred to in existing literature as a determinant of successful evolution of IRs. Specifically, it is predicted that the more efficient the communication between partners, the more successful the relationship will be (Cummings 1984; Gyenes 1991; Mohr and Spekman 1994; O'Callaghan 1986). An explanation for this prediction is that communication difficulties are a main cause of problems and conflicts among participants (Mohr and Nevin 1990). Etgar (1979) further points out that conflict is a consequence of inefficient interorganizational communication, which generates misunderstandings, incorrect interorganizational strategies, and frustrations.

While interorganizational communication seems to be crucial, there is a lack of research that has examined it, and hence it is difficult to recommend efficient communication strategies for participants in an IR. Moreover, Mohr and Nevin (1990) suggest that rules of thumb such as *more communication, improved communication,* and *open communication* are not only simplistic but probably inaccurate. However, the following communication strategies have been mentioned in the literature: interorganizational coordination, communication quality, information exchange, and participative decision making, each of which require further elaboration.

Interorganizational coordination, defined as the process by which participants in an IR seek to work together in a joint effort, was found by Narus and Anderson (1987) and Morgan and Hunt (1994) to be a positively related factor, in as far as the most successful IRs demonstrate the highest levels of coordination in the activities carried out by IR participants. Stern and El-Ansary (1992) also suggest that coordination is especially important in relationships with channels of distribution. Furthermore, a hotel's efforts to coordinate with travel agents, including actions such as providing them with up-to-date and timely information on each of the aspects influencing IR efficiency (such as prices, rooms available, and sales promotions), as well as responding to travel agents' requests and questions in a prompt fashion, are seen to contribute to the success of relationships between these two sectors (Knight 1994; Schulz 1994). As a result, the following hypothesis can be made:

> H3a: Relationships between hotel companies and travel agents with the highest levels of coordination are expected to be the most successful.

Though existing literature acknowledges that *communication quality* plays a vital role in the successful evolution of IRs, the concept of the term is somewhat imprecise. Mohr and Spekman (1994) associate communication quality with the exchange of accurate, timely, adequate, credible, and complete information. Similarly, Morgan and Hunt (1994) view it as relevant, timely, and reliable. In the relationship between hotels and travel agents, which are explored in this study, Schulz (1994) and Knight (1994) suggest that hoteliers should provide travel agents with adequate and timely information about facilities and services offered by the hotel, prices, sales promotions, and reservation procedures. Such communication will improve a hotel's relationship with travel agents significantly, which suggests another hypothesis:

> H3b: Relationships between hotel companies and travel agents with the highest levels of communicaton quality are expected to be the most successful.

Defined as the extent to which participants share critical information (Mohr and Spekman 1994), *information exchange* is identified as a characteristic of successful IRs (Devlin and Bleackley 1988;

Mohr and Spekman 1994). An explanation for this prediction is that partners need to exchange information regularly about IR perform-ance and progress, in order to assess the suitability of making some changes in the relationship or terminating it (Devlin and Bleackley 1988). Participants should further have access to any information relevant to the making of strategic decisions for the IR (Devlin and Bleackley 1988; Mohr and Spekman 1994). In this case, a hotel should provide travel agents with information about prices, reser-vation strategy, and service quality, to enable them to negotiate with customers directly (Knight 1994; Schulz 1994). Therefore, a positive correlation between IR success and information exchange can be predicted:

> H3c: Relationships between hotel companies and travel agents with the highest levels of information exchange are expected to be the most successful.

According to Devlin and Bleackley (1988), an efficient decision making process in any IR requires a formal authority and power structure, enabling all partners to *participate* in major decisions such as the establishment of roles, responsibilities, and expectations. Moreover, Mohr and Spekman (1994) suggest that partners should work together to plan all related activities. With regard to the re-lationship between hotels and travel agents, Vallen and Vallen (1991) also state that these two types of companies should make joint decisions about issues such as commissions, number of room reservations through travel agents, and joint publicity. Accordingly, the following hypothesis can be made:

> H3d: Relationships between hotel companies and travel agents with the highest levels of participation are expected to be the most successful.

Interorganizational Conflict. There will always be disagreements or conflicts between IR participants (Dwyer et al 1987). Interorganizational conflict is a fairly normal and common feature of relationships between organizations. On the basis of past research (Anderson and Narus 1990; Borys and Jemison 1989; Gaski 1984; Gyenes 1991; Morgan and Hunt 1994), it is the way organiz-ations resolve disputes that really influences IR success. Essentially, when conflicts are resolved amicably, such conflicts may actually increase efficiency. However, hostility resulting from conflicts not being resolved amicably can lead to dissolution. Therefore, partici-pants' positive attitude towards conflicts can be seen as a contribu-tory factor for the successful evolution of IRs, meaning that when disagreements are perceived as either a means to avoid future dis-putes or to provide productive discussion, the relationship will be successful (Frazier 1983; Morgan and Hunt 1994).

Drawing on the list of conflict resolution techniques suggested by March and Simon (1958), three sets utilized by IR participants can be identified (Mohr and Spekman 1994): constructive techniques, which imply an amicable conflict resolution and include techniques such as joint problem solving and persuasion; destructive techniques, including domination and harsh words, which resolve disputes with hostility; and other techniques, such as outside arbitration and smoothing/avoiding issues, which, while useful under certain circumstances, when utilized repeatedly may contribute to IR dissolution. As a result, additional hypotheses can be made:

> H4a: Relationships between hotel companies and travel agents with the most use of constructive conflict resolution techniques, including joint problem solving and persuasion, are expected to be the most successful.
> H4b: Relationships between hotel companies and travel agents with the least use of destructive conflict resolution techniques, including domination and harsh words, are expected to be the most successful.
> H4c: Relationships between hotel companies and travel agents with the least use of other conflict resolution techniques, such as outside arbitration and smoothing/avoiding issues, are expected to be the most successful.

Interorganizational Power and Dependence. Resource dependence theorists regard IR as an organizational strategic response to conditions of uncertainty and dependence (Pfeffer and Salancik 1978). Such a response is made by seeking to reduce uncertainty and manage dependence by deliberately structuring their relationships with other organizations. The literature further considers that successful IRs are characterized by partners having similar relative dependence and power (Frazier 1983; Heide and John 1988). This notion refers to a partner's perception of its dependence relative to its partners' dependence on the relationship (Anderson and Narus 1990). Relative power will thus be a partner's perceived difference between its own and its partners' power. As a general rule, it is assumed that whenever a partner perceives itself as being relatively more dependent than the rest of the partners, it will make no effort to develop a strong and long-term relationship. As a consequence, for an IR to be successful each of the partners should have a similar relative power and dependence (Bucklin and Sengupta 1993; Ganesan 1994; Hallén, Johanson and Seyed-Mohamed 1991).

Mohr and Spekman (1994) also suggest that successful IRs exhibit high interdependence among partners (that is, partners perceive mutual benefits from interacting). However, these authors did not find empirical evidence in the relationship between manufacturers and dealers in the personal computer industry. Considering relative dependence and power and interdependence factors, a final hypothesis can be made:

H5: Relationships between hotel companies and travel agents with similar relative dependence between partners and the highest levels of interdependence are expected to be the most successful.

Study Method. The study focused on hotels and limited the unit of analysis to those operating in the United States. These, 900 in total, are listed in the directory of the American Hotel and Motel Association (1994). Their sales and marketing vice-presidents were deemed the most qualified people to provide information about the corporate level relationship, between them and travel agency companies. Their hotel and agency properties are in multiple locations and are linked to their respective headquarters by ownership, management contract, or franchising. According to Crawford-Welch (1991), the response rates in mailing surveys in the hospitality industry range from 10.5 to 30.7. By adopting a modified version of the total design method of Dillman (1978), a high response rate was expected in this study, and thus a sample of 360 individuals was established. Due to the low response rate of the first mailing, 150 hotel companies were added to the initial sample. Therefore, the final sample consisted of 510 individuals.

Simple random sampling was used owing to the homogeneity of the population (Salant and Dillman 1994). From the total sample, 112 questionnaires were returned (22.0%), with 103 being usable (20.2% effective response rate). Obtaining this figure of usable questionnaires indicates us to state that 95 times out of 100 the estimate will fall within a range of ±9.13% (Salant and Dillman 1994).

Out of the 103 participants, 26 had more than 20 properties, 46 had a total of 6 to 20, and 31 had between 2 and 5. With regard to the clientele strategy, 45 hotel companies indicated business and leisure as their primary clientele, while 41 reported business clientele and 17 indicated leisure clientele. Participants in this study were primarily first-class hotel chains (50 companies), followed by economy (41 companies) and luxury (17 companies).

The percentage of reservations that hotel companies received from travel agencies ranged based on the characteristics of the hotel company. First, hotel chains with more than 20 properties reported, on average, 23% of reservations through this source, while those with 6–20 hotels indicated 20%, and those with fewer than 6 hotels reported 22%. Second, leisure hotel chains made more reservations (27%) through agencies than business hotels (18%) and leisure/business hotel chains (23%). Third, luxury hotels made significantly more reservations (29%) from agents than economy hotels (15%) and first class hotels (23%).

Measurement Method. A self-administered, mail survey questionnaire was used (Babbie 1995). Three steps were adopted in developing the questionnaire. An initial instrument was first developed, after reviewing the IR literature, with some modifications introduced. For example, "we pay commissions promptly and on time" was included to measure the trust of hotels in travel agents, and "we provide the travel agent with what they need to sell, such as information about quality levels" were added to the information exchange scale. Further, such statements as "we participate in goal setting and forecasting with the manufacturer" and "we help the manufacturer in its planning activities" were dropped from the original Mohr and Spekman's participation scale or restated. For instance, "manufacturer" was replaced by "hotel company" and "buyer" was substituted by "travel agency", as appropriate for the special features of the relationship between hotel and travel agency companies. Such special features were identified by examining the literature on hospitality management (Angelo and Vladimir 1994; Emmer, Tauck, Wilkinson and Moore 1993; Knight 1994; Koss 1992). The revised questionnaire was pretested in a series of personal interviews with two directors of sales and marketing in US hotel companies, similar in profile to the target respondents, and three professors in the School of Hospitality Management at Florida International University. Each of the participants was first asked to complete the questionnaire by considering one of the hotel companies they worked for. After analyzing the returned questionnaires, some changes were made in the questionnaire and each participant was interviewed in order to explain the objectives of the study as well as the structure of the instrument. The participants were then asked to make suggestions to improve measurement reliability, some of which justified changes in the questionnaire.

Several units of analysis have been used in literature to identify the determining factors for successful IRs. Mohr and Spekman (1994) focused on the relationship between a particular computer distributor and one of its suppliers, which was selected, at random and by the authors, from a list of all of the potential suppliers. Ganesan (1994), in his study on the relationship between sellers and buyers, allowed each party to choose a particular partner. The same unit of analysis was used by Anderson and Narus (1990), who examined the relationship between distributors and manufacturers in more than 110 industries.

Each of these alternatives was assessed by three of the participants in the pretest of the questionnaire. As a result, Mohr and Spekman's (1994) unit of analysis was discarded, because the phone calls to hotel companies increased the research costs and because the random selection of partners did not guarantee the existence of intense relationships. On the other hand, the Anderson and Narus' (1990) and Ganesan's (1994) unit of analysis was believed to generate a majority of intense relationships.

A mixture of these two units of analysis was develped for this study. Specifically, respondents were asked to indicate from a list of the top ten travel agency companies worldwide (Travel Weekly,

1994), the ones with own they have the most, the second, and the third volumes of business. The list included American Express Travel Related Services, Carlson Travel Network, Japan Travel Bureau International, Liberty Travel, Maritz Travel, Omega World Travel, Rosenbluth International, Thomas Cook Travel US, US Travel, and IVI Business Travel International. In order to guarantee that data regarding relationships with different levels of business, being used as a measure of success, were collected, three forms of the same questionnaire were developed. Each form referred to a different travel agent in relation to which the respondent was asked. One third of the sample were asked to report on the travel agent with whom they had the most business experience, another third, the agent with the second and the final third on the agent with whom they had the third-most volume of business.

Data Collection. The final questionnaire, enclosed with a postage-paid preaddressed return envelope, was mailed to the sales and marketing vice presidents of the 360 hotel companies initially included in the sample. The instrument had a cover page explaining the goals of the survey, providing instructions for completion, and requesting participation. In line with Dillman's (1978) total design method, three weeks after the first mail-out, a new cover letter, questionnaire, and postage-paid preaddressed return envelope were sent out to all members of the sample group who had not as yet responded.

Because of the unexpectedly low response rate of the first mailing, two new steps were included in the process. First, a random sample of 100 hotel companies was drawn from the non-respondents to the first mailing (316). This was followed up by phone calls to motivate their participation. Second, 150 additional hotel companies were selected at random as new individuals in the sample, making the final sample a total of 510 hotel companies. Two mailings with the questionnaire, a cover letter, and a postage-paid preaddressed return envelope were carried out for the new individuals in the sample. Of the 103 participants, 28 answered the questionnaire related to the travel agency with whom they had the most experience, 38 the second, and 37 the third most.

Measurement Scales. A five point Likert scale ranging from "strongly disagree" to "strongly agree" was used to measure managerial perceptions about items related to the following determinants of success: trust, commitment, relative dependence, interdependence, coordination, communication quality, information exchange, and participation. Conflict resolution techniques used with the travel agent were also measured using items with five-point "very frequently/very infrequently" scales. Table 1 shows all of the scales included in the questionnaire.

In this study, reliability was measured by the coefficient alpha (Cronbach 1951). Except for the so-called "relative dependence and interdependence" dimension, the Cronbach alpha values ranged

Table 1. Measurement Scales

Interorganizational trust: Extent to which respondents agree with the following:
    We trust that the agent's decisions will be beneficial to us.
    The relationship is marked by a great harmony.
    We pay commissions promptly and on time.
    The travel agent cannot be trusted at times.
    The travel agent can be counted on to do what is right.
    The travel agent has high integrity.
Commitment towards the relationship: Extent to which respondents agree with the following:
    We are very committed to continue.
    We intend to maintain the relationship indefinitely.
    The relationship deserves our maximum effort to maintain it.
    We have a strong sense of loyalty to this travel agent.
    We are continually on the look out for other travel agents.
Relative dependence and interdependence: Extent to which respondents agree with:
    If we wanted to, we could switch to another travel agent easily.
    If the travel agent wanted to, it could switch to another hotel easily.
Coordination: Extent to which respondents agree with the following:
    Our activities with the travel agent are well coordinated.
    We plan and schedule the sales with the travel agent.
Communication quality: Extent to which respondents agree with each of the following aspects of the communication:
    Our communication with the travel agent is timely, accurate, adequate, complete, and credible.
Information exchange: Extent to which respondents agree with the following:
    We share proprietary information with the travel agent.
    It is expected that any information which might help the other party will be provided.
    We provide the travel agent what they need to sell (e.g. information about quality levels).
Participation: Extent to which respondents agree with the following:
    The travel agent seeks our advice and counsel.
    Suggestions by us are encouraged by the travel agent.
    We seek advice from the travel agent.
Conflict resolution techniques: How frequently each of the following techniques is used:
    Smoothing over the problem, persuasive attempts by either party, joint problem solving, harsh words, outside arbitration, and travel agent-imposed domination.
Success of the relationship: Extent to which respondents agree with the following:
    The agent is an excellent company to do business with.
    The time and effort spent in developing and maintaining the relationship has been worthwhile.
    We are satisfied with the following aspects of the relationship: Total sales from the travel agent, profit on sales for the travel agent, cooperative advertising support, promotional support (coupons, displays), off-invoice promotional allowances, and compatibility of travel agent clientele with our properties.

from 0.57 to 0.93. Specifically, dimensions such as communication quality (α=0.93), participation (α=0.78), coordination (α=0.72), and trust (α=0.71) had either excellent or acceptable alpha values (George and Mallery 1995). The original "commitment" scale consisted of five items and the initial Cronbach alpha was only 0.52. After the item "we are continually on the look out for other travel agents" was eliminated, the Cronbach alpha increased to 0.83; thus, this item was dropped in final analysis. The three items of the "information exchange" scale reached an alpha value of 0.53, which would increase slightly to 0.57 by dropping the item "we provide the travel agent what they need to sell, such as information about quality levels"; however, due to the theoretical relevance of this item and its scarce impact on the alpha value, all of the items were kept as a scale for hypothesis testing. The "conflict resolution techniques" scale had five items that were designed to cover a spectrum of possibilities. As each item refers to a different technique, traditional reliability analysis might not be appropriate. However, a Cronbach alpha of 0.65 indicates that these items measure the same dimension: "conflict resolution". This value would be 0.70 after dropping the item "joint problem solving", which was still kept for further analysis owing to its relevance for hypothesis testing.

In order to measure IR success, respondents were asked about the success of the relationship between their hotel company and the same travel agent for which they previously answered questions on the determining factors for successful IRs. Specific data on quantitative performance indicators were not used, because they reflect a short-term orientation (Stafford 1994), and because many benefits of the relationship are difficult to track quantitatively (Bucklin and Sengupta 1993; Stafford 1994). Thus, qualitative measures of performance were adopted as indicators of success. Such measures associate IR success with participants overall satisfaction about the relationship, including satisfaction on specific performance indicators such as the total sales from travel agent and the profit on sales for the travel agent (Anderson 1990; Anderson and Narus 1984, 1990; Shamdasani and Sheth 1995; Van de Ven and Ferry 1980). A five point Likert scale ranging from "strongly disagree" to "strongly agree" was utilized to measure perception about a set of items which are presented in Table 1.

Specifically "success of the IR" was measured by a scale consisting of eight items. This dimension had a Cronbach alpha value of 0.86, which is considered very good. This value is even higher than the 0.80 that was obtained by Mohr and Spekman (1994) by using two objective measures of dyadic sales volume, along with an indicator of one partner's satisfaction with the other across several aspects of the relationship, including the general nature of personal dealings, the level of promotional support, and profitability.

Results of F tests of difference between mean values show a significant positive association between the form of the questionnaire and the average value of the answers to all of the items included in

Table 2. Results of *F* Tests of Difference among the Mean Values of Answers[a]

Variables in the Scale "success of the relationship"	Questionnaire about the First Agent		Questionnaire about the Second Agent		Questionnaire about the Third Agent	
	Mean	SD	Mean	SD	Mean	SD
The agent is an excellent company to do business with ($F = 1.915$, $P = 0.153$)	4.286	0.810	4.132	0.811	3.892	0.843
The time and effort spent in developing and maintaining the relationship has been worthwhile ($F = 2.437$, $P = 0.093$)	4.286	0.713	4.210	0.704	3.919	0.759
We are satisfied with:						
Total sales from the agent ($F = 4.371$, $P = 0.015$)	3.786	0.876	3.395	0.945	3.081	1.010
Profit on sales for the agent ($F = 1.949$, $P = 0.148$)	3.929	0.813	3.579	0.919	3.513	0.901
Cooperative advertising ($F = 0.250$, $P = 0.780$)	2.786	1.258	2.632	0.998	2.595	1.142
Promotional support ($F = 0.070$, $P = 0.932$)	2.714	1.213	2.632	0.998	2.622	1.019
Off-invoice promotional allowances ($F = 1.002$, $P = 0.371$)	2.786	1.166	2.576	0.948	2.568	1.015
Compatibility of agent clientele with our properties ($F = 2.307$, $P = 0.105$)	3.929	1.086	3.763	0.852	3.405	1.117

[a] A five point Likert scale ranging from 5 (strongly agree) to 1 (strongly disagree) was used to measure managerial perceptions about each variable.

the "success of the IR" scale (Table 2). Specifically, respondents to the questionnaire asking for the travel agency with whom the hotel company had the most experience reported the highest mean value in all of the items measuring the success of the relationship; this was followed by those answering with respect to the travel agent with whom they had the second most experience, and then by those relating to the travel agent with the third most experience.

Validity Tests. According to Hambrick (1981), content validity was established through the rigorous process by which the questionnaire was developed (this process was previously described). Moreover, the results of the confirmatory factor analyses conducted in this study suggest the construct validity. According to Venkatraman and Grant (1986), construct validity was also established through the use of expert opinions. In this study, as already noted, the questionnaire was pretested in a series of personal interviews. Further, the convergent validity is established as the results of *F* tests of difference between mean values indicate that the more experience with the travel agent, the higher is the mean value of all of the items measuring the success of the relationship (Table 2).

Data Analysis and Results

In order to condense the set of variables into a few underlying constructs or factors, a confirmatory factor analysis (CFA based on maximum likelihood) was conducted for trust, commitment, communication quality, information exchange, participation, conflict resolution techniques, and success of the IR. For those dimensions with fewer than three items (coordination, and relative dependence and interdependence) summary variables were created. Specifically, mean values of both items of the scale were used for coordination and interdependence, and the difference between the values of both items was defined as the summary variable for relative dependence. Kaiser-Meyer-Olkin's (KMO) test of sphericity and Barlett's test of adequacy provided support for each of the factor analyses conducted in this study.

Trust. The factor analysis yielded a two-factor solution accounting for 61.4% of the total variance. In social sciences, a factor solution accounting for 60% of the total variance is considered satisfactory (Hair, Anderson and Tatham 1987). Thus, the total variance accounted for by these factors is considered a good value. The first factor "extent to which the travel agent is trustworthy", with an eigenvalue of 2.57, consisted of items measuring the trust that the hotel company has in the travel agent ("the travel agent has high integrity", "the travel agent can be counted on to do what is right", and "the travel agent cannot be trusted at times"). This factor accounted for 42.9% of the variance, and its Cronbach coefficient was 0.73. The second factor, "overall trust in the relationship", with an eigenvalue of 1.11, comprised three items related to overall trust in the relationship ("the relationship is marked by a great harmony", "we pay commissions promptly and on time", and "we trust that the agent's decisions will be beneficial to us"). Although the Cronbach coefficient for this factor was only 0.52, it was decided to keep this factor for further analyses in order to test the hypothesis H1. This two-factor solution was confirmed by the chi-square statistic, which was 3.2228 with 4 degrees of freedom ($P = 0.5213$). Generally speaking, a non significant chi-square statistic indicates an adequate fit of the measurement scale. However, the chi-square statistic is sensitive to sample size and model complexity; therefore, rejection of a model on the basis of this evidence alone is inappropriate (Bagozzi and Yi 1988).

Commitment. One factor comprising all the items selected after the reliability analysis was obtained as solution to the factor analysis for the commitment scale (Table 1). The factor had an eigenvalue of 2.71 and accounted for 67.8% of the total variance, which is considered good. The Cronbach value for the items in the factor was also 0.83. The overall fit of the measurement scale was verified by considering that the chi-square statistic was not significant. Specifically, the chi-square was 1.5862 with 2 degrees of freedom ($P = 0.4524$).

Communication Quality. The factor analysis yielded one factor integrating all of the items measuring communication quality (Table 1). This factor showed an eigenvalue of 3.95 and accounted for 79.0% of the total variance, which is a good value. This scale is also reliable as its Cronbach alpha (0.93) is excellent. However, the chi-square value (17.3095 with 5 degrees of freedom, $P = 0.004$) does not suggest a reasonable fit of the measurement scale. The small number of degrees of freedom did not allow to estimate other measures of fit compensating for sample size, such as the goodness-of-fit index (GFI).

Information Exchange. The one-factor solution of the factor analysis comprised the three variables included in the initial "information exchange" scale (Table 1) and had an eigenvalue of 1.58. This factor explained 52.6% of the total variance and showed a Cronbach alpha of 0.53. Though these values make further analyses questionable, the factor was kept with a view to testing the hypothesis H3c. As the number of degrees of freedom was not positive (d.f.=0), the chi-square could not be estimated; therefore, the overall fit of the measurement scale can not be determined.

Participation. One factor including all the items of the original scale was obtained as solution of the factor analysis (Table 1). It had an eigenvalue of 2.08 and accounted for 69.4% of the variance. The Cronbach alpha was also good (0.78), making the factor reliable. The overall fit of the measurement scale can not be established owing to the lack of degrees of freedom (d.f.=0).

Conflict Resolution Techniques. A factor analysis with varimax rotation was conducted and two factors were yielded, both explaining a total variance of 66.3% (38.4% the first factor and 27.9% the second factor). The first factor referred to severe conflict resolution techniques (travel agent-imposed domination, harsh words, outside arbitration) and showed an eigenvalue of 2.30. The second factor, with an eigenvalue of 1.67, included soft techniques (smoothing over the problem, persuasive attempts by either party, joint problem solving). Both factors, which are reliable (Cronbach alpha was 0.75 for the first factor and 0.67 for the second), were kept for further analyses. This two-factor solution was confirmed by the chi-square statistic, which was 4.3104 with 4 degrees of freedom ($P = 0.3656$).

Success of the IR. The factor analysis with varimax rotation generated two factors accounting for 69.5% of the total variance, which is considered a good value. The first factor (overall success), with an eigenvalue of 4.5 and explaining 51.9% of the variance, was made up of all of the items of the original "success of the IR" scale, except for those refering to marketing support by the travel agent ("we are satisfied with the promotional support—coupons, displays", "we are satisfied with the off-invoice promotional allowances", "we are satisfied with the cooperative advertising support"), which made up the second factor (satisfaction with marketing support). This second factor had an eigenvalue of 1.41 and accounted for 17.60% of the total variance. Cronbach coefficients for both factors were very good, being 0.82 for the first factor and 0.89 for the second. This two-factor solution can be reasonably confirmed by means of the chi-square statistic, which was 29.8824 with 13 degrees of freedom ($P = 0.06$); moreover, the goodness-of-fit index was of 0.94 and the adjusted goodness-of-fit index was of 0.93, which are considered good values (Bagozzi and Yi 1988).

Hypothesis Testing

In principle, the set of hypotheses might be subject to a structural equation analysis with latent variables. A simple two-step procedure was chosen here: CFA followed by multiple regression. In accordance with previous studies (Kohli 1989; Mohr and Spekman 1994), multiple linear regression analysis is one appropriate approach to address the hypotheses. Regression analysis shows the effects of one variable (independent) over another variable (dependent). This statistical technique implies two main requisites about the distribution of each variable and the association between the variables (Hedderson 1991).

First, regression applies best to an analysis in which both the dependent variable and the independent variable are normally distributed non-categorical variables. In this study, they are continuous and results of Kolmogorov–Smirnov's tests of normality indicate that all of the variables are normally distributed (measures ranged from 0.169 to 0.454, with significance levels lower than 0.00). Moreover, kurtosis and skewness values were between $+1.4$ and -1.1. Second, regression also assumes that the effect of the independent variable is linear (that is, the effect of a unit difference in an independent variable is the same at all points in the range of the variable). In this study, the effect of the independent variables on the dependent variable (the success of the relationship between hotel companies and travel agents) can be assumed to be linear owing to theoretical constructs, previous empirical studies, and the high correlations between variables.

Two multiple regression analyses were run separately, one with "overall success" as the dependent variable, and the other with "satisfaction with marketing support". Independent variables are the results of the confirmatory factor analyses and the other summary variables. Each hypothesis will be addressed according to the results of both multiple regression analyses (Table 3).

> H1: Relationships between hotel companies and travel agents with the highest levels of interorganizational trust are expected to be the most successful.

As can be seen in Table 3, Beta coefficients indicate that "extent to which the travel agent is trustworthy" and "overall trust in the relationship" were to a considerable extent positively associated with both "overall success" and "satisfaction with marketing support". This means that more successful relationships with travel agents exhibited higher levels of trust, in comparison with the less successful relationships. Beta values also suggest that "overall trust

Table 3. Beta Coefficients from Simultaneous Multiple Regression Analyses

Independent Variable	Dependent Variables[a]	
	Overall Success	Satisfaction with Marketing Support
Communication Quality	0.19* (1)	0.29* (4)
	(adjusted R^2=0.334)	(adjusted R^2=0.019)
Commitment	0.16* (2)	0.02
	(adjusted R^2=0.117)	
Severe Conflict	−0.24*** (3)	−0.14
Solving Techniques:	(adjusted R^2=0.034)	
Harsh Words		
Outside Arbitration		
Agent Imposed Domination		
Coordination	0.22* (4)	0.01
	(adjusted R^2=0.043)	
Extent to which the	0.23** (5)	0.24* (5)
Agent is Trustworthy	(adjusted R^2=0.022)	(adjusted R^2=0.029)
Soft Conflict	0.21** (6)	0.05
Solving Techniques:	(adjusted R^2=0.025)	
Smoothing over the Problem		
Persuasive Attempts		
Joint Problem Solving		
Overall Trust in the	0.16** (7)	0.27** (3)
Relationship	(adjusted R^2=0.014)	(adjusted R^2=0.021)
Relative Dependence	−0.16* (8)	−0.19* (2)
	(adjusted R^2=0.015)	(adjusted R^2=0.036)
Information Exchange	0.11	0.19
Participation	0.55	0.32** (1)
		(adjusted R^2=0.229)
Interdependence	−0.02	−0.12
Adjusted R^2	0.60	0.33

[a]Values enclosed in parentheses represent the stage at which the variable was entered in the hierarchical or stepwise analysis, along with the additional adjusted R^2 explained by each variable added to the model.
*$P < 0.05$, **$P < 0.001$, ***$P < 0.0001$.

in the relationship" has a stronger association with "satisfaction with marketing support" than for "overall success". "Extent to which the travel agent is trustworthy" has a similar effect on both measures of success.

> H2: Relationships between hotel companies and travel agents with the highest levels of partners' commitment are expected to be the most successful.

Beta values indicate that commitment had a positive effect on both "overall success" and "satisfaction with travel agent marketing support" (Table 3), meaning that, as was foreseen, more successful relationships with travel agents exhibited higher levels of commitment. However, the association between commitment and "satisfaction with marketing support" was not significant ($P = 0.87$).

H3a: Relationships between hotel companies and travel agents with the highest levels of coordination are expected to be the most successful.

As shown in Table 3, Beta coefficients suggest that "overall success" and "satisfaction with marketing support" were influenced positively by coordination, meaning that more successful relationships with travel agents seem to exhibit higher levels of coordination. However, no significant association was found between coordination and "satisfaction with marketing support" ($P = 0.92$).

H3b: Relationships between hotel companies and travel agents with the highest levels of communicaton quality are expected to be the most successful.

Results show a significant positive association between communication quality and both "overall success" and "satisfaction with marketing suppport". Beta values also suggest that communication quality has a stronger association with "satisfaction with marketing suppport" than for "overall success". That is, as was foreseen, communication quality seems to characterize more successful relationships with travel agents.

H3c: Relationships between hotel companies and travel agents with the highest levels of information exchange are expected to be the most successful.

Table 2 shows that information exchange was positively associated with both "overall success" and "satisfaction with marketing support". Thus, true to expectations, more successful relationships with travel agents seem to exhibit higher levels of information exchange, compared with less successful ones. However, Beta values were not significant ($P = 0.21$ for "overall success" and $P = 0.19$ for "satisfaction with marketing support).

H3d: Relationships between hotel companies and travel agents with the highest levels of participation are expected to be the most successful.

In accordance with the hypothesis statement, the results of the study suggest that participation in decision making influenced positively on "overall success" and "satisfaction with marketing support", so that more successful relationships with travel agents seem to exhibit higher levels of participation (Table 3). However, the association between "overall success" and participation in decision making was not significant ($P = 0.55$).

H4a: Relationships between hotel companies and travel agents with the most use of constructive conflict resolution techniques, including joint problem solving and persuasion, are expected to be the most successful.

H4b: Relationships between hotel companies and travel agents with the least use of destructive conflict resolution techniques, including domination and harsh words, are expected to be the most successful.

H4c: Relationships between hotel companies and travel agents with the least use of other conflict resolution techniques, such as outside arbitration and smoothing/avoiding issues, are expected to be the most successful.

As shown in Table 3, results of multiple regression analyses indicated that the factor with the techniques "travel agent imposed domination", "harsh words", and "outside arbitration" was significantly negatively associated with overall success; and the factor with the techniques "smoothing over the problem", "persuasive attempts", and "joint problem solving" was significantly positively associated with overall success. However, no significant association was found with satisfaction with marketing support. Thus, the findings partially support the content of H4a, H4b and H4c.

H5: Relationships between hotel companies and travel agents with similar relative dependence between partners and the highest levels of interdependence are expected to be the most successful.

Results in Table 3 reveal no significant association between interdependence and either of the factors explaining the success of the relationship. With regard to relative dependence, measured as the difference in one partner's dependence on the other partner, the findings suggest the content of H5, to the extent that relative dependence had a significant negative association ($P < 0.05$) with both "overall success" and "satisfaction with marketing support" (Table 3). Therefore, considering that the lower the values of the variable "relative dependence", the more similar is the relative dependence, it might be said that successful relationships seem to exhibit similar relative dependence.

CONCLUSION

Empirical results from this study provide support for the majority of dimensions suggested in existing interorganizational literature as determining factors for successful IRs: trust, commitment, coordination, communication quality, information exchange, participation, usage of constructive resolution techniques, and similar relative dependence. The combined effect of the variables used in this study to measure these determining factors for successful IRs accounted for 60% of the overall success of the relationship between hotel companies and travel agents operating in the United States, and 33% of these hotel companies' satisfaction with marketing support by travel agents.

The practical implications to be drawn from this study are concerned with the manner in which hotel company managers should confront the future of their relationships with travel agencies. Specifically, the findings of this study suggest that in order to have successful relationships with travel agency companies, hotels should communicate with them in a timely, accurate, adequate, complete, and credible manner; show more commitment or dedication to maintaining this relationship; show a strong sense of loyalty; use joint problem solving, persuasive atempts and smoothing over the problem as the primary conflict resolution techniques; plan and schedule the sales with them; establish and maintain relationships with trusting and high-integrity travel agents; pay commissions promptly and on time; be less dependent on any one travel agency company for their business and be able to switch to other ones; provide them with what they need to sell (such as information regarding facilities, services, and special promotions); and seek advice from them.

The implementation of the aforementioned strategic actions by hotel companies should translate into more profitable business relationships. Potential benefits include more sales from travel agencies, appropriate commission levels, additional and improved promotional and advertising support by travel agencies, and compatibility of travel agent clientele with hotel companies' properties. Furthermore, transaction costs are expected to be reduced in as far as problems associated with opportunist behavior by travel agents and information asymmetries are avoided.

Another major practical implication is that knowledge of factors contributing to the success of the relationship between hotel companies and travel agencies could aid, not only in the ongoing management of existing relationships, but also in the selection of agencies as potential partners. Specifically, the results suggest that agents should be trusting, show a cooperative attitude, and be committed to the relationship with the hotel company. Similarly, hotel companies which are perceived as trusting, cooperative and committed to their relationships with travel agents, are expected to receive more offers from them to establish long-term business relationships. Thus, these conditions could represent major sources of competitive advantage for both travel agency and hotel companies which are interested in establishing business relationships. Moreover, hotel companies and travel agents should balance their relative dependence with a view to creating and developing profitable business relationships. As a result, it seems to be crucial that hotel companies establish relationships with a range of travel agents.

Generalization of study results is limited by the population and sample selected, which consist of hotel companies operating in the United States. The data reported here represent only one partner's (hotel companies) view of the relationship, at a corporate level, between hotel companies and travel agencies operating in this country. Another limitation of this study refers to the actual economic value of the success of the relationship. For example, the data do not allow conclusions on whether or not hotel companies reporting more successful relationships with travel agents are really having greater shares of agents' business. Similarly, the financial benefits that travel agents obtain by having successful relationships with hotel companies cannot be assessed.

Further, the scales measuring "information exchange" and "overall trust" showed questionable reliability values (0.53 and 0.52, respectively). These rates, although not unacceptable, could be higher if more items related to "information exchange" and "trust" were included in the questionnaire. However, the objective was to ensure the examination of the association between success of the relationship and most of the factors discussed in the literature. Thus, in order to not overwhelm respondents with too many questions, a limited number of items were included in the questionnaire.

As to future research directions, by collecting data from only hotel companies, this study suggests a number of factors contributing to the success of the relationship between hotel companies and travel agents. As the data represents only one partner's view of the relationship, a new study of the success of the relationship between hotel and travel agency companies from the latter's perspective is encouraged. Moreover, future research on this relationship should emphasize the need to be dyadic. More generally speaking, future research on IRs in the tourism industry should be designed in order to collect comparable data from all of the participants.

For a better understanding of successful IRs, the effect of additional factors should be examined in future research. Formalization of the relationship (Bresser 1988; Bucklin and Sengupta 1993; Heide 1994), flexibility of the relationship (Harrigan and Newman 1990), importance of the relationship for the parties involved (Bucklin and Sengupta 1993; Hall 1991), and frequency of transactions (Hall 1991) are factors that might be examined to enhance understanding of success differentials across interorganizational relationships. Other factors might be suggested by utilizing qualitative research techniques, such as case analyses. Specific studies should be also carried out to identify the nature and causes of each of the determinants of successful evolution of IRs. For instance, it would be interesting to describe the type of interorganizational communication that is associated with IR success. As regards conflict resolution techniques, it would be important to identify the types of conflicts affecting the success of IRs. Determinants of trust, commitment, and relative dependence would further contribute to improve present knowledge about successful IRs.

Finally, in order to improve the present understanding of IRs in the tourism industry, a study to examine relationships that hotel companies have with airlines, rental, recreational companies, tourism agencies, and other hotels should be undertaken. Although these, including travel agencies, operate independently and frequently compete with each other, they all form part of an overall system, in which all organizations interacting with and within tourism must work appropriately in order to provide tourists with a pleasant overall experience.

REFERENCES

American Hotel, and Association Motel
  1994 Directory of Hotel and Motel Companies. Michigan: American Hotel and Motel Association.
Anderson, E.
  1990 Two Firms, One Frontier: On Assessing Joint Venture Performance. Sloan Management Review 31(2):19–30.
Anderson, E., and B. Weitz
  1989 Determinants of Continuity in Conventional Industrial Channel Dyads. Marketing Science 8:310–323.
  1992 The Use of Pledges to Build and Sustain Commitment in Distribution Channels. Journal of Marketing 29:18–34.
Anderson, J., and J. Narus
  1984 A Model of the Distributor's Perspective of Distributor-Manufacturer Working Relationships. Journal of Marketing 48:62–74.
  1990 A Model of Distributor Firm and Manufacturer Firm Working Partnerships. Journal of Marketing 48:42–58.
Angelo, R. M., and A. N. Vladimir, eds.
  1994 Hospitality Today: An Introduction. Michigan: The Educational Institute of the American Hotel and Motel Association.
Babbie, E., ed.
  1995 The Practice of Social Research. California: Wadsworth.
Bagozzi, R. P., and Y. Yi
  1988 On the Evaluation of Structural Equation Models. Journal of the Academy of Marketing Sciences 16(1):74–94.
Barney, J. B., and M. H. Hansen
  1994 Trustworthiness as a Source of Competitive Advantage. Strategic Management Journal 15:175–190.
Biong, H.
  1993 Satisfaction and Loyalty to Suppliers Within the Grocery Trade. European Journal of Marketing 27:21–38.
Borys, B., and D. B. Jemison
  1989 Hybrid Arrangements as Strategic Alliances: Theoretical Issues in Organizational Combinations. Academy of Management Review 14:234–249.
Bresser, R. K. F.
  1988 Matching Collective and Competitive Strategies. Strategic Management Journal 9:375–385.
Bucklin, L. P., and S. Sengupta
  1993 Organizing Successful Co-marketing Alliances. Journal of Marketing 57:32–46.
Child, J., and D. Faulkner, eds.
  1998 Strategies of Co-operation: Managing Alliances, Networks, and Joint Ventures. Oxford: Oxford University Press.
Crawford-Welch, S.
  1991 An Empirical Examination of Mature Service Environments and High-performance Strategies within those Environments: The Case of the Lodging and Restaurant Industries. PhD dissertation. Virginia Polytechnic Institute and State University.
Cronbach, L. J.
  1951 Coefficient Alpha and the Internal Structure of Tests. Psycholometrika 16:297–334.
Cummings, T.
  1984 Transorganizational Development. Research in Organizational Behavior 6:367–422.
Devlin, G., and M. Bleackley
  1988 Strategic Alliances: Guidelines for Success. Long Range Planning 21:18–23.
Dillman, D. A., ed.
  1978 Mail and Telephone Surveys. New York: Wiley.

760   SUCCESSFUL BUSINESS RELATIONSHIP

Dwyer, F. R., P. H. Schurr, and S. Oh
    1987 Developing Buyer-Seller Relationships. Journal of Marketing 51:11–27.
Emmer, R. M., C. Tauck, S. Wilkinson, and R. G. Moore
    1993 Marketing Hotels: Using Global Distribution Systems. The Cornell
    Quarterly 34(6):2–11.
Etgar, M.
    1979 Sources and Types of Intrachannel Conflict. Journal of Retailing 55:61–78.
Frazier, G. I.
    1983 Interorganizational Exchange Behavior in Marketing Channels: A
    Broadened Perspective. Journal of Marketing 47:68–78.
Ganesan, S.
    1994 Determinants of Long-Term Orientation in Buyer–Seller Relationships.
    Journal of Marketing 58:1–19.
Gaski, J. F.
    1984 The Theory of Power and Conflict in Channels of Distribution. Journal of
    Marketing 48:9–29.
George, D., and P. Mallery, eds.
    1995 SPSS/PC+ Step by Step: A Simple Guide and Reference. Belmont CA:
    Wadsworth.
Gyenes, L. A.
    1991 Build the Foundation for a Successful Joint Venture. Journal of Business
    Strategy 12(6):27–32.
Hair, J. F. Jr, R. E. Anderson, and R. L. Tatham, eds.
    1987 Multivariate Data Analysis. New York: Mcmillan.
Hall, R. H., ed.
    1991 Organizations: Structures, Processes, & Outcomes. Englewood Cliffs NJ:
    Prentice-Hall.
Hallén, L., J. Johanson, and N. Seyed-Mohamed
    1991 Interfirm Adaptation in Business Relationships. Journal of Marketing
    55:29–37.
Hambrick, D. C.
    1981   Strategic Awareness Within Top Management Teams. Strategic
    Management Journal 2:263–279.
Harrigan, K. R.
    1985 Strategies for Joint Ventures. New York: Lexington.
    1988 Strategic Alliances and Partner Asymmetries. Management International
    Review 28:53–72.
Harrigan, K. R., and W. H. Newman
    1990 Bases of Interorganization Co-operation: Propensity, Power, Persistence.
    Journal of Management Studies 27:417–434.
Hedderson, J., ed.
    1991 SPSS/PC+ Made Simple. Belmont CA: Wadsworth.
Heide, J. B.
    1994   Interorganizational Governance in Marketing Channels. Journal of
    Marketing 58:71–85.
Heide, J. B., and G. John
    1988 The Role of Dependence Balancing in Safeguarding Transaction-Specific
    Assets in Conventional Channels. Journal of Marketing 52:20–35.
Hotel Motel Management
    1995 Technology. Hotel and Motel Management 210:19–40.
Johnston, R., and P. R. Lawrence
    1988 Beyond Vertical Integration: The Rise of the Value-Adding Partnership.
    Harvard Business Review 66:94–101.
Knight, M. B.
    1994 Build Partnership with Travel Agents. Successful Hotel Marketer 7(1):1.
Kohli, A.
    1989   Effects of Supervisory Behavior: The Role of Individual Differences
    Among Salespeople. Journal of Marketing 53:40–50.
Koss, L.
    1992   Hoteliers, Travel Agents Urged to Work Together. Hotel & Motel
    Management 207(13):8.

Lynch, R. P., ed.
  1993 Business Alliances Guide: The Hidden Competitive Weapon. New York:
    Wiley.
March, J. G., and H. A. Simon, eds.
  1958 Organizations. New York: Wiley.
Mohr, J., and R. Nevin
  1990   Communications Strategies in Marketing Channels: A Theoretical
    Perspective. Journal of Marketing 54:36–51.
Mohr, J., and R. Spekman
  1994   Characteristics of Partnership Success: Partnership Attributes,
    Communication Behavior, and Conflict Resolution Techniques. Strategic
    Management Journal 15:135–152.
Morgan, R. M., and S. D. Hunt
  1994 The Commitment-Trust Theory of Relationship Marketing. Journal of
    Marketing 58:20–38.
Narus, J., and J. Anderson
  1987 Distributor Contributions to Partnerships with Manufacturers. Business
    Horizons 30:34–42.
O'Callaghan, R.
  1986 Sistemas Inter-organizacionales. Nueva Arma Competitiva. Alta Dirección
    128:257–262.
Pekar, P. Jr, and R. Allio
  1994 Making Alliances Work: Guidelines for Success. Long Range Planning
    27(4):54–65.
Pfeffer, J., and G. Salancik, eds.
  1978   The External Control of Organization: A Resource Dependence
    Perspective. New York: Harper & Row.
Poon, A., ed.
  1998   Tourism, Technology and Competitive Strategies. New York: CAB
    International.
Provan, K. G., and J. B. Gassenheimer
  1994 Supplier Commitment in Relational Contract Exchanges with Buyers: A
    Study of Interorganizational Dependence and Exercised Power. Journal of
    Management Studies 31(1):55–68.
Rao, H.
  1994   The Social Construction of Reputation: Certification Contests,
    Legitimation, and the Survival of Organizations in the American Automobile
    Industry: 1895–1912. Strategic Management Journal 15:29–44.
Salant, P., and D. A. Dillman, eds.
  1994 How to Conduct your Own Survey. New York: Wiley.
Schulz, C.
  1994 Hotels and Travel Agents: The New Partnership. The Cornell Quarterly
    35(2):45–50.
Shamdasani, P. N., and J. N. Sheth
  1995 An Experimental Approach to Investigating Satisfaction and Continuity in
    Marketing Alliances. European Journal of Marketing 29(4):6–23.
Stafford, E. R.
  1994   Using Co-operative Strategies to Make Alliances Work. Long Range
    Planning 27(3):64–74.
Stern, L., and A. El-Ansary, eds.
  1992 Marketing Channels. Englewood Cliffs NJ: Prentice-Hall.
Travel Weekly.
  1994 Top 50 Travel Agencies of 1994. Travel Weekly (July 28):5.
Vallen, J. J., and G. K. Vallen, eds.
  1991 Check-in Check-out. Iowa: C. Brown.
Van de Ven, A. H., and D. I. Ferry, eds.
  1980 Measuring and Assessing Organizations. New York: Wiley.
Venkatraman, N., and J. H. Grant
  1986 Construct Measurement in Organizational Strategy Research: A Critique
    and Proposal. Academy of Management Review 11(1):71–87.

762   SUCCESSFUL BUSINESS RELATIONSHIP

Williamson, O. E., ed.
    1985 The Economic Institutions of Capitalism. New York: Free Press.
Wray, B., A. Palmer, and D. Bejou
    1994   Using Neural Network Analysis to Evaluate Buyer-Seller Relationships.
    European Journal of Marketing 28(10):32–48.

*Assigned 8 June 1998. Submitted 18 November 1998. Submitted 1 March 1999. Submitted 8
April 1999. Accepted 2 June 1999. Final version 27 July 1999. Refereed anonymously.
Coordinating Editor: Josef A. Mazanec.*

[6]

ELSEVIER

Available online at www.sciencedirect.com

SCIENCE @ DIRECT•

Tourism Management 25 (2004) 669–683

TOURISM MANAGEMENT

www.elsevier.com/locate/tourman

Chaos, crises and disasters: a strategic approach to crisis management in the tourism industry

Brent W. Ritchie[a,b,*]

[a] *School of Service Management, Faculty of Management and Information Science, University of Brighton, 49 Darley Road, Eastbourne BN20 7UR, UK*
[b] *Centre for Tourism Research, University of Canberra, ACT 2601, Australia*

Received 1 April 2003; accepted 17 July 2003

Abstract

This paper outlines and discusses a strategic and holistic approach to crisis management for the tourism industry. It notes the growing importance of crisis and disaster management for the tourism industry before exploring the definitions and nature of crises and disasters. The paper then proposes a strategic approach to their management from proactive pre-crisis planning through strategic implementation and finally evaluation and feedback. A discussion of crisis and disaster management literature and studies conducted in the tourism field are also introduced. It notes that although crises and disasters cannot be stopped their impacts can be limited by both public and private sector managers. The paper concludes that the understanding and subsequent management of such incidents can be vastly improved through the extension and application of crisis and disaster management theory and concepts from other disciplines, coupled with the development of specific tourism crisis management research and frameworks.
© 2003 Elsevier Ltd. All rights reserved.

Keywords: Crisis; Disaster; Tourism

1. Introduction

Faulkner (2001) notes an increasing number of disasters and crises which affect the tourism industry, ranging from natural to human influenced incidents. In recent years the global tourism industry has experienced many crises and disasters including terrorist attacks, political instability, economic recession, biosecurity threats and natural disasters. Lee and Harrald (1999, p. 184) state that "natural disasters can disrupt the supply and distribution chains for even the best prepared businesses...service businesses are increasingly vulnerable to electrical, communication and other critical infrastructure failures." This vulnerability can also be exposed through human induced behaviour most evident by September 11, 2001 and the Bali Bomb Attack, which dramatically impacted upon the tourism and travel industry. Faulkner (2001) argues that there is a lack of research on crisis or disaster phenomena in the

tourism industry, on the impacts of such events on both the industry and specific organisations, and the responses of the tourism industry to such incidents. This lack of interest and research is somewhat surprising considering that crisis management, disaster recovery and organisational continuity are important competencies for managers in both the public and private sector (Lee & Harrald, 1999, p. 184).

This paper aims to address these deficiencies and explore crisis and disaster management for the tourism industry by considering a strategic and holistic approach to crisis and disaster management. However, the article also notes the difficulty in responding to chaotic situations, which are often unpredictable and difficult to control. Nevertheless, this article stresses that chaos and change are an important part of public and private sector management which should be embraced and considered in modern tourism management. The paper begins by defining crises and disasters to improve our understanding of these phenomena before outlining the desire for management control over these incidents. The paper then suggests that a strategic approach to crisis management can be beneficial and proposes such an

*Corresponding address: Centre for Tourism Research, University of Canberra, ACT 2601, Australia.

E-mail address: Brent.Ritchie@canberra.edu.au (B.W. Ritchie).

0261-5177/$ - see front matter © 2003 Elsevier Ltd. All rights reserved.
doi:10.1016/j.tourman.2003.09.004

670   *B.W. Ritchie / Tourism Management 25 (2004) 669–683*

approach for the tourism and travel industry. The paper outlines key aspects of a strategic and holistic approach drawing on the crisis management literature and previous research in the tourism field. Finally the paper discusses future research avenues which could contribute to better understanding, planning and management of crises and disasters in an increasingly complex and disaster prone world.

2. Importance of crisis/disaster management for tourism

According to some authors the current state of the world is directly responsible for an increase in disasters and crises (Brammer, 1990; Blaikie, Cannon, Davis, & Wisner, 1994; Berke, 1998). As Richardson (1994) notes our environment has become a more crowded world and as the population increases pressures such as urbanisation, the extension of human settlement, and the greater use and dependence on technology have perhaps led to an increase in disasters and crises. The globalisation of the tourism industry has led to a rapid expansion of tourism businesses on an international scale in order to expand their market share and profitability. However, this process has also opened businesses up to a wider set of 'global risks' involved in running businesses at such a scale, as globalisation is often seen as complex and chaotic (Jessop, 1999). Greater exposure to political, economic, social and technological change in countries often removed from the bases of tourism companies requires tourism managers to effectively deal with crises and disasters (often located a substantial distance away). The world is also becoming more interdependent and connected so that small-scale crises in one part of the world can have a significant impact on other parts of the world. Political instability, or the outbreak of war in one part of the world can dramatically reduce tourist travel patterns to other parts of the world as experienced by the Gulf War of 1991 and the Iraq conflict in 2003. Tourism is therefore highly susceptible to external factors and pressures in the wider operating environment.

However, tourism is also an important economic sector for many countries and many destinations are dependent upon tourism for their growth and survival. This puts increasing pressure on managers and planners concerned with tourism to consider the impact of crises and disasters on the industry and develop strategies to deal with the impacts to protect tourism business and society in general. There is a need to understand such incidents and examine strategies that can be used to stop or limit their impacts on a growing and important industry sector. Crisis and disaster management should be a core competency for tourism destination managers as well as business managers. This paper proposes that understanding the nature of crises and disasters is a first

step in considering how to manage and reduce the impacts of such incidents.

3. Understanding crises and disasters

A number of authors have attempted to understand crises and disasters by first defining crises and disasters, explaining the nature of crises and disaster and their lifecycle or anatomy to help improve our understanding of such phenomena, and finally, by stressing the complexity and chaotic nature of incidents which pose challenges in managing or preventing crises or disasters.

3.1. Definitions

A number of authors have attempted to define a crisis to help improve their understanding of this phenomenon. Pauchant and Mitroff (1992, p. 15) believe that a crisis is a "disruption that physically affects a system as a whole and threatens its basic assumptions, its subjective sense of self, its existential core." Selbst (1978 in Faulkner 2001, p. 136) defines a crisis as "any action or failure to act that interferes with an organisation's ongoing functions, the acceptable attainment of its objectives, its viability or survival, or that has a detrimental personal effect as perceived by the majority of its employees, clients or constituents." Selbst's focus on perceptions implies that if an organisation's publics or stakeholders perceive a crisis, a real crisis could evolve from this misconception, illustrating that perception management is an important consideration in managing crises.

Faulkner (2001) considers the principal distinction between what can be termed a 'crisis' and a 'disaster' to be the extent to which the situation is attributable to the organisation itself, or can be described as originating from outside the organisation. Thus, a 'crisis' describes a situation "where the root cause of an event is, to some extent, self-inflicted through such problems as inept management structures and practices or a failure to adapt to change", while a "disaster can be defined as "where an enterprise...is confronted with sudden unpredictable catastrophic changes over which it has little control" (Faulkner, 2001, p. 136).

3.2. Nature and anatomy of crises and disasters

Crises can range, according to Coombs (1999) from small-scale organisational issues ranging from staff illness, staff challenges/breakdowns, malevolence and organisational misdeeds to external factors such as natural disasters (earthquakes, floods and fires) and terrorist incidents. However, for the purposes of this paper focus will be made on large-scale crises or

B.W. Ritchie / Tourism Management 25 (2004) 669–683   671

disasters that have the ability to cause the most damage to destinations and organizations.

Parsons (1996) suggests three types of crises:

1. *Immediate crises*: where little or no warning exists therefore organisations are unable to research the problem or prepare a plan before the crisis hits.
2. *Emerging crises*: these are slower in developing and may be able to be stopped or limited by organisational action.
3. *Sustained crises*: that may last for weeks, months or even years.

Strategies to deal with these different crisis situations will vary depending on time pressure, the extent of control and the magnitude of these incidents. The threat, time pressure and intensity of these incidents can lead to the development of a crisis or disaster continuum to help classify and understand such incidents and, more importantly, illustrate to managers when an 'issue' or a 'problem' can develop into a 'crisis.' Burnett (1998) outlines a crisis classification matrix (Fig. 1) which uses a sixteen cell matrix based on threat-level (high versus low), response options (many versus few), time pressure (intense versus minimal) and degree of control (high versus low).

Burnett (1998) suggests that problems or issues found in level 1 or the level 0 cell would not be classified as a crisis but would enable general strategic management responses as part of the normal management function. The most challenging problems are found in the lone level 4 cell as the time pressure is intense, the degree of control is low, the threat-level high and response options are few in number. Several of level 2 or 3 cells could develop or be classified as crises although Burnett (1998) does not state which ones specifically.

Previous crisis management research has also focussed on producing prescriptive models concerning the stages of crises to assist understanding and future proactive and strategic management of crises (see Richardson, 1994, 1995). In some cases these models or frameworks have been applied to real life case studies providing descriptive models. Fink (1986) and Roberts (1994) both developed slightly different models to explain the lifecycle of crises (see Table 1) suggesting that crises and disasters go through series of progressive stages. This classification based on lifecycle or anatomy is useful as it may illustrate to managers what strategies could be considered or developed at the various stages of a crisis or disaster and how to stop crises moving into the next stage. Using this lifecycle model, Faulkner (2001) developed the first tourism specific disaster management framework and subsequently applied this framework to the Katherine Floods in Australia making some modifications based on application to the case study (see Faulkner & Vikulov, 2001). Miller and Ritchie (2003) applied Faulkner's (2001) disaster framework to the 2001 Foot and Mouth Outbreak in the UK, but further testing and the development and application of theoretical frameworks for crisis and disaster management is required in the tourism industry.

Understanding crises and disasters, their lifecycle and potential impacts and actions can help in the development of strategies by organisations to deal with such incidents. By understanding these phenomena more effective strategies can be developed to stop or reduce the severity of their impacts on business and society, despite their complexity.

3.3. Dealing with complexity

However, despite the obvious need to understand and control the impacts of such incidents this is not simple for managers because of the chaotic nature of crises and disasters and the uncertainty that surrounds them. As

	Time pressure	Intense		Minimal	
Threat Level	Degree of control	Low	High	Low	High
	Response options				
Low	Many	(4) Level 2	(3) Level 1	(2) Level 1	(1) Level 0
	Few	(8) Level 3	(7) Level 2	(6) Level 2	(5) Level 1
High	Many	(12) Level 3	(11) Level 2	(10) Level 2	(9) Level 1
	Few	(16) Level 4	(15) Level 3	(14) Level 3	(13) Level 2

Source: Burnett (1998:483).

Fig. 1. A crisis classification matrix.

672   *B.W. Ritchie / Tourism Management 25 (2004) 669–683*

Table 1
Crisis and disaster lifecycle

Faulkner's (2001) stages	Fink's (1986) stages	Roberts (1994) stages
1. Pre-event		*Pre-event*: where action can be taken to prevent disasters (e.g. growth management planning or plans aimed at mitigating the effects of potential disasters)
2. Prodromal	*Prodromal stage*: when it becomes apparent that the crisis is inevitable	
3. Emergency	*Acute stage*: the point of no return when the crisis has hit and damage limitation is the main objective	*Emergency phase*: when the effects of the disaster has been felt and action has to be taken to rescue people and property
4. Intermediate		*Intermediate phase*: when the short-term needs of the people must be dealt with—restoring utilities and essential services. The objective at this point being to restore the community to normality as quickly as possible
5. Long term (recovery)	*Chronic stage*: clean-up, post-mortem, self-analysis and healing	*Long-term phase*: continuation of the previous phase, but items that could not be addressed quickly are attended to at this point (repair of damaged infrastructure, correcting environmental problems, counselling victims, reinvestment strategies, debriefings to provide input to revisions of disaster strategies)
6. Resolution	*Resolution*: routine restored or new improved state	

Source: after Faulkner (2001, p. 140).

Burnett (1998, p. 476) notes crises are difficult to resolve due to time pressure constraints, limited control and high uncertainty. Previous research has illustrated the difficulty in identifying the stages of a crisis, particularly for those that are long running or sustained, as the case of political instability in Israel (see Beirman, 2002a). Furthermore, identifying stages of a crisis is difficult when the crisis or disaster is spread geographically over a large area, as was the case with the Foot and Mouth Outbreak in the UK. Different regions were simultaneously in the emergency, intermediate and resolution stage of a crises while others were totally unaffected by the disease complicating management of the outbreak (see Miller & Ritchie, 2003).

Complexity and chaos theory may provide some insights into crisis and disaster management for organisations in the tourism industry. Crises and disasters illustrate chaotic situations and illustrate the complex interrelationships between human and natural systems (Faulkner, 2001). Understanding the relationship between cause and effect and the implications of decisions and actions is a complicated process. This is illustrated in the case of the Foot and Mouth Outbreak which started out as a farming crisis and ended up as a disaster for the tourism industry because of the way that it was handled (see Miller & Ritchie, 2003 for more information). Similarly, the SARS virus and its spread

throughout the world also illustrates the complex relationship between human and natural system. The boundaries between human action or inaction and the development of disaster/crisis phenomena is becoming increasingly difficult to distinguish because of this increasing complexity. Many stable systems can be influenced by small changes that can impact upon their stability. Here the 'ripple effect' is worth noting. Heath (1998, p. 9) stated that "the ability of a crisis to cause other crisis situations because these crises seem to fan outward" severely impacting other systems through their interdependence. Heath (1998) believed that effective and well planned crisis management strategies were needed to prevent or limit the 'ripple effect' or outward chaos associated with crisis incidents not only between organisations but also across different industrial sectors (agriculture, tourism).

4. A strategic and holistic approach to crisis planning and management

Organisations of all shapes and sizes all have to deal with change at some point in their lifecycle, and all destinations will have to deal with a disaster at some stage (Faulkner, 2001). Kash and Darling (1998, p. 179) claim that it is no longer a case of 'if' an organisation

B.W. Ritchie / Tourism Management 25 (2004) 669–683 673

will face a crisis; it is rather a question of 'when', 'what type' and 'how prepared' the organisation is to deal with it. Fink (1986, p. 7) believes that all businesses are on the edge of chaos stating "anytime you (i.e. managers) are not in crisis, you are instead in pre-crisis, or prodromal model." A core competency of managers is therefore to deal with and manage such change. Smallman (1996) notes there is a need for managers to move from a current dominant reactive paradigm to a proactive, holistic approach to dealing with chaos and change. Although, as previously noted, it is difficult to predict or control crises or disasters, managers are still able to reduce risk and prepare so that they can deal with such incidents more effectively than without any preparation. Developing organisational strategy can help organisations and destination to avoid or limit the severity of rapid change induced by crises or disasters.

Strategy has been defined by Johnson and Scholes (1993) as "the direction and scope of an organisation over the long term: ideally, which matches its resources to its changing environment, and in particular, its markets, customers or clients to meet stakeholder expectations."

Strategic planning and management is usually concerned with four main elements (Richardson & Richardson, 1992; Johnson & Scholes, 1993; Viljoen, 1994):

- *strategic analysis*: examining the macro or micro operating environment;
- *strategic direction and choice*: developing and selecting strategic directions and specific generic strategies to achieve organisational goals;
- *strategy implementation and control*: developing suitable organisational structures, human and financial resource strategies, providing leadership to control and allow for the implementation of specific strategies; and,
- *strategic evaluation and feedback*: continuous improvement is an important part of strategic planning and management and organisations learn how to improve the effectiveness of strategies through evaluation and monitoring.

The effective management of crises and disasters is vital for the tourism industry, which is often impacted negatively by external political, economic, social and technological factors often beyond the industry's immediate control. However, the emphasis of this paper is on controlling and managing complex incidents by public and private sector managers in the tourism industry, rather than other management or planning functions such as increasing market share, profitability, etc.

Fig. 2 sets out a strategic framework for the planning and management of crises and disasters for public or private sector organisations. The model suggests that a strategic management and planning approach to crisis and disaster management can be beneficial for tourism planners and managers. In particular, the model outlines three main stages in managing such incidents strategically: prevention and planning, implementation, evaluation and feedback. Within each stage various management tasks or activities are illustrated. Although not designed to be comprehensive due to space and time limitations, for the purposes of this paper the aspects illustrated in the model are considered by the author as the most common attributes in managing crises and act as discussion points within this paper. They are discussed in more detail with examples from the management and tourism field later in this section.

However, understanding and classifying crises and disasters, including the type of incident, its scale and magnitude (discussed in the previous section) will impact upon strategy development and implementation. Specific strategies will have to be developed to deal with an evolving crisis or disaster as it progresses through its lifecycle. A crisis with a long drawn out emergency phase may require quite different strategies than a crisis which quickly progresses through the intermediate, long term and finally to the resolution stage. A sustained crisis will require different strategies than an immediate crisis. Nevertheless, there appears are clear similarities between the lifecycle of a crisis and the strategic management framework including:

- a pre-event stage allowing the development of strategy and plans;
- a stage immediately before or after a crisis or disaster occurs which requires the implementation of strategies to deal with its impacts;
- continued implementation of strategies to control or reduce the severity of the crisis/disaster; and,
- a long term recovery or resolution phase allowing for evaluation and feedback into future prevention and planning strategies for destinations and businesses.

However, at all stages of the strategic management process there needs to be flexibility, evaluation and potential modification to strategy development and implementation depending on the nature of the crisis/disaster (its magnitude, scale and time pressure) and stakeholder response to strategies. Authors such as Kash and Darling (1998) believe that although crisis management is a requirement for organisations, and although business leaders recognise this, many do not undertake productive steps to address crisis situations. Managers who do take productive steps will be in a much better position to respond when a crisis or disaster effects an organisation or destination. The remainder of this section of the paper addresses the main elements of a proposed strategic management framework with reference to the literature on crisis management and

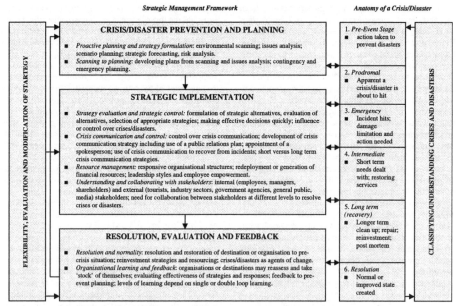

Fig. 2. Crisis and disaster management: a strategic and holistic framework.

provides, where applicable, specific tourism literature and examples. However, to date the literature directly related to crisis management in the tourism industry is scarce, although it is growing due to recent incidents of terrorism, war and the SARS outbreak (for recent books on the subject see Beirman, 2002b; Glaesser, 2003).

4.1. Crisis and disaster prevention and planning

At the pre-event and prodromal stage of a crisis or disaster activities can be undertaken by public and private sector organisations and managers to develop strategies and plans to stop or limit the impacts of a crisis or disaster (ranging from employee strikes, terrorist attacks, economic recessions, etc.).

Although organisations are able to design pre-crisis strategies to help with crisis management they are often unable to prevent a crisis from occurring. However, the real challenge is to recognise crises in a timely fashion and implement coping strategies to limit their damage (Darling, Hannu, & Raimo, 1996). Authors such as Burnett (1998) and Kash and Darling (1998) note that decisions undertaken before a crisis occurs will enable more effective management of the crisis, rather than organisations being managed by the crisis and making hasty and ineffective decisions. Proactive planning through the use of strategic planning and issues

management will help reduce risk, time wastage, poor resource management and reduce the impacts of those that do arise (Heath, 1998).

A number of techniques have been identified by researchers and practitioners to help in the proactive planning and strategy development for the prevention or reduction of crises and disasters through sensing potential problems (Gonzales-Herrero & Pratt, 1998). Authors such as Darling (1994) and Kash and Darling (1998) suggest that developing processes to deal with future crises as they arise are more efficient than continually scanning for all potential impacts. Problem recognition through environmental scanning and collecting data on the political, economic, social and technological environment can provide information on possible trends and their likely impacts on the organisation. Other tools identified by Kash and Darling (1998) include:

- *strategic forecasting*: allowing for predictions based on potential crisis or disaster situations and could include opinion based quantification, extrapolation of trends, simulation and cause and effect methods. Examples include the forecasting of the impact of the 1997–1998 Asian Economic Crisis to determine its impact on outbound travel to Australia.
- *contingency planning*: these are alternative plans which can be implemented if a crisis or disaster hits

B.W. Ritchie / Tourism Management 25 (2004) 669–683 675

and impacts upon the strategic direction of an organisation. These are helpful for less certain situations and can help resolve crisis situations quickly if they were to occur. Examples include contingency plans for impending war or the possible striking of key airline workers. Plans may include removing some destinations from tour operator itineraries or moving tasks from frontline to management staff for the duration of the strike.

- *issues analysis*: this is similar to contingency planning but it alerts managers to evolving trends in the external environment which can be used in developing strategies to use the trend to its advantage. Examples include the increasing environmental awareness of consumers. If hotels do not consider implementing waste reduction and energy efficient practices they may lose their market share to rival hotels who do implement such strategies.
- *scenario analysis*: which are detailed attempts to describe a potential end state if certain decisions were made by an organisation. The scenario is hypothetical but able to create discussion over decisions which can then be turned into contingency or emergency plans. Examples could include management succession plans or business take-over scenarios in the hotel sector.

For natural disasters proactive planning could also consider:

- *risk analysis and hazard mapping*: such as history of natural disasters in the area and likelihood of reoccurrence.
- *integrated emergency planning*: including pre-planning of advance warning systems, creation of a disaster management command centre, prepared coordination between emergency services and tourism authorities.

These techniques signify the need for managers and planners to gather information on potential issues or problems and what plans or strategies they would implement if a crisis or disaster occurs. Understanding the type of disaster or crisis a destination or organisation is susceptible to, and the nature of such an incident is invaluable to the creation of suitable plans and strategies which can prevent or limit the impact of such an incident. In short, moving from simply 'scanning to planning' is required through developing contingency and integrated emergency plans. If a potential crisis or disaster is identified then strategies may be implemented to stop it occurring. If however, this cannot occur then the crisis enters the prodromal stage and into the next phase of strategic crisis management: the implementation of strategies and plans to deal with the impacts.

However, despite the importance of proactive planning research conducted by Gonzalez Herrero (1997)

discovered in nation wide research that tourist organizations in the USA are better prepared to prevent and cope with business crises than comparable organizations in Spain. Only around 29% of Spanish organizations had crisis plans compared with 78% in the USA. Absence of formal planning was also discovered by Henderson (1999a, b. 2002) in research concerning crisis management of the tourism industry in Asia, despite the industry being subject to uncertainty, risk and external factors. Barton (1994) also noted the need for crisis management strategies in the hospitality sector, while facility managers could also benefit from crisis and disaster management (Barton & Hardigree, 1995). Furthermore, adventure tourism operators also need to deal with crises and incidents often concerning risk management as Beeton (2001) notes with respect to horseback tourism.

4.2. Strategic implementation

As an 'issue' develops into a crisis or disaster for managers it enters the prodromal phase of its lifecycle. If managers are aware of the impending crisis or disaster (through the use of proactive scanning) and have developed contingency or emergency planning procedures, they are able to implement strategies to stop a crisis/disaster from occurring or to limit its impacts on business and society. However, the implementation phase can also be complex and chaotic and complicate any specific strategy implementation. Implementation therefore requires flexibility, constant monitoring concerning:

- the evaluation, selection and implementation of appropriate strategies;
- implementing an effective crisis communication and control strategy;
- controlling or reallocating resources to deal effectively with such incidents; and,
- identifying and working collaboratively with key stakeholders in the tourism and other industry sectors.

Regular meetings (perhaps even daily) are required to assess the effectiveness of strategies, the response of various stakeholders to strategies and to review the development of the crisis or disaster as it evolves over its lifecycle.

4.2.1. Strategic evaluation and strategic control

This activity provides for the thorough evaluation of the possible strategies that are available to the organisation and the selection of those that will best fit its needs. However, the paradox of strategy selection and implementation is that decisions have to made quickly to limit the damage caused by a crisis or disaster, yet the nature of a crisis and its long term impacts may not be

676   *B.W. Ritchie / Tourism Management 25 (2004) 669–683*

fully known by an organisation. This requires the organisation to decide and act under intense time pressure and is what differentiates crisis management from normal strategic management (Burnett, 1998). Strategic alternatives will hopefully be generated from the proactive pre-event planning and environmental scanning. However, these may have to be modified in responding to crises of different magnitudes and threats and their impacts upon various stakeholders. Strategic options need to be evaluated and chosen quickly so that the organisation can gain control of the situation (Heath, 1998).

If response occurs in the emergency phase then important decisions on the handling of the crisis can be rushed resulting in hasty and inefficient decisions made in the midst of a crisis. Miller and Ritchie (2003) note this with respect to the Foot and Mouth Outbreak where the consideration of strategies to deal with the outbreak occurred after the crisis hit. In particular, the debate over whether to vaccinate animals was made in the emergency phase of the crisis which slowed the response of governmental agencies limiting the effectiveness to contain the spread of the outbreak. A lack of response to previous terrorist threats was noted by Hall (2002) with respect to the airline industry prior to September 11, 2001 while reports of terrorist activity in Indonesia prior to the Bali Bombing were ignored by local authorities.

However, some situations exist where organisations are unable to control a crisis or disaster, in cases where the crisis is widespread geographically or being dealt with by other organisations and is thus too far removed from making needed change. Again the Foot and Mouth Outbreak provides an example of these issues. Ritchie, Dorrell, Miller, and Miller (2003) note that decisions made at the national level over the handling of the outbreak were slowly filtered down to the regional and local level however they would change day by day as policies were developed during the outbreak, illustrating the complexity and chaotic nature of the incident. An example related to terrorism is the case of American Airlines who had to very carefully consider their strategies and advertising immediately after September 11, 2001 in order to rebuild confidence in air travel (Britton, 2003) which was difficult during an ongoing investigation by authorities into the terrorist incident. American Airlines strategy was in some ways restricted by government regulations and public perceptions and sentiment.

4.2.2. Crisis communication and control

Crisis management literature emphasises the need to have a detailed communication strategy as the media can encourage the flow and the intensity of a crisis or even turn an incident into a crisis (Keown-McMullan, 1997). Barton (1994) believes that the implementation of

a strategic crisis communication plan can help limit the damage from a crisis and allow an organisation to concentrate on dealing with the crisis at hand. Marra (1998, p. 461) notes that poor communication strategies can often make the crisis worse as a deluge of questions are often asked from a wide range of stakeholders including reporters, employees, stockholders, government officials and public residents.

Responding quickly to demands of the media and publics is important as the media have deadlines to work to and are looking for quick sources of information. If the crisis team does not fill the void, someone else will (Coombs, 1999). Zerman (1995, p. 25) agrees stating that "the mass media has the power to make a break a business." Sensationalist media coverage of the 1980 Mt. St. Helens disaster and the 1985 East Kootenay forest fires were noted as contributing to confusion during the emergency phase as the media were blamed for misleading public opinion concerning the severity of the disasters. This also impacted upon the long term recovery phase for the destination (see Murphey & Bayley, 1989). Beirman, (2002a, p. 169) notes that the media reporting of the more recent Palestinian–Israeli conflict has given the false impression that Israel is enmeshed in violence, severely damaging the tourism industry at an important time for pilgrimage tourism in 2000/2001. In the Foot and Mouth Outbreak, the British Tourist Authority felt that the media was very intense for the first 3 months and at times their reporting was hostile, sometimes neutral but rarely friendly leading to misinformation and a severe decline in tourism (British Tourist Authority (BTA), 2001). This hostility was also noted by Britton (2003) who believed that the hostility of the media towards the airline sector before September 11, 2001 also influenced the way the crises was handled by American Airlines.

However, in contrast to this Hall (2002) notes that the media, through the issue-attention cycle, can bring issues to the attention of government and policy makers because of the power and influence they have over public opinion, and in fact can help speed up the recovery process. Soñmez, Apostolopoulos, and Tarlow (1999) agree and note that the media are very important to help rebuild the image and restore confidence in a destination or organisation. Nevertheless, despite the importance of dealing with the media difficulties have been noted in managing them as it is unlikely that there will be a time delay between the start of any crisis and media coverage (Ashcroft, 1997).

Crisis communication and control is mainly concerned with providing correct and consistent information to the public and enhancing the image of the organisation or industry sector faced with a crisis. An emphasis on communication and public relations is required to limit harm to an organisation in an

B.W. Ritchie / Tourism Management 25 (2004) 669–683   677

emergency that could ultimately create irreparable damage. Co-operation with the media is considered vital because the media provides information to the public (Berry, 1999), illustrating the need to keep the media briefed frequently so misinformation is reduced. Regular two-way communication is the best way of developing a favourable relationship with publics (Coombs, 1999, p. 134).

Consistency of response is also noted as a key element in crisis communication. The ability to provide a consistent message to all stakeholders will build credibility and preserve the image of an organisation instead of tarnishing reputations through providing inconsistent messages (Coombs, 1999). Barton (1994) believes that many issues are overlooked by crisis managers regarding crisis communication, namely to focus on identifying the audience, developing goals for communicating effectively and creating strong positive messages.

Henderson (1999a, p. 108) states that "National Tourist Organisations with their responsibility for general destination marketing, research and development have an important role to play in the process of travel and tourism crisis management, representing and acting on behalf of the industry as a whole." However, Henderson (1999a) found that in the case of the Asian Economic Crisis, the Singapore Tourist Board implemented reactive strategies which took time to implement reducing their effectiveness. Herrero (1999) explains how numerous tourist enterprises and organizations have managed to reduce the negative impact of crisis situations thanks to the previous design of a communications plan. Soñmez et al. (1999) noted the importance for marketers to have a prepared crisis communication and marketing plan, as the cost of this will be far less than the costs associated with a downturn in visitor confidence and visitation due to a slow response. As Soñmez et al. (1999, p. 8) note "it is imperative for destinations to augment their crisis management plans with marketing efforts, to recover lost tourism by rebuilding a positive image."

4.2.3. Resource management

Throughout crisis implementation an organisation or destination area has to reorganise or reconfigure itself to deploy and control resources. These resources can include financial or human resources and may include the formation of crisis management units or teams within an organisation or at a destination level. They can also include the provision of support services for victims of disasters and for media. However, some authors believe that strategies alone will not be effective if an organisation does not have an adaptive, flexible, or responsive organisational culture and needs strong leadership to control strategy implementation. As Marra (1998, p. 472) states in regard to crisis communication strategy "a good strategy, will, in most cases,

lead to successful crisis management. Poor strategy, in turn, will worsen a crisis. Excellent crisis public relations skills, however, cannot save bad management, poor policies, and weak strategy." These aspects are considered in this section of the paper.

Leadership in dealing with a crisis or disaster has been mentioned by a number of key authors (Faulkner, 2001; Turner, 1994; Cassedy, 1991). Leadership is required within a specific organisation, within an industry sector, and at a destination level to provide direction and guidance in dealing with incidents as well as a spokesperson to deal with the media. According to Heath (1995, p. 13) "in crisis and disaster response management…time is too limited for consensus driven decision-making processes that include all those involved." Heath (1995) was referring to the delay by the Japanese government in responding to the Kobe earthquake, and suggests that fast leadership and the ability to make quick decisions is needed. This is easier to do if there is a pre-crisis unit or management team at an organisation, industry or destination level.

Cassedy (1991) suggests the need for a team leader to co-ordinate and control a crisis management team, which should help identify and develop crisis management strategies to deal with incidents. They should meet regularly to reflect and redesign the strategy as the environment changes and a pre-planned team can also respond to crises quickly and implement strategies more effectively. Essentially the team should be cross-functional providing input from all parts of a respective business, industry or destination to more effectively cover issues and problems likely to be encountered. Parsons (1996) suggests at an organisational level a steering group of senior executives should be involved but only one, preferably a senior director, should be nominated as a spokesperson.

Because tourism is an industry which comprises many individual businesses from a wide range of sectors, and public sector organizations at the international, national, regional and local level, an integrated approach to crisis and disaster management is required. Within the tourism industry established and large companies may have such a crisis management team on permanent staff. However, the tourism and travel industry is characterised by a large number of small or micro businesses and may rely on industry organisations to provide support during a crisis or disaster who can help integrate emergency planning. In fact local or regional plans should be augmented with national level disaster and crisis strategies. For instance, the Federation of Tour Operators (FTO) in Britain have a designated crisis management team who help members deal with crises and disasters and use their experience to provide leadership to the industry. They also provide workshops with the Association of British Travel Agents (ABTA) on effective crisis management for industry members.

At the destination level there are many examples of teams or crisis management units that have been developed to deal with tourism crises and disasters. Again the team should comprise representatives from local government, travel and tourism industry professionals and community leaders. Soñmez et al. (1999) suggest that any group can be divided into teams to share tasks including:

- a *communications/public relations team* to represent the destination and provide accurate information;
- a *marketing/promotional team* to manage the recovery marketing process including any required re-imaging or branding activities;
- an *information co-ordination team* to assess the damage done to help aid recovery; and,
- a *financial or fund raising team* to estimate the cost of recovery and develop fund raising or lobbying government to fund the ongoing crisis management activities.

The development of Fiji's Tourism Action Group (TAG) during the military coups illustrates the advantages of forming such a group. Fiji's tourist industry responded faster than expected during the most recent coup because of the implementation of a task force which was established in 1987 after the first coup. The British Tourist Authority (BTA) set up an Immediate Action Group (IAG) during the Foot and Mouth Outbreak consisting of internal BTA staff from a range of departments to help implement strategies to recover from the outbreak. The IAG role was also to source funding to aid in the recovery marketing effort from both public and private sector sources and succeeded in gaining additional funding to provide recovery marketing and branding initiatives. At an international level the World Tourism Organisation formed a Tourism Recovery Committee to deal with the impacts of September 11, 2001 on the tourism industry. This group comprised key business leaders from the tourism industry and representatives from member countries. Among their many tasks was to collect information on the impact of the crisis, share ideas and jointly consider strategies to correct misinformation and perceptions that consumers held about travel destinations.

These groups often provide a lobbying role to government and industry to source funding to provide support facilities including establishing communication strategies to deal with consumer and industry inquiries. The establishment of phone information lines is a well known strategy for dealing with crises and disasters (Ashcroft, 1997). Phone lines can provide assistance and information for the general public, media but also the tourism industry itself. The use of websites is also a useful tool and one that was used by the BTA to aid in the recovery throughout the Foot and Mouth Outbreak.

It provided information to consumers that the majority of the countryside was open, but also provided information for the tourism industry on government policy concerning the outbreak and recovery and compensation packages. The ability to fund resources to deal with disasters has been noted by Heath (1995) as an important factor in dealing more effectively with natural disasters. However, despite the sourcing or reallocation of human or financial resources for strategy implementation, some authors believe that other organisational factors may be better predictors of successful crisis management implementation.

Smallman and Weir (1999) note that the move towards holistic and proactive crisis management may require organisations to communicate more effectively and consider their organisational culture. In other words, undertaking proactive planning and implementation of strategies may not actually help organisations deal with incidents if their communication styles are autocratic and organisational culture is introverted. Tribe (1997) suggests that organisational structure and culture tend to evolve reactively and that rigid management structures may not be so appropriate for the twenty-first century. Management may need to substitute bureaucratic organisational structures for freer structures which may help position the organisation closer to the outside environment, allowing for improved monitoring of change and sensing potential crises and disasters before they occur. Movement away from bureaucratic organisational structures and styles also allows more flexibility and may empower frontline staff to make decisions and alert management of potential crises or disasters before they occur. Furthermore, empowered frontline staff may provide valuable information concerning whether strategies implemented to deal with crises or disasters are actually working effectively.

Marra (1998) notes that many of the crisis communication studies and literature overstate the importance of developing communication plans and strategies as many organisations do not manage crises well, despite having detailed plans. While subsequently organisations with no crisis communication plans have dealt with crises very effectively. Other variables are perhaps more able to determine the success of crisis communication strategies, namely the underlying communication culture of an organisation and the level of autonomy or power of the public relations department within an organisation (Marra, 1998).

4.2.4. Understanding and collaborating with stakeholders

As illustrated in the above discussion, understanding and working with key internal and external stakeholders are required to plan and manage crises and disasters in the tourism industry. According to Freeman (1984, p. 46) "stakeholders are those group(s) or organisation(s)

B.W. Ritchie / Tourism Management 25 (2004) 669–683   679

that can affect or are affected by the achievement of an organisation's objectives." Sautter and Leisen (1999, p. 326) note "if [tourism] players proactively consider the interests of all other stakeholders, the industry as a whole stands to gain significant returns in the long term." In the case of crisis and disaster planning and management, understanding the impact of a crisis or disaster on internal (business units, staff, managers, shareholders) and external (other agencies and organisations, general public, media, tourists) stakeholders and the relationship between these stakeholders is critical. This is because of the inter-relationship and dependency between these groups or individuals and a need to develop suitable strategies resolve any crisis or disaster. As discussed previously, because of the nature of tourism it is especially important that crisis or emergency management plans are integrated. Collaboration is required between different organisations, government departments, emergency personnel, media organisations and other stakeholders. This has been noted by Kouzmin, Jarman, and Rosenthal (1995) with respect to the emergency services in Australia. The authors argue that there are long-standing deficiencies in strategic and operational planning and forecasting approaches for disaster management and urge more co-operation and co-ordination between the various emergency services. In particular, it appears as though destinations should have a multi-disciplinary or multi-agency approach to crisis and disaster management for tourism.

The type of crisis or disaster and its magnitude will impact upon stakeholders in different ways. For example, airline strike action which will obviously impact upon the day to day management of an organisation and could impact on consumers (such as tourists). However, other incidents may only impact upon internal stakeholders within an organisation such as other departments or managers and shareholders. For large-scale disasters and crises the impacts will be felt by external stakeholders such as the general public, tourists, other sectors of the tourism industry and other industries. The media are an important stakeholder in communicating information concerning a crisis or disaster to various publics (including tourists) and are also important in restoring confidence in an organisation or destination when a crisis or disaster is entering the long-term recovery or resolution phase. Yet despite this little research has been undertaken on crisis communication or the management of key stakeholders during tourism crises.

4.3. Resolution, evaluation and feedback

The final stage of dealing with crises and disasters strategically is the evaluation and feedback stage as a destination or organisation begins to recover from a

crisis and normality begins to occur. The main goal of an organisation or destination is to control the crisis or disaster and reduce its severity or to stop it completely. However, as discussed previously, crises and disasters are chaotic and complex and their impacts can make long lasting changes to systems, but these changes they can be positive or negative. In fact some organisations or destinations may benefit from a crisis or disaster as travellers change their travel patterns. Examples include the US market visiting the Caribbean in greater numbers during the 1991 Gulf War and avoiding Europe and the Middle East.

Several authors note the ability of crises or disasters to act as turning points for destinations and businesses (Faulkner, 2001; Burnett, 1998; Kash & Darling, 1998). As Faulkner (2001, p. 137) notes "crises and disasters have transformational connotations, with each such event having potential positive (e.g. stimulus to innovation, recognition of new markets, etc.), as well as negative outcomes." Burnett (1998) suggests that crises create heroes or leaders who emerge to help direct a destination or organisation facing such crises back to normality or an improved state. An improved state is possible because of the ability of an organisation or destination to learn from crises and disasters, make policy changes, and adapt and modify strategies that did not work effectively. Therefore, at the resolution stage of crisis and disaster management a feedback loop back to proactive planning and prevention is possible.

However, the ability of organisations to learn is determined by the extent of their interest in learning from incidents and perhaps their organisational culture. Ritchie et al. (2003) suggest that although major tourism policy changes were made at the national level after the Foot and Mouth Outbreak in Britain very few changes were made at the local level researched, because of an attitude that these incidents cannot be forecast, an inability to think long term and a perception that such events are out of their control. Educational theory and loop learning may provide some insights on the nature of organisational learning from crises (see Kolb, 1984; Richardson, 1994). Double loop learning requires a paradigmatic shift as a result of the experience and so emergent knowledge is produced and ultimately new understanding is derived compared to single loop learning (Figs. 3 and 4). The distinction between a crisis and a disaster means that those who precipitate a crisis are better placed to reflect on mistakes that caused the problems and institute a paradigmatic shift in thinking. Conversely, and as evidenced by history, those who suffer the effects of a disaster react to events and are contained to single loop actions, if not single loop thinking, unless a larger body can enforce the necessary changes to prevent the events repeating themselves.

Organisations may make changes to their organisational structures, creating crisis management teams,

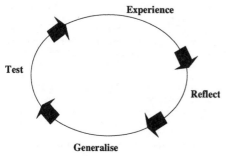

Source: Kolb (1984)

Fig. 3. Single loop learning.

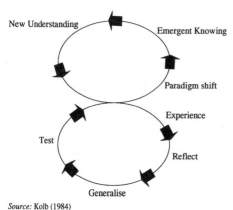

Source: Kolb (1984)

Fig. 4. Double loop learning.

providing more resources for their public relations team, update contingency plans or reduce their reliance on certain market segments. During the Asian Economic Crises in 1997–1998 the Australian Tourist Commission (the national marketing organisation) realised that their over reliance on the growing Asian market may have been flawed. However, they were quickly able to redistribute their resources and increase their marketing effort to traditional, but sometimes neglected markets of New Zealand, Europe and North America. The benefit of hindsight will allow destinations and organisations to develop even better crisis management strategies and plans and may help them understand the differences between 'problems' and crises. Soñmez and Backman (1992) noted that it was not until Hurricane Hugo hit South Carolina, USA in 1989 that the Myrtle Beach

tourism crisis management manual was developed. Britton (2003) acknowledged that September 11, 2001 was a unique experience for American Airlines and they have learnt enormously from rebuilding image after terrorist attacks. In the public sector, policy structure changes, as a response to incidents, can be beneficial for reducing potential future crises and disasters. For instance, after September 11, 2001 an Office of Homeland Security was formed in the USA, and in Australia a Tourism Working Group was established to develop strategies to deal with future crises (Hall, 2002).

However, mechanisms need to be put in place so this reflection and feedback loop can help improve future strategies to effectively deal with such incidents. Debriefing is one mechanism which can help disaster or crisis managers collect data on how they coped with these incidents and what improvements can be made and should be integrated into crisis and disaster management.

5. Conclusion and future research directions

This paper has outlined the importance of understanding crises and disasters for the tourism industry because the industry is highly susceptible to change and crises/disasters. However, a small but growing body of research on crisis and disaster management has been conducted in the tourism industry. This may be due, in part, to the chaotic and complex nature of these incidents and an inability by some managers and researchers to understand such phenomena. However, an analysis of the nature of crises and disasters can provide insights for how these may be managed. This is particularly important in the context of a fragmented industry such as tourism which is often impacted by external factors. A strategic, holistic and proactive approach to crisis management in the tourism industry is required through:

- developing proactive scanning and planning;
- implementing strategies when crises or disasters occur; and,
- evaluating the effectiveness of these strategies to ensure continual refinement of crisis management strategies.

Flexibility and continual monitoring is required by organisations and destinations to design and implement effective strategies to deal with chaos and change. As noted previously in this paper organisations should take a holistic approach to managing crises and may have to reconfigure their management structure, consider aspects related to resource allocation and organisational culture, all which may influence the effectiveness of crisis management. Furthermore, there is a need for co-operation between a wide number of stakeholders both

B.W. Ritchie / Tourism Management 25 (2004) 669–683   681

Table 2
Potential research disciplines, theories, and concepts for crisis management

Discipline and sub-fields	Theories or concepts
Business management (including strategic management and business failure)	Organisational culture and its contribution to (in)effective crisis management in the tourism industry
Public relations and communication/information management	Communication theory and the use of communication to control crises between internal and external stakeholders in the tourism industry
Geography and natural hazards/disaster management	Leadership styles and their contribution to (in)effective crisis management in the tourism industry
Environmental management	Organisational learning from crises and disasters in the tourism industry
Planning (including integrated emergency planning and risk management)	Stakeholder collaboration and planning in crises or disasters associated with the tourism industry
Political science (including terrorism, political instability, security and crisis management)	

internal and external to the organisation to effectively plan and manage crises and disasters. Leadership is required to provide direction to the industry in times of crisis and to bring stakeholders together at an organisational and destination level for integrated crisis/disaster management. In particular, spokespeople are needed to effectively deal with the media particularly for tourism crises or disasters.

Future research and the development of theoretical or conceptual frameworks are required on crisis and disaster management generally, but particularly focussing on the tourism industry. In particular, there is a need for researchers to move beyond simplistic prescriptive models which may provide check lists or information on *what* managers should do before, during or after crises toward descriptive models which develop and/or test models, concepts or theories related to crisis management to examine *why* crises were managed (in)effectively in the tourism industry. Theories or concepts from other discipline areas could shed further light on crisis management for the tourism industry are illustrated in Table 2 along with research fields which are related to crisis and disaster management in tourism.

There is also a need for research following different paradigmatic positions to improve our understanding of crisis and disaster management in the tourism industry, including:

• chaos and complexity theory applied to crises and disasters;
• positivistic approaches to quantify levels of preparedness and reactions of the industry to crises and disasters and help predict incidents through computer stimulation modelling;

• phenomenological approaches to explore attitudes and opinions of managers in the public and private sector towards crisis and disaster management; and,
• case study approaches are needed to test models and concepts surrounding crisis management in the tourism industry.

These research approaches should provide additional insights into crises and disasters helping the tourism industry to understand chaos and change. This will hopefully allow the industry to embrace these incidents as an everyday part of life and begin to plan and manage them in a strategic and holistic way, potentially reducing their impacts on business and society. As crises and disasters increase this will be a key skill for both tourism managers and planners in both the public and private sector.

Acknowledgements

The author would like to acknowledge the assistance of the School of Service Management, University of Brighton who provided some time release to develop this article as well as the constructive comments from the anonymous reviewers of this paper. However, any interpretation or omissions are the sole responsibility of this author.

References

Ashcroft, R. (1997). Crisis management: Public relations. *Journal of Managerial Psychology, 12*(5), 325–332.
Barton, L. (1994). Crisis management: Preparing for and managing disasters. *Cornell Hotel and Restaurant Administration Quarterly, 35*(2), 59–65.

Barton, D., & Hardigree, D. (1995). Risk and crisis management in facilities: Emerging paradigms in assessing critical incidents. *Facilities, 13*(9/10), 11–14.

Beeton, S. (2001). Horseback tourism in Victoria, Australia: Co-operative, proactive crisis management. *Current Issues in Tourism, 4*(5), 422–439.

Beirman, D. (2002a). Marketing of tourism destinations during a prolonged crisis: Israel and the Middle East. *Journal of Vacation Marketing, 8*(2), 167–176.

Beirman, D. (2002b). *Restoring tourism destinations in crisis: A strategic marketing approach*. Oxon: CABI Publishing.

Berke, P. (1998). Reducing natural hazard risks through state growth management. *Journal of the American Planning Association, 64*(1), 76–87.

Berry, S. (1999). We have a problem...call the press! (crisis management plan). *Public Management, 81*(4), 4–15.

Blaikie, P., Cannon, T., Davis, I., & Wisner, B. (1994). *At risk: Natural hazards people's vulnerability and disasters*. London: Routledge.

Brammer, H. (1990). Floods in Bangladesh: A geographical background to the 1987 and 1988 floods. *Geographical Journal, 156*(1), 12–22.

British Tourist Authority (BTA), (2001). *BTA corporate information*. London (online). Available at: http://www.tourismtrade.org.uk/coporate)info.htm. (Accessed 02 January 2002).

Britton, R. (2003). *Rebuilding credibility after a crisis*. Keynote presentation at Tourism and Travel Research Association (TTRA) conference St Louis, MO, 15th June.

Burnett, J. J. (1998). A strategic approach to managing crises. *Public Relations Review, 24*(4), 475–488.

Cassedy, K. (1991). *Crisis management planning in the travel and tourism industry: A study of three destinations and a crisis management planning manual*. San Francisco: PATA.

Coombs, T. (1999). *Ongoing crisis communication: Planning, managing and responding*. Thousand Oakes, CA: Sage.

Darling, J. (1994). Crisis management in international business: Keys to effective decision making. *Leadership and Organization Development Journal, 15*(8), 3–8.

Darling, J., Hannu, O., & Raimo, N. (1996). Crisis management in international business: A case situation in decision making concerning trade with Russia. *The Finnish Journal of Business Economics, 4*, 12–25.

Faulkner, B. (2001). Towards a framework for tourism disaster management. *Tourism Management, 22*(2), 135–147.

Faulkner, B., & Vikulov, S. (2001). Katherine, washed out one day, back on track the next: A post mortem of a tourism disaster. *Tourism Management, 22*(4), 331–344.

Fink, S. (1986). *Crisis management: Planning for the inevitable*. New York: American Association of Management.

Freeman, R. (1984). *Strategic management: A stakeholder approach*. Boston: Pitman.

Glaesser, D. (2003). *Crisis management in the tourism industry*. London: Butterworth-Heinemann.

Gonzalez Herrero, A. (1997). Preventive marketing: Crisis reporting in the tourism sector. *Estudios Turisticos, 1997*(133), 5–28.

Gonzales-Herrero, A., & Pratt, C. (1998). Marketing crises in tourism: Communication strategies in the United States and Spain. *Public Relations Review, 24*(1), 83–97.

Hall, C. M. (2002). Travel safety, terrorism and the media: The significance of the issue-attention cycle. *Current Issues in Tourism, 5*(5), 458–466.

Heath, R. (1995). The Kobe earthquake: Some realities of strategic management of crises and disasters. *Disaster Prevention and Management, 4*(5), 11–24.

Heath, R. (1998). *Crisis management for managers and executives*. London: Financial Times Management.

Henderson, J. C. (1999a). Managing the Asian financial crisis: Tourist attractions in Singapore. *Journal of Travel Research, 38*(2), 177–181.

Henderson, J. C. (1999b). Tourism management and the Southeast Asian economic and environmental crisis: A Singapore perspective. *Managing Leisure, 4*(2), 107–120.

Henderson, J. (2002). Managing a tourism crisis in Southeast Asia: The role of national tourism organisations. *International Journal of Hospitality & Tourism Administration, 3*(1), 85–105.

Herrero, A. G. (1999). Product commercialization and crisis planning in the tourist sector: Corporative image and consumer-centred marketing. *Papers de Turisme, 24*, 6.

Jessop, B. (1999). Reflections on globalisation and its (il)logic(s). In K. Olds, P. Dicken, P. F. Kelly, L. Kong, & H. W. Yeung (Eds.), *Globalisatoon and the Asia-Pacific: Contested territories* (pp. 19–38). London: Routledge.

Johnson, G., & Scholes, K. (1993). *Exploring coporate strategy*. Oxford: Butterworth-Heinemann.

Kash, T. J., & Darling, J. (1998). Crisis management: Prevention, diagnosis and intervention. *Leadership & Organization Development Journal, 19*(4), 179–186.

Keown-McMullan, J. (1997). Crisis: When does a molehill become a mountain? *Disaster Prevention and Management, 6*(1), 4–10.

Kolb, D. (1984). *Experiential learning*. New Jersey: Prentice-Hall.

Kouzmin, A., Jarman, A. M. G., & Rosenthal, U. (1995). Inter-organizational policy processes in disaster management. *Disaster Prevention and Management, 4*(2), 20–37.

Lee, Y. F., & Harrald, J. R. (1999). Critical issue for business area impact analysis in business crisis management: Analytical capability. *Disaster Prevention and Management, 8*(3), 184–189.

Marra, F. (1998). Crisis communication plans: Poor predictors of excellent crisis public relations. *Public Relations Review, 24*(4), 461–474.

Miller, G., & Ritchie, B.W. (2003). A farming crisis or a tourism disaster? An analysis of the foot and mouth disease in the UK. *Current Issues in Tourism*, forthcoming.

Murphey, P., & Bayley, J. (1989). Tourism and disaster planning. *The Geographical Review, 79*, 26–46.

Parsons, W. (1996). Crisis management. *Career Development International, 1*(5), 26–28.

Pauchant, T., & Mitroff, I. (1992). *Transforming the crisis prone organization*. San Francisco, CA: Jossey-Bass Publishers.

Richardson, B. (1994). Crisis management and management strategy—Time to "loop the loop?". *Disaster Prevention and Management, 3*(3), 59–80.

Richardson, B. (1995). Paradox management for crisis avoidance. *Management Decision, 33*(1), 5–18.

Richardson, B., & Richardson, R. (1992). *Business planning: An approach to strategic management* (2nd ed.). London: Pitman.

Ritchie, B.W., Dorrell, H., Miller, D., & Miller, G.A. (2003). Crisis communication and recovery for the tourism industry: Lessons from the 2001 foot and mouth disease outbreak in the United Kingdom. *Journal of Travel and Tourism, Marketing*, forthcoming.

Roberts, V. (1994). Flood management: Bradford paper. *Disaster Prevention and Management, 3*(3), 44–60.

Sautter, E., & Leisen, B. (1999). Managing stakeholders: A tourism planning model. *Annals of Tourism Research, 26*(2), 312–328.

Smallman, C. (1996). Challenging the orthodoxy in risk management. *Safety Science, 22*(1-3), 245–262.

Smallman, C., & Weir, D. (1999). Communication and cultural distortion during crises. *Disaster Prevention and Management, 8*(1), 33–41.

Soñmez, S. F., Apostolopoulos, Y., & Tarlow, P. (1999). Tourism in crisis: Managing the effects of terrorism. *Journal of Travel Research, 38*(1), 13–18.

B.W. Ritchie / Tourism Management 25 (2004) 669–683 683

Soñmez, S. F., & Backman, S. J. (1992). Crisis management in tourist destinations. *Visions in Leisure and Business*, *11*(3), 25–33.

Tribe, J. (1997). *Corporate strategy for tourism*. Suffolk: International Thomson Business Press.

Turner, D. (1994). Resources for disaster recovery. *Security Management*, *28*, 57–61.

Viljoen, J. (1994). *Strategic management: Planning and implementing successful corporate strategies* (2nd ed.). Melbourne: Longman.

Zerman, D. (1995). Crisis communication: Managing the mass media. *Information and Computer Security*, *3*(5), 25–28.

[7]

Improving the Accuracy of Hotel Reservations Forecasting: Curves Similarity Approach

ZVI SCHWARTZ AND STEPHEN HIEMSTRA

This study developed and tested a new type of an extrapolative forecasting model that improves the forecasting models of daily occupancy levels in a hotel by focusing on the shape of past booking curves. By applying a dissimilarity measure to identify past booking curves with a similar shape, the identified similar curves were then used to project future reservations. The study examined 10 forecasting horizons ranging from 1 to 99 days in advance. The results indicate that the curves similarity model is considerably more accurate than the three benchmark models tested. These results are statistically and practically significant. In addition, this study shows that under certain conditions a model that combines two independent models might produce a forecast that is more accurate than that of its components.

Accurate reservation forecasting is of growing concern to the hotel industry. This need for improved accuracy (Metz 1991; Schmidgall 1989) is a direct result of intensifying competition and shrinking profit margins. Many hotel managers consider the implementation of an efficient pricing policy, such as a yield management program, to be an effective response to changes in the competitive environment. For optimal results, these pricing policies need an accurate daily reservation forecast. Often, a long forecasting horizon is required, since hotel personnel begin using daily predictions many days before the actual date of stay (often as early as 90 days ahead). An understanding of demand distribution over time is necessary to develop room allocation policies that lead to optimal revenue levels, and according to Kimes (1989), this is especially true for the hospitality industry, where the phenomena have not been thoroughly analyzed. (Profit maximization through units allocation is desirable in service industries with constrained capacity, a perishable product, and a high potential revenue from each additional sold unit [marginal contribution]. Among the various industries in this category, airlines and car rental companies assume a leading role in studying the patterns of demand over time and in developing effective price optimization algorithms for their products.)

Furthermore, the accuracy of the reservations forecast has a substantial role in the effectiveness of decisions in other areas. An accurate forecast is necessary for examining marketing mix efforts or making financial (cash flow), purchasing, scheduling, maintenance, and training decisions.

The goal of this study was to develop and test a forecasting model that can be used by hotel managers to produce

Zvi Schwartz is the owner of TechnoLodge in Wildwood, Missouri. Stephen Hiemstra is in the Department of Restaurant, Hotel, Institutional and Tourism Management at Purdue University in West Lafayette, Indiana.

accurate forecasts of daily occupancy levels. It focused on extrapolative quantitative models that use information about past daily occupancy levels and about reservations on hand. This approach was dictated by the type of hotel data that are usually available and by the desire to develop a model that could be adopted by the industry as an effective managerial tool. The overall objective was to develop a forecasting model that was not only more accurate but also had no visible disadvantages (theoretical or practical) that were likely to prevent managers from using it.

The outline of this article is as follows. The next section reviews previous efforts to forecast airline and hotel reservations. It outlines the unique structure of hotel reservations data and discusses the adequacy of various types of forecasting models. The section that follows focuses on the methodology. It develops the curve similarity model and describes the three extrapolative benchmark models, the data sets, the hypotheses, the samples, and the statistical test. The results are reported in the fourth section. The empirical tests indicate that, compared to all other models tested in this study, the curves similarity approach results in more accurate forecasts that are statistically significant. The article concludes with implications for practitioners in the lodging industry and with recommendations for further research.

PREVIOUS APPROACHES: A LITERATURE REVIEW

Hotel room forecasting, like tourism or other types of forecasting, can be based on a number of different models and varying specifications. The choice of model and specification depends on the specific nature of the forecasted variable, the objective of the forecasting procedures, the implicit theories of consumer demand upon which they are based, and the nature of the available data (Witt and Witt 1995; Sheldon and Var 1985; Uysal and Crompton 1985; Crouch 1994). Explanatory models based on utility theory are usually preferable if the objective is to understand the primary factors associated with past trends. However, time series models often have been found to yield superior forecasts (Martin and Witt 1989; Witt and Witt 1991, 1995).

Despite the importance of accurate hotel reservation forecasts, only a few studies on the topic have been published. Yesawich (1984) used a general judgment-based approach to project annual occupancy levels. This method is most adequate for strategic planning.

Relihan (1989) reviews the yield management approach to hotel room pricing and devotes a section to a discussion on forecasting demand. He states that some hotels' systems employ sophisticated statistical analyses of reservations history. Relihan predicts that "in the not-too-distant future, a new type of computer system will be able to teach itself the rules" (p. 43); he is most likely referring to neural networks. He explains that, currently, in airline research departments, regression analysis is typically used to find a set of formulas, depicted as curves, that best represent the airline's entire reservation history. He notes that "other statistical methods can even use non-numerical data, substituting logical operators to develop rules for expert systems in a process called rule induction."

Andrew, Cranage, and Lee (1990) test the use of the Box-Jenkins approach and exponential smoothing in forecasting hotel occupancy rates. Their study shows that these methods can be effectively used to predict monthly occupancy levels for one period ahead.

In exponential smoothing, the new forecast is the previous forecast plus a portion (α) of the last forecast error. It is similar to a moving average in that it smoothes historical observation to eliminate randomness.

The Box-Jenkins approach is a systematic procedure that divides the forecasting problem into three stages. In the first stage, the forecaster identifies a tentative ARMA model, which is a mixed model of autoregression and moving average elements. A trend is removed by taking a successive differencing of the data. Identifying a tentative model is really choosing values for p and q for the ARMA (p,q) model. If $p,q \neq 0$, then the process is a mixed AR and MA. Choosing an appropriate order of p and q without trying all possible combinations is achieved by examining the autocorrelation coefficients and the partial autocorrelations. Parameters are estimated in the second stage. Computer algorithms identify the "best" values, and through diagnostics checks, the forecaster verifies that the model has removed all patterns. If the error is still not random, a new model needs to be identified. In the third stage, the computer algorithm applies the identified model and the estimated parameters to forecast future values of the series.

There are several reasons to question whether it is adequate to adopt the findings of Andrew, Cranage, and Lee to the challenging task of forecasting daily occupancy levels. First, note that they tested their models using *monthly* average occupancy levels, while this study was concerned with predicting *daily* occupancies.

A major concern with using Box-Jenkins is related to the lack of automation. Granger and Newbold (1986) say that

> The identification and diagnostic checking phases of the Box-Jenkins cycle require manual intervention. . . . [I]t would be desirable for some routine forecasting purposes to eliminate such a requirement. (p. 178)

Many hotels update their occupancy forecast every day, and some hotels do it even more often. These daily forecasts require more than a "re-run" of the predetermined model. Despite the dynamic operating environment and the considerable amount of information that is continuously added to the reservation database, they also require that someone frequently monitor the adequacy of the model's parameters and re-calibrate the model. The calibration phase of the Box-Jenkins method requires a statistical skill level rarely found among hotels' managers, and it is very time-consuming. It involves plotting and reading various charts and analyzing the results of several statistical tests. The model must be modified and tested until a satisfactory level of accuracy is reached. It seems unrealistic, then, to suggest a labor-intensive forecasting model, such as Box-Jenkins, for this routine forecasting task.

At first glance, the exponential smoothing model seems to be the answer to this problem. It is a fully automatic procedure that is quick and inexpensive to operate. A survey by Mentzer and Cox (1984) found that managers were most satisfied with exponential smoothing since it is considerably accurate and easy to understand and use. However, Granger and Newbold (1986) identify a major drawback of this fully automated approach, noting that exponential smoothing procedures generally postulate a single model from which forecasts are to be generated. Its eventual form is not dictated through identification and diagnostic checking of the data. They suggest that for a routine task, such as sales forecasting, a stepwise autoregression be adopted (p. 178). It is a fully automatic model that contains a mechanism for discriminating among various possible forms of forecast function.

The nature of hotel reservations data indicate that airline forecasting might be more relevant than tourism forecasting, especially since Witt and Witt (1995) have reviewed and summarized previous tourism forecasting efforts and concluded that no single forecasting method performs consistently best across different situations. (This finding on tourism parallels the conclusion of numerous forecasting studies. See, for example, McNees [1982] and Zarnowitz [1984] on explanatory methods and Makridakis et al. [1982] and Makridakis and Hibbon [1979] on extrapolative methods.) Furthermore, hotels and airlines share three significant characteristics:

- *A unique structure of the data.* Unlike most data on tourist arrivals or departures, hotel occupancy data, like airline seat data, comprise two distinctive time series sets that lead to the same point. These two sources of information (reservations on hand and previous stays) are discussed later in this section.
- *A limited capacity.* The size of the hotel, like the size of an airplane, imposes an "artificial" limit on the possible number of occupied rooms. This cap influences the effectiveness of the forecasting models. Methods that work well with unrestricted tourist flow would not necessarily be as effective in dealing with distributions that are capped.
- *Forecast periods and forecast horizons.* Tourism forecasts usually deal with long periods, namely, months and years. However, room occupancy (and airline seat) forecasts are often for a long horizon (i.e., more periods ahead). Hotels often forecast up to 60 periods (days) into the future.

These differences imply that lessons learned from specific tourism forecast studies might not be as relevant to forecasts of daily hotel occupancy as those learned from airline forecasting.

In a pathbreaking study on airline reservations forecasting, Lee (1990) describes the uniqueness of the reservations data set. A typical set includes hundreds of historical daily booking figures, that is, the accumulated reservations on hand for a given date. Graphically, these numbers are illustrated by booking curves. Suppose a hotel has information on past reservations and occupied rooms as well as information on reservations for future stays. Starting with day 1, and for every day of stay up to the current day, there are daily records on how reservations are accumulating as time draws closer to the date of stay. For any given date of stay N, there are N complete advanced booking curves that can be analyzed. When the forecasting horizon is of M periods' (days) length, there are also M incomplete booking curves. The booking curve of day N + 1 is incomplete, since there are no reservation records from the last day of this series, N + 1. The advanced booking curve of the desired date of stay N + M lacks reservation records for days N + 1, N + 2, . . ., N + M. Figure 1 illustrates N complete booking curves and three (M = 3) incomplete booking curves.

To forecast the total reservations on day N + M, the hotel can use information from the incomplete curve N + M or analyze the set of N complete curves. These two alternatives are demonstrated in Figure 2 where, for simplicity, we assume N = 3 and we assume a forecasting horizon of only one period (M = 1). The historical booking curve is the bold line representing all past occupancy figures or numbers of rooms occupied. The advanced booking curve of the forecasted day is the bold line titled "incomplete curve." It shows the reservations on hand for the forecasted day at various days before the date of stay.

Lee shows that when combining information from advanced booking curves with information from the historical booking curve, the accuracy of the forecast is improved. So, by means of reducing the forecast error, a combination of models provides a partial, indirect solution to the problem of accuracy deterioration as the time horizon increases.

Lee suggests the following mathematical term to relate current, on-hand bookings at t days before the day of stay to total bookings on hand on the day of stay.

$$B_d(0) = B_d(t) + BTC_d(t) = B_d(t) + \int_{s=t}^{0} B_d(s)ds,$$

$$t = M, M - 1, \ldots, 0$$

where

$B_d(0)$ = the total booking on the day of stay d,
$B_d(t)$ = the booking at time t days before the day of stay d, and
$BTC_d(t)$ = the number of bookings to come.

In his combined model (the full information model), Lee views the booking process as a time series of historical bookings. He assumes a simple fully automated moving average ($MA_{n=3}$) process for the historical booking figures as well as for the bookings-to-come element ($AVGBTC_{(t)}$). The model incorporates information from the booking curve as an independent variable where only the last number of bookings on hand is used.

FIGURE 1
N COMPLETE AND M INCOMPLETE ADVANCED BOOKING CURVES

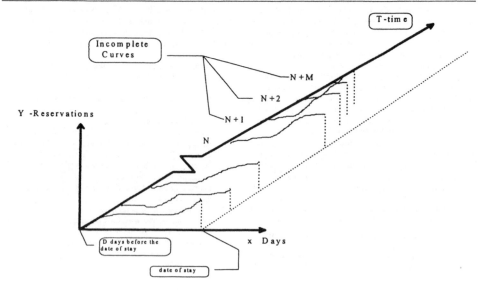

FIGURE 2

TWO INFORMATION SOURCES:
HISTORICAL AND ADVANCED BOOKING CURVES

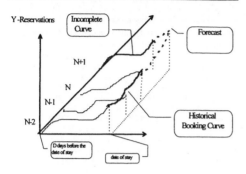

METHODOLOGY

This study hypothesized that the shape of the booking curve provides useful information that can be used to further improve the accuracy of the forecast. It developed a new type of model that captures the shape of past booking curves. The performance of this curves similarity model (model 1) was expected to surpass that of alternative extrapolative forecasts of daily reservations.

Traditional time series models were used as benchmark models to test the effectiveness of the curves similarity approach. Following Lee's findings, these benchmark models used information from the two independent sources. An effort was made to choose the adequate extrapolative models for each source. The historical curve was modeled with the semi-automated approach. Instead of using a fully automated model (e.g., moving average or exponential smoothing), which is easy to implement but which lacks a good theoretical foundation, or a "manual method" (Box-Jenkins), which is too labor intensive for this routine application, the stepwise AR was followed. This model (model 2) is the compromised model, which was mentioned earlier as the recommended approach for a routine procedure. The advanced booking curve is modeled as a high order polynomial model (model 3), since no better functional form (i.e., Lee's synthetic modeling approach) was found. Finally, model 4 is a weighted average combination of model 2's and model 3's predictions.

Model 1: Curves Similarity Approach

The curves similarity method identifies a set of complete advanced booking curves, which are similar to the incomplete curve of day $N + M$. A selection of similar curves involves comparing the available part of the incomplete booking curve of day $N + M$ to the relevant part of the complete curves. Once the similar curves (days) have been identified, their actual bookings or number of occupied rooms are used to forecast the bookings at the end of the forecasted period, i.e., day $N + M$. An example is given in Appendix A.

A visual identification of similar curves is very time consuming and therefore is not a practical method. (A hotel that

uses a reservation data set of two years and forecasts 60 days in advance must compare 60 incomplete curves to 730 complete curves [that is, 42,180 comparisons] every time managers wish to update the property's occupancy forecast.) Instead, a computerized comparison of the curves can be applied. There are various ways to formalize the curves comparison. The model developed for this study compares the incomplete curve of the forecasted day to each one of the complete curves. The result of each compared pair is a score that indicates the degree of the shape divergence. The (dis)similarity measure compares various points along the curves. The first pair of points is the most recent number of reservations on hand. Then, additional points along the curves are also compared.

This dissimilarity measure, S_i, is given by

$$S_i = \sqrt{\begin{aligned} (D_{N+M}{}^M - D_i{}^M)^2 + (D_{N+M}{}^{M+K} - D_i{}^{M+K})^2 \\ + (D_{N+M}{}^{M+2K} - D_i{}^{M+2K})^2 \\ + (D_{N+M}{}^{M+3K} - D_i{}^{M+3K})^2 \end{aligned}}$$

where

i	$= 1, \ldots, N$ and $K > 0$,
$D_{N+M}{}^M$	= the recorded reservations for day $N + M$ at M days before the date of stay,
Day $N + M$	= the final (missing) day of the forecasted (incomplete) booking curve,
$D_i{}^M$	= the recorded reservations for day i at M days before the date of stay,
Day i	= one of N days that have complete booking curves, and
$D_{N+M}{}^{M+K}$	= the recorded reservations for day $N + M$ at $(M + K)$ days before the date of stay.

The method proceeds by choosing all booking curves where the score of the dissimilarity measure meets the criterion Ψ. ($Z_i = \{Y_i | S_i \le \Psi\}$ [i.e., the group of selected booking curves Z_i is a subset of the population of booking curves Y_i.] Each of the Z_i's booking curves scored S_i, which is smaller or equal to Ψ.) The decision on the magnitude of Ψ and K (the degree of curve similarity and how disperse the observations are) should be made by the forecaster. This study uses $K = 10$, that is, when a forecast is made on day t, it uses data recorded on days t, t-10, and t-20.

Model 2: Stepwise Autoregression Model (AR)

This time series model was applied to the historical booking curve (Figure 1). This particular stepwise AR method was chosen because it provides a high degree of automation. The stepwise autoregressive method (SAS Institute 1993, p. 423) combines time trend regression with an autoregressive model. The number of lags is determined by the program in a stepwise procedure. Unlike other time series approaches (such as Box-Jenkins), this method does not require the user to estimate the model and its parameters. As such, it can be easily used by a reservation manager to produce quick forecasts of multiple time series. The autoregressive model is given by

$$\hat{Y}_t = a + b_1 Y_{t-1} + b_2 Y_{t-2} + \ldots + b_k Y_{t-k} + e_t$$

$$e_t \sim N(0, \sigma^2).$$

Model 3: High Order Polynomial Model (HOPM)

A visual inspection of hundreds of advanced booking curves revealed strong nonlinearity. Following the synthetic model approach suggested by Lee (1990), we attempted to identify a functional form that fits the shape of the advanced booking curves. Three types of functional forms were examined, the first being

$$\hat{Y}_t = \alpha \cdot Ln(t)$$

where

$\hat{Y}_t$ = the estimated number of reservation on hand at day t,
t = 1, 2, . . ., 150,
t = 1 = 150 days before the date of stay,
α = a parameter, and
Ln(t) = the natural logarithm of t.

The second type is a basic growth (logit) model.

$$\hat{Y}_t = \frac{\partial}{1 + \ell^{\beta + \lambda \cdot t}}$$

where

$\hat{Y}_t$ = the estimated number of reservation on hand at day t,
t = 1,2, . . .,150,
t = 1 = 150 days before the date of stay,
ℓ = a constant — the base of the natural logarithm (equals 2.71828),
∂ = the hotel capacity (i.e., the number of available rooms), and
β and λ = parameters.

To achieve a better fit, the logit model was modified to

$$\hat{Y}_t = S + \frac{\partial - S}{1 + \ell^{\beta + \lambda \cdot t}}$$

where

S = the actual number of reservation on hand at t = 1.

None of the tested functional forms had a good fit. The reason seems to be the large jumps (bends), which are caused by large group bookings. Instead, a high order polynomial model (HOPM) was chosen as the modeling tool for the advanced booking curves. It is a flexible, curvilinear response model that is easy to handle as a special case of the general linear regression model (Neter, Wasserman, and Kutner 1990). Each advanced booking Curve Y_i was modeled as a HOPM.

$$Y_i = a_i + b_i x + c_i x^2 + d_i x^3 + e_i x^4 + \epsilon_i$$

where i = 1, . . ., N and x is the day. The nonlinear ordinary least square method was used to estimate the parameters a, b, c, d, and e. The forecast was carried out as follows: First a HOPM was fitted to the available part of the incomplete booking curve. Then the estimated parameters were used in the formula to predict the bookings for the given forecasting horizon. An example is given in Appendix B.

Model 4: Weighted Average of AR and HOPM Predictions (AR&HOPM)

The prediction of the previous two models (AR& HOPM) were averaged to produce a better forecast. The combined prediction $\hat{Y}_{(4)}$ is given by

$$\hat{Y}_{(4)} = \omega \hat{Y}_{(2)} + (1 - \omega) \hat{Y}_{(3)},$$

where

$\hat{Y}_{(2)}$ = the prediction of the AR model, and
$\hat{Y}_{(3)}$ = the prediction of the HOPM model and $0 \le \omega \le 1$.

To identify the best weights, the following procedure was followed. The initial value of ω was set to 0.5. Then ω = .4 and ω = 0.6 were also tested. If a significant improvement in the forecast accuracy was achieved, ω was increased (or decreased) by increments of 0.1 until no further improvement could be achieved.

Hypotheses

Based on the analysis, it was hypothesized that the curves similarity model would perform better than the other three tested models.

Ha: Model 1, which captures more information on the shape of past booking curves, is more accurate than the rest of the tested models.

Following the findings of Lee (1990), we predicted that a combination of two models would outperform its components.

Hb: Model 4, which combines two sources of information, is more accurate than either model 2 or model 3.

Data

The data set used for testing the alternative models included daily records of individual reservations in three hotels. Hotel A is a 500-room resort located in the southwest United States. Hotel B is a 1,400-room hotel located near a major airport in the Midwest. Hotel C is a 350-room facility geared to business travelers; it is also located in the Midwest. There are 171,592 records in the data set of hotel A, 235,711 records for hotel B, and 55,617 for hotel C. Each record is a single row of alpha-numeric symbols. Each one of the records holds 51 different predefined fields that store various types of information. For example, some fields contain information regarding the date of stay, date of reservation, and so forth. Other fields store guest information such as names, addresses, and telephone numbers. (A complete detailed description of the data cannot be provided due to the hotels' need for confidentiality.) Of the 51 fields, only a few were available for this study. The fields that were used were

1. The date the entry was recorded,
2. The date the guest checked in,
3. The checkout date,
4. Room count — the number of rooms rented,
5. Room nights — number of nights the guest(s) stayed, and
6. Room number.

For each hotel, a booking curve of up to 150 days before the date of stay was created for every given date of stay between August 16, 1991, and October 9, 1994. Booking curves of 150 days were chosen since visual inspections of the curves indicated that only negligible numbers of bookings were recorded more than 150 days before the date of stay. As a result, a total of 1,151 curves for every hotel were available for analysis.

A typical curve includes one or more bends. Some of the bends result from large changes in the number of booked rooms and represent large groups that book during a short period. This study examined the patterns of total reservations in the hotel, that is, market segments were not separately analyzed. Ten different forecasting horizons were examined: 1, 2, 3, 7, 14, 21, 30, 45, 60, and 99 days into the future. These forecasting horizons were selected so that different rates of reservation accumulation on the booking curve would be adequately covered. Note that during early periods (many days before the date of stay), the reservations accumulated very slowly. Few reservations were recorded between 150 and 60 days before the date of stay. The first forecasting horizon was 99 days, which allowed for some information to accumulate (between 150 — or the first day of the series — and 99 days before the date of stay). The days closer to the date of stay show an accelerated rate of bookings and were given closer attention (1, 2, and 3 days before were each examined).

Samples

While the HOPM was fitted and tested on all 1,151 curves, the other three models were tested on samples of the curves of 45 different days. These samples were used in testing the curves similarity model (1), the AR model (2), and the combined model (4). The use of samples was necessary because the process of fitting models and forecasting is very time consuming.

Following Churchill's recommendation (Churchill 1991, p. 586), "pilot" runs were used to estimate σ. The variable measured was the absolute percentage error of the models' prediction. (See the discussion on the selected error measures.) The value of 10.3 emerged as representing the various results. Desiring a 95% confidence level, we set Z to 1.96. H, the precision element was set to 3% (allowing the estimate to be within ±3% of the true population forecast error). The sample size is given by

$$n = \frac{Z^2}{H^2} \sigma^2 = \frac{1.96^2}{0.03^2} \, 0.103^2 = 45$$

Since this procedure did not guarantee an optimal sample size, it was followed by reliability tests. The purpose of these reliability tests was to ensure that the sample size of 45 curves per hotel was sufficient. We first tested the reliability of the sample with the results of model 3. Recall that the HOPM, unlike the other three models, was applied to the entire population of booking curves (1,151 curves) in each hotel. The accuracy of model 3, when it was applied to the entire population of curves was compared to its accuracy when applied to the sample of 45 curves. The difference in the accuracy (using the mean absolute percentage error as the error measure) was not significantly different from 0 ($P < .001$). Thus, these results indicate that the sample size of 45 curves was reliable when model 3 was applied.

The second test compared the accuracy of each of the other three models. These models were applied to three different sets of 45 randomly selected booking curves. There were 30 different predictions that could be compared, since each model could be tested on 10 different forecasting horizons. We compared the accuracy of nine of these predictions in each of the three sample sets (three predictions per model) and found no significant difference among the three sample sets. This is a strong indication that the sample size of 45 booking curves generates reliable results.

The 45 days were randomly selected. A vector of uniformly distributed random numbers was generated using the RANDOM function in Microsoft Excel 5 (Microsoft Corporation 1993, p. 601).

Error Measurements

The comparison of forecasting models is based on the magnitude of the residual error. The selection of the best error measure is not simple, and forecasting experts often disagree as to which measure should be used (Anderson, Sweeney, and Williams 1990, p. 664; Berenson and Levine 1992, p. 790). A list of the most common measures of accuracy is given by Wheelwright and Makridakis (1985, p. 46) and includes mean error (ME), mean absolute deviation (MAD), mean squared error (MSE), standard deviation of error (SDE), percentage error (PE), mean percentage error (MPE), and mean absolute percentage error (MAPE).

The ME and MPE measures are not very useful, because positive errors are canceled by negative errors, and the mean is always close to zero. The MAD and the MAPE measures average the absolute errors, so that positive errors do not cancel the negative ones. Thus, MAD and MAPE are preferred to ME and MPE. MSE and SDE are obtained by first calculating the square of each one of the errors. These two groups of measures (percentage error and squared error) are the most widely used in studies that compare the accuracy of different forecasting models (Carbone and Amstrong 1982). The drawback of the squared error group has to do with the required assumption about the error's cost structure. Fields (1992, p. 97) warns against unjustified adoption of MSE, explaining that, without knowing the appropriate cost consequences of a forecast error, MSE cannot be directly interpreted. Since there is no empirical evidence or a solid theoretical reason to assume that a typical cost of forecast error in the hotel industry is indeed squared, we decided not to use MSE or SDE.

MAPE was selected as the accuracy measure. It was preferred to MAD, since it is a relative measure and thus allows a meaningful comparison when the units have a different scale. (The three hotels differ in their capacity: 350, 500, and 1,400 rooms. Furthermore, each hotel's occupancy fluctuates significantly.) Absolute percentage error (APE) was used to test for statistical significance. In order to check the sensitivity of the results to the selected error measure, accuracy was also estimated with the MAD measure. The ranking of the different models using MAD was found to be identical to the order of the models when MAPE was used.

Test of the Statistical Significance

Various tests can be used to statistically verify the superiority of one forecasting model over another. This study used the Wilcoxon matched-pairs signed-ranks test. The test was suggested by Wilcoxon (1945) and is described in Daniel (1990) and Conover (1980). The Wilcoxon matched-pairs signed-ranks test is widely used in the forecasting literature because it does not require making an assumption that the population differences between the pairs of observations are distributed normally. This study falls under the category of a large sample size, since $n > 30$. A large sample approximation (Daniel 1990, p. 153),

$$Z = \frac{T - [n(n+1)]/4}{\sqrt{n(n+1)(2n+1)/24}},$$

was calculated for each pair of models compared for each forecasting horizon. Z, the statistic, was distributed approximately as the standard normal. Sufficiently small values of Z would cause a rejection of H_0. The number of observations (differences) in each test was $n = 45$, and T is the sum of ranks with positive signs (i.e., the sum of all the ranks where method A is more accurate than method B).

Hypotheses Ha and Hb state that some models are more accurate than others. Using the Wilcoxon test, only a pair of models can be tested each time. The accuracy of one model is compared to the accuracy of the second model for a specific forecasting horizon.

To test Ha, the accuracy of model 1 was compared to the accuracy of models 2, 3, and 4 in each of the tested forecasting horizons. Similarly, to test Hb, the accuracy of model 4 was compared to that of models 2 and 3. For both Ha and Hb, the formal null hypothesis is given by

H_0: $Md \geq 0$, where Md is the median of the population of APE differences.

RESULTS AND DISCUSSION

The performance of the four models in all 10 forecasting horizons (three hotels) is given in Table 1 and is summarized in Figures 3 through 5 for each of the three hotels.

Ha is concerned with the relative performance of the curves similarity model. The results in Table 1 show that the curves similarity approach (1) outperformed all three models. The MAPE of the curves similarity model is lower than the MAPE of the other three benchmark models for all forecasting horizons in each of the three hotels tested.

Note that the following discussion is focused on forecasting horizons of up to 45 days. In longer forecasting horizons (60 and 90 days), the accuracy of all models is quite poor. Consequently, a hotel cannot use forecasts when the expected forecast error is of such magnitude.

To formally test Ha, model 1 was compared to the accuracy of the best model among models 2, 3, and 4. The results of the Wilcoxon test are given in Appendix C. When model 1 was tested on hotel A's data, H_0 was rejected for every forecasting horizon. With a confidence level of 95% ($\alpha = .05$), one can conclude that model 1 (which uses information on the shape of past curves) is more accurate than all other tested models. The results were similar for hotels B and C. Again, model 1 outperformed the best among models 2, 3, and 4, with a confidence level of 95%. The single exception was in hotel C at a forecasting horizon of 45 days, where the confidence level was only 8%.

Since the results are statistically significant (95% confidence level) for all three hotels in all eight forecasting horizons with only one exception, one might conclude that a curve similarity model that incorporates information about the shape of past booking curves has a significant advantage in terms of forecast accuracy. These results are also practically significant. The average reduction in the MAPE gained by using the curves similarity model is 5.2%. This magnitude of improvement in the accuracy of the model is likely to have a considerable positive effect on the quality of various managerial decisions made by hotel managers.

The accuracy of the stepwise autoregression (model 2) deteriorates quickly, and the MAPE measure reaches the 20% level after only four days. When the prediction of the AR model was combined with the predictions of the HOPM (model 3), the combined forecast (model 4) was more accurate than each one of them individually.

Hb examined the advantage of incorporating two independent sources of information in a model that is a linear

TABLE 1

ACCURACY (MAPE) OF THE FOUR TESTED MODELS

	Forecasting Horizon (Days)									
	1	2	3	7	14	21	30	45	60	9 9
Hotel A										
AR	10.9	16.6	22.7	23.5	25.8	26.6	27.5	28.6	29.0	30.1
HOPM	5.2	7.1	7.9	10.2	17.0	20.1	35.4	56.0	84.9	363.0
AR&HOPM	5.0	6.4	7.2	9.4	15.6	18.0	24.2	28.3	29.0	30.1
Curves similarity	1.4	2.3	3.0	4.4	10.8	14.9	21.4	24.7	26.1	27.6
Hotel B										
AR	15.4	19.8	25.3	25.2	28.5	26.2	32.5	31.8	31.7	30.9
HOPM	20.8	21.8	22.5	26.5	33.8	38.5	43.9	53.8	66.3	368.0
AR&HOPM	11.9	13.4	14.5	16.6	20.5	21.74	24.0	27.0	29.4	30.9
Curves similarity	8.8	9.2	8.6	10.7	13.8	14.8	20.0	22.2	23.6	25.5
Hotel C										
AR	13.5	17.9	20.2	20.9	20.9	21.5	23.6	26.0	27.0	28.5
HOPM	17.1	18.8	22.5	26.3	30.8	34.7	45.8	57.7	75.1	6589.2
AR&HOPM	11.4	13.1	14.5	16.6	17.7	28.6	21.7	24.8	27.0	28.5
Curves similarity	3.1	5.5	8.6	7.9	11.3	11.5	17.7	23.5	22.5	24.3

FIGURE 3

THE MAPE OF FOUR FORECASTING MODELS FOR HOTEL A

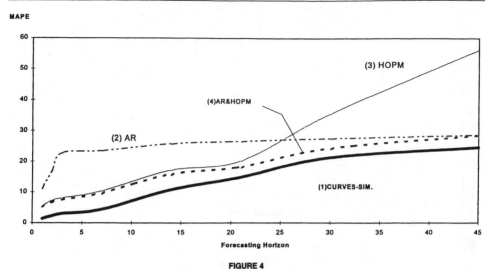

FIGURE 4

THE MAPE OF FOUR FORECASTING MODELS FOR HOTEL B

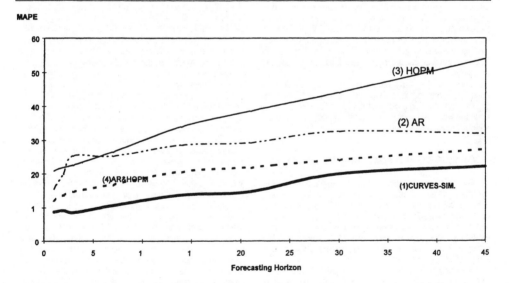

combination of the prediction of two models. The combined model (4) was compared and tested against the best noncombined model (2 or 3) in each forecasting horizon. The results of Hb's formal test are reported in Appendix D.

For hotel A, model 4 was more accurate in forecasting horizons of up to 21 days, and the result was statistically significant, with a confidence level of 10%. H_0 cannot be rejected for forecasting horizons of 30 and 45 days because of the relative accuracy of each one of the components of the combination. Recall that model 4 is a weighted average of the prediction of models 2 and 3. When the difference in accuracy between model 2 and model 3 is large, the combination cannot reduce the error. The weight of the much more accurate model is set close to 1, and the weight for the inac-

FIGURE 5
THE MAPE OF FOUR FORECASTING MODELS FOR HOTEL C

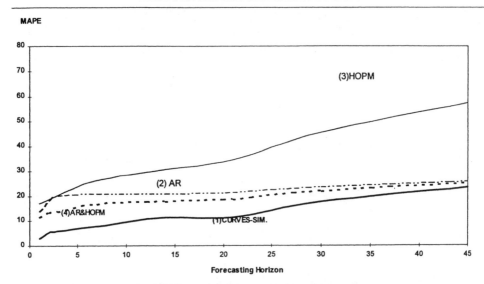

curate model is set close to 0. The combined forecast is very close to the prediction of the more accurate model, and no improvement can be gained by incorporating information from the much-less-accurate model. For hotel B, model 4 was significantly better than model 2 and model 3 only in forecasting horizons of 2, 3, 7, and 14 days. For hotel C, the improvement was statistically not significant for all forecasting horizons.

The conclusion is that Hb is partially rejected by the findings. The combined model is more accurate *only* when the gap between the two individual models' accuracy is not too wide and when the weights are modified to reflect the relative accuracy of each component.

CONCLUSION AND PRACTICAL IMPLICATIONS

This study showed that by incorporating information on the shape of past booking curves, one can significantly enhance the accuracy of traditional forecasting models. A model that identifies a current booking curve with similar past booking curves was developed. The results of the new model are more accurate than those of the traditional data extrapolation models, and the improvement is statistically and practically significant.

The study also demonstrated that historical reservations and previous booking curves can serve as two independent sources of information for the forecast. A different type of forecasting model was fitted to each source, reflecting the attributes of the data. It was shown that, as long as the difference in the accuracy of the base models is not too large, a weighted average of the two independent projections is more accurate than each one of its components. This finding is consistent with the theoretical literature on forecasting and with the results of applied studies in other fields.

The study has an important implication for managers in the lodging industry. Decision makers choosing an appropriate model for their daily reservation forecast should include a model that incorporates information on the shape of past booking curves in their consideration set. Such a model is expected to be more accurate than alternative time series approaches. Moreover, the use of information from the two independent sources — the advanced booking curves and the historical booking curve — should also be considered.

The accuracy of the forecast is essential to successful applications of a yield management system, which are designed to maximize the hotel's revenues and profits. Most hotels use the inventory control type of yield management algorithms (YMAs), where room rates are treated as constant (open or closed) and the optimization decision focuses on the number of rooms assigned to each room rate. The inventory control type of algorithms answer the following question: Which rates should be opened (or closed) every day, so that at the end of the period the revenue is maximized?

The inventory control type of YMAs require an estimate of the expected demand and an estimate of the expected revenue in each room rate category. These occupancy predictions are the "input" element in the revenue optimization model. Thus, inaccurate predictions lead to suboptimal decisions and decrease the hotel's revenue and profits (e.g., erroneously deciding to close a discount room rate based on an inaccurate estimate that the hotel will sell out). The demand for rooms is typically estimated by applying some sort of time series analysis to the reservation data. The results of this study indicate that the accuracy of the prediction can be enhanced significantly, thus improving the effectiveness of the revenue maximization algorithm.

Finally, information system managers should verify that the appropriate historical reservation data are recorded. An adequate data set would enable past booking curves to be reconstructed so that future forecasting efforts could benefit from the curves similarity approach.

FURTHER RESEARCH

Many questions remain unanswered, and there are several avenues for profitable research. Additional efforts may improve the way the shape of the curves is identified and compared. In this study we applied a rather "mechanical" approach, where coordinates of several points along the curves were used to identify each curve and to measure its resemblance to other curves. Early research efforts indicate that the coefficients of the HOPM may replace the coordinates in identifying and comparing curves. Moreover, neural networks algorithms might be more efficient in performing the pattern recognition task.

The results of this study are only a first step in improving the "input" of yield management systems, and a substantive research effort is still required to ensure that the occupancy forecast is adequate. Many inventory control algorithms require an occupancy forecast for each of the room rate categories. This study tested the accuracy of the hotels' overall occupancy, and effort should be directed to forecasting occupancy demand by rate categories. An additional challenge is presented by the variety of YMAs. Different mathematical maximization approaches were proposed in the yield management literature, and the solution methods differ because there are various ways to represent the inventory control problem mathematically. The problem can be formulated as a constrained revenue maximization problem where rooms are allocated such that the marginal revenue is equal across all segments (room rates). Probabilistic demand can be incorporated into the model, as was proposed by McDonnell-Douglas analysts (Belobaba 1989, p. 185). Glover, Glover, and McMillan (1982) developed a network model for Frontier Airlines that was later extended to include stochastic demand by Boeing researchers. Belobaba (1989) suggested an expected marginal revenue model that was developed for Western Airlines. Weatherford and Bodily (1992, p. 838) suggested this simple generic allocation rule:

Accept another discount customer (q1 $\longrightarrow$ q1 + 1) if

$$\text{PRspill} < \frac{R_1}{R_0}$$

where

q1 = the discount unit (decision variable that represents the number of discounts to accept),

PRspill = the probability that current demand plus the random full price demand will exceed capacity,

R_1 = the reduced price contribution, and
R_2 = the full price contribution.

Some of these algorithms require information beyond the occupancy figures. For example, some models require an estimation of the expected "leak" (i.e., the maximization model needs a prediction of how many low-rate segment customers would be willing to pay a higher room rate when their original low rate is no longer offered). Another group of

YMAs requires the assessment of probabilities besides the occupancy figures.

A limitation of all four models is the absence of a room rate variable. A lack of reliable information on quoted room rates prevents the inclusion of a price-quantity element in this study. It is expected that future research efforts may benefit from historical reservations data sets that include room rates information. The curves similarity model can handle information on room rates by modifying the similarity measure, S_i. This measure is expanded as follows:

$$S_i + \sqrt{(D_{N+M}^M - D_i^M)^2 + (D_{N+M}^{M+K} - D_i^{M+K})^2}$$
$$\overline{+ (D_{N+M}^{M+2K} - D_i^{M+2K})^2}$$
$$\overline{+ (D_{N+M}^{M+3K} - D_i^{M+3K})^2}$$
$$+ \vartheta \sqrt{(P_{N+M} - P_i)^2}$$

where the additional terms are

P_{N+M} = the average room rate of rooms booked for day N + M,
P_i = the average room rate of rooms booked for day i, and
ϑ = a scale parameter that would be used to adjust the scale of the new variable.

Adding explanatory variables to the extrapolative models might further improve the models by making them more robust in nonstable environments. Such variables might include competitors' room rates, marketing efforts, special events, group bookings, and so forth.

APPENDIX A

AN EXAMPLE OF CURVES SIMILARITY

Assume that the incomplete booking curve of 6/1/93 holds data up to 30 days before the date of stay. The booking curve is given in Figure 6.

FIGURE 6

INCOMPLETE BOOKING CURVE OF DAY 6/1/93 — 30 DAYS IN ADVANCE

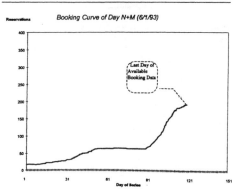

For simplicity, assume that there are only four complete booking curves available for comparison. (In reality a hotel should have hundreds of curves.) Since the forecasting horizon is 30 days, the available curves are for the following dates of stay: 4/28/93 to 5/1/93. The four complete booking curves are given in Figure 7.

By visually inspecting the curves, and without applying any formal measure of curves similarity, the curves of 4/28/93 and 5/1/93 are identified as most similar to the incomplete curve of 6/1/93. The predicted number of occupied rooms on 6/1/93 is calculated as the average final number of occupied rooms on 4/28/93 and 5/1/93.

$$\hat{Y} = (374 + 346) / 2 = 360.$$

APPENDIX B

AN EXAMPLE OF A HOPM

To forecast the number of occupied rooms on Tuesday, 6/1/93, 30 days before that day, and when 120 days of accumulating reservation records are available, the following steps are needed. The model is fitted to the first 120 days of reservation records (i.e., accumulative reservations for day 6/1/93 that were recorded between 1/2/93 and 5/2/93 are used to fit the model). The forecasted number of rooms on 6/1/93 is given by

$$\hat{Y}_{(6/1/93)} = a + b150 + c150^2 + d150^3 + e150^4$$

where

$\hat{Y}_{(6/1/93)}$ = the forecasted number of rooms on 6/1/93,
a = the number of reservations on hand at 1/2/93, and
$b,c,d,$ and e = the parameters of the fitted HOPM.

The figure 150 represents the length of the booking curve (1/2/93 to 6/1/93): 120 days of reservation records plus 30 days' forecasting horizon.

APPENDIX C

HYPOTHESIS A: THE RESULTS OF THE WILCOXON TEST

Model	Forecasting Horizon	Best Nonshape Model	P(Z) Hotel A	Hotel B	Hotel C
1	1	4	0.0000	0.0017	0.0000
1	2	4	0.0000	0.0290	0.0000
1	3	4	0.0000	0.0157	0.0000
1	7	4	0.0002	0.0014	0.0000
1	14	4	0.0049	0.0002	0.0012
1	21	4	0.0036	0.0238	0.0002
1	30	4	0.0019	0.0145	0.0000
1	45	4	0.0240	0.0023	0.9218

FIGURE 7

COMPLETE BOOKING CURVE OF DAYS 4/28/93 THROUGH 5/1/93

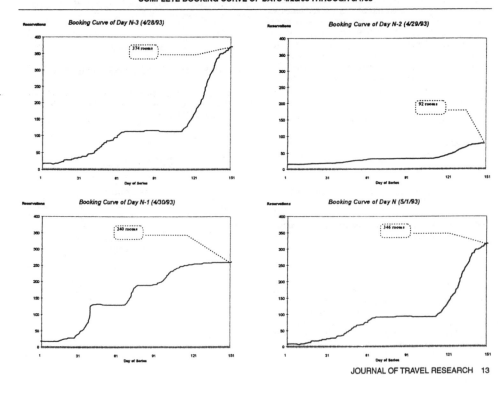

APPENDIX D
HYPOTHESIS B: THE RESULTS OF THE WILCOXON TEST

		Hotel A		Hotel B		Hotel C	
Model	Forecasting Horizon	Best Noncombined Model	P(Z)	Best Noncombined Model	P(Z)	Best Noncombined Model	P(Z)
4	1	3	0.0000	2	0.4842	2	0.5650
4	2	3	0.0047	2	0.0341	2	0.6922
4	3	3	0.0719	3	0.0007	2	0.6304
4	7	3	0.0003	2	0.1040	2	0.9216
4	14	3	0.0026	2	0.0000	2	0.9244
4	21	3	0.0017	2	0.5426	2	0.9233
4	30	3	0.2920	2	0.4528	2	0.9993
4	45	3	0.9997	2	0.8241	2	0.2959

REFERENCES

Anderson, D., D. Sweeney, and A. Thomas (1990). *Statistics for Business and Economics.* St. Paul, MN: West Publishing Company.

Andrew, W., D. Cranage, and C. Lee (1990). "Forecasting Hotel Occupancy Rates with Time Series Models: An Empirical Analysis." *Hospitality Research Journal,* 14 (2): 173–81.

Belobaba, P. P. (1989). "Application of Probabilistic Decision Model to Airline Seat Inventory Control." *Operations Research,* 37 (March–April): 183–98.

Berenson, M. L., and D. M. Levine (1992). *Basic Business Statistics: Concepts and Applications.* Englewood Cliffs, NJ: Prentice Hall.

Carbone, R., and S. Amstrong (1982). "Evaluation of Extrapolative Forecasting Methods: Results of a Survey of Academicians and Practitioners." *Journal of Forecasting,* 1: 215–17.

Churchill, G. A. (1991). *Marketing Research Methodological Foundations,* 5th ed. Chicago: The Dryden Press.

Conover, W. J. (1980). *Practical Nonparametric Statistics.* New York: John Wiley and Sons.

Crouch, G. I. (1994). "Guidelines for the Study of International Tourism Demand Using Regression Analysis." In *Travel, Tourism and Hospitality Research: A Handbook for Managers and Researchers,* 2d ed., edited by J. R. B. Ritchie and C. R. Goeldner. New York: John Wiley and Sons, pp. 583–96.

Daniel, W. W. (1990). *Applied Nonparametric Statistics.* Boston: PWS-KENT.

Fields, R. (1992). "The Evaluation of Extrapolative Forecasting Methods." *International Journal of Forecasting,* 8: 81–98.

Glover, R., L. Glover, and C. McMillan (1982). "The Passenger-Mix Problem in the Scheduled Airlines." *Interfaces,* 12: 73–79.

Granger, C. W. J., and P. Newbold (1986). *Forecasting Economic Time Series,* 2d ed. San Diego: Academic Press.

Kimes, S. E. (1989). "Yield Management: A Tool for Capacity-Constrained Service Firms." *Journal of Operations Management,* 8 (October): 348–63.

Lee, A. O. (1990). "Airline Reservations Forecasting: Probabilistic and Statistical Models of the Booking Process." Ph.D. diss., Flight Transportation Lab Report R 90-5, Massachusetts Institute of Technology.

Makridakis, S., A. Andersen, R. Carbone, R. Fildes, M. Hibon, R. Lewandowski, J. Newton, E. Parzen, and R. Winkler (1982). "The Accuracy of Extrapolation (Time Series) Methods: Result of a Forecasting Competition." *Journal of Forecasting,* 1 (2): 111–54.

Makridakis, S., and M. Hibon (1979). "Accuracy of Forecasting: An Empirical Investigation (with Discussion)." *Journal of the Royal Statistical Society,* A 142: 97–145.

Martin, C., and S. Witt (1989). "Accuracy of Econometric Forecasts of Tourism." *Annals of Tourism Research,* 16 (3): 407–28.

McNees, S. K. (1982). "The Role of Macroeconomic Models in Forecasting and Policy Analysis in the United States." *Journal of Forecasting,* 1 (2): 37–48.

Mentzer, J. T., and J. E. Cox (1984). "Familiarity Application and Performance of Sales Forecasting Techniques." *Journal of Forecasting,* 3 (1): 27–36.

Metz, C. L. (1991). "Tackling F&B's Profit Squeeze: Food and Beverage Departments Are Training Their Sights on Expenses as a Way to Boost Profits." *Lodging Hospitality,* 47 (12): 86–88.

Microsoft Corporation (1993). *User's Guide: Microsoft Excel Version 5.0.* Redmond, WA: Microsoft Corporation.

Neter, J., W. Wasserman, and M. Kutner (1990). *Applied Linear Statistical Models.* Illinois: Irwin.

Relihan, W. J. (1989). "The Yield Management Approach to Hotel-Room-Pricing." *The Cornell Hotel and Restaurant Administration Quarterly,* 30 (May): 40–45.

SAS Institute (1993). *SAS/ETS User Guide, Version 6,* 2d ed. Cary, NC: SAS Institute.

Schmidgall, R. S. (1989). "Forecasting for Profitability." *Bottomline* 4 (2): 20–23.

Sheldon, P., and T. Var (1985). "Tourism Forecasting: A Review of Empirical Research." *Journal of Forecasting,* (4): 183–95.

Uysal, M., and J. Crompton (1985). "An Overview of Approaches Used to Forecast Tourism Demand." *Journal of Travel Research,* 24 (Spring): 7–15.

Weatherford, L., and E. S. Bodily (1992). "A Taxonomy and Research Overview of Perishable-Asset Revenue Management: Yield Management, Overbooking, and Pricing." *Operation Research,* 40 (September–October): 831–43.

Wheelwright, Stephen C., and Spyros Makridakis (1985). *Forecasting Methods for Management.* New York: John Wiley and Sons.

Wilcoxon, F. (1945). "Individual Comparisons by Ranking Methods." *Biometrics:* 80–83.

Witt, S., and C. Witt (1991). *Modeling and Forecasting Demand in Tourism.* San Diego: Academic Press.

——— (1995). "Forecasting Tourism Demand: A Review of Empirical Research." *International Journal of Forecasting,* 11 (3): 447–75.

Yesawich, P. C. (1984). "A Marketing-Based Approach to Forecasting." *The Cornell Hotel and Restaurant Administration Quarterly,* 25 (November): 47–53.

Zarnowitz, V. (1984). "The Accuracy of Individual and Group Forecasts from Business Outlook Survey." *Journal of Forecasting,* 3 (1): 11–26.

[8]

INTERNATIONAL JOURNAL OF TOURISM RESEARCH
Int. J. Tourism Res. 4, 367–378 (2002)
Published online in Wiley InterScience (www.interscience.wiley.com). DOI: 10.1002/jtr.386

No Attraction in Strategic Thinking: Perceptions on Current and Future Skills Needs for Visitor Attraction Managers

Sandra Watson* and Martin McCracken

School of Management, Napier University of Edinburgh, New Craig, Craighouse Road, Edinburgh EH10 5LG, UK

ABSTRACT

This paper presents the findings from an exploratory study into managerial skill requirements in the Scottish visitor attraction sector. It provides an insight into the range, diversity and perceived importance of current and future skills. The main findings highlight a focus on operation skills, with 'soft' people skills also seen as being important in the future. However, less emphasis was given to strategic skills, either now or in the future. Given the intensely competitive environment for visitor attractions, this finding is rather concerning as strategic thinking has been presented in the literature and by tourism experts as essential to maintain commercial viability. Copyright © 2002 John Wiley & Sons, Ltd.

Received 5 July 2001; revised 10 January 2002; accepted 15 January 2002

Keywords: managerial skills; Scotland; visitor attractions; strategic; future.

INTRODUCTION

The visitor attractions sector in Scotland is becoming increasingly diverse, with globalisation adding to an already competitive environment. If the visitor attraction sector is going to continue to play a major

role in Scottish tourism, then there is a real need to examine the current skills and competences profiles of managers and identify if these will equip them to be successful in the future. Tourism Training Scotland (1998) identified a priority for the next 5 years as providing; 'management skills to equip the industry to be innovative in meeting the changes taking place in tourism and the broader business environment'. Although much research has been undertaken into current skills and knowledge, little work has been conducted on specifically identifying managerial skills and competence requirements in visitor attractions.

The visitor attraction sector of the Scottish tourism industry is facing a number of potential threats, which makes it difficult to sustain their competitiveness. These include a general downturn in the number of visitors to Scotland, with Scotland being considered an expensive destination offering comparatively poor value for money. The strength of sterling means that non-UK locations offer increasingly better value for money and these destinations are becoming more attractive given the availability of low-cost air transportation. The high cost of fuel is also seen as a deterrent for potential visitors, particularly to remote rural locations such as the Scottish Highlands and Islands. Additionally the lack of resources and funding in the public sector has been noted as a real issue, affecting visitor attractions ability to offer new products and operating services, and has resulted in a series of staff cuts (STB, 2000, pp. 158–159).

This paper reports on research examining the range and importance of current and future

*Correspondence to: S. Watson, School of Management, Napier University of Edinburgh, New Craig, Craighouse Road, Edinburgh EH10 5LG, UK.
E-mail: s.watson@napier.ac.uk

managerial competence and skills in the Scottish visitor attraction sector. It presents an overview of relevant literature, which was used to inform the design of a two-staged research study. The first stage explored the contextual issues that are influencing the managerial skills agenda, whereas the second focused on ascertaining the views of visitor attraction managers on the importance of managerial skills. The paper concludes with a discussion on the implications for managerial skills and competences.

LITERATURE REVIEW

The subject of management skills and competences and their potential role in contributing to organisational success have received much academic attention (Prahalad and Hamel 1990; Hamel, 1994). Stinchcombe (1990, p. 63) contends that the foundation of an organisation's capabilities is the competences of its individual members. The approach taken in the UK has been to develop agreed classifications of what managers 'do', demonstrated by skills, knowledge and understanding needed by managers. The ability of a manager to function successfully in the workplace is then measured against these competences. As Day (1988) articulates, it is related to 'the ability to put skills and knowledge into action'. The ability to exercise both technical expertise and management skills to identify and implement productivity improvements is clearly imperative to operational success. Jacobs (1989) proposes that attention needs to be paid to the development of both systems, and people in the operation. In support of this, the McKinsey 7-S framework, illustrates that organisational capability is influenced by the 'soft' elements of style, staffing, skills, and shared values, as well as the traditional 'hard' areas of strategy, structure and systems (Fifield and Gilligan, 1997).

Winterton *et al.* (2000) present a range of competences and capabilities that will be required of successful managers in the future. Critical competences include: technical knowledge; seeing and acting beyond local boundaries; learning and innovation; managing change; flexibility; a group orientated view of leadership, and transformational leadership.

Important competences cited are facilitation skills, communication across national boundaries, self-reliance, responsibility, self-monitoring and ability to learn from experience. Finally, the critical capabilities are presented as shared value, trust, honesty, sustainable development, influence, instinct and judgement, and learning.

Although the above discussion centres on generic managerial competences and skills, there has been a burgeoning interest in understanding what are the most important managerial skills and competences for managers in the tourist and hospitality industries. For example, Hay (1990) examines core managerial competences and characteristics, which are essential in a rapidly changing world, and Tas (1988) and Christou and Eaton (1997) identify the most important competences for hotel general management. In essence these surveys all identify 'soft' or 'human relation' associated competences as being the most significant. Ladkin (1999, p. 170) reports that when researchers have looked at what hotel managers do, four roles of entrepreneur, cost controller, marketeer, and service and quality control assurance can be identified. Additionally a Skills Task Force commissioned report designed to investigate the nature, extent and pattern of skill needs and shortages in the UK leisure sector, found that in the leisure sector there were major skills gaps among the existing workforce, including: entrepreneurial and management skills, information technology and customer care skills, and the training of volunteers (Keep and Mayhew, 1999, p. 2).

Also receiving attention in the literature has been research that attempts to identify the importance of managers possessing a balanced range of skills and competencies (Gamble *et al.*, 1994; Ladkin and Riley, 1996). Swarbrooke (2002) interprets the following as important for future success in managing visitor attractions: increased emphasis on quality enhancement; greater attention given to recruitment, staff development, appraisal and performance related pay, empowerment of staff, increased use of integrated computerised management information systems; increased professionalism of managers; greater emphasis on marketing; and a focus on ethical and social responsibility.

There appears to have been limited research

surrounding managerial skills needs in visitor attractions, although textbooks designed for university undergraduate courses, such as Theobald (1994) and Swarbrooke (2002), have included a chapter on employees' skill requirements. However, in the main the empirical work that exists on managerial skills is preoccupied with the hotel sector. Therefore a central objective in this study into skills needs for managers in the visitor attraction sector was to begin to redress the balance in the literature. In the next section the methodology and survey design addressed are described in more detail.

METHODOLOGY AND DATA COLLECTION

The study involved two main stages of primary research, utilising both qualitative and quantitative methodologies. In order to gain an understanding of both the context and range of managerial skills, the researchers adopted a 'methodologically pluralistic position' (Trow, 1957, p. 33; cited in Gill and Johnson, 1991, p. 127). This methodological pluralism is increasingly seen as being appropriate in explorative social science research because it overcomes the limitations and inherent bias in using a single method approach (Denzin and Lincoln, 2000).

A purposive sampling procedure (Jankowicz, 1991) was used in selecting interviewees, with individuals selected on the basis of their expert knowledge. Five key informants from organisations — either promoters or owners of Scottish visitor attractions — were drawn from the following organisations: Scottish Enterprise (national economic development agency); The Scottish Tourist Board (responsible for the strategic development of tourism); Historic Scotland (government agency responsible for the built heritage in Scotland); National Trust for Scotland (charitable organisation with over 100 built and natural properties); and the Ross and Cromarty Enterprise Company (a regional economic development organisation). Qualitative semi-structured interviews were conducted to obtain rich data on current and future key managerial skills in visitor attractions. The interviews, which lasted on average 1.5 h, were conducted by

both authors, tape recorded and subsequently transcribed in verbatim.

The second stage of the research involved developing a questionnaire to be issued to general managers at the top 20 attractions, based in Scotland, which charge admissions and the top 20 where admission was free. An additional nine new visitor attractions were included in the sample, which had opened since the Scottish Tourist Board data had been compiled in 1998, but were likely to feature in the next monitoring survey (STB, 1998). This purposive sample was selected to enable the researchers to examine the perceived skill requirements amongst managers of the most successful attractions in terms of visitor numbers. The authors used literature on skill requirements from generic and hospitality specific sectors, and the results from stage one of this research, to inform the questionnaire. In doing so, a deductive stance was adopted where attempts were made to see if the skill requirements reported elsewhere were relevant to this sample. A process of categorisation was undertaken and the skill statements were reworded to encompass the views from industry experts. The categorisation was intended to make the questions flow more logically, and form a basis for analysing the data.

The final survey instrument contained 45 skills/competence statements divided into seven categories. Table 1 provides a breakdown of items within each category in the questionnaire.

Respondents (general visitor attraction managers) were asked to rate the current and future importance of the skill on a five-point Likert Scale. The lowest rating equated to 'no' importance, and the highest option in terms of importance was labelled as 'essential'. The questionnaire also included seven factual and biographical questions and four open-ended questions addressing training and development issues in the visitor attraction.

After two mailings 25 useable questionnaires were received giving a response rate of 51%. Although the sample was limited, a response rate of 51% completed questionnaires can be considered good for a mail-based survey. The responses to the statements, which can be found in Tables 2 and 3, were analysed

Int. J. Tourism Res. **4**, 367–378 (2002)

Table 1. Skill/competence categories and number of items

Skill/competence category	Antecedents (from literature and interviews)	Number of items listed
Strategic/general management	External awareness, networking, understanding contradictions, benchmarking, maintaining shared values, knowledge management, commercial/ ecological awareness and decision-making	9
People management	Attracting, recruiting and leading employees, motivation, training and development, team building, involvement, openness trust, managing diversity and conflicts	11
Financial management	Pricing, budgeting, external funding, planning	4
Technological	Enhancing visitor experience, decision-making, promotion	3
Self-management	Influence, enthusiasm, self-reliance, learning, problem-solving, communications, creativity and innovation	8
Operational	Customer focus, marketing, quality enhancement, languages	7
Legal/ethical	Legislation, honesty, safety and security	3

using the same system as Tas (1988). Therefore those statements attaining a mean response rating of over 4.50 were described as 'essential', when a mean rating was between 3.50 and 4.49 it was deemed to be of 'considerable importance' and when the mean rating was between 2.50 and 3.49 the skill was rated as 'moderately important'.

KEY INFORMANT FINDINGS

According to the key informants, the environment in which visitor attractions operate is complex and changing which requires managers to be more externally aware, less insular and more adaptable.

Table 2 provides an overview of the ten key external influences raised by these industry experts and their potential implications for the skills required by visitor attraction managers. Generally the interviewees felt that the impact of globalisation, greater competition and demographic changes will require new ways of thinking and operating, particularly in relation to improved service quality, product development and selling, requiring greater innovation and creativity. For example the representative from Scottish Enterprise contended that 'Visitor attractions will have to get switched on to what the customer is looking for or else

they will die a death'. Similarly the Historic Scotland representative felt that 'the attraction sector tend[ed] to firefight and they are looking towards the next 2–3 or even 6 months but not longer term'.

Several of the representatives thought that if many of the smaller attractions were going to survive they would have to change their mindset towards competitors and start to work together and co-operate. The interviewee from Scottish Tourist Board summed up the view here when he pointed out that 'Small and medium visitor attractions should get away from seeing themselves as competitors and start to co-operate with each other.'

The key informants also recognised that increasing influence of the European Union would have a further impact upon both the position of tourism and the operation of visitor attractions. This can be seen in such areas as monetary union, legislative requirements and social policy. More specifically, at the national level, the interviewees hoped that the creation of the Scottish parliament would raise the profile of tourism in the political agenda and provide greater opportunity for lobbying and promotion of the sector.

The effects of changing demographics and work patterns were also cited, with several of the informants predicting the emergence of

Table 2. External influences on managerial skills

External influences	Managerial skill/competence requirements
Devolved Scottish parliament	Opportunity to collectively lobby
European Union Legislation (employment and health, safety and security)	Keeping up to date with relevant legislation
Monetary union	Marketing and pricing effectively
Lifelong learning	Awareness of training and development opportunities, managing more educated and diverse range of staff
Globalisation	Creativity and innovation, need to be commercially viable, understanding and meeting diverse customer needs, seeing and acting beyond local boundaries, benchmarking against international standards, networking, language skills
Increased leisure time	Understanding need to compete with a wide range of leisure providers (e.g. retail, cinemas, etc.), appropriate pricing strategy and effective marketing
New markets, e.g. ageing population, cash-rich–time-poor, decline of traditional family and increasing interest in culture and heritage	Understanding the composition and needs of diverse markets
Environmental and ecological awareness	Balancing commercial and ecological needs
Increasing availability and use of technology in society	Using technology to enhance visitor experience
Implications on working practices	Using internet to promote and sell the attraction Using technology in managerial decision making Computer literacy skills

new markets and greater competition for leisure time as a consequence. With this in mind attraction managers will be required to understand the composition and needs of potential new customers so they can offer them an experience to rival other leisure providers. The Scottish Tourist Board representative contended that 'If they [visitor attractions] are going to survive they have got to offer something that is different, something globally recognised but yet unique to attract the visitors to that location'. Interestingly the Historic Scotland representative felt that increasing ecological and environmental awareness would create new markets, which will ultimately influence the operation of visitor attractions. As she pointed put:

> People are now more interested in the natural environment and want to do more than laze about and learn more about the environment. The European tourist and particularly Germans are interested in Scottish and Celtic culture, and they want

to hear traditional music and see traditional crafts, and go to real attractions, not manufactured experiences.

Technological advances were also forwarded as being influential for visitor attraction managers' skills in two main ways. First, in relation to the actual promotion of the attraction, using Internet technology was felt to be becoming increasingly essential. However, as the Scottish Enterprise representative pointed out clearly some attractions in Scotland had not fully embraced Internet technology:

> Some are very good and are switched on and have very good and professional websites, and can use them effectively and can control the management information that comes from it. Others just don't use it which is a lost opportunity for them—in terms of being able to control things like sending out effective mail-shots, etc.

Secondly, technology can also play a huge

Table 3. Current skills for general managers in scottish visitor attractions

	Current Importance				
	Rank (overall)	Rank (category)	Skill category[a]	Mean[b]	SD
Keeping up to date with relevant legislation.	1	1	LE	4.76	0.52
To provide a safe and secure environment for visitors	1	1	LE	4.76	0.44
Understanding customer needs	2	1	OP	4.64	0.64
Understanding how to lead the organisation's employees	3	1	PM	4.60	0.65
Training and developing staff	3	1	PM	4.60	0.65
The ability to establish trust within organisation	3	1	PM	4.60	0.65
To be enthusiastic and committed to the attraction	3	1	SM	4.60	0.58
Meeting customer needs	4	2	OP	4.56	0.65
To motivate and enthuse employees	4	2	PM	4.56	0.65
To communicate effectively	5	2	SM	4.52	0.51
The ability to deal honestly in business	5	2	LE	4.52	0.59
Attracting and recruiting appropriate staff	6	3	PM	4.48	0.92
To encourage team-working	7	4	PM	4.40	0.71
Ensuring budgeting procedures are effective	8	1	FM	4.36	0.64
Sensitively managing visitors' problems	9	3	SM	4.32	0.69
To be willing to learn new skills to cope with change	9	3	SM	4.32	0.56
To use problem solving skills	9	3	SM	4.32	0.63
To be creative and innovative	10	4	SM	4.30	0.75
Marketing the attraction effectively	11	3	OP	4.28	0.79
Making decisions based on limited information	12	1	SGM	4.17	0.72
To encourage more staff involvement in the organisation	13	5	PM	4.16	0.85
The ability to identify skills shortages	13	5	PM	4.16	0.90
Enhancing merchandising for the attraction	13	4	OP	4.16	0.85
To be self reliant and recognise one's own abilities	13	5	SM	4.16	0.62
Understanding the need for the attraction to be viable	14	2	FM	4.13	1.25
Effectively managing diverse employee groups	15	6	PM	4.12	1.13
The ability to influence others	15	6	SM	4.12	0.53
Creating and maintaining shared values in the organisation	16	2	SGM	4.04	0.75
To ability to engender an open culture in the attraction	16	7	PM	4.04	0.84
The ability to manage conflicts in the organisation	16	7	PM	4.04	0.84
Ensuring the attraction meets quality standards	17	5	OP	4.00	1.25
Understanding factors in the external environment	18	3	SGM	3.96	0.75
Understanding the need for pricing strategy	19	3	FM	3.88	0.99
The ability to harness individual knowledge	20	4	SGM	3.84	2.73
Preparing business plans	21	6	OP	3.68	1.25
Using the Internet to promote and sell the attraction	22	1	TEC	3.64	1.38
Networking with other organisations and agencies	23	5	SGM	3.56	2.74
Bench-marking against international standards	24	6	SGM	3.36	2.74
Using technology in managerial decision-making	25	2	TEC	3.25	0.79
Using technology to enhance the visitor experience	26	3	TEC	3.24	0.93
Balancing commercial and ecological demands of the org	27	7	SGM	3.16	2.72
Ability to see and act beyond local boundaries	27	7	SGM	3.16	2.82
Securing funding from external sources	28	4	FM	3.13	1.19
Understanding the contradictions between stakeholders	29	8	SGM	2.96	2.72
Speaking a foreign language(s)	30	7	OP	2.80	1.04

[a] SGM = strategic/general management skills; PM = people management skills; OP = operational management skills; LE = legal/ethical awareness; SM = self-management skills; FM = financial management skills, TEC = technological skills.
[b] 2.50–3.49 = moderately important; 3.50–4.49 = considerable importance; 4.50 and above = essential.

                    Int. J. Tourism Res. **4**, 367–378 (2002)

part in enhancing the visitor experience at the attraction location. It was suggested that for modern 'experience' type attractions, using virtual reality and interactive media are vital to enrich visits. For example the representative from the National Trust for Scotland intimated that '…there is a lot of potential for technology to be used to record heritage—to provide virtual tours and open up new markets'. A more thorough analysis of the key influences on managerial skills as perceived by these industry experts can be gained from McCracken and Watson (2000).

The next section of this paper discusses the second part of the study, which sought to ascertain which skills and competences managers in Scottish visitor attractions perceived to be most important both now and in the future.

SURVEY FINDINGS

Attraction Characteristics

Of the 25 top attractions that returned completed questionnaires, the majority (14, or 56%) were located in Scotland's heavily populated central belt, which includes the cities of Glasgow, Edinburgh, Dundee and Stirling. Six attractions came from visitor attractions in the northeast. Three (12%) attractions were located in the northwest, and lastly two attractions were found in the south of Scotland.

The two largest attraction categories were interpretation and visitor centres, and museums and art galleries. Castles, historic houses, gardens and industrial and craft premises made up the remainder of the sample. Just over two-thirds (67%) charged an entrance fee to the attraction or some part of the site, for example, for a guided tour or special displays. On average the attractions in this sample employed around 70 full-time employees, with 80% employing less than 100 people.

Over three-quarters (76%) of those who completed the questionnaires were male. The average age of the male respondents was 43.5 years, whereas the females' average age was 29.3 years. Over one-third (34.8%) of the respondents are aged between 35 and 44. On average the visitor attraction managers had been working in the sector for just over 6 years and at their current place of work for around 4.5 years. In terms of qualifications, 45% of the sample were educated to degree level or above and 20% possessed diplomas in various disciplines.

Current managerial skills/competences

Table 3 provides the findings relating to the importance these managers attached to current managerial skills/competences. Eleven of the skills statements were perceived as being essential by the respondents, 26 were rated as being of considerable importance, and the remaining eight were moderately important. Joint top of the essential scale was, 'Keeping up to date with relevant legislation, for example, health, safety and employment' and to 'provide a safe and secure environment for visitors' with mean ratings of 4.76. Amongst the statements that were rated as being of considerable importance were 'attracting and recruiting appropriate staff', and being able to 'encourage team-working'. For those statements that were rated as being of moderate importance, being able to 'bench-mark against international standards' was at the top of this category. Bottom of the 45 skill statements was the ability for managers to 'speak a foreign language(s)'.

Future skills/competences

Respondents were asked to rate the skill statements in terms of their importance in the next 5 years. Table 4 provides the findings for this part of the questionnaire. Rated as most essential was the statement 'understanding how to lead the organisation's employees' ($M = 4.84$). Also rated as being essential by the managers and echoing their views on current skill needs was 'keeping up to date with relevant legislation'. Statements regarding 'marketing the attraction effectively' and 'being able to manage visitors' problems with understanding and sensitivity' were at the top of the considerable importance category. 'Ability to see and act beyond local boundaries—in a global tourism market', was placed at the top of the moderately important bracket. Rated

Table 4. Future skills for general managers in scottish visitor attractions

	Future Importance				
	Rank (overall)	Rank (category)	Skill category[a]	Mean[b]	SD
Understanding how to lead the organisation's employees	1	1	PM	4.84	0.37
Keeping up to date with relevant legislation	2	1	LE	4.80	0.41
Understanding customer needs	3	1	OP	4.76	0.52
To provide a safe and secure environment for visitors	3	2	LE	4.76	0.44
To motivate and enthuse employees	3	2	PM	4.76	0.46
Training and developing staff	4	3	PM	4.72	0.54
Meeting customer needs	4	2	OP	4.72	0.54
To be enthusiastic and committed to the attraction	5	1	SM	4.68	0.48
Establishing trust between staff and management	5	4	PM	4.68	0.48
Attracting and recruiting appropriate staff	6	5	PM	4.60	0.87
The ability to deal honestly in business	6	3	LE	4.60	0.50
To communicate effectively	6	2	SM	4.60	0.50
To encourage team-working	7	6	PM	4.56	0.58
Using the Internet to promote and sell the attraction	7	1	TEC	4.56	0.71
Marketing the attraction effectively	8	3	OP	4.48	0.65
Sensitively managing visitors' problems	8	3	SM	4.48	0.65
To be willing to learn new skills to cope with change	9	4	SM	4.44	0.58
To use problem-solving skills	9	4	SM	4.44	0.58
Encouraging more staff involvement in the organisation	10	7	PM	4.40	0.76
Effectively managing diverse employee groups	10	7	PM	4.40	0.76
Ensuring budgeting procedures are effective	10	1	FM	4.40	0.65
Enhancing merchandising for the attraction	11	4	OP	4.36	0.76
Identifying skills shortages in the organisation	12	8	PM	4.32	0.80
Understanding the need for the attraction to be viable	13	2	FIN	4.30	1.18
To be creative and innovative	14	5	SM	4.29	0.69
The ability to manage conflicts in the organisation	15	9	PM	4.28	0.79
Ensuring the attraction meets quality standards	16	5	OP	4.25	1.07
Understanding the need for pricing strategy	17	3	FIN	4.21	1.02
Understanding how factors in the external environment	17	1	SGM	4.21	0.78
The ability to influence others	18	6	SM	4.20	0.58
Making decisions based on limited information	19	2	SGM	4.17	0.72
To be self-reliant and recognise one's own abilities	20	7	SM	4.16	0.55
Using technology to enhance the visitor experience	21	2	TEC	4.08	0.91
The ability to engender an open culture in the attraction	21	10	PM	4.08	0.81
Using technology in managerial decision-making	22	3	TEC	3.96	0.95
Preparing business plans	23	6	FM	3.92	1.15
Securing funding from external sources	24	4	FM	3.88	1.15
The ability to harness individual knowledge	25	3	SGM	3.84	2.73
Networking with other organisations and agencies	26	4	SGM	3.68	2.75
Creating and maintaining shared values in the organisation	27	5	SGM	3.60	2.72
Bench-marking against international standards	28	6	SGM	3.56	2.79
Ability to see and act beyond local boundaries	29	7	SGM	3.48	2.80
Balancing commercial and ecological demands of the organisation	30	8	SGM	3.24	2.71
Speaking a foreign language(s)	30	7	OP	3.24	1.05
Understanding the contradictions between stakeholders	31	9	SGM	3.12	2.74

[a] SGM = strategic/general management skills; PM = people management skills; OP = operational management skills; LE = legal/ethical awareness; SM = self-management skills; FM = financial management skills, TEC = technological skills.
[b] 2.50–3.49 = moderately important; 3.50–4.49 = considerable importance; 4.50 and above = essential.

Table 5. Skills, training and development received or lacking in managers

Skills types	Training and development received (frequency)	Skills lacking (frequency)
Strategic/general management	3	1
People management	11	9
Self-management	10	1
Operations management	1	3
Legal/ethical management	4	1
Financial management	2	1
Technology	2	4
None	7	12

lowest overall was the ability to 'understand the contradictions between stakeholders'. The managers also felt that possessing the 'ability to speak a foreign language' would also be relatively low in importance in the future.

Training and development in the attractions

The respondents were also asked to comment on the training and development they had received in their present positions. Table 5 lists the various training and development activities that managers had received, as well as the types of training that they felt they were most lacking. These activities were categorised according to the specific skill sections that were presented in the main body of the questionnaire. The most popular types of training and development that these managers had received were 'people management' and 'self-management' related. Examples of 'people management' type activities were: appraisal skills training, discipline and grievance training, recruitment and selection training, and various other courses aimed at developing staff. In terms of 'self-management' the activities mentioned most commonly were related to management development activities provided by various suppliers, both in higher education and by private training and development organisations.

When questioned about skills/competence and training and development gaps in their organisations, almost 50% of the respondents felt that 'none' existed. This was not surprising given the fact that these general managers may be unlikely to criticise either their own operational and managerial skills level or that of

others in the attraction. For those who did feel there were skills lacking, most frequently they were related to 'people management'. The types of management skills gaps that were mentioned were: team thinking, communication skills, self-empowerment, leadership skills and motivational skills.

DISCUSSION

In many ways key influences having an impact on the skill portfolio of visitor attraction managers in Scotland are no different to those affecting managers of any business. There are, however, critical factors that make this industry unique, including its diversity, composition of ownership and the primary operational purpose and motivation. For example, attractions can be owned and managed by government agencies, charitable bodies or private businesses. Purpose, philosophy and missions may range from preservation, heritage or history to providing an educational or entertainment experience. Therefore the business may be driven by diverse and sometimes paradoxical motivations, such as the need to preserve a historical battle/burial site, but still providing a fitting visitor experience. Identifying a homogeneous set of skills to meet the business needs of visitor attractions is difficult. However, all the skill and competences presented were rated relatively high by the attraction managers. This portrays a high degree of agreement amongst the sample, with few skills identified as unimportant, either currently or in the future. With the diversity of the attractions, in relation to ownership, size, purpose and location, a greater divergence of views might have been expected.

The set of competences and skills that managers require are likely to be much wider than in other business environments. This is compounded further by the proliferation of small and medium sized enterprises (SMEs), and the geographical spread of visitor attractions in Scotland, which means that managers are often isolated and require to be more entrepreneurial. The industry experts consistently raised the need for attraction managers to be more commercially aware. The increased competitive environment evidenced by more investment in larger attractions and greater customer expectations has further compounded the importance of commercial viability in the sector. Therefore, a key dilemma faced by many attractions is the need to enhance commercial expertise, without losing the uniqueness and individual purpose of many of the visitor attractions.

The most interesting finding to emerge from this study was the generally low importance rating that these general attraction managers gave to those skills that were defined as 'strategic/general management' in nature. Almost 50% of the 'strategic/general management skills' were located within the moderately important category, with 33% remaining in that category when the managers rated the importance of skills for the future. This finding supports those of other researchers within the hospitality industry, who exposed an emphasis on operational type skills amongst similar managers in hotels (Geurrier and Lockwood, 1989). Interestingly the increasing requirement for strategic awareness amongst visitor attraction managers was also emphasised by the key informants. For example several highlighted the need for managers to form strategic alliances and have better awareness of how the global environment could have an impact upon their business.

In examining essential skills, it is interesting to note the predominance of 'legal and ethical concerns', with an emphasis on those skills to meet legislative requirements. Although these skills were not identified as being essential in the literature, they were raised as an area for attention through the key informant interviews. What was significant in the survey was the inordinate importance given to such skills. This is not to devalue the need to adhere to legislative considerations, but there did appear to be a preoccupation with such matters to the detriment of more longer term goals.

'People management' skills were also generally rated as being essential amongst the respondents in the sample. In the literature 'soft' or human relation skills were identified as being important (Jacobs, 1982; Geurrier & Lockwood, 1989; Christou & Eaton, 1997). This emphasis on people management skills appeared to increase when the respondents rated future skill requirements. For example, the ability to 'effectively manage diverse employee groups, including volunteers and seasonal workers' was also perceived to be an essential skill in the future.

As has been discussed previously, Winterton et al. (2000) highlighted the importance of certain personal competences for managers in the future. However, only possessing 'effective communications and enthusiasm and commitment' were rated as essential, currently and in the future, by the managers in this survey.

In terms of other operational skills those associated with 'understanding and meeting customer needs' were seen as being essential, both now and in the future. It was surprising, however, that currently, the 'use of technology to aid managerial decision making, and to enhance the visitor's experience', were rated as only moderately important skills. In both the literature (Keep and Mayhew, 1999; Winterton et al., 2000) and amongst the key informants interviewed the ability to use information technology was cited as being a critical skill. It is interesting to note that managers rated these skills higher in the future. For example 'using technology to promote attractions' was currently seen to be of considerable importance, but to be essential in 5 years time.

In terms of training and development provision in their visitor attractions, it can be seen that the managers felt there was a lack of skills of an essentially operational nature. This finding was not surprising given the high rating of these types of skills. This is also reflected in the literature that reports an emphasis on providing operational skills and competences for managers in the tourism industry (Geurrier and Lockwood, 1989; Christou and Eaton, 1997). However, other commentators, such as Ladkin (2000) and Swarbrooke (1995), strongly stress the need for more strategic training and development for managers. Also significant was the respondents' views that 'people management' training and development was needed. Given the attention that such issues have attained both from generic and industry based researchers (Keep and Mayhew, 1999; Winterton *et al.*, 2000) it would appear that this set of attraction managers appreciated the need to develop such skills.

However, of some concern was the finding that when asked about managerial skills gaps present in their sites, almost 50% of the sample felt that none existed. There also appeared to be evidence of a lack of training aimed at enhancing technological skills in these attractions and only a small minority of respondents reported a skill gap relating to technology. This may convey a rather complacent attitude towards training and development needs, or evidence that training has been highly effective at addressing such issues.

CONCLUSIONS

This exploratory study has highlighted a number of issues. First the key informants and the literature portray a range of managerial skill requirements for the future success of visitor attractions. Emphasis was placed on the need for attractions to be future-oriented, adaptable and flexible to meet the challenges in the competitive environment. In the main these were aligned to strategic activities, utilising technology as well as the ability to effectively manage human resources. However, the managers in this study appeared to have a bias for immediate and operational issues, although people management skills were high on their agenda. There appears to be little evidence of the importance of strategic thinking as a managerial competence.

Considering these findings it would appear that there is a gap between the perceptions of industry leaders and academic commentators and those actually managing visitor attractions. However, given the limited sample, further research is required to identify if this

apparent gap exists across the whole sector rather than just the more successful Scottish attractions studied.

REFERENCES

Christou E, Eaton J. 1997. Hospitality management competencies for graduate trainees: employers' views. *Journal of European Business Education* 7(1): 60–68.

Christou E, Karamanidis I. 1999. Hospitality management competencies revisited: industry and graduate contemporary perspectives. *Council for Hospitality Education, Hospitality Research Conference*, School of Management Studies for the Service Sector, University of Surrey; pp. 52–59.

Day M. 1988. Managerial competence and the charter initiative. *Personnel Management* **August**.

Denzin N, Lincoln Y (eds). 2000. *A Handbook of Qualitative Research*, 2nd edn. Sage Publications.

Fifield P, Gilligan C. 1997. *Strategic Marketing Management*. Butterworth-Heinmenn: Oxford.

Gamble PR, Lockwood A, Messenger S. 1994. European Management Skills in the Hospitality Industry. University of Surrey, **May**.

Gill J, Johnson P. 1991. *Research Methods for Managers*. Paul Chapman Publishing.

Guerrier Y, Lockwood A. 1989. Developing hotel managers—a reappraisal. *International Journal of Hospitality Management* 8(2): 82–89.

Hamel G. 1994. The concept of core competence. In *Competence-based Competition*, Hamel G, Heene A (eds). Wiley: New York; pp. 11–16.

Hay J. 1990. Managerial competencies or managerial characteristics. *Journal of Management Education and Development* 21(5): 305–315.

Keep E, Mayhew K. 1999. *The Leisure Sector*. Research Paper No. 6, Skills Task Force.

Jacobs, R. 1989. Getting the measure of management competence. *Personnel Management* **June**.

Jankowicz AD. 1991. *Business Research Projects for Students*. Chapman and Hall.

Ladkin A. 1999. Hotel general managers: a review of the prominent research themes. *International Journal of Tourism Research* 1: 167–193.

Ladkin A. 2000. Vocational education and food and beverage experience: issues for career development'. *International Journal of Contemporary Hospitality Management* 12(4): 226–233.

Ladkin A, Riley M. 1996. Mobility and structure in the career paths of UK hotel general managers: a labour market hybrid of the bureaucratic model? *Tourism Management* 17(6): 443–452.

McCracken M, Watson S. 2000. Impact of environmental trends for managers in Scottish visitor. *CHRIE Conference*, New Orleans, July.

Prahalad CK, Hamel G. 1990. The core competence of the corporation. *Harvard Business Review* **May-June**: 79–91.

STB 1998. The 1998 Visitor Attraction Monitor. Scottish Tourist Board: Edinburgh.

STB 2000. The 2000 Visitor Attractions Monitor. Scottish Tourist Board: Edinburgh.

Swarbrooke DJ. 2002. *The Development and Management of Visitor Attractions*, 2nd edn. Butterworth Heinmann: Oxford.

Stinchcombe AL. 1990. *Information and Organizations*. University of California Press: Berkeley, CA.

Tas RE. 1988. Teaching future mangers. *The Cornell Hotel and Restaurant Administration Quarterly* **29**(2): 41–43.

Theobald W. 1994. *Global Tourism: the Next Decade*. Butterworth Heinmann: Oxford.

Tourism Training Scotland. 1998. *Straight to Business: a Strategy and Action Plan for the New Millennium*. Tourism Training Scotland: Glasgow.

Trow M. 1957. A comment on participation observation and interviewing: a comparison. *Human Organisation* **16**(3): 33–35.

Winterton J, Parker M, Dodd M, McCracken M, Henderson I. 2000. *Future Skills Needs of Managers*. Department for Education and Employment: Nottingham.

Part II
Marketing

[9]

Research through Participant Observation in Tourism: A Creative Solution to the Measurement of Consumer Satisfaction/Dissatisfaction (CS/D) among Tourists

DAVID BOWEN

This study analyzes the rationale that led to the choice of participant observation as a practical research tool within a case study of tourist satisfaction and dissatisfaction on a small-group, soft-adventure, long-haul inclusive tour from the United Kingdom to Malaysia and Singapore. In particular, the advantages of participant observation are favorably contrasted with customer service questionnaires. The author also outlines some of the key problems and issues that were confronted through the technique and its special usefulness for tourism research. Although the focus of the research in this instance was tourist satisfaction/dissatisfaction, it is possible to envisage research into other tourist behavior and management questions. Consequently, it is hoped that other researchers and commercial organizations will attempt to more fully use the technique.

The short account below is extracted from a complete narrative of the period of participant observation on a small-group, soft-adventure, long-haul inclusive tour from the United Kingdom to Malaysia and Singapore. The narrative is closely bound to raw data—collected through observation and participation—although it also introduces a more detached conceptualization. Perhaps this initial narrative extract will enthuse the reader to examine the research technique that is the subject of this article—participant observation. For the purpose of anonymity, the names of the participants, the tour operator ("Expeditions"), and the specific tour ("Expeditions Malaysia" [EM]) are altered.

The extract centers on an experience in the unpromising surrounds of Kota Bahru in the extreme northeast of Malaysia. Here, the EM tourists engaged themselves in an activity that owed much to their own ingenuity and effort—although it was partly based on ideas within the *Lonely Planet* guidebook and a tour leader's suggestions.

The central idea was to get out of town to see the landing of a fish-catch by some local fisher-people. Accordingly, a deal was struck with a group of taxi drivers who duly, although not without some trouble, found the landing creek for the incoming fishing boats. Eventually, about twenty or so boats, slowly

driven by elongated propellers, motored their way alongside the crumbling stakes and short quays that lined the creek. It was early afternoon, extremely hot and shade-less apart from inside an open-fronted drinks-place—set with bare trestle tables and selling only locally produced soft drinks. The boats had nearly all moored, either to the stakes or to one another and all the tour group, with the exception of Donald, were in the drinks-place. Here was a memorable moment . . . although with regard to expectation it is worthwhile to highlight a conversation recorded in the field-notes.

Asif (the tour leader) asked:
"So what do you all want to do?"
No reply.
"So how long do you want to stay here?"
"All day."
General laughter.
"That's just how I like to take things too."
. . . The memorable moment was extended when Donald, who invariably ventured further afield than any other EM members, normally in great haste and earnestness, appeared on the opposite bank of the creek. He was in search of the ultimate photograph and appeared oblivious to the heat and the watching eyes. . . .

Asif spoke generally to the group: "I've asked before about what happened to all those crazy English people who came and planted rubber in Malaysia when no one wanted it—and then just caused an enormous boom—there's one of them over there! Just imagine Donald in a white pith helmet!"

. . . Asif suggested a rearrangement of the taxi groups . . . and six group members . . . continued on with the taxis a short distance across country roads to where there were reputed to be numerous good local traders selling batik, silver-ware workers and a

---

David Bowen is a field chair of tourism management at Oxford Brookes University in Oxford, England.

Journal of Travel Research, Vol. 41, August 2002, 4-14
© 2002 Sage Publications

renowned kite-maker called Ismail (a craft particular to the East Coast and especially Kota Bahru). Although contact with locals, even buyer-seller contact was not pronounced on the EM tour, this was an exception. Jane, Susi and Sinnead, stirred on by the stories told by Robbi, attempted some elementary haggling over prices in a number of batik places and Donald also attempted to do the same at Ismail the kite-makers place. This was perhaps inappropriate . . . Ismail's pride in his handicraft was such that he spent close on 30 minutes sewing-up two kites . . . in cardboard outer containers. The taxi drivers also entered into the spirit of the visit and bought miniature kites for themselves—Donald noticed this and believed that it rather suggested the specialness of their trip. So, a part of the pleasure from the afternoon at the fishing creek (and at the sellers' places) was derived not only from the familiarity with the people within the EM group but also from the tentative, transient relationships with the local seller-people and taxi drivers.

Just from this account, a convincing argument was suggested that the performance and involvement of the individual consumer—as well as the performance of other players, including the host population—exerted a key role in the creation of (tourist) consumer satisfaction and dissatisfaction (CS/D). Moreover, perhaps such performance was more important than expectation. Literally tens of other such accounts, throughout the tour, confirmed this suggestion—and many other suggestions. From participation and observation, the researcher was able to describe, analyze, and interpret tour group experience related to CS/D.

Of course, there is a considerable literature on (CS/D). This was originally conceived with reference to goods but was increasingly developed through the 1980s and 1990s within the field of services marketing (Glynn and Barnes 1995). Essentially, general theory on CS/D suggests that it is affected by six influences or "antecedents" that include expectation, performance, and disconfirmation (the difference between expectation and performance) (Oliver 1980), attribution (a consideration of the locus, stability, controllability, and importance of causal inferences by the consumers/ tourists) (Folkes, Koletsky, and Graham 1987), emotion (Mano and Oliver 1993), and equity (a sense of fairness) (Oliver and Swan 1989). Oliver (1993) interconnected these antecedents into an integrated model.

Two questions strongly suggested themselves—first, whether all six antecedents could be recognized within a tourism context and, second, how the antecedents contributed to the development of overall tourist satisfaction/dissatisfaction through time in an extended tourist experience. The relevance of the first question is vital to establish a connection between general research in the service industry and research in tourism as an example of a service industry. With regard to the second question, Brent Ritchie (1996, p. 67) in an assessment of the state of the art in tourism marketing/ marketing research, commented that

[we] need to make a much greater effort to understand how the total stream of travel/vacation services, each of varying importance to the traveller/vacationer, interact and accumulate.

Dimanche and Havitz (1994) also inferred that it was vital for concepts in consumer behavior to be understood and measured in terms of a *time continuum* rather than at just one point in time. Such an approach reveals an evolving *process*.

The interpretation of the narrative—intertwined with a literature review, interviews with a range of managers and directors, and posttour tourist interviews—created a model of influences on (tourist) CS/D for specific micro events (see Figure 1). A second model showed developing certainty with regard to tourist CS/D through the whole tourist experience (see Figure 2). The models are introduced here to give some immediate flavor of the conceptual understandings that were derived in large part from the participant observation. An explanation with some concrete findings is contained in the final section of this article. This supports the central argument of the study that the rationale and practice of participant observation are a valuable and appropriate research technique in tourism—specifically, tourist satisfaction and dissatisfaction.

Finally, by way of introduction, some essential details are as follows. The total length of the EM tour, including flights to and from England, Malaysia, and Singapore, was 14 days. The research was focused on a small group of 9 long-haul tourists (together with the researcher and a local Malaysian tour guide). The tour encompassed a variety of tourism environments—for example, the cities of Panang, Kuala Lumpur, and Singapore; the tropical rainforest of Taman Negara in central Malaysia; and the east coast Malaysia resort of Paya Beach on Tioman Island. Activities ranged across walks/boat journeys in the rainforest, snorkeling off the coast and islands, and cultural visits and experiences. For the most part, travel was by public transport—rail, ferry—although private minibus was also used on journeys that were not easily accessed by public transport. Accommodation was in two-star hotels.

The tourists mirrored the classic demographic and socioeconomic characteristics of this niche tourism market. The age range was from 28 through to 67 with an average age of 41. Of the participants, 5 were women and 4 were men, and there were two sets of partners. The participants were employed in a range of professional services. Experience with long-haul travel was varied although reasonably extensive—only one of the participants was on a first long-haul inclusive tour, while more than half had travel experience on between three and five continents and had been a member of an equivalent tour group within the preceding 18 months.

PARTICIPANT OBSERVATION—CHOICE

Reevaluation of Customer Service Questionnaires

In the initial stage of this research, it was considered that the objective of measuring tourist satisfaction might best be achieved through the conventional approach—most likely a before-and-after style customer service questionnaire (CSQ). Through time, however, persistent, disparate evidence from a variety of sources combined to dislodge such an approach.

Easterby-Smith, Thorpe, and Lowe (1991) gave a pragmatic and relevant summary of the strengths and weaknesses

6   AUGUST 2002

FIGURE 1
(TOURIST) CONSUMER SATISFACTION/DISSATISFACTION (WITHIN TOUR) FOR A SPECIFIC MICRO EVENT

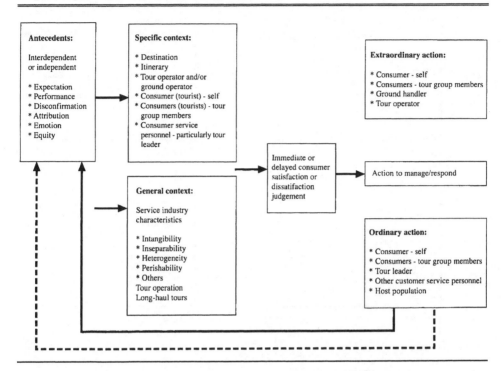

of the quantitative approach represented by CSQs. Their work was not focused on the tourism industry or CSQs generated by tour operators. To all intents and purposes, however, their general conclusions applied very closely to the conclusions reached from the study of a computed, statistically analyzed tour operator analysis of CSQ returns that were made available to the researcher—and a further study of several hundred noncomputed (original) returns:

> The main strengths are that: they [CSQs] can provide wide coverage of the range of situations; they can be fast and economical; and, particularly when statistics are aggregated from large samples, they may be of considerable relevance to policy decisions. On the debit side, these methods tend to be rather inflexible and artificial; they are not very effective in understanding processes or the significance that people attach to actions; they are not very helpful in generating theories; and because they focus on what is, or what has been recently, they make it hard for the policymaker to infer what changes and actions should take place in the future. (P. 32)

An emergent but persistent feeling of the researcher was that the whole process of CSQ analysis by tour operators pro-

duced a rather superficial understanding of behavior—even when an attempt was made to elicit a qualitative response. Moreover, it seemed that in numerous cases, the vast quantity of information that was produced and statistically analyzed was less important to the tour operators than the extraction of personal tourist details for future promotional mailouts. As a real attempt to understand the influences on CS/D and the processes through which it developed through time, the CSQs were largely inadequate. So, evidence from both primary and secondary sources eventually rejected the use of a CSQ in this tourist satisfaction research.

Paradoxically, a clear theme that arose from a range of interviews with senior managers and directors—particularly those who were more experienced—was the caution and doubt that they applied to CSQ responses. Nevertheless, they persisted with the staid and conventional CSQ approach—whether through force of habit, a fear of less established techniques, or a deference to objectivity and quantitative returns.

The good sense in the decision to reject CSQs was further evident within the EM tour itself. It was instructive to note the worn response of the tourists to a CSQ that was filled out on day 11 of 14 of the participant observation. The long-haul tourists, who, for the most part, had considerable knowledge of a range of tour operators and tourism experiences, should have represented a much more fertile source of detail. No less

FIGURE 2
TIME-CERTAINTY CS/D MODELS FOR TOURISTS: FOUR VARIANTS

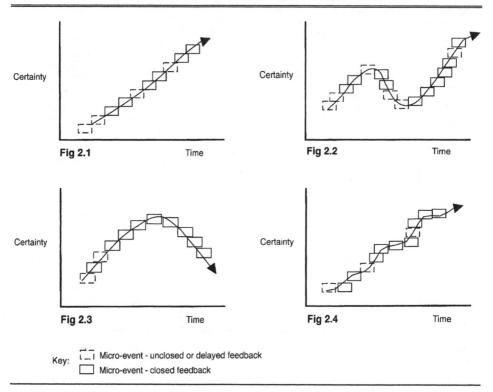

Fig 2.1   Time   Fig 2.2   Time

Fig 2.3   Time   Fig 2.4   Time

Key: ⌐_¬ Micro-event - unclosed or delayed feedback
        ☐ Micro-event - closed feedback

instructive was the less than enthusiastic demeanor of the tour group leader when faced with the task of distributing and collecting the CSQs. A cursory glance at the tourist responses suggested that the richness of the participant observation study eclipsed any hurried scribbling on a CSQ. By day 11 of 14, there had been considerable evidence of the power of participant observation in gauging the influences on satisfaction and changes in satisfaction *through* time— and not just at a *moment* in time represented by a CSQ.

Service and Tourism Characteristics

So far, this article has confined itself to the perceived weaknesses of conventional approaches. But what is special about tourism and tourists? What needs to be special about research that attempts to hone in on tourist satisfaction? An answer to this question needs in part to consider the service and tourism context within which tourists engage—and then to consider whether participant observation is particularly useful within this context.

A number of service characteristics are now broadly assumed to exist within the services marketing paradigm— intangibility, inseparability, heterogeneity, and perishability (Zeithaml, Parasuraman, and Berry 1985). With reference to

intangibility, services are viewed as performances or actions rather than objects. As regards *inseparability*—the term used to describe the simultaneous production and consumption of a service—the received argument is that goods are produced first, then sold and consumed, whereas most services are sold first and then produced and consumed simultaneously. The consumer and the producer participate in the production of the service. In addition, consumers themselves may interact with other consumers in the production process. Booms and Bitner (1981, p. 47) commented on this distinct "customer interface," and Bitner (1993, p. 359) suggested that the "evidence of service" so generated may accordingly involve both people (contact employees and other consumers) and the process of production alongside physical evidence. Meanwhile, the *heterogeneity* characteristic of services is largely connected with the vagaries of human interaction between and among service contact employees and consumers. Zeithaml and Bitner stated (1996),

Because services are performances, frequently produced by humans, no two services will be precisely alike. The employees delivering the service frequently *are* the service in the customer's eyes, and people may differ in their performance from day to day or even hour to hour. Heterogeneity also results because no two customers are precisely alike; each will have unique demands or experience the service in a unique way. (P. 20)

Finally, *perishability* refers to the service production characteristic of fixed time and space. Services cannot be saved, stored, resold, or returned. Perhaps this characteristic may seem to have the least relevant application to this research. However, it might be argued that consumers do feel the effect of perishability—inasmuch as it increases the tension to perform.

Of course, each consideration of context has attracted some skeptical thought. So, for example, it is argued that consumers chase after a bundle of benefits and do not concern themselves too much with whether a service is tangible or intangible. Likewise, Bitner (1993) clearly showed in her discussion of service mapping or blueprinting that some element of the service production is "invisible." Middleton (1994) also argued strongly against heterogeneity. Yet, strong counterarguments can disarm the skeptics.

So, the service character of the tourism industry produces a particular context for the tourism industry—with the qualification, of course, that there are wide intra-industry differences. Seaton and Bennett (1996) identified some further differences between tourism and other services—beyond the generic characteristics that distinguish services from goods. Seemingly relevant here is that tourism is a high-involvement, high-risk product to its consumers; tourism is a product partly constituted by the dreams and fantasies of consumers; and tourism is an extended product experience with no predictable critical evaluation point. Middleton (1994) also highlighted interdependence—subsector interlinkage of tourism products.

None of these extra differences are unique to tourism. Perhaps the uniqueness comes from the *combination* of some or all of the differences. Importantly, however, both the generic service characteristics and the supposedly special tourism characteristics—either singly or in combination—demand a response from consumers (tourists). Critically, the context so created seems to make it imperative that any *research* study is also responsive to the service climate. An inadequate recognition of the context limits the research even before it is commenced. This might seem to be a truism—but evidence, for example, from the overdependence on CSQs rather suggests that the truism is ignored. By contrast, participant observation is set *within* a context—a context that cannot be disregarded. Prior to the field research, it seemed logical that this would be a major strength in any exploration of tourist satisfaction. Contact with tourists in situ seemed to be the best research situation in an intangible, inseparable, heterogeneous, perishable, high-risk, high-involvement, interdependent, dream, and fantasy world.

Ryan (1995) made a particularly relevant and convincing appeal for the use of conversations in tourism research—and conversations are one of the key elements of participant observation. His research involved conversations with tourists in a hotel lounge and a beach restaurant in Majorca, Spain. The tourists were aware of his research purpose—which was not the case in the mode of participant observation that was

subsequently chosen for the EM tour—but the appeal nevertheless retained its relevance:

> If it is accepted that tourism is concerned with an experience of places and the interactions that occur at those destinations . . . then research that denies the opportunity for holiday-makers to speak of their own experiences in their own words—that seeks only reactions to a researcher dominated agenda—is itself limited. (P. 214)

So, the contention emerged that it was the participant observation method that truly discriminated in favor of the observation and consequent description, analysis, and interpretation of everyday tourism events.

Further Encouragement for Participant Observation—and the Specific EM Case

Agar (1986), with reference to ethnography, a close ally of participant observation, colorfully illustrated and then dismissed the questions that crowd in on nonpositivist, qualitative research:

> If you listen to discussions about social research, whether the speakers are professionals or laypersons, you hear the old bells tolling—"What's your hypothesis?" "What's the independent variable?" "How can you generalise with such a small sample?" . . . "Who did you use for a control group?" Those are important questions for some research, including, oftentimes, parts of an ethnographic study. But they simply miss the point of much of what goes into ethnography. (Pp. 70-71)

Johnson (1975) also drew attention to the naturalistic perspective and the contention that the tools of humanism such as experience, intuition, and empathy—crucial in participant observation—have an important role in the "fidelity" of research.

Meanwhile, Burgess (1984) encapsulated the key advantages of participant observation:

> The value of being a participant observer . . . is that researchers can utilise their observations together with their theoretical insights to make seemingly irrational or paradoxical behaviour comprehensible to those within or beyond the situation that is studied. Observations can also be used to support or refute ideas about human behaviour and to generate questions that can be used in future research. (P. 79)

The rationale for the choice of participant observation was further encouraged by a range of studies that had successfully used the technique in one way or another (Arnould and Price 1993; Penaloza 1994; Whyte 1981; Wolcott 1994), although only the former was applied specifically to a tourism context—river rafting.

Moreover, it seemed that the chosen study would match the preferred conditions for participant observation outlined by Jorgensen (1989):

Participant observation is most appropriate when certain minimal conditions are present:

— the research problem is concerned with human meanings and interactions viewed from the insiders' perspective;
— the phenomenon of investigation is observable within an everyday life situation or setting;
— the researcher is able to gain access to an appropriate setting;
— the phenomenon is sufficiently limited in size and location to be studied as a case;
— study questions are appropriate for case study; and
— the research problem can be addressed by qualitative data gathered by direct observation and other means pertinent to the field setting. (P. 13)

It is worthwhile considering the application of each of these in the EM case study. First, the research problem was to be viewed from the perspective of the consumer (tourist). The group size of 11 persons, including the tour leader and the researcher, seemed as if it would allow the necessary degree of rapport with the people, events, and overall setting.

Second, the tour was not created or manipulated by the researcher—other than any single tourist manipulated a tour. The researcher was constantly aware of the need to forge a balance between a passive and a proactive presence. The setting was, indeed, natural rather than artificial. With regard to the specific tour activities, the determined aim was to observe a tour that had a range of nonactive and active components and that would incorporate elements from each of the interdependent sectors commonly identified as forming the tourism industry. The EM tour was described in the brochure as a "leisurely tour" and an "easygoing adventure" and had time set apart for idle relaxation, beachcombing, and swimming as well as the rather more active mountain walking and jungle walking. Of course, not all tourist experiences with tour operators would yield themselves so easily to participant observation. Indeed, a setting that involved interaction with a small mobile group was perhaps the ideal for sustained study through time. This has been shown (in part) by the study of extraordinary experience in the (tourism) context of river rafting (Arnould and Price 1993). On the other hand, other studies (outside tourism) have not required the existence of a specific group of participants such as may be found in the present case study (Penaloza 1994; Whyte 1981; Wolcott 1994).

Third, access depended only on the twin limitations imposed on most tourists—time and money. The setting was open rather than closed. Access was not dependent on gatekeepers and consequent manipulation. In general, the setting was also visible rather than invisible. In the terms of Goffman (1959), it was "front-stage" rather than "backstage."

Fourth, the phenomenon was sufficiently limited in size and location to form a convenient single case study. Although there has been some management and academic argument as to when an inclusive tour starts and finishes in the mind of the consumer, each tour has a clear published departure date and return date. Observation could proceed between these times in the almost certain knowledge that every consumer would recognize them as the core, if not the whole, of the inclusive tour experience. Not only would a tour have generally distinct temporal limits, but it would also have clear limits with regard to its functioning, a predetermined size limit with regard to consumer numbers, and predetermined movement through geographical space. Jorgensen's (1989) condition was well met.

Fifth, it has been shown that a case study may be the preferred strategy when "how" or "why" questions are being posed. This was indeed the case in this study. Finally, Jorgensen's (1989) last condition was that the research problems were capable of being addressed by direct observation and other means within the field setting. Without entire surety, it seemed in advance that this would be the case.

The various conditions of Jorgensen (1989) appeared logical, workable, and comprehensive. Indeed, in the postfieldwork period, it was difficult to add new requirements or to suggest that any one of the requirements could realistically be omitted from the list.

PARTICIPANT OBSERVATION—PRACTICE

Complete Participation

Gold (1969, p. 30) devised a basic typology of field roles for participant observation—complete participant, participant as observer, observer as participant, and complete observer. The researcher eventually adopted the first role outlined by Gold—distinguished from the others by its covert rather than partially or completely overt nature. Dalton (1959) clearly described his reservations with regard to decisions concerning the covert/overt nature of participant observation:

> In no case did I make formal approach to the top management of any of the firms to get approval or support for the research. Several times I have seen other researchers do this and have watched higher managers set the scene and limit the inquiry to specific areas . . . the smiles and delighted manipulation of researchers by guarded personnel, the assessments made of researchers and their findings . . . all raised questions about who controlled the experiments. (P. 275)

Plainly, many of the decisions surrounding the research might have had to be confirmed with the tour operator management if they had been installed as the effective "gatekeepers" to the research—including fundamental elements such as the research questions or the choice of tour and destination. The researcher would have been in a favorable position to explain the research. Also, the previous interview contact with management effectively amounted to what Johnson (1975, pp. 63-64) described as a "progressive entry strategy." However, it was considered that the potential negative effects counterbalanced any positive gain.

Gold (1969) outlined two common potential problems that faced the covert participant observer:

> One, he may become so self-conscious about revealing his true self that he is handicapped when attempting to perform convincingly in the pretended role. Or two, he may "go native," incorporate the role into his self-conceptions and achieve self expression in the

role, but find he has so violated his observer role that it is almost impossible to report his findings. (P. 34)

The first problem was resolved by the almost complete predetermined coincidence of the researcher's actual and pretended role with regard to life circumstance. In the terminology of Gold (1969), the "mask of pretence" would be so closely bound that the risk of exposure and research failure would be very low. Indeed, because the researcher had decided to adopt the (true) identity of a university lecturer in marketing (but not tourism), it was felt that it was possible to legitimately and persuasively introduce an overt research interest in the posttour period. This was necessary for potential posttour clarification and extension. Such an approach paralleled that of Fine (1987). Importantly, too, insider participation appeared to match the perceived interpersonal skills of the researcher as a listener and questioner—the same skills highlighted as crucial for such study by Wolcott (1994). A tradition in qualitative research is that the personality of the scientist is a key research instrument (Gummesson 1991).

The second problem was overcome through a deliberate strategy of "immersion and resurfacing" (Dalton 1959, p. 283). Jorgensen's (1989) perspective, which celebrated the fusion of observation and participation, appeared to be powerfully convincing:

> Accurate (objective and truthful) findings are more rather than less likely as the researcher becomes involved directly, personally, and existentially with people in daily life. . . . The potential for misunderstanding and inaccurate observation increases when the researcher remains aloof and distanced physically and socially from the subject of study. Participation reduces the possibility of inaccurate observation, because the researcher gains through subjective involvement direct access to what people think, do, and feel from multiple perspectives. (P. 56)

During the extended management interviews, the researcher was able to identify appropriate tour group products with small numbers of consumers (10-20), which would facilitate the power of participant observation. Furthermore, during the course of each interview, managers had outlined the typical consumer in terms of standard social, economic, and demographic indices. The profile outlined by a number of tour operators was closely in line with the perceived profile of the researcher. This was important given the decision regarding the covert nature of the participant observation and the obvious need to establish, participate in, and sustain relationships with consumer insiders. The actual composition on the EM tour was almost exactly as predicted.

Wide Focus and Narrow Focus

There was a set prior intention as regards the specific means by which information would be observed and gathered. Initial observations were intended to be wide in focus. The aim was to become familiar with the functional workings of the tour group; the emergent patterns of everyday life in terms of activities, transport, and accommodation; characteristics of individuals within the group in terms of broad demographic, socioeconomic, and psychographic elements; and, finally, the initial relationships between the individuals

within the group. It was also necessary to become familiar with the macro setting of Malaysia. The choice of Malaysia as a destination that was new to the researcher was deliberate. It was important that the researcher paralleled the initial naïveté of the fellow consumers because the personal tourism experience of the researcher represented an additional source of access (beyond observation and conversation) to insider thoughts, feelings, and actions.

Given the time span of the tour, it was recognized that the wide focus would quickly have to be complemented with rather more closely focused observations, informal conversations, and casual questioning. Clearly, such conversations resembled those of ordinary everyday life. Accordingly, the researcher followed the dictum that was explained to Whyte (1981) by his informant in the classic "Street Corner Society":

> The next day Doc explained the lesson of the previous evening. "Go easy on that 'who,' 'what,' 'when,' 'where' stuff, Bill. You ask those questions and people will clam up on you. If people accept you, you can just hang around, and you'll learn the answers in the long run without even having to ask the questions." (P. 303)

It was found that there was hardly a truer word written in all the studies of participant observation. From day 1, there was an abundance of relevant listening opportunities.

The listening approach did not present a problem to the researcher. The general aim was to focus and then refocus (via observation, conversation, and questioning) on specific events and sets of events together with specific individuals and micro groups. Adapted from Burgess (1984), the focus of the participant observation was on the social situation in specific spaces and places at particular times, set within particular circumstances and with the involvement of specific actors. Such social situations allowed the exploration of established and even emergent research questions and propositions.

Trust

Of course, neither the wide focus period of observation nor the more detailed period of observation was accomplished without trust or at least what Johnson (1975, p. 142) called "sufficient trust"—a personal, commonsense judgment about what could be accomplished with a given person. Moreover, even sufficient trust changes over time, and the researcher was aware of the possibility that trust could erode—perhaps because of an overidentification with one individual or subgroup. However, such erosion did not occur or even threaten to occur. There was an absence of dominant individuals or isolated subgroups. This facilitated the progression of the research. The researcher was probably the closest person in the group to the tour leader, but it would be a fallacy to presume that this closeness was in any way thought of as overidentification. Such overidentification was not commented on by the other tourists either directly or indirectly during the fieldwork. Even if such was the case, there is a defense for the use of feeling/rapport as a legitimate approach within field research.

Trust, of course, is closely bound together with the establishment of relationships, and the researcher recognized that this required a need to blend together with other consumers and become fully engaged in events and conversations across the range of subgroups. It was anticipated that this would entail a heavy physical and psychological toll despite the low level of role conflict. This toll would be added to by the imperative to record. In reality, the physical burden was heavier than expected—on several occasions, one day of research and recording rolled into the next day. However, the psychological burden was less than expected—probably because of the very close coincidence of the actual and assumed identity of the researcher.

Method of Record—Field Notes

The main method of recording was through field notes compiled at the end of each day—or during significant other breaks during the day when the opportunity arose. In the terms of Burgess (1984, pp. 167-74), these consisted of a number of elements—"substantive field-notes," "method-ological field-notes," and "analytic memos." In the event, most of the notes were recorded at the end of the day, and the threefold split of the elements proved to be an extremely useful framework for thought.

These various types of field notes complemented the shuttle of observation and interaction during the participant observation. The determined object was to be a part of and apart from the emerging tourist experience through "guided introspection," in which the researcher asked (albeit covertly) the tourist consumers to think aloud about their thoughts, feelings, and actions; "interactive introspection," in which there was a two-way sharing of experiences between the researcher and the tourists; and "reflexivity within research," in which the focus of the research was on the tourist while nevertheless acknowledging in the writing the presence of the researcher (Wallendorf and Brucks 1993, pp. 340-42). There was an awareness that a thin line had to be negotiated between passivity and impassivity, reaction and proaction.

Other Methods

Notes were primarily recorded into a field notebook or other unobtrusive materials such as letter paper or postcard letters. Evidence from the management interviews strongly suggested that the researcher was capable of retaining information for some limited period of time, and the researcher remained of the opinion that a tape recorder had the effect of lowering concentration and acted as an unnecessary substitute for heightened awareness. Constant use of a tape recorder would have seemed to be unusual as well as impracticable. In any case, it was anticipated that many conversations would be broken and incomplete, thus facilitating a written record. This was exactly what happened. It was also decided not to use a camcorder. It was felt that pointing a camcorder in one direction would narrow the field of vision and would also tempt the researcher to delay both description and initial analysis until the post-fieldwork phase. This view was supported elsewhere. Finally, still photography did form part of the documentary evidence—it did not interfere with the observation and prompted later memories. Of course, photography was a perfectly normal tourist occurrence—as was the collection of tourism documents such as guides, brochures, maps, and so on that acted as an *aide-memoire*.

Retrospective Reworking and Beyond

Schwartz and Schwartz (1969, p. 90) recognized that there is a process of registering, interpreting, and recording observations so that observation is a continuous process of evaluation. This process may be very short and urgent within the field context or rather more leisurely during a period of "retrospective reworking." Schwartz and Schwartz believed that such retrospective reworking actually allowed for the expansion of observations—experience suggested that this belief was well founded.

The focus on individuals and mini-groups left the opportunity to develop life histories in the posttour period. The researcher envisaged that there would not be a difficulty in arranging to meet consumers. It was presumed that addresses would be exchanged and, accordingly, there would be the opportunity to pursue experiences relating both to the shared tour and other tourism experiences within an informal interview setting. Burgess (1984), with the use of an analogy from Read (1965, cited in Burgess 1984), went so far as to affirm that "it is essential to provide detailed cases of individuals' lives. For without that, the studies are devoid of material that brings a people to life" (p. 174). In the event, the extensive conversations during the tour itself allowed the researcher to develop considerable detail on the tourism careers of the tourists. But the post-fieldwork interviews were nevertheless carried through because it was felt that these would provide a further perspective on the tour—in effect, the interviews would provide a temporal source of triangulation. It was felt that the tourists might also engage in their own retrospective reworking. Hammersley and Atkinson (1983) succinctly argued this case:

> Once again, it is not a matter of accepting or rejecting data, but rather of knowing how to interpret it; there is a great temptation to assume that actions, statements, or interview responses represent stable features of the person or of settings. This may be correct, but it cannot be assumed. Actions are embedded in temporal contexts and these may shape them in ways that are important for analysis. (P. 194)

Analysis

Of course, the method of record only acts as the handmaiden to the subsequent process of analysis. In the very important writing process, it was intended to make use of each sort of "tale" that can be used in the writing of ethnography—"realist," "confessional," and "impressionist" (Van Maanen 1988, p. 47).

These tales covered the themes that emerged from the thoughts, feelings, and actions of the various actors during the successive unfolding of the events on the long-haul tour. Burgess (1984) has suggested that the presentation of data in chronological order is a compromise position. In this instance, however, this was certainly not the case. Chronological ordering and development were one key crux of the whole research—the development of tourist satisfaction through time. Although the research is by no means an example of grounded theory, some of the basic techniques of grounded theory proved useful during analysis—for example, the final model of tourist satisfaction development through time owed a debt to the axial coding framework of Strauss and Corbin (1990).

12   AUGUST 2002

PARTICIPANT OBSERVATION—
REVIEW AND CONCLUSION

Gilbert (1991) has criticized much work in tourism consumer behavior because it is general in nature or unsubstantiated empirically. This is not so in this particular work. A core of the research is the attempt to substantiate theory through a case study in an empirical context—through the use of participant observation. This places the work firmly within the emerging field of "critical ethnography" in which researchers have gone to the field to investigate consumers' experiences (Penaloza 1994)—what consumers think, feel, and do rather than what they *say* they think, feel, and do. In this research, the tourist thoughts on satisfaction poured out apace after a tentative beginning. The participant observation generated an immense amount of descriptive and analytical data that was later transformed into both a narrative and a number of interpretative models of tourist satisfaction/dissatisfaction (see Figures 1-2). It effectively confronted many inadequacies of much earlier tourist satisfaction research.

In the terms of Lilien and Kotler (1983, p. 204) the conceptualization (Figures 1-2) derived from the participant observation is "ambitious"—it identifies major variables, specifies fundamental relationships and exact sequences, and so addresses the time dimension. Figure 1 conceptualizes the process of CS/D formation for single micro events on the EM tour. Micro events are either closed or unclosed. In a closed micro event, there is an immediate judgment of consumer satisfaction. For example, one tourist (Frank) had a specific expectation that the tour leader should not be late to arrive at the initial airport rendezvous in Penang, Malaysia (following an internal flight from the international airport in Kuala Lumpur). However, the tour leader (Asif) arrived on the next internal flight—1 hour later. He also had an incomplete listing of tour group members. Frank felt insecure and rather afraid. These emotions interacted with Frank's expectation, his perceived performance of the tour leader and his immediate attribution of blame toward the tour leader. They were modified by Frank's consideration of the specific context and the general context—such as his view on the late arrival of the tour leader—so as to create a closed micro-event judgment of dissatisfaction. By contrast, other tourists were prepared to withhold judgment—and so delayed closure of the micro event until later on during the tour. They thought, felt, and responded differently regarding the tour leader's role and other elements of the specific context and the general context of the tour. The specific action that they took was to casually discuss the event with Asif—several days later—and to balance this specific micro event from the airport against a myriad of other micro events. So, a potentially different interpretation of the micro event emerged—the late arrival of Asif and the incomplete tour group list appeared more due to the inadequacies of the ground operator than the poor organization of Asif. By further contrast, one other tourist (Robbi) recounted that a similar situation occurred on his preceding tour in Thailand when the arrival of his own international, incoming flight was delayed. He was actually excited (the emotion antecedent) by the challenge of locating his tour group someplace within Bangkok. He was particularly impressed by the helpfulness of the local Thai people (the performance antecedent) and by his own resourcefulness (personal performance). He understood the nature of his flight delay (general context of tour operation). Thailand had

been a highly satisfying adventure from the start—from the first micro eventt. A graphical representation of the interaction of the antecedents of CS/D—a subpart of the conceptualization in Figure 1—is shown in Figure 3.

Actually, in broader terms—not just those related to specific examples of micro events—all of the antecedents (expectation, performance, disconfirmation, attribution, emotion, equity) were clearly recognizable through the participant observation. However, the *performance* antecedent appeared to be dominant. A vortex of influences has been conceived. The performance antecedent is at the core of the vortex and interacts—although not invariably—with the other antecedents. There are "actual interaction points" (e.g., when a performance creates an emotional response and so revises the emotion antecedent) and "potential but not actual interaction points" (e.g., when performance does not revise an expectation). The interactions occur continuously from one micro event to another.

Figure 2 illustrates a number of potential models to describe the development of overall certainty with regard to CS/D through time. In each, the tourist aggregates each micro-event experience. The actual model that best corresponded with the situation of the majority of the EM tourists was Figure 2.4. Certainty tended to reach specific plateaus following a series of micro events. Tourist action to manage or respond—despite the oncoming rush of new micro events—would then inform judgments on any outstanding, unclosed micro events. So, for example, following on from the late arrival of the tour leader at Penang Airport, a string of further logistical problems occurred throughout the tour. In Kota Bahru, in the extreme northeast of Peninsula Malaysia, the planned journey south to the island beach resort of Tioman was threatened by seeming problems between the tour leader and the local transport operator. The tourists themselves suggested various solutions, and eventually the daylong journey was completed in a small group of taxis. However, the most likely locus of blame for the problem only truly became evident during a telephone conversation between the tour leader and the ground operator—overheard by a number of the EM group—while on Tioman. The tour leader had some trouble getting through to the right person in the office of the ground operator. After some time, clearly exasperated and in response to a question on the other end of the telephone, the tour leader responded with the heaviest resignation: "Yes, I am a tour leader!" This comment seemed to encapsulate all that the tour leader had just occasionally hinted at in conversations with regard to a recently changed job situation. He was the most experienced tour leader employed by the ground operator but now felt less valued—following personnel and operational reorganization in middle and top management. Even the backup office of the ground operator did not appear to be sure about which tour leader was on the road with which tourists.

The tourists concluded that the real locus of blame for continuing logistical problems was not the tour leader. Of course, the impression should not be created that the basis of CS/D certainty rode on one chance telephone conversation. However, in combination with a whole range of other micro events, this occurrence encouraged the closure of related micro events and led to further certainty regarding tourist satisfaction or dissatisfaction with the tour leader and the whole EM tour.

JOURNAL OF TRAVEL RESEARCH   13

FIGURE 3
CS/D ANTECEDENTS—MICRO EVENT X

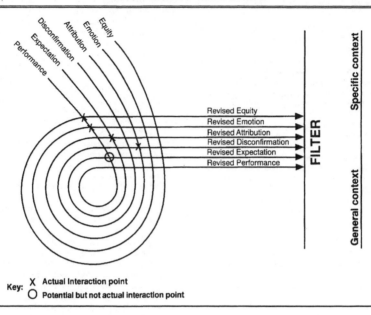

Key: X Actual Interaction point
     O Potential but not actual interaction point

So, participant observation allowed the development of conceptualization but was based within a real situation. It did *not* require an agenda to be set by the researcher and would not require an agenda to be set by management in any future practical application—beyond a flexible observational framework based on an open consideration of existing theory, knowledge, and practice. Geertz (1987, p. 16) commented on the possibilities that arise from "being there"—while not abandoning complete objectivity and embracing researcher sentiments. It allows the achievement of "thick" but nevertheless "interpretative" description (Geertz 1993, p. 20). In this participant observation, the consumer voices and, to a lesser although nevertheless important extent, the consumer service personnel voices were the key foundations of the whole technique and allowed a natural, unforced, and detailed evaluation of tourist satisfaction. To understand experience, one must move participant observation firmly away from the strictures of more conventional research techniques. As employed in this research, it was nonintrusive—even more so than other "in situ" techniques with their consequent heightened self-awareness (Stewart and Hull 1996).

Moreover, the tourist experience was observed and evaluated across the whole interdependent experience and not merely with reference to isolated attributes. This provided a holistic view that is crucial in any service industry such as tourism. From this point of view, the participant observation followed all but the initial and final stages of the Jafari tourist model (Jafari 1987). However, much early discussion during the participant observation related to life prior to "emancipation" or "distancing" from the ordinary world. Only the

"incorporation" stage was not covered within the participant observation—although views on CS/D in this stage were sought in the posttour interviews with the EM tourists.

A tour operator, with only the use of a CSQ, for example, *may* catch the point in time at which a process has evolved to an apex—*or may not*. Furthermore, the operator has not begun to understand the process itself—so fundamental for both strategic development and the understanding of a particular case. This is not to argue that all CSQ research is deficient. For example, there may be due need to use a CSQ so as to generate a statistical score on a particular attribute and to track its change with repeat measurements on separate occasions. Nor is this shift away from CSQs an attempt to decry the work of Parasuraman, Zeithaml, and Berry (1988) and the vast amount of research that has been conducted into the analysis of quality through the use of CSQs. However, a study of quality is not the same as a study of satisfaction. For example, the former represents a comparison of service expectations against industry expectations or managerial specifications. By contrast, judgments of customer satisfaction compare observed service experience against the customer's own specifications (Iacobucci, Grayson, and Ostrum 1994). Tourists on the EM tour had a definite intuitive awareness that quality was management driven and that satisfaction was consumer driven. Moreover, Iacobbucci, Grayson, and Ostrum (1994) also suggested that judgments of quality are more external and cognitive compared to those of satisfaction, which can be more internal and emotion based. This was supported on the EM tour by the influence of the role of emotion in the CS/D judgment. Both of these differences between the concepts of quality and satisfaction demand a more qualitative approach in satisfaction research.

Finally, evidence of the key experiential nature of tourism may require that information on tours should frequently be supplemented with experiential information. To get close to the tourist within the tourism context, the tour operator must search for new methods of data collection and analysis. The implementation of an experiential service event or service experience audit—based largely on participant observation—would create a more consumer-focused subsector and alleviate the problems that allow only a partial understanding of the tourist. Herein lies the opportunity for the tourism practitioner.

But there are opportunities, too, for the academic. The level of detail from the participant observation—which created the narrative and informed the conceptualization—would not be created by either quantitative or qualitative CSQs. Notwithstanding the work of Arnould and Price (1993), the general emphasis on CSQs may explain why there are still so very few attempts at analyzing satisfaction through time in an extended service. This applies both to tourism and other service contexts. Participant observation provides the chance to overcome the knowledge gap that is so created.

REFERENCES

Agar, Michael H. (1986). *Speaking of Ethnography.* Beverly Hills, CA: Sage.

Arnould, Eric J., and Linda L. Price (1993). "River Magic: Extraordinary Experience and the Extended Service Encounter." *Journal of Consumer Research,* 20: 24-45.

Bitner, Mary Jo (1993). "Managing the Evidence of Service." In *The Service Quality Handbook,* edited by Eberhard Scheuing and William Christopher. New York: AMACOM, chap. 29.

Booms, Bernard H., and Mary J. Bitner (1981). "Marketing: Strategies and Organisation Structures for Service Firms." In *Marketing of Services,* edited by James H. Donnelly and William R. George. Chicago: American Marketing Association, pp. 47-51.

Burgess, Robert G. (1984). *In the Field: An Introduction to Field Research.* London: Unwin Hyman.

Dalton, Melville (1959). *Men Who Manage.* London: Wiley.

Dimanche, Frederic, and Mark E. Havitz (1994). "Consumer Behaviour and Tourism: Review and Extension of Four Study Areas." In *Economic Psychology of Travel and Tourism,* edited by John C. Crotts and W. Fred van Raaij. New York: Haworth.

Easterby-Smith, Mark, Richard Thorpe, and Andy Lowe (1991). *Management Research.* London: Sage.

Fine, G. A. (1987). *With the Boys.* Chicago: University of Chicago Press.

Folkes, Valerie S., Susan Koletsky, and John L. Graham (1987). "A Field Study of Causal Influences and Consumer Reaction: The View from the Airport." *Journal of Consumer Research,* 13: 534-39.

Geertz, Clifford (1987). *Works and Lives: The Anthropologist as Author.* Stanford, CA: Stanford University Press.

——— (1993). *The Interpretation of Cultures: Selected Essays.* London: Fontana.

Gilbert, D. C. (1991). "An Examination of the Consumer Behaviour Process Related to Tourism." In *Progress in Tourism, Recreation and Hospitality Research,* edited by C. P. Cooper. London: Belhaven.

Glynn, William J., and James G. Barnes (1995). *Understanding Services Management.* Chichester, UK: Wiley.

Goffman, E. (1959). *The Presentation of Self in Everyday Life.* Garden City, NY: Doubleday.

Gold, R. L. (1969). "Roles in Sociological Field Observations." In *Issues in Participant Observation,* edited by G. J. McCall and J. L. Simmons. Reading, MA: Addison-Wesley.

Gummesson, Evert (1991). *Qualitative Methods in Management Research.* London: Sage.

Hammersley, Martyn, and Paul Atkinson (1983). *Ethnography: Principles in Practice.* London: Tavistock.

Iacobucci, Dawn, Kent A. Grayson, and Amy L. Ostrom (1994). "The Calculus of Service Quality and Customer Satisfaction." In *Advances in Services Marketing and Management Research and Practice,* vol. 3, edited by Teresa A. Swartz, David E. Bowen, and Stephen W. Brown. London: JAI, pp. 1-67.

Jafari, Jafar (1987). "Tourism Models: The Sociocultural Aspects." *Tourism Management,* 8 (2): 151-59.

Johnson, John M. (1975). *Doing Field Research.* London: Free Press.

Jorgensen, Danny L. (1989). *Participant Observation: A Methodology for Human Studies.* London: Sage.

Lilien, Gary L., and Philip Kotler (1983). *Marketing Decision Making.* New York: Harper & Row.

Mano, Haim, and Richard L. Oliver (1993). "Assessing the Dimensionality and Structure of the Consumption Experience: Evaluation, Feeling, and Satisfaction." *Journal of Consumer Research,* 20: 451-66.

Middleton, Victor T. C. (1994). *Marketing in Travel and Tourism.* 2d ed. Oxford, UK: Butterworth Heinemann.

Oliver, Richard L. (1980). "A Cognitive Model of the Antecedents and Consequences of Satisfaction Decisions." *Journal of Marketing Research,* 17: 460-69.

——— (1993). "A Conceptual Model of Service Quality and Service Satisfaction: Compatible Goals, Different Concepts." *Advances in Services Marketing and Management,* 2: 65-85.

Oliver, Richard L., and John E. Swan (1989) "Consumer Perceptions of Interpersonal Equity and Satisfaction in Transactions: A Field Survey Approach." *Journal of Marketing,* 53: 21-35.

Parasuraman, A., Valarie A. Zeithaml, and Leonard L. Berry (1988). "SERVQUAL: A Multiple Item Scale for Measuring Consumer Perceptions of Service Quality." *Journal of Retailing,* 64 (1): 12-40.

Penaloza, Lisa (1994). "*Atravesando Fronteras*/Border Crossings: A Critical Ethnographic Exploration of the Consumer Acculturation of Mexican Immigrants." *Journal of Consumer Research,* 12: 32-54.

Ritchie, J. R. Brent (1996). "Beacons of Light in an Expanding Universe: An Assessment of the State-of-the-Art in Tourism Marketing/Marketing Research." *Journal of Travel and Tourism Marketing,* 5 (4): 49-84.

Ryan, Chris (1995). "Learning about Tourists from Conversations: The over 55s in Majorca." *Tourism Management,* 16 (3): 207-15.

Seaton, A. V., and M. M. Bennett (1996). *Marketing Tourism Products.* London: International Thomson Business Press.

Stewart, William P., and Bruce R. Hull (1996). "Capturing the Moments: Concerns of *In Situ* Leisure Research." *Journal of Travel and Tourism Marketing,* 5 (1/2): 3-20.

Strauss, Anselm, and Juliet Corbin (1990). *Basics of Qualitative Research: Grounded Theory Procedures and Techniques.* London: Sage.

Van Maanen, John (1988). *Tales of the Field—On Writing Ethnography.* Chicago: University of Chicago Press.

Wallendorf, Melanie, and Merrie Brucks (1993). "Introspection in Consumer Research: Implementation and Implications." *Journal of Consumer Research,* 20: 339-59.

Whyte, William Foote (1981). *Street Corner Society: The Social Structure of an Italian Slum.* 3d ed. Chicago: University of Chicago Press.

Wolcott, Harry F. (1994). *Transforming Qualitative Data: Description, Analysis and Interpretation.* London: Sage.

Zeithaml, Valarie A., and Mary Jo Bitner (1996). *Services Marketing.* London: McGraw-Hill.

Zeithaml, Valarie A., A. Parasuraman, and Leonard L. Berry (1985). "Problems and Strategies in Services Marketing." *Journal of Marketing,* 49: 33-46.

[10]

Beyond "Commonsense Segmentation": A Systematics of Segmentation Approaches in Tourism

SARA DOLNIČAR

Market segmentation is an accepted tool in strategic marketing. It helps to understand and serve the needs of homogeneous consumer subpopulations. Two approaches are recognized: a priori and data-driven (a posteriori, post hoc) segmentation. In tourism, there is a long history of a priori segmentation studies in industry and academia. These lead to the identification of tourist groups derived from dividing the population according to prior knowledge ("commonsense segmentation"). However, due to the wide use of this approach, there is not much room for competitive advantage to be gained by using a priori segmentation. This article (1) reviews segmentation studies in tourism, (2) proposes a systematics of segmentation approaches, and (3) illustrates the managerial usefulness of novel approaches emerging from this systematics. The main aim is to offer academics and practitioners a menu of exploratory techniques that can be used to increase market understanding.

Keywords: market segmentation; segmentation systematics; a priori; a posteriori segmentation

A REVIEW OF SEGMENTATION STUDIES

The *Journal of Travel Research* is the major outlet for segmentation studies within the field of tourism. To evaluate the representation of different forms of segmentation studies in this field, all articles on segmentation published in the *Journal of Travel Research* in the past 15 years have been reviewed and can conceptually be grouped into four kinds of segmentation approaches: pure commonsense segmentations, purely data-driven segmentations, combinations of both where typically one commonsense segment is chosen and further split up into data-driven subgroups, and a sequence of two commonsense segmentations.

The first group of studies includes Baloglu and McCleary (1999), who investigate differences between visitors and nonvisitors of a certain destination with regard to the image of this particular tourist region; Goldsmith and Litvin (1999), contrasting heavy users and light users; Kashyap and Bojanic (2000), exploring systematic differences between business and leisure tourists with respect to value, quality, and price perceptions; Smith and MacKay (2001), who are interested in age differences in pictorial memory performance for advertising message targeting; Israeli (2002), who profiles the perceptions of destinations from the perspective of

disabled versus nondisabled visitors; Klemm (2002), investigating one particular ethnic minority in the United Kingdom and describing in detail their vacation preferences and interests; McKercher (2001), exploring systematic differences between tourists who spend their main vacation at a destination on one hand and tourists who only travel through this same town or city on the other hand; Meric and Hunt (1998), profiling the ecotourist; Court and Lupton (1997), grouping tourists initially by their intention to visit a destination and then searching for significant differences between those commonsense groups; and finally, Arimond and Lethlean (1996), who group visitors to a campground according to the kind of site rental taken and investigate differences. In terms of the share of pure a priori studies among all segmentation articles published, these commonsense segment descriptions amount to more than half of all investigations (53%).

Only one representative of the second group in its pure form (data-driven segmentation) could be identified among the articles reviews: Bieger and Lässer (2002) construct or identify data-driven segments among the Swiss population. The starting point is the entire population of Switzerland and not a particular group within this population. Groups are constructed/identified on the basis of different travel motivations. This very strict definition of data-based segmentation leads to the conclusion that only this one study can be included for our purposes, amounting to 5% of the studies published over the past 15 years.

The third group is commonly thought of as data-driven segmentation. However, strictly speaking, the publications described in this paragraph have a different starting point. The starting point is already a subgrouping of the population of tourists. This essentially means that commonsense segmentation is conducted first. Next, one of the groups emerging from this first step is chosen. In the third step, a data-driven segmentation is then conducted using data for the selected commonsense segment only. The danger of this approach is that market structure analysis is restricted to a selection of customers, thus limiting the horizon and risking the possibility that new potential market segments will not be

---

Sara Dolničar is an associate professor in the School of Management, Marketing & Employment Relations, at the University of Wollongong.

Journal of Travel Research, Vol. 42, February 2004, 244-250
DOI: 10.1177/0047287503258830
© 2004 Sage Publications

JOURNAL OF TRAVEL RESEARCH 245

FIGURE 1
A SYSTEMATICS OF SEGMENTATION APPROACHES

Which group is described first?	
A subgroup of the total tourist population determined by an a priori or commonsense criterion	A subgroup of the total tourist population determined by data-driven segmentation on multivariate basis
CONCEPT 1 = commonsense = a priori segmentation	CONCEPT 2 = data-driven = a posteriori = post-hoc segmentation

Which groups are explored next?			
A subgroup of the total tourist population determined by an a priori or common sense criterion		A subgroup of the total tourist population determined by data-driven segmentation on multivariate basis	
CONCEPT 3 = commonsense / commonsense segmentation	CONCEPT 4 = data driven / commonsense segmentation	CONCEPT 5 = commonsense / data-driven segmentation	CONCEPT 6 = data-driven / data-driven segmentation

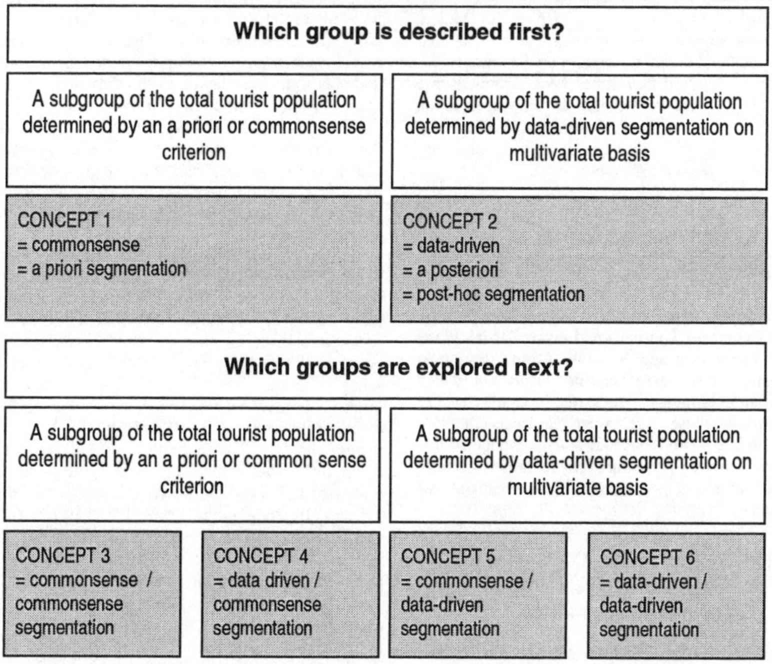

detected at all. Examples from the literature review include Silverberg, Backman, and Backman (1996), who emphasize the group of nature-based tourists only and further split these tourists up into data-driven segments according to the benefits they are seeking. Furthermore, Dodd and Bigotte (1997) choose the special interest group of winery visitors and derive data-driven segment within this group on the basis of demographic profiles. Visitors of a cultural-historical event in Italy were chosen by Formica and Uysal (1998) as the starting point for their data-driven study based on motivations. By doing so, the authors investigate a posteriori segments within another group of tourists clearly defined by a specific vacation activity, namely attending the event. Kastenholz, Davis, and Paul (1999) concentrate in their investigation on visitors of rural areas only. On the basis of this subgroup selection, the authors study the existence and nature of benefit groups. Moscardo et al. (2000) select the commonsense segment of visitors of local friends and relatives as their initial segment. Within this group, patterns of behavior are investigated in a data-driven manner. Focusing on senior motor coach travelers only as an initial a priori segment, Hsu and Lee (2002) group those travelers according to 55 motor coach selection attributes. Thus, 32% of all segmentation studies published in the *Journal of Travel Research* are found to follow this pattern of describing subgroups that might be of managerial interest.

One study reports on two market segments, which are derived by initially choosing a common sense segment and—in a second step—splitting this segment up by another a priori criterion. This study was conducted by Field (1999) and explores domestic versus foreign students within the segment of student travelers. Horneman et al. (2002) has to be classified into this group as well, because the initial subsegment on which their study focuses is the group of senior travelers. In a second step, the authors derive six segments based on answers to specific questions (most preferred holiday choice). This accounts for 11% of the segmentation studies.

A SYSTEMATICS OF SEGMENTATION APPROACHES

On the basis of the two fundamental segmentation approaches that are available, a systematics of conceptual approaches can be constructed. This systematics is outlined in Figure 1. It is based on sequential processing of the fundamental segmentation approaches. Clearly, this systematics can easily be extended further to represent simultaneous application of the two fundamental building blocks.

The publications described in the literature review would thus be assigned to Concept 1, Concept 2, Concept 5, and

246   FEBRUARY 2004

Concept 3, respectively. However, in addition to the classification of segmentation studies published in the *Journal of Travel Research,* two conceptual approaches to segmentation emerge that have so far not been empirically studied. Both these concepts use a data-driven segmentation as their starting point and build another grouping on this initial solution. This second solution can either be a commonsense grouping (Concept 4) or another data-driven segmentation (Concept 6). These two approaches are introduced as valuable extensions of the toolbox of the exploratory segmentation techniques and illustrated next.

ILLUSTRATING NOVEL SEGMENTATION CONCEPTS

Data from the Austrian National Guest Survey (conducted by the Institute of Tourism and Leisure Studies at the University of Economics and Business Administration in Vienna) collected in the summer seasons of 1994 and 1997 is used for illustrative purposes. The sample includes 14,571 respondents. Among these, 7,967 were questioned in 1994, and 6,604 in 1997. Personal interviews were conducted following a quota sampling procedure that identified destination regions, countries of origin, and segment of accommodation.

Segmentation Concept 4: The Usefulness of Commonsense Segment Analysis Following Data-Driven Groupings of Consumers

Segmentation Concept 4 implies a data-driven segmentation in the first stage of analysis and a commonsense segmentation in the second step. In the first step, psychographic segments are constructed on the basis of the survey data set. The data basis for this task consists of 22 binary statements about the motivation for taking this particular vacation.

The respondents are grouped using topology representing networks (TRNs) (Martinetz and Schulten 1994). Clearly, any other partitioning technique or modeling approach appropriate to the data could be used at this point. TRNs belong to the family of unsupervised neural networks. The number of groups has to be predefined and starting points for the iterative process have to be picked at random (or provided on the basis of previous calculations). Then, the TRN network processes the data on a row-by-row basis, assigning respondents to starting points. For each case, the closest starting vector is identified, declared the winner and allowed to adapt vector values of the segment representatives toward the input vector values. Additionally, all other starting points are updated in a way that monitors proximity (nearly located starting points are allowed to adjust to a higher extent). This latter step is responsible for the topological ordering of groups at the end of the partitioning process. The Austrian National Guest Survey data was analyzed by picking the best starting points from 100 random draws. Training of the TRN network was allowed for 100 epochs (indicating that each respondent was presented to the algorithm 100 times for the purpose of learning the data representation) and Euclidean distance was used as a proximity measure. TRN32 (available at http://charly.wu-wien.ac.at/software/) was used to undertake this calculation.

This process was repeated 10 times with different numbers of segments (from three to seven). Based on the stability of the solutions within each number of segments (number of pairs of respondents assigned to the same segment repeatedly), the six-cluster solution turned out to yield the best results with regard to compliance of repeated calculations and was therefore chosen as the data-driven segmentation solution for this particular data set.

The resulting market segments among tourists visiting Austria during the summer seasons of 1994 and 1997 are illustrated in Figure 2, where the line indicates the total sample average and the bars give the proportion of respondents within each particular segment that agree with each statement.

Psychographic Segment 1 contains 19% of the respondents and is characterized by a high interest in relaxing during the vacation. In addition, the locals, the natural environment, the safety, and the sustainability of the destination play an important role for these tourists. The second group interested in relaxing is Segment 4 (20%). In this case, relaxation seems to be the only driving force of the vacation with no other statements accepted more often than is the case on average. Segments 2 (18%) and 6 (13%) have to be interpreted with care. The first agrees with all statements above average, the latter with none. These segments thus have to be understood as a mix between actual responses and answer patterns. Psychographic Segment 3 (13%) is very distinct and defines the sports-oriented holiday-makers who love sun and water and appreciate a challenge. Finally, Segment 5 (18%) includes the culture-interested respondents.

In the second step, it is informative for managers to investigate the differences within one of these segments over time, for example, the identification of the sports tourist who spends the vacation in Austria during summer. Splitting the data-driven segments that way is a commonsense approach based on year, which is apparently most useful to a lakeside resort that caters to a high proportion of these holiday-makers and needs to know how this group develops over time. A simple cross-tabulation of data-driven segment membership and year is constructed for this purpose and a chi-square test is computed. This procedure results in a highly significant result ($p = .000$). The proportion of sports tourists is shown to increase from 42% in 1994 to 58% in 1997.

Besides this purely quantitative trend, a number of qualitative differences between the sports tourists of 1994 and 1997 can be identified. The average age of this segment increased by 2 years from 42 to 44 years (ANOVA $p = .000$). So did the number of overnight stays; in 1994, these holiday-makers spent 10 nights in Austria, 8.5 days in the region, and 8.1 days at the destination, whereas in 1997 these numbers significantly increased (ANOVA $p = .003, .000,$ and $.000$) to 10.8, 9.6, and 9 nights, respectively. With regard to vacation activities pursued by this segment, the picture remains fairly stable over time. The only significant shift that can be detected is that there seems to be less interest in mountaineering but more interest in hiking.

Clearly, these commonsense segments could be further compared in detail to study how tourists with this particular motivational background differ with regard to other descriptive pieces of information. Such a breakdown could be highly useful to management (in terms of information sources used, amount of money spent, activities pursued, accommodation chosen, shopping behavior, etc.).

JOURNAL OF TRAVEL RESEARCH 247

FIGURE 2
PSYCHOGRAPHIC PROFILES OF DATA-DRIVEN MARKET SEGMENTS

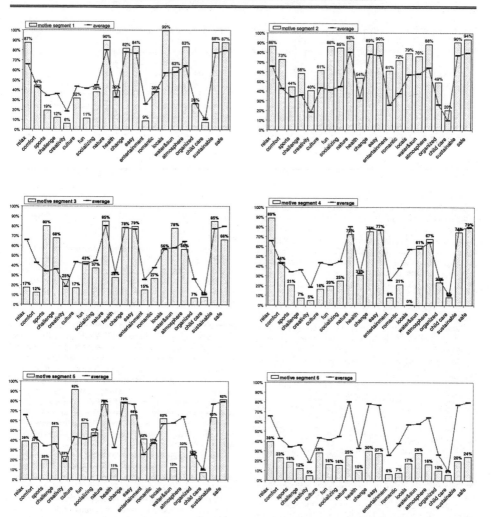

By following Concept 4, destination management in this example avoids mixing sports tourists from two consecutive waves by averaging background information over all of the members of this psychographic segment. Note that the same results would not have been achieved by separately partitioning the data by years. Thus, the decision makers not only learn about the potentially interesting target market of sports tourists but also gain insight into quantitative and qualitative changes occurring in this group over time.

Segmentation Concept 6: The Usefulness of Two Consecutive Data-Driven Consumer Groupings

In case of Concept 6, two data-driven segmentation studies are conducted sequentially. This does not lead to the same result as increasing the initial number of segments. As illustration, the data-driven segments from Step 1 in Concept 4 are used as a starting point again. The focus of interest

FIGURE 3
PSYCHOGRAPHIC SEGMENTS 1 AND 3 AMONG SPORTS TOURISTS

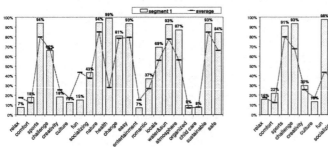 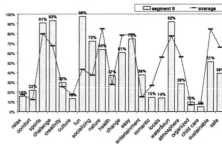

remains the segment of sports-interested tourists. Therefore, in the second step, only these tourists are studied, accounting for 13% of the total visitors to Austria in summer. This is achieved by constructing another data-driven segmentation based on this subsample alone and using the same psychographic criteria (clearly, for the second data-driven segmentation another segmentation base could be chosen as well). Again, TRN is used as a partitioning method and cluster numbers from 3 to 12 are explored with regard to stability of results. The maximum stability is reached in the 10 clusters solution. The resulting segments vary in size from 7% of the sample to 12%. For the purpose of the present segmentation study, not all 10 of them will be described in detail. However, 2 will be chosen as potentially interesting niche segments for destinations catering for sports tourism and aiming at differentiating themselves. The psychographic profiles of these 2 segments are given in Figure 3. Segment 1 is unique due to the high agreement among members (99%) that taking care of their health and beauty is very important to them during this vacation. The extraordinary feature of Segment 9 is that the one thing that seems to matter more than anything else is fun.

Further analysis shows that the resulting market segments after two steps of data-driven segmentation significantly differ with regard to age (ANOVA $p = .000$), the number of persons on the trip (ANOVA $p = .000$), the number of nights spent in Austria (ANOVA $p = .003$), the daily expenditures per person (ANOVA $p = .004$), and the expenditures for sports and entertainment (ANOVA $p = .000$). The differences and significances of the ordinal-scaled background variables on the segments of interest are given in Table 1.

Segment 1 (health-oriented sports tourist) is the oldest group of summer sports tourists in Austria. The average age is 49 years, which is 5 years more than the average among all sports tourists studied. The segment is attractive from the perspective of the duration of stay. Together with Segment 4, this group stays 1 day longer than the average (12 days). With regard to expenditures, however, this segment lies in the average range. These tourists have much prior experience with Austria as a holiday destination and therefore cannot be surprised easily. Three quarters of the members of this group state that their vacation has been just as they expected it to be.

With regard to vacation activities, Segment 1 specifies visiting spas significantly more often than the average. They also identify hiking and going for walks as part of their vacation entertainment.

Segment 9 (fun-driven sports tourists) is the youngest group, with an average age of 36 years. The fun-driven sports tourists have the shortest duration of stay among the constructed groups. The shorter duration of stay, however, is compensated by the highest daily expenditures per person. Members of Segment 9 spend 20% more money at the destination every single day. This can be distilled even further to expenditures on sports and entertainment. In this category of expenditures, Segment 9 spends 134% more than the average sports tourist in Austria. From the perspective of a sports or entertainment organization at the destination, this segment thus seems to be an optimal target for marketing action. Segment 9 has average prior experience with Austria, more often feels positively surprised by the vacation experience, and has a high proportion of groups of friends traveling together. With regard to vacation activities, this group is far more active than the sports tourist average in Austria. As a target group for evening entertainment, this group is excellently suited.

Using Concept 6 helps to detect two highly interesting niche markets among sports tourists—markets that have unique characteristics and therefore lend themselves perfectly to targeted marketing action. These segments could not have been the result of a one-stage data-driven segmentation process because other features dominating the total sample would have led to a different grouping.

CONCLUSIONS

Market segmentation is one of the most crucial long-term strategic marketing decisions a destination or organization makes. It is therefore of utmost importance to explore the market structure as thoroughly as possible to derive the most promising market segments with regard to the attractiveness of the segment and the matching potential of the segment's needs and the destination's or organization's strengths. The competitive advantage that can be gained from thorough

JOURNAL OF TRAVEL RESEARCH   249

TABLE 1

BACKGROUND INFORMATION ON THE SEGMENTS OF INTEREST

	Segment 1	Segment 9	Average	Pearson χ^2 p Value	Bonferroni Corrected
Intention to revisit Austria in summer				.000	.001
Very probable	34	33	33		
Probable	37	35	39		
Not probable	18	26	21		
How often in Austria before				.000	.000
Never	5	14	13		
Once	9	7	9		
Twice and more	86	79	78		
The vacation was				.000	.000
Better than expected	22	31	25		
As expected	75	66	73		
Worse than expected	3	3	2		
On vacation with friends				.000	.000
No	83	63	81		
Yes	17	37	19		
Sex				.004	ns
Male	59	72	63		
Female	41	28	37		
Tennis				.000	.000
Not at all	96	75	89		
Sometimes	3	15	8		
Often	1	10	2		
Cycling				.000	.000
Not at all	53	42	55		
Sometimes	22	23	19		
Often	25	35	26		
Swimming				.000	.000
Not at all	40	17	33		
Sometimes	30	37	35		
Often	30	46	32		
Spas				.005	ns
Not at all	80	92	89		
Sometimes	13	5	8		
Often	7	2	3		
Windsurfing				.000	.000
Not at all	97	78	93		
Sometimes	1	13	4		
Often	2	9	3		
Boating				.000	.001
Not at all	84	64	74		
Sometimes	14	31	22		
Often	1	5	4		
Mountaineering				.004	ns
Not at all	81	73	79		
Sometimes	8	16	10		
Often	10	11	11		
Hiking				.000	.000
Not at all	14	34	20		
Sometimes	15	31	23		
Often	70	35	56		
Going for walks				.000	.001
Not at all	8	16	10		
Sometimes	29	43	32		
Often	62	41	58		
Going out in the evening				.000	.000
Not at all	36	32	33		
Sometimes	34	34	37		
Often	29	34	30		

250   FEBRUARY 2004

market structure analysis is not fully exploited at present, with more than half of the segmentation studies published in the *Journal of Travel Research* within the past 15 years simply splitting tourists up by commonsense information and describing the resulting a priori segments. Most probably, the proportion of such studies in the industry is far higher than 53%.

In this article, a systematics of possible one- and two-step segmentation concepts is proposed. By considering a wider variety of possibilities available for exploratory market structure investigations, management can gain deep insight into the market structure from various perspectives. This leads to an improved basis for market research-driven decisions. The proposed systematics excludes three-step concepts as well as simultaneous combinations of the two fundamental building blocks: data-based and commonsense segmentation. However, such an extension is straightforward and bears potential for additional insights.

The two segmentation concepts, which—to the author's knowledge—have so far not been empirically conducted, were illustrated using Austrian National Guest Survey data. In the case of Concept 4 (data-driven segmentation followed by commonsense segmentation), an initial grouping was formed on the basis of motives for the vacation. In a second step, the sports-focused segment was selected and systematic differences between the sports tourists in 1994 and 1997 have been explored. Concept 6 was illustrated by using the same initial psychographic segmentation. The second data-driven segmentation was conducted selecting the sports tourists only and splitting them up into 10 subgroups, 2 of which have been found to be very distinctly profiled and thus market niches, which might be of high interest to a tourist destination or organization that can serve these particular needs well. For both of these concepts, the managerial usefulness of the approach was outlined, where the main advantage is that another perspective of market structure analysis is added that cannot be achieved by either one of the other approaches in the systematics used to date.

REFERENCES

Arimond, George, and Stephen Lethlean (1996). "Profit Center Analysis within Private Campgrounds." *Journal of Travel Research*, 34 (4): 52-58.

Baloglu, Seyhmus, and Ken W. McCleary (1999). "U.S. International Pleasure Travelers' Images of Four Mediterranean Destinations: A Comparison of Vistors and Nonvistors." *Journal of Travel Research*, 38 (2): 144-52.

Bieger, Thomas, and Christian Lässer (2002). "Market Segmentation by Motivation: The Case of Switzerland." *Journal of Travel Research*, 41 (1): 68-76.

Court, Birgit, and Robert A. Lupton (1997). "Customer Portfolio Development: Modeling Destination Adopters, Inactives, and Rejecters." *Journal of Travel Research*, 36 (1): 35-43.

Dodd, Tim, and Veronique Bigotte (1997). "Perceptual Differences among Visitor Groups to Wineries." *Journal of Travel Research*, 35 (3): 46-51.

Field, Arthur M. (1999). "The College Student Market Segment: A Comparative Study of Travel Behaviors of International and Domestic Students at a Southeastern University." *Journal of Travel Research*, 37 (4): 375-81.

Formica, Sandro, and Muzaffer Uysal (1998). "Market Segmentation of an International Cultural-Historical Event in Italy." *Journal of Travel Research*, 36 (4): 16-24.

Goldsmith, Ronald E., and Stephen W. Litvin (1999). "Heavy Users of Travel Agents: A Segmentation Analysis of Vacation Travelers." *Journal of Travel Research*, 38 (2): 127-33.

Horneman, Louise, R. W. Carter, Sherrie Wei, and Hein Ruys (2002). "Profiling the Senior Traveler: An Australian Perspective." *Journal of Travel Research*, 41 (1): 23-37.

Hsu, Cathy H. C., and Eun-Joo Lee (2002). "Segmentation of Senior Motorcoach Travelers." *Journal of Travel Research*, 40 (4): 364-74.

Israeli, Aviad A. (2002). "A Preliminary Investigation of the Importance of Site Accessibility Factors for Disabled Tourists." *Journal of Travel Research*, 41 (1): 101-4.

Kashyap, Rajiv, and David C. Bojanic (2000). "A Structural Analysis of Value, Quality, and Price Perceptions of Business and Leisure Travelers." *Journal of Travel Research*, 39 (1): 45-51.

Kastenholz, Elisabeth, Duane Davis, and Gordon Paul (1999). "Segmenting Tourism in Rural Areas: The Case of North and Central Portugal." *Journal of Travel Research*, 37 (4): 353-63.

Klemm, Mary S. (2002). "Tourism and Ethnic Minorities in Bradford: The Invisible Segment." *Journal of Travel Research*, 41 (1): 85-91.

Martinetz, Thomas, and Klaus Schulten (1994). "Topology Representing Networks." *Neural Networks*, 7 (5): 507-22.

McKercher, Bob (2001). "A Comparison of Main-Destination Visitors and through Travelers at a Duel-Purpose Destination." *Journal of Travel Research*, 39 (4): 433-41.

Meric, Havva J., and Judith Hunt (1998). "Ecotourists' Motivational and Demographic Characteristics: A Case of North Carolina Travelers." *Journal of Travel Research*, 36 (4): 57-61.

Moscardo, Gianna, Philip Pearce, Alastair Morrison, David Green, and Joseph T. O'Leary (2000). "Developing a Typology for Understanding Visiting Friends and Relatives Markets." *Journal of Travel Research*, 38 (3): 251-59.

Silverberg, Kenneth E., Sheila J. Backman, and Kenneth F. Backman (1996). "A Preliminary Investigation into the Psychographics of Nature-Based Travelers to the Southeastern United States." *Journal of Travel Research*, 35 (2): 19-28.

Smith, Malcolm C., and Kelly J. MacKay (2001). "The Organization of Information in Memory for Pictures of Tourist Destinations: Are There Age-Related Differences?" *Journal of Travel Research*, 39(3): 261-66.

[11]

ARTICLES

Effects of Ad Photos Portraying Risky Vacation Situations on Intention to Visit a Tourist Destination: Moderating Effects of Age, Gender, and Nationality

Leif E. Hem
Nina M. Iversen
Herbjørn Nysveen

ABSTRACT. This study investigated the power of fear evoked by ad photos in tourism ads. The basic assumption was that ad photos portraying a risky vacation situation could influence tourists' attitudes towards a destination and thereby their willingness to visit the place. A positive or negative change in attitude valence caused by risky vacation pictures de-

Leif E. Hem, Nina M. Iversen, and Herbjørn Nysveen are affiliated with the Norwegian School of Economics and Business Administration.

Address correspondence to: Leif E. Hem, Associate Professor, Norwegian School of Economics and Business Administration (NHH), Breiviksveien 40, 5045 Bergen, Norway (E-mail: leif.hem@nhh.no).

Journal of Travel & Tourism Marketing, Vol. 13(4) 2002
http://www.haworthpress.com/store/product.asp?sku=J073

10.1300/J073v13n04_01

1

pends on the tourist's level of tolerance to various perceived vacation risks. The prediction was that some tourist segments are risk seekers and thereby react more positively to risky vacation pictures, while others are risk averse and thereby react more negatively. The study results clearly indicated that overall fear created by risky vacation photos had a negative effect on intention to visit a tourist destination. However, age and nationality were found to moderate this effect. *[Article copies available for a fee from The Haworth Document Delivery Service: 1-800-HAWORTH. E-mail address: <docdelivery@haworthpress.com> Website: <http://www. HaworthPress.com> © 2002 by The Haworth Press, Inc. All rights reserved.]*

KEYWORDS. Evoked fear, perceived vacation risks, nature-based adventure tourism

INTRODUCTION

The importance of the revenue from tourism is evident in the strong competition between countries for the growing body of travelers (see, e.g., Riege & Perry 2000). Tourism is increasingly becoming a global industry and the main devices to attract tourists from distant markets are carefully targeted tourism advertising campaigns. Many countries spend enormous sums every year on tourism promotion. Yet, as media costs continue to accelerate, advertising managers have become increasingly concerned about the communication value of their commercial messages (Aaker & Joackimstahler 2000: 12). To obtain cost efficiency one common advertising message is often used to captivate a global audience. Taking into consideration the divergent characteristics of segments across nationalities and country cultures, one common message is unlikely to work successfully everywhere. Consequently, much attention is devoted to methods of pre-testing advertising stimuli (e.g., Vakratsas & Ambler 1999). Much of this pre-testing practice has its origin in a general preoccupation with the consumer as a cognitive information processor in the sense that only beliefs are measured (MacKenzie & Lutz 1989). However, in the past few years, interest in the nature and effects of consumers' affective reactions to advertising stimuli has rekindled (Haugtvedt et al. 1994). An example of such affective reactions is *fear*. The emotion of fear is also the basic component of advertisements playing on fear-appeals (e.g., Rogers 1975). In this paper, some factors are addressed that marketers should consider when designing tourism-advertising campaigns that may evoke fear.

Tourism advertisers commonly play on perceived vacation risks to evoke excitement and the desire for holiday adventures. This is especially true for tourist destinations trying to attract adventure tourists. However, little is known about how such risky advertising messages work across divergent tourist segments. While ad photos portraying a risky vacation situation may excite some individuals, others may merely experience feelings of fear. The latter type of tourist will most likely avoid visiting the destination. It is often assumed that one general fear-appeal message will have the same effect on activation of feelings of excitement in all markets. This assumption unlikely to be true, as different country populations may be more or less risk-averse. In highly risk-averse markets, a feeling of fear is a more likely response. Consequently, due to the negative impact that activation of fear can produce on intention to visit a place, the undifferentiated use of fear-appeals in tourism advertising can be a vulnerable strategy. Hence, tourist destinations that intend to attract tourists by use of fear-appeal ads can benefit from a better understanding of *to whom* and *in what situations* perceived vacation risks would not excite but rather frighten. Based on such understanding, advertising campaigns can be better targeted regarding perceived vacation risks.

This study focuses on the impact of evoked fear on intention to visit a tourist destination. The particular research setting is how perceived vacation risks, as portrayed in tourism advertisements, can create feelings of fear. The present study is conducted as an analysis of advertising material from the tourist region of "Fjord Norway." The Fjord Norway tourism product mainly offers nature-based vacations and Fjord Norway is profiled as "a touch of adventure." This commercial message is depicted in catalogues as well as in other printed materials. Photos of tourists situated on the edge of steep and dramatic natural attractions are commonly used. The characters are typically involved in daring exercises that create "thrills." In this way, the Fjord Norway advertising campaign plays on risky vacation experiences that are closely targeted to adventure tourists.

In the next sections of the paper the existing literature is reviewed, the main study variables are discussed, and some research hypotheses are outlined, after which the research methodology is described. Finally, the study findings are reported, conclusions are drawn and implications for tourism marketers are discussed.

LITERATURE REVIEW

In this section, a literature review is presented addressing the divergent types of perceived vacation risks, the role of fear in adventure tourism promotion, and the potential effects of fear-appeals in advertising. Based on the literature review some research hypotheses are proposed.

Divergent types of perceived vacation risks: It is widely acknowledged that not only perceived risk, but also the perception of safety that potential travelers associate with a tourist destination help them form a lasting destination image. It is also widely acknowledged that such destination images are critical in the destination choice process (Crompton 1979; Gartner & Hunt 1987). This implies that risks connected to tourism destinations are highly predictive of travel decisions and future travel behavior (Sonmez & Graefe 1998). When perceived risks are involved in tourism decision-making, the element of risk has the potential to severely alter more typical decision processes (Sonmez & Graefe 1998). Nevertheless, many tourist destinations play on perceived risk in their advertising campaigns. The Scottish tourism board promotes Scotland as a mix of risky and safe experiences (i.e., golf in scenic surroundings contrasted with a rough drama illustrating a Viking battle). Similarly, the New Zealand tourism board profiles New Zealand as a destination for risky adventure sports. These examples show that tourism advertising can evoke many types of perceived risks. These can be perceptions of (i) a risky country (e.g., due to terrorism, natural catastrophes, war, etc.), (ii) a risky vacation destination (e.g., due to drugs, alcohol, and crime), (iii) a risky holiday activity (e.g., adventure sports) or (iv) a risky tourist attraction (e.g., steep mountains, waterfalls, and rocks). It is likely that all these types of risks could be portrayed, either intentionally or unintentionally, in tourism advertising.

Cheron and Ritchie (1982) have elaborated on perceived risk. They view it as a multidimensional psychological phenomenon that influences individual perception and deception processes. They also acknowledge that the concept of perceived risk is made up of many different types of risks. Roehl and Fesenmaier (1992) have applied perceived risk to a tourism context and identified seven types of risks in vacation experiences. These include (1) equipment risk–the possibility of mechanical, equipment or organizational problems while on vacation; (2) financial risk–the possibility that a vacation will not provide value for the money spent; (3) physical risk–the possibility of physical danger, injury, or sickness while on vacation; (4) psychological risk–the possibility that a vacation will not reflect a person's self-image; (5) satisfaction risk–the possibility that a vacation will not provide personal satisfaction; (6) social risk–the possibility that a vacation will affect others opinions of a person; and finally (7) time risk–the possibility that a vacation will take too much time or even turn out to be a waste of time. Some risk dimensions are perceived to be more important than others are. The perceived importance of various types of risks varies across individuals and situations. A single tourist will pay most attention to what he/she perceives as the most important risks (Slovic 1972).

These examples of perceived vacation risks show the importance of addressing the effects of perceived risks on activation of fear in tourism promotion. However, the existing literature does not provide guidelines for managing the relationship between feelings of excitement and feelings of fear activated by scary photos in tourism promotion. Nor does it provide guidelines as to how to design optimal fear-appeal advertisements that can turn negatively perceived vacation risks into beliefs about positive and exciting tourism experiences. In the next section some factors are discussed that should be considered when fear-appeals are used in tourism promotion.

The role of fear in adventure tourism promotion: Few studies address the needs, motivations and expectations that underlie promotional campaigns and advertising material intended for adventure tourists. This is surprising considering that this is a remarkably increasing tourism segment. MacArthur (1989: 3) discusses the concept of adventure and notes that it requires three elements: "freedom of choice; intrinsic rewards; and an element of uncertainty, for instance when the experience outcome is uncertain or its risks are unpredictable." The EIU Travel and Tourism analyst gives the following definition of an adventure holiday: "An adventure holiday can be defined as one that contains an element of personal challenge, through controlled risk, daring and/or excitement, often in an inaccessible environment" ("Market Segments": 38). A common element within the two definitions described is the *risk* factor. Thus, experiences or activities that produce sensations and excitement define tourism adventures.

Zuckerman (1994: 313) has described the concept of sensation seeking. He defines it as "need for varied, novel, and complex sensations and experiences and the willingness to take physical or social risks for the sake of such experiences." It seems that sensational "thrills" are the main vacation benefits sought by adventure tourists. The way adventure tourists pursue sensations is by actively seeking calculated risks when participating in vacation activities. There is, however, a fine line between feelings of excitement and feelings of fear caused by such risks. If, for instance, tourism ads produce feelings of fear instead of feelings of excitement, they may sway the persuasion of the ad in an unfavorable way. The notion that fear-appeal ads can trigger such emotions is discussed next.

Effects of fear-appeals in advertising: The concept of fear is defined as a state of emotion (Gnoth et al. 2000; Plutchik 1980), and fear leads people to seek ways of coping with a perceived threat in an attempt to remove the danger (Rogers 1975; Tanner et al. 1991). Therefore, for most people fear has a significant effect on behavior. For decades, marketers have tried to take advantage of the emotional response of fear on consumer behavior by using threats of danger as appeals in advertisements (Janis & Feshback 1954). This advertising gimmick, with fear used to create persuasion, is termed fear-appeals. A wide range of studies shows significant effects of fear used in this way (see, e.g., Sutton 1982; Boster & Mongeau 1984 for a review).

There are inconsistent findings in research on fear-appeals regarding how this device works. Yet most studies show that fear is positively related to persuasion. Two meta-analytical literature reviews on fear-appeals conclude that higher levels of induced fear are associated with greater persuasive effectiveness (Sutton 1982; Boster & Mongeau 1984). An alternative view, which is commonly applied by practitioners, is that moderate fear-appeals are more persuasive than weak or strong ones. Weak fear-appeals are thought to create too little tension or drive, while strong fear-appeals are thought to create too much tension or drive. This belief is derived from the curvilinear theory posited by Janis (1967), which proposes that the fear/persuasion relationship is best represented by an inverted U-shaped curve. The inverted U-shaped curve indicates that moderate levels of fear are optimal. Ray and Wilkie (1970) have pointed out that in many cases moderate levels of fear heighten drive. The resulting effect is greater interest in the commercial message as well as in the marketed product.

The impact of fear-appeals on persuasion can be conceptualized as either *negative* or *positive*. *Negative* persuasion refers to fear-appeals where social marketers try to battle social problems such as AIDS or abuse of drugs, alcohol or cigarettes. They try to change such destructive behavior by using ads that create feelings of fear. Ads designed to reduce social ills are usually built on fear-appeals that underline the negative consequences of the issue at hand.

Positive persuasion of fear-appeals is the purposeful use of perceived risks to stimulate "an optimal level of fear." This means stimulation of an optimal balance-point between excitement and fear. The concept of an optimum stimulation level (OSL) is a closely related theoretical term that may explain aspects of positive persuasion. Hebb (1955) and Leuba (1955) introduced the OSL concept in the psychology literature. When an individual's optimal level of stimulation is met this produce a positive emotional response (e.g., excitement or sensation). People vary with respect as to when they experience optimal stimulation (e.g., Raju 1980; Zuckerman 1979). One person tolerates only a little stimulation before he/she experiences excitement, while another person requires extensive stimulation to experience the same level. OSL can therefore be conceptualized as a continuum with extremely arousal tolerant individuals (risk seeking individuals) at one end of the scale and extremely arousal intolerant individuals (risk averse individuals) at the other (e.g., Steenkamp & Baumgartner 1992). When, for instance, an ad message does not meet an individual's OSL level the ad is perceived as dull. On the other hand, when an individual's OSL level is exceeded by an ad message, the result is strong excitement or even feelings of fear, either of which produces a negative emotional response.

Whether fear-appeals enhance or inhibit persuasion often depend on characteristics of the recipients of the message. In one study, Burnett and Oliver (1979) observed that personality traits, product usage, and socioeconomic variables moderate the effectiveness of fear-appeals. Individual tourist characteristics determine what is the "optimal level of fear." To match individuals' "optimal level of fear," tourism ads should be carefully targeted to the particularities of selected market segments. Some tourists only get kicks from the idea of participating in fairly dangerous leisure activities such as extreme whitewater rafting, hang-gliding or mountain climbing. Others prefer the notion of rest and relaxation in a safe milieu. Characteristics that are found to distinguish tourists on preferences for holiday activities are for example age, gender, nationality, cultural factors, individual knowledge, and personal competencies (e.g., Pessemier & Handelsman 1984; Priest 1992). This article addresses to what extent age, gender and nationality impact the activation of fear from tourism ads, and whether or not the activated fear influences intention to visit a tourist destination.

To date research has not given marketers a complete understanding of the effect of fear-appeals on behavior (see Rotfeld 1988: 34). Attempts to provide communication guidelines for fear-appeals have pro-

duced conflicting results (Leventhal 1970; Sutton 1982). Although little
has been done on examining effects of fear-appeals in general, even less
has been done on use of fear-appeals in tourism promotion. Hence, the
need for theoretical and pragmatic guidance is great. To address this
topic, some research hypotheses concerning use of fear-appeals in tourism ads are developed next. These hypotheses were later tested on tourists from various countries considering a visit to "Fjord Norway."

RESEARCH HYPOTHESES

In the previous sections, several theoretical variables such as perceived vacation risks, adventure tourism and fear-appeals were presented and discussed. Below some potential relationships between
these constructs are postulated. Some relationships are not clearly defined in existing literature, and therefore some hypotheses have to be
outlined partly through logical argumentation. Figure 1 shows the main
hypothesized effects of a scary ad photo (portraying a risky vacation situation) on intention to visit a tourist destination.

One basic assumption is that an ad photo portraying some risky nature-based attractions or activities can potentially evoke feelings of
fear. For instance, photos of tourists situated on the edge of a steep and
dramatic cliff, or people involved in daring exercises, are expected to
induce some level of fear (see, e.g., Sutton 1982; Boster & Mongeau
1984). Therefore, it is proposed that tourism ad photos portraying in-

FIGURE 1. Summary of Hypotheses

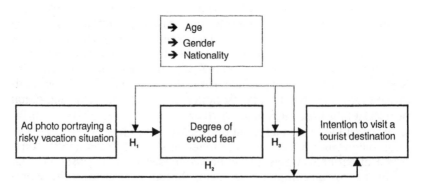

creasing levels of vacation risks produce stronger feelings of fear, and vice versa:

H_1: *Ad photos portraying risky vacation situations have a positive effect on the degree of evoked fear.*

It is well known that perceived risks connected to a destination are critical in the destination choice process (Crompton 1979; Gartner & Hunt 1987), and that such risks are highly predictive of travel decisions (Sonmez & Graefe 1998). Moreover, it is highly likely that an ad photo portraying a risky vacation situation can influence tourists to perceive a destination as risky. Risky tourism ad photos that evoke feelings of fear that are too strong are prone to create uncertainty, which again discourages tourists from choosing a destination (Key 1972). When the evoked fear exceeds a potential tourists' acceptance level (OSL), the destination is simply excluded from the "choice set" in the prior screening phase (see Goodall et al. 1988; Um & Crompton 1987; Goodall 1991; Gartner 1993). The destination is not transferred to the "decision set" (Gartner 1993) to be evaluated on an attribute-by-attribute basis. Systematic trade-off evaluations between destination benefits and attributes are not undertaken, as the destination is simply perceived as too risky. Therefore, the direct effect between risky tourism ad photos and intention to visit a tourist destination is hypothesized to be negative:

H_2: *Ad photos portraying risky vacation situations have a negative effect on intention to visit a tourist destination.*

Tourism ads are marketing devices used to impact overall product attitudes through piecemeal product evaluations. Overall product attitudes are again strong predictors of behavioral intentions to choose a product (e.g., Batra & Ray 1986; Kahle & Holmer 1985; Park & Young 1986; MacKenzie, Lutz & Belch 1986). Theoretical models predict an advertising effect on behavioral purchase intentions that is mediated by the ads' effect on the overall product attitude (Fishbein & Ajzen 1975; Mitchell & Olson 1981). The ad message is thought to influence overall product attitudes by stimulating systematic evaluations of emotional benefits and product attributes.

It seems likely that ad photos evoking strong feelings of fear may sway the valence of an overall destination attitude in a negative direction. Unfavorable affective evaluations underlie this judgment process. Ad photos evoking strong fear can create unfavorable affective piecemeal evaluations that impact the overall destination attitude negatively. Because behavioral intentions are derived from the overall destination attitude, tourists' intentions to visit are thereby reduced. Therefore, increasing levels of evoked fear impact the destination attitude negatively, which reduces tourists' intentions to visit the tourist destination.

> H_3: *Increasing degree of evoked fear impacts intention to visit a tourist destination negatively.*

Proposed moderating effects of age, gender, and nationality: Whether fear-appeals enhance or inhibit persuasion often depends on characteristics of the recipients of the ad message. Therefore, some proposed relations of a set of segment variables are outlined. The effects of these segment variables are discussed in relation to the elicitation of fear and to intention to visit a tourist destination. Burnett and Oliver (1979) observed that several characteristics, including (1) age, (2) gender and (3) nationality, moderate the effectiveness of fear-appeals. The impact of these segment variables on the advertising effects of fear-appeals is outlined below. Because limited a priori theory exists, concise hypotheses are not expressed for the moderating variables. Instead, the discussed relationships are stated as general propositions. In Figure 1 the proposed relationships are depicted as dotted lines.

Age: Marketers of Fjord Norway assume that older tourists visit this destination largely to experience nature-based attractions with scenic views and relaxing environments, while younger tourists look for more excitement. Thus, increasing age has a positive effect on intention to visit Fjord Norway when the area is portrayed as a nature-based tourism destination and a negative effect on intention to visit when portrayed as an adventure tourism destination.

Age is extensively used as an important moderating variable in many studies of advertising effects (see, e.g., Burnett and Oliver 1979). The moderating effect of age is also found in studies of "optimum stimulation levels" (OSL). This literature indicates that younger individuals have higher optimum stimulation levels and that higher age is negatively associated with OSL (Pessemier & Handelsman 1984; Zuckerman et al. 1978). It can therefore be argued that younger tourists handle perceived vacation risks better and are more tolerant towards feelings of fear. Moreover, risky tourism ad photos may evoke higher levels of fear among older tourists than among younger tourists. Therefore, age is thought to moderate the effects of H_1, H_2, and H_3.

Gender: The moderating effect of gender is found in studies of sensation seeking and optimum stimulation levels. This literature indicates that younger males have higher OSL scores than women (Zuckerman et al. 1978; Zuckerman 1994; Nell 1998). There is data that shows the highest sensations seekers are males aged 16–20 (Nell 1998). Therefore, gender is thought to moderate the effects of H_1, H_2, and H_3, since women evoke more fear than men.

Nationality: Nationality forms an individual's cultural heritage as well as their personal knowledge and skills. These national characteristics also distinguish tourists in their preferences for holiday activities (e.g., Pessemier & Handelsman 1984; Priest 1992). It is also likely that individuals vary in activation of fear according to their country of origin. People from countries where nature is similar to that portrayed in the photos of Fjord Norway will probably perceive the tourism destination as less risky, meaning that the photos will evoke less fear. Thus, nationality is believed to moderate the level of evoked fear and thereby to moderate H_1, H_2 and H_3.

RESEARCH METHODOLOGY

In this section, the research methodology underlying the study of effects of scary ad photos is presented. Primary research was considered necessary to test the stated hypotheses. As the hypotheses are correlational, a field study research design was found appropriate.

Research setting: The present study was conducted as an analysis of advertising material from Fjord Norway, which is a tourist destination located on the Southwest coast of Norway. The Norwegian fjords have been ranked as one of the top 20 attractions in the world, and the scenic views of Fjord Norway are breathtaking and unique. Consequently, this destination attracts substantial numbers of international tourists. Scary photos of tourists situated on the edge of steep and dramatic nature attractions are commonly used to signal "a touch of adventure" in order to promote this destination.

Instrument, questionnaire and measurements: This paper addresses advertising effects of ad photos portraying risky vacation situations; hence, actual advertisements from the region were employed. As advertisements are symbolic representations of attractions, nature-based attractions are most easily communicated visually (cf. Wells et al. 1998). Therefore, the selected ads include photos of some of the most characteristic and breathtaking sites in "Fjord Norway." The stimuli were divided into four groups of photos. *Group 1: ad photos displaying a risky vacation situation*–(a) one man on the edge of the cliff "Prekestolen" (the pulpit chair), (b) two men balancing on the "Kjærag rock" and (c) one girl sitting on the edge of a mountain looking down on "Geirangerfjorden (the Geiranger Fjord)." *Group 2: safe photos*–a photo displaying children playing in a field of flowers situated by "Hardangerfjorden (the Hardanger Fjord)." *Group 3: a collage of risky and safe photos*–a mix of two risky and four safe photos. *Group 4: a collage of safe photos*–a mix of six safe photos. Each respondent evaluated each of the six photos/collages as a within subject design. All photos are presented in Figure 2.

A questionnaire was developed that included all the ad photos, as well as the scales for measuring "evoked fear." The main dependent variable was "intention to visit" Fjord Norway. This variable was captured by use of two Likert-type scales, which are frequently used in attitude research (e.g., Fishbein & Ajzen 1975). One scale was positively

FIGURE 2. Photos Used as Stimuli in the Study

Photo 1

Photo 2

stated and one was negatively stated. The items were "the photo makes me want to visit" and "the photo makes me not want to visit." The latter scale was reversed in the data analysis. Factor analysis revealed that these two items loaded strongly on one factor (eigenvalue = 1.10, total variance = 22.1%) and Cronbachs alpha indicated reliable measures (α = .75). Three items were used to measure evoked fear. The items were "the photo signals danger," "the photo signals lack of security" and "the photo makes me scared" (see similar measures but in other contexts in Laroche et al. 2001: 304; Tanner et al. 1991: 44). Factor analysis revealed that one factor captured the fear dimension (eigenvalue = 3.09, total variance = 61.8%) and Chronbachs alpha indicated reliable measures (α = .92). An additive measure was constructed by aggregating the scores on each item and dividing the aggregated

FIGURE 2 (continued)

Photo 3

scores by number of items (i.e., $S = \sum_{i=1}^{n} S_i / n$, where S = score, S_i = score item, and n = number of items). Seven-point scales, with end points 1 = totally disagree and 7 = totally agree, were used to measure both "intention to visit" and "evoked fear." Information on the demographic variables age, gender and nationality was also collected.

Sampling: Questionnaires were mailed to subjects who applied for the Fjord Norway Travel Guide 2001. Respondents received the questionnaire together with the travel guide. They were requested to complete it and return it by mail using a pre-paid envelope. A lottery was conducted and a traditional Norwegian sweater was drawn as compensation for participation. To avoid biasing respondents, the compensation was announced at the end of the questionnaire. In an attempt to

Photo 4

cover the main market segments of tourists in Fjord Norway, the nationality composition of respondents was controlled. The aim was to include the most respondents from the three most significant markets, the
UK, Germany, and the USA (see Table 1).

The origin of respondents in the obtained sample was more widespread. Subjects came from the US (11.4%), Japan (1.8%) and from
several countries in Western Europe (Germany = 37.6%; UK = 15.8%;
Italy = 15.0%; France 11.9%; other European countries = 3.8%). The
typical subject was around 40 years of age, with less of younger (4% <
20 years) and older subjects (4% > 70 years). The sample was comprised of somewhat more woman (51.5%) than men (48.5%). Table 1
indicates that the main national markets were covered reasonably well
although the German market was somewhat overrepresented. Of the

FIGURE 2 (continued)

Collage 5

424 questionnaires collected, 38 questionnaires were removed from the sample due to major non-response biases or obvious careless responses. Data from a total of 386 fully completed questionnaires were used to run analyses. The sample was obviously self-selected, but because there were sufficient variation in the data set across respondents, examinations of the data were still allowed.

RESULTS

Table 2 shows the mean values of "evoked fear" and "intention to visit" across respondents for each of the six photos. An analysis of variance was undertaken to test the three proposed hypotheses based on the mean value evaluations. The results are presented in Table 3.

Collage 6

Hypotheses H_1 and H_2 postulated direct effects of ad photos on "evoked fear" and "intention to visit." The results showed support for both H_1 and H_2. Photos 1, 2 and 4 ("the risky photos") evoked a higher level of fear compared to photo 3 ("the safe photo") as well as to photos 5 and 6 ("the collages") ($F = 176.3$, $p < .00$). Furthermore, "the risky photos" were found to reduce intention to visit compared to "the safe photo" and to "the collages" ($F = 3.8$, $p < .00$).

Table 4 shows that the ad photos, which were chosen to portray a risky vacation situation, were perceived as such. Pair-wise comparisons of the six photos showed that there were no significant differences in evoked fear across photos 1, 2, and 4 ("the risky photos"). However, comparisons showed that "the risky photos" evoked significantly higher levels of fear compared to "the safe photo" and "the collages"

Managing Tourism Firms

18   *JOURNAL OF TRAVEL & TOURISM MARKETING*

TABLE 1. Geographic Nationality of Respondents (N = 386).

Nationality	Numbers	Percent frequency	Actual segments 2001 (%)
1. UK	61	15.8	17.6
2. Germany	145	37.6	17.6
3. USA	44	11.4	13.0
4. Japan	7	1.8	6.9
5. Spain	10	2.6	6.1
6. France	46	11.9	6.0
7. Italy	58	15.0	3.1
All other European countries	11	2.8	28.8
Africa + South America	4	1.0	0.1
Others (Asia, Australia, etc.)	-	-	0.8
Total	386	100.0	70.8

TABLE 2. Mean Value of Perception of Fear and Intention to Visit.

	Perception of fear	Intention to visit
Photo 1	3.60	5.87
Photo 2	3.74	5.79
Photo 3	1.36	5.99
Photo 4	3.82	5.77
Photo 5	1.42	6.14
Photo 6	2.58	6.09

Seven-point scales were used (1 = totally disagree and 7 = totally agree).

(photos 3, 5, and 6). Based on this finding it is argued that use of risky photos in tourism ads can evoke increased levels of fear. Results from the pair-wise comparison also revealed significant differences in the level of evoked fear across the collage of safe photos (photo 5) and the collage of risky and safe photos (photo 6). It can be argued that "the risky photos," when presented alone, will evoke the highest levels of fear. Collages with a mix of risky and safe photos may also evoke fear, but at a significantly lower level. The lowest level of fear was evoked by "the safe photo" and by "the collage of safe photos." These two photos (photo 3 and 5) activated significantly less fear than the others. No significant difference in evoked fear was generated between "the safe photo" and "the collage of safe photos."

TABLE 3. Results.

	df	F	p
Main effects			
Ad photo			
Fear	5	176.3	0.00
Intention	5	3.8	0.00
Fear			
Intention	18	33.5	0.00
Moderating effects			
Ad photo on Fear			
Photo	5	19.5	0.00
Photo × Age	36	1.6	0.02
Photo × Gender	6	0.1	0.99
Photo × Nationality	90	5.2	0.00
Ad photo on Intention			
Photo	5	1.4	0.21
Photo × Age	36	1.5	0.04
Photo × Gender	6	1.5	0.19
Photo × Nationality	90	10.9	0.00
Fear on Intention			
Fear	18	9.4	0.00
Fear × Age	110	1.5	0.00
Fear × Gender	19	1.1	0.35
Fear × Nationality	152	5.7	0.00

Hypothesis H_3 postulated a negative effect of evoked fear on intention to visit. An F-test supported this hypothesis ($F = 33.5$, $p < .00$). The results of a simple regression analysis also strongly supported this hypothesis (Adjusted $R^2 = 0.18$; $F = 508.6$, $p < .00$; Standardized Beta coefficient $= -.43$, $p < .00$). Thus, it follows logically that the use of scary ad photos evoking fear generally reduces the intention to visit a tourist destination.

Moderating effects of H_1: Age ($F = 1.6$, $p < .02$) revealed a moderating effect of ad photo on evoked fear. Younger persons experienced less fear than older ones when they were exposed to "the risky photos." This difference in responses across age groups does not occur for "the safe photos." Nationality was also found to moderate the effect of ad photo on evoked fear ($F = 5.2$, $p < .00$). Gender, however, did not show this moderating effect ($F = 0.1$, $p = .99$). When these three moderating variables were included in the analysis the main effect of ad photos on evoked fear was still significant ($F = 19.5$, $p = < .00$).

TABLE 4. Perceived Fear Across Photos. Pair-Wise Comparisons.

	Photo 1	Photo 2	Photo 3	Photo 4	Photo 5	Photo 6	F-value	p-values
Perceived fear	3.60	3.74	1.36	3.82	1.42	2.58	176.3	.00

Pairwise comparisons

		Mean differences	Significance
Photo 1	2	0.14	0.93
	3	2.24	0.00
	4	0.22	0.66
	5	2.18	0.00
	6	1.02	0.00
Photo 2	3	2.38	0.00
	4	0.08	0.99
	5	2.32	0.00
	6	1.16	0.00
Photo 3	4	2.46	0.00
	5	0.06	1.00
	6	1.22	0.00
Photo 4	5	2.40	0.00
	6	1.24	0.00
Photo 5	6	1.16	0.00

Moderating effects of H_2: The analyses revealed a moderating impact of age (F = 1.5, p = .04) and nationality (F = 10.9, p < .00) on the effect of ad photo on "intention to visit." Age had a positive moderating effect on intention to visit when subjects were exposed to "the risky photos," but not when respondents were exposed to the safe photos. Gender did not show a moderating impact on this effect (F = 1.5, p = .19). It should be noted that when one included the moderating variables, the main effect of ad photos on intention to visit was not significant (F = 1.4, p = .21).

Moderating effects of H_3: Age (F = 1.5, p < .00) and nationality (F = 5.7, p < .00) moderated the main effect of evoked fear on intention to visit. The negative effect of evoked fear on intention to visit was more significant for younger than for older respondents. Gender (F = 1.1, p = .35) did not show this moderating effect. The main effect of fear on intention to visit was still significant (F = 9.4, p < .00) when the moderating variables were included.

DISCUSSION

The findings show that tourism marketers should be highly aware of the pitfalls associated with the use of ad photos portraying risky vacation situations. Based on findings from the present study, this seems to be especially important when the task is to promote nature-based destinations and the ad photos themselves can be perceived as risky (given the strong support for Hypotheses H_1, H_2, and H_3). It was found that "intention to visit" the Fjord Norway was influenced negatively by evoked fear from ads portraying risky nature attractions and people in risky vacation situations. This finding is important for the designers of ads being used in international tourism promotion, especially when one attempts to attract divergent international tourist segments. Rather than activating motivations to travel, scary ad photos can instead evoke feelings of fear. For many tourist segments, evoked fear reduces the chance that the place advertised would be considered as a potential holiday destination. The evoked fear even inhibits favorable destination attribute evaluations. Both these effects reduce tourists' intentions to visit a tourist destination.

The general effect of evoked fear is, however, moderated by segment characteristics such as age and nationality. Younger tourists experienced less fear than older tourists did when they were exposed to "the risky photos" (H_1). However, the moderating impact of age on the effect of ad photo on intention to visit (H_2) and the moderating impact of age on the effect of evoked fear on intention to visit (H_3) seems to be opposite of what was expected. Younger tourists seem to be most impacted by the evoked fear from the risky photos in the sense that they were more discouraged to visit Fjord Norway. The risky photos impact older tourists less probably because they emphasize other criteria than fear in their evaluations of intentions to visit. Most likely older tourists had a stronger attitude towards Fjord Norway and thereby were more resistant to changes imposed by evoked fear from risky ads (Fishbein & Ajzen 1975; Heilman et al. 2000). However, given that older tourists experienced higher fear than younger tourists did when they were exposed to "the risky photos" (H_1) this effect may influence "intention to visit" after several exposures. Nationality is also shown to moderate the main effects in this study. However, the variation within and between nations blurs the picture of the direction of the moderating effect. No moderating effects were found for gender. The reason could be that the subjects participating were a bit too old and therefore, the effects found for younger men by Nell (1998) did not appear.

Managerial implications: From a managerial point of view the reported findings indicate that managers should carefully consider the pitfalls of utilising risky photos when designing ads to promote naturebased destinations. This is especially important since "intention to visit" the destination was influenced negatively by evoked fear from ads portraying risky nature attractions and people in risky vacation situations. Varying need for arousal across tourist segments should direct the extremity of the fear-appeals. Therefore, knowledge about your target segment(s) seems to be utmost important. The main challenge in tourism promotion is, thus, to design a mix of advertising stimuli that highlights positive vacation risks and conceals negative vacation risks. Before this mix is laid out, marketers should express concisely the optimal balance-point between dimensions of perceived risks and dimensions of perceived safety at a destination. This balance point is termed "an optimal level of fear," and is conceptualized as a fine-tuned equilibrium between feelings of excitement/sensations and feelings of fear. Identification of these balance points of primary target segments is essential as input for marketers who design promotional campaigns based on fear-appeals. Marketers should therefore prevent activation of fear, but also prevent activation of dullness by avoiding, respectively, too risky and too trivial photos. These effects can be estimated by pre-testing advertising stimuli.

Theoretical implications: The study findings support the importance of understanding feelings of fear when promoting a tourist destination. To gain more insight, the theoretical understanding of fear should be improved as well as practices in measuring it. Such improvements will extend the understanding of how fear and fear-appeals impact product evaluations and purchase intentions in general, and how they impact evaluations of tourist destinations in particular. Marketers typically believe that moderate fear-appeals are more persuasive than weak or strong ones. This belief is derived from the curvilinear theory (Janis 1967), which proposes that the fear/persuasion relationship is best represented by an inverted U-shaped curve. This notion is also in accordance with the OSL perspective (Steenkamp & Baumgartner 1992; 1995). Herein only the linear relationship between fear and persuasion has been investigated. An interesting topic for the future would be to design a study that particularly addresses whether or not fear behaves in accordance with the theory of the inverted U-shaped curve. Finally, the effects of age and nationality illustrate the importance of including segment characteristics as covariates in future studies on effects of fear and fear-appeals.

Limitations and further research: The present study obviously has weaknesses that should be considered in future studies. Herein subjects were exposed to "one shot" evaluations of six photos describing only a limited part of the Fjord Norway tourism product. There is little doubt that consumers' evaluations are influenced by active marketing activities, as usually will be the case in "real life" (see Heilman et al. 2000). Future research should therefore utilise other ad photos portraying other risky and safe vacation situations. Future studies should also use more as well as improved items to measure the concept of fear. After the 11th of September 2001, terrorism has frightened tourists around the world, making the importance of fear more salient than ever. More research is needed to isolate the effects of different fear and risk dimensions. The particular effect of fear-appeals in tourism advertising should be more thoroughly investigated to differentiate it from the impact of other types of vacation risks. In this study only the moderating effects of the segment variables age, gender and nationality were investigated. Other segment characteristics, such as lifestyle characteristics, may just as easily impact the effects of fear. This study showed moderating effects of nationality, which call for further studies on the effects of cultural differences in reactions to evoked fear.

REFERENCES

Aaker, D. A. & Joackimsthaler, E. (2000). *Brand Leadership*. New York: The Free Press, 350 p.

Batra, R. & Ray, M. L. (1986). Situational effects of advertising repetition: The moderating influence of motivation, ability, and opportunity to respond. *Journal of Consumer Research*, 12 (March), 432-45.

Boster, F. J. & Mongeau, P. (1984). Fear-arousing persuasive messages. *Communications Yearbook*, 8, 330-375.

Burnett, J. J. & Oliver, R. L. (1979). Fear appeal effects in the field: A segmentation approach. *Journal of Marketing Research*, 16 (May), 181-90.

Cheron, E. J. & Ritchie, J. R. (1982). Leisure activities and perceived risk. *Journal of Leisure Research*, 14, 139-54.

Crompton, L. (1979). Motivations for pleasure vacation. *Annals of Tourism Research*, 6, 408-24.

Fishbein, M. & Ajzen, I. (1975). *Belief, Attitude, Intension and Behavior: An Introduction to Theory and Research*. Reading: MA: Addison-Wesley.

Gartner, W. C. (1993). Image Formation Process. *Journal of Travel & Tourism Marketing*, 2 (No. 2/3), 191-215.

Gartner, W. C. & Hunt, J. D. (1987). An analysis of state image change over a twelve-year period (1971-1983). *Journal of Travel Research*, 16 (Fall), 15-19.

Gnoth, J., Zins, A. H., Lengmueller, R. & Boshoff, C. (2000). Emotions, mood, flow and motivation to travel. *Journal of Travel & Tourism Marketing*, 9 (3), 23-34.

Goodall, B. (1991). Understanding holiday choice. *Tourism Recreation and Hospitality Management*. Ed. C. Cooper. Belhaven Press; London, pp. 58-77.

Goodall, B., Radburn, M. & Stabler, M. (1988). Market opportunity sets for tourism. Geographical Paper No. 100. Department of Geography, Reading, from Goodall 1991.

Haugtvedt, C. P., Schumann, D. W., Schneider, W. L. & Warren, W. L. (1994). Advertising repetition and variation strategies: Implications for understanding attitude strength. *Journal of Consumer Research*, 21 (June), 176-189.

Hebb, D. O. (1955). Drives and the C. N. S. (Central Nervous System). *Psychological Review*, 62, 243-54.

Heilman, C.M., Bowman, D. & Wright, G.P. (2000). The evolution of brand preferences and choice behaviors of consumers new to a market. *Journal of Marketing Research*, 37, 139-155.

Janis, I. (1967). Effects of fear arousal on attitude change: Resent developments in theory and experimental research. In V. L. Smith & W. R. Eadington (Eds.), *Advances in Experimental Social Psychology*, Vol. 3. New York: Academic Press, Inc., 166-224.

Janis, I. & Feshbach, S. (1954). Personality differences associated with responsiveness to fear-arousing communications'. *Journal of Personality*, 23. 154-166.

Kahle, L. R. & Homer, P. M. (1985). Physical attractiveness of the celebrity endorser: A social adaptation perspective. *Journal of Consumer Research*, 11 (4), 954-61.

Key, H. (1972). Do we really know the effects of using "fear" appeals? *Journal of Marketing*, 36 (April), 55-57.

Laroche, M., Taffoli, R., Zhang, Q. & Pons, F. (2001). A cross-cultural study of the persuasive effect of fear appeal messages in cigarette advertising: China and Canada. *International Journal of Advertising*, 20, 297-317.

Leuba, C. (1955). Toward some integration of learning theories: The concept of optimal stimulation. *Psychological Report*, 1, 27-33.

Leventhal, H. (1970). *Findings and theory in the study of fear communications*. In L. Berkowitz (Ed.), *Advances in Experimental Social Psychology*, Vol. 5, New York: Academic Press, Inc., pp. 119-186.

MacKenzie, S. B. & Lutz, R. J. (1989). An empirical examination of the structural antecedents of attitude toward the ad in an advertising pre-test context. *Journal of Marketing*, 53 (April), 48-65.

MacKenzie, S. B., Lutz, R. J. & Belch, G. E. (1986). The role of attitude toward the ad as a mediator of advertising effectiveness: A test of competing explanations. *Journal of Marketing Research*, 23 (May), 130-43.

Market Segments: The UK Adventure Holiday Market (1992). *EIU Travel and Tourism Analyst*, 3, 37-51.

McArthur, S. (1989). Working hard to be a solo man: An investigation of the facets and ramifications of group size, as it relates to adventure tourism in whitewater rafting. Unpublished integrated project, School of Resource Science and Management, University of New England, Northern Rivers, Lismore.

Mitchell, A. A. & Olson, J. C. (1981). Are product beliefs the only mediator of advertising effects on brand attitude? *Journal of Marketing Research*, 18 (August), 318-32.

Nell, V. (1998). Why Younger Men Drive Dangerously: An Evolutionary Perspective. *The Safety & Health Practitioner*. Borehamwood, 16 (October), 19-23

Park, C. W. & Young, S. M. (1986). Consumer response to television commercials: The impact of involvement and background music on brand attitude formation. *Journal of Marketing Research*, 23 (February), 11-24.

Pessemier, E. & Handelsman, M. (1984). Temporal variety in consumer behavior. *Journal of Marketing Research*, 11 (November), 435-44.

Plutchik, R. (1980). *Emotion: A psychoevolutionary synthesis*, New York: Harper and Row.

Priest, S. (1992). Factor exploration and confirmation for the dimensions of an adventure experience. *Journal of Leisure Research*, 24, 127-39.

Raju, P. S. (1980). Optimum stimulation level: Its relationship to personality demographics and exploratory behavior. *Journal of Consumer Research*, 7 (December), 272-282.

Ray, M. L. & Wilkie, W. L. (1970). Fear: The potential of an appeal neglected by marketing. *Journal of Marketing*, 34 (January), 54-62.

Riege, A. M. & Perry, C. (2000). National marketing strategies in international travel and tourism. *European Journal of Marketing*, 34 (11/12), 1290-1304.

Roehl, W. S. & Fesenmaier, D. R. (1992). Risk perceptions and pleasure travel: An exploratory analysis. *Journal of Travel Research*, 32 (Spring), 17-26.

Rogers, R. W. (1975). A protection motivation theory of fear appeals and attitude change. *Journal of Psychology*, 91, 93-114.

Rotfeld, H. J. (1988). Fear appeals and persuasions: Assumptions and errors in advertising research. In James Leigh & Claude R. Martin, Jr. (Eds.), *Current Issues and Research in Advertising*, Ann Arbor: The University of Michigan, pp. 21-40.

Slovic, P. (1972). Convergent validation of risk taking specificity and the generality of risk taking behavior. *Journal of Personality and Social Psychology*, 22, 128-43.

Sonmez, S. F. & Graefe, A. R. (1998). Determining future travel behavior from past travel experience and perceptions of risk and safety. *Journal of Travel Research*, 37 (2), 171-77.

Sutton, S. R. (1982). Fear-arousing communications: A critical examination of theory and research. In Richard Eiser (Ed.), *Social Psychology and Behavioral Medicine*. London: John Wiley & Sons, Inc.

Steenkamp, J.-B. E. M. & Baumgartner, H. (1992). The role of optimum stimulation level in exploratory consumer behavior. *Journal of Consumer Research*, 19 (December), 434-448.

Steenkamp, J.-B. E. M. & Baumgartner, H. (1995). Development and cross-cultural validation of a short form of CSI as a measure of optimum stimulation level. *International Journal of Research in Marketing*, 12, 97-104.

Tanner, J. F., Hunt, J. B. & Eppright, D. R. (1991). The protection motivation model: A normative model of fear appeals. *Journal of Marketing*, 55 (July), 36-45.

Um, S. & Crompton, J. (1987). *A cognitive model of pleasure travel destination choice*. Department of Recreation and Parks, Texas A&M University, Texas.

26   *JOURNAL OF TRAVEL & TOURISM MARKETING*

Vakratsas, D. & Ambler, T. (1999). How advertising works: What do we really know? *Journal of Marketing*, 63 (January), 26-43.

Wells, W., Burnett, J., & Moriarty, S. (1998). *Advertising. Principles and Practice.* New Jersey: Prentice Hall, Englewood Cliffs (2nd ed.)

Zuckerman, M. (1994). *Behavioural expressions and biosocial basis of sensation seeking.* Cambridge: Cambridge University Press. Vol. 8.

Zuckerman, M. (1979). *Sensation seeking: Beyond the optimal level of arousal.* LEA, Publishers. Hillsdale, New Jersey.

Zuckerman, M., Eysenck, S. & Eysenck, H. J. (1978). Sensation seeking in England and America: Cross-cultural, age and sex comparisons. *Journal of Consulting and Clinical Psychology*, 46, 139-49.

SUBMITTED: 03/08/02
FIRST REVISION: 06/12/02
SECOND REVISION: 09/16/02
ACCEPTED: 09/20/02
REFEREED ANONYMOUSLY

[12]

The Nature of Independent Travel

KENNETH F. HYDE AND ROB LAWSON

Independent travel is an important and growing sector of worldwide tourism. This study examines the extent of travel planning by independent travelers, the extent to which travel plans are actioned, and the temporal sequence in which vacation elements are chosen. In-depth case studies were completed on 20 international travel parties who were first-time visitors to New Zealand. Travel parties were interviewed at both the beginning and the end of their vacations. Using an inductive-deductive process of research, a series of propositions was developed and tested using pattern-matching procedures. The study demonstrates that the motivations for independent travel are reflected in the decision processes adopted by independent travelers. Three characteristics are identified that distinguish the nature of independent travel: the traveler experiences an evolving itinerary, the traveler is willing to take risks in selecting vacation elements, and the traveler possesses a desire to experience the unplanned.

Keywords: *independent travel; travel planning; decision making; information search*

A continuing trend in international tourism is the growth in independent travel and the relative decline in package travel (Chesshyre 2002; Pryor 2001; Scutte 1997).

To the travel industry, a *package traveler* is a vacation traveler who has booked his or her air travel and accommodation—and perhaps other elements of the vacation—through a travel retailer. This traveler has purchased a product bundle, or package. To the travel industry, *independent travelers* are all tourists who are not package travelers; they are all the vacation travelers who have not booked an air travel and accommodation package with a travel retailer. By this definition, those vacation travelers who have booked only air travel with the travel retailer would be considered independent travelers; those vacation travelers who have booked their travel or accommodation through the Internet would also be considered independent travelers.

According to the "travel styles" definitions used by Tourism New Zealand (2002), the package traveler sector consists of tour group travelers and all other travelers who have booked their accommodation and internal transportation arrangements for the destination prior to departure. Tourism New Zealand views independent travelers as those with no travel bookings other than an international air ticket, as well as those with additional bookings that were not purchased as part of a travel retailer package. Backpackers are one sector of this independent travel market. Morrison, Hsieh, and O'Leary (1993) define independent travelers as those "who make their own transportation and accommodation arrangements, choosing not to buy prearranged packages or tours."

However, a definition of independent travel should be based on a tourist's behavior rather than the choice of distribution channel through which his or her vacation was purchased. What is important in a definition of independent travel is whether the elements of the vacation have been prebooked (from any source) prior to departure. The term *independent traveler* should apply to those travelers who have flexibility in their itinerary and some degree of freedom in where they choose to travel within a destination region. Package travelers are likely to have limited choice in the towns and cities they will visit within a destination region once their vacation is booked, whereas independent travelers are likely to have considerable choice in the towns and cities they will visit in the destination region, even after the vacation has been booked.

Independent travel may have accounted for some 78% of British overseas travelers in 1989, some 72% of French travelers, and some 58% of German travelers (Morrison, Hsieh, and O'Leary 1993). Among international tourists to New Zealand during 2001-2002, 92% of British, 90% of Australian, and 75% of American visitors were independent travelers (Tourism New Zealand 2002).

The World Tourism Organisation (1993, p. 21) has suggested that "the homogeneous group package tour developed so extensively during the 1960's, 1970's and into the 1980's . . . has become outmoded. It is not in line with the trend toward individual expression." Quest (1990, p. 137) claims, "The decline of the package tour may be due to the fact that it has become unfashionable," and "as more people travel overseas . . . they become more sophisticated in their demands, more importantly, they have the confidence to travel independently." Poon (1993) suggests that changing demographics and lifestyles have resulted in greater demand for choice and flexibility in vacations. Poon describes a growing group of *new tourists*, "consumers who are flexible, independent, and experienced travellers, whose values and lifestyle are different from those of the mass tourists" (p. 114).

The choice between the independent travel mode and the package travel mode is influenced by sociodemographic characteristics (such as age and gender of the traveler), travel characteristics (such as length of stay, size of travel party, and previous travel experience), country of origin, and travel destination (Hsieh et al. 1993; Hsieh, O'Leary, and Morrison

Kenneth F. Hyde is the academic director of marketing for the Manukau Institute of Technology, Auckland, New Zealand. Rob Lawson is a professor of marketing at the University of Otago, Dunedin, New Zealand.

Journal of Travel Research, Vol. 42, August 2003, 13-23
DOI: 10.1177/0047287503253944
© 2003 Sage Publications

14   AUGUST 2003

1994; Morrison, Hsieh, and O'Leary 1993; Sheldon and Mak 1987).

Despite the prevalence and importance of independent travel, surprisingly few of the leading texts, encyclopedias, or handbooks of tourism take space to explore this phenomenon.

It aids us little to simply assume that the essence of independent travel is "independence" or that independent travelers sometimes adopt "flexible itineraries." Independent travelers are likely to vary in the amount of preplanning of their vacation. There is likely to be a continuum in the degree of preplanning. At one extreme of this continuum may be travelers who have researched and preplanned (though not prebooked) a great deal of their vacation; at the other extreme may be travelers who have neither researched nor preplanned any of their vacation itinerary.

Research is required that investigates and describes the fundamental nature of the independent vacation in terms of planning, decision making, and behavior. Both commercial operators and public organizations within the tourism industry need to understand the type and extent of vacation planning undertaken by the independent traveler and the extent to which such travel plans are implemented (Coventry 1996). No item of research has sought to describe the nature of the independent vacation as a worthy subject of research in itself.

This article describes research that seeks to demonstrate the information search, planning, and decision making of travelers on an independent vacation. It then seeks to draw conclusions regarding the defining characteristics of independent travel. The research uses a case study methodology to investigate these issues and a pattern-matching technique to test a series of propositions relating to the nature of the independent vacation.

The background to the study draws on three fairly distinct areas of tourism research. First, a review of existing literature identifies a number of theorists who have described the motivational bases for independent travel. Second, existing research on tourist information search is summarized since this has often used independent travelers as its subjects. Third, several recent studies are summarized that recognize the multifaceted nature of travel planning and decision making. From this literature review, a number of research questions arise regarding independent travelers' information search, travel planning, and decision making.

The Motivational Bases
of Independent Travel

A considerable amount has been written in the tourism literature emphasizing the different motivational bases between the package traveler and the independent traveler.

In his exposition on the tourism phenomenon, Krippendorf (1987) suggests that travel offers the individual a *sense of freedom* and self-determination not available in everyday life. It might be that independent travel offers greater opportunities for this very sense of freedom sought by many tourists.

In addition, many people may be born with a sense of curiosity and a need to explore the world around them (Mayo and Jarvis 1981). Anderson (1970) describes the "Ulysses factor," which is a basic motivation of some tourists to explore, a curiosity for new places and people. Anderson appears to describe the characteristics of an independent traveler, saying, "He is not looking for anything in particular and is not greatly concerned with what he discovers. It is in this sense that he is a true explorer" (p. 179).

Gray (1970) recognized a clear distinction between two types of tourism. He identified *wanderlust* as a basic trait of some individuals that causes them to leave familiar things behind and seek out exciting new places and new cultures. This is contrasted with *sunlust*, which is a desire for a single-destination, stay-put vacation involving rest and the best of amenities.

Similar dichotomies have been identified many times in the literature with slightly different terminologies and exposition of motives. For example, a tourist's choice between package travel and independent travel might be a result of the balancing of two opposing motivational forces. According to Mayo and Jarvis (1981), in any traveler's behavior, we observe a balance between the traveler's *need for complexity* and *need for consistency* (i.e., a balance between a desire for novelty and a desire for routine). The individual chooses a vacation that represents the best balance of complexity and consistency that is consistent with his or her needs.

In his parsimonious view of tourism behavior, Plog (1973, 1991) identifies two personality types among tourists. The *psychocentric* traveler is safety seeking and prefers the familiar, and the *allocentric* traveler is adventure seeking and prefers the exotic. This distinction applies not only to a traveler's choice of destination but also to his or her choice of travel mode (Plog 1991). Plog's typology has received mixed empirical support (see Smith 1990; Madrigal 1995; Griffith and Albanese 1996).

The work of Lee and Crompton (1992) suggests that a tourist's choice of destinations may be influenced by a genetic predisposition toward seeking more or less novel experiences, a factor these writers term *novelty seeking*. Novelty-seeking tourists are likely to prefer the unusual, the adventuresome, a change of pace, and excitement. Novelty-avoiding tourists are likely to prefer a familiar, planned vacation experience.

Cohen (1972) described a typology of four alternative tourist roles, according to the traveler's desire for novelty or familiarity. The *organised mass tourist* purchases a package tour, as he or she seeks to minimize exposure to the unfamiliar. The *individual mass tourist* takes short sightseeing trips to provide a blend of familiarity and novelty. The *explorer* travels on a self-guided tour and tries to get off the beaten path while maintaining comfortable accommodation and reliable transportation. The *drifter* forgoes tourist establishments and seeks to envelop himself or herself in the host's culture. Keng and Cheng (1999) found support for Cohen's typology in their study of Singaporean tourists.

Finally, Poon (1993) draws a distinction between the *old tourist* and the *new tourist*. Old tourists search for the sun, are cautious, and follow the masses; it does not matter where they travel because the vacation is treated as an escape from the stress of urban life. According to Poon, new tourists are more spontaneous, with a lower level of vacation planning and a desire to do what comes on the spur of the moment. New tourists want to be different from the crowd and experience something different; they are adventurous.

A number of sectors of the independent travel market have been studied, including the adventure travel sector (Sung, Morrison, and O'Leary 2000), the bicycle travel sector (Ritchie 1998), and, in particular, the backpacker sector (Ateljevic and Doorne 2001). Riley (1988) describes the backpacker as a long-term budget traveler. He or she is a youth traveler driven by hedonistic and self-development motives who is often at an important junction in life such as the junction between the end of study and the commencement of a career. Loker-Murphy and Pearce (1995) define backpackers as travelers on an extended independent vacation, staying in budget accommodation, with an emphasis on informal and participatory vacation activities that expose them to the culture of the destination country. Many of these tourists are students or young professionals. They represent Cohen's (1972) explorers and drifters.

But we must be careful not to view all independent travelers as backpackers; backpackers are merely *a subset* of all independent travelers. In a study of independent travelers to New Zealand, Parr (1989) reports that such travelers are not solely budget travelers; rather, they include travelers adopting a very wide range of accommodation types and transportation modes. What these varied travelers hold in common is not a particular level of expenditure on vacations but a *lack of prebooking of vacation elements*. Parr found in her study that a full 62% of independent travelers arrived in New Zealand without any prior booking of vacation elements. Interestingly, 90% of the independent travelers studied by Parr traveled alone or as couples.

Tourist Information Search

While this research provides a good foundation for understanding the needs and wants of the independent traveler in relation to others, it does not help unravel the nature of information search, planning, and decision making undertaken by this type of tourist. This is likely to involve many more decision points and to be a complex and fragmented matter compared to those vacations taken by a package traveler.

Studies of tourists' information search and travel planning have often been studies of the independent traveler. Such studies are of two types: those that examine the sources of information used by tourists and those that examine the amount of search undertaken (Fodness and Murray 1997, 1998, 1999). From even the earliest studies, it appears that *personal* sources of information, particularly friends and relatives, constitute the major source of information in most tourist decision making (Gitelson and Crompton 1983; Nolan 1976). However, the choice of information source may vary by stage of the vacation and by type of traveler.

Travelers en route to their destinations are known to make use of travel information centers and other people to learn about attractions and activities; such information can influence an independent traveler's length of stay and choice of attractions and activities in the destination area (Fesenmaier, Vogt, and Stewart 1993). Travelers *at their destination* seek information from personal sources, such as employees of accommodation facilities and fellow travelers, and are also influenced by commercial signage (McDonough and Ackert 1986).

Travelers taking routine trips to familiar destinations use past experience and advice from family and friends in their travel planning. In contrast, travelers traveling longer distances, taking longer vacations, or visiting new and unfamiliar destinations are more likely to use *destination-specific literature* and to seek a greater volume of information (Etzel and Wahlers 1985; Gitelson and Crompton 1983). Those

travelers who want security and comfort are likely to use travel agents and tour operators; those seeking to explore new destinations tend to use printed material such as *guidebooks and brochures* (Snepenger 1987).

Fodness and Murray (1997, 1998, 1999) were able to demonstrate segmentation of the traveler population based on the amount of information search undertaken for the vacation. Amount of information search undertaken was related to the length of the vacation, as well as number of destinations and attractions visited. In their study of travel information search and planning, Schul and Crompton (1983) identified *active search* and *passive search* groups. Active searchers displayed variety in their choice of attractions and activities and preferred vacations that were an escape from the ordinary.

Travel Planning and Decision Making

By definition, independent travelers have not prepurchased the elements of their vacation. But have they preplanned those vacation elements? Morrison, Hsieh, and O'Leary (1993) suggest that independent travelers may have prearranged itineraries or flexible itineraries. What proportion of the independent vacation elements is planned prior to arrival at the destination versus the proportion of vacation elements chosen while on vacation? How flexible are the itineraries of independent travelers? Does the commercial tourism operator at the destination have the opportunity to influence these travel plans and travel behaviors?

The following studies provide some insight into travel planning and decision making for multidestination vacations. The elements of the vacation of central interest are the choice of subdestinations, travel routes, attractions, and activities. From her study of independent travelers, Parr (1989, p. 108) concluded that "some knew exactly what they wanted to do. . . . [Others] had little idea of what they wanted to see and do." In their study of visitors to Alachua County, Florida, Crotts and Reid (1993) found that most visitors had decided on recreational activities prior to arrival. But those travelers who made their activity decisions *after* arrival were typically long-haul and international visitors. In a study of travel planning by visitors to New Zealand, Tsang (1993) found that more than 40% of travelers had *no* preplanning of vacation activities, and only a minority of visitors had preplanned their length of stay in each subdestination.

Recognizing that much of the research on tourist decision making has assumed a single-destination choice, Leu, Crompton, and Fesenmaier (1993) presented a typology of multi-destination vacations. Stewart and Vogt (1997) called on researchers to investigate the decision processes by which an itinerary of multiple destinations is chosen. Tideswell and Faulkner (1999) employed regression analysis of Queensland Visitor Survey data to reveal a number of factors correlated with multidestination tourism: long-haul travel, access to a motor vehicle, having multiple purposes for the trip, and consulting many information sources prior to the trip. Taplin and McGinley (2000) demonstrated that multiperiod linear programming could be used to model the sequence of day-to-day route choices made by car tourists in multidestination tourism.

Clearly, tourist vacation decision making involves a complex series of decisions in which choices of the different elements in the vacation evolve in a temporal sequence

16   AUGUST 2003

(Dellaert, Ettema, and Lindh 1998). What is required is research that reveals the most common temporal sequences used by travelers. Very little research has been published on the temporal sequence of tourist decision making while on vacation.

Jeng (1997) asked respondents to imagine a 2- to 4-day domestic vacation trip and consider which vacation elements they might plan before departure. Jeng identified a set of *core* decisions made before departure, including date of trip, primary destination, location of overnight stay, and travel route. He identified a set of *secondary* decisions, made before departure but considered to be flexible, including choice of attractions and activities and secondary destinations. Third, he identified a set of en route decisions, including where to dine, shop, and stop and rest.

Woodside and his colleagues have provided two useful frameworks for understanding the multifaceted nature of multidestination vacations. Woodside and MacDonald (1993) presented a general systems framework for understanding a tourist's choice of vacation elements—including choice of destination, choice of accommodation, transport mode, travel route, subdestinations, attractions, and activities. According to Woodside and MacDonald, these travel decisions can be interdependent.

Woodside and King (2001) refer to the concept of a purchase consumption system (PCS), a sequence of purchases the consumer undertakes in which the purchase of one item may lead to the purchase of others. In the context of a vacation, this concept provides a framework for understanding the interrelated nature of vacation decisions: destination choices, activity choices, choice of attractions, accommodation choices, transportation mode and travel route to the destination, retail shopping purchases, dining choices, and transportation mode and travel route around the destination. Woodside and King demonstrated in their study of vacationers in the Big Island of Hawaii that several decisions within a customer's leisure-travel PCS are dependent on prior purchases of products. Some product purchases were not planned before the start of the trip. During each of the three stages of the vacation—before trip, during trip, and after trip—there was information search and decision making.

Woodside and King (2001) go on to describe the temporal sequence of decision making for their tourists. In level 1 decisions, destination choice and choice of attractions and activities were made. In level 2 decisions, accommodation and mode/route to the destination were decided. In level 3 decisions, retail purchases, dining choices, and routes taken between subdestinations were chosen. Woodside and King advocate continued research to develop an understanding of the sequence of decision-making processes used by vacationers.

The current research examined in detail the vacations of 20 independent travel parties who were visiting an international destination for the first time. The research sought to establish the following:

1. extent of pretrip information search;
2. extent of pretrip travel planning;
3. timing of information search—pretrip versus on vacation;
4. sources of information used both pretrip and on vacation;
5. percentage of pretrip travel plans that are actioned;
6. factors influencing the amount of information search, amount of planning, and percentage of plans actioned;

7. temporal sequence in the choice of vacation elements— namely, choice of subdestinations, route, attractions, and activities.

METHOD

Qualitative research methods have become increasingly common in tourism research (Riley and Love 2000; Walle 1997). Qualitative methods produce in-depth information on a small number of individuals and look beyond simple snapshots of events, people, or behaviors (Bonoma 1985; Patton 1991).

Typically, research on tourist information search and decision making has adopted a one-shot survey methodology. Questionnaires are distributed or interviews conducted at a single point in the vacation—either pretrip or posttrip or at some ad hoc point during the vacation. Such approaches to understanding tourist information search and decision making will of necessity suffer from the limitations of consumer recall. This is especially a problem when the research is seeking to understand the timing and sequence of decision events; the tourist who has been surveyed at a single point in the vacation might not reliably recall the chronology and details of the decision process.

What is required to understand the decision-making processes of independent travelers is a research methodology that collects data at more than one point in the vacation. Case study is a suitable methodology.

According to Yin (1994), case study is the preferred research methodology when "how" or "why" questions are being posed. Case study is especially useful for investigating the sequence or process of a phenomenon (Eisenhardt 1989). Case study does not yield trustworthy estimates of population characteristics. Rather, depth of understanding is based on a detailed knowledge of the particular and its nuances in context (Stake 1994).

While case study research can typically claim high levels of external validity, stringent procedures should be followed to ensure the reliability and internal validity of the data gathered. Such procedures may include testing rival explanations, seeking negative cases, triangulating methods and sources, and subjecting the data and findings to peer review (Lincoln and Guba 1986; Patton 1991).

Furthermore, case study has traditionally been viewed as an inductive, theory-building endeavor. But it can be argued that a combination of induction and deduction is desirable in case study; it is desirable that theories are not only built but also tested (Hyde 2000).

Pattern matching is an approach to theory testing in case study research (Campbell 1975; Wilson and Wilson 1988). In pattern matching, the model to be tested is expressed as a set of independent outcomes that are predicted to occur. Likewise, a countermodel is put forward that prescribes a pattern of competing outcomes. The case data gathered are compared to the predictions of the model and predictions of the countermodel. Support is demonstrated for the model if case data match the predicted pattern of outcomes of the model more closely than they match the predicted pattern of outcomes for the countermodel. If the results fail to show the entire pattern as predicted, the initial propositions need to be

JOURNAL OF TRAVEL RESEARCH 17

modified. In summary, pattern matching is a theory-testing procedure that actively employs rival explanations and exposes case evidence and conclusions to independent peer review.

In the current study, data gathering occurred in three phases. First, a series of propositions regarding independent travelers' information search, planning, and decision making was developed inductively from exploratory research, interviews, and published literature. Second, these propositions were tested and revised in a pilot set of interviews. Third, a final set of 19 propositions was tested in a series of in-depth interviews with 20 independent travel parties, using pattern-matching methodology.

These propositions (presented in full in the Results section) considered the content and extent of pretrip vacation planning, the most influential information sources in the preparation of pretrip vacation plans, when detailed information search occurred (pretrip vs. on vacation), when choice of attractions and activities occurred, the basis for choice of attractions and activities, the percentage of pretrip plans that were actioned, the temporal sequence in which vacation elements (subdestinations, route, attractions, and activities) were decided upon, the motivational and emotional aspects of the independent vacation experience, and whether the independent traveler enjoyed a vacation in which vacation elements were largely unplanned.

The discussion that follows describes this third and final phase of the research program, the theory-testing phase.

An initial interview was conducted with 32 travel parties within 24 hours of their arrival in New Zealand, an international destination they had not visited before. The interviews sought to probe and record content of cognitive sets *at these points in time*, rather than retrospectively.

New Zealand is a destination consisting of two main islands, the North Island and the South Island, and some smaller offshore islands. The North Island and the South Island are each approximately the size of Florida. Multi-destination trips are the primary form of vacation for visitors (Oppermann 1994). It is common for tourists to travel a circuit route around each of the main islands. The primary attractions are geographically dispersed, and travelers must choose a route connecting their selection of subdestinations. New Zealand has one of the highest length of stay and intranational dispersion of tourists of any international destination (Oppermann 1992).

The population from which the study sample was drawn was defined as follows: (1) independent travel parties, (2) who were first-time visitors to New Zealand, (3) traveling alone or as a couple, and (4) *not* visiting friends and relatives. The selection of travel parties was designed to maximize diversity within the sample. A stratified purposeful sampling method was used (Patton 1991). Three strata were judged critical to diversity in the study population, namely, nationality of the traveler, travel party size, and mode of transportation. All initial interviews were conducted in the city of Auckland, the major gateway for inbound international tourism to New Zealand. The sample was sought by intercepting tourists at two locations: the busiest tourist information center in the country and the busiest motor home rental depot in the country. The initial interviews were conducted during the peak summer visiting period of December and January. An interview protocol was followed (Yin 1994). The protocol required the interviewer to probe the following:

- planned vacation elements (i.e., where travelers planned to go on their vacations and what they planned to see and do),
- planned travel route,
- number of hours spent reading written sources of information to plan the vacation,
- number of personal sources of information consulted in planning the vacation, and
- which sources of information had most influenced their vacation plans.

Of the interviews, 28 were conducted in English, and 4 were conducted in Japanese. All interviews were tape-recorded and transcribed in full. A process of data triangulation (Patton 1991) was employed involving the interview transcript, quantitative measures (length of vacation planning time, length of vacation, number of vacation elements planned), and responses to two checklist items. The checklist items asked respondents if they would have liked more detailed information about New Zealand before they arrived and asked if they wanted all the details of their vacation itinerary planned. Interview transcripts were examined for each travel party to identify the list of planned vacation elements (subdestinations, attractions, and activities).

Arrangements were made for each travel party to recontact the researcher by telephone for a second interview, to be conducted at the end of their New Zealand vacation. Of the 32 travel parties participating in the first interview, 20 parties reported back for a second interview.

In the second interview, an interview protocol was followed that probed the following:

- subdestinations visited (i.e., locations involving at least one overnight stay);
- travel route followed;
- attractions and activities experienced;
- for each unplanned vacation element, why the traveler had chosen this element;
- amount and type of information search conducted while on vacation; and
- for planned vacation elements that were not actioned, how the traveler felt about failing to see or do that.

Respondents invariably spoke with enthusiasm and at length about the details of their vacation experiences. A number of travel parties referred to their trip diaries when speaking to the interviewer.

Again, a process of triangulation was applied with multiple data sources as follows: the interview transcript, responses to a checklist, and a map of the travel route taken. The checklist queried the following:

- sources of information used on the vacation,
- length of time that vacation elements were planned in advance,
- length of time that information on subdestinations was sought in advance,
- whether the traveler considered undertaking any spontaneous vacation elements, and
- whether the traveler considered that part of the adventure of the vacation was taking chances with his or her choice of attractions and activities.

18   AUGUST 2003

Each of four judges examined the 19 propositions against summaries and excerpts of transcript from each of the 20 cases. Each judge examined whether a proposition or its counterproposition was better supported by data. In total, 4 × 20 judgments were put to bear on *each proposition*. Wilcoxon matched-pairs signed-ranks tests were employed to test the level of agreement among judges.

RESULTS

The 20 travel parties came from a diverse range of countries, occupations, and age groups. Travelers came from continental Europe ($n = 7$), North America ($n = 3$), Australia ($n = 2$), Scandinavia ($n = 2$), Great Britain ($n = 2$), East Asia ($n = 2$), and the Middle East ($n = 2$). This matches well the diversity of international visitors to New Zealand. They traveled by a diverse range of transportation modes—rental car, motor home, purchase of a car, bus, train, flight, and hitchhiking. Accommodation types used included four-star hotels, motels, youth hostels, and tents. The length of travelers' vacations varied between 10 and 88 days.

Extent of Pretrip Information Search

The travelers studied displayed considerable variation in the amount of pretrip information search; amount of reading completed to research the vacation itinerary varied from 0 to 40 hours for any one individual or travel party.

Extent of Pretrip Travel Planning

On average, travel parties had fewer than seven specifically planned vacation elements. This number is not dissimilar to the size of cognitive sets found in other purchase decisions, including choice of vacation destination (Woodside and Sherrell 1977). Almost half of these specifically planned elements were subdestinations. Many fewer attractions or activities had been specifically planned. A minority of travel parties had a preplanned travel route.

Travelers' vacations consisted of a mean of 32.8 elements. In other words, some 80% of vacation elements had been neither specifically nor generally planned. This finding provides some indication of just how flexible independent vacation itineraries might be.

The Timing of Information Search

Studies by Crotts and Reid (1993) and Jeng (1997) suggested that domestic consumers vacationing in familiar destinations undertake most of their information search and travel planning prior to departure. The current study of international travelers to an unfamiliar destination has presented a very different result. For the travelers studied, a majority of information search and planning occurred *after arrival* at the destination. Travelers made detailed plans for choice of attractions and activities for the immediate *24-hour* period only. Only as travelers approached a subdestination did they seek detailed information on that subdestination and its attractions and activities.

The Sources of Information Used Both Pretrip and En Route

For these travelers, the most influential information sources in the preparation of vacation plans were travel guides and brochures. Of the travel parties, 80% had read a travel guide prior to arrival at the destination. While on vacation, these travelers were eager for information about local subdestinations, attractions, and activities from any source.

The Percentage of Pretrip Travel Plans That Are Actioned

No previous longitudinal studies were located describing the percentage of a traveler's plans that are put into action. The information presented here appears unique in this regard. Of the vacation elements these travelers had specifically planned, almost all—a mean of 72.9%—were actioned. This indicates that knowledge of a traveler's specific vacation plans may provide an accurate prediction of actual vacation behaviors.

The Factors That Influence Amount of Information Search, Amount of Planning, and Percentage of Travel Plans Actioned

Of the constructs studied, *amount of information search* was identified as being most central to predicting other aspects of travel behavior. Amount of information search was the strongest predictor of the amount of travel planning and percentage of travel plans that are actioned. A low-search group of travelers was identified, who were more likely to be backpackers (Fisher's exact test, $p = .077$) in their 20s ($\chi^2 = 6.173$, $df = 2$, $p = .046$), from English-speaking countries (Fisher's exact test, $p = .088$), and traveling alone (Fisher's exact test, $p = .030$). These travelers had few specific plans. What plans they had tended to feature a selection of *activities*, and yet these activities were readily substitutable. High-search travelers tended to be couples, from non-English-speaking countries, in their 30s, and not backpacking. They had many specific plans—especially a selection of "must-see" subdestinations—and were highly likely to action these plans. Notwithstanding this, even individuals who did the most planning experienced a vacation in which the majority of elements were indeed *unplanned*.

The Temporal Sequence in Which Vacation Subdecisions Are Made

In this study of independent travelers to New Zealand, the decision sequence observed for choice of vacation elements was as follows: subdestinations → travel route → attractions and activities.

Several findings point to subdestinations as being the central element in planning the vacation itinerary. Most specifically planned elements were subdestinations. High levels of information search were associated with precise planning of subdestinations but bore no relationship to degree of planning of attractions or activities. Most planned subdestinations were actioned. Several findings point to the conclusion that alternative activities are substitutable. Individuals who had the highest number of planned activities were *least* likely to action these plans.

Test of Propositions

Propositions were tested using a pattern-matching procedure. The following propositions were supported:

Proposition 1: An integral element in independent travel is the enjoyment the traveler experiences from not planning the details of the vacation ($z = -3.864$, $p = .000$).

Proposition 2: Vacation planning consists of a set of planned vacation elements. For some travelers, this set will consist of 8 to 16 elements; for other travelers, this set will consist of fewer than 4 elements ($z = -3.823$, $p = .000$).

Proposition 3: The most influential information sources in the preparation of planned vacation elements are printed sources (i.e., travel guides and brochures) ($z = -2.595$, $p = .010$).

Proposition 8: The decision sequence displayed by these travelers is subdestinations → travel route → attractions and activities ($z = -3.920$, $p = .000$).

Proposition 9: Travelers make detailed plans for choice of attractions and activities for the immediate 24-hour period only ($z = -2.314$, $p = .021$).

Proposition 10: Only as travelers approach a subdestination do they seek detailed information on that subestination and its attractions and activities ($z = -3.320$, $p = .001$).

Proposition 11: In addition to planned vacation elements, travelers will consider other attractions and activities ($z = -3.920$, $p = .000$).

Proposition 13: Choice of attractions and activities is based on balancing the pleasures expected from experiencing the attraction or activity versus the constraints of time and expense ($z = -3.920$, $p = .000$).

Proposition 14: Almost all planned attractions and activities will be actioned ($z = -2.636$, $p = .008$).

Proposition 18: Travelers will take advantage of serendipitous opportunities to experience some attractions and activities they had neither planned nor actively researched ($z = -3.920$, $p = .000$).

Proposition 19: The independent vacation is like experiencing the "fun of the fairground," a freewheeling experience of going from place to place, relatively unaware of what each subdestination offers, extracting as much as possible from each place (given the constraints of time and expense) and taking advantage of serendipitous opportunities ($z = -3.920$, $p = .000$).

Evidence in support of these propositions can be seen in the case data. Excerpts from two sample cases follow.

Case 1: Mike and Carol

Arrival interview. Mike and Carol were American citizens who lived and worked in Riyadh, Saudi Arabia. He was a 50-year-old mining engineer, and she was in her 40s. They booked their flight to New Zealand 8 weeks prior to arrival. They had booked a motor home for their vacation and would be joined for a short time by their son and his girlfriend. Between them, they had undertaken 20 hours of research for the vacation, including reading picture books and a guidebook and watching a travel video. Carol had done much more research than Mike, speaking with New Zealanders in Riyadh

and compiling a list of things to see and do in the North Island. (She had not prepared a list for the South Island.) Carol was interested in pottery and crafts. Table 1 lists the planned and unplanned elements of their vacation. They had 11 planned vacation elements, including just one subdestination.

> I purposely don't read up on where I'm going. I just follow my nose. And that way I'm not disappointed, because I've read about something that didn't make it. (Mike)

> And I, on the other hand, like to spend time with the books, researching, making a list of things. (Carol)

Departure interview. Their vacation was 22 days long. They stayed in motels. They actioned 82% of their planned vacation elements. Their vacation consisted of 38 elements in total, of which 87% was unplanned. They considered that they had planned the details of their vacation just 48 hours in advance. They considered their most useful information sources to be their guidebook, visitor information centers, and brochures. They considered that they took advantage of some spontaneous opportunities to do unplanned things and that part of the adventure of the vacation was taking chances.

> We had made absolutely no plans for the South Island. . . . But the constraint was that we had to have the kids to Christchurch only 3 days later on the 28th. So we had to make a short circle for the kids. (Mike)

> The lady that ran the motel as we were checking out in the morning—"How have you enjoyed your trip so far?" etc. etc., as they all ask . . . "Where are you heading today?" "Well I think we have to start heading north." And I said to her we really wanted to see Milford Sound but it's going to have to be another trip. And she said, "Why don't you just fly in?" And I said, "Well, it's pretty expensive was why." And she said, "But you really ought to do it." And I said, "It's only money." So we did, we flew in. She got us within 20 minutes. (Mike)

> She was on the phone. This was a snap decision. And in 20 minutes we were at the airport, getting on a plane flying. (Carol)

> We were certainly aware of the most popular places through the planning and that kind of thing. But it's interesting the little out-of-the-way places you find doing it Mike's way. You just go and if something looks interesting, then you search that out. (Carol)

Case 2: Francois and Edith

Arrival interview. Francois and Edith were from Switzerland. They were career people in their 30s. They appeared to be relatively wealthy, upper-middle-class people who were well traveled. New Zealand was their only destination on this vacation, and they had booked their flight to New Zealand 52 weeks prior to arrival. Francois had undertaken more than 40 hours of research for the vacation, including studying two travel guidebooks, but was reluctant to commit himself to an itinerary. He had planned a route for the couple to tour both

TABLE 1

**PLANNED AND UNPLANNED VACATION ELEMENTS—
CASE 1: MIKE AND CAROL**

Specifically Planned Elements	Generally Planned Elements
Whitewater rafting	Head north •
Blackwater rafting •	Caves •
Caving •	Geothermal area •
Abseiling	Trekking •
Mt. Cook •	Crafts and pottery •
Glaciers •	
Six items/67% actioned (•)	Five items/100% actioned (•)

Actual Vacation Elements

Sheepworld	Turangi	Milford Sound
Takapuna	Mountain trek •	Boat trip
Russell	Palmerston North	Haast
Swim with dolphins	Nelson	Fox glacier
Taupo Bay	Greymouth	Franz Josef
Kauri trees	Pancake rocks	Reefton
Warkworth	Christchurch	Paraparaumu
Otorohanga	Arts center	Mt. Egmont
Waitomo Caves	Botanical gardens	Taumaranui
Caving •	Twizel	Taupo
Blackwater rafting •	Mt. Cook •	Paeroa
Rotorua	Pottery •	Waiheke Island
Waimangu	Queenstown	

38 items/13% planned (•)

TABLE 2

**PLANNED AND UNPLANNED VACATION ELEMENTS—
CASE 2: FRANCOIS AND EDITH**

Specifically Planned Elements	Generally Planned Elements
Coromandel •	South Island •
Rotorua •	Nature •
Volcanic activity •	
Three items/100% actioned (•)	Two items/100% actioned (•)

Actual Vacation Elements

Coromandel •	Paekakariki	Nelson
Tapu		Wellington
Cathedral		
Whitianga	Cable car	Collingwood
Tauranga •	Blenheim	Motueka
Rotorua	Waipara	Wanganui
Walk	Christchurch	Waitara
Kauri forest	Crayfish	Orewa
Thermal area •	Cathedral	Whangarei
Maori village	Waitati	Mangonui
Old bath house	Dunedin	Opononi
Paradise Valley	Gore	Dargaville
Gisborne	Kingston	Kauri museum
Wairoa	Queenstown	Maritime museum
Napier	Ross	Aquarium
Dannevirke	Westport	

Forty-four items/7% planned (•)

the North and South Islands, but where they were to stop or what they were to do would be left flexible. They had just three specifically planned items, including two subdestinations. Table 2 lists the planned and unplanned elements of their vacation. They had booked a motor home for their vacation. Francois said he would not have liked any more information on New Zealand and definitely did not want the details of his vacation planned.

> *Question:* Have you learned a lot about New Zealand from the guidebooks?
> *Francois:* I don't know, it's very theoretical. One says so, one says so. So I think you have to, to see each day how it's going on.

Departure interview. Francois and Edith stayed in New Zealand for 24 days. In addition to traveling by motor home, they took a train journey. They stayed in camping grounds and motels. All three of their specifically planned vacation items were acted on. Their vacation consisted of 44 elements, of which 93% was unplanned. Even the travel route that they had planned prior to arrival was not strictly adhered to; they were willing to make changes to this route. Their primary source of information while on vacation was their travel guidebook, but they were also influenced by signage and by the motor home company's discount book. They considered that they made detailed vacation plans only for the immediate 24-hour period, chose where to go and what to do based on the enjoyment expected, and took advantage of some spontaneous opportunities to do unexpected things.

All life is planned. We work the whole day. It's planned. You have to. So the holidays we have just the direction, we read there's good way to drive to see something and is good. . . . We traveled 2 to 4 hours per day, so we stop here or there. When we say, "Today is enough," OK, then we look for a place. (Francois)

CONCLUSIONS

A number of theorists have recognized the motivational bases for independent travel. Krippendorf (1987) suggested that travel offers the individual a sense of freedom and self-determination. Anderson (1970) described the "Ulysses factor" as the motive for some tourists to explore the world around them. Gray (1970) recognized wanderlust as a trait of some individuals, which causes them to seek out exciting new places and new cultures. Plog (1973, 1991) identified the allocentric traveler as someone who is adventure seeking and preferring the exotic. Lee and Crompton (1992) suggested that novelty-seeking tourists prefer the unusual and the adventuresome. This study has demonstrated that these motivations for independent travel are directly reflected in the decision processes of independent travelers.

Compared to most other examples of consumer decision making, vacation decision making is a particularly complex and multifaceted matter, involving a series of decisions on multiple elements of the vacation itinerary. This study has

JOURNAL OF TRAVEL RESEARCH 21

identified and described the decision processes particular to independent travel.

For the travelers studied, an integral element in independent travel was the enjoyment experienced from *not* planning the details of their vacation. Some vacation elements were planned before arrival, but many other vacation elements were only learned about after arrival. The travelers also took advantage of serendipitous opportunities to experience some vacation elements they had neither planned nor actively researched. This is analogous to the three categories of retail purchase that consumers make—planned, unplanned, and impulse purchases (Solomon 2002).

The most influential information sources in the preparation of travel plans were travel guides and brochures. The number of hours of information search conducted correlated significantly with the number of specifically planned vacation elements, degree of planning of a travel route, and the percentage of specifically planned vacation elements that were actioned. Almost all plans to visit specific subdestinations were actioned.

High-search travelers were more likely to be couples, more likely to be in their 30s, more likely to be from non-English-speaking countries, but less likely to be backpackers.

For the travelers studied, alternative activities were relatively substitutable, yet alternative subdestinations were much less substitutable. The choice of subdestinations appears central to the travel decision process.

The temporal sequence of decision making displayed by the independent travelers in this study was as follows: subdestinations → travel route → attractions and activities. Only as travelers approached a subdestination did they seek detailed information on that subdestination and its attractions and activities. The travelers studied appeared hungry for information from many different sources while on vacation.

For these travelers, the independent vacation was like experiencing the "fun of the fairground," a freewheeling experience of going from place to place, relatively unaware of what each subdestination offered, extracting as much as possible from each place (given the constraints of time and expense) and taking advantage of serendipitous opportunities.

It appears that three characteristics distinguish the nature of independent travel:

1. travelers experience an evolving itinerary, rather than a planned itinerary;
2. travelers are willing to take risks in their selection of vacation elements; and
3. travelers possess a desire to experience the unplanned.

These characteristics of independent travel are likely to be displayed when

1. the vacation is a multidestination vacation,
2. forward bookings of accommodation and transportation have not been made,
3. the traveler lacks familiarity with the destination, and
4. levels of risk are perceived to be low or irrelevant.

This research has investigated travelers to an international destination, but this does not necessarily imply that independent travel is restricted to international tourism. Multidestination tourism can occur at a number of levels of abstraction: (1) a tour through several countries, (2) a tour through a single international destination, or (3) domestic tourism. It appears that such multidestination tourism is likely to become independent travel when the above listed conditions exist. A critical element appears to be a *lack of familiarity* with the destination. Otherwise, in the instance of the traveler who is familiar with the destination, the percentage of planned elements is likely to rise (Oppermann 1997). Provided the vacation is of sufficient duration, there may come a point in the chronology of the vacation when even individuals who do the most planning begin to experience unplanned, freewheeling independent travel.

Managerial Implications

Recent years have seen rapid growth in the number of entrepreneurial businesses established to cater to the needs of the rapidly growing independent traveler sector. A number of these businesses have been established in locations far from traditional tourist travel routes. Many small settlements now have entrepreneurs with businesses catering to the needs of the independent traveler. Experience has taught a number of lessons regarding the likely success of such entrepreneurial ventures.

For destination regions that attract substantial numbers of independent travelers, the understanding of independent traveler decision processes is crucial. The results of this research have provided insight into the extent of travel planning by independent travelers, the extent to which such plans are actioned, and the temporal sequence in which vacation elements are chosen. The research has suggested that many independent travelers do not make their choice of attractions and activities until they arrive in a region or on the day that they are driving to that region. This suggests that effective local distribution of the tourism product is very important to smaller, start-up enterprises. In addition to having the product on sale from their business premises, such businesses should consider if other parties would be willing to act as booking agents for them, including information centers, local moteliers and hoteliers in their region, and operators of businesses similar to their own.

If the business is located some distance from the traditional tourist travel routes, the business operator must question how the tourist could reach it more easily. Transport links, road signage, and cooperative promotional activities with other operators in the region should be considered.

The business targeting independent travelers needs to consider at what point the travelers actively research their vacation. Some travelers are "planners." Long before they have left their home, they have actively researched what is on offer in the destination. They may have looked at travel guidebooks, brochures produced by travel wholesalers, and publications from destination marketing organizations. They may have visited Web sites, including general travel Web sites for a destination, or searched the Web for specific attractions and activities, transport, and accommodation options. Entrepreneurial tourism businesses are thus likely to benefit from promotional activities such as the hosting of writers of travel guides, sales calls to travel wholesalers, and paid advertising space in destination guides and airline in-flight magazines.

But the current research has also emphasized the importance of promotional activities at a very local level. Operators of attractions and activities, at least in New Zealand, would be advised to concentrate a good proportion of the

22   AUGUST 2003

marketing budget on localized activities such as brochures and guides for a city or region and distribution of their promotional material widely within their own region.

Implications for Future Research

The conclusions regarding independent travel developed here would benefit from wider testing with vacations in different destinations, both international and domestic. Of particular note is the need to test the conclusions of this study regarding the temporal sequence of decision making among vacation elements. This is especially so, as Woodside and King (2001) found a different sequence of decision making for their visitors to the Big Island of Hawaii. The current study has identified that, for a group of travelers to New Zealand, subdestinations are central to their decision making and that attractions and activities do not play a central role in shaping the vacation itinerary. Yet the sequence of travel decision making may be different in other destinations where "icon" attractions—such as Niagara Falls or the Kilauea volcano—are likely to play a more central role.

As use of the Internet becomes more prevalent, it may be valuable to repeat the research conducted here and examine if use of the Internet leads to an increase in the proportion of vacation elements planned by the independent traveler prior to arrival at the destination.

Future research could be undertaken into the effects of perceived risk in determining the amount of prevacation information search and planning undertaken by the independent traveler. Research could be undertaken into the extent of risk taking in the decisions made by tourists. Research could also be undertaken to see if the novelty-seeking scale developed by Lee and Crompton (1992) might assist in identifying individual consumers with a greater or lesser desire for independent travel.

While many instances of consumer behavior can be described adequately using linear models of decision making, independent vacation decision making cannot be. Research activity should continue into describing these decision processes.

REFERENCES

Anderson, J. R. L. (1970). *The Ulysses Factor.* New York: Harcourt Brace.

Ateljevic, I., and S. Doorne (2001). " 'Nowhere Left to Run': A Study of Value Boundaries and Segmentation within the Backpacker Market of New Zealand." In *Consumer Psychology of Tourism, Hospitality and Leisure*, vol. 2, edited by J. A. Manzanec, G. I. Crouch, J. R. B. Ritchie, and A. G. Woodside. Wallingford, UK: CABI, pp. 169-86.

Bonoma, T. V. (1985). "Case Research in Marketing: Opportunities, Problems, and a Process." *Journal of Marketing Research*, 22 (May): 199-208.

Campbell, D. T. (1975). " 'Degrees of Freedom' and the Case Study." *Comparative Political Studies*, 8 (2): 178-93.

Chesshyre, T. (2002). "Independent Spirit? This Is for You." *The Times*, February 9, 4.

Cohen, E. (1972). "Towards a Sociology of International Tourism." *Social Research*, 39: 164-82.

Coventry, N. (1996). "Focus on F.I.T." *Inside Tourism*, 98: 1.

Crotts, J. C., and L. J. Reid (1993). "Segmenting the Visitor Market by the Timing of Their Activity Decisions." *Visions in Leisure and Business*, 12 (3): 4-7.

Decrop, A. (1999). "Qualitative Research Methods for the Study of Tourist Behaviour." In *Consumer Behavior in Travel and Tourism*, edited by A. Pizam and Y. Mansfeld. Binghamton, NY: Haworth.

Dellaert, B. G. C., D. F. Ettema, and C. Lindh (1998). "Multi-Faceted Tourist Travel Decisions: A Constraint-Based Conceptual Framework to Describe Tourists' Sequential Choices of Travel Components." *Tourism Management*, 19 (4): 313-20.

Eisenhardt, K. M. (1989). "Building Theories from Case Study Research." *Academy of Management Review*, 14 (4): 532-50.

Etzel, M. J., and R. G. Wahlers (1985). "The Use of Requested Promotional Material by Pleasure Travellers." *Journal of Travel Research*, 23 (Spring): 2-6.

Fesenmaier, D. R., C. A. Vogt, and W. P. Stewart (1993). "Investigating the Influence of Welcome Centre Information on Travel Behaviour." *Journal of Travel Research*, 31 (3): 47-52.

Fodness, D., and B. Murray (1997). "Tourist Information Search." *Annals of Tourism Research*, 24 (3): 503-23.

——— (1998). "A Typology of Tourist Information Search Strategies." *Journal of Travel Research*, 37 (November): 108-19.

——— (1999). "A Model of Tourist Information Search Behaviour." *Journal of Travel Research*, 37 (February): 220-30.

Gitelson, R., and J. L. Crompton (1983). "The Planning Horizons and Sources of Information Used by Pleasure Vacationers." *Journal of Travel Research*, 21 (Winter): 2-7.

Gray, H. P. (1970). *International Travel—International Trade.* London: Heath Lexington.

Griffith, D. A., and P. J. Albanese (1996). "An Examination of Plog's Psychographic Travel Model within a Student Population." *Journal of Travel Research*, 34 (June): 47-51.

Hsieh, S., J. T. O'Leary, and A. M. Morrison (1994). "A Comparison of Package and Non-Package Travelers from the United Kingdom." *Journal of International Consumer Marketing*, 6 (3-4): 79-100.

Hsieh, S., J. T. O'Leary, A. M. Morrison, and P. H. S. Chang (1993). "Modelling the Travel Mode Choice of Australian Outbound Travellers." *Journal of Tourism Studies*, 4 (1): 51-61.

Hyde, K. F. (2000). "Recognising Deductive Processes in Qualitative Research." *Qualitative Market Research: An International Journal*, 3 (2): 82-89.

Jeng, J. (1997). "Facets of the Complex Trip Decision Making Process." In *28th Travel and Tourism Research Association Annual Conference Proceedings.* Norfolk, VA: Travel and Tourism Research Association.

Keng, K. A., and J. L. L. Cheng (1999). "Determining Tourist Role Typologies: An Exploratory Study of Singapore Vacationers." *Journal of Travel Research*, 37 (May): 382-90.

Krippendorf, J. (1987). *The Holiday Makers: Understanding the Impact of Leisure and Travel.* Oxford, UK: Heinemann Professional.

Lee, T., and J. L. Crompton (1992). "Measuring Novelty Seeking in Tourism." *Annals of Tourism Research*, 19: 732-51.

Leu, C., J. L. Crompton, and D. R. Fesenmaier (1993). "Conceptualization of Multi-Destination Pleasure Trips." *Annals of Tourism Research*, 20: 289-301.

Lincoln, Y. S., and E. G. Guba (1986). *Naturalistic Inquiry.* Newbury Park, CA: Sage.

Loker-Murphy, L., and P. L. Pearce (1995). "Young Budget Travellers: Backpackers in Australia." *Annals of Tourism Research*, 22 (4): 819-43.

Madrigal, R. (1995). "Personal Values, Traveler Personality Type, and Leisure Travel Style." *Journal of Leisure Research*, 27 (2): 125-42.

Mayo, E. J., and L. P. Jarvis (1981). *The Psychology of Leisure Travel.* Boston: CBI.

McDonough, M. H., and G. A. Ackert (1986). *Information and Travel Decisionmaking: Tourism Information Series No. 8.* East Lansing: Michigan State University, Corporate Extension Services.

Morrison, A. M., S. Hsieh, and J. T. O'Leary (1993). "Travel Arrangement Classifications for European International Travellers." In *Spoilt for Choice: Decision Making Processes and Preference Changes of Tourists: Proceedings of the Institute of Tourism and Service Economics International Conference, November, University of Innsbruck*, edited by R. V. Gasser and K. Weiermair. Thaur, Germany: Kulturvel, pp. 221-35.

Nolan, S. D. (1976). "Tourists' Use and Evaluation of Travel Information Sources: Summary and Conclusions." *Journal of Travel Research*, 14 (Winter): 6-8.

Oppermann, M. (1992). "Travel Dispersal Index." *Journal of Tourism Studies*, 3 (1): 44-49.

——— (1994). "Length of Stay and Spatial Distribution." *Annals of Tourism Research*, 21 (4): 834-36.

——— (1997). "First-Time and Repeat Visitors to New Zealand." *Tourism Management*, 18 (3): 177-81.

Parr, D. (1989). "Free Independent Travellers." Unpublished master of applied science thesis, Lincoln College, University of Canterbury, New Zealand.

Patton, M. Q. (1991). *Qualitative Evaluation and Research Methods.* 2d ed. Newbury Park, CA: Sage.

Plog, S. C. (1973). "Why Destination Areas Rise and Fall in Popularity." *Cornell Hotel and Restaurant Administration Quarterly*, November, 13-16.

——— (1991). *Leisure Travel: Making It a Growth Market . . . Again!* New York: John Wiley.

Poon, A. (1993). *Tourism, Technology and Competitive Strategies.* Wallingford, UK: CAB International.

Pryor, C. (2001). "Japanese Pack for a Longer Stay." *The Australian*, August 14, 5.

Quest, M. (1990). *Howarth Book of Tourism*. London: Macmillan.

Riley, P. J. (1988). "Road Culture of International Long-Term Budget Travelers." *Annals of Tourism Research*, 15: 313-28.

Riley, R. W., and L. L. Love (2000). "The State of Qualitative Tourism Research." *Annals of Tourism Research*, 27 (1): 164-87.

Ritchie, B. W. (1998). "Bicycle Tourism in the South Island of New Zealand: Planning and Management Issues." *Tourism Management*, 19 (6): 567-82.

Schul, P., and J. L. Crompton (1983). "Search Behaviour of International Vacationers: Travel-Specific Lifestyle and Sociodemographic Variables." *Journal of Travel Research*, Fall, 24-30.

Scutte, C. (1997). "ASTA Panelists Offer Pointers on Booking Independent Travel." *Travel Weekly*, 56: 24.

Sheldon, P. J., and J. Mak (1987). "The Demand for Package Tours: A Mode Choice Model." *Journal of Travel Research*, Winter, 13-17.

Smith, S. L. J. (1990). "A Test of Plog's Allocentrism/Psychocentrism Model: Evidence from Seven Nations." *Journal of Travel Research*, 28 (Spring): 40-43.

Snepenger, D. J. (1987). "Segmenting the Vacation Market by Novelty-Seeking Role." *Journal of Travel Research*, 26 (Fall): 8-14.

Solomon, M. R. (2002). *Consumer Behavior: Buying, Having, and Being*. 5th ed. Upper Saddle River, NJ: Prentice Hall.

Stake, R. E. (1994). "Case Studies." In *Handbook of Qualitative Research*, edited by N. K. Denzin and Y. S. Lincoln. Thousand Oaks, CA: Sage.

Stewart, S. I., and C. A. Vogt (1997). "Multi-Destination Trip Patterns." *Annals of Tourism Research*, 24 (2): 458-61.

Sung, H. Y., A. M. Morrison, and J. T. O'Leary (2000). "Segmenting the Adventure Travel Market by Activities: From the North American Industry Providers' Perspective." *Journal of Travel and Tourism Marketing*, 9 (4): 1-20.

Taplin, J. H. E., and C. McGinley (2000). "A Linear Program to Model Daily Car Touring Choices." *Annals of Tourism Research*, 27 (2): 451-67.

Tideswell, C., and B. Faulkner (1999). "Multidestination Travel Patterns of International Visitors to Queensland." *Journal of Travel Research*, 37 (May): 364-74.

Tourism New Zealand (2002). *New Zealand International Visitor Survey: Results for the 12 Months to June 2002*. Wellington: Tourism New Zealand.

Tsang, G. (1993). "Visitor Information Network Study." Unpublished master of commerce thesis, University of Otago, Dunedin, New Zealand.

Walle, A. H. (1997). "Quantitative versus Qualitative Tourism Research." *Annals of Tourism Research*, 24 (3): 524-36.

Wilson, E. J., and D. T. Wilson (1998). " 'Degrees of Freedom' in Case Research of Behavioral Theories of Group Buying." *Advances in Consumer Research*, 15: 587-94.

Woodside, A. G., and R. I. King (2001). "An Updated Model of Travel and Tourism Purchase-Consumption Systems." *Journal of Travel and Tourism Marketing*, 10 (1): 3-27.

Woodside, A. G., and R. MacDonald (1993). "General System Framework of Customer Choice Processes of Tourism Services." In *Spoilt for Choice: Decision Making Processes and Preference Changes of Tourists: Proceedings of the Institute of Tourism and Service Economics International Conference, November, University of Innsbruck*, edited by R. V. Gasser and K. Weiermair. Thaur, Germany: Kulturverl, pp. 30-59.

Woodside, A. G., and D. Sherrell (1977). "Traveller Evoked, Inept, and Inert Sets of Vacation Destinations." *Journal of Travel Research*, 16 (1): 14-18.

World Tourism Organisation (1993). *Tourism to the Year 2000: Qualitative Aspects Affecting Global Growth*. Madrid, Spain: World Tourism Organisation.

Yin, R. K. (1994). *Case Study Research: Design and Methods*. 2d ed. Thousand Oaks, CA: Sage.

[13]

ELSEVIER

Available online at www.sciencedirect.com

SCIENCE @ DIRECT•

Tourism Management 26 (2005) 549–560

TOURISM MANAGEMENT

www.elsevier.com/locate/tourman

The relationship between brand equity and firms' performance in luxury hotels and chain restaurants ☆

Hong-bumm Kim[a,1], Woo Gon Kim[b,*]

[a] College of Hospitality & Tourism, Sejong University, Kwang-jin Gu, Gun-ja Dong 98, Seoul 143-747, Republic of Korea
[b] School of Hotel and Restaurant Administration, Oklahoma State University, 210 HESW, Stillwater, OK 74078-6173, USA

Received 27 February 2004; accepted 4 March 2004

Abstract

There is a growing emphasis on building and managing brand equity as the primary drivers of a hospitality firm's success. Success in brand management results from understanding brand equity correctly and managing them to produce solid financial performance. This study examines the underlying dimensions of brand equity and how they affect firms' performance in the hospitality industry—in particular, luxury hotels and chain restaurants. The results of this empirical study indicate that brand loyalty, perceived quality, and brand image are important components of customer-based brand equity. A positive relationship was found to exist between the components of customer-based brand equity and the firms' performance in luxury hotels and chain restaurants. A somewhat different scenario was delineated from the relationship between the components of customer-based brand equity and firms' performance in luxury hotels and chain restaurants.
© 2004 Elsevier Ltd. All rights reserved.

Keywords: Customer-based brand equity; Firms' performance; Chain restaurants; Luxury hotels; Brand awareness

1. Introduction

Brands have been increasingly considered as primary capital for many businesses. Financial professionals have developed the notion that a brand has an equity that may exceed its conventional asset value. Indeed, the cost of introducing a new brand to its market has been approximated at $100 million with a 50 percent probability of failure (Ourusoff, 1993; Crawford, 1993). Long-standing brand power, instead of management strategies for short-term performance, has been re-evaluated by many American companies. In addition, some firms seeking growth opportunities have preferred to acquire existing brands, thus establishing brand

management as a formal component of corporate strategy. For example, instead of developing a new luxury hotel brand, Marriott International Inc. decided to acquire an existing luxury hotel chain, the Ritz-Carlton, in 1995. Thus, the concept and measurement of brand equity has interested academicians and practitioners for more than a decade, primarily due to the importance in today's marketplace of building, maintaining and using brands to obtain a definite competitive advantage.

A brand symbolizes the essence of the customers' perceptions of the hospitality organizations. The term "brand" has multiple connotations. At one end of the spectrum, brand constitutes a name, a logo, a symbol, and identity, or a trademark. At the other end, brand embraces all tangible and intangible attributes that the business stands for (Prasad & Dev, 2000).

Although numerous local or global brands of different product categories have been employed to measure the brand equity, literature on brand equity within the hospitality industry has not been fully investigated. Only recently, Prasad and Dev (2000) demonstrated that brands would be a quick way for hotel chains to identify and differentiate themselves in

☆ This work was supported by Korea Research Foundation Grant (KRF-2001-041-C00424).

*Corresponding author. School of Hotel and Restaurant Administration, Oklahoma State University, 210 HESW, Stillwater, OK 74078-6173, USA.

E-mail addresses: kimhb@sejong.ac.kr (H.-b. Kim), kwoo@okstate.edu (W.G. Kim).

[1] College of Hospitality & Tourism, Sejong University, Kwang-jin Gu, Gun-ja Dong 98, Seoul 143-747, Republic of Korea. Tel.: +822-3408-3172; fax: +822-3408-3312.

0261-5177/$ - see front matter © 2004 Elsevier Ltd. All rights reserved.
doi:10.1016/j.tourman.2004.03.010

550   H.-b. Kim, W.G. Kim / Tourism Management 26 (2005) 549–560

the minds of the customers. They showed a method for converting customers' awareness of a brand and their view of a brand's performance into a brand equity index. The computation of brand equity allows top managers of hospitality companies to compare the strength of brands in a competitive set, to track a hotel brand's equity over time, and to formulate remedial marketing strategies (Prasad & Dev, 2000).

A hospitality company can use an endorsed brand extension strategy to extend the power of well-accepted brand identity to a number of diverse concepts differentiated by market segment (Jiang, Dev, & Rao, 2002). The endorsed brand strategy puts a well-established name on a cluster of products or services. By endorsing a range of products, the lead brand can lend its good name and image to the entire brand family (Muller, 1998). In service marketing, the company brand is the primary brand, whereas in packaged goods marketing the product brand is referred to as the primary brand (Low & Lamb Jr., 2000). In the hospitality industry, customers often base their purchase decisions on their perceptions of a company's brand (e.g., Marriott, Hilton, Hyatt, McDonald's, Burger King, Wendy's, Chili's, Applebee's, and TGI Friday's). That is, customers develop company brand associations rather than the brand association of product items.

A strong brand increases the consumer's attitude strength toward the product associated with the brand. Attitude strength is built by experience with a product. The consumer's awareness and associations lead to perceived quality, inferred attributes, and eventually, brand loyalty (Keller, 1993). This perspective is labeled as customer-based brand equity (Shocker, Srivastava, & Ruekert, 1994). The advantage of conceptualizing brand equity from this perspective is that it enables marketing managers to consider how their marketing programs improve the value of their brands in the minds of consumers (Keller, 1993). As a result, effective marketing programs on branding foster greater confidence of consumers. This confidence induces consumers' loyalty and their willingness to pay a premium price for the brand.

A strong brand provides a series of benefits to a service firm, such as greater customer loyalty and higher resiliency to endure crisis situations, higher profit margins, more favorable customer response to price change, and licensing and brand extension opportunities (Keller, 2001). For example, adding the "by Marriott" name tag on distinctive brand names aids the Marriott corporation in maintaining the differentiation, lowers operating risk, limits new-product introduction costs, and results in an improvement in corporate performance (Muller, 1998).

There have also been some assertions concerning the positive correlation between brand equity and a firm's performance (Park & Srinivasan, 1994; Aaker, 1996).

The rationale of the hotel industry, for example, is quite straightforward—hotels with strong brand equity are expected to command higher occupancy and average room rates, due to high customer satisfaction and a positive price–value relationship. It will result in higher operational performance, RevPAR[2] (Prasad & Dev, 2000). Little empirical research, however, actually demonstrated the correlation between brand equity and corporate performance in hospitality brands.

The purpose of this study is to examine the possible relationship between customer-based brand equity and firms' performance in the hospitality industry through an empirical study. Logical reasoning behind the study hypothesizes that the more customers are satisfied, the more they prefer the brand and the more they return. This should translate into higher sales revenue. The study's results could offer a diagnostic decision-making tool to help top hotel managers maximize the value of their brands.

2. Literature review

2.1. Different perspectives of brand equity

The issue of brand equity has emerged as one of the most crucial topics for marketing management in the 1990s (Leuthesser, 1988; Keller, 1993; Cobb-Walgren, Ruble, & Donthu, 1995; Lassar, Mittal, & Sharma, 1995; Aaker, 1996; Dyson, Farr, & Hollis, 1996). Brand equity has been considered in many contexts: the added value endowed by the brand name (Farquhar, 1989); brand loyalty, brand awareness, perceived quality, brand associations, and other proprietary brand assets (Aaker, 1991); differential effect of brand knowledge on consumer response to the marketing of the brand (Keller, 1993); incremental utility (Simon & Sullivan, 1993); total utility (Swait, Erdem, Louviere, & Dubelaar, 1993); the difference between overall brand preference and multi-attributed preference based on objectively measured attribute levels (Park & Srinivasan, 1994); and overall quality and choice intention (Agarwal & Rao, 1996). These numerous definitions imply that brand equity is the incremental value of a product due to the brand name (Srivastava & Shocker, 1991).

There have been three different perspectives for considering brand equity: the customer-based perspective, the financial perspective, and the combined perspective. The customer-based brand equity subsumes two multi-dimensional concepts of brand strength and brand value (Srivastava & Shocker, 1991). Here, brand strength is based on perceptions and behaviors of customers that allow the brand to enjoy sustainable and differentiated competitive advantages. Brand value

---
[2] Revenue Per Available Rooms.

is the financial outcome of the management's ability to leverage brand strength via strategic actions to provide superior current and future profits. Brand equity is defined as "a set of brand assets and liabilities linked to a brand, its name and symbol that add to or subtract from the value provided by a product or service to a firm and/or to that firm's consumers (Aaker, 1991)". Blackston (1995), on the other hand, has referred to brand equity as brand value and brand meaning, where brand meaning implies brand saliency, brand associations, and brand personality and where brand value is the outcome of managing the brand meaning. Keller (1993) has also defined brand equity as the differential effect of brand knowledge on consumer response to the marketing of the brand. Within the marketing literature, operationalizations of customer-based brand equity usually fall into two groups (Cobb-Walgren et al., 1995; Yoo & Donthu, 2001): consumer perception (brand awareness, brand associations, perceived quality) and consumer behavior (brand loyalty, willingness to pay a high price). Brand equity has been operationalized by Lassar et al. (1995) as an enhancement of the perceived utility and desirability that a brand name confers on a product. According to them, customer-based brand equity indicates only perceptual dimensions, excluding behavioral or attitudinal dimensions, such as loyalty or usage intention, which differs from Aaker's (1991) incorporated definition. The four dimensions of brand equity—brand loyalty, brand awareness, perceived quality, and brand image—suggested by Aaker (1991, 1996) have been broadly accepted and employed by many researchers (Keller, 1993; Motameni & Shahrokhi, 1998; Low & Lamb Jr., 2000; Prasad & Dev, 2000; Yoo & Donthu, 2001).

Financial perspective is based on the incremental discounted future cash flows that would result from a branded product's revenue over the revenue of an unbranded product (Simon & Sullivan, 1993). The asset representing the brand is included in the firm's assets on the balance sheet. The financial perspectives also adopt the financial market value-based technique to estimate a firm's brand equity (Simon & Sullivan, 1993). One of the most publicized financial methods is used by Financial World in its annual listing of worldwide brand valuation (Ourusoff, 1993). Financial World's formula calculates net brand-related profits and assigns a multiple based on brand strength. Obviously, the stronger the brand, the higher the multiple applied to earnings. Brand strength is defined as a combination of leadership, stability, trading environment, internationality, ongoing direction, communication support, and legal protection. Based on the financial market value of the company, their estimation technique extracts the value of brand equity from the value of a firm's other assets. The methodology separates the value of a firm's securities into tangible and intangible assets and then carves brand

equity out from the other intangible assets. The realization that the full value of brand-owning companies was neither explicitly shown in the accounts nor always reflected in stock market value led to a reappraisal of the importance of intangible assets in general, and brands in particular. Leading brand-owning companies have used the brand finance methodology. The approach is based on a discounted cash flow (DCF) analysis of forecasted, incremental cash flows earned as a result of owning a brand–the brand's contribution to the business.

Lastly, comprehensive perspectives incorporate both customer-based brand equity and financial brand equity. This approach has appeared to make up for the insufficiencies that may exist when only one of the two understandings is emphasized. Dyson et al. (1996), for instance, described a survey research system designed to place a financially related value on the consumer-based equity of brand images and associations. Motameni and Shahrokhi (1998) proposed global brand equity valuations, which combine brand equity from the marketing perspective and brand equity from the financial perspective.

2.2. Brand equity research in the hospitality industry

Relatively limited empirical evidence can be found with respect to the consumer-based equity of service brands (Smith, 1991) due to the fact that most studies have been concerned with the goods or have applied a non-altered framework to suggest brand equity value. Muller and Woods (1994), for example, emphasized brand management rather than product management in the restaurant industry, outlining a clear concept of the restaurant, dependability of brand name, and developing brand image. Muller (1998) suggested three key issues that a service brand should focus on in order to build equity and acceptance in the marketplace: quality products and services, execution of service delivery, and establishing a symbolic and evocative image. He insisted that, through the combination of these three elements in restaurant-brand development, the opportunity would come for charging price premium and enhancing customer loyalty. Murphy (1990) identified generic brand strategies such as simple, monolithic, and endorsed in the restaurant industry.

A recent study by Prasad and Dev (2000) is a good example of understanding and estimating brand equity in the lodging industry. They developed a customer-centric index of hotel brand equity considering customers as the source of all cash flow and resulting profits. Here, the customer-centric brand equity index is a measure for converting customers' awareness of a brand and their view of a brand's performance into a numerical index. Another study by Cobb-Walgren et al. (1995) focused on a consumer-based, perceptual measure of brand equity. The study employed the perceptual components of Aaker's (1991) definition of brand equity, as advocated by Keller (1993)—brand awareness, brand associations and perceived quality. Two sets of brand, from service category (hotels) and from product category (household cleansers), were employed to examine the effect of brand equity on consumer preferences and purchase intentions.

Table 1 summarizes previous related research on brand equity from a customer-based, financial, and comprehensive perspective.

3. Method

3.1. Survey framework and hypothesis

Two separate surveys were conducted to collect data for luxury hotels and chain restaurants. The hotel data were collected from Korean travelers for departure. In order to maintain the consistency of the data gathering process, graduate students majoring in hospitality and tourism management were trained. Trained graduate students conducted intercept surveys at Kimpo airport, South Korea. The main reason of selecting an airport for a survey site was that most luxury hotels were reluctant to do surveys for customers inside their hotels. Travelers, immediately after entering the gate of the departure lounge of the airport, were interviewed at various times of the day on three weekdays and the weekends over a three-week period in 2002. Every effort was made to get a representative sample. Respondents were approached and informed about the purpose of the study in advance of being given the questionnaire. At the beginning of the questionnaire, one screening question was asked to identify if respondents had stayed at a luxury hotel in the last two years. Those who met this criterion were given a copy of the self-administered questionnaire. Instructions included in the cover letter stipulated that the questionnaire be completed and returned directly to the students who had administered the survey. A total of 840 Korean travelers were approached, of which 602 (71.7%) responded and completed the questionnaires. Of these, 89 were excluded, since they had not been fully completed. Thus, a total of 513 questionnaires were used for further analysis. A method of increasing the response rate was the use of monetary incentives. The high response rate of 71.7% was partly attributed to the US$3 gift certificates offered in return for participation. Previous studies showed the effectiveness of using various monetary incentives in improving mail survey response rates (Brennan, Hoek, & Astridge, 1991; Brennan, 1992).

In order to measure brand equity and performance of chain restaurant firms, the respondents were selected from the city of Seoul, because most international fast food and chain restaurants are located in Seoul. The data were collected through a self-administered questionnaire using an intercept approach in a large shopping mall from June 15, 2002 to June 28, 2002. The subjects were selected from the stream of shoppers entering the mall between the hours of 1 p.m. and 6 p.m., Monday, Wednesday, and Saturday at a single location. Shoppers were asked to participate in a study conducted as part of a university project. Subjects were shoppers selected via a non-probability sampling technique. Those who agreed to participate were given a self-administered questionnaire, which they were instructed to complete and return directly to survey administrators. The surveyed sample represents a diverse group of 950 adults. A total of 409 questionnaires were returned by the shoppers, of which 394 were usable and represented a response rate of 41.5%.

The basic conceptual framework of this study is to examine the relationship between customer-based brand equity and a firm's performance in the hotel and chain restaurant industry. Evidence for this conjecture can be found in the research of Prasad and Dev (2000) who have proposed the straightforward rationale that hotels with strong brand equity, based on customers' positive evaluations of brand attributes, will command higher occupancy percentage and daily room rates, resulting in higher Revenue Per Available Room (RevPAR). Here, four dimensions of brand equity, namely brand loyalty, brand awareness, perceived brand quality, and brand image, are assumed to construct the context of brand equity.

The primary hypothesis of this study was formulated as follows:

Hypothesis. Customer-based brand equity and these four components in the hospitality industry will have a significant relationship with the performance of the firms of the corresponding brands.

In this study, we extend the aforementioned hypothesis to examine how the relationship between brand equity and firms' performance varies in the different categories of the hospitality industry—hotel and chain restaurants. The reason for selecting these two categories mainly stems from the fact that lodging and restaurants are representative sectors reflecting the characteristics of the hospitality industry properly. Additionally, in these sectors several different brands compete heavily with each other in order to have a competitive advantage by constructing definite brand equity. For the lodging category, 12 brands of luxury hotels located in Seoul, Korea were chosen to receive survey responses. For the restaurants, 13 brands of fast food and chain restaurants in Korea were selected to provide the database of responses. The detailed brands

Managing Tourism Firms

H.-b. Kim, W.G. Kim / Tourism Management 26 (2005) 549–560

Table 1
Previous research on brand equity

Researchers	Concept	Measurement
Customer-based perspectives		
Aaker (1991, 1996)	Brand awareness Brand loyalty Perceived quality Brand associations	Perceptual and behavioral conceptualization
Srivastava and Shocker (1991)	Brand strength	Brand strength (customers' perception and behavior) + fit = brand value (financial outcome)
Keller (1993, 2001)	Brand knowledge	Brand knowledge = brand awareness + brand image
Blackston (1995)	Brand meaning	Brand relationships model: objective brand (personality characteristics, brand image) + subjective brand (brand attitude)
Kamakura and Russell (1993)	Brand value	Brand value = tangible value + intangible Value: Segmentwise logit model on single-source scanner panel data
Swait et al. (1993)	Total utility	Equalization price measuring
Park and Srinivasan (1994)	Difference between overall preference and preference on the basis of objectively measured attribute levels	Brand equity = attribute based + non-attribute based
Francois and MacLachlan (1995)	Brand strength	Intrinsic brand strength Extrinsic brand strength
Lassar et al. (1995)	Performance Social image Commitment Value Trustworthiness	Evaluate only perceptual dimensions Discover a halo across dimensions of brand equity
Agarwal and Rao (1996)	Overall quality Choice intention	Brand perception/brand preference/brand choice paradigm
Yoo and Donthu (2001)	Brand loyalty Perceived quality Brand awareness/associations	Validating Aaker's conceptualization
Cobb-Walgren et al. (1995)	Brand awareness Perceived quality Brand associations	Relationship with brand preference and usage intentions (Aaker, 1991)
Prasad and Dev (2000)	Brand performance Brand awareness	Hotel brand equity index = satisfaction + return intent + value perception + brand preference + brand awareness
Financial perspectives		
Simon and Sullivan (1993)	Incremental cash flows which accrue to branded products	Brand equity = intangible assets−(nonbrand factors + anticompetitive industry structure)
Comprehensive perspectives		
Farquhar (1989)	Added value with which a given brand endows a product	Respective evaluation on firm's, trade's, and consumer's perspective
Dyson et al. (1996)	Brand loyalty Brand attitude	Consumer value model: proportion of expenditure × weight of consumption
Motameni and Shahrokhi (1998)	Global Brand Equity (GBE)	Brand strength (customer, competitive, global potency) × brand net earnings

of the two categories selected are Ritz-Carlton, Inter-continental, Westin Chosun, Marriott, Hyatt, Hilton, Lotte, Radisson Plaza, Ramada Renaissance, Sheraton Walker-hill, Shilla, and Swiss Grand among the luxury hotels, and Burger King, Pizza Hut, Little Ceasars Pizza, Hardee's, Jakob's, KFC, Lotteria, McDonald's, Popeye's, Subway, Sbarro, Ponderosa, and Sizzler among the fast food and chain restaurants.

3.2. Measures

For a better illustration of questionnaire design, the Appendix contains a summary of scale items and the scale reliability for the luxury hotels and chain restaurants. Measures of brand equity consist of the four dimensions of brand loyalty, brand awareness, perceived quality, and brand image. The reasoning for including brand loyalty as a component of consumer-based brand equity comes from the importance of customer satisfaction in developing a brand (Aaker, 1991). If customers are not satisfied with a brand, they will not be loyal to the brand, but search for another. This study employed six measurement items of brand loyalty, with a seven-point Likert scale anchored from 1 (strongly disagree) to 7 (strongly agree); "I regularly visit this hotel (restaurant)", "I intend to visit this hotel (restaurant) again", "I usually use this hotel (restaurant) as the first choice compared to other ones", "I am satisfied with this visit", "I would recommend this hotel (restaurant) to others", and finally "I would not switch to another hotel (restaurant) the next time".

Brand awareness, another component of brand equity, refers to the strength of a brand's presence in the customer's mind (Aaker, 1996). Three scale items were employed to measure brand awareness such as top-of-mind brand, unaided brand recall, and brand recognition (Kapferer, 1994; Francois & MacLachlan, 1995; Yoo & Donthu, 2001). "Write down the name of a luxury hotel (a chain restaurant) located in Seoul that first comes to your mind" is an example of the top-of-mind brand test, while "List three other names of luxury hotels (and chain restaurants) located in Seoul that come to your mind at this moment" constitutes unaided brand recall. To measure brand recognition, the respondents were asked to choose the brand names of which they were aware of from a list of selected luxury hotels (and chain restaurants). Since these items are open-ended or multiple choice questions, the Likert-type scale cannot be applied. Haley and Case (1979) insisted that brand awareness should be considered differently from other attitude scales of the Likert-type, and employed a 5-point scoring of open-ended questions to measure brand awareness, such as "top of mind (4)", "second unaided mention (3)", "other unaided mention (2)", "aided recall (1)", and "never heard of (0)". In this study we employed a 7-point rather than a 5-point

scaling. The respondents' answers were coded as 1 for "unrecognized brand in the aided recall", 2 for "recognized brand in the aided recall", 4–6 for "recalled brand without aid", and 7 for "top-of-mind brand" in order to transfer them to approximate metric scales. Respondents were asked to list three brands instead of two to derive a recalled brand without aid. The three "recalled brand without aid" were coded as 6 for "first recalled brand without aid", 5 for "second recalled without aid", 4 for "third recalled without aid", reflecting their orders. One interval (3) was put between "without aid" and "aided" recall to clearly distinguish the two and to make our scale with a neutral point, as is generally preferred in formulating attitude scales.

The third component of brand equity—perceived quality—was measured by a performance-based approach that focused only on customer perception rather than considering customer expectation as well. That is, our measurement scheme is much similar to that of SERVPERF than the well-known SERQUAL's approach (Lee & Hing, 1995; Parasuraman, Zeithml, & Berry, 1985; Fick & Ritchie, 1991; Bojanic & Rosen, 1993; Bolton & Drew, 1991; Cronin & Taylor, 1992; Saleh & Ryan, 1991). This study employed 10 seven-point Likert scale items for the chain restaurants and 11 items of the same type for the luxury hotels, such as 1 for "strongly disagree" and 7 for "strongly agree".

The final measure—brand image—requires the development of scale items specific to a product category (Dobni & Zinkhan, 1990; Low & Lamb Jr., 2000). For example, Timex watches are associated with functionality, whereas Rolex watches are associated with prestige (Park, Milberg, & Lawson, 1991). According to the pretest framework suggested by Low and Lamb Jr. (2000), this study developed different scale items for each category. For delineating appropriate brand image construct by pretest, 27 respondents of the purposive sample were asked to express any feelings, ideas, or attitudes that they could associate with fast food and chain restaurants. Similarly, another purposive sample of 28 respondents was gathered to derive suitable measures of brand image for luxury hotels. The open-ended responses were tabulated, and the most frequently mentioned responses (14 items for both fast food and chain restaurants and luxury hotels) were selected as the scale items for their respective category. In addition, three other variables such as "long history", "differentiated from other brands", and "familiar to me" were supplemented to both categories (Aaker, 1991; Keller, 1993). All of these items concerning brand image were measured on a seven-point Likert scale with 1 for "strongly disagree" and 7 for "strongly agree". Here, we presume that a high scale point of brand image indicates that the brand not only has a positive image to the customer but also exhibits a greater level of brand image strength in comparison with others.

H.-b. Kim, W.G. Kim / Tourism Management 26 (2005) 549–560 555

There are several possible tools to measure a hospitality firm's performance. Such profitability measures as return on equity (ROE), return on sale (ROS), and return on asset (ROA) are the most popular ratios to measure financial performance for hospitality operators and investors. However, such profitability measure as ROE and ROS are strongly related to the management ability of a firm rather than to the level of direct earnings from customers or buyers. This study used only sales as a firm performance measure in order to examine mainly the direct influence of customers' use without considering any expense or investment scale of the company. Therefore, common financial performance measures such as ROS, ROE, and ROA are not included in this study.

The sales amount used in this study indicates the revenue directly occurred, which concerns the main products, such as room, food & beverage, banquet, and other facilities for luxury hotels. In order to solve problems of comparability caused by different scale of selected hotels, the Revenue Per Available Room (RevPAR) rather than total sales was used. The RevPAR for 12 selected hotels from 1998 to 2001 was calculated by multiplying occupancy percentage and average room rates that were obtained from an existing database of the Korea Hotel Association.

The sales information in the same period in 13 selected international chain fast food and chain restaurants was obtained from the Korean Restaurant Association. This study used sales per unit, because the scales of restaurant companies are not identical. Sales per unit were calculated by dividing total sales amount by the number of units available during the survey period.

4. Results

The resulting respondents of the restaurants' sample consisted of 174 men (44.2%) and 220 women (55.8%), where the average age was 25.3 years old. In case of hotels, the samples included 303 men (59.1%) and 210 women (40.9%), whose average age was 35.4 years old. Factor analysis was first employed to examine the validity of brand equity structure, which consists of four underlying dimensions including brand loyalty, brand awareness, perceived quality, and brand image. Factor analysis with principal components and Varimax rotations produced one factor in both sample categories, which had eigenvalue greater than 1.0 and a factor loading of 0.50 or greater. Only one factor solution in each product category exhibits positive construct validity of the brand equity structure.

The results in Table 2 show that brand equity is a principal factor in each category, where the four dimensions of brand equity are loaded significantly

Table 2
Brand equity structure—Factor analysis[a]

Brand equity	Factor loadings	
	Chain restaurants	Luxury hotels
Brand loyalty	0.774	0.866
Brand awareness	0.545	0.309[b]
Perceived quality	0.741	0.881
Brand image	0.834	0.865
Eigenvalue	2.140	2.370
Variance explained	53.5%	59.3%

[a] Principal component factor analysis was employed in each category with iterations: Varimax rotation in SPSS/PC routine.
[b] Although brand awareness in luxury hotels appeared to have relatively low value of factor loading, it was included in the table for explanatory purpose.

except for brand awareness in hotels. It generally supports the assertion that the four dimensions are valid underlying variables of brand equity. It is of interest to notice that brand image and brand loyalty are loaded highly in the brand equity of chain restaurants, whereas perceived quality, brand loyalty, and brand image are loaded highly in that of hotels.

The results imply that all four dimensions are found to construct brand equity in chain restaurants, where perceived quality is most important and brand awareness is least significant for establishing brand equity in luxury hotels. In this study, the factor scores of brand equity in the two categories were further employed to analyze the relationship between the entire context of brand equity and firms' performance.

Next, regression analyses were employed for both hotels and restaurants in order to examine the relationship between brand equity and firms' performance. We checked the normality of the error term of the variate with a visual examination of the normal probability plots of residuals. Since the plot does not show a substantial or systematic departure, the regression variate was found to meet the normality assumption (Hair, Anderson, Tatham, & Black, 1992). In addition, the null hypothesis that each variable is normally distributed was tested using the Kolmogorov–Smirnov One-sample Test. This conservative procedure tests the goodness-of-fit of the data to a normal distribution with the parameters estimated from the data. The test confirmed that both hotel and restaurant data fit a normal distribution. Here, brand equity was presumed to be a predictor variable and was first considered as one independent variable measured in its entirety, and then as four independent variables of underlying dimensions constructing the brand equity. The Revenue Per Available Room (RevPAR) for luxury chain hotels was used as a dependent variable, while sales per unit for the chain restaurants was entered as a response variable.

Table 3
Impact of brand equity on firms' performance—4 stepwise regression analyses

	Chain restaurants		Luxury hotels	
	Standardized regression coefficients (*t*-values)	Tolerance value	Standardized regression coefficients (*t*-values)	Tolerance value
Dependent variable:				
Firms' performance[a]				
Independent variable:				
Brand equity[b]	0.757 (2.591)[c]		0.789 (4.060)[d]	
R^2	0.573		0.622	
F	6.715		16.482	
Significance level	0.001		0.001	
Brand loyalty	—		0.958 (4.919)[d]	0.387
Brand awareness	0.835 (3.392)[d]	0.542	0.897 (4.588)[d]	0.576
Perceived quality	0.730 (2.498)[c]	0.422	0.476(2.432)[c]	0.603
Brand image	—		—	
R^2	0.697		0.706	
Adjusted R^2	0.573		0.588	
F	10.795		11.506	
Significance level	0.001		0.001	

[a] Sales per restaurant unit in restaurants and RevPAR (Revenue Per Available Rooms) in hotels.
[b] As an input variable of entire brand equity, a factor score coefficient from the factor analysis as depicted in Table 2 was employed to examine its impact on the firms' performance.
[c] Significant at 0.05 level.
[d] Significant at 0.01 level.

The results from stepwise regression analyses in Table 3 show how brand equity itself, or the four underlying dimensions constructing brand equity, affects performance of chain restaurants and luxury hotel firms. When considering brand equity in its entirety as an independent variable, the results show that brand equity has a significant positive relationship with its performance in both fast food and chain restaurants ($R^2 = 0.573$) and in luxury hotels ($R^2 = 0.622$). This result supports our prior assertion that customer-based brand equity can be a critical factor for influencing firms' performance in the hospitality industry. In order to detect the presence of multicollinearity, the tolerance value is calculated and presented in Table 3. Tolerance is the amount of variability of the selected independent variable not explained by the other independent variables. Thus, very small tolerance values denote high collinearity. A common cutoff threshold is a tolerance value of 0.10. (Hair et al., 1992). Since all significant variables in Table 3 have much higher tolerance values than 0.10, no significant collinearity is found.

Other results from stepwise regression analyses show that among the four underlying dimensions, brand awareness and perceived quality appear to be significant independent variables that influence the performance of fast food and chain restaurant firms. It is surprising that brand loyalty and brand image, which are loaded highly to construct brand equity in fast food and chain restaurants, do not appear to support a positive relationship with firms' performance. One plausible conclusion is that brand awareness may be an important criterion for customers making low-involvement purchasing decisions, thus explaining why brand awareness appears to be a significant variable to fast food and chain restaurants' performance. That is, when we consider the relationship between brand equity and performance in fast food and chain restaurants, brand awareness and perceived quality seem to dominate the other two underlying dimensions of the brand equity, even though all four underlying dimensions are found to be important elements constructing brand equity from factor analysis.

In case of luxury hotels, however, the result of stepwise regression analysis shows that brand loyalty, brand awareness, and perceived quality have a significant positive effect on firms' performance. It is noteworthy that brand awareness appears as a significant variable affecting firms' performance, even though it is not loaded highly in the context of brand equity. The result implies brand awareness by itself may be not sufficient but somewhat spurious to establish the context of brand equity, particularly in luxury hotels. It shows, however, a hotel company must design its marketing mix to get its brand into the prospect's awareness set, which is finally transferred to the choice set. This result provides fairly convincing evidence of the effect that

H.-b. Kim, W.G. Kim / Tourism Management 26 (2005) 549–560   557

customer-based brand equity has on firms' performance in the hospitality industry, where brand loyalty, brand awareness, and perceived quality from the customers' perspective affect firms' performance in the luxury hotel business.

In summary, overall brand equity, delineated from four underlying dimensions, has shown a significant positive effect on performance in both chain restaurants and luxury hotels. The nature of the relationship between each underlying dimension of the brand equity and firms' performance, however, differs, while brand awareness and perceived quality are significant for performance in chain restaurants, and brand loyalty, brand awareness, and perceived quality are found to have significantly positive effects on performance in luxury hotels. The finding demonstrates that brand awareness, among all the other elements, is the most important dimension of hospitality brand equity in having a positive effect on firms' performance, even though it is rather insignificant or of relatively low importance in constructing brand equity itself.

5. Summary and conclusions

Previous research shows that brand equity can be expressed numerically from a financial perspective and also from the customers' perception and attitude. This study focused on identifying the underlying dimensions of customer-based brand equity and their relationship with firms' performance in the hospitality industry sectors of chain restaurants and luxury hotels, where customer-based brand equity is assumed to be constituted by brand awareness, brand loyalty, perceived quality, and brand image.

The findings generally confirm our original hypothesis that brand equity is best understood as a composite context represented by four underlying dimensions, and has a positive effect on its firms' performance. Although brand awareness was not loaded highly as a customer-based brand equity factor for both chain restaurants and luxury hotels, it was found to have a significantly positive relationship with firms' performance in both categories. In the case of luxury hotels, brand loyalty, brand awareness, and perceived quality significantly affected the corporate performance, as compared with chain restaurants where brand awareness and perceived quality were related with corporate performance. This shows that the relationship between brand equity and corporate performance is not the same in different sectors of the hospitality industry.

The results imply that hospitality firms like chain restaurants or luxury hotels should significantly consider brand loyalty, perceived quality, and brand image when attempting to establish definite brand equity from the customers' viewpoint. Additionally, increasing brand awareness through various promotional and communication strategies may be integral for increasing sales revenue. Heavy and successive promotional activities through the mass media seem to vastly prevail in the competitive markets of hospitality firms. But advanced methods of building brands, which do not rely on mass media, have been developed recently. These changes in the communication environment have led to more creative ways to approach customers. Besides TV commercials or magazine advertising, support activities, and charity involvement in social, cultural, sports, or other kinds of public events can improve a firm's brand awareness.

One of the most important conclusions that may be drawn from this study lies in the fact that perceived quality of a specific brand is found to significantly affect firms' performance in the hotel and restaurant business. This may stem from the rationale that luxury hotels and chain restaurants require better service delivery systems to customers. The results imply that brand awareness alone is not enough to generate satisfactory firms' performance and perceived quality should be managed carefully to produce good financial results.

It is noteworthy that brand loyalty had a significantly positive effect on performance of only luxury hotel firms. It seems that brand loyalty in fast food and chain restaurants may not be a detrimental factor affecting a firm's performance in comparison to other factors, such as brand awareness and perceived quality. The fact that brand loyalty is not significant in chain restaurants seems logical since there may be a definite value in variety when eating out; however, there may be no necessary value in variety when staying in luxury hotels. Brand loyalty will be considered as a repeat purchase behavior under conditions of strong sensitivity. A luxury hotel guest who repeatedly tends to stay at the same brand hotel and who attaches great importance to hotel brands in his or her choice is said to be brand loyal (Odin, Odin, & Valette-Florence, 2001). Loyal customers are less likely to switch to a competitor solely because of price, and loyal customers also make more frequent purchases than comparable non-loyal customers (Bowen & Shoemaker, 1998). These results show that brand loyalty, a component of brand equity that determines whether the customer is committed to the brand, can make a significant contribution in improving the operational performance of hotel companies. It is very rare that a single purchase by each customer is sufficient for the attainment of long-term financial profitability, so hotel marketers should remember the importance of repeat purchases and customer satisfaction. Brand-loyal customers rarely buy as a simple reaction to the stimulus of promotion. They may be satisfied, intend to visit again, or recommend to others through customers' learning, which is built up from

558   H.-b. Kim, W.G. Kim / Tourism Management 26 (2005) 549–560

experience of various services, from word-of-mouth reports from other customers, and from recollections of advertising and promotions. Most of the time, promotion can reinforce the existing behavior of existing customers. Most repeat purchases, however, are made on the basis of long-term views and attitudes. This type of buying is what most hotel companies are aiming at; it is, in essence, brand loyalty. The result of the study implies that to build a brand loyalty and eventually good performance, a hotel company has to get into the black box of dealing with customer attitudes, such that they are, first of all, satisfied, have intentions to visit the hotel again, and recommend it as a first-choice hotel to others.

In conclusion, the results of this study imply that strong brand equity can cause a significant increase in profitability and a lack of brand equity in hospitality firms can damage potential cash flow. That is, if a marketer in hospitality firms does not make efforts to improve customer-based brand equity, then the marketer should expect declining income over time.

As with any study, this one contains a number of limitations that should be surmounted in future research. First, this study did not investigate every possible extraneous effect that could affect or influence a firm's performance besides brand equity. These may include, for instance, sales promotions, management strategies, and innovative activities. Hopefully, future studies will incorporate these variables into their research scope. Second, this study was constrained to respondents from a single country, and this may well limit generalizations that may be made to the hospitality industry in other countries. A third limitation is the sampling framework. The quality of the data used in this research may be vulnerable due to the non-probability sampling method for hotels and restaurants. It may be that those respondents included in this study did not truly represent populations of customers in luxury hotels and chain restaurants. The results of this study will be more representative if the research is conducted through random sampling. More systematic and probability sampling would bring higher reliability and validity to the data and findings.

Future research may contrive a more sophisticated measure of financial performance, such as Return on Sale (ROA), Return on Equity (ROE), and Return on Asset (ROA). The financial ratios may represent a hospitality firm's performance better than operational performance, such as sales and RevPAR in this study. Finally, future research may develop a more hybrid and composite scale for approximating customer-based brand equity in multiple service industries including hospitality brands. In light of these considerations, it is hoped that the findings of this study will provide a firm basis on which to undertake additional research work.

Appendix. List of scale items for hotels and restaurants

A. *Brand equity questionnaire for luxury hotels*

I. *Brand loyalty scale: Cronbach's alpha=0.861 (strongly agree 7 ... strongly disagree 1)*
1. I regularly visit this hotel (mean = 3.03)
2. I intend to visit this hotel again (4.70)
3. I usually use this hotel as my first choice compared to other hotels (4.01)
4. I am satisfied with the visit to this hotel (4.71)
5. I would recommend this hotel to others (4.56)
6. I would not switch to another hotel the next time (3.47)

II. *Perceived quality scale: Cronbach's alpha=0.907 (strongly agree 7 ... strongly disagree 1)*
7. The staff treated you as a special and valued customer (mean = 5.01)
8. The hotel has up-to-date equipment (5.12)
9. The appearance of staff members (clean, neat, appropriately dressed) (5.29)
10. The hotel staff exhibits a good manner (5.21)
11. The hotel provides its services at promised times (5.02)
12. The hotel staff handles complaints of customers effectively (4.78)
13. The hotel staff actively communicates with customers (4.67)
14. Attractiveness of the hotel (4.73)
15. The knowledge and confidence of the staff (4.69)
16. The quality of food and beverages (4.93)
17. The hotel staff anticipates your specific needs and serves you appropriately (4.17)

III. *Brand image scale: Cronbach's alpha=0.909 (strongly agree 7 ... strongly disagree 1)*
18. It is comfortable (mean = 4.73)
19. It offers a high level of service (4.93)
20. It has a very clean image (5.13)
21. It is luxurious (5.14)
22. It is expensive (4.81)
23. It is a suitable place for high class (0.93)
24. I become special by visiting this hotel (4.35)
25. The staff is very kind (4.98)
26. It is big and spacious (4.95)
27. It is quiet and restful (4.71)
28. Service is sometimes excessive to me (4.06)
29. It has a long history (4.43)
30. It has a differentiated image from other hotel brands (4.53)
31. Its brand is familiar to me (4.42)

IV. *Brand awareness (no Cronbach's alpha is available due to the conversion of 3 original items to one-scale measure by transferring "do not know at all" to "1",*

H.-b. Kim, W.G. Kim / Tourism Management 26 (2005) 549–560   559

"aided recall" to "2", "unaided recall" to "4–6", and "recalling top-of-mind brand" to "7")

32. Write down the name of a luxury hotel in Seoul that comes first to your mind (top-of-mind brand)
33. List three other names of luxury hotels in Seoul that come to your mind at this moment (unaided brand recall)
34. Of the following 12 luxury hotels, please circle the name of the hotel name(s) you do not know (recognized and unrecognized brand in the aided recall)

B. Brand equity questionnaire for chain restaurants

I.   *Brand loyalty scale: Cronbach's alpha=0.860 (strongly agree 7 … strongly disagree 1)*
1.   I regularly visit this restaurant (mean = 3.53)
2.   I intend to visit this restaurant again (4.70)
3.   I usually use this restaurant as my first choice compared to other restaurants (3.71)
4.   I am satisfied with the visit to this restaurant (4.45)
5.   I would recommend this restaurant to others (4.08)
6.   I would not switch to another restaurant the next time (3.65)

II. *Perceived quality scale: Cronbach's alpha = 0.916 (strongly agree 7 … strongly disagree 1)*
7.   The physical facilities (e.g., building, sign, room décor, illumination) are visually appealing (mean = 4.50)
8.   The restaurant staff gives customers individual attention (3.45)
9.   The appearance of staff members (clean, neat, appropriately dressed) (3.67)
10. The restaurant has operating hours convenient to all their customers (3.95)
11. The staff provides its prompt services at promised times (3.93)
12. The staff handles complaints of customers effectively (3.85)
13. The staff is always willing to help customers (4.10)
14. The knowledge and confidence of the staff (3.54)
15. The food quality of the restaurant is good (3.68)
16. The restaurant insists on error-free service (4.04)

III. *Brand image scale: Cronbach's alpha = 0.804 (strongly agree 7 … strongly disagree 1)*
17. It is crowded (mean = 4.16)
18. It is noisy (4.56)
19. The price is reasonable (3.51)
20. Service is prompt (4.18)
21. It is conveniently located (4.67)
22. It has a differentiated image from other restaurant brands (4.06)
23. It tastes good compared with price (3.91)

24. Employees are very kind (3.90)
25. It has a very clean image (3.98)
26. It has cheerful and enchanting atmosphere (4.40)
27. There are many events (3.08)
28. I feel comfortable to visit alone (3.15)
29. It has a long history (3.71)
30. Its brand is familiar to me (4.05)

IV. *Brand awareness (No Cronbach's alpha is available due to the conversion of 3 original items to one-scale measure by transferring "do not know at all" to "1", "aided recall" to "2", "unaided recall" to "4–6", and "recalling top-of-mind brand" to "7")*
31. Write down the name of a chain restaurant in Seoul that comes first to your mind (top-of-mind brand)
32. List three other names of chain restaurants in Seoul that come to your mind at this moment (unaided brand recall)
33. Of the following 13 chain restaurants, please circle the name of the restaurant name(s) you do not know (recognized and unrecognized brand in the aided recall)

References

Aaker, D. A. (1991). *Managing brand equity*. New York: The Free Press.
Aaker, D. A. (1996). Measuring brand equity across products and markets. *California Management Review, 38*(3), 102–120.
Agarwal, M. K., & Rao, V. R. (1996). An empirical comparison of consumer-based measures of brand equity. *Marketing Letters, 7*(3), 237–247.
Blackston, M. (1995). The qualitative dimension of brand equity. *Journal of Advertising Research, 35*(4), RC2–RC7.
Bojanic, D. C., & Rosen, L. D. (1993). Measuring service quality in restaurants: An application of the SERVQUAL instrument. *Hospitality Research Journal, 18*(1), 3–14.
Bolton, R. N., & Drew, J. H. (1991). A longitudinal analysis of the impact of service changes on customer attitudes. *Journal of Marketing, 55*(1), 1–9.
Bowen, J. T., & Shoemaker, S. (1998). A strategic commitment. *Cornell Hotel and Restaurant Quarterly, 39*(1), 12–25.
Brennan, M. (1992). Techniques for improving mail survey response rates. *Marketing Bulletin, 3*, 24–37.
Brennan, M., Hoek, J., & Astridge, C. (1991). The effects of monetary incentives on the response rate and cost-effectiveness of a mail survey. *Journal of the Market Research Society, 33*(3), 229–241.
Cobb-Walgren, C. J., Ruble, C. A., & Donthu, N. (1995). Brand equity, brand preference, and purchase intent. *Journal of Advertising, 24*(3), 25–40.
Crawford, M. (1993). *New products management*. IL: Homewood.
Cronin Jr., J. J., & Taylor, S. A. (1992). Measuring service quality: A reexamination and extension. *Journal of Marketing, 56*(3), 55–68.
Dobni, D., & Zinkhan, G. M. (1990). In search of brand image: A foundation analysis. In M. E. Goldberg, & R. W. Pollay (Eds.), *Advances in consumer research. Association for consumer research* (pp. 110–119). UT: Provo.
Dyson, P., Farr, A., & Hollis, N. S. (1996). Understanding, measuring, and using brand equity. *Journal of Advertising Research, 36*(6), 9–21.

Farquhar, P. H. (1989). Managing brand equity. *Marketing Research,* *1*(1), 24–33.

Fick, G. R., & Ritchie, J. R. (1991). Measuring service quality in the travel and tourism industry. *Journal of Travel Research, 30*(2), 2–9.

Francois, P., & MacLachlan, D. L. (1995). Ecological validation of alternative consumer-based brand strength measures. *International Journal of Research in Marketing, 12*(4), 321–332.

Hair, J., Anderson, R., Tatham, R., & Black, W. (1992). *Multivariate data analysis* (2nd ed). New York: Macmillan Publishing Company.

Haley, R. I., & Case, P. B. (1979). Testing thirteen attitude scales for agreement and brand discrimination. *Journal of Marketing, 43*(4), 20–32.

Jiang, W., Dev, C., & Rao, V. R. (2002). Brand extension and customer loyalty: Evidence from the lodging industry. *Cornell Hotel and Restaurant Administration Quarterly, 43*(4), 5–16.

Kamakura, W. A., & Russell, G. J. (1993). Measuring brand value with scanner data. *International Journal of Research in Marketing, 10*(1), 9–22.

Kapferer, J. N. (1994). *Strategic brand management.* New York: Free Press.

Keller, K. L. (1993). Conceptualizing, measuring, and managing consumer-based brand equity. *Journal of Marketing, 57*(1), 1–22.

Keller, K. L. (2001). Building customer-based brand equity. *Marketing Management, 10*(2), 14–19.

Lassar, W., Mittal, B., & Sharma, A. (1995). Measuring consumer-based brand equity. *Journal of Consumer Marketing, 12*(4), 4–11.

Lee, Y., & Hing, N. (1995). Measuring quality in restaurant operations: An application of the SERVQUAL instrument. *International Journal of Hospitality Management, 14*(3), 293–310.

Leuthesser, L. (1988). *Defining, measuring, and managing brand equity. Summary of marketing science institute conference, Report no. 88-104.* Cambridge, MA: Marketing Science Institute.

Low, G. S., & Lamb Jr., C. W. (2000). The measurement and dimensionality of brand associations. *Journal of Product and Brand Management, 9*(6), 350–368.

Motameni, R., & Shahrokhi, M. (1998). Brand equity valuation: A global perspective. *Journal of Product and Brand Management, 7*(4), 275–290.

Muller, C. C. (1998). Endorsed branding. *Cornell Hotel and Restaurant Administration Quarterly, 39*(3), 90–96.

Muller, C. C., & Woods, R. H. (1994). An expected restaurant typology. *Cornell Hotel and Restaurant Administration Quarterly, 35*(3), 27–37.

Murphy, J. (1990). Assessing the value of brands. *Long Range Planning, 23*(3), 23–29.

Odin, Y., Odin, N., & Valette-Florence, P. (2001). Conceptual and operational aspects of brand loyalty: An empirical investigation. *Journal of Business Research. 53*(2), 75–84.

Ourusoff, A. (1993). Who said brands are dead? *Brandweek, 34*(32), 20–33.

Parasuraman, A., Zeithml, V. A., & Berry, L. (1985). A conceptual model of service quality and its implications for future research. *Journal of Marketing, 49*(4), 41–50.

Park, C., & Srinivasan, V. (1994). A survey-based method for measuring and understanding brand equity and its extendibility. *Journal of Marketing Research, 31*(2), 271–288.

Park, C. W., Milberg, S., & Lawson, R. (1991). Evaluation of brand extensions: The role of product feature similarity and brand concept consistency. *Journal of Consumer Research, 18*(2), 185–193.

Prasad, K., & Dev, C. S. (2000). Managing hotel brand equity: A customer-centric framework for assessing performance. *Cornell Hotel and Restaurant Administration Quarterly, 41*(3), 22–31.

Saleh, F., & Ryan, C. (1991). Analyzing service quality in the hospitality industry using the SERVQUAL model. *The Service Industries Journal, 11*(3), 324–343.

Shocker, A. D., Srivastava, R. K., & Ruekert, R. W. (1994). Challenges and opportunities facing brand management: An introduction to the special issue. *Journal of Marketing Research, 31*(2), 149–158.

Simon, C. J., & Sullivan, M. W. (1993). The measurement and determinants of brand equity: A financial approach. *Marketing Science, 12*(1), 28–52.

Smith, J. W. (1991). Thinking about brand equity and the analysis of customer transactions. In E. Maltz (Ed.), *Managing brand equity: A conference summary* (pp. 17–18). Cambridge, MA: Marketing Science Institute.

Srivastava, R. K., & Shocker, A. D. (1991). *Brand equity: A perspective on its meaning and measurement.* Cambridge, MA: Marketing Science Institute.

Swait, J., Erdem, T., Louviere, J., & Dubelaar, C. (1993). The equalization price: A measure of consumer-perceived brand equity. *International Journal of Research in Marketing, 10*(1), 23–45.

Yoo, B., & Donthu, N. (2001). Developing and validating a multidimensional consumer-based brand equity scale. *Journal of Business Research, 52*(1), 1–14.

[14]

Tourist Attractions and Attracted Tourists:
How to satisfy today's 'fickle' tourist clientele?

Mike Peters
and
Klaus Weiermair

Abstract
What are basic management principles in the creation of man made tourist attractions? In answering this question, the paper addresses first the topic regarding new forms of tourism behaviour. Subsequently, it discusses general changes in tourism and leisure behaviour, which can be observed globally, and distinguishes between global and local/regional changes in tourism behaviour. Through a discussion of the species of 'new tourists' and 'new tourism', this paper makes an attempt to derive its implications for attraction management which as of late has become an important issue on the tourism policy agenda in most European Alpine destinations. At the end three core elements of tourism management: imagination, attraction and perfection, will be analysed in connection with man made attractions. It is believed that the latter requirements carry important messages for attraction and/or event management and managers.

Associate Professor Mike Peters is at the Institute of Tourism and Service Economics, University of Innsbruck, Austria.
Professor Klaus Weiermair is Head of the Institute of Tourism and Service Economics, University of Innsbruck, Austria.

Introduction

Although cyclical and secular swings in the popularity and attractiveness of specific touristic regions and destinations have always existed, such notions as: destination life cycle, reengineering or relaunching of old tourism destinations, tourism trend research, and animation and theming in tourism belong to a more recent tourism vocabulary.

A number of reasons are probably responsible for these developments; some of them are of a more general nature, involving overall changes in consumer behaviour elsewhere, some are more specific to the tourism industry. First of all we notice the worldwide disappearance of the typical loyal customer who, irrespective of relative price and quality adheres to traditional, habitual, and repetitive purchasing decisions and behaviour. Prompted by more and easier accessible purchasing information, by an ever increasing rate of introductions of new product/services, and their fast and global market diffusion, customers have become choosy, fickle, and disloyal to their traditional suppliers. Tourism has been no exception in this regard, but while the notion of shortened product life cycles has been discussed for some time (Poon, 1993; Weiermair & Auer, 1998), its application to the tourism industry was not obvious (Agarwal, 1997; Butler, 1980). Since both, tourism services and tourists in a specific tourism destination may change over time, it is not easy to decipher destination life cycles the same way as you may analyse and manage simple product life cycles (Cooper, 1990).

Also tourism, particularly in its first and pioneering phase, is usually more concerned with the tangible aspects of its evolution e.g. the creation of new tourism sites in terms of hotels and traditional touristic infrastructure and less with the creation of intangible benefits in terms of 'vacation or tourism experiences' (Ritchie & Crouch, 1993).

While physical surroundings and tourism infra- and supra structure may age and became outdated, the aging of their intangibles in terms of service concepts and service philosophies may often be the more important depreciation element which can cause the decline of destination attractiveness. Throughout Europe, but particularly Central Europe, where tourism has declined in saturated markets (Weiermair, 1997), destination attractiveness has been questioned and much emphasis is currently being placed on making tourist destinations more attractive through innovative investments in technology, human resources, and new tourism events, theme parks, and the like. A call has been made for increasing attractiveness of tourist sites through appropriate management of tourist attractions (Scherrieb, 1998).

As Jago and Shaw pointed out, there no widely accepted definitional framework for the terms 'special events', 'festivals', 'hallmark events', 'major-events' and/or 'mega-events' exists (Jago & Shaw, 1998). All of them as well as the entire tourism industry contain 'man made attractions' as the common element, which can provide the stimulation for customers to travel. Swarbrooke proposed another typology of attractions (Swarbrooke, 1995). He differentiated:

- Natural environment attractions

- Man-made structures not designed to specifically attract visitors

- Man-made structures specifically designed to attract visitors

- Special events.

Whilst special events are of limited duration, tourist attractions do not have to be of temporary nature. Similarly events can also be used as primary attractions, around which to create theming, image building, and packaging (Getz, 1997).

A short profile of today's tourist and/or modern tourism

Even from an economic perspective, tourism can be first analysed as a demand phenomenon. As such, one has to delve deep into theories or theoretical constructs, which help explain consumer preferences for leisure products in general, and tourism products/services in particular. This section does not pretend to discuss the variety of approaches and/or theories which have been proposed to explain tourism or leisure behaviour, for such an exercise would fill an entire book. Rather a modest attempt will be made to stylise a few facts about today's tourism, and its changes over time and across national boundaries, and to speculate on possible causes for these changes towards 'post-modern tourism' using theoretical constructs, where available.

The quantitative dimensions of the postwar growth behaviour in tourism are well documented for most parts of the world (for example: WTO, OECD, EUROSTAT). Frequently historical figures are used to extrapolate growth trajectories for global and regional tourism (Edwards, A., 1992; Hailin Qu &

Hanqin Qiu Zhang, 1997). As long as the underlying preference function of tourists remain stable, purely statistical or simple economic and/or econometric explanatory and forecasting approaches can provide reasonably good estimates of underlying trends. In this context it should be pointed out that the economists' frequently used explanatory variables of income, price of tourism services, price of related substitute goods or services and available time for leisure consumption are in reality only constraint variables which allow us to merely make conjectures, and develop hypotheses with respect to the relationship of these economic variables and the amount of tourism activities consumed (an excellent overview on demand models is delivered by Crouch and Shaw, 1992).

Such demand models of tourism consumption prove far less useful when there are profound underlying structural changes in tourism and leisure behaviour based on new values, attitudes and/or preferences of tourists. According to some authors, such changes have occurred over the past ten years (Weiermair, 1998). This is evidenced by the uneven and at times contradictory tourism growth within and across regions, and the fast growth in visitor numbers of some tourist attractions and destinations versus the maturity or decline of others.

What accounts for these structural changes are radical departures in consumer behaviour. Where before the combination of a 'puritan ethics' and economic constraints guided consumer decision making in all arenas including tourism, today's motivating forces are not only less and less the result of rational economic decision making but may indeed be the tourist's 'reflection of deeper needs, needs which be himself does not even understand may not be aware of or may not wish to articulate' (Lundberg, 1976).

Many authors describe today's tourist behaviour and/or modern tourism as an 'escape' or 'flight' from daily routine phenomena where escape and self actualisation motives dominate but where behaviour is also still rooted or at least partially influenced by traditional norms and considerations of daily life (Crompton, 1979). Thus, spill-over leisure/familiarity concepts combine with compensatory concepts to explain tourism behaviour (see, for example: Cohen, 1988). The hybrid customer or tourist who seems to defy simple segmentation principles, becomes much more easy to define once we accept the co-existence of contradictory values, norms and behaviour. The accumulation of post war wealth has conditioned modern men towards consumerism and materialism, but at the same time set free the critical conditions for the experience of leisure, e.g. perceived freedom and intrinsic motivation. What is different, in many of the most developed countries today, is the dominance of intrinsic over extrinsic motivating factors, and the search and acquisition of emotional stimuli in many ordinary activities of consumption. Shopping centres become shopping experiences, destinations become stages for holiday adventures, and more generally leisure consumption becomes a state of mind (Opaschowski, 1993; Scherrieb, 1998).

Opaschowski (1993) pointed out, the psychological foundation of this new ethic in consumer behaviour goes back to the times of the romantic period in history (p. 13). According to this ethic, pleasure and animation take precedence over the functional and useful, even though the 'iron cage of economic necessities' must equally be populated alongside with the luxurious castles of dreams and pleasures.

Thus, the call for dream holidays, for holidays which make all those things possible, which ordinary daily routine cannot, is becoming more important in leisure and tourism. Often these dreams reflect social and personal deficits at home, which make people want to live in 'holiday dream worlds'.

These trends can also be observed in alpine tourism, but only a few studies report on changing tourism behaviour and quality perception of alpine tourists (see, for example: Fuchs and Weiermair, 1998). To find out more about the images of the alps, alpine holidays, and alpine cities, particularly in the context of excursion and short-term holidays, focus group interviews were carried out, for example in the city of Munich, with the

Perceived freedom and intrinsic motivation are strong elements shaping the choices of contemporary consumers.

objective to learn more about information and leisure behaviour of Germans in nearby sending regions (ITD, 1998). The focus groups were divided in younger (22-40 years of age) and elder potential travellers (41-60 years of age). Asked about their travel motives all young potential travellers named 'animation and fun', on the other side, asked about their negative associations with vacations in alpine regions, they all missed 'originality'. This supports former studies, which indicate consumers' holiday preferences to change towards having fun, gaining new experiences and breaking away from every day life (see, for example: ADAC, 1991; ÖGAF, 1996).

Technical advances and close adherence to the psychological needs of today's stressed out and lonesome individual have produced artificial or virtual dreamworlds in the form of theme or fantasy parks, hotels and/or clubs. Today these are not only competing very successfully with ordinary vacation destinations, but they have also become the benchmark against which the management of tourist attractions must be evaluated.

To summarise, we seem to be observing a global trend towards a new form of tourism, in which animation, fun and adventure, properly staged and ideally packaged individually form key elements of success (see, for example: Isenberg, 1995; Mikunda, 1997; Youngkhill, Dattilo, & Howard, 1998).

Global vs. regional patterns of behaviour in travel decision making and destination choice

As pointed out above, a trend in terms of new tourist types and novel tourism behaviour has been observed. There has been equally much discussion about globalisation of the tourism industry and its impact on future developments in tourism (Weiermair & Peters, 1998). Thus, an emerging key question is the global dispersion of this new form of tourism: Is there a convergence of tastes and preference in tourism on a world wide scale through or without the extension of national to international travel, and does this lead to similar international practices and tools in tourism management, particularly as regards tourist attractions?

Given the multiplicity of travel motives, travel products and activities, not to speak of travel experiences which, to a certain degree, all can embed new tourism behaviour, it becomes next to impossible to decipher the quantitative importance of these trends and localise them on a global scale. But if theming and theme parks are an important indication and expression of this 'new tourism', it however becomes much easier to observe

its growth and global distribution, as this sub-branch of tourism provides relatively good statistics. On a global scale the top 50 of the world's most visited parks hosted more than 242.8 million guests 1997. The majority of leisure parks is found in the U.S.A and Japan (Of the world's top 50 parks, 26 are in North America and 9 in Japan, but Europe and South-America appear to be at the moment the fastest growing markets.

Although attendance at the world's top 50 most visited parks dropped in 1998 by nearly 9.5 million visitors, or 4%, the top parks still hosted over 233.395.188 visitors which represents record levels in recent years. Weather and the economy

Is there a global convergence of tourists' tastes and preferences?

were cited as the reasons for the present decline (Amusement Business, 21/28/1998).

In Austria and Switzerland, two of the most tourism intensive countries in the world, little has been done in terms of theme park creations because of local opposition to these developments. Sagging tourism figures combined with the risk taking of emerging types of entrepreneurs or tycoons in tourism are presently leading to the creation of a new wave of fantasy parks. However not all of these theme parks will imitate earlier American success stories like Disneyland or the Magic Kingdom.

The difficulty which many European, Asian or South American park developments face is finding a proper balance between their own local traditions, local history, and local myth, and colour and a professional American style management or orchestration of such theme parks or themed tourist events/attractions. Often management tools and tourism goals are judged negatively as the pejoratively used terms of *McDonaldisation* and *Walt Disneysation* suggest. In the next chapter we will try to strip these terms of their cultural bias and report principles on successful management production, which are necessary to satisfy today's experience and adventure oriented tourist, irrespective of cultural context and cultural belonging.

Key principles in the design and operation of tourist attractions

A number of books have been written in the last couple of years which have all focused on frontier management practices in the field of service operations and service marketing (Bieger, 1998). In addition a number of tourism specific areas have shown how some of these management tools can be applied to tourism (see, for example: Kunst & Lemmink, 1995; Poon, 1993). For the sake of simplicity and in order to reduce the task to manageable proportion we will discuss three core elements which are common to most successfully managed tourist attractions, events and/or fantasy parks. They include

- Imagination
- Attraction
- Perfection

The first and probably most important managerial or entrepreneurial task is to create new products, services or better yet 'experiences' based on consequent observations of tourists' behaviour or market research dealing with human needs, problems, and problem solutions using psychological and/or other qualitative market research tools (for example focus groups). We are speaking of a

new generation of entrepreneurs and pioneers, who, in addition to having vision of future services, can translate these with modern software and service quality concepts into commercialised products. They must understand and respond to tourists' vacation dreams which constitute an amalgam of sun lust, comfort and convenience, contrast and adventure, peacefulness and nature, as well as animation and fun. Often many of these visions emerge from children's fairy tales, accounts of religious history, sites of famous personalities or important historical happenings. E.g. today, there exist three competing Santa Claus villages in Canada, Sweden and Finland.

Assuming visionaries in tourism are equally distributed around the globe along with a normal distribution of tourist location and natural tourist attractions, the next most important question becomes how to apply psychological foundations of service (quality) experience and learning to the selling of service perception, service consumption and service recollection (Kunst & Lemmink, 1995).

It is here that a number of lessons can be learnt from professional theme park-, event- or club operations, for the process involves a number of steps and skills which are often absent in mainstream tourism operations. 'Imagineers' know how to stimulate and animate through 'theming' and visualisation. By descending to the markets' most common denominator with respect to intellectual and aesthetic demand, tourism managers and operators of tourist attractions can build a much safer bridge between consumers' (tourists') quality expectations and their perceptions of performance quality.

In most jurisdiction and in most tourist destinations but notably in the context of urban tourism, tourist attractions have become

increasingly managed yielding man made as opposed to natural tourist attractions. One of the prime reasons for this development lies in the fact that holiday products or services are in their entirety inaccessible to the imagination, unless they can be somehow reduced and simplified. Attraction management is therefore largely concerned with the strategy and implementation of imaginisation (Judd, 1995).

It is important to integrate the tourist intellectually and emotionally into the service production process (Normann, 1991). Many traditional managers of tourist attractions, such as e.g., museums, art galleries, religious monuments, or even natural parks, merely provide the physical integration of the client with the service. The latter often are people who may be specialists in the domain of the attraction, e.g. art critics or curators, clergy or rangers who often may deliver a very elitarian interpretation of the offered attractions, their jobs and/or their role in society. The notion that art should only be shown and marketed to the educated art lover, religious monuments shown to the informed tourist or nature shared with the ecologically minded traveller implies either discrimination and/or at worst poor customer segmentation. How art treasures, historical buildings or other man made and natural attractions are presented in order to appeal to wide audiences/clients is one of the most important skills in the process of attraction management. Tourism or leisure cultures if they are to exist on a broad basis, require a demystification of the traditional comprehension of culture. Wanting to share culture with others from a different cultural background may in itself be determined by a lot of ethnic and socioeconomic variables. Generally speaking, either very primitive or very evolved host cultures seem to be able to share cultural values and activities with foreigners, whilst cultures in transition suffer from identification problems and therefore often produce hostility towards foreign tourists (Bachleitner & Luger, 1996). There is a growing discipline within management which specialises in intercultural management, and which certainly could be applied to the creation and management of leisure cultures. This brings us already close to the third success criterion: perfection.

The most successful service operations including those in tourism are the ones which are orchestrated, planned and processed like a screenplay with a well written script (Lovelock, 1991). Nothing is left to chance, the whole process from the first service encounter to the last is rehearsed and important strategic points of interaction with the customer (tourist) are reinforced through special quality controls. Entrepreneurs should use management tools, such as service blueprinting and/or flowcharting diagrams to optimise flows and to follow the principles of value chain management.

This exercise involves on the one hand the use of logistics and operation research methods to smoothen the process of service delivery, and to minimise, e.g. waiting queues, on the other hand it involves the setting of quality standards in terms of behavioural standards for service (contact) personnel. Above all, it requires again a sound knowledge of which service quality elements or attributes are to be used in which combination and for which service acts within the service chain. For example, how should high tech and high touch or traditional and modern elements in the interior decoration, the appearance of the service personnel, or in the choice of goods and services to be provided be blended to achieve the highest degree of customer satisfaction?

Service quality and customer satisfaction research in tourism provides us with valuable insights into the varying importance of various quality attributes and/or service interaction points, and as such can be used as a valuable guide for the operation of tourist attraction (Weiermair & Fuchs, 1998).

Possible lessons for the management of tourist attractions

Though national cultural differences prevail, there seems to exist a global overarching trend towards certain forms of leisure cultures in which well orchestrated leisure attractions, such as theme or fantasy parks play an important role. What does the experience concerning the management of tourist attractions, notably those in the U.S.A., suggest for example for European Alpine destinations?:

• Each tourism receiving country should carefully examine which relevant themes, events or attractions lend themselves to the construction and/or development of leisure parks.

• Irrespective of the nature of such leisure or theme parks, professionals in tourism should learn about the process of managing complex service chains, for this knowledge cannot only be applied to major tourist attractions but is equally valid for most tourism enterprises.

• Even small- and medium-sized tourism enterprises can learn from the managerial know how of successful attraction/theme park entrepreneurs: on the one hand service providers should understand consumer problems and consumer behaviour in order to fulfil their expectations, and more than this, to surprise them with an extraordinary service

experience. On the other hand service elements which do not increase customers' value, should be excluded.

• Complexity of the tourism product and/or tourism attraction calls for the development of service management instruments which allows entrepreneurs to analyse complex service processes (e.g. flowcharting, waiting-queue management and blueprinting). The entrepreneur furthermore has to learn to write a script which serves the right service/product at the right time and location, in the right quantity, and quality.

• Much needs to be done to professionalise the structuring of service enterprises and the management of the service encounter in terms of designing tourism products and service delivery systems (which involves also architectural questions).

• Alpine tourism managers have to distinguish between core and peripheral services because they have to identify the stimulus which may attract potential tourists (in order to create a favourable image).

Market researchers often carry out surveys in their destinations/cities and/or regions. But this is the wrong way to identify 'new' needs and desires of potential tourists, because they already have chosen their destination. It is more effective to analyse the consumer in sending regions, not only those who are just aware but also familiar with the tourist destination, and to explore their motivations. Tourist attractions could induce tourists to visit a destination for the first time: according to Milmann and Pizam (1995) awareness by itself does not necessarily lead to a more positive image of a destination and an increased likelihood of visiting it. Thus, it would be more

Managing Tourism Firms

efficient to invest in means of moving customers directly into the stage of destination familiarity.

The increasing importance and success of attractions and theme parks underline the need for more research in the field of the development of holistic tourism products/experiences. Thus, it seems useful not only to extract and concentrate on primary travel motives of tourists but to analyse a composite of motives and understand their interdependencies and correlations (Dann, 1981, Pearce, 1988; Plog, 1994). On the supply side, questions of ownership control, entrepreneurship and strategy development of tourist attractions, as well as resource protection and sustainable management could be the focus of future tourism research studies. A number of trends in tourist attractions were identified by Pearce (1999), who derived a recommendation for marketing research and studies in business strategy, which could be of benefit to owners/operators and audiences as well as a growth area for tourism researchers.

Alpine tourism in Europe has lost a good part of its competitiveness. This requires increasing product differentiation and specialisation, and innovative product development (Smeral, Weber, Fuchs, Auer, & Peters, 1998). Man-made products can be seen as an effective stimulus to attract tourists and to redefine and reposition the image of many European Alpine regions.

References

ADAC (Ed.) (1991). *Städtetourismus: Eine Orientierungshilfe für Klein- und Mittelstädte.* München: ADAC Zentrale.

Agarwal, S. (1997). The resort cycle and seaside tourism: An assessment of its applicability and validity. *Tourism Management, 18*(2), 65-73.

Amusement Business (1998). 21/28.

Bachleitner, R., & Luger, K. (1996). Zur Sozialkritik am Tourismus. In K. Weiermair, M. Schipflinger, & M. Peters, (Eds.). *Alpine tourism: Sustainability - reconsidered and redesigned* (pp. 397-402). Innsbruck: ITD Series.

Bieger, Th. (1998). *Dienstleistungs-management.* Bern: Haupt.

Butler, R.W. (1980). The concept of a tourist area cycle of evolution: Implications for management of resources. *Canadian Geographer, 24*, 5-12.

Cohen, E. (1988). Authenticity and commodization in tourism. *Annals of Tourism Research, 15*, 371-356.

Cooper, C.P. (1990). Resorts in decline. The management response. *Tourism Management, 11*(2), 63-67.

Crompton, J. (1979). Motivations for a pleasure vacation. *Annals of Tourism Research, 6*, 408-424.

Crouch, G. I., & Shaw, R.N. (1992). International tourism demand: A meta-analytical integration of research findings. In P. Johnson, & B. Thomas (Eds.), *Choice and demand in tourism.* London: Mansell.

Currie, R.R. (1997). A pleasure-tourism behaviours framework. *Annals of Tourism Research, 24*(4), 884-897.

Dann, G. (1981). Tourist motivation: An appraisal. *Annals of Tourism Research, 8*(2), 187-219.

Edwards, A. (Ed.) (1992). *International tourism forecasts to 2005.* London: The Economist Intelligence Unit.

Fitzsimmons, J.A., & Fitzsimmons, M.J. (1998). *Service management: Operations, strategy, and information technology* (2nd ed.). New York: McGraw-Hill.

Fuchs, M., & Weiermair, K. (1998). Qualitätsmessung vernetzter Dienstleistungen am Beispiel des alpinen Wintertourismus. *Tourismus Journal, 2*(2), S.211-235.

Getz, D. (1997). *Event management & event tourism.* New York: Cognizant Communication Offices.

Hailin Qu & Hanqin Qiu Zhang (1997). The projected inbound market trends of 12 tourist destinations in South-East Asia and the Pacific 1997-2001. *Journal of Vacation Marketing, 3*(3), 247-263.

Isenberg, W. (Ed.) (1995). *Kathedralen der Freizeitgesellschaft.* Bensberg: Thomas-Morus-Akademie.

ITD - Institute of Tourism and Service Economics (1998). *Focusbefragung über das Reiseverhalten in Reisesendeländern,* unpublished. Innsbruck: University of Innsbruck.

Jago, L.K., & Shaw, R.N. (1998). Special events: A conceptual and definitional framework. *Festival Management & Event Tourism, 5*, 21-32.

Judd, D. (1995). Promoting tourism in US cities. *Tourism Management, 16*(3), 175-187.

Kunst, P., & Lemmink, J. (1995). *Managing service quality.* Den Haag: Paul Chapman Publishing.

Lovelock, Ch. (1991). *Services marketing.* London: Prentice-Hall.

Lundberg, D.E. (1976). *The tourist business.* Boston: CBI Publishing.

Mikunda, Ch. (1997). *Der verbotene Ort oder Die inszenierte Verführung.* Düsseldorf: Econ.

Milman, A., & Pizam, A. (1995). The role of awareness and familiarity with a destination: The Central Florida case. *Journal of Travel Research, XXXIII*(3), 21-27.

Nash, D. (1996). *Anthropology of tourism.* New York: Pergamon Press.

Normann, R. (1991). *Service management.* Chisester: John Wiley & Sons.

ÖGAF (Ed.) (1996). *Gästebefragung Österreich.* Wien: Österreichische Gesellschaft für angewandte Freizeitforschung.

Opaschowski, H.W. (1993). *Freizeitökonomie. Marketing von Erlebniswelten.* Opladen: Leske & Budrig.

Opaschowski, H. W. (1993). Wir schaffen Glückseligkeit. In W. Isenberg (Ed.), *Kathedralen der Freizeitgesellschaft: Kurzurlaub in Erlebniswelten. Trends, Hintergründe, Auswirkungen* (Bensdorfer Protokolle, 83) (pp. 11-34). Bensberg: Thomas-Morus-Akademie.

Pearce, P. (1988). *The Ulysses factor: Evaluating visitors in tourist settings.* New York: Springer.

Pearce, P. (1999). Marketing and management trends in tourist attractions. *Asia Pacific Journal of Tourism Research, 3*(1), 1-10.

Plog, S.C. (1994). Developing and using psychographics in tourism research. In J. Ritchie, & C. Goeldner (Eds.), *Travel, tourism and hospitality research* (pp. 209-231). New York: Wiley.

Poon, A. (1993). *Tourism, technology and competitive strategies.* Wallingford, UK: CAB International.

Ritchie, J.R.B., & Crouch, G.I. (1993). Competitiveness in international tourism: A framework for understanding and analysis. In AIEST (Ed.), Editions AIEST Vol. 35. *Competitiveness of long haul tourist destinations* (pp. 23-71). St. Gallen: Niedermann.

Scherrieb, H.R. (1998). *Freizeit- und Erlebnisparks in Deutschland.* Würzburg: VDFU.

Smeral, E., Weber, A., Fuchs, M., Auer, W., & Peters, M. (1998). *The future of international tourism.* Vienna: WIFO.

Swarbrooke, J. (1995). *The development & management for visitor attractions.* Oxford: Butterworth Heinemann.

Weiermair, K., & Auer, W. (1998). Structural changes of alpine tourism and resultant adaptation problem of tourism enterprises. *Journal of International Hospitality, Leisure & Tourism Management, 1*(4), 79-91.

Weiermair, K., & Fuchs, M. (1998). Quality dimensions in alpine tourism and their assessment by tourists and tourism entrepreneurs. In institut d'administration des entreprises, Université d'Aix-Marseille (Ed.), *5th international research seminar in service management* (pp. 839-859). Aix-en-provence: institut d'administration des entreprises, Université d'Aix-Marseille.

Weiermair, K., & Peters, M. (1998). Entrepreneurial small- and medium-sized tourism enterprises: Threats and opportunities in a globalized world. In K.S. Chon (Ed.), *Tourism and hotel industry in Indo-China & Southeast Asia* (pp. 235-243). Houston: University of Houston.

Weiermair, K. (1997). On the concept and definition of quality in tourism. In P. Keller (Ed.), AIEST Editions, Vol. 39, *Quality management in tourism* (pp. 33-58). St. Gallen: Niedermann.

Weiermair, K. (1998). The effect on environmental context and management on the performance characteristics of cultural events: The case of the 700 year Exhibition in Stams and Meran. *Festival Management & Event Tourism, 5*(1) & *5*(2), 85-91.

Youngkhill, L., Dattilo J., & Howard, D. (1998). The complex and dynamic nature of leisure experience. *Journal of Leisure Research, 26*(3), 195-211.

[15]

Cultural Differences between Asian Tourist Markets and Australian Hosts, Part 1

YVETTE REISINGER AND LINDSAY W. TURNER

This article analyzes five language groups of Asian tourists to Australia: Indonesian, Japanese, Korean, Mandarin, and Thai. The cultural differences between Asian tourists and Australian service providers are identified. The dimensions of the identified differences are determined by principal components analysis. The results indicate that in 73 (62.4%) of 117 areas of measurement, there are significant differences between Asian and Australian samples. The Japanese are the most distinct from the Australian sample, followed by the Korean sample. The implications of the results for tourism industry managers and marketers are discussed prior to the causal analysis of satisfaction presented in part 2, which shows that marketers cannot rely on perceptions of service alone to generate Asian tourist satisfaction but must also consider specific cultural values and rules of social behavior. Part 2 will appear in the May 2002 issue.

Currently, the international tourism industry is faced with an increasing number of inbound travelers from Asia. The Asian tourist market has become the largest source of international tourists to Australia during the past decade. The Asian market represented nearly 50% of the total international market share in 1995-1997 (Bureau of Tourism Research [BTR] 1995-1997) and 42.6% in 1998 (BTR 1998b). The Asian market (excluding Japan), the number-one source of international tourists to Australia, currently represents 24.3% of the international market. The Japanese market, the second-largest source, represents 18.3% of market share. The Japanese market is the largest single source, followed by New Zealand, Europe (excluding the United Kingdom/Ireland), United Kingdom and Ireland, and the United States (BTR 1998b) (see Table 1). Among the Asian markets (excluding Japan), Singapore is the largest source of visitors, with 23.0% of Asian market share, followed by Taiwan, Hong Kong, Malaysia, Indonesia, China, South Korea, and Thailand (BTR 1998b) (see Table 2).

The Asian market also has shown the strongest annual growth in tourist arrivals to Australia at an average rate of 31.2% in 1994, at a time when the average growth in international tourist arrivals from other regions was between 5% and 12% (Australian Tourist Commission [ATC] 1994). A downturn in this growth occurred in 1998 due to the Asian financial crisis. There was an overall decline of 55%, with South Korean, Taiwanese, Indonesian, Malaysian, Thai, and Hong Kong arrivals showing significant reductions. Singapore and China maintained growth. Increases in tourist arrivals to 2000 have been returning to growth in all Asian markets.

The Japanese and other Asian markets are also the two major markets generating tourists to Queensland (BTR 1998a, 1998b), the major holiday state for international tourists in Australia. The percentage of Japanese tourists visiting Queensland in 1995 increased to 78%, South Korean to 70%, Taiwanese to 68%, Hong Kong to 46%, Chinese to 43%, Singapore to 39%, and Malaysian to 28% (Bureau of Tourism Research [BTR] 1996). In 1996, the Japanese represented nearly 25% of all international arrivals to the Gold Coast, the major holiday destination in Queensland (BTR 1998b).

The economic downturn in Asia was not so severe as to suggest that the Asian crisis has dramatically diminished tourism flows to Australia, and with appropriate new transition policies, the Asian countries, which experienced economic growth rates for more than three decades, will emerge again (McKay 1998).

According to predictions, the Asian market will be the largest source of international tourists to Australia beyond the year 2000. Arrivals from Asia (excluding Japan) will represent more than 30% of the total international market share (ATC 1994). Japan will remain the single most important source of tourists to Australia. Arrivals from Japan will represent more than 20% of market share (ATC 1994). The South Korean market will also continue to grow. Australia was always the second most popular non-Asian destination after the United States for the Korean market (Prideaux 1998). This market, traditionally characterized by group travel, currently experiences an increase in fully independent travel to Australia (McAllan 1997). The Singapore market will also grow and will provide a high number of repeat visitors. It is predicted that during the next 5 years, China may become one of the prime sources of Asian outbound tourism due to its booming economy, emergence of an upper-middle-upper class, and liberalization of border controls and currency regulations. Hong Kong will be the region's most consistent source of inbound tourism to Australia. Hong Kong is the most mature market in North East Asia and has a well-traveled population (McAllan 1997). Australia's other Southeast Asian markets of Indonesia, Thailand, and Malaysia will also continue to provide a steady source of tourists with a predicted combined arrival figure of about 350,000 by the year 2000.

Yvette Reisinger is an associate professor in the Department of Management/Tourism at Monash University in Melbourne, Australia. Lindsay W. Turner is an associate professor in the School of Applied Economics at Victoria University of Technology in Melbourne, Australia.

Journal of Travel Research, Vol. 40, February 2002, 295-315
© 2002 Sage Publications

TABLE 1
INTERNATIONAL TOURIST ARRIVALS TO AUSTRALIA BY MAJOR COUNTRIES OF ORIGIN, 1995 TO 1998

Ranking	Country	Arrivals (in thousands)			Percentage
		1995	1997	1998	
1	Asia (excluding Japan)	962.0	1,276.2	937.9	24.3
2	Japan	737.7	813.9	704.4	18.3
3	New Zealand	490.7	685.7	640.5	16.6
4	Europe (excluding United Kingdom/Ireland)	378.6	438.2	467.2	12.1
5	United Kingdom and Ireland	335.4	435.9	448.4	11.6
6	United States	287.9	329.6	353.2	9.6
7	Other countries	174.5	273.7	239.2	6.2
8	Canada	55.0	64.8	68.1	1.8
Total		3,421.8	4,318.0	3,858.9	100.0

Source: Bureau of Tourism Research (1997, 1998a, 1998b).

TABLE 2
ASIAN TOURIST ARRIVALS TO AUSTRALIA BY MAJOR
COUNTRIES OF ORIGIN, 1995 TO 1998 (EXCLUDING JAPAN)

Country	Arrivals (in thousands) 1995	Country	Arrivals (in thousands) 1997	Country	Arrivals (in thousands) 1998	Asian Market Share (%)
Singapore	168.5	Singapore	239.3	Singapore	215.6	23.0
South Korea	160.6	South Korea	233.8	Taiwan	135.0	14.4
Taiwan	138.3	Indonesia	160.4	Hong Kong (SAR)	130.4	13.9
Hong Kong	117.3	Taiwan	153.2	Malaysia	101.8	10.9
Indonesia	107.6	Hong Kong (SAR)	151.7	Indonesia	82.6	8.8
Malaysia	94.4	Malaysia	143.7	China	73.3	7.8
Thailand	72.5	Thailand	68.6	South Korea	62.3	6.6
China	n.a.	China	65.9	Thailand	44.6	4.8
Other Asia	102.8	Other Asia	59.6	Other Asia	92.3	9.8
Total	962.0		1,276.2		937.9	100.0

Source: Bureau of Tourism Research (1997, 1998a, 1998b).

The turnaround in the proportion of Asian versus non-Asian inbound travel to Australia will affect the development of new marketing strategies, which need to be tailored to the Asian tourist market. The recent increase in Asian inbound tourism to Australia has caught the Australian tourism industry unprepared (March 1997). Australians do not distinguish between the Asian markets and have no knowledge of their cultural attributes (Prideaux 1998). Consequently, Australia will face challenges learning about the Asian tourist market and developing responsive and culture-oriented marketing programs. Success in retaining and even increasing Asian market share in Australia will depend on responding quickly to the needs of the distinct Asian markets. The Asian market niche with the greatest potential is the middle class from Malaysia, South Korea, and Thailand (Crotts and Ryan 1997), not the wealthy elite from Japan, Hong Kong, Singapore, and Taiwan on which the Australian tourism industry traditionally has concentrated in the past. Thus, it will be important to understand the cultural orientation of these newly emerging markets. This will be vital for the purpose of marketing and, in particular, market segmentation and the design of advertising campaigns (Mok and Armstrong 1995). The ability to respond to each market's peculiarities and to adopt not just global marketing programs but regional programs will provide a challenge (McAllan 1997).

The tourists' perceptions of those who take care of them during their holiday may enhance tourists' holiday experiences or discourage them from repeat visitation. These perceptions are extremely important, particularly to Asian tourists. As Dimanche (1994) noted, marketers need to know more about how cultural differences affect tourist behavior. The influence of cultural differences on destination perceptions and the local people who have direct contact with tourists is of particular significance.

Asian tourists come to Australia for a relatively short time, mostly in organized tour groups (BTR 1998b), and have limited contact with local people. They develop their perceptions of locals through direct face-to-face contact with service providers who are often the only contact points with tourists. As Riley (1995) noted, tourist and host behavior could, therefore, be explained within the context of the service encounter. The cultural differences between international tourists and service providers may affect their social experiences and, consequently, satisfaction with each other. Consequently, by understanding cultural differences, local providers can develop and offer new cultural features of a tourism product, which is value added to the core product. It is very important for a tourist destination like Australia to educate its tourism industry employees about the cultural background of its international visitors, particularly Asian visitors. Moreover, it is imperative for all Western providers to understand and address the needs of culturally different tourist markets. Developing tourism products to meet Westerners' perceptions of Asian tourists' needs might preclude the delivery of the experience that Asian tourists may seek (Crotts and Ryan 1997). Consequently, the growth of the Asian markets with different cultural backgrounds represents a challenge and opportunity not only for the Australian but also the international tourism marketplace.

RESEARCH OBJECTIVES

The main research objectives of this study are the following:

1. to identify the key cultural differences between the Asian tourist markets and the Australian host population, as a representative of Western culture;
2. to determine the key dimensions of these differences and their indicators; and
3. to identify major cultural themes that should be included in every promotional strategy aiming at the Asian tourist market.

Culture, in this article, refers to a stable and dominant cultural character of a society shared by most of its individuals and remaining constant over long periods of time. Culture does not refer to the subcultures of many ethnic groups living in a society, which may be distinguished by religion, age, geographical location, or some other factor, nor the individuals' character, which can be influenced by environmental forces and easily changed over time (Hofstede 1980).

We admit that individual Asian markets are heterogeneous with respect to sociocultural characteristics. We also believe that any cultural grouping is heterogeneous at a particular scale and that there are regional as well as individual differences in any culture, including Japan (Iverson 1997). In this study, all Asian samples, except the Japanese (100% of Japanese tourists are from Japan), are represented by more than a single country. For instance, the Mandarin-speaking market is represented by tourists from Mainland China, Singapore, Taiwan, Hong Kong, and a very small percentage from Malaysia and Vietnam. The South Korean market is represented by 99.4% of tourists from South Korea and 0.6% from Japan. Similarly, the Thai market is represented by 98% of tourists from Thailand and 2% from Japan and China. The Indonesian market is represented by 93.4% of tourists from Indonesia and 6.6% from Hong Kong and India. However, the issue of the regional differences is not analyzed here. The aim of the study is to analyze various Asian cultures from a broad national perspective, as opposed to a regional or an individual perspective, and to recognize a national dominant cultural character of the major Asian markets that distinguishes them from the Australian population. Similarly, the Australian sample is composed of hosts of different origins such as Britain and New Zealand, with 96% of the Australian sample born in Australia and 4% born in the United Kingdom and New Zealand.

The two distinct groups, tourists and hosts, were chosen for the study because these groups are the major tourism players. Hosts in this study are nationals of the visited country who are employed in the tourism industry and provide a service to tourists (e.g., front-office employees, bus drivers,

shop assistants, waitresses, custom officials). Knight (1996) referred to hosts as those who provide tourism services (e.g., shelter, accommodation, and food), are in direct contact with tourists, and derive direct benefits from the tourists. Nettekoven (1979) referred to them as "professional hosts" who are employed in the places of most frequent tourist visitation. These places offer maximum opportunities for a direct tourist-host contact. As a result, hosts represent the first contact points with tourists. Consequently, cross-cultural differences in the interpersonal interaction in the tourism context are most likely to be apparent in these two groups, tourists and hosts.

One may, of course, argue that the interaction between local providers and international tourists is itself affected by business practices and tourism transactions that shape the nature of the tourist-host contact; thus, the variations in this contact may not be necessarily attributed to the nature of cultural differences. However, the provider's business practices as well as the tourist's perceptions of these practices are by themselves culturally determined. The provider's service behavior is subjected to the influence of a provider national culture; the tourist's perceptions of the provider's behavior are subjected to the influences of a tourist national culture. Thus, the variations in their interpersonal interaction are attributed to the cultural differences in their perceptions of what constitutes the socially and culturally appropriate service behavior. This is supported by the literature review findings, which show that the cultural differences in interaction patterns between guests and service providers lead to different perceptions of the guests' treatment (Sheldon and Fox 1988).

HYPOTHESES

The findings of the literature review show that there are differences in cultural values, rules of social behavior, perceptions, social interaction, and satisfaction among various nationalities. Therefore, it is hypothesized that there are significant differences in these measurement groups between Asian and Australian populations in the tourism context. These differences can be grouped into dimensions of cultural differences between Asian tourists and Australian hosts.

LITERATURE REVIEW

Culture

According to Tylor (1924), culture is the "complex whole which includes knowledge, beliefs, art, morals, law, customs, and any other capabilities and habits acquired by man as a member of society" (p. 1). Culture is a way of life of a particular group of people (Harris and Moran 1979) and it holds human groups together (Benedict, cited in Kluckhohn 1944). Culture represents patterns of behavior associated with particular groups of people (Barnlund and Araki 1985), "standards for deciding what is . . . , what can be, . . . what one feels about it, what to do about it, and how to go about doing it" (Goodenough 1961, p. 522). Culture is a guide to behavioral interpretation (Kim and Gudykunst 1988). It is a way of feeling and thinking (Harris 1988) and doing things (Sapir-Whorf 1921) and a means through which human needs are met (Malinowski 1939) and values are communicated (Dodd, Hattersley, and Swan 1990).

Culture includes systems of values (Hofstede 1980), symbols and meanings (Kim and Gudykunst 1988) that influence experiences, help to communicate, develop attitudes toward life (Geertz 1973), and allow for interaction that is understood by the group (Foster 1962). Culture also represents "the sum of peoples' perceptions of themselves and of the world" (Urriola 1989, p. 66). The similarity in these perceptions indicates the similarity of peoples' cultures and sharing and understanding of meanings (Samovar, Porter, and Jain 1981). Hofstede (1980) argued that culture is " the collective programming of the mind which distinguishes the members of one human group from another" (p. 5). Kluckhohn and Kelly (1945) argued that culture is an information system. Hall (1965) viewed culture as a communication system. Language, "the symbolic guide to culture" (Sapir 1964, p. 70), "transmits values, beliefs, perceptions, norms" (Samovar, Porter, and Jain 1981, p. 141) and facilitates man's perceptions of the world (Sapir 1964). Consequently, differences in language can create different ways of communication.

Culture includes the observable elements, such as the observable characteristics of behavior, material arts, and social arrangements, and nonobservable elements such as the beliefs, attitudes, and values held by most people in a society (Sussmann and Rashcovsky 1997). Triandis (1972) added other elements, such as role perceptions, stereotypes, categorizations, evaluations, expectations, memories, and opinions. Members of a similar culture have similar values; conform to similar rules and norms; develop similar perceptions, attitudes, and stereotypes; use common language; and participate in similar activities (Samovar, Porter, and Jain 1981; Triandis 1972). However, "when the similar behavior patterns obtained in one culture differ from the similar patterns obtained in another, we infer the existence of some differences in subjective culture" (Triandis 1972, p. 9). These differences indicate that individuals belong to different cultures (Landis and Brislin 1983, p. 187). Consequently, culture can be referred to as differences between groups of people who do things differently and perceive the world differently (Potter 1989).

Culture exists at various levels of society: civilizations culture (Eastern vs. Western), national culture (American and French), ethnic culture (Chinese and Malay), occupational culture (lawyers, doctors), organizational culture (IBM, McDonald's), and industries culture (hotels) (Pizam 1993).

Hofstede (1980) identified four basic dimensions on which national cultures vary from each other: (1) power distance, the extent to which society accepts inequality in power and the way in which interpersonal relationships develop in hierarchical society; (2) uncertainty avoidance, the extent to which culture encourages risk taking and tolerates uncertainty and the extent to which people feel threatened by ambiguous situations; (3) individualism-collectivism, the extent to which culture encourages individuals to be concerned about own goals and needs as opposed to collective goals and needs; and (4) masculinity-femininity, the extent to which "masculine" values such as assertiveness, materialism, and lack of concern for others prevail over the "feminine" values such as quality of life, concern for others, and harmonious human relations.

Although Hofstede's (1980) work has a wide managerial application, it was criticized for (1) not identifying all dimen-

sions (e.g., Confucian dynamism was missing); (2) putting too much emphasis on sexism in the masculine/feminine dimensions; (3) defining the individualism/collectivism dimensions primarily in relationship to the private self, as opposed to one's family; (4) being culture bound; and (5) including all employees of only one company (IBM) in a single industry. In addition, Hofstede mistakenly assumed that culture corresponds with national territory and that cultures are homogenous. In fact, many cultures (e.g., the United States, Australia, and Canada) have a wide range of national ethnic cultures.

Kluckhohn and Strodtbeck (1961) differentiated cultures by their value orientations toward five universal relationships: (1) toward humans: human beings may be perceived as good, a mixture of good and evil, or evil; (2) toward nature: humans may be subjected to nature, live in harmony with nature, or control nature; (3) toward activity: cultures may be "being," "becoming," or "doing"; (4) toward time: past, present, and future; and (5) toward relationships among people: lineal (hierarchical relationship), collateral (group relationship), and individualism (the individual goals take primacy over group goals).

Hall (1983) differentiated cultures in terms of (1) context: the level of information included in a communication message—low context cultures versus high context cultures; (2) space: ways of communicating through handling of personal space; (3) time: different perceptions and orientations toward time—monochronic cultures versus polychronic cultures; and (4) information flow: the structure and speed of messages between individuals.

Cultural Differences

The cultural dimensions, on which national cultures vary, indicate the existence of differences between cultures. The main cultural differences were found to be in cultural values; social categories such as role, status, class, hierarchy, attitudes, perceptions, patterns of interaction, relationships, verbal (language and paralanguage: intonation, laughing, crying, questioning) and nonverbal (body language such as facial expressions, head movements, gestures, use of space, use of physical distance between people); communication (Bochner 1982); and service (Wei, Crompton, and Reid 1989).

The cultural differences may be small and supplementary or large and incompatible (Sutton 1967). When the differences are small, people are not separated by cultural distance. When the differences are large, people are separated by large cultural distance (Sutton 1967). Large cultural differences may create cultural conflicts between a host population and tourists (Wei, Crompton, and Reid 1989). These conflicts are related to value systems, lifestyles, individual behavior, expectations, traditions, safety levels, and moral conduct (Mathieson and Wall 1982). The main sources of cultural conflict are (1) cultural ethnocentrism, (2) communication process as related to language and interpretation, (3) poor quality of service and lack of understanding and appreciation of international service standards and visitors' expectations, and (4) lifestyle differences and differences in customs, particularly in relation to accommodation and food (Wei, Crompton, and Reid 1989). Cultural conflicts can emerge not only when a number of visitations to a destination is growing but also when a destination attracts a steady flow of tourists (Wei, Crompton, and Reid 1989). They occur because international tourists and hosts are, in most cases, socially unskilled in a foreign

JOURNAL OF TRAVEL RESEARCH   299

culture. However, the cultural conflicts may be significantly minimized when tourists and hosts are aware of the cultural differences between each other. Consequently, it is important to understand the target culture and the reasons for cultural dissimilarity.

The greatest cultural differences were found among Asian and Western cultures (Samovar and Porter 1991), particularly in network patterns (Yum 1985), self-presentation (Tu 1985), self-disclosure (Ting-Toomey 1991), expressing emotions (Schrerer, Wallbott, and Summerfield 1986), feelings of responsibility for other people (Argyle 1972), understanding of morality (Retting and Pasamanick 1962), accepting compliments (Barnlund and Araki 1985), perceptions of social interaction (Kim and Gudykunst 1988), formality (Samovar and Porter 1988), and understanding of what constitutes friendship (Wei, Crompton, and Reid 1989).

Cultural Differences in Values

Of particular importance are differences in cultural values (Sutton 1967; Taft 1977). Value has been defined as "an enduring belief that a specific mode of conduct or end-state of existence is personally and socially preferable to an opposite mode of conduct or end-state of existence" (Rokeach 1973, p. 5). Values are individual attributes that contribute to the development of attitudes (Samovar and Porter 1988), perceptions, needs, and motivations of people (Bailey 1991). They provide a set of rules for behavior (Samovar and Porter 1988) and are standards of conduct (Williams 1968) and factors for resolving conflicts and decision making (Rokeach 1973). People from different cultures possess different values (Segall 1986). The differences in values reflect differences in behavior (Rokeach 1973), perceptions of social status, goals, interests, activities, and willingness to cooperate or compete (Amir 1969). People with similar values are perceived to be more similar than those who perceive their values to be dissimilar (Feather 1980b; Obot 1988). As a result, values can differentiate cultural groups (e.g., Hofstede 1980).

Values have been shown to be useful in the analysis of the consumer's motives (Munson 1984) and understanding leisure and travel behavior (Pitts and Woodside 1986). On the basis of values, one may differentiate individuals with similar leisure/recreation choice criteria and travel behavior (Pitts and Woodside 1986). Values also have been shown to be useful market segmentation variables. They define market segments desiring similar product benefits (Vinson and Munson 1976). Values enrich segment descriptions and other socioeconomic segmentation variables (Dhalla and Mahatto 1976). Boote (1981) found that personal values are better market segmentation variables than demographic characteristics. Values also have been used to explain variations in the behavior of consumers of different cultural groups. Values are particularly useful in describing individuals who visit a specific destination or attractions versus those who do not visit. Consequently, by examining values, marketers can learn about the visitors and what they seek in their activities (Pitts and Woodside 1986).

Cultural Differences in Rules of Social Behavior

Rules of social behavior guide and direct behavior (Fridgen 1991). They indicate how people ought or ought not to behave (Argyle and Henderson 1985). They govern verbal and nonverbal behavior. They are important components of relationships (Argyle and Henderson 1985). They are developed to understand the meanings of behavior, make social interaction easier (J. Cohen 1972) and more understandable to others (Y. Kim 1988), and achieve harmony of interaction (Moghaddam, Taylor, and Wrigth 1993). Rules set expectations and standards for evaluation (Noesjirwan and Freestone 1979).

Although there are rules of behavior that are universal, there are many rules that vary according to dominant culture (Mann 1986; Triandis 1972). For instance, there are different ways of defining interpersonal relations and attributing importance to social interactions (Wagatsuma and Rosett 1986); establishing and maintaining relations; greetings; self-presentations (Argyle 1967); beginnings of conversation; degree of expressiveness, frankness, intensity, persistency, intimacy, and volume of interaction (Jensen 1970); understanding of what constitutes friendship (Wei, Crompton, and Reid 1989); expressing dissatisfaction and criticism (Nomura and Barnlund 1983); describing reasons and opinions; exaggerations; and telling the truth (Argyle 1978). There are differences in physical distance; gestures; eye and body movement; standing; looking; touching; expressing politeness, dislike, and negative opinions; joking; showing warmth; addressing people; apologizing; farewelling; use of time; perceiving sense of shame; feelings of obligations; responsibility; avoiding embarrassment; confrontation; taking initiatives; responses; external appearance; even entertaining guests or eating and drinking habits (Argyle 1972, 1978; Dodd 1987; Gudykunst and Kim 1984; Hall 1983).

In the tourism context, cultural differences in social behavior were found in the amount of leisure time spent on various activities among nations (Ibrahim 1991), patterns of recreation (Rodgers 1977), leisure and travel behavior (Sussmann and Rashcovsky 1997; Pizam and Sussmann 1995; Pizam and Jeong 1996), vacation travel preferences (Richardson and Crompton 1988; Ah-Keng 1993), importance of food (Sheldon and Fox 1988), benefits derived from traveling (Woodside and Lawrence 1985), sources of information used when deciding about vacation destinations (Mihalik, Uysal, and Pan 1995), tipping (Lynn 1997), purchasing arts (Thompson and Cutler 1997), and complaining behavior (Huang, Huang, and Wu 1996).

Cultural differences (and similarities) were found in the traveling behavior of the Asian markets (March 1997). The differences included the following: (1) ability and desire to speak English (Indonesians speak better English than Koreans), (2) eating patterns dependent on religious factors (Koreans have strong preference for their own cuisine; Indonesians require halal food), (3) level of adventurous spirit (Koreans are more adventurous than Japanese), (4) degree of overseas travel experience, (5) consumer expectations from overseas travel, and (6) different traveling patterns and demands in terms of desired accommodation (luxury versus budget), purpose of travel, seasonality due to different school holiday calendars, and shopping behavior (big versus moderate spenders). The similarities included (1) tendency for group travel, (2) desire for luxury and brand-name products, and (3) tendency not to give direct feedback to the service provider about service quality. It was found that when deciding about their vacation destinations, the Japanese relied more heavily on the print medium as an information source, while the

300   FEBRUARY 2002

Germans relied more on word-of-mouth advice from family and friends (Mihalik, Uysal, and Pan 1995). In response to unsatisfactory service in a hotel, Americans were more likely to stop patronizing the hotel, complain to hotel management, and warn family and friends. Japanese, on the other hand, were more likely to take no action (Huang, Yung, and Huang 1996). Pizam and Sussmann (1995) noted that behavioral differences between tourists from Japan, France, Italy, and the United States were attributable to cultural influences. Ibrahim (1991) reported that these differences were caused by the differences in value systems.

Differences in rules of behavior may cause social interaction difficulties because members of different cultures may misunderstand and misinterpret the rules of other cultures. Stringer (1981) noted that in bed-and-breakfast establishments, even different customs of handling cutlery and eating habits caused irritation. Consequently, an analysis of the rules governing contact with foreigners is important (Argyle et al. 1986) and can facilitate the improvement of social relationships (Argyle 1981).

Cultural Differences in Perceptions

Perceptions are "the impressions people form of one another and how interpretations are made concerning the behavior of others" (Hargie 1986, p. 47). Cultural differences cause different nationalities to perceive differently (Mayo and Jarvis 1981) and interpret causes differently (Segall et al. 1990). Alhemoud and Armstrong (1996) found that Kuwaiti University students and English-speaking foreigners living in Kuwait had significantly different perceptions of tourism attractions in Kuwait. Foreigners were more impressed with cultural attractions, while the students favored manufactured attractions. Several empirical studies have been conducted on the cultural differences in perceptions (Samovar and Porter 1991).

Perceptions of local people are a very important part of the total tourism product. They may enhance tourist holiday experiences and contribute to the success of the tourist destination (Hunt 1975) or deter visitation. Hoffman and Low (1981) found that tourists' perceptions of residents were the single most important factor determining tourists' repeat visitation. They noted that tourists would not return to destinations where they would not feel welcomed, and they would likely tell others of their less than satisfying experiences.

A primary way in which visitors form perceptions and make judgments about their hosts is interacting with service personnel (Wei, Crompton, and Reid 1989). Service providers play an important role in influencing the customer's perceptions (Zeithaml, Parasuraman, and Berry 1990). The cultural differences influence the interaction processes between a service provider and a visitor during service delivery (Wei, Crompton, and Reid 1989). Armstrong, Mok, and Go (1997) found significant differences in perceptions of service quality in the Hong Kong hotel industry between European, Asian, and English Heritage cultural group clusters (representing tourists from 28 countries). Sheldon and Fox (1988) showed that cultural differences lead to different perceptions of what constitutes proper guests' treatment. When providers deal with the culturally different customer, the differences between what guests expect and what providers think the guests expect (Zeithaml, Parasuraman, and Berry 1990) may be large.

Cultural differences also shape different attitudes of hosts to the tourists they serve (Richter 1983). Many studies identified cultural differences in perceptions of international tourists by local hosts by nationalities (Pizam and Sussmann 1995; Richardson and Crompton 1988). Residents of host destinations perceived the tourists to be different than themselves in a variety of behavioral characteristics and lifestyles (Pizam and Telisman-Kosuta 1989). The Japanese tourists were perceived as traveling in groups, bowing to everybody, heavily spending and constantly photographing (Cho 1991), taking short holidays to avoid separation with the family, and expecting the infrastructure for larger groups (Ritter 1987). Koreans were perceived as loyal to their sociocultural identity, unwilling to accept non-Korean ways of living, fond of Confucian philosophy, traveling in groups, spending freely (Cho 1991; Business Korea 1991), and conducting their trips in a loose and unplanned manner relative to the Japanese and Americans, who travel in a rigid and meticulous manner (Pizam and Jeong 1996). The local residents perceived the tourists to be different from themselves in the destinations where the majority of tourists were foreigners and only minimally different in the destinations where the majority were domestic tourists (Pizam and Telisman-Kosuta 1989).

National cultures have an important intervening effect on tourist behavior (Pizam and Jeong 1996). However, Dann (1993) criticized the practice of using nationality as a discriminant variable for explaining the differences in tourist behavior. According to Dann, many tourists possess multiple nationalities, and their country of birth may be different from their country of nationality. Many tourists from the United States, Canada, or Australia are also pluralistic in their cultures.

Cultural Differences in Social Interaction

Tourist-host social interaction occurs as the tourist travels, stays in hotels, dines, visits tourist attractions, goes shopping or to nightclubs, talks to tour guides, and so forth. This interaction may take the form of observation of members of the other group without any communication, friendly greetings, inquiries at the front office, business transactions at stores, or even prolonged intimate association (Cook and Sellitz 1955). In the cross-cultural setting, this interaction refers to the direct face-to-face encounters between tourists and hosts who are members of different cultural groups, speak different languages, and have different values and perceptions of the world (Bochner 1982; Sutton 1967). This type of contact is experienced by tourists when they travel from a home culture to the host culture and by hosts when they serve tourists from a foreign culture.

Although the contact hypothesis indicates that the contact between tourists and hosts from different cultures can lead to enhancement of tourists' and hosts' attitudes toward each other, learning about each other's culture, fostering social interaction (Bochner 1982), positive attitude change (Pearce 1982), exchange of correspondence and gifts, development of personal relationships (Smith 1957), friendships (e.g., Boissevain 1979; Pearce 1988), and satisfaction (e.g., Stringer 1981), the same contact also may generate negative feelings. For example, it may develop negative attitudes, stereotypes, and prejudices; and increase tension, hostility, suspicion, and often violent attacks (Bochner 1982; Pi-Sunyer 1978).

The outcomes of the social interaction between tourists and hosts from different cultures depend on the degree of

JOURNAL OF TRAVEL RESEARCH   301

"interculturalness" in the encounter, that is, the extent of similarity and differences between participants (Levine 1979). Consequently, large cultural differences do not allow for effectively dealing with members of other cultures (Kim and Gudykunst 1988). According to Pearce (1982), there is always an opportunity for misunderstanding and interaction difficulties when there is a meeting of cultures that differ in interpersonal conduct.

Fontaine (1983) listed difficulties in culturally and linguistically different countries due to differences in word use, styles of interaction, and rules governing these interactions. Craig (1979) found differences in understanding of appropriate qualities in interpersonal behavior. Qualities (such as being yourself, open, friendly, outspoken, informal, and truthful in interpersonal relations) admired in most Western cultures are less likely to be admired in Eastern societies that view Westerners as lacking grace, manners, and cleverness (Craig 1979). The understanding of friendship is also different. Americans regard friendships as superficial and without obligation. Chinese understand friendships in terms of mutual obligations and reciprocation (Wei, Crompton, and Reid 1989).

The tourist-host interaction can be analyzed in terms of the service encounter (Riley 1995). In the tourism and hospitality industry that deals with intangible elements of its product, it is the nature and quality of the service encounter that establishes and confirms customer expectations about it. Shostack (1985) defined service encounter as "a period of time during which a consumer directly interacts with a service" (p. 243) and when the customer makes judgments about the service. The service encounter is usually termed the moment of truth (Normann 1984) because it provides the opportunity for customers to experience either conformation or disconfirmation of their expectations, which, in turn, contributes to their satisfaction (Smith and Houston 1983). The customer's perception of this encounter is a crucial component in the evaluation of the quality of the service (Bitner 1990). Service quality is highly dependent on the performance of service providers (Elliott 1995). The providers play a major role in creating a positive impression for the customer (Bejou, Edvardsson, and Rakowski 1996). Saleh and Ryan (1991) emphasized the providers' ability to empathize with the customer as indicated by the term "the service of conviviality." Gronroos (1990) believed that both the instrumental (*what* the customer gets from the service) and expressive performance (*how* the customer gets the service) of service quality are needed to satisfy customers.

The interaction patterns between guests and service providers are influenced by cultural differences (Sheldon and Fox 1988). Sheldon and Fox (1988) noted that Chinese hosts believe that by escorting their guests everywhere and providing them with a very tight itinerary, they provide their guests with courteous and high-quality service. Japanese hosts take care of the affairs of their guests in advance and even fulfill their needs beyond expectations (Befu 1971), believing that the hosts know best what the guests' needs are. Western tourists may view such hospitality as uncomfortable, intrusive, or lacking trust.

Satisfaction

Satisfaction is a state of mind in which customers' needs, wants, and expectations are being met or exceeded, resulting in repurchase and loyalty (Anton 1996). Westbrook (1981) defined satisfaction as a psychological outcome deriving from an experience. Pizam, Neumann, and Reichel (1978) defined it as the result of the comparison between a tourist's experience and expectations. Pearce (1988) suggested that fulfillment of expectations depends on how much people value the outcome of their experiences. Hughes (1991) proposed to analyze satisfaction in terms of the degree of fit between the tourist expectations and the ability of the environment to meet these expectations, implying that when the tourist's cultural environment fits the host's cultural environment, the optimal fit is achieved. When the host's environment cannot meet the tourist's expectations, mismatch can lead to feelings of stress, anxiety, and dissatisfaction.

The availability of high-quality service substantially influences consumer satisfaction (Anton 1996; Wuest, Tas, and Emenheiser 1996). Service providers play a key role in satisfying customer expectations (Zeithaml, Parasuraman, and Berry 1990). Of particular importance is the extent to which service providers understand the nature of the tourists' needs (Saleh and Ryan 1991). Crotts and Ryan (1997) noted that it is vital to address the cultural needs of different tourist markets to preclude the delivery of experiences according to the providers' perceptions of tourists' needs.

The studies above suggest that significant cultural differences exist among the international tourist markets, and more investigation in the area of cultural differences between various nationalities in the tourism context is warranted. As Feather (1980b) and Sutton (1967) noted, the analysis of the cultural backgrounds of different nations and different groups within each nation is necessary to determine where differences in value priorities between these groups occur. "The whole question of which value discrepancies are the important ones for different groups and how these discrepancies are handled both between and within societies is one of great theoretical and practical importance" (Feather 1980b, p. 2).

METHODOLOGY

Sample

A sample of 618 Asian tourists visiting the Gold Coast region, Australia's major tourist destination, were personally interviewed in their own language, along with 250 Australian service providers. Asian tourists were surveyed in a variety of locations on the Gold Coast, where there is a large concentration of Asian tourists. The total population of Asian tourists was divided into five mutually exclusive and exhaustive strata (Asian language groups), which represented distinct Asian tourist markets: Indonesian, Japanese, Korean, Mandarin, and Thai. The selection of cultural language groups was based on the statistical data showing the arrivals of international tourists to Australia from major countries of origin. A representative sample of respondents was chosen from each stratum. The sample elements were not selected in proportions that reflected the size of each major Asian tourist market on the Gold Coast; rather, the emphasis was on getting a maximum number of respondents from different language groups. An attempt was, however, made to choose respondents from a wide variety of sociodemographic backgrounds. This was done to ensure the samples representativeness of the central tendency of their culture. The respondents

302 FEBRUARY 2002

were equivalent in their characteristics in terms of the purpose of travel and length of stay on the Gold Coast. Australian hosts were randomly selected from a variety of sectors of the tourism and hospitality industry on the Gold Coast such as accommodation, transportation, or entertainment in the same time period. Again, disproportionate samples were taken from each stratum because proportionate samples would have resulted in small samples. The study was conducted over the period 1994 to 1995.

Instrument

Five measurement groups of cultural values, rules of social behavior, perceptions of service, forms of interaction, and satisfaction with interaction were measured by a structured questionnaire. Personal values were measured using the Rokeach Values Survey (RVS) (Rokeach 1973). The RVS was assessed as the best available instrument for measuring values because it is "based on a well-articulated conceptualization of value" and is successful in "finding specific values that differentiate various political, religious, economic, generation and cultural groups" (Braithwaite and Law 1985, p. 250). The RVS has been used in numerous studies to measure human values (e.g., Feather 1980a, 1980b, 1980c, 1986a, 1986b; Ng et al. 1982), and it has identified cultural differences between countries, including differences between Western and Asian countries. The 36-item RVS scale produced a Cronbach alpha value of .9497 that indicated that the RVS was a very reliable instrument. In respect of validity, all items were adapted from the RVS (Rokeach 1973). Rokeach (1973) selected only those values that were considered to be important across culture, status, and sex (Rokeach 1971).[1] The respondents were asked to indicate the importance of specific values by rating them on a 6-point scale, ranging from 1 (*not important*) to 6 (*extremely important*).

Rules of social interaction were measured using Argyle et al.'s (1986) list of 34 rules of social behavior, which also has been widely used and assessed as a reliable and valid measure of the rules of social relationships. Only the rules that were applicable to tourist-host interaction were included; the rules that governed family invitations, social visitation, or sexual activity were excluded. The rules specific to Asian cultures, such as the clear indication of intentions, conforming to rules of etiquette and the status of the other person, having a sense of shame, and avoiding embarrassment, were included. These rules were chosen from the literature on interpersonal relations in Asian cultures and focus group discussions with Asian students. The Cronbach alpha was .9048, indicating that the instrument was highly reliable. The respondents were asked to indicate the importance of specific rules on a 6-point Likert-type scale, ranging from 1 (*not important*) to 6 (*extremely important*).

Perceptions of service were measured using a 22-item SERVQUAL instrument (Parasuraman, Zeithaml, and Berry 1985, 1988), which also has been widely applied in empirical studies in various disciplines, including the hospitality and tourism industry, and assessed as reliable and highly valuable (Fick and Ritchie 1991; Luk et al. 1993; Albrecht 1992; LeBlanc 1992; Saleh and Ryan 1991). However, the SERVQUAL scale was modified by eliminating all positive and negative statements, including the word *should*, which made comparison of responses difficult. Only the words describing service (adjectives) were used. Also, the scale

was supplemented by additional items to reflect the distinctive features of high-quality service as perceived by Asian visitors (e.g., the ability of hosts to speak an Asian language, treat tourists as guests, know Asian culture and customs). These distinctive items of service were identified on the basis of the literature review about service quality. The responses were measured on a 6-point Likert-type scale, ranging from 1 (*least important*) to 6 (*extremely important*). Cronbach alpha for the 29-item perception scale was .9567, indicating a high reliability of the instrument.

Tourist-host interaction was measured using a list of various forms of interaction, such as playing sport together, having a close relationship, or sharing a meal. These items were adapted from several studies' direct and indirect measures of social contact (Black and Mendenhall 1989; Vassiliou et al. 1972; Feather 1980b; Kamal and Maruyama 1990; Gudykunst 1979; McAllister and Moore 1991). Again, the responses were measured on a 6-point scale ranging from 1 (*least preferred*) to 6 (*most preferred*). The Cronbach alpha for the scale was high at .8558.

Satisfaction with interaction was measured using a list of various components of satisfaction with social interaction, such as satisfaction with language spoken, conversation, or time spent together. The items were measured on a 6-point scale ranging from 1 (*dissatisfied*) to 6 (*extremely satisfied*). The Cronbach alpha for the scale was high at .8876.

The Cronbach alpha was also computed for the host survey and was .9462 for the values scale, .8418 for the rules scale, .9230 for the perceptions scale, .7513 for the interaction scale, and .8394 for the satisfaction scale.

The instrument also included a section on sociodemographic characteristics of respondents.

Procedure

The instrument was translated into Asian languages and back translated to the English language by a professional translating agency. The instrument was pretested twice in two pilot studies to ensure that it was clear and understandable: once on a sample of 20 Australian tourists and 20 providers and the second time on a sample of 50 Asian tourists. Professional native Asian-language-speaking interviewers were hired to collect data. In total, the data collection process resulted in surveying 870 respondents: 250 Australian hosts and 618 Asian tourists from five language groups (106 Indonesian, 108 Japanese, 172 Korean, 130 Mandarin speaking, and 102 Thai).

Data Analysis

Because of the smaller individual sample sizes, there was a need to reduce the number of variables analyzed. Thus, the analysis focused only on the variables that statistically differed between Asian and Australian populations. These differences were identified by the Mann-Whitney U-Test.

The basic dimensions of the cultural differences (the gap scores) were determined by principal components analysis. Only the raw scores for those variables that differed were factor analyzed, as from a marketing perspective the interest lay in what cultural aspects were different rather than similar. Although an analysis of the entire set of variables would be interesting, the number of variables to case size would have been too large. R-type factor analysis was used (instead of Q-type) to analyze relationships among the variables (instead

Managing Tourism Firms

of cases) and to identify groups of variables forming latent dimensions (factors) not easily observed. Principal components analysis was chosen (instead of common factor analysis) to minimize the number of factors needed to account for the maximum portion of the variance represented in the original set of variables and to reduce the specific and error variance as a proportion of the total variance. Oblique rotation was chosen to obtain several theoretically meaningful interrelated factors, as opposed to orthogonal rotation, which reduces the number of variables to a smaller set of independent factors regardless of how meaningful the resulting factors are. Only the factors having latent roots (eigenvalues) greater than 1 and factor loadings greater than 0.6 were considered significant. Comrey in Hair et al. (1995) suggested that loadings in excess of 0.63 (40% of overlapping variance) are very good and in excess of 0.70 (50% of overlapping variance) are excellent.[2]

RESULTS

Profile of the Respondents

The Asian sample tended to be older than the Australian sample with the majority (55%) of the former being older than 30 years of age and 60% of the later being younger than 30 years of age. The Asian sample had a high percentage of those with higher and postgraduate degrees (45%), while the Australian sample had a very high percentage with a high school education only (60%). One-third of the Asian tourists (31%) had completed high school only. The largest groups of Asian tourists (17.8%) were represented by administrators and managers, followed by professionals (14.6%), educators (14.4%), and sales representatives (12.8%). The largest groups of Australian providers were represented by food and beverage employees (19.6%), front-office staff (18.4%), sales representatives (17.6%), housekeepers (17.6%), transport employees (8%), tour guides (7.2%), and entertainers (6.4%).

The largest group of Asian tourists was Korean (28%), followed by Japanese (17.5%), Thai (16.3%), Indonesian (16.2%), and Singaporean (11.5%) nationalities. Nearly 80% of all Asian respondents came to Australia for the purpose of holiday. The majority of them (41%) were on their first trip to Australia, while 36% had visited Australia once before. The majority of the Asian tourists (80%) stayed in Australia for more than 5 days, and 24% stayed for 7.

About 11% of Asian tourists did not speak English at all, while the majority of the Australian hosts (63%) did not speak an Asian language at all. The major sociodemographic characteristics of the Asian and Australian respondents are presented in Tables 3 and 4.[3]

Results of the Mann Whitney U-Test

The results of the Mann Whitney U-Test identified significant differences in all five measurement groups (cultural values, rules of behavior, perceptions of service, forms of interaction, satisfaction with interaction) between the total Asian and Australian populations, with 73 out of 117 (62.4%) areas of measurement showing significant cultural differences between the Australian and the total Asian samples (see Tables 5 and 6).[4]

TABLE 3

MAJOR SOCIODEMOGRAPHIC CHARACTERISTICS OF ASIAN TOURISTS

Asian Tourists	Percentage
Age	
Younger than 18 years	3.4
18-24	18.9
25-31	23.0
32-38	21.0
39-45	15.5
46-52	10.7
53-59	4.9
60 and older	2.6
Education	
Primary school	3.7
High school	30.7
Diploma	20.1
University degree	38.8
Postgraduate degree	6.6
Occupation	
Manager/administrator	17.8
Professional	14.6
Semiprofessional	7.4
Tradesperson	3.4
Clerk	10.0
Salesperson/service worker	12.8
Machine operator/driver	1.6
Laborer	1.3
Homemaker	8.3
Student	14.4
Unemployed	5.2
Retired	3.2
Country of residence	
Korea	28.0
Japan	18.0
Indonesia	16.5
Thailand	16.2
Singapore	12.5
Nationality	
Korean	28.0
Japanese	17.5
Thai	16.3
Indonesian	16.2
Singaporean	1.5
Language spoken	
Indonesian	17.2
Japanese	17.5
Korean	27.8
Mandarin	21.0
Thai	16.5
Purpose of visitation	
Holiday	79.6
Business	5.3
Study	8.9
Visiting friends and relatives	5.3
Sport	0.8
Previous visitation	
Never	40.6
One time	8.6
Two times	36.4
Three times	5.2
Four times and more	3.2
Length of stay	
1 day	1.5
2 days	0.8
3 days	2.8
4 days	4.7

(continued)

TABLE 3 Continued

Asian Tourists	Percentage
5 days	10.2
6 days	12.6
7 days	24.3
8 days	13.4
9 days	6.0
10 days	23.8
Knowledge of English	
1 (not at all)	11.3
2	21.2
3	21.7
4	20.7
5	12.9
6 (fluent)	12.1
Differences in behavior	
1 (very similar)	2.8
2	11.0
3	21.5
4	28.8
5	15.4
6 (totally different)	20.6

TABLE 4

MAJOR SOCIODEMOGRAPHIC
CHARACTERISTICS OF AUSTRALIAN HOSTS

Australian Hosts	Percentage
Age	
Younger than 18 years	1.2
18-24	39.2
25-31	18.0
32-38	12.8
39-45	9.6
46-52	13.2
53-59	5.2
60 and older	0.8
Education	
Primary school	1.2
High school	60.0
Diploma	25.6
University degree	12.8
Postgraduate degree	0.4
Occupation	
Front office	18.4
Food and beverage	19.6
Retail	17.6
Tour guide	7.2
Custom	0.0
Transport	8.0
Entertainment	6.4
Travel operations	1.2
Ride operations	4.0
Housekeeping	17.6
Knowledge of Asian language	
1 (not at all)	63.2
2 (very little)	21.2
3	9.2
4	2.0
5	2.4
6 (fluent)	2.0
Differences in behavior	
1 (very similar)	4.0
2	5.2
3	18.8
4	30.8
5	23.2
6 (totally different)	18.0

The Mann Whitney U-Test also identified significant differences in all five measurement groups between the individual Asian language groups and the Australian sample. The Japanese were the most distinct from the Australian hosts. Of 117 areas of measurement, 83 significant differences were found between Australian hosts and Japanese tourists, 74 between the Korean sample, 64 between the Indonesian and Thai samples, and 53 between the Mandarin sample (see Table 5).[5]

Results of the Principal Components Analysis

The analysis identified several cultural dimensions in the total Asian sample and each Asian language group. In the total Asian sample, five dimensions were identified: perceptions of communication, values of family/competence, interaction, rules of feeling display, and satisfaction. The dimension of communication reflects the tourists' need for adequate communication with hosts and the hosts' ability to be informative, give adequate explanations, listen to tourists, and anticipate and understand tourists' needs. The dimension of family/competence reflects the importance of family and cues that describe the person's capabilities to succeed, such as being intellectual, independent, self-controlled, and polite. The dimension of interaction describes the preferences for forms of social interaction such as being invited home or playing sport together. The dimension of feeling display indicates disclosing personal feelings in public such as criticizing in public or showing respect. The dimension of satisfaction shows the components of satisfaction with social interaction between tourists and hosts (see Table 7).

In the Indonesian sample, four dimensions were identified: perceptions of responsiveness, perceptions of attention, interaction, and satisfaction. The dimension of responsiveness consists of variables that describe the hosts' capacity to respond to tourists' needs and provide required service, the cues associated with timing of service provision, physical appearance of service providers, and the hosts' ability to solve problems. The dimension of attention consists of variables that describe the hosts' ability to pay attention to tourists, anticipate and understand their needs, be concerned about tourists, and listen to them. The dimension of interaction describes the preferences for forms of social interaction. The dimension of satisfaction relates to satisfaction with the hosts' knowledge of Indonesian culture and language.

In the Japanese sample, five dimensions were identified: perceptions of helpfulness, values of competence, interaction, greetings, and satisfaction. The dimension of helpfulness consists of variables that describe the providers' ability to help tourists, respond to their needs including being punctual, accurate, able to solve problems, trustworthy, respectful, hospitable, polite, confident, communicative, informative, and professional. The dimension of competence consists of variables that describe the cues associated with accomplishment, such as being intellectual, logical, obedient, self-respectful, wise, and independent. The dimension of interaction describes the preferences for social interaction. The

JOURNAL OF TRAVEL RESEARCH   305

TABLE 5

NUMBER OF SIGNIFICANT DIFFERENCES BETWEEN AUSTRALIAN HOSTS AND ASIAN LANGUAGE GROUPS

Group Indicators	Max	Total Asian	Indonesian	Japanese	Korean	Mandarin	Thai
Cultural values	36	18	14	26	26	12	14
Rules of interaction	34	22	24	22	18	18	20
Perceptions of service	29	23	18	23	20	15	24
Forms of interaction	11	7	5	8	7	6	3
Satisfaction	7	3	3	4	3	2	3
Total	117	73	64	83	74	53	64

dimension of greetings is related to the way in which people greet each other, such as addressing by first name or shaking hands. The dimension of satisfaction relates to the satisfaction with friendship and time spent together.

In the Korean sample, five dimensions were identified: perceptions of communication, rules of feeling display, perceptions of performance, interaction, and satisfaction. The dimension of communication reflects the tourists' needs for adequate information and explanations, for someone to listen to them, and the hosts' ability to speak the Korean language and have some knowledge of the Korean culture. The dimension of feeling display is related to rules of social behavior and concerns of disclosing personal feelings in public. The dimension of performance consists of variables that describe the cues associated with providing high-quality service as perceived by the Korean tourists, that is, being responsive, respectful, punctual, and neatly dressed. The dimension of interaction describes the preferences for social interaction. The dimension of satisfaction relates to satisfaction with providers and friendship.

In the Mandarin sample, five dimensions were identified: perceptions of punctuality, interaction, perceptions of understanding, rules of feeling display, and satisfaction. The dimension of punctuality focuses on the timing and responsiveness of service. The dimension of interaction describes the preference for forms of social interaction. The dimension of understanding is related to the hosts' ability to anticipate and understand individual tourists' needs, pay attention to tourists, and speak the Asian language. The dimension of feeling display concerns disclosing personal feelings in public. The dimension of satisfaction relates to satisfaction with providers and time spent together.

In the Thai sample, five dimensions were identified: perceptions of courtesy, perceptions of understanding, rules of feeling display, satisfaction, and interaction. The dimension of courtesy consists of variables that describe the hosts' ability to treat tourists as guests and behave toward tourists in a respectful and polite manner. It entails the need to be trustworthy, considerate, and friendly. The dimension of understanding consists of variables that describe the hosts' ability to understand and anticipate tourists' needs, pay attention to tourists, listen to them, and keep them informed. The dimension of feeling display reflects cues associated with disclosure of personal feelings in public. The dimension of satisfaction relates to satisfaction with conversation, providers, and friendship. The dimension of interaction describes the preferred forms of social interaction.[6]

DISCUSSION

The interpretation of the identified dimensions in the total Asian sample, based on the findings of the literature review, is presented below. The interpretation of the identified dimensions in each Asian language group is not presented due to the limited space. However, several references to distinct Asian groups are made.

Total Asian Market

Communication. As high uncertainty avoidance cultures, all Asian markets do not tolerate ambiguity and taking risk. They are concerned about communication difficulties in Australia. Asian languages such as Japanese, Korean, or Mandarin have several different levels used by various social classes and genders. For example, DeMente (1991b) reported that there are different levels of the Korean language used by various social classes in a Korean hierarchical society: (1) an extremely polite form used when addressing superiors, (2) an intimate form for addressing close friends or equals, and (3) a rough form used when speaking to people on a lower social level. Also, all Asian markets use indirect smoothing strategies to manage conflicts (Kim and Gudykunst 1988). This is in contrast to Australians, who tolerate ambiguity and risk and do not avoid conflicts.

As members of high context cultures, Asian people communicate in an indirect, implicit way by using numerous nonverbal cues such as body language, facial expressions, or eye gaze. Australians, who belong to a low uncertainty and low context culture, have only one language used by all social classes and genders. They communicate in a more direct, explicit way by emphasizing words and verbal expressions.

Family/competence. Asians are very much family oriented. Family needs and security are the concern of all its members. The relationships between the family members are of a dependence nature. Each member of the family depends on the other for security and protection. In Australia, this type of dependency does not occur. Family ties are looser; people are taught to be self-reliant and independent. Also, in Asian high power distance cultures, societies have a well-developed social hierarchy. Proper education and intellectual achievements are important to get a good job and belong to the "right social class." For example, in the masculine Japanese culture, emphasis is placed on professional competence, intellectual achievements, and wisdom (Zimmerman 1985). In Australian low power distance culture, education and intellectual achievements are not of such importance. Austra-

TABLE 6

THE MANN-WHITNEY U-TEST OF THE DIFFERENCES IN CULTURAL VALUES, RULES OF SOCIAL INTERACTION, PERCEPTIONS OF SERVICE, FORMS OF INTERACTION, AND SATISFACTION WITH INTERACTION BETWEEN AUSTRALIAN HOSTS ($N = 250$) AND TOTAL ASIAN TOURISTS ($N = 618$)

	z-test
Cultural Values	
A comfortable life	−1.4703
An exciting life	−1.1237
A sense of accomplishment	−1.8044
A world of peace	−1.4887
A world of beauty	−0.5049
Equality	−2.8793**
Family security	−2.8891**
Freedom	−6.5026***
Happiness	−3.2357**
Inner harmony	−2.1927*
Mature love	−3.4440***
National security	−1.3962
Pleasure	−2.0275*
Salvation	−5.5966***
Self-respect	−6.7442***
Social recognition	−1.6728
True friendship	−2.4880*
Wisdom	−0.0306
Ambitious	−2.2367*
Broad-minded	−0.4982
Capable	−1.1952
Cheerful	−1.7364
Clean	−2.7369**
Courageous	−1.1777
Forgiving	−0.1657
Helpful	−0.0107
Honest	−3.1904**
Imaginative	−1.0280
Independent	−3.7725***
Intellectual	−2.1053*
Logical	−0.7708
Loving	−2.6717**
Obedient	−1.0057
Polite	−3.3062***
Responsible	−0.0102
Self-controlled	−2.4574*
Rules of social interaction	
Should address by first name	−5.6758***
Should shake hands	−6.8501***
Should look in the eye	−9.5694***
Should think about own needs	−0.4808
Should express opinion	−0.5112
Should show intentions clearly	−5.8349***
Should obey instructions	−6.3291***
Should criticize in public	−7.0109***
Should compliment other	−7.9697***
Should apologize if not at fault	−0.4428
Should compensate if at fault	−3.0403**
Should repay favors	−0.6371
Should take others' time	−3.2099**
Should develop relationship	−5.6425***
Should touch the other person	−1.2410
Should acknowledge birthday	−2.5842**
Should be neatly dressed	−1.2572
Should conform to etiquette	−3.9182***
Should conform to social status	−2.0481*
Should swear in public	−5.4757***
Should not make fun of other	−0.3453

TABLE 6   Continued

	z-test
Should avoid arguments	−6.6947***
Should avoid complaining	−2.9989**
Should avoid embarrassment	−0.6598
Should have a sense of shame	−5.6699***
Should ask for financial help	−0.6472
Should ask for advice	−1.4431
Should ask personal questions	−5.2496***
Should respect others' privacy	−6.3187***
Should show interest in others	−7.1359***
Should show respect to other	−8.1729***
Should show affection	−1.2262
Should show emotions	−3.9084***
Should talk about sensitive issues	−0.8220
Perceptions	
Neatly dressed	−5.2277***
Perform service required	−6.2694***
Responsive to tourists' needs	−6.6850***
Require help	−1.2015
Prompt service	−7.5167***
Service on time	−7.5816***
Find solutions to problems	−5.0824***
Answer questions	−4.5351***
Provide accurate information	−6.4345***
Friendly	−0.9894
Polite	−3.0413**
Respectful	−5.0529***
Considerate	−3.2617**
Treat as guests	−4.8425***
Trustworthy	−3.7197***
Confident	−0.4764
Concerned about welfare	−5.4387***
Approachable	−3.5354***
Easy to find	−7.7714***
Easy to talk to	−2.9905**
Keep tourists informed	−4.8190***
Listen to tourists	−5.7517***
Give adequate explanations	−3.2087**
Understand tourists' needs	−5.6261***
Anticipate tourists' needs	−5.0024***
Offer individualized attention	−4.2763***
Know Asian culture/customs	−0.4982
Speak Asian languages	−0.3821
Know Australian history/culture	−0.7542
Forms of interaction	
Invite home	−9.8994***
Play sport together	−3.6514***
Share recreation facilities	−0.5862
Take part in family parties	−7.9068***
Have close relationship	−7.8447***
Share a meal	−5.6582***
Chat on a street	−0.0996
Talk in shops	−0.5012
Exchange gifts	−2.4978*
Have business contact only	−2.6874**
Have no contact at all	−0.6818
Satisfaction	
With tourists/hosts	−4.9786***
With conversation	−0.2667
With friendship	−0.8191
With time spent together	−3.4804***
With knowledge of others' language	−1.9804*
With knowledge of others' culture	−0.3272
With service provided	−0.7144

*$p < .05$. **$p < .01$. ***$p < .001$.

JOURNAL OF TRAVEL RESEARCH   307

TABLE 7

**RESULTS OF THE PRINCIPAL COMPONENTS ANALYSIS IN THE TOTAL ASIAN
SAMPLE FOR THE VARIABLES THAT DIFFERED BETWEEN AUSTRALIAN HOSTS
AND ALL ASIAN TOURISTS (SIGNIFICANT FACTOR LOADINGS ONLY)**

	Factor	Loading	Variables Included in the Factor
F1	Communication	0.75601	Give adequate explanations
		0.75519	Anticipate tourists' needs
		0.74292	Understand tourists' needs
		0.73079	Listen to tourists
		0.72124	Offer individualized attention
		0.67482	Keep tourists informed
F2	Family/competence	0.76365	Family security
		0.74741	Intellectual
		0.70615	Independent
		0.65336	Self-controlled
		0.61418	Polite
F3	Interaction	0.85795	Have close relationship
		0.82800	Invite home
		0.82584	Take part in parties
		0.82131	Play sport together
		0.81233	Share a meal
		0.77885	Exchange gifts
F4	Feeling display	0.76020	Should criticize in public
		0.74455	Should show respect to others
		0.72936	Should ask personal questions
		0.72554	Should conform to social status
		0.71870	Should respect others' privacy
		0.71268	Should address by first name
		0.66947	Show emotions clearly
F5	Satisfaction	0.75012	With time spent together
		0.65842	With tourists/hosts
		0.63060	With knowledge of others' language

lian society regards education as a right instead of privilege and often disregards social position. Society values more sport heroes and financially wealthy people than intellectualists. On the other hand, the Thai people do not commit themselves seriously to hard work or education, which are essential for success (Komin 1990). Australians have more sense of achievement and internal motivation to work hard, self-actualization, and self-reliance.

Interaction. As members of collectivistic cultures, Asian people are oriented toward group interests and needs (Hsu 1953). The social relations are perceived in terms of social usefulness (Hsu 1971) and are characterized by group activities, keeping up with "in groups," sharing and doing things together, dependence on each other, group loyalty and consensus, inclusiveness, and collaterality. For example, Ahmed and Krohn (1992) identified characteristic elements in Japanese behavior, including traveling in groups and taking group photos. Similarly, the Korean culture emphasizes group travel (Kim and Prideaux 1996; Prideaux 1998). Also, in Asian cultures, an individualistic behavior is regarded as an expense to others (Hsu 1971). In contrast, Australians, who belong to a more individualistic culture, are concerned about the individual's needs and well-being. They place greater emphasis on egalitarian, exclusive relationships and "doing one's own things." The concept of privacy is strong and relationships within groups looser. Solitude is perceived positively, and other people's privacy is respected. Consequently, Austra-

lian society is seen as a selfish social phenomenon, in which an individual person's gain is a loss for the whole group.

In addition, as members of high power distance cultures, Asian people are obedient and submissive to a group leader, authority, and elders. Superior-subordinate hierarchical relationships dictate respect to higher ranking authorities reflected in the forms of being loyal to them, obeying them, fulfilling their instructions, and showing total respect and gratitude. Since Australians belong to a low power distance culture, the concepts of group loyalty and obedience to authority and seniority are extremely weak.

All Asian societies are also supposed to hold together and function harmoniously. For example, Komin (1990) noted that in Thailand, polite, cool, and superficial relationships are preferred with strangers because they guarantee a harmonious society. All social relationships in Asian societies conform to formal rules of appropriate behavior (Hsu 1972) that cover every aspect of conduct, including eating, drinking, seating, entertaining, greeting, and apologizing. As a result of very strict forms of social behavior, Mandarin-speaking societies use a third party in personal dealings (DeMente 1991c). This custom is not known in Australian society where the focus is on quick and direct face-to-face dealings.

Furthermore, all Asian societies are very much family dependent and give precedence in all things to the family, for them being invited to a home is an honorable event. For example, Japanese appreciate being invited to restaurants and nightclubs (DeMente 1991a). Since cuisine is regarded as an important element of the Korean holiday experience

(Prideaux 1998), they also appreciate being invited to restaurants for a meal.

Moreover, an important aspect of social relations in the Japanese, Korean, and Mandarin-speaking societies is the tradition of gift giving and reciprocating. This tradition creates and nurtures relationships with people. Gifts are always tailored to hierarchical position, age, and gender of the receiver and donor and are given as expressions of apology, appreciation, gratitude, or remembrance. In Japan, gifts are purchased for those who stayed at home (Morsbach 1977). Gifts are the tangible way of saying "thank you" (DeMente 1991c). Brand names are important. There are various types of gifts. Small thank-you gifts for hospitality and gifts for honored guests are common in Japan (DeMente 1991a; Zimmerman 1985). However, in Australia gift giving often seems to be inappropriate, and the donor can be suspected of a bribe. Also, the Australian style of expressing gratitude verbally with a simple "thank you," whether casual or emotional, is treated in Mandarin-speaking societies as insincere (DeMente 1991c).

Feeling display. As members of high uncertainty avoidance and formal cultures, Asians do not display their feelings in public in order not to cause disagreement and conflict. They do not swear and do not ask personal questions. Komin (1990) noted that the Thai are reluctant to ask personal questions if these could in any way imply a criticism and make others uncomfortable. However, questions regarding age and earnings, which are impolite to ask in Australia, are regarded as polite in Thailand because they offer a quick way of establishing a person's status (Komin 1990). By complying with formal rules of social behavior, keeping emotions under control, and being self-restrained and reserved, they save one's own and other's face and maintain social harmony. The concept of "saving face" prescribes using respectful language, being extremely polite, avoiding criticism and excessive complimenting, and not damaging one's own or others' reputation (DeMente 1991b). Failure to keep emotions under control may mean loosing face, respect, and status and causing humiliation on both sides. Wei, Crompton, and Reid (1989) noted that the Chinese are expected to possess dignity, reserve, patience, and sensitivity to customs. To behave properly in the Mandarin-speaking societies, the most common way is "to do nothing" and "say nothing" (DeMente 1991c). Such practice is totally irrational and unacceptable from an Australian viewpoint. Australians, who belong to a low uncertainty and informal culture, are unrestrained in their behavior and have less control over their verbal and nonverbal expressions. They openly disagree, criticize each other, and swear in public. Rules of social behavior play a minor role in their lives. They are not concerned about destroying someone else's reputation and saving one's own and other's face. The focus is on solving problems and conflicts rather than avoiding them. Australian people are also encouraged to ask questions and employ critical thinking to challenge and disagree.

Furthermore, in Asian cultures people use smaller interpersonal distance than in Australia. Sitting and standing occurs in very close proximity. However, physical contact such as holding hands, leaning on shoulders, touching knees or feet, and linking arms is usually avoided in public. In contrast, Australians use larger interpersonal distance, touch less, and prefer to sit side by side less.

Satisfaction. Satisfaction with interpersonal relations in collectivistic Asian cultures depends on the development of an atmosphere of closeness and cooperation. Friendship for Asian people implies obligations. For example, Wei, Crompton, and Reid (1989) reported that for Chinese, friendship implies mutual obligations and reciprocation. In Thailand, the determination of friendship depends on who one is, whom one knows, and one's wealth (Komin 1990). Also, Asian people tend to fit every person they meet into a social hierarchy. In more individualistic Australia, the satisfying social relationships are exclusive and based on mutual interests and activities rather than social hierarchy. Australians tend to find out what a person is like. Social relationships do not imply any obligations on the parties involved. Australians regard friendship as being relatively superficial. Also, the development of satisfying social relationships in Asia takes a longer time than in Australia. For example, the Japanese require a long time to get to know people well and to develop an atmosphere of trust (*shinyo*) (Ziff-Levine 1990), comfort (*amae*) (Nakane 1973), and complete acceptance. In contrast, it is easier to develop relationships with Australians and get along well with them in a relatively short period of time.

In terms of satisfaction with service, service in Asia is of a higher standard, personalized, and more customer oriented. Although in Australia the service quality is high, there is still much scope for improvement to match the Asian standard. For example, the Australian service providers are seen by Koreans as being too slow (Prideaux 1998), and the local cuisine also has a poor image (Kim 1997). Koreans do not regard Australians as friendly and welcoming (Kim 1997). In fact, they have an image of Australia as a racist country (Prideaux 1998).

Furthermore, as members of high uncertainty avoidance cultures, Asian people are worried about the exposure to language difficulties when traveling overseas. Although their English language skills are improving, they are unhappy about the Australians' inability to communicate with Asian tourists. According to Indonesians and Koreans, the Australian hosts' knowledge of the guests' culture and language is imperative to be able to respond to the guests' standards of behavior and needs. One of the major problems for Koreans visiting Australia is language difficulties and lack of appreciation of distinctive Korean culture (Prideaux 1998). Thus, "Koreans are dependent on tour guides to navigate them through a country which has no public signage in Korean and few tourism workers who speak the language" (Prideaux 1998, p. 98). As a result, Australia has failed to provide a product that lives up to the promotional images of the country (Prideaux 1998).

Although Thai people have a great sense of humor, they do not appreciate sarcasm, which is accepted in Australia. They also do not pay much attention to time constraints. In Thailand, conversations between people are relaxed. However, they require conformity to rules of social conduct (Komin 1990).

The analysis of the cultural dimensions identified in each Asian language group points to several characteristic dimensions in each group. These dimensions are briefly presented below.

In the Indonesian sample, two characteristic dimensions were identified: perceptions of service responsiveness and attentiveness. In terms of responsiveness, Indonesians believe that service may occur over an extended time period. Being in a hurry is an indication of impatience (Geertz 1967). In contrast, in Australia time commitments are more important and must be kept. There is more focus on punctuality and efficiency of service provision. Also, in Indonesia physical appearance and appropriate dress should reflect social position and age. This is in contrast to Australian culture, in which clothing style is more casual. In respect of attentiveness, Indonesians believe that people must pay attention to correct behavior and the nature and forms of obligations, which are specified by a system of social hierarchy. In contrast, Australian society is more egalitarian, and peoples' behavior depends less on social position and age.

In the Japanese sample, three characteristic dimensions were identified: perceptions of service helpfulness, competence, and greetings. In Japan, helpfulness is seen in terms of being punctual, informative, trustworthy, respectful, and polite. Punctuality is regarded as a measure of professionalism and competence. Australian society regards punctuality as relative to the importance of the occasion. Also, the Japanese require precision and accuracy (Turcq and Usunier 1985) of information. In contrast, Australians are not concerned with detail to such a degree and are not worried if problems are not solved immediately. Furthermore, in Japan the concept of trustworthy service is relative and depends on social situations and time. The sincere and trustworthy person strives for harmony with surroundings and a group through self-restraint (*enryo*) (Dace 1995). Australians, in contrast, are more direct and open. They tend to "lay all cards on the table." In Japan, respect for others and one's self is shown through fulfilling work obligations and complying with the rules of social etiquette (Ahmed and Krohn 1992). In Australia, where people value equality, respect is gained through individual achievements.

Japanese politeness is an expression of social etiquette rather than a feeling of kindness or regard. It requires no damage to one's own and others' reputation, avoidance of conflict, and controlling emotions (Lebra 1976). For Australians, manners are less comprehensive. An essential element of the Japanese polite character is an apologetic and humble attitude and consideration to the effects of one's own behavior on others (Ziff-Levine 1990). However, the Japanese apologize not only when they want to admit guilt but also to avoid friction and offense and demonstrate humility and regret (DeMente 1991a), which may often seem to be illogical to Australians. Also, in a Japanese culture confidence and loud behavior are regarded with suspicion and as rude (Condon 1978). In contrast, Australians regard confidence as a sign of strength. Moreover, the Japanese tend to listen to and obey orders without questioning them. This is again in contrast to Australians who are unfamiliar with the concepts of obedience and listening to superiors.

In Japan, competence is seen to be dependent on personal qualities such as being self-controlled, logical, obedient, and self-respectful. Self-controlled means being disciplined, emotionally restrained, and able to comply with rules of formal behavior. In Australian culture, no corresponding aspects of life seem to be related. Australians are not concerned about controlling their own behavior and complying with rules of socially accepted behavior. The Japanese way of logical thinking is intuitive and flexible. In contrast, the Australian way of thinking is objective and absolute. The Japanese way of being obedient is shown by willingness to comply with the social order and respect for others, and it does not have an

equivalent in Australia either. Furthermore, respecting one's self in the Japanese context requires saving one's own and other's face. In Australia, self-respect is gained by collecting financial wealth and standing against authority.

In Japan, individuals are addressed by second names, titles, or functions. The Japanese use first names only with family members and childhood friends and feel embarrassed when called by their first names (DeMente 1991a). Australian informality of calling people by their first names is regarded as rude. In Japan, name cards (*meishi*) are exchanged at the beginning of conversation to indicate the titles, positions, and ranks of the owners. The exchange of name cards is followed by a bow. There are different kinds and grades of Japanese bows, depending on age, rank, and social position (DeMente 1991a; Zimmerman 1985). The Japanese do not practice shaking hands, as favored by many Australians. However, since the Japanese have recently become used to dealing with Western businessmen, they politely accept handshaking (DeMente 1991a).

In the Korean sample, only one characteristic dimension was identified: perceptions of service performance. In a relatively feminine culture such as Korea, society is committed to personal relations (Q. Kim 1988), quality of life, and social harmony. However, Koreans also believe in masculine values such as inequality among people (Q. Kim 1988), performance, and intellectual achievements. Respect is gained through intellectual achievements and hard work. Punctuality is a measure of professionalism. Koreans do not appreciate the waste of time that occurs if meal service is slow (Prideaux 1998). In Australia, people are more money and possession oriented, and more emphasis is placed on performance, growth, and assertiveness. However, Australians also support feminine values such as equality and welfare of others. Furthermore, in Korea, there are specific customs concerning appropriate dress and physical appearance, which are prescribed by law for different social classes. This is again in contrast to Australian culture, in which clothing style is more casual and depends less on social position or age.

In the Mandarin-speaking sample, two characteristic dimensions were identified: perceptions of punctuality and understanding. Mandarin-speaking societies expect people to adhere to a full, heavy schedule and be on time or early for meetings and appointments (DeMente 1991c). Being late is regarded as lacking sincerity, concern for the other, and professionalism. This is in contrast to the Australian style of work, which is more relaxed and in which delays can be justified. Also, the Chinese are socially and psychologically dependent on others (Hsu 1953). The inherent need to care about foreign visitors in the Mandarin cultures results in a national responsibility for giving constant attention to and helping foreigners to cope with the different customs, to a degree that may become annoying for Western visitors (Wei, Crompton, and Reid 1989). Chinese escort their guests constantly to not only ensure that visitors do not have contact with Chinese, who may offer a different view of their political reality, but to fulfill all needs of the visitors (Wei, Crompton, and Reid 1989). In Australia, people know best what their needs are and how these needs can be satisfied.

In the Thai sample, two characteristic dimensions were identified: perceptions of courtesy and understanding. The Thai people are very attentive and try to please everyone. The Thai say whatever is required to conform to norms of respect and politeness and avoid unpleasantness and conflict. For

Australians, truth is absolute and does not depend on a situation. The Thai people rarely say "please" or "thank you" as the Thai words of politeness carry the "please" element. As a result, in English the Thai may appear to be demanding something, whereas in Thai they make a polite request (Komin 1990). Also, the Thai use the smile instead of polite words (Komin 1990). In Australia, words such as please and thank you are used commonly. Furthermore, in Thailand, respect is shown to all of higher status and age and also to objects of everyday life such as books, hats, umbrellas, elephants, and rice, which are associated with knowledge, the head, royalty, religion, and life (Komin 1990). In contrast, Australians are less respectful, and they do not have as many sacred symbols.

MARKETING IMPLICATIONS

The cultural differences between Asian and Australian populations presented in the study point to the development of specific marketing strategies aimed at the Asian tourist market. Promotional advertising aiming at all Asian tourists should focus on the opportunity to develop close human relations between tourists and Australian people. Travel itineraries should be developed and structured around socializing with Australian people and other travelers. As a base for the development of social relations, attention should be paid to (1) the dependent nature of Asian social relations, (2) the hierarchical structure of Asian societies and the ability of the hosts to comply with authority and seniority, and (3) social etiquette, which demands the providers treat Asian tourists according to their age, social positions, and ranking. For example, special care, respect, and courtesy should be shown to elders, and obedience to any higher-ranking superiors. Appropriate seating arrangements in buses and restaurants and hotel room allocations should be made according to age and social ranking. Australian providers should identify their professional status by wearing formal work uniforms and badges with names and positions displayed. Preferably, an older person should represent management, as this person would be seen of high social status and professional experience. Similarly, an older person is a better tour guide choice because he or she is seen as knowledgeable and experienced. The hotel management should welcome and farewell Asian tourists at the airport or hotel, creating an atmosphere of social order and indicating that the management has a sense of responsibility and respect.

The hierarchy and seniority system and the compliance with basic rules of social etiquette should be emphasized in advertising. All Asian tourists should be addressed by their titles and last names, except Thai tourists who should be called by their titles and first names. Tourists should wear badges with their names and titles. Although Japanese and Korean tourists do not expect foreigners to know exactly how to bow, Australian providers should show some inclination to conform to their custom of bowing, instead of handshaking, to show their politeness and respect of tourists. In addition, exchanging business cards (*meishi*) with English text on one of the sides, indicating the social status of the person introduced, followed by a bow would fulfill the Japanese custom of introduction. The Thai tourists should be greeted with a smile instead of "hello" and a handshake. Advertising to Japanese and Korean tourists should incorporate pictures

of bowing. Advertising to Thai people should show people with a smile on their faces.

Marketers should emphasize the time spent in Australia as a means of developing social relations with Australians and consider that the average Asian tourist values the importance of time spent on socializing and devoting personal time to other people. Conversations should comply with the rules of formal etiquette. Providers should not feel offended when asked about their age or salary earnings. In fact, they should ask tourists these questions to establish their social status. Ironic and sarcastic comments or jokes, common in Australia, should be avoided. The Australian relaxed, casual, and slow-pace lifestyle, which offers much time for socializing, should be promoted, in particular, to Indonesian and Thai tourists. The aspect of "having a good time, fun, and pleasure" should be the focus of promotional messages aiming at the Thai market.

Given the sensitivity and importance of face saving to all Asian tourists, caution has to be exercised in personal dealings with Asian tourists involving openly displaying feelings and expressing opinions to prevent conflict and disagreement in interpersonal relations between providers and tourists. Special care should be taken not to insult and damage the reputation of the tourist, even if criticism is constructive and negative feelings justified. It is important not to offend any tourist, not to swear in front of them, and not to criticize or talk about sensitive issues. However, personal questions related to tourist social status are permitted. The providers should strive to be considerate and take into account the effects of one's own behavior on the tourists' feelings. If there are any differences in opinions, providers should find a suitable way of expressing their own views that do not offend and harm a tourist. Failure to do so will result in conflict and may cause humiliation and loss of dignity and social status on both sides. Consequently, providers should practice self-control, coolness of manners, nonassertiveness, and humility.

The promotional strategies aiming at the Japanese and Korean markets should emphasize the educational and intellectual aspects of travel to Australia to enhance the tourists' intellectual and cultural experiences. The value of knowledge and wisdom should be used as criteria for the enhancement of the Japanese and Korean tourist's social status and their recognition among fellow nationals.

Commercial advertising should be directed toward Asian families so as to appeal to all its members rather than the individual tourist. Special offers for extended families should be proposed and large family tours organized. The advertising messages should promise the fulfillment of family needs including security. The safety of airlines, high quality of the Australian infrastructure and recreation facilities, low crime rate, and clean and unpolluted environment can be highlighted in promotional brochures. The competence and professionalism of Australian service providers needs to be stressed specifically to the Japanese market. Focus should be on the ability of the providers to fulfill professional obligations, being respectful and obedient. By doing this, the cultural predisposition of Asian tourists to avoid risk can be overcome, without loosing interest in traveling to Australia.

Marketing strategies aiming at Asian tourists should also focus on a team spirit and promote group activities such as group traveling, sightseeing, picnics, barbecues, and recreational activities. Individual activities may not be popular among Asian tourists who prefer to feel "in-group." Tour

JOURNAL OF TRAVEL RESEARCH   311

guides, front office staff, airline staff, and restaurateurs should never leave the Asian tourists on their own as they demand constant attention. In particular, the Mandarin-speaking tourist groups should not be separated even for a short period of time because of the inherent need for support and dependence.

All Asian tourists would be particularly pleased if Australian hosts were to follow their custom of gift giving. Small welcome and farewell gifts should be given to tourists on their arrival and departure as a means of showing an appreciation for coming to Australia. An appropriate gift should be given, such as a box of golf balls, a boomerang, or koala toys. Every gift should be artistically wrapped as the Japanese and Koreans, in particular, value external presentation. Gifts should be given in order of seniority. In addition, a small gift in the form of Australian fruit or a bottle of wine should be available in each hotel room. A lot of discretionary time for purchasing gifts for each family member should be included in the travel itineraries for Asian tourists. Australian tour operators should organize special shopping tours.

Advertising aiming at all Asian tourists should focus on hosts performing acts of kindness that bind tourists and make them feel obliged (Lebra 1976), such as gift giving, experiencing a sporting game, and sharing an interest in Asian art, food, or other elements of culture. The Asians appreciate being invited to a nightclub or out for dinner. Being invited home is regarded as an honorable and rare event, and it can shorten significantly the time necessary for the development of relations. This later aspect may be important for hosts dealing with visiting Asian tour operators.

Australian providers should be anxious to provide the best service they can, particularly to the Japanese. Those who provide services to the Japanese, Korean, and Mandarin-speaking tourists should be punctual. Of importance is the effective dissemination of information to passengers and corrective action during service breakdown (Laws 1990). When the service cannot be delivered to tourists on time, providers should provide an explanation for the service delay, apologize politely, and compensate for lack of promptness and efficiency, even if it is not their fault. Compensation in the form of a personal written apology or a small gift would be appropriate and eliminate the potential for offense and frictions in human interactions with Asian tourists. Any waiting time should be entertaining to give tourists a feeling of getting the most of every moment of their holiday. For example, the Japanese tourists, who value education and intellectual achievements, could be shown educational books or videotapes of Australia while waiting at the airport or in the hotel lobby. Also, serving Japanese or Chinese tea before the meal would show the tourists that the order is being fulfilled and would give them a feeling of smooth service delivery. However, Australian providers should be less concerned about being punctual and delivering service on time to Indonesian and Thai tourists. Indonesian and Thai tourists should not be hurried. They require relaxed and flexible service.

Every promotional campaign aiming at the Asian tourist market should emphasize Australian genuine hospitality, concern for tourists, and ability to anticipate and understand their needs. Promoting Australian hosts' commitment to personalized service would enhance the Asian tourist's interest in traveling to Australia.

Australian providers should learn some basic phrases and principles of the Asian languages to be used in different social situations with people of different social standing in order to be perceived as communicative and informative. Just a small ability in speaking Asian languages would help to greet and farewell tourists, inquire politely about their trip or health, make polite casual comments, and be able to respond to their queries. Australian providers should not expect that all Asian tourists speak the English language. The Japanese, Korean, and Mandarin-speaking tourists would be particularly grateful to hosts for having a degree of competence in their mother tongues, which would also enhance tourist satisfaction with Australian providers. Since the Japanese rely more on print media (Mihalik, Uysal, and Pan 1995), visitor guides, brochures, and magazines translated into Japanese should be made available to all Japanese and Australian travel agents, foreign and domestic libraries, public and private, and all other points of tourist information. The provision of multilingual signs and services would also assist all Asian tourists.

Learning Asian languages should be complemented by learning the nonverbal aspects of communication, including body language, gestures, and eye gazing. It would be advisable to understand the customs of Asian greeting, entertaining, gift giving, and eating and drinking habits. The different principles of truth and sincerity also need to be understood. Australian providers need to be alert for signals that reveal the true meanings of the Asian words and expressions. They should learn how to recognize what is unsaid and intentions behind the Asian words and say only what has to be said to conform to rules of politeness, respect, and avoidance of conflict. Straightforwardness should be avoided as it might be regarded by Asian tourists as rude and would not be reciprocated. Australian providers must be careful in interpretation of subjective assessment provided by Japanese tourists in the host country (Iverson 1997) and not be complacent.

Special efforts need to be made to learn about the Asian guests' country of origin, its history, traditions, music, food, and everyday life. This is particularly important to Korean and Indonesian tourists. This would not only be an indication of the hosts' willingness to please Asian tourists but also would show an interest and appreciation of their culture and enhance the tourists' ego and pride.

CONCLUSION

Several conclusions can be drawn from the findings of the study. First, the study supports evidence from past research results that there are cultural differences between Western and Eastern societies. The cultural differences identified in the study appear to be consistent with the general Eastern/Western differences discussed in the literature review. Second, the study indicates that these differences do exist between Australian and Asian populations in the tourism industry. Consequently, the study contributes to the body of knowledge concerning cross-cultural differences between the international tourist markets in the tourism industry. Third, the study indicates that cultural differences are very useful constructs for international tourism promotion, and they can provide very accurate criteria for targeting and positioning. As a result, tourism marketers should take into account the cultural backgrounds of international tourists to identify specific profiles of the market segment and determine how a destination should position itself in the international marketplace to appeal to international tourists. Fourth, the study implies the need for multicultural education and training. As the tourism industry becomes more culturally diverse, future tourism and hospitality managers should understand their customers from different cultural backgrounds. Cultural awareness, communication, and interpersonal skills will be necessary to avoid and/or reduce tensions and develop understanding among international tourists and hosts with different cultural values. Cross-cultural awareness studies should be incorporated into tourism and hospitality programs offered at tertiary institutions. Although the number of Australian students studying Asian languages and cultures is increasing, there is a necessity for more subjects tailored to the Australian tourism industry needs, including Asian cultures, cultural behaviors and expectations in host cultures, cross- and intercultural interactions and communication, and cultural confrontation. Cultural training programs would help the providers to understand one's own culture and the culture of the tourist, appreciate the differences between cultures, and, as a result, accept, respect, and communicate with the culturally different tourist.

Most important, the study suggests a solution to the problem facing the Australian tourism industry of maintaining growth in inbound tourism from Asia beyond the year 2000. The study suggests that to respond better to the Asian tourist markets and avoid potential problems of negative perceptions and dissatisfaction with hosts, tourism industry officials should reassess their marketing practices and focus more on the cultural differences between tourists and hosts and the impact of these differences on the tourist's psychological needs and experiences.

FURTHER RESEARCH

It would be of considerable interest to analyze the items on which there were no significant differences, which was not possible due to the sample size in this study. The intervening impact of the "gap" between tourists' expectations and providers' perceptions of tourists' expectations on the identified variations could also be addressed. The questions of to what degree cultural differences determine social interaction between Australian hosts Asian tourists and their satisfaction needs is to be addressed. To find the answer to this question, a model involving interaction and satisfaction as dependent variables is developed in part 2, separately for each Asian language group. These models allow for comparisons of the complex relationships between cultural differences, social interaction, and satisfaction with this interaction across different Asian language groups. The extent of the cultural influences on tourist interaction and satisfaction varies between the different Asian markets. Consequently, different promotional strategies may have to be developed for distinct markets, and these are discussed further in part 2.

NOTES

1. The RVS items could also be translated into Asian languages, concept equivalence could be achieved, and the Australian and Asian values could be compared. Although there is an Eastern equivalent of the RVS developed on the basis of 40 important Chinese values (Chinese Culture Connection 1987), this instrument could not be used in the study as it would not permit adequate mea-

surement of Western values and, consequently, the comparison between Asian and Australian values.

2. Two statistical packages were used for data input, namely, the SPSS for Windows Release 6.0 (Norusis 1993) and the GB-STAT for Windows Version 5.0 (Friedman 1994).

3. The sociodemographic characteristics of the individual language groups are available from the authors of this article.

4. Eighteen out of 36 areas of measurement showed significant differences in cultural values, 22 out of 34 in rules of social interaction, 23 out of 29 in perceptions of service, 7 out of 11 in forms of interaction, and 3 out of 11 in satisfaction with interaction.

5. The tables with the significant differences between the individual Asian language groups and the Australian sample are available from the authors of this article.

6. The results of the principal components analysis for each Asian language group are available from the authors of this article.

REFERENCES

Ah-Keng, K. (1993). "Evaluating the Attractiveness of a New Theme Park: A Cross-Cultural Comparison." *Tourism Management*, 14 (3): 202-10.

Ahmed, Z., and F. Krohn (1992). "Understanding the Unique Consumer Behavior of Japanese Tourists." *Journal of Travel and Tourism Marketing*, 1 (3): 73-86.

Albrecht, K. (1992). *The Only Thing That Matters*. New York: Harper Business.

Alhemoud, A., and E. Armstrong (1996). "Image of Tourism Attractions in Kuwait." *Journal of Travel Research*, 34 (4): 76-80.

Amir, Y. (1969). "Contact Hypothesis in Ethnic Relations." *Psychological Bulletin*, 71 (5): 319-42.

Anton, J. (1996). *Customer Relationship Management: Making Hard Decisions with Soft Numbers*. Upper Saddle River, NJ: Prentice Hall.

Argyle, M. (1967). *The Psychology of Interpersonal Behavior*. Harmondsworth, UK: Penguin.

——— (1972). "Nonverbal Communication in Human Social Interaction." In *Nonverbal Communication*, edited by R. Hinde. London: Royal Society and Cambridge University Press.

———(1978). *The Psychology of Interpersonal Behavior*. 3d ed. Harmondsworth, UK: Penguin.

——— (1981). "Intercultural Communication." In *Social Skills and Work*, edited by M. Argyle. London: Methuen.

Argyle, M., and M. Henderson (1985). "The Rules of Relationships." In *Understanding Personal Relationships*, edited by S. Duck and D. Perlman. Beverly Hills, CA: Sage, pp. 63-84.

Argyle, M., M. Henderson, M. Bond, Y. Iizuka, and A. Contarello (1986). "Cross-Cultural Variations in Relationship Rules." *International Journal of Psychology*, 21: 287-315.

Armstrong, R., C. Mok, and F. Go (1997). "The Importance of Cross-Cultural Expectations in the Measurement of Service Quality Perceptions in the Hotel Industry." *International Journal of Hospitality Management*, 16 (2): 181-90.

Australian Tourist Commission (1994). *Tourism Market Potential Targets 1994-2000*. Sydney: Australian Tourist Commission.

Bailey, J. (1991). *Managing Organizational Behaviour*. Brisbane, Australia: John Wiley.

Barnlund, D., and S. Araki (1985). "Intercultural Encounters: The Management of Compliments by Japanese and Americans." *Journal of Cross-Cultural Psychology*, 16: 9-26.

Befu, H. (1971). *Japan: An Anthropological Introduction*. New York: Harper and Row.

Bejou, D., B. Edvardsson, and J. Rakowski (1996). "A Critical Incident Approach to Examining the Effects of Service Failures on Customer Relationships: The Case of Swedish and U.S. Airlines." *Journal of Travel Research*, 35 (summer): 35-40.

Bitner, M. (1990). "Evaluating Service Encounters: The Effects of Physical Surrounding and Employee Responses." *Journal of Marketing*, 54 (April): 69-82.

Black, J., and M. Mendenhall (1989). "A Practical but Theory-Based Framework for Selecting Cross-Cultural Training Methods." *Human Resource Management*, 28 (4): 511-39.

Bochner, S. (1982). *Cultures in Contact: Studies in Cross-Cultural Interaction*. New York: Pergamon.

Boissevain, J. (1979). "The Impact of Tourism on a Dependent Island: Gozo, Malta." *Annals of Tourism Research*, 6 (1): 76-90.

Boote, A. (1981). "Market Segmentation by Personal Values and Salient Product Attributes." *Journal of Advertising Research*, 21 (February): 29-35.

Braithwaite, V., and H. Law (1985). "Structure of Human Values: Testing the Adequacy of the Rokeach Value Survey." *Journal of Personality and Social Psychology*, 49: 250-63.

Bureau of Tourism Research (1995-1997). *International Visitor Survey 1995, 1996, 1997.* Canberra, Australia: Bureau of Tourism Research.
——— (1996). *International Visitor Survey.* Canberra, Australia: Bureau of Tourism Research.
——— (1998a). *Australian Tourism 1998 Data Card.* Canberra, Australia: Bureau of Tourism Research.
——— (1998b). *International Visitor Survey December Quarter 1998.* Canberra, Australia: Bureau of Tourism Research.
Business Korea (1991). "The Way of Korean Traveling, Koreans are so Strange?" *Business Korea,* 9 (2): 29.
Chinese Culture Connection (a team of 24 researchers) (1987). "Chinese Values and the Search for Culture-Free Dimensions of Culture." *Journal of Cross-Cultural Psychology,* 18 (June): 143-64.
Cho, S. Y. (1991). "The Ugly Koreans are Coming?" *Business Korea,* 9 (2): 25-31.
Cohen, J. (1972). *Behavioral Science Foundations of Consumer Behavior.* New York: Free Press.
Condon, J. Jr. (1978). "Intercultural Communication from a Speech Communication Perspective." In *Intercultural and International Communication,* edited by F. Casmir. Washington, DC: University Press of America.
Cook, S., and C. Sellitz (1955). "Some Factors Which Influence the Attitudinal Outcomes of Personal Contact." *International Sociological Bulletin,* 7: 51-58.
Craig, J. (1979) *Culture Shock! What Not to Do in Malaysia and Singapore, How and Why Not to Do It.* Singapore, Japan: Times Books International.
Crotts, J., and C. Ryan (1997). "Introduction." *Journal of Travel and Tourism Marketing,* 6 (1): 1-7.
Dace, R. (1995). "Japanese Tourism: How Knowledge of Japanese Buyer Behavior and Culture Can Be of Assistance to British Hoteliers in Seeking to Develop This Valuable Market." *Journal of Vacation Marketing,* 1 (3): 281-88.
Dann, G. (1993). "Limitation in the Use of Nationality and Country of Residence Variables." In *Tourism Research: Critiques and Challenges,* edited by D. Pearce and R. Butler. London: Routledge.
DeMente, B. (1991a). *Japanese Etiquette and Ethics in Business.* Chicago: NTC Business.
——— (1991b). *Korean Etiquette and Ethics in Business.* Chicago: NTC Business.
——— (1991c). *Chinese Etiquette and Ethics in Business.* Chicago: NTC Business.
Dhalla, N., and W. Mahatto (1976). "Expanding the Scope of Segmentation Research." *Journal of Marketing,* 40 (April): 34-41.
Dimanche, F. (1994). "Cross-Cultural Tourism Marketing Research: An Assessment and Recommendations for Future Studies." *Journal of International Consumer Marketing,* 6 (3/4): 123-34.
Dodd, A., M. Hattersley, and L. Swan (1990). "Curriculum: Action on Reflection." In *People, Culture and Change: Coming of Age,* edited by L. Lovat and D. Smith. Wentworth Falls, NSW, Australia: Social Science Press.
Dodd, C. (1987). *Dynamics of Intercultural Communication.* Dubuque, IA: William C Brown.
Elliott, K. (1995). "A Comparison of Alternative Measures of Service Quality." *Journal of Customer Service in Marketing and Management,* 1 (1): 33-44.
Feather, N. (1980a). "Similarity of Values Systems within the Same Nation: Evidence from Australia and Papua New Guinea." *Australian Journal of Psychology,* 32 (1): 17-30.
——— (1980b). "Value Systems and Social Interaction: A Field Study in a Newly Independent Nation." *Journal of Applied Social Psychology,* 10 (1): 1-19.
——— (1980c). "The Study of Values." *Journal of Asia-Pacific and World Perspectives,* 3: 3-13.
——— (1986a). "Value Systems across Cultures: Australia and China." *International Journal of Psychology,* 21: 697-715.
——— (1986b). "Cross-Cultural Studies with the Rokeach Value Survey: The Flinders Program of Research on Values." *Australian Journal of Psychology,* 38 (3): 269-83.
Fick, G., and J. Ritchie (1991). "Measuring Service Quality in the Travel and Tourism Industry." *Journal of Travel Research,* 30 (2): 2-9.
Fontaine, G. (1983). "Americans in Australia: Intercultural Training for the Lucky Country." In *Handbook of Intercultural Training 3,* edited by D. Landis and R. Brislin. New York: Pergamon.
Foster, G. (1962). *Traditional Cultures and the Impact of Technological Change.* New York: Harper and Row.
Fridgen, J. (1991). *Dimensions of Tourism.* East Lansing, MI: Educational Institute of the American Hotel and Motel Association.
Friedman, P. (1994). *GB-STAT Statistical Package Version 5.0.* Silver Spring, MD: Dynamic Microsystems.
Geertz, C. (1967). "Indonesian Cultures and Communities." In *Indonesia,* edited by R. McVey. New Haven, CT: Hraf.
——— (1973). *The Interpretation of Culture.* New York: Basic Books.
Goodenough, W. (1961). "Comment on Cultural Evolution." *Daedalus,* 90: 521-28.

Gronroos, C. (1990). *Service Management and Marketing: Managing the Moments of Truth in Service Competition.* Lexington, MA: Lexington Books.
Gudykunst, W. (1979). "The Effects of an Intercultural Communication. Workshop on Cross-Cultural Communication: Attitudes and Interaction." *Communication and Education,* 28 (3): 179-87.
Gudykunst, W., and Y. Kim (1984). *Communicating with Strangers: An Approach to Intercultural Communication.* Reading, MA: Addison-Wesley.
Hair, J., R. Anderson, R. Tatham, and W. Black (1995). *Multivariate Data Analysis with Readings.* Englewood Cliffs, NJ: Prentice Hall.
Hall, E. (1965). *The Silent Language.* Greenwich, CT: Fawcett.
——— (1983). *The Dance of Life: The Other Dimensions of Time.* New York: Doubleday.
Hargie, O. (1986). *A Handbook of Communication Skills.* London: Routledge.
Harris, M. (1988). *Culture, People, Nature: An Introduction to General Anthropology.* 5th ed. New York: Harper and Row.
Harris, M., and R. Moran (1979). *Managing Cultural Differences.* Houston, TX: Gulf.
Hoffman, D., and S. Low (1981). "An Application of the Profit Transformation to Tourism Survey Data." *Journal of Travel Research,* 20 (2): 35-38.
Hofstede, G. (1980). *Culture's Consequences: International Differences in Work-Related Values.* Beverly Hills, CA: Sage.
Hsu, F. (1953). *Americans and Chinese: Two Ways of Life.* New York: Akerland-Schuman.
——— (1971). "Psychosocial Homoeostasis and Jen: Conceptual Tools for Advancing Psychological Anthropology." *American Anthropologists,* 73 (1): 23-44.
——— (1972). *Americans and Chinese: Reflections on Two Cultures and Their People.* Garden City, NY: Doubleday Natural History Press.
Huang, C., C. Yung, and J. Huang (1996). "Trends in Outbound Tourism from Taiwan." *Tourism Management,* May: 223-28.
Huang, J. H., C. T. Huang, and S. Wu (1996). "National Character and Response to Unsatisfactory Hotel Service." *International Journal of Hospitality Management,* 15 (3): 229-43.
Hughes, K. (1991). "Tourist Satisfaction: A Guided Cultural Tour in North Queensland." *Australian Psychologist,* 26 (3): 166-71.
Hunt, J. (1975). "Image as a Factor in Tourism Development." *Journal of Travel Research,* 13 (3): 1-7.
Ibrahim, H. (1991). *Leisure and Society: A Comparative Approach.* Dubuque, IA: W. C. Brown.
Iverson, T. (1997). "Japanese Visitors to Guam: Lessons from Experience." *Journal of Travel and Tourism Marketing,* 6 (1): 41-54.
Jensen, J. (1970). *Perspectives on Oral Communication.* Boston: Holbrook.
Kamal, A., and G. Maruyama (1990). "Cross-Cultural Contact and Attitudes of Qatari Students in the United States." *International Journal of Intercultural Relations,* 14: 123-34.
Kim, E. (1997). "Pre-Visit Expectations of Australia." *Journal of Travel and Tourism Marketing,* 6 (1): 11-20.
Kim, Q. (1988). "Korea's Confucian Heritage and Social Change." *Journal of Developing Societies,* 4 (2): 255-69.
Kim, S., and B. Prideaux (1996). "Korean Inbound Tourism to Australia a Demand Side Analysis." Occasional Paper, Department of Business Studies, University of Queensland, Brisbane, Australia.
Kim, Y. (1988). *Communication and Cross-Cultural Adaptation: An Integrative Theory.* Intercommunication Series. Philadelphia: Multilingual Matters.
Kim, Y., and W. Gudykunst (1988). *Theories in Intercultural Communication.* International and Intercultural Communication Annual 12. Newbury Park, CA: Sage.
Kluckhohn, C. (1944). *Mirror for Man.* New York: McGraw-Hill.
Kluckhohn, C., and W. Kelly (1945). "The Concept of Culture." In *The Science of Man in the World of Crisis,* edited by R. Linton. New York: Columbia University Press, pp. 78-106.
Kluckhohn, C., and F. Strodtbeck (1961). *Variations in Value Orientations.* New York: Harper and Row.
Knight, J. (1996). "Competing Hospitalities in Japanese Rural Tourism." *Annals of Tourism Research,* 23 (1): 165-80.
Komin, S. (1990). "Culture and Work-Related Values in Thai Organizations." *International Journal of Psychology,* 25 (5/6): 685-704.
Landis, R., and R. Brislin (1983). *Handbook of Intercultural Training 2 and 3: Issues in Training Methodology.* New York: Pergamon.
Laws, E. (1990). "Effectiveness of Airline Responses to Passengers during Service Interruptions: A Consumerist Gap Analysis." Paper presented at the Tourism Research into the 1990s Conference, Durham University, December 10-12.
LeBlanc, G. (1992). "Factors Affecting Customer Evaluations of Service Quality in Travel Agencies: An Investigation of Customer Perceptions." *Journal of Travel Research,* 30 (spring): 10-16.
Lebra, T. (1976). *Japanese Patterns of Behavior.* Honolulu: University Press of Hawaii.
Levine, D. (1979). "Simmel at a Distance: On the History and Systematics of the Sociology of the Stranger." In *Strangers in African Societies,* edited by W. Shack and E. Skinner. Berkeley: University of California Press, pp. 21-36.

Luk, S., C. Leon, F. W. Leong, and E. Li (1993). "Value Segmentation of Tourists' Expectations of Service Quality." *Journal of Travel and Tourism Marketing*, 2 (4): 23-38.

Lynn, M. (1997). "Tipping Customs and Status Seeking: A Cross-Country Study." *International Journal of Hospitality Management*, 16 (2): 221-24.

Malinowski, B. (1939). "The Group and the Individual in Functional Analysis." *American Journal of Sociology*, 44: 938-64.

Mann, L. (1986). "Contributions to Cross-Cultural Psychology: An Introduction." *Australian Journal of Psychology*, 38 (3): 195-202.

March, R. (1997). "Diversity in Asian Outbound Travel Industries: A Comparison between Indonesia, Thailand, Taiwan, South Korea and Japan." *International Journal of Hospitality Management*, 16 (2): 231-38.

Mathieson, A., and G. Wall (1982). *Tourism: Economic, Physical and Social Impacts.* New York: Longman.

Mayo, E. Jr., and L. P. Jarvis (1981). *The Psychology of Leisure Travel: Effective Marketing and Selling of Travel Service.* Boston: CBI.

McAllan, G. (1997). "Focus on Asia." *Australian Tourist Commission Newsletter*, May: 7.

McAllister, I., and R. Moore (1991). "Social Distance among Australian Ethnic Groups." *Sociology and Social Research*, 75 (2): 95-100.

McKay, J. (1998). "The End of the Asian Miracle?" *Monash University Magazine*, 1 (autumn/winter): 25.

Mihalik, B., M. Uysal, and M. C. Pan (1995). "A Comparison of Information Sources Used by Vacationing Germans and Japanese." *Hospitality Research Journal*, 18 (3): 39-46.

Moghaddam, F., D. Taylor, and S. Wrigth (1993). *Cross-Cultural Perspective.* New York: Freeman.

Mok, C., and R. Armstrong (1995). "Leisure Travel Destination Choice Criteria of the Residents." *Journal of Travel and Tourism Marketing*, 4 (1): 99-104.

Morsbach, H. (1977). "The Psychological Importance of Ritualized Gift Exchange in Modern Japan." *Annals of the New York Academy of Sciences*, 293: 98-113.

Munson, J. (1984). "Personal Values: Consideration in Measurement and Application to Five Areas of Research Inquiry." In *Personal Values and Consumer Psychology*, edited by R. Pitts and A. Woodside. Lexington, MA: Lexington Press, pp. 13-29.

Nakane, C. (1973). *Japanese Society.* New York: Penguin.

Nettekoven, L. (1979). "Mechanisms of Intercultural Interaction." In *Tourism: Passport to Development?*, edited by E. DeKadt. London: Oxford University Press, pp. 135-45.

Ng, S., A. Hossain, P. Ball, M. Bond, K. Hayashi, S. Lim, M. O'Driscoll, D. Sinha, and K. Yang (1982). "Human Values in Nine Countries." In *Diversity and Unity in Cross-Cultural Psychology*, edited by R. Rath, H. Asthana, D. Sinha, and J. Sinha. Lisse, the Netherlands: Swets and Zeitlinger.

Noejirwan, J., and C. Freestone. (1979). "The Culture Game." *Simulation and Games*, 10 (2): 189-206.

Nomura, Y., and D. Barnlund (1983). "Patterns of Interpersonal Criticism in Japan and the United States." *International Journal of Intercultural Relations*, 7 (1): 1-18.

Normann, R. (1984). *Service Management: Strategy and Leadership in Service Businesses.* New York: John Wiley.

Norusis, M. (1993). *Statistical Package for Social Sciences (SPSS) for Windows: Professional Statistics 6.0.* Chicago: SPSS.

Obot, I. (1988). "Value Systems and Cross-Cultural Contact: The Effect of Perceived Similarity and Stability on Social Evaluations." *International Journal of Intercultural Relations*, 12: 363-79.

Parasuraman, A., V. Zeithaml, and L. Berry (1985). "A Conceptual Model of Service Quality and Its Implications for Future Research." *Journal of Marketing*, 49 (fall): 41-50.

——— (1988). "SERVQUAL: A Multiple-Scale Item for Measuring Consumer Perceptions of Service Quality." *Journal of Retailing*, 64 (spring): 12-40.

Pearce, P. (1982). *The Social Psychology of Tourist Behaviour.* International Series in Experimental Social Psychology, Vol. 3. New York: Pergamon.

——— (1988). *The Ulysses Factor: Evaluating Visitors in Tourist Settings.* New York: Springer Verlag.

Pi-Sunyer, O. (1978). "Through Native Eyes: Tourists and Tourism in a Catalan Maritime Community." In *Hosts and Guests*, edited by V. Smith. Philadelphia: University of Pennsylvania Press.

Pitts, R., and A. Woodside (1986). "Personal Values and Travel Decisions." *Journal of Travel Research*, 25 (summer): 20-25.

Pizam, A. (1992). "Managing Cross-Cultural Hospitality Enterprises." In *The International Hospitality Industry: Organizational and Operational Issues*, edited by P. Jones and A. Pizam. London: Wiley, pp. 205-25.

Pizam, A., and G. Jeong (1996). "Cross-Cultural Tourist Behavior: Perceptions of Korean Tour Guides." *Tourism Management*, 17 (4): 277-86.

Pizam, A., Y. Neumann, and A. Reichel (1978). "Dimensions of Tourist Satisfaction with a Destination Area." *Annals of Tourism Research*, 5 (3): 314-22.

Pizam, A., and S. Sussmann (1995). "Does Nationality Affect Tourist Behavior?" *Annals of Tourism Research*, 22 (4): 901-17.

Pizam, A., and N. Telisman-Kosuta (1989). "Tourism as a Factor of Change: Results and Analysis." In *Tourism as a Factor of Change: A Socio-Cultural Study 1*, edited by J. Bystrzanowski. Vienna, Austria: European Coordination Centre for Documentation in Social Sciences, pp. 149-56.

Potter, C. (1989). "What Is Culture: And Can It be Useful for Organizational Change Agents?" *Leadership and Organization Development Journal*, 10 (3): 17-24.

Prideaux, B. (1998). "Korean Outbound Tourism: Australia's Response." *Journal of Travel and Tourism Marketing*, 7 (1): 93-102.

Retting, S., and B. Pasamanick (1962). "Invariance in Factor Structure of Moral Value Judgments from American and Korean College Students." *Sociometry*, 25: 73-84.

Richardson, S., and J. Crompton (1988). "Vacation Patterns of French and English Canadians." *Annals of Tourism Research*, 15 (3): 430-35.

Richter, L. (1983). "Political Implications of Chinese Tourism Policy." *Annals of Tourism Research*, 10: 347-62.

Riley, M. (1995). "Interpersonal Communication: The Contribution of Dyadic Analysis to the Understanding of Tourism Behaviour." *Progress in Tourism and Hospitality Research*, 1 (2): 115-24.

Ritter, W. (1987). "Styles of Tourism in the Modern World." *Tourism Recreation Research*, 12 (1): 3-8.

Rodgers, H. (1977). *Rationalizing Sports Policies.* Strasbourg, France: Council of Europe.

Rokeach, M. (1971). "Long-Range Experimental Modification of Values, Attitudes and Behavior." *American Psychologist*, 37: 523-64.

——— (1973). *The Nature of Human Values.* New York: Free Press.

Saleh, F., and C. Ryan (1991). "Analyzing Service Quality in the Hospitality Industry Using the SERVQUAL Model." *Service Industries Journal*, 11 (3): 324-45.

Samovar, L., and R. Porter (1988). *Intercultural Communication: A Reader.* Belmont, CA: Wadsworth.

——— (1991). *Communication between Cultures.* Belmont, CA: Wadsworth.

Samovar, L., R. Porter, and N. Jain (1981). *Understanding Intercultural Communication.* Belmont, CA: Wadsworth.

Sapir, E. (1964). *Culture, Language, and Personality: Selected Essays.* Berkeley: University of California Press.

Sapir-Whorf, E. (1921). *Language: An Introduction to the Study of Speech.* New York: Harcourt, Brace.

Scherrer, K., H. Wallbott, and A. Summerfield (1986). *Experiencing Emotions: A Cross-Cultural Study.* Cambridge: Cambridge University Press.

Segall, M. (1986). "Culture and Behavior: Psychology in Global Perspective." *Annual Review of Psychology*, 37: 523-64.

Segall, M., P. Dasen, J. Berry, and Y. Poortinga (1990). *Human Behavior in Global Perspective: An Introduction to Cross-Cultural Psychology.* Pergamon General Psychology Series. London: Pergamon.

Sheldon, P., and M. Fox (1988). "The Role of Foodservice in Vacation Choice and Experience: A Cross-Cultural Analysis." *Journal of Travel Research*, 27 (3): 9-15.

Shostack, G. (1985). "Planning the Service Encounter." In *The Service Encounter*, edited by J. Czepiel, M. Solomon, and C. Surprenant. Lexington, MA: Lexington Books, pp. 243-54.

Smith, H. (1957). "The Effects of Intercultural Experience: A Follow-Up Investigation." *Journal of Abnormal and Social Psychology*, 54: 266-69.

Smith, R., and M. Houston (1983). "Script Based Evaluation of Satisfaction and Services." In *Marketing of Services*, edited by L. Berry, L. Shostack, and G. Upah. Chicago: American Marketing Association.

Stringer, P. (1981). "Hosts and Guests: The Bed and Breakfast Phenomenon." *Annals of Tourism Research*, 8 (3): 357-76.

Sussmann, S., and C. Rashcovsky (1997). "A Cross-Cultural Analysis of English and French Canadians' Vacation Travel Patterns." *International Journal of Hospitality Management*, 16 (2): 191-207.

Sutton, W. (1967). "Travel and Understanding: Notes on the Social Structure of Touring." *International Journal of Comparative Sociology*, 8 (2): 218-23.

Taft, R. (1977). "Coping with Unfamiliar Cultures." In *Studies in Cross-Cultural Psychology 1*, edited by N. Warren. London: Academic Press.

Thompson, C., and E. Cutler (1997). "The Effect of Nationality on Tourist Arts: The Case of the Gambia, West Africa." *International Journal of Hospitality Management*, 16 (2): 225-29.

Ting-Toomey, S. (1991). "Intimacy Expressions in Three Cultures: France, Japan, and the United States." *International Journal of Intercultural Relations*, 15: 29-46.

Triandis, H. (1972). *The Analysis of Subjective Culture.* New York: Wiley Interscience.

Tu, W. (1985). "Selfhood and Otherness in Confucian Thought." In *Culture and Self: Asian and Western Perspectives*, edited by A. Marsella, G. DeVos, and F. Hsu. New York: Tavistock, pp. 231-51.

Turcq, D., and J. Usunier (1985). "Les Services au Japon: l'Efficacité: Par la Non-Productive." *Revue Française de Gestion*, May-June: 12-15.

Tylor, R. (1924). *Primitive Culture.* Cloucester, MA: Smith.

Urriola, O. (1989). "Culture in the Context of Development." *World Marxist Review*, 32: 66-69.

Vassiliou, V., H. Triandis, G. Vassiliou, and H. McGuire (1972). "Interpersonal Contact and Stereotyping." In *The Analysis of Subjective Cul-*

ture, edited by H. Triandis, V. Vassiliou, G. Vassiliou, Y. Tanaka, and A. Shanmugam. New York: John Wiley.

Vinson, D., and M. Munson (1976). "Personal Values: An Approach to Market Segmentation." In *Marketing: 1776-1976 and Beyond*, edited by K. Bernhardt. Chicago: American Marketing Association, pp. 313-18.

Wagatsuma, H., and A. Rosett (1986). "The Implications of Apology: Law and Culture in Japan and The United States." *Law and Society Review*, 20 (4): 461-98.

Wei, L., J. Crompton, and L. Reid (1989). "Cultural Conflicts: Experiences of U.S. Visitors to China." *Tourism Management*, 10 (4): 322-32.

Westbrook, R. (1981). "Sources of Consumer Satisfaction with Retail Outlets." *Journal of Retailing*, 57 (3): 68-85.

Williams, R. Jr. (1968). "The Concept of Value." In *Encyclopedia of the Social Sciences*, edited by D. Sills. New York: Macmillan and Free Press.

Woodside, A., and J. Lawrence (1985). "Step Two in Benefit Segmentation: Learning the Benefits Realized by Major Travel Markets." *Journal of Travel Research*, 24 (summer): 7-13.

Wuest, B., R. Tas, and D. Emenheiser (1996). "What Do Mature Travelers Perceive as Important Hotel/Motel Customer Service?" *Hospitality Research Journal*, 20 (2): 77-93.

Yum, J. (1985). "The Impact of Confucianism on Communication: The Case of Korea and Japan." 35th Annual Conference of the International Communication Association, Honolulu.

Zeithaml, V., A. Parasuraman, and L. Berry (1990). *Delivering Service Quality*. New York: Free Press

Ziff-Levine, W. (1990). "The Cultural Logic Gap: A Japanese Tourism Research Experience." *Tourism Management*, 11 (2): 105-10.

Zimmerman, M. (1985). *How to Do Business with the Japanese: A Strategy for Success*. New York: Random House.

[16]

PERGAMON

Tourism Management 23 (2002) 367–378

TOURISM
MANAGEMENT

www.elsevier.com/locate/tourman

Benefit segmentation of Japanese pleasure travelers to the USA and Canada: selecting target markets based on the profitability and risk of individual market segments

Soo Cheong Jang[a], Alastair M. Morrison[a,*], Joseph T. O'Leary[b]

[a] *Department of Hospitality and Tourism Management, Purdue University, Room 156, Stone Hall, West Lafayette, IN 47907 1266, USA*
[b] *Department of Forestry and Natural Resources, Purdue University, West Lafayette, IN 47907, USA*

Received 7 August 2000; accepted 26 June 2001

Abstract

Many previous research studies have offered alternative approaches to segmenting travel markets, but few have provided any decision rules for selecting target markets. This study used factor-cluster analysis to define three benefit-based segments of the Japanese outbound travel market (novelty/nature seekers, escape/relaxation seekers, and family/outdoor activity seekers). The demographic and trip-related characteristics of these markets were compared. Four criteria were then used (profitability, risk, risk-adjusted profitability index, and relative segment size) to reach a decision on the choice of the optimum target market. © 2002 Elsevier Science Ltd. All rights reserved.

Keywords: Benefit segmentation; Japanese travelers; Target market selection; Profitability; Risk

1. Travel market segmentation and targeting

The primary goal of market segmentation is to identify the segments that are most interested in specific goods and services and to focus marketing efforts on them in the most effective way. Market segmentation allows travel marketers to understand the needs and wants of different travel groups and to efficiently communicate with them. Kotler (1999) defines market segmentation as the subdividing of a market into distinct subsets of customers, where any subset may conceivably be selected as a target market to be reached with a distinct marketing mix. In other words, market segmentation makes it possible to find homogeneous smaller markets thereby helping marketers to identify marketing opportunities and to develop products and services in a more tailor-made manner.

One important issue with market segmentation is how best to subdivide travel markets. Many alternative segmentation criteria have been suggested in the tourism literature and these include geographic characteristics (Reid & Reid, 1997), demographics (Taylor, 1987; Anderson & Langmeyer, 1982), psychographics (Silverberg, Backman, & Backman, 1996; Schewe & Calantone, 1978), expenditure (Mok & Iverson, 2000; Legoherel, 1998; Spotts & Mahoney, 1991; Pizam & Reichel, 1979), benefits (Yannopoulos & Rotenberg, 1999; Shoemaker, 1989, 1994; Woodside & Jacobs, 1985; Haley, 1968), activities (Hsieh, O'Leary, & Morrison, 1992), and communication channels (Hsieh & O'Leary, 1993). But what is the most effective segmentation criterion? It is clear from this brief review that there is not one criterion or variable with which all past researchers agree. However, several authors have suggested that benefit segmentation is one of the best segmentation bases (Morrison, 1996; Loker & Perdue, 1992). According to Haley (1968), the rationale behind this segmentation approach is that benefits sought by consumers are the fundamental reasons for the existence of true market segments and they determine the consumers' behavior much more accurately than do other descriptive variables such as demographic and geographic characteristics. Some tourism researchers also claim that benefit segmentation is a more appropriate approach for defining destination segments and

*Corresponding author. Tel.: +1-765-494-7905; fax: +1-765-494-0327.

E-mail addresses: jangs@purdue.edu (S.C. Jang), alastair@cfs.purdue.edu (A.M. Morrison), jto@fnr.purdue.edu (J.T. O'Leary).

developing marketing strategies because it identifies travelers' motivations and the satisfaction of what they need and want from their travel trips (Ahmed, Barber, & Astous, 1998).

Market targeting is the next step after the travel market has been segmented (Kotler, 1999). Before the choice of segments is made, the relative profitability of each potential target market must be considered. The ultimate objective of market segmentation is usually to make the most money from the selected target markets. Suppose a destination has two types of travelers: one is teenaged travelers staying in campgrounds, pursuing outdoor activities and spending relatively small amounts of money; the other is middle-aged travelers visiting cultural attractions, purchasing many souvenirs while lodging at upscale hotels. To which of these two markets should priority and limited resources be allocated (Legoherel, 1998)? The answer depends on the strategic direction of the destination, its resources and priorities. However, the choice will in some part be based on the expected economic returns compared to the costs of attracting each market. The criterion of substantiality must also be met: a segment must be large enough to be profitable (Kotler, 1999). Thus, potential profitability is one of the most important criteria in selecting target markets. The risk level associated with potential earnings is another factor that must be taken into account when comparing potential profitability and the choice of a market segments. Even though the expected economic earnings may be great, this may be meaningless if the chance of earning them is low. Therefore, profitability and risk play a vital role in evaluating the attractiveness of each segment and selecting the best target market.

2. Study objectives

To date, there has been no reported research on the evaluation of travel market segments in terms of profitability and risk. To fill this research gap, while providing a potentially useful benefit segmentation of an important long haul travel market, the research team decided to analyze Japanese pleasure travelers and to assess the profitability and risk level of the resulting benefit segments. Japan is an important origin country for primary destinations in both the USA and Canada in terms of economic contributions. This study makes a unique contribution to the tourism research literature by identifying benefit segments of Japanese travelers to the USA and Canada and then evaluating the resulting segments using the profitability and risk concepts. The five major objectives of this study were to:

1. Identify the benefit segments of Japanese pleasure travelers to the USA and Canada.

2. Profile the benefit segments.
3. Determine if there were statistical differences among the segments in terms of socio-demographic and trip-related characteristics.
4. Evaluate the benefit segments on the basis of profitability, risk, and market size.
5. Identify the optimum benefit segment.

3. Review of related research studies

3.1. Benefit segmentation in travel and tourism

A number of studies have been conducted using benefits as a segmentation base in travel and tourism. Frochot and Morrison (in press) reviewed several of these articles published in academic journals. After discussing the basic principles of benefit segmentation and the methodological issues associated with segment identification, they explained the potential advantages and disadvantages of using benefit segmentation. They argued that benefit segmentation is most helpful in designing and modifying facilities and attractions, vacation packaging, activity programming, and service quality measurement. However, explaining that trends, fashion, and other factors influence the benefits sought from destinations, they identified the instability of benefit segments over time as one of the limitations of this approach. The periodic updating of the benefit segmentation analysis was recommended. The other perceived disadvantage was the difficulty of generalization of the outcomes. Since most benefit segments are specific to a certain destination or the case being analyzed, the results of one study cannot be directly applied in other research.

Gitelson and Kerstetter (1990) examined the relationship between socio-demographic variables, benefits sought and subsequent behavior. Using factor analysis, they identified four benefits sought by North Carolina visitors: relaxation, excitement, social, and exploration. Women rated the relaxation dimension as more being more important than the men. No significant differences existed between benefits sought and level of education, while the income variable was significantly different for the exploration factor.

Yannopoulos and Rotenberg (1999) conducted a benefit segmentation study on the near-home tourism market. Using data collected from residents of Upper New York State, these researchers segmented the market into five clusters, which were named intangible amenities, active materialists, entertainment and comfort, cultured materialists, and entertainment and shopping. This research study indicated that age and household income were significant but gender, education, and composition of household were not significantly different across the five clusters.

S.C. Jang et al. / Tourism Management 23 (2002) 367–378 369

3.2. Japanese travel market studies

There have been several segmentation studies on Japanese travelers using travel motivations, which are generally accepted as having a direct relationship with the benefits sought (Frochot & Morrison, 2000). Cha, McCleary, and Uysal (1995) conducted one of the most frequently cited of these studies, investigating the travel motivations of Japanese overseas travelers using factor-cluster analysis. The study revealed six distinct motivation factors: relaxation, knowledge, adventure, travel bragging, family, and sports. Based on these motivation factors, Japanese pleasure travelers were segmented into three clusters, labeled as sports, novelty, and family/relaxation seekers. Age and education levels were significantly different among the three clusters, but gender, occupation, and income were not.

Andersen, Prentice, and Watanabe (2000) studied the travel motives of Japanese independent travelers to Scotland. According to this analysis, having new experiences (novelty), leaning about new cultures (understanding), and viewing scenery were the important motives. Using cluster analysis, Japanese independent travelers were separated into three segments: careerists, collectors, and mainstreamers. Careerists were the segment seeking to improve their careers through foreign travel, reflecting the Japanese "workaholic" culture in the blurring of leisure and work. Collectors were characterized as seeking prestige and collecting experiences, partly in the tangible form of souvenirs. The mainstreamers had a generally weaker endorsement of motives. The researchers stressed the need for target marketing and image differentiation in promoting to the three identified segments.

Milner, Collins, Tachibana, and Hiser (2000) studied Japanese visitors to Alaska during the summer of 1996 and winter of 1997. They reported that the Japanese were motivated to see particular items such as mountains, tundra, various polar animals, and the Midnight Sun in summer. In winter, motivations included seeing the Northern Lights, attending special events such as dog sledding, and cruising.

3.3. Evaluation of segment attractiveness

Very little research has been done on the evaluation of segment attractiveness to assist with target market selection. McQueen and Miller (1985) recommended the assessment of market attractiveness based upon profitability, variability, and accessibility. They used the relative weighted population size and expenditures of each group to assess profitability. Loker and Perdue (1992) proposed a systematic approach to evaluating segments using a ranking procedure. They assessed segment attractiveness in terms of profitability, accessibility, and reachability by ranking each segment on its

relative performance on the three evaluation criteria. The overall ranks were determined by summing the scores for each segment across the three criteria. Profitability was measured by the percentages of total expenditure related to the percentage of respondents, the percentage of person-nights, and average expenditures per person-night.

Kastenholz, Davis, and Paul (1999) conducted a very similar type of segment assessment for rural tourism in Portugal. A composite index of segment attractiveness from a revenue-generating perspective was constructed. The index consisted of three criteria; the size of the segment as measured by the percentage of study respondents in the segment, the number of persons in the travel party, and the average expenditures per person per day of cluster members. The clusters were then ranked on their relative performance on each of there three criteria, then a composite score was calculated by simply adding the rankings on each criterion across each segment.

The weakness of these previous studies with respect to target market selection was their lack of a comprehensive understanding about the profitability of the resulting market segments. Specifically, these studies only used the relative size of the market segments for target market selection. Additionally, the studies disregarded the probability or risk associated with each segment's potential profitability. This study attempted not only to analyze segment profitability but also risk, in evaluating segment attractiveness. This research is different because the results suggest quantifiable profitability and risk criteria for target market selection that have not been employed to date in tourism marketing research.

4. Methodology

4.1. Data source

The data used in this study were from the Pleasure Travel Markets Survey for Japan (PTAMS Japan) that was collected by the Coopers and Lybrand Consulting Group in 1995 under the joint sponsorship of the Canadian Tourism Commission, the US Travel and Tourism Administration (now Tourism Industries), and Secretaria de Turismo, Mexico. After samples were randomly selected by using the birth date method, a total of 1200 in-home interviews were conducted in seven major cities in Japan including Tokyo and Osaka. All respondents were Japanese, aged 18 years or older, who took overseas vacations of four nights or longer during the past 3 years or were planning to take such a trip in the next 2 years. The questionnaire collected a wide range of information including socio-demographic characteristics (age, gender, marital status, education, occupation, income, etc.), trip-related characteristics (type of trip, travel expenditures, the number of person in travel party, use of package tours, etc.), benefits sought, activities, information sources, destination images, and levels of satisfaction.

The population of this study was Japanese pleasure travelers to the USA and Canada. The sample consisted of 505 travelers who engaged in pleasure travel to the two countries during the three years prior to the survey. The sample included travelers to Mainland USA (143; 28.3%), Hawaii (142; 28.1%), Guam/American Samoa (42; 8.3%), and Canada (178; 35.3%).

The attitudinal scales used in PTAMS Japan were developed based on research conducted in the early 1970s as part of the Canadian Travel and Motivation surveys. An independent university research team tested the reliability of these scales in the mid 1990s, and the coefficients were found to be very high.

4.2. Analysis

The data analysis was completed in four steps. First, 42 benefit statements were grouped using factor analysis to find the underlying constructs associated with the travel benefits sought. Principal Components Analysis with a Varimax rotation was used with a predetermined cut-off Eigenvalue of one. Only factor loadings > 0.4 were retained and, with the exception of two items, all the factors satisfied the 0.4 criteria and were included in the factor identification. Cronbach's Alpha, the most commonly used reliability measure, was applied to test the reliability of factor. The factors with alphas > 0.6 were retained for further analysis. An alpha of 0.6 and higher indicates that there is a reasonable level of internal consistency among the items making up the factor (Hair, Anderson, Tatham, & Black, 1998).

Second, a cluster analysis was prepared to segment the market into homogeneous groups based upon the identified benefit factors. Third, socio-demographic and trip-related profiles of travelers in each cluster were developed and compared using χ^2 tests and Analyses of Variance (ANOVA) to determine if there were statistical differences among the clusters. Finally, the four measures of profitability, risk, risk-adjusted profitability index (RPI), and relative segment size (RSS) were developed and used to determine the attractiveness of each cluster. ANOVA was employed to provide the basis for the profitable market segments.

4.3. Evaluation of market segments

New measures of profitability were used to evaluate segment attractiveness. Profitability usually refers to the difference between revenues and expenses. The total revenue earned by a destination is the sum of every traveler's expenditures. The total expenses include the costs of destination development, infrastructure, environmental preservation, product development, and marketing. Profitability measures how much profit can be earned. Although the profitability measure is quite straightforward, it is difficult to get accurate and comprehensive expense data for a destination. Revenue side data are directly computed because traveler expenditure information is usually readily available. But expense side data are often very limited or complicated to apply directly. For example, destination development costs are generally large and occur at the very beginning of development. It is difficult to decide how much of the costs should be allocated on an annual basis. Even a slight variation in the calculation technique can have a great impact on profitability, thereby providing different information for target market selection decisions. Thus, even though the computation of profit can be made only with total revenues and total costs known, it may be reasonable to use expenditure data as a proxy for profitability. Given the situation of unknown costs for a destination, the best estimate is that expenditure levels are closely related to potential profits. Under the same levels of marginal costs and marginal revenues, the higher the expenditures, the higher are the total revenues, and the greater the profit (Maurice & Thomas, 1999). Therefore, expenditure per party, expenditure per traveler, and expenditure per traveler per night were used as profitability proxies in this study.

Risk is another difficult concept to measure. Risk literally refers to the probability that some unfavorable event will happen. In this study, risk was assumed to be the uncertainty that a market segment may have less profit potential than the mean potential. Risk reduces the reliability of the market segment. The greater the probability of low profit potential, the riskier the segment. The risk concept has been well developed in the finance field. One common way used in finance is to employ the standard deviation, a measure of the tightness of the probability or frequency distribution. The smaller the standard deviation, the tighter the distribution and the lower the total risk of the market (Brigham & Gapenski, 1988). Thus, the *risk* associated with segment profitability in this study can also be measured by looking at how far the expenditure observations are from their mean. A small standard deviation will be obtained when the expenditure observations are close to the mean; this increases the chance that the profitability, or mean expenditure, will actually be attained. If the standard deviation is very large, this will introduce greater uncertainty about the expected profitability. Because a normal distribution can be completely described by its expected value or mean and standard deviation, the expenditure distribution for each segment was tested for normality and were all found to be normal.

S.C. Jang et al. / Tourism Management 23 (2002) 367–378

Another useful measure of risk is the *coefficient of variance* (CV), which is the standard deviation divided by the expected value (in this study, the mean expenditure). The CV indicates the relative risk per unit of expenditure, and it provides a more meaningful basis for comparison when the mean expenditures of the market segments are not the same (Brigham & Gapenski, 1988). The standard deviation simply measures the dispersion of the expected expenditures around the mean and provides information on the extent of possible deviations of the actual profitability from the expected, while the CV serves as a risk-to-profitability ratio and is intended to relate the total risk to the mean profitability. Where differences in expected profitability exist among market segments, the CV is a better risk measure than the standard deviation (Brigham & Gapenski, 1988). Therefore, this study used the CV as the way to measure profitability risk.

One method that reflects profitability and risk at the same time is the RPI, which is the mean expenditure divided by the standard deviation times one hundred. The RPI shows the relative profitability after risk, and it provides a method to compare market segments and select the most potentially profitable segment when the risks of each segment are not the same.

The last evaluation technique is the RSS, which is calculated as the mean expenditure multiplied by the probability of the occurrence of a specific segment. RSS refers to the probability-added mean expenditure of a specific segment and represents the relative economic size of the market segment. Thus, the higher the RSS, the better chance marketers have. RSS and RPI were used for the overall evaluation of the market segments and for target market selection in this study.

5. Results

5.1. Factor analysis: the definition of benefits sought

Eleven benefit factors were found with Eigenvalues $\geqslant 1$, and they accounted for 63.0% of the total variance. Three of these factors were dropped due to low Cronbach's alphas, ranging from 0.39 to 0.49. The remaining eight factors explained 49.9% of the variance and are shown in Table 1.

The first factor was named *nature and environment*, containing the five benefits of environmental quality, air, water and soil, standards of hygiene and cleanliness, personal safety, nice weather, and interesting rural countryside. The second factor, *knowledge and entertainment*, was comprised of visiting a place I can talk about when get home, going to places I have not visited before, opportunities to increase one's knowledge, going places my friends have not been, and having fun, being entertained. The third factor was labeled as *history and*

culture with the two benefits of historical, archaeological, and military places and arts and cultural attractions. *Outdoor activities* was the fourth factor, including outdoor activities, roughing it, visits to appreciate natural ecological sites, and unique and different native groups. The fifth factor, *family and relaxation*, was comprised of being together as a family, doing nothing at all, activities for the whole family, shopping, and just relaxing. The sixth factor was labeled as *escape* since it incorporated escaping from the ordinary, getting away from the demands of home, and getting a change from a busy job. The seventh factor was named *value* because of the high loadings of the best deal I could get and a destination that provides value for holiday money. *Lifestyle* was the eighth factor, comprising experiencing new and different lifestyles, experiencing a simpler lifestyle, and trying new foods.

5.2. Cluster analysis: the definition of market segments

Two different types of cluster analysis techniques were employed to identify groups of travelers based on similarities in benefits sought. The eight benefit factors extracted in the factor analysis were used as clustering variables. First, a hierarchical cluster analysis was performed. This helped to determine the number of clusters and identify outliers. The agglomeration coefficient and dendrogram revealed that a three-cluster solution was most appropriate and that there were nine outliers among the observations. Second, a non-hierarchical method, the K-Means clustering technique, was applied with the cluster centers from the hierarchical results as the initial seed points after the outliers were deleted (Hair et al., 1998). The three clusters had 136 (27.4%), 152 (30.7%), and 208 (41.9%) out of the remaining 496 observations.

To delineate the three clusters and to label them, the mean importance scores for each benefit factor were computed and these are presented in Table 2. Cluster 1 had the highest importance ratings for five benefit factors including nature and environment and knowledge and entertainment. Cluster 2 placed the highest importance on escape, while Cluster 3 had the highest scores for both outdoor activities and family and relaxation. An examination of the mean importance scores for each benefit factor and individual items suggested the labels of Cluster 1, 2, and 3 as *novelty/ nature seekers*, *escape/relaxation seekers*, and *family/ outdoor activities seekers*, respectively.

Table 2 also shows that the respondents rated value as the most important benefit. Four other benefit factors (nature and environment, knowledge and entertainment, family and relaxation, and escape) were also given relatively high importance. History and culture, outdoor activities, and lifestyle were not highly rated. This result is partly supported by prior research (Yuan &

Table 1
Factor analysis of benefit sought items of Japanese pleasure travelers to the USA and Canada[a]

Factors	Loading	Eigen value	Variance explained (%)	Reliability alpha
Nature and environment		3.15	7.5	0.75
Environmental quality, air, water and soil	0.78			
Standards of hygiene and cleanliness	0.74			
Personal safety	0.61			
Nice weather	0.49			
Interesting rural countryside	0.45			
Knowledge and entertainment		3.06	7.3	0.75
Visiting a place I can talk about when get home	0.74			
Going to places I have not visited before	0.70			
Opportunities to increase one's knowledge	0.65			
Going places my friends have not been	0.65			
Having fun, being entertained	0.50			
History and culture		2.61	6.2	0.65
Historical, archaeological, military places	0.76			
Arts and cultural attractions	0.73			
Outdoor activities		2.56	6.1	0.73
Outdoor activities	0.78			
Roughing it	0.76			
Visits to appreciate natural ecological sites	0.48			
Unique or different native groups	0.46			
Family and relaxation		2.56	6.1	0.76
Being together as a family	0.68			
Doing nothing at all	0.66			
Activities for the whole family	0.66			
Shopping	0.58			
Just relaxing	0.56			
Escape		2.50	5.9	0.80
Escaping from the ordinary	0.81			
Getting away from the demands of home	0.77			
Getting a change from a busy job	0.71			
Value		2.27	5.4	0.69
The best deal I could get	0.74			
Destination that provides value for money	0.69			
Availability pre-trip and in-country tourist info	0.56			
Outstanding scenery	0.45			
Lifestyle		2.24	5.3	0.72
Experiencing new and different lifestyle	0.79			
Experiencing a simpler lifestyle	0.76			
Trying new foods	0.46			
Total variance explained			49.9	

[a] Two benefit items were removed for the low factor loadings. Three factors including nine items were deleted due to the low reliability alphas.

McDonald, 1990; Cha et al., 1995) in a sense that there emerged a common factor, knowledge.

Cross-tabulations were performed to provide sociodemographic and trip-related profiles of the three clusters. The profile of each cluster can be summarized as follows.

5.2.1. Cluster 1 (novelty/nature seekers)

This segment consisted of travelers with a cultural appreciation, who are seeking new knowledge, are concerned with environmental quality, and want to experience new foods and lifestyles. They also pursued the best deal they could get and tended to like shopping.

S.C. Jang et al. / Tourism Management 23 (2002) 367–378 373

Table 2
Mean importance scores of benefits sought among the three clusters[a]

Benefit factors/items	Cluster 1 (n = 136)	Cluster 2 (n = 152)	Cluster 3 (n = 208)	Mean (n = 496)
Nature and environment	2.93	2.68	2.67	2.74
Environmental quality, air, water and soil	3.04	3.03	2.88	2.97
Standards of hygiene and cleanliness	3.13	2.98	2.92	3.00
Personal safety	2.73	2.44	2.51	2.55
Nice weather	3.13	3.04	3.00	3.04
Interesting rural countryside	2.60	1.92	2.05	2.16
Knowledge and entertainment	3.12	2.93	2.35	2.74
Visiting a place I can talk about when get home	3.14	2.84	2.21	2.66
Going to places I have not visited before	3.30	3.13	2.50	2.91
Opportunities to increase one's knowledge	3.42	2.89	2.44	2.85
Going places my friends have not been	2.40	2.39	1.75	2.13
Having fun, being entertained	3.32	3.38	2.85	3.14
History and culture	2.85	1.54	1.73	1.98
Historical, archaeological, military places	2.89	1.47	1.78	1.99
Arts and cultural attractions	2.82	1.61	1.69	1.97
Outdoor activities	2.01	1.63	2.03	1.90
Outdoor activities	1.91	1.82	2.37	2.07
Roughing it	1.71	1.55	2.05	1.80
Visits to appreciate natural ecological sites	2.62	1.81	2.05	2.13
Unique or different native groups	1.81	1.37	1.65	1.61
Family and relaxation	2.72	2.60	2.74	2.69
Being together as a family	2.29	1.81	2.49	2.23
Doing nothing at all	2.92	2.95	2.69	2.83
Activities for the whole family	2.18	1.84	2.59	2.25
Shopping	3.21	3.20	2.80	3.04
Just relaxing	3.09	3.20	3.04	3.10
Escape	2.76	2.79	2.53	2.67
Escaping from the ordinary	2.79	2.86	2.51	2.70
Getting away from the demands of home	2.56	2.26	2.20	2.32
Getting a change from a busy job	2.92	3.23	2.88	3.00
Value	3.26	2.93	3.06	3.08
The best deal I could get	3.46	3.07	3.38	3.31
Destination that provides value for money	3.07	2.66	2.91	2.88
Availability pre-trip and in-country tourist info	2.98	2.76	2.74	2.81
Outstanding scenery	3.54	3.22	3.21	3.30
New Lifestyle	2.35	2.34	1.88	2.15
Experiencing new and different lifestyle	2.45	2.59	1.89	2.26
Experiencing a simpler lifestyle	2.18	2.34	1.90	2.11
Trying new foods	2.43	2.09	1.84	2.08

[a] Respondents were asked to rate all benefits on a Likert scale from 1 to 4, where 1 = not important at all and 4 = very important. Importance scores in bold text represent the highest importance scores on the benefit factors or items across the three clusters. Nine observations were deleted because of outliers.

They were a somewhat older group than the other two and were either white-collar workers, unemployed, housewives, or had part-time jobs. Two-thirds of them are married. They were most likely to have traveled with wives, husbands, girlfriends, or boyfriends in the summer or fall, visiting big cities in Mainland USA or Canada.

5.2.2. Cluster 2 (escape/relaxation seekers)

Travelers belonging to this segment were eager to get away from their ordinary lives and busy jobs. They tended to be white-collar workers, college students, or specialists, and the majority of them were single in their 20s and 30s. Visiting either big cities or beach resorts, they traveled to Hawaii and Canada with friends. Their travel trips were relatively evenly spread among the four seasons of the year.

5.2.3. Cluster 3 (family/outdoor activities seekers)

The members of this cluster enjoyed being together with family and doing outdoor activities such as hiking or climbing. In their 20s or 30s, they tended to be married and either white-collar workers, unemployed or housewives. They like to travel to beach resorts and sports and outdoor activity venues in Hawaii and Canada during the summer and winter.

The χ^2 analyses and one-way ANOVAs were used to identify whether significant differences existed among the clusters (Table 3). Among the socio-demographic variables, significant differences were found for age, marital status, and occupation. People in their 20s represented the highest proportions of the travelers in all three clusters. However, Cluster 2 (escape/ relaxation seekers) had the largest share in their 20s, at 51.3%. Cluster 1 (novelty/nature seekers) had a much larger proportion in the 40s, 50s, and 60s (together representing 49.3%). The age distributions were consistent with the findings for marital status. Half of those in Cluster 2 were single, compared to 32.4% in Cluster 1 and 32.7% in Cluster 3 (family/outdoor activity seekers). White-collar workers were the largest occupational group for all three clusters. Cluster 2 had a particularly high proportion of white-collar workers (30.9%). Another large group was those who were unemployed or housewives, especially in Cluster 3 (22.6%).

Among the trip-related characteristics, significant differences were found among the three clusters for travel companion, number of people in travel party, season of trip, region, and type of trip. The highest percentage of respondents in Clusters 1(35.2%) and 3 (49.0%) were traveling with wives, husbands, girlfriends, or boyfriends. Friends represented the highest proportion in Cluster 2 (33.8%). The number of people included in the travel party was the highest in Cluster 3 (2.09 persons), compared to 1.5 in Cluster 1 and 1.52 in Cluster 2. The season of trip seemed to be related to the travel region and type of trip. Cluster 1 preferred summer (41.9%) and fall (30.9%) and was strongly represented by visitors to Mainland USA (40.4%) and Canada (42.6%). Cluster 1 was more likely to visit big cities (46.3%). Cluster 2 tended to be more indifferent about the season of trip and the highest proportion visited Hawaii (33.6%) where beach resort facilities are available. A significant share of the travelers in Cluster 3 went in summer (34.6%) and winter (33.2%). They traveled to Hawaii (33.7%) and Canada (33.7%) and showed preferences for trips to beach resorts (37.5%), sports and outdoor activity places (18.8%), and cities (18.8%).

5.3. Evaluation of market segments and target market selection

5.3.1. Profitability

To identify the most profitable market segment, the three clusters were evaluated based upon their mean expenditures. Mean expenditures were measured in terms of mean expenditure per travel party, mean expenditure per person, and mean expenditure per person per night. It was expected that the most profitable segment would have the highest expenditure in the all three spending categories. Table 4 shows the results and indicates that statistical differences were found for all the expenditure categories across three clusters. With the highest mean expenditures in all three categories, Cluster 1 initially appeared to be the most profitable segment. Cluster 3's expenditures per travel party were higher than Cluster 2's but were lower in the other two expenditure categories. Even though Cluster 1 consistently showed superiority in mean expenditures, these results were not sufficient in deciding if it was the best segment from a profitability standpoint. The uncertainty needed to be gauged along with these profitability results.

5.3.2. Risk

The risk or uncertainty was measured through the CV, which indicates the relative risk (Table 5). Cluster 1 appeared the least risky segment, both in terms of the expenditure per travel party and expenditure per person. However, Cluster 2 had the lowest CV for expenditure per person per night. The length of stay (number of nights) tended to vary more for Cluster 1, but was more stable for Cluster 2. In order to make a choice, it was necessary to consider profitability and the risk simultaneously. A measure combining profitability and risk needed to be used.

5.3.3. Risk-adjusted profitability index (RPI)

A RPI was created and applied to assist in making the final decision on segment choice. As shown in Table 6, Cluster 1 had the highest RPI in two expenditure categories, while Cluster 2 led in expenditure per person per night. It is suggested that expenditures per party and per person provide better decision guidelines for destination marketers. Expenditure per person per night represents more useful information for hotels and restaurants, as they can serve visitors in each cluster with the appropriately priced products and services. Thus, the highest RPI scores in expenditures per travel party and per person indicated that Cluster 1 was the segment generating the greatest expenditures for a destination, even after considering the risk. Thus, Cluster 1 was confirmed as the most profitable segment from a destination marketer's viewpoint.

S.C. Jang et al. / Tourism Management 23 (2002) 367–378 375

Table 3
Socio-demographic and trip-related profile of three clusters of Japanese pleasure travelers to the USA and Canada

Characteristics	Cluster 1 ($n = 136$) Novelty/nature seekers	Cluster 2 ($n = 152$) Escape/relaxation seekers	Cluster 3 ($n = 208$) Family/outdoor activities seekers	χ^2 or F	Sig.
Socio-demographic					
Age				χ^2 : 43.6	0.000
18–19	2.9%	3.9%	3.4%		
20–29	33.1%	51.3%	35.6%		
30–39	14.7%	22.4%	31.7%		
40–49	20.6%	10.5%	16.3%		
50–59	19.1%	7.9%	9.1%		
60–	9.6%	3.9%	3.8%		
Gender				χ^2 : 3.3	0.189
Male	29.4%	34.2%	38.9%		
Female	70.6%	65.8%	61.1%		
Marital status				χ^2 : 18.6	0.001
Single	32.4%	50.0%	32.7%		
Married	65.4%	49.3%	67.3%		
Other	2.2%	0.7%	0.0%		
Education				χ^2 : 16.6	0.164
Primary school (grades 1–7)	2.2%	3.3%	1.4%		
Some high school	29.4%	19.9%	22.1%		
High school (grade 12)	8.1%	16.6%	12.0%		
Tech. or vocational school	16.2%	13.9%	11.1%		
Some college or university	15.4%	21.2%	16.8%		
College or university	26.5%	24.5%	34.6%		
Advanced degree	2.2%	0.7%	1.9%		
Occupation				χ^2 : 26.9	0.043
College student	12.5%	13.8%	9.1%		
White-collar worker	24.3%	30.9%	24.5%		
Blue-collar worker	2.9%	7.2%	3.4%		
Administrator/Manage	8.8%	4.6%	8.2%		
Specialist/Freelancer	6.6%	13.2%	15.4%		
Self-employed	5.1%	6.6%	4.3%		
Part-timer	15.4%	4.6%	10.1%		
Unemployed/Housewife	20.6%	15.8%	22.6%		
Other	3.7%	3.3%	2.4%		
Income				χ^2 : 13.7	0.323
Less than ¥3 million	6.8%	7.2%	4.2%		
¥3.0–¥4.9	10.2%	19.6%	25.4%		
¥5.0–¥6.9	19.3%	21.6%	18.3%		
¥7.0–¥9.9	22.7%	24.7%	19.7%		
¥10.0–¥11.9	14.8%	11.3%	10.6%		
¥12.0–¥14.9	14.8%	5.2%	10.6%		
¥15 million or over	11.4%	10.3%	11.3%		
Trip-related					
Travel companion				χ^2 : 33.2	0.003
Traveled alone	10.2%	13.1%	6.1%		
Wife\husband\girlfriend\boyfriend	35.2%	24.8%	49.0%		
Father\Mother	7.0%	2.1%	3.5%		
Other relatives	3.9%	5.5%	2.0%		
Friends	21.1%	33.8%	22.2%		
Organized group\club	8.6%	7.6%	4.5%		
Business colleagues	13.3%	12.4%	12.1%		
Number of people in travel party	1.54	1.52	2.09	F : 9.66	0.000
Number of nights in USA or Canada	7.08	7.71	7.35	F : 0.22	0.802

(continued on next page)

Table 3 (*continued*)

Characteristics	Cluster 1 ($n = 136$) Novelty/nature seekers	Cluster 2 ($n = 152$) Escape/relaxation seekers	Cluster 3 ($n = 208$) Family/outdoor activities seekers	χ^2 or F	Sig.
Package tour				χ^2 : 1.32	0.517
Yes	66.9%	71.1%	65.4%		
No	33.1%	28.9%	34.6%		
Season of trip				χ^2 : 26.2	0.000
Spring (Mar–May)	16.2%	16.4%	14.4%		
Summer (June–Aug)	41.9%	32.2%	34.6%		
Fall (Sept–Nov)	30.9%	28.3%	17.8%		
Winter (Dec–Feb)	11.0%	23.0%	33.2%		
Region				χ^2 : 33.1	0.000
Mainland USA	40.4%	24.3%	23.6%		
Hawaii	14.7%	33.6%	33.7%		
Guam/American Samoa	2.2%	11.2%	9.1%		
Canada	42.6%	30.9%	33.7%		
Type of trip				χ^2 : 92.3	0.000
A visit to friends or relatives	13.2%	9.9%	9.6%		
A trip to Cities	46.3%	27.8%	18.8%		
A beach resort trip	17.6%	38.4%	37.5%		
A trip to a mountain resort	2.9%	1.3%	5.3%		
A culture, history or heritage trip	9.6%	0.7%	1.4%		
A sports and outdoor trip	2.9%	8.6%	18.8%		
A trip to an exhibition	0.7%	2.0%	1.4%		
A trip to an amusement park	0.7%	4.0%	2.4%		
Other	5.9%	7.3%	4.8%		

Table 4
Comparison of segment profitability (unit: ¥10,000)[a]

Expenditure category	Cluster 1 ($n = 136$) Novelty/Nature seekers	Cluster 2 ($n = 152$) Escape/Relaxation seekers	Cluster 3 ($n = 208$) Family/outdoor activities seekers	F	Sig.
Mean expenditure/travel party	**68.1**	51.7	62.2	4.6	0.01
Mean expenditure/person	**49.2**	37.8	34.9	18.1	0.000
Mean expenditure/person/night	**7.8**	6.0	5.8	9.27	0.000

[a] Numbers in bold text represent the highest expenditure across the three clusters.

Table 5
Comparison of coefficient of variance (CV) for segment profitability risk[a]

Expenditure category	Cluster1 ($n = 136$) Novelty/nature seekers	Cluster2 ($n = 152$) Escape/relaxation seekers	Cluster3 ($n = 208$) Family/outdoor activities seekers
Mean expenditure/travel party	**0.62**	0.84	0.73
Mean expenditure/person	**0.47**	0.54	0.55
Mean expenditure/person/night	0.74	**0.56**	0.61

[a] Numbers in bold text represent the lowest expenditure across the three clusters.

5.3.4. Relative segment size (RSS)

Another important consideration in segment selection was the relative market size. A measure of RSS was used to compare the three segments. Table 7 shows that Cluster 3 consistently had the highest RSS in all three expenditure categories. This implies that the expected total market size of Cluster 3 was the greatest, even though this group's profitability (Table 4) was not

Table 6
Comparison of risk-adjusted profitability index (RPI)[a]

Expenditure category	Cluster1 (n = 136) Novelty/nature seekers	Cluster2 (n = 152) Escape/relaxation seekers	Cluster3 (n = 208) Family/outdoor activities seekers
Mean expenditure/travel party	**162.4**	118.7	136.2
Mean expenditure/person	**214.9**	184.8	182.7
Mean expenditure/person/night	135.1	**179.9**	162.9

[a] Numbers in bold text represent the highest RPI across the three clusters.

Table 7
Comparison of relative segment size (RSS) (unit: ¥10,000)[a]

Expenditure category	Cluster1 (n = 136; 27.4%) Novelty/nature seekers	Cluster2 (n = 152; 30.7%) Escape/relaxation seekers	Cluster3 (n = 208; 41.9%) Family/outdoor activities seekers	Sum (n = 496)
Mean expenditure/travel party	18.2	15.8	**26.5**	60.5
Mean expenditure/person	13.2	11.6	**14.9**	39.7
Mean expenditure/person/night	2.1	1.8	**2.5**	6.4

[a] Numbers in bold text represent the largest RSS across the three clusters.

ranked the highest. The RSS figures in Table 7 were obtained by multiplying the mean expenditures (Table 4) for each cluster by the probability of occurrence (e.g., 136/496 for Cluster 1).

5.3.5. Target market selection

The RPI and RSS results identify potentially high profit generating segments from different viewpoints and can be interpreted in alternate ways according to who is doing the marketing. If the organization or destination is large and industry with more of a mass marketing strategy, the largest market segment (Cluster 3) would be the one to pursue. Marketers in smaller organizations or destinations pursuing niche-marketing strategies may prefer to target the most profitable segment (Cluster 1). Overall, given the intensely competitive situation in tourism today, Cluster 1 seems to be the most realistic choice of segments for most marketers. From this evaluation process, it is clear that some subjective decision criteria are required in making a final choice. However, the process has value in contributing quantifiable evaluation criteria for establishing segment attractiveness and selecting target markets.

6. Conclusions

Many prior research efforts using similar methodologies have not differentiated Japanese pleasure travelers to the USA and Canada on the basis of benefits sought. Using factor-cluster analysis, this study produced three, non-homogeneous benefit-sought groups (novelty/nature seekers, escape/relaxation seekers, and family/outdoor activities seekers). Differentiated marketing

strategies need to be applied to effectively appeal to each of these groups.

Significant differences among the three groups were found for age, marital status, occupation, travel companions, number of people included in the travel party, season of trip, region, and type of trip. These socio-demographic and trip-related characteristic differences can help marketers develop the most effective strategies including product and service development, pricing, distribution channels, and advertising.

Although the benefit segmentation applied in this study was effective and provided useful information for marketing, it is just one of many alternate segmentation bases for differentiating travelers. Future research on market segmentation should incorporate other variables such as activities and satisfaction. To further test the segment evaluation criteria proposed in this study, follow-on studies could explore international travelers of other nationalities and combine these with different segmentation bases.

It is important that marketing strategies be developed by incorporating economic return on investment criteria. Marketing strategies that do not consider profitability and risk cannot be successful in the long term. This study thus attempted to establish quantifiable profitability and risk evaluation criteria to determine segment attractiveness and to assist with target market selection. The profitability and risk analyses revealed that Cluster 3 (family/outdoor activities seekers) was the largest market segment with the greatest potential appeal to mass marketers. Cluster 1 (novelty/nature seekers) was the most profitable segment and would be more attractive to smaller and niche marketers.

378 *S.C. Jang et al. / Tourism Management 23 (2002) 367–378*

References

Ahmed, S., Barber, M., & Astous, A. (1998). Segmentation of the Nordic Winter Sun seekers market. *Journal of Travel and Tourism Marketing, 7*(1), 39–63.

Anderson, B., & Langmeyer, L. (1982). The under-50 and over-50 travelers: A profile of similarities and differences. *Journal of Travel Research, 20*(4), 20–24.

Andersen, V., Prentice, R., & Watanabe, K. (2000). Journey for experiences: Japanese independent travelers in Scotland. *Journal of Travel and Tourism Marketing, 9*(1/2), 129–151.

Brigham, E., & Gapenski, L. (1988). *Financial management: Theory and practice* (5th ed.). New York, NY: The Dryden Press.

Cha, S., McCleary, K., & Uysal, M. (1995). Travel motivations of Japanese overseas travelers: A factor-cluster segmentation approach. *Journal of Travel Research, 34*(1), 33–39.

Frochot, I., & Morrison, A. (2000). Benefit segmentation: A review of its applications to travel and tourism research. *Journal of Travel and Tourism Marketing, 9*(4), 21–45.

Gitelson, R., & Kerstetter, D. (1990). The relationship between sociodemographic variables, benefits sought and subsequent vacation behavior: A case study. *Journal of Travel Research, 28*(3), 24–29.

Hair, J., Anderson, R., Tatham, R., & &Black, W. (1998). *Multivariate data analysis* (5th ed.). Upper Saddle River, NJ: Prentice-Hall, Inc..

Haley, R. (1968). Benefit segmentation: A decision-oriented research tool. *Journal of Marketing, 32*(3), 30–35.

Hsieh, S., & O'Leary, J. (1993). Communication channels to segment pleasure travelers. *Journal of Travel and Tourism Marketing, 2*(2/3), 57–75.

Hsieh, S., O'Leary, J., & Morrison, A. (1992). Segmenting the international travel market by activity. *Tourism Management, 13*(2), 209–223.

Kastenholz, E., Davis, D., & Paul, G. (1999). Segmenting tourism in rural areas: The case of north and central Portugal. *Journal of Travel Research, 37*(4), 353–363.

Kotler, P. (1999). *Marketing management: Analysis, planning, implementation, and control* (10th ed.). Englewood Cliffs, NJ: Prentice-Hall, Inc..

Legoherel, P. (1998). Toward a market segmentation of the tourism trade: Expenditure levels and consumer behavior instability. *Journal of Travel and Tourism Marketing, 7*(3), 19–39.

Loker, L., & Perdue, R. (1992). A benefit-based segmentation of a nonresident summer travel market. *Journal of Travel Research, 31*(1), 30–35.

McQueen, J., & Miller, K. (1985). Target market selection of tourists: A comparison of approaches. *Journal of Travel Research, 24*(1), 2–6.

Maurice, S., & Thomas, C. (1999). *Managerial economics* (6th ed.). Boston, MA: Irwin/McGraw-Hill.

Milner, L., Collins, J., Tachibana, R., & Hiser, R. (2000). The Japanese vacation visitor to Alaska: A preliminary examination of peak and off season traveler demographics, information source utilization, trip planning, and customer satisfaction. *Journal of Travel and Tourism Marketing, 9*(1/2), 43–56.

Mok, C., & Iverson, T. (2000). Expenditure-based segmentation: Taiwanese tourists to Guam. *Tourism Management, 21*, 299–305.

Morrison, A. (1996). *Hospitality and travel marketing* (2nd ed.). Albany, NY: Delmar Publishers.

Pizam, A., & Reichel, A. (1979). Big spenders and little spenders in US tourism. *Journal of Travel Research, 18*(1), 42–43.

Reid, L., & Reid, S. (1997). Traveler geographic origin and market segmentation for small island nations: The Barbados case. *Journal of Travel and Tourism Marketing, 6*(3), 5–22.

Schewe, C., & Calantone, R. (1978). Psychographic segmentation of tourists. *Journal of Travel Research, 16*(3), 14–20.

Shoemaker, S. (1989). Segmentation of the senior pleasure travel market. *Journal of Travel Research, 27*(3), 14–21.

Shoemaker, S. (1994). Segmenting the US travel market according to benefits realized. *Journal of Travel Research, 32*(3), 8–17.

Silverberg, K., Backman, S., & Backman, K. (1996). A preliminary investigation into the psychographics of nature-based travelers to the Southeastern United States. *Journal of Travel Research, 35*(2), 19–28.

Spotts, D., & Mahoney, E. (1991). Segmenting visitors to a destination region based on the volume of their expenditures. *Journal of Travel Research, 29*(4), 24–31.

Taylor, G. (1987). Foreign pleasure travel by Americans. *Journal of Travel Research, 25*(3), 5–7.

Yannopoulos, P., & Rotenberg, R. (1999). Benefit segmentation of the near-home tourism market: The case of upper New York state. *Journal of Travel and Tourism Marketing, 8*(2), 41–55.

Yuan, S., & McDonald, C. (1990). Motivational determinants of international pleasure time. *Journal of Travel Research, 24*(2), 42–44.

Woodside, A., & Jacobs, L. (1985). Step two in benefit segmentation: Learning the benefits realized by major travel markets. *Journal of Travel Research, 24*(1), 7–13.

[17]

A General Theory of Tourism Consumption Systems: A Conceptual Framework and an Empirical Exploration

ARCH G. WOODSIDE AND CHRIS DUBELAAR

A tourism consumption system (TCS) is defined as the set of related travel thoughts, decisions, and behaviors by a discretionary traveler prior to, during, and following a trip. The central proposition of a theory of TCS is that the thoughts, decisions, and behaviors regarding one activity influence the thoughts, decisions, and behaviors for a number of other activities. Using exit interview travel data and quick clustering analysis, this article empirically examines seven basic TCS propositions pertaining to decisions made once the destination has been selected. The findings support and extend the basic propositions specifically indicating clear patterns in the behaviors of visitors to Prince Edward Island, Canada. The authors conclude by recommending that this approach is useful for tourism marketers and practitioners in general. Suggestions are provided for analyzing TCS to increase the effectiveness of tourism marketing strategies.

The purpose of this article is to suggest a framework for a theory of tourism consumption systems (TCSs) and an exploratory empirical examination to illuminate this framework. A tourism consumption system is defined as the set of related travel thoughts, decisions, and behaviors by a discretionary traveler prior to, during, and following a trip. The central proposition of a theory of TCSs is that the thoughts, decisions, and behaviors regarding one activity influence the thoughts, decisions, and behaviors for a number of other activities, implying that behavioral patterns should be visible in the consumption of tourism offerings.

A deep understanding of tourism behavior needs to extend beyond theories and focus on information search and destination choice for which ample models already exist (e.g., see Bello and Etzel 1985; Fodness and Murray 1999; Woodside and Lysonski 1989). The "defining moments" (i.e., events vividly and automatically retrieved from memory) of a trip may not relate, per se, to unique features of a destination area. Thus, the theory of TCS focuses on achieving deep understanding of the multiple immediate and downstream relationships among events prior to, during, and following a discretionary trip rather than predicting and explaining destination choice. In particular, this article focuses on the actions and decisions subsequent to the choice and details the patterns of behavior, highlighting the regularity and striking differences present in groups that travel to the same destination.

TOURISM CONSUMPTION SYSTEMS

Decisions and behaviors by travelers and tourists represent a rich mosaic of relationships among multiple sets of variables. These variables include the following:

- background variables (demographic, psychographic, and social);
- destination marketing and related service marketing influences—for example, destination advertising Web sites and offers to provide inquirers with free visitor information guides (VIGs) and the information and persuasiveness of these VIGs; related service marketing influences include event and attraction marketing and advertising by car rental firms, restaurants, and accommodations;
- prior trip behavior, information search, and current trip planning;
- choices and behaviors regarding destinations, transportation modes, travel routes, accommodations, visiting attractions, restaurants and foods, durable purchases, and local-area destinations;
- micro and macro evaluations and satisfactions (i.e., regarding individual and global consumption events occurring during the trip); and
- conations (e.g., willingness and intentions to repeat the tourism-related consumption events, such as visiting the same destination in the future).

For example, air versus car travel from home to a major destination is likely to influence the use of destination-area transportation mode, places visited, and event participation in the local destination vicinity. Also, travelers' use versus nonuse of VIGs (made available by many local and regional

Arch G. Woodside is a professor of marketing in the Carroll School of Management at Boston College in Boston. Chris Dubelaar is a senior lecturer in the Department of Marketing at Monash University in Melbourne, Australia. The authors thank the four JTR reviewers and Charles R. Goeldner for the helpful comments and suggested revisions on earlier drafts of this article. They gratefully acknowledge Roberta MacDonald, University of Prince Edward Island, Charlottetown, and the Marketing Agency, Prince Edward Island, for the data files used to empirically explore the propositions in this article.

Journal of Travel Research, Vol. 41, November 2002, 120-132
DOI: 10.1177/004728702237412
© 2002 Sage Publications

JOURNAL OF TRAVEL RESEARCH   121

FIGURE 1
MODEL OF DISTANCE, USE OF ADVERTISING INFORMATION, AND FIRST/PRIOR VISIT
BEHAVIOR ON PRIME MOTIVE, TRAVELER DESTINATION BEHAVIORS, AND OUTCOMES

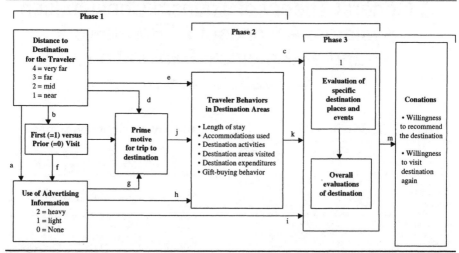

Note: Figure 1 includes 13 propositions of direct relationships. Each proposition is identified by a lowercase letter. For example, P_a: the greater the distance to the destination for the traveler, the greater the use of advertising information; P_b: the greater the distance to the destination for the traveler, the greater the likelihood of a first visit to a destination.

tourism boards around the world) is likely to have many influences beyond the destination choice decision. For example, use of VIGs may influence choice of accommodations and restaurants, attractions and events, and gift-buying behavior (Woodside, Trappey, and MacDonald 1997).

Any given discretionary trip is complex in the many related thoughts, decisions, behaviors, and evaluations that occur prior to, during, and following the trip. The discretionary traveler's thoughts, actions, and attitudes are likely to be influenced by seemingly minor events that often trigger substantial investments in time and money. Consequently, complexity and nuance need to be captured in modeling and empirically examining discretionary trips.

While related, the concept of TCS differs from Solomon's (1988, 1999) view of consumption constellations. "Consumption constellations [are] sets of products and activities used by consumers to define, communicate, and perform social roles" (Solomon 1999, p. 562). TCS refers to the related thoughts, actions, and behaviors of discretionary travelers prior to, during, and following their trips. Unlike consumption constellation research, the primary focus of the study of TCSs is not on social roles reflected by the combined use of several seemingly unrelated products-services and brands. TCS focuses on direct and indirect relationships occurring between all variables relevant for a discretionary trip. Earlier theoretical work by Clawson and Knetsch (1966) emphasizes such a systems view.

Clawson and Knetsch (1966, pp. 33-36) advocated a broad view in describing the "total recreation experience" as five related but distinctly different phases:

1. an outdoor recreation experience begins by anticipation, including planning;
2. travel to the actual site ("in almost every instance some travel is required, even if it is only a short walk or bicycle ride to a local playground," p. 34);
3. on-site experience and activities (even though this experience is what many seem to think is the total outdoor recreation experience, it "may be less than half of the total," p. 33);
4. travel back, which is unlikely to be a duplicate of the travel to the site ("Even when the route is the same, the recreationists are different. . . . If travel back is from a vacation, memories of the vacation and anticipation of the job are certainly different from the thoughts on the outbound trip," p. 34);
5. recollection and sharing of recollections with friends, relatives, and associates.

Clawson and Knetsch (1966) concluded their five-phase theory of the total recreation experience by recommending that "all in all, each phase of the total experience seems to merit serious, if not equal attention in research, in planning, and in operations" (p. 36). The following theoretical development builds on the contributions of Clawson and Knetsch.

Issues and Propositions in Tourism Consumption Systems

Figure 1 summarizes an example set of specific TCS issues. The following questions represent initial issues posed by a theory of TCS. How is the distance traveled associated with whether or not it is a first visit or how the visitor used the information available? How are each of the above associated with motivations for the travel and behavior in the area? How are the above associated with evaluations and conations of the area?

Figure 1 is not intended to be a complete view of TCS. The figure reflects both direct and indirect relationships supported in travel, tourism, and consumer research literatures (for earlier versions and discussions of similar frameworks, see Clawson and Knetsch 1966; Woodside and MacDonald 1994; Woodside 2000). For simplicity and ease of discussion, Figure 1 is divided into three phases:

- *Phase 1:* prior and during travel relationships affecting traveler behaviors in destination areas
- *Phase 2:* during and post travel relationships
- *Phase 3:* post travel relationships affecting future behaviors

The one-directional arrows in Figure 1 summarize several hypotheses regarding TCSs. To increase clarity by simplifying this introduction to TCSs, we did not include feedback loops in Figure 1. However, several feedback loops are likely to be found in real-life TCSs. For example, the length of stay and accommodations used in the destination areas may be revised based on the visitor's evaluations of specific destination experiences. The prime motive for the trip reported by the traveler may be revised based on the experiences evaluated during the trip. The view reflects the mental model (i.e., set of implicit or explicit assumptions) (see Senge 1990) advocated by Weick (1995): "the creation of meaning is an attentional process, but it is attention to that which has already occurred.... People discover their own intentions" [and frequently revise their beliefs and attitudes based on their observations of outcomes to their own behavior] (pp. 25-37).

> *Proposition 1:* Travel party characteristics influence (a) trip-related use of information, (b) prior visits to the destination area, (c) destination evaluation, (d) prime motives, and (e) behaviors in destination areas.

As shown by the initial five arrows in Figure 1, travel party characteristics are hypothesized to influence most planning and doing variables in TCSs. Several studies confirm the strong influences of travel party characteristics on information search and use strategies implemented by discretionary travelers (e.g., see Fodness and Murray 1998, 1999; Snepenger et al. 1990). In general, the planning and doing behaviors of travelers are heavily influenced by the composition of the traveling party (McIntosh and Goeldner 1990).

> *Proposition 2:* Prior visits to the primary destination area influence (f) search/use of advertising information and (g) the prime motive for a trip to the destination.

"Destination-naive" (Snepenger et al. 1990) travelers search and use information more extensively than repeat visitors to the destination. Extensive use of VIGs is more likely to occur among first-time visitors compared to repeat visitors. "Experiencing a different culture" is more likely to be seen as a primary motivation for the trip to the destination among first-time compared to repeat visitors; the opposite re-

lationship is expected for "visiting friends and family members" as a primary trip motivation. While these propositions appear intuitive, their confirmation and relative strengths need to be examined empirically. Otherwise, valuable information into the nuances of such relationships and downstream impacts on evaluations and conations may go unnoticed.

A strategic outcome from examining the impacts of first-time and repeat destination visits is achieving deep "sensemaking" (Weick 1995) into the multiple modes of planning, behaviors, and evaluations by different visitor segments. Consequently, such deep sensemaking may result in using multiple unique destination marketing strategies for uniquely defined target markets. An example of such a strategy might be marketing Prince Edward Island (a small Canadian Atlantic maritime province) as a future destination by providing free copies to Japanese schoolchildren of *Akage No Anne* (*Red-Haired Anne*, the Japanese translation of *Anne of Green Gables*) and marketing "relaxation and escaping from overwork" to repeat visitors from Canadian origins.

> *Proposition 3:* Use of information influences (h) prime motives for the trip to the destination, (i) visit behaviors in the destination area, and (j) evaluations of destination places and events.

Information use influences previsit expectations of what the traveler might do, as well as not do, in the destination area. For example, VIGs sent by Nevada and Las Vegas versus Prince Edward Island will stress different motivations for visiting and different behaviors available while in the respective destination areas.

Heavy versus light users of destination information (e.g., VIGs) often stay longer, do more activities in the destination area, spend more money, are more satisfied with their visits, have a more positive overall attitude about the destination area, are more willing to visit the destination in the future, and are more willing to recommend a trip to the destination to friends (Woodside, Trappey, and MacDonald 1997). These findings occurred for both first-time and repeat visitors. Tourism strategy implication: getting VIGs into the hands of repeat and first-time visitors may be have high positive impacts for both the visitors and the destination tourism industry.

> *Proposition 4:* Prime motives for the trip to the destination influences travelers' destination behaviors (arrow k in Figure 1).

While a given destination rarely can be all things to all visitors (the mistake of a "We have it all" marketing strategy), visitors often can be segmented meaningfully into a few groups according to their principal reason for selecting the destination. Lengths of stay, expenditure amounts, and accommodations used are likely to vary by visitors segmented according to their primary motive for visiting the destination. For example, visitors attracted to the destination to experience a culture different from their own might be expected to tour local destination areas, stay overnight in bed-and-breakfast accommodations, eat more often at restaurants, and have greater destination-related expenditures compared to visitors motivated primarily to visit friends and relatives. However, stating the seemingly obvious does not inform on the strength of such relationships. Consequently, the several

JOURNAL OF TRAVEL RESEARCH   123

relationships implied by arrow k in Figure 1 need to be examined empirically.

Proposition 5: Visitor behaviors in the destination area influence their evaluations with respect to the destination (l in Figure 1).

Visitors may be segmented according to their destination-area behaviors. Visitors experiencing versus not experiencing certain behaviors are likely to evaluate destination places and events differently. For example, related to visitors experiencing nightclubs during their stays in Charlottetown, Prince Edward Island (PEI), versus visitors experiencing historical sites, the first visitor segment may have lower evaluations overall of Charlottetown versus the second segment. While some overlap of segment membership may occur, membership in the two destination-area behavior segments may be mostly unique.

The issues here focus on the following questions. What do visitors actually do in the destination area, and how do their behaviors influence their evaluations of specific destination places and events, as well as their overall evaluations of the destination? What specific destination behaviors influence positive and negative evaluations about the destination area?

Studies of visitors to four Mediterranean countries (Turkey, Egypt, Greece, and Italy) (Baloglu 2000) support the hypothesis that participating versus not participating in specific destination behaviors influences visitors' evaluations concerning the destinations. Consequently, Baloglu (2000) advocated adopting Woodside's (1982) recommendation to create destination positioning strategies based on visitors' experiences that they subsequently evaluate very positively.

The point is worth noting that three levels of traveler evaluations occur related to a discretionary trip:

- Prior to starting the current trip, some evaluations occur about specific places, attractions, accommodations, local destination area touring, and events in a destination area (micro evaluations), as well as an overall assessment of the destination region (macro evaluation).
- During the trip, both micro and macro evaluations are subject to revisions based on the experiences and benefits realized (Woodside and Jacobs 1985).
- After the trip is completed, both micro and macro evaluations are likely to undergo further revisions based on reflections and discussions about what happened during the trip and the meanings of these happenings (see Arnould and Price 1993).

To reduce complexity and achieve simplicity, Figure 1 emphasizes only the second and third levels of evaluations—micro and macro trip-related evaluations occurring while still in progress, as well as after most of the trip experiences are complete. Also, micro evaluations based on direct experiences have the greatest impact on macro evaluations—such as global attitude toward the destination—and conations (for reviews on this rationale, see Peter and Olson 1999, chap. 6; Fazio and Zanna 1987; Smith and Swinyard 1982).

Proposition 6: Visitor evaluations of their experiences in the destination area influence their overall evalua-

tions with respect to the destination (arrow m in Figure 1), and postexperience evaluations influence conations (arrow n in Figure 1).

While the consumer behavior literature (see Peter and Olson 1999) provides strong rationales for the propositions displayed by evaluation-conation arrows m and n in Figure 1, Weick (1995, pp. 192-93) states the case vividly in a travel context:

> People discover what they think by looking at what they say, how they feel, and where they walk. The talk makes sense of walking, which means those best able to walk the talk are the ones who actually talk the walking they find themselves doing most often, with most intensity, and with most satisfaction. How can I know what I value until I see where I walk? People make sense of their actions, their walking, their talking.

Thus, while potential visitors' evaluations are likely to show expectations on how much visitors will like their experiences in a destination region (e.g., "It should be fun!" and "The region looks beautiful [in the photographs]."), such evaluations are only preliminary. These preliminary evaluations are subject to substantial revisions following actual visits and participation in activities in the destination region. Related to this theoretical view, Howard and Sheth (1969) proposed the use of "attitude" and "attitude'" (attitude prime) to distinguish preexperience brand attitude from postexperience brand attitude'. Also, proposition 6 is grounded in Smith and Swinyard's (1983) hypothesis and empirical results that only after purchasing and using a product or service are anything resembling beliefs and attitudes formed.

Proposition 7: Multiple paths occur in traveler behaviors within destination areas.

An additional proposition not shown in Figure 1 is worth discussing: travelers visiting a destination region may be segmented usefully by their behavior while in the destination region. One sequence of steps, a single behavioral path, is unlikely to dominate most discretionary travelers' behaviors in a destination region. For some segment of visitors, gift buying may dominate destination areas visited (see Kim and Littrell 1999) and vice versa. Traveling local heritage roadways may affect accommodation choices.

What causes some travelers to tour outlying regions within the destination region while others travel only within a very limited geographic area in the destination region? The segmentation issue: what is the personal (demographic-psychographic) and trip-related profile of each visitor segment? Such issues are of theoretical and practical importance. Learning the nuances in triggering behavior paths that include visits to outlying tourism-dependent destination regions may be helpful in planning strategies to influence such behaviors. Many examples exist of outlying tourism-dependent local destination areas that earn only a small fraction of the tourism revenues received by the main regions visited by tourists—for example, the eastern versus the western side of the Big Island of Hawaii and the outer Prince and King Counties versus Queen County in PEI.

METHOD

The Database

A secondary database was used to examine hypotheses related to the arrows in Figure 1. The extensive data file (i.e., face-to-face interviews with 2,239 travel parties) from the 1992 PEI exit survey was used. The "Marketing Agency" (a provincial government-sponsored organization) and Roberta MacDonald, University of Prince Edward Island, provided these data to us. The only use of the data made prior to the study reported here was a government descriptive report profiling visitors' demographics, attitudes, and behaviors (Marketing Agency 1993) and a study on the impact of PEI's 1992 advertising campaign on attitudes, behaviors, and traveler expenditures (see Woodside, Trappey, and MacDonald 1997).

The data were collected using a 12-page questionnaire. The data collected included motives of the current trip to PEI; the number of previous trips and their purposes; the length of time since the last trip to PEI; visitors' perceptions of the PEI visitor information guide and whether or not they received the guide before or after entering PEI; their awareness and extent of use of the VIG; their evaluations of the visual appeal, ease of use, and amount of information in the VIG; and their mode of entry into PEI (e.g., ferry, air, cruise ship—at the time of the study, no "fixed link" [i.e., bridge] had been constructed that attached PEI to the Canadian mainland). Additional data collected included the following topics: type of accommodations used on PEI, evaluations of the accommodations used, participation in each of 15 activities while in PEI and evaluations of activities done, visits to each of 10 attractions in PEI and evaluations of these attractions, the destination areas visited in PEI and overnight stays there, the perceived quality of PEI's road signage, evaluations of PEI on 10 image items, expenditures in Canadian dollars while in PEI (including credit card purchases and spending by children), the proportions of total PEI expenditures by eight categories, the travel party size and description, and demographic information (age, marital status, education, employment outside the home, life cycle stage, annual household income, and origin by province, state, and country). Additional details on the specific questions in the questionnaire are available elsewhere (see Woodside, Trappey, and MacDonald 1997).

Questionnaire administration procedure. The interviews were completed during the tourism seasonal period (May 22 to October 5, 1992) when more than 95% of leisure travelers visit PEI. The questionnaire was administered at all points of exit from PEI (ferries, airports, and cruise ships) in matching proportions to total trip visits for each travel mode.

A quota sampling procedure was used to ensure that the proportions of Canadian, U.S., and European respondents matched the population of visitors from these three origins: 65% of completed interviews were with Canadians, and 31% were respondents from the United States; previous to the study, two-thirds of PEI leisure visitors were estimated to be Canadians, and about 30% were estimated to be Americans.

The only exception to the quota-sampling rule involved Japanese visitors. Because profiles of Japanese visitors were an objective for the study, nearly 1% of the total respondents were Japanese visitors. Japanese visitors are estimated to represent less than 0.2% of total leisure visitors. To ensure a high cooperation rate (88% achieved), native Japanese interviewers conducted interviews with Japanese respondents in Japanese.

Response rate. The overall cooperation/completion interview rate was 94%. Due mainly to some nonresponses to some of the questions, the useable number of responses to test the propositions was close to 88% of the completed interviews.

Assessment of data collection method. The exit-intercept method used for data collection offers several advantages. First, the 94% cooperation and 88% useable response rates are considerably higher than reported in "inquiry conversion" studies (i.e., survey research studies with respondents being contacted by mail or telephone several months after they had requested advertised free information about a destination). Reported response rates in inquiry conversion studies average less than 60% (see Woodside and Dubelaar 1999).

Second, exit-intercept interviews are likely to minimize memory problems in retrieving details of the trip in responding to questions asked in the survey instrument. Also, unlike mail and telephone procedures, all respondents are answering the questions at the same time during their trip; thus, confounding of responses caused by varying lengths of time since the trip and completing the questionnaire is eliminated.

Also, we can be close to certain that the respondents in exit-intercept studies actually visited the destination on their current trip—they are face-to-face with the interviewer. Thus, "telescoping" does not occur. Telescoping by the respondent includes moving events in memory forward in time to report a visit to the destination that is the focus of the study. Telescoping may occur in some instances because the respondent wants to be helpful and enjoys telling about a trip made some years ago to the destination being asked about. The most important advantage of the exit-intercept method may be the ability to compare responses to acquirers of advertising information (e.g., free VIGs) with nonacquirers of such information. Such a comparison is a quasi-experiment design of advertising effectiveness research of tourism marketing programs (e.g., see Woodside, Trappey, and MacDonald 1997).

The disadvantages include the higher research costs compared with mail and telephone interviews and the inability to randomly stop travelers to ask for their participation in the study for destinations that many travelers can enter and exit without stopping. As an island with limited entry-exit access at the time of the study, natural stops and queuing aided the data collection procedure for the PEI study.

Data analysis. Because this study is intended to be exploratory in examining systems of relationships between leisure travel behaviors, "quick clustering" (Kamen 1970) is the main data analysis method used for examining the propositions. Quick clustering includes correlation analysis followed by creating maps showing the highly significant relationships between the variables under examination. For each of the variables examined, ordinal and interval variables were developed to permit the calculation of Pearson product-moment correlations. All the correlations included in the quick clustering maps in the Findings section are significant statistically ($p < .01$). While some of the reported correlations appear small (e.g., $r = .10$, $p < .01$), "tipping point" analysis (not shown in the findings, but see Gladwell 1996; McClelland 1998) indicates that the correlation coefficient understates the significance of the relationship being described between the two variables. The rationale for tipping analysis: behavioral scientists have observed that societal variables make little impact on a dependent variable until they reach a certain critical level (e.g., McClelland 1998; for a related discussion, also see Bass, Tigert, and Lonsdale 1968). Consequently, a linear correlation coefficient underestimates the strength of such relationships. Thus, rather than concluding that a small correlation that is highly significant is indicative of an unimportant relationship, a relevant path relating the two variables should be noted.

Unique Aspects about the Research Setting

The links among travel party characteristics and prime motive for the trip to the destination area and the behaviors in the destination area may be rather distant in time as well as place. For example, the reading by young schoolgirls of the Japanese translation of *Anne of Green Gables* (a novel of an orphaned girl who is adopted by a sister and brother and grows up on Prince Edward Island, Canada, written by Lucy Maude Montgomery and translated by Muraoka 1952) creates a deep-seated attraction to visit PEI. Muraoka's translations of the series of Anne books have been reprinted more than 100 times in Japan (Cole 1993). This subtle link results in more than 1,000 Japanese visitors to PEI annually. These "pilgrimages" (Cole 1993) by young Japanese women and their travel companions occur usually 5 to 10 years after their reading the Anne book series.

The PEI provincial government maintains houses furnished in the time period of the Anne series; guided tours are offered to visitors of the grounds and houses. The Anne musical is the primary performing arts attraction offered each year in Charlottetown. While not all discretionary trips to PEI relate to the Anne book series, many Canadians, Americans, and Europeans are also motivated to visit the province because of their childhood reading of *Anne of Green Gables* (Marketing Agency 1993). Consequently, travel party composition factors often influence behavior: search and use of information, perceptions and evaluations of specific destination places and events, and the overall evaluations of destinations. The destination experiences of walking the paths, touring houses mentioned in the Anne books series, and attending the Charlottetown (capital of PEI) summer festival of the musical *Anne of Green Gables* are the activities completed by Japanese visitors. Their evaluations of their experiences are very positive.

Limitations

The findings below describe empirical associations only. Cause-and-effect relationships are not tested scientifically in the study; formal treatment and test groups and treatments were not included in the design of the study. The study is limited by the use of secondary data that were not collected by the primary researchers with the analysis presented in mind. However, the primary researchers (PEI's Marketing Agency) did plan on collecting detailed data on all aspects of leisure travel behavior involving visiting PEI.

The data collection procedure was retrospective and mostly self-reports. The data were collected at one point toward the end of visitors' stays in PEI. Even though the data are mostly self-reports, we can be certain that the respondents had actually been to PEI during the time frame of the study since the data were collected face-to-face at PEI exit locations. Not all the details presented in Figure 1 are described empirically in this report. For example, local-area travel routes and the use of transportation modes in PEI are not described in this report. Data were not collected on these two variables in the primary study. The reported empirical study is intended to explore associations, not to test causal paths. Tests of alternative models that explain dependent relationships are possible using partial correlations and path analysis (see Pedhazur 1982). The results of the quick clustering method employed in this report suggest the value in examining the relative impacts of direct and indirect paths of influence on identifiable dependent variables.

FINDINGS

Phase 1 Findings

Figure 2 shows findings relevant for variables in the first four boxes in the left-hand side of Figure 1. To increase clarity and partially to reduce complexity, we show only distance as a chronic traveler characteristic in Figure 2. Because the PEI visitor information guide is not published in Japanese and its availability was not advertised in Japan in 1991-1992, the responses by Japanese visitors are excluded from the analysis resulting in Figure 2.

Several different ordinal scales indicating physical distance from PEI were used for computing an index of distance. We used kilometers from the center of each origin to the center of PEI and employed five distance zones:

1 = Canadian Atlantic maritime provinces
2 = Quebec and Ontario provinces and U.S. New England states
3 = U.S. Mid-Atlantic states
4 = Other U.S. states (mostly Midwest states)
5 = European countries

For purposes of data analysis, binary coding was used for first visit (FV = 1) versus prior visits (PV = 0) and for each prime motive for the trip that included visiting PEI (e.g., family visit = 1 if prime visit; 0 for family visit if other prime motive ticked). For use of the VIG, two variables were estimated: reporting receiving the VIG before the trip (coded 1 if yes, 0 if no) and level of use of the VIG ($0 = none$, $1 = light$, $2 = heavy$).

Note in Figure 2 that as predicted in the first set of propositions (proposition 1), the travel party characteristic (i.e., distance) strongly relates to first versus prior visits ($r = .58$, $p < .001$). This finding reflects the useful conclusion for tourism marketing strategy that two distinct visitor segments occur for PEI—the first-time distant traveler and the local repeat-visit traveler. Distance and receiving the VIG are related positively ($r = .11$, $p < .01$); distant travelers tend to do their homework more so than nearby travelers.

Figure 2 shows very strong relationships of distance with prime motives for visiting PEI. The distant travelers come to

FIGURE 2
DISTANCE, PRIOR VISITS, AND EVALUATION

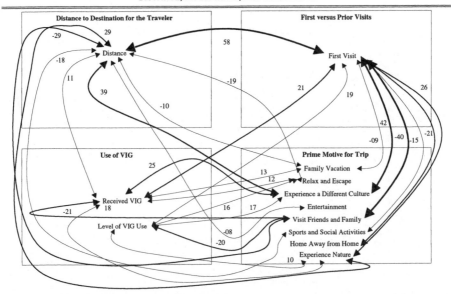

Note: Pearson product-moment correlations shown with decimal point omitted; for all *rs*, *p* < .001. Thick lines are used to emphasize several strong associations. VIG = visitor information guides.

PEI for two prime motives: experience a different culture and experience nature. Nearby originating travelers come to PEI for two different prime motives: visit friends and family and for sports and social activities. Such findings indicate the value of using two distinct strategies to position the destination in the minds of prospective visitors—depending on their geographic distance. By analogy, "You have a friend in Pennsylvania" may be a useful positioning message for only one segment of the nearby visitors to this state; such a message is likely to be less effective for most visitors from distant origins.

Figure 2 includes a significant negative relationship between use of the VIG and visiting friends and relatives (*r* = –.20, *p* < .001). Given the substantial positive impacts of using versus not using the VIG on increasing expenditures, the image of PEI, and satisfaction with the visit *even among nearby visitors*, some marketing effort may be worthwhile in attempting to eliminate this negative relationship. "Visit PEI again for the very first time—New Experiences Guaranteed by Reading This Guide" may aid in increasing VIG readership among nearby Atlantic maritime province visitors.

Proposition 3 receives strong support: use of VIG information is associated with (h) prime motives for the trip to the destination, (i) visit behaviors in the destination area, and (j) evaluations of destination places and events.

Additional findings are worth noting in Figure 2. As prime motives, "family vacation" and "relax and escape" connect substantially less with key travel variables compared

to the other motives in Figure 2. Thus, tourism consumption systems analysis provides valuable insights into how motives connect visitors segmented by distance with destination behaviors (e.g., see Figure 3). Proposition 4 is supported: prime motives for the trip to the destination influence travelers' destination behaviors.

To increase clarity, Figure 3 includes only two of the possible eight prime motives (see Figure 1 for the eight prime motives). Figure 3 shows how these two prime motives are linked with travel behaviors in the destination region as well as the number of previous visits and other phase 1 variables.

Several findings in Figure 3 warrant discussion. First, consider the negative relationship between number of previous visits and use of advertising information (*r* = –.37, *p* < .001). Conclusion: more frequent visitors tend to use advertising information infrequently compared to first-time and less frequent visitors. While frequency of visits is not associated with destination expenditures, use of advertising information is strongly associated with destination expenditures (*r* = .23, *p* < .001).

For destinations having two primary markets by frequency of visits (i.e., first-time visitors represent 57% and repeat visitors 43% of PEI visitors), increasing the perceived usefulness of information such as VIGs to repeat visitors is likely to increase the total expenditures in the destination region. One exception to this proposition is gift-buying behavior. Use of advertising information is associated negatively with gift-buying behavior (*r* = –.13).

JOURNAL OF TRAVEL RESEARCH 127

FIGURE 3
EMPIRICAL RESULTS FOR PHASE 1

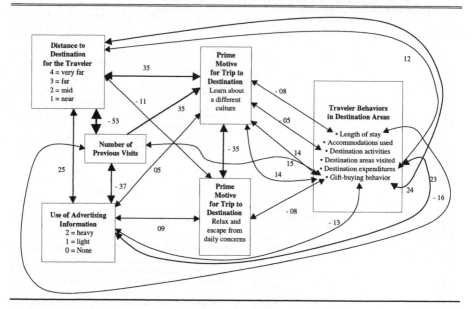

The dominant relationship concerning gift-buying behavior shown in Figure 3 is the positive connection with distance to the destination ($r = .24$, $p < .001$). Similarly, a positive link occurs between gift buying and learning about a different culture as the prime motive for visiting PEI.

Phase 2 Findings

Two issues of particular interest are related to distant and mainly first-time visitors versus nearby and mainly repeat visitors to PEI:

- Do these two market segments engage in different behaviors during their visits?
- Do these two market segments evaluate their experiences differently?

The answers from the data analysis present surprising findings. The two customer segments do often participate in different activities. The more distant and mostly first-visit customers consistently evaluate the activities less positively compared to nearby customers. The lower evaluations of specific activities done in PEI imply negative distance and conative (e.g., willingness to recommend and definitely visit again) linkages. Consequently, the findings provide strong support for proposition 2.

Table 1 includes the correlation of participating in each activity with a distance index. The revised distance index includes Japanese respondents to compare these visitors by activities and postexperience evaluations with those of nearby and middle distance visitors. The i distance index includes the following ordinal assignments:

1 = respondents living in the Canadian maritime provinces ($n = 595$)
2 = other Canadian respondents and Americans living in the New England states ($n = 906$)
3 = Americans living beyond the New England states and Europeans ($n = 544$)
4 = Japanese ($n = 150$)

Nearly all correlations are significant statistically. The activities that visitors from distant homes are most prone to do include the following:

- Visit museums and historical or cultural sites
- Attend lobster suppers
- Sightseeing

The activities that visitors from nearby origins are most prone to do include the following:

- Golfing
- Enjoying nightlife
- Water sports

Note in Table 2 the substantial drops in being "very pleased" with the activity engaged in for visitors from nearby versus more distant origins. The majority of participants in most activities were very pleased only for the nearby customer segment. Possibly, visitors from more distant origins

TABLE 1

CORRELATIONS OF VISITORS' DISTANCE INDEX AND ACTIVITIES DURING VISIT IN PRINCE EDWARD ISLAND

Activity	Correlation	$p <$
Going to the beach	.08	.000
Water sports (swimming, windsurfing, boating)	−.14	.000
Golfing	−.16	.000
Other active sports	−.09	.000
Spectator sports	−.11	.000
Harbor cruise or land tour	.11	.000
Sightseeing within cities/towns (on your own)	.22	.000
Sightseeing outside cities or towns (on your own)	.18	.000
Antique/handcraft shopping	.05	.011
Shopping in general	−.01	.541
Visiting museums and historical or cultural sites	.31	.000
Attending live theater	.22	.000
Attending lobster suppers	.26	.000
Eating local cuisine	−.03	−.120
Enjoying nightlife	−.16	.000

Note: The distance index includes 1 = respondents living in the Canadian maritime provinces; 2 = other Canadians and U.S. New England states respondents; 3 = other U.S. residents and Europeans; 4 = Japanese.

TABLE 2

SHARE OF RESPONDENTS "VERY PLEASED" WITH THE ACTIVITY FOR EACH OF THE VISITOR DISTANCE SEGMENTS (IN PERCENTAGES)

Activity	Each Distance Segment			
	1	2	3	4
Going to the beach	54	47	42	4
Water sports (swimming, windsurfing, boating)	55	45	14	0
Golfing	60	47	35	1
Other active sports	54	35	28	0
Spectator sports	74	31	29	0
Harbor cruise or land tour	45	40	48	0
Sightseeing within cities/towns (on your own)	53	43	54	3
Sightseeing outside cities or towns (on your own)	56	50	61	45
Antique/handcraft shopping	45	34	34	3
Shopping in general	31	24	25	0
Visiting museums and historical or cultural sites	52	47	49	3
Attending live theater	85	62	66	54
Attending lobster suppers	70	56	61	9
Eating local cuisine	49	36	38	0
Enjoying nightlife	49	41	46	0

Note: Sample sizes vary substantially by activities. For example, total responses evaluating the beaches were 1,322, but only 131 watched spectator sports. Respondents are included only if they participated in the activity and evaluated the activity. See Tables 3 and 4 for an example.

have more experiences in these activities at a greater number of alternative destinations versus PEI, and comparisons to such alternatives result in PEI ratings below being very pleased.

Tables 3 and 4 show examples of more detailed information than is summarized in Table 2. A striking finding in Table 4 is that while 85% of the Japanese visitors reported attending PEI lobster suppers, only 9% were "very pleased."

Given that the overall majority of visitors do not report being very pleased with the PEI beaches, going to PEI beaches is less of a key driver than other PEI activities (see Table 3). However, those visitors who strongly agree that "PEI's beaches are superior" are significantly more likely to "definitely visit PEI again" (see additional findings below). Thus, making sweeping conclusions regarding visitors' evaluations of their destination activities may be misleading; for example, visitor experiences on PEI beaches are a positive driver for nearby customers but not a key driver for visitors from more distant origins.

Through the 1990s, PEI's general marketing strategy included the message, "Warmest beaches north of the Carolinas." However, based on the findings in Tables 1 and 2, emphasizing beach activities to visitors from distant origins may be counterproductive.

Figure 4 reflects the negative relationships between distance to origins and visitors' evaluations of PEI activities, as well as the positive relationships with doing specific activities on PEI with overall evaluations with respect to PEI.

Note in Figure 4 that none of the variables shown was found to be associated with perceiving PEI as an expensive destination. Visits to PEI museums were related negatively to evaluating PEI as having no nightlife and being boring and old-fashioned.

Figure 5 summarizes key linkages among activities done by visitors in PEI. For example, length of stay (i.e., number of nights in PEI) is associated positively with staying in bed and breakfast accommodations but is unrelated to staying in hotels. Visiting Charlottetown is not included in Figure 5 because nearly all travelers visit this city (the capital of the PEI) during their visit. Thus, visits to Charlottetown are not influenced and do not influence doing the activities included in Figure 5.

As shown in Figure 5, New London and Kensington are found to be activity hub cities. Note that this observation applies in particular to New London.

Phase 3 Findings

What evaluations by visitors are the positive and negative principal drivers to visiting PEI and being willing to recommend PEI to friends? Figure 6 summarizes the findings that help answer this question.

Sightseeing in the cities and visiting PEI museums are associated strongly with both conations in Figure 6. Antique and craft shopping and the local PEI cuisine are the secondary positive drivers linked to the two primary activity drivers as well as directly with visiting PEI again. Evaluating the beaches is not associated directly with the two conations (see Figure 6 for additional details).

Note that as might be expected, global PEI evaluations regarding PEI are associated most strongly with visiting PEI again and with willingness to recommend PEI to friends. The combined factor that includes having no nightlife and being boring and old-fashioned is the largest negative driver toward recommending PEI to friends ($r = −.42, p < .001$). The

JOURNAL OF TRAVEL RESEARCH   129

TABLE 3
DETAILED EXAMPLE OF EVALUATIONS BY SEGMENTS: GOING TO THE BEACH

Distance Segment	Postexperience Evaluation (%)				
	Very Disappointed	Disappointed	Pleased	Very Pleased	Number
1 = Canadian maritime	0	2	44	54	283
2 = Other Canada and U.S. New England	0	1	52	47	627
3 = Other U.S. states and Europe	0	3	55	42	314
4 = Japan	1	9	86	4	98
Total	0	2	53	44	1,322

Note: Chi-square = 94.75, *df* = 9, *p* < .000; shares of each distance segment reporting going to the beach: segment 1 = 48% (i.e., 283 of 595), segment 2 = 69%, segment 3 = 58%, and segment 4 = 65%.

TABLE 4
DETAILED EXAMPLE OF EVALUATIONS BY SEGMENTS: LOBSTER SUPPERS

Distance Segment	Postexperience Evaluation (%)				
	Very Disappointed	Disappointed	Pleased	Very Pleased	Number
1 = Canadian maritime	1	1	28	70	140
2 = Other Canada and U.S. New England	1	1	42	56	432
3 = Other U.S. states and Europe	1	2	37	61	243
4 = Japan	0	5	87	9	127

Note: Chi-square = 134.15, *df* = 9, *p* < .0000. Participation in lobster suppers: segment 1 = 23%, segment 2 = 48%, segment 3 = 45%, and segment 4 = 85%.

FIGURE 4
DISTANCE, PRIOR VISITS, AND EVALUATIONS

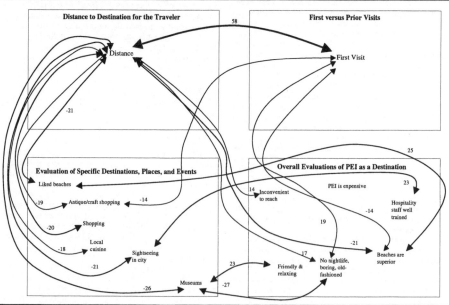

Note: PEI = Prince Edward Island.

130   NOVEMBER 2002

FIGURE 5
KEY RELATIONSHIPS BETWEEN ACTIVITIES

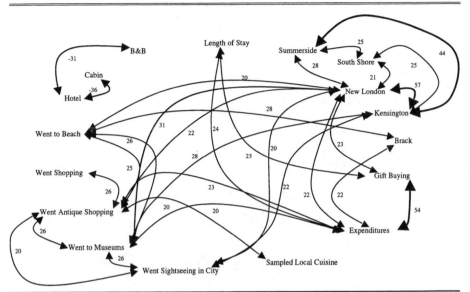

Note: Pearson product-moment correlations shown with decimal point omitted; for all *rs*, *p* < .001. Thick lines used to emphasize several strong associations.

overall image that PEI is friendly and relaxing is the largest positive image driver for recommending PEI to friends (*r* = .45, *p* < .001). The findings support proposition 5: visitor behaviors in the destination areas influence their evaluations with respect to the destination. Proposition 6 is supported: visitor evaluations of their experiences in the destination area influence their overall evaluations with respect to the destination, and postexperience evaluations influence conations. Figure 6 shows detailed results supporting proposition 6.

Notice the strong secondary influence shown in Figure 6 of PEI's hospitality staff being perceived as well trained. Visitor evaluations of destination hospitality quality are found to have strong direct influences on both conative factors in Figure 6.

Proposition 7 is supported: multiple paths do occur in traveler behaviors within PEI. Multiple ways occur for increasing and decreasing conations. The complexity in the quick clustering maps (shown in Figures 2-6) threatens to overwhelm the viewer with equivocality rather than uncertainty. Some paths, starting with distance and ending with the two conations in Figure 6, show net gains (computed by multiplying the directionality of arrows for a given path), and some paths show a net loss, that is, reductions in conations.

Thus, the following question has multiple, rather than one, useful answers: does distance from origin increase or decrease visitors' intentions to return and favorable word-of-mouth communications? The most accurate answer is that the impact of distance to the destination on visitor conations depends on the activities and evaluations that occur along the

way. Doing or not doing certain activities affects how the distance of visitors' origins relates to their conations concerning the destination (cf. Etzel and Woodside 1982).

CONCLUSIONS AND RECOMMENDATIONS FOR TOURISM STRATEGIES

Viewing leisure travel behavior as a consumption system may help deepen understanding of the streams of thoughts and actions by travelers prior to, during, and after travel. For specific destinations and industries (e.g., hospitality, car rental, and retail stores), learning the details that culminate in, as well as block, visits and purchases with respect to their services may be useful.

Viewing tourism behavior as consumption systems enables us to focus on understanding multiple decisions and actions rather than only the destination choice decision (cf. Moutinho 1987; Woodside and Lysonski 1989). Such a systems perspective shows the complexities that unfold within leisure travel. While not all visitors to a destination from a given origin are the same, most likely a dominant customer behavior segment needs to be identified for planning marketing strategies to attract visitors from each major origin. Analysis of visitors by their tourism consumption systems provides the marketing strategist with deep profiles of different customer segments demographics, trip planning activities, trip behaviors, evaluations of trip services experienced,

JOURNAL OF TRAVEL RESEARCH 131

FIGURE 6
RELATIONSHIP BETWEEN EVALUATION OF SPECIFIC DESTINATIONS, PLACES, AND EVENTS
WITH OVERALL DESTINATION EVALUATIONS AND CONATIONS

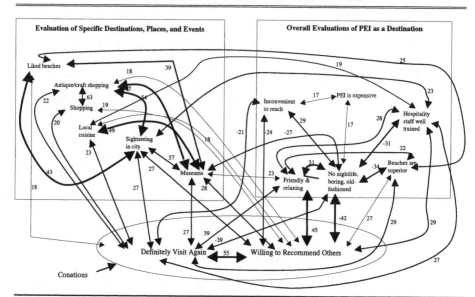

Note: Pearson product-moment correlations shown with decimal point omitted; for all *rs*, *p* < .001. Thick lines used to emphasize several strong associations. PEI = Price Edward Island.

global evaluations of services and destinations, and conations—and how these variables are linked together.

Consequently, the product and communication strategies for destination marketers and marketers of tourism services can focus on (1) the trip activities actually done by each segment and (2) the experiences they evaluate very positively. For example, many PEI visitors from the Canadian maritime provinces actually participate in water sports and evaluate these experiences very positively. While communicating the activities and benefits of water sports to these PEI visitors is likely to be an effective strategy, PEI attractions and activities other than water sports are more appealing to PEI's other customer segments. Promoting PEI water sports to Americans from the midwestern and southern states may actually hurt rather than help build a favorable image toward the destination.

A regional destination, such as PEI, cannot afford to have one positioning strategy for all relevant market segments. However, promoting a regional destination as "having it all" needs to be avoided—this shopworn message does not match the benefits sought or experienced by visitors (see Woodside and Jacobs 1985).

Creating a limited number of product-market strategies is recommended. Designing unique tourism products and experiences that can be delivered for each of three to six market segments builds well onto what is known about alternative

tourism consumption systems. Interestingly enough, if we identify the tourism segment as the unit of analysis we wish to study in order to select the appropriate strategies implied above, Finn and Kayande (1997) suggested that we can substantially reduce the costs of data collection by being more efficient in how we design our studies. This implies that we need not survey 2,000 respondents face-to-face to collect the data we need; instead, we can survey fewer people with a more focused instrument and achieve the same degree of accuracy.

REFERENCES

Arnould, E. J., and L. L. Price (1993). " 'River Magic': Hedonic Consumption and the Extended Service Encounter." *Journal of Consumer Research*, 20: 24-35.
Baloglu, Seyhmus (2000). "A Path-Analytical Model of Visitation Intention Involving Information Sources, Socio-Psychological Motivations and Destination Images." In *Consumer Psychology of Tourism, Hospitality and Leisure*, edited by A. G. Woodside, G. I. Crouch, J. A. Mazanec, M. Oppermann, and M. Y. Sakai. Cambridge, UK: CABI Publishing.
Bass, Frank M., Douglas J. Tigert, and Robert T. Lonsdale (1968). "Market Segmentation: Group versus Individual Behavior." *Journal of Marketing Research*, 5 (August): 268-72.
Bello, Dan, and Michael Etzel (1985). "The Role of Novelty in the Pleasure Travel Experience." *Journal of Travel Research*, 24 (1): 20-26.
Clawson, Marion, and Jack L. Knetsch (1966). *Economics of Outdoor Recreation*. Washington, DC: Resources for the Future Series, Johns Hopkins University Press.
Cole, Sally (1993). "Japanese Make Pilgrimage to PEI to Celebrate the Amazing 'Anne' Link." *The Guardian*, July 31: 2.

132   NOVEMBER 2002

Etzel, Michael J., and Arch G. Woodside (1982). "Segmenting Vacation Markets: The Case of the Distant and Near-Home Travelers." *Journal of Travel Research*, 20 (Spring): 10-14.

Fazio, Russell H., and Mark P. Zanna (1987). "Attitudinal Qualities Relating to the Strength of the Attitude-Behavior Relationship." *Journal of Experimental Social Psychology*, 14: 398-408.

Finn, Adam, and Ujwal Kayande (1997). "Reliability Assessment and Optimization of Marketing Measurement." *Journal of Marketing Research*, 34 (2): 262-75.

Fodness, Dale, and Brian Murray (1998). "A Typology of Tourist Information Search Strategies." *Journal of Travel Research*, 37 (November): 108-19.

——— (1999). "A Model of Tourist Information Search Behavior." *Journal of Travel Research*, 37 (February): 220-30.

Gladwell, M. (1996). "The Tipping Point." *The New Yorker*, 72: 32-39.

Howard, John A., and Jagdish N. Sheth (1969). *The Theory of Buyer Behavior*. New York: John Wiley.

Kamen, Joseph (1970). "Quick Clustering." *Journal of Marketing Research*, 7 (2): 199-204.

Kim, Soyoung, and Mary A. Littrell (1999). "Predicting Souvenir Purchase Intentions." *Journal of Travel Research*, 38 (4): 153-62.

Marketing Agency (1993). *Summary Profile of PEI Visitors*. Charlottetown, Prince Edward Island: Marketing Agency.

McClelland, David C. (1998). "Identifying Competencies with Behavioral-Event Interviews." *Psychological Science*, 9 (5): 331-39.

McIntosh, R. W., and Charles R. Goeldner (1990). *Tourism: Principles, Practices, Philosophies*. New York: John Wiley.

Moutinho, Luiz (1987). "Consumer Behavior in Tourism." *European Journal of Marketing*, 21 (10): 2-44.

Muraoka, Hanako (1952). *Akage No Anne* [Red-haired Anne]. Tokyo: Mikasa-Shobou.

Pedhazur, E. J. (1982). *Multiple Regression in Behavioral Research*. New York: Holt, Rinehart & Winston.

Peter, J. Paul, and Jerry C. Olson (1999). *Consumer Behavior*. New York: McGraw-Hill.

Senge, Peter (1990). *The Fifth Discipline*. New York: Doubleday.

Smith, Robert E., and William R. Swinyard (1982). "Information Response Models: An Integrated Approach." *Journal of Marketing*, 46: 81-93.

——— (1983). "Attitude-Behavior Consistency: The Impact of Product Trial versus Advertising." *Journal of Marketing Research*, 20: 257-67.

Snepenger, D. K., K. Meged, M. Snelling, and K. Worrall (1990). "Information Search Strategies by Destination-Naïve Tourists." *Journal of Travel Research*, 29 (Summer): 13-16.

Solomon, Michael R. (1988). "Mapping Product Constellations: A Social Categorization Approach to Symbolic Consumption." *Psychology & Marketing*, 5 (3): 233-58.

——— (1999). *Consumer Behavior*. 4th ed. Upper Saddle, NJ: Prentice Hall.

Weick, Karl E. (1995). *Sensemaking in Organizations*. Thousand Oaks, CA: Sage.

Woodside, Arch G. (1982). "Positioning a Province Using Travel Research." *Journal of Travel Research*, 20: 2-6.

——— (2000). "Introduction: Theory and Research on the Consumer Psychology of Tourism, Hospitality and Leisure." In *Consumer Psychology of Tourism, Hospitality and Leisure*, edited by A. G. Woodside, G. I. Crouch, J. A. Mazanec, M. Oppermann, and M. Y. Sakai. Wallingford, UK: CABI Publishing, pp. 1-17.

Woodside, Arch G., and Chris Dubelaar (1999). "Meta-Analysis of Advertising Conversion Research Findings: Testing the Self-Generated Validity Hypothesis Regarding Sponsor Identity." In *Marketing in the Third Millennium: Proceedings—ANZMAC99* [CD]. Sydney: School of Marketing, University of New South Wales.

Woodside, Arch G., and Laurence W. Jacobs (1985). "Step Two in Benefit Segmentation: Learning the Benefits Realized by Major Travel Markets." *Journal of Travel Research*, 23 (Fall): 14-24.

Woodside, Arch G., and Steven Lysonski (1989). "A General Model of Traveler Destination Choice." *Journal of Travel Research*, 27 (4): 8-14.

Woodside, Arch G., and Roberta MacDonald (1994). "A General Systems Framework of Customer Choice Processes of Tourism Services." In *Spoilt for Choice*, edited by R. Gasser and K. Weiermair. Vienna: Kultur Verlag, pp. 30-59.

Woodside, Arch G., Randolph J. Trappey III, and Roberta MacDonald (1997). "Measuring Linkage-Advertising Effects on Customer Behaviour and Net Revenue: Using Quasi-Experiments of Advertising Treatments with Novice and Experienced Product-Service Users." *Canadian Journal of Administrative Sciences*, 14 (2): 214-28.

Part III
The Internet and IT

[18]

Available online at www.sciencedirect.com

SCIENCE @ DIRECT°

International Journal of
Hospitality
Management

ELSEVIER   Hospitality Management 24 (2005) 281–294

www.elsevier.com/locate/ijhosman

Effect of information technology on performance in upscale hotels

Sunny Ham[a,*], Woo Gon Kim[b], Seungwhan Jeong[c]

[a]*Hospitality and Tourism Management, University of Kentucky, 121 Erikson Hall, Lexington, KY 40506, USA*
[b]*School of Hotel and Restaurant Administration, Oklahoma State University, USA*
[c]*Department of Tourism Information Science, Ansan College of Technology, Korea*

Abstract

Improving productivity is the primary role of information technology (IT) in the lodging industry, while information resources have long played a crucial role in conducting successful lodging operations. A number of studies devoted much effort to investigate the relationships between IT investment and business productivity and performance, but the outcomes were not consistent. This study examines the effect of IT applications on their performance in lodging operations. The survey was conducted in upscale hotels to identify the relationship between IT usage and the performance of lodging operations. Front-office applications, restaurant and banquet management systems, and guest-related interface applications significantly and positively affected performance of lodging operations; however, guest-related interface applications were not significant. The findings of this study will benefit the lodging industry by providing critical information to management to assist in deciding whether a lodging operation should strategically invest in IT or not and in determining specific areas of focus for IT investment.
© 2004 Elsevier Ltd. All rights reserved.

Keywords: Information technology; Performance; Lodging operations; Upscale hotels

*Corresponding author. Tel.: +1-859-257-4332; fax: +1-859-257-1275.
E-mail addresses: sham2@uky.edu (S. Ham), kwoo@okstate.edu (W. Gon Kim), jsh1767@ansantc.ac.kr (S. Jeong).

0278-4319/$ - see front matter © 2004 Elsevier Ltd. All rights reserved.
doi:10.1016/j.ijhm.2004.06.010

282 *S. Ham et al. / Hospitality Management 24 (2005) 281–294*

1. Introduction

Information, coupled with technological developments, has been a critical ingredient for the hospitality business, while serving as a key success factor for effective lodging industry operations in the 21st century (Winston, 1997). Hospitality industries have identified effective implementation of information technology (IT) as a vital component of the effort to promote and achieve their goals for successful description, promotion, distribution, amalgamation, organization, and delivery of hospitality products and services and have demonstrated a positive and significant relationship between the use of IT and the development of a competitive advantage (Cho and Olson, 1998; Clemons, 1986; McFarlan, 1984; Porter, 1985).

The impact and importance of IT in the infrastructure of the hospitality industry have had solid strategic implications for industry leaders. Increasing reliance on IT systems is the wave of the future and is expected to continue to alter operations significantly (Hospitality Technology, 2003). Both academic researchers and industry personnel have paid attention to the already substantial impacts IT has had and to the potential for even more dominant contributions to the hospitality and tourism industry. Implementation of IT systems has resulted in decreased costs, greater productivity and increased revenues in the lodging industry (Siguaw et al., 2000; Huo, 1998), improving customer service and business operations (Sweat and Hibbard, 1999; Barcheldor, 1999; Van Hoof et al., 1996).

Over the last decade, hospitality researchers dedicated their efforts to determining the effects of using IT on performance or productivity. A number of studies investigated the effect of using IT on productivity using numeric scale measurements and found a positive relationship between IT investment and company productivity and performance (Alpar and Kim, 1990; Mahmood and Mann, 1993; Rai et al., 1997); other researchers reject this conclusion (Barua et al., 1995; Weil, 1992). Researchers realized that the relationship between IT investment and corporate performance is complex and multifaceted. A key element in any analysis of IT applications is the actual user of the IT tools implemented to support service delivery. Hotel employees are uniquely positioned to assess increases or decreases in hotel performance due to their involvement with the implementation of IT applications to achieve their goals. This study examines employee perceptions of the effect of IT applications on their performance in lodging operations. Since the roles and types of IT applications differ from division to division, there is a need for management to determine how well specific IT applications contribute to the performance in these diverse components of the industry. Therefore, this study addresses the need to differentiate the impacts of IT implementation by service division of hotel operations as well as evaluating the overall performance. Specifically, the study examines the effect of IT on the performance of lodging operations in two ways: (1) this study utilizes a measurement scale in evaluating performance change presumably caused by the use of IT and (2) this study evaluates the effect of four categories of IT systems separately on the performance of lodging operations. The four categories of IT systems include front-office applications, back-office applications, restaurant and banquet management systems, and guest-related interface applications.

The results of this analysis will benefit the lodging industry by providing industry personnel definitive information to assist in deciding whether a lodging operation should strategically invest in IT or not and in determining specific areas of IT application that positively affect industry performance. Further, research in this area provides a basis for comparison with other means of analyzing performance, such as financial report analyses and customer satisfaction and loyalty.

2. Literature review

2.1. IT in the lodging industry

Technology is gradually becoming a critical source of sustainable competitive advantage in the hospitality industry, particularly in the areas of description, promotion, distribution, amalgamation, organization, and delivery of hospitality products. Use of IT, more than ever before, is a major prerequisite in forming strategic alliances, developing innovative distribution methods, and communicating with consumers and partners while satisfying consumer demand (Chaffney, 2000). Customers and partners alike tend to place greater importance on organizations which utilize IT to a greater extent than their competitors (Hewson, 1996). Much more attention should be paid to IT subjects because of constantly changing condition, especially in the current situation hotels are forced to confront and deal more effectively with the speed and competition, and increasing customer expectations (Aksu and Tarcan, 2002).

Hospitality literature supports the essential role of IT in refining customer service (Sweat and Hibbard, 1999), improving operations (Barcheldor, 1999), increasing revenues, and minimizing costs (Huo, 1998). A number of researchers have identified a positive and significant relationship between the use of IT and the development of a competitive advantage (Cho and Olson, 1998; Clemons, 1986; McFarlan, 1984; Porter, 1985). Cho and Olson (1998) recommended that IT be extensively adopted within the lodging industry and noted the visible evidence of the acceptability and widespread use of IT in many aspects of the service industry in general and in the lodging industry in particular. Given the benefits that IT provides to the lodging industry, the extensive use of technology would appear to be an inevitable conclusion (Siguaw et al., 2000).

As noted above, using information technologies resulted in notable advantages in competition, cost reduction, efficiency, and information-sharing. The types of information technologies used within lodging segments vary significantly. Internet, intranet, e-mail connections, electronic trade, central reservation systems, and Web applications are some examples of IT applications that have been broadly implemented throughout the industry. In a rapidly growing trend, lodging establishments are benefiting significantly from the newer IT applications. For example, hotels are using IT to market their goods and services, to receive

284
S. Ham et al. / Hospitality Management 24 (2005) 281–294

reservations, and to evaluate customer complaints/suggestions (Aksu and Tarcan, 2002).

Armijos et al. (2002) studied technology investment in the lodging operations and provided valuable data on the use of IT in these endeavors. Average capital expenditures for technology as a percentage of total revenues increased from 4.26% in 2000 to 4.98% in 2001, while technology operating expenditures as a percentage of total revenues increased from 5.59 to 6.26% in the same period. While these increases are minimal, they reflect an increase in the perceived value of technology implementation as well as sustained increases in expenditures related to technology, which have been spurred by new technological developments.

2.2. Linkage between IT investment and hotel productivity and performance

IT investment has been found to contribute to increased company productivity and performance (Alpar and Kim, 1990; Mahmood and Mann, 1993; Rai et al., 1997). Banker et al. (1990) studied the use of point-of-sale and order-management IT in Hardee's fast food stores. In the 89 stores studied, approximately half had introduced the new technology. Those stores adopting the IT performed significantly better than other outlets in terms of cost control and profitability. However, the conclusions of studies that found positive relationships between IT investment and company productivity and performance have not been uniformly accepted by researchers in the field (Barua et al., 1995; Weil, 1992).

Roach (1991) identified the contradictory findings noted above as a so-called "productivity paradox." The paradox outlined by Roach is that service industries were spending more on IT but productivity levels tended to be worse than those in other industries. In a later study, David et al. (1996) tested the validity of the productivity paradox of hotel-industry technology by sending questionnaires to chief financial officers of the large hotel companies. While all respondents believed that installing computer application in the front office would improve productivity in that area of operations, the respondents, in most cases, expected little productivity enhancement from back-office systems. In the estimation of most respondents, guest-operated technology did not improve productivity, and some respondents reported guest-operated systems such as in-room information, vending, and entertainment, as well as automated check-in and check-out devices, seemed actually to decrease productivity. The resultant findings indicated that technology expenditures do not always provide direct or measurable economic benefit to the hotel companies. The finding did not show a clear relationship between the use of IT and productivity of the lodging operations.

This study intends to clarify the effect of IT usage on performance in the lodging industry. Hotel employees were asked to evaluate the impact of IT use on performance in distinct and diverse service areas which have implemented IT tools to achieve their goals. The IT applications of the lodging operations are divided into four categories: front-office applications, back-office applications, restaurant and banquet management systems, and guest-related interface applications.

The following hypotheses were developed and subsequently tested.

H1: The usage level of front-office IT applications correlates positively with performance of lodging operations.

H2: The usage level of back-office IT applications correlates positively with performance of lodging operations.

H3: The usage level of restaurant and banquet management systems IT applications correlates positively with performance of lodging operations.

H4: The usage level of guest-related IT applications correlates positively with performance of lodging operations.

The next section of this paper describes the methodology for examining the effect of the use of these four categories of IT applications in lodging operations. Finally, this paper concludes with a discussion of the findings and recommendations for the lodging industry to utilize the results of the study to fulfill its strategic objectives. Future research would be suggested.

3. Methodology

3.1. Sample and data collection

The research sample consisted of employees of 13 five-star hotels and eight four-star hotels in Seoul, Korea. The subjects of this study were hotel employees with defined levels of experience in the current work environment. Previous studies focused on hotel guest perceptions as the basis for the study. However, due to hotel employee's extensive involvement in implementing IT applications to improve the performance of the hospitality organization, hotel staff rather than hotel guests are considered to be in a better position to assess increases or decreases in productivity of employees or hotel's overall performance. The hotels were upscale, full-service commercial hotels located in the city of Seoul. In terms of types of hotels, most were international chain hotels while a few were domestic hotels. The list of 13 international hotel chains selected includes: Sheraton Walker-Hill, Ritz-Carlton, Inter-Continental, Westin Chosun, Marriott, Hyatt, Hilton, Radisson Plaza, Ramada Renaissance, Sofitel, Novotel, Swiss Grand, and Holiday Inn Crown Plaza, while the remaining eight domestic hotels include Lotte, Amiga, Shilla, Koreana, Rivera, Royal, New World, and Olympia. Out of these eight, three hotels are five-star hotels, and the remaining five are four-star hotels. Thirty questionnaires were distributed for the purpose of pilot testing the questionnaire in May 2002. A letter from the Korean Hotel Association assisted in gaining the participation of all 21 hotels in the study. Questionnaires were sent to the human resource director in each hotel along with an instruction sheet. Employees were asked to complete the survey during their breaks or before/after their shifts. The instrument was administered to a cross section of employees including the front-desk, reservation, restaurants and cocktail lounges, and back-office. These employees were selected for

286   *S. Ham et al. / Hospitality Management 24 (2005) 281–294*

inclusion in the survey due to their relatively high usage of IT. In order to select employees knowledgeable about IT applications and hotel performance in each hotel and to capitalize on employment experience, only hotel employees who had worked more than 3 years in each hotel property were included in the survey. Human resource directors in each hotel returned the completed surveys to the researchers. The survey was conducted from August 10 through August 31, 2002. Out of 1000 questionnaires administered, 710 surveys were returned with a response rate of 71%. Among the returns, 648 questionnaires were usable, representing an effective response rate of 64.8%.

3.2. Survey instrument

After an extensive literature review and a series of in-depth interviews with expert panels, the questionnaire was developed by the researchers. Expert panels included information systems managers, room division managers, restaurant managers, controllers, and vendors of hotel application systems such as Property Management System (PMS), Point-of-Sale (POS), sales and catering, in-room entertainment system, and back-office functions. Based on the comments collected during the pilot testing period, items that were not clearly stated were revised, and a complete questionnaire was developed. The final instrument used for this study was a self-administered questionnaire composed of three sections measuring level of IT applications, hotel performance, and demographic information.

The first section measured the hotel employees' evaluation of different levels of technology applications in four different areas of hotel operations, which contained front-office applications, back-office applications, restaurant and banquet management systems, and guest-related interface applications. Front-office applications were measured by five items, including reservation system, check-in/check-out, room status and housekeeping management, in-house guest information functions, and guest accounting modules. All items concerning usage of IT systems were rated on a 5-point, Likert-type scale ranging from 1 (very low) to 5 (very high). Six items were used to measure back-office applications, including personnel, purchasing module, accounting modules (account receivable, account payable, and payroll), inventory module, sales and catering, and generating financial reports and updating statistics. Restaurant and banquet management systems were measured by four items such as menu management system (recipe management), sales analysis (sales forecasting, menu-item pricing), beverage-control system, and cost control (pre-costing and post-costing applications). Five items were used to measure guest-related interface applications, including call-accounting system, electronic locking system, energy management systems, guest-operated devices (in-room entertainment, in-room vending, and guest information services), and auxiliary guest services (automated wake-up call system and voice mail).

The second section measured the effectiveness of technology applications in enhancing the performance of hotel operations. Based on the financial performance measurement (Brown and Dev, 1997) and panel experts' opinion, five items were used to measure the hotel performance: (1) the use of technology enhances annual

S. Ham et al. / Hospitality Management 24 (2005) 281–294 287

sales amount; (2) the use of technology enhances reduced operating costs; (3) the use of technology enhances increased occupancy rate; (4) the use of technology enhances greater levels of repeat business; (5) the use of technology enhances positive word of mouth. During pretesting process, we tested the major assumption that hotel employees who worked more than 3 years in the current property were able to evaluate operational and financial performance of the property. Most respondents did not show much difficulty in answering items related to hotel performance because they were exposed to many meeting with their managers and top managers concerning the performance of the hotel. A five-point Likert type scale anchored from 1 (strongly disagree) to 5 (strongly agree) was used for each question. The last section included six demographic items: gender, age, education, department, years of experience, and current position.

4. Results

4.1. Descriptive characteristics of the respondents

Descriptive characteristics of the respondents were summarized in Table 1. Among the 648 respondents, 310 respondents (47.8%) were male, and 338 respondents were female (52.2%). About one-fourth of the hotel employees were under 29 years of age, another one-half fell into the category between 30 and 39 years old, another one-fifth of respondents' age was 40–49 years old, the remaining 25 respondents (3.9%) were more than 50 years old. Approximately one-fourth of respondents reported between 3 and 4 years of work experience in the current property, 14.2% reported between 5 and 6 years, 31.0% reported between 7 and 10 years, and 29.6% indicated 11 years or more in the current location. Educational levels were high. Respondents who graduated from high school accounted for 7.6%, respondents who had completed the associate's degree numbered 46.3%, while respondents who had graduated from college or above were 46.1% of the survey population. Approximately 69% of respondents worked for five-star hotels, while the remaining 31% worked for four-star hotels. Approximately one-third of respondents worked in room departments, 37% worked in food and beverage departments, and the remaining 29.5% worked in the back-office.

4.2. Dimensions in IT applications and hotel performance

Initially, a factor analysis was utilized to derive the dimensions of IT application in terms of usage level and hotel performance. The two primary uses for factor analysis are summarization and data reduction. In summarizing the data, factor analysis derived underlying dimensions that describe the data in a much smaller number of concepts than the original individual variables (Hair et al., 1998). The analysis was conducted to understand the underlying dimensions of gathered responses in IT applications usage level and to apply the categorized factors to the subsequent multiple regression analysis as independent variables. In addition, factor analysis

Table 1
Descriptive characteristics of respondents

Variable	Frequency	%
Gender		
Male	310	47.8
Female	338	52.2
Age		
Under 29	168	25.9
30–39	321	49.5
40–49	134	20.7
50 or above	25	3.9
Education		
High school graduate	49	7.6
Associate degree	300	46.3
College	252	38.9
Graduate school	47	7.2
Department		
Room	213	32.9
Food and beverage	240	37.0
Back office	191	29.5
Years of experience in the current property		
3–4 years	163	25.2
5–6 years	92	14.2
7–10 years	201	31.0
11 or above	192	29.6
Position		
Entry level	223	34.4
Supervisor	237	36.6
Assistant manger	155	23.9
Manager	33	5.1

was conducted to determine the dimensions of hotel performance and to apply the categorized factors to the subsequent multiple regression analysis as dependent variables. Principal component analysis was used to identify the underlying dimensions of IT application usage level and the hotel performance. Factors with eigenvalues greater than 1.0 were retained. The attributes with factor loadings of 0.50 or greater were included in a factor. The results of dimensions in IT application usage level are presented in Table 2, while the results of dimensions in hotel performance are presented in Table 3.

Tables 2 and 3 show each variable loading and eigenvalues, percent of variance explained, and the alpha value of the four factors of usage level of IT applications and hotel performance dimensions, respectively. Reliability analysis (Cronbach's

S. Ham et al. / Hospitality Management 24 (2005) 281–294   289

Table 2
Factor analysis of usage level of IT applications

Factors	Loadings	Eigenvalues	Percent of variance	Alpha
Factor 1: Front-office applications		5.47	34.9	0.92
Reservation system	0.81			
Check-in/check-out	0.80			
Room status and housekeeping management	0.75			
In-house guest information functions	0.71			
Guest accounting modules	0.73			
Factor 2: Back-office applications		3.29	16.4	0.81
Personnel	0.76			
Purchasing module	0.78			
Accounting modules (A/R, A/P, payroll)	0.75			
Inventory module	0.76			
Sales and catering	0.76			
Generating financial reports and updating statistics	0.73			
Factor 3: Restaurant and banquet management systems		2.53	12.6	0.63
Menu management system (recipe management)	0.77			
Sales analysis (sales forecasting, menu item pricing)	0.70			
Beverage control system	0.74			
Cost control	0.68			
Factor 4: Guest-related interface applications		1.99	9.9	0.74
Call accounting system	0.64			
Electronic locking system	0.85			
Energy management systems	0.72			
Guest-operated devices (e.g., in-room entertainment and vending)	0.60			
Auxiliary guest services (automated wake-up call system, voice mail)	0.59			
Total variance explained			73.80	

Alpha) was conducted to test the internal consistency of each factor. Cronbach's coefficient alpha for each set of measures was computed to test reliability and internal consistency. Cronbach's alpha is most often used to test the reliability of a multi-item scale. The cut-off point is generally known as 0.6 (Hair et al., 1998). Cronbach's coefficient alpha for the five front-office application items was 0.92, for the six back-office application items 0.82, for the four restaurant and banquet management system items 0.63, the five guest-related interface items 0.74, and the

Table 3
Factor analysis of hotel performance

Factor	Loadings	Eigenvalues	Percent of variance	Alpha
Factor: Hotel performance		3.65	10.15	0.93
Use of technology enhances reduced operating costs	0.84			
Use of technology enhances positive word of mouth	0.83			
Use of technology enhances greater levels of repeat business	0.82			
Use of technology enhances increased occupancy percentage	0.81			
Use of technology enhances annual sales amount	0.80			
Total variance explained			76.36	

five hotel performance items 0.93. Since all the alpha values are in between 0.63 and 0.93 and all above 0.6, the estimates of reliability and internal consistency were high.

4.3. IT applications affecting performance of hotels

Multiple regression analysis was conducted to identify whether IT applications had significant effects on performance of hotels. Four factors were generated from the factor analyses and they were included in the regression models as independent variables. The four independent variables were front-office applications, back-office applications, restaurant and banquet management systems, and guest-related interface applications. The dependent variable of the model was performance of hotels. Table 4 presents the results of the regression analysis.

According to the R^2 value of the regression model in Table 4, 59.9% of the variation of the performance of hotels was explained by the four independent variables together. The significant F-ratio ($F = 46.94$, $p = 0.000$) indicated the satisfactory level of the "Goodness-of-Fit" of the regression model. Front-office applications ($t = 4.127$, $p = 0.000$), back-office applications ($t = 2.111$, $p = 0.035$), and restaurant and banquet management systems ($t = 3.453$, $p = 0.000$) were found to be significant IT applications affecting the performance of hotels. The only IT applications that were not significant were guest-related interface application. In terms of hypotheses, the results suggest that H1, H2, and H3 be accepted and H4 be rejected.

The standardized β-value was used to investigate the relative importance of each of the four independent variables in contributing to the performance of upscale hotels. From the results, front-office IT applications ($\beta = 0.317$) was the single most important determinant factor in explaining performance of upscale hotels with the highest β value, followed by restaurant and banquet management systems ($\beta = 0.267$) and back-office applications ($\beta = 0.142$).

Table 4
Factors affecting hotel performance

	β	t	p
Independent variables			
Factor 1: Front-office applications	0.32	4.13	0.00
Factor 2: Back-office applications	0.15	2.11	0.04
Factor 3: Restaurant and banquet management systems	0.27	3.45	0.00
Factor 4: Guest-related interface applications	0.05	1.49	0.16
Constant	3.42	24.29	0.00
R^2	0.60		
F	46.94		
P	0.00		

5. Conclusions

This study was intended to determine the effect of IT usage on the performance of upscale hotels in four distinct service areas, which have implemented IT to achieve their goals in lodging operations. In order to achieve the study purpose, the following analyses were conducted. First, descriptive analyses of the data were conducted for all variables. Second, factor analyses were utilized to derive the dimensions of the respondent hotels' IT applications usage level and the performance of hotels. Finally, a multiple regression analysis was performed to identify whether certain IT applications had significant effects on the performance of hotel operations. The research sample was comprised of employees of 13, five-star hotels and eight, four-star hotels. The sampled hotels were upscale commercial hotels. A self-administered questionnaire was utilized to gather data, and the effective response rate was 64.8%.

In regard to the personnel assessment of hotel performance in relation to level of IT applications, three IT applications, front-office IT applications, back-office IT applications, and restaurant and banquet management systems were found to significantly affect the performance of upscale hotels. Front-office applications ($\beta = 0.317$) were the most significant IT applications affecting performance of upscale hotels, and restaurant and banquet management systems with the second and back-office applications with the third. Only guest-related interface applications were not significant in affecting the performance of upscale hotels.

Since previous studies generated inconsistent results about the relationship between the use of IT and performance of lodging operations, the findings of this study were compared with those from previous studies. The empirical results of this study are consistent with those of the previous study by David et al. (1996), which mentioned "productivity paradox of hotel-industry technology." They included three IT applications in their study: front-office applications; back-office applications; guest-related interface applications. They reported that front-office applications improved productivity in the front office. The results of this study demonstrated that installing computer applications in the front office, including reservations management, rooms-management, and guest-accounting modules, is a good strategy to improve performance of hotels.

Back-office applications, in this study, were identified to significantly affect performance of hotels, which is in contrast to the findings of the previous study by David et al. (1996). David et al. (1996) stated that, in most cases, the respondents expected little productivity enhancement from back-office IT applications. However, the improvement was not great though, in many cases, the respondents noted a slight improvement in productivity as a result of installing certain back-office computer modules. Combining the current and previous studies, it is quite convincing that installing back-office applications, such as personnel, purchasing modules, accounting modules, and financial reporting modules, may not contribute the improvement of short-term performance of hotels, but are expected to improve performance of hotels in the long run.

The unique finding of this study showed that restaurant and banquet management systems have a significant impact on the performance of hotel operation. Thus, hotel information system managers should invest more resources in adopting cost control applications, menu & recipe management applications, beverage control, and sales forecasting and menu pricing applications to improve the performance of food and beverage outlets in upscale hotels.

The only IT applications not significantly affecting the performance of upscale hotels were guest-related interface applications. Guest-related technologies were not improving performance of hotels. The result was coincident with David et al. (1996). They showed that guest-operated systems, such as in-room information, vending, entertainment, automated check-in and check-out devices, seemed actually to decrease productivity. Therefore, we can surmise that the IT applications used by guests may provide guest satisfaction with the facilities of hotels, but was not perceived to improve the performance of hotels.

Hotel executives recognize that IT is an essential component of their businesses and that much more attention should be paid to the impact of IT investment decisions, because of the constantly changing industry conditions. Investment in IT and training of employees would be a strategy established at a corporate level to pursue the business success on a long-term basis.

6. Limitations and suggestions for future research

Since the data of the study was collected from upscale hotels in Korea, the results of the study may not be directly applied to upscale hotels in other countries as well as other types of hotels. The results of this study may vary with service levels, size, and geographic locations of hotels, suggesting future research opportunities. In addition, a similar study could be conducted in the United States or in other countries, which will make it possible to find a difference among nations or continents.

The employees of hotels evaluated the IT usage and the impact of its usage level on their hotel performance. The usage of IT systems in four areas, front-office applications, back-office applications, restaurant and banquet management systems, and guest-related interface applications, were evaluated utilizing 5-point rating scale and the performance of hotel operations in relative to the use of IT were measured by answering the five-item performance dimensions, enhancing annual sales amount, reducing operating costs, increasing occupancy rate, elevating levels of repeat customers, and positive word of mouth.

Hotel employees are in good positions to rate the changes in performance through implementation of IT applications. In the long-term, hotel owners and investors expect IT adoption to contribute to bottom-line profitability of hotel performance. Therefore, a more sophisticated overall performance measures may include financial (operating income, sales, cash flow, and return on investment) and operational indicators (RevPAR, market share, occupancy), and customer-perspective indicator (guest satisfaction score and customer loyalty) via use or adoption of new IT systems.

References

Aksu, A.A., Tarcan, E., 2002. The Internet and five-star hotels: a case study from the Antalya region in Turkey. International Journal of Contemporary Hospitality Management 14 (2), 94–97.

Alpar, P., Kim, M., 1990. A macroeconomic approach to the measurement of information technology value. Journal of Management Information Systems 7 (5), 55–69.

Armijos, A., DeFranco, A., Hamilton, M., Skorupa, J., 2002. Technology trends in the lodging industry: a survey of multi-unit lodging operations. International Journal of Hospitality Information Technology 2 (2), 1–17.

Banker, R., Kauffmann, J., Morey, R., 1990. Measuring gains in operational efficiency from international technology: a study of positran deployment at Hardee's Inc. Journal of Management Information System 7 (2), 29–54.

Barcheldor, B., 1999. Hospitality and travel: a trip to Grandma's goes high tech. Information Week, September 27, p. 189.

Barua, A., Krieble, H., Mukhopadhyay, T., 1995. Information technologies and business value: an analytic and empirical investigation. Information Systems Research 6 (1), 3–23.

Brown, J., Dev, C., 1997. The franchisor—franchisee relationship: a key to franchise performance. Cornell Hotel and Restaurant Administration Quarterly 38 (6), 30–38.

Chaffney, D., 2000. Internet Marketing. Prentice-Hall, London.

Cho, W., Olson, M., 1998. A case study approach to understanding the impact of information technology on competitive advantage in the lodging industry. Journal of Hospitality and Tourism Research 22 (4), 376–394.

Clemons, E., 1986. Information systems for sustainable competitive advantage. Information & Management 11 (3), 131–136.

David, J., Grabski, S., Kasavana, M., 1996. The productivity paradox of hotel-industry technology. Cornell Hotel and Restaurant Administration Quarterly 37 (2), 64–70.

Hair, J., Anderson, R., Tatham, R., Black, W., 1998. Multivariate Data Analysis, fifth ed. Upper Saddle River, New Jersey.

Hewson, D., 1996. To the seaside via hyperspace. The Sunday Times, May 26, p. 10.

Hospitality Technology, 2003. 2002 Hospitality technology lodging industry technology study, obtained from http://htmagazine.com/2002_LITS/.

Huo, Y., 1998. Information technology and the performance of the restaurant firms. Journal of Hospitality and Tourism Research 22 (3), 239–251.

Mahmood, M., Mann, G., 1993. Measuring the organizational impact of information technology investment: an exploratory study. Journal of Management Information Systems 10 (1), 97–122.

McFarlan, F., 1984. Information technology changes the way you compete. Harvard Business Review 62 (3), 98–103.

Porter, M., 1985. Competitive advantage: creating and sustaining superior performance. Free Press, New York.

Rai, A., Patnayakuni, R., Patnayakuni, N., 1997. Technology investment and business performance. Communication of the ACM 40 (7), 89–97.

Roach, S., 1991. Services under siege-the restructuring imperative. Harvard Business Review 69 (5), 82–92.

Siguaw, J., Enz, C., Namasivayam, K., 2000. Adaptation of information technology in US Hotels: strategically driven objectives. Journal of Travel Research 39 (2), 192–201.

Sweat, J., Hibbard, J., 1999. Customer disservice. Information Week, June, pp. 65–78.

Van Hoof, H., Verbeeten, M., Combrink, T., 1996. Information technology revisited- International lodging industry technology needs and perceptions: a comparative study. Cornell Hotel and Restaurant Administration Quarterly 37 (6), 86–91.

Weil, P., 1992. The relationship between investment and information technology and firm performance: a study of the value manufacturing sector. Information Systems Research 3 (4), 307–333.

Winston, M., 1997. Leadership of renewal: leadership for the twenty-first century. Global Management 31, 31.

[19]

Available online at www.sciencedirect.com

SCIENCE @DIRECT®

International Journal of
Hospitality
Management

ELSEVIER

Hospitality Management 23 (2004) 381–395

www.elsevier.com/locate/ijhosman

Factors affecting online hotel reservation intention between online and non-online customers

Woo Gon Kim*, Dong Jin Kim

School of Hotel and Restaurant Administration, Oklahoma State University, 210 Human Environmental Science West, Stillwater, OK 74078, USA

Abstract

This study examined the differences between demographic and behavioral characteristics of customers who purchased products online and customers who did not. Additionally, this study investigated determinants that explain a customer's online reservation intention. To meet the purpose of this study, the researchers surveyed customers from eight hotels in Korea. The data were analyzed using χ^2 analysis, factor analysis, and multiple regression analysis. The two types of respondents differed in regard to their age, educational background, weekly browser usage, and the number of years of Internet use. Furthermore, the results showed that the determinants affect the respondents' online reservation intentions differently according to their past online purchasing experience.
© 2004 Elsevier Ltd. All rights reserved.

Keywords: Online reservation; Online purchase experience; Information technology; Information search; Hospitality industry

1. Introduction

Experts anticipate that the Internet, with its recent noticeable increases in users and functions, will greatly transform hospitality organizations. For example, Olsen and Connolly (2000) argued that hospitality firms will experience significant transformations because of the increased customer base available on the Internet. Dev and Olsen (2000) discussed the role of information

---

*Corresponding author. Tel.: +1-405-744-8483; fax: +1-405-744-6299.
E-mail addresses: kwoo@okstate.edu (W.G. Kim), dongjk@okstate.edu (D.J. Kim).

0278-4319/$ - see front matter © 2004 Elsevier Ltd. All rights reserved.
doi:10.1016/j.ijhm.2004.02.001

382 *W.G. Kim, D.J. Kim / Hospitality Management 23 (2004) 381–395*

technology (IT) and suggested that the Internet will provide great opportunities for future sales. Rayman-Bacchus and Molina (2001) stated that information and computer technology, especially the Internet, have changed the socio-economic context of tourism and, furthermore, that it will stimulate further changes.

Though electronic commerce (e-commerce) is in its infancy, purchasing via the Internet is one of the most rapidly growing forms of shopping (Levi and Weitz, 2001). Forrester Research (2001) reported that Internet sales by consumers totaled $48.3 billion in 2000, while online hotel sales represented $3.7 billion in the same time period. Poel and Leunis (1999) revealed that hotel reservations were ranked second after concert tickets in terms of the average consumers' propensity to buy a specific product or service.

Hospitality corporations have responded to the opportunities offered by e-commerce by developing web sites to take full advantage of the practical and creative business uses of the Internet. The Internet is an alternate distribution channel that can be compatible with existing channels (Rayman-Bacchus and Molina, 2001). The use of web sites in hospitality organizations goes beyond simply promoting and selling products to consumers. The adoption of web sites also provides the hospitality firms with important business opportunities and competitive edges.

Using the Internet as a reservation method can benefit the hospitality firms and also the customers by reducing costs and providing real-time information to both parties. According to Cobanoglu (2001), business travelers still use travel agents as their favorite hotel reservation resource followed by toll free reservation numbers, and then calling the hotel directly. Use of online hotel reservation system follows the previous three media in terms of favor. However, experts in IT predict that within several years the Internet will be one of the most important sources for hotel reservations and services (Cline and Warner, 2001). The number of online hotel reservations in 2001 accounted for 4.9% of total reservations made, and this percentage is expected to more than triple over the next 3 years. While the proportion of online reservations is increasing, only 64% of hospitality firms currently handle such transactions (Cline and Warner, 2001). Because an explosive increase in the number of online hotel reservations is expected, hotel marketers need to understand the determinants of customers' online hotel reservation intentions.

Despite the recent growing use of the Internet as a new reservation method, to the best of our knowledge, the factors that affect online hotel reservation intention have not yet been investigated.

Considering the above information, this study aims to:

1. Examine the differences in demographic and behavioral characteristics between customers with previous online purchase experience and customers without any such experience.
2. Investigate the factors that affect hotel reservation intentions of online and non-online customers.

W.G. Kim, D.J. Kim / Hospitality Management 23 (2004) 381–395 383

Based on the above objectives, research questions are as follows:

Research Question 1: Do customers who make online reservations differ from non-online customers with regard to demographic and behavioral characteristics (i.e., gender, age, income, education, weekly browser usage, and years of the Internet use)?
Research Question 2: Do the determinants affect the customer's online reservation intention differently according to one's past online purchase experience?

2. Literature review

As the importance of the Internet for the hospitality organizations grew and became more broadly accepted, researchers tried to find sociodemographic and behavioral characteristics of online customers. Bonn et al. (1998) argued that individuals who purchased travel online were likely to share sociodemographic characteristics. They investigated differences in the propensity to use the Internet based on the subjects' sociodemographic and behavioral characteristics and found that gender did not significantly affect the customer's information search behavior via the Internet, but age, income, and education level did. Similarly, Weber and Roehl (1999) provided a profile of people who used the Internet to search for travel information or to purchase travel arrangements. Their study found that the respondents who searched for travel information or who purchased travel products online reported higher incomes, higher status occupations, and more years of experience with the Internet than those who did not search or purchase online. The findings of these studies suggest that managers of hospitality organizations should understand the differences between sociodemographic and behavioral characteristics between online and non-online customers before implementing their promotion strategies.

Previous researchers have also examined what current and potential online customers like to see from hospitality and travel web sites. In an earlier study, Murphy et al. (1996) found 32 common features in the hotel reservation sites found through search engines; those features were then divided into four categories: promotion, service, interactivity, and management. Jarvenpaa and Todd (1997) used a conceptual approach to examine consumer attitudes toward early features of online shopping. The shopping factors identified by online customers were compiled into four categories: product perceptions, shopping experience, customer service, and consumer risks. Chu (2001) conducted focus group interviews to identify Internet users' needs and expectations toward airline/travel web sites. The results revealed that consumers were more willing to purchase low-involvement products via the Internet than high-involvement products. When asked what they expected to see from an airline/travel web site, the respondents identified informative, interactive, and attractive factors.

Jeong et al. (2001) investigated consumer perceptions of hotel web sites. They found that potential online customers only moderately liked online reservation web

384   *W.G. Kim, D.J. Kim / Hospitality Management 23 (2004) 381–395*

sites. They concluded color combination, ease of use, navigation quality, information completeness, accuracy, and currency were crucial factors for increasing sales via the Internet. Out of the six key drivers of online transaction intentions, information completeness turned out to be the most critical for online customers' satisfaction with web site information. Also, they discovered that color combination, information currency, accuracy, completeness, and navigation quality did have significant influences on customer's perception of the hotel product. Yoon (2002) investigated the antecedents and consequences of trust and satisfaction in online purchase decisions. The antecedents included in the study were transaction security (i.e., security warranty phrases and clarity of refund policy), web site properties (i.e., adequacy of product description and width of product selections), navigation functionality (i.e., usefulness of help functions and overall operational efficiency) and personal variables (i.e., familiarity with e-commerce and previous satisfaction with e-commerce). The author found that the four antecedent dimensions influenced online customer's purchase intentions, whereas web site trust and satisfaction operate as the mediating variables.

The above studies focused on the online behavior of customers in the hospitality; however, studies that are more generally focused on consumer online behavior also inform this study. To better understand online purchasing behavior, theoretical foundations were developed from Internet-related studies of consumer's perspectives. Jeong and Lambert's (2001) empirical results showed that consumers' perceived quality of information about products and services on the web was most crucial in predicting their decision-making. In their study of the four constructs of information quality (i.e., perceived usefulness, perceived ease of use, perceived accessibility, and attitudes), perceived usefulness and attitudes were powerful indicators in predicting the customers' purchase behavior.

In another study, Shim et al. (2001) proposed an Online Prepurchase Intentions Model based on the Interaction Model of the prepurchase consumer information search (Klein, 1998) and the Theory of Planned Behavior (Ajzen, 1985, 1991). They concluded that consumers' intentions to use the Internet for purchasing were influenced by their attitudes (i.e., payment security, privacy, safety, etc.), perceived behavioral control, and Internet purchase experience. Based on empirical findings, Shim et al. (2001) argued that the information search was the single most crucial element leading to purchase via the Internet.

In yet another study, Liang and Huang (1998) tested the ability of a transaction cost model to explain online consumers' purchasing decisions. The researchers included search, comparison, examination, negotiation, order and payment, delivery, and post-service into the online transaction process. Results showed that transaction costs determined the consumer's acceptance toward Internet shopping. The authors also argued for a learning effect in electronic shopping based on their finding that the determinants of customer acceptance for the online web shoppers were different from those of the non-online ones. According to their findings, uncertainty was the most significant construct for online shoppers, while asset specificity was the most significant for non-online shoppers.

Finally, Szymanski and Hise (2000) determined that consumer's perceptions of online convenience, product information, site design, and financial security were the dominant factors in consumer assessments of satisfaction. After examining web sites of retailers, Kagan et al. (2000) concluded that consumers wanted such advanced functions as checking real-time availability and tracking completed orders although current web sites that had only basic transaction functions. The results also indicated that consumers wanted greater assurances of confidentiality and privacy. These findings are consistent with other studies that showed that issues such as privacy (Kelly and Rowland, 2000) and return policies (Wood, 2001) substantially influenced customer's perceptions of safety regarding online shopping.

In summary, the review of the literature revealed online customer decision-making is an important area of study for the hospitality industry and, furthermore, that a body of knowledge exists in the area of consumer online decision-making. However, no study was found that described the differences in the factors that affect hotel reservation intentions of online and non-online customers.

3. Methods

To answer the research questions, survey data were collected from the customers in eight hotels in Korea and analyzed. The following sections describe the measurement and analysis, and the subjects for this study.

3.1. Measurement and analysis

In this study, a questionnaire comprising 19 determinants was designed to measure the online shopper's perceived importance toward each determinant. The determinants pertaining to online hotel reservation were developed from previous studies by Jarvenpaa and Todd (1997) and Weber and Roehl (1999), as well as from a focus group interview. The focus group consisted of five hotel managers in charge of online reservations, and five hotel guests who primarily reserved their rooms online. The determinants of online hotel reservation intention used in the study are shown in Table 1.

The questionnaire consisted of three sections. The first section measured customer's perceived importance of online hotel reservation. The respondents were asked to rate the importance of each determinant using a 5-point Likert scale (1 = least important; 5 = most important). The second section measured respondent's past online purchase experiences (1 = yes, 2 = no) and online reservation intention of hotel products and services using a 7-point Likert scale (1 = most unlikely, 7 = most likely). The third section was designed to obtain the respondent's demographic and behavioral characteristics: gender, age, income, education level, browser use per week, and number of years of Internet use.

According to a recent study by Shim et al. (2001), past purchase experience via the Internet was one of the most important factors (i.e., attitude, behavioral control, and purchase experience) in predicting Internet purchase intention. Liang and Huang

386   *W.G. Kim, D.J. Kim / Hospitality Management 23 (2004) 381–395*

Table 1
Determinants of online hotel reservation intention used in the study

Determinants	Jarvenpaa and Todd (1997)	Weber and Roehl (1999)	This study
Freedom from hassles	√		√
24-h accessibility	√	√	√
Easy payment procedures		√	√
Appropriate product/service information		√	√
Real-time location of available rooms			√
Ease of comparing hotels	√		√
Ease of contacting hotels	√	√	√
Ease of finding what I want	√		√
Variety of choices	√	√	√
Ease of acquiring hotel-related information	√		√
Ease of understanding policy			√
Ease of placing orders	√	√	√
Credibility of online transaction	√	√	√
Reliability of provided pictures	√		√
Reliability of products/services information	√	√	√
Reduced purchase-related costs	√		√
Discounted price	√	√	√
Ease of canceling	√	√	√
Security of sensitive information	√	√	√

(1998) indicated that non-online and online consumers had different considerations while purchasing electronically. Until recently, the percentage of hotel reservations made online was extremely low in Korea, so limiting the subjects of a study exclusively to guests who made online hotel reservations would produce insufficient data for quantitative analysis. Therefore, for the purpose of this study, respondents who had any past online purchase experience related to airlines, hotels, or time-share resorts were considered to have past online purchase experience. Online purchase experiences with airlines and time-share resorts were included due to the similarity of hotel products in terms of the characteristics of high risk, relatively high price, and intangibility. Online reservation intention was used as the best proxy of real reservation behavior.

The collected data were analyzed using Statistical Package for Social Science (SPSS) version 10.0. First, χ^2 analysis was conducted to find out the differences of demographic and behavioral characteristics of customers who had purchased products online and those who had not. Factor analysis was utilized to determine the underlying structure of the original 19 determinants toward online reservations. Finally, multiple regression analysis was employed to investigate the causal effect of extracted factors on the online reservation intention.

3.2. Sampling

Fifty-five questionnaires were distributed for the purpose of pre-testing in May 2001. Based on the comments collected during the pre-testing period, a complete

W.G. Kim, D.J. Kim / Hospitality Management 23 (2004) 381–395   387

questionnaire was designed. A quota-sampling method was adopted for data collection. The number of questionnaires distributed in each hotel was based on the number of rooms in that hotel. The questionnaires were distributed to Korean hotel guests who stayed in eight five-star hotels in Seoul when they checked in at their hotels. The front desk clerks encouraged the guests to complete the form with a prepared speech. The guests were asked to either return the completed questionnaires to the front office or leave them in their room for housekeeping personnel to collect. The questionnaires were collected from May 11 through May 25, 2001. Most hotels were business hotels, mainly due to their location in the city of Seoul, therefore, most respondents were business clients. Out of 500 questionnaires that were distributed, a total of 262 (52.4%) questionnaires were returned. Of the returned questionnaires, 7 were eliminated because of an excessive amount of missing data. After elimination, 255 questionnaires (51.0%) were coded and analyzed for the empirical investigation.

4. Results

4.1. Sample characteristics

The χ^2 analyses were conducted to investigate differences in the respondent's demographic and behavioral characteristics (i.e., gender, age, income, education level, browser use per week, and the number of years of Internet use) between the online and non-online groups. Table 2 provides the results of χ^2 analyses.

Among the 255 respondents, 135 respondents (52.9%) indicated that they had purchased airline, hotel, or time-share services via the Internet and 120 respondents (47.1%) indicated that they had not. Neither the respondent's gender nor their income showed statistical significances, suggesting that the online purchase experience was not significantly different in terms of their gender and income. On the other hand, the respondent's age revealed significant results ($\chi^2 = 7.125$, $p = .028$), suggesting that the online purchasers and non-online purchasers differ according to the respondent's age. Furthermore, the two groups varied in regard to their educational backgrounds ($\chi^2 = 6.748$, $p = 0.080$). Similarly, the two groups differed in terms of the respondents' browser use per day ($\chi^2 = 18.290$, $p = 0.000$) and the years of Internet use ($\chi^2 = 18.625$, $p = 0.000$). Approximately 64% of the respondents who used a browser 5 days or more per week had past online purchase experience, and 76% of those who had used the Internet for more than 3 years also had past online purchase experience. On the other hand, approximately 66% of the respondents who used browsers 2 days or less per week did not have any past online purchase experience, and 64% of those who had used the Internet for less than 1 year did not have any online purchase experience. Overall, respondents with past online purchase experience showed higher browser usage and more years of Internet use.

Most of the results of the χ^2 analyses are consistent with the results of Bonn et al. (1998) and Weber and Roehl (1999). However, Weber and Roehl's (1999) empirical

Table 2
Respondent profiles and the results of χ^2 analysis

Variable	Past online purchase experience		χ^2	P
	Yes ($n = 135$)	No ($n = 120$)		
Gender			0.399	0.528
Male	65 (55.1%)	53 (44.9%)		
Female	69 (51.1%)	66 (48.9%)		
Age			7.125	0.028
20–29	59 (44.7%)	73 (55.3%)		
30–39	53 (60.2%)	35 (39.8%)		
40 or over	20 (64.5%)	11 (35.5%)		
Annual income			0.686	0.709
Less than $18,500	72 (52.2%)	66 (47.8%)		
$18,501–$37,000	39 (56.5%)	30 (43.5%)		
$37,001 or more	23 (48.9%)	24 (51.1%)		
Education			6.748	0.080
High school	5 (38.5%)	8 (61.5%)		
2-year college	61 (46.6%)	70 (53.4%)		
4-year college	53 (62.4%)	32 (37.6%)		
Graduate school	15 (60.0%)	10 (40.0%)		
Browser use per week			18.290	0.000
Less than 2 days	29 (34.1%)	56 (65.9%)		
3–4 days	43 (60.6%)	28 (39.4%)		
5 days or more	63 (63.6%)	36 (36.4%)		
Internet use			18.625	0.000
Less than 1 year	28 (36.4%)	49 (63.6%)		
1–2 years	39 (52.0%)	36 (48.0%)		
2–3 years	32 (59.3%)	22 (40.7%)		
More than 3 years	34 (75.6%)	11 (24.4%)		

results found that online purchasers and non-online purchasers differed in income, while this study found that income was not a significant variable. The limited number of income categories in this study compared to the study by Weber and Roehl (1999) could partially explain why income was not found to be a significant variable in this study. In this study, income was categorized into smaller number categories because of sample size. Additionally, customers had less access to the Internet and online shopping was not widely accepted by the average consumer some years ago. At that time, income could be an important factor that differentiated online purchasers and non-purchasers. However, at present, online shopping is widely accepted and gaining popularity among almost all consumers regardless of income level, so online purchase behavior now correlates with technological familiarity (e.g., browser use per week and the years of Internet use).

W.G. Kim, D.J. Kim / Hospitality Management 23 (2004) 381–395 389

Table 3
Results of factor analysis

Factor[a]	Mean	SD	Factor loading	Eigen value	Variance explained %
FACTOR 1: Convenience (0.71)[b]				5.57	13.53
Freedom from hassles	3.70	0.97	0.756		
24-h accessibility	3.69	1.00	0.742		
Easy payment procedures	3.23	0.94	0.587		
Appropriate product/service information	3.45	0.96	0.494		
Real-time location of available rooms	3.46	0.96	0.415		
FACTOR 2: Ease of information search (0.74)				1.64	13.06
Ease of comparing hotels	3.53	1.07	0.823		
Ease of contacting hotels	3.35	1.08	0.775		
Variety of choice	3.51	1.03	0.525		
Ease of finding what I want	3.53	1.01	0.501		
Ease of acquiring hotel-related information	3.20	0.95	0.479		
FACTOR 3: Transaction (0.71)				1.52	12.80
Ease of understanding policies	3.00	0.89	0.729		
Ease of placing orders	3.20	0.92	0.724		
Credibility of online transaction	3.02	0.90	0.613		
FACTOR 4: Information credibility (0.65)				1.45	8.98
Reliability of provided pictures	2.94	0.96	0.843		
Reliability of products/services information	3.12	0.91	0.714		
FACTOR 5: Price (0.70)				1.19	8.90
Reduced purchase-related costs	2.98	0.75	0.853		
Discounted price	2.77	0.69	0.797		
FACTOR 6: Safety (0.61)				1.05	8.06
Ease of canceling	2.92	0.96	0.792		
Security of sensitive information	2.85	0.94	0.570		
Total variance explained					65.33

[a] Principal component factors with iterations: Varimax rotation.
[b] Reliability score (Cronbach's α) for each factor grouping is shown in parentheses.

4.2. Factor analysis

Prior to multiple regression analysis, the 19 determinants were factor analyzed using principal component analysis with orthogonal varimax rotation in order to identify the structure of determinants related to online hotel reservation. Table 3 presents the results relevant to the question of which determinants are important to explain the total variances in all the variables. The number of factors was determined by retaining only the factors with an eigenvalue of 1 or higher.

390   *W.G. Kim, D.J. Kim / Hospitality Management 23 (2004) 381–395*

The first factor, *convenience*, included five items: freedom from hassles, 24-h accessibility, easy payment procedures, appropriate product/service information, and real-time location of available rooms. The second factor, *ease of information search* consisted of five items: ease of comparing hotels, ease of contacting hotels, variety of choice, ease of finding what the customer wants, and ease of acquiring hotel-related information. The third factor, *transaction* included: ease of understanding policies, ease of placing orders, and credibility of online transaction. The fourth factor was related to *information credibility*, and the fifth factor was related to *price*. Finally, the sixth factor was related to *safety* which included ease of canceling and security of sensitive information.

As seen, all factor loading scores were higher than 0.40 and the six extracted factors accounted for 65.33% of the variation in the original 19 items. Cronbach's α coefficients of all factor dimensions were higher than 0.60 and were found to be reliable (Hair et al., 1995).

4.3. Multiple regression analysis

To determine the importance of each factor to online reservation intention, two multiple regression analyses were conducted based on the earlier findings of the χ^2 analysis that online and non-online groups are heterogeneous. Online reservation intention was the dependent variable, while the six determinant factors were the independent variables. All variables were entered at the same time. Table 4 reports the results of the multiple regression analyses.

For the online group, five factors such as *convenience*, *ease of information search*, *transaction*, *price*, and *safety* significantly influenced online reservation intention. *Convenience* turned out to be the most important factor followed by *transaction*, *safety*, *ease of information search*, and *price*. Overall, the regression results explained

Table 4
Regression results: factors affecting online reservation intention

Factor	Past online purchase experience			
	Yes ($n = 135$)		No ($n = 120$)	
	Std. β	t	Std. β	t
FACTOR 1: Convenience	0.317	3.622***	0.245	2.428**
FACTOR 2: Ease of information search	0.236	2.708***	0.136	1.378
FACTOR 3: Transaction	0.244	2.850***	0.160	1.630
FACTOR 4: Information credibility	0.076	0.871	0.151	1.488
FACTOR 5: Price	0.211	2.450**	0.178	1.820*
FACTOR 6: Safety	0.241	2.812***	0.200	2.010**
	Adjusted $R^2 = 0.492$		Adjusted $R^2 = 0.426$	
	$F = 6.294$***		$F = 3.626$***	

*$p < 0.10$, **$p < 0.05$, and ***$p < 0.01$.

49.2% (adjusted R^2) of the variance in online reservation intention. On the other hand, only three factors such as *convenience, price,* and *safety* were the significant factors for the non-online group. The adjusted R^2 was 0.426, suggesting that 42.6% of the variation of online reservation intention was explained by the regression equation.

As the results show, *convenience, price,* and *safety* were significant factors for both groups. It is essential to note the significant differences in determinant factors between the two groups. The results of the regression analyses indicated that online and non-online groups did not give the same importance to each determinant relative to making an online reservation. Unlike the non-online group, the online group considered *ease of information search* and *transaction* to be more important factors than *price*. Among the five significant factors, *price* was the least important factor for the online group. Hence, we conclude that *price* was a more important factor than *ease of information search* and *transaction* for first time online reservation users. However, as customers become more familiar with online reservations, *price* becomes a less important factor than *ease of information search* and *transaction*.

5. Conclusion

This study empirically investigated the differences in demographic and behavioral characteristics of customers who purchased products online and those who had not. Online purchasers and non-online purchasers did not differ by gender and income. In terms of age and education level, people over the age of 30 and/or people who were highly educated were more likely to make reservations using the Internet. The results of this research also verified that online purchasers and non-online purchasers differed in their weekly browser usage and in the number of Internet use. Respondents with past online purchase experience reported higher weekly browser usage and more years of Internet use than those who did not have any experience with online purchasing.

A major objective of this study was to identify different determinants that explain a customer's online reservation intention for the online group and the non-online group. As the multiple regression results suggested, the significant factors that affected online reservation intention in both the online group and the non-online group were *convenience, safety,* and *price. Ease of information search* and *transaction* were the significant factors affecting online reservation intention only in the online group. On the other hand, the online group considered *ease of information search* and *transaction* to be more important than *price*.

Based on the study findings, online hotel marketers need to take into consideration two different strategies depending on the life-cycle stage of the online reservation site. When online reservation systems are designed for the first time users (e.g., the introductory stage), *convenience, price,* and *safety* factors should be emphasized. However, when the online customer base reaches the growth stage, *information search* and *transaction* functions should be highlighted and integrated into the structure of online hotel reservation systems. As the number of hotel guests who have previous online purchase experience increases, most hotel online reservation systems should strengthen and emphasize *ease of information search* and *transaction function*. In other words, when online hospitality marketers focus on retaining existing online hotel reservation guests rather than creating new online guests, *information search* and *transaction* functions should be emphasized.

Ease of information search may include the following: customers should be able to find important contact information within two clicks on the hotel web site. Frequently requested information should be displayed on the first page with hyperlinks. Eventually, online reservation systems should offer sufficient information for customer's reservation decision-making. The availability of a virtual property tour would enable customers to better understand the hotel facilities. In terms of *transaction* features, ordering functionality should be designed simply and clearly. Improving the credibility and reliability of online transaction can include establishing a fast and stable reservation system and providing accurate information about hotel products, services, and facilities. Cancellation, refunds, and other general policies should be clearly explained and easily understood by online customers.

An effective relationship between marketing and information systems departments should be established. Jeong and Lambert (2001) addressed the need for web researchers to pay special attention to customer's web behavior patterns and their attitudes toward online reservation systems before and after using them. The results of this study suggest that important factors affecting hotel reservation intentions for the customers who have purchased online differ from those customers who have not purchased online. Over time, information that is frequently requested by the customers is likely to change. Consequently, to better meet the changing needs of the customers, the marketing department should establish a close working relationship with the information systems department.

To acquire a competitive advantage, methods of data collection, analysis, interpretation, and implementation must be taken into consideration. Each time hotel guests make online reservations, they are asked to enter the number of rooms, duration of their stay, their address, name, phone number, credit card number, etc. Online hotel reservation systems facilitate the collection of information on customer characteristics and online behavior. Consequently, hospitality marketers can build guest databases easier than ever before and implement customized promotional activities that meet specific needs and wants of respective customers. Examples of such promotional activities include introducing packaged products, sending electronic hotel newsletters, and sending catalogs and direct mail to appropriate market segments.

The physical distance between the customer and organization in online shopping makes online customers more concerned about the security of their sensitive information and the safety of using their credit cards. To alleviate customers' privacy concerns, a focus should be placed on determining and mediating the major issues. Marketing managers must develop strategies to assure customers of the security and safety of online transactions. In addition, hotel employees who are building and maintaining a guest database should receive formal training on protecting the privacy of sensitive guest information.

6. Limitations and suggestions for future research

The following limitations should be taken into consideration in interpreting the findings of this study. The first limitation is associated with the sampling method. The sampling method used in this study was a quota-sampling method, which is a non-probability sampling method. Thus, the study was restricted to generalization rather than specific application of the findings.

The second limitation regards the attributes that were studied. Some seemingly important attributes of online purchasers and non-online purchasers were not included in this study, such as motivations, attitudes, and benefits. Hence, these other important attributes should be examined in future research.

The third limitation is in regards to 'intention' itself. According to Banks (1950) and Katona (1960), more than 60% of the subjects who said they would buy actually did so. The results of their studies revealed that, while a relationship does exist between intent and action, buying intention does not always accurately reflect actual behavior. Future research should investigate the factors that affect actual online reservation behavior instead of reservation intention. Since the number of online hotel reservations was extremely low in Korea at the time of the survey, past online purchase experience in this study included airlines, hotels, and time-share resorts. However, future research should focus exclusively on customer experiences and behaviors pertaining to online hotel reservations.

Additional suggestions for future research should include a "technology glossary". To the non-online customers, "technology glossaries" such as "freedom from hassles" and "appropriate information" might be perceived differently. Hence, the term "technology glossary" should be chosen carefully with detailed explanation when a survey instrument is designed, and particularly when the respondents are unfamiliar with the terms, which non-online customers are.

Since online reservation is a relatively new phenomenon, many issues need to be addressed. First, there is a need for additional research on the physical components of online reservation systems, such as color combination and pictorial attributes. According to the study by Jeong et al. (2001), aesthetic quality such as color combination is an important component that affects customer's perceptions of overall web site quality. Additional research is needed to explore in more detail the physical components of online reservation web sites. Thus, future researchers should investigate which color combinations improve customers' overall perceptions of web site quality, and which pictorial attributes increase customers' attention while viewing an online reservation web site.

This study investigated determinants affecting online reservations. However, those factors could vary according to property characteristics such as size, type, and location. Those determinants could also vary according to the customer's cultural background. Therefore, future research should investigate if determinants differ

394   *W.G. Kim, D.J. Kim / Hospitality Management 23 (2004) 381–395*

depending on the characteristics of property and cultural characteristics of respondents. In addition, some researchers (e.g., Shim et al., 2001; Jeong and Lambert, 2001) investigated online customer's behavior patterns. However, it would be useful to further investigate online customer's behavior patterns.

Finally, the indication from this study that customers' intentions to purchase online and the characteristics of income and experience differ depending on the level of Internet acceptance has implications for developing more precise theories on customer use of the Internet.

In conclusion, noticeable increases in Internet users and functions provide opportunities for those in the hospitality to transform how they interact with customers. This study provides information that can be useful in the transformation process and offers implications for future practice and research. In today's changing hospitality industry such information can provide the basis for sound decision-making and success.

References

Ajzen, I., 1985. From intention to action: a theory of planned behavior. In: Kuhl, J., Beckman, J. (Eds.), Action Control: From Cognitions to Behaviors. Springer, New York, NY.

Ajzen, I., 1991. The theory of planned behavior. Organizational Behavior and Human Decision Processes 50 (2), 179–211.

Banks, S., 1950. The relationship between preference and purchase of brands. Journal of Marketing 15 (4), 145–157.

Bonn, M.A., Furr, H.L., Susskind, A.M., 1998. Using the Internet as a pleasure travel planning tool: an examination of the sociodemographic and behavioral characteristics among Internet users and nonusers. Journal of Hospitality and Tourism Research 22 (3), 303–317.

Chu, R., 2001. What online Hong Kong travelers look for on airline/travel websites? International Journal of Hospitality Management 20 (1), 95–100.

Cline, R.S., Warner, M., 2001. Hospitality e-business: the future. The Bottomline [Online]. Available: http://www.hftp.org/Members/BottomLine/current/ebusiness.htm [July 16, 2001].

Cobanoglu, C., 2001. Analysis of business travelers' hotel selection and satisfaction. Ph.D. Dissertation, Oklahoma State University.

Dev, S.C., Olsen, M.D., 2000. Marketing challenges for the next decade. The Cornell Hotel and Restaurant Administration Quarterly 41 (1), 41–47.

Forrester Research, 2001. NRF/Forrester Online Retail Index. Forrester Research, Inc., Cambridge, MA. Available: http://www.forrester.com/NRF/1,2873,0,00.html [October 15, 2001].

Hair, J.F., Anderson, R.E., Tatham, R.L., Black, W.C., 1995. Multivariate Data Analysis 4th Edition. Prentice-Hall International, London.

Jarvenpaa, S.L., Todd, P.A., 1997. Consumer reactions to electronic shopping on the World Wide Web. International Journal of Electronic Commerce 1 (2), 59–88.

Jeong, M., Lambert, C.U., 2001. Adaptation of an information quality framework to measure customers' behavioral intentions to use lodging Web sites. International Journal of Hospitality Management 20 (2), 129–146.

Jeong, M., Oh, H., Gregoire, M., 2001. An Internet Marketing Strategy Study for the Lodging Industry. American Hotel & Lodging Foundation, Washington, DC.

Kagan, A., Post, G., Noel, M.C., 2000. Selling the web: web features used by retailers. The Journal of Applied Business Research 16 (1), 15–26.

Katona, G., 1960. Powerful Consumer: Psychological Studies of the American Economy. McGraw-Hill, New York, NY, pp. 80–83.

W.G. Kim, D.J. Kim / Hospitality Management 23 (2004) 381–395 395

Kelly, E.P., Rowland, H.C., 2000. Ethical and online privacy issues in electronic commerce. Business Horizons 43 (3), 3–12.

Klein, L.R., 1998. Evaluating the potential of interactive media through a new lens: search versus experience goods. Journal of Business Research 41 (3), 195–203.

Levi, M., Weitz, B.A., 2001. Retailing Management 4th Edition. McGraw-Hill, New York, NY.

Liang, T., Huang, J., 1998. An empirical study on consumer acceptance of products in electronic markets: a transaction cost model. Decision Support Systems 24 (1), 29–43.

Murphy, J., Forrest, E.J., Wotring, C.E., Brymer, R.A., 1996. Hotel management and marketing on the Internet: an analysis of sites and features. The Cornell Hotel and Restaurant Administration Quarterly 37 (3), 70–82.

Olsen, M.D., Connolly, D.J., 2000. Experience-based travel: how technology is changing the hospitality industry. The Cornell Hotel and Restaurant Administration Quarterly 41 (1), 30–40.

Poel, D.V.D., Leunis, J., 1999. Consumer acceptance of the Internet as a channel of distribution. Journal of Business Research 45 (3), 249–256.

Rayman-Bacchus, L., Molina, A., 2001. Internet-based tourism services: business issues and trends. Futures 33 (7), 589–605.

Shim, S., Eastlick, M.A., Lotz, S.L., Warrington, P., 2001. An online prepurchase intentions model: the role of intention to search. Journal of Retailing 77 (3), 397–416.

Szymanski, D.M., Hise, R.T., 2000. E-satisfaction: an initial examination. Journal of Retailing 76 (3), 309–322.

Weber, K., Roehl, W.S., 1999. Profiling people searching for and purchasing travel products on the World Wide Web. Journal of Travel Research 37 (3), 291–298.

Wood, S.L., 2001. Remote purchase environments: the influence of return policy leniency on two-stage decision processes. Journal of Marketing Research 38 (2), 157–169.

Yoon, S., 2002. The antecedents and consequences of trust in online-purchase decisions. Journal of Interactive Marketing 6 (2), 47–63.

[20]

PERGAMON

Tourism Management 24 (2003) 241–255

TOURISM MANAGEMENT

www.elsevier.com/locate/tourman

Information supply in tourism management by marketing decision support systems

Karl W. Wöber

Institute for Tourism and Leisure Studies, Vienna University of Economics and Business Administration, Augasse 2-6, Vienna 1090, Austria

Received 3 July 2002; accepted 4 August 2002

Abstract

The importance of information and efficient information management is steadily increasing due to the evolution of new technologies and high-capacity storage media but also because growing market dynamics raise information needs. A marketing decision support system (MDSS) can be of particular importance as it supports organizations in collecting, storing, processing, and disseminating information, and in the decision-making process by providing forecasts and decision models (Little, 1979). The following article provides insights into a successful implementation of a MDSS in tourism. Based on findings on the analysis of the system's protocol files, it discusses the information needs in tourism management.
© 2002 Elsevier Science Ltd. All rights reserved.

Keywords: Marketing decision support systems (MDSS); Tourism statistics; Internet

1. Introduction

Operators in tourism management, compared to other management sectors, are confronted with a vast field of complex aims, requiring different plans of action. The special working requirements of the services sector are a result of its business peculiarities. Problems in strategic, and frequently operational planning, are characterized by their complexity, often being inter-mingled, non-transparent, individualistically dynamic and requiring the achievement of multiple goals. The vast amount of information or complex weighting of the different sectors can present an insurmountable problem for human resources. As a result there are high expectations of decision-makers' trouble-shooting abilities.

In order to solve complex problems, decision-makers need to have a factual knowledge of the industry (declarative knowledge) and the methodology used (procedural knowledge). The wealth of knowledge is drawn from two pools; that obtained from the "storage" of already existing experiences, and by generating knowledge in the respective field. Combining these two pools creates an arena for problem solving.

1.1. Declarative knowledge—decision basis in tourism planning

Currently, information gains more and more importance, leading legitimately to the development of a fourth economic sector—the information sector. Information also plays a vital role in tourism for entrepreneurs and managers who spend the whole day involved in information processing. In the tourism industry there is no lack of market research data, on the contrary, there is a rather uncontrolled growth of various data sources, each having different survey purposes and survey designs. Tourism surveys of national and international market research institutes are published in ever shorter intervals and the level of itemization of market data increases rapidly. Information collected by these means has indicated data which can be organized into the following groups (Seitz & Meyer, 1995):

1. information on markets and environment,
2. information on customer behavior,
3. information on competition in the industry, and
4. internal information for executive boards.

The first three information groups are predominantly non-discretionary from a manager's point of view as the

E-mail address: karl.woeber@wu-wien.ac.at (K.W. Wöber).

0261-5177/02/$ - see front matter © 2002 Elsevier Science Ltd. All rights reserved.
PII: S 0 2 6 1 - 5 1 7 7 (0 2) 0 0 0 7 1 - 7

242 K.W. Wöber / Tourism Management 24 (2003) 241–255

information can very rarely be directly influenced by an individual company. Information from these groups are similar in nature and scope for most sectors represented in the tourism industry (hotel trade, restaurant trade, tour operators, travel agents, common carriers, pressure groups, etc.). In the fourth group however, there is a larger scope for variety (Hebestreit, 1992, p. 92).

Due to high costs for primary market research many tourism managers abandon market research in general (Seitz & Meyer, 1995, p. 18). Even the larger businesses and tourism organizations lack market research departments and employees rarely work exclusively on market research items. This results again in an inconsistent development of marketing aims and strategies, as businesses as often as not grope in the dark for their direction.

In Europe the most frequent or highly recognized of the commissioned tourism studies are either publicly financed, directly by national or local authorities, or indirectly by government agencies. This method of procuring market research, is important and often a condition for its development, as the expensive primary studies cannot be financed by the numerous small or medium-scale businesses. The resulting *obligation to pass on information,* created by the above-mentioned research financing, has led to a wider search—in regional tourism organizations, and other bodies representing tourism—to find means of successfully sharing and communicating information.

Traditional data resources in tourism market research are reports, records and statistics which may be presented either in printed format or are electronically driven (CD-ROM). Computer-based information systems (databases) are currently a rarity, but usually can be found either in connection with the official statistical data of a country or a region (e.g. http://www.oestat.gv.at/—Statistics, Austria) or international institutions (e.g. http://www.world-tourism.org/—World Tourism Organization, http://europa.eu.int/comm/eurostat/—Eurostat, database of the European Union). The information available by this method is rarely used since it ignores the special information requirements of the end-user (managers), or is simply inaccessible due to high fees, complicated application procedures or is simply not user friendly. The lack of practical relevance, of these information systems, can be explained by their bias toward representing the economic interest of the sponsors and data collectors and/or by the universal requirements the systems have to meet in the collection, storage and search of statistical data from other industries.

Market research results are mainly available in print and they can be obtained either in bookshops, on-line (see e.g. http://www.studien.at/) or directly from the author. From the consumer's perspective this way of passing on secondary information has a number of disadvantages:

- Due to the complex design of market research reports the surveyed data is not up to date anymore.
- Data from different sources cannot be easily compared especially if it has been surveyed for different purposes.
- Information contained in reports is often of limited relevance for the particular problem.
- Presentation of data is either not detailed enough, not significant enough, or supplementary information is missing which prevents a faultless interpretation of results.
- Often only very specific data from a more comprehensive study is required and thus the cost–benefit-ratio becomes unattractive.

There is usually an over-abundance of available information leaving managers to cope with determining which is the best source. Often the entrepreneur has to rely on external consultants and market research specialists resulting in additional costs.

1.2. Procedural knowledge—decision basis in tourism planning

"The big problem with management science models is that managers practically never used them". More than 20 years ago John Little described the discrepancy between the scientific development of planning instruments, models, level of itemization and the fact that, when available, the knowledge gathered is rarely put into practice. This is caused by the numerous, often poorly documented assumptions of model architects, which was denoted as *model platonism* by Hans Albert (Albert, 1967). As a response to this problem Little suggested that the manager is included in the model (Little, 1970). He postulated in his article on the *Decision Calculus,* on-line models with the following features: robustness, ease of control, simplicity, completeness of relevant detail and suitability for communication.

The communication problem is of vital importance in the every day life of managers' daily events. It is still common practice to employ various levels of change rather than continually observe the changes in market share and volume. Many entrepreneurs do not even know terms such as market segmentation or market positioning and they do not regard them as essential. They keep on looking for measures to expand seasonal business but lack knowledge of methods that will measure their success. Corporate planning only takes place if external financing is required and supporting documents have to be submitted to the lender (Phillips & Moutinho, 1998, p. 68). Heuristic forecasting methods are hardly ever used, accordingly quantitative methods

K.W. Wöber / Tourism Management 24 (2003) 241–255   243

are never used. Models of strategic market planning—portfolio analyses and analyses of the lifecycle of a product—employed in other industries are hardly ever used in tourism management.

The grounds for the poor employment of methodological processes in tourism management can be divided into two groups; technological development and insufficient training.

Issues related to the *technological development* of existing information processing and transmission systems are:

- Data required for the application of tourism models is either not up-to-date or unsuitable.
- Standard software is not able to support the relatively complex tasks in tourism management.
- Specially developed software is too expensive for single tourism businesses.

Issues related to the insufficient training of tourism managers are:

- Managers have little knowledge of existing methods or available data.
- Managers are confronted with various data sources and different results and they do not know how to cope with this situation.
- Managers do not know which data sources and models are suitable.

2. The transmission of market research data in the Internet

Due to the vital role of tourism in many countries and regions in Europe a number of programs concerning tourism promotion have been installed. Government and private tourism organizations have been established in order to strengthen a tourism destination. Usually the aim is to increase the added value of a region. The major tasks of these bodies are:

- to provide consumers with information about the destination,
- to coordinate and implement sales promotion measures,
- tourism advertising,
- support in sales and distribution, and
- to coordinate and implement market research projects.

For most of their tasks (except the coordination and implementation of market research projects) these tourism promoting bodies provide efficient methods. The actual effect of the last item mentioned has been lost in the past due to inefficient instruments relating to the transmission and utilization of declarative and procedural knowledge. Now with the development of cheaper

hard- and software many tourism organizations are reconsidering their promotion policy.

In almost all industries systems are being developed in order to support investment and marketing planning (Wierenga & van Bruggen, 2000). Also the tourism industry has developed decision support systems and the most important applications are: (1) systems supporting marketing decisions in national tourism organizations (Mazanec, 1986; Rita, 1993), (2) travel counselling systems for shipping clerks (e.g. Hruschka & Mazanec, 1990), (3) systems supporting regional planning regarding the optimal selection of locations in which to invest (Calantone & di Benedetto, 1991; Walker et al., 1999), (4) systems providing tourism portfolio analyses (Mazanec, 1994, 1998; Wöber, 1998), (5) simulation tools for forecasting travel behavior in certain regions (Middelkoop, 2001). In Austria in 1982, the Austrian Society of Applied Research in Tourism (ASART) started a project aiming at the development of a marketing information system for the national tourism organization in Austria (Austrian National Tourist Office). The first version of the tourism marketing information system (TourMIS) consisted of a database installed in a host system of the Scientific Computer Center Vienna and an optimization programme for the advertising budget of the Austrian National Tourist Office (Mazanec, 1986). Though the programmes were adapted in 1991 in favor of PC-software, and hence became accessible for a greater number of people (mainly employees of tourism organizations in the federal provinces), the area-wide information supply for top managers in the tourism industry did not begin until 1999 when the internet version (www.tourmis.wu-wien.ac.at) was introduced.

3. Tourism marketing information system

The major aim of TourMIS is an optimal information supply and decision support for the tourism industry. The first step is to provide on-line tourism survey data, as well as evaluation programmes to transform data into precious management information. TourMIS predominantly comprises:

1. a *database* containing tourism market research data (declarative knowledge),
2. various program modules (*method-base*, procedural knowledge) converting acknowledged methods/models into simple surfaces, and
3. various administrative programmes which assist the maintenance of the database and track and control the information search behavior of users.

The internet supports the transport and presentation of animated and unanimated pictures, sound and video recordings and text and numerical data and is

244   *K.W. Wöber / Tourism Management 24 (2003) 241–255*

expandable. A high-performance SQL-database and a functionally designed user interface for TourMIS based on hypertext and Perl (Practical Extraction and Reporting Language) permits the development of interactive applications. The programme modules contained in the method-base are developed according to the specific requirements of tourism managers. The internet offers a number of advantages against the old PC-solution. Since changes in the database have immediate worldwide effect the speed of information transmission can be reduced to the availability of the information source. For example, TourMIS makes the monthly projections of Statistics Austria available within only a few seconds to all regional managers of the Austrian National Tourist Office regardless of whether they are located in New York, Sydney, Tokyo or Madrid. Anybody provided with access to the internet and entitled to use TourMIS may access data and information, make calculations or simulations send or receive data—without tiresome postal procedures, danger of loss, delays and costs. All these advantages have led to a significant expansion in the number of users.

3.1. Conditions for the use of the system

In the beginning TourMIS was provided with strict access control and used to be only accessible to certain users. In this respect the application did differ from traditional internet offers. However, the present concept is also not an *Intranet*. Unlike the Intranet which supports internal information management systems TourMIS is not owned by a certain organization but is open to all authorized tourism organizations, societies, tourism consultants, companies, tourism training centers, pressure groups, etc. in Austria and abroad. By covering the maintenance costs, a consortium of 12 of the most important initiators of market research projects in Austria (Austrian National Tourist Office, nine provincial tourism organizations, the two special interest associations for Hotel Trade and Restaurant Trade of the Federal Chamber of Commerce, Federal Ministry for Economic Affairs and Labour Tourism and Recreational Commerce Section) guarantee the continuous updating of the comprehensive database. Since 2000 this initiative has provided the Austrian tourism industry with free access to overall data and functions (with some exceptions) of TourMIS. The necessary hardware resources are situated at the Institute for Tourism and Leisure Studies at the University of Economics and Business Administration in Vienna where a major part of the necessary maintenance work is carried out.

3.2. The TourMIS database

In the beginning TourMIS contained data that was strongly influenced by the internal interests of its commissioner, the Austrian National Tourist Office. In this respect international tourism statistical data, empirical tourism studies and economic indicators for the most important markets of origin for the Austrian tourism industry have been collected in TourMIS. The PC-version, developed in the early 1990s, contained more than 10,000 time series. The periodicity of information was generally based on annual data, however the most significant time series have also been recorded for periods of less than a year.

Over the years the database has continually expanded. Due to the increasing importance of overseas markets further information has been required. Unequal needs of provincial tourism organizations led to additional statistics regarding the federal provinces and Vienna, being city and federal province at the same time, acquired an exceptional position. Furthermore data on the Austrian and international city tourism has been added. This information was collected at the branch offices of the Austrian National Tourist Office, transmitted by fax and data was entered manually into the marketing information system in order to be available to users. Later based on international co-operation (European Cities' Tourism, European Travel Commission), the first on-line maintenance agreements with local tourism organizations were initiated. The most important available data sources of TourMIS are indicated in Tables 1 and 2. Besides the basic information search functions the method-base has also been continually upgraded. In this respect the system more and more meets the requirements of an efficient decision support tool. In the next paragraphs the most important data sources and the facilities for analysis and reporting are discussed.

3.2.1. National tourism statistics Austria

One of the first data sources which was installed in TourMIS was the official tourism statistics in Austria. Data generated from the registration with accommodation suppliers is one of the fundamental supports of the official inbound tourism statistics in Austria. Accommodation statistics are divided into two different kinds of survey: the accommodation for inbound travel and the accommodation capacity (Statistik Austria, 2001). The data on arrivals and overnights are surveyed for 50 generating countries related to 13 different accommodation types and 1600 municipalities (= report communities) on a monthly basis. Thus the official travel survey offers 25 million data points per annum which can be transformed into precious information for tourism managers. From the data material important information on tourism development, trends in markets of origin and accommodation types, evaluation of the competing situation can be derived. For example, for each of the 1600 municipalities the database allows the user to regularly monitor the development of the

K. W. Wöber / Tourism Management 24 (2003) 241–255   245

Table 1
Data sources in TourMIS

Source	Feature	Evaluation	Period	Update	Data format
Statistik Austria	Bednights, arrivals, capacity (suppliers and beds)	50 countries of origin (markets), 13 types of accommodation—for Austria and her 9 provinces	Since 1960	Monthly	Secondary data in time series format
Austrian Guest Survey	250 variables incl. intention to revisit, guest satisfaction, type of travel, means of transport, duration of stay, travel motive, expenses, selection of accommodation, activities, net income of the household, profession, education, etc.	16 countries of origin (markets)—for Austria and her 9 provinces	Since 1991	Each third year	Primary data
ETC (European Travel Commission)	Bednights, arrivals, capacities (beds)	21 countries of origin (markets)—for 33 destinations (countries) in Europe	Since 1990	Annually	Secondary data in time series format
ECT (European Cities' Tourism)	Bednights, arrivals, capacities (beds)	21 countries of origin (markets)—for 80 European cities	Since 1983	Annually	Secondary data in time series format
Number of visitations in Austrian attractions (Austrian National Tourist Office)	Number of visits for 240 Austrian attractions	Federal provinces of Austria	Since 1998	Annually	Secondary data in time series format
Austrian Hotel and Restaurant Panel	60 variables incl. net product, fixed and working assets equity and debt capital, cash flow, profitability figures, etc.	Location, size, category and type of business.	Since 1982	Annually	Primary data

Table 2
Automatic selection of analyzing methods

Measurement	Measurement		
	Not specified	Nominal	Metric
Metric	Descriptive statistics	Mean value comparison	
Nominal	Frequency	Cross tabulation	Mean value comparison
Nominal multiple response question	Multiple response-frequency	Multiple response-cross tabulation	

average duration of stay, the seasonality, market shares, guest-mix structure, and, in connection with the capacity statistics, the occupancy rate.

TourMIS presently offers official tourism statistics only at the provincial basis which nevertheless requires maintenance work of 11,700 data sets per month. The necessary data transfer from the host system of Statistik Austria (ISIS) to TourMIS takes place automatically each time after the arrival of new data segments and in accordance with various maintenance routines.

The information supply of TourMIS users takes place by means of predefined tables and reports created for the user in real time operations. Table formats conform to the data material. The design of a single table or a single report is of vital importance. The content and design of tables or reports plays an important role in the user's perception of the system's usefulness and usability (Wöber & Gretzel, 2000). Only if the information supply meets the users' needs will the system achieve its aim of providing a high-performance usage of market data and improve the information supply in tourism management.

Therefore, all available TourMIS tables and reports are created in close collaboration with the tourism industry. The query results are presented in the form of tables, texts and graphics or in a data format offering

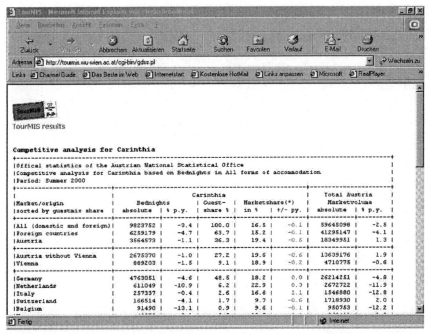

Fig. 1. Competitive analysis for Austrian regions.

the chance for further processing with another standard software product (e.g. spreadsheet programmes). The major advantages of TourMIS compared to the official database supply offered by Statistik Austria are:

- no particular database knowledge is required by the user,
- the data transformations and calculations implemented in the method-base of TourMIS allow for adequate problem reporting, and
- the user interface refers to a familiar technical terminology.

Especially for the requirements of the managers in the provincial tourism organizations TourMIS offers tables with more detailed analyses. Fig. 1 presents an example for competitive analyses in TourMIS for destination management organizations. The table compares the seasonal results of one federal province (Carinthia) with the results of all other federal provinces in Austria. The table shows all bednights broken down into different markets of origin arranged in accordance with their significance and the changes against the previous year. The comparison with the developments in other (competitive) destinations permits an evaluation of the

market share development in Carinthia. The analysis in Fig. 1 indicates for example that Carinthia could defend its position regarding the three most important markets (Germany, Netherlands, Italy), shown in the increase of market shares, despite the fact that Carinthia experienced a severe loss in bednights. On the other hand, an apparent success regarding the increased demand of American guests (+7.7%) has to be put into perspective since the other federal provinces outperformed Carinthia in this segment. Due to the comparative analysis and a simple and informative presentation of the statistics (using sorting features and different colors to distinguish between market share gains (green) and losses (red)) the data material is upgraded. The analysis presented in Fig. 1 may be used for historical or current data, for each Austrian province, based either on arrivals or bednights for each of the 13 different accommodation types. Therefore there are at the end of a season 270 new tables available for interpretation.

The opportunities for implementing tools which use official tourism statistics for benchmarking analyses, the implementation of early warning systems and forecasting tourism trends is obvious. Due to the refinancing interests of data collection authorities and the lack of

K.W. Wöber / Tourism Management 24 (2003) 241–255   247

financial resources in the tourism industry, however, the data analysis for smaller tourism regions or report communities has been prevented in the past. This factor must be regretted since it can be assumed that the evaluation of key success factors in tourism marketing will significantly improve when they are measured in smaller regional units. Also tourism managers, especially those operating on a regional level, usually have only very little influence in the organization of nation-wide surveys. Therefore, many of the statistical series are based on administrative regions that are not always congruent with actual regional use and by tourists and subsequent flows.

3.2.2. Number of visitations in Austrian attractions

The collection of statistical data on leisure-time activities and especially the measurement of visitor arrivals in attractions are a rather complex project. It is rarely executed internationally on a systematic or continuous basis. The major problems lie in the delimitation of the study object and the methods of measurement. Since the early 1990s, the Austrian National Tourist Office has collected and distributed information on the visitation numbers in Austrian attractions. In close collaboration with the nine provin-

cial tourism organizations a list of 240 Austrian attractions is checked for completeness and up-dated on an annual basis.

Since 2001 this maintenance procedure is carried out on-line in TourMIS. Here the market research specialists at the respective provincial tourism organizations enter their information into the system. Due to the newness of the database the reporting facilities are still very limited. The present tables either provide simple time series for a single attraction or list all attractions for one or more federal province(s) arranged according to frequency of visits. (see Fig. 2).

3.2.3. Austrian guest survey

Since 1988 alternating every third year, a comprehensive visitor survey in Austria has been carried out. The Austrian Guest Survey is one of the most important sources of information in tourism market research. It provides vital information on guest profiles, customer satisfaction, information and booking behavior, type of travel, destination, means of transport, accommodation, activities, visitor expenditures and other current topics. The Austrian Guest Survey is financed and coordinated by a consortium of authorities responsible for tourism promotion in Austria (Austrian National Tourist Office

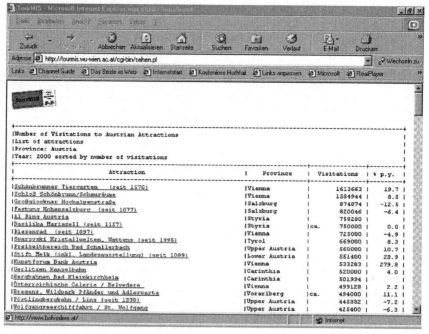

Fig. 2. Number of visitations in Austrian attractions.

and nine provincial tourism organizations), the Chamber of Commerce and the Federal Ministry for Economic Affairs and Labour (Tourism and Recreational Commerce Section).

Since the Austrian Guest Survey is a primary study it presents some features which complicate the information diffusion in TourMIS compared to the above-mentioned secondary data sources. The main reasons for these additional difficulties are:

(1) the much wider scope of the study,
(2) the required data analyses are more demanding, and
(3) interpretation possibilities are limited by the sample size and characteristics.

The Austrian Guest Survey has more than 200 features which are partially modified for each survey. Considering the scope of the study and that only descriptive evaluation is possible the Austrian Guest Survey offers more than 1 million findings per survey. Traditional forms of report (market research report, press releases, etc.) cover just a small part of the real investigation and evaluation potential. Thus important questions managers would raise remain unanswered although theoretically the answers exist.

Data of primary analyses are available unprocessed (disaggregated data format). Regarding the Austrian Guest Survey there are 10,000 interviews per survey, all of the features being available in quantitative form. However, information processing requires the application of analytical methods ranging from calculating simple mean values to complicated data mining procedures. The necessary methodological knowledge has to be obtained from statistics experts who create costs which, in most cases, cannot be covered by the tourism industry. Therefore, due to a lack of know-how or lacking financial support, many questions managers raise remain unanswered although data actually would be available.

Contrary to a census, as found in official statistics, sample surveys do not integrate all elements of the whole picture into the study. The major aim in statistics is to draw reliable conclusions regarding to the totality from a limited number of elements. The previously mentioned evaluation procedures take more effort and interpretation depends on the features of the sample (sample size and sampling technique).

To know whether a study result may be regarded reliable requires expert know-how. On the other hand, sometimes, statisticians have not enough technical knowledge to evaluate the fault tolerance for certain problems in the tourism industry. Thus information processing by means of electronic media becomes very interesting for primary surveys. The challenge is to combine expert know-how from two different fields: statistics and tourism. The aim is to create an arena for

practitioners allowing them to access all possible evaluations concerning a data item, without considering the necessary procedures of analysis (Fig. 3). TourMIS offers help in the selection of simple, descriptive evaluation methods. Depending on the level of measurement of the features selected by the user the appropriate evaluation method is applied (see Table 2).

In addition the user may select only a certain part of the overall data set for evaluation (e.g. data of a certain province or market). In order to prevent interpretation errors due to unreliability of results, those values based on a small sample are only indicated after informing the user about the problem.

The analysis takes place in real time (Fig. 4). TourMIS provides the facilities to evaluate more than one survey, at the same time offering two alternatives: longitudinal and cross section analyses. The first application informs the tourism manager about changes in the guest behavior over a specified period of time. Query support is provided by offering only variables surveyed unmodified over the overall selected period of time (i.e. the standard questionnaire programme). The latter application increases the sample size (for 4 surveys more than 45,000 interviews) which makes answers to detailed questions possible (assuming a particular time invariance, of course). This function permits for example reliable results about the share of side expenses of Italian guests in the federal province of Salzburg during a particular season.

3.2.4. Comparison of hotel and restaurant groups

The database supports regional planners and tourism managers in their decisions as well as managers in the hospitality industry. The results of the past 10 years of a project which has been executed by the ASART and commissioned by the Austrian Hotel and Restaurant Association situated within the Austrian Federal Chamber of Commerce are presented in TourMIS. In this project operating data and annual financial statements for hotels and restaurants in Austria are compared on an annual basis. Information collected directly from the businesses with a high level of itemization is supplemented with comprehensive, compressed data stored at cooperative industry related organizations such as the Wirtschaftsförderungsinstitut der Austrian Federal Economic Chamber- und Tourismusbank and BÜRGES Förderungsbank of the Austrian Federal Ministry of Economic Affair and Labour (Wöber, 2001). In connection with the design and evaluation of continually repeated surveys a number of new approaches for the diagnosis and comparison of industry groups are developed. TourMIS presently provides the following applications:

• Industry information for more than 1300 hotels and restaurants per year since 1991.

K.W. Wöber / Tourism Management 24 (2003) 241–255   249

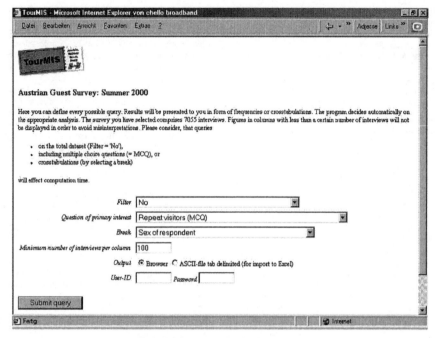

Fig. 3. Defining a query—Austrian Guest Survey.

- Various functions supporting key ratio analyses in the hotel and restaurant industry.
- The chance for hotel and restaurant managers to participate on-line in the most significant hotel and restaurant panel survey in Austria.

Information about more than 50 different key ratios is provided in the form of arithmetic mean and median values for 30 distinguished industry groups (Fig. 5). Within the industry groups additional evaluations for businesses of excellent profitability (best practice enterprises) are available.

For the hotel and restaurant panel database TourMIS users are provided with the following query and analyzing facilities:

- Evaluation of a key ratio for all industry groups referring to a certain year.
- Comparison of all key ratios for a particular industry group.
- Development of a key ratio uncovering the main industry developments.
- Benchmarking analysis for a particular hotel or restaurant (only provided when managers are actively participating in the study).

The quality of information based on the results of the survey is strongly influenced by the number of participating businesses. Due to the chance for interaction in the internet the first results may be obtained straight after entering business data. In this context the problem of how to prevent participants from entering incorrect data occurs. TourMIS offers a number of plausibility controls during data entry and records data in a second, temporary database. At regular intervals experts determine which records are qualified to be stored in the general database.

3.2.5. International tourism statistics

Several international umbrella organizations have decided to collect tourism statistics from various countries and to observe the economic development of tourism (WTO, WTTC, OECD, Eurostat). The availability of this data is unfortunately restricted and publications are due to complicated data collection procedures, obsolete and access to data is relatively expensive. The European Travel Commission (ETC[1]), the umbrella organization of national tourism organizations,

---
[1] see http://www.etc-europe-travel.org/.

250

K.W. Wöber / Tourism Management 24 (2003) 241–255

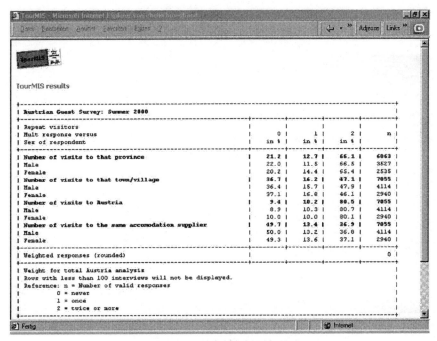

Fig. 4. Query Result –Austrian Guest Survey.

and European Cities Tourism (ECT[2]), the umbrella organization of European city tourism organizations, have set themselves the target of representing the interests of tourism practitioners. Both organizations have taken advantage of TourMIS for some years now in order to collect official statistics of their members (currently 33 countries and more than 80 cities in Europe). Once a year market research experts collect bednight and arrival data of national and cities' tourism organizations broken down into the major markets of origin as well as into the number of accommodation suppliers and beds in their region.

Due to differing definitions and survey methods applied by the various countries and cities the collected data material is not readily available or comparable (Wöber, 2000). Official statistics are only of limited use for the calculation of market volumes and market shares. Therefore comparative analyses have to be executed based on observations of relative changes but not on the basis of absolute values (Fig. 6).

As with the decision 90/665/EEC of December 1990 of the European Council a milestone has been

laid down regarding the development of a community methodological framework of the compilation of Community tourism statistics.[3] Since 1997 the development of an information system for tourism statistics has been in progress.[4] Unfortunately free access to the information system implemented by EUROSTAT is restricted to data suppliers and organization of the European Union. But experience with TourMIS shows that worthwhile discussions on diverse survey methods, definitions and harmonizing methods depend on the number of participants. Participation is necessary in order to gain acceptance for new directives and changes.

---

[2] see http://www.europeancitiestourism.com/.

[3] Council of the European Union (editor), Council Directive 95/97/EEC of 23 November 1995 on the collection of statistical information in the field of tourism, Official Journal nr. L291 of 6 December 1995, p. 1.
[4] Commission of the European Communities (editor) Report to the Council, the European Parliament, the Economic and Social Committee and the Committee of Regions on the Application of the Directive of the Council 95/97/EEC on the compilation of statistical data in the field of tourism, 17 January 2001, p. 3.

K.W. Wöber / Tourism Management 24 (2003) 241–255

251

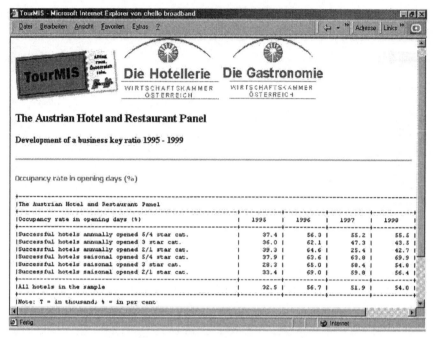

Fig. 5. Development of business key ratios in hotels and restaurants in Austria.

4. Analysis of the user behavior of TourMIS

How do we know that we have successfully implemented a system? Researchers have not really agreed on an indicator for successful implementation (Eierman, Friedman, & Adams, 1995). One appealing approach is a cost–benefit study. In this evaluation, one totals the costs of developing a system and compares them with the benefits resulting form the system. In theory, this sounds like a good indicator of success, but in practice it is difficult to provide meaningful estimates. Obtaining the cost side of the ratio is not too much of a problem if adequate records are kept during the development of the system. However, an evaluation of the benefits of a computer-based information system is difficult. How can the value of improved information processing be measured? With transactions processing and some operational control systems, it is usually possible to show tangible savings. For example, many transactions systems have resulted in increased productivity in processing paperwork without a proportional increase in cost. Operational control systems, such as those used to control inventories in large hotels and restaurants,

may reduce inventory balances, saving storage and investment costs while maintaining existing service levels.

For systems that aid a decision-maker, it is much more difficult to estimate the benefits. For a marketing information system, like TourMIS, use of the system is voluntary. A manager or other user receives a report but does not have to use the information on it or even read the report. In particular systems that provide on-line retrieval of information from a database can be classified as voluntary since the use of such a system is frequently at the discretion of the user. For this type of system where use is voluntary, it is generally accepted that high levels of use is a sign of successful implementation (Davis, 1989; Venkatesh & Davis, 2000). In this case the economic or personal success of its users is indirectly measured by the frequency of usage. Several authors have shown that the frequency of usage is determined by the perceived usefulness (textual component) and the ease of use (technical component) (Davis, 1989, Wöber & Gretzel, 2000).

The acceptance of TourMIS can be determined by means of constantly updated and on-line available

252   *K.W. Wöber / Tourism Management 24 (2003) 241–255*

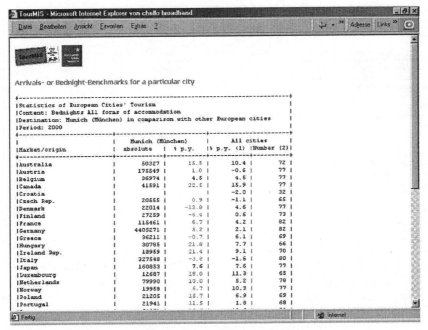

Fig. 6. Destination benchmarking—example for Munich.

access statistics. Contrary to other internet applications the accesses to websites is not counted but the number of virtually answered queries is. Results of the TourMIS statistics are therefore not influenced by website characteristics (number of graphics or distortions due to the application of window techniques), but do represent the "genuine user acceptance". In addition, the comprehensive protocol system permits the analysis of queries broken down into various user groups, information sources and the type of query (e.g. textual options for the compilation of tables and reports, data queries, etc.).

The community of TourMIS users has continually developed. In 1998, there were only 50 registered users at the Austrian National Tourist Office and at the end of 2001 more than 1000 registered TourMIS users have been counted. The distribution of user groups indicates that TourMIS is not only favored by tourism managers (44.6%), but also by employees, students and pupils of education and research institutes (31.6% of all queries) and other non tourism professionals or private persons (23.8%). The distribution of various user groups is presented in Table 3.

The right-hand column of Table 3 shows the average number of queries per user in 2001 and there-

fore indicates the frequency of use for a specific TourMIS user group. The employees of provincial tourism organizations use TourMIS most (92 queries per user) due to the comprehensive data material available on the federal provinces. The students, as the largest user group, show a relatively low number due to only temporal interest (for a seminar paper or a diploma thesis they need access to data material only once). The number of accommodation providers and F&B managers using the system is, considering the number of existing businesses, very low. A reason for this is probably that the most interesting information source for this user group (the Austrian hotel and restaurant panel database) is a relatively new data set that is simply not known by the managers. Overall, 34.538 queries have been processed in 2001, signifying an increase of 35.5% in comparison to the previous year (25,492 queries). Table 4 presents the significance of the various data sources for information supply.

About half of all queries are made regarding the official tourism statistics in Austria. The industry appears to be very interested in the development of the major markets of origin and accommodation types in the federal provinces (on average approx. 50 queries per

K.W. Wöber / Tourism Management 24 (2003) 241–255   253

Table 3
Origin of TourMIS users

User groups	Queries				
	Users in (%)[a]	2000	2001	2001 in (%)	Per user[a]
National tourism organizations	11.3	4844	4957	14.4	44
Branch offices of national tourism organizations	5.7	3541	2970	8.6	52
Provincial tourism organizations	4.5	3072	4132	12.0	92
City tourism organizations	6.1	1125	1488	4.3	24
Regional tourism organizations	2.8	78	204	0.6	7
Accommodation suppliers	4.9	392	679	2.0	14
Restaurants	1.9	177	348	1.0	18
Tour operators	1.9	180	304	0.9	16
Travel agencies	1.8	24	327	0.9	18
Common carriers	0.4	193	67	0.2	17
Culture, sport and leisure suppliers	1.0	90	197	0.6	20
Other tourism suppliers	2.3	161	442	1.3	19
Universities, polytechnics	9.0	1850	4790	13.9	53
Other educational institutions	2.2	105	220	0.6	10
Students	20.4	3027	5429	15.7	27
Management or tax consultants	6.9	644	2669	7.7	39
Public institutions, pressure groups	2.9	625	1110	3.2	38
Other organizations/businesses	8.6	4938	3064	8.9	36
Private persons	5.4	426	1141	3.3	21
Total	100.0	25,492	34,538	100.0	35

[a] Per December 31, 2001.

Table 4
Usage of TourMIS sources (sorted by number of queries in 2001)

Sources	2000	In (%)	2001	In (%)	00–01 in (%)
Statistik Austria monthly data	6510	25.5	6919	20.0	6.3
ECT	4568	17.9	6449	18.7	41.2
ETC	3773	14.8	6452	18.7	71.0
Statistik Austria seasonal data	3120	12.2	5105	14.8	63.6
Statistik Austria annual data	3398	13.3	4495	13.0	32.3
Austrian Guest Survey	2185	8.6	2240	6.5	2.5
Austrian Hotel and Restaurant Panel	1938	7.6	2094	6.1	8.0
Number of visitors[a]			784	2.3	
Total	25,492	100.0	34,538	100.0	35.5

[a] New source in 2001.

day). Regarding the official statistics for Austria most queries are made in connection with information concerning monthly statistics (20% of all queries). The international data sources ECT and ETC gained 18.7%, respectively and they rank behind the official Austrian statistics. The significant increase of queries regarding these two international data sources as well as the tendency towards English queries, however, indicate a growing international interest in TourMIS.

The assessment of demand of information certainly needs a more detailed investigation than simply monitoring the current use of market research resources. However, in TourMIS "demand of information" not only refers to the principal (statistical) sources, but also

to the sort of data transformations (analysis) and formats of automatically generated reports available to the users. The functional characteristics and the design of the system have always been developed in close collaboration with the affected managers. For instance, concerning the development of the decision support tools part of the international data sources in the system, the developers have met more than 20 times in form of working group meetings and seminars with representatives (CEOs and research directors) of European Cities Tourism and the European Travel Commission. The involvement of the managers in the design and operation of the information system resulted in favorable user attitudes and perceptions of the information system and led to higher levels of use. In the beginning only a few members were able and willing to actively contribute to this project by entering their data on a regular basis. Today, more than 100 managers working in different tourism destination marketing organizations, based in more than 30 different European countries, and speaking more than 15 different languages, are obviously convinced by the significance of the project and the value of the system as they regularly and voluntarily enter their data into the system.

5. Conclusions

Generally speaking tourism managers benefit from access to the internet in two ways: the internet provides the opportunity to communicate and serves as a platform for new distribution channels. The present article does not deal with new distribution channels and new booking systems in the tourism industry. This undoubtedly important topic has been discussed in an number of publications and symposia (Sheldon, 1997; Werthner & Klein, 1999). The present article introduced TourMIS, an on-line accessible decision support tool for tourism and hospitality management which has been successfully used by more than 1000 users for 3 years. According to Ritchie and Ritchie for the development of an industry supported destination marketing information system, information must be both generally accessible and widely advertised so that managers are aware of the benefits it offers (Ritchie & Ritchie, 2002, p. 451). In lieu of a more preferable cost–benefit analysis, the success of TourMIS was analyzed by studying actual system use observed from various log files generated by the system. The merits of this form of evaluation lie in the objectivity of the findings, the cost-effective procedure, and the comparability of the estimates when the analysis are performed on a regular basis.

The major reason for the poor application of management science models and methodologies in tourism management is the insufficient education of practitioners and the inadequacy of problem solving features of standard software solutions. The development of simple, affordable (shareware) programs, downloadable for every tourism manager, is the first step into a new era of dialogue between research and practice. Within a short time, for internal diagnosis, forecasts and simulations on the net there will be high-performance computer languages available which are now being developed by major international software producers.

Technological progress will also offer benefits for the electronic transmission of tourism market research data. Interdisciplinary research projects will be challenged with tourism research, research in statistics and commercial information technology. For example there are still a number of problems to be solved in order to be able to jointly use ecoscopic and demoscopic tourism data within a marketing information system. These combination options require a constant standardization of information sources as well as new approaches towards the methodological processing of data gained from various studies (Froeschl, 1997).

Another vital research initiative will be the development of information systems about themselves? Optimizing the knowledge presentation of "service quality in information services" has been neglected in the past. By applying and accepting decision support systems the significance of this field of research will increase. In this respect, another open research question refers to the role of user tracking data commonly generated from system protocols, and how this information can effectively be used. Thus data on the user behavior offers not only information on necessary improvements in the data processing of tourism market research results (Wöber & Gretzel, 2000), but also on the future focus of tourism market research.

The sudden explosion of data and the growing need for information challenges basic research as far as data reduction and decision support methods are concerned. Therefore existing concepts for qualitative forecasts and market reaction models and their calibration options in a marketing information system have to be reconsidered. In this respect projects which aim at a systematic and regular compilation of experiences experts made with regard to various technical subjects (e.g. short-term development of singular markets of origin) are considered to be promising. It is their aim to provide an improved evaluation of future market developments and eventually to integrate the findings into the strategic planning of national and regional tourism organizations and businesses.

Another necessary development regards already existing data collections and the processing of the European cities' statistics. In this respect this author has observed many shortcomings relating to the international comparability of the data. The improved communication possibilities provided by the new medium stimulates critical discussions and behavioral learning among all participants. Within European Cities Tourism, among other things, new initiatives to evaluate one city's major competitors have been released due to the managers' increased awareness of the importance of this problem.

The trend towards globalization in research, where the internet plays a vital role, refers also to tourism research. To those critics who refer to the internet as uncontrolled growing, complicated and in its applications too playful, supporters used to point out that one

K.W. Wöber / Tourism Management 24 (2003) 241–255   255

day smart and profitable applications would be found. That is where we stand now. The new areas of responsibility regional and national tourism managers are confronted with today, not only suggest short-comings in education but also promise new opportunities for the next manager generations to acquire status.

References

Albert, H. (1967). *Marktsoziologie und entscheidungslogik.* Berlin: Neuwied am Rhein.

Calantone, R. J., & Benedetto di, C. A. (1991). Knowledge acquisition modeling in tourism. *Annals of Tourism Research, 18*(2), 202–212.

Davis, F. D. (1989). Perceived usefulness, perceived ease of use, and user acceptance of information technology. *MIS Quarterly, 13*, 318–340.

Eierman, M. A., Friedman, F., & Adams, C. (1995). DSS theory: A model of constructs and relationships. *Decision Support Systems, 14*, 1–26.

Froeschl, K. A. (1997). *Metadata management in statistical information processing.* Wien, New York: Springer.

Hebestreit, D. (1992). *Touristik Marketing. Grundlagen, Ziele, Basis-Informationen, Instrumentarien, Strategien, Organisation und Planung des Marketing von Reiseveranstaltern. Ein Handbuch für Praktiker.* Berlin: Berlin Verlag.

Hruschka, H., & Mazanec, J. A. (1990). Computer-assisted travel counseling. *Annals of Tourism Research, 7*(2), 208–227.

Little, J. D. C. (1970). Models and managers. The concept of a decision calculus. *Management Science, 16*(8), 466–485.

Mazanec, J. A. (1986). A decision support system for optimizing advertising policy of a national tourist office. Model outline and case study. *International Journal of Research in Marketing, 3*, 63–77.

Mazanec, J. A. (1994). International tourism marketing—adapting the growth share matrix. In J. Montana (Ed.), *Marketing in Europe, case studies* (pp. 184–203). London: Sage.

Mazanec, J. A. (1998). International tourism marketing: A multi-factor portfolio model. In H. Hartvig-Larsen (Ed.), *Cases in marketing* (pp. 115–141). London: Sage.

Middelkoop, M. van (2001). *Merlin: A Decision Support System for Outdoor Leisure Planning. Development and Test of a Rule-based Microsimulation Model for the Evaluation of Alternative Scenarios and Planning Options.* Ph.D. thesis, Technical University Eindhoven, Netherlands.

Phillips, P. A., & Moutinho, L. (1998). *Strategic planning systems in hospitality and tourism.* Wallingford: CABI.

Rita, P. (1993). *A knowledge-based system for promotion budget allocation by National Tourism Organizations.* Doctoral thesis, College of Cardiff, University of Wales.

Ritchie, R. J. B, & Ritchie, J. R. B. (2002). A framework for an industry supported destination marketing information system. *Tourism Management, 23*, 439–454.

Seitz, E., & Meyer, W. (1995). *Tourismusmarktforschung.* München: Vahlen.

Sheldon, P. (1997). *Tourism information technology.* Wallingford: CABI.

Statistik Austria (2001). *Tourismus in Österreich.* Wien: Statistik Austria.

Venkatesh, V., & Davis, F. D. (2000). A theoretical extension of the technology acceptance model: Four longitudinal field studies. *Management Science, 46*, 186–204.

Walker, P. A., Greiner, R., McDonald, D., & Lyne, V. (1999). The tourism futures simulator: A systems thinking approach. *Environmental Modelling & Software, 14*, 59–67.

Werthner, H., & Klein, S. (1999). *Information technology and tourism—a challenging relationship.* Wien, New York: Springer.

Wierenga, B., & van Bruggen, G. (2000). *Marketing management support systems. Principles, tools and implementation.* Boston: Kluwer.

Wöber, K. W. (1998). TourMIS: An adaptive distributed marketing information system for strategic decision support in national, regional, or city tourist offices. *Pacific Tourism Review, 2*(3/4), 273–286.

Wöber, K. W. (2000). Standardizing European city tourism statistics. *Annals of Tourism Research, 27*(1), 51–68.

Wöber, K. W. (2001). *Betriebskennzahlen im österreichischen gastgewerbe.* Bilanzjahr 1999. Wien: Österreichischer Wirtschaftsverlag.

Wöber, K. W., & Gretzel, U. (2000). Tourism managers' adoption of marketing decision support systems. *Journal of Travel Research, 39*(2), 172–181.

Part IV
Pricing

[21]

An executive summary for managers and executive readers can be found at the end of this article

Consumer evaluations of price discounts in foreign currencies

Michael A. Callow
Assistant Professor of Marketing, Department of Business Administration, Morgan State University, Baltimore, Maryland, USA

Dawn B. Lerman
Assistant Professor of Marketing, Graduate School of Business, Fordham University, New York, NY, USA

Keywords *Pricing, Consumer behaviour, Marketing strategy, Italy, United States of America*

Abstract *Today's consumers are becoming increasingly exposed to foreign markets through travel or via the Internet. They are facing new challenges in these less familiar shopping environments. One such challenge is the comparison of prices in a foreign currency. This issue is addressed by examining how consumers from different countries evaluate such price discounts. Hypotheses are developed regarding the impact of currency denomination familiarity on consumers' attitudinal response to changes in prices. The results of an experimental study conducted in Italy and the USA support the proposition that consumers who are more familiar with the foreign currency's denomination will be more influenced by price differentials than those consumers who are less familiar with the foreign currency's denomination. The implications of the findings for pricing strategies in regional trade zones, international tourism, and global e-marketing are discussed.*

Introduction

Until recently, researchers have treated international pricing primarily as an economic issue. Prior research in this topic has focused on four main areas (Stottinger, 2001):

(1) microeconomic issues (e.g. price elasticities of demand);

(2) export pricing issues (e.g. price escalation);

(3) internal pricing issues (e.g. transfer pricing); and

(4) consumer-oriented issues (e.g. consumer reference prices).

International markets

There may be a tendency to assume that culture is not a major determinant of pricing in international markets. More recently, however, several researchers have started to question this assumption and to explore the role that culture plays in consumer responses to price. Studies in this area have focused on a variety of issues, including cultural comparisons in price sensitivity (Ackerman and Tellis, 2001; Li and Gallup, 1995), value consciousness (Maxwell, 2001), price haggling (Fang, 1999; Kramer and Herbig, 1993), face-saving considerations (Zhou and Nakamoto, 2001), gift giving (Ahuvia and Wong, 1998; McGowan and Sternquist, 1998), price-quality signals (Agarwal and Teas, 2001), the visual appeal of numbers (Suri *et al.*, 2001), and consumers' attribution for higher than expected prices (Maxwell, 1999). These studies indicate significant differences by which consumers from different cultures evaluate and respond to prices, and suggest that further research into cross-cultural pricing issues is needed.

The Emerald Research Register for this journal is available at
http://www.emeraldinsight.com/researchregister
The current issue and full text archive of this journal is available at
http://www.emeraldinsight.com/1061-0421.htm

The purpose of this research is to examine the impact of unfamiliar currencies on the consumer's attitudinal response towards price reductions. More specifically, it looks at how consumers from two countries (the USA and Italy) are influenced by price discounts in foreign currencies. We argue that consumers have different reference points based on their pricing experiences and that these reference points will affect their evaluations when comparing prices in foreign currencies. This issue is of growing importance to both academics and practitioners, given the recent launch of the euro in much of the European Union and the continued rise in global tourism and international e-commerce. As such, this paper develops a conceptual framework for the effect of currency unfamiliarity on the consumer's attitudinal reaction towards price discounts and reports on an experimental study conducted in the USA and Italy.

Conceptual framework

Research

The aim of this research is to determine whether there is a significant difference between consumers from countries with high denomination currencies (HDCs) and low denomination currencies (LDCs) when they compare prices in a foreign currency. In particular, we expect that any change in evaluations resulting from a price reduction is influenced by the degree of congruency between the consumer's and the foreign country's currency denomination. Denomination refers to the quantity of currency units that would be needed to provide an equivalent value relative to other currency units. In HDCs (e.g. the Turkish lire), consumers are accustomed to inexpensive goods priced in the thousands or millions of units. In LDCs (e.g. the US dollar), everyday inexpensive items are generally priced in single-digit or double-digit numbers. An underlying assumption to be tested in this study is that consumers will respond in different degrees to price reductions when the pricing information is given in either a high or a low currency denomination. In other words, how will a UK consumer shopping for a particular brand react to a price comparison of $5 in the USA compared with an approximately equivalent price comparison of ¥595 in Japan?

Value of goods and services

A national currency constitutes part of the culture's symbolic system that is used in the marketplace to communicate the value of goods and services (Callow and Lerman, 2003). The currency's denomination, in turn, has a significant impact on how consumers evaluate prices. For instance, Raghubir and Srivastava (2002) found that consumers will either over-spend or under-spend when purchasing in foreign currencies, depending on whether the exchange rate is a multiple or a fraction of an equivalent unit in the home currency. Indeed, the information-processing model suggests that consumers are influenced not only by the price of the product at the time of choice but also by previous experiences (Monroe and Lee, 1999). According to this literature, consumers develop acceptable price ranges for products based on a subjective or psychological judgment scale that is influenced – among other things – by previous pricing experience. Consumers are therefore expected to rely on previous price discount experiences when evaluating future price discounts in their domestic currency. Thus, a US consumer would be conditioned to evaluate a $2 discount on an ink-jet cartridge based on the original price and on previous discounts, much in the same way as a South Korean consumer would be conditioned to evaluate a roughly equivalent 2,350 won discount.

Price is seen as an objective information cue used by consumers to evaluate a product offer (Jamal and Goode, 2001). Previous research suggests that consumers rely on extrinsic information cues such as price compared to intrinsic information cues when shopping around for products (cf. Rao and Monroe, 1989; Han and Terpstra, 1988). Pricing research suggests that discounting tactics tend to have a positive effect on consumer perceptions of product value (cf. Della Bitta *et al.*, 1981; Berkowitz and Walton, 1980; Suri *et al.*, 2000). Monroe (2003) proposes that pricing information may be used to infer the quality of a product as well as the monetary cost or sacrifice needed to make the purchase. Consumers engage in a trade-off between the perceptions of quality and the cost to judge the product's perceived value. Product managers therefore use price discounts as a tactic to diminish the perceived monetary sacrifice of the purchase, and avoid the pitfall of lessening the perceived quality of the product by relying on a temporary – rather than permanent – reduction in price. To our knowledge, however, there is no empirical research that has examined the effects of price discounts in currencies that are unfamiliar to the consumer.

Subjective criterion

We propose that price becomes somewhat more of a subjective criterion to consumers when it is displayed in a foreign currency whose denomination is unfamiliar. Indeed, the money illusion effect proposes that consumers do not always act rationally when dealing with economic transactions, since they are sometimes biased towards nominal monetary values (e.g. the face value of the discount) instead of real monetary values (e.g. the percentage discount) (Shafir *et al.*, 1997). Dehaene and Marques (2002) suggest that consumers are better at estimating prices in a familiar currency than in an unfamiliar currency. We therefore expect the money illusion effect to be more relevant when dealing with an unfamiliar currency denomination as opposed to one that is more familiar.

Familiarity with the currency denomination
In discussing consumer expertise, Alba and Hutchinson (1987, p. 411) make a clear distinction between expertise and familiarity. Whereas expertise relates to a person's ability to perform product-related tasks successfully, familiarity is defined as "the number of product-related experiences that have been accumulated by the consumer". For the purpose of our study, currency familiarity is the extent to which the consumer is accustomed to a particular currency denomination.

Domestic currency

Consumers are very familiar with their domestic currency and are expected to be somewhat familiar with currencies that use similar denominations. In other words, we expect consumers to react more to price discounts when the foreign currency denomination is congruent with the consumer's domestic currency denomination, and to have less of a reaction when faced with price discounts in a currency denomination that is incongruent with their own. A lack of familiarity will leave travelers having to calculate the worth of monetary reductions that are in multiples or fractions of their current currency. For example, a US consumer traveling in Europe will have a relatively easy time evaluating prices in euros, since the value of the dollar (an LDC) is currently almost at par with the euro. Americans should therefore feel comfortable evaluating price discounts in euros, since they are visually familiar with the absolute differential in monetary amounts between the original price and the reduced price. However, if traveling to an HDC country, the US consumer will be less familiar with the visually high absolute monetary discount in the foreign currency and will therefore be less certain when evaluating this type of discount. We therefore propose that congruency between the domestic and foreign currencies leads to a greater degree of attitude adjustment towards the reduced price. In terms of our study of US (LDC) and Italian (historically HDC) samples, we hypothesize the following:

H1a. Attitude change following a reduction in price will be greater among Americans when prices are displayed in low denomination currencies than in high denomination currencies.

H1b. Attitude change following a reduction in price will be greater among Italians when prices are displayed in high denomination currencies than in low denomination currencies.

Price reductions

We also expect that consumers from incongruent currency denominations will have different attitudinal responses to price reductions depending on the denomination of a third foreign currency. In other words, pricing evaluations are less likely to change among HDC consumers than LDC consumers when prices are displayed in a foreign LDC. At the same time, we would expect that LDC consumer attitudes would be less influenced than HDC consumer attitudes when evaluating price discounts in an HDC setting. Thus,

H2. Americans will have a greater attitude change following a reduction in price in a low denomination currency compared with Italians.

H3. Italians will have a greater attitude change following a reduction in price in a high denomination currency compared with Americans.

In addition, we expect that variations in the real monetary amount of the discount (i.e. $5 versus $30 discount) may also be affected by the currency denomination's perceived degree of familiarity. Consumer attitudes will be more influenced by higher discounts than lower discounts when the prices are displayed in congruent denominations. In other words, a $30 price differential will have a more significant impact on a US consumer's attitude towards a particular offer than a $5 price differential. At the same time, this would mean that consumers faced with price reductions in a less familiar denomination level are less likely to pick up on substantial versus small discounts compared with consumers who are more familiar with the denomination level. Thus,

H4a. Americans will be less influenced than Italians by the absolute amount of the discount when prices are displayed in an HDC.

H4b. Italians will be less influenced than Americans by the absolute amount of the discount when prices are displayed in an LDC.

Method

Experimental design

The above hypotheses were tested using a $2 \times 2 \times 2$ between-subjects experimental design, run in a classroom setting using student samples from the USA and Italy. The methodological design needed to: create stimuli that manipulated the currency denomination and discount amount of a price for a product in a foreign market; include subjects from a high-denomination and a low-denomination currency; measure each subject's attitudinal reaction towards the price differential; and, measure any potential covariates.

Experimental design

A nationality (USA vs Italy) × denomination (HDC vs LDC) × discount (high vs. low) design was used to test the hypotheses. The subjects were presented with the following scenario: "You are on vacation in a foreign country. This is your first visit to this country. You have decided to purchase a compact camera to take pictures during your vacation. You will be making the purchase in *dhoveps*, the local currency." A camera was chosen as the product category, since it is of general interest to the student population, it is relevant to the travel scenario, it is widely available in both the USA and Italy, and it is priced comparably in both countries. The term dhovep was selected from among non-word stimuli used in experiments by Dorfman (1994), since the letter combination was foreign to both English and Italian speakers.

The subjects were given the dhovep's exchange rate relative to their own currency. For instance, a US respondent in the HDC condition was given an exchange rate of 2,420 dhoveps to the US dollar, whereas someone in the LDC condition was given an exchange rate of 2.42 dhoveps to the dollar. For the Italians, the HDC condition was 2.42 lire to the dhovep and the LDC condition was 2,420 lire to the dhovep. Subjects were also told in the scenario at the beginning of the experiment that they did not take a calculator with them on the trip and therefore that they could not use one.

Exchange rate

After learning the exchange rate, respondents were then told that the salesperson at the store recommended the PXR-M70, since it was the most popular brand of compact camera sold in the store. The students were shown a promotional flyer that included a picture of the camera, a description of its features, and its price in dhoveps (equivalent to US$90 and 198,174 lire). This meant that for the Americans the original price was dvp. 217.80 for the congruent condition and dvp. 217,800 for the incongruent condition. The Italians were shown a price of dvp. 81,890 for the congruent condition and dvp. 81.89 for the incongruent condition. The respondents were then asked to evaluate the offer.

Once they had finished evaluating the offer, they were told that they had decided to visit another store before making a purchase decision. They were informed that the salesman at the new store recommended the same camera. The respondents were once again shown the promotional flyer, but this time at a price that was either 5 percent or 30 percent lower than the price at the original store (the subjects were not told the percentage discount: instead they were shown just the new price in dhoveps). The Americans under the congruent condition were therefore shown a new price of either 206.91 or 152.46. Those under the incongruent condition were shown a new price of either 206,910 or 152,460. The Italians under the congruent condition were shown a reduced price of 77,790 or 57,320, whereas those under the incongruent condition were shown a price of 77.79 or 57.32. The participants were then asked to evaluate this new offer.

The original questionnaire was drafted in English and then translated into Italian. The accuracy of the Italian version was verified by using a back-translation procedure (Hui and Triandis, 1985).

Selection of subjects

Undergraduate students

Undergraduate students were recruited from a US ($n = 86$, mean age = 21.4, male = 35 percent) university and an Italian ($n = 86$, mean age = 23.37, male = 60 percent) university to take part in the experiment. The US sample was selected for the dollar's LDC status, whereas the Italian sample was included for the lire's HDC status. It should be noted that the Italian experiments were conducted in February 2002, at the same time as the nation was in the midst of a dual-currency system transitioning from the lira (an HDC) to the euro (an LDC). However, at the time of the study, the euro was still a relatively unfamiliar currency in comparison with the lire for the Italian consumer, and consumer prices were still being displayed in lires as well as euros. A shortage of euro notes also meant that consumers were still making most cash purchases in lire. It is therefore more than likely that the Italians were still using the lira as a frame of reference for evaluating prices at the time of the experiment. Italy was also chosen because it had the highest currency denomination of the other European countries joining the euro.

Dependent variables
To measure the consumer evaluation of the offer four variables were used. The first variable measured the perceived value of the product itself (Zeithaml, 1998). Subjects were asked to rate the overall value of the camera on a seven-point scale anchored by "low value"(1) and "high value" (7).

Perceived fairness

To measure the perceived fairness (Campbell, 1999) and perceived expensiveness (Slonim and Garbarino, 1999) of the price two additional scales were included. Perceived fairness was measured using two items. The first item used the words "fair" and "unfair" as anchors to a seven-point scale. The second item asked the respondents whether they agreed with the statement "This price is fair." Pearson's correlation coefficient was 0.73 ($p < 0.01$) for the US sample and 0.55 ($p < 0.01$) for the Italian sample. One item with the anchoring words "expensive" and "inexpensive" was used to measure perceived expensiveness. Higher scores on this seven-point scale reflect a higher sense of inexpensiveness, whereas lower scores reflect a higher sense of expensiveness.

Purchase intention was measured using two items. The first item was a seven-point Likert-type scale that asked subjects whether they agreed with the statement "I would buy this camera." The second item asked if they would purchase the camera, using the anchors "definitely not" and "definitely would." The correlation coefficients for the two-item scales were 0.58 ($p < 0.01$) for the US sample and 0.42 ($p < 0.01$) for the Italian sample.

Evaluation

In order to measure the respondents' evaluation of the price discount, their responses to the original promotional flyer were subtracted from their responses to the discounted promotional flyer. This was done to gauge the degree and direction of any change in attitude for each respondent. Thus, a score of 0 would mean that there was no change in evaluations, a positive number would mean an increase in evaluations, and a negative number would mean a decrease in evaluations (see Table I).

Results
The data were analyzed using ANOVA. Figure 1 graphs the estimated marginal means for each dependent variable.

H1a proposes that the US subjects will have a greater change in attitude when the two prices are compared in the lower-denomination currency compared with the higher-denomination currency. In contrast, *H1b* posits that the Italian subjects will have a greater attitudinal change when the two prices are compared in the higher-denomination currency compared with the lower-denomination currency. The nation × denomination interaction was

	US					Italian			
	n	mean	s.d.	Min.	Max.	*n*	mean	s.d.	Min.	Max.
Purchase intention	86	0.95	2.21	−5	8	85	0.88	2.08	−4	8
Price fairness	86	1.64	1.88	−2	7	86	1.26	1.96	−4	9
Price expensiveness	86	1.62	2.01	−5	7	86	1.40	2.29	−4	9
Product value	85	1.09	1.66	−5	6	86	0.35	1.51	−4	6

Table I. Descriptive statistics for dependent variables

(a) Perceived expensiveness

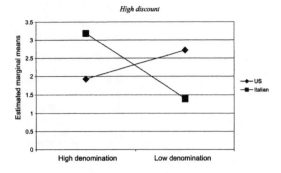

(b) Perceived fairness

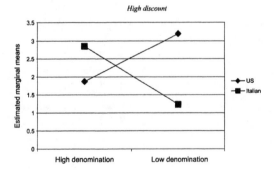

(continued)

Figure 1. Estimated marginal means for expensiveness, fairness, value, and purchase intention

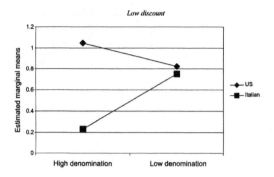

(c) Perceived value

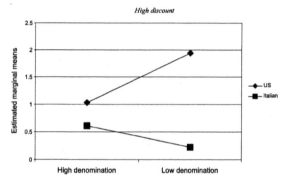

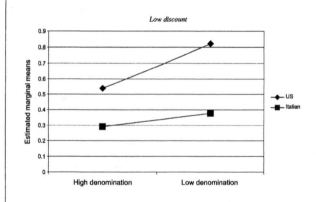

(*continued*)

Figure 1.

(d) Purchase intention

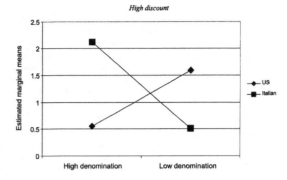

Figure 1.

statistically significant for expensiveness ($F(1,158) = 6.33, p < 0.05$), fairness ($F(1,158) = 4.22, p < 0.05$), and purchase intention ($F(1,158) = 7.48, p < 0.01$). The interaction was not significant for value ($F(1,157) = 2.29$, $p = 0.13$). Planned comparisons revealed higher scores of purchase intention ($F = 4.76, p < 0.05, X_{LDC} = 1.44, X_{HDC} = 0.42$) and value ($F = 2.97$, $p = 0.08, X_{LDC} = 1.38, X_{HDC} = 0.78$) in the LDC condition compared with the HDC condition for the US sample, thus providing support for *H1a*. However, there was no statistically significant difference between the two denominations for price fairness ($F = 2.17, p = 0.14, X_{LDC} = 2.01, X_{HDC} = 1.46$) and expensiveness ($F = 0.73, p = 0.39, X_{LDC} = 1.82, X_{HDC} = 1.45$).

Italian data

The Italian data indicate higher values for the HDC condition compared with the LDC condition for expensiveness ($F = 7.13, p < 0.01, X_{HDC} = 2.14, X_{LDC} = 0.93$), providing support for *H1b*. Purchase intention was only marginally significant ($F = 2.85, p = 0.09, X_{HDC} = 1.33, X_{LDC} = 0.52$) and fairness was not statistically significant ($F = 2.04, p = 0.15, X_{HDC} = 1.54, X_{LDC} = 0.99$) between the HDC and LDC conditions among the Italian sample.

H2 predicts that attitudinal change will be greater among the Americans than the Italians when prices are compared in an LDC, whereas *H3* states that the Italian sample's evaluations will be more altered by the price reduction than the US when prices are shown in an HDC. The planned comparisons revealed statistical support for *H2* for expensiveness ($F = 9.40$, $p < 0.01$, $X_{USA} = 1.83$, $X_{ITA} = 0.93$), fairness ($F = 7.09$, $p < 0.01$, $X_{USA} = 2.01$, $X_{ITA} = 0.99$), and value ($F = 3.97$, $p < 0.05$, $X_{USA} = 1.38$, $X_{ITA} = 0.30$). There was marginal support for purchase intention ($F = 3.73$, $p = 0.06$, $X_{USA} = 1.44$, $X_{ITA} = 0.52$). Under the HDC condition, however, the results were insignificant for expensiveness ($F = 0.78$, $p = 0.38$, $X_{USA} = 1.45$, $X_{ITA} = 2.13$), fairness ($F = 0.04$, $p = 0.84$, $X_{USA} = 1.46$, $X_{ITA} = 1.54$), and value ($F = 2.10$, $p = 0.15$, $X_{USA} = 0.78$, $XITA = 0.45$), but marginally significant for purchase intention ($F = 3.25$, $p = 0.07$, $X_{USA} = 0.42$, $X_{ITA} = 1.33$). Thus, *H2* was supported and *H3* was not supported.

Degree of familiarity

The last set of hypotheses examines the impact of the degree of familiarity of the denomination on the discount differential. According to *H4a*, US respondents will be less influenced than the Italians by the real magnitude of the discount amount when the pricing information is presented in an HDC. *H4b* suggests that the Italian subjects will be less influenced than the US by changes in the discount amount when the price reduction is presented in an LDC.

The contrasts for the high denomination data reveal statistically significant simple effects of discount for the Italian sample for purchase intention ($F = 4.06$, $p < 0.05$, $X_H = 2.19$, $X_L = 0.50$), fairness ($F = 20.01$, $p < 0.01$, $X_H = 2.87$, $X_L = 0.23$), and expensiveness ($F = 8.55$, $p < 0.01$, $X_H = 3.28$, $X_L = 1.28$), but not for value ($F = 0.18$, $p = 0.67$, $X_H = 0.59$, $X_L = 0.35$). In each case, the mean values for these variables are greater under the high discount condition (X_H) compared with the low discount condition (X_L). At the same time the simple effects of discount for the US sample was statistically insignificant for purchase intention ($F = 0.14$, $p = 0.71$, $X_H = 0.57$, $X_L = 0.27$), fairness ($F = 2.25$, $p = 0.14$, $X_H = 1.86$, $X_L = 1.02$), expensiveness ($F = 2.43$, $p = 0.12$, $X_H = 1.82$, $X_L = 1.02$), and value ($F = 0.78$, $p = 0.38$, $X_H = 0.98$, $X_L = 0.49$). For the US sample, then, there is no perceived preference for the higher discount over the lower discount under the high denomination condition. There is therefore general support for *H4a*.

Low denomination data

In terms of the low denomination data, contrast analysis reveals significant simple effects of discount for the US sample for fairness ($F = 21.59$, $p < 0.01$, $X_H = 3.23$, $X_L = 0.84$), expensiveness ($F = 9.37$, $p < 0.01$, $X_H = 2.85$, $X_L = 1.02$), and value ($F = 5.99$, $p < 0.05$, $X_H = 1.96$, $X_L = 0.86$), but not for purchase intention ($F = 0.59$, $p = 0.44$, $X_H = 1.68$, $X_L = 1.27$). Inspection of the means reveals that the US sample in this instance had significantly higher evaluations for the high discount condition relative to the low discount condition. As for the Italian sample, the simple effects of discount were not significant for purchase intention ($F = 0.00$, $p = 0.98$, $X_H = 0.48$, $X_L = 0.47$), fairness ($F = 0.87$, $p = 0.35$, $X_H = 1.22$, $X_L = 0.73$), expensiveness ($F = 2.56$, $p = 0.11$, $X_H = 0.23$, $X_L = 0.34$), or value ($F = 0.11$, $p = 0.74$, $X_H = 0.23$, $X_L = 0.37$). These results indicate that the Italian sample, unlike the US sample, showed no discernible preference for the high discount over the low discount under the low denomination condition. The data therefore support *H4b*.

Discussion

This study examines the role of consumer familiarity with a currency's denomination level on price comparisons in a foreign currency. In general, our results suggest that currency denomination does play a significant part in shaping the consumer's attitudinal reaction to price reductions.

Unfamiliarity with the currency's denomination

The results provide some support for the notion that consumers will tend to respond more favorably to foreign price discounts when the currency's denomination is similar to their own. Among the US sample, the changes in evaluation for value and purchase intention were greater for the lower denomination currency than for the higher denomination currency. In contrast, the Italian sample revealed greater change in perceived expensiveness of the price discount for the HDC compared to the LDC, and was marginally more influenced to purchase the product under the HDC condition.

US versus Italian preference for discounts in a foreign currency

Comparisons

Cross-national comparisons of the data revealed that, under the LDC condition, the US respondents had a more positive change in attitude towards the discounted camera's value, its inexpensiveness and price fairness than the Italians. This supports our hypothesis that the Americans would be more comfortable than the Italians when evaluating price discounts in a currency whose denomination level is more similar to the dollar than the lira. However, when evaluating price discounts under the HDC condition, there were no significant differences between the Americans and Italians. According to our hypothesis, we expected the Italians to have a stronger reaction to the price differential than the Americans. One possible explanation is that the Americans were influenced by the nominal value (Raghubir and Srivastava, 2002) of the price differential. In other words, despite the unfamiliarity of the denomination level, the US respondents may gauge a price discount in the thousands of dhoveps as being somewhat significant by its sheer numerical size (note, however, that the Americans were still more influenced by the discount in the LDC condition).

The discount effect

High/low denomination

A comparison of the real amount of the price differential on the respondents' evaluations of the new offer revealed that in some instances a higher discount fared no better than a lower discount. The US subjects under the high denomination condition who were shown a 30 percent discount had similar attitudinal reactions to the price reduction to those who were shown a 5 percent discount. However, under the low denomination condition the Americans were more influenced by the 30 percent discount compared with the 5 percent discount. At the same time, the Italian respondents exhibited no evaluative differences between the two discounts under the low denomination currency, yet had more positive reactions to the 30 percent discount than to the 5 percent discount under the high denomination currency. It seems, therefore, that the size of the discount is more effective when consumers are familiar with the foreign currency's denomination level.

Managerial implications

These findings have strategic implications for pricing in regional zones, on the Internet, and in international tourism. Consumers shopping in foreign environments evaluate prices depending on the relationship of that currency's denomination with their own. In particular, our results suggest that incongruent denomination levels reduce the effectiveness of price reductions. Marketers may therefore want to consider alternative strategies when pricing for consumers from non-congruent currency denominations. Our results indicate that the size of the price reduction is less effective in changing attitudes when the consumer is unfamiliar with the denomination level. This suggests that the price discount strategy is an ineffective tool under these circumstances.

Limitations

There are several limitations to this study. First, the study was based on one product category. This study used a moderately priced consumer durable. It may be the case that the effectiveness of price discounts may differ from one product category to another. Second, the data were collected from university students. However, by using a more homogeneous sample such as students, we hope to have controlled for various extraneous variables of education level, age, and income that could have potentially confounded our results. Students are also an important part of the consumer society that travels abroad.

Pricing strategies

Future research

Future research is needed to further explore the role of the currency's denomination level on pricing strategies targeting international consumers. It would be interesting to determine which types of price reduction strategies are more effective when the consumer's currency denomination and the price currency denomination are incongruent. Finally, it would be worthwhile to explore the consumers' learning effect when faced with incongruent currencies over an extended period of time.

References

Ackerman, D. and Tellis, G. (2001), "Can culture affect prices? A cross-cultural study of shopping and retail prices", *Journal of Retailing*, Vol. 77 No. 1, Spring, pp. 57-82.

Agarwal, S. and Teas, R.K. (2001), "Quality cues and perceptions of quality, sacrifice, value, and willingness-to-buy: an examination of cross-national applicability", working paper, No. 37-1b, Iowa State University of Science & Technology, Ames, IA.

Ahuvia, A. and Wong, N. (1998), "The effect of cultural orientation in luxury consumption", in Arnould, E.J. and Scott, L.M. (Eds), *Advances in Consumer Research*, Vol. 25, Association for Consumer Research, Ann Arbor, MI, pp. 29-32.

Alba, J.W. and Hutchinson, J.W. (1987), "Dimensions of consumer expertise", *Journal of Consumer Research*, Vol. 13 No. 4, pp. 411-35.

Berkowitz, E.N. and Walton, J.R. (1980), "Contextual influences on consumer price responses: an experimental analysis", *Journal of Marketing Research*, Vol. 17 No. 3, pp. 349-58.

Callow, M. and Lerman, D. (2003), "Cross-cultural pricing issues", in Rugimbana, R. and Nwankwo, S. (Eds), *Cross-Cultural Marketing*, Thomson Learning, London.

Campbell, M.C. (1999), "Perceptions of price unfairness: antecedents and consequences", *Journal of Marketing Research*, Vol. 36, May, pp. 187-99.

Dehaene, S. and Marques, J.F. (2002), "Cognitive euroscience: scalar variability in price estimation and the cognitive consequences of switching to the euro", *Quarterly Journal of Experimental Psychology*, Vol. 55 No. 3, pp. 705-31.

Della Bitta, A.J., Monroe, K.B. and McGinnis, J.M. (1981), "Consumers' perception of comparative price advertisements", *Journal of Marketing Research*, Vol. 18 No. 4, pp. 416-27.

Dorfman, J. (1994), "Sublexical components in implicit memory for novel words", *Journal of Experimental Psychology: Learning, Memory, and Cognition*, Vol. 20 No. 5, pp. 1108-25.

Fang, T. (1999), *Chinese Business Negotiating Style*, Sage, Thousand Oaks, CA.

Han, C.M. and Terpstra, V. (1988), "Country-of-origin effects for uni-national and binational products", *Journal of International Business Studies*, Vol. 19 No. 2, Summer, pp. 235-55.

Hui, H.C. and Triandis, H.C. (1985), "Measurement in cross-cultural psychology: a review and comparison of strategies", *Journal of Cross-Cultural Psychology*, Vol. 16, June, pp. 131-52.

Jamal, A. and Goode, M. (2001), "Consumers' product evaluation: a study of the primary evaluative criteria in the precious jewellery market in the UK", *Journal of Consumer Behaviour*, Vol. 1 No. 2, pp. 140-55.

Kramer, H.E. and Herbig, P.A. (1993), "The *suq* model of haggling: who, what, when, why?", *Journal of International Consumer Marketing*, Vol. 5 No. 2, pp. 55-69.

Li, D. and Gallup, A.M. (1995), "In search of the Chinese consumer", *Chinese Business Review*, Vol. 22, September/October, pp. 19-23.

McGowan, K.M. and Sternquist, B.J. (1998), "Dimensions of price as a marketing universal: a comparison of Japanese and US consumers", *Journal of International Marketing*, Vol. 6 No. 4, pp. 49-65.

Maxwell, S. (1999), "Biased attributions of a price increase: effects of culture and gender", *Journal of Consumer Marketing*, Vol. 16 No. 1, pp. 9-23.

Maxwell, S. (2001), "An expanded price/brand effect model: a demonstration of heterogeneity in global consumption", *International Marketing Review*, Vol. 18 No. 3, pp. 325-44.

Monroe, K.B. (2003), *Pricing: Making Profitable Decisions*, 3rd ed., McGraw-Hill/Irwin, New York, NY.

Monroe, K.B. and Lee, A.Y. (1999), "Remembering versus knowing: issues in buyers' processing of price information", *Journal of the Academy of Marketing Science*, Vol. 27, pp. 207-25.

Raghubir, P. and Srivastava, J. (2002), "Effect of face value on product valuation in foreign currencies", *Association for Consumer Research Conference*, Atlanta, GA, October, pp. 16-20.

Rao, A.R. and Monroe, K.B. (1989), "The effect of price, brand name, and store name on buyers' perceptions of product quality: an integrative review", *Journal of Marketing Research*, Vol. 26, August, pp. 351-7.

Shafir, E., Diamond, P. and Tversky, A. (1997), "Money illusions", *The Quarterly Journal of Economics*, Vol. 112, May, pp. 341-74.

Slonim, R. and Garbarino, E. (1999), "The effect of price history on demand as mediated by perceived price expensiveness", *Journal of Business Research*, Vol. 45 No. 1, May, pp. 1-14.

Stottinger, B. (2001), "Strategic export pricing: a long and winding road", *Journal of International Marketing*, Vol. 9 No. 1, pp. 40-63.

Suri, R., Anderson, R.E. and Kotlov, V. (2001), "Comparison of the popularity of 9-ending prices in the USA and Poland", Gilly, M.C. and Meyers-Levy, J. (Eds), *Advances in Consumer Research*, Vol. 28, Association for Consumer Research, Valdosta, GA, p. 141.

Suri, R., Manchanda, R.V. and Kohli, C.S. (2000), "Brand evaluations: a comparison of fixed price and discounted price offers", *Journal of Product & Brand Management*, Vol. 9 No. 3, pp. 193-206.

Zeithaml, V.A. (1998), "Consumer perceptions of price, quality, and value: aA means-end model and synthesis of evidence", *Journal of Marketing*, Vol. 52, July, pp. 2-22.

Zhou, Z. and Nakamoto, K. (2001), "Price perceptions: a cross-national study between American and Chinese young consumers", Gilly, M.C. and Meyers-Levy, J. (Eds), *Advances in Consumer Research*, Vol. 28, Association for Consumer Research, Valdosta, GA, pp. 161-8.

Further reading

Zaichkowsky, J.L. (1994), "The personal involvement inventory: reduction, revision, and application to advertising", *Journal of Advertising*, Vol. 23, December, pp. 59-70.

■

This summary has been provided to allow managers and executives a rapid appreciation of the content of this article. Those with a particular interest in the topic covered may then read the article in toto to take advantage of the more comprehensive description of the research undertaken and its results to get the full benefit of the material present

Executive summary and implications for managers and executives

Consumers do struggle with foreign currencies

Work looking at pricing in international markets has tended to focus on the practical issues associated with exchange rates, internal pricing and a range of microeconomic issues. However, with the growth of international trade and especially international trade in consumer goods, the question of how consumers behave when faced with an unfamiliar currency is important. For Europeans there is an added consideration in that the debate over creating a single currency and the impact of that currency's introduction remains an important political debate.

Callow and Lerman observe that a national currency ". . . constitutes part of the culture's symbolic system that is used in the marketplace to communicate the value of goods and services." The implication of this statement is that a foreign currency is unfamiliar and is less effective in communicating the value of goods and services. Even where the consumer is capable (or even expert) in dealing with the unfamiliar currency, their lack of familiarity with the currency makes it difficult to many quick judgements about value.

Dealing with lots of noughts

Callow and Lerman make a distinction between "high denomination currencies" (e.g. Turkish lira) and "low denomination currencies" (e.g. the US dollar). The assumption here is that a consumer from a low denomination country will have more difficulty dealing with transaction using a high denomination currency than with a low denomination currency. This argument is supported by the suggestion that ". . . consumers do not always act rationally when dealing with economic transactions since they are sometimes biased towards nominal monetary values . . . instead of real monetary values." Thus the surplus of noughts in some currencies suggests to the consumer that something is at a higher value than is actually the case.

Again we should remind ourselves that expertise in dealing with the currency is not the issue here. Indeed the issue relates to non-conscious behaviour and assumptions about value rather than the practical and mathematical issues associated with dealing in a foreign currency.

Are we being ripped off?

When we deal with an unfamiliar currency we often suspect that we are being "ripped off". Indeed one of the complaints that followed the introduction of the Euro in countries such as Italy and Germany was that traders were taking advantage of consumer unfamiliarity to increase prices (and this may not have been universally true but there is ample anecdotal evidence to suggest that traders did behave in the manner).

For the unfamiliar consumer there is no doubt that this worry about value (we are not entirely sure whether we are getting the best value) will influence the way in which we respond to the presentation of prices, the promotion of sales promotions and the use of discounts. Callow and Lerman focus on the issue of discounting which, as well as giving us specific information about one pricing situation, also gives us further insight into the behaviour of consumers when using unfamiliar currencies. And, as the authors point out, the growth of international travel and the use of the Internet to purchase goods and services makes understanding consumer behaviour in such situations more important to marketers.

Does high or low denomination affect consumer reaction to discounting?
Callow and Lerman use an experimental approach to assess whether consumers respond differently to discounts in currencies of a different order to the one which they find familiar (e.g. consumers from low denomination counties using high denomination currencies). By using an experimental approach the authors examine the response of consumers from the USA (low denomination) and Italy (formerly high denomination). In the latter example there may be questions asked as to whether the country could be described as truly high denomination since the research was conducted after the switch to the Euro (a low denomination currency) when the former currency was operating in parallel with the new currency.

The outcome of the study seems to suggest that the use of high denomination currencies by consumers from low denomination countries presents more challenges (although we should remember that the high denomination Italians had had a bit of practice dealing in a low denomination currency since the switch to the Euro). It is clear however that consumers do not have the same understanding or grasp of discounting in an unfamiliar currency – regardless of denomination.

However, this difficulty understanding the discount offer is increased where the consumer is dealing with a doubly unfamiliar situation (foreign currency and different scale of denomination). As the authors put it "... currency denomination does play a significant part in shaping the consumer's attitudinal reaction to price reductions."

One interesting finding is the impact that unfamiliarity has on how the consumer views the scale of price reduction. What seems to emerge is a situation where increasing the level of discount has a diminishing value in terms of consumer response and that a lack of familiarity with the currency medium in which the discount is presented increases this diminution in value. Put bluntly, marketers should think carefully about the degree of discount offered – increasing the discount will not necessarily achieve the objective of increasing sales. A small discount can be just as effective as a large discount.

As international trade continues its growth, the way in which consumers deal with pricing in foreign currencies will grow in importance. The work here from Callow and Lerman provides a useful start for marketers who want to understand how currencies affect consumer response to the offers we make.

(A précis of the article "Consumer evaluation of price discounts in foreign currencies". Supplied by Marketing Consultants for Emerald.)

[22]

The Influence of Selected Behavioral and Economic Variables on Perceptions of Admission Price Levels

SEONG-SEOP KIM AND JOHN L. CROMPTON

It has been suggested that there is a need to include variables other than traditional economic variables in models designed to assess visitors' reactions to admission prices. This study explored the influence of selected behavioral and nontraditional economic factors in influencing visitors' reactions. Analyses were undertaken on responses from five data sets that addressed pricing issues in the Texas state park system. Generally, the economic factors were more useful predictors than the behavioral factors. Especially useful were perceptions of value for the admission price and importance of admission price to a day visit. Ownership of an annual pass and level of loyalty were also useful predictors of price perceptions.

A challenge confronting tourism marketers is how to ameliorate participants' resistance to increases in price. Several authors have suggested the need for an assessment of the factors that influence attitude toward price, especially relating to an individual's level of acceptance of a price and the effect of level of acceptance on visitation rates (Crompton and Lamb 1986; Fedler and Miles 1989; Howard and Selin 1987; Kerr and Manfredo 1991; McCarville 1992).

A number of conceptualizations of how individuals learn about prices and how they process that information have been proposed (Monroe, Powell, and Choudhury 1986), but the model depicting price information processing that has been most widely recognized in the consumer behavior field is that developed by Jacoby and Olson (1977). The analyses reported in this study were guided by an adaptation of the Jacoby and Olson model, which is described in Figure 1. The study's objective was to assess the relative influence of selected behavioral and economic variables on perceptions of price levels. The guiding proposition was that perception of an admission price would be explained and predicted by selected behavioral and economic factors. The elements of intention to visit and visitation behavior shown in Figure 1 were not considered in this study.

O-price refers to the physical objective price. This is the stimulus entrance price to which visitors are exposed (see Figure 1). However, visitors' senses are selectively activated by the price stimulus, and their interest in and level of involvement with the stimulus is likely to determine the extent to which they meaningfully absorb the information (Assael 1995). *Encoding* is the interpretation and assignment of meaning an individual gives to the physical price. It has been defined as the process by which we select and assign a

word or visual image to represent a perceived object (Schiffman and Kanuk 1994). Thus, although individuals received the same external stimulus (O-price), perceptions of it are likely to be changed in the encoding process as individuals adapt it to fit an existing set of beliefs (Schoell and Guiltinan 1995; Zeithaml 1982). For example, if the entrance price to a park is $5, information acquired in the past or a visitor's existing financial status makes it likely that some will interpret the price as being relatively expensive, while others consider it to be inexpensive.

This process of adapting the O-price to fit an existing set of beliefs leads to different *psychological evaluations* of an admission price. The central construct in the psychological evaluation is the reference price since it establishes a reference point for the evaluation. It is the internally held standard that visitors use to evaluate new price information.

Reference price has been operationalized both by a single criterion and by multiple criteria (Jacobson and Obermiller 1989). Single-criterion definitions include "last price paid" (Gabor 1977; Uhl 1970), "the average price" (Monroe 1973), and "anticipated or expected price" (Assael 1995; Helgeson and Beatty 1987; Jacobson and Obermiller 1989; Lattin and Bucklin 1989; Winer 1986). Multiple criteria to operationalize the concept of the reference price have been used by (1) Jacoby and Olson (1977), who considered reference price to be an amalgam of "fair price," "price most recently charged," "price last paid," and "price normally paid"; (2) Klein and Oglethorpe (1987), who defined it as a combination of "aspiration price" (the most you are willing to pay), "market price," and "historical price"; and (3) Diamond and Campbell (1989), who recognized two categories of definition: definitions relating to previous payment experience (e.g., average price paid and price last paid) and definitions such as fair price and the most you would pay.

In addition to reference price, psychological evaluation of a price is likely to be influenced by a number of *behavioral and economic* factors (Zeithaml 1984).

Seong-Seop Kim is in the Department of Hotel and Tourism Management at Sejong University in South Korea. John L. Crompton is in the Department of Recreation, Park and Tourism Sciences at Texas A&M University in College Station, Texas.

Journal of Travel Research, Vol. 41, November 2002, 144-152
DOI: 10.1177/004728702237414

FIGURE 1
A MODEL OF PROCESSING OF PRICE STIMULI AND INFLUENCING FACTORS

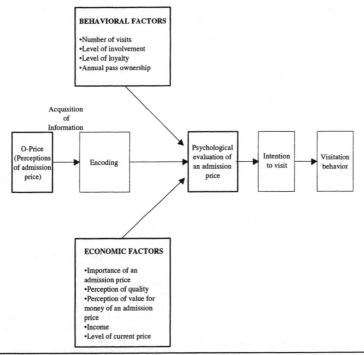

Note: This study is concerned with those parts of the model shown with a darker boundary.

BEHAVIORAL FACTORS

Major *behavioral* factors influencing psychological evaluation of price are likely to include number of visits, level of involvement, level of loyalty, and ownership of an annual pass (see Figure 1).

Frequent visitors to an attraction may react negatively to price increases because this may diminish the number of times they can go (Cockrell and Wellman 1985). Furthermore, frequent visitors may expect discounts in return for their repeated visitation. Thus, they may resist a price increase if it is not accompanied by a quantity discount in the format of an annual pass.

On the other hand, past experience may reinforce visitors' positive beliefs toward an attraction and result in less resistance to price increases (Bovaird, Tricker, and Stoakes 1984; Reiling and Kotchen 1996). Thus, LaPage (1995) argued that repeat visitation is evidence of agreement with entrance prices, and Grimes, Pinhey, and Campos (1976) reported that experienced campers were more willing to pay higher amounts for camping facilities than inexperienced campers. Similarly, Kerr and Manfredo (1991) reported that frequency of visitation of park and recreation areas was positively correlated with attitude toward payment. These studies suggest that experienced visitors are more likely to accept price increases and be less sensitive to them. Thus, level of visitation is likely to affect reaction to price increases.

Level of involvement is often measured by ownership of products relating to the activities of interest. Those owning multiple products may report negative responses toward current admission prices or an increase in price because these indicators of high involvement suggest that these individuals are likely to be frequent users and thus directly affected (Kim, Scott, and Crompton 1997). Again, however, an antithetical reaction may also occur. People who are highly involved with state parks may consider them to be a more central activity in their lives. Acceptance level theory postulates that there is a latitude range of acceptable prices (Sherif 1963). This range will vary among visitors but is likely to be larger for highly involved visitors (Fedler and Miles 1989; Howard and Selin 1987). Thus, these visitors are likely to react more positively to price increases and be less sensitive to price changes than low-involved individuals.

Loyalty is defined as "committed behavior that is manifested by propensity to participate in a particular recreation service" (Backman and Crompton 1991, p. 205). In this

146   NOVEMBER 2002

article, behavioral measures of loyalty were operationalized as positive opinion leadership, intention to revisit, and continued future use.

In Backman and Crompton's (1991) study, price sensitivity was not highly correlated with loyalty. Nevertheless, it has been argued by others that loyal participants are more likely to be supporters of price increases because they receive valued benefits from their participation (Howard, Edginton, and Selin 1989). Vogt and Watson (1998, p. 6) concluded, "Loyalty is often the necessary condition for customer demand to be maintained when slight price changes occur." On the other hand, loyal visitors may reject a price increase if they are required to pay the increased price on every visitation and there is no quantity discount. Thus, people who are highly loyal to state parks may show negative reactions to price increases.

Those who own an annual pass are likely to be frequent visitors and supporters of the state park system. Vogt and Watson (1998) found those intending to buy an annual camping pass were more likely to consider a price acceptable and were not as sensitive to a price change. It seems likely that they would adopt a neutral attitude toward a daily admission price if they were not required to pay it. In contrast, those who do not own an annual pass may react negatively toward an entrance price increase because they are required to pay it on every visit to a park.

ECONOMIC FACTORS

The economic factors that are likely to substantially influence perception of price include importance of the admission price in making a decision to go on a visit, perception of the attraction's quality, perception of value for money of an admission price, income level, and current price (see Figure 1).

The data sets used in the analyses in this study measured *importance of admission price* in the decision to visit. This was considered to be an indicator of price sensitivity since it is reasonable to conjecture that those who regard admission price as being important in the decision to visit are more likely to respond negatively to price increases.

Quality is an important determinant in perception of price. There is a linkage between perception of quality and price because visitors are likely to consider quality when they evaluate price (Crompton and Lamb 1986; Manning et al. 1996; McCarville 1992). An attraction perceived as being high quality is likely to be considered as worthy of being priced relatively high, and visitors are likely to be willing to pay more than those who judge an attraction as not being of high quality (McCarville 1990, 1992).

McCarville (1992) noted that *good value for money* occurs when users receive more benefits from services than their perceived costs. Perceived value will affect perception of price and level of visitation (Crompton and Lamb 1986; Gregersen and Lundgren 1996; LaPage 1995; McCarville 1990, 1992; Richer 1998). Crompton and Lamb (1986) suggested that perceptions of good value of a service may reduce users' resistance to price increases. Similarly, LaPage (1995) stated that visitors' willingness to pay depends on the value they perceive for the price paid.

Many studies have reported that *income level* is a key variable in predicting visitation (e.g., Ashley, 1990; Crompton

and Lamb 1986; Grimes, Pinhey, and Campos 1976; King and Richards 1977; Loomis 1980; Philipp 1995). Perceptions of price may differ among income levels (Grimes, Pinhey, and Campos 1976). Low-income people may perceive more financial constraints in visiting an attraction than other groups because of lack of vehicles and the cost of travel (Ashley 1990; Loomis 1980; Philipp 1995). Price awareness or sensitivity tends to be inversely related to income level, although those with very low incomes tend not to be especially aware of pricing levels (Morris and Morris 1990).

Finally, *level of current price* may influence perceptions of price increases. Most resistance to new entrance prices is likely to be found at higher levels of price. Howard and Cable (1980) reported that respondents showed increased resistance when prices of swimming lessons were gradually increased along a low, medium, and high continuum. Christensen and Richer (1998) reported that willingness to pay gradually dropped with increases in the suggested user prices for entrance to a wilderness area. A study of estimation of site demand conducted by Leuschner and Cook (1987) similarly reported that an increase in wilderness fees led to a decrease in number of visitations. These findings are consistent with traditional economy theory indicating that as price increases, demand will decrease.

DESCRIPTION OF DATA SETS

Five data sets that were specifically designed to address pricing issues in Texas state parks were analyzed in this study. They were all commissioned during the 1990s by the Texas Parks and Wildlife Department (TPWD).

The survey procedures used in deriving the first four of the five data sets were similar, with an initial questionnaire being either mailed to a sample of respondents or handed to a sample of park visitors on site. In all four cases, follow-up procedures consisted of a reminder card mailed 2 days after the initial contact and two follow-up questionnaires mailed 2 and 4 weeks after the initial contact.

Data set 1 was derived from a sample of 3,200 names that were chosen randomly from a list of those holding a current Texas driving license, which was made available by the Texas Department of Transportation. The effective sample size from the mail survey was 2,688 after 512 uncontactable people were excluded. The total response rate was 40.7%.

The sample for data set 2 comprised visitors to nine Texas state parks. Visitors were personally handed the survey as they entered the park and were asked to return it in the prepaid envelope provided. The effective sample size was 2,373, and the overall response rate was 67.8% ($n = 1,610$).

Data set 3 was derived from a mail survey comprising 2,964 individuals who had responded to a previous survey of park visitors conducted by the TPWD. The overall response rate was 56%.

The sample in data set 4 was drawn from two subsets of respondents sampled from data sets 2 and 3. They were resurveyed some 2 years after the original contact. An overall response rate of 54.8% was obtained ($n = 880$).

Data set 5 was collected using computer-assisted telephone interviewing technology. The stratified sample was selected from 10 economic regions of Texas, which were defined by the state's comptroller. Response rates from the

JOURNAL OF TRAVEL RESEARCH 147

TABLE 1

**RESULTS OF PRINCIPAL COMPONENT FACTOR ANALYSIS WITH VARIMAX ROTATION
FOR THE BEHAVIORAL ITEMS MEASURING INVOLVEMENT IN DATA SETS 3 AND 4**

| | Data Set 3 | | | | | Data Set 4 | | | | |
| | Factor Loadings | | | | | Factor Loadings | | | | |
Behavioral Involvement Item	Factor 1	Factor 2	Commun-alities	M	SD	Factor 1	Factor 2	Commun-alities	M	SD
Number of pieces of equipment owned	.50		.26	6.32	2.36	.52		.30	6.65	2.27
Number of books owned about parks, the outdoors, conservation, or camping	.64		.45	6.33	12.46	.52		.54	8.54	22.15
Number of subscriptions to park, outdoor, conservation, or camping magazines	.82		.68	0.98	1.45	.81		.66	1.13	1.42
Number of memberships in park, outdoor, conservation, or camping organizations	.79		.63	0.60	1.01	.80		.68	0.77	1.16
Expenditures spent on visiting parks, wildlife, and natural areas		.84	.72	368	823		.71	.52	434	1,445
Number of miles traveled to visit parks, wildlife, and natural areas		.85	.74	1,047	2,345		.79	.62	1,133	4,862
KMO (Kaiser-Meyer-Olkin)			.68					.69		
Eigenvalue	2.24	1.22				2.26	1.03			
Variance explained (%)	37.4	20.3				37.7	17.2			
Reliability alpha for each dimension	.61	.63				.64	.61			
Total scale reliability alpha			.66					.65		

Note: Factor 1—Ownership. Factor 2—Travel-Related Behavior.

10 regions ranged from 57% to 67%, and a total of 3,000 responses were collected.

PRICE VARIABLE

In the mail surveys, the dependent variable, perceptions of the admission price (O-price) to state parks, was operationalized by the question, "Daily admission fees to Texas state parks currently range from $3 to $5 per vehicle. Is this much too low, too low, about right, too high, much too high, or don't know?" Responses were recorded on a 5-point Likert-type scale. The wording was adjusted slightly for the on-site sample (data set 2) and the phone survey (data set 5) to reflect their different contexts; in the case of the phone survey, it was reduced to a 4-point scale: *too low, about right, too high,* and *don't know.*

BEHAVIORAL AND ECONOMIC VARIABLES

Number of day and overnight visits were recorded in an open-ended question. Six items were used to measure behavioral involvement adapted from Kim, Scott, and Crompton (1997). These items appeared in data sets 3 and 4. The six-item measures were transformed into z-scores because distributions of individual items varied widely, and the items'

units of measurement were different. The z-scores were used in a principal components factor analysis. The results (see Table 1) produced a consistent two-factor solution that reflected ownership and travel-related behavior. Grand means of the z-scores on these two dimensions were included in the regression analyses.

Behavioral loyalty was measured by five items. Table 2 shows results of the principal components factor analyses undertaken on the items in each of the three data sets in which they appeared. A one-factor solution consistently emerged. Grand means of the five items were used in the multiple regression analyses in data sets 2, 3, and 4.

Importance of admission price in a decision to visit was operationalized by 5-point Likert-type scales ranging from *not at all important* to *extremely important.* Five-point scales were also used to measure perceptions of quality (*very low quality* to *very high quality*), perceptions of value for money of the admission price (*very poor value* to *very good value*), and level of current price (*much too low* to *much too high*). Household income level was operationalized by six categories ranging from under $15,000 to more than $75,000.

RESULTS

Results from the five multiple regression models developed from the five data sets are reported in Tables 3, 4, 5, 6, and 7. Not all the behavioral and economic variables listed in

TABLE 2

RESULTS OF PRINCIPAL COMPONENT FACTOR ANALYSES WITH VARIMAX ROTATION ON FIVE LOYALTY SCALE ITEMS USED IN DATA SETS 2, 3, AND 4

Loyalty Item	Data Set 2				Data Set 3				Data Set 4			
	Factor Loadings	Commun-alities	M	SD	Factor Loadings	Commun-alities	M	SD	Factor Loadings	Commun-alities	M	SD
I would encourage my friends and relatives to come to this park	.83	.69	4.46	.76	.82	.68	4.30	.88	.83	.69	4.39	.83
If this park was closed, it makes no difference to me since I would simply go to another park	.57	.33	3.32	1.32	.38	.40	3.46	1.35	.37	.33	3.37	1.43
I will not come back to this park often because it would get boring	.72	.51	4.13	1.03	.64	.41	4.21	1.02	.60	.36	4.21	.98
If another nearby park was cheaper, I would probably go to it	.61	.37	3.48	1.12	.63	.40	3.39	1.21	.59	.34	3.47	1.17
After I leave this park on this trip, I will say positive things about it to others	.80	.64	4.51	.75	.77	.59	4.32	.89	.78	.61	4.51	.79
KMO (Kaiser-Meyer-Olkin)	.74				.67				.67			
Eigenvalue	2.54				2.22				2.14			
Variance explained (%)	50.8				44.3				42.8			
Total scale reliability alpha	.71				.66				.62			
Grand mean	3.98				3.94				3.99			

TABLE 3

MULTIPLE REGRESSION OF SELECTED INDEPENDENT VARIABLES ON PERCEPTION OF AN ADMISSION PRICE (DATA SET 1)

Independent Variable	β	t-Value	p-Value	Adjusted R^2
Importance of the admission price on a day visit	.33	5.61	.000	.22
Perception of value for money of the admission price	−.27	−4.56	.000	

Note: Tolerance is higher than .93; variance inflation factor is lower than 1.08.

TABLE 4

MULTIPLE REGRESSION OF SELECTED INDEPENDENT VARIABLES ON PERCEPTION OF AN ADMISSION PRICE (DATA SET 2)

Independent Variable	β	t-Value	p-Value	Adjusted R^2
Perception of value for money of the admission price	−.51	−22.19	.000	.33
Level of current prices	.16	7.22	.000	
Income	−.09	−4.00	.000	
Projected number of overnight visits	.09	3.88	.000	
Paid types[a]	−.06	−2.63	.009	

Note: Tolerance is higher than .84; variance inflation factor is lower than 1.01.
a. Dummy variable (0 = per visit payers, 1 = annual pass holders).

Figure 1 were included in all five data sets. Table 8 summarizes the variables that were available in each data set and records those shown to be significant in Tables 3 through 7. The adjusted R^2s were .22, .33, .34, .37, and .13, that is, the percentages of the variability in the dependent variables that were accounted for by the independent variables.

Behavioral variables were generally relatively weak predictors. Level of behavioral involvement was significant in only one of the three regression models in which it was included, while level of behavioral loyalty had a negative relationship with perception of admission price in two of the three data sets, indicating that loyal people perceived admission prices to be lower. Ownership of an annual pass was significant in two of the three regression models in which it was included, indicating that people who paid the per visit price perceived admission prices to be higher than did annual pass holders.

In general, economic factors were better predictors than behavioral factors. Importance of admission price on a day visit was positively correlated with perception of admission price in three regression models. Perception of value for money of admission price was negatively associated with perception of admission price in five regression models. Income was a significant predictor in only one of the four data sets, and it indicated that lower income people had more negative perceptions of admission prices. Level of current price was incorporated into only one of the models, and it showed a positive relationship with perception of admission price.

DISCUSSION

Previous studies have reported that level of prior participation may influence price expectation or attitude toward the price because visitors establish a reference price through their experience (Cockrell and Wellman 1985; Gregersen and Lundgren 1996; McCarville 1996). Some studies have identified a negative relationship between level of participation and acceptance level of price (McDonald, Hammitt, and Dottavio 1985), while others have reported a positive relationship (Kerr and Manfredo 1991; LaPage 1995; Reiling and Kotchen 1996). Results of this study indicated that number of day or overnight visits was not significantly correlated to perceptions of admission price levels, implying that visitors' attitudes toward price were not affected by level of participation.

TABLE 5

MULTIPLE REGRESSION OF SELECTED INDEPENDENT VARIABLES ON PERCEPTION OF AN ADMISSION PRICE (DATA SET 3)

Independent Variable	β	t-Value	p-Value	Adjusted R^2
Perception of value for money of admission prices	−.38	−10.70	.000	.34
Importance of the admission price on a day visit	.23	6.87	.000	
Travel-related behavior dimension of behavioral involvement	.11	3.56	.000	
Paid types[a]	−.09	−3.17	.002	
Level of behavioral loyalty	−.09	−2.84	.005	

Note: Tolerance is higher than .68; variance inflation factor is lower than 1.46.
a. Dummy variable (0 = per visit payers, 1 = annual pass holders).

TABLE 6

MULTIPLE REGRESSION OF SELECTED INDEPENDENT VARIABLES ON PERCEPTION OF AN ADMISSION PRICE (DATA SET 4)

Independent Variable	β	t-Value	p-Value	Adjusted R^2
Perception of value for money of admission prices	−.37	−9.88	.000	.37
Importance of the admission price on a day visit	.28	7.68	.000	
Level of behavioral loyalty	−.12	−3.40	.001	

Note: Tolerance is higher than .71; variance inflation factor is lower than 1.40.

There is some evidence to suggest that low-involved respondents have higher price expectations than highly involved respondents (McCarville, Crompton, and Sell 1993). Thus, it was considered possible that those reporting low involvement with state parks may be especially sensitive to admission prices, but a significant relationship of this

150   NOVEMBER 2002

TABLE 7

MULTIPLE REGRESSION OF SELECTED INDEPENDENT VARIABLE ON PERCEPTION OF AN ADMISSION PRICE (DATA SET 5)

Independent Variable	β	t-Value	p-Value	Adjusted R^2
Perception of value for money of admission prices	−.36	−12.66	.000	.13

Note: Tolerance is higher than .98; variance inflation factor is lower than 1.02.

nature emerged in only one of the three data sets in which it was tested.

This study provided evidence to reinforce the intuitive belief that people who are behaviorally loyal to state parks are likely to be more favorable to accepting current admission prices or a price increase. This may be explained by the assimilation and contrast effect, which suggests that highly loyal visitors to state parks are more likely to assimilate an entrance price and thus accept the pricing structure because they are most cognizant of the positive benefits they receive from state parks and better understand the rationale for the pricing policy (Howard, Edginton, and Selin 1989). There may also be a perception that they enjoyed a bargain price in the past. The results also offer empirical verification for the intuitive notion that per visit payers are likely to be more sensitive to admission prices than annual pass holders because they pay on every visit (Vogt and Watson 1998).

The perceived importance of admission price when making a decision to visit a state park for a day visit was a relatively consistent predictor of perception of admission price levels, suggesting that people who perceive admission price to be an important factor when visiting state parks are likely to be sensitive to changes in price. This finding is consistent with other studies that have discussed the effect of price sensitivity on attitude toward price levels (Gabor and Granger 1964; Kamen and Toman 1970; Morris and Morris 1990; Nagle and Holden 1995).

Perception of value for money of the admission price also was a strong predictor of attitude toward current price levels, suggesting that those who perceive the admission price to be a good value for money are likely to be less sensitive to a price change. This is supported by other studies in which perception of good value for money resulted in greater willingness to pay or decreased resistance to price increases (Crompton and Lamb 1986; Dodds and Monroe 1985; Dodds, Monroe, and Grewal 1991; Garvin 1987; Kerin, Jain, and Howard 1992; LaPage 1995; McCarville 1992; Monroe and Chapman 1987; Nagle and Holden 1995; Richer 1998; Szybillo and Jacoby 1974).

The literature is replete with studies indicating that low-income visitors tend to show stronger resistance to the imposition or raising of admission prices (Bamford et al. 1988; Grimes, Pinhey, and Campos 1976; Loomis 1980; Philipp 1995; Reiling and Kotchen 1996; Thompson and Tinsley 1979). However, in this study, income level was not a good predictor of perceptions of admission price. Several factors may have contributed to this apparently anomalous finding. The $3 to $5 levels of admission prices at Texas state parks may not have been sufficiently high to dissuade low-income individuals from visiting them. Even low-income visitors

TABLE 8

SUMMARY OF THE RESULTS

Independent Variables	Data Sets									
	1		2		3		4		5	
	A	B	A	B	A	B	A	B	A	B
Behavioral factors										
Number of day visits	✓		✓				✓	✓	✓	
Number of overnight Visits	✓		✓	+	✓		✓		✓	
Level of behavioral involvement					✓	+	✓		✓	
Level of behavioral loyalty			✓		✓	−	✓	−		
Own an annual pass			✓	−	✓	−	✓			
Economic factors										
Importance of admission price on a day visit	✓	+			✓	+	✓	+		
Importance of admission price on an overnight visit	✓	*			✓	*	✓	*		
Perception of quality									✓	
Perception of value for money of admission price	✓	−	✓	−	✓	−	✓	−	✓	−
Income	✓		✓	−	✓				✓	
Level of current price			✓	+						

Note: A: ✓ indicates independent variables tested in each subhypothesis. B: + represents positively significant independent variables at the .05 level; − represents negatively significant independent variables at the .05 level; * represents variable that was not included in the final regression model because of multicollinearity. R^2 values are as follows: data set 1 = .22, data set 2 = .33, data set 3 = .34, data set 4 = .37, and data set 5 = .13.

may have considered the range of the admission prices as being within their latitude of acceptance. Another factor may be that low-income visitors were not concerned about levels of current admission prices or price increases because they knew that they could not visit state parks frequently due to other financial constraints such as lack of a vehicle or money for travel.

There was some tentative support for the notion that perception of admission price is influenced by the level of the current price. Others have reported that resistance increases with higher levels of the current price (Christensen and Richer 1998; Howard and Cable 1980; Leuschner and Cook 1987; Manning et al. 1996). People may be more resistant to an increase in the level of admission prices at higher price levels because of a belief that public park services should provide benefits and enjoyment to visitors at only nominal cost or without charge since they have already been paid for through taxes (e.g., Clawson and Knetsch 1966; Cockrell and Wellman 1985; Ellerbrock 1982; Harris and Driver 1987; McCarville, Driver, and Crompton 1992). This "public goods" position that public park and leisure resources are a communal good and thus should be subsidized with public funds is viewed by some as being a reasonable argument against raising fees to high levels (Hendon 1981; Howard and Crompton 1984).

The analyses reported here offer insight into the influence of behavioral and economic variables in psychologically evaluating price. This extends the findings from previous

JOURNAL OF TRAVEL RESEARCH 151

studies that have been confined to an economic conceptualization or measured only the effect of actual prices on acceptance level. This broader design was an attempt to react to suggestions by others that factors in addition to economic variables need to be included in models to reduce the unexplained variance of visitors' reactions toward admission prices or their changes (Fedler and Miles 1989; Gratton and Taylor 1995; Howard and Cable 1980; Howard and Selin 1987; Kerr and Manfredo 1991).

All of the samples were derived from populations of Texans, which suggests that generalizability beyond the state may be questionable. However, there does not appear to be any reason to assume that these findings would not be equally applicable to other state park systems having similar day use fee ranges and structures. Certainly, the findings add to this body of literature, and as more studies of this nature are reported, more confidence can be placed on the generalizability of the patterns that emerge.

REFERENCES

Ashley, F. B. (1990). "Ethnic Minorities' Involvement with Outdoor Experiential Education." In *Adventure Education*, edited by J. C. Miles and S. Priest. State College, PA: Venture Publishing.

Assael, H. (1995). *Consumer Behavior and Marketing Action*. 5th ed. Cincinnati, OH: South-Western College Publishing.

Backman, S. J., and J. L. Crompton (1991). "The Usefulness of Selected Variables for Predicting Activity Loyalty." *Leisure Sciences*, 13 (3): 205-20.

Bamford, T. E., R. E. Manning, L. K. Forcier, and E. J. Koenemann (1988). "Differential Camping Pricing: An Experiment." *Journal of Leisure Research*, 20 (4): 324-42.

Bovaird, A. G., M. J. Tricker, and R. Stoakes (1984). *Recreation Management and Pricing: The Effect of Charging Policy on Demand at Countryside Recreation Sites*. Brookfield, VT: Gower.

Christensen, N., and J. R. Richer (1998). "Maximum and Appropriate Price for Day Use in the Desolation Wilderness." Paper presented at the 7th International Symposium on Society and Resource Management, May, University of Missouri, Columbia.

Clawson, M., and J. L. Knetsch (1966). *Economics of Outdoor Recreation*. Baltimore: Johns Hopkins University Press.

Cockrell, D., and J. D. Wellman (1985). "Democracy and Leisure: Reflections on Pay-as-You-Go Recreation." *Journal of Park and Recreation Administration*, 3 (4): 1-10.

Crompton, J. L., and C. W. Lamb Jr. (1986). *Marketing Government and Social Services*. New York: John Wiley.

Diamond, W. D., and L. Campbell (1989). "The Framing of Sales Promotions: Effects on Reference Price Change." *Advances in Consumer Research*, 16: 241-47.

Dodds, W. B., and K. B. Monroe (1985). "The Effect of Brand and Price Information on Subjective Product Evaluations." *Advances in Consumer Research*, 12: 85-90.

Dodds, W. B., K. B. Monroe, and D. Grewal (1991). "Effects of Price, Brand, and Store Information on Buyers' Product Evaluations." *Journal of Marketing Research*, 28 (August): 307-19.

Ellerbrock, M. (1982). "Some Straight Talk on User Fees." *Parks and Recreation*, 16 (1): 59-62.

Fedler, A. J., and A. F. Miles (1989). "Paying for Backcountry Recreation: Understanding the Acceptability of Use Fees." *Journal of Parks and Recreation Administration*, 14 (2): 35-46.

Gabor, A. (1977). *Pricing: Principles and Practice*. London: Heinemann.

Gabor, A., and C. Granger (1964). "Price Sensitivity of the Consumer." *Journal of Advertising Research*, 4 (December): 40-44.

Garvin, D. A. (1987). "Competing on the Eight Dimensions of Quality." *Harvard Business Review*, 65 (November-December): 101-9.

Gratton, C., and P. Taylor (1995). "From Economic Theory to Leisure Practice via Empirics: The Case of Demand and Price." *Leisure Studies*, 14 (4): 245-61.

Gregersen, H. M., and A. L. Lundgren (1996). "User Fees as a Park Management Tool: A Framework for Analysis." In *Recreation Fees in the National Park Service: Issues, Policies, and Guidelines for Future Action*, edited by A. L. Lundgren. St. Paul: University of Minnesota Press, pp. 123-33.

Grimes, M. D., T. K. Pinhey, and D. E. Campos (1976). "Pay as You Play: An Analysis of Attitudes Toward a Fee-for-Use Approach to Outdoor Recreation." In *Scientific Research in the National Parks Conference*

Proceedings, edited by R. M. Linn. Washington, DC: National Park Service, pp. 1013-19.

Harris, C. C., and B. L. Driver (1987). "Recreation User Fees: Pros and Cons." *Journal of Forestry*, 85 (5): 25-29.

Helgeson, J. G., and S. E. Beatty (1987). "Price Expectation and Price Recall Error: An Empirical Study." *Journal of Consumer Research*, 14: 379-86.

Hendon, W. S. (1981). *Evaluating Urban Parks and Recreation*. New York: Praeger.

Howard, D. R., and S. Cable (1980). "Determining Consumers' Willingness to Pay for Park and Recreation Services." *Trends*, 25 (2): 42-44.

Howard, D. R., and J. L. Crompton (1984). "Who Are the Consumers of Public Park and Recreation Services? An Analysis of the Users and Nonusers of Three Municipal Leisure Service Organizations." *Journal of Park and Recreation Administration*, 2 (3): 33-48.

Howard, D. R., C. R. Edginton, and S. W. Selin (1989). "Determinants of Program Loyalty." *Journal of Park and Recreation Administration*, 6 (4): 41-51.

Howard, D. R., and S. Selin (1987). "A Method for Establishing Consumer Price Tolerance Levels for Public Recreation Services." *Journal of Parks and Recreation Administration*, 5 (3): 48-59.

Jacobson, R., and C. Obermiller (1989). "The Formation of Reference Price." *Advances in Consumer Research*, 16: 234-40.

Jacoby, J., and J. C. Olson (1977). "Consumer Response to Price: An Attitudinal, Information Processing Perspective." In *Moving Ahead with Attitude Research*, edited by Y. Wind and P. Greenberg. Chicago: American Marketing Association, pp. 73-86.

Kamen, J., and R. Toman (1970). "Psychophysics of Prices." *Journal of Marketing Research*, 7 (February): 27-35.

Kerin, R. A., A. Jain, and D. J. Howard (1992). "Store Shopping Experience and Consumer Price-Quality-Value Perceptions." *Journal of Retailing*, 68 (4): 376-97.

Kerr, G. N., and M. J. Manfredo (1991). "An Attitudinal Based Model of Pricing for Recreation Services." *Journal of Leisure Research*, 23 (1): 37-50.

Kim, S., D. Scott, and J. L. Crompton (1997). "An Exploration of the Relationships among Social Psychological Involvement, Behavioral Involvement, Commitment, and Future Intentions in the Context of Birdwatching." *Journal of Leisure Research*, 29 (3): 320-41.

King, D. A., and M. T. Richards (1977). "Determinants of Choice in Outdoor Recreation." In *Outdoor Recreation: Advances in Application and Economics*, edited by J. M. Hughs. GNT WO-2. Washington, DC: USDA Forest Service, pp. 91-97.

Klein, N. M., and J. E. Oglethorpe (1987). "Cognitive Reference Points in Consumer Decision Making." *Advances in Consumer Research*, 14: 183-87.

LaPage, W. F. (1995). "New Hampshire's Self-Funding State Parks." *Different Drummer Magazine*, 2 (3): 29-32.

Lattin, M. J., and R. E. Bucklin (1989). "Reference Effects of Price and Promotion on Brand Choice Behavior." *Journal of Marketing Research*, 26: 299-310.

Leuschner, W. A., and P. S. Cook (1987). "A Comparative Analysis for Wilderness User Fee Policy." *Journal of Leisure Research*, 19 (2): 101-14.

Loomis, J. B. (1980). "Monetizing Benefits under Alternative River Recreation Use Allocation Systems." *Water Resources Research*, 16 (1): 28-32.

Manning, R. E., W. LaPage, K. Griffall, and B. M. Simon (1996). "Suggested Principles for Designing and Implicating User Fees and Charges in the National Park Service." In *Recreation Fees in the National Park Service: Issues, Policies, and Guidelines for Future Action*, edited by A. L. Lundgren. St. Paul: University of Minnesota Press, pp. 134-36.

McCarville, R. E. (1990). "The Role of Cognitive Processes in Explaining Reactions to Price Changes for Leisure Services." *Journal of Park and Recreation Administration*, 18 (3): 74-86.

——— (1992). "Successful Pricing in the Eye of the Beholder." *Parks and Recreation*, 27 (December): 36-40.

——— (1996). "The Importance of Price Last Paid in Developing Price Expectations for a Public Leisure Service." *Journal of Park and Recreation Administration*, 14 (4): 52-64.

McCarville, R. E., J. L. Crompton, and J. A. Sell (1993). "The Influence of Outcome Messages on Reference Prices." *Leisure Sciences*, 15 (2): 115-30.

McCarville, R. E., B. L. Driver, and J. L. Crompton (1992). "Persuasive Communication and the Pricing of Public Leisure Services." In *Influencing Human Behavior*, edited by M. J. Manfredo. Champaign, IL: Sagamore Publishing, pp. 263-92.

McDonald, C., W. Hammitt, and F. D. Dottavio (1985). "An Individual's Willingness to Pay for a River Visit." In *Proceedings of the 1984 National River Recreation Symposium*. Baton Rouge: Louisiana State University, pp. 605-18.

Monroe, K. B. (1973). "Buyer's Subjective Perceptions of Price." *Journal of Marketing Research*, 10: 73-80.

Monroe, K. B., and J. D. Chapman (1987). "Framing Effects on Buyers' Subjective Evaluations." *Advances in Consumer Research*, 14: 193-97.

Monroe, K. B., C. P. Powell, and P. K. Choudhury (1986). "Recall versus Recognition as a Measure of Price Awareness." *Advances in Consumer Research*, 13: 594-99.

Morris, M. H., and G. Morris (1990). *Market Oriented Pricing: Strategies for Management*. Lincolnwood, IL: NTC Business Books.

Nagle, T. T., and R. K. Holden (1995). *The Strategy and Tactics of Pricing: A Guide to Profitable Decision Making*. 2nd ed. Englewood Cliffs, NJ: Prentice Hall.

Philipp, S. (1995). "Race and Leisure Constraints." *Leisure Sciences*, 17 (2): 109-20.

Reiling, S. D., and M. J. Kotchen (1996). "Lessons Learned from Past Research on Recreation Fees." In *Recreation Fees in the National Park Service: Issues, Policies and Guidelines for Future Action*, edited by A. L. Lundgren. St. Paul: University of Minnesota Press, pp. 49-70.

Richer, J. R. (1998). "Monitoring Visitor Response to the Adventure Pass Program." Paper presented at the 7th International Symposium on Society and Resource Management, May, University of Missouri, Columbia.

Schiffman, L. G., and L. L. Kanuk (1994). *Consumer Behavior*. 5th ed. Englewood Cliffs, NJ: Prentice Hall.

Schoell, W. F., and J. P. Guiltinan (1995). *Marketing*. Englewood Cliffs, NJ: Prentice Hall.

Sherif, C. W. (1963). "Social Categorization as a Function of Latitudes of Acceptance and Series Range." *Journal of Abnormal and Social Psychology*, 67 (2): 148-56.

Szybillo, G. J., and J. Jacoby (1974). "Intrinsic versus Extrinsic Cues as Determinants of Perceived Product Quality." *Journal of Applied Psychology*, 59 (1): 74-78.

Thompson, C., and A. Tinsley (1979). "Income Expenditure Elasticities for Recreation: Their Estimation and Relation to Demand for Recreation." *Journal of Leisure Research*, 10 (2): 265-70.

Uhl, J. (1970). "Consumer Perception of Retail Food Price Changes." Paper presented at the First Annual Meeting of the Association for Consumer Research, Amherst, MA.

Vogt, C. A., and A. E. Watson (1998). "Brand Loyalty as an Indicator of Fee Support by Desolation Wilderness Visitors." Paper presented at the 7th International Symposium on Society and Resource Management, University of Missouri, Columbia.

Winer, R. S. (1986). "A Reference Price Model of Brand Choice for Frequently Purchased Products." *Journal of Consumer Research*, 13: 250-56.

Zeithaml, V. A. (1982). "Consumer Response to In-Store Price Information Environments." *Journal of Consumer Research*, 8 (March): 357-69.

——— (1984). "Issues in Conceptualizing and Measuring Consumer Response to Price." *Advances in Consumer Research*, 11: 612-16.

[23]

Pergamon

S0261–5177(96)00016–7

Tourism Management. Vol. 17, No. 4, pp. 247–254. 1996
Copyright © 1996 Elsevier Science Ltd
Printed in Great Britain. All rights reserved
0261-5177/96 $15.00 + 0.00

Pricing policy in nature-based tourism

Jan G Laarman

Department of Forestry. Box 8008, North Carolina State University, Raleigh, NC 27695, USA

Hans M Gregersen

Department of Forest Resources, 115 Green Hall, 1530 N. Cleveland Ave, University of Minnesota. St Paul, MN 55108, USA

Visitors to publicly owned national parks, wildlife reserves and other natural areas pay entrance fees and other charges for their access and use. What principles and criteria contribute to an appropriate pricing policy? The answers to this are complex because of multiple pricing objectives, visitor categories, visitor activities, fee instruments and philosophical positions. In this review paper, these issues are examined from the perspective of public agencies that are working to improve their pricing practices. Pricing is a potentially powerful tool to move towards greater efficiency, fairness and environmentally sustainable management. To date, this tool is underutilized. Copyright © 1996 Elsevier Science Ltd

Keywords: national parks, willingness to pay, fees, contingent valuation, pricing, revenue sharing

A small but rapidly growing segment of the world's tourism industry is nature-based tourism (NBT). This refers to travel motivated totally or in part by interests in the natural history of a place, where visits combine education, recreation and often adventure. It is certain that NBT provides substantial flows of hard currencies to several economies of the developing world.[1–3] It is also certain that only a small share of the money spent by visitors in NBT goes towards protecting the attractions they go to see.

A main attraction for NBT is publicly owned national parks, wildlife reserves and other protected areas.[4–5] Yet entrance fees and other charges for access to such areas frequently are below amounts visitors are willing and able to pay, and below amounts required to finance park operating budgets. The perverse result is that relatively poor countries subsidize visits of persons from relatively wealthy countries, who comprise a large proportion of all NBT participants. Moreover, the generation of only small revenue flows from parks and reserves provides governments with little political or fiscal rationale to augment funding for them in strategies of national development. The vicious circle is one of low fees, inadequate revenue and deficient public investment – followed by continued low fees, revenue and investment.

Although these principles are readily grasped in the abstract, only a few analyses examine them empirically.[6–7] Pricing and revenue allocation in NBT are seriously neglected in public policy, especially for the many governments around the world struggling with fiscal problems. Our paper has three objectives:

- to review briefly the economist's concept of willingness to pay as a basis for NBT pricing;
- to examine administrative criteria in NBT pricing from the perspective of a government agency; and
- to discuss the elements of success in NBT pricing at policy and project levels.

What price to access nature? Willingness to pay

Demand for NBT as willingness to pay

National parks, biological reserves and other natural attractions for NBT are valued for their existence and their use. Existence values explain the demand for preserving sites; use values reflect the demand for visiting them.

The choice to visit or not visit a particular site for NBT is determined by an individual's willingness to pay (WTP) for it in relation to the competing uses of his or her income. Demand studies indicate that WTP varies with income, education, occupation, demographic aspects and psychographic profiles.[8]

Additionally, WTP is higher or lower in relation to a site's attributes, or 'qualities'. These attributes comprise attraction factors and infrastructure factors. The special amenities of the Galapagos Islands, Serengeti Plain and other 'jewels of nature' explain high WTP. These sites have high scarcity value. Few persons will pay as much for access to 'ordinary' sites, ie those for which several alternatives provide roughly similar experiences. The WTP also reflects the presence and quality of ground transportation, accommodations, guide service and cooperative governments. The attraction factors and infrastructure factors jointly determine the amount of satisfaction provided by the tourism visit, and thus the WTP for it.

Determining WTP: travel costs and contingent valuation

Willingness to pay (WTP) is different in concept from ability to pay. Both can be different from the amount an individual actually pays (ie for access and use of NBT sites). The focus of demand studies is the WTP. Most studies of WTP rely on one of two analytical methods: travel costs and contingent valuation.

Decades ago, the economist Harold Hotelling inferred that the use value of a recreation site is given by the transportation, food, lodging and other costs to travel to and experience the site. Clawson and Knetch[9] built on this idea to relate travel expenditures to the numbers of persons visiting different recreation sites from different origins. The inverse relationship between travel costs and visitation rates is a demand curve. An individual's willingness to pay a fee for access or use (or both) can be derived from this relationship. In practice, however, the travel-cost approach is employed more often to value and defend NBT as a land use than to guide pricing, eg for the Monteverde Cloud Forest in Costa Rica.[10]

While the travel-cost method is grounded in observed market behavior, the contingent valuation method poses hypothetical 'what if' questions about how individuals would respond to specified fee types or amounts. Representative applications include contingent valuation studies at Nairobi National Park,[11] Tikal National Park[12] and several parks in Costa Rica.[13–14]

The answers on WTP are contingent upon the situations described by the interviewer. The choices – or contingencies – have to be realistic, well described and clearly understood by respondents. Through years of experience and hundreds of surveys, the limitations of contingent valuation are by now familar.[15] However, they are no less a constraint in applied work.

The administrative framework: perspectives of the public agency

The economist's answer on WTP is only a starting point for the administrator of the public agency (eg for national parks and wildlife), who has numerous interests to serve and criteria to weigh. The matter of setting fees for NBT is complex because of multiple pricing objectives, visitor categories, NBT activities and fee instruments. Importantly, the context of charging fees is often surrounded by philosophical and legislative debates. In countries where access to nature has been considered 'every person's right', the discussion of new or higher fees is bound to stir controversy.

Pricing objectives

The agency's perspective on a new or elevated fee begins with reasons to impose it. Here we identify 10 pricing objectives, realizing that our list may be incomplete:

(1) The revenue goal is an obvious one for private NBT suppliers, and for public suppliers whose budgets are constrained. Even where fee collections must be turned over to a national treasury, budget allocations often reflect the amount of revenue generated.

(2) The collection of revenue from NBT indicates that natural areas have financial value. Demonstrating through user fees that visitors pay their way wholly or in part is important in political discussions of land use.

(3) If revenues from fees can be made to increase, this may enable public agencies to gain increasing independence from outside influences. In the example of Peru, an estimated 90% of financial input for the country's protected areas is from external sources.[16] The acceptance of external funds can be inseparable from external influence on policy making. Conversely, greater financial autonomy may lead to greater policy autonomy.

(4) Fees can be designed to reduce subsidization of groups perceived to receive unfair advantages, eg non-residents who pay no taxes for financing the NBT sites they visit. Conversely, fee policy may deliberately subsidize target groups or activities, especially if natural history is considered a merit good. In each context, defining what is just and meritorious is subjective, resting on political and administrative judgments.

(5) If fees are made high enough, they will discourage low-income visitors (except as they are

Pricing policy in nature-based tourism: J G Laarman and H M Gregersen

Table 1 Guiding principles for fee policy in NBT

Principle	Rationale
Fees supplement but do not replace general sources of revenue	Even for heavily visited sites, fee revenue rarely covers total costs, especially capital costs. Heavy dependence on fee revenue reduces visitor diversity and the scope of attractions that can be offered. Yearly fluctuations in fee revenue make fees an unstable income source
At least a portion of fee revenues should be set aside ('earmarked') for sites that generate them	Earmarking increases management's incentives to set and collect fees efficiently. Visitors may be more willing to pay fees if they know that fees are used on site
Fees should be set on a site-specific basis	National guidelines specify fee objectives and policies, yet management goals and visitor patterns vary across NBT sites, requiring local flexibility in assessing the type and amount of fee
Fee collection is not justified at all sites	Fees are not cost-effective at places with low visitation demand and high collection costs
Fee systems work best when supported by reliable accounting and management	Administrative decisions about fees require acceptable data on costs and revenues of providing NBT for different sites and activities

Source: Adapted from Lindberg and Huber[19] (pp 103–104).

granted access through other policies). This can be a deliberate step to restrain total visitation, and to ration it to a selected socioeconomic element (eg the relatively high-spending tourists).

(6) Fees can be a management tool to relieve crowding if fees are elevated during peak times and for congested sites. However, evidence on off-peak pricing to shift use patterns is inconclusive, possibly because even 'high' fees have been modest in most cases to date.

(7) Fee policy for publicly owned NBT sites can be designed to stimulate private business and regional economic development. Low fees contribute to high visitation. This increases the total number of persons who spend for hotels, guide and transport services, and other goods and services. However, the visitors may include many who travel on low budgets, eg backpackers, students and nearby residents. Also, low fees at public sites make it difficult for private businesses to compete in direct production of similar NBT activities.

(8) Among recreation managers, a frequent assumption is that NBT visitors are more respectful of their surroundings if they have to pay for them. Those arguing this position assert that vandalism, littering and other negative behaviors decrease when visitors pay for use. This proposition merits more study than it has received to date, especially in a cross-cultural international context.

(9) The levy of one or more fees helps the public agency to educate its visitors. At the time of fee collection, information can be presented verbally or in writing to explain why fees are being collected. This gives the agency an opportunity to win visitor support for programs and special needs. Supplementary information may address natural history, risks and liability and other topics to enhance visitors' enjoyment and safety. Even though such information can be presented separately, its combination with fee payments is efficient for the agency, and helps visitors understand what they receive in exchange for their money.

(10) As a corollary of the preceding point, policy discussions of new or increased fees help to educate public agencies about their visitors. Proposals to increase fees require forecasts of acceptability, cost recovery and consequences for visitation patterns. Moreover, implementation of a new fee is wisely accompanied by monitoring and evaluation to determine actual impacts. The information collected for feasibility and later for evaluation provides profiles on visitor numbers, composition and likes and dislikes.

Hence pricing objectives are many, competing and varying from one area to another. Administrators are challenged to articulate their pricing objectives, and to make them feasible to attain. *Table 1* offers guiding principles.

Pricing strategies

The strategy of how to set fees emerges from pricing objectives in combination with information about visitors' WTP. The strategy should change through time as visitor demand increases, and as administrators acquire experience with different types of fees. *Table 2* shows an evolution that begins with small charges, and moves towards increasingly higher ones.

'Token charges' are below supply costs, do not deter use and do not raise significant revenues. However, the approach establishes a pricing policy (ie access is not completely free), and may improve

Table 2 An approximate evolution of pricing strategies in NBT

Objectives	Experience
Introduction of token charges	Nominal fees become accepted as a way to impute value to visitation
Fees for revenue	'Reasonable' fees become accepted as a necessary budget supplement
Fees to offset costs	Fees are set to recover some or all of operating costs
Fees as management tools	There are many discussions but few test cases of using differential pricing to affect use patterns (eg fees varying by season, day of the week, and site)
Fees for profit	Profit can be appropriate even in public agencies, eg to build capital reserves and replace facilities. Yet there is little evidence to date of profit-making behavior in most parks agencies

Source: Adapted from LaPage, W F 'Financing the wilderness with user taxes' in Martin, B H (ed) *Fees for Outdoor Recreation on Lands Open to the Public: Conference Proceedings* Appalachian Mountain Club, Gorham, NH (1984) 95.

data collection and analysis (eg on visitor numbers, periods of peak use, etc).

'Going-rate charges' reflect that pricing of a given NBT attraction should be equivalent to charges at comparable attractions after adjusting for differences in site quality, travel costs, visitors' incomes and other demand factors. This is a market-oriented strategy. However, implementation is made difficult by the uniqueness of certain NBT attractions. Also, because marketed-oriented pricing has not been widely practiced in the public sector, going-rate fees typically depart from frameworks of visitor supply and demand. Even fees at private nature reserves, which generally charge more than public reserves, are often subsidized by grants and other external financial support.[17]

'Cost-based charges' are self-explanatory. The approach is straightforward to explain and defend in concept. Usually, cost-based approaches imply fees that are higher than token charges and going-rate charges. Various manuals guide the collection and analysis of cost data, but a complete cost accounting is challenging. In most practice to date, the costs of ecological impacts and congestion are omitted as too difficult to quantify. Even costs of operation and maintenance can be difficult to completely define

and estimate. In application, then, many cost-based charges are underestimates.

Fees, taxes and contributions

Various types of fees and charges are assessed in exchange for access to and use of NBT sites (*Table 3*). In a public agency, the choices are determined by cultural and legal norms, administrative costs and human imagination. Criteria governing the form and method of payment include the following:

- The system of fees and charges should be clear about which persons will pay what amounts; there should be no room for ambiguity.
- Fair fees reflect (1) ability to pay, and (2) payment in proportion to the benefits received. Efficient fees reflect payment in proportion to the costs of management and administration.
- Fee instruments should not distort economic efficiency, eg approaches should avoid large taxes in sectors such as transportation, hotels etc.
- The choices among alternative fee instruments should weigh expected revenues against expected costs of fee collection and administration.

Where ability to pay is an issue, approaches which combine different kinds of fees and charges can be

Table 3 Categories of fees and charges in NBT

Fee type	Observation
General entrance fee	'Gate fees' allow either free or priced access to facilities beyond the entry point
Fees for use	Examples: fees for visitor centers, parking, camp sites, guide services, boat use, trail shelters, emergency rescue, etc
Concession fees	Charges (or revenue shares) are assessed on individuals and businesses which sell food, accommodations, transportation, guide services, souvenirs and other goods and services to NBT visitors
Royalties and profit shares	Can be charged on sales of guidebooks, postcards, tee-shirts, souvenirs, books, films, photos, etc
Licenses and permits	For tour operators, guides, researchers, wildlife collectors, mountain climbers, river rafters, etc. The concept can be extended to individual campers, bikers, etc
Taxes	Examples: room taxes, airport taxes, vehicle taxes, excise taxes on sports and outdoor equipment, etc
Voluntary donations	Include cash and in-kind gifts, often through 'friends of the park' organizations

Source: Adapted from Sherman and Dixon[7] (pp 109–112).

attractive. For example, fees for general entry to a nature park can be kept low so that few persons are excluded at the gate. Inside the gate, individual services and facilities are priced at their cost of provision. This has obvious political appeal, but faces the drawback that collection of different fees at the same site can be costly for management and irritating for visitors.

Taxes levied on equipment (fishing gear, camping equipment, boats, diving equipment, cameras, etc) can generate substantial revenues in industrialized countries.[18] Yet this approach is less feasible in most developing countries, where foreign visitors typically enter the destination countries carrying equipment from their home countries.

Taxes collected at airports, hotels and other facilities may be able to generate substantial revenues for allocation to national parks and other NBT sites. However, the funding of NBT sites from such broad-based taxes is less fair than collecting payments from NBT users.

Licenses and permits for mountain climbing, river rafting, safari opportunities, reef diving, etc, can be sold to high bidders through auctions. The successful bidders are expected to comply with agreements which specify conditions of access, liability and permit revocation. The auction approach is most viable where (1) administrative structures are efficient and honest, (2) access to NBT sites can be controlled, (3) numbers of allowed entries are restricted, and (4) revenue considerations rank high among pricing objectives. Clearly, only a few NBT attractions meet all of these conditions. Furthermore, auctioning is often opposed by small tour operators, who fear that their larger competitors will apply political influence and bribes to capture all the permits.

Particularly in recent years, voluntary contributions of cash, land and labor have been increasingly important resources for NBT. From the criterion of meeting varying ability to pay, voluntary contributions are superior to mandatory fees. Tapping voluntary contributions is politically correct in 'green societies', and can be remunerative. As reported by Lindberg and Huber,[19] The Nature Conservancy solicited US$150 thousand for the Charles Darwin Research Station in the Galapagos Islands by mailing an appeal for contributions to visitors who signed the station's guest book. In Costa Rica, several private organizations have raised substantial funding for that country's protected areas through external grants and gifts.

More generally, the international conservation organizations direct what must be a large financial transfer from industrialized to developing countries for wildlife, national parks and other resources valuable for NBT. It is highly appropriate for these organizations to pay for existence value, which is widely enjoyed by citizens of all countries. It is less

appropriate for them directly or indirectly to subsidize on-site visitation, which is a private rather than public good. Even more importantly, the recipient country may be expected to accept that 'he who has the gold makes the rules'. The philanthropy of cross-country nature protection is little explored. Nor is much known about possible neocolonial influences in 'nature sectors' where foreign contributions are significant.

Multi-tiered pricing

Multi-tiered pricing occurs when fees vary by category of visitor. Fees are often reduced for children, students, handicapped and retired persons – particularly for residents.

When WTP is lower for residents than non-residents, two-tiered pricing yields more revenue than either a high or low fee alone.[6] More generally, a public agency which aims to make as much revenue as possible charges different fees to different visitors in relation to their varying WTP. This promotes not only revenue objectives, but possibly also social equity.

However, multi-tiered pricing is not free of dilemmas. When carrying capacity is limited so that some visitors have to be excluded, the public agency makes more revenue by selling access to non-residents over residents. The trade-off between revenue versus local use has no answer except in a political framework.

Explanations for multi-tiered fees sometimes confuse social merit, fairness and ability to pay. Reduced fees for students may reflect an assumption that students have low incomes, even though some are from wealthy families. Ecuador's fee to visit the Galapagos Islands is many times higher for non-residents (foreigners) than residents (nationals), even though some Ecuadorians are wealthy and many foreigners are not.

In summary, multi-tiered pricing is highly imperfect as a policy instrument. It attempts to discriminate among individuals on the basis of broad but mythical averages, ie foreigners are rich, students and retirees are poor, etc. Furthermore, criteria for differential pricing are not solely fiscal, but also legal, political and cultural. For these reasons, the performance of multi-tiered pricing may depart from the economist's expectation of high revenue generation.

Public attitudes about fees

The charging of fees to access nature touches fundamental questions regarding which among a country's resources should be provided 'free' or at only nominal prices. In many settings, access to public wildlands has been everyone's right, particularly for dispersed uses of lands not privately claimed. If the use of public lands is everyone's right, then is it justifiable for a government to deny access to individuals who cannot or will not pay a fee?

It can be politically popular to favor free access. Some environmental organizations maintain that access to nature promotes self-reliance, independence and even democracy.[20] Moreover, nature-based activity fits the philosophies of 'green societies'. That NBT is perceived to be compatible with environmental protection provides an argument for subsidizing it. To the preceding premises can be added the concern for equity, ie that low-income people should not be excluded from nature appreciation, particularly in light of the alleged virtues it bestows.

This is a formidable list of cultural and psychological obstacles in the way of elevating fees for NBT. Even when governments are under pressure to adopt enterprise-like behavior, political leaders have been reluctant to increase fees in fear of public protest. Moreover, the natural resources agencies have been notably timid on this matter. Discussions to increase fees correlate well with periods of falling budget appropriations, but do not lead to long-term and sustained policy efforts.

Indeed, the models of NBT pricing in western societies may be poor examples for developing countries. To date, wealthy societies have seemed quite willing to subsidize NBT, despite mild undercurrents to the contrary. For example, fee revenues collected by the USA's National Park Service are equivalent to only 5–6% of the agency's expenditures.

This contrasts with the starker reality of low-income countries. Chronic shortages of public revenues imply that NBT visitors should pay, especially when they are (rich) foreigners. It is no surprise that fees for NBT are most differentiated and market-oriented in Costa Rica, Ecuador, East Africa and elsewhere in the developing world.

In the presence of public resistance to fees, administrators have several strategies to counteract it:[21]

- Visitors are less reluctant to pay fees when they know how and why their fees are used. Some evidence suggests that visitors are happier to pay when informed that their fees contribute to on-site management. Conversely, visitors should be informed of services that will be discontinued if fees are not collected.
- Support for fees increases when they are for 'quality' improvements. Visitors are sensitive to the quality of toilets, trails, maps, signs and other infrastructure.
- Visitors are less opposed to fees which offset costs than fees which control entry or ration use. Hence the way that fees are described can shape attitudes.
- Fee increases are more palatable in regular small increments than in large jumps, even when fees are comparatively low.
- Support for increased fees is only partly related to an individual's income and past amounts of use.

More important is the past level of the fee for a particular type of activity in a particular place, ie a conditioned expectation.

The preceding observations from North America may be less relevant elsewhere, particularly in cross-cultural settings. For example, a study at Tikal (Guatemala) indicated no relationship between WTP higher fees and information that fees would be returned for park management.[12] More generally, the subject of public support for higher fees traverses difficult ground in psychology and communications. Comparatively little is known about this, especially when pricing is linked with emotional subjects such as nature protection and customary rights.

As indicated, one avenue to win support for fees is to open the issue for public education. The premise is that people will act rationally when presented with justifiable reasons for paying higher fees. Opposite to this strategy is hiding fees, particularly when they are high, so that visitors are unaware of them. For instance, high fees to view mountain gorillas in Central Africa have been included in the prices of tour packages.

Other indirect revenues include taxes for overnight lodging, transportation services etc. The fees and taxes are attached to expenditures such as hotel bills and airline tickets, where they are less conspicuous and less avoidable than if levied separately. Moreover, indirect methods transfer a part of the costs of fee collection from public agencies to private businesses. To be weighed gainst these apparent advantages, cooperation is unlikely where businesses are obliged to collect fees and taxes, but derive no benefit from them. Finally, indirect fees and taxes – where they are large – can distort prices in ways that hurt the larger economy.

Revenue sharing with local communities

There is no shortage of advice on the 'how to' aspects of cultivating local support for NBT in communities near protected areas.[22–24] One of many strategies is to encourage governments to share entrance and user fees with the communities. The revenues at any particular NBT site are insignificant for a national treasury, but can be important locally. Where it can be made to function, revenue sharing is a focal point for cooperation between parks administrators and local residents.

Yet revenue sharing is not widely practiced. In studies of 28 protected areas in Africa, Asia, and Latin America, Wells and Brandon[25] reported only three examples of it for Kenya, Nepal and Mexico. Revenue sharing is simple in concept, but governments have been reluctant to pursue it. In the first place, revenue sharing has to be supported by top-level authorities for revenue collection. Understandably, they can be highly unsympathetic to proposals which reduce inflows to the treasury. Second, revenue sharing works best when officials in parks and wildlife agencies invite community leaders to discuss NBT pricing and revenue disposition. Not every parks administrator is open to this, and the process can be long and difficult. For example, revenue sharing at Ranomafana National Park (Madagascar) extends to 160 villages, demanding an enormous effort in organization and dialogue.[26]

Perhaps most importantly, successful revenue sharing requires mutual trust between the government and local residents. Trust is often in short supply, particularly in respect of collecting and handling money. Typically, each side regards the other as incompetent and corrupt.

None of these obstacles is insurmountable. If revenue sharing spreads more widely in the future, local communities are likely to play a larger role in decisions about NBT pricing. Communities will want NBT to generate high and continuing yields of revenue. They can be expected to attempt to influence fee policy in ways that come close to market-oriented pricing.

Success in NBT pricing: final suggestions

In this review paper, we assert that pricing is a potentially powerful tool to move towards greater efficiency, fairness and environmentally sustainable NBT. To date, this tool is underutilized. We conclude with a few suggestions to advance pricing practice for administrators who take the issue seriously.

Money-making behavior is not part of the usual administrative culture for public authorities in charge of parks and wildlife. Most professional rewards are tied to program development, not entrance receipts. Perhaps the majority of sites for NBT cannot become self-financing, even under the most intelligent of pricing strategies. It is easy to understand why too much pressure to generate revenues would be an unfortunate distraction. Nor do visitors expect public nature reserves to be managed as businesses.

While we accept these qualifications, they do not stop us from arguing the importance of pricing. The proposition that contact with nature bestows social benefits cannot be accepted at face value. Even where the premise is valid, it does not warrant free or nearly free access to publicly owned natural attractions. These attractions are not costless to provide, and the concept of 'user pays' is perfectly appropriate for NBT as a private good (even when it is supplied through a public agency). For socially meritorious individuals (students, local residents, etc), the public agency can make exceptions to a pricing rule. There is ample precedent for this.

Regarding the amount of revenue to be collected, a politically defensible position is cost recovery. The provision of services at their cost (marginal-cost

pricing) is a standard pillar of public finance. The costs to be recovered through user fees are an agency's expenditures to provide for NBT, not its total outlay for park protection and maintenance. The total outlay contributes existence value for the world, but visitors should not be charged for it. Rather, visitors should pay for their direct use, eg capital and operating costs of trails, interpretive centers, guide services and the like. Because many costs are indivisible, the accounting to separate user costs from all other costs is not easy. However, practice should be subordinated to principle, not the other way around.

In some cases, the agency's direct costs to support visitation may be high in relation to small numbers of visitors. Then, the agency has over-built its infrastructure in relation to user demand. Costs cannot be recovered through any reasonable level of fees. This indicates inefficient public spending, and obligates the agency to re-think how it should allocate its budget.

The elements of successful fee setting contain few surprises. The agency must be clear about its pricing objectives. It must be particularly mindful of how its fees affect businesses in the tourism sector. It must have reliable information about visitors' WTP. It must realize that visitors and tourism businesses are more accepting of small but regular fee increases than of large jumps. It must actively discuss its fee policy with revenue authorities, tour and hotel operators and local communities.

These guidelines are easily written but less easily followed, as illustrated by recent events in Costa Rica. In late 1994, the country's natural resources agency announced that daily park entrance fees for non-residents would rise from US$1.25 to US$15.00. The new fee is well above the middle range of WTP indicated by previous studies.[13] The steep increase provoked immediate protests, especially by tour operators. Newspapers interviewed angry tourists who claimed they were being exploited. In the town of Cahuita, where livelihoods depend on visitors to the adjacent national park, local people protested the fee increase by taking control of the park entrance. In just one year, non-resident visitation to Costa Rica's national parks fell by 47%. Critics attribute this to the new entrance fee, although that cannot be proved. More certain is that the fee increase has been exceptionally controversial, and that few people in the tourism sector were prepared for it.[27]

The preceding example takes us to our final issue, collaboration. One definition of success in NBT pricing is shared agreement (or not too much disagreement) that the types and amounts of fees contribute to national objectives for tourism and nature conservation. The focus on fees is an excellent means to promote a dialogue about these objectives. Various parties are invited to the table:

park managers, revenue authorities, tour and hotel operators, managers of private NBT reserves and leaders of communities near NBT sites. The government's aim is to create a climate of good will by giving each party a voice in the deliberations. Just as importantly, the authorities hear all arguments for and against different fee proposals. In the end, the choices among alternatives are no less difficult, but they are informed.

Acknowledgements

The background research for this paper was funded by the Environmental Policy and Training (EPAT) project, funded by the United States Agency for International Development (USAID), and administered by the Midwestern University Consortium for International Assistance (MUCIA), USA.

References

[1]Boo, E *Ecotourism: The Potentials and the Pitfalls* World Wildlife Fund, Washington, DC (1990)
[2]Whelan T (ed) *Nature Tourism: Managing for the Environment* Island Press, Washington, DC (1991)
[3]International Resources Group, Inc 'Ecotourism: a viable alternative for sustainable management of natural resources in Africa' US Agency for International Development, Bureau for Africa, Washington, DC (1992)
[4]McNeely, J A *Economics and Biological Diversity* International Union for the Conservation of Nature and Natural Resources, Gland, Switzerland (1988)
[5]Dixon, J A and Sherman, P B *Economics of Protected Areas* Island Press, Washington, DC (1990)
[6]Lindberg, K 'Policies for maximizing nature tourism's ecological and economic benefits' World Resources Institutes, Washington, DC (1991)
[7]Sherman, P B and Dixon, J A 'The economics of nature tourism: determining if it pays' in Whelan T (ed) *Nature Tourism: Managing for the Environment* Island Press, Washington, DC (1991) 89–131
[8]Ryel, R and Grasse, T 'Marketing ecotourism: attracting the elusive ecotourist' in Whelan T (ed) *Nature Tourism: Managing for the Environment* Island Press, Washington, DC (1991) 164–186
[9]Clawson, M and Knetch, J L *Economics of Outdoor Recreation* Johns Hopkins University Press, Baltimore, MD (1965)
[10]Tobias, D and Mendelsohn, R 'Valuing ecotourism in a tropical rainforest reserve' *Ambio* 1992 **20** (2) 91–93
[11]Abala, D O 'A theoretical and empirical investigation of the willingness to pay for recreational services: a case study of Nairobi National Park' *Eastern Africa Economic Review* 1987 **3** (2) 111–119
[12]Barry, C C 'Nature tourism and its development in Guatemala: assessing current trends and future potential' MS thesis, University of North Carolina, Chapel Hill, NC (1992)
[13]Baldares, M J and Laarman, J G 'User fees at protected areas in Costa Rica' in Vincent, J R (ed) *Valuing Environmental Benefits in Developing Economies* Michigan State University, East Lansing, MI (1991) 87–108
[14]Hanrahan, M, Solorzano, R and Echeverria, J 'Valuation of non-priced amenities provided by the biological resources within the Monteverde Cloud Forest Reserve' Tropical Science Center, San Jose, Costa Rica (1992)
[15]Mitchell, R C and Carson, R T *Using Surveys to Value Public Goods: The Contingent Valuation Method* Resources for the Future, Washington, DC (1989)
[16]Barzetti, V (ed) *Parks and Progress: Protected Areas and Economic Development in Latin America and the Caribbean* International Union for the Conservation of Nature and Natural Resources and Inter-American Development Bank, Washington, DC (1993)
[17]Alderman, C L 'A study of the role of privately owned lands used for nature tourism, education, and conservation' Conservation International, Washington, DC (1990)
[18]Prosser, N S 'A successful excise tax: the Dingell-Johnson Program' in Martin, B H (ed) *Fees for Outdoor Recreation on Lands Open to the Public: Conference Proceedings* Appalachian Mountain Club, Gorham, NH (1984) 115–118
[19]Lindberg, K and Huber, R M Jr 'Economic issues in ecotourism management' in Lindberg, K and Hawkins, D E (eds) *Ecotourism: A Guide for Planners and Managers* Ecotourism Society, North Bennington, VT (1993) 82–115
[20]Gould, E M Jr 'Culture and guides to action' in Martin, B H (ed) *Fees for Outdoor Recreation on Lands Open to the Public: Conference Proceedings* Appalachian Mountain Club, Gorham, NH (1984) 10–14
[21]Driver, B L 'Public responses to user fees at public recreation areas' in Martin, B H (ed) *Fees for Outdoor Recreation on Lands Open to the Public: Conference Proceedings* Appalachian Mountain Club, Gorham, NH (1984) 45–48
[22]Drake, S P 'Local participation in ecotourism projects' in Whelan T (ed) *Nature Tourism: Managing for the Environment* Island Press, Washington, DC (1991) 132–163
[23]West, P C and Brechlin, S R (eds) *Resident Peoples and National Parks* University of Arizona Press, Tucson, AZ (1991)
[24]Brandon, K 'Basic steps toward encouraging local participation in nature tourism projects' in Lindberg, K and Hawkins, D E (eds) *Ecotourism: A Guide for Planners and Managers* Ecotourism Society, North Bennington, VT (1993) 134–151
[25]Wells, M and Brandon, K *People and Parks: Linking Protected Area Management with Local Communities* World Bank, World Wildlife Fund, and US Agency for International Development, Washington, DC (1992)
[26]Peters, W J Jr 'Attempting to integrate conservation and development among resident peoples at Ranomafana National Park, Madagascar' PhD thesis, North Carolina State University, Raleigh, NC (1994)
[27]Chase, L 'National park entrance fees in Costa Rica' Dept of Agricultural, Resource, and Managerial Economics, Cornell University, Ithaca, NY (1995)

[24]

Available online at www.sciencedirect.com

SCIENCE ⓓ DIRECT®

Tourism Management 26 (2005) 529–537

TOURISM
MANAGEMENT

www.elsevier.com/locate/tourman

ELSEVIER

The perceived importance of price as one hotel selection dimension

Tim Lockyer*

Department of Tourism Management, Waikato Management School, The University of Waikato, Private Bag 3105, Hamilton, New Zealand

Received 4 September 2003; accepted 3 March 2004

Abstract

A review of the literature reveals numerous research projects which have considered the factors important in the selection of hotel/ motel accommodation. These projects adopted a closed question approach and almost uniformly reported that cleanliness was the most important attribute, with price being rated far less important (Hosp. Res. J. 19(4) (1996) 113). Taking a fresh approach, this research focuses specifically on gaining an understanding of the impact of price in accommodation selection, and to do this three focus groups were established comprising 42 participants who were asked to participate in both open and closed questions.

Of particular interest was that although the findings from the closed questions were very similar to other research (Int. J. Contemp. Hosp. Manage. 6(14) (2002) 294), the focus group discussion identified quite a different perspective: that price should not be considered along with other attributes but needs special consideration. The research identified 'trigger points' which play an important part in the potential guest purchase decision process.
© 2004 Elsevier Ltd. All rights reserved.

Keywords: Accommodation; Price; Focus group; CATPAC; Consumer behaviour

1. Introduction

Understanding the factors that are important in the selection of hotel and motel accommodation by guests is an interesting and important area of research. A better understanding of the influence of the many factors involved in the guest selection process helps managers more effectively tailor and develop their facilities and staff so that they are able to achieve and maintain the highest possible occupancy, resulting in a positive impact on profitability. This issue has attracted the attention of a number of researchers, for example Dolnicar and Otter (2003) reviewed 21 studies undertaken over the period of 1984–2000 looking at factors influencing occupancy. From the 21 journal articles Dolnicar and Otter (2003) extracted 173 attributes. These included such factors as: Image, Service, Price/ Value, Hotel, Room, Food and Beverage, Security and others. In addition there has also been research into the impact of different segments of the market for example: American Business Travellers (Weaver & Oh, 1993), Motor Coach Tour Operators (Schaefer, Illum, & Margavio, 1995), Leisure Business Meetings Conven-

tions (Dube and Renaghan, 1999), and Business Guests (Lockyer, 2002).

Callan (1996) summarised a number of research projects that had been conducted and of particular interest is the finding that within many of these, the standard of housekeeping and cleanliness was rated as the most important in the selection of accommodation by guests.

The importance of cleanliness has also been identified more recently by Lockyer (2000, 2002). In these studies it is important to note that 'Price or Room Rate' was not rated highly by potential guests as a deciding factor in the selection of accommodation. Research has also shown that there is a 'gap' between what accommodation managers *believe* is important and what guests *say* is important in the selection of accommodation (Lockyer, 2002). The importance of this has become evident when discussing research findings from the guest perspective with industry management. Where research indicates that accommodation guests gauge cleanliness and related items as the most important, on the other hand, industry indicates almost uniformly that price is the most influential factor in guest selection (Lockyer, 2002). This view from industry can be understood if some time is spent in the reservation department of a hotel or motel—many of the inquiries from

*Tel.: +64-7-838-4466; fax: +64-7-838-4331.

E-mail address: lockyer@waikato.ac.nz (T. Lockyer).

0261-5177/$ - see front matter © 2004 Elsevier Ltd. All rights reserved.
doi:10.1016/j.tourman.2004.03.009

530 *T. Lockyer / Tourism Management 26 (2005) 529–537*

potential guests include, as one of the first questions, an inquiry about price. As a result this is a predominant issue in the minds of accommodation management staff.

The evident difference between what guests perceive as important (Cleanliness) and what industry management perceive as important (Price) prompted this research, with the objective of better understanding the role of price in the purchase decision of hotel and motel accommodation, and understanding why such differences seem to exist. The identification of such a mismatch raises the secondary question; is previous research into factors affecting occupancy appropriate? It therefore seems justified to look at previous research methods used (Kitzinger & Barbour, 1999). For example: Saleh and Ryan (1992) used factor analysis; Dube and Renaghan (1999, 2000) used frequency tables; Weaver and Oh (1993) used mean values and group comparisons; Tsaur and Gwo-Hsiung (1995) used descriptive statistics, to illustrate a few. Each of these researchers has developed some form of list of attributes, using a variety of methods, and then asked potential guests to rank the identified attributes. This approach has raised a number of problems, as identified by Callan (1996) where cleanliness is identified as the most important attribute. The potential customer participating in the research has no or little idea before staying in a particular establishment as to the level of its cleanliness. However, cleanliness is a factor which has an impact on whether the guest returns and on levels of repeat business.

The decision as to which hotel or motel to select is potentially complex. In the consumer behaviour literature stages can be described as "Need Recognition", "Search for Information", "Alternative Evaluation", "Purchase" and "Outcome" (Engel, Blackwell, & Miniard, 1990, p.28). This purchase decision process has lead to a number of models to try to better understand this procedure, leading in turn to a variety of means of measuring and modelling perceptions and behaviours of potential customers (Galloway, 1999). One, proposed by Engel, Blackwell and Miniard (1990, p. 482), gives a model of consumer behaviour purchase and outcomes which emphasises the impact that such items as environmental influences (culture, social class, personal influence and family) and individual differences (motivation and involvement, knowledge, attitude, personality, lifestyle, demographics) have on the decision process. This implies that to simply ask a potential guest to rank or indicate in some other way the importance of items derived from a list of attributes is inadequate because it does not take into consideration the many factors which influence the decision process. Such approaches are focused on information search and the evaluation of a series of alternatives with little recognition of implicit needs, past experience or the presence of significant other factors that can influence decision making. As a result there is a fundamental flaw not only in method of the research but also of logic.

After some consideration of the best way to understand factors influencing the price decision, it was thought that a focus group approach would better investigate the influences that impact on the purchase decision and the role of price in that process. The use of focus groups has an established pedigree in social anthropology, media/cultural studies and health research. One advantage of this approach is that it gives the ability to explore a specific set of issues and involves a form of collective activity (Kitzinger & Barbour, 1999). Focus groups also provide participants the opportunity to explore experiences, opinions, wishes and concerns. In taking part in a focus group participants have the ability to generate their own questions, frames and concepts and to pursue their own priorities. Points of view are constructed and expressed as participants wish. Statistical representation is not the aim of most focus groups, but their membership may comprise a structured rather than random sample, containing demographic diversity (Kuzel, 1992). As a result a better understanding of consumer behaviour can be developed.

2. Methodology

As indicated focus groups were used for this research using a modified nominal group technique. It was the original objective to establish three focus groups each with 15 persons, one with persons with low hotel or motel use, one with medium use and one with high use, but this was abandoned as it was felt that diversity would assist in the discussion (Kitzinger, 1995). For a content analysis to be generalisable to some population the sample for the analysis should be randomly selected (Neuendorf, 2002). As there was no reason to believe that the views of those living in Hamilton would be any different from people living in any other part of New Zealand, the population was defined as all people living in Hamilton aged 18 or older. The recruiting of participants was undertaken in two steps. The initial step was to select names randomly from the Hamilton phone book. After a lot of phone calls very little progress was made in recruiting the number of people required for the focus groups. On answering the phone people seemed interested, but reluctant to participate. The next step involved placing flyers in the mailboxes of randomly selected areas of the city. These flyers gave an introduction to the research, details about what the participants would receive (NZ$50 book voucher and refreshments) and the intended nights that the research would take place, along with a phone

T. Lockyer / Tourism Management 26 (2005) 529–537   531

number if they were interested. This produced a good response from potential participants, resulting in three focus groups with a total of 42 persons participating. The focus groups took place on three consecutive nights in an appropriately set out room at the University.

Each of the focus groups was exposed to the same steps as follows:

1. A quantitative survey containing 49 questions using a seven-point Likert scale from 1 = very extremely unimportant 7 = extremely important, plus 0 = not applicable/don't know/have no opinion. The questions were a slightly modified set as used previously by Lockyer (2002) (see Table 2 for details of the items included). In addition demographics and information regarding the usage of hotel or motel accommodation by participants were gathered.
2. Adaptation of nominal group technique. Each participant was supplied with an A3 sheet of white paper and asked the following questions:

   a. When thinking about booking a motel or hotel what are the most important factors you consider? (List 3 or 4).
   b. When you look at a picture of a hotel or motel what are the things you notice first? (List 3 or 4).
   c. Describe at what point in the selection process the price becomes important?
   d. Where would you rate price in the selection criteria on a scale 1 = most important 10 = least important.

3. Each of the sheets of paper from the previous step was displayed on the wall. From the questions "a" and "b" common themes were identified. Each of these themes were used as discussion points, executed in an interactive manner, encouraging as much participation as possible from all participants. Each participant was given a number for identification, and was encouraged to say the number before their comment (sometimes they forgot). This gave the ability to identify comments and participants. Then questions "c" and "d" were also discussed, culminating in a very open discussion of other issues and interests relating to the selection of accommodation. This part of the focus group was recorded so that it could be accurately transcribed. Although the different occurrences revealed some variation, there were considerable similarities. Each of the following factors was discussed at some point in the discussion: price, location, facilities, safety, cleanliness, choice and service.
4. The final part of the research involved the participants completing the same 49 question survey as was administered in stage 1. The purpose of this was to identify whether the discussion had changed the views of the participants.

SPSS was used to evaluate the closed questions in stages 1 and 4 above. For the content analysis resulting from stages 2 and 3 (above) TextSmart™ and CATPAC was used. In using content analysis there is always some concern about the reliability of the findings; this has been defined as the extent to which a measuring procedure yields the same result (Carmines & Zeller, 1979). When using content analysis the interceder reliability becomes very important. For this reason two different computer programs were used, each of which take a quite different approach. CATPAC reads the text, uses an artificial neural network to develop relationships between words and produces a summary of the main ideas in the text. The output of this is displayed as a three-dimensional conceptual map. TextSmart™ which is primarily for the analysis of open-ended survey responses, uses cluster analysis and multi-dimensional scaling techniques to automatically analyse keywords and groups text into categories. Thus it can code without the use of a user-created dictionary, which has the effect of reducing coding biases.

3. Data analysis

As detailed earlier the research involved three groups with a total of 42 participants. Of this number, 71.4 per cent were female and 28.6 were male. As illustrated in Table 1 the largest age group of participants (26.2 per cent) was aged between 40 and 49, the next largest group (23.8 per cent) were aged between 30 and 39. The second part of Table 1 provides details of the number of times the participants have stayed in accommodation in the past 12 months. As is illustrated, the largest number was 19.0 per cent who stayed three times, 16.7 per cent once, and 14.3 per cent twice. The final part of Table 1 lists a selection of the participant's employment; this is presented as a representative sample.

The first part of the data analysis used the data collected in stages one and four of the focus group meeting as detailed in the methodology, that is, the quantitative questionnaires. The objective was to determine whether the focus group discussion had influenced the responses. Coefficient alphas were computed to obtain internal consistency estimates of reliability for the survey completed before the focus group discussion and the same survey was completed after the focus group discussion. For the survey conducted at the beginning of the focus group meeting the Alpha = 0.740 while the survey conducted at the end of the survey had an Alpha = 0.945. This indicates that the focus group did have some impact on the way in which the second survey was answered, although as illustrated in Table 2 the changes were fairly minor. The first column in Table 2 lists the 49 items that were included in the survey. As previously discussed the

Table 1
Age, number of stays in a motel or hotel in the past 12 months and example of employment of focus group participants

Age	Frequency	Per cent
Below 20 years	1	2.4
20–29 years	8	19.0
30–39 years	10	24.8
40–49 years	11	26.2
50–59 years	9	21.4
60 years or over	3	7.1
Total	42	100.0

Number of times stayed in paid accommodation in the past 12 months

0	4	9.5
1	7	16.7
2	6	14.3
3	8	19.0
4	3	7.1
5	2	4.8
6	1	2.4
7	4	9.5
9	1	2.4
10	2	4.8
12	1	2.4
15	3	7.1
Total	42	100.0

Employment of participants

Tutor/teacher	7	16.7
Accountant	4	9.5
Engineer	3	7.1
Retired	3	7.1
Manager	2	4.8
Mother	2	4.8
Administrator	1	2.4
Architectural practice manager	1	2.4
Consultant	1	2.4
Baker	1	2.4
Bank manager	1	2.4
Builder	1	2.4

questions used a seven-point Likert scale from 1 = very extremely unimportant to 7 = extremely important, plus 0 = not applicable/don't know/have no opinion. All 42 focus group participants completed both surveys. The two rows of figures in the square brackets [ ] are the descending rating of the survey items from the two surveys. These give an indication of movement of the items, for example "non-smoking rooms" went from fifth to fourth in ranking. The other columns provide the mean, standard deviation, mean difference and *t*-value. These indicate the way in which the views of the participants changed from the start to the end of the focus group discussion.

Cleanliness in both surveys was rated at the top and Room rate/Price was about one third down the results. Although during the focus discussion there was a lot

said about Room rate/Price in the second survey it had moved by two steps in importance from a mean of 5.86 to a mean of 6.05. Overall there was very little movement between the two surveys except for items such as "Efficiency of front desk" which moved from number 10 (mean 6.03) in the first survey to number three (mean 6.28) in the second. On the other hand, the item "Safety and Security of hotel/motel & surrounding area" went from number three before the focus group discussion to number 13 afterwards. Although there were 49 items in the surveys there were just five items where the difference was statistically significant ($p < 0.05$) and these are indicated in Table 2. Of interest is that in each case the items became more important, with the first three relating to guest staff interaction: "Efficiency of front desk" (from number 10 to 3), "Sympathetic handling of complaints" (from number 15 to 9), "Room service availability" (From number 37 to 31), and the last two relating to facilities "Laundry and dry cleaning service" (from number 44 to 34), "Access to Gym facilities" (from number 47 to 45). Although during the focus group discussion there were a lot of comments made about the importance of price (as will be discussed later), this item only changed its rating from number 14 to 12.

To this point the research has not revealed anything new. Results are very much in keeping with the findings from other research, cleanliness is rated at the top and price as a lot less important.

3.1. "Price" focus group discussion

As previously indicated the focus group discussion was based on open questions and participants involved in writing responses on flip chart papers which were then displayed on the wall and used as a basis for further discussion. Firstly the participants were asked to list the three most important items in the selection of accommodation. Fig. 1 gives a simple percentage representation showing the major responses and the percentage of times indicated by respondents.

Each of the three columns "first, second and third" were derived by adding together how many times each item was mentioned across the three focus group occurrences and then converting into percentages. Fig. 1 presents a simple representation of the percentages. "Price" was indicated 43 per cent of the time as the first most important item in the selection of accommodation. One way of viewing Fig. 1 is as a three-step decision model in relation to a purchase decision, almost as 'trigger points', just as when looking at Maslow's (1954) work on the hierarchy of needs when physiological needs are met then movement can progress. A useful way to look at Fig. 1 may be in the same light, and this stepping process in the making of decisions became more evident in the Focus Group

T. Lockyer / Tourism Management 26 (2005) 529–537 533

Table 2
Comparison between the two surveys at the beginning and end of the focus group discussion

	First survey		Second survey			
	Rating	Mean std. dev.	Rating	Mean std. dev.	Mean difference	t-value
Cleanliness of hotel	[1]	6.48 (0.80)	[1]	6.36 (0.93)	0.12	0.80
Effective room locking systems	[2]	6.26 (1.08)	[2]	6.33 (0.82)	−0.07	−0.41
Safety and Security of hotel/motel & surrounding area	[3]	6.24 (0.89)	[13]	5.98 (1.25)	0.27	1.40
Soundproofing between bedrooms	[4]	6.17 (1.01)	[6]	6.12 (0.94)	0.05	0.42
Non-smoking rooms	[5]	6.12 (1.10)	[4]	6.20 (1.10)	−0.07	−0.44
Comfort of mattress and pillow	[6]	6.12 (0.83)	[10]	6.07 (0.78)	0.05	0.53
Enthusiasm, willingness and commitment of staff to attend to guest needs	[7]	6.12 (0.80)	[11]	6.05 (0.76)	0.07	0.65
Accuracy of wake up call	[8]	6.10 (1.25)	[8]	6.10 (1.23)	0.00	0.00
Message handling	[9]	6.07 (0.98)	[14]	5.98 (1.08)	0.10	1.00
Efficiency of front desk (check in, check out, and billing)	[10]	6.03 (0.95)	[3]	(6.28 0.78)	−0.25	−2.04*
Standard of bedroom maintenance	[11]	6.02 (0.90)	[7]	6.12 (0.89)	−0.10	−0.78
Bathroom and showers (good heat control & water pressure)	[12]	6.00 (0.94)	[5]	6.17 (0.73)	−0.17	−1.42
Courteous, polite, well mannered staff	[13]	5.95 (0.94)	[15]	5.98 (0.81)	−0.02	−0.23
Room rate/Price	[14]	5.86 (0.98)	[12]	6.05 (0.76)	−0.19	−1.39
Sympathetic handling of complaints	[15]	5.79 (0.86)	[9]	6.10 (0.82)	−0.31	−2.31*
Availability of parking	[16]	5.79 (1.09)	[17]	5.86 (0.98)	−0.07	−0.49
Good quality bath towel and wash cloth	[17]	5.74 (1.13)	[16]	5.95 (0.85)	−0.21	−1.65
Convenient to tourist destination	[18]	5.73 (1.16)	[18]	5.83 (0.97)	−0.10	−0.63
Adequate lighting for reading in bedrooms	[19]	5.60 (1.17)	[21]	5.55 (0.94)	0.05	0.34
Clear signs to rooms and facilities	[20]	5.58 (1.11)	[24]	5.45 (1.06)	0.13	1.40
Services provided as ordered and prompt	[21]	5.56 (0.92)	[19]	5.59 (0.81)	−0.02	−0.23
Quiet air-conditioning in bedrooms	[22]	5.51 (1.00)	[20]	5.59 (1.07)	−0.07	−0.49
Food service efficiency	[23]	5.49 (1.05)	[28]	5.22 (0.94)	0.27	1.92
Tea and coffee making facilities in bedroom	[24]	5.43 (1.17)	[25]	5.43 (0.99)	0.00	0.00
Internal décor—ambiance	[25]	5.38 (1.10)	[22]	5.52 (1.04)	−0.14	−1.00
Special rates or inclusive package available	[26]	5.24 (1.14)	[26]	5.41 (0.95)	−0.17	−1.10
Attractiveness of bedroom	[27]	5.20 (1.10)	[27]	5.24 (0.92)	−0.05	−0.44
Good reputation of hotel/motel	[28]	5.19 (0.99)	[23]	5.50 (1.25)	−0.31	−1.87
Dressing table with good mirror and light	[29]	5.10 (1.01)	[36]	4.80 (1.26)	0.30	1.78
Quality television and video	[30]	5.02 (1.28)	[32]	5.02 (0.95)	0.00	0.00
Flexible hours of opening—food and beverage facilities	[31]	4.98 (1.14)	[33]	4.90 (1.28)	0.07	0.39
Direct dial telephone in bedrooms	[32]	4.95 (1.28)	[41]	4.61 (1.36)	0.34	1.83
Star rating of the motel/hotel	[33]	4.90 (1.20)	[35]	4.85 (0.91)	0.05	0.26
Access to cooking facilities	[34]	4.88 (1.33)	[29]	5.12 (1.00)	−0.24	−1.15
Room rate inclusive of breakfast	[35]	4.88 (1.27)	[30]	5.10 (1.32)	−0.22	−1.60
Work area in bedroom (with separate lighting)	[36]	4.74 (1.23)	[42]	4.59 (1.27)	0.15	1.06
Room service availability	[37]	4.62 (1.08)	[31]	5.10 (1.05)	−0.48	−3.19**
Free newspaper	[38]	4.61 (1.46)	[37]	4.76 (1.58)	−0.15	−0.83
Spa available	[39]	4.53 (1.26)	[40]	4.68 (1.27)	−0.15	−0.92
Staff recognise returning guests	[40]	4.52 (1.50)	[39]	4.69 (1.33)	−0.17	−1.16
Restaurant available	[41]	4.49 (1.60)	[38]	4.73 (1.38)	−0.24	−1.46
Computer internet connection in room	[42]	4.46 (1.66)	[43]	4.54 (1.34)	−0.07	−0.40
Pool available	[43]	4.40 (1.25)	[44]	4.51 (1.23)	−0.11	−0.67
Laundry and dry cleaning service	[44]	4.24 (1.56)	[34]	4.86 (1.34)	−0.62	−3.64**
Sky television in room	[45]	4.22 (1.46)	[47]	3.95 (1.34)	0.27	1.51
Relaxing lounge and bar	[46]	4.20 (1.19)	[46]	4.07 (1.29)	0.12	0.96
Access to Gym facilities	[47]	4.02 (1.35)	[45]	4.37 (1.30)	−0.34	−2.40*
Bar available	[48]	3.61 (1.39)	[48]	3.68 (1.46)	−0.07	−0.68
Mini bar in room	[49]	3.38 (1.31)	[49]	3.64 (1.28)	−0.26	−1.54

Note: *t-test two tailed probability <0.05; **t-test two tail probability <0.01; standard deviations are in parentheses; a negative indicates that the first survey results are rated lower than the second survey.

discussion. What is also of particular interest is "Cleanliness" and that from being rated as the most important factor (Table 2) in this study and many others (Callan, 1996) in Fig. 1 it is almost the least mentioned factor.

As indicated, once the participants had completed the first open questions the sheets of paper were displayed on the wall, and the focus group discussion was subsequently based on these items. During the discussion records were made by a research assistant using

534   *T. Lockyer / Tourism Management 26 (2005) 529–537*

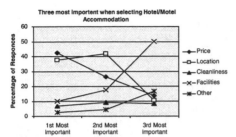

Fig. 1. The three most important factors in the selection of accommodation, displayed as percentages.

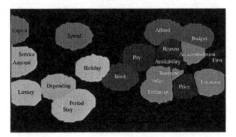

Fig. 2. Category map of price and importance in the section of accommodation.

shorthand and all the discussions were recorded onto a digital recorder. These two sources were used to produce an accurate record of the focus group discussion.

TextSmart™ was one of the two content analytical tools used to evaluate the findings from the focus group discussion. Fig. 2 is the category map for the discussion directly relating to price as a factor in the selection of accommodation. It should be noted in Fig. 2 that the various colours represent the categories. The grouping and relationships are important, as these show associations between words. For example while "Expect" and "Spend" (red colour) are in the same category group there is some spatial difference between them. The grouping around "Availability" indicates close relationships of the words and the relationships between different categories.

Each of the themes in the discussion were related to a specific question and person in the focus group. The first task undertaken was to 'cleanse' the data. The purpose was to minimise irregularities by using a number of tools including spelling correction, development of alias and exclusion lists in order to attain some common meaning in words, such as using, for example, one word 'price' for 'prices', 'price' and 'priced' and removing unnecessary words such as 'am', 'it', and 'I', etc. Care must be taken during this process to ensure that the underlying meaning of the text is not changed.

To assist with this the changes are done in a live interactive environment where the results of any change can be immediately seen, and inappropriate changes can be undone. During this process the categories (as illustrated in the various colours) are created. As already stated, these visualisation features of the software are used where the colours illustrate category plots of word associations. Also a process of "brushing" allows for the verification and integration of the data using on-screen functions to highlight specific words, responses and categories.

Table 3 gives a detailed description of each of the categories in Fig. 2. The colours down the left-hand column correspond to the category map colours (Fig. 2); the words in italics also relate directly to Fig. 2. For example the first category discussed contains the words "*Availability and First*" and then draws from the focus group discussion the underlying meaning and supporting evidence.

CATPAC was also used to analyse the focus group responses in relation to price. CATPAC uses the theory of neural networks to establish patterns within written text (Hample, 1996). CATPAC reads and analyses text by using a neural pathway; this is achieved by running a scanning window through the text. The software seeks to simulate what happens in the human brain. As messages, thoughts or re-lived memories pass from brain cell to brain cell, a biochemical electromagnetic pathway is established (memory track). Every time there is a thought within the brain the biochemical/electromagnetic resistance along the pathway carrying that thought is reduced. The more frequently patterns or maps of thought are repeated, the less resistance there is to the links being developed. As a result the brain is very good at pattern recognition (Caudill & Butler, 1990). Neural network software seeks to imitate this function. CATPAC establishes patterns within written text. The software can read rows of text and learn the underlying concepts of clusters of meaning which it reports in the form of a dendogram (Hample, 1996).

When CATPAC first starts, the researcher loads exclusion words. These are words such as 'I', 'me' and 'am' which occur in text but have no underlying meaning. By loading these words they are not included in the CATPAC analysis. CATPAC then loads three main starting parameters: (1) Unique Words 25, (2) Window Size 7 and (3) Slide Size 1. As a result initially CATPAC selects 25 unique words for the neural network connection; when developing the connections it scans seven words at a time, and increments by one word, meaning that initially it considers words 1–7, then 2–8, etc. To draw meaning from the text these parameters are changed, according to experience and the type of text being analysed. Because the text generally comprised short statements made by the focus group participants and after some experimentation, a

T. Lockyer / Tourism Management 26 (2005) 529–537 535

Table 3
Category map key and discussion

Dark blue	*Availability First:* That the first thing potential guests do is to confirm availability of accommodation. In the focus group discussion this was a very early and strongly made point. "If there is no accommodation there is no point in asking any other questions", "No point in finding out price if there's no room"
Brown	*Reason Pay Price:* The focus group strongly emphasised that there was a strong relationship between the price and the reason for staying in the accommodation. The example was given that if it was necessary to attend a funeral or someone was admitted into hospital at short notice the amount that people would pay changes significantly. Each of these words is separated but is also closely related to availability. "Tend to pay more for one off ..."
Green	*Afford Budget:* In the focus group there was a lot of discussion on this point. It became very clear that there was an expectation of an amount that people were prepared to pay and that through this an "initial budget had been decided". When enquiring of accommodation providers this was an important concern
Light blue	*Business Accommodation Value Different:* The focus group emphasised the point that the importance of price for many potential business guests is different than non-business guests. The discussion emphasised that because many business guests stay in accommodation which are paid and often selected by others price has a lower priority, "Depends whether it is business or pleasure. I don't mind so much if it is on business but I would be looking at it a lot more carefully if I was taking my family ..."
Orange	*Location:* This is interestingly placed between "Price" and "First". From the focus group discussion there was a strong relationship drawn between these three items, with the discussion emphasising an almost linear relationship between price and location, that if you wish to stay in a particular location then you would probably have to pay more. That staying further away may reduce the cost of the accommodation but does increase transport cost and time, and that it may therefore be better to pay a higher price, "Location, depending on what you're doing and where you're going and your purpose", "When you're staying at a hotel you don't want to spend all your time traveling"
Yellow	*Holiday Period Stay Luxury:* From the discussion there was strong evidence of a greater importance of a holiday and the desire for as much luxury as can be afforded
Red	*Expect Spend:* Although these two factors are disjointed it does indicate an expectation in the purchases decision. "You often want to spend less on it but sometimes the situation will dictate what you have to spend"
Pink	*Amount Service Depending:* From the discussion it was evident that the participants felt a strong relationship between the amount that is paid for accommodation and the level of service received. Again it is of note that this relationship did not appear in the structural equation model, "That the service should be consistent"
Purple	*Book:* This factor is related both to pay and holiday

Table 4
Frequency of words in CATPAC analysis

Word	Freq	Per cent
Price	84	26.2
First	26	8.1
Look	24	7.5
Pay	22	6.9
Holiday	20	6.2
Hotel	20	6.2
Want	20	6.2
Stay	18	5.6
Budget	16	5.0
Reason	16	5.0
Cost	14	4.4
Good	14	4.4

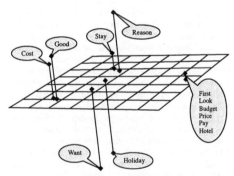

Fig. 3. Spacial map of CATPAC analysis.

setting of 12 unique words was selected as most appropriate. Table 4 lists these words and their frequency of occurrence. Also a scanning window of 15 words was selected. This large window was selected as the import file from the focus group discussion which was based on open dialogue. Each time the window moves through the text the programme looks for relationships between words and develops simulated neural connections. The special model produced through CATPAC is illustrated in Fig. 3. The value of this plot is that it indicates a spacial relationship between words. The grouping of the six items on the right of Fig. 3 were so closely related and grouped that it was impossible to separate them into individual items, and as a result they have been grouped together. Fig. 3 gives four specific groupings:

1. "First, Look, Budget, Price, Pay Hotel". With reference to the text and Fig. 3 and Table 3 the TextSmart™ category map, it is evident that price has a close relationship to the selection, and this is related to the amount that is perceived as the correct amount to pay for the accommodation.

2. "Stay, Reason". The reason for the stay has an important relationship to what a person is willing to spend. With reference to the text it is clear that this also has a time element.
3. "Want, Holiday". This relates to what the potential guest is looking for from the accommodation and how this relates to the accommodation.
4. "Good, Cost". A relationship between cost and getting value for money.

It needs to be noted that Fig. 3 does not give a quantifiable indication of strength, but does give valuable insight into the word groupings.

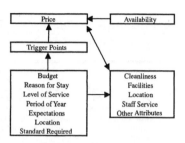

Fig. 4. Model of the influence of price on accommodation selection.

4. Discussion

To answer the research question, this study comprised a number of both qualitative and quantitative components. The quantitative was a survey conducted at the start and end of the focus group meeting. This comprised 49 statements that the participants rated for importance on a seven-point Likert scale. The analysis of the two surveys is contained in Table 2. The questions selected followed those used in a number of previous studies (Lockyer, 2002), each of which endeavoured to understand the factors that are important to potential guests in accommodation selection (Callan, 1996). It came not as a surprise that "Cleanliness" was rated the most important factor, and that "Price" was rated a lot less important.

As the object was to understand the impact that room rate/price has on the selection of accommodation; the findings imply that this variable is of little importance.

The next stage of the research was to ask the participants to write down the three most important factors when selecting hotel or motel accommodation. From the answer to the previous question, it could have been assumed that cleanliness would be listed as the most important. However, price was listed as the first most important factor (see Fig. 1). Also of particular interest was that cleanliness was rated the lowest ranking of the five emergent categories. This is somewhat contradictory, but does indicate that price has a complex relationship with the selection of accommodation. Again the research to this point does not give any real understanding of the influence price has in the purchase process.

The rest of the focus group discussion was dominated by a modified nominal group technique. It was through this discussion and the analysis of the comments made by participants that a new understanding of the impact price has on the purchase of accommodation began to develop. The analysis of the discussion involved the use of two content analysis tools, TextSmart™ (Fig. 2 and Table 3) and CATPAC (Table 4 and Fig. 3), plus close

examination and analysis of the text from the focus group discussion. It was at this stage of the research that previous notions of price were significantly changed giving evidence that the understanding of price and its impact involves comprehension and analysis of what is referred to as trigger points.

Fig. 4 represents an accumulation of the findings and highlights the impact that the trigger points have on the decision process.

As illustrated in Fig. 4 the research suggests price as a factor in the selection of accommodation within three influencing variables. The first is availability, shown in Fig. 4 as having its own 'space'. It was of particular interest to note how strongly the focus group members emphasised this point. A statement which summarised the discussion on this point was: "If there are no rooms available there is no point in asking about price". This was also strongly evident from the TextSmart™ analysis, (at the top of Table 3).

The next section in Fig. 4 illustrates the impact that the trigger points have on the selection process. It became very clear through the focus group discussion and analysis that factors such as budget, reason for stay and level of service desired are critical issues and are often considered as part of an early decision process: "Usually before I ring I've done a lot of research". The researcher was surprised at how definite these trigger points were, and how clearly the focus group participants were able to articulate them, for example: "Often we've been using motel rooms because we've been away for sports events and therefore it's a cost factor in terms of everybody that's involved in the sports event and trying to keep it down to a reasonable price"; "How long you're going to spend in the room, are you going to relax in the room or are you dropping your things and doing something else"; "It also depends who's paying— if it was business I'd probably go for the top range if I could" (refer to Table 3 for more details). What also struck the researcher was how well-defined each of the trigger points were and how in examples given by the participants, either just one or multiple factors are used in the evaluation process. For example if a family

T. Lockyer / Tourism Management 26 (2005) 529–537   537

member is sick in hospital and a short notice overnight stay in a hotel or motel is required to visit them, there is far less concern over price than if the stay was for many other reasons. This is of particular interest to accommodation industry management, as the currently used yield management models do not reflect these trigger points accurately.

The last area in Fig. 4 is cleanliness, facilities, location, etc. The research indicates there is a relationship between these areas and the expectation of guest selection of accommodation and to price, both through the trigger points and also as a direct influence. However, many of these influences are more related to repeat business rather than for the first stay.

This research has confirmed the complexity of the accommodation purchase decision and suggests that previous research into the question of the factors influencing the selection of accommodation is flawed through creating listings of items that ignore relationships between those items. The understanding of the impact that price has on the selection of accommodation needs consideration of trigger points. As suggested by Fig. 4 these trigger points are used by guests in a large number of different ways. This has significant implications for management in hotels and resorts. Although tools such as yield management can take into account such items as time of year and level of demand, many of the other attributes are not considered. As a consequence, there is a much greater need among management to have a more inclusive decision making model when considering the occupancy in their establishment.

Acknowledgements

This research was sponsored through the contestable research fund of the Waikato Management School of the University of Waikato, and Professor Chris Ryan, Waikato Management School for his continued support.

References

Callan, R. J. (1996). An appraisement of UK business travelers' perceptions of important hotel attributes. *Hospitality Research Journal, 19*(4), 113–127.

Carmines, E. G., & Zeller, R. A. (1979). *Reliability and validity assessment.* CA, Beverly Hills: Sage.

Caudill, M., & Butler, C. (1990). *Naturally intelligent systems.* London: Bradford Books.

Dolnicar, S., & Otter, T. (2003). Which hotel attributes matter? A review of previous and a framework for further research. In: T. Griffin, & R. Harris (Eds.), *Asia Pacific Tourism Association nineth annual conference,* Sydney, Australia (pp.176–188).

Dube, L., & Renaghan, L. M. (1999,). How hotel attributes deliver the promised benefits. *Cornell Hotel and Restaurant Administration Quarterly, 5*(40), 89–95.

Dube, L., & Renaghan, L. M. (2000,). Creating visible customer value—how customers view best-practice champions. *Cornell Hotel and Restaurant Administration Quarterly, 1*(41), 62–72.

Engel, J. F., Blackwell, R. D., & Miniard, P. W. (1990). *Consumer behaviour* (6th Ed.). London: The Dryden Press.

Galloway, L. (1999). Hysteresis: A model of consumer behaviour? *Managing Service Quality, 5*(9), 360–371.

Hample, S. (1996). RU ready for AI? *American Demographics, May,* 60pp.

Kitzinger, J. (1995). Introducing focus groups. *British Medical Journal, 311,* 299–302.

Kitzinger, J., & Barbour, R. S. (1999). Introduction: the challenge and promise of focus groups. In R. S. Barbour, & J. Kitzinger (Eds.), *Developing focus group research politics, theory and practice.* London: Sage Publishing.

Kuzel, A. J. (1992). Sampling in qualitative inquiry. In B. F. Crabtree, & W. L. Miller (Eds.), *Doing qualitative research* (pp. 31–44). Newbury Park, CA: Sage.

Lockyer, T. (2000). A New Zealand investigation into the factors influencing consumers' selection of business hotel accommodation. *Australian Journal of Hospitality Management, 7*(2), 11–23.

Lockyer, T. (2002). Business guests' accommodation selection: The view from both sides. *International Journal of Contemporary Hospitality Management, 6*(14), 294–300.

Maslow, A. H. (1954). *Motivation and personality.* New York: Harper and Row.

Neuendorf, K. A. (2002). *The content analysis guidebook.* London: Sage.

Saleh, F., & Ryan, C. (1992). Client perceptions of hotels. *Tourism Management, June,* 163–168.

Schaefer, A., Illum, S., & Margavio, T. (1995). The relative importance of hotel attributes to motorcoach tour operators. *Journal of Hospitality and Leisure Marketing, 3,* 65–80.

Tsaur, S. H., & Gwo-Hsiung, T. (1995). Multiattribute decision making analysis for customer preference of tourist hotels. *Journal of Travel and Tourism Marketing, 4,* 55–69.

Weaver, P. A., & Oh, H. C. (1993). Do American business travellers have different hotel service requirements? *International Journal of Contemporary Hospitality Management, 5*(3), 16–21.

[25]

Restaurant Tipping and Service Quality

A Tenuous Relationship

by Michael Lynn

Conventional wisdom suggests that table servers can judge how well they're doing by the size of their tips. As it turns out, however, that may not be true.

Tipping is nearly ubiquitous in the U.S. restaurant industry. As a result, many restaurant managers give the custom little thought. However, others see it as a useful management tool. Consider the following quotations:

- "By eliminating tipping, it [a service-charge system] would take away all incentive to put out that effort at providing good service." —*Bernard Schreiner, who owned Schreiner's Restaurants, in Fond du Lac, Wisconsin*[1]

[1] Quoted in: "Waitstaff Compensation: Tips vs. Service Charges," *Current Issues Report* (Washington, DC: National Restaurant Association, June 1988), p. 7.

Michael Lynn, Ph.D., is an associate professor of consumer behavior and marketing at the Cornell University School of Hotel Administration (wml3@cornell.edu).

- "This program will be monitored by your charge tip averages. Tip averages are the most effective way to measure a server's capabilities and progress within the restaurant."
 —*Internal document that announced a servers' contest at Houston's Guadalajara Restaurant*

- "I want to know when someone gets a small tip because the customer is telling us that he didn't get good service and we can then remedy the situation."—*The late Thad Eure, Jr., who was proprietor of Raleigh's Angus Barn*[2]

As the above quotations illustrate, some restaurateurs rely on tips to **(1)** motivate servers to deliver good service, **(2)** measure server performance, and **(3)** identify dissatisfied customers. All of those uses of tips assume that service quality has a large effect on the size of tips that consumers leave. This article examines and challenges that assumption.

The notion that tips are given in response to service quality finds support in psychologists' theories about the need for equity in interpersonal relationships and in consumers' self-reports about their tipping behavior. Some psychologists, for instance, tell us that people are socialized to feel anxiety or distress when their relationships with others are inequitable.[3] A relationship is inequitable when the benefits one person receives from the relationship are not proportionate to the benefits he or she delivers to the relationship partner. Since inequitable relationships are distressing, the theory goes, people strive to maintain a balance between the benefits delivered and received in their rela-

tionships. This theory is relevant to tipping, because restaurant customers get service and give tips in relationships with servers. To keep those relationships equitable, customers should give bigger tips when they get better service.[4]

Reinforcing the psychological theory are consumers' self-reports. When asked why they leave tips, consumers most often reply that they tip to reward workers for services rendered. For example, a recent national survey found that 54.5 percent of respondents reported that the *best* explanation for why they do or do not tip restaurant table servers had to do with the quality of service received. No other explanation received anywhere near this level of endorsement.[5]

Despite the aforementioned reasons for believing that customers reward better service with larger tips, there are also good reasons for questioning this belief. First, researchers have found that equity motivations are weak in traditional economic relationships between buyers and sellers.[6] Tipping is an economic payment that occurs in the context of a commercial exchange, so it is possible that equity concerns affect tipping less than they do purely social actions. Second, researchers have demonstrated that people are poor at identifying

the causes of their own actions.[7] Thus, one should regard with skepticism consumers' reports that they tip as a reward for good service. Finally, people feel strong social pressure to tip 15 to 20 percent of the bill size.[8] Such social pressure may prevent consumers from leaving a small tip even when they are dissatisfied with the service.

Testing the Relationship

Several researchers (including this author) have tested the different expectations outlined above by empirically examining the relationship between tip sizes and evaluations of the service or dining experience. However, many of these studies are unpublished, and those studies that have been published (including an earlier version of this one) appeared in academic journals that are rarely read by restaurant managers. This article summarizes extant research in a meta-analysis of the service-tipping relationship with the purpose of informing restaurant managers about the actual nature of that relationship.[9] Meta-analysis is a way of statistically combining and comparing the results of different studies. By statistically testing data from many tipping studies, this meta-analysis permits stronger and more generalizable conclusions about the nature of the relationship between tip size and service quality than can be obtained from any of the individual studies alone.

A thorough search uncovered eight published and six unpublished studies that have examined the relationship between tipping and evalu-

[2]Thad Eure, Jr., "Fixed Service Charges? — No," *Restaurants USA*, Vol. 7, No. 2 (February 1987), p. 25.

[3]See: J.S. Adams, "Inequality in Social Exchange," in *Advances in Experimental Social Psychology*, Vol. 2., ed. L. Berkowitz (New York: Academic Press, 1965); and Elaine Walster, Ellen Berscheid, and G. William Walster, "New Directions in Equity Research," *Journal of Personality and Social Psychology*, Vol. 25 (1973), pp. 151–176.

[4]See: Melvin L. Snyder, "The Inverse Relationship between Restaurant Party Size and Tip Percentage: Diffusion or Equity?," *Personality and Social Psychology Bulletin*, Vol. 2 (Summer 1976), p. 308; and Michael Lynn and Andrea Grassman, "Restaurant Tipping: An Examination of Three Rational Explanations," *Journal of Economic Psychology*, Vol. 11 (June 1990), pp. 169–181.

[5]Tibbett L. Speer, "The Give and Take of Tipping," *American Demographics*, February 1997, pp. 51–55. Also see: Susan Adelman, "How Your Customers Decide What to Tip," *NRA News*, June–July 1985, pp. 43–44.

[6]For example, see: Richard L. Oliver and John E. Swan, "Consumer Perceptions of Interpersonal Equity and Satisfaction in Transactions: A Field Survey Approach," *Journal of Marketing*, Vol. 53 (1989), pp. 21–35.

[7]For example, see: David G. Myers, *Social Psychology* (New York: McGraw-Hill, 1990), pp. 103–106.

[8]Lynn and Grassman, *op. cit.*

[9]A previous version of this meta-analysis appeared in: Michael Lynn and Michael McCall, "Gratitude and Gratuity: A Meta-Analysis of Research on the Service–Tipping Relationship," *Journal of Socio-Economics*, Vol. 29, No. 2 (June 2000), pp. 203–214.

Exhibit 1

Fourteen tipping studies

The studies constituting the basis for the meta-analysis described in the accompanying article are listed below.

Charly Baune, "The Economics of Tipping at Waldo's Pizza" (unpublished paper, St. Cloud State University, 1992).

Orn Bodvarsson and William Gibson, "Gratuities and Customer Appraisal of Service: Evidence from Minnesota Restaurants," *Journal of Socio-Economics*, Vol. 23, No. 3 (1994), pp. 287–302.

April H. Crusco and Christopher G. Wetzel, "The Midas Touch: The Effects of Interpersonal Touch on Restaurant Tipping," *Personality and Social Psychology Bulletin*, Vol. 10 (December 1984), pp. 512–517.

Kevin Kilkelly, "An Economic Study on Restaurant Tipping," (unpublished paper, St. Cloud State University, 1992).

Michael Lynn, "The Effects of Alcohol Consumption on Restaurant Tipping," *Personality and Social Psychology Bulletin*, Vol. 14 (March 1988), pp. 87–91.

Michael Lynn and Andrea Grassman, "Restaurant Tipping: An Examination of Three Rational Explanations," *Journal of Economic Psychology*, Vol. 11 (June 1988), pp. 169–181.

Michael Lynn and Jeffrey Graves, "Tipping: An Incentive/Reward for Service?," *Hospitality Research Journal*, Vol. 20, No. 1 (January 1996), pp. 1–14.

Michael Lynn and Bibb Latane, "The Psychology of Restaurant Tipping," *Journal of Applied Social Psychology*, Vol. 14 (November/December 1984), pp. 551–563.

Michael Lynn and Gabriella Petrick, "Tipping at Coyote Loco" (unpublished data set, Cornell University, 1996).

Michael Lynn and Paul Strong, "Tipping at Anti Pasto" (unpublished data set, University of Houston, 1992).

Joanne M. May, "Tip or Treat: A Study of Factors Affecting Tipping Behavior" (unpublished master's thesis, Loyola University, 1978).

Connie Mok and Sebastian Hansen, "A Study of Factors Affecting Tip Size in Restaurants," *Journal of Foodservice Marketing*, Vol. 3, No. 3/4 (1999), pp. 49–64.

Mustafa Olia, "Restaurant Tipping" (unpublished paper, St. Cloud State University, 1991).

Rosenthal.[10] A more detailed description of the methods employed in this meta-analysis can be found in a previous version of this study published in the *Journal of Socio-Economics*.[11] A more detailed description of the studies included in the meta-analysis is presented in Exhibit 2.

Tenuous Correlation

A graphic depiction of the 24 correlations between tip sizes and service evaluations in this meta-analysis is presented in Exhibit 3 (overleaf). The significance test associated with those correlations combined to produce an overall z-score of 5.82. The probability of getting a z-score this large by chance alone (i.e., if there were no positive relationship) is less than 1 in 10,000. Thus, the data indicate that tip sizes do increase somewhat with ratings of the service or dining experience. However, the correlation between tips and evaluations of the service or dining experience had a mean of only .11. Since the absolute value of a correlation can range from 0 to 1, an average correlation of .11 is quite small and indicates that tips in these studies were only weakly related to evaluations of the service or dining experience.

Realizing that correlation coefficients may not be meaningful to restaurant managers unfamiliar with statistics, I present other depictions of the tipping–service relationship in Exhibits 4 and 5. Exhibit 4 displays the median-, minimum-, and maximum-tip percentages left for different levels of rated service at

ations of the service or dining experience that preceded the tip. Those studies are listed in Exhibit 1. The studies, which involved 2,645 dining parties at 21 different restaurants, provided 24 independent tests of the tipping–service relationship. The results of each of those tests were used to calculate two statistics— namely, a correlation coefficient, *r*, that reflects the size of the observed tipping–service relationship, and a z-score, which reflects the statistical significance of the relationship. I then analyzed the resulting 24 correlation coefficients and 24 z-scores using meta-analytic formulas and procedures advocated in books by Brian Mullen and Robert

[10]Brian Mullen, *Advanced Basic Meta-Analysis*, (Hillsdale, NJ: Lawrence Erlbaum Associates, 1989); and Robert Rosenthal, *Meta-Analytic Procedures for Social Research*, (Newbury Park, CA: Sage Publications, 1991). See also: Michael Lynn and Brian Mullen, "The Quantitative Integration of Research: An Introduction to Meta-Analysis," *Journal of Hospitality and Tourism Research*, Vol. 21, No. 3 (1997), pp. 121–139.

[11]Lynn and McCall, 2000.

RESTAURANT MANAGEMENT

Exhibit 2
Descriptive summary of tipping–service studies

Study and source	Data available?	Method	Type of service evaluation	Restaurant name[1]	Restaurant location	Sample size	Correlation coefficient[2]	Z-score
Baune (1992); unpublished	No	Exit interviews	Customer rating of service	Waldo's Pizza	St Cloud, MN	94	.23	2.18
Bodvarsson and Gibson (1994); journal	Yes	Exit interviews	Customer rating of service	Embers	St. Paul, MN	98	.23	2.23
				Chi-Chi's	St. Paul, MN	99	.06	0.55
				Baker's Square	St. Cloud, MN	100	.23	2.31
				Alvies[a]	St. Cloud, MN	100	-.02	-0.18
				Red Lobster[b]	St. Cloud, MN	100	.22	2.16
				Pirate's Cove	St. Cloud, MN	100	-.14	-1.41
				Persian	St. Cloud, MN	100	.10	0.94
Crusco and Wetzel (1984); journal	No	Server records and customer survey	Customer rating of dining experience	Unknown	Oxford, MS	114	.13	1.38
Kilkelly (1992); unpublished	No	Exit interviews	Customer rating of service	Perkins	Sauk Rapids, MN	100	.12	1.18
Lynn (1988); journal	Yes	Server records	Noncustomer rating of service	Mother's	Columbus, OH	207	.10	1.38
Lynn and Grassman (1990); journal	Yes	Exit interviews	Customer rating of service	Red Lobster[c]	Columbia, MO	103	.33	3.35
Lynn and Graves (1996: Study 1); journal	Yes	Exit interviews	Customer rating of service	Bennigan's	Houston, TX	106	.16	1.59
				Olive Garden	Houston, TX	67	.29	2.41
Lynn and Graves (1996: Study 2); journal	Yes	Server records	Customer rating of dining experience	Red Lobster[c]	Columbia, MO	174	.22	2.86
Lynn and Latane (1984: Study 1); journal	Yes	Exit interviews	Customer rating of service	IHOP	Columbus, OH	169	.12	1.50
Lynn and Petrick (1996); unpublished	Yes	Restaurant records and customer survey	Customer rating of service	Coyote Loco	Ithaca, NY	130	.09	1.03
Lynn and Strong (1992); unpublished	Yes	Server records	Noncustomer rating of service	Anti Pasto	Houston, TX	202	.01	0.14
May (1978); thesis	No	Server, restaurant, and observer records	Noncustomer rating of service	Unknown	Chicago, IL	184	.01	0.13
Mok and Hansen (1999); journal	Yes	Exit interviews	Customer rating of service	Chili's	Houston, TX	98	.33	3.30
Olia (1991); unpublished	No	Exit interviews	Customer rating of dining experience	Alvies[a]	St. Cloud, MN	50	-.06	-0.39
				La Casita	St. Cloud, MN	50	-.19	-1.29
				Red Lobster[b]	St. Cloud, MN	50	-.01	-0.03
				Ember's	St. Cloud, MN	50	.18	1.18

[1] Restaurants with a common superscript (a, b, or c) are the same restaurant.
[2] Correlations between bill-adjusted tips and evaluations of the service or dining experience.

Exhibit 3

Twenty-four correlations between tip sizes and service evaluation in this meta-analysis (by size)

		.18			
		.16	.29		
		.13	.23		
	.09	.12	.23		
-.06	.06	.12	.23		
-.19	-.02	.01	.10	.22	.33
-.14	-.01	.01	.10	.22	.33

Note: This graph shows that, when sorted by size, the frequency of tipping–service correlations forms a roughly bell-shaped curve centered around values of .10 to .19. Note that all of the values are relatively small, given that correlations can range from -1.0 to 1.0.

five selected restaurants. Exhibit 5 plots the tip percentages and service ratings of 98 dining parties at one of the restaurants. I chose these particular studies in part because the tipping–service relationships from those studies are among the strongest in the literature. Nevertheless, readers will notice that the average (or median) tip increases only slightly as service ratings increase. Increasing service ratings from 3 to 5 (on a five-point scale) raises the median tip by less than 3 percent of the bill in all four of the studies where sample sizes make this comparison meaningful. In two of four studies, the increase is less than 1 percent of the bill as the service rating goes from middling (3) to superior (5). Readers will also notice that the range in tips at each level of rated service is quite large. The studies found that consumers leave tips of 5 percent (or less) and tips of 20 percent (or more) at any given level of service. Since these are the strongest relationships that have been documented, the tipping–service relationship can only be described as weak.

What's a Manager to Do?

The good news in this analysis is that—consistent with restaurant managers' assumptions, psychologists' theories, and consumers' self-reports—the studies showed a positive and statistically significant relationship between tips and service evaluations. The unsettling news is that the relationship was weak in the sense that differences between service levels in the average (or median) tip were small while differences within service levels in the tips left by different dining parties were large. Those findings have disheartening implications for restaurant managers who seek to use tips to motivate servers, measure server performance, or identify dissatisfied customers.

Motivating servers. I think it's fair to say that most restaurant managers rely on tips as an incentive for servers to deliver good service. In fact, one of managers' most common objections to replacing voluntary tips with automatic service charges is that it would entail the loss of this incentive—as emphasized by one of the quotations presented at the beginning of this article.[12] However, the weak relationship between tips and service evaluations in this meta-analysis raises serious concerns about the efficacy of using tips as incentives.

Even though tip levels generally did increase with service evaluations, that increase was so small relative to the range of tips that in practice restaurant servers would be hard pressed to notice it. In other words, most servers won't be able to detect improved tips as a consequence of excellent service. I base this conclusion on the work of Jacob Cohen, who suggested that the correlation between two variables has to have a value of .30 or larger to "be visible to the naked eye of a careful observer."[13] All but two of the correlations between tips and service evaluations in this meta-analysis were smaller than this .30 value. Thus, it is doubtful that servers would see the effects of spending the extra effort to deliver good service on their tip incomes. Consistent with this argument, a survey of the tipped employees in a five-star hotel found that 47 percent saw no relationship between the quality of their service and their earnings.[14] Another survey of waiters and waitresses from 12 different restaurants

---

[12]National Restaurant Association, June 1988, *op. cit.*; and Thad Eure, Jr., *op. cit.*
[13]Jacob Cohen, "A Power Primer," *Psychological Bulletin,* Vol. 112 (1992), pp. 155–159.
[14]Boas Shamir, "A Note of Tipping and Employee Perceptions and Attitudes," *Journal of Occupational Psychology,* Vol. 56 (1983), pp. 255–259.

Exhibit 4
Median, minimum, and maximum tips at each level of customer-service rating for selected restaurants

Service rating (scored from 1 to 5)	IHOP[a] (Lynn & Latane, 1984) $r = .12$	Bennigan's[b] (Lynn & Graves, 1996) $r = .16$[c]	Olive Garden[b] (Lynn & Graves, 1996) $r = .29$[c]	Red Lobster[b] (Lynn & Grassman, 1990) $r = .33$[c]	Chili's[b] (Mok & Hansen, 1999) $r = .33$[c]
1 "Poor"	$n = 6$	$n = 6$	$n = 0$	$n = 0$	$n = 1$
Median tip	10.3%	13.8%	—	—	0
Tip range	0 to 25%	5 to 25%	—	—	—
2 "Below average"	$n = 13$	$n = 9$	$n = 0$	$n = 0$	$n = 2$
Median tip	14.3%	13.3%	—	—	18.9%
Tip range	0 to 20%	0 to 20%	—	—	18 to 20%
3 "Average"	$n = 21$	$n = 14$	$n = 9$	$n = 3$	$n = 18$
Median tip	13.1%	15.0%	14.2%	0	13.9%
Tip range	0 to 48%	7 to 22%	10 to 18%	0 to 8%	5 to 20%
4 "Above average"	$n = 78$	$n = 32$	$n = 18$	$n = 23$	$n = 39$
Median tip	15.1%	13.3%	14.2%	9.5%	15.8%
Tip range	0 to 43%	0 to 43%	0 to 18%	3 to 20%	4 to 42%
5 "Excellent"	$n = 51$	$n = 45$	$n = 40$	$n = 77$	$n = 38$
Median tip	14.0%	15.2%	16.3%	10.9%	16.4%
Tip range	0 to 57%	5 to 32%	10 to 33%	3 to 25%	8 to 37%

Here's an example of how to read the table above:
In the 1984 Lynn and Latane study (second column), six respondents gave the IHOP a poor service rating (score = 1). Nevertheless, their median tip was 10.3 percent of their bill. While some customers stiffed the server, others tipped as high as 25 percent.

[a] Originally scored using a 10-point scale, IHOP's service ratings were converted to a 5-point scale for this table. The scale ranged from 1 = poor service to 5 = excellent service.

[b] Service was rated on several dimensions and the average of all the ratings was rounded to the nearest whole number, 1 to 5.

[c] The "r" value represents the correlation between percentage of tip and service ratings at each individual restaurant. The value of r may vary from 0 to 1. Thus, r values of .1, for instance, show only a weak correlation.

found that only 50 percent thought that servers who routinely received larger-than-average tips did so because they provided good service.[15] This inability of servers to see the relationship between tips and service is important because tips will not motivate servers to deliver good service if the servers do not believe that better service results in larger tips.

Given that the meta-analysis suggests that tips provide only a modest incentive to deliver good service, managers should consider supplementing customer tips with

[15]Mary Harris, "Waiters, Customers, and Service: Some Tips about Tipping," *Journal of Applied Social Psychology*, Vol. 25 (1995), pp. 725–744.

other means of evaluating and rewarding server effort. Managers should personally observe their servers' work, hire mystery diners to evaluate servers, or ask customers to evaluate servers on comment cards or in post-dining interviews. Furthermore, managers should use monetary bonuses, work schedules, station sizes, preparation and clean-up assignments, or other incentives to reward those servers who receive the best evaluations.[16]

[16]Customer evaluations can themselves be problematic. One study, for instance, found that customers focus most on outstandingly good or poor performance and barely notice merely good service. See: Kate Walsh, "A Service Conundrum: Can Outstanding Service Be Too Good?," *Cornell Hotel and Restaurant Administration Quarterly*, Vol. 41, No. 5 (October 2000), pp. 40–50.

Measuring servers. Many restaurant managers already reward their better servers with larger stations, more desirable work schedules, and other perks. However, some of those managers use tip averages to help identify their best performers. The weak relationship between tips and service uncovered in this meta-analysis suggests that such a use of tip records may not be appropriate. The results of this meta-analysis do not provide definitive conclusions about the validity of using servers' tip averages as a way of separating good from bad servers, because tips and service levels can be more strongly related when averaged and compared across servers than when taken separately and compared across dining parties as was done in this study.[17] Nevertheless, these results do mean that managers cannot safely assume that tip averages are a good measure of a server's ability or performance. Reinforcing this cautionary note are the results of a study that found the self-rated service abilities of 47 waiters and waitresses from one restaurant were only weakly related to their tip averages (correlation = .27).[18] Given the weak relationship between tips and service in that study and in the present meta-analysis, I suggest that restaurant managers use other means of measuring servers' abilities and performances.

Customer triage. Many managers believe that small tips are an indication that customers are dissatisfied and that they need to be placated. However, the research reviewed in this article suggests otherwise. Consumers who rated the service as excellent sometimes left tips of 5 percent or less, so one cannot conclude that small tips always mean that the customer was dissatisfied with the service. Furthermore, consumers who rated the service as poor sometimes left tips of 20 percent or more—so not everyone who is dissatisfied with the service leaves a small tip. In general, the weak relationship between tips and service evaluations means that tips are a poor indicator of customer satisfaction

Exhibit 5

Scatter plot of tip percentage against service evaluations

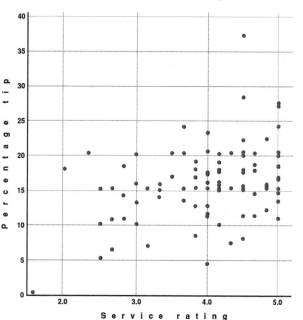

Each point on the graph shows a given party's service evaluation and percentage tip at a Chili's restaurant (N = 98). The plot shows the absence of a strong relationship between tip percentage and service evaluation. (Correlation *r* = .33).

Source of data: Connie Mok and Sebastian Hansen, "A Study of Factors Affecting Tip Size in Restaurants," *Journal of Foodservice Marketing*, Vol. 3, No. 3/4 (1999), pp. 49–64.

[17]Cheri Ostroff, "Comparing Correlations Based on Individual-level and Aggregated Data," *Journal of Applied Psychology*, Vol. 78 (1993), pp. 569–582.

[18]Michael Lynn and Tony Simons, "Predictors of Male and Female Servers' Average Tip Earnings," *Journal of Applied Social Psychology*, Vol. 30 (2000), pp. 241–252.

or dissatisfaction. To better identify dissatisfied customers whose problems need to be addressed, restaurant managers need to observe their customers and train their servers to read customers' nonverbal cues.

This study confirmed that tips are positively related to service, as most people believe, but that the relationship is so weak as to be meaningless. This suggests that while tips are a reward for service, they are not a good way to motivate servers, measure server performance, or identify dissatisfied customers. Restaurant managers need to find and use other means of accomplishing those tasks. CQ

[26]

0261-5177(95)00006-2

Tourism Management, Vol. 16, No. 3, pp. 217–224, 1995
Copyright © 1995 Elsevier Science Ltd
Printed in Great Britain. All rights reserved
0261-5177/95 $10.00 + 0.00

Pricing practices in tourist attractions

An investigation into how pricing decisions are made in the UK

H Anthea Rogers

School of Business, Oxford Brookes University, Wheatley Campus, Oxford OX33 1HX

This article reports findings from a survey on pricing practices in tourist attractions carried out in the UK in 1991–92. It focuses on the decision makers involved; the procedural practices employed; the assumptions and uncertainty underpinning the information base; current price structures; and price dynamics, and briefly examines the role of price in the context of the marketing mix. It provide benchmarks for participants in the industry as well as a framework for further academic research. It suggests the sector is overly cautious and conservative in its approach and that for some participants further experimentation with price changes and price levels could raise total revenues obtained from entry charges.

Keywords: pricing practices, pricing procedures, price structures, price dynamics, price sensitivity, tourist attractions

Pricing tourist attractions became headline news in the UK national press in 1993; Buckingham Palace, the jewel in the crown of British tourism, opened its doors to the public for the first time at an admission charge that many regarded as well below the market level. Later in the year the announcement that an 'all-in' entry charge was to be introduced at Windsor Castle again brought the issue of admission charges and price structures to the fore of public discussion at a time when the future growth and long-run viability of the sector is being questioned.

The controversy surrounding the issues highlighted the fact that there has been little empirical work done to elucidate the processes and procedures used by decision makers when setting admission prices for tourist attractions. The lack of a research base to inform the debate inevitably means that commentators on the sector and sometimes even the participants involved face considerable difficulties in identifying best practice or assessing price decisions in an objective manner. Benchmarks need to be established in order to further the analysis. This research project was undertaken to elicit information on the procedural practices and methodologies used when determining charges for entry to tourist attractions.

The approach adopted involved a situational review by means of a sample postal questionnaire of attractions with formal entry charges. The intention was to establish an information base on pricing procedures and practices by exploring the methodology and approaches used, highlighting the assumptions underpinning the decision making and indicating, where relevant, whether variables such as size, ownership or type of attraction exerted a significant influence on behavioural practices.

The survey

Structure

An initial sample was drawn from a list of 4575 tourist attractions registered with the English Tourist Board (ETB) on the basis of category type. The structured sample was compiled by:

- initially excluding categories such as churches and chapels that were unlikely to have a formal entry charge;
- selecting two contrasting Tourist Board Regions – the South East and Cumbria – that contained in aggregate nearly 10% of all registered attractions.

Table 1 Structure of sample

Factor	No of attractions: 84	Percentage of overall sample
Size[a]		
Small	31	36.9
Medium	33	39.3
Large	20	23.8
Category		
Historic house	20	23.8
Museum	31	36.9
Heritage centre	8	9.5
Farm/wildlife park	10	11.9
Other	15	17.9
Ownership		
Privately owned	24	28.6
Partnership	5	6.0
Private ltd company	7	8.3
Public ltd company	5	6.0
Trust/charity	32	38.1
Local authority/government	8	9.5
Other	3	3.6

Source: Sample Survey 1991–92.
Note: [a]Small denotes less than 50 000 visitors per annum although the majority actually received under 25 000 per annum; medium denotes 51 000 to 199 000 visitors per annum; large denotes 200 000+ per annum.

The ETB was able to provide, via their information department, readily accessible contact names and data from which a structured 'type of attraction sample' could be constructed;

- compiling a sample of 104 attractions randomly from within the listed type categories with the intention of achieving a 20% sample from within these regions;
- piloting a trial run (24) which achieved a high response rate and confirmed that the questionnaire was robust;
- mailing the remaining questionnaires from which an 80% response was achieved, although a proportion of these (13) had not been fully completed and so were abandoned;
- examining the profile of respondents, which revealed that the size distribution appeared relatively unbalanced compared with the national norm and so additional large attractions were selected from other tourist boards, primarily the Heart of England and London Tourist board areas.

The final sample of fully completed questionnaires includes 84 attractions that are, in the author's view, sufficiently representative of the sector as a whole to draw general conclusions from their responses.

The breakdown in terms of type of attraction, size and ownership is indicated in *Table 1*. For this survey the perspective of the decision maker was regarded as the significant criterion for classification. Though it was initially thought that the questionnaire would be anonymous virtually all of the respondents sent promotional material with their

returns. Categories and size were checked against the data but in nearly all cases the view of the respondent regarding classification was respected since it is their perspective on these variables that would influence their decision making.

Content

Factual information was sought on: responsibility for the price decision and the person(s) involved; the objectives set for price; the mechanics of arriving at a decision, including the time and effort devoted to the process; the information base used; the role of price in the marketing mix; the pricing structures used; the role of costs; the significance of competitors' policies and actions; the dynamics of price levels and the training of personnel involved with price decisions.

The survey did not set out to test any hypothesis regarding behaviour differences within the sector as this would have required substantial enlargement of the sample and neither time nor resources permitted this. Cross-tabulations have been undertaken and are included as part of the information base. Where statistically significant cross-correlations were feasible these have been reported.

One would expect that, as a service industry, the whole of the attractions sector would be highly market orientated in their approach and that the role of price as a component of the marketing mix would be carefully monitored and appraised.[1] Open-ended questions were asked in order to elicit information on price awareness and price sensitivity of visitors and the perceived role of price as a competitive variable. The survey also focused on the attitudinal perspectives of the decision-makers and Likert[2] preferential scales were used as an exploratory vehicle. Opportunities were provided for qualitative statements to be made in addition to closed formatted responses. Careful attention was paid to the sequencing of questions: initially factual procedures and processes were examined; philosophical and attitudinal issues were introduced towards the end. There is no guarantee, however, as a postal questionnaire was used that respondents did not answer the questions in reverse order!

Attractions are the central core of the tourism industry: they provide the motivation for travel, accommodation and other support sectors. Estimates indicate that there are approximately 5500 units charging for entry but they compete with others that allow free entry. The sector is diverse and fragmented in terms of size, ownership and type. It ranges from small owner-managed enterprises to large units owned and operated by multinational companies. There are altruistic organizations with charity status. Some attractions have grown from small beginnings out of an owner's hobby while others have been purpose built involving extensive infrastructure development with the inevitable high

Table 2 Association between size and responsibility for pricing

Responsibility[a]	Small No	%	Medium No	%	Large No	%	Total No	%
Individual on their own (category 'X')	9	11	6	7	0	0	15	18
Individual after consultation (category 'Y')	5	6	14	17	10	12	29	35
Group decision (category 'Z')	17	20	13	15	10	12	40	47
Totals of whole sample	31	37	33	39	20	24	84	100

Note: [a]All percentages based on total sample. Chi-square = 11.5957; df = 4; P 0.025.

Table 3 Individual with overall responsibility for price decision in category 'Y' and segmented by size

Responsible individual	Small No	%[a]	Medium No	%[a]	Large No	%[a]	Total No	%[b]
Owner	2	40	5	36	4	40	11	38
Managing director	2	40	5	36	4	40	11	38
Marketing director/manager	1	20	1	7	1	10	3	10
Finance director/accountant	0	0	0	0	1	10	1	3
Operations director/manager	0	0	3	21	0	0	3	10
	5	100	14	100	10	100	29	100

Notes: [a]% given in relation to size segmentation; [b]% given in relation to category 'Y' segment.

Table 4 Individuals involved and associated with group decision making

Individual involved	Small (17) No	%[a]	%[b]	Medium (13) No	%[a]	%[b]	Large (10) No	%[a]	%[b]	Total No	%[a]
Owner	7	17.5	41.2	3	7.5	23.0	2	5.0	20.0	12	30.0
Managing director/manager	1	2.5	5.9	5	12.5	38.5	5	12.5	50.0	11	27.5
Marketing director/manager	2	5.0	11.8	4	10.0	30.8	10	25.0	100.0	16	40.0
Finance director/accountant	3	7.5	17.6	6	15.0	46.1	9	22.5	90.0	18	45.0
Operations director/manager	2	5.0	11.8	5	12.5	38.5	7	17.5	70.0	14	35.0
External adviser	2	5.0	11.8	1	2.5	7.6	1	2.5	10.0	4	10.0
Other	8	20.0	47.2	4	10.0	30.8	3	7.5	30.0	15	37.5

Notes: [a]% based on respondents (40) taking group decisions (ie category 'Z' – see *Table 2*); [b]individuals involved with group decisions according to size distribution within category 'Z'.

fixed costs associated with substantial capital outlays. Whereas theme parks offer stimulation and exhilaration, idyllic country gardens in contrast offer peace and tranquillity. The diversity hides the common objective of offering pleasurable experiences to visitors and in aggregate the attractions are big business in terms of consumer expenditure, attracting spending from domestic and overseas visitors.

So how do these diverse concerns take decisions regarding admission and entry charges?

The decision makers

A range of personnel accepts responsibility for price decision making. In 18% of the organizations sampled the price decision centred solely around *one individual* and of these 67% were owners and 33% were professional managers. These units were exclusively small or medium-sized concerns and very few of these used external advisers (*Table 2*). Nearly

35% of decisions were actually taken by *an individual after consultation with others* and in 76% of these concerns overall responsibility for pricing was accepted either by owners (38%) or managing directors (38%). Marketing directors/managers ranked third, being responsible for price in 10% of the concerns (see *Table 3*). The consultative process involved the managing director in 62% of these units; marketers and operations managers were each consulted by 47% of the units. External involvement was small except in the case of some non-profit-making organizations where interested stakeholders had an input.

Group decision making was the norm for 47% of the units surveyed and within these groups the role of the accountant figured most prominently (45%) followed by marketers (40%), operations staff (35%) and owners (30%) (see *Table 4*). External advice was taken in 10% of these cases. The role of marketers and accountants increased as organizations grew and in the largest organizations marketers were involved in all decisions and accountants in 90% of these group decisions.

Training in pricing procedures

Only 14.3% of those involved in pricing decisions had participated in any formal training: historic houses accounted for 6%, heritage centres 2.5%, wildlife and museums each with 1.2% of the overall total. Heritage centres had the highest proportion of trained price decision makers (28%) per category type, closely followed by historic houses with 25%. Looking at organizations that had no staff with specific training in pricing procedures, trusts or charity status encompassed nearly 40% of this total and private limited companies 28.5% followed by local authorities with 25%. In all, 25% of the staff from large organizations had received formal training in pricing.

Pricing objectives

This aspect was explored at the end of the survey, in order to minimize the chance of distortion, although in reality it would loom large at the beginning of the price decision process and be a major determinant of approach and procedures. A wide variety of objectives was revealed reflecting the diversity of the sector. Most of the responses were qualitative in nature and pose problems in terms of classification. They were generally seen as synonymous with the overall aims of the organization and so could be broadly categorized as 'profit' and 'non-profit' orientated. No organization used the term maximization when referring to the relationships between price, profit or revenue although the maximization of 'enjoyment' for visitors was a recurrent theme. It is interesting to speculate whether the classic questionnaire problem was at work here in the sense that respondents answered in terms of what they thought they ought to be doing from an ethical point of view or whether in terms of economists' models they are actually 'satisficers' rather than maximizers. Further research would be necessary to provide a definitive answer to this tantalizing issue. The concept of 'value for money' was frequently mentioned as an underpinning rationale and where revenue generation or fund raising was specifically identified as a significant objective it was frequently justified with explanations encompassing preservation or conservation. A historic house wished 'to provide funds to maintain the property' while another historic property saw 'revenue generation as a means of conserving national heritage for posterity'.

An industrial tourism unit saw their attraction as a public relations exercise and many attractions in rural areas saw themselves as offering opportunities for city dwellers to enjoy the countryside and at the same time be given insights into rural life from the past. Educational opportunities also figured prominently in the replies and linked strongly with value-for-money concepts. An implied, but not overtly expressed, common focus appeared to be visitor numbers in that this was regarded as a performance measure by many decision makers.

Primary influence on pricing

The responses to questions regarding the factors taken into account when pricing decisions are made are set out in *Table 5*. They confirm that price decisions are multifaceted and complex, requiring more than one approach to be used. Very few of the respondents, 6%, felt that influences other than those recorded in *Table 5* needed to be specifically mentioned. The exceptions were concerns with active or diverse stakeholders such as publicly owned organizations or those with trust status.

Significantly, 65% of all respondents listed 'what the market will bear' as a primary influence: breaking down this average, 72% of trusts and charities listed this as important but in contrast only 50% of local authorities; historic houses and heritage centres listed this in 75% of their responses but for only 55% of museums did this figure prominently. Overall 51% of respondents declared costs as a primary influence, this average concealing that 80% of plcs gave this a high rating but only 37% of local authorities; 65% of museums relied on costs in contrast with historic houses and heritage centres where only 25% of the respondents from both categories listed costs as significant to their decision making. Competitors' prices were closely monitored and taken into account by 23% of respondents, a surprisingly low proportion in view of the fact that many participants in the industry regard it as a highly competitive environment. On the whole it would appear that small attractions were less influenced by 'what the market would bear' and twice as likely to take the prices of competitors into account as are large concerns. Although the current sample is not robust enough to confirm this in a statistically significant sense it intimates that large concerns are the price leaders and that smaller concerns are price followers. Price following is recognized as a means of coping with the complexity of price decision making and from the perspective of the small concern may well reduce information provision costs considerably. The implications for medium and large concerns are that as trend setters their sector-wide responsibilities are significant.

Price structures

Analysis of the price structures used reveals that 'all-in' inclusive admission charges are the norm (80%); 87% of attractions charged per adult with

Pricing practices in tourist attractions: H A Rogers

Table 5 Primary influences on pricing decisions

Category	Costs No	Costs %ᵃ	Competitors' prices No	Competitors' prices %ᵃ	What market will bear No	What market will bear %ᵃ	Other No	Other %ᵃ	Total responses No	Total responses %ᵃ
Size										
Small	18	58	9	29	14	45	2	6	43	139
Medium	14	42	7	21	25	75	1	3	47	142
Large	11	55	3	15	16	80	2	10	32	160
Total responses and as % overall sample	43	51	19	23	55	65	5	6	122	145
Ownership										
Private individuals	8	33	8	33	15	62	0	0	31	129
Partnerships	3	60	2	40	3	60	0	0	8	160
Private ltd company	6	85	3	43	5	71	0	0	14	200
Public ltd company	4	80	1	20	3	60	0	0	8	114
Trust or charity	17	53	5	16	23	72	2	6	47	147
LAs/govt	3	37	0	0	4	50	3	37	10	125
Other	2	66	0	0	2	66	0	0	4	133
Total responses and as % of overall sample	43	51	19	23	55	65	5	6	122	145
Type of attraction										
Historic house	5	25	5	25	15	75	2	10	27	135
Museum	20	65	7	23	17	55	1	3	45	145
Heritage centre	2	25	1	13	6	75	1	12	10	125
Farm/park	6	60	4	40	6	60	1	10	17	170
Other	10	66	2	13	11	73	0	0	23	153
Total responses and as % of overall sample	43	51	19	23	55	65	5	6	122	145

Notes: ᵃbased on responses against number of concerns within category size, ownership category and type category.

reductions for children and OAPs; 71% offered discounts for parties and only a small number offered variations in entry fees according to season (11%), month (2%), day of week (6%) or time of day (4%). Virtually none of the small concerns used these variations. Flexible pricing was chiefly used in concerns where the decision maker had received training in pricing procedures. The lack of price flexibility might be explained by the fact that the majority of respondents subsequently stated that they were uncertain about the responsiveness of visitors to price or price sensitivity so that a conservative approach could be rationalized as a valid policy to adopt.

Price dynamics

Some 40% of respondents had maintained the same overall structure for five or more years, indicating very little desire or perceived need to experiment with alternative charge or admission structures. In view of the price experimentation that has been undertaken in other sectors of the tourism industry (eg hotels) this stance is surprising. Large organizations appeared to have modified price levels within the last two years more than smaller concerns and though 40% overall routinely increased prices in line with inflation over 50% of large concerns did this automatically.

The information base

In any decision-making situation the information base available is crucial to the effectiveness of decisions, a minimum level being essential to avoid guesswork. In view of the fact that over 65% of respondents declared 'what the market will bear' as a primary determinant of their pricing strategy the customer profile information base used to underpin such a rationale appears to be restrictive in terms of the decision-making support it can offer. The importance of a researched information base has been stressed by many authors including Gabor, who stated: 'Research can be of effective help in the solution of the pricing problems of service establishments'.[3] Specific questions were asked regarding the type of data collected and patterns of collection. The source of visitors and the frequency of their visits was the best informed area (see *Table 6*).

Large concerns were more active in data collection and account for the majority of 'regular' collections: 65% of large units regularly collected information on where their visitors came from and the frequency of these visits; 25% monitored visitor income levels while 40% built socio-economic profiles. The neglect of this area by smaller units was to be expected since data collection is expensive in time and resources but the variance in proactivity between large and medium-sized units is more difficult to explain.

Table 6 Data collection

Factor	Regularly %[a]	Sometimes %[a]	Never %[a]	No reply %[a]
Where visitors come from	39	48	13	0
Their income levels	8	8	62	22
Socio-econ groups	13	14	52	20
Frequency of visits	32	33	27	7

Note: [a]% of total sample.

Price sensitivity

Decisions on entry charges have to be made within the context of the marketing mix and the sensitivity of visitors to price changes and price levels. A range of questions, open and scaled, was therefore included in the survey to reveal the attitudes and understanding of decision makers regarding the perceived demand functions facing their attractions and the role of price in the marketing mix.

First a set of open questions asked respondents to predict percentage changes in attendances if prices were increased or decreased by 10% and 20% respectively. A surprisingly large proportion of the decision makers (45%) felt unable to make any prediction regarding the likely impact on visitor numbers of a suggested percentage change in price, the majority of these declaring frankly that they would be unable to make any such prediction because of the limited information base and the uncertaintly involved. However, 24% believed that there would be no change at all in visitor numbers, indicating that in their view visitors were not price sensitive. Only 31% of respondents felt able to make a prediction regarding the likely effect on visitor numbers following a given percentage price change. Though only an approximate measure of price elasticity, since time scales were not specified, the replies indicate that the perceived demand elasticities for tourist attractions are highly inelastic (see *Table 7*).

For a theoretical 10% increase in price 76% of the respondents thought that the most likely effect on visitor numbers would be a fall of less than 5%; while a price decrease of an equivalent percentage was judged by 85% of the respondents as likely to lead to a rise in visitor numbers of less than 5%. A theoretical rise in price of 20%, which would in practice be substantial, was anticipated by 37% of the respondents to lead to less than a 5% fall in visitors while a 20% fall in price was judged by 59% of respondents to lead to an estimated 5% increase in visitors.

These replies indicate that the perceived demand functions facing tourist attractions are regarded as highly inelastic by the decision makers involved in setting prices. The inclusion of the 24% who believed that there would be no change in the levels of

visitor numbers reduces the elasticities in the above four change situations to -0.149, -0.325, -0.124 and -0.212 respectively. Practitioners believe themselves to be operating on inelastic demand functions and the implications for pricing strategy are strategically interesting. The elasticities associated with price rises have marginally higher values than those associated with price falls, suggesting a possible kink in the demand curve. Practitioners in the industry may see themselves operating in a local oligopolistic market structure where price decreases are matched by competitors but price rises largely ignored. In classic oligopolistic style prices may therefore be kept rigid, partly because of the fear of a price war amongst competitors but in addition this may be reinforced if alternative non-price competitive variables can be used as part of the marketing mix.

However, the inelastic demand functions as perceived would lead to increases in revenue if prices were raised and it is interesting to speculate in this scenario why these attractions do not at least experiment with raising prices.

Tentative explanations that can be advanced are that:

- the apparent lack of experience in using price as a dynamic competitive variable leaves many operators unaware of the potential impact on revenue;
- the lack of training in pricing techniques leaves decision makers incognizant of the role of price as a market variable;
- the preoccupation with visitor numbers as a measure of performance reduces the strategic role of price as a generator of profits and higher rates of return;
- the image of 'expensive' is regarded as highly

Table 7 Responsiveness of visitor numbers to given percentage price changes

Price change (%)	Visitor number change (%)	Elasticity d
Rise of 10	Decrease 2.63	-0.263
Rise of 20	Decrease 11.52	-0.576
Fall of 10	Increase 2.19	-0.219
Fall of 20	Increase 7.52	-0.376

Note: Calculated from changes predicted by the 31% who felt able to make quantitative estimates.

Pricing practices in tourist attractions: H A Rogers

Table 8 Perceptions on price and other aspects of the marketing mix

Statement	Strongly Disagree 1 (%)	Disagree 2 (%)	Neutral 3 (%)	Agree 4 (%)	Strongly agree 5 (%)	Mean	SD
The 'product' on offer is the most important influence on the number of visitors we receive per annum	1.2	6.1	1.2	48.8	42.7	4.26	0.86
Our location does not influence the number of visitors we receive	37.3	38.6	3.6	14.5	6.0	2.13	1.24
Admission prices do not influence the number of visitors we receive	6.0	42.9	23.8	25.0	2.4	2.75	0.98
Pricing decisions are very difficult to make	3.6	26.5	13.3	45.8	10.8	3.34	1.10
The 'right' price is crucial for our successful operation	1.2	10.7	23.8	47.6	16.7	3.68	0.92
Pricing decisions have to be taken on a trial and error basis	9.5	44.0	16.7	28.6	1.2	2.68	1.03
Our advertisements always set out our admission prices very clearly	28.9	25.3	14.5	20.5	10.8	2.59	1.38
Visitors to our attraction are not price sensitive	9.6	44.6	26.5	18.1	1.2	2.57	0.94
I am happy with the procedures used to set prices in our organization	2.4	6.0	16.7	64.3	10.7	3.75	0.82

undesirable from a marketing-mix perspective;
• entry charges are part of the total revenue received and need to be suboptimized to encourage additional spending in other areas within the attraction.[4]

A generalized explanation may not be feasible but the attitude of decision makers and their perceptions in this context was investigated further by presenting a series of statements for appraisal using a traditional Likert five-point scale, rated in terms of strong disagreement, disagreement, neutrality, agreement or strong agreement. These were made up of positive and negative statements to reduce the chance of acquiescence bias and as significant correlations between cross-check questions was observed the validity of responses is accepted as reflecting attitudinal perspectives. The responses are recorded in *Table 8.*

Non-price components of the marketing mix were regarded as influential: the product was seen as central for 91% of respondents, with a low standard deviation of 0.86, and 77% thought that location was an important issue although the range of views on this aspect of the marketing mix was wider since 20% believed that for their attraction location was not important. Though price decisions were seen as difficult by the majority of decision makers there was concord that they were regarded as crucially important. A greater degree of controversy surrounded the issue as to whether price should be set out in advertisements: a mean score of 2.59 combining with a standard deviation of 1.38, 55% believed that it should not be included, 30% that it should and 15% were uncertain. The replies to this statement correlated significantly to attraction type. The issue of pricing being a trial-and-error activity was disputed by 54% but almost 3% agreed with this tenet reflecting the uncertainty that had been indi-

cated previously when examining price responsiveness. The most consistent response in this group of questions was to the final statement where 75% agreed with the statement and only 8% indicated a degree of unhappiness or self-doubt regarding the procedures used. It is left to the reader to judge whether this response is justified in terms of performance, or whether the post-decision rationalization reflects an understandable unwillingness to admit inadequacy or complacency in the context of difficult and complex decision making.

Conclusions

Overall the evidence seems to suggest that the sector is cautious and conservative in its approach to pricing decisions although there is recognition of the importance of price as a facet of the marketing mix. This view is posited on the evidence that though a large number of people are involved in price setting the information base used by the majority appears limited and there is a general unwillingness to experiment with more strategic or dynamic pricing policies. The role of price 'as an active and purposeful management tool both strategically and operationally' has been identified by Normann[5] as a feature of successful service businesses. Kotler[6], too, stresses how 'price is not revised enough to capitalise on market changes'. This may indicate that much of the industry, though apparently competitive on a regional or national level, is in reality oligopolistic on a local basis and that the reluctance to compete on price reflects classic oligopoly behaviour at this local market level. It is difficult to reconcile the stated perceptions of low price responsiveness with the apparent reluctance to raise price levels or experiment with more dynamic price structures. However, it has to be recognized that revenue obtained via entry charges is only a proportion of total revenue for most attractions and that restrained entry charges might well induce additional expenditure within individual attractions on food, beverage, souvenirs etc leading to other benefits for profit and non-profit-orientated organizations. None of the respondents recorded this joint pricing as influential even though opportunities were provided for them to add additional points and information regarding their pricing objectives and strategies. The lack of formal training may also encourage a conservative approach in the face of uncertainty.

Returning to the opening issue regarding the publicity given to pricing decisions in leading UK attractions, this study has highlighted the processes and procedures used within this diverse and challenging industry. The evidence seems to suggest that many participants, though stating that their underpinning rationale is primarily what the market will bear, in fact operate in a real world of such imperfect information and high uncertainty that discovering what the market will bear is extremely difficult and time consuming. The reality for small and many medium-sized enterprises is that they are forced into following their competitors and using cost-based procedures. In this context the price that is set by the market leaders or 'Jewels in the crown' becomes not merely their own individual decision but simultaneously sets the ceiling under which other participants in the sector are forced to operate. Their responsibility is onerous in terms of the effect on the performance and profitability of the sector as a whole.

The inevitable conclusion is that the strategic base for pricing warrants further research and attention by both academics and practitioners.

Acknowledgements

The author wishes to express gratitude to all respondents who completed the questionnaires and to Oxford Brookes University (then Oxford Polytechnic) for financially supporting the cost of the survey.

Further reading

Holloway, J and Plant, R V *Marketing for Tourism* Pitman, UK (1988)

Middleton, V T C *Marketing in Tourism and Travel* Heinemann, Oxford (1988)

Witt, S F and Moutino, L (eds) *Tourism Marketing and Management Handbook* Prentice Hall (1989) [In particular the sections on 'Pricing in Tourism' by A Meidan and 'Tourism marketing mix' by J Cohen.]

Normann, R *Service Management: Strategy and Leadership in Service Business* Wiley, Chichester (1991)

Schlissel, M R and Chasin, J 'Pricing of services: An interdisciplinary review' *Service Industries J 1991* **11** (3) 271–286

Rogers, L 'Service industry pricing' in *Pricing for Profit* Basil Blackwell, Oxford (1990) Ch 9

References

[1]Cooper, C, Fletcher, J, Gilbert, D and Wanhill, S *Tourism Principles and Practice* Pitman, London (1993) Ch 18, 214, Ch 20, 228

[2]McDougall, G H C and Munro, H in Brent-Ritchie, J R and Gouldner, C R (eds) *Travel, Tourism and Hospitality Research* Wiley, Chichester (1987)

[3]Gabor, A *Pricing: Concepts and Methods for Effective Marketing* 2nd edn, Gower, Aldershot (1988) 195

[4]Guiltinan, J 'The price bundling of services: a normative framework' *J Marketing* 1987 **52** (2) 74–85

[5]Normann, R *Service Management: Strategy and Leadership in Service Business* Wiley, Chichester (1991) 125

[6]Kotler, P *Marketing Management: Analysis, Planning, Implementation, and Control* 8th edn Prentice-Hall (1994) 474

[27]

Tourism Economics, 1997, 3 (3), 265–279

The economics of tipping: tips, profits and the market's demand–supply equilibrium

Zvi Schwartz

TechnoLodge, 16500 Lancaster Estates Drive, Wildwood, MO 63040, USA.
Tel: +1 314 273 5577. E-mail:technolodge@cdmnet.com.

Research indicates that the size of a tip is rarely correlated with the quality of the service rendered. These findings empirically refute the widely accepted economic argument that tipping is an efficient quality-control mechanism. This study provides an alternative explanation to the existence of tipping. It develops a microeconomics tipping model and demonstrates that tips affect the firm's profitability through changes in the market's demand–supply equilibrium when consumer segments differ in their demand functions and their propensity to tip. This demand–supply framework can serve as a useful tool for managers who wish to select an appropriate tipping policy for their firms.

Tipping is a special form of voluntary payment, usually occurring after face-to-face service has been provided. Despite its voluntary nature, tipping has a significant worldwide economic impact involving billions of dollars annually.[1] A 1991 change in the US tax law led to renewed debate among hospitality practitioners and academics on the desirability of tipping. Hospitality firms have some control over tipping: managers can forbid tipping or limit the amount of tips their employees are allowed to collect. Moreover, they can enforce a certain 'tip', for example by including a 15% service charge in the check. To optimally shape the firm's tipping policy, the manager must understand how tips affect the firm's performance. However, most studies regard tipping as a social phenomenon, focusing on why people tip and what factors affect the size of the tips. The findings of these studies are of limited use to an employer concerned with the effect of tipping policy on the firm's income. This paper develops an economic model of tipping which shows that tipping policy can have a substantive effect on firms' profitability by changing the market equilibrium.

The study extends the theoretical microeconomics literature by showing how the traditional demand–supply models of a segmented consumer market (both for a monopolist and a competitive market) can be expanded to include tipping behaviour. The models demonstrate that in many cases the equilibrium with tips is significantly different from that without tips. The results suggest an economic explanation for why tipping exists. It is shown that in various market conditions, tips increase the firms' profitability. This is an alternative explanation to the traditional economic explanation that tipping is an efficient service-quality monitoring system; a theory which is not supported by empirical tests. Finally, this article provides a methodological framework for practitioners who wish to evaluate the effect of tipping on the market equilibrium and consequently on their profits.

The paper is organized as follows. The next section reviews the literature on tipping. It discusses previous studies on the determinants of tip size, customers' reasons for tipping, and what purpose is served by tipping. The third section describes the demand–supply model for a segmented consumer market. Two types of firms are examined: a monopolist firm and a firm which is too small to control prices. For each type, we show how tips are accounted for in the demand–supply models. Using these models, we simulate a market and outline the results in the fourth section. We show how the firm's profitability depends on the combination of two factors: the difference between the customers' propensity to tip and the difference between the customers' demand functions. The paper concludes by outlining the managerial implications of its findings.

Literature review

Tips are a major portion of many service providers' income,[2] and according to several publications,[3] the size of the tip can be effectively manipulated by the server. Relying mostly on field experience and anecdotal evidence, these publications claim that tippee-controlled factors, such as smiling faces drawn on the backs of the customers' checks, affect the size of the tip. Academic studies[4] tested these claims and most often support their validity.

Other empirical studies tested the effect of *exogenous* factors on tipping. They indicate that factors beyond the server's control also affect the tip. Among them are the size of the restaurant bill and the server's physical appearance.[5] Less obvious factors include customers' beliefs about weather conditions, the amount of sunshine, the payment method, the size of the restaurant party and the tipper's gender.[6] Cross-country differences in the prevalence of tipping were shown to reflect cross-country differences in tolerance for status, power differences between people and feminine values,[7] the nation's level of neuroticism[8] and the value of status and prestige.[9]

Considerable attention is given to the question: Why does the custom of tipping exist? There are several conflicting speculations regarding the *origin* of the tipping custom, some going back as far as the Roman era. These theories, however, fall short of explaining why the phenomenon remains a viable kind of an economic transaction.

The traditional microeconomics explanation[10] argues that customers monitor the service quality more efficiently than the firm. The size of the tip is linked to the quality of the service, and tipping is adopted by management as a less expensive monitoring mechanism. Some of the savings in the 'production' costs are passed on to the customers. Hence, both the consumer and the firm benefit from the tipping/quality-control arrangement. Empirical studies, however, do not support this theory. Lynn and Graves[11] tested the connection between tip size and the perceived service quality in a pair of carefully designed studies. The authors concluded that tips provide an incentive which is *too weak* for the managers to rely upon. Other studies indicate that servers may not even be aware of a link between the service quality and the tip, further undermining the validity of the service-quality argument.

This study shows that tips affect firms' profitability through changes in the market's demand–supply equilibrium. It demonstrates that firms can greatly benefit from tipping, thus providing an alternative to the empirically refuted quality–control argument.

The model

In this section we develop a demand–supply model that describes how market equilibrium is affected by the customers' tipping behaviour. The model examines two types of firms: a monopolist firm, and a firm which is too small to control market prices. The market demand is composed of two segments that differ in their willingness to pay and propensity to tip. We begin our analysis by describing the traditional demand–supply models for a segmented consumer body. The building blocks for these models can be found in the microeconomics literature.[12] This section shows how tips are incorporated into the demand–supply models and examines the tips' impact on the aggregated demand, the firm's supply curve and the market equilibrium. The following section uses these demand–supply models to examine the affect of the tips on the firm's profitability.

Consider a restaurant that faces a demand composed of two homogenous market segments, denoted by 1 and 2. The segments differ in their willingness to pay. The consumers of segment 2 have a 'stronger' demand; that is, they have a higher willingness to pay. Their demanded quantity per given price is higher than that of segment 1's consumers. The demand functions (D_1 and D_2) of both segments are linear:

$$D_1 : P_1 = \alpha_1 - \beta_1 \, q_1 \tag{1}$$

$$D_2 : P_2 = \alpha_2 - \beta_2 \, q_2 \tag{2}$$

Where q_1, q_2 denote the quantity demanded by segments 1 and 2 respectively. p_1, p_2 denote the price paid by segments 1 and 2 respectively, and β_1, β_2 denote the slope of the demand curves D_1 and D_2. An aggregated market demand is given by:

$$D: \begin{cases} Q = q_2 = \dfrac{\alpha_2 - P_2}{\beta_2} & P \geq \alpha_1 \\[3mm] Q = q_1 + q_2 = \dfrac{\alpha_1\beta_2 + \alpha_2\beta_1 - P(\beta_1 + \beta_2)}{\beta_1 + \beta_2} & P \leq \alpha_1 \end{cases} \tag{3}$$

Total cost, TC, is given by:

$$TC = F + VQ^2 \tag{4}$$

where F denotes the fixed cost and V denotes the variable cost.

No tips

In the benchmark scenario, customers do not tip, and Equations (3) and (4) are sufficient to derive the market equilibrium. The model assumes that a monopolist restaurant cannot tell the consumers apart since there is no exogenous signal of each consumer's demand function. Furthermore, in a restaurant setting, even if the groups were distinguishable, setting a different price for each consumer segment would be difficult and most likely illegal. Since price discrimination is not possible, the monopolist sets the marginal cost, *MC*, equal to the total marginal revenue, *MR*, where *MR* is the horizontal summation of the marginal revenue curve of segment 1 and the marginal revenue curve of segment 2. Hence,

$$
MR = \begin{cases} \alpha_2 - 2\beta_2 Q & Q \leqslant \dfrac{\alpha_2 - \alpha_1}{\beta_2} \\[3mm] \dfrac{\alpha_1\beta_2 + \alpha_2\beta_1 - 2\beta_1\beta_2 Q}{\beta_1 + \beta_2} & Q \geqslant \dfrac{\alpha_2 - \alpha_1}{\beta_2} \end{cases} \tag{5}
$$

and

$$
MC = 2VQ \tag{6}
$$

When the *MC* line intersects the upper part of the *MR* line (*MC*$_1$ in Figure 1), the restaurant sells $Q_a{}^*$. If the *MC* line intersects the lower part of the *MR* line (*MC*$_3$ in Figure 1), then the restaurant sells $Q_b{}^*$. When the *MC* line intersects both parts of the *MR* function (*MC*$_2$ in Figure 1), the restaurant sells either $Q_a{}^*$ or $Q_b{}^*$, depending on which quantity generates a higher profit.

Thus, to maximize profits the restaurant sells either:

$$
Q_a^* = \frac{\alpha_2}{2(V + \beta_2)} \tag{7}
$$

or

$$
Q_b^* = \frac{\alpha_1\beta_2 + \alpha_2\beta_1}{\beta_1 + \beta_2} \Bigg/ \left[2\left(V + \frac{\beta_2 + \beta_1}{\beta_1\beta_2} \right) \right] \tag{8}
$$

Figure 1 shows the market equilibrium, P^* and Q^*, for *MC*$_3$.

When the restaurant is too small to control market prices, a market equilibrium is reached when demand equals supply, ie. $MC = P$. Using Equations (3) and (6) we arrive at:

$$
Q^* = \begin{cases} \dfrac{\alpha_2}{2V + \beta_2} & Q \leqslant \dfrac{\alpha_2 - \alpha_1}{\beta_2} \\[3mm] \dfrac{\alpha_1\beta_2 + \alpha_2\beta_1}{\beta_1 + \beta_2} \Bigg/ \dfrac{\alpha_1\beta_2 + \alpha_2\beta_1}{\beta_1 + \beta_2} & Q \geqslant \dfrac{\alpha_2 - \alpha_1}{\beta_2} \end{cases} \tag{9}
$$

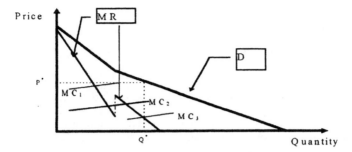

Figure 1. The monopolist's market equilibrium – *MC* intersects the lower part of the *MR* line.

Both segments tip the same amount

When the restaurant's patrons tip their servers, the demand functions of the basic model are no longer adequate and must be modified to reflect the tips. The consumers consider the total amount they pay when they make their purchase decision. From the customer's perspective, the cost of an item is comprised of the item's menu-price as well as the expected tip. For example, when an item on the menu is priced at \$10, the customer's perceived price, *P*, is \$11 (*P* = \$10 + 10% tip). Thus, we modify the demand curves, (3) and (4), as follows:

$$P_1 = \frac{\alpha_1 - \beta_1 q_1}{1 + T_1} \tag{10}$$

$$P_2 = \frac{\alpha_2 - \beta_2 q_2}{1 + T_2} \tag{11}$$

where $T_1, T_2 \leqslant 0$ and usually $T_1, T_2 < 1$.

When both segments tip the same, that is, $T_1 = T_2 = T$, the new aggregated demand function, *D*, is given by

$$D: \begin{cases} Q = q_2 = \dfrac{\alpha_2 - P_2(1 + T)}{\beta_2} & P \geqslant \dfrac{\alpha_1}{1 + T} \\[4mm] Q = q_1 + q_2 = \dfrac{\alpha_1 \beta_2 + \alpha_2 \beta_1 - P(\beta_1 + \beta_2)(1 + T)}{(\beta_1 + \beta_2)} & P \geqslant \dfrac{\alpha_1}{1 + T} \end{cases} \tag{12}$$

A monopolist firm maximizes profits when marginal cost = marginal revenue or *MC* = *MR*. However, *MC* and *MR* are different from (5) and (6) since both are adjusted to reflect the tip. *MR* is derived from the adjusted demand function (12):

$$
MR = \begin{cases} \dfrac{\alpha_2 - 2\beta_2 Q}{1 + T} & Q \leqslant \dfrac{\alpha_2 - \alpha_1}{\beta_2} \\[4mm] \dfrac{\alpha_1\beta_2 + \alpha_2\beta_1 - 2\beta_1\beta_2 Q}{(\beta_1 + \beta_2)(1 + T)} & Q \geqslant \dfrac{\alpha_2 - \alpha_1}{\beta_2} \end{cases} \tag{13}
$$

In the long term, servers' payroll is adjusted to reflect their income from tips.[13] That is, employers who operate in an efficient market consider tips to be an integral part of servers' compensation. The higher the tips, the smaller the salary. Thus, tips reduce the restaurant's operating costs. The (smaller) total cost for the restaurant is given by

$$
TC = F + VQ^2 - TPQ \tag{14}
$$

Where TPQ is the amount of tips the servers receive.[14] This tip element, TPQ, includes the function P, which has two distinctive sections. As a result, the MC function has also two different forms depending on where it intersects the MR line:

$$
MC = \begin{cases} Q\left(2V + \dfrac{\beta_2 T}{1 + T}\right) - \dfrac{\alpha_2 T}{(1 + T)} & Q \leqslant \dfrac{\alpha_2 - \alpha_1}{\beta_2} \\[4mm] 2Q\left(V + \dfrac{2\beta_1\beta_2 T}{1 + T}\right) - \dfrac{\alpha_1\beta_2 + \alpha_2\beta_1}{(\beta_1 + \beta_2)(1 + T)} & Q \geqslant \dfrac{\alpha_2 - \alpha_1}{\beta_2} \end{cases} \tag{15}
$$

As in the case without tips, MC might intersect the upper, the lower, or both parts of the MR line. Hence, to maximize profits the restaurant sells either Q_a^* or Q_b^*:

$$
Q_a^* = \frac{\alpha_2}{2(V + \beta_2)} \tag{16}
$$

$$
Q_b^* = \frac{\alpha_1\beta_2 + \alpha_2\beta_1}{\beta_1 + \beta_2} \bigg/ \left[2\left(V + \frac{\beta_2 + \beta_1}{\beta_1\beta_2}\right)\right] \tag{17}
$$

Note that both quantities, Q_a^* and Q_b^* are identical to those sold by a monopolist firm in an equilibrium without tips [(16) = (7) and (17) = (8)]. When the restaurant is too small to control market prices, the restaurateur equates supply and demand, ie $MC = P$. Using Equations (15) and (12) we arrive at:

$$
Q^* = \begin{cases} \dfrac{\alpha_2}{2V + \dfrac{\beta_2(1 + 2T)}{1 + T}} & Q \leqslant \dfrac{\alpha_2 - \alpha_1}{\beta_2} \\[4mm] \dfrac{\alpha_1\beta_2 + \alpha_2\beta_1}{\beta_1 + \beta_2} \bigg/ \left(2V + \dfrac{\beta_2 + \beta_1}{\beta_1\beta_2}\dfrac{1 + 2T}{1 + T}\right) & Q \geqslant \dfrac{\alpha_2 - \alpha_1}{\beta_2} \end{cases} \tag{18}
$$

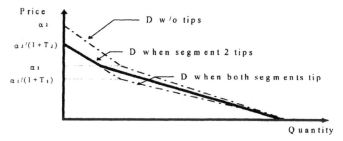

Figure 2. The aggregated demand function for markets with and without tipping.

The segments differ in their propensity to tip

Now, suppose that the 'stronger' segment, 2, is also a better tipper. To simplify the mathematical representation, we assume that segment 1 never tips and that, on an average, segment 2 adds a tip of $T_2\%$ to the stated price. Note that this simplification does not affect the results since we investigate how the *difference* between the segments' propensity to tip affects the restaurant's profitability. The demand functions of segments 1 and 2 are given by Equations (2) and (11) respectively, and the aggregated demand is:

$$D: \begin{cases} Q = q_2 = \dfrac{\alpha_2 - P_2(1 + T_2)}{\beta_2} & P \geqslant \alpha_1 \\[4mm] Q = q_1 + q_2 = \dfrac{\alpha_1\beta_2 + \alpha_2\beta_1 + \alpha_2\beta_1 - P[\beta_2 + \beta_1(1 + T_2)]}{\beta_1 + \beta_2} & P \leqslant \alpha_1 \end{cases} \tag{19}$$

The aggregated demand functions for markets with and without tipping are shown in Figure 2.

MR is given by:

$$MR = \begin{cases} \dfrac{\alpha_2 - 2\beta_2 Q}{1 + T_2} & Q \leqslant \left(\dfrac{\alpha_2}{1 + T_2} - \alpha_1\right)\dfrac{1}{\beta_2} \\[4mm] \dfrac{\alpha_1\beta_2 + \alpha_2\beta_1 - 2\beta_1\beta_2 Q}{\beta_2 + \beta_1(1 + T_2)} & Q \geqslant \left(\dfrac{\alpha_2}{1 + T_2} - \alpha_1\right)\dfrac{1}{\beta_2} \end{cases} \tag{20}$$

Total cost is:

$$TC = F + VQ^2 - T_2 P Q_2 \tag{21}$$

and marginal cost, MC, is:

$$MC = Q\left(2V + \dfrac{\beta_2 T_2}{1 + T_2}\right) - \dfrac{\alpha_2 T_2}{(1 + T_2)} \quad \text{for} \quad Q \leqslant \left(\dfrac{\alpha_2}{1 + T_2} - \alpha_1\right)\dfrac{1}{\beta_2} \tag{22}$$

or

$$MC = Q\left(V + \frac{\beta_1 T_2(1 + T_2)}{\beta_2 + \beta_1(1 + T_2)}\right) + \frac{\beta_1 T_2}{\beta_2 + \beta_1(1 + T_2)}\left[\alpha_2 - \frac{\alpha_1\beta_2 + \alpha_2\beta_1}{\beta_1 + \beta_2(1 + T_2)}\right]$$

for $Q \geqslant \left(\dfrac{\alpha_2}{1 + T_2} - \alpha_1\right)\dfrac{1}{\beta_2}$

To maximize profits the restaurant sells either

$$Q_a^* = \frac{\alpha_2}{2(V + \beta_2)} \tag{23}$$

or

$$Q_b^* = \left\{\frac{\alpha_1\beta_2 + \alpha_2\beta_1}{\beta_1 + \beta_2(1 + T_2)} - \frac{\beta_1 T_2}{\beta_1 + \beta_2(1 + T_2)}\left[\alpha_2 - 2(1 + T_2)\frac{\alpha_1\beta_2 + \alpha_2\beta_1}{\beta_1 + \beta_2(1 + T_2)}\right]\right\} \Big/$$

$$2\left[V + \frac{\beta_1\beta_2}{\beta_1 + \beta_2(1 + T_2)}\left(1 + \frac{T_2(1 + T_2)\beta_1}{\beta_1 + \beta_2(1 + T_2)}\right)\right] \tag{24}$$

When the restaurant does not control market prices, the market clears at $MC = P$. Using Equations (22) and (19) we calculate the quantity sold in an equilibrium:

$$Q^* = \frac{\alpha_2}{2V + \dfrac{\beta_2(1 + 2T_2)}{1 + T_2}} \quad \text{for} \quad Q \leqslant \left(\frac{\alpha_2}{1 + T_2} - \alpha_1\right)\frac{1}{\beta_2} \tag{25}$$

or

$$Q^* = \left\{\frac{\alpha_1\beta_2 + \alpha_2\beta_1}{\beta_1 + \beta_2(1 + T_2)} - \frac{\beta_1 T_2}{\beta_1 + \beta_2(1 + T_2)}\left[\alpha_2 - 2(1 + T_2)\frac{\alpha_1\beta_2 + \alpha_2\beta_1}{\beta_1 + \beta_2(1 + T_2)}\right]\right\} \Big/$$

$$\left[2V + \frac{\beta_1\beta_2}{\beta_1 + \beta_2(1 + T_2)}\left(1 + \frac{T_2(1 + T_2)}{\beta_2}\frac{\beta_1\beta_2}{\beta_1 + \beta_2(1 + T_2)}\right)\right]\right\}$$

$$Q \geqslant \left(\frac{\alpha_2}{1 + T_2} - \alpha_1\right)\frac{1}{\beta_2}$$

The restaurant's profit Π, is the difference between its total revenue and its total cost:

$$\Pi = TR - TC = P^*Q^* - TC \tag{26}$$

The following section uses a numerical example to simulate a market, and explores the relations between the size of the tip, the demand and the restaurant's profitability. The tips (T_1, T_2 and T) range between 0 and 25%. The initial parameters of the demand functions are set as follows:

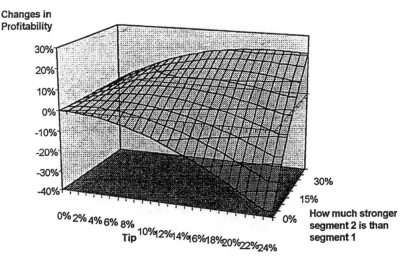

Figure 3. The effects of differing segment demand and propensity to tip on the monopolist firm's profits.

$$D_1: P_1 = 100 - 10q_1$$

and

$$D_2: P_2 = 100 - 10q_2.$$

We investigate how the difference between the segments' demands affects profits by letting segment 2's demand be up to 40% higher than segment 1, ie $100 \leq \alpha_2 \leq 140$. Total cost, (4), is set at:

$$TC = 50 + 20Q^2,$$

that is, the fixed cost is 50 and the variable cost is 20.

Results and discussion

A monopolist firm

When both segments tip the same amount, ie $T_1 = T_2 = T$, *the monopolist firm's profits are not affected by the size of the tip.* This result holds true for any level of incongruity in the segments' willingness to pay. The proof is as follows. The restaurant's profits when both segments do not tip are:

$$\Pi_{no\ tip} = TR{-}TC = P^*Q^*{-}F{-}VQ^{*2}.$$

From (16) and (17) we know that $Q^* = Q^{**}$, hence, the restaurant's profits, when both segments tip, are

$$\Pi_{both\ tip} = TR{-}TC = P^{**}Q^*{-}F{-}VQ^{*2}+TP^{**}Q^*.$$

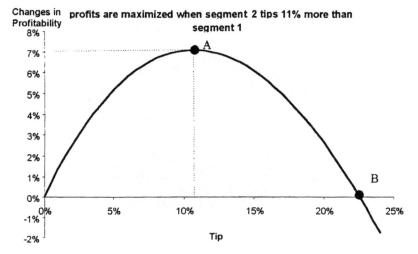

Figure 4. A monopolist firm faces two segments that differ in their tipping and demand functions.

The difference in profits is,

$$\Pi_{no\ tip}-\Pi_{both\ tip} = Q^*[P-^*\ P^{**}(1 + T)].$$

From (3) and (12) we get $P^* = P^{**}(1 + T)$, and

$$\Pi_{no\ tip}-\Pi_{both\ tip} = Q^*[\ P^{**}(1 + T)-P^{**}(1 + T)] = 0\ (Q.\ E.\ D).$$

When the segments differ in their propensity to tip, the monopolist's profits are different from its profits without tips (and from its profits when both segments tip the same amount). The monopolist firm can either increase or decrease its profitability. The outcome depends on a combination of the following factors:

- The difference between the segments' willingness to pay
- The difference between the segments' propensity to tip

Figure 3 is a graphical representation of these somewhat complex relations. When both segments have the same demand function (ie a 0% difference on the Y axis), a tipping incongruity reduces the firm's profitability.

The more segment 2 tips, the lower the restaurant's profits are. For example, a 15% tip by segment 2 reduces the restaurant's profits by 16%. Hence, a monopolist firm facing segments that differ in their propensity to tip but not in their demand can improve its profitability by adopting a 'no tipping' policy.

A positive shift of segment 2's demand curve would increase the desirability of tips to the employer. When segments 2's demand is 20% stronger than that of segment 1, the 'optimal' tipping level is 11%. That is, the restaurant maximizes profits when segment 2 tips 11%. At this level of tipping (point A in Figure 4) the restaurant's profits are 7% higher than its profits when both segments tip equally. Any deviation from this 'optimal' tipping level (in both directions) reduces the restaurant's profits. If segment 2 tips above 22% (point B in Figure 4) profit will be lower than profit when both segments do not tip or tip equally. These results indicate that:

For a monopolist who faces a segmented market where the segments differ in their demand function, there is an 'optimal' level of difference in the segments' propensity to tip. The larger the difference between the segments' demand functions, the higher this 'optimal' level of tipping difference. As a segment's demand gets stronger, both the tip (needed to maximize profits) and the highest profit (attainable by the monopolist firm) increase.

A non-monopolist firm

A restaurant which is too small to control market prices is likely to benefit from tips. The degree to which tipping impacts on profits depends on the difference between the segments' demand functions. The improvement in profitability from tips is slightly smaller when the segments differ in their willingness to pay. The higher the tip, the higher the restaurant's profits. Thus, for a non-monopolist firm:

When both segments tip equally, the profits increase with the tip and decrease as the gap between the segments' demand functions grows. Figure 5 shows that the improvement in profitability from tips shrinks slightly when the segments differ in their willingness to pay.

When the segments differ in their propensity to tip, the results are very

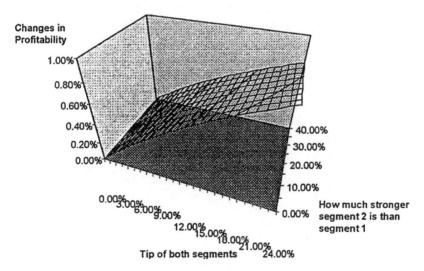

Figure 5. The correlation between the firm's profit margin, the size of the tip and the difference between the segments' demand functions, when both segments tip equally.

Table 1. Market conditions and the recommended tipping policy.

	Monopolist		Competition	
	Effects on firms' profitability	Recommended tipping policy	Effects on firms' profitability	Recommended tipping policy
Segments tip the same.	(1) The tip has no effect.	N/A	(1) Large tips and smaller differences between the segments' demand lead to higher profits.	Encourage tipping.
The segments differ in their propensity to tip.	(2) When both segments have the same demand, the larger the difference between the segments' tipping, the lower the profit.	Abolish tipping.	(2) When both segments have the same demand, the larger the difference in the segments' tipping, the lower the profit.	Abolish tipping.
	(3) When segments' demands differ, higher profits are attainable when the stronger segment is also a better tipper. The larger the difference between the demands, the larger the attainable profit increase.	Try to establish the difference between the tips that maximizes profits.	(3) When segments' demands differ, higher profits are attainable when the stronger segment is also a better tipper. The greater the difference between the demands, the larger the attainable profit increase.	Try to establish the difference between the tips that maximizes profits.

similar to those of the monopolist firm (Figure 3). When the segments have the same willingness to pay, the more segment 2 tips, the lower the restaurant's profits are. As we move along the Y axis (increasing the demand of segment 2), the highest attainable profit increases. These higher profits require a larger tip by segment 2.

In equivalent tip levels, the profit's improvement rate attainable by the non-monopolist firm is slightly higher than the one attainable by the monopolist firm. For example, when the difference in the segments' willingness to pay is 20%, the 'optimal' tipping level is 11% – the same as for the monopolist firm. However, the maximum increase in profitability is 7.43%. This is slightly higher than the 7.02% increase attainable by the monopolist firm.

Managerial implications

Managers should realize that tipping policy affects profitability through its effect on market demand–supply equilibrium. The findings of this study contradict economists' belief that tips have no substantial direct impact.[15] Our theoretical analysis demonstrates that in more realistic situations, where segments differ in their demand and tipping behaviour, tips do affect the firm's profitability. In several cases, the resulting change in profits is even larger than the change in tips (ie a one per cent change in tips is associated with a larger than one per cent change in profits). Moreover, the profit margins of hospitality firms are small because of the industry's inability to differentiate efficiently. Hence, even a minor change in profitability, due to an adjustment in tipping policy, is significant to a hospitality firm.

This study provides a methodological framework to assess the effect of tips on firms' profits. To apply this framework efficiently, management must have a solid understanding of the market. First, it must be able to quantify its supply function through analysis of its costs structure. A typical cost function includes both fixed and variable elements: $TC = F + f(V)$. V, the variable component, is a function of the quantity sold, ie $V = g(Q)$.

Managers must be able to tell whether a firm has a monopoly (or is close to having one) by studying the competition. Finally, they must be able to assess their customers' demand function and tipping behaviour. While numerous segmentation techniques have been tested, this task of formalizing the price–quantity relation by consumer segment is still a challenging one. It is further complicated as one needs to identify each segment's propensity to tip. Large hospitality firms (ie hotel and restaurant chains) gather and analyse this type of information as part of their ongoing market research efforts. Unfortunately, obtaining the required information is more difficult for smaller hospitality firms. Independent small units are therefore less likely to take advantage of a controlled tipping policy which is designed specifically to maximize profits through its impact on the market's demand–supply equilibrium.

The outcome of the market analysis (segments' demand and propensity to tip, supply function and competitive status) indicates what the firm's tipping policy should be.[16] Our results and recommendations for a tipping policy are reported in Table 1. Note that establishing a specific gap in tips

(Recommendation 3 in Table 1) might be beyond a firm's ability. In such cases, managers should estimate how abolishing tipping or adding a service charge to checks would affect profits. Management can use this model to identify and select the most profitable course of action.

Conclusions

Empirical studies indicate that the size of the tip is rarely correlated with the quality of service, contradicting the widely accepted economic theory that tipping is an efficient quality-control mechanism. In an attempt to find an alternative explanation to the existence of tipping, this study examined the effects of tips on profitability through the market's demand–supply equilibrium. The paper develops a microeconomics model where tips are incorporated into both the demand and the supply functions. Using the model to simulate a market for monopolist and non-monopolist firms, we show that tips have a significant effect on the profitability of both type of firms when there are differences between the consumer segments' demand functions and between their propensities to tip.

The framework developed here can be used by managers to select an appropriate tipping policy. Information on the firm's market position, the demand for its product, and its cost function is combined with information on the tipping behavior of the customer segments. The resulting market equilibrium (with tipping) anticipates the impact that various levels of tips would have on the market equilibrium and the firm's income. Thus, the model is useful in evaluating the direct economic payoffs of a tipping policy.

As for every economic theoretical model, further studies are desirable. Empirical tests are of major importance in establishing the validity of the model. Theoretical modelling efforts in related fields, such as game theory, might prove fruitful in providing more solid economic explanations as to why tipping continues to exist.

Endnotes

1. K. McCrohan and R. Pearl, 'An application of commercial panel data for public policy research: estimates of tip earnings', *Journal of Economic and Social Measurement*, Vol 17, No 3–4, 1991, pp 217–231; R. Pearl, *Tipping Practices of American Households: 1984*, Final Report to the Internal Revenue Service Under Contract TIR 82-21, Survey Research Laboratory, University of Illinois, Champaign, IL, 1985.
2. D. Schmidt, 'Tips: the mainstay of many hotel workers' pay', *Monthly Labor Review*, Vol 108, 1985, pp 50–51.
3. For example, MenuTree Books, *Maximum Tips: How to Get the Most Out Of Waiting Tables*, SFO Press, San Francisco, CA, 1986; M. Rockett, *How to Make Outrageously Great Tips*, Proof Positive Productions, Edmonton, 1994.
4. A. Crusco and C. Wetzel, 'The Midas Touch: the effects of interpersonal touch on restaurant tipping', *Personality and Social Psychology Bulletin*, Vol 10, 1984, pp 512–517; K. Garrity and D. Degelman, 'Effect of server introduction on restaurant tipping', *Journal of Applied Social Psychology*, Vol 20, 1990, pp 168–172; M. Harris, 'Waiters, customers, and service: some tips about tipping', *Journal of Applied Social Psychology*, Vol 25, No 8, 1995, pp 725–744; M. Lynn and K. Mynier, 'Effect of server posture on restaurant tipping', *Journal of Applied Social Psychology*, Vol 28, No 8, 1993, pp 678–685; B. Rind and P. Bordia, 'Effect of Server's 'Thank You' and personalization on restaurant tipping', *Journal of Applied Social Psychology*, Vol 25, No 9, 1995

pp 445–451; B. Rind and P. Bordia , 'Effect on restaurant tipping of male and female servers drawing a happy, smiling face on the backs of customers' checks', *Journal of Applied Social Psychology*, Vol 26. No 3. 1996, pp. 218–225; R. Stephen and L. Zweigenhaft, 'The effect on tipping of a waitress touching male and female customers', *Journal of Social Psychology*, Vol 126, 1986, pp 141–142; K. Tidd and S. Lockard, 'Monetary significance of the affiliative smile: a case for reciprocal altruism', *Bulletin of the Psychometric Society*, Vol 11, 1978, pp 344–346.

5. J. May, *Tip or Treat: A Study of Factors Affecting Tipping Behavior*, thesis (MS), Loyola University, Chicago, IL, 1978; Lynn and Mynier, *op cit*, Ref 4; J. Hornik, 'Tactile stimulation and consumer response', *Journal of Consumer Research*, Vol 19, 1992, pp 449–458.

6. Crusco and Wetzel, *op cit*, Ref 4; M. Cunningham, 'Weather, mood and helping behavior: quasi experiments with the Sunshine Samaritan', *Journal of Personality and Social Psychology*, Vol 37, 1979, pp 1947–1956; Lynn and Mynier, *op cit*, Ref 4; B. Rind, 'Effect of beliefs about weather conditions on tipping', *Journal of Applied Social Psychology*, Vol 26, No 2, 1996, pp 137–147; J. Stilman and W. Hansley, 'She wore a flower in her hair: The effect of ornamentation on non-verbal communication', *Journal of Applied Communication Research*, Vol 1, 1980, pp 31–39.

7. M. Lynn, G. Zinkhan and J. Harris, 'Consumer tipping: a cross-country study', *Journal of Consumer Research*, Vol 20, 1993, pp 478–488.

8. M. Lynn, 'Neuroticism and the prevalence of tipping: a cross-country study', *Personality and Individual Differences*, Vol 17, 1994, pp 137–138.

9. M. Lynn, 'Tipping customs and status seeking: A cross-country study', *International Journal of Hospitality Management*, Vol 6, 1997, pp 221–224.

10. O. Bodvarson and W. Gibson, 'Gratuities and customer appraisal of service: evidence from Minnesota restaurants', *Journal of Socio-Economics*, Vol 23, No 3, 1994, pp 287–302; N. Jacob and A. Page, 'Production, information costs, and economic organization: the buyer monitoring case', *American Economic Review*, Vol 70, No 3, 1980, pp 476–478; P. Earl, *Microeconomics for Business and Marketing*, Aldershot, Hants, UK, 1995; D. Hemenway, *Prices and Choices: Microeconomic Vignettes*, Ballinger, Cambridge, MA, 1988.

11. M. Lynn and J. Graves, 'Tipping: an incentive/reward for service?', *Hospitality Research Journal*, Vol 20, No 1, 1996, pp 1–14.

12. For example, T. Blumental, D. Levhari, G. Ofer and A. Sheshinski, *Price Theory*, Academon, Jerusalem, 1971; J. Henderson and R. Quandt, *Microeconomic Theory: A Mathematical Approach*, McGraw-Hill International, Tokyo, 1980; F. Warren-Boulton, *Vertical Control of Markets: Business and Labor Practices*, Ballinger, Cambridge, MA, 1978.

13. Hemenway, *op cit*, Ref 10.

14. Total costs are adjusted by changing the firm's variable cost. Alternatively, one could change the fixed costs. The results of both approaches are almost identical. While the figures are slightly different, the relations among the various factors and the firm's profitability are the same.

15. Hemenway (*op cit*, Ref 10, p. 95) says: 'Overall, the custom of tipping probably has had only the most minor effect on the total price of most purchases.'

16. Note that these recommendations are based solely on the market equilibrium framework. Behavioural and managerial factors, which are beyond the scope of this microeconomics analysis, should be considered as well.

[28]

Tourism Analysis, Vol. 4, pp. 19–27, 1999
Printed in the USA. All rights reserved.

EXPLAINING AND PREDICTING WILLINGNESS TO PAY IN TOURISM: A METHODOLOGICAL FRAMEWORK AND EMPIRICAL ILLUSTRATION

ANDREAS H. ZINS

Institute for Tourism and Leisure Studies, Vienna University of Economics and Business Administration, Augasse 2-6, A-1090 Vienna, Austria

Leisure attractions sometimes undergo redesign processes in order to maintain or advance the present attraction level. In this study an excursion rack railway had to be reconsidered basically due to the cost-caused negative profitability. Alternative scenarios had to be evaluated applying three different research methods: 1) a multiattribute attitudinal approach, 2) a conjoint task, and 3) two measures to assess the willingness to pay. The cross-validation of the different measurement techniques using structural equation models (SEM) discovered useful results about the psychometric relationships. The conjoint task appeared to deliver the least biased results. However, the free-rider effect could not be quantified satisfactorily, maybe due to the very particular situation of a product and service that had not been changed for more than 100 years.

Leisure railway services   Product redesign   Conjoint analysis
Structural equation models

The main research question focuses on the potential market response in view of alternative management decisions. Of course, the closure of the leisure facility would entail a particular change of the attractiveness of the mountain and of the neighboring communities for both target segments: overnight tourists as well as day-trippers. The consequences of such a decision have to be evaluated rather at the political level of regional development than from an entrepreneurial point of view.

Major stakeholders (the federal railway company, the province, the community, private companies) are strongly interested in the adoption of alternative product–service combinations. The introduction of a new transportation technology would entail not only different service benefits to the potential customers but also different fixed and variable costs. The basic product and additional services provided through the rack railway have to undergo radical change. The basic managerial inquiry focuses, therefore, on the potential market response in view of alternative management decisions:

- Is it possible to change a traditional product/service substantially without losing market share?
- What are the critical features to consider for developing a new product?

Address correspondence to Andreas H. Zins. Tel: +43-1-31336-4999; Fax: +43-1-317-12-05; E-mail: andreas.zins@wu-wien.ac.at; WWW: http://www.wu-wien.ac.at/inst/tourism/fac/zins

20   ZINS

- Is it appropriate to follow a single-product or a multiproduct strategy?
- Which combination would yield the best opportunities to attract a broad market potential?

From a methodological perspective the following questions are raised:

- Which measurement approach provides the most consistent results (compare Bonifield, Jeng, & Fesenmaier, 1997)?
- Are there relevant cues to identify the free-rider behavior?

Different Methodologies

Attitudes represent the central explanatory variables in numerous consumer behavior models (Bettman, 1979, p. 17; Engel, Blackwell, & Miniard 1993, p. 48; Howard & Sheth, 1969, p. 30). Based on the strong relationship to behavioral aspects they are very common in the tourism and leisure context (Carmichael, 1992; Goodall, 1991; Mazanec, 1994; Moutinho, 1987; Walmsley & Jenkins, 1992; Woodside & Carr, 1988; Woodside & Lysonski, 1989). They are useful in explaining preferences and buying intentions (Ajzen & Fishbein, 1980). Attitudes are multidimensional in nature; hence, the measurement process basically applies multiattribute models.

An alternative way of revealing the consumer–product relationship is to decompose overall utility or preference evaluations into prespecified and transparent product elements. This approach is commonly known as the conjoint analysis and is widely accepted in the marketing science (Green & Srinivasan, 1990; Green & Wind, 1984). While the application for commercial projects cannot be easily surveyed, the scientific literature is more and more inclined to discuss methodological problems (Carroll & Green, 1995; Louvière, 1996). The assumption of independent attributes, for example, is only transferred from the measurement level to the analytical level whereby interaction effects are neglected (Green & Srinivasan, 1990). In tourism and leisure settings, the use of the conjoint technique is not so widespread; maybe this is due to the fact that products and services are in most cases very complex and compound (Louvière, 1984). Applications can be quoted for analyzing different products and services, for example: in the hospitality field (Ding, Geschke, & Lewis, 1991; Filiatrault & Ritchie, 1988; Purdue, 1995; Renaghan & Kay, 1987; Wind, Green, Shifflet, & Scarbrough, 1989); when designing travel packages (Carmichael, 1992; MacKenzie, 1992; Muehlbacher & Botschen, 1988; Oppermann & Schubert, 1994; Rosenthal, 1997); when forming destination alliances (Hill & Shaw, 1995); when structuring and analyzing the decision-making process (Bonifield et al., 1997; Dellaert, Borgers, & Timmermans, 1997; Dellaert, Prodigalidad, & Louvière, 1998; Molin, Oppewal, & Timmermans, 1997; Woodside & Carr, 1988); or in the field of leisure facilities (Toy, 1989). A similar application in the field of rail transportation is documented by Meffert and Perrey (1997). The problem of free riding was addressed only once in connection with revealing preferences for ecological tourism products (Woehler, 1993).

A simple conjoint design was preferred for this study in order to meet the particular situation (see Sample section). Nine product alternatives (cf. Table 1 for product features) had been developed and graphically illustrated by applying a fractional factorial design. Respondents were asked to sort them according to their preferences. The list of features was kept strictly limited to those of predominant interest. The relative influence of those four features on the overall utility perception is a research objective when applying conjoint analysis, although there were many more varied options for the mode of transportation. Traditional steam locomotives, diesel (or electric) engines using the existing track, and the construction of a new cabin cableway at a somewhat different location were thought to represent the major possible changes.

Table 1
Alternative Product Features for the Conjoint Design

Features			
Mode	steam	diesel	cableway
Reservation	yes	no	
Operating season	year around	summer	
Price in US$	14.50	22.70	31.80

EXPLAINING AND PREDICTING WILLINGNESS TO PAY   21

The alternative multiattribute measurement of preferences involved a list of 20 attitudinal statements (see Table 2) describing the multifaceted relationship between the individual and the facility of the rack railway. For comparability with the conjoint design these statements cover the most crucial attributes: nostalgia, image, comfort, velocity, reservation, convenience, landscape, environmental impacts. The original list of items (factors)—later condensed—will be used for cross-validating the conjoint results and for explaining the psychometric properties of the partworth utilities.

Special emphasis had to be drawn on the free-rider problem. Pampered by the long-lasting tradition of state-subsidized operation paired with socially staggered fares it was expected that the tendency to preserve the present conditions would be rather high and the willingness to pay rather low. In order to compare constrained (conjoint task) and unconstrained measures for the willingness to pay, two additional questions were integrated into the questionnaire: one direct variable that mea-

sures the unconstrained willingness to pay in terms of currency units (WTP) and a Likert-type scale that measures the willingness to pay more to preserve the nostalgic steam locomotives (cf. Table 2, ATT17).

The analysis of the actual fares paid gives the following structure: 50% of the passengers accept the full fare; 33% ride at a 50% discount (retired people, families, special environmental ticket); about 11% are in favor of an even higher reduction; 5% use a combination ticket including railway transportation to the location.

The nominal fare for an up- and downhill ride amounted to US$21.80 in the previous year. Taking into account that 75% of the customers are riding both ways while 20% are transported uphill and only 5% downhill (at—of course—reduced rates), the maximum average revenue per capita would be US$19.20. Actually, the average revenue amounts to US$14. The gap of 27% is lost by granting different price reductions. As special fares for children and/or families are quite common, this offer was considered separately in the

Table 2

List of Attitudinal Statements Toward the Rack Railway

Variable Name	Statement	Mean Rating
ATT01	The rack railway is the main attraction of Puchberg.	1.65
ATT02	The smoke and the steam are constitutional for the nostalgic experience of the rack railway.	1.35
ATT03	The rack railway is highly attractive for Puchberg.	1.55
ATT04	In my opinion, the rack railway is a pure technical facility to climb the mountain; it is an equivalent to cableway.	2.81
ATT05	The Schneeberg mountain is directly associated with the rack railway.	1.81
ATT06	I perceive the rack railway as a cultural monument.	1.27
ATT07	The rack railway in its present design is outdated.	3.49
ATT08	When riding with the rack railway, the nostalgic character is predominant.	1.57
ATT09	When riding with the rack railway, the experience of the landscape plays the major role.	1.79
ATT10	The smoke of the rack railway pollutes the environment.	2.96
ATT11	The smoke of the railway is unpleasant to the passengers and hikers.	3.40
ATT12	The change from steam to diesel or electricity is expected to improve the velocity.	2.96
ATT13	Such a change will entail the loss of identity of the rack railway.	1.33
ATT14	The smoke and the steam of the rack railway is an inseparable feature of Puchberg.	1.47
ATT15	The comfort of the wagons should be increased together with the overall modernization of the rack railway.	2.63
ATT16	The old steam trains should coexist with modern trains in order to preserve the nostalgic character of the railway.	1.62
ATT17	I am ready to pay more for a steam train than for a modern one.	1.99
ATT18	To avoid waiting time I would prefer seat reservation from at home.	1.88
ATT19	More trains per day could defuse the problem of waiting time.	1.77
ATT20	The present value-for-money relationship is reasonable.	1.67

Likert scale ranging from 1 "applies exactly" to 4 "does not apply at all."

questionnaire. The levels of the price feature were set up according to these relationships: the lowest category reflects the grand mean of actual fares paid and compares favorably to the fares of comparable mountain rails; the middle category is slightly above the nominal full fare; and the highest price is considered to represent the upper limit acceptable for the core target group of nostalgia lovers. As the middle price level reflects the actual nominal fare, it is assumed that demand will be more elastic up to this point. Hence, it can be supposed that the smaller price level spacing between categories 1 and 2 will fall into the steep region of the utility function. The difference between categories 2 and 3 has a larger attribute range, which coincides with a flatter slope of the utility function. This may contribute to a higher internal validity as Darmon and Rouziès (1989) found out with synthetic data.

Sample

Data were gathered by means of a mailed questionnaire because the study had to be carried out during the nonoperation period (winter season). A prior analysis of actual passengers had revealed that hiking and experiencing nostalgic trains were among the predominant motivations riding on this excursion railway. Both had about equal importance. Hence, two samples of target groups were identified: first, those loving nostalgic railways and, second, those loving nature and hiking. In total, 389 questionnaires were returned; 375 of them had the conjoint task completed and could be used for methodological comparisons. Both target groups have equal shares in the sample; 88% of the respondents had used the train before. No significant differences occurred between the two target groups in this respect with the exception that hikers had a higher overall frequency of prior usage. The obviously high percentage of market penetration does not seem to be biased as this leisure facility has a high attraction level among the total population within a catchment area of about a 1-hour car ride.

Results

Attitudes and Willingness to Pay

The multiattribute approach delivers the base orientation of preference (Likert scale ranging from 1 "applies exactly" to 4 "does not apply at all"). The top six attitudinal items (scale means from 1.27 to 1.57; Table 2) focus on the nostalgic image and character of the rack railway. These perceptions make up the top priorities of the potential customers. In turn, the most refused statements address negative aspects such as pollution, overaging, and speed (scale means from 3.49 to 2.96). Other statements reveal that the rack railway in the present outlook is perceived to be a unique facility that cannot be replaced easily. Nevertheless, some responses show evidence for possible improvements: more trains per day, coexistence of modern and traditional trains, and optional reservation from at home.

Ninety percent of the respondents find the value-for-money relationship reasonable (Table 2, ATT20). Seventy-nine percent are inclined to pay even more to ride on a steam train (Table 2, ATT17). These findings are indifferent across age groups, identified target groups, and actually granted fares. One out of two customers ride on the rack railway at a reduced fare. Their attitude concerning an extra charge for steam locomotives does not differ from those of the "regular" passenger. Investigating differences between the two top-box ratings of the steam preference and the value-for-money attitude does not result in significant contrasts.

Additional information can be drawn from the "willingness-to-pay" variable (WTP), which measured the amount in currency units. The mean value is US$19.90, the median US$19.20. The upper quartile value amounts to US$23.20, slightly above the actual nominal full fare of US$21.80. While 50% of the passengers had to ride at the full fare, 30% of the respondents acknowledged being ready to pay exactly the full fare. Only an additional proportion of about 15% is even ready to pay more. It could be assumed that both groups—actual full-fare passengers and those 45% of respondents accepting the full fare or even more—would overlap entirely. However, only less than 60% of the latter group is made up by full-fare passengers: inconsistency or different free-riding behavior? Moreover, the average WTP is independent from fare that had been actually paid the last time. Both groups, full-fare and reduced-fare passengers, do not differ significantly in terms of stated WTP; and this is again below the actual full fare. Although both groups do not differ in terms of their value-for-money evaluation, they show a different relative adaptation between their past financial contribution and their stated willingness to pay. Two possible effects can be assumed. 1) Reduced-fare passengers overstate their willingness to pay because they are sure to be granted reductions in the future. 2) Full-fare passengers intentionally underestimate their WTP in order to avoid further price increases in view of the unstable situation of the rack railway.

The elasticity between those potential customers willing to pay more for steam trains and those who are not can elucidate the price sensitivity. The relationship between acceptable price and the "steam preference" is not strictly linear. This, again, gives rise for detecting the phenomenon of free ridership. The range between lowest and highest mean of the WTP variable is about 16% of the lowest level. Means are different between the four categories of the "steam preference" ($p < 0.001$, $\eta^2 = 0.063$); however, even the highest mean (US\$21.40) does not exceed the actual full fare.

Preference Analysis With Conjoint Measurement

The utility functions are estimated at the individual level and aggregated afterwards. On average, the following partworth utilities are thus derived (Fig. 1). The importance weights of the attributes are calculated as a ratio between the absolute range of the partworths per feature and the sum of these ranges. Thus, the mode of transportation is responsible for 60% of the overall preference building. The price factor accounts for 24% whereas the options for reservation and a year-around operation are only of minor utility.

Three simulation cards (product alternatives) were defined to analyze the preferences for realistic products. The features are: 1) traditional steam locomotives, summer season with optional reservation at US\$22.70; 2) diesel locomotives, summer season without optional reservation at US\$15.50; 3) cabin cableway, year-around operation without reservation at US\$14.50. The potential market share applying the logit-estimation (comparable to the BTL method) shows a significant dominance of the existing steam alterna-

tive. When reducing the potential future market to only two concurrent alternatives (nostalgic steam trains at US\$31.80 and modern diesel trains at US\$15.50) the derived market share for the nostalgic trains is between 50% and 60% according to the estimation algorithm.

Incorporating Attitudes, Partworth Utilities, and WTP Into a Structural Equation Model

A third and integrated approach should analyze the psychometric structures between attitudes, derived benefits from the conjoint task, and the stated willingness to pay. Linear structural equation models were calibrated using the ML method under AMOS 3.6 (Arbuckle, 1995). First of all, the factor pattern of the attitudes was analyzed. Five factors were identified representing attitudinal domains such as "regional attraction," "nostalgia," "comfort," "environment," and "price sensitivity for steam" (Fig. 2). Respondents who think that both the mountain and its historic excursion train contribute to the attractiveness of the region closely tie this attractiveness to the nostalgic character of the rack railway (standardized correlation: 0.67). In a consistent way, the preference for nostalgia correlates positively with the price sensitivity for steam (corr.: 0.37). On the other hand, improvements of comfort and environmental impacts are quite opposite to the former preference domains.

The initial MODEL A introduced the stated willingness-to-pay measure (WTP in currency units) as the dependent variable. The model ($\chi^2 = 67.457$, $df = 38$) fits the data very well (GFI = 0.968, TLI = 0.955, RMSEA = 0.046); yet the explanation of the variation in the WTP variable does not exceed 5%. The main effect is exercised by the single component factor representing the willingness to pay more for supporting the nostalgic steam trains. The regression weight with the WTP variable (open, currency unit format) is negative (standardized: -0.22). Other attitudinal factors—especially the nostalgia preference—are indirectly backing this relationship. This means that the more customers support the conservation of the status quo combined with the nostalgic character of the facility the more they seem to be ready to pay. The direction of the relationship appears to

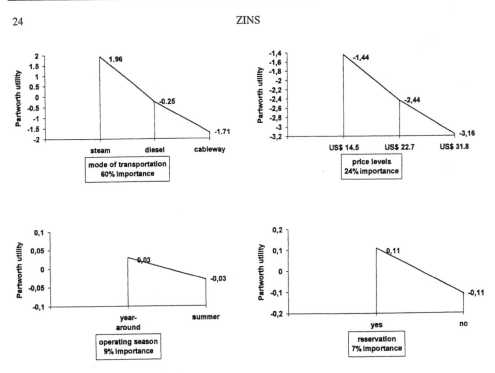

Figure 1. Partworth utilities for four product features.

be correct; yet, the noise or "free-rider bias" is considerable, as the explanatory power of the model is very weak.

The introduction of the benefits derived from the conjoint experiment extended the SEM approach to MODEL B. The partworth utilities for "steam" and "price" should act as mediator variables between attitudes and the willingness-to-pay variable. The partworth variables "operation season" and "reservation" could not improve the model. Figure 2 depicts the standardized correlation coefficients for the significant paths and the squared multiple correlations. Fit parameters for MODEL B amount to: $\chi^2 = 103.447$, $df = 56$ (GFI $= 0.960$, TLI $= 0.941$, RMSEA $= 0.048$). Significant relationships can be observed between various attitudinal factors and the partworth utility for the steam alternative. A strong emphasis on nostalgia coincides with a higher preference for steam locomotives. Perceived negative environmental impacts seem to weaken the favorable attitude towards steam engines. Finally, the readiness to pay

more for the maintenance of the nostalgic attraction correlates positively with the derived benefits from steam locomotives (corr.: –0.15). The more utility is attributed to the steam alternative the higher is the accepted price level (corr.: 0.21). However, a significant correlation between the Likert-type price readiness and the conjoint price level could not be corroborated, whereas a medium-size link to the WTP (in currency units) from both—conjoint price level and price readiness—with consistent signs could be confirmed. Nevertheless, the overall degree of explanation remains—with and without derived utility scores—rather poor.

Discussion and Implications

Which of the approaches reveals the real customer preferences? Neither is superior, and competing arguments for validity can be pointed out. The multiattribute measurement resulted in a five-dimensional attitudinal space. The nostalgic ele-

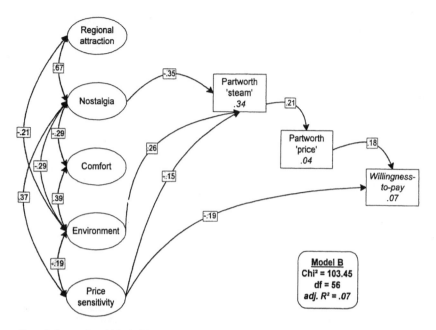

Figure 2. Structural model for "willingness to pay" (without measurement model).

ments affiliated to the rack railway were most emphasized. The environmental impacts were considered less relevant. Several attributes concerning convenience and comfort had been rated in between. A vast majority supports the preservation of the traditional steam locomotives in order to maintain the identity of the rack railway as well as of the mountain and the community. While 90% of the respondents appreciate the current value-for-money relationship, an overwhelming majority of 79% are ready to pay more to maintain the nostalgic steam attraction.

These findings coincide in general with the indirect preference measurement via conjoint analysis. Yet, the majority for conserving the status quo is not that convincing when taking the forced trade-offs into account. When accepting this overwhelming wish to preserve, the problem of finding the appropriate price has to be resolved. Again, looking at the attitudinal results, 79% of the potential customers can be identified to accept higher fares for traditional steam trains. Now, taking the stated willingness to pay (WTP in currency units)

reliable and valid, those 79% are ready to pay only 20% more than the average per capita revenue. This, in turn, is 15% below the actual full fare. Obviously, these findings are contradictory. Maybe the stated WTP is biased in such a way that the respondents did not want to uncover the real amount of the acceptable price in order to avoid a considerable price increase. Usually, the opposite phenomenon can be observed, so respondents overestimate their WTP because these statements have no real-life consequences.

The biased and erroneous response behavior referring to the WTP is revealed by applying structural equation models. Attitudes toward the rack railway together with the derived benefit scores from the conjoint analysis explain only 7% of the variation of the WTP. This weak explanatory power for WTP is directly supported only by the other—stated or derived—price preferences. No direct influence from the "steam" benefit to the WTP could be detected; no significant correlation between the Likert-type willingness to pay and the constrained price preference derived from the conjoint analysis could be established. When comparing full-fare passengers with reduced-fare passengers—who stated the same WTP on average (US$20)—the free-rider behavior becomes more obvious. The model's R^2 goes down to 5% for the full-fare group whereas for the reduced-fare passengers it doubles to 14%. This indicates that the entire response behavior of the latter group appears to be much more consistent than for the full-fare group.

A second conceptual bias is unveiled by the structural equation model (Fig. 2). The attitudinal factors have strong ties to the derived conjoint benefit "steam" only and no direct influence on the partworth for "price." Therefore, it can be argued that the whole multiattribute scale is able to illustrate the doubtless high preference for the traditional steam operation ($R^2 = 34\%$) but is weak in discriminatory power. In view of the partly weak and partly insignificant relationships in the model, the heterogeneity of the constrained and unconstrained preference assessment becomes evident.

In turn, the outcome of the conjoint measurement gives a more realistic insight into the preference structure. On average, we can conclude that the mode of transportation contributes 60% to the overall utility perception. The price levels account for 24%. The cost situation for steam operation suggested curbing the demand. The demand analysis, however, delivered controversial results. Therefore, a single-product strategy does not seem to be feasible. To design a two-product operation it is necessary to find the optimal product bundles. If "optimal" means profit maximizing, different investment and operating costs have to be considered. It is not the purpose of this study to discuss these constraints in detail.

To sum up, the attitudinal approach and the willingness-to-pay approach in particular yielded very inconsistent results. Generally, the conjoint task is designed to simulate consumption decisions more realistically. Therefore, it is argued that the derived preference weights and benefits as well as the simulated market shares are more reliable than the stated attitudes. This conclusion is opposite to the results found by Bonifield et al. (1997). In their study of motivational bundles and trade-offs the authors concluded that the conjoint task through its complexity introduced more error than

the conventional methods (p. 45). The comparison of the three methodological approaches on the individual level in this study showed that considerable noise and systematic error due to the free-rider phenomenon exist. This free-riding behavior appears to be nonuniformly distributed among the various target groups. When asked for the value for money or for the willingness to pay, no dramatic changes could be inferred when compared to the actual situation of accepted price levels. However, the 79% majority in favor of the maintenance of the nostalgic steam trains, who simultaneously intended to pay more, diminishes to an overall share of 50% or 60% when respondents are forced to make trade-offs. Nevertheless, the conjoint task lacks some realistic assumptions for this application, which should be overcome in similar situations: the method is not robust against inertia (i.e., the persistence of a preference) (for a unique leisure attraction that has been inherited for several generations). The conjoint task did not incorporate the possible change from a one-product to a multiproduct strategy. Respondents had been rarely exposed to a market situation where more than one product alternative (e.g., steam and diesel or electric locomotives in parallel operation) existed. Therefore, implicitly it can be assumed that the respondents had a hypothetical situation in mind where only one type of the leisure attraction could be realized. As a consequence, the simulated market shares for different simultaneous alternatives have to be treated with caution.

References

Ajzen, I., & Fishbein, M. (1980). *Understanding attitudes and predicting social behavior.* Englewood Cliffs, NJ: Prentice-Hall.

Arbuckle, J. L. (1995). *Amos users' guide.* Chicago, IL: SmallWaters Coproration.

Bettman, J. R. (1979). *An information processing theory of consumer choice.* Reading, MA: Addison-Wesley.

Bonifield, R. L., Jeng, J.-M., & Fesenmaier, D. R. (1997). Comparison of approaches for measuring traveler motivations. *Tourism Analysis, 1*(1), 39–47.

Carmichael, B. (1992). Using conjoint modeling to measure tourist image and analyse ski resort choice. In P. Johnson & T. Berry (Eds.), *Choice and demand in tourism* (pp. 93–106). London: Mansell.

Carroll, J. D., & Green, P. E. (1995). Psychometric methods in marketing. Research: Part I, conjoint analysis. *Journal of Marketing Research, 32,* 385–391.

Darmon, R. Y., & Rouziès, D. (1989). Assessing conjoint analysis internal validity: The effect of various continuous attribute level spacings. *International Journal of Research in Marketing, 6*, 35–44.

Dellaert, B. G. C., Borgers, A. W. J., & Timmermans, H. J. P. (1997). Conjoint models of tourist portfolio choice: Theory and illustration. *Leisure Sciences, 19*. 31–58.

Dellaert, B. G. C., Prodigalidad, M., & Louviere, J. J. (1998). Using conjoint analysis to study family travel preference structures: A comparison of day trips and 1-week holidays. *Tourism Analysis, 2*(2), 67–75.

Ding, S., Geschke, U., & Lewis, R. (1991). Conjoint analysis and its application in the hospitality industry. *Journal of the International Academy of Hospitality Research, 2*, 2–29.

Engel, J. F., Blackwell, R. D., & Miniard, P. W. (1993). *Consumer behavior* (7th ed.). Fort Worth, TX: The Dryden Press.

Filiatrault, P., & Ritchie, J. R. B. (1988). The impact of situational factors on the evaluation of hospitality services. *Journal of Travel Research, 26*, 29–37.

Goodall, B. (1991). Understanding holiday choice. In P. Cooper (Ed.), *Progress in tourism. Recreation and hospitality management* (Vol. 3, pp. 58–77). London: Belhaven.

Green, P. E., & Srinivasan, V. (1990). Conjoint analysis in marketing: New developments with implications for research and practice. *Journal of Marketing, 54*, 3–19.

Green, P. E., & Wind, Y. (1984). Conjoint analysis of price premiums for hotel amenities. *Journal of Business, 57*(1/2), 111–132.

Hill, T., & Shaw, R. N. (1995). Co-marketing tourism internationally: Bases for strategic alliances. *Journal of Travel Research, 34*, 25–32.

Howard, J. A., & Sheth, J. N. (1969). *The theory of buyer behavior*. New York: Wiley.

Louvière, J. J. (1984). Using discrete choice experiments and multinomial logit choice models to forecast trial in a competitive retail environment: A fast food restaurant illustration. *Journal of Retailing, 60*(4), 81–107.

Louvière, J. J. (1996). Conjoint analysis. In R. P. Bagozzi (Ed.), *Advanced methods of marketing research* (pp. 223–259). Cambridge, MA: Blackwell Business.

MacKenzie, J. (1992). Evaluating recreation trip attributes and travel time via conjoint analysis. *Journal of Leisure Research, 24*(2), 171–184.

Mazanec, J. A. (1994). Consumer behavior. In St. Witt & L. Moutinho (Eds.), *Tourism marketing and management handbook* (2nd ed., pp. 293–299). New York: Prentice Hall.

Mazanec, J. A. (1999). Simultaneous positioning and segmentation analysis with topologically ordered feature maps: A tour operator example. *Journal of Retailing and Consumer Services, 6*(4), 219–235.

Meffert, H., & Perrey, J. (1997). Nutzensegmentierung im Verkehrsdienstleistungsbereich—theoretische Grundlagen und empirische Erkenntnisse am Beispiel des Schienenpersonenverkehrs. *Tourismus Journal, 1*(1), 13–40.

Molin, E. J., Oppewal, H., & Timmermans, H. J. P. (1997). *Modeling family decision making: A conjoint based approach.* Working paper, Urban Planning Group, Eindhoven University of Technology.

Moutinho, L. (1987). Consumer behavior in tourism. *European Journal of Marketing, 21*(10), 3–44.

Muehlbacher, H., & Botschen, G. (1988). The use of trade-off analysis for the design of holiday travel packages. *Journal of Business Research, 17*(2), 117–131.

Oppermann, R., & Schubert, B. (1994). Konzeption der Dienstleistung 'Studienreise' mittels Conjoint-Analyse. *der markt, 33*(1), 23–30.

Purdue, R. R. (1995). Traveler preferences for information center attributes and services. *Journal of Travel Research, 33*, 2–7.

Renaghan, L. M., & Kay, M. Z. (1987). What meeting planners want: The conjoint-analysis approach. *Cornell Hotel and Restaurant Administration Quarterly, 28*(1), 67–76.

Rosenthal, J. (1997). Touristische Umweltgütezeichen. *Tourismus Journal, 1*(1), 41–70.

Toy, D. (1989). Strategic marketing for recreational facilities: A hybrid conjoint analysis. *Journal of Leisure Research, 21*(4), 276–296.

Walmsley, D. J., & Jenkins, J. M. (1992). Cognitive distance: A neglected issue in travel behavior. *Journal of Travel Research, 31*, 24–29.

Wind, J., Green, P. E., Shifflet, D., & Scarbrough, M. (1989). Courtyard by Marriott: Designing a hotel facility with consumer-based marketing models. *Interfaces, 19*(1), 25–47.

Woehler, K. (1993). Internalisierungsbereitschaft externer Kosten umweltvertraeglicher Angebote bei Urlaubern. In G. Langer & K. Weiermair (Eds.), *Tourismus und Landschaftsbild. Nutzen und Kosten der Landschaftspflege* (pp. 213–242). Wien: Kulturverlag.

Woodside, A. G., & Carr, J. A. (1988). Consumer decision making and competitive marketing strategies: Applications for tourism planning. *Journal of Travel Research, 26*, 2–7.

Woodside, A. G., & Lysonski, S. (1989). A general model of traveler destination choice. *Journal of Travel Research, 27*, 8–14.

Part V
Managing Staff

[29]

Sustaining Tourism Employment

Peter M. Burns
The Business School, University of London, Stapleton House, 277-281 Holloway Road, London N7 8HN

This paper addresses some of the problems that arise out of the special characteristics history and circumstances have given to employment in the tourism sector. Impetus for the paper was provided by field work conducted in Sri Lanka and the Cook Islands as part of a Tourism Master Planning Consultancy, and my own experiences as a working chef during two periods in London. The findings provide a suitable stage for examining the perceived wisdom surrounding the nature of tourism employment. In particular, we emphasise that while tourism jobs provide value-added for both employer and holidaymaker through so-called 'people skills', these important skills seem not to be counted when remunerating employees. The role of expatriates in training is looked at, as is the role of government. We conclude with some concrete ideas about ways in which quality of experience at the workplace can be added for tourism employees. Without this, the long- term sustainability of this 'people industry' will be vulnerable.

Introduction

In a sense, the issues about sustaining tourism's employment could act as a metaphor for the debate about sustainable tourism. Both agendas are dominated by issues of 'worthwhileness'. There is evidence supportive of each side of the divide (for there is indeed a divide), ranging from polemics like Turner & Ash's *The Golden Hordes* (1975), Bryden's chilling analysis of the discredited Zinder Report (1973: 155), to the seemingly uncritical acceptance of tourism as having intrinsic worth by such commentators as Peters (1969), Foster (1985) and Burkart & Medlik (1989). There are also the questions of definition. Tourism itself has a number of definitions. It has been described as an 'industry' (Medlik, 1991 *passim*), a 'system' (Christie-Mill & Morrison, 1985: xix) and very often as a 'phenomenon'. Given that definitions vary according to the underlying purpose for the definition, and that the purpose of this article is to explore tourism's key human resource: the workforce, the most appropriate definition for tourism is that by Jafar Jafari (1981):

> A study of man [sic] away from his usual habitat, of the industry which responds to his needs, and the impacts that both he and the industry have on the host socio-cultural, economic, and physical environments.

This is a definition that takes account of tourism's *problematique* in terms of human and environmental issues. Having taken a working definition of tourism, the next problem to be addressed is that of defining what is meant by 'tourism employment'. While the following text will describe many of the characteristics relating to employment in tourism, it is clear that different sectors have very different forms of employment. These range from the clear cut divisions of labour

0966-9582/93/02 0081-16 $1.80/0
JOURNAL OF SUSTAINABLE TOURISM

and heavily unionised airline sector, the clearly defined contracts and conditions of service by international corporations such as Ramada Renaissance and Sheraton, the minimum wage, short contract, insecure conditions that characterise much of catering work to the prostitutes working bars in any one of a number of tourist traps around the world. However, it is generally understood that almost any discussion about tourism and employment will be dominated by hotel and catering , after all, it constitutes the largest component of the sector. So, while our working definition here of 'tourism employment' is not a complex one (let it simply be all direct employment created by the tourist spend), the issues are, in themselves, very complex. While most of the examples drawn upon will be from the hotels sector, the issues raised will be underpinned by reference to the wider net of employment through tourism, including the marginal and informal.

Empirical evidence gathered through field research in several developing countries and through working in the hotel sector of the tourism industry over several years has led me to conclude that, with a few noteworthy exceptions, tourism employers seem to exhibit little concern over sustaining or developing their workforce. Sustainability seems to rely on de-skilling tactics (Gabriel, 1988), where jobs become de-skilled through purchasing supplies with little or no value-added, or through the greater use of technology. This is discussed by Riley & Jones (1992: 300) who assert that

> The character of this change is almost universally de-skilling...it is easier to make numerical micro [labour cost] adjustments in the unskilled workforce than in the skilled, so it is always in the interest of managers to de-skill!

For the hotel sector in the developed world, this last point is evidenced in at least two ways, firstly by the rise of fully prepared dishes in catering packs by companies such as Brake Brothers and Young's Seafood, and secondly by the rise in Hi-Tec hotel and catering products such as those to be seen at major catering exhibitions (such as London's 'Hotelympia'). Such phenomena are described by Riley (1991: 234) who cites Chivers (1973) on *technological substitution* and Alpert (1986) on *simplification or standardisation of the product.*

One result of this de-skilling process is the resultant minimum requirements in terms of induction and training. Wood (1992: 300) notes that corporate hospitality organisations actively pursue low pay strategies, with Riley (1991) noting that 'on-the-job-training capacity [remains] mainly for the unskilled'. This training, of course, is not with the intention of upgrading or extending skills with career progression in mind, it is simply 'job instruction' for the range of simple tasks that make up the working life of the 'unskilled' hotel worker. During my work as a temporary chef in London during 1982–85 and 1988–90, I did not encounter a single experience of 'induction'. Interviews, often conducted standing up in a corner of the kitchen, were restricted to questions about 'having my own knives', 'having my own chef's uniform' and 'not making any trouble'. In common with others, I was rarely asked about previous experience, the possession of a set of knives and a white jacket seemed to be sufficient prerequisite. The implication was that one would only be there for a short time anyway.

Certainly, these personal experiences bear out Riley's skill model (Riley, 1991: 236–8) where low pay policies place a reliance on the labour surplus resulting from decreasing the proportion of skilled to unskilled employees. Employee behaviour is characterised by job hopping to accumulate skills, and an acknowledgement that seniority is not formally rewarded (all the temporary chefs I worked with received the same hourly rate: reward for seniority came about through the allocation of 'cushy' or 'interesting' (i.e. skilful, such as chaude–froide decoration) jobs. Younger chefs, (up to their early twenties) or much older 'burnt-out' chefs (in their mid to late fifties) were given the more repetitive tasks such as 'turning' potatoes or the 'hot' tasks such as large scale sauteeing of meat for sauced dishes.

Along with this, low levels of union membership estimated by Byrne (1986 in Wood, 1992: 103–4) at less than 6% in the UK, and a management style that divides to rule (Gabriel, 1988: 46), leads to the conclusion that such employers accept high labour turnover as inevitable. Wood (1992: 95–103) discusses the rather confused issues concerning labour turnover, citing the view that many managers don't see turnover as a problem. My experiences in the UK and Third World have yet to reveal any sustained effort to either calculate the full cost of turnover, or to acknowledge, come to terms with, and consequently address, the underlying causes. In 1977, Raoul Salmon, speaking of his home, Tahiti, noted that

> Labour is unskilled [and] poorly motivated...To work in a hotel is considered uninteresting and being underpaid...Hotels cannot keep their staff very long...The same turnover is true of training for hotel jobs...Half the people starting do not finish. (in Farrell, 1977: 16)

Interviews with operators during early 1988 revealed a similar pattern. By relying on a young, often female (Enloe, 1989: 35; Bagguley, 1987) and de-skilled workforce, the opportunity for enhancing the tourist 'product' through the value-added resulting from a stable workforce is lost. The past decades of phenomenal tourism growth in all receiving areas (whilst fully acknowledging visitor arrival blips at specific destinations) has allowed operators to rely on a constant turnover of tourists...the one time visitor, in a sense mirroring the constant turnover of tourism staff (this last point being something of a theme in government tourism reports and Master Tourism Plans, e.g. the Cook Islands Master Tourism Plan, 1992). However, as the axiom from the restaurant trade has it: *a business cannot survive without repeat business.*

This message must be acknowledged by operators as part of their commitment to national success in bringing the right kind and the right numbers of tourists in for the right kind of holiday experience especially given the growing sophistication and increased level of information flows. Governments for their part must show a commitment to educating and training the workforce at all levels. This commitment is not met with the establishment of the type of hotel schools that only serve to provide international companies and expatriate managers with a compliant, service-oriented workforce, but tourism education centres that not only teach vocational skills, but educate workers into dealing with the complex issues arising from being involved in an economic sector that earns its bread from hedonism and the cashing in of stark differences between rich and poor; to use MacCannell's argument:

> In the name of tourism, capital and modernized peoples have been deployed to the most remote regions of the world...In short, tourism is not just an aggregate of merely commercial activities; it is also an ideological framing of history, nature, and tradition; a framing that has the power to reshape culture to its own needs. (1992: 1)

Tourism and Employment Generation

In simple terms, there is little doubt about tourism's ability to create employment opportunities, and it is this potential that many governments seize upon as their main reason for encouraging and promoting tourism as an economic sector (Enloe, 1988: 35; Burkart & Medlik, 1989: v; Edgell, 1990: 26); after all, unemployment and under-employment (Todaro, 1982: 197–8), whether as urban drift or displaced workers from restructuring economies, is a characteristic of many developing nations or regions (Harrison, 1993: 176). There is little argument against those who see tourism as a generally labour intensive industry (Edgell, 1990; Burkart & Medlik, 1989), with the main demand in quantitative terms being for semi-skilled or unskilled workers

> Tourism requires large numbers of workers with minimal skills...[an employment study in New Brunswick]...revealed that of the 80% of employees in the tourist labour force in the accommodation and food services categories, only 4% were in managerial or professional occupations. (Mathieson & Wall, 1990: 80)

For a developing country, or depressed region in a developed country, which has tourism as an employment generating strategy, one may ask where the 4% management team is likely to come from. One suspects that they would be imported. Aside from these formal jobs, tourism, with its dependency on the value-added of personal service creates the conditions for a range of 'labour-only' petty entrepreneurs, '...outside the commercial interest or competitive capacity of dominant sector firms' (Britton, 1982: 345), what Sri Lankan officials for instance, term 'own account' workers. In its widest sense, the tourism sector can thus provide income opportunities for individuals with no capital but an ability to make conversation with tourists in the tourists' native language. These 'go-betweens' such as taxi drivers, woodcarvers, shop touts and so called 'unofficial guides' can make a living from tourism. Under these conditions, tourism's ability to generate a range of employment opportunities can be seen as significant (whatever the arguments about the boundaries or parameters of what constitutes a tourism job (Johnson & Thomas, 1990)).

However, in the enthusiasm for promoting tourism as a labour intensive sector, it must not be forgotten that it is also capital intensive. Tourism projects that have anything significant to offer in terms of employment requires capital for both project development and infrastructure support, a point clearly not acknowledged by Edgell (1990), who asserts:

> Tourism employment is concentrated mainly in the services sector…Thus, much labor is used with relatively little capital (p. 26).

While the evidence varies as to whether the labour to capital ratio is 'better' or 'worse' than for other industrial sectors, tourism should not be viewed as a cheap option (the recent Master Tourism Plan for the Cook Islands assumed a construction and development cost of about NZ$3,000,000 for a 30 roomed Polynesian style resort. With an average national direct employment staff/room ratio of 1:1, this is in the region of NZ$100,000 capital investment for each job created). Christie-Mill & Morrison (1985:230) note that the capital/labour output ratio will decline over time as the initial infrastructural costs decline and as experience of the operators increases. This view however, is problematic in that it doesn't account for long-term environmental sustainability, i.e. costs that have to be met over time if the project and its environment is not to suffer decline or neglect.

Patterns of Employment

In considering the ability of tourism to generate employment, we must also examine the nature of these jobs. In numerical terms, the highest requirement is for semi or unskilled jobs. However, apart from the low level of skills, there is the factor of seasonality, and the effect this has on jobs. Seasonality often means the development of part-time employment with consequential opportunity cost in career or self development for employees. In many countries, even those with a strong record of trade unionism, tourism workers (especially those in the hotel sector) are non unionised. This can be seen as a direct consequence of another phenomenon related to tourism employment in the hotel sector: that of core and periphery workers. By this I mean that while many jobs are semi or unskilled, some key jobs, such as head waiters, chefs, accountants and engineers are highly specialised. These workers tend to have different employment patterns than most of the workforce. They form a 'core' of year-round employees. Hudson & Townsend (1992) note that these core employees will usually be male. This is an example of the ways in which male and female employees not only have clearly differentiated roles, but are treated differently. Riley & Jones (1992) term the notion of core–periphery workers as 'the two workforces', '…with some people having very strong tenure and others having very loose job tenure' (1992: 300). Many jobs traditionally associated with females, such as room maid or receptionist can be seen to reflect what (probably male) managers interpret as a motherly, caring role. Enloe (1989: 34–35) brings a feminist perspective to the notion of 'low skill':

> Since the eighteenth century, employers have tried to minimise the cost of employing workers in labour-intensive industries by defining most jobs as 'unskilled' or 'low-skilled' — jobs in other words that workers naturally know how to do. Women in most societies are presumed to be naturally capable at cleaning, washing, cooking, serving. Since tourism companies

need precisely those jobs done, they can keep their labour costs low if they can define these jobs as women's work. In the Caribbean in the early 1980s, 75% of tourism workers were women.

(A notion which of course breaks down when certain male-dominated societies wish to inhibit the contact between female local employees and foreign male guests. This leads to a situation where so called 'room boys' are employed as the unskilled operatives in the housekeeping department).

Unlike employment in the manufacturing sector, labour in the tourism industry is part of a service 'product'. If that part of the ambience in a hotel or restaurant that relies on the mood of the staff is not right, then the product is not right (Urry, 1990:79). This places added responsibility on the management that has not only to reach financial targets expected by owners, but, to some extent, create formal and informal compensation measures to counteract: 'poorly paid service workers [enhancing] the almost sacred quality of the visitors' gaze upon some longed for and remarkable tourist site' (Urry, 1991: 67). These measures may range from elaborate uniforms and job titles, unofficial free meals on duty, to turning a blind eye to petty pilfering. Gabriel (1988: 3). A reliance on the smiling and being 'good' to the customers creates something of a paradox, for while on the one hand employees are treated as 'unskilled', on the other hand the employing organisation gains benefit from the value-added to the product by 'service skills' (Bull, 1991: 146).

The social and financial divide between 'hosts' and 'guests' are much sharper in the developing world than they are in the North — the 'symbolic boundaries between work and leisure' (Urry, 1990) are not as blurred. Gabriel (1988) in Urry (1991: 77) notes that for those working in guest contact areas, especially where money, and therefore tips, may change hands, much of the smiling and graciousness is false: 'pretending to offer service with a smile when in reality no one means it. We know, the management knows this, even the customers know this, but we keep pretending'. This is not to say that many service workers don't get real satisfaction from both doing a professional job and making their customers happy (Farrell, 1982: 240).

Farrell (1982) in his study of tourism in Hawaii, asks if employment in tourism leads to a *servant class*. He notes that a 1978 Hawaii State survey that asked employees if tourist jobs were demeaning found that most people in the industry were happy in their work, but that there were factors that affected the attitude towards such work. These included: strength of ethnic identification; employee perception of tourists and their attitudes; local community vision of tourism; socio-economic aspirations of the employees' families; degree of specific anti-tourism influenced exercised by peers, parents or teachers; the level of economic/cultural disparity between visitor and worker, and the manner in which employees are treated by industry managers (Farrell, 1982: 241). However, another picture of tourism employment emerges from Cynthia Enloe (1989: 34):

Hawaiians refer to the big hotels owned by the Americans and Japanese as 'the new plantations': Caucasian men are the hotel managers, Hawaiian men and women are the entertainers, Hawaiian men the coach drivers and Filipino women the chambermaids.

The social and cultural relationships between employer and employee in Hawaii are particularly complex.

The Characteristics of Tourism Employment

Tourism employment has characteristics that engender certain generalisations. The first is that while there is an obvious relationship between tourism expenditure and employment generation, increasing tourism revenues does not necessarily increase the number of jobs: several factors enter the equation such as productivity gains through technology, using high prices as a factor in creating or maintaining exclusivity or isolation, the relative increase of dependency on imported goods as the tourist sector moves up-market. Secondly, the particular nature of tourism in a given locale (including levels of service, extent of luxury or simplicity, labour costs) will determine the level and type of employment. Patterns of employment and the nature of that employment will inevitably change as a tourist destination changes as a result of fashion or different marketing strategies. Thirdly, local availability of skills (or skill shortages) has an effect on employment characteristics: a high level of general education and training means less reliance on expatriate management and technical skills.

A fourth generalisation is that tourism employment may challenge or even distort traditional/conventional work patterns. It may take people away from other productive sectors of the economy, particularly agriculture (Bryden, 1973: 18, 35). This newly created employment, perhaps carried out within the context of leisured and hedonistic lifestyles of the tourist, may well be fundamentally different from what has gone before. Other changes in patterns of employment might occur. Such properties operate on a twenty-four hour basis. This creates the opportunity for the introduction of part time work. Some of these part time positions may be filled by people already in employment, or by people leaving one sector of the economy to join the tourism economy, thus making a further contribution to labour shortages elsewhere.

A further generalisation is that tourism employment patterns may be in conflict with traditional life patterns. For instance, staff may be required to work when they would normally be at church, temple or mosque. Shift work, and night duty may cause jealousy between partners. This jealousy can be further exacerbated in a society traditionally dominated by males if women get promoted into positions of power and responsibility. This was seen to be a particular problem in the case of The Regent of Denerau, a luxury resort in Fiji, which first encountered just this problem in the early 1980s. Such conflicts in traditional gender roles may be further complicated by societal attitudes towards the very notion of young female employees having contact with foreign male guests. Even within a country, attitudes may vary between rural and city communities. Field work enquiries about the lack of female employees in virtually any positions in hotels and resorts outside Sri Lanka's capital, Colombo, led to the conclusion that rural dwellers had a deep mistrust of women working in hotels — 'We know what goes on in there!' said one respondent. This is in direct contrast to the luxury hotels based in Colombo, where women have a record of successful and progressive career patterns. A final generalisation is that where much of the employment in tourism is seasonal, it could be argued that it encourages those who only seek a part time or seasonal commitment to work (Mathieson & Wall, 1990: 81).

Hudson & Townsend (1992: 56) ask whether such employment characteristics are 'an unavoidable corollary of reliance upon tourism'? They develop their question:

> While some undesirable aspects can be improved (for instance, by developing complementary summer and winter activities to avoid the problems of seasonality), others pose more intractable problems, as job characteristics are closely tied to the organisation and character of the tourism industries. Indeed, given the intensely competitive character of these highly labour-intensive industries, there are very powerful pressures to increase competitiveness by cutting labour costs.

However, as Hudson & Townsend go on to observe, cutting labour costs may have an effect on competitiveness regarding quality of service. This dichotomy between cutting labour costs to improve productivity and the risk of losing competitive edge through losses in quality is well debated by Riley & Jones:

> Quality speaks of skill, of continuity, of a stable workforce, the very opposite of the economic and technological cost-cutting pressures. Here then is the dilemma for the strategist. If the economics are at odds with the qualitative needs for skill development and continuity, how is skill to be maintained and how stable should the organization be? (1992:300)

The answer presented to us revolves around the key issue of motivating a diverse and constantly shifting workforce, 'the need to motivate is an unrelenting task' (Riley & Jones, 1992).

Supply and Demand in Tourism Employment

Employment created by tourism is generally categorised into three types:

- Direct employment such as that resulting from tourism spending in hotels, restaurants, travel/ tours tourist retail outlets.
- Indirect employment still in the tourism supply sector but not resulting directly from the tourism spend, such as agriculture, fisheries, manufacturers.
- Induced employment resulting from local people spending income earned from engaging in the tourism industry. Construction work directly related to tourism, such as the building of a new resort or airport, is sometimes included in this category.

Thus the perceived wisdom is that tourism has an ability to create a wide range of job opportunities, and this remains a key factor in governments engaging in tourism and tourism development. This alerts us to the importance of accurate workforce predictions. However, Bull (1991: 134) notes:

> if the destination starts with unemployment and low incomes, tourism will create employment and raise incomes [this will lead to] reduction in government spending on welfare...increased tax revenues [and create] increased opportunity to save.

The extent to which countries will benefit from these opportunities depends on the sophistication of their economy, particularly the strength of cross sectoral economic linkages (the more expenditure on local produce and locally produced goods, the more employment will be created). What Bull does not address at this stage is the opportunity cost in creating tourism jobs, and for developing countries; this opportunity cost should certainly include the social cost of bringing into the formal sector those who were previously not in paid employment (Bryden, 1973: 73). Bull does however, note that different capital/labour ratios will pertain according to the relative stage of development and consequential use of technology. He also makes the very important point that:

> these labour ratios are more significant in the travel and tourism sector because of the element of service, i.e. staff value added is part of the product [and so] labour inputs are more complicated than accountants would have us believe [thus] tourism employment remains high where consuming tourists are willing to pay. (Bull, 1991: 137)

As alluded earlier, there exists a very complex relationship between management strategies, which in the developed world (but not so in the East and Asia (Wood, 1992: 299) tend towards keeping a downward pressure on labour costs and the proportion of skilled to unskilled labour in the sector. A consequence of this is the development of very weak internal labour markets which depend on the use of a high proportion of unskilled operatives, that can be brought on-line or laid-off according to the vagaries of the tourist season and hotel occupation rates. This is borne out to some extent by the field work research, one of which, the Cook Islands, had many of the characteristics relating to low pay, less than adequate compensation for workers and an almost complete lack of training, while the other, Sri Lanka, experienced similar (and positive) benefits for employees (and the high proportion of indigenous ownership) as Wood (1992: 299) describes for Thailand. In both cases, 'service' is seen as an honourable part of Buddhist culture.

The magical multiplier

These two pieces of field work that acted as the catalyst for this article both make predictions concerning future workforce requirements. The Cook Islands study bases its predictions on a modified employee to rooms employment multiplier. The Sri Lanka study, with its complex industrial base and varied touristic offerings, predicts workforce requirements using an employment multiplier based on tourist night targets. Both studies attempt to avoid the exaggerated forecasts associated with the detailed 'human resource planning' approach to predicting national labour supply. This approach is limited due to the unreliability of the statistics that have to be used for projections. An added complication is that as different markets emerge, with consequential differing demands, the profile of a nation's workforce will change with its general style of tourism. Thus highly specific 'manpower forecasts' of the traditional type often seen in Tourism Master Plans are now generally thought to be unreliable (e.g. Belt, Collins' World Bank Master Plan for Fiji in 1973, and more recently, the Tourism Council of the South Pacific's Master Plan for the Solomon Islands, 1990).

What these plans for Fiji and the Solomon Islands didn't do in their predictions is to take account of the acknowledged characteristics of tourism employment: part-time, casual; seasonal, and with high turnover. Both the Cook Islands and Sri Lanka employment multipliers are modified by taking into account these effects by calculating notional Full Time Equivalents (FTEs) (Burns, 1993). Farrell (1982: 324), produces detailed evidence that casts doubt over traditional methods in arriving at employment multipliers. He reports Merrill (1974) as 'challenging the usual notion of room to job ratios used to project employment'. Merrill's investigation into the job impact of new hotel rooms in Hawaii, where the received wisdom was that 1.77 jobs would be created from each new room, showed that of the 76 new jobs created by 100 new rooms, only 34 provided the *prime income* (by a head of household) for families. The remainder of the jobs were taken up by spouses of household heads who had employment elsewhere; Merrill termed these secondary jobs. Thus Merrill classified job-holders not jobs, and used the term primary job to mean the prime source of income for a household. Secondary job meant that the income derived was supplementary to that household even if it was the prime source of income for the employee. Using a 1973 survey, Merrill reported that 34 heads of families with primary jobs in hotels supporting 84 persons and that 42 employees with secondary employment in hotels benefited 156. Merrill's findings in Hawaii uncovered quite a different pattern in the relationship between rooms and jobs. Only 76 hotel jobs were created, and distributed in previously unacknowledged ways, but these jobs directly benefited 240 persons (Merrill in Farrell). Detailed surveys of this type are problematic on a national basis, the reality is that consultants have only limited amounts of time (typically six to twelve weeks), and this level of detail is not possible. However, the notion of classifying jobs as supporting primary or secondary incomes is worth further study.

Role of Expatriates in Training

Field work in Sri Lanka and the Cook Islands revealed dramatic differences in the position and importance of expatriates in the tourism workforce. On the one hand, we have Sri Lanka where expatriates are almost non-existent. Nearly all senior positions in the sector are filled by nationals. Evidence suggested three reasons for this: first, the sheer amount of education and training going on in Sri Lanka; secondly, the importance attached to training is a reflection of a culture that clearly views education as important in its own right and thirdly, there is the increasing flow of nationals who have gained senior management experience as expatriates themselves (notably in the Gulf), and are now returning to fill senior positions. On the other hand, the case of the Cook Islands matches the position in very many other countries at a similar stage of development. Expatriates hold virtually every position of importance, from General Manager of a resort to assistant patisseur. Ankomah (1991: 435) discusses in detail the reliance on management contracts for hotels (72% in Sub-Saharan Africa, 47% in Latin America, 60% in Asia compared to 2% in Europe). There exists then, something of a dependency culture in which countries are persuaded that the industry cannot function without expatriates. In a sense, this is true, but the solution to this apparent conundrum is apparently not forthcoming. Discussions about replacing foreigners with nationals, whilst on the agenda at government level, seem to be diluted at a more practical level. Immigration officers with responsibility for work permits seem convinced of calamity if the operators do not get their Swiss pastry chef, or Australian general manager. Expatriates form a powerful lobby backed up by a strong support network. It is this then that sets the framework for failure of many countries to train their nationals adequately for the very topmost positions. Perhaps this failure can, to some extent, be attributed to a failure in communication between expatriate management and the indigenous workforce. Inadequacies in work performance indicate the non technical background of the workers, but at the same time evidences the inadequate training and induction of workers to the tasks and operations of the establishment. In other words, it reveals the inadequacies of expatriate personnel to handle inter-cultural situations for which they in turn have had little preparation or guidance.

Many managers take the simplistic view that technological development is a task of transferring knowledge and skills, without realising its cultural and social implications. Managers put the blame for work performance failure on the receiving end (workers) for its (their) incapacity to receive what is given, rather than stopping to ask where the inadequacy of the 'donor' performance lies. Perhaps expatriate workers in the private sector should receive induction courses with attention being given to both the economy and culture of the nation. Courses should ensure that all expatriates are motivated to carry out knowledge and skills sharing. Expatriate managers with responsibilities for training have had as little preparation as those on the receiving end. In other words, workers cannot be expected to manage culturally-alien demands made on them any better than the expatriate personnel can be expected to manage in what is for them, a similarly alien environment. Riley & Jones (1992: 310) acknowledge that the culture of transnational hotels is Western European so that '...training takes on the additional burden of culture transfer as well as teaching skills and knowledge'. They continue: '[this must be] a part of any training strategy because the easy route of imposing, without thought, American-European management style and definitions of skill and quality will lead to frustration'.

This situation can be exacerbated when the dominant culture also defines the motivation and reward system. Pacific Islanders, for instance, who find personal motivation through Family, Church and sharing, may be puzzled when exhorted to work harder for the benefit of a foreign hotel or in order to gain some individual reward. While the social structure outside the world of work cannot be replicated, the 'family-feeling' phenomenon sometimes manifested in an integrated resort hotel could be used, along with ethnographic knowledge, to formulate culturally appropriate motivation. This could be in the form of individual bonuses being accumulated for distribution to a whole village (where village–resort ties are strong), or for support to village or resort sports teams. Macauley & Hall (1992) report the Ka'anapali Beach Hotel as introducing a whole range of social and cultural strategies that eventually reduced labour turnover by 58.9% to an annual rate of 15%, the lowest on the island of Maui (the next lowest is 40%, with many other properties report turnover in excess of 100% per year), sick leave abuse reduced by 58% and donations to two major charities concerned with preserving the cultural traditions of the Hawaiian people increased by over 100% In a Western European context, the whole notion of developing a positive culture at the work place is discussed at length by Lockwood, Gummerson, Hubrecht & Senior in Teare & Olsen (1992: 312–38).

Conclusions

We started this article by arguing that there were parallels to be drawn between the debates on defining tourism and defining what constitutes tourism employment. In the same way, we see the pattern of solutions mirroring the 'solutions' put forward for the *problematique* of tourism. That is to say, in looking for answers about the consequences of tourism, we have to look to the ways in which it is developing, the extent to which touristic developments match the host country's cultural environment. Equally, it is clear that while there are different employment practices in different countries, many of the characteristics of tourism employment could be considered global, the involvement of the consumer in the place and country of production (i.e. the tourist in the resort or hotel) means that this is much more so than say, for mining (child labour being used in Colombia) or for the garment industry (where harsh, sweatshop employment conditions in Sri Lanka are causing grave social concern). In resolving the *problematique* of tourism's employment, if it is to provide a quality work experience, which in turn will positively affect the tourists' holiday, we should be looking for culturally appropriate solutions which can be sustained through profound changes in recruitment, employment, training and staff retention patterns. In the same way that providing 'solutions' for tourism has concentrated on the symptom, not the cause (how can we more effectively move more tourists, accommodate them etc. rather than developing a view about appropriateness of different types of tourism, the structure of tourism, and carrying capacity), the 'answers' to human resource problems are sought in divisive individual reward (or sanctions) systems rather than in the underlying causes of a demotivated and ineffective workforce. The Basil Fawltey 'panic and blame it on the staff' management style strikes a familiar chord with many of us.

However, system changes of this magnitude will have to operate on two levels. On the first, governments have to develop strategies that balance the sometimes conflicting needs of national welfare (foreign exchange, technology exchange, 'development') and local desire (which may simply be 'to be left in peace') to create a favourable investment climate or framework for development. If this economic strategy is underpinned by the development of a favourable cultural environment, where local populations understand the implications of tourism, appropriate development is likely to be supported. At the second level, tourism operators (be they local entrepreneurs or transnational corporations) have to develop in-house schemes that motivate the workforce into being long-term partners in achieving company goals and objectives.

In order to achieve societal goals through tourism, governments might consider:

- Recognising the role that social anthropology has to play in this most powerful form of production, by ensuring that cultural issues are integrated into training programmes.
- Ensuring that national training policy includes strategies for management development, not just skill training for operatives.
- Establishing training programmes for expatriate managers which would include cultural orientation and a knowledge of the way in which tourism is expected to help in the fulfilment of national goals.
- Developing tourism awareness programmes that inform the local population about the nature of tourism thus providing a platform for informed decision making.
- (In conjunction with the above point): monitoring the image of the destination country being portrayed in the generating countries by tour operators.
- (As a part of working with tour operators): encouraging them to develop cultural awareness programmes as part of their holiday product.
- Re-examining the perceived wisdom about long term employment of expatriates in tourism. Expatriates often form a powerful lobby that does not always work for the interests of indigenous peoples.
- Ensuring foreign companies have clearly spelt out arrangements for training locals to take over expatriate jobs, these strategies may include work shadowing and overseas exposure to back up in-house training. The granting of work permits could be conditional upon the strength of the strategies.

On the part of the various tourism enterprises, they might consider:

- Acknowledging the need for retraining the workforce as source markets and the destination profile changes.
- Consideration of the true economic and opportunity costs of maintaining reliance on part-time, seasonal, casual and generally de-skilled workers. While this makes some financial sense, it hardens the common perception of employment in the sector as being less than a first choice career choice.
- Acting to break the familiar pattern of staff poaching or migration by establishing attractive career opportunities; staff poaching is a manifestation of short sighted employment practices.
- Recognising that competence at work, best developed through training, will increase job satisfaction and thus enhance the (elusive) 'value-added' factor.

- Taking example from the best employment practices in other sectors and working towards offering clearly understood employment conditions and compensation packages and sound, consistent and fair management practices.
- Recognising that culture, along with the environment, is tourism's key resource. All training should be underpinned by a respect for these two aspects.
- Recognising the importance and true extent of the relationship between a resort and surrounding habitations by ensuring that the resort is seen as a community asset rather than an imposition — this may mean setting up formal links with the wider community, supporting community projects, and encouraging visits from locals.
- Considering the relevance of schemes, such as Total Quality, Quality Circles, and Staff as Internal Customer, which appear to have worked in other sectors of the international business community.
- Setting of (and reward for) clear, measurable performance and quality standards.
- *And by remembering that owners and managers need training too!*

These employment practices need not necessarily be expensive or elaborate, one owner of a small resort (twenty five rooms) in the Cook Islands, described his weekly meetings with all employees to discuss budgets, targets, forecasts and coming events for the week. This involvement of the staff in the affairs of the business has encouraged them to work with owners and managers towards success. The manager of a much larger (inland) resort hotel in Sri Lanka described strategic policies for integrating his business (which was of dominant economic significance in the immediate area) with the wider community , this included a promise to buy produce from local petty agricultural producers at full market rates...and using the resort transport to visit the poorer areas where farmers could not transport their produce; ensuring support to the local municipal in their town clean-up campaigns, and regularly supporting local religious events (including the use of the resort's transport and facilities).

Many of the above points will not require financial input, but will demand time and commitment from owners and managers (which is what they, in turn, demand from their employees). Some measures will require budgets, these being pension contributions, incentive schemes, contributions to village/community funds (if employees are mostly from one area). Sustaining the tourism workforce then is about much more than instituting effective personnel practices. As is clearly demonstrated above, it involves total commitment not only to those who contribute their labour to the means of production, but also to those whose who live their life under the shadow of tourism. Sustaining tourism's employment is just one piece of the jigsaw that is tourism. In the final analysis, it is as much about better tourism planning and cultural sensitivity as it is about planning human resources.

References

Alpert, W.J. (1986) *The Minimum Wage in the Restaurant Industry*. New York: Praeger.

Ankomah, Paul (1991) Tourism skilled labor: The case of Sub-Saharan Africa. *Annals of Tourism Research* 18, 433–42.

Bagguley, P. (1987) Flexibility, restructuring and gender: Changing employment in Britain's hotels, Lancaster Regionalism Group. In R. Wood (ed.) *Hospitality Industry Labour Trends: British and International Experience in Tourism Management* (1992), pp. 297–304.

Belt, Collins and Associates (1973) *Fiji's Ten Year Tourism Master Plan*. Washington DC: World Bank.

Britton, Stephen (1982) Political economy of Third World tourism. *Annals of Tourism Research* 9, 331–58.

Bryden, J. (1973) *Tourism and Development: A Case Study of the Commonwealth Caribbean*. Cambridge: Cambridge University Press.

Bull, A. (1991) *The Economics of Travel and Tourism*. Melbourne: Pitman Publishing.

Burkart, A.J. and Medlik, S. (1989) *Tourism: Past, Present and Future* (2nd edn). Oxford: Heinemann.

Burns, Peter (1993) *Tourism's Human Resources: Case Studies From the Developing World*. London: University of North London Press.

Chivers, T.J. (1973) The proletarianization of the service worker. *Sociological Review* 21 (4), 663–5.

Christie-Mill, R. and Morrison. A. (1985) *The Tourism System: An Introductory Text*. New Jersey: Prentice Hall.

Cook Islands Master Tourism Plan (1992–2001). Funded by Asian Development Bank, undertaken by ESG Consultants (London) for Government of the Cook Islands.

Edgell, David L. (1990) *International Tourism Policy*. New York: Van Nostrand Reinhold.

Enloe, Cynthia (1989) *Bananas, Beaches and Bases: Making Feminist Sense of International Politics*. London: Pandora.

Farrell, B. (ed.) (1977) *The Social and Economic Impact of Tourism on Pacific Communities*. Santa Cruz: Center for Pacific Studies.

Farrell, B. (1982) *Hawaii: The Legend That Sells*. Honolulu: University of Hawaii Press.

Foster, Douglas (1985) *Travel and Tourism Management*. Basingstoke: Macmillan.

Gabriel, Y. (1988) *Working Lives in Catering*. London: Routledge.

Harrison, Paul (1993) *Inside the Third World: The Anatomy of Poverty* (3rd edn). London: Penguin.

Hudson, Ray and Townsend, Alan (1992) Tourism employment and policy choices for local government. Peter Johnson and Barry Thomas (eds) *Perspectives on Tourism Policy*. London: Mansell.

Jafari, J. (1981) Editor's page. *Annals of Tourism Research* 8 (1).

Johnson, P. and Thomas, B. (1990) Employment in tourism: A review. *Industrial Relations Journal* 21, 36–48.

Lockwood, A., Gummesson, E., Hubrecht, J. and Senior, M. (1992) Developing and maintaining a strategy for service quality. In R. Teare and M. Olsen (eds) *International Hospitality Management: Corporate Strategy in Practice*. London: Pitman.

Mathieson, A. and Wall, G. (1990) *Tourism: Economic, Physical and Social Impacts*. Harlow: Longman.

MacCannell, Dean (1992) *Empty Meeting Ground: The Tourist Papers*. London: Routledge.

Macauley, F. and Hall, S.J. Ethics, the internal customer and quality. Paper delivered at the Second Annual Conference on Human Resource Management in the Hospitality Industry, 8th December 1992, Brighton University.

Medlik, S. (1991) *Managing Tourism*. Oxford: Butterworth-Heinemann.

Merrill, W. (1974) Hotel employment and the community in Hawaii. PhD Dissertation, University of Edinburgh.

Peters, M. (1969) *International Tourism*. London: Hutchinson.

Riley, Michael (1991) An analysis of hotel and labour markets. In C. Cooper (ed.) *Progress in Tourism, Recreation and Hospitality Management* Vol. 3. London: Belhaven.

Riley, Michael and Jones, Peter (1992) Labor strategy in international hotel management. In Richard Teare and Michael Olsen (eds) *International Hospitality Management: Corporate Strategy in Practice*. London: Pitman.

Salmon, Raoul (1977) Development of tourism in French Polynesia: Promises and problems. In Bryan Farrell (ed.) *The Social and Economic Impact of Tourism on Pacific Communities*. Santa Cruz: Center for Pacific Studies.

Todaro, M. (1982) *Economics for a Developing World*. London: Longman.

Tourism Council of the South Pacific (1990) *Solomon Islands Tourism Master Plan*. United Nations Development Project, Suva.

Turner, l. and Ash, J. (1975) *The Golden Hordes*. London: Constable.

Urry, J. (1990) *The Tourist Gaze*. London: Sage Publications.

Wood, Roy (1992) *Working in Hotels and Catering*. London: Routledge.

[30]

PERGAMON

Tourism Management 23 (2002) 551–556

**TOURISM
MANAGEMENT**

www.elsevier.com/locate/tourman

Research note

Mintzberg, managers and methodology: some observations from a study of hotel general managers

Suchada Chareanpunsirikul[a], Roy C. Wood[b],*

[a] *Department of Tourism and Hotel Studies, School of Humanities, Bangkok University, Rama 4 Road, Klong-Toey, Bangkok 10110, Thailand*
[b] *The Scottish Hotel School, University of Strathclyde, 94 Cathedral Street, Glasgow, Scotland G4 0LG, UK*

Abstract

Mintzberg's model of managerial roles is well established in the canon of management theory despite being derived from an 'unrepresentative' small and precisely chosen sample of senior executives. There are a number of applications of Mintzberg's model in the hospitality literature, most focused on (generally successful) attempts at replication of his findings. This paper queries conventional applications of Mintzberg's model in the context of the international hotel industry, the commentary deriving from a mixed method study of general managers of luxury hotels in Thailand. The study examined the utility of Mintzberg's framework in the Thai context with specific reference to general managers' time allocations to Mintzberg's ten managerial roles. The study also considered cross-cultural issues in time allocations to these roles by Thai and non-Thai general managers. A number of issues emerged that posed interesting challenges to the application of Mintzberg's model in the hospitality context. © 2002 Published by Elsevier Science Ltd.

1. Introduction

This paper reports an analysis of managerial time allocations to specific activities and managerial work roles. The ten-fold model of work roles devised by Mintzberg (1973) based on his research into five chief executives was used as a template for the study.

A manager's job in any organisation is busy and demanding. Mintzberg argued that managers' activities were scattered, short-term attempts at coping rather than deliberative, analytical and logical activities as earlier classical management writers had suggested. Rather than engaging in 'traditional' management functions (for example, planning, organising, commanding, co-ordinating and controlling) Mintzberg found that managerial activities did not generally approximate to this model. Instead, managerial roles emerged according to the wider characteristics of managerial work: namely brevity, variety and fragmentation. Ten such roles were identified, described under three general categories: interpersonal, informational and decisional.

The interpersonal role arose from the manager's formal authority and occurred when a manager dealt

with others as a figurehead, leader or liaison. The informational role involved the manager's receiving, storing and sending information as a monitor, disseminator or spokesman. The decisional role involved making decisions about organisational activities as an entrepreneur, disturbance handler, resource allocator or negotiator (see Fig. 1). In addition, Mintzberg argued that all ten roles are present in all managerial jobs because the formal authority in managerial jobs leads to certain kinds of interpersonal relations inside and outside the organisation. From these comes access to information which enables managers to make decisions and plan strategies for their units.

2. Management roles in the hospitality industry

Applications of Mintzberg's ten-role model have a respectable tradition in studies of organisational behaviour in the hospitality industry (see Ley, 1978; Arnaldo, 1981; also Ferguson & Berger, 1984; Shortt, 1989). Ley (1978) conducted an empirical study with eight hospitality managers in the United States. His study focused on the effectiveness of innkeepers in terms of Mintzberg's ten managerial work roles. Ley (1978, p. 69) additionally analysed the purpose of each activity as a means to judge the relationship between managerial

*Corresponding author. Tel.: +44-141-548-3945; fax: +44-141-552-2870.

E-mail address: r.c.wood@strath.ac.uk (R.C. Wood).

0261-5177/02/$ - see front matter © 2002 Published by Elsevier Science Ltd.
PII: S 0 2 6 1 - 5 1 7 7 (0 2) 0 0 0 1 6 - X

INTERPERSONAL ROLES	
Figurehead	Symbolic head; obliged to perform a number of routine duties of legal and social nature.
Leader	Responsible for the motivation of subordinates; responsible for staffing and training.
Liaison	Maintaining self-developed network of outside contacts/informers who provide information and favours.
INFORMATION ROLES	
Monitor	Through seeking and receiving a variety of special information, develops thorough understanding of organization and environment.
Disseminator	Transmits information received from outsiders and subordinates to members of the organization.
Spokesperson	Transmits information to outsiders on organization's plans, policies, actions, results; serves as expert on organization's industry.
DECISIONAL ROLES	
Entrepreneur	Searches organization and its environment for opportunities to bring about change.
Disturbance Handler	Responsible for corrective action when organization faces important, unexpected disturbances.
Resource Allocator	Responsible for the allocation of organizational resources of all kinds
Negotiator	Responsible for representing the organization at major negotiations

Fig. 1. Mintzberg's ten managerial work roles (Mintzberg, 1973).

effectiveness and time allocations to the ten work roles. In doing so, managers who were judged to be highly effective, effective or less effective could be compared according to the time they allocated to specific work roles or to major role groupings (interpersonal, informational and decisional). The significance of Ley's study will be returned to later.

In another relevant study, Arnaldo (1981) conducted a postal questionnaire of 194 hotel managers in America. He asked each of them about their personal details; about the measures which were used to judge their effectiveness; and to rate each of Mintzberg's ten roles against their own use of time and their perceived importance. A critical problem with the last part of this is that managers have been consistently shown to have a very limited ability to judge their own use of time, a problem more generally noted in diary research methods (see Stewart, 1967; Clark, Riley, Wilkie & Wood, 1998). In addition, the tendency of managers to consistently perceive each of Mintzberg's roles in a like way seems highly unlikely. Arnaldo concluded that the leader role was perceived as both the most important and the most time consuming. Similarly, he found the entrepreneurial role to be important although relatively less time-consuming.

2.1. Applications to the present study

The study reported here examined hotel general managers' perceived and actual time allocations to Mintzbergian managerial work roles in the context of Thai and non-Thai general managers of luxury hotels in

Thailand and was principally concerned with the cross-cultural implications of Mintzbergian analysis. In respect of the latter, the extent to which Mintzberg's analysis could be deemed ethnocentric was of interest. The analyses referred to earlier were all conducted in the west. In short, the study was concerned with whether Mintzberg's model applies to non-western managerial cultures. Parallel to this concern was the understanding that the nature of the international hotel industry is such that in many 'non-western' countries, international hotel chains employ expatriate rather than indigenous senior managers for their units. Within reasonable limits therefore, and employing appropriate sampling techniques, such countries provide useful locations for comparing the styles and role performance of indigenous and non-indigenous managers.

3. Methods employed

The form of the study was as follows. Eight subjects, hotel general managers, were identified from a larger sample based on their willingness to participate in the research. All the managers were in command of 'luxury' hotels. In the Thai context these are classified as Group 1 (on a five-point scale) and charge a single room rate of 3000 baht per night (approximately £100 at the time of the research). The sample comprised seven males and one female manager. The properties they managed consisted of five city hotels and three resort hotels. These hotels were classified as one Western chain, one Asian chain, one international chain, two independent hotels and three national hotel groups. Four managers were Thai, and four non-Thai.

In order to compare the subjects' perceptions of time allocation with their actual time allocations they were asked to complete a questionnaire prior to a period of observation. The purpose of this questionnaire was to assess subjects' perceptions of their time allocations to Mintzberg's roles with a view to identifying subsequently whether or not perception and practice coincided. This questionnaire was adapted from Ley's (1978) 77-item management activity survey (MAS) which was based on the activities contained in Mintzberg's ten managerial roles. Each hotel general manager in the observation was asked to rate on a 7-point scale his or her time allocation to each item.

Observation of the daily activities of these managers was then undertaken to determine actual time allocations to the ten managerial work roles of Mintzberg. Structured observation enables the researcher to make detailed and comprehensive recordings of activity through 'shadowing' subjects. The observation period was five consecutive working days spent with each general manager. For reasons of confidentiality, the researcher was excluded from private meetings or

S. Chareanpunsirikul, R.C. Wood / Tourism Management 23 (2002) 551–556   553

sensitive communications during the observation period. However, it was possible to observe around 70% of each manager's daily activities which, as previous research predicts, were diverse and fragmented. That during the course of each working day, general managers encounter a great variety of activities means that their desk work is frequently interrupted by telephone calls or by subordinates coming to their office. All of the general managers studied agreed that they could control such interruptions. They could ask their secretaries to screen telephone calls or close the office door, but normally they did not want to do this, except when they had work which required a great deal of concentration, which was rarely. As a result, all the general managers in the observation were in favour of an 'open door' policy.

4. Principal findings

The key areas of interest were:

- the degree of alignment between managers' perceptions of their time allocation to certain roles and their actual time allocations; and
- whether Mintzberg's framework made sense in the case of non-western managers and, relatedly the nature of any similarities and differences in managerial role performance according to culture.

4.1. Actual and perceived time allocations

From previous studies it might be expected that hotel managers in the sample would perceive the leader role as the most important and allocate their time accordingly. Mintzberg (1973, p. 92) described the leader role as 'responsible for the motivation and actuation of subordinates; responsible for staffing, training and associated duties'. In terms of perception, the results of this research show that three of the sample *perceived*

the leader role as the most important in terms of time allocation, with two of these placing this equal with the resource allocator role. Two managers perceived most time to be spent on the disseminator role and three gave the entrepreneur role.

The results of the observation show that the managers' actual time allocations to the leadership and entrepreneur roles were low, although this was less so in the case of the former. For the leadership role, the average perceived value for all eight managers was 2.3 compared to an average actual value of 4.5. For the entrepreneurial role the difference was far greater, the average perceived value being 3, and the average actual value 8.6 (see Table 1). Those managers who perceived the leader and entrepreneur role as most important and time consuming actually allocated relatively little time to them. The time allocation to the entrepreneur role ranged from 7th to 10th positions.

The relatively low percentage of time allocation to the leader role has parallels with Ley's study. Ley (1978) noted that although all innkeepers perceived both the leader and entrepreneur roles to be important, no innkeeper devoted proportionally more time to the leader role than to each of the other work roles. This finding contradicted the work of other researchers such as Mintzberg (1973), and in the hospitality context, Arnaldo (1981) and Kim (1994), who found that the role of leader consumed a high percentage of managers' time.

All the hotel general managers in the sample allocated most of their working time to the monitor role. The disseminator was the second most important role for six of the eight general managers, the remaining two allocating most time to the figurehead role. Perhaps ironically, one possible explanation for these findings has its roots in the concept of leadership. The leadership style observed in the structured observation could best be described as 'participative and achievement-oriented' rather than 'autocratic' (a style that seemed less attractive to these managers). The general managers who allocated a low percentage of time allocation to

Table 1
Perceived and actual time allocations to managerial roles

| Manager | 1 | | 2 | | 3 | | 4 | | 5 | | 6 | | 7 | | 8 | |
Roles	P	A	P	A	P	A	P	A	P	A	P	A	P	A	P	A
Figurehead	3	2	4	3	8	3	2	2	6	4	6	3	4	4	5	3
Leader	4	4	1	5	1	6	4	6	2	3	2	4	4	3	1	5
Liaison	6	5	7	4	4	4	8	4	2	3	4	6	6	6	6	4
Monitor	5	1	6	1	4	1	2	1	5	1	3	1	8	1	7	1
Disseminator	2	3	2	2	3	2	4	3	1	2	1	2	3	2	3	2
Spokesman	9	7	9	7	9	8	9	5	9	9	9	10	9	8	8	7
Entrepreneur	1	8	2	9	4	9	1	7	4	8	7	8	1	10	4	10
Disturbance handler	8	9	9	8	4	5	7	8	8	10	7	5	6	9	5	9
Resource allocator	6	6	4	7	1	7	6	9	3	6	4	7	2	5	1	8
Negotiator	10	10	10	10	10	10	10	10	10	5	9	8	10	7	10	6

leadership and exhibited such a style allocated the majority of their time to the monitor and disseminator roles.

4.2. Applications of managerial roles to Thai managers

The results of this research tentatively suggest that Mintzberg's framework is applicable to the work of hotel general managers in Thailand, at least in the large luxury sector. Both Thai and non-Thai general managers performed some of Mintzberg's ten managerial roles in their daily operation. The only areas in which there were noticeable differences between Thai and non-Thai managers in time allocations to roles related to the negotiator, spokesman and disturbance handler roles. Specifically:

- Thai general managers spent more time on the negotiator role than non-Thai general managers, the average actual average time allocations being 6.5 and 10; and
- non-Thai general managers' allocated more time to the spokesman (6.75/8.5) and disturbance handler (7.5/8.25) roles than did Thai general managers.

Differences of time allocations to some work roles could indicate differences in terms of cultural approach on the part of the Thai managers. It is generally recognised that local managers will observe local cultural norms and procedures in the conduct of their responsibilities. In contrast, expatriate managers are either unaware or deliberately ignore such conventions, bringing with them their own culture and that of their organisations. Thai work culture is extensively dependent on negotiation, whereas the mediation of 'disturbances', often through deployment of the spokesman role is not uncommon among expatriate managers whose cultural orientation is more directive (see Schell & Marmer Soloman, 1997).

5. Some reflections of methodology

Mintzberg's (1973) study of managerial roles has been one of the most influential in business research, so much so that it is easy to forget that it was based on observing only five chief executive officers (CEOs) each for a period of 1 week (Stewart, 1998). Perhaps what is most remarkable about Mintzberg's work is the extent to which it has been applied in subsequent studies, not least in the hospitality industry. Here, the samples have generally been much larger but the level of management studied lower than was the case in the original research. Findings have by no means been consistent, as is the case with the present study. Variation in findings has, however, been defined in range: divergence from Mintzberg's model has been discerned empirically without fundamentally challenging the construction of the model. Four such categories or types of variation are worth commenting on.

The first concerns those assumptions underlying the ability of research subjects to estimate the time they allocate to particular tasks of interest to the researcher. In general, such estimates have been regarded as unreliable (Stewart, 1998). In the hospitality field however, Ley's (1978) use of a detailed and lengthy questionnaire inventory of activities was useful in focusing subjects' attention on the range and minutiae of such activities. Despite adoption of a revised version of this instrument in the present study, the differences between perceived and actual time allocations to roles were considerable (notwithstanding issues of accuracy attendant on the observation of such roles to which we shall turn shortly). Some studies have elicited reasonable congruence between perception and reality, others have not. It is by no means certain that Ley's approach is any more reliable than the often derided 'diary methods' employed in the studies of managerial activity and role performance. It is clear that the methods employed to assess perceptions of these elements are crude by most standards: less clear is what can be done to improve this aspect of methodology. One radical proposition is that perception of time allocated by managers to particular activities and functions is less important than how they prioritise these roles.

This is the second theme here. It is too problematic because it is again by no means clear that subjects in research of this nature perceive Mintzberg's roles in the same way. Indeed, a remarkable feature of Mintzberg-based studies is the extent to which congruency of these perceptions is taken for granted. A cynic might observe that both this and the previous issue cannot be resolved at a methodological level as the problem is one of a priori theorising. Thus, it might be argued that in accepting Mintzberg's model of managerial role performance, it is both inevitable and necessary that applications will produce difference between perceptions of time and perceptions of the meanings of roles. Without such difference there would be nothing to study or measure! In this view, Mintzberg's model is little more than a descriptively trivial device of little serious analytic use.

The counter argument to this view is that if we are to understand what managers 'do' then we need models that can be operationalised. This does not imply slavish adherence to the model, but instead active research to probe its boundaries and improve upon it. Thus far, research in the hospitality field has confined itself to examining the substantive boundaries of Mintzberg's model that is as noted earlier, the range and extent of variations in findings according to the context of study. A key conclusion of the present study is that what is required in addition is a probing of the interpretative

S. *Chareanpunsirikul, R.C. Wood / Tourism Management 23 (2002) 551–556* 555

boundaries of Mintzberg's framework. Much of the apparent success of Mintzberg-based studies is based on avoidance of questions of interpretation. The findings of these studies are less certain precisely because they do not examine the interpretative flexibility of subjects' perceptions of their roles. Accordingly, some examination of the perceptions of these roles is required if future studies are to avoid further simple iterations of the substantive variations in Mintzberg's model according to research context.

This exercise needs to be closely linked to the third set of issues considered here, namely those means employed to verify managers' perceptions of their time allocation to particular roles and activities. In this study, as with others, direct observation was used and behaviours classified according to Mintzberg's framework. As a matter of course, however, such classification entailed a high degree of improvisation on the part of the researcher on how to classify particular activities. The core problem here is one of contingency. If a manager takes a telephone call, it is necessary to ascertain what the call was about in order to make an effective classification according to the role performance framework. Contingency also arises in terms of the consistency with which the researcher applies categories of behaviour. In terms of personal commitment and awareness, the strains on the researcher are considerable, not unlike those that occur in much ethnographic research (see Mars & Nicod, 1984 for an interesting reflection upon these issues in the hotel context). The only defence against these problems is constant vigilance, a reasonably rigorous framework for allocating behaviours and a tendency on the part of subjects to a certain obviousness of behaviour. The importance of the latter should not be underestimated. In the hospitality studies noted earlier, dominant patterns of time allocation and role behaviour were readily evident and this is also apparent in other, more general studies (Stewart, 1998).

The final consideration is the role of culture as a source of variation in findings of Mintzbergian studies. This, as it were, is the core substantive (as opposed to interpretative) theme here. The role of culture in producing variations in managerial behaviour is well documented (the classic model derives, of course, from Hofstede, 1984). Indeed, the assertion that management behaviour is likely to be affected by localised culture seems passé. Of greater interest in the context of international studies is the particular position of expatriate labour.

In the hospitality sector, the use of expatriate labour remains extensive despite efforts in many countries at 'indigenisation' of management. It was the presence of such managers in Thailand that allowed the construction of this research in a manner designed to capture proposed facets of role performance that might differ between indigenous and expatriate managers. In as much as objectivity is possible in Mintzbergian studies, the findings of this study, described earlier, were to a degree predictable, the indigenous managers operating more according to local cultural imperatives than their expatriate colleagues. The latter were, in reality, far more likely to adopt a 'western' approach to management (i.e. a USA/UK style), delegating 'cultural work' to an indigenous subordinate.

In arguing for the broad applicability of Mintzberg's model, and subject to the caveats itemised above, a key methodological issue remains the extent to which it is possible to capture the complexity of managerial role performance in an increasingly internationalised economy. Variation is not according to local culture alone but to the increasing interpenetration of practices as a result of people from different cultural milieu working for the same organisation. So far this issue remains largely unexplored and perhaps offers the best way forward for further studies of the hospitality sector according to a Mintzberg rubric.

6. Conclusions

The results from the observation confirm previous research findings that general managers' work activities are fragmented (Stewart, 1967; Mintzberg, 1973; Ley, 1978). This present study has examined Mintzberg's ten managerial work role model in the context of Thai and non-Thai hotel general managers of Thai luxury hotels. The results confirm that the work of a hotel general manager involves brevity, variety and fragmentation. Few significant differences were noted in the behaviours of the managers in this sample suggesting that, although a blunt instrument, Mintzberg's model has some utility. This utility is, however, constrained by several unanswered questions about the application of Mintzbergian methodology, questions worthy of investigation in further study.

References

Arnaldo, M. J. (1981). Hotel general managers: A profile. *Cornell Hotel and Restaurant Administration Quarterly, 22,* 53–56.

Clark, M., Riley, M., Wilkie, E., & Wood, R. C. (1998). *Researching and writing dissertations in tourism and hospitality.* London: International Thomson Business Press.

Ferguson, D. H., & Berger, F. (1984). Restaurant managers: What do they really do? *Cornell Hotel and Restaurant Administration Quarterly, 25,* 26–36.

Hofstede, G. (1984). *Culture's consequences: International differences in work-related values.* London: Sage.

Kim, S. M. (1994). Tourist hotel general managers in Korea: A profile. *International Journal of Hospitality Management, 13,* 7–17.

Ley, D.A. (1978). An empirical examination of selected work activity correlates of managerial effectiveness in the hotel industry using a structured observation approach. Unpublished Ph.D. thesis, University of Michigan, USA.

Mars, G., & Nicod, M. (1984). *The world of waiters*. London: George Allen & Unwin.

Mintzberg, H. (1973). *The nature of managerial work*. New York: Harper & Row.

Schell, M. S., & &Marmer Soloman, C. (1997). *Capitalising on the global workforce: A strategic guide for expatriate management*. New York: McGraw-Hill.

Shortt, G. (1989). Work activities of hotel managers in Northern Ireland: A Mintzbergian analysis. *International Journal of Hospitality Management, 8*(2), 121–130.

Stewart, R. (1967). *Managers and their jobs*. London: Macmillan.

Stewart, R. (1998). Managerial behaviour. In M. Poole, & M. Warner (Eds.), *The handbook of human resource management* (pp. 184–200). London: International Thomson Business Press.

[31]

Available online at www.sciencedirect.com

SCIENCE 🍦 DIRECT®

PERGAMON

Tourism Management 25 (2004) 45–59

TOURISM
MANAGEMENT

www.elsevier.com/locate/tourman

The impact of national culture on the transfer of "best practice operations management" in hotels in St. Lucia

Christine A. Hope*

School of Management, Bradford University, Emm Lane, Bradford, West Yorkshire BD9 4JL, UK

Received 8 August 2002; accepted 2 December 2002

Abstract

This article briefly outlines the convergence vs. divergence debate before describing research into the potential impact of national culture on the transfer of "best practice operations management" to hotels in St. Lucia. The main focus of the paper is on the findings of fieldwork, which supports the contention that national culture does potentially create a barrier to the successful transposition of approaches developed elsewhere. In the case of St. Lucia high uncertainty avoidance and leanings towards high power distance appeared to hinder the adoption of teamworking, empowerment and communication. In addition, attitude towards time and punctuality also mitigated against the provision of a reliable service as and when required. However, with training and supportive HR practices, the end results achieved by International Chains did demonstrate the value of operating "people friendly" policies in line with "best practice".

© 2003 Elsevier Science Ltd. All rights reserved.

Keywords: Globalisation; Human resource management; Hotels; St. Lucia

1. Introduction

Often referred to as the convergence vs. divergence debate, arguments are still on-going as to whether or not, with increasing globalisation, organisations and cultures are becoming more and more alike. The research of Foster and Minkes (1999) seems to support convergence at an organisational structure level, but divergence at the micro, or operational level. McGaughey and De Cieri (1999) pointed out that Adler argues that studies at the macro-level support convergence whilst those at a micro-level support divergence, but they believe that this is too simplistic. This debate is relevant to the research described here, insofar as supporters of convergence would argue that it is possible to identify one best way of operating in a given industry. Supporters of divergence, however, would argue that because of differences in the beliefs, values and attitudes of people of different cultures, operational practices need to be adapted in order to work successfully.

An examination of core operations management textbooks (Chase, Aquilano, & Jacobs, 2000; Hope &

---

*Tel.: + 44-1274-234358; fax: +44-1274-546866.

E-mail address: c.a.hope@bradford.ac.uk (C.A. Hope).

Mühlemann, 1997; Meredith & Shafer, 2001; Russell & Taylor, 2000; Slack, Chambers, & Johnston, 2001) written in the English language lends support to the existence of "best practice" as the underlying messages in most of them is very similar. For a fuller discussion of "best practice" operations management, please see Hope and Mühlemann (1998, 2001). Hope and Mühlemann (2001), Morden (1999) and Rodrigues (1998) have all argued that adaptations may need to be made when transferring "best practice" between nations because of the impact of national culture and have suggested how differences have implications for managers. Roney (1997) identified problems encountered when attempting to introduce TQM into a manufacturing context in Poland, which could be attributed to national cultural differences. Similarly, Huyton and Ingold (1995) reported that the Ritz Carlton faced operational problems in Hong Kong despite trying to operate in the same manner that had won them the Malcolm Baldrige Award for Quality in the USA. Teare (1993) explained how the Hyatt chain does recognise the need to adapt procedures when operating in different countries. However, research, particularly in the service sector has not been extensive, and although evidence clearly exists which supports the argument that national

0261-5177/03/$ - see front matter © 2003 Elsevier Science Ltd. All rights reserved.
doi:10.1016/S0261-5177(03)00059-1

46 *C.A. Hope / Tourism Management 25 (2004) 45–59*

culture does have an impact on the successful transfer of "best practice", knowledge is still sketchy regarding just what nuances of culture impact on which aspects of "best practice".

McLaughlin and Fitzsimmons (1996), in a paper discussing strategies for globalising service operations concluded:

> "With globalization, the impact of cultural adaptation will need to be central to our study of operational topic areas such as joint venturing, materials management, purchasing, new product development, layout and process design, supervision and motivation, training, work force scheduling, environmental management and labour-management relations. These are all key areas of front room and back room management that are likely to require adaptation from country to country as services are globalised" (pp. 55–56).

Proponents of contingency theory on the other hand question whether national culture impacts on managerial practices. They argue that organisation design and organisational culture is linked to other factors such as size, nature of the industry and other operational conditions and that these are the major factors which dominate management. Child and Kieser (1979) in a study of German and UK firms found evidence which suggested that factors such as size, etc. did affect the *structure* of firms, as per contingency theory, but that the relationship between these factors and managers' roles was less consistent. They found that their data suggested that the cultural factor had most bearing upon modes of individual conduct and interpersonal relationships.

Child and Tayeb (1983) compared the contingency approach with that held by radical theorists and political economists and those arguing the cultural (or divergence) perspective. They seem to conclude that they are all valid to a point, but are interlinked:

> "We therefore arrive at the conclusion that it is an error to disregard factors identified by any of the three theoretical perspectives" (p. 54).

The research reported in this paper attempts to contribute to the debate by considering the impact of "best practice operations management" in hotels in St. Lucia and was partly confirmatory and partly exploratory in nature. Theory and prior research does suggest that cultural differences will impact on operations (Huyton & Ingold, 1995; Purcell, Nicholas, Merrett, & Whitwell, 1999; Roney, 1997) and in that sense the study was intended to provide further confirmation that this is the case—in other words, that it is not possible to identify one mode of operating which may be labelled "best practice". However, the fieldwork itself was to be undertaken in St. Lucia where knowledge of the

characteristics of the culture is limited and in that sense the research was exploratory.

1.1. Background: cultural dimensions

It is an accepted fact that there are different cultures throughout the World (Adler, 2002; Schneider & Barsoux, 1997; Warner & Joynt, 2002). The societies in which we grow up have their own sets of rules about the way we behave and interact with others. These rules or norms are not written down and we are often not even conscious of them. A great deal of research has been undertaken in an attempt to understand just what *culture* is and how the various national cultures differ. Space does not permit a full review of this literature here, suffice it to say that various "cultural dimensions" have been identified by quite a number of researchers (Hall & Hall, 1990; Hofstede, 1980, 1994; Schein, 1985; Tayeb; Triandis, 1995; Trompenaars & Hampden-Turner, 1997). There is no definitive list of these although common themes and overlaps occur (Hope, Mühlemann, & Potter, 2000). Examples of these dimensions include: collectivist vs. individualist—this relates to whether we place importance on loyalty to the in-group or, on the other hand, we value and reward individuals and ties between individuals are loose; and high vs. low uncertainty avoidance—defined as "the extent to which the members of a culture feel threatened by uncertain or unknown situations" (Hofstede, 1994, p. 113); low vs. high power distance—"the extent to which the less powerful members of a society expect and accept that power is distributed unequally" (Hofstede, 1994, p. 28).

The purpose of this research was neither to measure where St. Lucia lies on these various cultural dimensions, nor to use one particular set of dimensions to analyse results. Rather an attempt was made to bear in mind Tayeb's (2001) strictures:

> "…national culture is a complex construct and we simplify them at our own peril. But regrettably, many authors of cross cultural studies have a tendency to focus on a few dimensions and ignore various aspects of cultures which might have equally significant bearings on people's values, attitudes and behaviours" (p. 95).

When analysing the results therefore, all the dimensions with which the author was familiar were borne in mind and contextual information was also sought in an effort to keep as open a mind as possible. In particular the author was aware at all times of the danger of her own "cultural baggage" (i.e. white British) acting as a filter and for example great efforts were made when conducting interviews to confirm understanding of what was said by the interviewees. For example, the author would summarise her understanding of what she had

C.A. Hope / Tourism Management 25 (2004) 45–59   47

been told and ask the interviewees to confirm or clarify her interpretation. The author also sought to further confirm understanding by discussing her perceptions of the interviews with two St. Lucians who could be described as "informed" and "independent" of the hotel industry.

2. Propositions

As already mentioned, the study reported here was intended to be partly exploratory in nature. Although literature on Caribbean culture does exist (Beckford, 1972; Coke, 1995; Emmanuel, 1993; Khan, 1987; Smith, 1965), the trend in sociological, economic, administrative and political literature of these islands has been to treat them as one single entity (Beckford, 1972; Bernal, Figueroa, & Wilter, 1984; Mills, 1970). Hofstede (1980, 1994) included Jamaica in his study and Trompenaars and Hampden-Turner (1997) examined Curaçao; however, St. Lucia has not been included in the studies of culture and therefore only fairly broad assumptions could be made a priori about cultural characteristics. It was therefore not possible to develop a set of detailed propositions before conducting the fieldwork, linking cultural traits to expected problem areas. However, following the framework developed in Hope and Mühlemann (2001) a number of operational areas were identified where culture was thought likely to impact on operations in hotels. These aspects of management were grouped under two headings. These are presented in Table 1.

The basic premise was that if national culture did not impact on "best practice" techniques, then where these were in place, their implementation would not cause problems and management would not feel impelled to adapt them for local conditions. Where "best practice" was not being followed, the reason why would be investigated. This could be because:

1. national culture "clashed" with the approach and adaptations had been made,
2. there was a lack of awareness of "best practice" management techniques,
3. of factors relating to the external environment.

This final reason would include possible restrictions to operations management due to non-availability of finance, import restrictions, climatic conditions, employment law, etc. It could be argued, however, that these are only decision constraints which are similar to constraints anywhere in the World and that they are not fundamental differences as may be argued is the case of culture. For example, exchange constraints are merely a form of cash constraint; import restrictions are a form

Table 1
Management aspects

(1) Management of employees within hotels
  (a) Selection
  (b) Training
  (c) Empowerment
  (d) Team-working
  (e) Appraisal
  (f) Reward

(2) Management of processes
  (a) Standard operating procedures
  (b) Total quality management
  (c) Planned maintenance
  (d) Equipment/working conditions

of constraint on availability. All operations face resource constraints of one kind or another.

Often, when hotels are located in Lesser Developed Countries (LDCs), there is resentment towards the foreign management (Bastin, 1984; Girvan and Jefferson, 1971; Lewis, 1970; Williams, 1983). Frequently there are large wage differentials and expatriates take all the top managerial jobs. In addition, in ex-colonies, especially with a history of slavery, the situation is likened to neo-colonialism and locals resent having to *serve* the rich tourists (Krippendorf, 1987). It was recognised that these factors would have to be taken into account before necessarily attributing problems to *culture*. Having said that, it could be argued that it is precisely because of historical factors, such as slavery, that values relating to power distance, individualism, fate and time are in conflict with imported practices (Coke, 1995; Emmanuel, 1993; Khan, 1987).

It could also be hypothesised that locally owned and managed hotels would have less employee problems as there would be more likelihood of adaptations to management practices in order to conform to local cultural norms. Following this logic, most problems should be encountered where the hotel owners were foreign and standard procedures were implemented which were designed in a country with the greatest cultural divergence from St. Lucia.

3. Methodology

Child and Tayeb (1983) discussed research design in the context of the three theoretical perspectives discussed earlier. They identified two extreme approaches: *ideographic*—basically there are so many variables and the situation is so complex that it is impossible to make meaningful comparative studies—each combination of characteristics/features is unique and it is only possible to study one case at a time; and *nomothetic*—it is possible to simultaneously consider culture, contingency and political-economy. They advocated the middle road and concluded that using carefully matched samples:

"...it may nevertheless be possible to identify some particular influences emanating from each" (p. 64).

Tayeb (2001) more recently warned that

"To know something is there, non-cultural factors in this case, is necessary but not sufficient—you have to design it out of your investigation. In the absence of such designs in many published studies, their author's assertions about the influence of culture are pure conjecture, and not factually based propositions" (p. 97).

To the extent that only one type of industry setting was to be studied on one island, it was felt that industry culture was being controlled for, as would the context. The one main variable that was different in the cases to be studied would be nationality of ownership.

The actual research method adopted was dependent upon two main factors:

1. type of access granted to the researcher by the hotels that agreed to take part,
2. the time made available to the researcher to meet employees.

The main aims of any method employed would be to establish:

1. What operational procedures were followed?
2. What problems existed?
3. extent of adoption/awareness of "Best Practice" techniques and
4. existence of external factors impacting on operations management.

As, prior to arriving on St. Lucia, it had not been possible to establish the extent of cooperation that would be forthcoming from the hotels, two data collection instruments were prepared. Structured interviews for hotel managers were developed based on the management areas listed in Table 1. They were intended to establish:

1. the approaches/techniques adopted,
2. problems encountered and reasons for them.

In addition questions aimed at gathering background information regarding such aspects as location/availability of suppliers, links to the market (tour operators/agents) educational provision and labour laws were included, however all hotels were expected to face the same external conditions.

Questionnaires to be completed by front line employees or for use as an interview guide were also developed. These were divided into four parts. The first part contained 29 questions to establish the nature of the job, the second part (27 questions) was intended to find out how the employees felt about their work, the third part asked for suggestions for improved ways of doing the job (3 open questions) and the final part (13 questions) asked about their age, education and experience. Both the set of questions in the structured interview and the questionnaires were pilot tested for clarity and content within the International Operations Management Research Group at the University of Bradford. A copy of the questionnaire may be found in Appendix A.

3.1. Sample

On a prior visit to St. Lucia, contact had been made with the Permanent Secretary at the Ministry of Tourism and the President of the St. Lucia Hotel and Tourism Association (SLHTA) and their help enlisted. It was agreed that the fieldwork should be undertaken at the end of May, after the Jazz Festival, when occupancy was expected to be relatively low. The fieldwork was to be undertaken over a two-week period and it was thought realistic to include four hotels in this time period. The SLHTA initially approached and sought the co-operation of a number of hotels. The preferred sample was four large (by St. Lucia standards) All-Inclusive hotels, with ownership based in the USA, the Caribbean, Europe and St. Lucia. Unfortunately, this did not prove possible and the sample actually used included three large All-Inclusive hotels (Europe was dropped) and one medium sized St. Lucian hotel that did not operate on an All-Inclusive basis. All hotels catered for holiday-makers and had links with various international tour operators. Scheduling the actual visits took place on arrival in St. Lucia and proved a little difficult. Requests were made for the researcher to spend 2 days at each hotel interviewing the General Manager, three or four other managers and between 10 and 15 front-line staff members. This did not prove possible and the actual sample of staff interviewed is presented in Table 2. Questionnaires were left at each hotel for distribution to employees. At Hotel A each manager interviewed agreed to distribute questionnaires to employees in their section. Completed questionnaires were collected by the Executive Assistant to the General Manager and returned by post. The response rate was approximately 50%. At Hotel B a similar procedure was followed except that the questionnaires were ready for collection at the end of the week. The response rate was just over 65%. At Hotel C, 60 questionnaires were delivered to the Training Manager after the visit together with stamped addressed envelopes. The response rate was 22%, however interviews had been conducted with two teams of front-line employees at this hotel. At Hotel D the General Manager was reluctant to

C.A. Hope / Tourism Management 25 (2004) 45–59 49

Table 2
Staff interviewed and questionnaire response

	Hotel A	Hotel B	Hotel C	Hotel D
Characteristics	American All-Inclusive	St. Lucian All-Inclusive	Caribbean All-Inclusive	St. Lucian
Interviewees	General Manager HR Director Executive Housekeeper Front office Manager Assistant Engineer	Catering Manager Assistant Housekeeper Front-desk Manager Engineering Manager	General Manager Rooms Division Manager Assistant Engineer Training Manager Personnel Coordinator Front Office Manager Housekeeping team Front office team	General Manager
Returned questionnaires	28	39	13	11
Response rate	50%	65%	22%	18%

take 60 questionnaires for distribution to staff and it is probable that the 11 responses reflect a higher response rate than 18%. Some of these were collected by Reception, others were posted back.

3.2. Analysis

All the interviews were taped and transcriptions made. These were then analysed/coded using the QSR Nudist 4.0 software package.

As, due to the nature of the study, the size of sample was relatively small, it was not deemed appropriate to use a sophisticated statistical package to analyse the responses to the questionnaire. Consequently, the responses to 67 questions were coded and entered into the Microsoft Excel Spreadsheet package and the answers to the remaining five open questions were simply tabulated in Microsoft Word.

Before coding the interview transcripts, a set of nodes was developed within Nudist based upon the theoretical expectations, the structure behind the interviews plus nodes for the cultural dimensions individualism/collectivism, uncertainty avoidance, high/low context language, time, and power distance. This original set of nodes was added to whenever text within the transcripts was encountered which did not seem to be covered by the original set. Text could also be coded to more than one node. When all transcripts had been coded they were re-analysed against the augmented set of nodes. Printouts of all the text coded to each node were then studied and sections of text that illustrated good practice, bad practice, problems and external factors were highlighted in different colours. The transcripts of the nodes were then grouped together under each of the headings listed in Table 1. The node transcripts for each group were then re-examined and evidence of best practice was extracted and collated. The same process

was followed to identify and collate evidence of limitations/problems. Finally, evidence of the effect of external factors was collated.

Analysis of the questionnaires mainly involved either the calculation of an average score for individual questions for each hotel or calculation of the percentage responses in any "class" of response. Differences between actual work practices and preferences were also calculated, i.e. between scores on related questions in parts 1 and 2 of the questionnaire.

The results from the quantitative analysis of the responses on the questionnaires together with the comments made to the open questions on the questionnaires were studied to see if the findings from the interviews were supported.

Copies of a report of the findings were sent to each of the General Managers of the hotels who took part in the study. They were asked to contact the author if they felt that the findings were inaccurate in any way. Two responses were received, neither indicated that the findings were disputed nor inaccurate. One manager commented on the quality and value of the report and the potential usefulness of the findings.

4. Findings

The findings indicate that culture had an impact on the successful transfer of "best practice". The cultural factors related to "power distance" and "risk avoidance" seem to create barriers to empowerment and team working in line with Emmanuel's (1993) conclusions regarding authoritarianism. There was a reluctance to accept the added responsibility and risk involved with empowerment. In discussion with locals who possessed some knowledge of the cultural literature, it was suggested to the researcher that slavery could provide an explanation for current behaviour/attitudes. When slaves were told to do a task, they would want to make absolutely certain that they understood *exactly* what was required. Doing something wrong resulted in punishment. On the other hand, there was absolutely no incentive to do *more* than was required. This manifested itself today as some reluctance to act without specific and detailed instructions (i.e. low-context language). This interpretation supports Khan's (1987) conclusions relating to the psychological insecurity of the "Caribbean man".

The role of supervisor was also seen as quite clear-cut—their role was to supervise (and not get their hands dirty by "lending a hand"). They would "check up" on front-line staff—there was no trust for instance that chambermaids could be relied upon to do it right. It seemed that once you were the equivalent of an "overseer", you became one of "them"—the power relationship was very distinct. It was also expected that promotion came with seniority.

Employees from two hotels mentioned that there was lack of respect for the employees. This manifested itself by complaints about poor equipment/working conditions/hours of work. Although all the hotels had numerous and frequent "Best Employee" type awards, lack of space to do the job, split shifts, six day working, low pay and the bad "attitude" of supervisors were seen as "not respecting them as people". One of these hotels was locally owned and managed, the other was part of the Caribbean chain and the General Manager was from Europe. The problem seemed greater in the smaller locally owned and run hotel. In the other hotel it did not seem to be a major problem as this hotel was ranked joint first with the hotel that was part of the US chain when employees were asked, "Do you like your job?" This lack of respect may be linked to the "power-distance" dimension and clearly does not follow "best practice". On the other hand, it may simply be evidence of poor practice human resource management.

Although some writers have noted a tendency to individualism in the Caribbean (Coke, 1995) there was some evidence of *collectivism* particularly in the social context, e.g. family and friends would often get together to build the house of one of their members. Also when asked in the questionnaire whether they would prefer to work in a team, the average score in all hotels indicated a preference for team working. One could argue that *collectivism* should aid team working, however communication problems existed *between* departments indicating a lack of team work between different teams, i.e. people in other departments were not "in-group". Despite one of the hotels stressing team-working, calling staff team members, the employees in that hotel, when asked "What really annoys you at work?" mentioned the lack of cooperation

from other departments—usually involving a lack of information.

With respect to communication per se, on the positive side employees seemed quite happy to tell their boss if he/she was wrong. The majority of employees also stated that they would admit a mistake to their boss. This ranged from 64% in the locally owned and managed hotel to 92% in the Caribbean owned hotel. However, there was clear evidence of a preference for instructions to be detailed—exhibiting a tendency towards high risk avoidance and demonstrating a "low-context" language, as mentioned earlier.

Relationships clearly dominated time. Although there was no evidence of parallel tasking (as opposed to sequential), it was more important that you stop and talk to someone you passed in the street who came from your village, than to arrive on time for a pre-arranged appointment. Being on time was not a priority—thus supporting Coke's (1995) view of Caribbean society. There was some evidence that this could affect schedules and time keeping of employees, but it was not always clear whether late arrival of employees was due to attitude or the poor transport services on the Island. The attitude towards time might also explain why farmers found it difficult to plan the staggering of crops—one General Manager complained that although they tried to buy local produce, it was difficult because the farmers would for example plant all their tomatoes at the same time, rather than staggering them. The result was that tomatoes grown locally were only available for part of the year.

Table 3 presents a selection of quotes made either during interviews or on the questionnaires that either provide evidence of the adoption of "best practice" or barriers to the implementation of "best practice". The categories down the left-hand side represent some of the nodes identified during the coding process which was explained earlier in the paper in the analysis section.

5. Conclusions

As Tayeb (2001) has pointed out, researchers looking at the impact of culture are rarely in the ideal position of having the resources to conduct a large-scale study. The research reported here was clearly limited in scope and was intended as an exploratory or pilot study. One of the underlying principles of "best practice operations management" is that there should be quality of design and conformance to design. In order to produce a good or service consistently, which meets design specifications "first-time, every time", it is necessary to design and manage the delivery or production process to do so. In this research, the focus has been on the delivery process—"how" the service is delivered, not the "what"

C.A. Hope / Tourism Management 25 (2004) 45–59 51

Table 3
Illustrative quotes from interviews and questionnaires

	Examples of best practice	Limitations/problems
Selection	"Before, we used to hire a lot of skilled workers and we had problems…their mannerisms were not what the hotel should be like, they were not smiling people, they were not friendly people, but they knew how to do the job. So we switched it around and we said, hire the friendly and train the skill—we can train the skill".	"…interviewing everyone for a job. I found that you know like they couldn't express themselves much or tell you what they did before. …people didn't like express themselves a lot, they didn't have like no eye contact.…You tried to talk to them and you bring up everything so that they can have like a conversation with you. It was really hard".
Training	"We have a cross training programme in effect,…like we have a lot of people in the laundry training in the kitchen, we have housekeeping, room attendants training in the kitchen, waiters from the restaurant and bar they train in the kitchen…"	"I think in terms of coaching, I think you have to spend more time than anything else in terms of time to talk to people. …reminding why the standard is there. …but in general it's a cultural thing, I really believe that the culture is just not encouraging discipline and accountability and so the guys…the waiters that I have asked 3 times now, …I said this is now the 3rd time that I am asking you not to walk from here to there with your shirt hanging out, he says, "Yes boss, you right I know, I'm sorry", and probably in two weeks he's gonna do it again because the whole country runs around including the Prime Minister with the shirt hanging out".
Empowerment	"Now they have to make the decisions—they have to live with it and get the results every month, which has made them incredibly efficient actually. …I always tell them listen, I'm here to make sure you do your job but I'm not here to do yours. I've no intentions to do that what so-ever".	"Everybody expects to have a supervisor. The supervisor only expects to supervise but not necessarily do much. …I could never quite figure out what the supervisors were doing! …Others just don't understand why there's no longer a supervisor, because it's just a society thing".
Team-working	"We call them team members, we do not look at them as our people employed within the resort as staff, simply because we want them to feel like they are part of a team…like today, I have a new lady that just joined us, …well she has been introduced to the rest of the team and she is being coached and trained by some people that are responsible for her while she's there. …If one team member has finished off the upper rooms, you find it is so rewarding to see them going from one station to another because they have built that camaraderie between them, they all pitch in and help the team members."	"Some of the local managers really have a bad attitude …and they don't care how busy it is, they wouldn't get their hands dirty, they would not lift a spoon off the table, because I have a right, am in charge, I have a title". "I wouldn't say they were team oriented—because I'm still trying to instil that into them".
Appraisal	"After every six months of what you've been doing, there is an evaluation that is done and we will assess one's ability, one's readiness—whether one is ready or not to go on and accept more responsibility and that is sent on to our head Office on a regular basis".	"Once a year we do evaluations, that's usually before the salary increases at the end of the year. We meet with them one on one and tell what the supervisors say".
Rewards	"I think a lot of emphasis has been put on staff and staff morale and all—the communication aspects—from manager to line staff for instance—really really different".	"And then another thing—we are human and we like to be recognised—a little bit of recognition goes a long way". "No one tell us if we do good or anything".
Standard operating procedures	"Each department has its own copy—we call it a SOP—Standard of Operating Procedures … so we have a step by step procedure that we follow. It is very detailed".	"To be honest, I have never even looked at it (SOP manual)".
TQM: excellent communication	"Management—line staff—like we know, communication is very important, and I think—I've seen that—I've witnessed that. …Like they have taken a decision and if it's going to affect staff, immediately you find that managers would tell their staff. … I think that the downwards communication—because I think it's so good, that people feel confident enough to bring their problems to the managers if there is a problem".	"… people are thinking that sometimes department heads and maybe the general manager are too off limits".

Table 3 (*continued*)

	Examples of best practice	Limitations/problems
Planned maintenance	"We do have planned maintenance policies. We—for example, we know that most times the paint job that's done would normally last for as much as six months, we normally do not wait to see it actually being chipped off the wall for us to be able to have them go in and do a touch up in the rooms".	"Whoever is responsible for servicing, sometimes is short of telling us and you sometimes have to order and sometimes have to wait—but that seldom happens. Like when we had our marble machine—when we have pads for them, for the floor—sometimes the padding goes very low and the guy who's using it, we monitor it, but sometimes he would say very late that its going low and then we have to wait. Maybe it would finish before the supply comes".
Equipment/ working conditions	"We realised that if we go for example to M… faucets that's one example, M… faucets, one insert would fit the shower or the sink faucet, so the M… faucet is a little more expensive but the part and back up service is so reliable that we have decided to go M…, and gradually we are changing the whole hotel into M…, so if we get a drip we don't have to worry about—is it shower or is it sink, just pick up a part and insert and one fits all".	"Not getting the equipment to do what you want to do at the moment—but there is a substitute, and the substitute itself is not even available—it's annoying you because, you cannot get that done before that time since you don't have the material to do it—so you find that itself annoys you".

or end product. As such, issues relating to cultural differences between customer and provider and between customers have not been addressed in this research. However, the research has provided some evidence to support the contention that cultural differences do have an impact on the management of operations in hotels in St. Lucia.

In some ways the results were surprising and to an extent contrary to expectations. The locally owned and smallest of the hotels had the least happy employees and it was clear to the author that there were operational inefficiencies and a lack of "best practice" implementation, e.g. the practice of checking, double checking and even triple checking that employees did what they were supposed to do was the norm. The employees clearly did not feel as though they were valued. As this was the smallest of the hotels studied, some of the problems could have been seen as due to lack of resources, however as one employee stated: "… nobody appreciates us, so what more can I say …"—how much does it cost to give praise and thanks in appreciation for a good job well done? The most likely explanation for the problems observed in this hotel was a lack of understanding of the role of management in implementing "best practice"—the emphasis was on the end product rather than the processes.

There was ample evidence of knowledge and a clear understanding of "best practice operations management" across most of the ten management aspects covered in the interviews in the larger three hotels, but the adoption and implementation of certain aspects did falter and initial resistance to some approaches could be explained by cultural differences. "Best practice" in service operations management advocates the provision of training, support and rewards to employees, and ensuring excellent communication between employees. The employees of the two hotels that had most closely followed and successfully implemented "best practice" came out top when employees were asked "do you like your job?" Two factors in particular seemed to improve the acceptance and successful transfer of "best practice" type approaches: a greater emphasis on training and senior management who "practised what they preached". There is evidence to suggest, therefore, that "best practice" is transferable and will lead to improved service quality in hotels on the Island. However, the training may have to be tailored to local conditions and take into account cultural differences, and true empowerment may be difficult to achieve. Nevertheless, providing that standard operations procedures are implemented sensibly, taking into account the local context and culture, the basic tenets of "best practice operations management" do appear to be transferable— *with care and effort*.

Acknowledgements

The author wishes to acknowledge the help of the management and employees of the four hotels who took part in this study and for the support of Ms Berthia Parle, President of the St. Lucia Hotel and Tourism Association and Veronica Guard, Permanent Secretary at the Ministry of Tourism, Civil Aviation and International Financial Services, St. Lucia.

Appendix A

The copy of the questionnaire is given below

C.A. Hope / Tourism Management 25 (2004) 45–59 53

Questionnaire Survey

Improving Ways of Working in Hotels
St. Lucia
May/June 2000

Project Leader: Dr Christine A Hope

The International Operations Management Research Group
THE MANAGEMENT CENTRE
UNIVERSITY OF BRADFORD
Emm Lane
Bradford
West Yorkshire
BD9 4JL
UK
Tel: + 44 1274 234358
Fax: + 44 1274 546866
Email: c.a.hope@bradford.ac.uk

Research Group Members: Professor Alan Mühlemann, Dr Christine Hope, Dr Roger Beach, Dr Zoe Radnor, Dr Margaret Webster, Ms Tamsin Potter, Ms Andrea Cullen, Ms Josephine Braithwaite.

54   *C.A. Hope / Tourism Management 25 (2004) 45–59*

The questionnaire is divided into four parts. **The first part is about the nature of your job as it is now. The second part is about how you feel about your work. In the third part I am going to ask you for suggestions about improved ways of doing your job. Finally I would like to know a little more about you.**

Part 1: Your job

1. What is your job title? ....

2. Do you work the same hours every week?   Yes ☐ No ☐

3. How many hours a week do you usually work?

     1 – 20   ☐

     21 – 40   ☐

     41 – 20   ☐

     More than 60 ☐

4. Do you work shifts?   Yes ☐ No ☐

5. At the beginning of the week do you know how many hours you are going to work each day?

    Yes ☐   Approximately ☐   No ☐

6. Do you have some control over how many hours you work each week?   Yes ☐ No ☐

7. How were you trained to do your present job? (*Please tick as many boxes as apply*)

     My supervisor taught me   ☐

     A fellow worker showed me   ☐

     I was given written instructions   ☐

     I was left to do the job how I wanted ☐

     I already knew how to do the job   ☐

     Other (please specify) ....

8. If a checklist exists for your job (i.e. a list of tasks which you should follow):

     do you always use it?   ☐

     did you used it to begin with?   ☐

     do you sometimes use it?   ☐

     there is no checklist?   ☐

9. If you think of a better or quicker way to do the job, do you:

     use the better/quicker way?   ☐

     stick with the way you were told/taught to do the job? ☐

10. Are there any training courses which you can go on?   Yes ☐ No ☐

11. If the answer to the previous questions was yes, do you have to go on them?

    Yes ☐ No ☐

12. Can you ask to go on training courses?   Yes ☐ No ☐

13. How are you rewarded (e.g. by fixed rate per hour/day/week/salary)?

    ....

14. Is there any extra pay/incentive for good performance (e.g. bonus)?   Yes ☐ No ☐

15. Does your pay depend on the performance of others?   Yes ☐ No ☐

16. Do you usually work: on your own? ☐   in a team? ☐

17. Do you have any say about who you work with?   Yes ☐ No ☐

18. Does anyone check your work after you have done it?

    Always ☐   Sometimes ☐   Never ☐

19. If you have problems at work is there someone you can ask for help?   Yes ☐ No ☐

20. If the answer to the previous question was yes, who?

    Colleague ☐   Supervisor ☐   Manager ☐

21. Are you encouraged to think of a better way to do your job?   Yes ☐ No ☐

22. Is it considered acceptable to tell your boss if you think they are wrong or unfair?

    Yes ☐   No ☐

23. Do you have more than one person who can tell you what to do?   Yes ☐ No ☐

24. Do the instructions of the managers sometimes contradict each other?   Yes ☐ No ☐

25. In your job, do you know what you are supposed to be doing?

    Always ☐   Usually ☐   Rarely ☐   Never ☐

26. Do you talk about your work problems with your fellow workers (i.e. not the bosses)?

    Yes ☐ No ☐

27. If you did something wrong by mistake

    would you not tell anyone at work? ☐

    would you tell a colleague?   ☐

    would you tell a boss?   ☐

28. If you think of a better way to do the job

    do you not tell anyone at work   ☐

    do you tell a colleague   ☐

    do you tell a boss   ☐

29. Do you have the correct equipment/tools to do your job?

    Yes ☐   For most things I do ☐   No ☐

Part 2

**In this part of the questionnaire, I am trying to find out how you would _prefer_ to work.
Please tick the box which most closely matches how you feel about the situation described.**

30. Are you happy with the number of hours you work?   Yes ☐   Reasonably happy ☐   No ☐

31. If your hours are not fixed, would you like to know in advance when you will be working and

    for how long?   Yes ☐   No ☐   Not applicable ☐

32. Do you prefer to work as part of a team or alone?   Alone ☐   Part of a team ☐

33. If you are in a team, do you prefer to work with friends?

    Yes ☐ No ☐   Doesn't matter ☐

34. If you work in a team, would you prefer to pick who you work with?   Yes ☐   No ☐

35. Do you prefer to have a fixed rate of pay or would you prefer pay to be linked to how well

    you do your job?   Fixed rate of pay ☐   Linked to performance

36. If you are working in a team would you be happy to have your pay linked to the performance

    of the team?   Yes ☐   No ☐   Doesn't matter ☐

37. Are you happy with the way you are currently being rewarded?

    Yes ☐   Reasonably happy ☐   No ☐

38. Do you think the way you are currently being rewarded is fair?   Yes ☐   No ☐

39. Would you like more opportunities to receive more training now to help you to do your job

    well?   Yes ☐   No ☐

40. Would you like more opportunities to develop more skills?   Yes ☐   No ☐

41. Would you have liked to receive more training when you started the job? Yes ☐   No ☐

42. Would you like to have clearer instructions about what you should be doing?

    Yes ☐   No ☐

43. Do you feel you are given too much advice?   Yes ☐   No ☐

44. Would you like to have more say in how you do your job?   Yes ☐   No ☐

45. If you have problems at work, are you happy with the way your manager or supervisor supports

    you?   Yes ☐   Reasonably happy ☐   No ☐

46. If you make suggestions, do you feel that management takes any notice?

    Yes ☐   To some extent ☐   No ☐

47. Do you like your job?   Yes ☐   No ☐   It's OK ☐

(48–51) Which of the following situations do you prefer? (Please circle : 1—Not at all; 2—Prefer not to; 3—Have no preference; 4—Would like to a certain extent; 5—Would really like)

48. Dealing with new challenges/situations every day   1   2   3   4   5

49. Knowing what you will be doing each day   1   2   3   4   5

50. Having a great deal of variety in the job   1   2   3   4   5

51. Being able to do different jobs each week/month   1   2   3   4   5

52. What three things do you like best about your job?

    ....

    ....

    ....

C.A. Hope / Tourism Management 25 (2004) 45–59   57

53. What three things do you like least about your job?

    ....

    ....

    ....

54. Would you like more responsibility in your job?   Yes ☐   No ☐

55. Would you like to be given the authority to use your own judgement more when dealing with

    customers?   Yes ☐   No ☐

56. Usually, do you like dealing with hotel guests?   Yes ☐   No ☐

Part 3

In this part I have asked a few questions to give you an idea of the type of thing I am looking for, but please make any suggestions you can think of which would help you to do your job better and to enjoy what you do more.

57. What three things do you think make it difficult for you to do your job well?

    ....

    ....

    ....

58. If you could change three things about the way you have to do your job, what would they be?

    ....

    ....

    ....

59. If your manager asked you for three suggestions about how they could help you, what would you say?

    ....

    ....

    ....

Part 4

About You. Please remember that only I will see these answers and also that I am not asking for your name.

60. How old are you? ....

61. Are you male or female?   Male ☐   Female ☐

62. Were you born on St. Lucia?   Yes ☐   No ☐

63. If the answer to the previous question was No, in which country were you born?

    ....

58   *C.A. Hope / Tourism Management 25 (2004) 45–59*

Education up to the age of 18 years.

64. Were you educated on St. Lucia?   Yes ☐   No ☐

65. If the answer to the previous question was No, in which country were you educated?

   ....

66. Have you been to College or University?   Yes ☐   No ☐

67. If yes, where? ....

68. How did you find out about your present job?

   In an advertisement   ☐

   From a friend who works here   ☐

   From a relative who works here   ☐

   Other (please specify) ....

69. Do any of your relatives work at this hotel?   Yes ☐   No ☐

70. How long have you been working at this hotel? ....

71. Have you worked in any other hotels?

   No   ☐

   1 other hotel   ☐

   2–3 other hotels   ☐

   more than 3 other hotels   ☐

72. What job would you like to be doing in:

   1 year ....

   5 years ....

   10 years ....

Thank you very much for filling in this questionnaire.

If there is anything else you can think of which you would like to tell me, please do so. Also, if any questions were unclear, please let me know.

....

....

....

....

....

....

....

C.A. Hope / Tourism Management 25 (2004) 45–59   59

References

Adler, N. J. (2002). *International dimensions of organizational behavior* (4th Ed.). Ohio: South Western.

Bastin, R. (1984). Small island tourism: Development or dependency? *Development Policy Review, 2*(1), 79–90.

Beckford, G. (1972). *Persistent poverty*. Oxford: Oxford University Press.

Bernal, R., Figueroa, M., & Wilter, M. (1984). Caribbean economic thought: The critical tradition. *Social Economic Studies, 33*(2), 5–96.

Chase, R., Aquilano, N., & Jacobs, F. (2000). *Production and operations management* (8th Ed.). New York: McGraw-Hill.

Child, J., & Kieser, A. (1979). Organizational and managerial roles in British and West German companies: An examination of the culture-free thesis. In C. J. Lammers, & D. J. Hickson (Eds.), *Organizations alike and unalike. International and Interinstitutional Studies in the Sociology of Organizations* (pp. 251–271). London: Routledge & Kegan Paul.

Child, J., & Tayeb, M. (1983). Theoretical perspectives in cross-national organizational research. *International Studies of Management and Organization, XII*(4), 3–70.

Coke, F. (1995). Barriers to excellence. In N. M. Cowell, & I. Boxill (Eds.), *Human resource management: A Caribbean perspective*. Kingston Jamaica: Canoe Press.

Emmanuel, P. (1993). *Governance and democracy in the Commonwealth Caribbean: an introduction*. Barbados: Institute of Economic Research.

Foster, M. J., & Minkes, A. L. (1999). East and West: Business culture as divergence and convergence. *Journal of General Management, 25*(1), 60–71.

Girvan, N., & Jefferson, O. (Eds.) (1971). *Readings in the political economy of the Caribbean*. Jamaica: New World Group.

Hall, E. T., & Hall, M. R. (1990). *Understanding cultural differences*. Maine: Intercultural Press.

Hofstede, G. (1980). *Culture's consequences: International differences in work-related values*. London: Sage Publications.

Hofstede, G. (1994). *Cultures and organizations: Intercultural cooperation and its importance for survival*. London: Harper Collins Business.

Hope, C. A., & Mühlemann, A. P. (1997). *Service operations management: Strategy, design and delivery*. Hemel Hempstead: Prentice-Hall.

Hope, C. A., & Mühlemann, A. P. (1998). Total quality, human resource management and tourism. *Tourism Economics, 4*(4), 367–386.

Hope, C. A., & Mühlemann, A. P. (2001). The impact of culture on best practice production/operations management. *International Journal of Management Reviews, 3*(3), 199–218.

Hope, C. A., Mühlemann, A. P., & Potter, T. L. (2000). Culture—a critical review and framework for further research. *Proceedings of the 50th annual AIEST congress, China*, Vol. 42. St. Gallen: AIEST.

Huyton, J. R., & Ingold, A. (1995). The cultural implications of total quality management—the case of the Ritz Carlton Hotel, Hong Kong. In R. Teare, & C. Armistead (Eds.), *Services management: New directions, new perspectives*, Cassell.

Khan, J. (1987). *Public management: the Eastern Caribbean experience*. Holland: Foris Publications.

Krippendorf, J. (1987). *The holiday makers*. Oxford: Butterworth-Heinemann.

Lewis, V. (1970). Comment on multinational corporations and development underdevelopment in mineral export economies. *Social and Economic Studies, 19*(4), 529–533.

McGaughey, S. L., & De Cieri, H. (1999). Reassessment of convergence and divergence dynamics: Implications for international HRM. *International Journal of Human Resource Management, 10*(2), 235–250.

McLaughlin, C., & Fitzsimmons, J. A. (1996). Strategies for globalizing service operations. *International Journal of Service Industry Management, 7*(4), 43–57.

Meredith, J. R., & Shafer, S. M. (2001). *Operations management for MBAs* (2nd ed.). New York: Wiley.

Mills, G. E. (1970). Public administration in the commonwealth Caribbean bureaucracies: Evolution, conflicts and challenges. *Social and Economic Studies, 19*(1), 5–25.

Morden, G. (1999). Models of national culture—a management review. *Cross Cultural Management, 6*(1), 19–44.

Purcell, W., Nicholas, S., Merrett, D., & Whitwell, G. (1999). The transfer of human resource and management practice by Japanese multinationals to Australia: Do industry, size and experience matter? *International Journal of Human Resource Management, 10*(2), 72–88.

Rodrigues, C. A. (1998). Cultural classifications of societies and how they affect cross-cultural management. *Cross Cultural Management, 5*(3), 29–39.

Roney, J. (1997). Cultural implications of implementing TQM in Poland. *Journal of World Business, 33*(2), 152–168.

Russell, R. S., & Taylor, B. W. (2000). *Operations management* (3rd ed.). New York: Prentice-Hall.

Schein, E. H. (1985). *Organisational culture and leadership*. London: Jossey-Bass Publishers.

Schneider, S. C., & Barsoux, J-L. (1997). *Managing across cultures*. Hemel Hempstead: Prentice-Hall.

Slack, N., Chambers, S., & Johnston, R. (2001). *Operations management* (3rd ed.). London: Pitman.

Smith, M. G. (1965). *The plural society in the British West Indies*. Berkley: University of California Press.

Tayeb, M. (2001). Conducting research across cultures: Overcoming drawbacks and obstacles. *International Journal of Cross Cultural Management, 1*(1), 91–108.

Teare, R. (1993). Designing a contemporary hotel service culture. *International Journal of Service Industry Management, 4*(2), 63–73.

Triandis, H. C. (1995). *Individualism and collectivism*. Boulder: Westview Press.

Trompenaars, F., & Hampden-Turner, C. (1997). *Riding the waves of culture: understanding cultural diversity in business* (2nd ed.). London: Nicholas Brearley Publishing.

Warner, M., & Joynt, P. (Eds.) (2002). *Managing across cultures: Issues and perspectives* (2nd ed.). London: Thomson Learning.

Williams, E. (1983). *From Columbus to Castro: The history of the Caribbean 1492–1969*. Great Britain: Stepmundsbury Press Ltd.

[32]

PERGAMON

Tourism Management 22 (2001) 157–165

TOURISM MANAGEMENT

www.elsevier.com/locate/tourman

An investigation of employees' job satisfaction: the case of hotels in Hong Kong

Terry Lam[a,*], Hanqin Zhang[a], Tom Baum[b]

[a]*Department of Hotel & Tourism Management, The Hong Kong Polytechnic University, Hung, Hung Hom, Kowloon, Hong Kong*
[b]*Scottish Hotel School, The University of Strathclyde, Curran Building, 94 Cathedral Street, Glasgow G4 0LG, Scotland, UK*

Received 13 August 1999; accepted 28 January 2000

Abstract

High employee turnover in the hotel industry has become one of the major concerns for Hong Kong hotel managers. Many studies have found that turnover is related to job satisfaction, and the importance of job facets perceived by employees. The study examines the relationship between demographic characteristics of hotel employees and job satisfaction, and also examines the importance of job variables. The study findings show that there are significant differences between demographic variables of employees and the six Job Descriptive Index (JDI) categories. It is suggested that training and development programmes, particularly for newcomers and well-educated employees, and a total quality management approach may help improve job satisfaction with the job. © 2001 Elsevier Science Ltd. All rights reserved.

Keywords: Job satisfaction; Demographic characteristics; Job descriptive index; Hong Kong

1. Introduction

The hotel industry is a service and people-oriented business. To be successful in a competitive market, it is important that hotel managers know how their employees feel at work and what they want. The amount of effort that an employee expends toward accomplishing the hotel's goals depends on whether the employee believes that this effort will lead to the satisfaction of his or her own needs and desires. In this context, the key to facilitating motivation lies with managers' good understanding of what their employees want from work (Simons & Enz, 1995).

Hong Kong employees' morale in all industries ranks the lowest of all workers in the world and has been going downhill for the last 24 years (International Survey Research, 1995). The deterioration of employees' morale has caused detrimental impacts on productivity, job satisfaction, and commitment. The hospitality industry in Hong Kong has been troubled with high turnover and employee morale problems. The problems seem to be an

<hr>

* Corresponding author. Fax: + 852-2362-9362.
E-mail addresses: hmterry@polyu.edu.hk (T. Lam), hmhanqin@polyu.edu.hk (H. Zhang), t.g.baum@strath.ac.uk (T. Baum).

inalienable feature of this industry worldwide (Woods, 1992). The competitive business environment requires, as an imperative, strong management and stable, eager to serve, and highly committed employees, working as a team to run the business. The unpublished employee turnover figures of Hong Kong hotels show that turnover is high every year. Table 1 shows that the highest rate was reached in 1998 with 86 per cent. Many hotel managers regard the high turnover rate as a regrettable "fact of life" about which they can do nothing (Johnson, 1980).

Most of the literature on employee turnover suggests that labour turnover is a "hidden" cost for most organizations. Additional recruitment and training costs must be incurred as well as a resulting decrease in productivity. In the early 1980s, some studies suggested that total turnover costs run from a minimum of US$50 for a new kitchen helper to several thousands for a top executive (Lungberg & Armatas, 1980). In addition, the intangible costs of turnover are notable in the areas of employees' morale, employee productivity, reputation and goodwill of an organization (Hogan, 1992) that may result in loss of customers, quality of products and services (Johnson, 1981).

There have not been many research studies of employee turnover in the Hong Kong hotel industry,

Table 1
The employee turnover of Hong Kong hotels from 1995 to 1998 (October)[a]

Year	Range of annual turnover	Average of annual turnover
1998	10.73–86.81 (Jan.–Oct.)	27.29 (Jan.–Oct.)
1997	13.46–63.59	30.61
1996	10.51–52.14	26.50
1995	18.65–64.89	32.0

[a]Source: Unpublished employee turnover rates of Hong Kong hotels provided by Hong Kong Hotels Association.

though the topic has been a focal issue for discussion for many years. However, job satisfaction factors are likely to play a major role in influencing labour turnover in the hotel industry. The objectives of this study are:

1. to investigate the importance of job aspects as perceived by employees,
2. to assess the employees' job satisfaction levels towards the job aspects, and
3. to examine the relationship between employees' demographic characteristics and job satisfaction towards the job aspects.

2. Job satisfaction

Job satisfaction has been considered in a variety of ways, and is defined differently in various studies. Katzell (1964) argues that if there is consensus about job satisfaction, it is the verbal expression of an incumbent's evaluation of his/her job. On this basis, it is an affective or hedonic tone, for which the stimuli are events or conditions experienced in connection with jobs or occupations. Locke (1976) defined job satisfaction as a pleasurable or positive emotional state resulting from the appraisal of one's job or job experiences. Robbins and Coulter (1996) stated that job satisfaction is an employee's general attitude towards his or her job. When people speak of an employee's job attitude, they are likely referring to his/her job satisfaction. Ivancevich and Donnelly (1968) argue that almost every writer has defined job satisfaction in his own way although this leads to, basically, an identical definition.

Mobley and Locke (1970) conducted five studies to explore the relationship between the importance of a job aspect and the degree of satisfaction towards that aspect. The results indicated that value attainment and frustration produce, respectively, more satisfaction and dissatisfaction when the value was more important than when it was less important. However, Ewen (1967) and Mikes and Hulin (1968) have typically found that the sum of the weighted scores of importance did not predict ratings of overall job satisfaction any better than the sum of un-

weighted satisfaction ratings. In most previous studies of the importance of aspects of the job, results show that facet satisfaction or overall job satisfaction can be predicted from a combination of facet importance and facet-description variables (e.g. Butler, 1983; Mastekaasa, 1984; Locke, Fitzpatrick & White, 1983). That is, there is a stronger relationship between, on the one hand, facet-description, and on the other, facet satisfaction or overall job satisfaction for employees who rated aspects of the job highly than those who rated them low. Rice, Gentile and McFarlin (1991) also supported findings that the relationship between the level of importance attached to aspects of the job and facet satisfaction was generally stronger among employees placing high importance on the job facet than among those placing low importance on it.

3. Impact of demographic characteristics on job satisfaction

Past empirical studies in the disciplines of social science, psychology and management have shown that age has significant effects on job relationships (Warr, 1990; Rhodes, 1983; Farris, 1971). However, one study found such a relationship in women but not in men (Shott, Albright & Glennon, 1963). Both De La Mare and Sergean (1961) and Cooper and Payne (1965) investigated the relationship between degree of job satisfaction and age. The latter is measured in terms of frequency, and duration of absence. The results indicate that age among blue-collar workers was positively related to both of the variables. Gibson and Klein (1970) found similar results in their study of 2067 blue-collar employees and suggested that there was a positive relationship between overall job satisfaction and age. The findings were claimed valid as effect of tenure was controlled so that it could not distort the results. Gibson and Klein suggested that there are three reasons for the positive relationship. Firstly, older people seem to have a different relationship to authority than younger people. Secondly, they have higher needs to be directed and to accept orders, and thirdly, cognitive structures are different from those of younger people.

Herzberg, Mausner, Peterson and Capwell (1957) stated that overall job satisfaction is related to age with a U-shaped relationship, and explained that this relationship is due to the newness of the job. Satisfaction dropped when job expectations are not met. However, increasing maturity and work experience finally cause the employee to adjust his/her work expectations to a more realistic level. When these new adjusted expectations are met, job satisfaction begins to rise. Other than the U-shape model, Sterns, Marsh and McDaniel (1994) noted that there were highly diverse hypothesized models of the relationship between age and job satisfaction in the literature

T. Lam et al. / Tourism Management 22 (2001) 157–165   159

that include J-shaped functions (e.g. Saleh & Otis, 1964), positive linear functions (e.g. Hunt & Saul, 1975), negative linear functions (e.g. Muchinsky, 1978), and no significant relationship (e.g. Ronen, 1978).

An employee's satisfaction with an organization is closely related to length of service. Smith, Gregory and Cannon (1996) state that there was a significant difference in overall job satisfaction based on tenure in companies in the hospitality industry. Higher satisfaction levels of new employees with less than six months of employment were found which might be related to the pleasure of obtaining a new job. Overall satisfaction drops for employees of more than six months, and the greatest level of job turnover occurs during this period. Smith et al. (1996) argue that high turnover may be due to lack of job satisfaction among employees. However, it should be noted that the sampling ratio between hourly paid employees to salaried employees in their study is six to one and the high sampling mix of temporary employees may bias the results. Gibson and Klein (1970) report a negative and linear relationship between satisfaction and company tenure whereby the degree of job satisfaction decreases as length of service increased. Hulin and Smith (1965) reported positive, monatomic relationships between satisfaction with the work itself, and pay and company tenure.

Shea, Paines and Spitz (1970) found that marital status seems to have little influence on job satisfaction. Both married and non-married women in both black and white groups expressed the same degree of satisfaction with their jobs when occupational category was controlled. Having said that, Wild (1970) studied job satisfaction of 2159 female workers and 236 female ex-workers of electronic companies, and reported that job dissatisfaction was more prevalent among single workers. Research has consistently showed that married employees are more satisfied with their jobs than their unmarried co-workers (Keller, 1983; Federico, Federico & Lundquist, 1976). It may be that conscientious and satisfied employees are more likely to be married or that marriage changes employees' expectations of work. However, status other than single or married have rarely been studied. It is not clear whether the divorced, widowed, or couples who live together without being married, have an impact on an employee's performance and satisfaction.

Vollmer and Kinney (1955) found that the higher an employee's educational level, the more likely these was to be dissatisfaction. This was explained on the basis that employees with a higher educational background would expect more in terms of financial compensation, benefits, and supervision than the ones with a lower educational background. However, Sinha and Sarma (1962) studied the relationship between attitude towards union membership and job satisfaction on a sample of 100 workers in India, and found that there was no relationship between job satisfaction and educational levels. Although there are different arguments about the influence of educational levels on job satisfaction, it appears that employees with higher education have higher expectations of salary, incentives, and recognition. Higher expectations generate higher tension to perform. If the higher expectations can be fulfilled, higher job satisfaction will result.

4. Job satisfaction studies in Hong Kong

It appears that concern for worker's attitude has been minimal in the hospitality industry in Hong Kong. Nevertheless, some studies about Hong Kong employees' work attitude were identified. Chau (1977) sought to observe and interpret the attitudes and beliefs of workers in Hong Kong by replicating Whitehill and Takezawa's (1968) study. The study focused on employment continuity, economic and personal involvement, organizational identification, status transfer, and motivational sources. Three hundred and sixty production temporary and permanent workers from three manufacturing companies in Hong Kong were studied. The results showed that a relatively large percentage of Hong Kong workers, when compared to their American and Japanese counterparts, listed monetary rewards as their primary goals. The latter placed more emphasis upon job responsibilities and achievement as sources of motivation.

Chau (1980) studied attitudes towards work, job satisfaction, aspirations and life styles of woman executives in Hong Kong. Among 66 full-time women executives, 62 seemed to be very satisfied with their human relations at work in general. Among all variables, opportunity for self-actualization was rated and considered as the most important variable. The author found that if pay was below the women's expectations, money would become more important than interesting work. However, if pay was above their expectations, then an interesting job became more important.

5. Research methodology

The research design of this study was descriptive and quantitative in nature. According to the Hong Kong Tourism Association (HKTA, 1999), the 88 hotels in Hong Kong are classified into three categories, i.e. 44 belong to high tariff, 32 medium tariff, and 12 are hostels/guesthouses. It appears that the population variance in this study in terms of job satisfaction within strata is little but that between strata it is larger. A stratified sampling method was used to select the sampling units, as there is a requirement for greater reliability and a larger sample for some strata than for others (Alreck & Settle, 1995). The human resources managers of randomly selected hotels from each category were approached to determine whether they would permit the survey to be conducted. Five hotels agreed to help, of which 2 were high tariff, 2 medium tariff, and one a hostel. A sampling frame consisted of two sets of employee lists provided by the 5 participating hotels; one set contained existing employees and the other employees who had resigned during the three months before the survey was conducted. Samples of 200 existing and 200 resigned employees were randomly identified. In order to ensure a quality of equal probability of selection method (EPSEM) samples (Babbie, 1995), the sample ratio among the hotel categories was maintained at 2 (high tariff): 2 (medium tariff): 1 (hostel). The questionnaires were distributed through the human resource managers, and were collected directly by the researchers to ensure confidentiality of the information provided. Altogether 288 complete and usable questionnaires were collected, representing response rates of 86 and 58 per cent of the existing and the resigned employees, respectively.

The job descriptive index (JDI) initially developed by Smith, Kendall and Hulin (1969) was used. It was later revised by constructing an additional job in general (JIG) scale to reflect the global, long-term evaluation of the job (Balzer et al., 1997). The revised instrument was used in this study to measure job satisfaction perceived by employees in relation to the six facets of a job: Work Itself, Promotion, Pay, Supervision, Co-workers, and Job In General. The internal reliability estimates for the sub-scale of the revised JDI and the JIG were high with coefficient alpha, α ranging from 0.86 to 0.92 (Balzer et al., 1997).

The research instrument comprised of three sections. The first section consisted of ninety items, of which eighteen items came under the category of work, supervision, co-worker, and job in general and nine items under each category for pay and promotion factors. Respondents were asked to circle "Y" besides an item if it described the way which he/she saw the job, and "N" for an item which he/she did not. A question mark "?" was circled when the respondent could not decide. The former employee respondents were asked to recall the perceptions of the jobs they previously had in the hotels. The second section measured the relative importance of each of the five JDI components using the following 5-point scale: *most important* (1), *important* (2), *average* (3), *less important* (4), *and least important* (5). Demographic data about the respondents were collected in the last section. Since all of the target respondents were Chinese, the Chinese version of the JDI used in Mok and Woon's study (1987) was adopted, and the JIG category was translated into Chinese by using a blind translation-back-translation method as described by Brislin (1976).

Statistical package for the social sciences (SPSS) was used to analyse the data. An absolute frequency (N) and an adjusted frequency (per cent) were computed for the demographic items, and the relative importance of the five categories of JDI. One-way Analysis of Variance (ANOVA) and Independent-samples t-test were used to assess for significant difference of JDI mean scores among demographic variables. Duncan's Multiple-Range (Hair, Anderson, Tatham & Black, 1998) test was used to find out outstanding groups for nature of each demographic item. Lastly, the independent-samples t-test was used to investigate the mean JDI score differences between the existing and the resigned employees.

6. Results and discussion

Table 2 profiles the respondents' demographic characteristics. Sixty per cent were existing employees. About 85 per cent were between 21 and 35 years of age. A large proportion of the sample (81.2 per cent) was single. Just over half (52.6 per cent) were female. Over 53 per cent had completed matriculation or above, indicating that a large number of the sample was well educated, and 46 per cent had worked in hotels for less than six months.

Table 3 shows that 42.2 per cent of the respondents considered that pay was a more than average category contributing to job satisfaction in hotels. The finding is supported by Chau's (1977) report on production workers' motivation in Hong Kong. In Chau's study, monetary rewards were considered by workers as the primary goal. The finding in this study was also found congruent to many studies that reward is important (Charles & Marshall, 1992; Simons & Enz, 1995). The reasons for the higher degree of importance attached to pay as perceived by hotel employees in Hong Kong are likely to be twofold. Firstly, very high living standards have encouraged employees to pursue higher income to support their living. Secondly, it is within their culture that Chinese people wish to earn more and save more for any possible contingency in the future. Thus money appears to be very important compared to other job aspects for Chinese employees.

Table 3 shows that 31.7 per cent of the respondents indicated that promotion was the most important job aspect among the five categories of JDI. Promotion is linked to pay increase. It seems that the same argument holds as it does for pay in that employees believe that fortune will come along with promotion. The traditional compensation structure of the hotel industry has been that employees' incomes essentially rely upon customers' tips on top of their low basic salary. However, the economic downturn and the slump of inbound tourism in Hong Kong decreased employees' incomes from tips at the time the survey was being conducted. Promotion is, therefore, one important means to ensure a pay increase.

About 35 per cent of the sample ranked supervision as the least important to them. This finding does not support Scanlan's (1976) hypothesis that the nature of

T. Lam et al. / Tourism Management 22 (2001) 157–165

supervision was the first determinant of job satisfaction. A possible explanation of the result is that Hong Kong employees have accepted traditional autocratic or parent-type management in the hotel industry. They rarely complain of poor management, at least in public. Culturally, Chinese employees are concerned for the other's "face" that often leads to a non-confrontational style of conflict management such as avoiding, obliging, and compromising (Ting-Toomey, 1988). This attitude towards supervision would be expected to result in pass-

ivity, conformity, and obedience (Triandis, 1990; Westwood & Chan, 1992). Thus it may be concluded that employees were not concerned about the nature of supervision and would try to maintain a harmony-working environment by not jeopardizing other people's face.

Table 4 shows the group means of demographic variables and also describes the results of analysis of variance (ANOVA) that determine the relationship between the JDI scores and demographic characteristics. Type I error rate was set at 0.05 for the ANOVA and t-test, i.e. those factors with significant level (p-value) less than 0.05 indicate that they produce significant effect on the dependent variable. For the variables of age, educational level, length of employment, and marital status statistically significant differences were found. Post-hoc Duncan test was used to further identify which group indeed differs from others. Within the JDI's six categories, significant differences were found among the age groups. As found by Duncan post-hoc test, employees in the age group 21–25 were more satisfied with co-workers than the others. However, the group of age over 50 was generally satisfied with promotion, supervision, work itself, and the job in general, but not with pay. A majority of this age group of employees has lower education and is in the lower levels of the organizational hierarchy. The employees were generally not satisfied with their low incomes. As was discussed before, a portion of their incomes might come from customers' tips for service. This shrinkage was due to the slump of inbound tourism that hit Hong Kong at the time of the survey. On the other hand, it appears that this particular age group of employees usually have lower expectations of promotion, supervision and the work itself, and were more willing to accept their situation. Thus the respondents reported more satisfaction on those attributes.

The results in Table 4 show that there are significant differences (p-value < 0.05) between educational levels and the six JDI categories. Employees with primary school education level were more satisfied with co-workers, work, and the job in general, but not with promotion compared to the other groups. The finding indicates that employees with low education levels are dissatisfied with their promotional path and career development. Perhaps given an increasing number of

Table 2
Profile of study sample

Item and response category	$N = 287$	
	N	Percentage
Status		
Resigned	115	40.1
Existing	172	59.9
Age		
16–20	32	11.1
21–25	126	43.9
26–35	88	40.7
36–49	32	11.1
50 or above	9	3.1
Marital status		
Single	233	81.2
Married	54	18.8
Sex		
Female	151	52.6
Male	136	47.4
Highest level of formal education completed		
Primary school	17	5.9
Junior high school	37	12.9
Senior high school	80	27.9
Matriculation	63	22.0
Technical institute/college	48	16.7
University	42	14.6
Length of employment		
6 months or less	134	46.7
Over 6 months to 2 years	79	27.5
Over 2 years to 5 years	34	11.8
Over 5 years to 10 years	23	8.0
More than 10 years	17	5.9

Table 3
Relative rankings of each of the JDI categories ($n = 287$)

Rankings	Work n (%)	Supervision n (%)	Pay n (%)	Promotion n (%)	Co-workers n (%)
1. Least important	59 (20.6)	*101 (35.2)*	48 (16.7)	50 (17.5)	29 (10.1)
2. Less important	52 (18.1)	40 (13.9)	64 (22.3)	66 (23.0)	65 (22.6)
3. Average	*82 (28.6)*	27 (9.4)	54 (18.8)	40 (13.9)	*84 (29.3)*
4. Important	49 (17.1)	65 (22.7)	37 (12.9)	*91 (31.7)*	45 (15.7)
5. Most important	45 (15.6)	54 (18.8)	*84 (29.3)*	40 (13.9)	64 (22.3)
Total	287 (100)	287 (100)	287 (100)	287 (100)	287 (100)

Table 4
Analysis of demographic effects on JDI category scores (max. score is 54 for each category)

Demographic variables	Co-workers	Pay	Promotion	Supervision	Work	Job in general
Age						
1. 16–20	32.84	20.00	18.56	37.22	33.13	31.59
2. 21–25	37.73	16.52	21.49	35.55	23.67	22.10
3. 26–35	29.15	20.07	17.07	30.73	30.91	25.99
4. 36–49	29.53	15.38	15.13	30.56	23.53	30.81
5. 50 or above	30.00	6.00	48.00	48.00	47.00	36.00
ANOVA						
Main effect probability	0.000[a]	0.004[a]	0.000[a]	0.000[a]	0.000[a]	0.000[a]
Differ.	2 > 1,3–5	1–4 > 5	2 > 4	5 > 1,2,3,4	5 > 1–4	1,4,5 > 2
(Duncan)			5 > 1,2,3,4		1,3 > 4,2	5 > 3
Educational level						
1. Primary school	37.41	15.88	16.00	35.94	32.24	43.41
2. Junior high school	38.89	25.40	24.16	43.54	35.03	33.68
3. Senior high school	32.68	18.60	18.05	31.29	26.53	26.48
4. Matriculation	31.83	19.75	21.05	33.24	27.94	26.78
5. Technical institute	30.00	11.17	16.63	35.15	22.77	14.13
6. University	34.55	13.24	23.48	30.43	26.67	22.05
ANOVA						
Main effect probability	0.000[a]	0.000[a]	0.000[a]	0.000[a]	0.000[a]	0.000[a]
Differ.	1 > 3,4,5	2 > 1,3–6	2,6 > 1,3,5	2 > 1,3–6	1 > 3,5,6	1–4,6 > 5
(Duncan)	2 > 3–6	3,4 > 5	4 > 1		2 > 3–6	1 > 2–6
	6 > 5	4 > 5,6			4 > 5	2 > 3–6
Length of employment						
1. 6 months or less	36.65	11.94	19.70	34.46	26.35	24.98
2. 6 months – 2 years	29.47	22.84	17.59	33.51	27.46	21.65
3. 2 years – 5 years	32.82	29.06	21.12	30.49	27.88	34.09
4. 5 years – 10 years	34.04	18.83	33.65	44.56	41.65	31.52
more than 10 years	26.30	19.06	13.65	26.29	19.59	26.59
ANOVA						
Main effect probability	0.000[a]	0.000[a]	0.000[a]	0.000[a]	0.000[a]	0.000[a]
Differ.	1 > 2,3,5	2–5 > 1	1,3 > 5	1,2 > 5	1–4 > 5	3 > 1,2,5
(Duncan)	3 > 5	3 > 1,2	4 > 1,2,3,5	1–4 > 5	4 > 1–3,5	4 > 2
	4 > 2,5					
Marital status						
1. Single	33.24	17.36	18.71	33.28	26.43	24.20
2. Married	34.09	18.30	25.19	37.59	32.98	32.48
t-Test sig. level	0.491	0.614	0.000[a]	0.016[a]	0.000[a]	0.000[a]

[a] Significant at the 0.05 level. The higher the scores of a category of JDI, the higher degree of the satisfaction is perceived by an employee towards that category.

well-educated graduates from hotel schools every year in Hong Kong, the hotel industry is demanding employees with higher education levels. As employees advance their career to upper levels in the hotel, they are required to earn higher qualifications. In the past, promotion was linked closely to seniority and hands-on experience. Thus, employees with primary level education are not satisfied with promotion when they realise that they might have reached the ceiling in terms of their career.

Low satisfaction with the job in general and pay was found among employees who had graduated from technical institutes, and universities. This may imply that employees from the educational institutes perceive that they have made a greater investment in their education, and that their pay-off should be greater. The implication is supported by equity theory (Ronen, 1986; Scholl, Cooper & McKenna, 1987) that employees' return should be commensurate with their investment. Otherwise, they will be dissatisfied. Thus, the employees will expect more in terms of favourable working conditions more understanding supervision as well as higher pay than employees from high schools, (Vollmer & Kinney, 1955). When their expectations could not be met, the disconfirmation of expectations might cause the employees disappointment towards the job, and their pay. In order to narrow the disconfirmation of expectations, hotels may consider focusing efforts on training and development of this group of highly educated employees. Such strategic measures can facilitate not only the employees' vertical promotion prospects in their hotels, but

Table 5
Comparison of mean JDI scores by employee status

JDI components	Resigned employees	Current employees	t-Test sig. level
Co-workers	33.39	33.40	0.992
Pay	12.19	21.12	0.000[a]
Promotion	21.29	19.02	0.060
Supervision	34.18	34.03	0.914
Work itself	28.43	27.15	0.314
Job in general	20.57	29.23	0.000[a]

[a]Significant at the 0.01 level.

also their lateral transferability to other companies. Thus, they may be more satisfied with their jobs.

Satisfaction among the six categories of JDI varied significantly with length of employment. Workers who had worked over 10 years at hotels scored lower satisfaction for the attributes of co-workers, promotion, supervision, and work itself. This is contrary to Mok and Woon's (1987) study, which reported that workers with more than ten years of employment were most satisfied.

Employees who had worked in hotels for more than ten years were least satisfied with promotion, pay, and work. It is likely that this category of employees did not find many opportunities for career advancement in the hotels. The reasons for limited advancement are threefold. Firstly, the employees do not have the required know-how, skill, or ability. Secondly, the limited expansion of hotels may have deterred their advancement, and finally, according to the Peter Principle (Laurence & Hull, 1996), the employees might have attained a ceiling of capability so that they could not advance to the next level. With limited advancement, the employees likely faced low pay, repetitive work and unchallenging jobs. On the other hand, employees who had joined hotels for six months or less scored lower satisfaction with pay than other categories of employees. This group of new employees generally had high expectations of pay and incentives. Yet, most of them are used to being paid a low basic salary because they are encouraged to earn tips by providing personal quality service to hotel guests. The result of the study clearly indicates that their expectations were unmet.

The relationship of the JDI category scores and the employee status is reported in Table 5. Only pay, and job in general showed significant differences in the relationship with job satisfaction between current and resigned employees. It may imply that the employees' low satisfaction towards pay and job may lead to employee turnover in hotels. The result appears to be compatible with Chau's (1977) reports that production workers considered monetary rewards as their primary goal in Hong Kong.

7. Conclusion and implications

First, findings from this study show that well-educated hotel employees were not satisfied with their jobs. In general, they are more aggressive and have a higher degree of unmet expectations than the others. To trade-off their normative unmet expectations, hotels may provide job rotation opportunities, particularly, for well-educated employees with potential. New environment, new knowledge and learning of new information as a result of a job rotation programme may produce high motivation. Importantly, the exposure to different job functions can help them develop, and prepare for promotion in the future.

Second, the well-educated employees and those with more than 10 years of service were particularly dissatisfied with their hotel work. It seems that the prevailing autocratic management style in the Hong Kong hotel industry may become obsolete and ineffective due to the gradual change of social culture and upgrading of the educational qualification of employees. Studies have shown that employees nowadays look for a sense of personal power together with the freedom to use that power (Van Oudtshoorn & Thomas, 1993). They expect a high degree of job involvement and decision making at work. Hotels may consider implementing total quality management as well as empowering their employees. One of the examples is to provide a higher degree of autonomy for employees, within operative guidelines, to handle guest demands and complaints on the spot without referring them every time to higher levels in the hierarchy.

Third, pay was considered as the most important category attributing to job satisfaction, followed by promotion. Strategically, hotels should focus efforts on training and development for employees to improve their promotional prospects. On-the-job training of technical skills as well as off-the-job learning on supervision and management for supervisory employees are important to enhance their competency and promotability.

Fourth, pay was the most important category contributing to satisfaction. However, employees were not satisfied with their monetary rewards. It was found that almost all hotels in Hong Kong were compelled to freeze their employees' annual salary increments and/or cut their salary as a result of the economic setback. Others laid off their employees. However, it is suggested that hotels should revise their employees' salary packages and make them more competitive as soon as the poor economic situation has recovered. The money saved from salary freezes, wage cuts or employee redundancy should be utilized to invest in employee training so as to improve their skills and knowledge so that employees will become satisfied, loyal and committed to their hotels. Productivity will be enhanced and that will provide monetary payoffs for the hotel in the long-term.

In conclusion, the study findings show that there are significant differences between demographic characteristics of hotel employees and the six JDI categories. It is important that hotel management understands the impact of the demographic characteristics on employees' satisfaction and turnover rate. This study may have provided the relevant information for hotel management to consider.

Several limitations of this study should be considered together with the conclusion drawn above. Firstly, the small sample size may limit the generalization of this study. Secondly, Hong Kong was in a period of economic downturn at the time of the study was conducted and employee redundancy measures undertaken by hotels became a focal issue. Employees were concerned about extrinsic rewards such as pay, and bonuses to support their living standards more than any intrinsic incentives under such circumstances. The data obtained in this study might have been biased by current economic factors. It is suggested that a similar study can be conducted in the future when the economic recession in Hong Kong has been reversed so that possible impacts of economic factors on employees' job satisfaction can be measured. Thirdly, most of the demographic variables show different effects on employees' job satisfaction. This may imply that the relationship may be biased by different organizational characteristics such as organizational culture, departmental functions, size and age of hotel. The findings, therefore, may be contaminated by the different organizational characteristics found in the participating hotels. It is suggested that any future study should include the variable of hotel classification in the statistical analysis.

References

Alreck, P. L., & Settle, R. B. (1995). *The survey research handbook* (2nd ed.). Chicago: IRWIN.

Babbie, E. R. (1995). *The practice of social research* (7th ed.). Belmont, CA: Wadsworth Publishing Co.

Balzer, W. K., Kihm, J. A., Smith, P. C., Irwin, J. L., Bachiochi, P. D., Chet, R., Sinar, E. F., & Parra, L. F. (1997). *Users' manual for the job descriptive index and the job in general scales*. Bowling Green: Bowling Green State University.

Brislin, R. W. (1976). Comparative research methodology: Cross-cultural studies. *International Journal of Psychology, 11*(3), 215–229.

Butler, J. K. (1983). Value importance as a moderator of the value fulfillment-job satisfaction relationship: Group difference. *Journal of Applied Psychology, 68*, 420–428.

Charles, K. R., & Marshall, L. H. (1992). Motivational preferences of Caribbean Hotel workers: An exploratory study. *International Journal of Contemporary Hospitality Management, 4*(3), 25–29.

Chau, T. (1977). Workers' attitudes in Hong Kong: A comparison with other countries. *Hong Kong Manager*, 8–13.

Chau, T. (1980). Woman executives in Hong Kong. *Hong Kong Manager*, 8–12.

Cooper, R., & Payne, R. (1965). Age and absence: A longitudinal study in three firms. *Occupational Psychology, 39*, 31–43.

De La Mare, G., & Sergean, R. (1961). Two methods of studying changes in absence with age. *Occupational Psychology, 35*, 245–252.

Ewen, R. B. (1967). Weighting components of job satisfaction. *Journal of Applied Psychology, 51*, 68–73.

Farris, G. F. (1971). A predictive study of turnover. *Personnel Psychology, 24*, 311–328.

Federico, S. M., Federico, P., & Lundquist, G. W. (1976). Predicting women's turnover as a function of extent of met salary expectations and biodemographic data. *Personnel Psychology, 29*, 559–566.

Gibson, J. L., & Klein, S. M. (1970). Employee attitudes as a function of age and length of service: A reconceptualisation. *Academy of Management Journal, 13*, 411–425.

Hair Jr., J. F., Anderson, R. E., Tatham, R. L., & Black, W. C. (1998). *Multivariate data analysis* (5th ed.). New Jersey: Prentice-Hall.

Herzberg, F., Mausner, B., Peterson, R. O., & Capwell, D. F. (1957). *Job attitudes: A review of research and opinion*. Pittsburgh: Psychological Service of Pittsburgh.

HKTA, Hong Kong Tourist Association. (1999) *Annual Digest Statistics*, 180.

Hogan, J. J. (1992). Turnover and what to do about it. *Cornell Hotel and Restaurant Administration Quarterly, 33*(1), 40–45.

Hulin, C. L., & Smith, P. C. (1965). A linear model of job satisfaction. *Journal of Applied Psychology, 49*, 209–216.

Hunt, J. W., & Saul, P. N. (1975). The relationship of age, tenure, and job satisfaction in males and females. *Academy of Management Journal, 18*, 690–702.

International Survey Research. (1995). http://www.isrglobalsurveys.com/main/asp.

Ivancevich, J. M., & Donnelly, J. H. (1968). Job satisfaction research: A manageable guide for practitioners. *Personnel Journal, 47*, 172–177.

Johnson, K. (1980). Staff turnover in hotels. *Hospitality*, 28–36.

Johnson, K. (1981). Towards an understanding of labour turnover? *Service Industries Review, 1*(1), 4–17.

Katzell, R. A. (1964). Personal values, job satisfaction, and job behavior. In H. Borav, *Man in a work at work* (pp. 341–363) (Chapter 15).

Keller, R. T. (1983). Predicting absenteeism from prior absenteeism, attitudinal factors, and nonattitudinal factors. *Journal of Applied Psychology, 68*, 536–540.

Laurence, J. P., & Hull, R. (1996). *The Peter principle*. London: Souvenir press.

Locke, E. A. (1976). The nature and consequences of job satisfaction. In M. D. Dunnetter, *Handbook of industrial and organizational psychology* (pp. 1297–1349). Chicago: Rand-McNally.

Locke, E. A., Fitzpatrick, W., & White, F. M. (1983). Job satisfaction and role clarity among university and college faculty. *Review of Higher Education, 6*, 343–365.

Lungberg, D. E., & Armatas, J. P. (1980). *The management of people in hotels, restaurants and clubs* (4th ed.). Dubuque, Iowa: Wm. C. Brown.

Mastekaasa, A. (1984). Multiplicative and additive models of job and life satisfaction. *Social Indicators Research, 14*, 141–163.

Mikes, P. S., & Hulin, C. L. (1968). Use of importance as a weighting component of job satisfaction. *Journal of Applied Psychology, 52*, 394–398.

Mobley, W. H., & Locke, E. A. (1970). The relationship of value importance to satisfaction. *Organizational Behavior And Human Performance, 5*, 463–483.

Mok, C., & Woon, C. C. (1987). *Research report on causes of employee turnover: An analytical investigation in Hong Kong*. Hong Kong Polytechnic.

Muchinsky, P. M. (1978). Age and job facet satisfaction: A conceptual reconsideration. *Aging and Work, 1*, 175–179.

Rice, R. W., Gentile, D. A., & McFarlin, D. B. (1991). Facet importance and job satisfaction. *Journal of Applied Psychology, 76*(1), 31–39.

Rhodes, S. R. (1983). Age-related differences in work attitude and behaviors: A review and conceptual analysis. *Psychological Bulletin, 93*, 328–367.

T. Lam et al. / Tourism Management 22 (2001) 157–165   165

Robbins, S. P., & Coulter, M. (1996). *Management*. Upper Saddle River, NJ: Prentice-Hall.

Ronen, S. (1978). Job satisfaction and the neglected variable of job seniority. *Human Relations, 31*, 297–308.

Ronen, S. (1986). Equity perception in multiple comparison: A field study. *Human Relations*, April, 333–346.

Saleh, S. D., & Otis, J. L. (1964). Age and level of job satisfaction. *Personnel Psychology, 17*, 425–430.

Scanlan, B. K. (1976). Determinants of job satisfaction and productivity. *Personnel Journal, 55*, 12–21.

Scholl, R. W., Cooper, E. A., & McKenna, J. F. (1987). Referent selection in determining equity perception: Differential effects on behavioral and attitudinal outcomes. *Personnel Psychology*, 113–127.

Shott, G. L., Albright, L. E., & Glennon, J. R. (1963). Predicting turnover in an automated office situation. *Personnel Psychology, 16*, 213–219.

Shea, J. R., Paines, H. S., & Spitz, R. S. (1970). *Dual careers*; vol. 1. Manpower Research Monograph No. 21. Washington, DC: Manpower Administration, US Department of Labor.

Simons, T., & Enz, C. A. (1995). Motivating hotel employees. *Cornell Hotel and Restaurant Administration Quarterly, 36*(1), 20–27.

Sinha, D., & Sarma, K. C. (1962). Union attitudes and job satisfaction in Indian workers. *Journal of Applied Psychology, 46*, 247–251.

Smith, K., Gregory, S. R., & Cannon, D. (1996). Becoming an employer of choice: Assessing commitment in the hospitality workforce. *International Journal of Contemporary Hospitality Management, 8*(6), 3–9.

Smith, P. C., Kendall, L. M., & Hulin, C. L. (1969). *The measurement of satisfaction in work and retirement: A strategy for the study of attitudes*. Chicago: Rand McNally & Co.

Sterns, A. A., Marsh, B. A., & McDaniel, M. A. (1994). *Age and job satisfaction: A comprehensive review and meta-analysis*. Paper presented at the Ninth Annual Conference of the Society of Industrial and Organizational Psychology, Nashville, TN.

Ting-Toomey, S. (1988). Intercultural conflict styles: A face-negotiation theory. In Y. Y. Kim, & W. B. Gudykunst, *Theories in intercultural communication*. Beverly Hills, CA: Sage.

Triandis, H. C. (1990). Cross-cultural studies of individualism and collectivism. In J. Berman, *Nebraska symposium on motivation, 1989*. Lincoln: Nebraska University Press.

Van Oudtshoorn, M., & Thomas, L. (1993). *A management synopsis of empowerment. Empowerment In Organizations, 1*(1).

Vollmer, H. M., & Kinney, J. A. (1955). Age, education and job satisfaction. *Personnel, 32*, 38–44.

Warr, P. (1990). Age and employment. In H. C. Triandis, M. D. Dunnette, & L. M. Hough, *Handbook of industrial and organizational psychology*, vol. 4 (pp. 485–550). Palo Alto, CA: Consulting Psychologists Press.

Westwood, R. I., & Chan, A. (1992). Headship and leadership. In R. I. Westwood, *Organizational behaviour: Southeast Asian perspectives*. Hong Kong: Longman.

Whitehill, A., & Takezawa, S. (1968). *The other worker*. Honolulu: East-West Center Press.

Wild, R. (1970). Job needs, job satisfaction, and job behaviour of women manual workers. *Journal of Applied Psychology, 54*, 157–162.

Woods, R. H. (1992). *Managing hospitality human resources*. East Lansing, MI: Educational Institute of the American Hotel and Motel Association.

[33]

 Pergamon

www.elsevier.com/locate/atoures

Annals of Tourism Research, Vol. 30, No. 2, pp. 446–464, 2003
© 2003 Elsevier Science Ltd. All rights reserved
Printed in Great Britain
0160-7383/03/$30.00

doi:10.1016/S0160-7383(02)00101-9

PAY DETERMINATION
A Socioeconomic Framework

Michael Riley
Edith Szivas
University of Surrey, UK

Abstract: The article attempts to form a conceptual framework for understanding how pay levels and differentials are determined in tourism employment. This is constructed from the application of economic, structural, and psychological theories to known structural, and behavioral features of the industry. It identifies factors that work in concert to exert deflationary or inflationary pressures on the level of pay. The attractiveness of tourism, mobility, and the tolerance of low pay feature strongly, but at the heart of the notion is that the socioeconomic factors are synthesized into fundamental managerial assumptions which are maintained by industry norms. The outcome is a framework replete with deflationary influences. **Keywords:** pay, wage, labor markets, pay satisfaction. © 2003 Elsevier Science Ltd. All rights reserved.

Résumé: La détermination de la paie : un cadre socioculturel. L'article est une tentative de former un cadre conceptuel pour comprendre comment on détermine les niveaux et les écarts salariaux dans les emplois du tourisme. Ce cadre se construit à partir d'une application de théories psychologiques, structurelles et économiques aux caractéristiques de structure et de comportement de l'industrie. L'article identifie les facteurs qui fonctionnent ensemble pour exercer des pressions déflationnistes ou inflationnistes sur le niveau de paie. L'attrait du tourisme, la mobilité et la tolérance d'un bas niveau salarial figurent fortement dans la question, mais au cœur de l'idée, on trouve que les facteurs socioéconomiques sont synthétisés dans des suppositions fondamentales de gestion qui sont soutenues par les normes de l'industrie. Le résultat est un cadre fortement constitué d'influences déflationnistes. **Mots-clés:** paie, salaire, marché du travail, satisfaction salariale. © 2003 Elsevier Science Ltd. All rights reserved.

INTRODUCTION

This paper attempts to create a conceptual framework for understanding pay determination in tourism. It is constructed from known and conspicuous behavioral and structural features of the industry. The analysis uses syntheses of selected economic and psychological theories to explain how these features influence both levels and differentials. The analysis acknowledges that there are problems with empirical approaches: that the macro level is handicapped by a paucity of

---

Michael Riley (PhD) is Professor of Organizational Behavior in the School of Management, University of Surrey (Guildford GU2 7HX, UK. Email <m.riley@surrey.ac.uk>). His research interests include behavioral studies and tourism labor markets. The research interests of **Edith Szivas** (PhD), Lecturer in Tourism at the same institution, include development, labor markets, and transitional economies in relation to tourism.

useful data and the micro level is confined to specific sectors of the industry. The analysis uses empirical studies without depending upon them. The absence of data does not disable the arguments. Accepting that pay determination is not solely an economic phenomenon makes it possible to construct an explanation that focuses on the *processes* that produce a level of pay and on the structures which maintain it.

The analysis takes as a starting point the fact that, broadly speaking, tourism pay is relatively low, has narrow differentials and a tendency to resist inflation (Riley, Ladkin and Szivas 2002:39–60; Lee and Kang 1998). To an extent, this generalization is unfair because there is evidence that some occupations and organizations experience high remuneration. Furthermore, the accusation of low pay depends on perspective. From subsistence level, pay in tourism might not seem low at all. It is, in a sense, all too easy to take a "developed economy" view as the accepted wisdom. Notwithstanding this, it is the fact that levels of pay appear to be perennially low despite the inevitability that they must, at some time, have confronted shortages of labor that leads the analysis towards *deflationary pressures or processes.*

In the light of this, the analysis explores three such pressures. One, as there are no economic benefits, but some perils attached to job tenure, there is little incentive to keep existing staff. Two, stemming from the above, market mechanisms dominate over institutional mechanisms to the extent that even when institutional mechanisms are in place they are subservient to the market. Three, workers have "target" earnings that are bounded by the rationality of similar skills and by industrially prescribed promotion channels. The effect of this is to exclude external propitious comparisons and to give industrial norms a determining influence on pay. These pressures impact on managers' assumptions when setting a rate of pay, make workers complicit in the maintenance of low pay, and reside both in the behavior of the market and in intra-organizational processes. The heart of the argument is that *unconnected factors act in concert upon the assumptions and expectations of both managers and workers.* The argument goes further to suggest that when this takes place in the context of industrial sector communities, then pay becomes both an economic phenomenon and a cultural one—a norm of the industry that, in turn, maintains the economic status quo. Occupational and industrial communities are a structural feature of the social organization of tourism employment and, as such, are "players" in the pay determination process.

The theoretical perspective used, is somewhat eclectic and selective involving a number of disciplines, but is justified by the focus on one specific yet diverse industry. The analysis assumes sufficient commonality among sectors of tourism to make an industrial framework possible (Riley, Ladkin and Szivas 2002:61–69). The discussion makes one particular contribution to the debate on tourism and employment growth: that if there were an absence of wage inflation, then the pressure for increased labor productivity would be diminished.

PERSPECTIVES ON THE DETERMINANTS OF PAY

The approach to constructing a framework will be to pursue the arguments through five *perspectives*, or different ways of seeing the influences on pay. An obvious place to start is with job attributes and the link to labor market characteristics.

Perspective One: Job Attributes

Hage (1989) argued that the attributes of any job determine the character of the labor market it resides in (with the corollary that to alter a job is to alter its market). Four job attributes are particularly important in terms of effects they engender: one, human capital is simply the amount of education and experience required by a job or possessed by an individual; two, skill specificity or the degree to which the job skills are unique to an organization; three, the degree to which personal qualities, such as personality traits and appearance, count in a job; and, four, the ease with which the output of the job can be measured by management. Each attribute affects the character of the market. At its simplest, the lower the human capital requirements the larger the labor market. By contrast, the higher the specificity, the smaller the market. Similarly, the more personal qualities count in selection the larger will be the market given that they are randomly distributed in society. Furthermore, the more management is able to specify and measure the job the easier it is to recruit and train, which again enlarges the market. The consequent economic logic of all this is that management need pay less as the size of the market increases.

From Adam Smith onwards, the attractiveness of a job and the ease with which it can be learned has been accepted as influencing the reward it carries. The principal issue for tourism is the *combined* effects of attractiveness and easily acquired skills. There are two aspects of this argument: that increasing attractiveness itself makes the labor market larger (subject to human capital constraints) and that where personal traits are a selection criterion, it combines with attractiveness to produce both low pay and pay differentials among people in the same occupation. The real issue of this combined effect is its persistence over time, with people being attracted to jobs with low pay. The commonest explanations involve limited occupational choice and compensatory factors. Thus, economic theories talk of the opportunity costs and rational information-based decisions. Whether individuals' action is on the basis of alternative costs and benefits or follow rational interpretation of market prospects or both is never clear.

Usually complex choice is associated with only high human capital careers, but Williams and Leppel (1994) show that it is even less clear in blue-collar markets where only medium-term vocational education decisions have to be made. It is at least a possibility that, given any level of remuneration, the decisive factors could be non-economic. Although tourism occupations have a number of attractive features (such as glamour, travel, variety, and people orientation), the actual source of attractiveness is, with one exception, immaterial. Attractiveness influences pay through enlarging the market and through that part of attractiveness rooted in the desire for learning. *These two influences draw the same response from management: that of offering lower pay.* When attractiveness is considered against a background of relatively low skills that can be acquired easily, then the effect of these two processes is amplified. For the worker, attractiveness attaches a cost to a tourism occupation.

Normally workers can use organization specific human capital to improve earnings by staying on to take advantage of the organization's need to keep them for their acquired specific skills (Mincer and Jovanovic 1981). This is unlikely to be the case with tourism employment for two reasons. First, employers pay less for a job where tenure will be short because of the learning and consequent advancement process. Learning can be part of the attraction of a job. Rosen (1972) points out that the capacity of a job to teach has a downward effect on the rate of pay. He argues that certain jobs are seen as opportunities to learn and thus employers assume short tenure and offer a rate that represents the role the job is playing in a recognized career progression. He suggests that, in theory, there is always a virtual wage that is above the actual market rate and which represents the rate firms would have to pay if they recruited fully trained and experienced people. By not recruiting fully trained workers, employers forego productivity in favor of lower labor costs. Second, even organization specific skills can be acquired quickly and hence only a limited monetary advantage accrues to the individual. According to human capital theory, experienced workers should have higher pay than the less experienced because they are more productive. This argument is somewhat weakened by the debate over whether "experience" differentials can be explained by "productivity differentials" (Medoff and Abraham 1981). In any case, it is doubtful whether this applies to tourism because the real implication of easy-to-learn skills is that productivity is not strongly related to job tenure. Therefore, there is little incentive to reward tenure. *This is a deflationary influence on levels of pay.*

The arguments so far have been concerned with explanations of the level of pay, not with pay differentials. Although difficult to locate empirically, pay differentials need explanation. Human capital theory suggests that the pay of an individual is primarily attributable to acquired education and experience. It goes on to suggest that rewards to those similarly endowed would be the same across industries and organizations (Becker 1975). By this argument, those who invest in education and those who have more experience should earn more than those who do not. However, arguments have already been made that this may not be the case. Furthermore, if, as in tourism, personal attributes count, then this distorts human capital effects and may produce pay differentials among jobs within an organization and between the same jobs in different organizations. An interesting augmentation of this argument comes from Stinchcombe (1963) who suggests that pay differentials can be explained by differentiating jobs in terms of whether they are "talent additive" or "talent complementary". In the latter case, the individual's output is more than just another person's worth of work. It is disproportionately higher and thus attracts a higher rate of pay. It is easy to imagine a case for some managers, maitre'ds, and chefs of a charismatic persuasion coming into this category.

Perspective Two: Industrial Structure

Notwithstanding the arguments on job attributes, explanations of pay must also come from the industrial structure. The relationship among structural–organizational factors and pay is through mobility and career opportunity. Heightened opportunity can depress basic pay rates and differentials while mobility lessens the power of tenure. The capacity of any industry to provide opportunities is dependent on its size and structure characteristics (Ghiselli 1969). Structure is the enabling factor, which either encourages or discourages job change, location change, and the seeking of advancement

Essentially, the structural arguments relate to employment concentrations. In this respect, the industry has a dual character with many instances of high density, including in resorts, airports and large organizations, as well as in many more geographically fragmented small concentrations such as, hotels, restaurants, visitor attraction centers, and car rental offices. To these components can be added the ownership structure. In tourism, ownership is often concentrated in large organizations but with staff dispersed in a fragmented structure. In these circumstances, management has a choice either to reward all staff in the same way or allow for local circumstances. In terms of pay, the important structural variables are size of company, size of operating unit, and geographical dispersion.

Research suggests that size of company has the greater influence on the rate of pay. One argument to support this assertion is that large companies, because of the opportunities for advancement they offer, attract better workers who are more productive (Evans and Leighton 1989). If the size variable is taken together with the degree of functional specialization within the organization, then this simultaneously forms the opportunity structure. It creates hierarchical levels and specialisms with pay differentials attached. These act as an incentive to all forms of mobility. However, in the light of assumptions of short tenure, it is difficult to see why large companies should, in terms of pay as a recruitment incentive, be any different from small ones. Getting the best people out of an abundant market may not take much of a differential. By contrast, Nolan and Brown (1983) suggest that management is always discriminating even when the market is oversupplied. One arbiter of management's attitude to the labor market is productivity. In their study, they used manufacturing where labor is a direct input to productivity and where tenure is valued. If, individual performance does not affect output, then the case for being discriminating in the marketplace is diminished (another deflationary pressure).

It could be argued that where organizations share a labor market and have occupations in common, then they would display similar pay structures. However, organizational analysis suggests that this may not be true. Contingency theory argues that there is no one effective organization structure and that there is constant adaptation (Donaldson 1996). One outcome of this is that there are differences in the importance allotted to the same job in different organizations. This creates market pay differentials that have no market explanation as they are conceived entirely for intra-organizational purposes. The study by Talbert and Bose (1977) in the retail industry shows the influence of differential value on the same occupation. Such intra-organizational differentials are evidence that management is not passive in the face of market forces even when a surplus exists.

Although it is not possible to regard all tourism occupations as belonging to one single labor market, it is argued that all segmented ones share the structure of the industry and are open to similar influences. Empirical evidence on careers demonstrates that they are pursued across sectors, occupational and organizational borders through ladders created by skill structures (Maillat 1984; Ladkin and Riley 1996). Riley (1991), building on Rosen's idea—that links learning, tenure, and pay—postulates a model of skill and mobility that contains two features: the desire to learn and the existence of an alternative market. Workers acquire skills through deliberate mobility among firms. The argument is that whenever limited on-the-job training opportunities co-exist with a constrained degree of opportunity to change occupation *within* the firm, then high labor turnover follows. By this means the industry renews its skill base. The downside for employees is that it encourages management to assume that short tenure is always the case. At the heart of this model is the transferability of skills across tourism sectors and beyond (a hotel receptionist can become a travel agent clerk and a dental receptionist, or a hotel chef can use the same skills in institutional catering). A more important issue arises when the alternative market has some strong differentiation. If that characteristic is "social hours" of work, which, can be contrasted with the "unsocial hours" of some tourism occupation, then occupations, which share skills across such markets possess what might be called conspicuous opportunity costs. The key factor here is that if an alternative market that can attract workers away exists, then it may constitute an inflationary pressure on tourism pay. The alternative argument would be that such an exit avenue creates more mobility which has the opposite effect.

Perspective Three: Organizational Structure

What distinguishes some sectors of the industry from conformity to the mobility dominated model is the structural device organizations use to offset its effects. This "devise" is the adoption of a strong internal market. Although there is considerable evidence that hotels, irrespective of size or ownership, tend to operate weak internal labor markets (Simms, Hales and Riley 1988), such sectors as airlines have strong internal markets. It might be surprising to some that even large hotel chains appear to have weak internal markets. But, notwithstanding corporate ownership, the hotels themselves live in local labor markets and seek the advantages from such local markets. In theoretical terms, the most powerful motivation for setting up a strong internal market is skill specificity (Doeringer and Piore 1971) and it could be argued that airlines and possibly tour operators contain some fairly unique skills. However, a more likely explanation lies in the need to manage large numbers of people concentrated in one location. These circumstances push management towards a bureaucratic solution involving clear hiring standards, formal promotion criteria, restricted ports of entry, and established pay differentials among jobs. In other words, mechanisms are based on managerial criteria not external market forces. Once pay is set by internal criteria, the influence of the external market is curtailed. One consequence of this is a stable workforce. Trade unions could be part of that strong internal market in which case the negotiation process influences the pay differentials set through job evaluation. The essential argument here is that strong internal labor markets exert an inflationary pressure, because they reward tenure, reduce competition, and push employee pay referents towards groups similarly managed (Cappelli and Sherer 1988). Institutionally determined pay attracts like-for-like comparisons.

The issue of having a stable workforce has to contend with the nature of demand. While it is true that for large parts of the tourism industry, consumer demand is seasonal, the arguments concerning uncertainty go beyond this notion of variable, but reasonably predictable demand patterns (Krakover 1998). Riley, Gore and Kelliher (2000), in arguing a case for economic determinism in human resource management, put forward two aspects of the same argument. First, short-term fluctuations in demand determine labor productivity in that managers seek to control labor costs by manipulating supply through numerical and earnings flexibility. Even within bureaucratically managed sectors, measures of flexibility are incorporated into union agreements. Second, constant daily concern to match supply with fluctuating demand leads to a short-term "mentality" which, in real terms, means "leave it to the market to set the rates of pay".

Fundamentally, weak internal labor markets are the devise that allows recruitment and labor turnover fluctuations to match supply with demand. Another is the use of earnings variation in the form of overtime or flexible pay systems, such as tipping and its variants. Such short-term devises exert a deflationary pressure when the market is plentiful (Fry 1979). Gowler and Legge (1970) have argued convincingly that systems which relate pay and performance directly, of which tipping would be an example, absorb the conflict occurring when supply and demand are temporally mismatched. Feelings of resentment about having to work harder are ameliorated by the fairly instant return. Furthermore, people who work under this kind of pay system simply get used to fluctuations in workload and in earnings. It would be a mistake to underestimate the importance of this micro-effect, because its real value comes from the time effects that accompany the obsession with earnings. Camerer, Babcock, Loewenstein and Thaler (1997) in their study of cabdrivers illustrate the effect of this very precisely in that it bequeaths a "limited horizon" perspective whereby the labor supply calculus boils down to time parameters no larger than the day. It is this short-term horizon that takes the workers attention away from basic pay; less prosaically, the poem *The Poor Wake Up Quickly* captures the effect perfectly (Enright 1968:37). A focus on varying earnings takes the worker's attention away from aspiration towards a higher platform. *In aggregate terms, this earnings focus acts as a deflationary pressure.*

Perspective Four: Wider Issues

Three wider issues are of import to the analysis: business pricing, gender, and the minimum wage. Confining the arguments to managerial responses to the labor market ignores the importance of how management thinks about business. Accepting that uncertainty of consumer demand is a strong motive for controlling labor costs, the same argument is augmented by general pricing approaches at the industry level. The tourism industry, by necessity, forward prices for consumers and builds in flexibility through discounting and incentives. The contrast between the long-term thinking on consumer pricing and the short-term contingency thinking on labor pricing only adds strength to the deflationary pressure of the latter.

Discussion of low pay cannot avoid the role of gender. One central argument is that when an occupation has a high proportion of women, that causes pay to be low. Substantive proof of this comes at two levels: that many low paid occupations are conspicuously populated by women and that intra-occupational differentials often favor men; this is offered as indirect proof that the job could carry higher pay if it wanted to (Hernandez 1996). Attached to this idea are a bundle of issues to do with attachment to the market and discrimination. While not rejecting these arguments, this analysis assumes the more fundamental position that the economic system produces low paid jobs irrespective of who does them. The fact that high proportions of the occupants of such jobs are women, or for that matter young people, do not cause the level of pay. It tempers the discrimination argument and points the finger at the nature of jobs (Murgatroyd 1982). This is a hard stance to maintain when women suffer greater levels of discrimination and, by inference, tourism may be one of the culprits (Bonjour and Gerfin 2001). However, this does not alter the basic tenet that jobs are priced by the economic process, not the likely incumbents.

The literature on the minimum wage has as its main theme the question of whether or not minimum wage regulation reduces employment, and the answer is both contradictory and inconclusive (Card and Krueger 1995). In relation to pay, the key question is whether a base level minimum causes a "knock-on effect". This takes the form of, one, rates rising above the minimum as the conditions of competition change; two, differentials in the same organization above the base rate rise as a consequence; and, three, rates of pay in jobs which are not covered by the regulation but which are close in skill and proximity come under pressure to rise. As workers covered by minimum wage regulation usually do not have negotiating power, any knock-on effect is due to market shortage. Minimum wages could have the effect of enlarging the market by absorbing the unemployed. What evidence exists suggests that minimum wages are more a spur to productivity increases than an inflationary pressure on pay.

Perspective Five: Satisfaction

Notwithstanding the structural arguments, a comprehensive explanation has to address the psychological issues. For one thing, any exploration of the attractiveness of tourism has to confront not just the fact of low pay, but that it is tolerated and often exists along side high job satisfaction. Two theoretical relationships are salient here: that between pay satisfaction and job satisfaction and that between level of pay and pay satisfaction. However, before exploring these relationships, two issues need to be set aside, one, the individual's general attitude towards money. The "value placed on money" is accepted as a distinct variable, independent of wealth and level of pay (Furnham and Argyle 1998). Tang (1995), for example, found that a high value on money produced low pay satisfaction, irrespective of the level of pay. Two, the affect of performance on satisfaction is not considered here because it has been addressed in the structural arguments relating to productivity and individual differentials.

From the perspective of established models that connect satisfaction, commitment, and labor turnover, pay is usually seen as part of satisfaction (Brown and McIntosh 2000; Price and Mueller 1981). If pay is part of satisfaction, then incidence of low pay and high job satisfaction are hard to explain. However, there is evidence that some low paid workers, in their evaluation of their lot, separate pay and job and are thus able to maintain dissatisfaction with pay and high job satisfaction (Riley, Lockwood, Powell-Perry and Baker 1998). Other explanations involve compensating factors. The fact that some kind of trade-off takes place seems likely (Shapira 1981). The service work itself suggests compensating attributes that may be "traded" for pay. These include workers recognising intrinsic value in service work (particularly its variety and scope for autonomy) and valuing the small working groups in which it is normally conducted and certain fringe benefits. As a consequence of this, they seek satisfaction from such attributes, despite low pay. This may be a rationalization based on perceived life-chances or on worse alternatives. There is a distinct feeling of "not factory" in their expectations (Shamir 1975). This notion of compensation assumes that pay is conceived as being a part of the evaluation of the job. Therefore, to an extent, how the individual defines "job" is as important as how they construe satisfaction with it. To add to the complexity pay satisfaction itself has been shown to be multidimensional (Carraher 1991; Judge 1993) with implications for how it is perceived (Carraher and Buckley 1996). In this context, the role of the pay system and the pay structure are prominent variables (Heneman, Greenberger and Strasser 1988). One further complication is the degree to which satisfaction with the organization is part of the individual's calculus (Chiu 1999; Shaw, Duffy, Jenkins and Gupta 1999). If it is, then that opens the possibility of a relationship between pay and organizational satisfaction, distinct from job satisfaction.

One argument that cannot be ignored is that pay, despite being relatively low, is not considered as such by recipients. This brings to the fore the level of pay and how its justice is evaluated. The literature is consistent in showing that lower paid workers express higher satisfaction with pay than those paid more (Brown and McIntosh 1998; Cappelli and Sherer 1988). However, the explanation for this does not rely on a split of pay from job satisfaction, as after a point money becomes less important to satisfaction and hence the higher paid consider other aspects more salient. The idea behind this is that the crossover point is "target earnings". Once these earnings are reached, other job attributes take over in the satisfaction calculus. At this point, research becomes problematic, because target earnings are subjectively determined and are hard to measure; and thus research often has to adopt proxy measures, such as expected earnings or mean earnings (Drakopoulos and Theodossiou 1997).

Despite this, there is substance in the idea that pay satisfaction is influenced by aspiration. Considerable support for the idea that people set their own "target level" and that this can be estimated comes from the direct study of feelings of underpayment. Mirowsky (1987) found that such feelings were in fact detached from actual pay but related to a social norm based on what people ought to earn in a specified category or class. He argues that the needs and status of groups play a role in the formation of the benchmark. This is not to deny the workings of equity-driven pay-on-pay comparisons that promote like-on-like comparisons that lead to low aspiration. This argument moves comparison to another level of abstraction where consensus and social norms play a role in pay satisfaction through judgements of the distribution of earnings (Alves and Ross 1978). This line of argument is the basis on which it may be said that low paid workers are complicit in maintaining their situation. The evocation of social norms is a more diffused argument than the commonly applied reference group theory with its taxonomies of pay referents (Goodman 1974). Furthermore, Blau (1994) has extended this work by showing that pay referents are of differential importance. The pragmatic problem for tourism is that there is a dearth of research on the comparative processes and the identity of "significant others" used by tourism workers. It is a matter of speculation.

Speculation, however, is not without the circumstantial evidence of tourism workers living and working in occupational communities. Large employment concentrations isolated from the general population by unsocial hours of work, common skills and shared identity all point towards to the preconditions for an occupation community (Salaman 1974). Against this background, the suggestion that pay comparisons are kept within industry boundaries seems reasonable and leads towards the argument that pay levels are maintained by a cultural norm as well as by economic imperatives. What is being evoked here is not a full blown comparative system that reference group theory would predict, but a gentler form of using pay referents simply as a guide to expectation rather than as a strategic instrument for negotiation. If pay referents are constrained by pragmatic considerations and confined to sector cultures, then pay levels may be maintained by the assumptions of all people working on those sectors.

A case must exist for low pay being maintained by deflationary norms shared by both workers and managers in the industry. In other words, the forces that determine pay are embedded in the industrial cultures of tourism sectors that, in turn, share as many similar features as they have common job attributes and structures. The finding of Lee and Kang (1998), that tourism pay displays a narrow distribution is, indirect, modest support to the arguments above. The issue, which emerges from looking at such processes is whether pay is separated from job satisfaction. If it is, then the suggestion is that workers are less likely to push for pay increases. Other issues explore what level of earnings workers aspire to and whether the expected pay level is determined by industrial culture born out of a commonality of skills and re-enforced by an occupational community.

The Conceptual Framework

The conceptual framework attempts to explain pay determination and does so through five perspectives. Their synthesis draws on the prominent features of tourism employment identified as the attractiveness of jobs, transferable skills, the social-unsocial hours exchange, the fact that productivity is unhinged from performance, the need for flexibility of supply, the fragmented small-scale structure, the dominance of local labor markets, long forward pricing with short-term contingency, and the embeddedness of low pay in industry culture. The outcome of the interaction among the factors and individual decisions can be summarized as that tourism jobs have, in Hall's (1976) terms, a high context attraction-compensatory character; that there is considerable inducement for mobility; that, at least in terms of pay, there is no obvious reason for large firms to behave substantially differently from small ones; that the conflict between consumer price setting and demand responsive cost management forces labor to yield (labor is manipulated because it can be); and that most of the pressures identified in the analysis were deflationary, irrespective of actual level of pay. The central plank on which the framework is built is the relatively low levels of easily acquired skills leading management not to reward tenure. The *working principle* of the framework is that the factors consort together to impact on the assumptions made by managers about jobs and markets and by workers about their horizons. The management simply assumes that the labor market will provide, that there is no reason to reward tenure, that the need for flexibility is constant, and that there is a tolerance of low pay.

However, it is one thing to synthesize a set of factors but quite another to suggest how that synthesis takes place. The use of assumptions as the working principle needs to be substantiated. In this respect, the more important question is where the synthesis takes place. Given that the framework leads towards managerial decision-making and worker acceptance processes, the obvious place to look is cognition. It is in this schema that the holistic concepts that materialize as assumptions reside. The conceptual framework being advocated is depicted in a similar way in the minds of the players to that of Dutton (1993) where managers' behavior is assumptive. However, these assumptions are themselves the product of the process of social norm formation from experience of the environment. Here the evidence from the organizational culture literature is clear: that managers develop ways of thinking somewhat prescribed by organizational norms (Spender 1998). The basic process is problem identification and resolution. Solving the same or similar problems becomes a matter of mental habit. The same process exists on an industry level, with this as the *active principle* within the framework. This is very close to Spender's notion of industrial recipes where managers in different organizations within an industry share the same levels of uncertainty and incomplete information and come to the same interpretation of their problems so that what constitutes "common sense" is an industrial norm (Spender 1989).

One of the largest assertions of the framework is that there is "always" a large market available to recruiters, which implies that there is no such thing as a labor shortage (Riley 1991). This must be challenged because a genuine shortage is one possible inflationary pressure. In the first place, it has to be conceded that high velocity labor turnover can give the illusion of a shortage where none exists. Conversely, extreme instability can hide real shortages. A firm can be in a large market but it may not feel like one as far as recruitment is concerned (Manning 2000). However, the fact that if shortages have occurred but made no impression on aggregate earnings, the most likely explanation is the improvising ability of management to cope without raising pay (Alpert 1986; Riley 1990). One strategic option is the importation of labor (Choi, Woods and Murrmann 2000). Apart from this, the only other strong inflationary forces identified were those of a consumer desire for quality that eventually worked its way into a need for a stable workforce, and unionism.

Another assertion of the framework that needs to be qualified concerns productivity and pay. The impression may have been given that productivity does not count in terms of pay determination. This would not be entirely true, as the qualitative effects count. But if labor productivity is essentially determined by demand patterns, then the input of performance, whether high or low, is limited by the contingent throughput of tourists (Riley 1999). *It is this circumstance that unhinges productivity from pay levels.* Therefore, it could be suggested that the framework and its processes are really the product of size and maturity and would only be applicable to established mass tourism destinations. The logic is that norms take time to form and need re-enforcement. Thus, in circumstances of a new and isolated development, the distribution of rewards may be different from established employment concentrations. This may be true and is a subject worthy of research. However, even if reward distribution is unencumbered by deflationary processes, it will still be a product of cultural norms, whether industrialized or not.

CONCLUSION

The framework discussed in this paper is one dominated by deflationary pressures on labor pricing and by the heavy influence of industry norms on worker aspiration. While economic development is concerned with larger issues than wage inflation/deflation, the existence of a process for producing either is not without significance. The creation of new jobs alone does not lead automatically to the creation of wealth for the indigenous population. Examples of extended supply such as shift work, long hours, and double jobbing can be found alongside community-performed tasks and work sharing, as well as examples of conditional supply such as lifestyle constraints. In these circumstances, it is worth looking again at the motives of people who work in tourism and the way they supply their labor.

One of the issues raised in the analysis was that of "target wages", or the level of aspiration expressed by pay. The argument was that this was a relative value governed by "uninspiring" industry norms. This may be a disingenuous argument because the comparison used may not be relative but absolute, that is, against some "level of subsistence" or reserve wage. Though economists can express such a level in various ways, it is also a matter of individual definition (Sharif 1986). This creates a link between the individual's evaluation of their low pay and their standard of living that is independent of comparisons with others. What is an acceptable standard is self-defined and thus a motivational factor. This brings the arguments to the distinction between working poor and others. It might not be easy for the image of tourism to accept that some of its workers are "working poor", but it is a realistic view that they are.

Sharif (2001) argues that there are differences between the motives and behaviors that lie behind supplying labor of the working poor and working non-poor and that the classical explanation of the acceptance of low pay as being due to "irrational limited aspiration" is flawed. That is not to say that it would not be perfectly reasonable for any analysis to assume the normal supply curve for labor (upward-sloping then backwards bending)—which has at its lowest point on the curve the amount of pay capable of drawing the individual into a tourism job performed at the lowest level of effort—but to do so with caution. The assumption of this curve is that the low point represents some kind of subsistence level or reservation wage that is acceptable. There is in fact no guarantee that this point at which people take up work actually provides an acceptable standard of living. Sharif argues that when it does not, consideration should be given to an alternative supply curve that shows a negative relationship between wage rates and the amount of labor supplied (more is supplied for less pay). In this conception, the curve falls forward in a gentle downward slope. He argues that where the level of pay is the sole income and does not give a subsistence standard of living, workers put in extended hours to get as much as is possible from what is available. This would apply just as well to a self-defined subsistence level. By contrast, where tourism is based on community activity or a family firm, then everyone cooperates to give each member a share of the pot. In these circumstances, people give their labor knowing their share is not optimal and may not be meeting their personal target earnings. In both cases, there is a "distress" element to the selling of labor. There can be conflicts within internal divisions of an indigenous population sharing a fairly fixed amount of reward (van den Berge 1992). In other words distress selling is a two-way valve—having to work longer to scoop as much as possible from the pool and have to work extended hours for a fixed amount, simply to maintain the pool.

Distress selling carries both a condition and a consequence. The former is that the self-definition of an adequate standard is influenced by other sources of income and possibly capital. Often tourism incomes are mixed in with other sources. A full understanding of tourism incomes and their relationship to labor supply requires these other sources, such as agriculture, family, and community, to be considered. Indeed many tourism products are built out of capital owned by the poor. The consequence is the effect on the quality of tourism products of a workforce that is selling its labor in a distress condition. An unresponsive laborforce is a drag upon economic development (Miracle and Fetter 1970). The presence of deflationary pressures suggests that, at least theoretically, this form of extended labor supply can occur both in a developed and underdeveloped situation. If this is the case, there are issues concerning incentives which are complicated if there is a negative relationship between wages and supply.

Apart from institutional procedures—such as minimum wage legislation and unionism—the central inflationary drive appears to come only from the desire for higher quality driven by competition. Generally speaking, high quality is associated with consistency, which leads to the issue of having a stable workforce. The evidence that within tourism units, stable cohorts co-exist along with a mobile population is problematic for management. Both are needed, which begets the problem of how the stable proportion of the workforce is managed. Human resource management has the dilemma of handling simultaneously a stable and an unstable workforce. The operational management literature expresses the problem in terms of core and periphery workers and implies separate treatment often going to the extreme of outsourcing. The real choice is between a strong and a weak internal labor market.

If the conceptual framework discussed here is valid, then the stable elements of the workforce may well have their pay determined by the deflationary pressures maintained by the unstable. This issue returns the size variable to the fore because only concerted action by a number of large firms in the same local market is likely to have any affect. However, it has been argued within the framework that there is no real reason why large organizations should behave very differently from small ones. Against this is the argument that where large firms, operating in close proximity, each manage bureaucratically, then this has a knock-on stabilizing effect on the local labor market (Edwards 1979). What this represents is a move towards institutional ideas on management structure and control by firm. The rationale for such behavior is purely internal and makes no concessions to external factors (Tolbert and Zucker 1999). The relevance of such a theoretical approach depends upon the *coexistence* of a degree of bureaucracy and a strong internal labor market. The case of these two conditions coexisting in tourism, where information technology has enabled management to use bureaucratic controls but without a strong internal labor market, is rare.

To summarize, the framework does not claim to be comprehensive. However, it does claim to fit the circumstances of tourism *where easily acquired, transferable skills co-exist and engender weak internal labor markets in organizations that economically are bound to a rate of throughput*. It could be relevant to other industries with similar characteristics. The framework goes beyond economic theory to show how economic, structural, and psychological factors act in concert. It also shows that the problems and solutions exist at different levels of abstraction. The sociological argument that (economic) decision-making becomes embedded within the social relationships and culture of organizations can be extended (Brinton and Nee 1998). The argument here is exactly the same, but the domain of such embeddedness is *not organization but industry*. For that reason, the roots are deeper and cannot be disturbed by organizational change. In other words, the problems and the solutions are located in different places.

The task of substantiating the framework requires research in four areas. One would be concerned with the substantive structural and pay factors. Another would examine how the synthesis takes place in the minds of the players (Phillips 1996). A third would be concerned with the extent of institutional influences on pay and a fourth would look at the tolerance of low pay. The problem of validating in substantive terms is one of confronting limited wage data and one of having to align that data to mobility patterns. In a sense, the study of mobility would be initially more indicative of how the framework functions than differentials, although the latter are clearly necessary. In the respect of the psychological approach, two possible study areas suggest themselves. The first is to conduct research on how managers perceive the labor market (their working principle of how it functions). This would connect the market view to organizational decision-making (Gore and Riley 2000). The second would find out the process of norm-formation on an industry-wide scale. It is time for the restoration of industrial culture as an important area of study. Knowing what managers and workers share offers a chance of understanding their assumptions about each other and the effects of these on decisions and their acceptance. In similar vein, the incursion of institutionalism into wage determination in circumstances of deregulated markets should be investigated. As part of this approach, more needs to be known about pay differentials within organizations. Finally, at a psychological level, it is essential to learn more about how the process of acceptance of low paid work and of low pay are related. ◪

Managing Tourism Firms

REFERENCES

Alves, W., and P. Ross
  1978   Who Should Get What? Judgements of the Distribution of Earnings. American Journal of Sociology 84:541–564.
Alpert, W.
  1986   The minimum Wage in the Restaurant Industry. New York: Praeger.
Becker, G.
  1975   Human Capital. New York: National Bureau of Economic Research.
Blau, G.
  1994   Testing the Effects of Level and Importance of Pay Referents on Pay Level Satisfaction. Human Relations 47:1251–1268.
Bonjour, D., and M. Gerfin
  2001   The Unequal Distribution of Unequal Pay: An Empirical Analysis of the Gender Wage Gap in Switzerland. Empirical Economics 26:407–427.
Brinton, M., and V. Nee
  1998   The New Institutionalism in Sociology. New York: Russell Sage Foundation.
Brown, D., and S. McIntosh
  1998   If You're Happy and You Know It....Job Satisfaction in the Low Wage Service Sector. Centre for Economic Performance. London School of Economics. Discussion Paper 405.
  2000   Job Satisfaction and Labour Turnover in the Retail and Hotel Sectors. In Policy Measures for Low-Wage Employment in Europe, W. Salverda, C. Lucifora and B. Nolan, eds., pp. 218–237. Cheltenham: Edward Elgar.
Camerer, C., L. Babcock, G. Loewenstein, and R. Thaler
  1997   Labor Supply of New York Cabdrivers: One Day at a Time. The Quarterly Journal of Economics 112:407–441.
Carraher, S., and M. Buckley
  1996   Cognitive Complexity and the Perceived Dimensionality of Pay Satisfaction. Journal of Applied Psychology 81:102–109.
Carraher, S.
  1991   On the Dimensionality of the Pay Satisfaction Questionnaire. Psychological Reports 69:887–890.
Cappelli, P., and P. Sherer
  1988   Satisfaction, Market Wages and Labor Relations: An Airline Study. Industrial Relations 27:56–73.
Card, D., and A. Krueger
  1995   Equilibrium Wage Differentials and Employer Size. Center for Mathematical Studies in Economics and Management Science. Discussion paper 860, October. North Western University Illinois.
Chiu, R.
  1999   Does Perception of Pay Equity, Pay Satisfaction and Job Satisfaction Mediate the Effect of Positive Affectivity on Work Motivation? Social Behaviour and Personality 28:177–184.
Choi, J., R. Woods, and S. Murrmann
  2000   International Labor Markets and the Migration of Labor Forces as an Alternative Solution for Labor Shortages in the Hospitality Industry. International Journal of Contemporary Hospitality Management 12:61–66.
Drakopoulos, S., and I. Theodossiou
  1997   Job Satisfaction and Target Earnings. Journal of Economic Psychology 18:693–704.
Doeringer, P., and M. Piore
  1971   Internal Labor Markets and Manpower Analysis. Lexington: Heath Lexington Books.
Donaldson, L.
  1996   The Normal Science of Structural Contingency Theory. In Studying Organization: Theory and Method, S. Clegg and C. Hardy, eds., pp. 165–174. London: Sage.

Dutton, J.
  1993 Interpretations on Automatic: A Different View of Strategic Issue Diagnosis. Journal of Management Studies 39:357–399.
Edwards, R.
  1979 Contested Terrain: the Tansformation of the Workplace in the Twentieth Century. London: Heinemann.
Enright, D.
  1968 Selected Poems. London: Chatto and Windus.
Evans, D., and L. Leighton
  1989 Why Do Small Firms Pay Less. Journal of Human Resources 24:299–318.
Fry, J.
  1979 A Labour Turnover Model of Wage Determination in Developing Economies. The Economic Journal 89:353–369.
Furnham, A., and M. Argyle
  1998 The Psychology of Money. London: Routledge.
Ghiselli, E.
  1969 The Efficacy of Advancement on the Basis of Merit in Relation to Structural Properties of the Organization. Organizational Behavior and Human Performance 4:402–414.
Goodman, P.
  1974 An Examination of Referents Use in the Evalation of Pay. Organizational Behavior And Human Performance 12:170–195.
Gowler, D., and K. Legge
  1970 The Wage Payment System. In Local Labour Markets and Wage Structures, D. Robinson, ed., pp. 168–214. London: Gower Press.
Gore, J., and M. Riley
  2000 A Study of the Perception of the Labour Market by Human Resource Managers n the UK Hotel Industry: A Cognitive Approach. Tourism and Hospitality Research 2:232–241.
Hage, J.
  1989 The Sociology of Traditional Economic Problems: Products and Labor Markets. Work and Occupations 16:416–445.
Hall, F.
  1976 Beyond Culture. New York: Anchor Books.
Heneman, R., D. Greenberger, and S. Strasser
  1988 The Relationship Between Pay-for-Performance Perceptions and Pay Satisfaction. Personnel Psychology 41:745–759.
Hernandez, P.
  1996 Segregacion ocupacional de la mujer y discriminacion salarial. Revista de Economia Aplicada 4:57–80.
Judge, T.
  1993 Validity of the Dimensions of the Pay Satisfaction Questionnaire: Evidence of Differential Prediction. Personnel Psychology 46:331–355.
Krakover, S.
  1998 Employment Adjustment Trends in Tourism Hotels in Israel. Tourism Recreation Research 23:23–32.
Ladkin, A., and M. Riley
  1996 Mobility and Sructure in the Career Paths of UK Hotels Managers: A Labour Market Hybrid of the Bureaucratic Model. Tourism Management 17:443–452.
Lee, C., and S. Kang
  1998 Measuring Earnings Inequality and Median Earnings in the Tourism Idustry. Tourism Management 19:349–358.
Manning, A.
  2000 Pretty Vacant: Recruitment in Low-Wage Labour Markets. Oxford Bulletin of Economics and Statistics 62(Special Issue):747–770.
Maillat, D.
  1984 Mobility Channels: An Instrument or Analysis and Regulating Local Labour Markets. International Labour Review 130:349–362.

Medoff, J., and K. Abraham
    1981   Are Those Paid More Really More Productive? The Case of Experience.
        Journal of Human Resources 16:186–216.
Mincer, J., and B. Jovanovic
    1981   Labor Mobility and Wages. *In* Studies in Labor Markets, S. Rosen, ed.,
        pp. 21–64. University of Chicago Press: Chicago.
Miracle, M., and B. Fetter
    1970   The Backward-Sloping Labour Supply Function and African Economic
        Behaviour. Economic Development and Cultural Change 18:240–251.
Mirowsky, J.
    1987   The Psycho-Economics of Feeling Underpaid: Distributive Justice and the
        Earnings of Husbands and Wives. American Journal of Sociology 92:1404–
        1434.
Murgatroyd, L.
    1982   Gender and Occupational Stratification. Sociological Review 30:572–602.
Nolan, P., and W. Brown
    1983   Competition and Workplace Wage Determination. Oxford Bulletin of
        Economics and Statistics 45:269–287.
Phillips, M.
    1996   Industrial Mindsets: Exploring the Culture of two Macro-Organizational
        Settings. *In* Cognition Within and Between Organizations, J. Meindl, C. Stub-
        bart and J. Porac, eds., pp. 475–508. London: Sage.
Price, J., and C. Mueller
    1981   Professional Turnover: The Case of Nurses. New York: SP Medical Books.
Riley, M.
    1990   The Labour Retention Strategies of UK Hotel Managers. The Service
        Industries Journal 10:614–618.
    1991   An Analysis of Hotel Labour Markets *In*: Progress in Tourism, Recreation
        and Hospitality Management. C. Cooper ed., vol 3, pp. 232-246 .London:
        Belhaven.
    1999   Re-defining the Debate on Hospitality Productivity. Tourism and Hospi-
        tality Research 1:182–186.
Riley, M., A. Lockwood, J. Powell-Perry, and M. Baker
    1998   Job Satisfaction, Organisation Commitment and Occupational Culture: A
        Case from the UK Pub Industry. Progress in Tourism and Hospitality Research
        4:159–168.
Riley, M., J. Gore, and C. Kelliher
    2000   Economic Determinism and Human Resource Management Practice in
        the Hospitality and Tourism Industry. Tourism and Hospitality Research
        2:118–128.
Riley, M., A. Ladkin, and E. Szivas
    2002   Tourism Employment: Analysis and Planning. Clevedon: Channel View
        Publications.
Rosen, S.
    1972   Learning and Experience in the Labor Market. Journal of Human
        Resources 7:326–342.
Salaman, G.
    1974   Community and Occupation. Cambridge: Cambridge University Press.
Shamir, B.
    1975   A Sudy of the Work Environment and Atitudes to Work of Employees in
        a Number of British Hotels. PhD dissertation in sociology, London School
        of Economics.
Shapira, Z.
    1981   Making Trade-offs between Job Attitutes. Organizational Behavior and
        Human Performance 28:331–355.
Sharif, M.
    1986   The Concept and Measurement of Subsistence: A Survey of the Litera-
        ture. World Development 14:555–577.
    2001   Inverted "S": The Complete Neo-classical Labour-Supply Function. Inter-
        national Labour Review 139:409–435.

Shaw, J., M. Duffy, D. Jenkins, and N. Gupta
  1999 Positive and Negative Affect: Signal Sensitivity and Pay Satisfaction. Journal of Management 25:189–206.
Simms, J., C. Hales, and M. Riley
  1988 Examination of the Concept of Internal Labour Markets in UK Hotels. International Journal of Tourism Management 9(3):3–12.
Spender, J.
  1989 Industry Recipes. Oxford: Blackwell.
  1998 The Dynamics of Individual and Organizational Knowledge. *In* Managerial and Organizational Cognition: Theory Methods and Research, C. Eden and J. Spender, eds., pp. 35–67. London: Sage.
Stinchcombe, A.
  1963 Some Empirical Consequences of the Davis–Moore Theory of Stratification. American Sociological Review 38:805–808.
Tang, T.
  1995 The Development of a Short Money Ethic Scale: Attitudes toward Money and Pay Satisfaction Revisited. Personality and Individual Differences 19:809–816.
Talbert, J., and C. Bose
  1977 Wage-Attainment Processes: The Retail Clerk Case. American Journal of Sociology 83:403–424.
Tolbert, P., and I. Zucker
  1999 The Institutionalization of Institutional Theory. *In* Studying Organization, S. Clegg and C. Hardy, eds. London: Sage.
van den Berge, P.
  1992 Tourism and the Ethnic Division of Labor. Annals of Tourism Research 19:234–249.
Williams, M., and K. Leppel
  1994 Modelling Occupational Choice in Blue-collar Labor Markets. Economics of Education Review 13:243–250.

Submitted 1 May 2001. Resubmitted 10 February 2002. Resubmitted 4 June 2002. Accepted 16 September 2002. Final version 7 October 2002. Refereed anonymously. **Coordinating Editor: Abraham Pizam**

Part VI
Sectoral Studies

[34]

Available online at www.sciencedirect.com

SCIENCE DIRECT•

Tourism Management 26 (2005) 185–201

TOURISM
MANAGEMENT

www.elsevier.com/locate/tourman

ELSEVIER

Managing gardens for visitors in Great Britain: a story of continuity and change

Joanne Connell

Department of Marketing, University of Stirling, Stirling Scotland FK9 4LA, UK

Received 14 May 2003; accepted 6 October 2003

Abstract

Garden visiting is a popular activity in Great Britain. This paper identifies the historical antecedents and accompanying development of garden visiting as a form of tourism and recreation, focusing on the management of gardens open to the public in both time and space. Such an approach reveals that many gardens have been established for some considerable time and visiting is by no means a new pastime. The paper reports on a survey of garden owners in Great Britain and uses historical reconstructions to assess the theme of continuity and change in garden management and visiting through time.
© 2003 Elsevier Ltd. All rights reserved.

Keywords: Garden visiting; Great Britain; Gardens; History

1. Introduction

Most conventional research on tourism issues has adopted either an historical or a contemporary theme-related methodology, but few studies have developed a mixed-methods approach where the historical patterns of development are interwoven with current issues to highlight and explain both continuity and change in tourism phenomenon. Garden visiting lends itself to this mode of analysis, as it is not an activity specific to the 20th and 21st centuries, but has an historical continuity traceable from the 16th century. In this paper, gardens are broadly defined as cultivated grounds open to the pleasure-seeking public, but the definition does not include urban parks, which are different in form and use.

This paper contends that contemporary garden visiting represents the historical evolution of a form of recreation deeply embedded in popular culture and seeks to understand current reasons for opening gardens to the public by examining the interconnections which exist in terms of *continuity* of the gardens as a visitor resource and *change* in the ways gardens are managed for visitors. Such an approach reveals that many gardens have been established for some considerable

time and visiting is by no means a new pastime but complements the rise of country house visiting, which has created a distinct tourism and recreation phenomenon (Hunt, 1964; Towner, 1996). Undeniably, most gardens were not created for visiting *per se*, being privately owned and consumed. Through time, gardens have adopted and adapted their facilities for this function—the consumption of pleasure by the public. To illustrate these points, the paper commences with a discussion on the origins of garden visiting, followed by an analysis of the first national study of gardens as visitor attractions in Great Britain to examine their evolution, operation and management approaches.

2. The early origins of garden visiting

The origins of present-day large-scale participation in country house and garden visiting as a discrete activity can be traced back to the early Victorian period in Great Britain. Prior to this time, visiting country houses was a pastime predominantly of the upper class (Towner, 1996), thus distinguishing between the practice and the scale of garden visiting. In other words, garden visiting existed as an elite pursuit long before it became a popular and widespread leisure activity. It is impossible to state with any degree of accuracy when and where

E-mail address: j.j.connell@stir.ac.uk (J. Connell).

garden visiting first emerged, as early activity is based in the private arena, and printed guides to gardens were given to visitors according to the owner's degree of interest in the visitor experience. Towner (1996), for example, outlines the growth in country house visits by the affluent classes across Northern Europe from the 16th century as the likely origins of this process. In Britain, the aristocracy, politicians, wealthy merchants and professionals created houses and gardens for periods of leisure, as an alternative to a full-time life in medieval towns. Gifford, McWilliam, and Walker (1984), for example, recorded the growth of pleasure villas around Edinburgh, as early as the mid-16th century. A major theme of social life centred on visiting the country estate of friends and associates, and the large Elizabethan house became a social and cultural centre (Girouard, 1978). Thomas (1983) and Hoskins (1988) argued that as a growing taste for gardening as recreation became prominent, pleasure gardens and parks became a central feature of country houses, and a stream of literature on gardening emerged, beginning with Hills's _The Profitable Arte of Gardening_ in 1568 (Strong, 1991). Such activities are prevalent in the later writings of literary figures such as Evelyn, in the 17th century and Pope in the 18th century. Diffusion and interchange of garden ideas was stimulated by emerging opportunities for foreign and domestic travel. Some of the initial influences on garden development in England arose from the Grand Tour. Travellers were eager to see for themselves the landscapes that were reflected in the admired Renaissance style (Crandell, 1993). The French and Dutch styles of formal garden, which had come to dominate the English garden until the early 1700s, were rejected in favour of designs inspired by nature. Designers such as William Kent and Lancelot 'Capability' Brown were engaged to create the most desirable parks and gardens of the time (Trevelyan, 1942; Horn, 1980). European travellers admired the new English parks in the 1700s (Hunt & Willis, 1975) and the park phenomenon was taken home. The dissemination of new styles and novel ideas in early British gardens was again a function of tourism and garden visiting on a micro-scale, initially with neighbours visiting each other.

2.1. The 18th and 19th centuries

Girouard (1978, p. 210) argued that walking or driving around the parkland or garden of one's own property or that of someone else was a significant part of aristocratic leisure time in the 18th century, commenting that "guests or visitors, having done the circuit of the rooms, did the circuit of the grounds". Polite visiting, as it was called, was generally undertaken by the urban elite and Ousby (1990) notes that many country houses and gardens attracted tourists travelling on circuits of the country or on short visits from the towns. Jane

Austen's work candidly reflects social trends of those times, and gardens are no exception. Her novel, _Pride and Prejudice_ (1813), features this form of polite tourism, where the heroine Elizabeth Bennett visits Pemberley, Lord Darcy's Derbyshire estate. In another part of the story, Mrs. Bennett is keen to show her guests that her garden was up-to-date with gardening fashions. A recent BBC television production of _Pride and Prejudice_ emphasised the importance of the garden setting in the novel, where producers consulted the Garden History Society in order to portray historical accuracy in garden scenes (Batey, 1996).

Certainly, landowners took pride in the presentation of their houses and gardens, and landscaping became a major preoccupation on many estates towards the end of the 18th century. Diaries from this time reveal that country house owners willingly opened up their grounds including Powis Castle and Warwick Castle (Gard, 1989). Motivations for opening included a desire to improve and inform the aspirations and tastes of the visitors (Fearnley-Whittingstall, 2002).

The visiting phenomenon described so far was of little relevance to the working class population. Mandler (1997) indicated that the Victorian era was the first age of mass country house visiting. It is contended that the growth of visits to country houses and gardens is mirrored by the growth of leisure generally, and countryside leisure more specifically. The factors that stimulated demand included: transport improvements and cheaper fares; increases in leisure time and disposable income; the desire to escape from urban life, and; changes in attitude to the rural environment. Such factors are well-documented in the rural recreation and tourism literature (e.g. Glyptis, 1991; Patmore, 1983; Clarke & Critcher, 1985), but never before linked with garden visiting. A number of owners opened up parkland to visitors for informal recreation after a sense of assumed personal responsibility. Opening houses to the public was not perceived as a way of generating revenue from the estate. Conversely, in many cases, the reality was that house owners viewed opening to the public as a financial and logistical burden, but pursued as an act of benevolence, based on the notion that the land-owning classes had a social obligation to provide space and opportunity for recreation. Many large cities were relatively close to some of the earliest estates open to the public; for example, Chatsworth House in Derbyshire was a wagon ride from Sheffield. Thomas Cook's first organised excursion to an historic house was to Chatsworth in 1849.

Constantine (1981) attributes the first increase in public interest in gardens in the 19th century to when the urban middle class began to emulate the upper class traditions of creating and enjoying gardens, and the rational recreation movement of late 19th century encouraged the working class to take up gardening as

J. Connell / Tourism Management 26 (2005) 185–201 187

a pursuit. A growing public interest in gardening and botany was also influential in the establishment of botanical gardens in the major cities during the early 1800s (Chadwick, 1966; Lasdun, 1991; Garrod, Pickering, & Willis, 1993). Through the late 19th century and into the early 20th century, park and garden visiting was an activity particularly advocated by social reformers and the enabling legislation of the mid-part of the century facilitated the setting out of urban parks for recreation (Clarke & Critcher, 1985; Billinge, 1996). The emerging paternalistic and health-promoting view of outdoor leisure (Taylor, 1995; Worpole, 1997) and the perception of the welfare benefits of outdoor recreation prevailed in social policy through to the 1930s and beyond.

2.2. Managing visitors in the 18th and 19th centuries

In the 18th century, garden visiting was simply a case of turning up on the doorstep, and, if the housekeeper approved, the head gardener would show the visitors around the garden. It was expected that visitors would provide a tip. Even before the age of mass garden visiting, William Shenstone of The Leasowes in Warwickshire, saw mid-18th century visitors as a nuisance and described them as 'Sunday starers'. An engraved inscription along the garden's circuit stated:

> "*And tread with awe these favour'd bowers, Nor wound the shrubs, nor bruise the flowers; So may your path with sweets abound So may your couch with rest be crown'd! But harm betide the wayward swain, Who dares our hallow'd haunts profane.*" (quoted in Fearnley-Whitingstall, 2002, p. 141)

Despite this apparent concern for visitor damage to the garden, Shenstone produced a descriptive brochure for visitors, one of the first garden owners to do so.

Gardens created in the 18th century were a major attraction of their time. The landscape gardens of the early part of the century, with their temples, grottos, follies and man-made pre-defined vistas, attracted the most visitors, and the more fanciful and outrageous, the more visitors would flock to such gardens. Porteous (1996, p. 87) commented that 18th century landscape gardens operated "a kind of outdoor theatre" and "a form of mood-management", creating emotional responses in visitors such as delight, anxiety, terror and reflection on experiencing the tranquil, unkempt and surprise elements of a garden.

Many gardens achieved fame at this time and guidebooks, plans and proper opening times as well as tea rooms, were all on offer to visitors by the end of the 18th century (Tinniswood, 1998). In terms of the motivation for these early garden visitors, Tinniswood (1998, p. 80) observed that, for most tourists, the fact that the garden "was famous and had lots to see was probably quite enough to make a visit worthwhile". Thus, garden visiting during this period was a popular pursuit and visiting the grand landscape parks such as Stourhead was *de rigeur* in fashionable circles (Owen, 1998).

Early attempts at managing visitors in both historic houses and gardens are identifiable from the 1870s and, similar to Shenstone's experience, show unease about wear and tear. First, a small number charged an entry fee as a means of controlling numbers, although most preferred not to implement this measure as many welcomed visitors to their properties out of a sense of benevolence. Second, some estates placed a strict entry limit on the number of tickets available each day. In some cases, the tickets were supplied without charge, which allowed owners to implement the limit more easily. Third, some estates adopted the notion of the timed ticket (Mandler, 1997). Such an approach remains a common strategy in the contemporary management of houses and gardens, particularly those belonging to the National Trust (see Benfield, 2001), where visitors arrive for a tour at a specified time and are thus only on-site for a given period of time. In Scotland, one of the first great estates to formalise visitor management was the Duke of Atholl's grounds at Dunkeld, Perthshire. Regulations for guides to grounds were set out clearly, where guides had to wear a badge, ensure that visitors signed the guest's book and that visitors were not allowed to wander freely, in an attempt to prevent wilful damage (Durie, 2003).

Mandler (1997) examined archive material relating to correspondence between the Head Gardener at Chatsworth (Thomas Speed) in 1883 and several of his colleagues in other gardens. This material is illuminating because it provides evidence about the attitude to, and nature of, visitor management in gardens in the late Victorian period. Thomas Speed asked his colleagues what arrangements they had introduced to control visitor numbers and the costs incurred in maintaining their garden for visitors. The responses ranged from those who charged a fee, such as Blenheim and Eaton (where visitors were charged one shilling each for entry), to those who were not charging, but considering doing so. One illuminating comment from George Glass, the gardener at Enville Hall in 1883, stated that the garden attracted large crowds and that management was required to cope with the numbers:

> "*I place a man at the entrance and he admits all who come. We do not allow any bottles or baskets to be taken in the grounds. They can be left at the gate. All parties are requested not to walk on the grass. I have a few men about the grounds just to see that parties are behaving themselves... We do not allow any picnics or games to be carried on inside the grounds, only to walk quietly around*" (Mandler, 1997, p. 197).

Belvoir Castle in Leicestershire, which charged only two old pence for entry, was quite different. The Head Gardener stated:

"The increased facilities offered by Railways bring a great invasion of visitors and I am sorry to say that no regulations exist to meet such circumstances...Should the Duke take up his residence at the Castle in the summer time he would find it annoying to have people all over the place" (Mandler, 1997, p. 198).

Many estate owners expressed concern about charging visitors in most instances. It was not the intention to prevent respectable working class people from visiting country houses at all and many landowners preferred to operate an informal system where there was no charge for entry but visitors could give tips to gardeners and servants. Others used the revenue generated to pay workers as guides, in some cases, retained workers who were too old for manual work (Durie, 2003). However, some workers were instructed not to accept tips, such was the spirit of benevolence.

Mandler (1997) argues that the regulation of visitors to country houses developed from the 1880s and changes in admission policies emerged. It was the accepted norm to charge for entry by 1900, and many raised their entry charges in an attempt to regulate visits and subsidise the costs of opening to the public. For some landowners, the realisation that greater professionalism was the key to more profitable house openings resulted in more innovative ways of purposely managing estates for visitors, including publication of an opening schedule and using entry fees to pay professional guides. As a result, visitor numbers increased and some enterprises became commercially profitable, such as Warwick Castle and Eaton Hall (Mandler, 1997). A substantial number of country house owners turned to the commercialisation of their estates after 1870 in the light of falling incomes as a result of agricultural depression and decreasing incomes from land, increasing costs of maintenance and an increasing tax burden, leading to many estates being rationalised, broken up or sold (Howkins, 1991). Mandler (1997) states that many houses in the late 19th century became luxurious homes—a base for entertaining in the country, kept in the private sphere and not considered in the wider sense as national heritage nor as something to share with visitors.

From the 1880s, the pattern of visiting and the meanings attached to open houses and gardens began to change as demand for access to the countryside and enjoyment of historic houses and parks intensified. However, fewer houses were open and the ones that remained so were more heavily regulated, with restricted visitor access, as privacy became more important in the Victorian era (Franklin, 1989). Changing tastes, stimulated by the Arts and Crafts movement, influenced visits to areas that typified rurality and the vernacular heritage. As Mandler (1997, p. 217) notes, these people "had fallen in love with the country, but not... with the country house". However, while the visitors were only interested in grounds, owners could maintain a sense of privacy in not having to open the house. Benevolent attitudes began to change towards the end of the 1800s with the political climate and landowners began to view visitors not as considerate and grateful as in previous times, but as a mob without the capacity to appreciate fine things.

2.3. The early 20th century

A succession of tax laws leading to higher levels of taxation and death duties dealt heavy blows to landowners in the early 20th century (Tinniswood, 1998; Gaze, 1988) and the costs of maintaining a house and garden in many instances could no longer be met through income. In addition, wartime led to the ruination of many fine properties through requisition and the loss of male heirs and estate workers in conflict (Mandler, 1997; Clemenson, 1982). Garden maintenance was often a low priority, as buildings demanded more urgent attention. Gardens are even more vulnerable to the vagaries of neglect than buildings as they deteriorate so rapidly through natural processes, and a great deal of money is often required to restore a garden to its former condition (Gaze, 1988). A good example of garden neglect is the Victorian gardens of Heligan House in Cornwall, which remained untouched from the First World War until restoration in the 1990s. The gardening staff, who signed up for the army together and entered the same platoon, did not return from the First World War. A sad reminder of the story of these workers is the discovery and conservation of their signatures on the privy wall in the Melon Garden, a list of names scribbled before their departure to the War (Samuel, 1998). Other gardens, which did not fall into such severe neglect, often needed new uses to revive them; for example, Sheffield Park Garden in East Sussex, which has been sympathetically extended and promoted to attract more visitors by the National Trust (Gaze, 1988). Nevertheless, the garden was not a static resource in decline everywhere. A new age of gardening commenced in the inter-war years in Britain, marked by houses and estates changing hands and new gardens being made. In many instances, the primary objective in the new styles of garden creation was satisfying the owner's love of plants. Creative imaginations made gardens that had the qualities to inspire and appeal to the emotions (typified by Hidcote, Great Dixter and Sissinghurst), a feature shared by the gardens of previous centuries, but containing new and different elements of style, design and planting. The garden at Sissinghurst created by Vita Sackville-West and

J. Connell / Tourism Management 26 (2005) 185–201 189

Harold Nicolson opened to visitors in the early 20th century, with Vita on hand to answer questions and striking up rapport with visitors (Fearnley-Whittingstall, 2002), demonstrating a love for the garden and the desire to share it with like-minded visitors. Such care for a garden and its appreciation by visitors is a continuing theme that has underpinned garden owner motivations for opening over many centuries.

3. Country houses and gardens in contemporary Britain

With inadequate incomes to support the maintenance of a country house coupled with high land prices as a result of demand for development land, some land-owners have cashed in and realised their capital assets since 1945 (Sayer, 1993). Consequently, many houses, and subsequently, their gardens, were neglected or lost, while others have transferred in ownership to conserva-tion organisations such as the National Trust, to be kept in perpetuity for future generations. The National Trust's first garden acquisition was Hidcote, Glouces-tershire, in 1948, and in 2000, seven out of the top 10 most visited Trust properties were gardens. Traditional estates have survived in a different form as a result of the adaptation process to changing economic and social conditions, and have been proactive in finding new sources of income through estate diversification and management of land as a business enterprise (Clem-enson, 1982; Wigan, 1998). A range of management strategies and activities materialised in the country house sector, which were more highly structured and planned than previous approaches to achieving financial buoyancy, one of these being opening gardens on a commercial and professional basis.

Opening to the public is a popular method of offsetting the costs of maintenance and repair, not just because revenue generated from ticket sales can be ploughed back into maintenance budgets, but also because a property managed on a commercial basis can be declared a business and associated tax benefits can be obtained (Littlejohn, 1997). However, Massing-berd (cited in Sayer, 1993, p. 10) comments that, according to the Historic Houses Association (HHA), many country house owners claim that insufficient revenue for maintaining and running a property is made through opening to the public. Evidence suggests that only a very small number of properties were true profit generators in the 1980s (Dartington Institute, 1987). Littlejohn (1997) explains that several variables can be identified, which are likely to determine the economic survival of a country house, including the attractiveness of parks and gardens, the proximity to centres of population, tourist areas or routes and marketing capability. Young (1981) argues that gardens as a

setting for a country house are no less important than the house itself. Littlejohn (1997, p. 170) comments that "gardens are undoubtedly a major, perhaps the major draw of country houses".

While much of the discussion so far has focused on country house gardens, as such properties form the precursor to the garden as a visitor attraction, it is by no means the only type of garden operating in the garden visit market. In fact, the opening of gardens other than those belonging to stately homes has a relatively long background if the emergence of the National Gardens Scheme (NGS) in 1927 is acknowledged (see Hunnin-gher, 2001). The Scheme was designed to raise funds for a single charity, The Queen's Nursing Institute, but has expanded in scope to raise money for a range of charities. In terms of participating gardens, 600 gardens took part in the first year of operation and about 5000 were included in the Scheme's guide—known as the *Yellow Book*—in 2002. The Scheme has encouraged a plethora of garden types to open, from ordinary, private residences, to Royal gardens, to garden visitor attrac-tions. What is particularly significant is that the Scheme has assisted in the creation of a new type of garden to visit, based on historical antecedents but different in terms of social stratification and space—that of the private residence. Many gardens are promoted in their own right, without the support of a stately home, and achieve very high visitor numbers. The best example of this type of garden is Wakehurst Place in West Sussex, which achieves the largest visitor figures for any National Trust property (285,142 visitors 2002) (The National Trust, 2003). Historically too, this was the case. Not all gardens were those attached to country houses and 18th century English 'pleasure gardens' such as Ranelagh and New Spring Gardens, both in London, were open to those who paid a subscription and were settings for banquets, masquerades, dancing and moon-lit concerts. They were designed to run at a profit from admission fees, refreshments and special events, and often employed a large staff to run these commercial ventures (Coke, 1991). While 18th century commercial pleasure gardens were arenas for entertainment and sensual pleasures for "rumbustuous" Georgian society (Brown, 1999, p. 42), they were to have a short longevity as the Victorians transformed gardens into spaces for quiet and respectable enjoyment. As Whitaker and Browne (1971, p. 25) noted, modern parks and gardens are often still guided by the regulations set out in Victorian times, encouraging disciplined use and appro-priate behaviour.

Similar to other leisure sub-sectors, the massive increase in demand and supply of recreational oppor-tunities in the post-war period fuelled the growth in garden visiting. In the 1960s, between one and two million people visited gardens (Hunt, 1964), when the first guide-book to national gardens was published.

190   *J. Connell / Tourism Management 26 (2005) 185–201*

Today, around 16 million visits are made to British gardens (Evans, 2001).

Gardens open to the public today are not confined to those belonging to country houses and reflect a diversity of ownership and management. Some of these gardens emanate from a country house backdrop, but operate as the sole attraction (such as Drummond Castle Gardens, Perthshire and the Lost Gardens of Heligan, Cornwall, where the associated houses are not open to the public), while others are more modern creations (for example, the Scottish Plant Collectors Garden in Perthshire, which links historical and contemporary themes in garden creation). The development of the garden as a visitor attraction reflects, to some extent, the evolution of the commercial leisure market and the emergence of sites created and/or managed for the visiting public. Therefore, to understand the extent to which historical continuity and change exists in the gardens open to the public in Great Britain, attention now turns to the first major study of garden visiting to be undertaken in the country, undertaken by the author. This paper adds another dimension to the study of garden visiting to that in Connell (2004), as it explores gardens open to the public and their management.

4. Gardens open in Great Britain: empirical research

This research set out to assess the scope of gardens open to the public in Great Britain and to develop baseline data given that little information currently exists on the subject of gardens in a recreational context. In view of the scale and diversity of gardens as visitor attractions, a quantitative approach using a questionnaire survey was deemed most appropriate as a wide geographic coverage could be achieved, thereby establishing base-line data for Great Britain.

The most suitable method of data collection was by means of a postal questionnaire survey. As a substantial population was required to meet the research objectives, face-to-face interviewing was impractical; so a balance between sample size, resources available and the need to gather as representative a sample as possible was required (Page, Forer, & Lawton, 1999). In this research, deriving base-line data required a blanket approach that could only be achieved through a postal survey, in line with the UK Visitor Attraction Monitor methodology.

The survey objectives were to gain an understanding of the use, perception and management of gardens as a recreational resource. Accordingly, the main sections in the questionnaire focused on: the characteristics and ownership of gardens; visitors to the garden; visitor management; aspects affecting visitor enjoyment; and future aspects likely to affect the management of the garden. A range of question types was included in the survey design. Most questions were of the closed type, with tick box answers, although open questions were also included to elicit informed answers about visitor management in gardens from respondents.

4.1. Selecting the sample

To avoid sampling error as much as possible, a database of all gardens open to the public on a regular and/or commercial basis was created, comprising 1223 gardens. It is estimated by the author that in Great Britain there are approximately 5000 gardens open to the public. Nearly four-fifths of these gardens are open for no more than a couple of hours a year. It was decided to exclude the large number of gardens in this category from the survey from a practical perspective, as there would be a danger of results being skewed by too many inappropriate gardens that are not managed for visitors.

The selection procedure was not designed to select a certain quota of garden categories, according to geographic location or type. Instead, as large a population as possible was sought with the aim of including all gardens open to the public on a regular basis. Accordingly, the survey population included all gardens defined as visitor attractions by national and regional tourism organisations, as well as all regularly opening smaller, private gardens in order to be as representative of gardens open to the public as possible. The survey population was constructed by using and cross-referencing a number of sources, including: *The Good Gardens Guide 2000* (King, 2000), an independent, annual guide to gardens in Great Britain, selected by inspection; the 'Yellow Books' of the National Gardens Scheme of England and Wales and Scotland's Garden Scheme; the Gardenvisit.com website (Gardenvisit. com, 2000); the British Tourist Authority list of gardens (BTA, 2000); the National Trust Handbooks (England and Wales, and Scotland); and Area Tourist Board promotional leaflets.

Of the 1223 questionnaires distributed, 593 forms were returned resulting in a 48.4% response rate. The response rate is considered to be favourable, as many postal surveys in tourism research appear to achieve a much lower return with 30% being common and acceptable for most purposes (see Page et al., 1999 in relation to surveys of tourism enterprises). Gardens responding to the survey were located across Great Britain, although many were located in the south of England. This pattern adequately reflects the supply of gardens and the original sample, with 15.3% of responses from Scotland and 5.1% from Wales; the remaining 79.6% were accounted for by English gardens (Fig. 1). Analysis of the data was conducted on two levels. The first comprised a basic frequency analysis to establish preliminary findings. Second, a number of

J. Connell / Tourism Management 26 (2005) 185–201   191

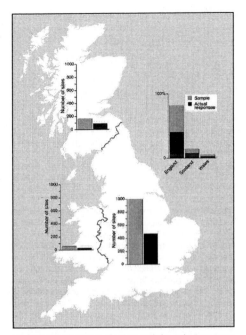

Fig. 1. Geographic location of survey population and response rates.

cross-tabulations were produced and chi-square tests were performed to test the degree of association between variables. The results will now be discussed.

5. The characteristics of gardens open in Great Britain

Respondents were asked to identify the most applicable description of their garden. While plantsman's[1] gardens formed the largest category (26%), the sample also comprised a significant number of historic gardens (24.6%). Other types of garden with special planting interests accounted for a further 6.7%, while another 16.6% had historic connections. Private gardens accounted for 51.1% of the sample, 13.3% were part of an historic house (not National Trust), and 11% were classed as private commercial gardens, broadly in line with the survey population. The sample included gardens which were part of a National Trust/National Trust for Scotland (NT/NTS) house (7.9% of the sample) and 5.1% were NT/NTS gardens (that is, without a house open to the public as part of the overall experience). There were a small number of other types of garden, such as nursery gardens (4.2%), where the

---
[1] Defined as garden containing specific planting interest.

garden has been created as an adjunct to a plant nursery enterprise or where such a business has been developed on top of a successful garden open to the public. Some 2.5% of the sample gardens formed part of another attraction (defined as not a historic house, but might include zoos and theme parks, with a garden sufficiently important to be recognised as an attraction in its own right). Gardens belonging to another organisation, such as local authorities or conservation organisations, formed 1.9% and botanical gardens accounted for 1.5% of the sample.

5.1. Garden ownership

In terms of ownership, 67.5% of respondents were the owners of the gardens. Nearly 32% of respondents were employed to manage the garden by organisations, such as the National Trust and other organisations, as well as private enterprise. The remaining 0.7% of respondents were Trustees. According to the English Tourism Council, the Scottish Tourist Board, Wales Tourist Board and the Northern Ireland Tourist Board (2000), 69% of England's 4500 visitor attractions are owned and operated by the private sector and not-for-profit sector. The gardens sector reflects this analysis and it too appears to be dominated by the private and not-for-profit sectors. In terms of length of time that the respondent had owned or managed the garden, responses showed a normal distribution. With a mean ownership of garden ownership between 11 and 20 years, a low turnover in garden ownership, along with a substantial investment period in the development of a garden, is reflected. This is particularly marked in private gardens, where most respondents had owned their gardens for more than 11 years, some as much as 40 years, indicating a continuity of ownership, development and management style.

5.2. Trends in the numbers of gardens open to the public through time

Fig. 2 illustrates the year of first opening to the public. While it is clear that some gardens have a long tradition of opening to the public, with 13 gardens open prior to 1900 and the earliest garden open was recorded in 1642, a marked number of gardens opened in the twentieth century. Gardens opening prior to 1900 tended to be almost entirely linked with a historic house (some of which have subsequently become National Trust properties) and Botanic gardens, which have their origins in the 1600s. The figures indicate a substantial increase in garden supply from 1970 onwards. In terms of methodology, it might be argued that the survey does not represent those gardens that opened then closed at some point. However, in a pool of over 1000 gardens, there will be a small number that enter and exit (similar

192   *J. Connell / Tourism Management 26 (2005) 185–201*

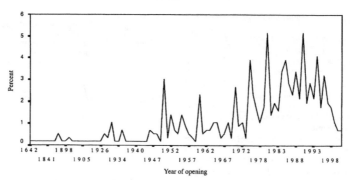

Fig. 2. Year gardens first opened.

to any other type of enterprise) over time. Some of these may be old, some more contemporary. However, the survey includes a substantive number of gardens that opened in each historic period, and thus it is not unreasonable to make inferences from such data.

The illustration in Fig. 2 indicates a series of phases in relation to gardens opening to the public for the first time, where a number of peaks of varying magnitude are noticeable. In the 1920s and 1930s, the time of the initial rise of the leisure society, gardens may have been built and opened to reflect growing mobility of the middle and upper middle class, particularly if one bears in mind the rising popularity of the car and the small increase in day trips to locations in rural areas (Towner, 1996). Cross-tabulating year of opening with main reason for opening indicates a statistical association ($P = <0.000$), and highlights a number of notable points. A larger than expected number of gardens opened in the period 1926–1950 for charity fund-raising. With the establishment of the National Gardens Scheme in England and Wales in 1927, the substantial number of gardens opening up at this time for charity follows suit.

The peak in the 1950s and 1960s again relates to increasing mobility, but it is also interesting to note from the cross-tabulation that revenue generation to fund maintenance was of greater importance as a main reason for opening (1951–1975), a reflection of the pressures on country house owners. Indeed, the latter assertion is supported by a three-way cross-tabulation between year of opening, category of garden and main reason for opening, which shows a greater than expected number of gardens as part of a historic house being opened in the period 1951–1975, when compared with other types of gardens. The highest number of National Trust gardens opened in the period 1951–1975, although gardens belonging to other conservation organisations tended to open in the post-1976 period. The post-1976 period is notable for the number of tourist-oriented and/or commercial-based gardens that opened—for exam-

ple, a higher number of private tourist gardens, nursery gardens and gardens open as part of another attraction opened during this time than any previous time.

The last quarter of the twentieth century was notable for the rise in the commercialisation of visitor attractions and Fig. 2 shows a considerable increase in the numbers of gardens opening to the public for the first time. Cross-tabulation indicates a greater number of gardens than expected opening as a business enterprise in the period 1976–2001, particularly significant in private gardens and private commercial gardens. Indeed, 73.5% of those gardens that were created as visitor attractions were opened in the post-1976 period. Thus, the eminence of the private sector in the supply of the garden experience by means of a business enterprise in the period 1976–2001 is established.

Fig. 2 indicates a decrease in the number of gardens opening to the public in the latter part of the 1990s. It may be argued that the reason for this decrease is related to the over-supply of gardens open to the public. Over-supply of formal leisure opportunities is a thorny issue in contemporary tourism and recreation, and has been witnessed across a range of recreation resources, particularly in the attractions sector (Mintel, 2002). Closures of visitor attractions do occur on a frequent basis, as reported annually in *Sightseeing in the UK*, and gardens are not exempt from this fate. Some 59 gardens out of a total of 859 attractions have closed between 1978 and 1999 (English Tourism Council et al., 2000, p. 34). It is clear that a relationship exists between the year of opening and visitor numbers, with gardens that have opened since 1976 tending to attract low visitor numbers (79.8% below 10,000 per year), compared with 25% of pre-1900 gardens attracting over 300,000 visitors per year. Whether this is indicative of a greater interest in heritage gardens, that historic gardens are better marketed by organisations such as the National Trust, or that newer gardens have certain characteristics desired by niche horticultural markets is an interesting

J. Connell / Tourism Management 26 (2005) 185–201 193

point. Certainly, the results indicate a significant relationship ($P = 0.000$) between the year of opening and visitor profile, with pre-1900 gardens being particularly appealing to those visitors seeking a pleasant day out, compared with visitors to post-1976 gardens, who show a stronger propensity to possess a gardening interest or horticultural specialism.

5.3. Reasons for opening gardens to the public

The main reason for opening the garden was for charity fund-raising (51.9%). A further 19.6% of respondents cited the main reason was as a means of maintaining the garden and another 11% as running a business enterprise (Fig. 3). Secondary reasons for opening were: to share the garden with others (18.6%); to complement another attraction, such as an historic house (8.6%); as a result of demand, often associated with requests to open for charity from the National Gardens Scheme (NGS) (5.6%), and to help with maintenance costs (3.2%). Gardens do appear to be quite unusual in that the number originally opening for charity fund-raising (for external charities, not the garden as a charity as in the case of some houses and gardens) is a feature unique to gardens in the attractions sector. The significance of charity openings is undoubtedly a manifestation of the success of the NGS. While attractions tend to open up for a variety of reasons, including preservation of heritage, generation of income and for entertainment (English Tourism Council, 2000), charity fund-raising is a factor that is peculiar to the garden sector.

The continuity and change theme is particularly marked in relation to reasons for opening. As discussed earlier, in an historic context, social obligations and benevolence typified the rationale for early garden owners (Mandler, 1997). Later, a dichotomy developed between those gardens required to operate as revenue generators and/or commercial enterprises, and those where owners desired purely to share a love of plants. Such a change is inherent in the survey results, which revealed that the main reason for the garden remaining open to the public had changed through time (20% of respondents). Financial reasons emerged as the main motivation in this respect, having developed from charity fund-raising purposes, with gardens not being financially viable without visitors to support their upkeep.

Private gardens overwhelmingly opened for charity fund-raising purposes (79.8%). Historic houses, National Trust properties, National Trust gardens and other conservation organisation gardens opened primarily as a means of maintaining the property/garden. Only 11.1% of gardens opened as a business enterprise: these gardens are mainly confined to gardens forming part of another attraction that is not an historic house (60% opened as a business enterprise), and nursery gardens, that is, those gardens run in conjunction with a nursery business (32%). This relationship is statistically significant ($P = 0.000$).

Few of the private gardens had changed their main reason for opening (84.4%), similar to gardens that form part of other attractions, National Trust properties and gardens, and other conservation organisation gardens. Gardens that changed their original objective for opening more significantly were botanic gardens (44.4% had changed their original remit for opening), nursery gardens (44.0%), and private tourist gardens (32.3%). This relationship is statistically significant ($P = 0.003$). An exploration of why these particular gardens developed new reasons for opening revealed that the overriding reason was linked to financial issues. Changes in motivation tended to be manifested in two major forms: first, botanic gardens, which originally opened as

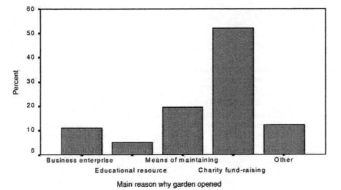

Fig. 3. Reasons for opening a garden to the public.

194   *J. Connell / Tourism Management 26 (2005) 185–201*

educative and scientific resources, are now under greater pressure to derive self-supporting income generation from visitors, and; second, nursery gardens, which had sometimes developed from a hobby had turned into fully fledged businesses with income generation as a new priority.

Only 9% of gardens were created as visitor attractions. However, 29% of owners considered their garden as a visitor attraction today, intimating that gardens tend to become a product for visitor consumption once they have been established for some years. In the survey, 64.8% of gardens were described as private gardens. Private gardens are the least likely category of garden to have been created as a visitor attraction (98.7% were not created as attractions). More commercial operations such as gardens that form part of other attractions and private tourist gardens were created as attractions (28.6% and 27.7%, respectively). The continuity and change theme is clear in this respect, with gardens remaining open to the public, but with a change in the rationale for opening and a particular emphasis on generating revenue. A facet not part of the remit in the 18th century, where gardens operated in a drastically different social and economic climate, creating sufficient income to maintain gardens has become a key motivation for garden owners. One way in which income can be produced is through the provision of visitor services.

5.4. Visitor services in gardens

It is clear that providing facilities to visitors, such as teas and guide-books, took place from the 18th century (Tinniswood, 1998; Fearnley-Whittingstall, 2002). In order to track the changes in visitor service provision through time, the questionnaire asked respondents to indicate what facilities were provided when the garden first opened. Table 1 shows the figures relative to the facilities provided today. The percentage change column denotes the large increase in services. The growth may be explained by a growing sophistication and increase in commercial opportunities related to both consumer

requirements and evolution of the business. In relation to the latter assertion, the life-cycle of the garden as a visitor attraction product is the primary consideration. Development, expansion and consolidation of the attraction and the addition of extra services to expand the commercial base of the enterprise, especially in the 1980s and 1990s, has been a major focus of activity for visitor attractions in Great Britain.

While 36.6% of respondents had not made any changes to service provision, 37.2% stated that additions had been made to attract more visitors and a further 12.1% of respondents replied that additions were necessary to maintain visitor numbers. Overall, the findings would appear to confirm the earlier argument relating to commercialisation of the garden as a leisure experience through time.

Table 2 accentuates the changes in service provision made to gardens according to the period of time in which gardens opened. Such figures indicate that the supply of visitor services in gardens increases through time. It is particularly interesting to note that some visitor services were well-developed in pre-1900 gardens, as discussed earlier. The provision of guide books, guided walks and events in gardens points to a high degree of interaction between the host and guest in gardens historically, which has declined hence, in line with an increase in services directed at the mass consumer-driven leisure market. However, what is also intriguing is that historic gardens have maintained the high level of social interaction, offering more guided walks, events and guide books than gardens opened in subsequent years.

It is notable that only a very small numbers of gardens have installed sophisticated audio-visual displays. The absence of capital-intensive information provision would seem to denote that many gardens are somewhat low key in their approach to visitor information. Those gardens where audio-visual displays were operating were in the heritage sector, particularly National Trust properties, accounting for over 50% of such gardens, and generally attracting large numbers of visitors. While

Table 1
Comparison of visitor services when gardens first opened and today

Service type	Service provided when garden first opened		Service provided today		Percentage change
	Percent	Frequency	Percent	Frequency	
Shop	14.2	83	38.1	225	+271.1
Plant sales	42.5	248	70.2	414	+166.9
Teas	52.6	308	76.8	453	+147.1
Toilets	62.2	363	81.4	480	+132.2
Car park	65.2	381	77.5	457	+119.9
Guide book	26.5	155	52.5	310	+200
Children's area	4.6	27	15.8	93	+344.4
Guided walks	15.2	89	41.9	247	+277.5
Events	13.3	78	42.4	250	+320.5

J. Connell / Tourism Management 26 (2005) 185–201

Table 2
Visitor services in relation to year of opening

Percentage within year of opening

	Pre-1900	1900–1925	1926–1950	1951–1975	1976–2001	p-value
Service provided when garden first opened						
Shop	0	0	5.8	12	18.2	0.026
Plant sales	7.7	0	17.3	18.8	58.2	0.000
Teas	15.4	11.1	34.6	47.8	61.1	0.000
Toilets	23.1	44.4	55.8	60.2	67.1	0.006
Car park	0	55.6	63.5	75.9	65.1	0.000
Guide book	30.8	0	30.8	34.3	23.6	0.05
Walks	30.8	11.1	5.8	14.3	15.9	0.17
Events	23.1	0	5.8	10.4	15.3	0.126
Children's area	0	0	0	1.5	6.9	0.033
Service provided today						
Shop	69.2	77.8	49.1	52.6	29.3	0.000
Plant sales	46.2	88.9	67.9	65.9	74.4	0.055
Teas	84.6	88.9	83.0	80.0	75.6	0.525
Toilets	92.3	88.9	84.9	88.1	78.2	0.08
Car park	53.8	88.9	84.9	89.6	72.1	0.000
Guide book	100	88.9	71.7	63.0	42.2	0.000
Walks	84.6	77.8	43.4	55.6	33.3	0.000
Events	76.9	66.7	54.7	59.3	31.9	0.000
Children's area	23.1	55.6	28.3	20.0	11.8	0.000

the emphasis on minimalist interpretation is not intended as a criticism, it is suspected that information provision relates strongly to the needs of the market and the environmental attributes of the gardens. Historically, the interaction between the head gardener and the visitor, on a one-to-one tour of the garden, formed the essence of the visitor experience, and guide-books produced by garden owners in the same period bridged the gap where such tours were not appropriate. In contemporary Britain, the influence of post-modernity in tourism experiences emphasis the importance of the interaction between gardener and visitor, where the process and practice of gardening is a marketable commodity to visitors. From a visitor perspective, being able to converse with a gardener or the garden owner can be a highlight of the visit. This is a mutual process as many garden owners like the experience of sharing their garden with visitors, talking to them about plants and design and providing hospitality. In some gardens, the emphasis on personalities and working practices in some gardens, such as at Sissinghurst in the 1920s, or today in the Lost Gardens of Heligan, highlights the form of tourist gaze (Urry, 1995) where visitors see an ordinary aspect of their life, namely, gardening, within a new context, such as a beautiful or famous garden. Smit's (1997) review of the garden restoration at Heligan is pronounced in its celebration of the people who have worked on the project, and those workers form part of the charm and appeal of that particular garden.

5.5. Visitor trends

As might be expected through a boom era in leisure time, spending and experiences, most garden owners reported an increase in visitor numbers since the garden first opened (49.7%), while 30.3% thought that numbers were static. The reasons cited for increases in numbers were varied. However, 34.9% considered that interest in gardens had increased within the general public, while another 34.9% considered that improved marketing of the garden had assisted in attracting more visitors (see Table 3). The results obtained seem to adequately reflect findings for all attractions by the English Tourism Council et al. (2001), who state that increases in visitor figures to attractions were explained by advertising (25%) and development of a new attraction/feature (12%). Where the garden results differ is in respect of the increased interest in gardens.

Gardens with visitor numbers of 2000 or less appear to be more vulnerable to changing visitor numbers, illustrated by a much lower rate of increase than other categories of garden and accounting for 54.1% of the gardens experiencing a decrease in visitor numbers over time. In addition, in terms of those gardens where the visitor numbers are staying static, 69.1% of such gardens are those with visitor numbers of 2000 or less ($p = 0.000$). Such figures are most likely explained by the limited market appeal of small, private gardens.

Decreases in numbers were reported by 14.8%, mostly accounted for by greater competition from other

196 *J. Connell / Tourism Management 26 (2005) 185–201*

Table 3
Reasons for increase in visitor numbers

Reasons for increase in visitor numbers	Frequency	Valid percent of gardens
More public interest in gardens	98	34.9
Improved marketing of garden	93	34.9
New attraction in garden	30	10.7
More visitors to the area	11	3.9
Other	44	15.7
Don't know	24	

Table 4
Reasons for decrease in visitor numbers

Reason for decrease in visitor numbers	Frequency	Valid percent of gardens
Competition from other attractions	45	53.6
Reduced openings	12	14.3
Reduction in visitors to the area	9	10.7
Most locals already visited	6	7.1
Other	12	14.3
Total	84	
Missing cases	14	

Table 5
Explanations of how garden visitors are changing

How garden visitors are changing	Frequency	Valid percent of respondents
Wider interest in gardens	38	27.9
More young people interested	28	20.6
Higher media profile	25	18.4
More family interest	16	11.8
Looking for high standards	7	5.1
More overseas visitors	4	2.9
Unsure	1	0.7
Other	17	12.5
Total	136	
Missing cases	44	

attractions (see Table 4). Competitors were viewed as other gardens, other visitor attractions, Sunday retailing (traditionally, a favourite day for visiting gardens) and a general perception of an increase in leisure opportunities. Competition is reflected in the finding of the English Tourism Council et al. (2001), who found that competition from Sunday retailing accounted for 11% of reasons for decreases and competition from new attractions (11%). The response given by some respondents, 'most locals already visited', denotes the local nature of the market for some of the gardens. The inference is that small, private gardens with minimal opening hours have limited appeal to visitors from outside the area (or an owner perception of this being the case).

5.6. Garden visitors

The description of the majority of garden visitors by owners in the sample was that the majority had a general interest in gardening (60.5%), although nearly a third visited simply as a pleasant day out. Fewer than 10% of visitors were classified as those possessing specialist horticultural knowledge. Contrary to the perceived image of garden visitors comprising older age groups, a mix of age groups were perceived by garden owners to visit their particular garden.

Respondents gave some indications about group visits to their garden. Coach groups appear as a significant feature in visit profiles, with 65.1% of gardens reporting that such groups visit their garden. School groups were not a large market sector, with only 23.3% of gardens receiving such visits. Family visits are of some significance too, with 51.5% of gardens stating that families visited their garden. However, this figure needs to be examined with the findings from the age profile in mind. Garden owners were asked if they thought garden visitors were changing and 25.5% replied in the affirmative, citing a wider interest in gardens as the main reason (see Table 5). However, 69.6% of respondents did not think that garden visitors were changing, emphasising stability of the market.

The traditional view of gardening as the pursuit of older people has, however, been challenged by the notion of 'instant gardens', which appeal to young, busy people who want to enjoy their gardens and use them as social spaces but have insufficient time, skill or patience to create a garden (Mintel, 2000; Euromonitor, 1999).

Similarly, the results appear to confirm that a younger audience for garden visiting is emerging. The results also indicate that the role of the media should be recognised in raising the profile, interest and participation in gardening. While it might appear that this is a new phenomenon, history informs us that, in fact, this is just a continuation of past trends, as the creation of gardens filtered through the social classes, and took on new spatial and temporal meanings. However, garden visiting is an activity dominated by AB occupational groupings (Connell, 2004); so perhaps through time the garden visitor profile has little changed.

5.7. Managing garden visitors

5.7.1. Admissions

One of the key aspects of managing visits to gardens in the 18th and 19th centuries related to admission charges. While it has already been established that the rationale for opening gardens has developed away from the spirit of benevolence to a more commercially based

J. Connell / Tourism Management 26 (2005) 185–201 197

approach by 1900 (Mandler, 1997), the entry charges today appear to be quite modest when compared with admission charges for visitor attractions in Great Britain, with 78.9% charging less than £3.00, with a mean average of £3.74 (standard deviation £1.30). In 2000, the average adult admission charge to British attractions was £3.52 (English Tourism Council et al., 2001, p. 27), although about 50% charge £3.00 or less. Around 19% of attractions do not charge for admission according to the English Tourism Council et al. (2001), however, the garden owners survey shows that 5.1% of gardens do not charge admission. The comparatively low rate is explained by the high propensity of gardens open for charity fund-raising where the owner does not operate on a profit basis, along with conservation organisation gardens (not National Trust) at 18.2%, and nursery gardens (24%). The more commercial enterprises tend to charge higher admission prices, including 33.3% of gardens that form part of other attractions, 25.8% of gardens forming part of an historic property (not National Trust) and 20% of private tourist gardens, charging more than £4.00. The historic context of garden admissions appears slightly different, where a smaller number of gardens open to the public in the 19th century, for example, attracted proportionately higher visitor numbers, and mechanisms for controlling visitor numbers through pricing were more prominently used. Few garden owners were concerned about controlling visitor numbers, with most gardens seeking to expand or at least maintain current numbers.

5.7.2. Visitor impacts

A crucial aspect of opening gardens in pre-1900 gardens related to the damage caused by visitors. To examine continuity and change in this instance, the survey revealed that just over 51% of garden owners reported damage to the garden caused by visitors, thus, is still an issue that creates problems for contemporary garden owners. In the light of the work by Benfield (2001), Garrod, Fyall, and Leask (2002) and the earlier conceptualisation of impacts and the visitor experience by Graefe and Vaske (1987), these issues are a valid line of inquiry, with an historical continuity traceable from the 18th century. In natural resource-based attractions, like gardens, there is an inevitable trade-off for owners and managers between maintaining the garden in pristine condition and inviting visitors into the garden. The most widely reported problem in the survey was general wear and tear, followed by theft of garden materials (plants, cuttings and statuary). Theft was cited as a significant problem in a small number of gardens, several of which were private gardens whose owners had decided not to open in future due to the severity of the problem. Such occurrences have been reported in the popular press. Corbett (1998, p. 65) noted the need in

Table 6
Types of limiting measures in place in gardens

	Frequency	Valid percent of gardens
Limit opening	4	4.6
Limit numbers	3	3.4
Limit group visits	3	3.4
Timed ticketing	3	3.4
Group tours only	2	2.3
Limit parking	1	1.1
Other	14	16.1
No plans to limit visitors	57	65.5
Total	87	
Missing cases	12	

some gardens to install theft detection systems and closed-circuit television to prevent the theft of antique garden statuary and garden furniture as well as trees and plants. The theme of mistreatment of gardens by visitors is a common one (Buchan, 1995; Whitsey, 1997; Lane Fox, 2000). Conversely, Nicolson (1996, p. 6) comments that garden visitors are "an appreciative and careful lot because they have gardens of their own, or wish they had". The survey findings emphasise Nicolson's view, as there appears to be low level of reported damage to gardens other than the predictability of wear and tear.

In relation to specific tasks, 60.8% of owners stated that tasks were required to reduce the effects of visitor use, including turfing (36.2%), litter collection (21.2%) and 27.8% stated that some areas in the garden required cordoning to stop visitors from entering. Only 15.4% of garden owners thought that there were sometimes too many visitors in the garden. Of those, 29.5% had introduced measures for limiting numbers, including limiting opening, limiting numbers, limiting group visits and timed ticketing (Table 6), standard techniques used by visitor attractions to manage visitors (Swarbrooke, 2001). It seems that carrying capacity problems are not a significant issue for most gardens, other than a few of the larger garden attractions which are perceived as being of a national or international notoriety, such as Sissinghurst (Benfield, 2001).

The history of managing visitors to garden indicates that a significant number of the measures in Table 6 are by no means new. The concept of timed ticketing and limiting numbers on a daily basis were well used techniques in the late 19th century, and before this time, it was common for visitors to be taken around a garden on a one-to-one basis or in a small group, thus limiting pressures on the garden, the garden staff and protecting the privacy of the household. In fact, more emphasis on ensuring good behaviour in gardens is evident in the 19th century, with stricter rules in place for visitors.

198 *J. Connell / Tourism Management 26 (2005) 185–201*

6. Future management issues and implications

6.1. Recognition of market changes

It is clear that a number of management issues underpin this research. For example, it is evident that gardens respond to market forces and there is an increasing recognition that different typologies of visitors constitute their markets. In particular, the use of segmentation, targeting and positioning are certainly techniques that some of the more sophisticated gardens use to nurture their markets (Connell, 2004). However, this recognition is a reflection of the historical evolution and growth of gardens, where even garden owners in the 18th century were conscious of introducing new styles, exotic plants and design features to be at the forefront of garden developments to impress neighbours and visitors, as well as to satisfy the owner's gardening interests.

If gardens wish to expand visitor numbers, the research has shown that the general interest visitor market is the most significant in terms of volume and value. The market for gardens reliant on the *Yellow Book* is limited to enthusiasts and more purposive visitors, as opposed to those looking for a pleasant day out or something to do on a sunny day. Planning for expansion is thus required and a consideration of how effective marketing may be achieved, and how a wider market may be reached, is necessary. The limited potential of the small private garden if operated as a commercial venture is likely to remain a problem. Recommended strategies for coping with the development and expansion of private gardens include clustering of similar attractions, expansion of visitor services and commercial appeal, and appropriate marketing through segmentation. Such approaches reflect the historical evolution of gardens as visitor attractions, where garden owners had to make choices about professionalisation, commercialisation and development of leisure space. For many garden owners, developing visitor services has resulted from recognition of visitor needs in the context of an increasing sophistication of the leisure market, and there are distinctive historical traits in the development of gardens open to the public that have informed the growth and development of the sector into its contemporary form.

6.2. Ownership issues

While gardens have developed as a form of enterprise in line with the general leisure trend towards greater commercialisation, on the whole the private owner is a dominant force in the sector. The survey research found that, in some cases, it was the desire of private garden owners to remain private and, indeed, some were planning to reduce opening times or close altogether.

One of the reasons for closure relates to the impacts caused by visitors to gardens, which confirms Garrod et al.'s (2002) suggestion that impacts are not confined to larger attractions or those with significant visitor numbers. Overcoming existing and potential impacts requires careful handling, through visitor management. To retain privacy, owners could consider the introduction of various initiatives, such as disallowing or discouraging visitor use of toilets in the house, providing owner guided tours rather than open access or ensuring that visitors are made aware that taking cuttings and seeds is inappropriate behaviour. Such approaches are clearly documented in the history of garden visiting.

Gardens run by the owner and /or volunteers and family members are not necessarily sustainable in the long-term as people lose interest and health and availability of goodwill place limitations on opening. In addition, because the costs of opening a garden can exceed the revenue gained from admission, a financial burden is placed on those participating in schemes such as the NGS, which may lead to doubts over the viability of opening for charity. Garden owners may need to consider the viability of opening and make decisions about enterprise development or closure.

6.3. Future trends

While the main remit of this paper has been to explore the interconnections between past and present, some mention of future trends is a valid place to end the discussion, mainly because future issues of concern indicate the permanence of the continuity and change theme in the garden sub-sector. Garden owners identified the most important issues in the future management of the garden in relation to visitors as maintaining high standards (18.4%), developing and improving the garden (14.1%) and finance limitations (11.7%). For just over 10% of gardens, increasing age and failing health was viewed as the most significant factor in keeping the garden open. Age and health factors mostly affect private gardens, which are often run directly by an ageing owner. In these instances, solutions to overcome the problems associated with passing on the garden to an heir are often considered, a theme reflected in earlier times. Formation of a private trusts is one way of ensuring the future survival of a garden (for example, The Trebah Garden Trust), or by donating the garden to an organisation such as The National Trust, although The National Trust is unlikely to accept a garden without a significant endowment, which will provide financial support for maintenance and running costs.

The empirical work reported in this paper suggests a range of old and new issues for garden owners in the future. Maintaining high standards, adding new

J. Connell / Tourism Management 26 (2005) 185–201 199

features, developing and improving gardens to retain and stimulate visitor interest and appreciation, and financial aspects have figured strongly through the centuries, emphasising the continuity of visiting-related issues. The more strongly commercial elements suggested by promotion, attracting visitors and competition from other attractions are more recent considerations for garden owners, and highlight the changing context of the garden as a leisure resource.

There is a danger that private gardens could be squeezed out of the marketplace as the experience on offer becomes outmoded and visitors abandon them for more facility-driven attractions, as suggested by the general literature on attractions (Stevens, 2000). Mintel (2002) state that attractions need to renew features and services to attract repeat visitation and that younger and more affluent visitors expect development and change. Accordingly, it is encouraging to see that garden owners acknowledge the need to develop their garden and add new features. In addition, gardens are somewhat unusual as contemporary visitor attractions in that there is a low-key approach to interpretation and visitor experiences. Where perhaps gardens differ from other attractions is in the retention of a high touch approach, where visitors are able to meet with garden owners or workers and talk about plants, design and the development of the garden and where visitors can apply knowledge and ideas gained to their own garden, in a meeting of the public and the personal. As argued earlier, such an approach is reminiscent of the historical evolution of garden interpretation and is important to maintain.

7. Conclusions

The British garden is an interesting example of historical evolution of a resource that has displayed distinct patterns of continuity and change through time and space. In some cases, historic houses created gardens for the consumption of the house owner, which in the fullness of time, have been extended to a small number of initial visitors and, later, the visiting public *en masse*. An historical perspective is important in understanding how a landscape-based resource, namely the garden, has been created, adopted as an element for personal consumption in the private sphere and then widened to include public consumption, reflecting wider changes in society. What should be stressed is that garden visiting and consumption is not a new post-modern phenomenon but has evolved through time, most notably in the late 19th and 20th century, as the attraction and appeal of garden environments developed as fashionable resources to visit and enjoy in the growing leisure time among the social classes.

Therefore, while this paper can only act as a broad overview of the historical evolution of the garden as a visitor resource, it has nonetheless highlighted the processes in a society where economic, social and political shifts have led to the reuse of private and to a lesser degree public garden settings, being developed as an integral aspect of the 'visitor industry' from the Victorian period. Major changes certainly occurred in the post-war years and the expansion in reuse of such gardens in the 1970s and 1980s was a key feature that added to the growing diversification of attractions seeking to appeal to day-trippers and visitors alike. Subsequent changes in the late 1990s are less clear and time will have to elapse before the extent to which patterns of opening, development and usage are following previous trends or setting new ones can be examined.

This paper has outlined the emergence, growth and maturity of garden visiting through the centuries in contemporary Britain, illustrating the historic customs, practice and trends of opening gardens to the public and the development of garden visiting into a major activity in contemporary times. The discussion has shown the importance of recognising the historic continuity of garden opening because it has shaped the contemporary use of gardens as visitor attractions. As Page (2003) argues, tourism is characterised by continuity and change in the form, nature and extent of tourist activity. A methodological approach incorporating an historical comparison with the present day is appropriate in a number of other areas of tourism research, but is little used other than to explain changing trends in tourism per se, and not to explain or engender a greater understanding of sub-sectors, where appropriate.

While Lowenthal (1985) argued that the past was a foreign place and that people in the past behaved differently and for different reasons, this paper posits that in respect to garden visiting, while modern practices and motivations may look superficially different, they are grounded in the past. In other words, the historical context provides a platform from which to better understand the scope and nature of gardens open to the public, and may even hold the key to solving contemporary problems.

References

Batey, M. (1996). As seen on TV. *The Garden History Society Newsletter, 46*, 2–3.

Benfield, R. W. (2001). "Good things come to those who wait". Sustainable tourism and timed entry at Sissinghurst Castle Garden, Kent. *Tourism Geographies, 3*(2), 207–217.

Billinge, M. (1996). A time and place for everything: An essay on recreation, re-creation and the Victorians. *Journal of Historical Geography, 22*(4), 443–459.

British Tourist Authority (2000). Promotional Activity—Gardens, http://www.visitbritain.com/corporate/gardens.htm. Accessed 5th December 2000.

Brown, J. (1999). *The pursuit of paradise. A social history of gardens and gardenin.* London: Harper Collins.

Buchan, U. (1995). Home and garden: A cup of tea and a taste of paradise. *Sunday Telegraph*, March 25th, 25.

Chadwick, G. F. (1966). *The park and the town.* London: Architectural Press.

Clarke, J., & Critcher, C. (1985). *The devil makes work. Leisure in capitalist Britain.* Basingstoke: Macmillan.

Clemenson, H. (1982). *English country houses and landed estates.* London: Croom Helm.

Coke, D. (1991). Pleasure-gardenIn. In G. Jellicoe, S. Jellicoe, P. Goode, & M. Lancaster (Eds.), *The Oxford companion to gardens* (pp. 441–443). Oxford: Oxford University Press.

Connell, J. (2004). The purest of human pleasures: The characteristics and motivations of garden visitors in Great Britain. *Tourism Management*, *25*(2). doi:10.1016/j.tourman.2003.09.21

Constantine, S. (1981). Amateur gardening and popular recreation in the 19th and 20th centuries. *Journal of Social History*, *14*, 389–403.

Corbett, S. (1998). Take care of the peonies and the crowds will take care of themselves. *Country Life*, *192*(46), 62–65.

Crandell, G. (1993). *Nature pictorialised.* Baltimore: John Hopkins University Press.

Dartington Institute (1987). *Employment generated by historic houses and gardens: A report to the historic houses association.* Dartington: Dartington Institute.

Durie, A. J. (2003). *Scotland for the holidays: Tourism in Scotland c1780–1939.* East Linton: Tuckwell Press.

English Tourism Council (2000). *Action for attractions.* Summary Leaflet, London: English Tourism Council.

English Tourism Council, Northern Ireland Tourist Board, VisitScotland and Wales Tourist Board (2000). *Sightseeing in the UK 1999.* London: English Tourism Council.

English Tourism Council, Northern Ireland Tourist Board, VisitScotland and Wales Tourist Board (2001). *Sightseeing in the UK 2000.* London: English Tourism Council.

Euromonitor (1999). Gardening in Europe—gardening equipment, *Global Market Information Database.* September 1999, Euromonitor.

Evans, M. (2001). Gardens tourism—is the market really blooming? *Insights, A153–159.* London: English Tourism Council.

Fearnley-Whittingstall, J. (2002). *The garden: An English love affair.* London: Weidenfeld and Nicolson.

Franklin, J. (1989). The victorian country houseIn. In G. E. Mingay (Ed.), *The rural idyll* (pp. 7–22). London: Routledge.

Gard, R. (Ed.), (1989). *The observant traveller. Diaries of travel in England, Wales and Scotland in the county record offices of England and Wales.* Association of County Archivists, London: HMSO.

Gardenvisit.com. (2000). http://www.gardenvisit.com. Accessed on 6th December 2000.

Garrod, B., Fyall, A., & Leask, A. (2002). Scottish visitor attractions: Managing visitor impacts. *Tourism Management*, *23*, 265–279.

Garrod, G., Pickering, A., & Willis, K. G. (1993). The economic value of botanic gardens: A recreational perspective. *Geoforum*, *24*(2), 215–224.

Gaze, J. (1988). *Figures in a landscape. A history of the National Trust.* London: Barrie and Jenkins.

Gifford, J., McWilliam, C., & Walker, D. (1984). *Edinburgh, the buildings of Scotland.* Harmondsworth: Penguin.

Girouard, M. (1978). *Life in the English country house.* London: Yale University Press.

Glyptis, S. (1991). *Countryside recreation.* Harlow: Longman.

Graefe, A. R., & Vaske, J. J. (1987). A framework for managing quality in the tourist experience. *Annals of Tourism Research*, *14*(3), 390–404.

Horn, P. (1980). *The rural world 1780–1850. Social change in the English countryside.* London: Hutchinson.

Hoskins, W. G. (1988). *The making of the English landscape.* London: Hodder and Stoughton.

Howkins, A. (1991). *Reshaping rural England: A social history 1850–1925.* London: Harper Collins Academic.

Hunningher, E. (2001). *Making gardens: The national gardens scheme.* London: Cassell.

Hunt, P. (Ed.), (1964). *The shell gardens book.* London: Phoenix House.

Hunt, J. D., & Willis, P. (1975). *The genius of the place.* London: Paul Elek.

King, P. (Ed.), (2000). *The good gardens guide 2000.* London: Bloomsbury Publishing.

Lane Fox, R. (2000). On the yellow book road. *Financial Times*, May 13th, 18.

Lasdun, S. (1991). *The English park: Royal, private and public.* London: Andre Deutsch Limited.

Littlejohn, D. (1997). *The fate of the English country house.* Oxford: Oxford University Press.

Lowenthal, D. (1985). *The past is a foreign country.* Cambridge: Cambridge University Press.

Mandler, P. (1997). *The fall and rise of the stately home.* New Haven: Yale University Press.

Mintel (2000). *Gardening review 2000.* London: Mintel.

Mintel (2002). *Visitor attractions in the UK.* London: Mintel.

Nicolson, N. (1996). Flying visits and passing glories. *Sunday Telegraph*, June 16th, 6.

Ousby (1990). *The Englishman's England: Taste, travel and the rise of tourism.* Cambridge: Cambridge University.

Owen, J. (1998). Gardening on a grand scale. *The Times*, April 4th.

Page, S. J. (2003). *Tourism management: Managing for change.* Oxford: Butterworth Heinemann.

Page, S. J., Forer, P., & Lawton, G. R. (1999). Small business development and tourism: *Terra incognita? Tourism Management*, *20*(4), 435–459.

Patmore, J. A. (1983). *Recreation and resources. Leisure patterns and leisure places.* Oxford: Blackwell.

Porteous, J. D. (1996). *Environmental aesthetics: Ideas, policies and planning.* London: Routledge.

Samuel, R. (1998). The lost gardens of Heligan. In R. Samuel (Ed.), *Island stories: Unravelling britain. Theatres of memory*, Vol. II (pp. 125–131).

Sayer, M. (1993). *The disintegration of heritage. Country houses and their collections 1979–1992.* Norwich: Michael Russell.

Smit, T. (1997). *The Lost Gardens of Heligan.* London: Gollancz.

Stevens, T. (2000). The future of visitor attractions. *Travel and Tourism Analyst*, *1*, 61–85.

Strong, R. (1991). Renaissance gardens. In G. Jellicoe, S. Jellicoe, P. Goode, & M. Lancaster (Eds.), *The Oxford companion to gardens* (pp. 164–165). Oxford: Oxford University Press.

Swarbrooke, J. (2001). Visitor attraction management in a competitive market. *Insights, A41–52.* London: English Tourism Council.

Taylor, H. (1995). Urban public parks, 1840–1900: Design and meaning. *Journal of Garden History*, *23*(2), 201–221.

The National Trust (2003). *Annual Report 2001/2*, www.nationaltrust.org.uk, Accessed 9th September 2003.

Thomas, K. (1983). *Man and the natural world: Changing attitudes 1500–1800 in England.* London: Allen Lane.

Tinniswood, A. (1998). *The polite tourist. A history of country house visiting.* London: The National Trust.

Towner, J. (1996). *An historical geography of recreation and tourism in the western world 1540–1940.* Chichester: Wiley.

J. Connell / Tourism Management 26 (2005) 185–201 201

Trevelyan, G. M. (1942). *English social history*. London: Longmans, Green and Co.

Urry, J. (1995). *Consuming places*. London: Routledge.

Whitaker, B., & Browne, K. (1971). *Parks for people*. New York: Winchester Press.

Whitsey, F. (1997). Gardening: Cutting thoughts on garden thieves. *Daily Telegraph*, July 12th, 6.

Wigan, M. (1998). *The Scottish Highland estate. Preserving an environment*. Shrewsbury: Swan Hill Press.

Worpole, K. (1997). The outdoor life. *Landscape Design*, March 1997, 25.

Young, J. (1981). *The country house in the 1980s*. London: George Allen and Unwin.

[35]

 Pergamon

www.elsevier.com/locate/atoures

Annals of Tourism Research, Vol. 27, No. 3, pp. 682–708, 2000
© 2000 Elsevier Science Ltd. All rights reserved
Printed in Great Britain
0160-7383/00/$20.00

PII: S0160-7383(99)00094-8

MANAGING HERITAGE TOURISM

Brian Garrod
University of the West of England, UK
Alan Fyall
Napier University, UK

Abstract: This article discusses the findings of a Delphi survey of owners and managers of historic properties, officers of heritage-based organizations, consultants, and academics from across the United Kingdom. The purpose of the study was to investigate the major constraints and imperatives relating to the long-term management of built heritage attractions. Three related issues were assessed: the fundamental mission of heritage attractions; the factors which impact upon decisions relating to charging for tourist entry; and the perceptions of heritage managers as to the respective roles of such attractions and public agencies in funding tourism management and heritage conservation programs. The paper then considers the significance of these issues in assessing potential strategies for moving heritage tourism toward sustainability. **Keywords:** heritage tourism, Delphi technique, mission, pricing, funding, sustainability, United Kingdom. © 2000 Elsevier Science Ltd. All rights reserved.

Résumé: La gestion du tourisme patrimonial. Cet article discute des résultats d'une enquête Delphi parmi des propriétaires et gérants des propriétés historiques, des comités directeurs d'organisations patrimoniales, des consultants et des universitaires de partout dans le Royaume-Uni. L'objet de l'étude était d'examiner les contraintes et impératifs liés à la gestion à long terme des attractions patrimoniales construites. On évalue trois questions apparentées: la mission fondamentale des attractions patrimoniales, les facteurs qui influent sur la tarification et les perceptions des gérants au sujet du rôle des attractions et des organismes gouvernementaux pour le financement de la gestion du tourisme et des programmes de sauvegarde. On considère ensuite l'importance de ces questions pour évaluer des stratégies éventuelles pour faire progresser le tourisme patrimonial vers la durabilité. **Mots-clés:** tourisme patrimonial, technique Delphi, mission, tarification, financement, durabilité, Royaume-Uni. © 2000 Elsevier Science Ltd. All rights reserved.

INTRODUCTION

The recent literature of tourism studies has been captivated with the notion of sustainable tourism. Rarely before has one single dimension of this research attracted so much attention and raised so much controversy. Indeed, a great many academic textbooks and journal articles focusing on the concept of sustainability have emerged over the past decade, some conceptualizing the main issues (Clarke 1997; Hunter 1995, 1997; Krippendorf 1987), some

---

Brian Garrod is Senior Lecturer in the Faculty of Economics and Social Science, University of the West of England (Coldharbour Lane, Bristol BS16 1QY, UK. Email ⟨brian.garrod@uwe.ac.uk⟩). **Alan Fyall** is Lecturer in the Marketing Cognate Group, Napier Business School, Napier University. Their current research focuses on development and implementation strategies for pursuing the objectives of sustainable tourism.

generally endorsing the concept (Cater and Goodall 1992; Eber 1992; Hunter and Green 1995; Inskeep 1991; Middleton and Hawkins 1998), and others censuring it (Hughes 1995; McKercher 1993; Wheeller 1994). There has also been a large number of collected works published on the theme of sustainable tourism (Bramwell, Henry, Jackson, Prat, Richards and van der Straaten 1996; Bramwell and Lane 1994; Briguglio, Archer, Jafari and Wall 1996; Cater and Lowman 1994; Hall and Lew 1998; Priestley, Edwards and Coccossis 1996; Stabler 1997).

Given this context, it is perhaps surprising that the heritage tourism sector has received relatively little attention from scholars interested in the concept of sustainable tourism. With a few notable exceptions (Anfield 1994; Cope 1995; Croft 1994; Johnson and Thomas 1995; van der Borg, Costa and Gotti 1996), the academic literature has preferred to concentrate on the cultural, educational, and practical conservation aspects of heritage tourism. Yet the heritage sector represents a highly significant component of tourism in many developed economies. In the United Kingdom, for example, the heritage sector has been described as "a major strength of the British market for overseas visitors" (Markwell, Bennett and Ravenscroft 1997:95) and is estimated to generate around 28% of all UK tourism expenditure annually (Carr 1994). The heritage sector has also been vaunted as a major potential growth area for tourism in the UK (Prentice 1993a). In view of the economic significance of heritage as a tourism "product", it is curious indeed that so little interest has been shown in assessing the conditions that must be met in order to secure its sustainability.

It is surprising that so little academic attention has been paid to exploring the relationship between heritage tourism and sustainability because the two concepts evidently share a common theme. Sustainable development has been defined as a process which ensures that "we pass onto the next generation a stock of [natural and built] capital assets no less than the stock we have now" (Pearce 1992:4). Heritage tourism, meanwhile, has been viewed simply as "tourism centred on what we have inherited, which can mean anything from historic buildings, to art works, to beautiful scenery" (Yale 1991:21). The pivotal concept in both of these definitions is clearly that of "inheritance", yet the connection between heritage tourism and sustainability still remains largely unexplored.

The purpose of this article is to investigate some of the possible reasons for this disparity. In particular, it is hypothesized that the notion of sustainable tourism is an "essentially contested concept" (Hall 1998), meaning that its definition and use is inherently a matter of dispute. As such, the term sustainable tourism has come to mean a great number of different things, according to the differing backgrounds and perceptions of those who are defining and employing it. This much is widely acknowledged in the literature (Garrod and Fyall 1998; Hunter 1997; McKercher 1993). However, the particular contribution of this article is to apply this analysis to the context of built heritage tourism. In short, it sets out to determine whether the relative slowness of the heritage tourism sector to catch on to the sustainability imperative can be explained by the distinctive institutional conventions and ideological imperatives of heritage managers. In so doing, the article considers the significance of three core issues: the fundamental mission of heritage attractions; the factors which impact upon decisions relating to charging entry fees; and the perceptions of managers as to the respective roles of heritage attractions and public agencies in funding such management and conservation programs.

MANAGING HERITAGE TOURISM

It has long been recognized that the ideological and institutional context of heritage tourism is fundamentally different from that of general tourism. In particular, it has been argued that a so-called "curatorial approach" still pervades the heritage sector (Leask and Goulding 1996). This implies a heritage mission that is primarily one of caring for the property and maintaining it in as pristine a state as possible, with issues such as financial solvency and public access entering into the decision-making process only as secondary considerations. In other words, the heritage mission tends to be perceived as comprising a conservation goal with financial and public access constraints. Indeed, many heritage managers do not even consider themselves to be in the "tourism business" (Croft 1994), preferring to view their role more as guardians of the national heritage than as providers of public access to it. The notion has even been advanced that some of these managers, particularly those in the museums and galleries sector, actually resent tourists for distracting them from their curatorial goals (Thomas 1998). One of the important consequences of this lack of attention to economic management issues by the heritage establishment has been the emergence of a considerable backlog of urgent maintenance and repair work, as access to traditional sources of public funding has been restricted by successive government spending cuts. The situation is now said to be critical with respect to historic buildings, which are especially prone to both natural decay and a wide range of negative tourist or user impacts (English Tourist Board 1991b).

Nevertheless, heritage managers have generally been reticent to explore more direct means of raising the revenues necessary to fund the maintenance and repair work the properties in their care inevitably require, whether they are open to the public or not. While the "user pays principle" is now widely recognized as a potential vehicle for promoting sustainability in the context of other major forms of tourism (Burns and Holden 1995; Forsyth, Dwyer and Clarke 1995; Laarman and Gregersen 1996), many heritage managers are apparently wary of adopting this principle. The effect is that users are presented with "token" admission prices which reflect only a part of the "full social costs" of their activities (Pearce, Markandya and Barbier 1989). The implications of this failure to recognize the "true" value of natural assets are well documented. The lack of representative prices tends to generate excessive demand for such assets, resulting in their physical overuse. Further, the absence of truly representative asset values tends to lead society to "underinvest" in their conservation, resulting in their physical deterioration. It might well be argued that these implications are equally valid in the context of built "heritage" assets.

Yet heritage managers generally remain unconvinced by the logic of the user pays principle. The literature suggests a number of reasons why this may be the case. First, it can be argued that heritage managers have tended to associate the pricing of access to heritage with its commodification, and the concern is that this will lead to the established "golden rules" of conservation (such as uniformity of concern) being displaced by contradictory commercial values (Newby 1994). It is argued that heritage has a value far beyond the price that can be put on it; a cultural value to society, both present and future, which one must not allow to become compromised by base commercial values. A second possible reason for the apparent lack of enthusiasm among heritage managers for charging for admission is that they find the notion difficult to reconcile with their ideological beliefs about the wider mission of the heritage sector (Curtis 1998; Glaister 1998; Leask and Goulding 1996). If potential visitors or tourists are prevented from experiencing the heritage property because it is too expensive, then whose heritage does the property represent and for whom is it being preserved? Charging anything more than a token price for admission is evidently a concept with which many heritage managers feel intensely uncomfortable; yet it would appear to have enormous potential as part of a strategy for moving the heritage sector toward sustainability. Not only does admission pricing offer the opportunity of managing tourist numbers, it also represents an important potential source of funds for managing their impact and for funding vital conservation programs.

Study Methods

With these research issues in mind, the authors conducted an initial postal survey of 300 managers and owners of built heritage properties, officers of organizations with a heritage remit, and heritage tourism consultants. The study took place during the summer of 1997 and the survey achieved a response rate of 28%, following a telephone reminder in September. The questionnaire used a Likert scale to elicit respondents' opinions on a range of issues relating to the management of built heritage tourism attractions, broadly defined as any property that attracts the public by virtue of its explicit connection with the past. The issues investigated included how the decision whether or not to charge admission prices is determined, how they are set in places where they are used, the types of visitation impact experienced at these attractions and the degree of severity of such impacts, and respondents' perceptions of what should be the fundamental mission of heritage attractions.

The initial survey generated some interesting and instructive findings with regard to management and pricing issues facing the heritage sector. Table 1 presents a summary of the major findings of the survey. Further details can be found in Fyall and Garrod (1998). On reviewing the results of the survey, a number of contextual issues were raised which it was felt required further exploration. In particular, how do pricing decisions fit into the overall mission of the heritage attraction? What are the major institutional constraints on the pricing of admission to heritage attractions? How far are present pricing practices contributing to, or perhaps detracting from, the sustainability of heritage attractions?

Issues such as these are probably too complex and abstract to be addressed using standard questionnaire techniques. First, they

Table 1. Principal Findings of the Initial Survey

Visitor Impacts

• Occasional overcrowding of parts of the site was considered to be a very important or extremely important problem by 62% of respondents; persistent overcrowding of parts of the site was considered to be a very important or extremely important problem by 48% of respondents.

• Almost all respondents reported some form of wear and tear due to visitors, including trampling, handling, humidity, temperature, pilfering and graffiti.

• Traffic congestion was deemed to be a relatively minor problem in comparison to the above; nevertheless the majority of traffic related problems were considered to be persistent rather than occasional.

• 82% of respondents reported the potential for management to compromise the authenticity of the heritage property as either a very important concern or extremely important concern.

Admission Pricing Practices

• Profit or surplus maximization was not widely employed in the heritage sector, while revenue maximization and revenue targeting were very widely employed; 48% of respondents considered the need to achieve revenue targets a very important or extremely important factor in their admission pricing strategy.

• The strategic use of admission pricing to influence the volume of visitors was not considered an important factor in influencing admission price decision-making; 53% of respondents considered the use of low admission prices to attract users unimportant; 67% considered the use of high admission prices to limit visitor volumes unimportant.

• Many managers did not consider admission pricing to be an essentially moral issue; 33% of respondents reported that they saw no need to keep prices low to avoid the exclusion of disadvantaged social groups.

The Heritage Mission

The following criteria were suggested for what makes a "successful" heritage attraction:

• The attraction must be inexpensive and visitor-friendly.
• It must be physically and intellectually accessible.
• It must balance the needs of the visitor and the conservation imperative.
• It must be able to maintain authenticity and the integrity of the site.
• It must deliver value for money.

require respondents to have specialist knowledge of the main concerns at stake and a good awareness of the major contextual issues relating to the study. Unless the survey is well targeted there is a risk that the respondents will not have sufficient expertise and familiarity with the issues at hand to provide meaningful responses to the questions posed. Second, such issues are not well disposed to being addressed within the framework of a standard postal questionnaire. With issues as complex and abstract as these, the respondents must be given every opportunity to address them at as deep a conceptual level as possible. Replies based on gut reactions or snap judgements are not likely to be especially valuable. It can be argued that traditional questionnaire-based survey techniques do not encourage the respondents to explore far enough beneath the surface of the issues being addressed.

In order to investigate these critical issues in greater depth, a follow-up study was undertaken using a version of the Delphi technique. The Delphi technique, originally developed in the early 50s (Dalkey and Helmer 1963), involves the formation of a panel of experts who are asked to perform some specialist task, such as forecasting a future variable or teasing out the critical elements of a practical problem. This takes place over a number of survey "rounds", which are usually conducted by mail, although studies have sometimes employed face-to-face interviews or computer-based conferences (Smith 1995). The purpose of the first round (known as the "scoping round") is to allow the panelists to establish the conceptual boundaries of the study; what the key issues to be considered are, and how they are to be framed. Subsequent rounds (known as "convergence rounds") seek to move the panel towards consensus on the issue at hand by circulating the results of each successive round back to the respondents, who are then asked to reappraise their responses in the light of those made by other panel members. As the technique progresses through a number of rounds, the panelists' responses can be expected to converge around a central value or key concept.

The major advantage of the Delphi technique is that it enables complex and polemical issues to be investigated over an extended period of time. The technique is iterative, so that respondents get to air their views and then to reconsider them in the light of those put forward by other panelists. Many researchers believe that this is preferable to the traditional "one shot" questionnaire where respondents are asked to make on-the-spot judgements in isolation from others (Pan, Vega, Vella, Archer and Parlett 1995). By enabling respondents to evaluate their responses against those of other experts, the Delphi technique attempts to achieve a higher quality of response on expert issues than a single round questionnaire is able to achieve. The panelists in a Delphi study do not meet one another and ideally should not know who else is sitting on the panel. The merit of this approach is that it encourages the panelists to express their expert opinions freely. Other research methods that attempt to synthesize expert opinion (such as focus groups) do not preserve the anonymity of their respondents and run the risk of generating findings that are biased either by the institutional loyalties of the individual participants or else by peer pressures arising among the group during the course of the study (Frechtling 1996).

The Delphi technique is well established as a tool of tourism research. It has been used in a range of contexts and in a number of different ways. The most common use of the technique in tourism is in forecasting future market conditions (Kaynak and Macaulay 1984; Liu 1988; Moeller and Shafer 1994; Yong, Keng and Leng 1989). Other studies, meanwhile, have applied the Delphi technique to resolving a specific issue, such as identifying the environmental impacts of an individual development (Green and Hunter 1992; Green, Hunter and Moore 1990a, 1990b) or determining appropriate marketing strategies for a particular destination (Pan et al 1995). It has also been suggested that the Delphi technique might be useful in estimating the non-market values associated with tourism (Grant, Human and Le Pelley 1998; Sinclair and Stabler 1997). Clearly this technique has considerable potential as a study method of both qualitative and quantitative tourism research.

Formation of the Panel and Study Format

Heritage tourism has traditionally involved individuals from a wide range of backgrounds, including conservators and curators, planners, operations managers, strategic experts, public relations experts, and marketing professionals. Therefore, it was felt that the panel should encompass as wide a range of professional expertise as possible. The final panel comprised heritage management consultants, local authority officers, heritage organization administrators, tourism academics, and museums officers in approximately equal numbers. A rather higher number of historic property managers sitting on the panel was considered appropriate given the applied nature of the issues being addressed.

While previous Delphi studies have sometimes included tourists in the panel (Green et al 1990a, 1990b), the present study does not. There were two main reasons for this. One, the focus of the study was on heritage managers' perceptions of the sustainability issue, which were felt to be important in explaining the relative slowness of the heritage sector to embrace the concept of sustainable tourism. While tourists' perceptions may have some bearing on heritage management practices, this is only likely to be an indirect influence (in as much as they may influence the perceptions of heritage managers). Two, the Delphi technique clearly relies on the opinions of experts; whether panelists drawn from the general public will possess sufficient expertise with regard to the specialist subject matter under investigation is a matter of some dispute in the Delphi literature (Hill and Fowles 1975; Masser and Foley 1987; Preble 1984). Therefore, the panel comprised individuals from the supply side of the heritage tourism sector. The panel was drawn from two separate sources. First, a number of respondents to the initial postal questionnaire expressed a willingness to be involved in a follow-up study. This questionnaire was aimed at owners of historic properties, managers of heritage attractions, heritage consultants, and those working in government or near-government organizations with a significant heritage remit. As such, the members of the panel drawn from the initial survey work represented a wide range of professional functions and expertise. Second, a number of academics, selected on the basis of their reputation as researchers in tourism, were included. The panelists were asked to commit themselves to completing three survey rounds; a scoping round and two convergence rounds. Table 2 illustrates the diverse backgrounds of the 17 members of the panel.

While the small panel size might be criticized for its lack of statistical representativeness, it should be borne in mind that the Delphi technique is not intended to serve as a substitute for a randomly sampled, statistically rigorous survey, but as a complement. Furthermore, previous research into the methodological basis of the technique tends to suggest that the absolute number does not determine the quality of the study findings, the balance of expertise represented on that panel does. Indeed, Delphi studies have been successfully undertaken with as many as 900 and as few as four panelists (Sinclair and Stabler 1997).

An important consideration in applying this research technique is to ensure that the panel members are permitted to employ their expertise effectively in exploring the subject matter of the study critically and in as much depth as possible. Many previous Delphi studies have been criticized for not making this allowance (Sackman 1975). Clearly panelists need to be given sufficient scope to interpret the questions according to their understanding of the issues involved and to apply their own perspectives to the problem set; otherwise they will either fail to address the issues in sufficient depth, or will become bored and disillusioned with the study (Martino 1972). Another consideration, actually common to many techniques of qualitative research, is the need to minimize the potential for bias to creep into the analysis because the different panel members, and they and the researchers, interpret the questions posed and the answers offered differently (Hill and Fowles 1975).

Table 2. Membership of the Delphi Panel

Membership	First Round	Second Round	Third Round
Heritage Management Consultant	2	2	1
Local Authority Officer	2	2	2
Heritage Organization Officer	2	2	2
Historic Property Manager	6	5	5
Academic	3	2	2
Museum/Working Museum Officer	2	2	2
Total	17	15	14

This may result in those involved in the study using the same words but speaking different languages. This eventuality is particularly relevant to the context of this study, given the comments made in the first section of this article regarding the conceptual flexibility of the notion of sustainable tourism.

Clearly a fine balance is required among the above considerations. The approach adopted by this study was to allow the panelists to define their own terms and to allow them every opportunity to explain their assumptions and reasoning within the framework of the questionnaire. Rather than to impose researcher-led definitions of key terms, such as sustainability, conservation, and heritage, the approach taken by the study was to allow the panel to define these terms for themselves and to ensure that these individual perspectives were highlighted and drawn to the attention of the other panelists. Given that the purpose of the study was to explore different perceptions of the sustainability concept and its application in the context of heritage tourism, it was considered that the imposition of a set of definitions of the key concepts would have frustrated this purpose. A common set of definitions would also have failed to capitalize on one of the major strengths of the Delphi technique: to enable the panel members to draw out and explore such differences, rather than to neglect them, as most other survey methodologies do. Thus, the questionnaires were left very "open" in style in order to facilitate this process. Panel members were also given copious feedback between study rounds, including a five-page document summarizing the responses of individual panelists to the questions posed in the scoping round.

The purpose of the Delphi study remained as the follow up on the initial postal survey, to provide a more qualitative context to the findings that had been generated and to fill in some of the gaps that had emerged in the coverage of the initial questionnaire. Accordingly, the following issues were isolated for further investigation: what heritage experts perceive the fundamental mission of heritage attractions to be; what they consider the major imperatives and constraints relating to the charging for admission to heritage properties to be over the next ten years; and how they perceive the respective roles of heritage attractions and government agencies in funding such management and conservation programs.

Study Findings

The scoping round began by asking panelists to offer their opinion as to what should be the fundamental mission of heritage attractions in general. It is clear from the responses that while the term sustainability was mentioned only by a small minority of panelists, there is nevertheless a substantial affinity between managers' perceptions of the fundamental mission of heritage attractions and the principles of sustainable development.

In order that the panelists might be able to reflect meaningfully upon their responses to the scoping round, the initial responses were synthesized under eight headings, each representing a different conceptual element of the heritage mission. As Table 3 shows, these conceptual elements demonstrate a strong resonance with the notion of sustainable development. First, there is a strong emphasis on conservation. If the use of heritage assets by the present generation is not to conflict with their potential use by future generations, then the fundamental task of the heritage sector must be to ensure an appropriate balance between the contemporary use of those assets and their conservation for the future. Access and relevance were also considered important elements in the mission. If heritage is to have meaning, either to the present or future generations, then it must be made accessible and relevant to those who wish to experience it. Again, a strong relationship with the principles of sustainable development is evident. The panelists also identified a need to recognize the importance of the local community in this mission—a requirement that is widely endorsed in the sustainable tourism literature.

Table 3. Typology of Elements in the Mission of Heritage Attractions

Conservation	The role of the heritage manager is to safeguard the heritage asset for posterity; to ensure that the use of heritage assets by the present generation does not compromise the ability of future generations to use and benefit from those assets; and to ensure that the present generation properly manages the heritage assets it holds in trust for the nation as a whole.
Accessibility	Heritage only has significance to the extent that it benefits people. If people are prevented from experiencing a heritage asset, it can no longer be considered part of their heritage. However, high levels of accessibility can lead to heritage assets becoming damaged. At the same time, conservation requirements can prevent the present generation from enjoying and benefiting from the heritage assets to the fullest extent.
Education	Education plays an important role in achieving accessibility. In order to appreciate the heritage asset, visitors must be able to understand its nature and significance, including why it should be conserved. This requires the use of an array of interpretational techniques, ranging from the very formal to the very informal. Education is most effective if it is also entertaining.
Relevance	Heritage attractions must be relevant to as wide an audience as possible; they should not be the preserve of a small minority of "heritage enthusiasts". Ideally, all visitors should leave with a better appreciation of why the heritage asset is relevant to them, the local area, and to the nation as a whole. Heritage attractions should also seek to be something with which the local community can identify, giving them a greater sense of place and pride.
Recreation	Part of the mission of heritage attractions must be to entertain visitors and provide a recreational opportunity. If they do not enjoy themselves then they will be less likely to make return visits or to recommend the attraction to others. Conservation requirements may limit the recreational potential of a heritage site.
Financial	Heritage attractions must be financially sound if they are to fulfil their overall mission. Finances need not, however, be generated entirely by charging for admission and some external funding, particularly for expensive conservation work, will inevitably be required.
Local Community	The heritage attraction should seek to work in harmony with the local community. Visitors should not be afforded use of the heritage asset at the expense of locals. Heritage attractions can also have important economic multiplier effects throughout the local community.
Quality	Heritage attractions must increasingly provide a high quality service to their visitors if they are to compete in the ever more crowded tourism marketplace. This includes providing a range of facilities, flexibility, a high standard of cleanliness, well-trained staff and adequate car parking. If a charge is made for admission then the heritage attraction should aim to exceed visitors' expectations.

In the two convergence rounds of the study, the panelists were asked to prioritize the eight elements identified in the scoping round. While several members stated that they found this task difficult, the degree of consistency evident in the rankings nevertheless indicates the development of a broad consensus. Indeed, a Spearman's rank correlation coefficient (r_s) of 0.9762 was recorded, indicating a very high level of agreement between the two sets of rankings (Table 4). The highest-ranked element in both rounds was conservation. The relatively low mean score attributed to conservation by almost all of the panelists suggests a widespread consensus on the importance of conserving heritage assets for the benefit of future generations. This contrasts with the considerably higher mean scores (and hence lower rankings) attributed to those elements relating to the contemporary use of the asset, such as recreation and relevance. The implication is that the importance of the heritage asset as an endowment for future generations is generally considered to outweigh its significance as an asset for contemporary use.

Whether this emphasis is to be considered consistent with sustainable development thinking is very much open to debate. As already discussed, sustainability is a highly contested concept and academics have identified a wide spectrum of philosophical positions on what it means in the context of tourism, ranging from the light green or "technocentric" to the deep green or "ecocentric" (Garrod and Fyall 1998; Henry and Jackson 1996; Hunter 1997). Deeper green viewpoints tend to place a greater emphasis on the importance of resource conservation over economic growth than lighter green perspectives. Some commentators might therefore argue that the higher priority that is accorded to conservation as compared with contemporary use is entirely consistent with sustainability, given the increasingly evident need to defend the interests of future generations against the highly adverse impacts associated with the contemporary use of heritage assets. Others, meanwhile, might choose to argue that conservation for the future is worthless in

Table 4. Prioritization of Elements in the Mission of Heritage Attractions

Mission	Second Round		Third Round		
	Mean Score	Rank	Mean Score	Rank	Change
Conservation	1.73	1	1.27	1	–
Accessibility	3.40	2	3.07	2	–
Education	4.60	4	4.00	3	↑
Relevance	5.33	6	5.07	6	–
Recreation	5.80	7	5.67	7	–
Finance	4.00	3	4.27	4	↓
Local Community	6.07	8	5.73	8	–
Quality	4.73	5	4.33	5	–
					$r_s = 0.9462$

itself. If each generation denies itself the use of heritage assets in order to conserve them for future generations, then no generation will ever allow itself to experience and engage fully with its heritage. The result will be to strip the heritage asset of its human dimension, consign its significance to the past, and deprive it of its fundamental identity. This latter view suggests rather less precedence being given to conservation as compared with other objectives relating to contemporary use (Bender and Edmonds 1992).

One can only speculate as to why conservation might be ranked so far above the other elements. Conceivably, the higher weighting that is generally accorded to conservation might be the result of the particularly strong notion of futurity that is often associated with heritage assets. Indeed, it is argued that the struggle between conservation and contemporary use is particularly evident in the case of heritage assets because the chain of bequest and inheritance is more explicit (Millar 1991). Alternatively, this heavy emphasis might be a reflection of the curatorial background of many of the respondents. A significant proportion of heritage attractions in the United Kingdom is owned by public sector authorities and organizations with trust status (Markwell et al 1997). Not only does this organizational context usually require managers to open the properties in their care to the public, at least occasionally, but it also confers a strong curatorial imperative upon them. They are charged with managing the nation's heritage on their behalf; if it is allowed to become damaged and degraded, then clearly they cannot be deemed to be acting responsibly (Cossons 1989; Cope 1995).

Another interesting feature of the rankings is that visitor or tourist education was ranked substantially higher than both relevance and recreation. While the panel recognized that education is more effective if it can be made entertaining, the panel still considered it more important to educate users than to offer them an entertaining recreational experience. Some writers have queried this view, arguing that the importance of education in the heritage mission has often been overplayed in the past (Berry 1994). Research into motivations suggests that they are not generally looking to be educated but to have a general leisure experience (Prentice 1993b). Indeed, it has been suggested that the motivation for visiting heritage attractions might better be likened to window shopping than knowledge gathering (Markwell et al 1997). There is a danger, therefore, that the heritage mission may overemphasize education at the expense of the more mundane role played by the heritage attraction in providing an opportunity for popular entertainment and recreation. On the other hand, the ranking of education above relevance might lend further support to the argument that users of heritage attractions often do not understand what they are gazing at (Urry 1990). Heritage clearly needs interpretation if it is to be of relevance to them. In this way, they may come to recognize the true value of the heritage asset experienced, including the need to maintain and conserve it (Moscardo 1996). Yet, as other writers have pointed out, heritage interpreters tend to be highly intelligent people, and there is a danger that the interpretation they provide will be comprehensible only to an educated elite of heritage devotees (Bramwell and Lane 1993).

Perhaps the most intriguing finding is that the mission of heritage attractions to the local community is ranked as least important of all the elements listed in Table 4. Much of what has been written about sustainable development in the context of tourism takes as its central theme the need to "maintain a balance" between the interests of the site, the user, and the host community (English Tourist Board 1991a). The latter is likely to experience many of the negative social and environmental impacts of heritage tourism, including traffic congestion, parking and access problems, and antisocial behavior on the part of tourists. On the other hand, the local community stands to benefit through the various economic multiplier effects generated by the attraction and the contribution of the heritage asset itself to the local social fabric and culture. If these impacts are not given sufficient weighting in the overall "balance", then the management of heritage attractions must surely be unsustainable.

Factors Influencing Pricing Strategy

The second task set before the Delphi panelists was to consider the principal factors likely to influence pricing strategy in the UK heritage tourism sector over the coming decade. Table 5 shows that the responses fell into four major categories: financial pressures, the state of competition, the user profile, and issues relating to the management of access. In the two convergence rounds, the panelists were asked to rank these factors according to their assessment of their likely importance. As with the previous exercise, while some reported that they found this task quite difficult and taxing, a remarkable degree of unanimity emerged in the responses. Table 6 illustrates the rankings achieved and shows that a Spearman's rank correlation coefficient (r_s) of 0.9835 was recorded, again indicating a very high level of agreement between the rankings achieved in each of the two convergence rounds.

Overall, it would appear that the commercial environment of the heritage tourism sector is set to become more difficult and challenging over the coming decade. The striking feature of Table 6 is that the highest ranked factors generally relate to the financial pressures experienced by heritage attractions. Indeed, the final rankings suggest that the most important influence on pricing strategy over the coming decade will be the need to cover further increases in maintenance and conservation costs. This expectation is widely echoed in the academic literature (Berry 1994; Cossons 1989) and is particularly significant in view of the considerable backlog of conservation and maintenance work that has already been referred to in this article. Meanwhile, the second highest ranked factor suggests that it will become increasingly difficult for heritage attractions to obtain external sources of revenue over the coming decade. Clearly the panel expects the unfavorable financial situation in which much of the heritage sector already finds itself to worsen over the next decade.

The heightened financial pressures faced by the heritage sector may also be a function of the increased competitive pressures, both internal and external, that are being brought to bear on heritage attractions. This notion is supported by the third and fifth highest ranked factors, which suggest that the competitive pressures experienced are likely to become more intense over the coming decade. Not only will there be heightened internal competition from within

Table 5. Typology of Factors Influencing Pricing Strategy

Financial Pressures
• *Increased operating costs*: particularly as maintenance and repair costs continue to mount.
• *Tighter external funding*: especially in terms of obtaining external funding from local authorities, business sponsorships, legacies and charitable organizations.
• *Enhanced role of ancillary activities in revenue generation*: ancillary activities, such as gift shops and tea rooms, are likely to play an increasingly important part in generating revenues for heritage attractions.

Competition
• *Increased competition from other leisure activities*: including theme parks, shopping malls, and multimedia entertainment complexes.
• *Increased competition within the market for heritage visits*: the market for heritage attractions itself looks set to become increasingly crowded.
• *Increasing international character of the market*: with international tourists becoming an ever more important market segment.

Visitor Profile
• *Reduced emphasis on the traditional family group*: as society changes there are likely to be fewer traditional family groups visiting attractions.
• *Increased participation by older people in the market*: with an ageing national population, a growing tendency towards early retirement and wider car ownership, the share of older people in the visitor profile is likely to increase.
• *Increased interest in nostalgia*: with the millennium drawing near there will be an increased interest in the nation's heritage.
• *Increasing visitor expectations*: especially with regard to the standard of presentation, interpretation and on-site facilities as visitors experience improved standards in other leisure market sectors.

Managing Access
• *Pricing will become more important as a tool for managing demand*: charging for admission will be required if carrying capacities are not to be exceeded.
• *Social pricing will be less important*: that is, strategic price-setting designed to allow people across all income brackets to visit is becoming an outdated concept.
• *Prohibitive pricing will be resisted*: token pricing will continue to be the norm.
• *Managing visitor impact will be more costly*: managing the impact of visitors will become more challenging and hence more costly. This will force heritage attractions to review their current pricing practices.

the increasingly congested heritage market, but this as a whole will also face greater external competition from other related leisure markets (such as theme parks, leisure centers, and shopping complexes). If individual heritage attractions do not compete successfully at both of these levels, then user numbers—and hence admission revenues—will surely continue to fall. The fourth and (jointly) sixth ranked factors suggest one possible response to the

Table 6. Factors Likely to Influence Pricing Strategy Over the Next Decade

Factor	Second Round		Third Round		
	Mean Score	Rank	Mean Score	Rank	Change
Financial Pressures					
Increased operating costs	3.53	1	3.14	1	–
Tighter external funding	4.73	3	3.86	2	↑
Enhanced role of ancillary activities in income generation	5.47	4	5.64	4	–
Competition					
Increased competition from other leisure activities	4.60	2	5.07	3	↓
Increased competition within the market for heritage visits	5.73	6	6.36	5	↑
Increasingly international market place	10.13	12	10.21	12	–
Visitor Profile					
Reduced emphasis on traditional family group	10.27	13	10.35	13	–
Increase share of older people in visit rates	7.47	9	9.00	9	–
Increased interest in nostalgia as millennium draws nearer	10.40	14	11.57	14	–
Increased visitor expectations regarding standards and facilities	5.53	5	6.64	6=	↓
Managing Access					
Pricing will become more important as a tool for managing demand	6.20	8	6.71	8	–
Social pricing will be less important	8.53	10	10.21	11	↓
Prohibitive pricing will be resisted by those managing heritage attractions	9.53	11	9.79	10	↑
Managing the environmental impacts of visitors will be more costly	6.00	7	6.64	6=	↑

$$r_s = 0.9835$$

problems of increased financial and competitive pressures: to attempt to increase spending by visitors in on-site gift and tea shops, restaurants, craft outlets, supplementary exhibits, and so on. This view seems quite common in the heritage sector. For example, it is argued that, as a benchmark, a heritage attraction should aim to double its adult admission revenue through secondary spending by users once they have come on-site (Markwell et al 1997).

There are, however, several reasons to question whether this strategy is entirely consistent with the sustainability of the heritage attraction. First, investment in such facilities can be very expensive and must surely be at the opportunity cost of investment in better interpretation, conservation programs, and management practices. Second, users can only spend on-site if they are first admitted to it. Under such conditions it is tempting for the heritage manager to set admission charges relatively low in order to encourage more people to visit their attraction, hoping that any loss of admission revenue can be made up through secondary spending. This is often seen as an attractive strategy because of the long-standing tendency of the heritage sector to judge the "success" of an attraction by the number of visitors it has admitted. Unfortunately, this tendency has been reinforced by the academic literature. For example, Yale (1991) explicitly correlates success with attracting greater numbers. It has also been reinforced by the industry itself, in the annual "league tables" based on visitor numbers produced by organizations such as the British Tourist Authority and English Heritage. The danger is that as numbers grow so too do resulting impacts on the heritage property and its surrounding area. In this case the short-term success of the attraction in achieving greater numbers might turn into long-term failure as the heritage assets that serve to promote visitations become damaged and degraded (English Tourist Board 1991b).

In contrast, while the potential for the use of admission charges in managing access was widely raised in the scoping round, the results of the two convergence rounds suggest that the panel does not consider the issue particularly significant. Indeed, none of the factors relating to the use of pricing as a tool for managing access was ranked in the top five. The general lack of enthusiasm for the use of pricing as a strategic tool for managing demand perhaps indicates the widespread tendency for heritage attractions to adopt "token" pricing strategies. This means the setting of "neutral" admission charges which are intended neither to encourage nor to discourage visitors. Opponents of admission pricing often propose alternative methods of managing access to heritage properties, such as timed tickets, limiting parking space, or adopting low key marketing strategies (Cadogan 1995). It should be noted, however, that these forms of physical restraint are just as liable to restrict access to the heritage property. While it could be argued in the context of other forms of tourism that admission pricing is socially inequitable in that it may serve to deter poorer social groups, while measures based on physical restraint have a more even impact across the social strata, care should be taken in applying this assertion to the context of the heritage sector. Users of heritage attractions are often from the more wealthy social groups in any case. Poorer members of society do not visit heritage attractions because they are too often inaccessible to them, either socially or physically. Moreover, the reality of the situation is that managers typically seem to be more concerned with admission prices *per se* deterring repeat visits than they are about *enhanced* admission prices excluding poorer people (Curtis 1998).

It is also relevant to note that of the four factors relating to the use of admission charges to manage access, the expectation that visitation impacts would impose increasingly significant costs was ranked highest. This tends to suggest that the panel expected heritage attractions to adopt a largely reactive strategy towards the sustainability issue, or to accept that more costly impacts are inevitable rather than to take strategic measures to moderate them. Perhaps this is to be expected given the stated mission of many attractions in the heritage sector to provide access to the general public. However, it is worrying because many writers on the subject of sustainable development argue that proactive strategies are needed in addressing the sustainability imperative.

This raises the question of the extent to which the duty of the heritage sector to provide access to the public should be considered unconditional. Given the damage that visitors can do to the fabric and ambience of a heritage site, and the higher priority given by the panel to conservation as opposed to contemporary use, it might be argued that charging for admission is the lesser of two evils. This may limit access to the heritage attraction, but at the same time this will reduce impacts on the fabric of the site and the local area, and perhaps provide additional funds for presentation, interpretation, management, and conservation works. As tourism practitioners are now beginning to recognize, free and unlimited access to a heritage asset can serve to destroy that asset, thereby limiting access for future generations. Where heritage assets are provided essentially as "free goods", there is always the danger of "free riding", leading to excessive and unsustainable use (Grant et al 1998).

Funding Priorities

The third question in the scoping round asked the panel to consider what they felt the criteria should be for setting the conservation-funding priorities of organizations such as the National Trust and English Heritage. The Delphi questionnaire asked the panelists to identify a range of possible criteria and to explain their reasoning. As Table 7 shows, the responses to the scoping round fell into four major categories: significance, risk elements, economic aspects, and management considerations. In the two convergence rounds the panelists were asked to rank the criteria established in the scoping round according to their importance. Table 8 illustrates the rankings achieved after the second and third rounds.

Table 7. Typology of Public Funding Priorities

Significance
• *Uniqueness*: significance can be defined in terms of an asset's intrinsic rarity value: a unique heritage asset should be conserved at almost any cost.
• *Relevance*: significance can be equated with relevance to the visitors, the local community, and the nation as a whole: a heritage asset that is not relevant to people has no meaning.
• *Public appeal*: can be used as a measure of significance. It can be argued that the public are the best judge of what is important to them.
• *Educational merit*: significance can also be defined in terms of the actual or potential educational merit of the asset in question.

Risk Elements
• *Irreversibility*: this conception of risk relates to the possibility that a heritage asset may be permanently lost if it is not appropriately conserved.
• *Visitor impact*: some heritage sites are under serious threat because of the pressure of visitor numbers and/or the behaviour of users.
• *Depreciation*: all heritage assets, regardless of whether or not they are open to the public, are inevitably vulnerable to the ravages of time.

Economic Aspects
• *Financial independence*: those attractions that are more likely to be able to generate their own funds in the future should be prioritized.
• *Complementary funding potential*: priority should be accorded to those attractions that are more able to attract matching funding from other funding sources.
• *Avoiding commercial pressures*: special consideration should be given to those attractions that find it hard to compete in the market without investment in ancillary facilities.
• *Multiplier effects*: public conservation funding should be awarded to those attractions that have the greatest potential to contribute to local economic development.

Management Considerations
• *Timeliness*: conservation funding should be channeled toward those attractions for which timely conservation will save greater conservation costs in the future.
• *Managerial prudence*: those attractions that have introduced parallel measures to prevent further deterioration should be considered more worthy of public conservation funding.
• *Consolidation*: priority should be given to those sites that, if conserved, enable the consolidation of existing holdings and more effective management over all.

The question of how to prioritize conservation funding proved to be the most controversial of the three issues addressed by the study. For this particular question, a Spearman's rank correlation coefficient (r_s) of 0.7890 is reported. While this figure in itself indicates a high degree of correlation between the two sets of rankings, the coefficient proved somewhat lower than that which was calculated for either of the two preceding questions. The implication is that the panelists were more than ready to refine their initial responses after further reflection. Evidently the members found the iterative

Table 8. Heritage Conservation Priorities for Funding Organizations

Priority	Second Round		Third Round		
	Mean Score	Rank	Mean Score	Rank	Change
Significance					
Those attractions that are most rare and/or unique	2.21	1	2.14	1	–
Those attractions that have the greatest relevance to visitors, the local community and the nation	4.57	3	2.93	3	–
Those attractions that are most heavily visited by the public	9.00	13	9.21	10	↑
Those attractions with the highest educational merit/potential	7.86	7=	7.43	5	↑
Risk Elements					
Those attractions that are likely to be permanently lost unless conserved	2.36	2	2.71	2	–
Those attractions under the heaviest pressure from visitor numbers	8.71	10	9.36	11	↓
Those attractions under the greatest threat from the natural elements	6.86	5	9.00	8=	↓
Economic Aspects					
Those attractions most able to generate their own funding in the future	9.71	14	11.21	14	–
Those attractions most able to attract matching funding from other sources	8.50	9	9.00	8=	↑
Those attractions that would find it hard to compete without investment in their ancillary services	8.93	12	8.36	7	↑
Those attractions with the greatest potential to contribute to local economic development	7.86	7=	8.00	6	↑
Management Considerations					
Those attractions for which timely intervention will save greater conservation costs in the future	4.64	4	4.86	4	–
Those attractions introducing parallel measures to prevent deterioration	8.79	11	10.07	13	↓
Those attractions that permit the consolidation of existing holdings	7.21	6	9.79	12	↓

$r_s = 0.7890$

Delphi process helpful in assisting them to form their opinions on this particular issue.

Table 8 shows that the highest ranked criterion related to the rarity value or uniqueness of the heritage asset in question. This would tend to suggest that those assets that are representative of a particular genre of which there are few other remaining examples should be conserved in preference to those where many good examples still exist. This is resonant of the traditional conservation viewpoint, that the conservator's duty is to preserve archetypal examples of what remains of significant heritage sites, buildings, and artifacts. Public appeal, as demonstrated by users' rates, was ranked much lower by the panel (13th in the second round, rising to 10th in the third round).

It could be debated whether this view is fully compatible with the principles of sustainable development. On the one hand, it might be argued that today's general public is not in a strong position to anticipate the needs and wants of future generations regarding heritage assets in general, and heritage tourism in particular. If this is true, then decisions about what is to be conserved for posterity and what is not are best placed in the hands of experts, who are in a much better position to choose on behalf of future generations. It does not necessarily follow that those heritage assets that have the greatest public appeal at present will be of relevance to people in the future. Nor does it necessarily follow that those heritage properties that currently have only a limited public appeal, or about which the general public knows or cares little, should be considered any less worthy of preservation for the future. This view is often put forward by the heritage establishment (Newby 1994).

On the other hand, it might be argued that the best way to judge the preferences of future generations is to examine those of the present generation. If persons making conservation decisions are drawn from the ranks of intellectuals and the social elite, then arguably they will not be in a good position to determine what kind of heritage the general public of the future will wish to inherit (Newby 1995). There is then a danger that the heritage sector will remain largely the province of middle class "heritage enthusiasts", and hence accessible and relevant only to a very narrow cross-section of society as a whole.

There are also a number of features (Table 8) which relate back to the previous study question on admission pricing strategy. First is that the panel did not generally feel that the pressures imposed by visitors on heritage attractions should be a major criterion for determining conservation funding. Perhaps the panelists assumed that the attractions facing the most pressure from users would be the most frequently visited locations and associated this with public appeal, which was itself not considered to be an important criterion for making decisions about conservation funding. It is unclear, however, where this leaves small, fragile sites that are put under intolerable pressure from even a small trickle of visitors.

Second, it was noticeable that the panel did not place a high priority on directing external conservation funding towards those attractions that would otherwise have to make further investments in their on-site ancillary services in order to raise the required funds internally. This may be viewed as a matter of some concern, given that one of the most significant impacts noted in the initial study was that of facilities (such as signs, stairways, ramps, toilet blocks, gift shops, and car parking facilities) on the authenticity of the heritage asset. Maintaining a high throughput of visitors may also have ramifications in terms of direct impacts, such as trampling, handling, pilfering, traffic congestion, and so on. It can be argued that this is hardly a sustainable strategy, especially in comparison to the low volume, high revenue strategy suggested by admission pricing (Fyall and Garrod 1996).

Third, and perhaps most significantly, the panel did not consider the ability of the attraction to generate its own funding in the future to be an important criterion for assessing conservation priorities. This suggests that the panel assumed the external funding of heritage conservation will always be required. Perhaps this is true, but it is of some concern that the panel considers the ability to generate independent funding so low an imperative for heritage attractions. If the panel's predictions of more difficult financial times ahead are correct, then heritage attractions will simply have to become ever more self-reliant as a survival tactic. Again the discussion turns back to the potential role of strategic pricing in pursuing the heritage mission.

CONCLUSION

Perhaps the most striking feature of this study was the emergence of a fairly close association between the fundamental elements of the heritage mission and the widely acknowledged principles of sustainable development. This judgement is supported by Cope (1995) and Phillips (1995), both of whom interpret the founding philosophies of the National Trust as being essentially synonymous with the principles of sustainable development. Nevertheless, it is evident from the Delphi ranking exercise that a number of important interpretational disparities remain in practice. These relate particularly to the balance that is to be achieved between conservation and contemporary use, the part that is to be played by education in the heritage mission, and the nature of the relationship among the heritage attraction, tourists, and the local community. Further exploration of these issues suggests that the proposed correlation between the heritage mission and the objectives of sustainable development may in fact be somewhat misleading. The results of the Delphi survey suggest that the heritage establishment tends to place more emphasis on conservation and education, and less on contemporary use and local community, than is evident in most other interpretations of the sustainability imperative. Whether this approach is capable of achieving genuinely sus-

tainable development is open to debate. Proponents of more ecocentric versions of sustainability might argue that this is entirely in
keeping with the sustainability imperative; if heritage properties
are not conserved, then they will ultimately become lost and unable
to be part of the heritage of future generations. Others adopting a
more technocentric perspective, however, might wish to argue that
futurity should not be achieved at the expense of equity in the pursuit of sustainable development. If the present generation is denied
access to the heritage property, then it will just as surely cease to
be a relevant part of their heritage.

    The survey also highlighted a number of important contextual
issues relating to the subject of pricing strategy among heritage
attractions. While previous studies have examined pricing practices
among attractions in a quantitative manner (Leask and Goulding
1996; Rogers 1995), none have attempted to interpret their results
in the light of a qualitative understanding of the prevailing constraints and imperatives of tourism management. What is particularly revealing about the findings of the Delphi study is that while
the panelists generally anticipated more difficult financial times
ahead for the heritage sector, elevated admission prices were not
generally thought to be a suitable strategic response. This might be
considered surprising given the enthusiasm for applying the so-
called "user pays principle" that is often expressed in the context of
other economic activities, including various tourism sectors.
Nevertheless, heritage managers tend to argue that elevated admission pricing usually runs counter to the fundamental mission of
heritage attractions, which explicitly includes providing public
access to the property or site concerned.

    Two alternative approaches to elevated admission prices were
proposed in the course of the Delphi study: the use of physical
restraints and attempting to increase visitors' secondary spending.
It is not clear why the former is considered acceptable while strategic admission pricing is not, as both would appear to restrict
access. The strategy of trying to increase secondary spending, meanwhile, carries with it a number of inherent dangers. One, the pursuit of secondary spending usually requires investment in additional
on-site facilities, such as gift shops, restaurants, and other ancillary
services. This kind of development is widely acknowledged to
detract from the authenticity of the heritage experience and can
divert investment away from vital repair, maintenance, and conservation work. Two, the strategy of attempting to increase secondary
spending is often only viable when visitor numbers are stable or
increasing. If the heritage property is approaching its carrying capacity, or has already exceeded it, then this strategy is likely to
prove counter-productive in the long run.

    The study also proved of significant value in exploring experts'
perceptions of what should be the conservation funding priorities of
major heritage organizations. Perhaps it was to be expected that
managers would consider factors such as rarity and uniqueness to
head the list of funding priorities. This approach places the respon-

sibility for selecting what is to be conserved and what is to be inherited firmly in the hands of experts and resonates strongly with the traditional curatorial approach to heritage management. Whether this is entirely consistent with sustainable development thinking is, however, open to debate. This article suggests that unless a wider range of stakeholders is involved in the decision-making process, heritage runs the risk of losing its relevance and meaning. It is hard to see how an attraction could be considered part of a "sustainable" heritage sector if this were allowed to happen.

Finally, the study generated a number of new insights into the relationship between conservation funding priorities and pricing practices. The establishment largely accepts that individual heritage properties will need some degree of external funding in order to pay for the repair, maintenance, and conservation work all such properties inevitably require. Nevertheless, it was not generally considered acceptable to prioritize properties that are most threatened by excessive visitation numbers, nor was it considered necessary to prioritize properties that would otherwise be forced to adopt pricing policies aimed at increasing secondary spending. What becomes clear is that the establishment is firmly wedded to what has been called the "curatorial" view of heritage management. This article suggests, however, that this approach is not entirely synonymous with the more generally accepted notion of sustainable development. If one thing is clear, it is that sustainable heritage management will not be achieved by maintaining the *status quo*. New management philosophies and practices will have to be adopted.■

Acknowledgments—The authors would like to thank the panelists who took part in this study for their participation and forbearance. Thanks are due to Luiz Moutinho and Richard O'Doherty for their insightful comments on early drafts of this article.

REFERENCES

Anfield, J.
    1994 Loving them to Death: Sustainable Tourism in National Parks. *In* Cultural Tourism, J. M. Fladmark, ed., pp. 199–213. London: Donhead Publishing.
Bender, B., and M. Edmonds
    1992 Stonehenge: Whose Past? What Past? Tourism Management 14:355–357.
Berry, S.
    1994 Conservation, Capacity and Cashflows: Tourism and Historic Building Management. *In* Tourism: The State of the Art, A. V. Seaton, ed., pp. 712–718. Chichester: Wiley.
Bramwell, B., and B. Lane
    1993 Interpretation and Sustainable Tourism: The Potential and the Pitfalls. Journal of Sustainable Tourism 1:71–80.
Bramwell, B., and B. Lane, eds.
    1994 Rural Tourism and Sustainable Rural Development. Clevedon: Channel View.
Bramwell, B., I. Henry, G. Jackson, A. G. Prat, G. Richards, and J. van der Straaten, eds.
    1996 Sustainable Tourism Management: Principles to Practice. Tilburg: Tilburg University Press.

Briuglio, L., B. Archer, J. Jafari, and G. Wall, eds.
  1996 Sustainable Tourism in Islands and Small States: Issues and Policies. London: Pinter.
Burns, P. M., and A. Holden
  1995 Tourism: A New Perspective. London: Prentice Hall.
Cadogan, G.
  1995 Buildings. *In* The National Trust: The Next Hundred Years, H. Newby, ed., pp. 117–134. London: The National Trust.
Carr, E. A. J.
  1994 Tourism and Heritage: The Pressures and Challenges of the 1990s. *In* Building a New Heritage: Tourism, Culture and Identity in the New Europe, G. J. Ashworth and P. J. Larkham, eds., pp. 50–68. London: Routledge.
Cater, E., and B. Goodall
  1992 Must Tourism Destroy its Resource Base? *In* Environmental Issues in the 1990s, A. M. Mannion and S. R. Bowlby, eds., pp. 309–323. Chichester: Wiley.
Cater, E., and G. Lowman, eds.
  1994 Ecotourism: A Sustainable Option? New York: Wiley.
Clarke, J.
  1997 A Framework of Approaches to Sustainable Tourism. Journal of Sustainable Tourism 5:224–233.
Cope, D.
  1995 Sustainable Development and the Trust. *In* The National Trust: The Next Hundred Years, H. Newby, ed., pp. 53–69. London: The National Trust.
Cossons, N.
  1989 Heritage Tourism—Trends and Tribulations. Tourism Management 11:192–194.
Croft, T.
  1994 What Price Access? Visitor Impact on Heritage in Trust. *In* Cultural Tourism, J. M. Fladmark, ed., pp. 169–178. London: Donhead Publishing.
Curtis, S.
  1998 Visitor Management in Small Historic Cities. Travel & Tourism Analyst 3:75–89.
Dalkey, N., and O. Helmer
  1963 An Experimental Application of the Delphi Method to the Use of Experts. Management Science 9:458–467.
Eber, S., ed.
  1992 Beyond the Green Horizon: Principles for Sustainable Tourism. Godalming: World Wide Fund for Nature.
English Tourist Board
  1991a Tourism and the Environment: Maintaining the Balance. London: English Tourist Board.
  1991b Heritage Sites Working Group: Final Report to the Tourism and the Environment Task Force. London: English Tourist Board.
Forsyth, P., L. Dwyer, and H. Clarke
  1995 Problems in the Use of Economic Instruments to Reduce Adverse Environmental Impacts of Tourism. Tourism Economics 1:265–282.
Frechtling, D.
  1996 Practical Tourism Forecasting. Oxford: Butterworth-Heinemann.
Fyall, A., and B. Garrod
  1996 Sustainable Heritage Tourism: Achievable Goal or Elusive Ideal? *In* Managing Cultural Resources for the Tourist, M. Robinson, N. Evans and P. Callaghan, eds., pp. 239–270. Sunderland: Business Education Publishers.
  1998 Heritage Tourism: At What Price? Managing Leisure 3:213–228.
Garrod, B., and A. Fyall
  1998 Beyond the Rhetoric of Sustainable Tourism? Tourism Management 19:199–212.
Glaister, D.
  1998 Charges Fear is Staved Off. The Guardian (March 18):18.
Grant, M., B. Human, and B. Le Pelley.
  1998 Who Pays for the Free Lunch? Destination Management and the "Free Good" Factor. English Tourist Board Insights (January):A95–A101.

Green, H., and C. Hunter
 1992 The Environmental Impact Assessment of Tourism Development. *In* Perspectives on Tourism Policy, P. Johnson and B. Thomas, eds., pp. 29–47. London: Mansell.
Green, H., C. Hunter, and B. Moore
 1990a Application of the Delphi Technique in Tourism. Annals of Tourism Research 17:270–279.
 1990b Assessing the Environmental Impact of Tourism Development: Use of the Delphi Technique. Tourism Management 11:111–120.
Hall, C. M.
 1998 Historical Antecedents of Sustainable Development and Ecotourism: New Labels on Old Bottles. *In* Sustainable Tourism: A Geographical Perspective, C. M. Hall and A. A. Lew, eds., pp. 13–24. Harlow: Longman.
Hall, C. M., and A. A. Lew, eds.
 1998 Sustainable Tourism: A Geographical Perspective. Harlow: Longman.
Henry, I. P., and G. A. M. Jackson
 1996 Sustainability of Management Processes and Tourism Products and Contexts. Journal of Sustainable Tourism 4:17–28.
Hill, K. Q., and J. Fowles
 1975 The Methodological Worth of the Delphi Forecasting Technique. Technological Forecasting and Social Change 7:179–192.
Hughes, G.
 1995 The Cultural Construction of Sustainable Tourism. Tourism Management 16:49–59.
Hunter, C.
 1995 On the Need to Re-Conceptualise Sustainable Tourism Development. Journal of Sustainable Tourism 3:155–165.
 1997 Sustainable Development as an Adaptive Paradigm. Annals of Tourism Research 24:850–867.
Hunter, C., and H. Green, eds.
 1995 Tourism and the Environment: A Sustainable Relationship? London: Routledge.
Inskeep, E.
 1991. Tourism Planning: An Integrated and Sustainable Development Aproach. London: Routledge.
Johnson, P., and B. Thomas
 1995 Heritage as Business. *In* Heritage, Tourism and Society, D. T. Herbert, ed., pp. 170–190. London: Mansell.
Kaynak, E., and J. A. Macaulay
 1984 The Delphi Technique in the Measurement of Tourism Market Potential: The Case of Nova Scotia. Tourism Management 5:87–101.
Krippendorf, J.
 1987 The Holiday Makers: Understanding the Impact of Leisure and Travel. Oxford: Heinemann.
Laarman, J. G., and H. M. Gregersen
 1996 Pricing Policy in Nature-Based Tourism. Tourism Management 17:247–254.
Leask, A., and P. Goulding
 1996 What Price our Heritage? A Study of the Role and Contribution of Revenue Management in Scotland's Heritage Based Visitor Attractions. *In* Managing Cultural Resources for the Tourist, M. Robinson, N. Evans and P. Callaghan, eds., pp. 239–270. Sunderland: Business Education Publishers.
Liu, J. C.
 1988 Hawaii Tourism in the Year 2000: A Delphi Forecast. Tourism Management 9:279–290.
Markwell, S., M. Bennett, and N. Ravenscroft
 1997 The Changing Market for Heritage Tourism: A Case Study of Visits to Historic Houses in England. International Journal of Heritage Studies 3:95–108.
Martino, J. P.
 1972 Technological Forecasting for Decisionmaking. New York: Elsevier.

Masser, I., and P. Foley
  1987 Delphi Revisited: Expert Opinion in Urban Analysis. Urban Studies
    24:217–225.
McKercher, B.
  1993 The Unrecognised Threat to Tourism: Can Tourism Survive
    "Sustainability"? Tourism Management 14:131–136.
Middleton, V. T. C., and R. Hawkins
  1998 Sustainable Tourism: A Marketing Perspective. Oxford: Butterworth-
    Heinemann.
Millar, S.
  1991 Heritage Management for Heritage Tourism. *In* Managing Tourism, S.
    Medlik, ed., pp. 115–121. Oxford: Butterworth-Heinemann.
Moeller, G. H., and E. L. Shafer
  1994 The Delphi Technique: A Tool for Long-Range Travel and Tourism
    Planning. *In* Travel, Tourism and Hospitality Research: A Handbook for
    Managers and Researchers, J. R. B. Ritchie and C. R. Goeldner, eds., pp.
    473–480. New York: Wiley.
Moscardo, G.
  1996 Mindful Visitors: Heritage and Tourism. Annals of Tourism Research
    23:376–397.
Newby, H.
  1995 The Next One Hundred Years. *In* The National Trust: The Next Hundred
    Years, H. Newby, ed., pp. 150–163. London: The National Trust.
Newby, P. T.
  1994 Tourism: Support or Threat to Heritage? *In* Building a New Heritage:
    Tourism, Culture and Identity in the New Europe, G. J. Ashworth and P. J.
    Larkham, eds., pp. 206–228. London: Routledge.
Pan, S. Q., M. Vega, A. J. Vella, B. H. Archer, and G. R. Parlett
  1995 A Mini-Delphi Approach: An Improvement on Single Round Techniques.
    Progress in Tourism and Hospitality Research 2:27–39.
Pearce, D.
  1992 Towards Sustainable Development through Environmental Assessment.
    CSERGE Working Paper PA 92–11. London: CSERGE.
Pearce, D., A. Markandya, and E. B. Barbier
  1989 Blueprint for a Green Economy. London: Earthscan.
Phillips, A.
  1995 Conservation. *In* The National Trust: The Next Hundred Years, H. Newby,
    ed., pp. 32–52. London: The National Trust.
Preble, J. F.
  1984 The Selection of Delphi Panels for Strategic Planning Purposes. Strategic
    Management Journal 5:157–170.
Prentice, R.
  1993a Heritage: A Key Sector of the "New" Tourism. *In* Progress in Tourism,
    Recreation and Hospitality, Vol. 5, C. Cooper and A. Lockwood, eds., pp. 309–
    324. London: Belhaven.
  1993b Tourism and Heritage Attractions. London: Routledge.
Priestley, G. K., J. A. Edwards, and H. Coccossis, eds.
  1996 Sustainable Tourism? European Experiences. Wallingford: CAB
    International.
Rogers, H. A.
  1995 Pricing Practices in Tourist Attractions: An Investigation into How Pricing
    Decisions are Made in the UK. Tourism Management 16:217–224.
Sackman, H.
  1975 Delphi Critique. Lexington: DC Heath and Company.
Sinclair, M. T., and M. Stabler
  1997 The Economics of Tourism. London: Routledge.
Smith, S. L. J.
  1995 Tourism Analysis: A Handbook (2nd ed.). Harlow: Longman.
Stabler, M., ed.
  1997 Tourism and Sustainability: Principles to Practice. Wallingford: CAB
    International.

Thomas, J.
    1998 Museums Resent Tourists. Tourism: The Journal of the Tourism Society
        97:19.
Urry, J.
    1990 The Tourist Gaze: Leisure and Travel in Contemporary Societies. London:
        Sage.
van der Borg, J., P. Costa, and G. Gotti
    1996 Tourism in European Heritage Cities. Annals of Tourism Research
        23:306–321.
Wheeller, B.
    1994 Ego Tourism, Sustainable Tourism and the Environment: A Symbiotic,
        Symbolic or Shambolic Relationship? *In* Tourism: The State of the Art, A. V.
        Seaton, ed., pp. 647–654. Chichester: Wiley.
Yale, P.
    1991 From Tourist Attractions to Heritage Tourism. Huntingdon: ELM
        Publications.
Yong, Y. W., K. A. Keng, and T. L. Leng
    1989 A Delphi Forecast for the Singapore Tourism Industry: Future Scenario
        and Marketing Implications. International Marketing Review 6:35–46.

Assigned 22 July 1998. Submitted 10 February 1999. Accepted 20 July 1999. Refereed anonymously. Coordinating Editor: Neil Leiper

[36]

INTERNATIONAL JOURNAL OF TOURISM RESEARCH
Int. J. Tourism Res. 7, 1–10 (2005)
Published online in Wiley InterScience (www.interscience.wiley.com). DOI: 10.1002/jtr.520

Satisfying the Basics: Reflections from a Consumer Perspective of Attractions Management at the Millennium Dome, London

Nigel Hemmington[1,*], David Bowen[2], Evgenia Wickens[3] and Alexandros Paraskevas[2]
[1]*School of Services Management, Bournemouth University, Poole BH12 5BB, UK*
[2]*School of Business, Oxford Brookes University, Department of Hospitality, Leisure and Tourism Management, Oxford OX3 0BP, UK*
[3]*Department of Tourism, Buckinghamshire Chilterns University College, High Wycombe HP13 5BB, UK*

ABSTRACT

The Millennium Dome, London, was supposed to be the centrepiece of UK celebrations marking the start of the twenty-first century. Unwittingly, it also emerged as the centrepiece of much media negativity and scrutiny — for the full length of its (projected) 1 year of opening. Four years after the doors closed, and with the perspective of time, this study reflects on the Millennium Dome as a case study of visitor attractions management — with data drawn from the consumer perspective at the time of opening. The focus of the primary research is on the satisfaction of visitors to the Millennium Dome. This was carried out when the attraction was weathering the media storm following its opening. Both quantitative and qualitative data was gathered from 530 exit questionnaires and 350 qualitative interviews. The quantitative data revealed visitor assessments of the experience of the Millennium Dome as a whole, and their assessments of its constituent parts (zones). The findings of the qualitative interviews led to the construction of a typology of meanings for visitors to the Millennium Dome. Even though time has elapsed since closure, both the quantitative and the qualitative findings still have a wider application in the interpretation of the visitor experience in attractions. Recommendations at the time indicated a need for management to focus on 'the basics' of the visitor experience with the addendum that a failure to do so could detract from 'the most amazing day out ever' or, indeed, 'a very special day' — and to ensure a closer match between marketing expectations and the reality of the experience. Reflection has not altered such often neglected but fundamental tenets. Copyright © 2005 John Wiley & Sons, Ltd.

Received 27 April 2004; Revised 21 October 2004; Accepted 30 October 2004

Keywords: The Millennium Dome; media negativity; visitor attractions management

THE CASE STUDY

The celebrations of the year 2000 served to highlight the role in tourism that is played by special events and the attractions that are developed alongside them. Governments around the world provided financial support for projects and attractions that celebrated the millennium; many of which were of a particularly transitory nature. In the UK, the Government-controlled Millennium Commis-

*Correspondence to: N. Hemmington, School of Services Management, Bournemouth University, Poole BH12 5BB, UK
E-mail: nrhemmington@bournemouth.ac.uk

sion, responsible for the commitment of lottery funds, part-funded a plethora of such events and attractions. The Millennium Dome, which was located in an area of redeveloped docklands on the River Thames east of the City of London, was the centre-piece of the UK celebrations — both as 1999 moved into 2000 and, subsequently, in the form of a year long visitor attraction.

The Millennium Dome soon achieved first place, in terms of visitors, among the new London attractions (followed by British Airways' London Eye, the National Portrait Gallery and the Stratford Cultural Quarter) that, according to the London Tourist Board, would increase UK visitor numbers by 3.9% to 26.5 million (Clarke, 2000). Also on an international level, industry reports placed the Millennium Dome among the major millennium special events including the Expo 2000 in Hannover, the Olympic Games in Sydney and the European Football Championships cohosted by Belgium and The Netherlands. This seemed to confirm the grand, if rather ethnocentric, claim (by some advocates) that the Millennium Dome could be an example to the rest of the world in the act of celebration.

The Millennium Dome, however, soon became the subject of political exploitation, attracting negative national and international media attention, not only during the perceived failings of the opening night, effectively 31 December 1999, but also during its subsequent operation. Although the core criticism was on the tremendous investment for its construction (US$1.29 billion) and its poor operational planning, the underlying feeling was that the Millennium Dome's promise of 'the most amazing day out ever' did not live up to visitors' expectations. NMEC (the New Millennium Experience Company — the company managing the Millennium Dome) originally set a target of 12 million visitors (an average of 33 000 per day) but in the first 2 months of its operation managed an average of 11 820 (January) and 19 639 visitors (February). The turmoil caused by the vociferous negative publicity and the poor attendance led to the change of the Millennium Dome's chief executive. New management, supported by further financial backing of US$43 million, eventually indicated that the main strategy to achieve the attrac-

tion's reversal of fortune was to go 'back to the basics' (Tylee, 2000): the very basics that had been ignored in the initial planning. Such a suggestion, however, had been clearly evident from quantitative and qualitative primary research carried out within the first month of the opening of the Millennium Dome — research that gained some good coverage in the general media and was also outlined in the English Tourism Council (now VisitBritain) publication *Insights* (Wickens *et al.*, 2000).

There is a paucity of research in visitor attraction management (Fyall, 2003), and given the importance of attractions to tourism in general (Gunn, 1988), it is remarkable that this area has received so little attention. This is particularly significant in the light of the number of visitor attraction developments in the UK around the time of the millennium and the subsequent number of business failures (Stevens, 2003). So, even though time has elapsed since closure of the Millennium Dome both the quantitative and the qualitative findings still have a wider application in the interpretation of the visitor experience in attractions — and also the response of attractions that are subject to especially close media attention.

THE CONSUMER AND SATISFACTION — A GENERAL PERSPECTIVE

There is a considerable literature on consumer satisfaction and dissatisfaction (CS/D). This originally was conceived with reference to goods but increasingly has been developed through the 1980s and 1990s within the field of services marketing (Glynn and Barnes, 1995). Specific consideration of CS/D for visitors within a tourism context is also now evident (Arnould and Price, 1993; Oh and Parks, 1997; Yuksel and Yuksel, 2001a,b; Bowen and Clarke, 2002).

Essentially, general theory on CS/D suggests the influence of six elements or 'antecedents'. These include expectation, performance, expectancy disconfirmation (the difference between expectation and performance), attribution (a consideration of the locus, stability, controllability and importance of causal inferences by the consumers/tourists/visitors), emotion and equity (a sense of fairness) (Folkes *et al.*, 1987; Oliver and Swan, 1989; Oliver, 1993; Mano and Oliver, 1993).

The antecedents that have received the greatest attention in an appraisal of satisfaction are expectation, performance and expectancy disconfirmation. There is a case for considering these antecedents separately — as independent variables. Overlap between the three — bound together in the antecedent 'expectancy disconfirmation' — is commonplace, however, both in the academic and trade literature. The study of expectancy disconfirmation has been connected to the establishment of standards and has involved elements of appraisal and comparison. Miller (1977) actually defined four types of expectation comparison standards — 'ideal' ('can be'), 'lowest tolerable level' ('must be'), 'deserved' ('should be') and 'expected' ('will be'). It was suggested that the latter was the most realistic form of expectation. With regard to appraisal and comparison the linkage of consumer expectations with outcomes goes back to Thibaut and Kelley (1959) and Kelley and Thibaut (1978) and their study of the social psychology of groups. Kelley and Thibaut (1978, pp. 8–9) summarised their framework in an overview:

> The outcomes for any participant in an ongoing interaction can be stated in terms of the rewards received and the costs incurred by the participant. . . . By rewards we refer to whatever gives pleasure and gratification to the person. Costs refer to factors that inhibit or deter the performance of any behaviour. . . .

In an application to consumer satisfaction, Oliver (1989, pp. 1–16) concluded that:

> Consumers are posited to hold preconsumption normative standards or to form expectancies, observe product (attribute) performance, compare product with their norms and/or expectations, form disconfirmation perceptions, combine these perceptions with expectation levels, and form satisfaction judgements.

Outcomes that are poorer than expected (a negative disconfirmation) were rated below a

reference point, whereas those better than expected (a positive disconfirmation) were evaluated above a given point. Expectations were confirmed when a product performs as expected. Accordingly, satisfaction is seen as the combination of expectation, performance, and disconfirmation — and dissatisfaction results when a subject's expectations were negatively disconfirmed.

On the other hand, a counter movement has queried such a cognitive approach by consumers (Botterill, 1987; Fournier and Mick, 1999) and has also emphasised the role of emotion (otherwise called 'affect'). Havlena and Holbrook (1986: 394) stated that:

> . . . though consumption experiences vary in their mix of utilitarian/hedonic, tangible/intangible, or objective/subjective components . . . the latter, more emotional aspects of consumption experiences occur to a greater or lesser extent in almost all consuming situations.

Additionally, it is necessary to take into account the relationship that may exist between direct experience and/or indirect experience (word of mouth communication) and specific management-generated communication via marketing programmes. Deighton (1984) argued that expectations formed via marketing, specifically the medium of advertising, were considered by consumers to be partisan and biased. Furthermore, consumers were only likely to accept such a partisan source of expectation after exposure to more objective information — such as experience or 'evidence' recalled from memory. Deighton (1984, p. 767), however, suggested that contrary to the classic tradition of advertising research, in which the communicator and receiver were viewed as adversaries, the advertiser was more typically a tempter rather than an adversary — and the consumer was 'a naive and fallible investigator seeking a tolerable understanding of the markets in which he/she must deal'. Hoch and Ha (1986), in an extension of Deighton's work, suggested that even though consumers might not believe the claims of advertisers they did not require very convincing evidence in order to start believing what advertisers told them. Consumers were motivated to search for hypothesis consistent information — confirmatory bias — rather than inconsistent information.

CONSUMER SATISFACTION/ DISSATISFACTION, ATTRACTIONS, EVENTS AND THE MEDIA

Inevitably, it must be noted that some of the CS/D theory was not developed with specific reference to services or to tourism or visitor attractions or special events — or any of these suffering as well as benefiting from close media scrutiny. Each tourism subsector within the broader frame of services will probably place a particular spin on such general theory. As an example, take special events. These are defined by Getz (1997, p. 4) in relation to customers or guests as '. . . an opportunity for a leisure, social or cultural experience outside the normal range of choices or beyond every day experience'. It would seem that the specific character of such events might have an effect on both the processes and the outcomes of the customers' judgement with regard to satisfaction or dissatisfaction.

Oliver (1989) showed that expectations are influenced by the product, the context and the individual. In this study of the Millennium Dome, the *context* was particularly influenced by politics and the media — a situation that is not uncommon in what Getz (1997) labelled 'major special events' and 'mega special events'. Other theoretical models of media effects suggest that people are active interpreters of news items in different ways. McQuail (1983) suggests that people choose what they watch and read and, in so doing, they control the media. Such models, however, ignore the media's ability to set the agenda by continually presenting one version of reality to their audience. Accordingly, Philo (1990) presents an alternative theoretical model in his attempt to understand the complex issues of media influence on different types of audience. He suggests that it is possible to talk of 'the cultural effects' on the audience — in some cases some members of the audience will take on media images in an uncritical fashion, in other cases, individuals will be able to understand the biased messages. He claims that the news may 'offer a preferred view of events, but we

cannot assume that its audience will all accept this interpretation'.

The present study aims at investigating the factors influencing overall visitor satisfaction by identifying aspects of the Millennium Dome experience that the visitors particularly enjoyed and those that they feel could be improved. A further aim is to evaluate the media influence in the formation of visitor's expectation and subsequent experience.

PROCEDURE

In seeking to identify, explore and understand visitor perspectives of the Millennium Dome it was decided that an interpretive approach to the research using qualitative methods would be most suitable. However, there was a need to balance the qualitative approach — which invariably involves a longer time period per interviewee but gathers data of greater depth — with the need for some rapidly assembled quantitative information. It was decided, therefore, that a combination of in-depth interviews and a relatively simple quantitative questionnaire would produce appropriate data for further investigation.

A questionnaire was designed according to the accepted standards (Moser and Kalton, 1971; Youngman, 1982). It was deliberately and visibly short (two sides of A4 paper), in order to encourage a high response rate, and included two distinct sections. The first section comprised a self-completion questionnaire, with pre-coded, tick-box style questions relating to the visitor assessment of the Millennium Dome experience. The second section comprised open-ended questions that were administered by researchers when they collected the first section from respondents. The qualitative interviews were conducted in the form of a conversation between the researcher and the visitor 'with the purpose of eliciting certain information from the respondent' (Moser and Kalton, 1971, p. 271). The responses were recorded in order to facilitate further analysis at a later stage (Strauss and Corbin, 1990).

The questionnaire was pilot tested with 30 visitors leaving the Millennium Dome at the Greenwich underground station. Experience of administering the questionnaire and analysis of the pilot data revealed the need for several changes in both format and content. In particular, it was discovered that many visitors were very keen to talk about their experience (both positive and negative) and that there was a clear opportunity to gather quite rich qualitative data. The qualitative section of the survey was, therefore, extended to take advantage of this opportunity. The pilot study also indicated that interviewing at the underground station was not good because interviews were interrupted by the arrival and departure of trains. As a consequence of this, permission was sought, and granted by NMEC, for the study to take place within the Millennium Dome site.

Researchers were located at the various exit points of the Millennium Dome and a convenience sample was selected from visitors as they left the attraction. A total of 530 exit questionnaires and 350 qualitative interviews were conducted during the period 14–30 January 2000. Visitors were selected at various times of day, and on both weekdays and the weekend. Not all visitors proceeded on to the open-ended questions (hence the discrepancy between completed questionnaires and completed qualitative interviews) but there were extremely few refusals to take part at all (approximately one in a hundred). Moreover, most respondents preferred that the interviewers assisted in completing the questionnaires, ticking the boxes and so forth. Each of the researchers was sensitised to issues in visitor satisfaction and general issues in tourism and so was able to both record and start the analysis within the field. The data from the quantitative questions were aggregated. The qualitative data were categorised and analysed using content analysis and hermeneutics. In order to ensure validity all four researchers read, sorted and re-read the data until they reached agreement on the categorisation of each answer.

FINDINGS AND ANALYSIS

The initial release of the results led to considerable media interest. Such urgency no longer remains — the Millennium Dome is, after all, closed — but meaningful reflective study is obviously based on such quantitative and qualitative data.

Statistics

The first part of the questionnaire indicated that the visitors had a reasonably clear opinion about their experience of the various Millennium Dome 'Zones' (specialised themed areas). The quantitative results in response to the question 'How did the Zones measure up to your expectations?' are shown in Table 1.

Some obvious satisfaction patterns emerge here. A number of zones clearly measured up to expectations and represented clear sources of satisfaction. These included the Central Arena Show and the Home Planet. Dialogue with the interviewees frequently recorded descriptions such as 'spectacular', 'brilliant' and 'superb' to characterise the Central Arena Show. By contrast, there were also zones that failed to measure up to expectation. This particularly applied to the Body zone and also to the Faith and Mind zones.

Further analysis of this section of the questionnaire showed that none of the respondents were able to visit all the zones in the Millennium Dome (Table 2). The Central Arena Show and the Body zone were the locations most visited. The high percentage visiting the much-hyped Body zone added further importance to the poor rating it received with regard to

Table 1. Visitor satisfaction by zone.

Zone	Poor %	Average %	Very good %
Body	53	31	16
Central Arena Show	6	9	85
Faith	38	48	16
Home Planet	4	12	84
Journey	5	35	60
Living Island	16	50	34
Mind	34	39	27
Money	24	48	28
Our Town Story	11	50	39
Rest	4	28	68
Play	3	31	66
Self-portrait	18	44	38
Shared Ground	13	47	40
Skyscrape	8	24	68
Talk	15	37	48
Work and Learn	20	52	28
Overall rating	16	46	38

expectation and satisfaction. This was the zone where visitors had very high expectations and were ultimately disappointed with what they saw.

During the weekdays, it was found that visitors might typically visit approximately seven zones. At the weekend, however, owing to the higher attendance that led to longer queues, this sometimes dropped to two or three zones. As one respondent inimically remarked: 'The Body + the Show + a Meal = The End'.

Respondents were also asked whether they considered the Millennium Dome to be good value for money and whether they would recommend the Millennium Dome to friends and relatives. A high number (60%) stated that the Millennium Dome was not good value for money. This finding was consistent with the

Table 2. Zones not visited.

Zone	Not visited %
Body	1
Central Arena Show	0
Faith	52
Home Planet	41
Journey	37
Living Island	34
Mind	38
Money	53
Our Town Story	87
Rest	59
Play	63
Self Portrait	67
Shared Ground	81
Skyscrape	45
Talk	65
Work and Learn	56

negative media coverage, which nourished the perception that the Millennium Dome was built with public money — 'approximately US$ 678 million came from the Millennium Commission (lottery money) that is considered public money' (O'Brien, 1999).

Paradoxically, 75% of visitors said that they would have recommended the Millennium Dome to friends/relatives, which suggests that the overall visitor experience was not a negative one. The results of later independent research (Rines, 2000) were consistent with these findings. The key to understanding visitor perceptions, however, is in the link between the low number of zones visited and the visitor perceptions of poor value for money. The visitors would have liked to be able to spend *more time* in the Millennium Dome. It is this that is reflected in the high potential referral rate. Visitors did not want to leave the Millennium Dome — they wanted to see more and to do this without the need for a feverish rush from zone to zone.

Visitor meanings

The main aim of the qualitative research was to explore the Millennium Dome's meaning to the visitors and their recommendations for potential improvements (that is, an identification of the areas of their dissatisfaction). Two questions sought to establish the meaning of the Millennium Dome to visitors — 'What does the Millennium Dome mean to you?' and 'What key words would describe your Millennium Experience?' With regard to the meaning of the Millennium Dome it was possible to categorise the results into four groups of responses (Table 3).

Table 3. Categorisation of visitor meaning.

Visitor voice	Interpretation	Narrative: visitor words/phrases
Very special day	Sacred	Amazing, fantastic, brilliant, exhilarating
	Symbolic	Excellent, stunning, spectacular, exciting, a landmark in time, just could not be topped
Good day out	Recreational	Interesting, informative, valuable, fun
	Diversional	Pleasant, enjoyable, thought-provoking
Ordinary	Mundane	Flat, average, disappointing, lacks depth
Meaningless	Workaday	Rubbish, waste, everything disappointing
	Profane	Means nothing

The Millennium Dome, London 7

The most positive responses viewed the Millennium Dome as particularly special and this group truly considered that they had 'one amazing day' — just as the marketing campaign had suggested. A range and variety of words, including superlatives and comparatives, were used to describe the whole and parts of the experience. The Millennium Dome was a one-off experience, even an experience of a lifetime and something not to be missed. The 'very special day' at the Millennium Dome held symbolic significance — so much so that the anthropologist would describe the day as a 'sacred journey' (Graburn, 1989); a decidedly special event to celebrate the turn of one century into another in Britain. Only a minority of the respondents, however, felt this way.

A considerable proportion of the respondents was less effusive and viewed the day in more mundane but nevertheless positive terms — 'a good day out'. From the point of view of the initial objective of the Millennium Dome it might be argued that such a response falls short of the original conception. A day that is substitutable and comparable with other experiences at other attractions, however, certainly can be viewed within the positive frame.

This is not the case for those respondents who viewed the Millennium Dome as an 'ordinary' experience — or worse still as a 'meaningless' experience. Although in a decided minority (approximately one-tenth of respondents) the opinions of these visitors most closely resembled the most vehement of media critics. For a visitor experience, again in the terms of the anthropologist, to be so negative as to be 'workaday' or 'profane' (Graburn, 1989) is indeed a disappointing indictment.

VISITOR RECOMMENDATIONS

Visitors to the Millennium Dome suggested a number of actions that management could quickly institute to deal with many of the aspects of visitor dissatisfaction. Their recommendations are loosely arranged along the path of a chronological visitor audit from pre-entry through to exit (Johns and Clark, 1994):

(1) create a period ticket for 2–3 days or allow reduced price entry for subsequent visits because it is not possible to see all the zones — there is a constant pressure to move on quickly to another zone;

(2) create a ticket for single parents together with one or two or three children;

(3) improve internal signposting — it is difficult to find the entrance to some zones;

(4) design a better (free) brochure to help plan the day. Provide this on site and at point of sale;

(5) provide better *in situ* descriptions of zones in order to allow more informed choice-making by visitors and also provide better explanations within the zones;

(6) improve information with regard to wait-times for entry to the zones;

(7) provide improvements in both planned and spontaneous entertainment for visitors waiting in queues;

(8) provide rest points — seating is in extremely short supply and the day becomes even more tiring as a consequence;

(9) ensure that all equipment is fully functional and maintained;

(10) extend opening hours beyond 6 pm — one amazing day should extend into the evening.

Later in 2000 the new chief executive of the Millennium Dome recognised the need to focus on the 'basics'. A number of operational changes were addressed (O'Brien, 2000).

(1) An 'on-the-spot' maintenance programme was introduced in early February to assure a 100% working order condition of all interactive games (Tylee, 2000).

(2) In February the wait time for the Body Zone was 2 hours on a 19000-attendance day. After the introduction of a time ticket system in early May, on a 32000-attendance day the maximum wait was reduced to 20 minutes.

(3) New ticket pricing aiming at repeat visitors was established.

(4) The opening times were extended by 2 hours to encourage more families to visit after school hours and make the Dome more attractive to corporate hospitality (Jardine, 2000).

(5) People flow was enhanced through new signage and directional arrows that sug-

Int. J. Tourism Res. **7**, 1–10 (2005)

gested ways for the public to move once in the Dome.

(6) New packages for key domestic short-break operators and transport services were agreed (TTG, 2000).

DISCUSSION AND CONCLUSION

It was possible to identify each of the six causal antecedents of satisfaction. Visitors had clear expectations of the Millennium Dome as informed by the voracious public debate and the (initial) hyped marketing of the Millennium Dome and were able to measure their experience against their expectations; the emotional element attached to satisfaction was clear from the well articulated meanings that the visitors attached to the Millennium Dome (Table 3); equity related both to a sense of fairness regarding price and time investments but also the wider picture relating to the overall actual cost and opportunity cost of the Millennium Dome to the tax-paying public; and, finally, visitors were also able to attribute blame, when blame was thought appropriate.

It is clear from the recommendations that the visitors had no problem with the concept of the Millennium Dome itself, or the different zones. Further studies have shown that the concept of the zones being designed by companies with a background in the live event industry using interactive displays (as opposed to the traditional static stand) was very successful and could tell the story of a brand (Rines, 2000).

Visitors did suggest, however, that more attention should be paid to the detail of the experience, particularly those that had to do with well-being (e.g. rest points) and many of the more functional aspects of the experience (e.g. ticketing and signposting). These findings suggest that no matter how innovative or sophisticated the concept, and no matter how positive or negative the publicity that it receives, visitor satisfaction will be mediated by factors that relate to the functional and well-being aspects of the experience. From this point of view nearly all visitors are insistent on the 'must be' and 'should be' elements of the Miller (1977) classification of expectations.

Several aspects of the findings also indicate a desire on the part of the visitors to engage effectively and meaningfully with the experi-

ence. These include the desire for more time, the need for better information, and the desire for more detailed descriptions of each of the zones. As Voase (2002) suggests, the emergence of 'thoughtful' consumers with an 'augmented ability to reflect, and increased readiness to engage' will create demands for information that enables visitors to interact meaningfully with attractions and their component parts. For many visitors passive engagement is no longer acceptable or desirable. The presence of active and thoughtful visitors who demand the tools for effective engagement with attractions is not a particularly new finding — but illustrates the need for attraction managers to remind themselves of established trends in behaviour.

The study also suggested that visitors' satisfaction would improve if there were a closer match between the marketing expectations and the reality of the experience. From a mere superficial interpretation of the meaning ascribed to the Millennium Dome and the key words and phrases that respondents used to describe the Millennium Dome, the marketing initiative should have emphasised the Millennium Dome as a very good day out that is fun and interesting — but 'not one amazing day'. There were strong views about keeping this strap-line created by the M&C Saatchi advertising agency for the Millennium Dome (Reynolds, 2000; Tylee, 2000), but eventually in June 2000 the campaign's strap-line changed to 'you've got a mind of your own; take it to the Dome' (Garrett, 2000). Some of the visitors, with inflated expectations fuelled by the Millennium Dome marketing campaign, were looking for the highest ('can be') comparison standards to be fulfilled — and were often, although not invariably, less than satisfied.

There are still lessons to be learned from the Millennium Dome experience, and perhaps the most important one is that no matter how innovative the concept is, aspects that relate to visitor well-being and the functional parts of the experience have to be managed effectively and be market-led. Designers created an impressive package of experiences but it was only after the launch that management considered the market and its needs. Government backing perhaps buoyed management into such a fundamental error. Even the Prime Minister himself later viewed such backing with some misgiving. With some hindsight, the PM '. . . would have listened to those who said "Do not try to run big visitor attractions"' (The Times, 2004). The initial target of 12 million visitors showed the confidence of the initial Millennium Dome management. Eventually, when replaced, management was forced to review the target and bring it down to 6 million visitors (The Economist, 2000).

A further lesson relates to the role of the media. Recent work by Beirmann (2003) on restoring tourism destinations in crisis has emphasised the crucial integrative role of the media in such work. The media, however, also can be hugely destructive as well as constructive in its effect — and especially so in any attraction/event that is closely bound with Government. The media has the power to create and destroy products/services/events by the way it visualises, portrays and writes about them. The media can be regarded as the gatekeeper of what is seen and heard — and can expose, underexpose or overexpose attractions/events such as the Millennium Dome to the public. The media can act as a major contributor to the public definition of the attraction/event and so influence travel-buying decisions. Once defined, it is very difficult to change the media opinion and engage in business repositioning — and especially so when the attraction/event has a short lifespan. In this respect, it will be informative to compare (from an objective research source, not the International Olympic Committee or the Greek Government) how negative international media attention in the build-up to the Athens Olympics affected the short-fall in attendance at Olympic venues (especially in the first week of competition). In the case of the Millennium Dome, only *actual tourist experience* could truly overcome widely held media negativity. Post visit shifts in opinion were a frequent occurrence among the 530 exit surveys in the Millennium Dome study — even though around 10% of visitors still considered the Millennium Dome to be 'meaningless' (very close to much of the media exposure). This rather suggests that the media influence on the tourist was closer to the view expressed by Philo (1990) rather than McPhail (1983) — tourists, as media consumers, did not control the media

effect but were capable in many instances of separating out the negative hype from the reality of the experience.

The Millennium Dome has long since vanished from the front-page of the national and international press. The lessons from the experience, however, remain highly relevant. It is important that the tourism industry develops and retains a collective memory for, as in other spheres, the past can inform the present and the future.

REFERENCES

Arnould EJ, Price LL. 1993. River magic: extraordinary experience and the extended service experience. *Journal of Consumer Research* 20: 24–45.

Beirmann D. 2003. *Restoring Tourism Destinations in Crisis: a Strategic Marketing Approach*. CABI Publishing: Wallingford.

Botterill DT. 1987. Dissatisfaction with a construction of satisfaction. *Annals of Tourism Research* 14: 139–140.

Bowen D, Clarke J. 2002. Reflections on tourist satisfaction research: past, present and future. *Journal of Vacation Marketing* 8(4): 297–308.

Clarke L. 2000. *London: a Market Profile*. Arthur Andersen's Hospitality and Leisure Services: London.

Deighton J. 1984. The interaction of advertising and evidence. *Journal of Consumer Research* 11: 763–770.

Folkes VS, Koletsky S, Graham JL. 1987. A field study of causal influences and consumer reaction: the view from the airport. *Journal of Consumer Research* 13: 534–539.

Fournier S, Mick DG. 1999. Rediscovering satisfaction. *Journal of Marketing* 63(October): 5–23.

Fyall A, Garrod B, Leask A. 2003. *Managing Visitor Attractions; New Directions*. Butterworth-Heineman: Oxford.

Garrett J. 2000. Dome turns criticism on its head in new ad. *Campaign* 23 June: 7.

Getz D. 1997. *Event Management and Event Tourism*. Cognizant Communication Corporation: New York.

Glynn WJ, Barnes JG. 1995. *Understanding Services Management*. Wiley: Chichester.

Graburn NH. 1989. Tourism: the sacred journey. In *Hosts and Guests*, 2nd edn, Smith VL (ed.). University of Pennysylvania Press: Philadelphia; 21–36.

Gunn C. 1988. *Vacationscape: Designing Tourist Regions*. Van Nostrand Reinhold: New York.

Havlena WJ, Holbrook MB. 1986. The varieties of consumption experience: comparing two typolo-

Int. J. Tourism Res. 7, 1–10 (2005)

gies of emotion in consumption behavior. *Journal of Consumer Research* **13**: 394–409.

Hoch SJ, Ha YW. 1986. Consumer learning: advertising and the ambiguity of product experience. *Journal of Consumer Research* **13**: 221–233.

Jardine A. 2000. Extra two hours a night for Dome to hit visitor targets. *Marketing* **9 March**: 1.

Johns N, Clark S. 1994. Quality auditing at visitor attractions. In *Insights*. English Tourist Board: London; A17–22.

Kelley HH, Thibaut JW. 1978. *Interpersonal Relations*. Wiley: New York.

Mano H, Oliver RL. 1993. Assessing the dimensionality and structure of the consumption experience: evaluation, feeling, and satisfaction. *Journal of Consumer Research* **20**: 451–466.

McQuail D. 1983. *Mass Communication Theory: an Introduction*. Sage: London.

Miller JA. 1977. Studying satisfaction, modifying models, eliciting expectations, posing problems, and making meaningful measurements. In *Conceptualisation and Measurement of Consumer Satisfaction and Dissatisfaction*, Hunt HK (ed.). Market Science Institute: Cambridge, MA; pp. 72–91.

Moser CA, Kalton G. 1971. *Survey Methods in Social Investigation*. Heineman: London.

O'Brien T. 1999. 1.3 billion buys a mega Millennium Dome. *Amusement Business* **111**(21): 1–3.

O'Brien T. 2000. Millennium Dome gets new life with Gerbeau. *Amusement Business* **112**(23): 1–3.

Oh H, Parks SC. 1997. Customer satisfaction and service quality: a critical review of the literature and research implications for the hospitality industry. *Hospitality Research Journal* **20**(3): 36–64.

Oliver RL. 1989. Processing of the satisfaction response in consumption: a suggested framework and research propositions. *Consumer Satisfaction, Dissatisfaction and Complaining Behaviour* **2**: 2.

Oliver RL. 1993. Cognitive, affective, and attribute bases of the satisfaction response. *Journal of Consumer Research* **20**: 418–430.

Oliver RL, Swan JE. 1989. Consumer perceptions of interpersonal equity and satisfaction in transactions: a field survey approach. *Journal of Marketing* **53**: 21–35.

Philo G. 1990. *Seeing and Believing: The Influence of Television*. Routledge: London.

Reynolds E. 2000. Dome's 'amazing' ad appeals to public's sense of wonder. *Marketing* **17 February**: 26.

Rines S. 2000. Story lines. *Marketing Week* **23**(10): 57.

Stevens T. 2003. The future of visitor attractions. In *Managing Visitor Attractions*, Fyall A, Garrod B, Leask A (eds). Butterworth-Heinemann: Oxford; 284–298.

Strauss A, Corbin J. 1990. *Basics of Qualitative Research*. Sage: London.

The Economist. 2000. Britain: another £29m down the drain. **27 May**: 60–61.

The Times. 2004. *Fallible Blair admits 'I am Labour's trust problem'*. **20 September**: 1.

Thibaut JW, Kelley HH. 1959. *The Social Psychology of Groups*. Wiley: New York.

TTG. 2000. Dome eyes trade deals. *Travel Trade Gazette UK and Ireland* **29 May**: 4.

Tylee J. 2000. Dome ad strategy in turmoil as Gerbeau goes back to basics. *Campaign* **11 February**: 4.

Voase R. 2002. Rediscovering the imagination: investigating active and passive visitor experience in the 21st century. *International Journal of Tourism Research* **4**(5): 391–400.

Wickens E, Paraskevas A, Hemmington N, Bowen D. 2000. Intelligence report: Millennium Dome — the perception and the reality. In *Insights*. English Tourism Council: London; A137–142.

Youngman MB. 1982. *Designing and Analysing Questionnaires*. Rediguide 12, University of Nottingham, School of Education.

Yuksel A, Yuksel F. 2001a. Measurement and management issues in customer satisfaction research: review, critique and research agenda: part one. *Journal of Travel and Tourism Marketing* **10**(4): 68.

Yuksel A, Yuksel F. 2001b. Measurement and management issues in customer satisfaction research: review, critique and research agenda: part two. *Journal of Travel and Tourism Marketing* **10**(4): 81–111.

[37]

 Pergamon

www.elsevier.com/locate/atoures

Annals of Tourism Research, Vol. 28, No. 3, pp. 638–657, 2001
© 2001 Elsevier Science Ltd. All rights reserved
Printed in Great Britain
0160-7383/01/$20.00

PII: S0160-7383(00)00064-5

SOUVENIR BUYING INTENTIONS FOR SELF VERSUS OTHERS

Soyoung Kim
University of Georgia, USA
Mary A. Littrell
Iowa State University, USA

Abstract: This research examines what influences tourists who want to purchase three categories of souvenirs and who are considering purchases for themselves vs. as gifts for family and friends. Female tourists traveling to Mexico completed a questionnaire and responded to photographic stimuli of three Mexican textile products. Findings suggested that the relationship between purchase intentions and some significant predictors, such as previous travel experience and attitude toward souvenirs, were affected by souvenir categories. However, the relationships were little influenced by the situational variable of buying for oneself vs. for others. When ethnic and recreational tourists were compared, relatively few differences were discovered. **Keywords:** Mexico, tourism shopping, gift buying. © 2001 Elsevier Science Ltd. All rights reserved.

Résumé: L'intention d'acheter des souvenirs pour soi-même ou pour d'autres personnes. Cette recherche examine ce qui influence les touristes qui veulent acheter trois catégories de souvenirs et qui pensent faire des achats pour eux-mêmes ou comme cadeaux pour la famille et des amis. Des touristes femmes qui voyageaient au Mexique ont rempli un question-naire et ont répondu à des stimuli photographiques de trois produits textiles mexicains. Les résultats suggèrent que les rapports entre les intentions d'achat et quelques indices significa-tifs tels que l'expérience des voyages et l'attitude envers les souvenirs étaient modifiés par les catégories de souvenirs. Pourtant, les rapports étaient peu influencés par le variable situa-tionnel d'acheter pour soi-même ou pour d'autres personnes. En comparant le tourisme ethnique au tourisme récréatif, on a trouvé relativement peu de différences. **Mots-clés:** Mexique, shopping de tourisme, achat de cadeaux. © 2001 Elsevier Science Ltd. All rights reserved.

INTRODUCTION

Shopping is seldom mentioned as the primary motive for undertaking a trip; however, it is a common and preferred tourist activity in many destinations (Cook 1995; Jansen-Verbeke 1991; Timothy and Butler 1995). US tourists who traveled abroad in 1997 reported shopping as their second most important activity (Travel Industry Association of America 1998). In addition, shopping opportunities are a major attraction drawing tourists to many less developed countries where the prices

---

Soyoung Kim is Assistant Professor at the University of Georgia (Department of Textiles, Merchandising, and Interiors, Athens GA 30602-3622, USA. Email <soyoung@cc.usu.edu>). Her research is directed toward tourist behavior and apparel shopping. **Mary Littrell** is Pro-fessor of Textiles and Clothing at Iowa State University. Her research focuses on ethnic product marketing, alternative trade, and small business/entrepreneurship.

of goods are generally low (Keown 1989). They often spend more money on shopping than on food, lodging, or other entertainment (Jansen-Verbeke 1991; Timothy and Butler 1995). Although their expenditure patterns have occasionally been studied, little is known about what influences tourists' souvenir purchase decisions.

Tourism souvenir research divides along two major paths. In one direction, researchers have explored artisan producers of souvenirs and have asked questions concerning the impact of product commercialization on artisans' products and their lives (Cohen 1992, 1993). Along a second path, researchers have focused on tourist consumers of souvenirs. The meanings that tourists attach to souvenirs (Bentor 1993; Gordon 1986; Littrell 1990; Morris 1991; Shenhav-Keller 1993; Wallendorf and Arnould 1988); linkages of product choice to tourism styles (Graburn 1989; Littrell et al 1994; Moscardo and Pearce 1999); definitions of souvenir authenticity (Cohen 1988; Littrell, Anderson and Brown 1993); and associations among age, gender, and souvenir behaviors (Anderson and Littrell 1995, 1996) have all been explored. Yet, delineating tourist characteristics that impact actual purchase intentions remains little examined.

Tourists frequently purchase gifts in addition to souvenir items for their own personal use (Rucker, Kaiser, Barry, Brummett, Freeman and Peters 1986). In a study of midwestern US tourists, nearly 70% purchased gifts for family and friends during their travels (Littrell et al 1994). The consumer behavior literature suggests that situational factors, such as a gift-giving, affect consumer decisions. Studies of gift-giving vs. buying for oneself reveal inconsistent findings. For example, Vincent and Zikmund (1976) found that consumers perceived greater risk in buying a wedding gift than if the same item was bought for themselves. Specifically applied to tourism, Rucker et al (1986) noted that tourists made more planned purchases for others than for themselves, indicating their higher involvement in the former type of situation. However, Heeler, Okechuchu and Reid (1979) found that college students sought less information in a gift-giving situation than in a personal situation. Despite the discrepant findings from previous gift-giving research, it appears that factors affecting intention to buy for self vs. others may not be parallel and warrant attention in the tourism venue.

This research integrated scholarship on tourism shopping, souvenirs, and gift buying by asking two questions. One, which characteristics of tourists serve as predictors of their purchase intentions for various categories of textile souvenirs? Two, are relationships between predictor variables and purchase intentions influenced by the situational variable of buying for oneself vs. buying for others? Tourists' souvenir purchase intentions were explored among US tourists intending to travel or having recently traveled to Mexico. Two groups, ethnic and recreational tourists, were chosen as they represented two common types identified in previous studies (Cohen 1979; Littrell et al 1994; Smith 1989). Ethnic and recreational themes are also prominently featured in Mexican tourism promotions. In addition, textile souvenirs were a particular focus, due to the high propensity to purchase local handcrafts and clothing when traveling (*Consumer Reports Travel Letter* 1995). Tourist characteristics considered relevant to souvenir purchase intentions included demographic characteristics, attitude toward other cultures, exposure to the host culture, and attitude toward souvenirs.

In addition to a scholarly goal of contributing to the research literature on tourism shopping and souvenirs, applied outcomes were also sought. First, better understanding of gift vs. self-directed purchase intentions held promise for assisting tourism retailers in developing targeted promotional strategies. Second, in order that findings not remain solely applicable to the souvenirs particular to a specific travel destination (in this case Mexico), purchase intentions were explored for three categories of them thought to hold relevance across tourism destinations.

Gordon (1986) projected that souvenirs can be categorized into five types. Pictorial images, such as postcards, photographs, and illustrated books about particular regions, are the most common type of souvenir. Piece-of-the-rock souvenirs are usually natural material or objects, such as rocks, shells, or pine cones, taken from a natural environment. Symbolic shorthand souvenirs are usually manufactured products which evoke a message about the place from which they came, such as a miniature Eiffel Tower from France or a lobster pot from Maine. Markers offer no reference to a particular place in themselves but are inscribed with words which locate them in place and time. For example, a t-shirt with little meaning in itself but marked "Grand Canyon" becomes a reminder of the place. Finally, local product souvenirs include a variety of objects such as local foods and crafts.

For this research, a t-shirt and local textile crafts, which represent two categories of Gordon's souvenir types (namely local product and marker) were initially identified for this study. Local crafts were further divided into two categories based on previous researchers' findings that tourists differentiate between and attach different value to textile souvenirs that portray strong cultural symbolism vs. those which are more generic but still exude qualities of hand-production (Littrell 1990; Slaybaugh, Littrell and Farrell-Beck 1990). At the end, tourists' purchase intentions for three product categories were examined: an ethnic product with cultural symbolism, a generic handcraft, and a symbolic marker.

SOUVENIR PURCHASE INTENTIONS

Previous research in the fields of tourism and consumer behavior provided guidance for selection of tourist characteristics to include in the study as possible predictor variables for souvenir purchase intentions. In addition, gift buying research provided further insights.

Demographically, while the associations between age and tourist behavior are evidenced by several studies (Anderson and Langmeyer 1982; Anderson and Littrell 1995, 1996; Littrell 1990), specific studies on the effects of age and other demographic variables on purchase intentions are limited. Littrell (1990) found that tourists' age was associated with the meaning they attached to textile crafts. Younger tourists associated the meaning of textile crafts with their shopping experiences which often involved action-oriented travel to remote villages. In contrast, older consumers seemed to value the aesthetic pleasure taken from owning, contemplating, and using a textile over time. In another study, distinctly varying souvenir-purchasing styles were noted among female tourists in different age groups (Anderson and Littrell 1995, 1996). For example, tourists in early adulthood tended to make mostly unplanned souvenir purchases and shop with their children. Older tourists, on the other hand, made planned purchases with their friends or husbands. The present study examined the effect of age on souvenir purchase decisions along with the effects of other demographic variables, including education, employment, income, and marital status.

The attitudes that tourists hold toward other cultures may influence their travel experience including souvenir purchase intentions. In this study, world-mindedness and consumer ethnocentrism were included as the two major dimensions of attitude toward other cultures that may relate to souvenir purchase intentions. Sampson and Smith defined world-mindedness as "a frame of reference, or value orientation, favoring a worldview of the problems of humanity, with mankind, rather than the nationals of a particular country, as the primary reference group" (1957:105). Its five dimensions included responsibility, cultural pluralism, efficacy, globalcentrism, and interconnectedness (Hett 1991). World-mindedness was found to have a highly negative association with ethnocentrism (Smith 1955).

Ethnocentrism may account partially for different evaluations of foreign products (Netemeyer, Durvasula and Lichtenstein 1991). Consumer ethnocentrism represents beliefs about the appropriateness and morality of purchasing foreign products. It provides consumers with feelings of belonging and with guidelines for purchasing behavior acceptable to an ingroup (those groups with which one identifies oneself). Highly ethnocentric consumers may consider the purchase of foreign products as wrong because it hurts the domestic economy, causes unemployment, and is unpatriotic. Therefore, they may devalue the quality of foreign products. In contrast, nonethnocentric consumers evaluate foreign products more objectively regardless of national origin (McIntyre and Meric 1994). Such ethnocentric bias may be also reflected in international tourists' perception of souvenir attributes and purchase decision making.

Cultural knowledge refers to one's knowledge about a culture—its language, dominant values, beliefs, and prevailing ideology (Wiseman, Hammer and Nishida 1989). Preexisting knowledge of the host culture has a positive impact on effective communication across cultures. That is, cultural knowledge minimizes a person's misunderstanding with people from another culture. In addition, previous cultural experience, according to Wiseman et al (1989), is an important factor influencing adaptation. They found that greater degrees of perceived knowledge of a specific culture were related to greater understanding of other cultures in general, and that by knowing another culture, people can learn the boundaries of their own culture and discover new cultural perspectives. The concept of exposure to the host culture, which can be measured by knowledge of the host culture and previous cultural experience, has not been studied in the context of international tourism. In this study, it was proposed that exposure to the host culture would affect tourists' attitude and behavior toward products from the culture.

Several studies have sought to identify the dimensions by which consumers evaluate souvenirs (Littrell 1987, 1990). In the latter study, international tourists were asked to describe the meanings associated with their favorite textile crafts acquired during travels. Responses were content analyzed resulting in five major categories: textile uses related shopping experiences, associations with place or culture, personal memories of travel, and intrinsic qualities. The importance of aesthetic qualities, including appealing colors and designs, was reconfirmed among midwestern US tourists. Additional criteria valued by these tourists related to product quality, use, and uniqueness. Whether a product was easy to pack or carry on a trip also held value to these shoppers (Littrell et al 1994). While evaluative criteria have been identified in several studies, little research has been carried out concerning attitudes toward the importance of souvenir attributes as related to tourists' intentions to purchase.

To understand the nature of gift giving, numerous studies have been conducted which provide insights on motivations of givers, popular gift choices, and the gendered nature of gifting behavior. The symbolic and motivational aspect of gifts has been of particular interest to researchers. For example, Sherry (1983) found that the primary reasons for gift giving are either altruistic (maximizing the pleasure of the recipient) or agonistic (maximizing the donor's personal satisfaction). Belk and Coon (1993) emphasized the importance of recognizing gift giving as an expression of unselfish or agapic love. Still other researchers, including Goodwin, Smith, and Spiggle (1990), have found that gift-giving motives are either obligatory or voluntary.

Clothing is a popular gift choice and among the most preferred by various consumer groups (Hyllegard and Fox 1997; Horne and Winakor 1991, 1995; Rucker et al 1986). On average, Americans spend $259 a year on this item, while they spend $79 on gifts of food (American Demographics 1993). As related to tourism, Rucker and her colleagues (1986) found that about 25% of the international tourists in their study reported that they had been asked to buy clothing for others during their visits to the United States. In their study, t-shirts were clearly the most popular type of clothing. Therefore, this and other textile types deserve special attention in studies dealing with gift-giving behavior.

Previous work on this subject has shown that gift exchange behavior is highly gendered. That is, women give more gifts than they receive and devote more attention than men to selection of gifts (Areni, Kiecher and Palan 1998; Beatty, Kahle, Utsey and Keown 1993; Caplow 1983; Otnes, Lowrey and Kim 1993). Given the prominent role of women in gift giving and the great importance they attach to shopping for it, therefore, it is important to understand their gift-giving behavior. As applied to the present study, the researchers attempted to understand the effects of this tendency and personal situations on female tourists' textile souvenir purchase intentions. Specifically, the relationships among purchase intentions and predictor variables were examined as they were influenced by buying for oneself vs. buying for others.

Study Methods

Research methods, including sampling, data collection procedures, and instrument development were designed to elicit responses that would answer the questions of this study. Female adults who had traveled to Mexico or were planning to do so in the near future were the population from which the sample was drawn. The rationale for selecting female adults as respondents was that they are the more frequent purchasers of souvenirs such as apparel and household textiles (Anderson and Littrell 1995; Jansen-Verbeke 1991; Littrell et al 1994). Mexico was chosen as it has traditionally been one of the prime destination countries for international tourism. In 1996 Mexico was ranked seventh as the most popular destination in the world, with 19.3 million US tourists and 2.1 million other inbound tourists spending at least one night in Mexico. Together they spent $6.9 billion, whereas Mexican outbound tourists spent only $3.4 billion abroad (Industry Sector Analysis 1998). Mexico is clearly a highly favored destination for US tourists.

Six Mexico government tourism offices and one marketing office in the United States provided mailing lists of names for individuals who had requested information concerning potential travel in Mexico. The merged mailing list contained approximately 2,900 persons throughout the country. From the list, male names, travel agencies, and names with insufficient address information were eliminated. A self-administered questionnaire and color photographic stimuli of Mexican textile products were then mailed to 900 females randomly selected from the list. Mailing followed the first three steps of the Dillman Total Design Method (Dillman 1978). Of the 900 questionnaires mailed, 51 were returned due to an inaccurate address or the recipient was of minor age. From the remaining 849 questionnaires, 336 were returned for a response rate of 40%. Of these, only adult women who had traveled to or were planning to travel to Mexico within one year were eligible for inclusion. A total of 277 eligible respondents were identified, and the analyses for this study were based on their responses.

The respondents' ages ranged from 18 to 76, with an average of 41 years. Most were Caucasian (83%). In terms of education, the majority (83%) of the sample completed high school and 30% had attended or graduated from college. About two-thirds were married and 71% were employed. More than 47% of the respondents had incomes of $50,000 or above; approximately 26% had incomes between $25,000 and $49,999. In 1996, 37% of the total US female population reported incomes of more than $50,000 (US Bureau of Census 1997). Thus, the sample for this study appeared to possess somewhat higher income levels than the total female population.

Stimuli were color photographs of three Mexican textile products selected to represent the three types of ethnic product, generic handcraft, and symbolic marker. Textile products were selected because they are small and easy to pack (Graburn 1989) and are common shopping items among tourists visiting Mexico (Adair 1996). An initial set of stimuli including 13 souvenirs formed the base for the final selection. Initial choice was based on the researchers' observations of markets and shops in Mexico and consultation with a cultural specialist in the state of Oaxaca. Three criteria for souvenir selection were used: one, that items be currently on the market and available to tourists; two, that they would be diverse in technique, color, function, design, theme, and price (Littrell 1990; Littrell et al 1993; Slaybaugh et al 1990); and, that they represent the three product types identified for the study.

For 8 out of 13 products, photographs as well as information about fiber content, size, and price were obtained from the 1996 catalog of FONART (Fondo Nacional para el Fomento de las Artes). This is a government organization that promotes craft development and marketing in Mexico and abroad. FONART has a network of stores that are located in the largest cities of Mexico, and features a wide selection of crafts from all over the nation. The researchers noticed that t-shirts and woven belts were not available in the catalog, but they were among major souvenir items in Mexico. Therefore, three t-shirts and a woven belt were purchased from stores or markets in Mexico. Pictures of these items were taken by a professional photographer in a manner to resemble the photographic style of the catalog.

A pretest of the 13 stimuli photographs was completed by a group of 24 women employed in faculty and staff positions at the researchers' university. Three Mexican textile souvenirs representing three different product types (woven rug as an ethnic product, placemat as a generic handcraft, and t-shirt as a symbolic marker) were selected using the two criteria: that items elicited diverse responses from participants related to purchase intention, and that product type be maintained for the final stimuli. Information on the fiber content, size, and price was presented in the questionnaire so respondents would have the same information as would be available in an actual purchase situation. The three products were a hand woven wool rug represented an *ethnic product* with color and design features native to the Oaxaca region of Mexico; a solid colored, coarsely textured set of placemats representing a *generic handcraft* with hand production qualities but lacking design linkages to a specific tourism region; and a t-shirt with the words "Quetzalcoatl [a chief Toltec and Aztec god] Mexico-Oaxaca" and a design of Quetzalcoatl images to represent a *symbolic marker* with visual imagery denoting a tourism destination (Gordon 1986).

A questionnaire was developed to measure the variables under investigation: travel activities, demographic characteristics (age, education, employment, income, and marital status), attitude toward other cultures, exposure to Mexican culture, attitude toward souvenirs, and intention to purchase souvenirs. The scale assessing tourists' preferences for ethnic or recreational activities was adapted from the tourism styles scale developed by Littrell and her colleagues (1994) and was used to form groups of tourists for further analysis in this research. Respondents were asked to rate the level of importance of 12 travel activities when traveling in other countries (1=very unimportant; 7=very important). Factor analysis confirmed the existence of the two dimensions that explained 63% of the total variance (Table 1). Factor 1, ethnic tourism, included three items favoring engrossment in the authentic life of communities (alpha=.75). Factor 2, recreational tourism, contained five items related to recreational activities such as attending sports and participating in night entertainment (alpha=.69). The mean scores for the two factors were 5.42 and 4.37, respectively. Using a median split method, respondents with the higher half of the ethnic tourism factor scores were placed in a group titled ethnic tourists (n=121; mean=6.28) and those high on the recreational tourism factor were placed in the recreational tourist group (n=152; mean=5.38). Of the 273 tourists, 72 respondents were included in both groups. Because separate regression analyses were run for each group of tourists, their inclusion in both analyses was not problematic. These 72 respondents also illustrated tourists for whom more than one set of activities was a priority.

A total of 12 questions were used to measure two dimensions of attitude toward other cultures. These included nine questions on world-mindedness and three on consumer ethnocentrism. The items measuring the former were adopted from previous studies (Bhawk and Brislin 1992; Wiseman, Hammer and Nishida 1989) as well as developed by the researchers (1=strongly disagree; 7=strongly agree). The items measuring consumer ethnocentrism were selected from the CETSCALE developed by Shimp and Sharma (1987). Principal component factor analysis with varimax rotation was performed on these

Table 1. Factor Analysis of Ethnic and Recreational Travel Activities

Factor Title and Items	Factor Loadings	Alpha
Ethnic		0.75
Visiting ethnic communities	0.85	
Attending ethnic or community festivals or fairs	0.79	
Meeting interesting people different than myself	0.78	
Recreational Tourism		0.69
Shopping	0.75	
Visiting recreational theme parks with rides and sports	0.74	
Bringing home souvenirs from the trip	0.70	
Participating night entertainment such as dancing or nightclubs	0.62	
Taking a complete package tour	0.50	

items to examine the dimensionality of the concepts. An eigenvalue of one was used for the purpose of extraction. In addition, an examination of scree-tests and conceptual clarity of items included within each factor determined the decision for the number of factors. As a result, three were generated that accounted for 51% of the total variance. Factor 1, labeled interest in other cultures, consisted of three items related to general interest in other cultures (alpha=.73) (Table 2). Factor 2 included three items from the CETSCALE and was labeled consumer ethnocentrism. The items reflected the attitude against purchasing foreign products (alpha=.71). Factor 3, open-mindedness, contained four items representing global worldview and cultural pluralism (alpha=.65). Open-mindedness appeared to be an outer-directed perspective on other cultures, while interest in other cultures represented a more emotional, inner-directed way of viewing other cultures.

Two measures of exposure to Mexican culture were knowledge of it and the frequency of travel in Mexico. Based on Wiseman et al's (1989) definition of cultural knowledge, two questions were asked for self-assessment of knowledge of Mexican culture and fluency of Spanish: "How knowledgeable are you about Mexico?" (1=not at all; 7=very knowledgeable) and "How well do you speak Spanish?" (1=not at all; 7=very well) (alpha=.69). Travel experience was measured through a single item question: "How many times have you traveled in Mexico prior to 1996?."

Table 2. Factor Analysis of Attitude toward Other Cultures

Factor Title and Items	Factor Loadings	Alpha
Interest in Other Cultures		0.73
I like to decorate my home or office with artifacts from other countries	0.81	
I love to travel abroad if I have time and money	0.76	
I am interested in the history and culture of other countries	0.75	
Consumer Ethnocentrism		0.71
American products are the first, last, and foremost	0.81	
Only those products that are not available in the United States should be imported	0.77	
It is not right to purchase foreign products, because it puts Americans out of jobs	0.71	
Open-Mindedness		0.65
Any healthy individual, regardless of race or religion, should be allowed to live wherever she/he wants to in the world	0.69	
We all have a right to hold different beliefs about God and religion	0.62	
Culturally mixed marriages are not wrong	0.59	
It would be better to be a citizen of the world than of any particular nation	0.54	

Attitudes toward souvenir attributes were measured based on Fishbein's (1967) attitude model. A consumer's favorable attitude suggests positive beliefs about the product and a tendency to behave in a positive manner toward it. Product attitude is, therefore, generally defined as a predisposition to respond to a particular product in a favorable or unfavorable manner (Kim 1995). According to Fishbein's (1967) attitude model, the two important concepts in measuring product attitude are evaluative criteria (or, the attributes of a product which the consumer finds to be important) and the perception of the attributes possessed by a particular product. The Fishbein model can be expressed in the following mathematical form:

$$A_B = \sum_{i=1}^{n} b_i e_i$$

where A_B=attitude toward the behavior, b_i=the belief that performing behavior B leads to consequence i, e_i=the evaluation of consequence i, and n=the number of salient consequences.

This model has been considered especially suitable for measuring attitude toward a product or brand (Schiffman and Kanuk 1983). Marketing researchers propose that the consumer's product attitude is defined as the summed set of beliefs about (or perception of) the product's attributes weighted by the evaluation of the importance of the attributes. Therefore, one should measure b_i and e_i separately in order to compute the score of the attitude toward the product. In the present study, b_i was referred to as perceived souvenir attributes and e_i as evaluative criteria for selecting souvenirs.

Perceived souvenir attributes were measured by asking respondents to react to photographic stimuli of three souvenir items. Evaluative criteria for these were measured by the product attribute items developed by Littrell et al (1994) as related to aesthetics, quality, use, uniqueness, and easy of transport during travel. Respondents viewed color photographs of three souvenir items and indicated their perception of the presence of 11 attributes for each souvenir (1=strongly disagree; 7=strongly agree). They were then asked to rate the importance of 11 criteria when selecting souvenirs as they travel (1=very unimportant; 7=very important).

Factor analysis of evaluative criteria resulted in three factors: aesthetics, uniqueness, and care and travel. The factors accounted for 57% of the total variance. Factor analysis was performed on perceived attributes separately for each Mexican souvenir item. A three-factor solution was employed in order to produce factors directly comparable with the three evaluative criteria factors. Only items loading on the same factor across the three souvenirs and on the identical factor of evaluative criteria were chosen to create a measure of attitude toward souvenirs, resulting in two items for each factor. Items for the aesthetics factor were "The design is appealing" and "The colors are appealing," while the items for the uniqueness factor included "It is new, innovative" and "The product is unique or one of kind." The items for the care and travel factor covered "It is easy to care for or clean" and "It is easy to pack or carry with me on the trip." Further, the three dimensions of attitude toward souvenirs in this study were measured using indices derived from a combination of the evaluative criteria factor and the perceived attributes factor. That is, evaluative criteria factor scores were multiplied with the associated perceptions of souvenir attributes and then summed to obtain an overall attitude score for each of the three souvenirs.

Intention to purchase textile souvenirs for self or for others were the dependent variables in this study. Within the context of consumer behavior, intention refers to the plan to acquire or use products and is used as an alternative measure to purchase behavior (Mullen and Johnson 1990). It is generally assumed that favorable results of consumers' internal processes in response to a product will lead to their actual purchase of the product. It was measured using two items. Respondents were asked to indicate the likelihood that they would purchase each souvenir item for themselves and for others as a gift (1=very unlikely; 7=very likely).

Study Results

A series of multiple regression analyses was performed to estimate the relationships between purchase intentions and predictor variables of demographic characteristics, attitude toward other cultures, exposure to Mexican culture, and attitude toward Mexican souvenirs. Intention to purchase souvenirs for oneself and for others were regressed separately on the same set of predictor variables. In addition, a separate regression equation was estimated for ethnic and recreational tourists as well as for each souvenir. The standardized regression and R^2 coefficients for each equation are presented in Tables 3–5. This regression models explained from 39% to 56% of the variance in purchase intentions.

With respect to demographic characteristics, only marital status was significantly associated with purchase intention. Among the ethnic group, married women held stronger intention to purchase a t-shirt for themselves. No other demographic characteristics were statistically significant in predicting purchase intentions for any of the three product categories, whether for self or for others. As to attitudes toward other cultures among the three factors, consumer ethnocentrism was the only variable that was significant in all three souvenir categories. It decreased ethnic tourists' intentions to purchase a generic handcraft (placemat) and a symbolic marker (t-shirt) as gifts, as well as recreational tourists' intention to purchase an ethnic product (rug) for themselves. On the other hand, open-mindedness increased an ethnic tourist's intention to purchase an ethnic product for others. Interest in other cultures was not significant in all souvenir categories. Knowledge of Mexican culture was also not significant in all three categories. However, greater travel experience showed negative effects on pur-

Table 3. Regression Analyses for an Ethnic Product (Rug)

	Ethnic		Recreational	
	Self	Others	Self	Others
Demographic Characteristics				
Age	.02	−.07	.13	−.02
Education	.04	−.09	−.13	−.05
Employment (1=employed)	−.13	.10	−.01	−.01
Income	−.10	.05	−.07	.03
Marital Status (1=married)	.08	.01	.02	−.03
Attitudes toward Other Cultures				
Interest in Other Cultures	.09	−.06	.01	−.04
Consumer Ethnocentrism	−.06	.01	−.17[a]	−.11
Open-Mindedness	.07	.25[a]	.10	.10
Exposure to Mexican Culture				
Knowledge	−.01	.11	.17	.18
Travel Experience	−.05	−.06	−.19[a]	−.09
Attitudes toward Souvenirs				
Aesthetics	.37[c]	.36[c]	.39[c]	.35[c]
Uniqueness	.37[c]	.27[b]	.28[c]	.22[b]
Care and Travel	.15	.26[b]	.12	.19[a]
R^2	56	44	47	39

[a] $p < .05$
[b] $p < .01$
[c] $p < .001$

chase intentions for a symbolic marker and an ethnic product among the recreational tourists.

Highly significant coefficients resulted between the ratings of purchase intention and attitude toward aesthetics for all three souvenirs. The latter was the only dimension that was significant in predicting both groups of tourists' intentions to purchase souvenirs for themselves and as gifts in all three souvenir categories. In addition, it had the strongest effects on purchase intentions among the three subscales. The positive coefficients indicated that those who held more favorable attitudes toward aesthetic qualities of color and design of souvenirs tended to have stronger purchase intentions regardless of the souvenir categories. Attitude toward uniqueness positively affected purchase intentions for an ethnic product (rug) and a generic handcraft (placemat). Both tourist groups intending to purchase these textile souvenirs for themselves or as gifts valued products that appeared new, innovative, unique, or one-of-a-kind. Moreover, attitude toward care and travel exerted a significant effect on purchase intention for a rug and a t-shirt. Whether a product was easy to care for and transport was important to both ethnic and recreational tourists intending to purchase rugs and t-shirts as gifts.

Table 4. Regression Analyses for a Generic Handcraft (Placemat)[a]

	Ethnic		Recreational	
	Self	Others	Self	Others
Demographic Characteristics				
Age	−.05	−.03	.03	.04
Education	−.02	−.10	−.05	−.08
Employment (1=employed)	−.04	.01	−.04	.01
Income	−.10	−.09	−.10	−.09
Marital Status (1=married)	.08	.08	−.01	−.01
Attitudes toward Other Cultures				
Interest in Other Cultures	−.04	−.07	−.08	−.04
Consumer Ethnocentrism	−.11	−.18[a]	−.06	−.07
Open-Mindedness	−.01	.07	.07	.04
Exposure to Mexican Culture				
Knowledge	.06	.06	.06	.13
Travel Experience	−.03	−.03	.04	.04
Attitudes toward Souvenirs				
Aesthetics	.39[c]	.30[b]	.48[c]	.41[c]
Uniqueness	.33[c]	.34[c]	.36[c]	.34[c]
Care and Travel	.18	.13	.01	.05
R^2	54	52	52	47

[a] $p<.05$
[b] $p<.01$
[c] $p<.001$

CONCLUSION

This research was designed to contribute to scholarly and applied understanding of what influences tourists when they are intending to purchase three categories of souvenirs and considering purchases for themselves vs. as gifts for family and friends. Purchase intentions were explored for two groups of tourists in relation to their demographic characteristics, attitude toward other cultures, exposure to Mexican culture, and attitude toward souvenirs.

The first research question wanted to find out which tourist characteristics serve as predictors of tourists' purchase intentions for various categories of textile souvenirs. Although Abraham-Murali and Littrell (1995) found that consumers' responses were different when discussing garments in general vs. when discussing specific garments in photographs, much of the previous research on souvenir shopping was conducted on broad categories of products. Importantly, the present study demonstrated that the relationships among some tourist characteristics and purchase intentions were inconsistent across the three different souvenir product categories examined.

For example, tourists' previous tourism experience had a slight negative effect on purchase intentions only for an ethnic product

Table 5. Regression Analyses for a Symbolic Marker (T-Shirt)

	Ethnic		Recreational	
	Self	Others	Self	Others
Demographic Characteristics				
Age	−.01	−.08	.14	−.14
Education	.09	.07	.05	.04
Employment (1=employed)	−.09	.07	.03	.10
Income	−.08	−.15	−.05	−.01
Marital Status (1=married)	.27[a]	.23	.10	.12
Attitudes toward Other Cultures				
Interest in Other Cultures	.04	−.05	.04	−.10
Consumer Ethnocentrism	−.09	−.25[b]	.01	−.14
Open-Mindedness	.10	.03	.08	.07
Exposure to Mexican Culture				
Knowledge	.07	.01	.03	.01
Travel Experience	−.13	−.16	−.24[b]	−.24[b]
Attitudes towards Souvenirs				
Aesthetics	.37[c]	.33[b]	.47[c]	.33[b]
Uniqueness	.13	.19	.14	.06
Care and Travel	.14	.21[a]	.07	.32[c]
R^2	41	44	42	46

[a] $p<.05$
[b] $p<.01$
[c] $p<.001$

(rug) and a symbolic marker (t-shirt). That is, the more times tourists had traveled to Mexico, the less likely they were to buy these two souvenirs, especially a symbolic marker. Considering that these two items were highly representative of and unique to the tourism area, perhaps tourists would buy these items on a first visit. Therefore, those who had traveled to the area before may have already purchased these products during their previous visits. Another possible explanation is that while these two products may be considered very unique by retailers due to their design features native to the tourism area, tourists' previous experience in Mexico may diminish the extent to which they are perceived as new and different. This suggests the importance of retailers offering some stock that changes regularly over time in order to attract the interest of repeat tourists. For a generic handcraft, tourism experience was not a significant predictor of purchase intentions.

Interestingly, tourists' attitude toward the uniqueness of a souvenir positively affected purchase intentions for an ethnic product and a generic handcraft, but not for a symbolic marker. An examination of the means for the factor, Attitude toward uniqueness, provided insights as to why the relationship between attitude toward the uniqueness of souvenirs and purchase intentions would differ among the souvenirs. The means showed that overall, respondents held highly positive attitudes toward the uniqueness of a symbolic marker or t-shirt (mean=20.58), compared to the other two souvenirs (mean=16.49 for an ethnic product; mean=17.05 for a generic handcraft). This may suggest that attitude toward the uniqueness of a souvenir does not affect purchase intentions when the souvenir is generally perceived to be highly unique. It would appear that a t-shirt with a label distinctive to Mexico might be more clearly unique to a specific site for tourists than would a rug or placements. Knowledge of uniqueness for handwoven Mexican products, such as rugs and placemats, may come through greater awareness and understanding of Mexican crafts.

While the characteristics discussed above showed inconsistent relationships with purchase intentions for different souvenir product categories, there were some variables that appeared to be unaffected by souvenir types. Most importantly, attitude toward the aesthetic properties of souvenirs appeared to most affect purchase intentions across all three categories. This indicates that among the three dimensions of attitude toward souvenirs, attitude toward the aesthetic qualities are the best predictor of purchase intention, irrespective of the souvenir type. This finding was consistent with the study of Eckman, Damhorst and Kadolph (1990) who found that, in their analysis of 21 previous studies, aesthetic criteria such as styling and color have the greatest impact on selection of women's apparel. This suggests that the purchase decision process for textile souvenirs may not differ from the decision process for other textile and clothing products. Accordingly, the notion that aesthetic criteria are the most important product attributes in making purchase decisions may also be generalized to textile souvenirs.

Findings regarding the relationships between attitude toward souvenirs and purchase intention warrant great attention from tourism promoters or retailers who are marketing souvenirs. Generally, they should stress the aesthetic qualities such as design, colors, and uniqueness of products to increase sales; however, they should also develop appropriate promotional strategies for different products. As already discussed, for some souvenirs such as a rug (ethnic product), it appeared that positive responses to the care and portability of the products were also important in making purchase decisions. For a rug, attitude toward care and portability was more important than attitude toward uniqueness in predicting purchase intention. Therefore, retailers of rugs should attempt to yield positive responses from tourists particularly regarding care and portability. Some Mexican weavers who recognize the importance of portability for tourists in making purchase decisions show how to better roll up and pack the rug. Other promotions such as care instructions or free delivery to hotels may be also appropriate in appealing to tourists who are concerned about the care and portability of souvenirs.

In relation to the first research question, when ethnic and recreational tourists were compared, relatively few differences were discovered. For both groups, their attitudes toward souvenir aesthetics and uniqueness were closely linked to purchase intentions. Such findings bode well for Mexican tourism attractions that encompass both ethnic and recreational activities. Store merchandising strategies that focus on product aesthetics and uniqueness would seem to appeal to both groups of tourists.

Among the few differences that distinguished the two groups, for ethnic tourists, consumer ethnocentrism significantly decreased intentions to purchase a generic handcraft and a symbolic marker. Perhaps these consumers who are loyal to US products recognized that the handwoven placemats and t-shirt are common at home while the rug, with its native designs is less duplicative of US merchandise. Further research is warranted for sorting out details of this relationship. In a second example, the negative impact of travel experience on purchase intentions was apparent only for recreational tourists. That is, previous travel experience decreased recreational tourists' desire to purchase souvenirs in two categories. What is not known from the present research are the products actually purchased by the two tourist groups during their past travels. In previous research, tourists involved in active, outdoor pursuits were frequent purchasers of t-shirts (Littrell et al 1994). The question for further research arises as to how seasoned tourists' previous purchases in a product category impacts future purchase intentions.

The second research question asked whether the relationships between purchase intentions and predictor variables are influenced by the purchase situation of buying for oneself vs. buying for others. The same set of variables was used to predict tourists' intentions to purchase souvenirs for themselves and for others as gifts. The results from the two sets of tests were very similar, with a few interesting exceptions. Most interestingly, tourists' attitude toward the care and portability of souvenirs was a more important predictor of purchase intention when the souvenirs were considered as gifts for others rather than for themselves. This suggests that tourists are less inclined to purchase a souvenir they perceive to be hard to pack or carry, especially if the souvenir is to be given as a gift. Nevertheless, the similar findings between the two situations indicate that overall, retailers probably do not need different strategies for attracting tourists to gift buying vs. buying for self.

There are several concerns related to this study that warrant further investigation. First, this study was carried out using Mexican products only. Future researchers may want to consider products from different places for generalization of the present research findings to tourism destinations in other parts of the world. Second, the question concerning why the relationships between variables differ among souvenir types could be studied more systematically using an experimental approach. To illustrate, using the same type of products with the same features but with different designs (like innovative vs. common) and different types of products with similar levels of uniqueness in designs would aid in identifying the determinants of the differing relationships. Finally, it should be noted that this research explored gift giving generally. Future research should investigate whether the relationship

654   SOUVENIR BUYING INTENTIONS

of the recipient (family member, close friend, neighbor), along with the recipient's age and past tourism experience, impact purchase intentions. ■

Acknowledgements—Partial support for this study came from the Louise Rosenfeld International Fund and the College of Family and Consumer Sciences, Iowa State University.

REFERENCES

Abraham-Murali, L., and M. A. Littrell
  1995   Consumers' Conceptualization of Apparel Attributes. Clothing and Textiles Research Journal 13:328–348.
Adair, M.
  1996   Mexico. New York: Macmillan.
American Demographics
  1993   Parting Gifts. American Demographics (July):28.
Anderson, B., and L. Langmeyer
  1982   The Under-50 and Over-50 Travelers: A Profile of Similarities and Differences. Journal of Travel Research 21:20–24.
Anderson, L. F., and M. A. Littrell
  1995   Souvenir-Purchase Behavior of Women Tourists. Annals of Tourism Research 22:328–348.
  1996   Group Profiles of Women as Tourists and Purchasers of Souvenirs. Family and Consumer Sciences Research Journal 25:28–56.
Areni, C. S., P. Kiecker, and K. M. Palan
  1998   Is it Better to Give than to Receive? Exploring Gender Differences in the Meaning of Memorable Gifts. Psychology and Marketing 15:81–109.
Beatty, S. E., L. R. Kahle, M. Utsey, and C. Keown
  1993   Gift-Giving Behaviors in the United States and Japan: A Personal Values Perspective. Journal of International Consumer Marketing 6:49–66.
Belk, R. W., and G. S. Coon
  1993   Gift Giving as Agapic Love: An Alternative to the Exchange Paradigm Based on Dating Experience. Journal of Consumer Research 20:393–417.
Bentor, Y.
  1993   Tibetan Tourist Thangkas in the Kathmandu Valley. Annals of Tourism Research 20:107–137.
Bhawuk, D. P. S., and R. Brislin
  1992   The Measurement of Intercultural Sensitivity Using the Concepts of Individualism and Collectivism. International Journal of Intercultural Relations 16:413–436.
Caplow, T.
  1983   Rule Enforcement without Visible Means: Christmas Gift Giving in Middletown. American Journal of Sociology 89:1306–1323.
Cohen, E.
  1979   A Phenomenology of Tourist Experiences. Sociology 13:179–201.
  1988   Authenticity and Commoditization in Tourism. Annals of Tourism Research 15:371–386.
  1992   Tourist Arts. In Progress in Tourism, Recreation and Hospitality Management, C. P. Cooper and A. Lockwood, eds., pp. 3–32. London: Belhaven Press.
  1993   The Heterogeneization of a Tourist Art. Annals of Tourism Research 20:138–163.
Consumer Reports Travel Letter
  1995   Traveler's Notes. Consumer Reports Travel Letter (October):234.
Cook, S. D.
  1995   1996 Outlook for Travel and Tourism Basics for Building Strategies. In Proceedings of the Travel Industry Association of America's Twenty-first Annual Outlook Forum, S. D. Cook and B. McClure, eds., pp. 5–18. Washington DC: Travel Industry Association of America.

Dillman, D. A.
  1978 Mail and Telephone Surveys: The Total Design Method. New York: Wiley.
Eckman, M., M. L. Damhorst, and S. J. Kadolph
  1990 Toward a Model of the In-Store Purchase Decision Process: Consumer
    Use of Criteria for Evaluating Women's Apparel. Clothing and Textiles
    Research Journal 8(2):13–22.
Fishbein, M.
  1967 A Behavior Theory Approach to the Relations between Beliefs about an
    Object and the Attitude toward the Object. *In* Readings in Attitude Theory
    and Measurement, M. Fishbein, ed., pp. 389-400. New York: Wiley.
Goodwin, C., Smith, K.L., and Spiggle, S.
  1990 Gift-Giving: Consumer Motivation and the Gift Purchase Process. *In*
    Advances in Consumer Research, R. Pollay and G. Gorn, eds., pp. 690-698.
    Provo UT: Association for Consumer Research.
Gordon, B.
  1986 The Souvenir: Messenger of the Extraordinary. Journal of Popular Cul-
    ture 20(3):135–146.
Graburn, N. H.
  1989 Tourism: The Sacred Journey. *In* Hosts and Guests: The Anthropology
    of Tourism (2nd ed.), V. Smith, ed., pp. 21-36. Philadelphia PA: University
    of Pennsylvania Press.
Heeler, R. F., Okechuchu, C. and Reid, S.
  1979 Gift vs. Personal Use Brand Selection. *In* Advances in Consumer
    Research, W. Wilkie, ed., pp. 325-328. Ann Arbor MI: Association for Con-
    sumer Research.
Hett, E. J.
  1991 The Development of an Instrument to Measure Global-Mindedness. Dis-
    sertation Abstracts International 52(6), 2099-A.
Horne, L., and G. Winakor
  1991 A Conceptual Framework for the Gift-Giving Process: Implications for
    Clothing. Clothing and Textiles Research Journal 9(4):23–33.
  1995 Giving Gifts of Clothing: Risk Perceptions of Husbands and Wives. Cloth-
    ing and Textiles Research Journal 13(2):92–101.
Hyllegard, K. H., and J. J. Fox
  1997 The Value of Gifts to College Students: The Impact of Relationship Dis-
    tance, Gift Occasion, and Gift type. Clothing and Textiles Research Journal
    15(2):103–114.
Industry Sector Analysis
  1998 Mexico: Travel and Tourism Market. Industry Sector Analysis (June 22):1.
Jansen-Verbeke, M.
  1991 Leisure Shopping: A Magic Concept for the Tourism Industry? Tourism
    Management 12:9–14.
Keown, C. E.
  1989 A Model of Tourists' Propensity to Buy: The Case of Japanese Visitors to
    Hawaii. Journal of Travel Research 27(3):31–34.
Kim, H.
  1995 Consumer Response toward Apparel Products in Advertisements Con-
    taining Environmental Claims. PhD dissertation in Textiles and Clothing.
    Iowa State University.
Littrell, M. A.
  1987 Tourist Consumers of Textile Handcrafts: An International Perspective.
    Paper presented at the annual meeting of the American Home Economics
    Association. Indianapolis IN.
  1990 Symbolic Significance of Textiles Crafts for Tourists. Annals of Tourism
    Research 17:228–245.
Littrell, M. A., L. F. Anderson, and P. J. Brown
  1993 What Makes a Craft Souvenir Authentic? Annals of Tourism Research
    20:197–215.
Littrell, M. A., S. Baizerman, R. Kean, S. Gahring, S. Niemeyer, R. Reilly, and
    J. Stout
  1994 Souvenirs and Tourism Styles. Journal of Travel Research 33(1):3–11.

656   SOUVENIR BUYING INTENTIONS

McIntyre, R., and H. J. Meric
  1994 Cognitive Style and Consumers' Ethnocentrism. Psychological Reports
        75:591–601.
Morris, W. F., Jr.
  1991 The Marketing of Maya Textiles in Highland Chiapas, Mexico. *In* Textile
        Traditions of Mesoamerica and the Andes: An Anthology, M. B. Schevill, J.
        C. Berlo and E. B. Dwyer, eds., pp. 403-433. Austin: University of Texas Press.
Moscardo, G., and P. L. Pearce
  1999 Understanding Ethnic Tourists. Annals of Tourism Research 20:416–434.
Mullen, B., and Johnson, C.
  1990 The Psychology of Consumer Behavior. Hillsdale NJ: L. Erlbaum.
Netemeyer, R. G., S. Durvasula, and D. R. Lichtenstein
  1991 A Cross-National Assessment of the Reliability and Validity of the CETS-
        CALE. Journal of Marketing Research 28:320–327.
Otnes, C., T. M. Lowrey, and Y. Kim
  1993 Gift Selection for Easy and Difficult Recipients: A Social Roles Interpret-
        ation. Journal of Consumer Research 20:229–244.
Rucker, M., Kaiser, S., Barry, M., Brummett, D., Freeman, C. and Peters, A.
  1986 The Imported Export Market: An Investigation of Foreign Visitors' Gift
        and Personal Purchase. *In* Developments in Marketing Science, N. K. Malho-
        tra and J. M. Hawes, eds., pp. 120-124. Greenvale NY: Academy of Market-
        ing Science.
Sampson, D. L., and H. P. Smith
  1957 A Scale to Measure World-Minded Attitudes. Journal of Social Psychology
        45:99–106.
Schiffman, L. G., and Kanuk, L.L.
  1983 Consumer Behavior (2nd ed.). Englewood Cliffs NJ: Prentice-Hall.
Shenhav-Keller, S.
  1993 The Israeli Souvenir. Annals of Tourism Research 20:182–196.
Sherry, J. F. Jr.
  1983 Gift Giving in Anthropological Perspective. Journal of Consumer
        Research 10:157–168.
Shimp, T. A., and S. Sharma
  1987 Consumer Ethnocentrism: Construction and Validation of the CETS-
        CALE. Journal of Marketing Research 24:280–289.
Slaybaugh, J., M. A. Littrell, and J. Farrell-Beck
  1990 Consumers of Hmong Textiles. Clothing and Textiles Research Journal
        8(2):56–64.
Smith, H. P.
  1955 Do Intercultural Experiences Affect Attitudes? Journal of Abnormal and
        Social Psychology 51:469–477.
Smith, V.
  1989 Introduction. *In* Hosts and Guests: The Anthropology of Tourism (2nd
        ed.), V. Smith, ed., pp. 1-17. Philadelphia PA: University of Pennsylvania Press.
Timothy, D. J., and R. W. Butler
  1995 Cross-Border Shopping: A North American Perspective. Annals of Tour-
        ism Research 22:16–34.
Travel Industry Association of America
  1998 Fast Facts. http://www.tia.org/press/fastfacts6.stm.
US Bureau of Census
  1997 Statistical Abstract of the United States. Washington DC: US Government
        Printing Office.
Vincent, M., and Zikmund, W.G.
  1976 An Experimental Investigation of Situational Effects on Risk Perception.
        In Advances in Consumer Research, B. B. Anderson, ed., pp. 125-129 Ann
        Arbor MI: Association for Consumer Research.
Wallendorf, M., and E. Arnould
  1988 My Favorite Things: A Cross-Cultural Inquiry into Object Attachment,
        Possessiveness, and Social Linkage. Journal of Consumer Research 14:531–
        547.

Wiseman, R. L., M. R. Hammer, and H. Nishida
  1989   Predictors of Intercultural Communication Competence. International
  Journal of Intercultural Relations 13:349–370.

*Submitted 25 August 1999. Resubmitted 19 April 2000. Accepted 26 April 2000. Refereed
anonymously. **Coordinating Editor: Valene L. Smith***

[38]

Pergamon

www.elsevier.com/locate/atoures

Annals of Tourism Research, Vol. 26, No. 3, pp. 613–631, 1999
© 1999 Elsevier Science Ltd. All rights reserved
Printed in Great Britain
0160-7383/99/$20.00+0.00

PII: S0160-7383(99)00024-9

MUSEUMS
A Supply-Side Perspective

Steven Tufts
York University, Canada
Simon Milne
Victoria University, New Zealand

Abstract: The educational and cultural mandates of museums are being transformed as institutions play an increasingly important part in urban economic development and tourism promotion strategies. In contrast to more common demand-side studies, this paper emphasizes the supply-side by focussing on everyday museum operations. It outlines the competitive responses being adopted by museums in Montreal, Canada, including shifts in sources of revenue, new technologies, labor practices and the development of networks. Study findings show that the restructuring of museum operations raises important questions concerning not only the traditional public mandate of museums, but also on its ability to enhance consumption experiences and to contribute to a diversified tourism product. **Keywords:** museums, funding, cultural attractions, organization. © 1999 Elsevier Science Ltd. All rights reserved.

Résumé: Les musées: une perspective de l'offre. Les mandats éducatifs et culturels des musées se transforment, jouant un rôle de plus en plus important dans des stratégies de développement économique urbain et de promotion de tourisme. Par contraste aux études plus nombreuses de la demande, cet article souligne le côté de l'offre en examinant le fonctionnement quotidien des musées. L'article présente des réponses compétitives adoptées par des musées à Montréal, au Canada: des changements de sources de revenu, de nouvelles technologies, de nouvelles politiques de travail et le développement de réseaux. Cette restructuration du fonctionnement des musées soulève des questions importantes concernant non seulement le mandat public traditionnel des musées mais aussi leur capacité pour améliorer les expériences du consommateur et contribuer à un produit diversifié du tourisme. **Mots-clés:** musées, financement, attractions culturelles, organisation. © 1999 Elsevier Science Ltd. All rights reserved.

INTRODUCTION

For much of the 20th century the generally accepted definition of the museum has been an institution which serves to collect, conserve, research, interpret and exhibit society's material culture (ICOM 1986; Weil 1990:57–58). Museums have traditionally been

Steven Tufts (Department of Geography at York University, 4700 Keele Street, North York, Ontario M3J 1P3, Canada. Email ⟨stufts@yorku.ca⟩) is conducting research on the impact of organized labor on urban tourism development. **Simon Milne** is Professor of Tourism, School of Business and Public Management, Victoria University, New Zealand. His research interests include sustainable tourism development and the economic restructuring of tourism industries.

spaces where a society can celebrate its past and form a sense of its cultural identity (Urry 1996). Over the last decade, however, there has been increasing attention to a "cultural revival" of heritage experiences as popular leisure and urban tourism activities (Hewison 1987). Politicians and planners have taken the opportunity to integrate museums into economic development initiatives in both large and small urban centers (Vaughan and Booth 1989; Zukin 1995). In simple terms, the role of the museum is evolving, with cultural institutions expected to perform a broader range of economic functions, often as part of complex urban redevelopment strategies (Bassett 1993; Bianchini 1990, 1993; Urry 1995; Watson 1991). While the Canadian government asserts that the "true value" of the museum is "measured in terms of our culture and heritage", it still stresses that museums "generate almost a billion dollars in revenue each year" (Communications Canada 1990:21).

The expanding role of cultural institutions in advanced capitalist economies has forced researchers to focus more on the links between the cultural and the economic. Sayer (1997) characterizes the "cultural turn" in much economic geographic research not so much as a result of a "culturalized economy" but rather as the "economization of culture". Although Sayer concedes that the relationship between culture and economy is "highly complex", he maintains "economic forces continue to dominate contemporary life" (1997:16). The purpose of museums reflects various cultural agendas (such as nation building and education); but the ability of institutions to adhere to public mandates and play a central role in the overall tourism product often is determined by the operating environment (including access to sources of funding). For the purposes of this paper, the Montreal museum sector is treated as a set of cultural institutions operating under increasingly complex and, at times, contradictory economic constraints. The treatment is, in

Table 1. 1993/94 Montreal Museum Survey—sample by Theme (N=26)

Type of Museum	Population[a]	Sample[b]	Coverage %
Historic Sites and Interpretation/Info Centres	21	9	43
Exhibition Centers and Galleries	12	4	33
Science and Nature	8	5	63
Art	7	5	71
Ecomuseums	3	1	33
Maisons de la Culture[c]	8	8	100
Other	2	2	100
Total	61	26	43

[a] Based on La Société des Musées Québécois 1993 membership listings.
[b] Discussions were held with museum directors and or other representatives.
[c] Les Maisons de la Culture (MdlC) are centers administered by the municipality of Montreal with the mandate of bringing cultural events to communities outside of the downtown city core. Interviews were held with the head of the department responsible for the MdlC and directors of two of the eight centers.

part, a response to the recent call for tourism research to adopt more rigorous approaches to studying restructuring in tourism-related sectors (Ioannides and Debbage, 1998). The focus on the "economic forces" currently affecting museums in the city is not meant to reduce these institutions to a purely economic function.

The growing importance of museums as cultural attractions has drawn the attention of tourism researchers for some time, but most of the work to date emphasizes demand side issues (Harrison 1997; Urry 1990). Following a brief review of how researchers have attempted to understand the importance of museums in urban settings, an outline is given of the "supply-side" operational context in Montreal in the 90s. Focus is on the search for new funding opportunities, the use of new information technologies, labor management, alliance formation, and museum agglomeration. The findings show that these institutions are being forced to adopt a range of strategies in an increasingly challenging environment in order to secure stable funding year to year and fulfil their public mandates.

The data are drawn from in-depth open interviews held with professionals (directors and curators) from 26 Montreal museums (Table 1). This sample was drawn from the 61 institutions in the Greater Montreal Area that are listed as members of La Société des Musées Québécois. The museums contacted during the, 1993–94 study period were predominantly the larger ones located in Montreal's major tourism areas (Figure 1). Smaller museums in suburban communities are deliberately under represented.

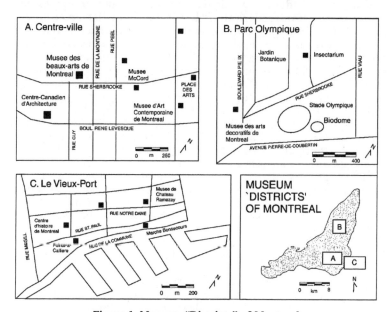

Figure 1. Museum "Districts" of Montreal

Discussions were also held with representatives from the Canadian and Quebec museum associations and recent issues of their respective journals, Muse and Musées were reviewed.

MUSEUMS IN THE URBAN ECONOMY

Museums have been used as the main attractions drawing tourists into the city. For example, the recent Renoir exhibit in Canada's National Gallery in Ottawa reportedly increased local hotel revenues by $4.8 million dollars (Calgary Herald 1997). However, the economic importance of museums in the local economy is much more complex than their ability to attract visitors with popular traveling exhibitions. Museums reflect an essential sense of a particular time and place unavailable elsewhere, and help to define the overall tourism product. Their unique architectural styles and permanent exhibits give tourists "something distinctive to gaze upon" (Urry 1990:128). Recent research has demonstrated that they expect "to learn something" when visiting museums (Jansen-Verbeke and van Rekom 1996) and to see an honest representation of a "good local place" (Harrison 1997). Regardless of the specific nature of the "pull factor" attracting visitors, planners have included museums in the overall promotion of urban destinations, leading researchers to classify these cultural institutions as primary elements of the tourism product (Jansen-Verbeke 1986).

Museums enable cities to "market" themselves, as cultural centers which both delight residents and tourists and appeal to professionals and investors (Kotler, Haider and Rein 1993; Kearns and Philo 1993). Harvey (1987), building on the work of Bourdieu (1984), argues that cultural consumption is often a means for capital to profit from upper and middle class attempts to reject mass culture. Elite classes differentiate themselves through the consumption of "cultural capital", high art, and antiquities which are often relatively inaccessible to lower classes (Fyfe and Ross 1996). Cultural institutions also provide a place for elites, who administer and frequent these non-profit institutions, to network and re-affirm their social position (Zukin 1995). In depressed urban economies, such as Montreal's, cultural amenities provide high-skilled professionals with an incentive to remain in a "liveable" city.

In the process of attracting tourists and nearby residents of different backgrounds to the city, museums become potential instruments for combining consumption activities with personal, lived experiences. To some extent the different components of the city (cultural attractions, shopping centers, and the like) converge, each offering the services and experiences of the other (Featherstone 1991). A tourist may enter a museum for a negligible admission fee, but during the visit include lunch, buy a souvenir, and take a taxi back to a nearby hotel. Thus, Ashworth and Tunbridge (1990) view the National Gallery and Canadian Museum of Civilization as the Ottawa–Hull region's effort to develop the Ottawa River waterfront's boutiques and restaurants. Similarly, on West Sherbrooke

Street in Montreal (Figure 1), gallery owners, antique dealers, high-end clothing retailers and museum professionals have formed an informal association to develop and promote the area as a place for the consumption of up-market consumer goods and a refined cultural aesthetic.

The synergy between cultural and consumption experiences creates spaces for both the tourist and resident groups to consume (Cohen 1995; Schurmer-Smith and Hannam 1994). Places of consumer activity are appropriated to exhibit culture while the aesthetic of culture is used simultaneously to promote consumption and inscribe products with various meanings. Zukin sees the processes of economic production and cultural consumption as increasingly inseparable:

> In fact, culture supplies the basic information—including symbols, patterns and meaning—for nearly all service industries. In our debased contemporary vocabulary, the word *culture* has become an abstraction for any economic activity that does not create material products like steel, cars or computers (Zukin 1995:11–12; emphasis in original).

The bulk of research into museums and urban development continues to focus on the attraction of tourists, the characteristics and behavior of museum visitors, and the consumption of cultural experiences. This focus on demand side issues has tended to neglect the evolving structure of the museum itself and the impacts of these changes on the surrounding urban setting. It is argued that by looking at the operating environment challenging museums, and the way they are responding to these issues, one can begin to understand better the evolving role that museums in particular, and the cultural sector in general, will play in the future urban economy.

Challenges in the 90s

For 30 years, Montreal has felt the impact of de-industrialization as economic activity has shifted westward to other Canadian cities, and core industries have slipped into decline (Leveillée and Whelan 1990; Whelan 1991). Montreal had experienced periods of infrastructural investment leading up to Expo '67 and again in preparation for the, 1976 Olympics, but fell behind other Canadian cities such as Toronto and Vancouver which developed rapidly in the 80s. The city has been actively exploiting its unique cultural heritage as a means of (re)developing its tourism market and fostering economic growth.

Through agencies such as the Greater Montreal Tourism and Convention Bureau, the city has been attempting to reinforce an image of the city as a major cultural destination. Museums have been a vital part of the agency's efforts to create a unique tourism product in its promotional campaigns. Montreal's Place des Arts, a complex of adjoining theatres, auditoriums and the Musée d'Art Contemporain is an example of a project aimed at tourists and elites, as well as developing the cities downtown central business district (Figure 1). Museums have also been placed at the center of attempts to use heritage tourism as a way to merge this and business development with the celebration of local architectural history and diverse cultural composition (see Chang, Milne, Fallon and Pohlman 1996). Part of the redevelopment of the urban heritage district in Old Montreal included the construction of a new archaeology museum and renovations to other museums in the area.

The federal government played an important role in the development of several of Montreal's new museums in the early 90s. In, 1986, Communications Canada funded research on the state of Canadian museums. In the wake of the studies a report and working paper were released which contained several recommendations for a revamped federal museum policy (Communications Canada 1986, 1988, 1990). After the 1988 federal election, some of the working paper's recommendations were adopted and the government began to invest money heavily into the financially troubled museum sector— assisting established institutions and financing the construction of new projects (Godfrey 1991). The result was an explosion in the number of museums throughout the country. The number of museums in Canada grew by nearly 25% between 1983 and 1994 (1,005 to 1,236), while visitation grew from just over 21 million to almost 25 million (Statistics Canada 1995). Montreal alone received $300 million in funding for nine new cultural attractions. Many of the new museum openings were planned to coincide with the celebration of the city's 350th birthday in the spring and summer of 1992 (Montreal Gazette 1992:February 29, E1). The visible investment in cultural institutions was perhaps also a means of the federal government to win favor with the majority of Quebec residents during the constitutional crisis of the early 90s. Although the federal government may have been encouraged to make such a visibly patrimonial investment in Montreal, it can be argued that the city's economy was genuinely in need of development assistance and was due for significant investment in new cultural attractions (Chang et al 1996).

Unfortunately, the museum building boom of the early 90s was not matched by a concomitant increase in government funding of annual operating budgets (Lacroix 1992). Federal expenditures on museums decreased by 4.1% between 1990–91 and 1994–95 to less than $225 million. Although provincial government expenditures on museums reached $293 million in 1992–93, levels of funding have also not been sustained as support declined to $277 million in 1994–95. Municipal governments only contribute approximately 5% to overall public expenditures on museums, but their contribution also decreased by 3.7% during this period as local funding focused on heritage sites. Across Canada, museums have had to sustain annual budgets with greater earned revenues (including corporate sponsorships, donations, foundations, as well as admission revenues). Nationally, earned revenues increased by 17.9% between 1990–91 and 1993–94 (Statistics Canada 1997).

The annual operating budgets of the 26 institutions in the survey totaled over $100 million in 1993–94. Although most museums received funding from a variety of sources, 9 museums were funded primarily by private sources (such as foundations) with the remainder depending largely on support from different levels of government (Table 2). Of the 26 institutions, 19 reported that the level of public funding had decreased from 1992–93. The museums supported primarily by private foundations reported that their endowments were stable, but their overall annual budgets were vulnerable to decreases in public funding as well. The budgetary constraints place museums in a difficult situation. Responses such as reducing personnel, limiting hours of operation, and sacrificing the quality of exhibits simply lead to reduced service, lower revenues from admission fees, and the ultimate failure to fulfil the museum's public mandate (interviews). There was consensus among those interviewed that funding annual operating budgets remains the most significant challenge to maintaining the quality of the museum experience.

While the Canadian museum sector has been able to attract the largest portion of corporate donations to the arts within the country (CBAC 1992), several of the professionals interviewed noted that corporate dollars are increasingly difficult to secure. For example, the city's premier art gallery, Musée des Beaux Arts, received over $1 million in corporate sponsorships for exhibits in 1987 but had no sponsorships in 1993. The director explained that the competitive environment facing several private sector corporations has limited their budgets for philanthropic projects. At the same time, the number of new museums established in Montreal in the 90s means more institutions are competing for these limited funds. While most of the directors and curators surveyed felt that these establishments were diverse enough to limit competition for visitors, it was noted that there is significant competition for corporate sponsors.

Similarly, the managers surveyed reported that individual donations were also increasingly difficult to secure. The largest museums actively solicited contributions from individuals in the form of membership programs. Those with annual budgets less than $500,000 did not have the resources to institute elaborate membership programs and as a result were not as able to pursue in-

Table 2. Funding Sources and Budgets of Surveyed Museums[a] (N=26)

Largest Funding Source	No.	Annual Operating Budget in Can$ (1993)	No.
Public (Federal)	1	$0–$250K	9
Public (Provincial)	6	$250K–$1m	5
Public (Municipal)	8	$1m–$10m	7
University	2	$10–$20m	2
Private	9	over $20m	3

[a] Source: 1993/1994 survey data.

dividual donations aggressively through telemarketing membership drives or other approaches. However, few of the smaller museums did have less formal "friends or supporters" associations which assisted with volunteers and fundraising efforts.

As government, corporate and individual support becomes increasingly difficult to find, museums are forced to look to visitors for revenue. The most obvious method of securing operating revenues is from admission fees. But this strategy is far from a panacea for museum administrators. Most view the establishment or increase of admission fees as being counterproductive (Table 3). Admission fees accounted for less than 5% of the overall operating budgets for 18 (most with annual budgets less than $10 million) of the 26 museums in the survey. The general feeling was that increasing fees would decrease visitorship (making current exhibits inaccessible or undesirable to a large part of the public). Only two of the museum administrators stated that they had plans to raise fees in the short term.

The resistance of administrators in Montreal to increase fees, however, does not mean that earned revenues have not become more important. Although Canadian museums in general may be less dependent on the "market" than their American counterparts, they are likely more dependent on earned revenues than those in most of Europe (Weil 1990). While private funding of various types can keep institutions alive in a period of public sector cuts, such a reliance is argued by many commentators to carry a considerable cost (Schurmer-Smith and Hannam 1994; Weil 1990). Corporate sponsors may be relatively conservative about the types of exhibits they will back and may also look to support mainstream material which will attract large audiences and maximize marketing spin-offs (Alexander 1996; Turgeon and Colbert 1992). A greater reliance on the market place may also tempt organizations to seek out the type of affluent audience that can afford higher admission charges. It can also be argued that corporate sponsorship will reduce the ability of museums to fulfil their educational role as mandated by the public. As Trigger, an anthropologist with strong connections to Montreal's McCord Museum of Canadian History, notes:

Table 3. The Role of Admission Fees and Other Revenues[a] (N=26)

Admission Rate		Fees as % of Budget		Future Admission Rate	
No Fees	8	0%	8	No fee	7
$1–$5	11	1%–5%	10	Future fee	1
$6–$10	5	6%–20%	0	Stable fee	14
$11>	2	21%–50%	8	Reduce fee	3
		>50%	0	Raise fee	1

[a] Source: 1993/1994 survey data.

Nor do I believe that museums can accept money from corporate
sponsors and pretend to maintain their academic freedom. How
many exhibitions do we see that portray corporate sponsors in a
critical light (Trigger 1988:8)?

Responding to the Changing Environment

The tightening of public and private sector financial support has
forced museums to re-evaluate several traditional practices.
Perhaps most significantly, exhibits are being popularized in order
to attract larger numbers of visitors as the museum is transformed
from "temple to big top" (Lind 1992:32; Urry 1990). New information technologies are being used to make exhibits more accessible to the public. Budget cuts have forced the re-evaluation of
staffing levels. The importance of increasing visitorship has also
encouraged museums to enter into formal and informal cooperative
relationships.

New Sources of Revenues. Montreal museums are attempting to
appeal to the mass audiences needed to attract corporate sponsors,
please foundations and government funding bodies, and guarantee
larger admission revenues. Nearly one quarter of the administrators
identified tour groups as their primary target audience (a reflection
of the importance of the tourism market). Surveyed museums
reported that tourists account for 40% to 60% of visitorship. But in
order to attract larger numbers of visitors, institutions are increasingly focusing on popular entertainment and neglect educational
aspects of the museum experience. In 1995, the Musée des Beaux
Arts sponsored *Moving Beauty*, an exhibit of rare automobiles which
was dismissed by critics because of its inappropriateness in a fine
arts museum. Nevertheless, the museum's board deemed the exhibit a necessary step in the attempt to lift it out of debt (Duncan
1995). The McCord Museum produced *That's Hockey* in 1996–97
aimed at the large number of Montrealers interested in the historical role the sport has played in shaping the city.

The cultural attractions in the survey had various themes (including science, heritage and art) but all used the word museum to
denote even what some may consider pure spectacle. The best
example in Montreal of this is the Musée Juste Pour Rire which
opened in 1993. Its initial admission fee was an unsustainable $18
per visit, and near death experiences, re-openings, and scaled down
admission fees have followed as the museum failed to attract the
interest of residents and tourists. Clearly some have more commercial appeal than others. For example, the Biôdome, a "nature"
museum with four indoor simulated natural environments (including the St Lawrence estuary), has been able to sustain admission
fees which are significantly higher than all of the heritage ones in
the survey. Indeed, the wide variety of Montreal attractions identifying themselves as "museums" in the 90s appears to mesh with
Urry's conclusion that "museums cannot be created about anything

anywhere. But a museum on almost any topic can be created some-where" (1990:134). This popularization process even calls into ques-tion the very definition of the more traditional museum (Weil 1990). Although several of the administrators were well aware of the popularization issue, they did not see it as a future problem in their "dignified" museum. But they were willing to point the finger at other institutions with "less integrity".

The commercialization of culture does not, however, always result in the debasement of cultural experiences or less educational value (Sayer 1997). Montreal museums are attempting to increase visitor-ship by attracting seniors and school children, with the latter often putting pressure on parents for return visits. Professionals and aca-demics have also been trying to come to terms with questions of representation in museum exhibitions and have explored ways of including voices from marginalized communities (Karp and Lavine 1991, Karp, Kreamer and Lavine 1992). Thus, museums elsewhere have been established to represent and attract ethnic groups, and gender issues have also been more closely scrutinized (Glaser and Zenetou 1994). One curator stated that her historical museum had recently attempted to appeal to and include native groups which have been marginalized through neglect and misrepresentation in past exhibits.

Several of the museums were actively seeking to increase sales of cultural products related to their exhibits. All of the 18 institutions in the survey which had boutiques cited the growing importance of gift sales, especially "high mark-up" items and several had aggres-sive plans to expand this part of their operation. Some of the larger ones (annual budgets greater than $10 million) report sales of up to $3 million per year. One science and nature participant in the sur-vey reported gift store revenues of $1 million, compared to admis-sion revenues of $5.5 million. Museums have also cooperated with institutions from across Canada to sell mail order products. These alternative revenue sources are not equally accessible to large and small operations. The former are likely to be at an advantage as they have the necessary visitor numbers to run successful retail business. Smaller museums have, however, also been innovative. One historical institution raised significant revenues by charging a small fee to couples wishing to use the indoor displays as backdrops for wedding photos.

New Technologies. Alternative advances are being used to make the museum experience more accessible to the general public. Several of them use videos or computers to enhance exhibits. But there are factors limiting the immediate integration of new technol-ogy. Some administrators noted that the costs of adding new tech-nologies can be prohibitive. For example, the $50,000 rental fee for an infra-red audio guide to complement tours can only be justified if attendance is substantial. In one case, a museum that evaluated the potential of an infra-red audio guide decided against its use and hired seven summer student guides for the same cost. Some commentators also argue that such technologies can reduce visitor interaction with the artifacts and other attendees (Goodes 1991, Alexander 1996).

The fastest growing area of applied technology in museums, however, lies in the display and dissemination of images. The World Wide Web is now an important way for museums to advertise exhibitions and provide visitors with information (Dumais 1996). The large Montreal institutions are using the Internet to attract residents and visitors from Canada and abroad. The Greater Montral Tourism and Convention Bureau lists most of the surveyed institutions on its website and 12 of them have also developed their own sites. Smaller establishments, with fewer resources, are less likely to develop their own sites. Some professionals feel that technological developments such as CD ROM and the Internet increase accessibility to museum holdings and will encourage visitation (Lambert 1995; Wertheim 1995). At the same time, such technology may also threaten visitorship levels if they are forced to compete with their own "virtual" exhibits. The impacts information technologies will have on the frequency of museum visits and visitor expectations of the "real" exhibit created by digital images have yet to be explored fully.

Labor Issues. The largest component of a museum's budget is often labor costs and this no doubt explains the rash of recent layoffs of staff by cash-strapped institutions throughout Canada (Bula 1994; Crew 1995). Attempts to manage government expenditures will continue to put pressure on a largely feminized workforce which is underpaid relative to other cultural industry workers (Frank 1996). In the Montreal survey, a total of 1,486 staff were employed by the 26 institutions, 62% on a full time basis (Table 4).

Table 4. Labor and Montreal Museums[a] (N=26)

Employees per Museum	No.	Type of Employment	No. Employed
1–4	3	Full-time	921
5–15	11	Part-time	565
16–50	5	Part-time (all year)	58
51–100	2	Part-time (seasonal)	501
>100	2		

Subcontracting Labour	No.	Subcontracting Trend	No.
No Subcontracting	11	Increasing	12
Security only	5	No Change	14
Other Subcontracting	10	Decrease	0

[a] Source: 1993/1994 survey data.

The majority of institutions have experienced declining or frozen employment levels as dictated by recent budget cuts.

Compared to the Canadian laborforce as a whole, the museum workers employed in the institutions surveyed had above average rates of unionization. The 11 establishments with unionized employees (accounting for 60% of the total sample) were mostly the larger publicly administered and funded museums. None of the primarily privately funded ones were unionized. A few administrators stated that unionization can create increased wage costs, barriers to subcontracting, and delays in implementing layoffs. For example, strike activity at Montreal's Biôdome throughout the 90s has closed the institution during peek visitor periods (Derfel 1995). One director stated that Montreal's city government has attempted to create paragovernmental administrative agencies for its municipal museums in order to avoid organization by strong city workers' unions.

The museums surveyed are moving towards more flexible labor relationships in order to cut wage bills. One large exhibition center has all but 20 of its 180 employees working on contract. While the use of sub-contracted labor for security, cleaning and other tasks is an established practice, there is also a trend toward outsourcing to specialized firms (operations such as marketing, research, and exhibit design). Over one-third of those interviewed plan to increase the use of sub-contracted labor further over the next five years, with the rest expecting little change. Managers are no longer merely overseers of collections but salespeople, accountants, market researchers, and educators (Mayer 1991). The director of a small art museum stated that finding permanent, full-time qualified professionals is difficult for financially troubled institutions which still need highly skilled people. There is also the practice of larger museums "poaching", professionals from smaller ones after they have gained the necessary experience.

The paid laborforce is supplemented by volunteer workers in 11 of the institutions surveyed. They are especially important to museums adjusting to financial pressures, but they are viewed as a complement to, not a substitute for, paid labor. For example, volunteers may assist with fundraising efforts or serve as informational instructors, but they are not often used to create exhibits or perform cleaning duties. One director emphasized that managing volunteers was a specialized skill given they are not easily recruited and must be used in tasks that make them feel productive and appreciated. Although the number of museums in Montreal grew substantially in the 90s, there is no evidence to suggest that there will be an equally impressive increase in employment opportunities. Reduced budgets, new communication technologies, and the existence of an extensive volunteer system limits the possibilities for dynamic full-time job growth.

Networks and Alliances. Economic geographers have become increasingly aware of how strategic firm alliances and network formation have become an essential feature of corporate power in advanced economies (Allen 1997; Axelsson and Easton 1992; Yeung 1994). Cooperation among museums has always been a part of everyday operations (such as exchange of artifacts and traveling exhibits). There is a significant amount of cooperation and networking among museums which at first appears to mimic inter-firm network relations such as joint marketing and externalized operations. Montreal institutions are part of national (Canadian Museums Association), provincial (La Société des Musées Québécois), and local (La Société des Directeurs des Musées Montréalais) organizations which jointly promote the richness and diversity of the museum sector through information networks and publicity campaigns.

National and provincial organizations are the more established and formal networks servicing the sector's collective lobbying, literary, and research and development needs. The local museum society is less formal than the larger groups but is viewed by the administrators interviewed as the most effective marketing and publicity tool through promotions such as Montreal's annual Museum Day (free admission in all of them). Some of those interviewed did, however, suggest that associations tend to exclude or marginalize small museums, and pay greater attention to the needs of the larger institutions which contribute the most in terms of financing.

Cooperation between museums and various governmental tourism agencies is at times just as important as networking among the former. For many, marketing initiatives beyond print media are only financially feasible with the assistance of joint publicity programs or subsidized tourism packages. Some of them were almost solely dependent upon the tourism maps, promotional packages, and web access provided by Montreal's tourism promotion bureau. Most work closely with the agency, but a significant minority complained that some museums were neglected in favor of more popular cultural attractions or other elements of the tourism product (such as accommodation and festivals).

Agglomeration and Museum Parks. Some commentators argue that a successful cultural tourism product depends on the complementarity of spatially clustered institutions even though these large attractions tend to be "bad neighbors" for residents, such as large crowds and traffic congestion (Ashworth 1995). Clusters of cultural institutions also tend to centralize in the inner city and often limit cultural resources in suburban areas. The municipal government in Montreal has attempted to develop several small museums/cultural institutions, Les Maisons de la Culture outside of the downtown core, in efforts to make culture and heritage accessible to suburban residents. Clustering of cultural institutions, however, allows visitors easy access from one museum to another, but more importantly allows several of them form a "synergy" which adds to a neighborhood architectural and artistic aesthetic (Jansen-Verbeke 1997).

There are three identifiable museum "districts" in Montreal: Vieux Montréal, Parc Maisonneuve, and Centre-Ville (Sherbrooke Street West) (Figure 1). Administrators of museums located within these areas are generally happy with their location. Over half of those operating outside the three districts stated that they would prefer to be in one of the agglomerations. The desire to enter these areas stems from the need to tap into areas of high tourist density (Law 1993). The initial formation of these agglomerations reflects different periods of infrastructural development. For example, the Parc Maisoneuve museum complex was developed in the wake of the, 1976 Olympics, while the Old Port re-emerged as an urban heritage site in the 90s (Chang et al 1996).

Spatial proximity fosters informal alliances among museums looking to economize their everyday operations. For example, a small Montreal art museum and a neighboring historical center share signage and visitors. Similarly, one museum in the survey was collaborating with two other nearby institutions to organize a large joint exhibit. Some difficulties arise concerning the division of responsibilities and costs, and as a result alliances are often based on long term relationships of trust and reciprocity established within the cultural sector community.

CONCLUSION

The evolving nature of Montreal's museum sector has several implications for the urban economy and the development of cultural institutions. The decline of both public and private support for museum operations during the 90s has made it increasingly difficult for Montreal museums to meet their traditional mandate of preserving culture and educating society. They are being pressured to produce a product which maximizes admission revenues and appeals to the marketing objectives of corporate sponsorship. Pressures to increase sales of culturally inscribed goods in museum boutiques tend to necessitate exhibits which appeal to broad-based tastes. Questions arise concerning the ability of a "popularized" museum experience to cater to the demands of cultural tourists. A popularized museum experience will not necessarily appeal to the tourist searching for an intense sense of local time and space (Harrison 1997) or "food for thought" (Jansen-Verbeke and van Rekom 1996). An oversupply of mediocre attractions or spectacles masquerading as museums will only increase the competition for corporate, individual, and state sources of revenue while debasing the overall cultural product. The key issue remains—how museums in this environment can deliver a cultural experience which sustains appeal to tourists and residents alike.

This research shows that small museums face a difficult future. While new communication technologies have provided some large museums with access to new media such as the Internet, these technologies are often beyond the reach of smaller museums. Museums with limited access to emerging technologies such as Internet and reduced financial resources will find it difficult to broaden their appeal to a wider audience. There are also problems for smaller museums in attracting multi-skilled professionals. While networking and alliances are evident in the sector and provide small establishments with a range of competitive options, larger counterparts dominate the agendas of the well-established formal bodies that represent museums. Of the nine participants in the survey with annual budgets below $250,000, five were primarily privately funded by endowments. The greater stability of their primary funding source may allow them to survive but expansion of exhibits and marketing programs will prove difficult.

The problems that face smaller museums are important on a number of fronts. They play an important role in supplying the tourism product with diversity and local flavor. Many small institutions in Montreal diversify their (and broader tourism) products with specialized themes that also embrace space and time specific experiences. Beyond the tourism focus, however, Weil (1990:40) also notes that the particular strengths of small museums—flexibility and freedom from the weight of large collections—make them very important in any attempts to move this community towards a more socially relevant role.

Larger museums, however, will also continue to face challenges in the present environment. Pressures to increase earned revenues and limit costs will potentially change the very nature of the museum experience itself. The development of Montreal's Marché Bonsécours into a place where traveling exhibitions are presented in a "warehouse" space staffed by contracted workers is perhaps the best example of a "flexible" museum. But this alternative setting does not reflect any well-developed sense of time and place. As large establishments, the core of the museum product, increasingly adjust to decreasing budgets by appealing to broader markets or adopting more "flexible" operations, the overall experience will be affected.

By examining Montreal museums from a supply-side perspective, this paper sheds light on the changing role of cultural institutions in urban economic development. The questions the paper begins to answer relate to the evolving nature of cultural institutions as places for leisure, education, and the celebration of local heritage versus a transition to an alternative consumption experience. It is necessary to examine how cities may restructure cultural institutions in order to boost consumption experiences and tourism activities, while still appealing to a sense of culture and place. While the predominantly demand-side approaches discussed here go someway toward explaining why cultural infrastructure has played an increasingly important role in urban tourism development, they are limited in their ability to explain how institutions such as museums are adjusting to the new role. To gain a better insight into cultural sectors as tourism products and broader urban socioeconomic structures, more empirical research is necessary on the supply-side. Furthermore, only a rigorous linking of supply- and demand-side

628 STEVEN TUFTS AND SIMON MILNE

perspectives can bring about a better sense of the changing nature of cultural sectors, and their importance for urban development. ■

Acknowledgments—Special thanks for the help of all museum professionals who took part in this survey. The research project was funded by Quebec's research funding agency (FCAR).

REFERENCES

Alexander, V.
1996 Pictures at an Exhibition: Conflicting Pressures in Museums and the Display of Art American. Journal of Sociology 10:797–839.
Allen, J.
1997 Economies of Power and Space. *In* Geographies of Economies, R. Lee and J. Wills, eds., pp. 59–70. London: Arnold.
Ashworth, G. J
1995 Managing the Cultural Tourist. *In* Tourism and Spatial Transformations: Implications for Policy and Planning, G. Ashworth and A. Dietvorst, eds., pp. 265–283. Wallingford: CAB International.
Ashworth, G. J., and J. E. Tunbridge
1990 The Tourist–Historic City. London: Belhaven.
Axelsson, B. and G. Easton, eds.
1992 Industrial Networks: A New View of Reality. London: Routledge.
Bassett, K.
1993 Urban Cultural Strategies and Urban Regeneration: A Case Study and Critique. Environment and Planning A 25:1773–1788.
Bianchini, F.
1990 Urban Renaissance? The Arts and the Urban Regeneration Process. *In* Tackling the Inner Cities, S. MacGregor and B. Pimlott, eds., pp. 215–250. Oxford: Clarendon Press.
1993 Remaking European Cities: The Role of Cultural Politics. *In* Cultural Policy and Urban Regeneration: The West European Experience, F. Bianchini and M. Parkinson, eds., pp. 1–20. Manchester: Manchester University Press.
Bourdieu, P.
1984 Distinction: A Social Critique of the Judgement of Taste. Cambridge: Cambridge University Press.
Bula F.
1994 Jobs Sacrificed in Museum's Back-to-Work Agreement. Vancouver Sun (November 16):B1.
CBAC
1992 Annual CBAC Survey of Corporate Donations, 1992 Council for Business and Arts in Canada. Toronto: CBAC.
Calgary Herald
1997 Renoir Show Pumped up Local Economies. Calgary Harald (November 29):C4.
Chang, T. S. Milne, D. Fallon, and C. Pohlman
1996 Urban Heritage Tourism, the Global–Local Nexus. Annals of Tourism Research 23:284–305.
Cohen, E.
1995 Contemporary Tourism: Trends and Challenges, Sustainable Authenticity or Contrived Post-Modernity. *In* Change in Tourism: People Places Processes, R. Butler and D. Pearce, eds., pp. 12–29. London: Routledge.
Communications Canada
1986 Report and Recommendations of the Task Force Charged with Examining Federal Policy Concerning Museums. Ottawa: Minister of Supply and Services.

1988 Challenges and Choices: Federal Policy and Program Proposals for Canadian Museums. Ottawa: Minister of Supply and Services Canada.
1990 Canadian Museum Policy: Temples of the Human Spirit. Ottawa: Minister of Supply Services Canada.
Crew R.
1995 Jeopardizing Canada's Past and Future. Toronto Star (April 15):H15.
Derfel A.
1995 Blue-Collars' Overtime Strike Closes Biôdome. Montreal Gazette (March 30):A3.
Dumais, M.
1996 L'internet: alors, on se branche? Musées 18(1):40.
Duncan A.
1995 Running on Empty. Montreal Gazette (October 21):H1.
Featherstone, M.
1991 Consumer Culture an Postmodernism. London: Sage.
Frank J.
1996 Canada's Cultural Labour Force. Canadian Social Trends (41):22–26.
Fyfe, G., and M. Ross
1996 Decoding the Visitor's Gaze: Rethinking Museum Visiting. *In* Theorizing Museums, Representing Identity and Diversity in a Changing World, S. MacDonald and G. Fyfe, eds., pp. 127–152. Oxford: Blackwell.
Glaser, J. and A. Zenetou, eds.
1994 Gender Perspectives: Essays on Women in Museums. Washington DC: Smithsonian Institute Press.
Godfrey S.
1991 Money for Museums a Priority, Masse Says. Montreal Gazette (June 9):C9.
Goodes, D.
1991 Qualified Democratization: The Museum Audioguide. Journal of Canadian Art History 142:51–73.
Harrison, J.
1997 Museums and Touristic Expectations. Annals of Tourism Research 24:23–40.
Harvey, D.
1987 Flexible Accumulation through Urbanisation: Reflections on the American City. Antipode 193:260–286.
Hewison, R.
1987 The Heritage Industry. London: Methuen.
ICOM
1986 Dictionary of Museology. Budapest: International Council of Museums.
Ioannides, D., and K. Debbage
1998 Introduction: Exploring the Economic Geography and Tourism Nexus. *In* The Economic Geography of the Tourist Industry, D. Ioannides and K. Debbage, eds., pp. 1–13. London: Routledge.
Jansen-Verbeke, M. C.
1986 Inner-City Tourism: Resources, Tourists Promoters. Annals of Tourism Research 13:79–100.
1997 Developing Cultural Tourism in Historical Cities: The Local Challenge in a Global Market. Discussion paper presented at the International Academy for The Study of Tourism conference, Malaysia, June.
Jansen-Verbeke, M. C., and J. van Rekom
1996 Scanning the Museum Visitor: Urban Tourism Marketing. Annals of Tourism Research 23:364–375.
Karp, I., C. Kreamer and S. Lavine, eds.
1992 Museums and Communities: The Politics of Public Culture. Washington DC: Smithsonian Institution Press.
Karp, I. and S. Lavine, eds.
1991 Exhibiting Culture: The Poetics and Politics of Museum Display. Washington DC: Smithsonian Institution Press.
Kearns, G. and C. Philo, eds.
1993 Selling Places: The City as Cultural Capital, Past Present and Future. Oxford: Pergamon Press.

630   STEVEN TUFTS AND SIMON MILNE

Kotler, P., D. Haider and I. Rein, eds.
    1993 Marketing Places: Attracting Investment, Industry and Tourism to Cities,
        States and Nations. New York: Free Press.
Lacroix, L.
    1992 Museums in Quebec: Twenty Years of Expansion—Twenty Years of
        Hardship? MUSE 10:116–119.
Lambert, J. B.
    1995 Virtual Galleries. Omni 174:25.
Law, C.
    1993 Urban Tourism: Attracting Visitors to Large Cities. London: Mansell.
Leveillée, J., and R. Whelan
    1990 Montreal: The Struggle to Become a "World City". *In* Leadership and
        Urban Regeneration: Cities in North America and Europe, pp. 152–170.
        Newbury Park CA: Sage.
Lind, M.
    1992 Reinventing the Museum. The Public Interest 109:22–39.
Mayer, C.
    1991 The Contemporary Curator: Endangered Species or Brave New Profession?
        MUSE 92:34–38.
Montreal Gazette
    1992 Nine Cultural Attractions Worth $300 Million Set to Open. Montreal
        Gazette (February 29):E1, E10.
Sayer, A.
    1997 The Dialectic of Culture and Economy. *In* Geographies of Economies, R.
        Lee and J. Wills, eds., pp. 16–26. London: Arnold.
Schurmer-Smith, P., and K. Hannam
    1994 Worlds of Desire, Realms of Power: A Cultural Geography. London:
        Arnold.
Statistics Canada
    1995 Government Expenditures on Culture Catalogue 87-206. Ottawa: Minister
        of Supply and Services.
    1997 Canada's Culture, Heritage and Identity: A Statistical Perspective
        Catalogue 87-211-XPB. Ottawa: Minister of Supply and Services.
Trigger, B.
    1988 Reply to Julia Harrison's "The Spirit Sings" and the Future of
        Anthropology. Anthropology Today 4(6):6–10.
Turgeon, N., and F. Colbert
    1992 The Decision Process Involved in Corporate Sponsorship for the Arts.
        Journal of Cultural Economics 161:41–51.
Urry, J.
    1990 The Tourist Gaze. London: Sage.
    1995 Consuming Places. London: Routledge.
    1996 How Societies Remember the Past. *In* Theorizing Museums, Representing
        Identity and Diversity in a Changing World, S. MacDonald and G. Fyfe, eds.,
        pp. 145–167. Oxford: Blackwell.
Vaughan, D. R., and P. Booth
    1989 The Economic Importance of Tourism and the Arts in Merseyside. Journal
        of Cultural Economics 132:21–34.
Watson, S.
    1991 Gilding the Smokestacks: The New Symbolic Representations of De-indus-
        trialized Regions. Environment and Planning D: Society and Space 9:59–70.
Weil, S. E.
    1990 Rethinking the Museum and other Meditations. Washington DC:
        Smithsonian Institute Press.
Wertheim, M.
    1995 Interactive Museums. Omni 142:150–154.
Whelan, R.
    1991 The Politics or Urban Redevelopment in Montreal: Regime Change from
        Drapeau to Doré. Quebec Studies 12:154–169.
Yeung, H.
    1994 Critical Reviews of Geographical Perspectives on Business Organizations

MUSEUMS 631

and the Organization of Production: Towards a Network Approach. Progress in Human Geography 184:460–490.
Zukin, S.
1995 The Cultures of Cities. New York: Blackwell.

Submitted 28 August 1997. Resubmitted 21 June 1998. Resubmitted 2 October 1998. Accepted 21 October 1998. Final version 18 November 1998. Refereed anonymously. Coordinating Editor: Myriam Jansen-Verbeke.

[39]

PERGAMON

Available online at www.sciencedirect.com

SCIENCE @ DIRECT•

Tourism Management 24 (2003) 401–410

TOURISM MANAGEMENT

www.elsevier.com/locate/tourman

Difference in shopping satisfaction levels: a study of tourists in Hong Kong

James Wong*, Rob Law

School of Hotel & Tourism Management, The Hong Kong Polytechnic University, Hung Hom, Kowloon, Hong Kong

Received 24 July 2001; accepted 11 October 2002

Abstract

Since the handover of sovereignty of Hong Kong to China and the financial turmoil experienced in 1997, the retail trade in Hong Kong has undergone a major restructuring. As sales to tourists account for more than 2% of the Gross Domestic Product of Hong Kong, it is beneficial to investigate the shopping satisfaction levels of visitors to Hong Kong. This study aims to explore travellers' expectations and perceptions of shopping in Hong Kong, compare the responses of Asian and Western travellers and recommend possible actions that would improve the position of the retail trade in Hong Kong. An analysis of the results revealed that significant differences exist between the expectations and perceived satisfaction of the seven tourist groups studied for service quality, quality of goods, variety of goods and price of goods. It was also noted that Western travellers were more satisfied with almost all the individual attributes than were Asian travellers. In the light of these empirical findings, theoretical and practical implications are discussed.
© 2003 Elsevier Science Ltd. All rights reserved.

Keywords: Shopping; Satisfaction levels; Tourists; Hong Kong

1. Introduction

Tourism is one of the main sources of revenue in Hong Kong. It accounted for about 5% of the Gross Domestic Product of Hong Kong in 1999 (HKTA, 1991–2000). The shopping of tourists has accounted for half of the total visitor expenditure over the past 10 years as shown in Table 1. In 2000, shopping accounted for more than HK$30 billion (50.2%) of total tourism receipts. The shopping expenditure of tourists, therefore, has a great impact on the local economy of Hong Kong. In recent years, the influence of the pegged exchange rate system and the emergence of other Asian competitors have led to a substantial challenge to Hong Kong's position as a 'Shoppers' Paradise'. The price competitive index of Dwyer, Forsyth, and Rao (2000) highlighted the fact that Hong Kong ceased to be a price competitive tourism destination with the drop in exchange rates in Malaysia, Thailand and South Korea

after 1997. Furthermore, a change in the composition of tourists visiting Hong Kong has in turn, induced a significant change in market structures. Since the handover of Hong Kong to China in 1997, there has been a continual increase in the number of visitors from the Mainland. As Qu and Li (1997) indicated, Hong Kong is the number one destination for the Mainland Chinese travelling abroad. In 2000, over 3.7 million visitors from the Mainland came to Hong Kong, an increase of 18.1% compared to 1999. This number accounted for almost half of the total number of Chinese visiting destinations outside of the People's Republic of China; it is presumed that this number will continue to increase over the forthcoming years.

As noted, the rapidly changing origin profile of travellers visiting Hong Kong has had a great impact on Hong Kong's tourism industry. This is because the majority of tourists' spending on shopping in Hong Kong is now by visitors from China, Taiwan and the USA, each accounting for 26.4, 21.5 and 11.4% of the total visitor spending, respectively. However, the proportions of total expenditure of visitors from different countries for which shopping accounts are found to be very different among different nationalities. Asian

*Corresponding author. Tel.: +852-2766-6528; fax: +852-2362-9362.

E-mail addresses: hmjames@polyu.edu.hk (J. Wong), hmroblaw@polyu.edu.hk (R. Law).

0261-5177/03/$ - see front matter © 2003 Elsevier Science Ltd. All rights reserved.
doi:10.1016/S0261-5177(02)00114-0

402 J. Wong, R. Law / Tourism Management 24 (2003) 401–410

Table 1
Percentage of shopping receipts among total tourism receipts in Hong Kong from 1991 to 2000

Year	Total tourism receipts ($ million)	Total receipts on shopping ($ million)	%
2000	61,514	30,880	50.2
1999	52,984	26,757	50.5
1998	55,251	26,023	49.0
1997	72,086	34,416	49.2
1996	84,520	40,850	49.5
1995	74,914	37,068	50.8
1994	64,263	32,452	51.9
1993	60,026	29,609	50.8
1992	48,390	24,802	53.1
1991	39,607	20,079	52.4

Source: HKTA: Statistical Review of Tourism 1991–2000.

visitors tend to spend a larger proportion of their total expenditure on shopping than Western visitors do. According to the Hong Kong Tourist Association (HKTA, 1991–2000), shopping accounted for 64.7% of the total expenditure of Mainland Chinese tourists and 59.1% of Taiwanese visitors' expenditure, while visitors from the USA and Australia spent most on accommodation (44.1 and 41.1%, respectively). Because of the changes in tourist composition and the differences between the spending patterns of Asian and Western tourists, it is important to investigate the shopping satisfaction levels of different travellers since the handover. It can be argued that a retail mix and provision that existed prior to 1997 might now be less effective. For example, Kozak (2001) found that the nationality of tourists has a significant effect on reported levels of satisfaction with a destination. Therefore, it was thought important to focus on the differences between the importance expectations and perceptions of shopping attitudes for each of the traveller groups. This will provide new information about the role of retail business in segmenting tourism markets, permitting strategies appropriate for travellers from each country, in order to improve the total tourism receipts for Hong Kong.

Just as customer satisfaction is essential to corporate survival (Pizam & Ellis, 1999), it is also important for destinations that compete in a worldwide market. As Summers (2001) has indicated, Hong Kong's competitiveness as a tourist destination is constantly challenged by the continued devaluation of neighbouring currencies and the development of new tourism infrastructure in competing destinations. Examples of these neighbouring countries include South Korea, Singapore, Thailand, Malaysia and Taiwan (Carben, 1991). Therefore, it is important to maintain a high level of service standard, an awareness of customer expectations and improvements in the services and products of the retail trade in Hong Kong. However, there have only been a limited number of studies on the shopping of tourists in Hong

Kong. For example, Heung and Qu (1998) noted that the retail trade had contributed a great deal to Hong Kong. Also, Mak, Tsang, and Cheung (1999) specifically investigated the shopping preferences of Taiwanese visitors. Recently, some attentions have been paid to hotel services and shopping. For example, Heung and Cheng (2000) investigated 200 tourists' levels of satisfaction with shopping in Hong Kong before the handover. Choi and Chu (2000) focused on the needs of Asian and Western travellers by identifying their perceptions of, and levels of satisfaction with, the services and facilities provided by hotels in Hong Kong. Despite this, little research has been done with respect to the levels of satisfaction of tourists from different countries solely with their shopping experiences while on vacation in Hong Kong since handover. This survey seeks to redress the balance. Specifically, the issues will be addressed by exploring the travellers' expectations and perceptions of shopping in Hong Kong and comparing the responses of Asian and Western travellers. As the tourists' shopping behaviour may be affected by a number of attributes, this paper will focus on the shopping market as a whole rather than to diversify the topic on each of the market segments. Recommending actions that might be used to improve the position of the retail trade in Hong Kong will be provided in the last section.

2. Literature review

Customer satisfaction always appears on top of the list of important issues that must be addressed by marketers (HR Focus, 1992). The concern for measuring customer satisfaction in the tourism industry has been precipitated by the need to position destinations competitively in the worldwide marketplace. In response to the need for a more reliable way of measuring customer satisfaction, many researchers have attempted to develop theoretical and methodological frameworks for measuring customer satisfaction. Peterson and Wilson (1992) pointed out that more than 15,000 academic and trade articles have been published on the topic of customer satisfaction over the past two decades. According to the study of Oh and Parks (1997), at least nine theories on customer satisfaction have been introduced in the literature. These include: (1) expectancy disconfirmation; (2) assimilation or cognitive dissonance; (3) contrast; (4) assimilation contrast; (5) equity; (6) attribution; (7) comparison level; (8) generalized negativity; and, (9) value precept. Among these theories, expectancy disconfirmation has received the widest acceptance because of its broadly applicable conceptualization. Oliver (1980) introduced the expectancy disconfirmation model in studies of customer satisfaction in the retail and service industries.

J. Wong, R. Law / Tourism Management 24 (2003) 401–410 403

According to this theory, customers purchase goods and services with pre-purchase expectations about anticipated performance. After purchasing and consuming the goods and services, the results are compared with the initial expectations. Disconfirmation arises if the results do not meet the expectations. Positive disconfirmation is a result of perceptions of performance being higher than expectation, whereas negative disconfirmation is a result of perceptions being lower than expectation. Customer satisfaction is therefore related to positive disconfirmation or confirmation (Barksy, 1992; Hill, 1986; Oliver, 1980). Furthermore, customer satisfaction has generally been found to lead to positive behavioral intentions such as return, repurchase, and purchase recommendation in many tourism and hospitality studies (Barksy, 1992; Bojanic, 1996; Chadee & Mattsson, 1995; Dube, Renaghan, & Miller, 1994; Pizam & Milman, 1993). As a result, measuring customer satisfaction is an important task for tourism marketers to carry out as it is directly linked to repeat business. The primary function of measuring customer satisfaction is to provide information; the information relates to how well a destination is currently meeting its tourists' needs. With this information, marketers can focus their efforts on improving the quality of products or services, thereby enhancing the overall competitive advantages of the destination.

Shopping experiences are an amalgam of perceptions of products and services. They comprise the sum of satisfaction level that shoppers have with the individual elements or attributes of all the products and services that make up the experience (Pizam & Ellis, 1999). Generally, there is no uniformity of opinion among researchers as to the components of the service experience encounter. Czepiel, Solomon, Suprenant, and Gutman (1985) suggested that customer satisfaction is a function of level of satisfaction for two independent elements, i.e. functional and performance-delivery elements; the product bought is a functional element, whereas the service provided by the retailer is a performance-delivery element. Two other methods of classification have been proposed; Lovelock (1985) proposed the use of core and secondary groupings and Lewis (1987) developed the use of essential and subsidiary factors. All of these classification systems include consideration of a combination of the customers' behaviour and environment elements. However, many researchers have suggested that a situation specific approach should be used, i.e. no universal elements should be measured. Thus, this study will draw on the most relevant shopping studies and shopping attributes applicable to the Hong Kong situation. The results of a study by Keown (1989) indicated that travellers perceived the outstanding shopping attributes of Hong Kong to be 'wide selection of merchandise', 'faster and efficient service', and 'good value for money'. Mak et al.

(1999) surveyed 100 Taiwanese tourists, asking them what their perceptions of shopping experiences in Hong Kong were. The results showed that the shopping attributes, 'variety of goods' and 'price' were rated higher in Hong Kong than in Singapore, whereas 'product quality', 'service quality', and 'reputation of stores' were rated lower. In a recent study of shopping satisfaction, Heung and Cheng (2000) identified four shopping attributes, i.e. tangible quality, service quality, product value, and product reliability. Among these four factors, tangible quality was not found to be significant in influencing a tourist's level of satisfaction with shopping. Therefore, this factor was excluded in the current survey and 'variety of goods' were substituted. As Hong Kong is one of the most famous shopping centres in the world, the 'variety of goods' available to visitors from different countries should be considered as an important factor. Besides, the term 'product value' was replaced with 'price of goods' as the dollar value of a commodity is much easier for the respondents to realize the actual value level. Furthermore, the term 'product reliability' was replaced with 'quality of goods' in this survey, to promote a better understanding of the questions among the respondents. Finally, service quality, variety of goods, price of goods, and quality of goods were selected as the attributes used to assess the tourists' shopping expectations and perceptions of Hong Kong.

3. Methodology

In November 2000, a large-scale international visitor survey was conducted in the departure hall of Hong Kong International Airport. A structured questionnaire consisting of three sections was developed to collect data through the use of personal interviews. The first section related to the trip profile of the tourists. The second section included a study of the individual tourists' shopping expectations and experiences. The respondents were asked to rate on a five-point Likert scale with a rating ranging from 1 = 'very unimportant' to 5 = 'very important' of their expectation towards the four main attributes of shopping. These included; 'service quality', 'quality of goods', 'variety of goods', and 'price of goods'. Besides, their shopping satisfaction level was measured by a five-point Likert scale ranging from 1 = 'very dissatisfied' to 5 = 'very satisfied' for these four main attributes. The last section was used to collect demographic data about the tourists such as gender, age, educational level and annual household income. As this survey was used for both Western and Asian travellers, the questionnaire was first developed in English and then translated by professional translators into Chinese. Both versions of the questionnaire were double-checked by project investigators to ensure that the meaning of the questions was the same. A pilot test was conducted to ensure the practicability, clarity, reliability, and comprehensiveness of the questionnaire.

A total of 1004 international visitors were successfully interviewed by means of a systematic sampling method. To conduct the survey in an efficient way, each interviewer was assigned a specific flight route based on the flights scheduled for the major cities of the target countries. An interviewer was given a random number every day to indicate the counting interval between target respondents. In order to ensure that the respondents were visitors and had stayed in Hong Kong, three initial filtering questions were asked to exclude Hong Kong residents, transit passengers, and others who were not residents of one of the seven target source markets: Chinese Mainland, Taiwan, Singapore, the United States of America, Canada, Australia, and Malaysia. One additional question was asked to identify whether the respondents had bought anything in Hong Kong.

4. Findings

Among the questionnaires collected from the 1004 respondents, 610 were found to be usable in this study, the rest were incomplete. Table 2 shows the demographic profile of the respondents. The gender distribution was 58.7% males and 41.3% females, respectively. The distribution between Eastern and Western travellers was also quite even. Among the 610 respondents, 284 (46.6%) were of Asian origin (including all travellers from Mainland China, Taiwan, Singapore, and Malaysia), and 326 (53.4%) were of Western origin (including all travellers from the USA, Canada and Australia). The three dominant age groups of the respondents were found to be 26–35 (31.4%), 36–45 (21.6%) and 46–55 (22.1%). More than 98% of the respondents had completed secondary education or higher. Only 7.8% of the respondents earned less than US$10,000 per year. The distribution of respondents among the other annual household income ranges was quite even.

Of the 610 respondents, all had purchased goods in the territory. Of these, 68% of the respondents had

purchased clothing or footwear, 51% had purchased jewellery, watches and gifts and 22% had purchased electrical or electronic products. These results are consistent with the official data published by the Hong Kong Tourist Association (now the Hong Kong Tourism Board). The respondents were asked to provide their reasons for buying these products in Hong Kong. The results as shown in Table 3 indicate that most

Table 2
Demographic profile of respondents (N = 610)

	N	%
Sex		
Male	358	58.7
Female	252	41.3
Age		
25 or less	49	8.0
26–35	191	31.4
36–45	132	21.6
46–55	135	22.1
56–65	61	10.0
66 or above	42	6.9
Country of residence		
Mainland China	72	11.8
Taiwan	120	19.7
Singapore	59	9.7
USA	195	32.0
Canada	59	9.7
Australia	72	11.8
Malaysia	33	5.3
Education level		
Less than secondary/high school	11	1.8
Completed secondary/high school	104	17.0
Some college or university	103	16.9
Completed college/university diploma/degree	291	47.7
Completed postgraduate degree	101	16.6
Annual household income		
Less than US$10,000	48	7.8
US$10,000–29,999	106	17.4
US$30,000–49,999	119	19.5
US$50,000–69,999	115	18.9
US$70,000–99,999	95	15.6
US$100,000 or more	127	20.8

Table 3
Summary of visitors' eight main reasons to buy goods in Hong Kong (N = 610)

Main Reasons	Chinese Mainland	Taiwan	Singapore	United States of America	Canada	Australia	Malaysia	Total count
Attractive price	33	49	34	98	39	41	19	313
Variety of goods	15	16	11	22	11	14	7	96
Good quality	19	8	3	33	13	9	/	85
Fashion/novelty	14	18	18	15	3	4	9	81
Unique/special/attractive	8	14	4	21	4	3	5	69
Preference	2	17	8	9	7	2	5	50
Not available in his/her own countries	7	5	4	17	7	4	2	46

J. Wong, R. Law / Tourism Management 24 (2003) 401–410   405

respondents specified 'attractive price' as their main reason ($n = 313$), followed by 'variety of goods' ($n = 96$), 'good quality' ($n = 85$) and 'fashion/novelty' ($n = 81$). Among the 610 respondents, 135 (47.5%) Asian travellers and 178 (54.6%) Western travellers expressed the opinion that the price of products in Hong Kong was attractive. This finding contradicts the results of other studies that claimed prices in Hong Kong were non-competitive compared to those found in other Asian countries due to the pegged exchange rate (Dwyer et al. 2000).

Paired sample *T*-tests were used to compare the overall mean scores for expected level of satisfaction with the mean scores for the perceived level of satisfaction for the four shopping attributes. The results show the overall results for the four shopping attributes have a significant *t*-value at the 0.05 level (Table 4). The tests of the shopping attributes show that there are differences between the expected and perceived levels of satisfaction. Among the four shopping attributes, two were found to be positively disconfirmed attributes with perception scores greater than expectation scores, and two were found to be negatively disconfirmed attributes with perception scores lower than expectation scores. The positively disconfirmed attributes were 'service quality' and 'variety of goods', while the negatively disconfirmed attributes were 'quality of goods' and 'price of goods'. The overall results indicate that the satisfaction levels of the tourists were much higher than they expected in terms of the service quality and variety of goods they found. However, room for improvement was still found with regard to travellers' satisfaction levels in the areas of 'quality of goods' and 'price of goods'.

In order to further investigate the negatively and positively disconfirmed attributes among travellers from different countries, a series of paired sample *T*-tests were applied to investigate if there was any statistical difference between the attitudes of travellers from different countries. Table 5 shows the results of these tests.

Factor 1 'Service quality'—Among the travellers from the seven countries investigated, the positively discon-firmed value only appeared in travellers from the USA, Canada, and Australia ($p < 0.05$). The Western travellers were found to have low expectation and high perception mean scores for this factor compared to those of Asian travellers. The positively disconfirmed value in the group of Australian tourists was as high as 0.79. However, the opposite result was found in the mean scores for expectation and perception of Asian travellers. The mean difference was −0.3 in the group of Taiwanese tourists. Therefore, a significant negatively disconfirmed value was found in the group of Taiwanese travellers ($p < 0.05$). Although negatively disconfirmed values were also found for this attribute for travellers from Mainland China, Singapore, and Malaysia, they were found to treat it as an indifferent shopping attribute, as a non-significant *t*-test value was obtained ($p > 0.05$).

Factor 2 'Quality of goods'—A very high mean expectation score of 4.36 was found for travellers from China. All Asian travellers showed negative mean differences; while Western travellers expressed positive mean differences between their expectations and percep-tions for this shopping attribute. The negatively disconfirmed values were found to be 0.35 and 0.27 ($p < 0.05$) within the groups of travellers from Mainland China and Taiwan, respectively. The travellers from all other countries treated 'Quality of goods' as an indifference shopping attribute ($p > 0.05$).

Factor 3 'Variety of goods'—All Western travellers had higher mean scores for perception than expectation of importance for this shopping attribute. However, all Asian travellers had lower mean scores for perception than expectation, except those from Malaysia. Therefore, a negative mean difference was found for travellers from these countries of residence. Only the positively discon-firmed values for travellers from the USA and Canada were found to be at a significant level ($p < 0.05$). A very high positively disconfirmed value of 0.34 was obtained for the Canadian travellers. Values for travellers from other countries yielded no significant *t*-values ($p > 0.05$).

Factor 4 'Price of goods'—All travellers from different countries showed negatively disconfirmed

Table 4
Paired sample *T*-tests—Mean differences between tourists' expectations of importance and satisfactions of shopping experience in Hong Kong ($N = 610$)

Factors	Expectation		Satisfaction		Mean Diff.	*t*-value	*p*
	Mean[a]	S.D.	Mean[b]	S.D.			
Service quality	3.70	0.97	3.88	0.85	0.18	3.600	0.000
Quality of goods	4.09	0.79	4.01	0.65	−0.08	−2.329	0.020
Variety of goods	4.10	0.81	4.17	0.69	0.07	1.971	0.049
Price of goods	4.15	0.84	3.65	0.91	−0.5	−10.950	0.000

[a] Expectation mean scale: 5 = very important expectation; 4 = important expectation; 3 = neutral; 2 = unimportant expectation; 1 = very unimportant expectation.
[b] Satisfaction mean scale: 5 = very satisfied; 4 = satisfied; 3 = neutral; 2 = dissatisfied; 1 = very dissatisfied.

Table 5
Paired sample T-tests—Mean differences between tourists' expectations of importance and satisfactions of shopping experience in Hong Kong based on different country of residences ($N = 610$)

Factors	Country of residence	Expectation		Satisfaction		Mean Diff.	t-value	p
		Mean[a]	S.D.	Mean[b]	S.D.			
Service quality	Chinese Mainland	3.99	0.83	3.82	0.72	−0.17	−1.229	0.223
	Taiwan	3.72	0.87	3.42	0.82	−0.30	−2.772	0.006
	Singapore	3.85	0.98	3.63	0.79	−0.22	−1.275	0.207
	United States of America	3.70	0.97	4.17	0.78	0.47	6.178	0.000
	Canada	3.59	0.91	4.00	0.79	0.41	3.661	0.001
	Australia	3.32	1.15	4.11	0.85	0.79	5.351	0.000
	Malaysia	3.82	1.04	3.64	0.93	−0.18	−1.063	0.296
Quality of goods	Chinese Mainland	4.36	0.54	4.01	0.52	−0.35	−3.729	0.000
	Taiwan	3.89	0.83	3.62	0.60	−0.27	−3.391	0.001
	Singapore	4.05	0.90	3.88	0.56	−0.17	−1.427	0.159
	United States of America	4.18	0.71	4.23	0.64	0.05	1.043	0.298
	Canada	4.03	0.83	4.10	0.71	0.07	0.574	0.568
	Australia	3.96	0.86	4.13	0.65	0.17	1.685	0.096
	Malaysia	4.06	0.90	3.88	0.60	−0.18	−1.099	0.280
Variety of goods	Chinese Mainland	4.17	0.73	4.11	0.64	−0.06	−0.587	0.559
	Taiwan	3.88	0.88	3.83	0.60	−0.05	−0.581	0.562
	Singapore	4.17	0.75	4.05	0.63	−0.12	−1.154	0.253
	United States of America	4.20	0.74	4.33	0.70	0.13	2.402	0.017
	Canada	3.93	0.78	4.27	0.69	0.34	3.016	0.004
	Australia	4.32	0.82	4.42	0.60	0.10	0.895	0.374
	Malaysia	3.91	0.95	4.09	0.72	0.18	1.000	0.325
Price of goods	Chinese Mainland	4.15	0.80	3.46	0.80	−0.69	−5.255	0.000
	Taiwan	4.13	0.86	3.14	0.84	−0.98	−8.858	0.000
	Singapore	4.19	0.80	3.58	0.81	−0.61	−4.327	0.000
	United States of America	4.16	0.82	4.03	0.79	−0.13	−1.839	0.067
	Canada	4.19	0.82	3.81	0.94	−0.37	−3.091	0.003
	Australia	4.15	0.93	3.69	1.00	−0.46	−3.279	0.002
	Malaysia	3.97	1.02	3.33	0.85	−0.64	−2.996	0.005

[a] Expectation mean scale: 5 = very important expectation; 4 = important expectation; 3 = neutral; 2 = unimportant expectation; 1 = very unimportant expectation.
[b] Satisfaction mean scale: 5 = very satisfied; 4 = satisfied; 3 = neutral; 2 = dissatisfied; 1 = very dissatisfied.

values for this shopping attribute. The highest mean difference score was found to be 0.98 for the group of Taiwanese tourists. All Asian travellers showed greater negatively disconfirmed values than Western travellers, ranging from 0.98 to 0.61; Western travellers showed negatively disconfirmed values ranging from 0.13 to 0.46. All values were at significant levels ($p < 0.05$) except for the value for travellers from the USA. This indicates that travellers from the USA were indifferent to this attribute ($p > 0.05$) even they had the highest satisfaction score on this factor, as their expectations were also high in value. Therefore, the statistical difference between the USA tourists' importance expectation and satisfaction of this shopping attribute is insignificant.

When the scores for travellers from all the seven countries investigated are compared, some important findings are noted. Analysis of variance (ANOVA) was used to categorize differences between groups from different countries, considering their levels of satisfaction for each of the shopping attributes. From the

ANOVA results shown in Tables 6 and 7, it can be seen that there are significant differences in the expectations and perceptions for all but one attributes among travellers from different countries. In terms of expectations, the mean scores for travellers from Mainland China, Taiwan and Singapore were found to be significantly high when compared to those for Australians for the 'service quality' attribute, with $p < 0.003$. Furthermore, for 'quality of goods', the mean scores for travellers from Mainland China and Singapore were also significantly higher compared to those of Australian travellers with $p < 0.002$. However, the expectations of Taiwanese travellers for the 'quality of goods' and 'variety of goods' attributes were found to be relatively low compared to those travellers from the USA and Canada ($p < 0.002$ and $p < 0.001$, respectively). The perceptions of Taiwanese travellers for all the shopping attributes investigated were also significantly lower than those travellers from the USA, Canada and Australia. It can be generally identified that the perceptions for all

J. Wong, R. Law / Tourism Management 24 (2003) 401–410   407

Table 6
Comparison of expectation importance of decision factor on shopping by different country of residence (N = 610)

Factors	Group 1 Mainland China (N = 72)	Group 2 Taiwan (N = 120)	Group 3 Singapore (N = 59)	Group 4 USA (N = 195)	Group 5 Canada (N = 59)	Group 6 Australia (N = 72)	Group 7 Malaysia (N = 33)	ANOVA Main effect probability	Differ (Tukey HSD)
Service quality	3.99 (0.83)	3.72 (0.87)	3.85 (0.98)	3.70 (0.97)	3.59 (0.91)	3.32 (1.15)	3.82 (1.04)	0.003	1,3 > 6
Quality of goods	4.36 (0.54)	3.89 (0.83)	4.05 (0.90)	4.18 (0.71)	4.03 (0.83)	3.96 (0.86)	4.06 (0.90)	0.002	1 > 2,6 2 < 4
Variety of goods	4.17 (0.73)	3.88 (0.88)	4.17 (0.75)	4.20 (0.74)	3.93 (4.32)	4.32 (0.82)	3.91 (0.95)	0.001	2 < 4,6
Price of goods	4.15 (0.80)	4.13 (0.86)	4.19 (0.80)	4.16 (0.82)	4.19 (0.82)	4.15 (0.93)	3.97 (1.02)	0.935	/

Note: Expectation mean scale: 5 = very important expectation; 4 = important expectation; 3 = neutral; 2 = unimportant expectation; 1 = very unimportant expectation.

Table 7
Comparison of satisfactory level of shopping experience by different country of residence (N = 610)

Factors	Group 1 Mainland China (N = 72)	Group 2 Taiwan (N = 120)	Group 3 Singapore (N = 59)	Group 4 USA (N = 195)	Group 5 Canada (N = 59)	Group 6 Australia (N = 72)	Group 7 Malaysia (N = 33)	ANOVA Main Effect Probability	Differ (Tukey HSD)
Service quality	3.82 (0.72)	3.42 (0.82)	3.63 (0.79)	4.17 (0.78)	4.00 (0.79)	4.11 (0.85)	3.64 (0.93)	0.000	1 > 2 1 < 4 2 < 4, 5, 6 3 < 4, 6 4 > 7
Quality of goods	4.01 (0.52)	3.62 (0.60)	3.88 (0.56)	4.23 (0.64)	4.10 (0.71)	3.96 (0.65)	3.88 (0.60)	0.000	1 > 2 2 < 4, 5, 6 3 < 4 4 > 7
Variety of goods	4.11 (0.64)	3.83 (0.60)	4.05 (0.63)	4.33 (0.70)	4.27 (0.69)	4.42 (0.69)	4.09 (0.72)	0.000	2 < 4,5,6 3 < 6
Price of goods	3.46 (0.80)	3.14 (0.84)	3.58 (0.81)	4.03 (0.79)	3.81 (0.94)	3.69 (1.00)	3.33 (0.85)	0.000	1 < 4 2 < 3, 4, 5, 6 3 < 4 4 > 7

Note: Satisfaction mean scale: 5 = very satisfied; 4 = satisfied; 3 = neutral; 2 = dissatisfied; 1 = very dissatisfied.

408   *J. Wong, R. Law / Tourism Management 24 (2003) 401–410*

four shopping attributes were comparatively higher for the tourists from the USA, Canada and Australia.

From the results of the questionnaires, it was found that there were differences in the attitudes to the four shopping attributes among travellers from the seven countries of residence examined. Independent samples *T*-tests were used to investigate if the scores for importance expectation and perception for the shopping attributes were statistically different from one group of tourists to another. In comparing Asian and Western tourists, the findings of independent samples *T*-tests indicate that Asian travellers had comparatively high expectations for 'service quality' ($p < 0.003$) and low expectations for 'variety of goods' ($p < 0.012$) compared to those of Western travellers, as shown in Table 8. Furthermore, the perceived levels of satisfaction for Asian travellers were found to be significantly lower than those of Western travellers for all shopping attributes, as shown in Table 9.

In all cases, Asian travellers were significantly less satisfied for all shopping attributes than Western travellers. Finally, it was found that over 30% of the travellers of Mainland China and Taiwan thought that the goods they purchased in Hong Kong were not good value for money; only 12% and 10% of the travellers from the USA and Canada had such negative feelings. The 'quality of goods' and 'price of goods' were found to have a great influence on the shopping experiences of Asian travellers, while the 'service quality' and 'variety of goods' only appeared to have a moderate effect on the overall shopping experience of Asian and Western visitors to Hong Kong.

5. Discussion

The results of this study highlight some important issues. Four main attributes were demonstrated to affect the satisfaction levels of tourists with their shopping experiences in Hong Kong. The results indicate that there are significant differences between the shopping behaviour of Asian and Western travellers. Retailers should therefore improve their approach when catering for travellers from different countries. They should be aware of national differences and provide a high standard of service for tourists of all nationalities. Some retailers may treat Western travellers better than Asian travellers because they perceive Western travellers to have greater spending power. This may, therefore, be the reason that service quality was found to be a positively disconfirmed attribute in the group of Western travellers. In the past, the spending power of the travellers from Mainland China was comparatively low. Even after 20 years of rapid growth, China is still a low-income country. According to the market price measure of per capita income, China (US$710) ranked 112th out of 206 countries in 1997 (Huang & Hanna, 2001). For this reason retailers often neglect this group of customers. Furthermore, many retailers tend to mix tourists from Mainland China with those from Taiwan. Generally, they tend to serve them in the same manner. However, many Taiwanese travellers do not like to be treated in the same way as Mainland Chinese travellers. Thus, these Taiwanese tourists were found to have a poor impression of service quality in Hong Kong. A significant dissatisfied difference was found in this group

Table 8
Independent samples *T*-tests for the expectation of importance factors in the decision to come shopping in Hong Kong (Eastern and Western Visitors)

Variables	Eastern, $N = 284$		Western, $N = 326$		Mean Diff.	*t*-value	*p*
	Mean	S.D.	Mean	S.D.			
Service quality	3.82	0.91	3.60	1.01	0.23	2.949	0.003
Quality of goods	4.06	0.81	4.10	0.77	−0.04	−0.638	0.524
Variety of goods	4.01	0.84	4.18	0.78	−0.16	−2.508	0.012
Price of goods	4.13	0.85	4.16	0.84	−0.03	−0.522	0.602

Note: Expectation mean scale: 5 = very important expectation; 4 = important expectation; 3 = neutral; 2 = unimportant expectation; 1 = very unimportant expectation.

Table 9
Independent samples *T*-tests for the satisfaction level of shopping experience in Hong Kong (Eastern and Western visitors)

Variables	Eastern, $N = 284$		Western, $N = 326$		Mean diff.	*t*-value	*p*
	Mean	S.D.	Mean	S.D.			
Service quality	3.59	0.81	4.13	0.80	−0.54	−8.223	0.000
Quality of goods	3.80	0.59	4.18	0.65	−0.38	−7.508	0.000
Variety of goods	3.98	0.64	4.34	0.68	−0.37	−6.826	0.000
Price of goods	3.33	0.84	3.92	0.88	−0.58	−8.349	0.000

Note: Satisfaction mean scale: 5 = very satisfied; 4 = satisfied; 3 = neutral; 2 = dissatisfied; 1 = very dissatisfied.

J. Wong, R. Law / Tourism Management 24 (2003) 401–410

409

of tourists. Retailers should pay attention to the consistency of their service standards. Also, the purchasing power of, and number of tourists from, Mainland China have improved and increased a great deal in recent years. Retailers should be aware of these changes in the market and provide their employees with suitable training on how to serve Mainland Chinese tourists.

As for the quality of goods, the importance expectations of the travellers from Mainland China were high compared to those of the other groups. The reason for this phenomenon may be due to misleading communications between the residents of Mainland China and their relatives in Hong Kong. Many people in Hong Kong exaggerate the quality of their living standard and the products available in Hong Kong. Also, many residents of Mainland China do not have any experience of travelling outside China. Most often the first destination they visit is Hong Kong. They have not been to Hong Kong before and tend to rely on second-hand information about it. It is common for them to 'over value' what they buy in Hong Kong. The situation is becoming much worse as there are some dishonest retailers and travel agencies in Hong Kong who co-operate in order to cheat the Mainland visitors. The number of reported complaints made by Mainland visitors has increased tremendously from 197 in 1998 to 316 in 2000, representing a rise of 60% which is much larger than the increase in percentage growth of Mainland visitors (The Sun, 2001). Furthermore, the number of unreported cases could be much more than the official data. Thus, a significant negatively disconfirmed attribute has resulted in the group of Mainland Chinese tourists. To reduce the difference between the expected and perceived quality of goods, appropriate promotional campaigns should be carried out to convey an accurate message to potential buyers in Mainland China and Taiwan. Quick and effective actions should be taken to stop any dishonest retailers trading once they have been reported. More information in the form of shopping guides and booklets should also be provided to tourists. Finally, a detailed compensation scheme should be set up and convenient ways should be provided to enable tourists claim back their losses.

For the attribute 'variety of goods', residents of the USA and Canada were found to be quite satisfied. This may be because many Western travellers find that the products in Asia are new to them. Also, the North American visitors' spending power is high compared to that of the residents of other countries. Therefore, this was found to be a positively disconfirmed attribute of shopping experience within these groups.

Although over half of the respondents ($n = 313$ or 51%) expressed that the price of products in Hong Kong was attractive, the 'price of goods' in Hong Kong was found to be a negatively disconfirmed shopping attribute in the underlying feeling of the travellers. A possible reason for this phenomenon is that the expectation of the travellers on the price of goods was much lower than what they experienced in Hong Kong. However, the price of goods was still comparatively lower than other destinations. The reason is that many retailers have kept their costs down by cutting manpower, salaries, and rental costs over the past few years. These cost savings are reflected in the current prices of goods. The prices of goods in Hong Kong are therefore remaining competitive in the tourist shopping business. No matter how, in the long run, retailers should ensure the quality of their goods and improve the quality of their service. Courtesy programs should be carried out to improve the attitude of front line staff towards tourists, especially towards Asian travellers.

6. Conclusions

Tourist shopping is the primary source of income for the tourism industry in Hong Kong. This study provides useful information about tourists' shopping preferences and patterns, which can be used for future tourism planning and control. The findings of this study indicate that there is a great deal of difference between the Asian and Western travellers' expectations and perceptions towards the shopping attributes. This cultural difference leads to negatively and/or positively disconfirmed attributes among them. Different perceptions of satisfaction were identified for the two major tourist groups (i.e. those from Asian and Western cultures). In this study, Asian travellers were found to be less satisfied with almost all of the shopping attributes investigated than Western travellers. If this state of affairs is allowed to continue, it will have serious implications for the Hong Kong tourism industry and economy. Remedial actions should be carried out to improve the situation. The development of any such actions should take into account national and cultural factors. Based on the results of this survey, it is suggested that further studies should be carried out to analyse the responses of the major national tourist groups such as those from Mainland China and the USA. Besides, an in-depth study on the difference of shopping satisfaction among different shopping market segments will add further insight to the full picture of the tourist retail business. Also, investigations of the expectations and perceptions of 'food and beverages', 'accommodation' and 'transportation' for each of the major tourist groups would contribute additional valuable information to the tourism industry in Hong Kong. Finally, it would be interesting to compare and contrast the findings with this study with a future study for repeated visits.

Acknowledgements

The authors wish to acknowledge the comments offered by the anonymous reviewers and the financial support provided by the Hong Kong Polytechnic University. Dr. Bob McKercher's provision of methodology details for the survey is also appreciated.

References

Barksy, J. D. (1992). Customer satisfaction in the hotel industry: Meaning and measurement. *Hospitality Research Journal, 16*(1), 51–73.

Bojanic, D. C. (1996). Consumer perceptions of price, value and satisfaction in the hotel industry: An exploratory study. *Journal of Hospitality and Leisure Marketing, 14*(1), 5–22.

Carben, R. (1991). Big business. *Asia Travel*, July, p. 47.

Chadee, D., & Mattsson, J. (1995). Measuring customer satisfaction with tourist service encounters. *Journal of Travel and Tourism Marketing, 4*(4), 97–107.

Choi, T. Y., & Chu, R. (2000). Levels of satisfaction among Asian and Western travellers. *International Journal of Quality and Reliability Management, 17*(2), 116–131.

Czepiel, J. A., Solomon, M. R., Suprenant, C. F., & Gutman, E. G. (Eds.) (1985). Service encounters: An overview. in *The service encounter: Managing employee customer interaction in service business* (pp. 3–15). Massachusetts: Lexington Books.

Dube, L., Renaghan, L. M., & Miller, J. M. (1994). Measuring customer satisfaction for strategic management. *The Cornell Hotel and Restaurant Administration Quarterly, 35*(1), 39–47.

Dwyer, L., Forsyth, P., & Rao, P. (2000). The price competitiveness of travel and tourism: A comparison of 19 destinations. *Tourism Management, 21*(1), 9–22.

Heung, V., & Cheng, E. (2000). Assessing tourists' satisfaction with shopping in the Hong Kong Special Administrative Region of China. *Journal of Travel Research, 38*(4), 396–404.

Heung, V., & Qu, H. (1998). Tourism shopping and its contributions to Hong Kong. *Tourism Management, 19*(4), 383–386.

Hill, D. J. (1986). Satisfaction and consumer services. *Advances in Consumer Research, 13*, 311–315.

HKTA. (1991–2000). *A statistical review of tourism.* Hong Kong: HKTA.

HR Focus. (1992). Quality, service, and people: Key issues for entrepreneurs. *HR Focus, 69*, 24.

Huang, Y., Hanna, D. (2001). Hidden markets. *Hong Kong Business*, February, 11–13.

Keown, C. (1989). Hong Kong tourists' shopping experiences. *Hong Kong Manager, 25*(4), 30–35.

Kozak, M. (2001). Comparative assessment of tourist satisfaction with destinations across two nationalities. *Tourism Management, 22*, 391–401.

Lewis, R. C. (1987). The measurement of gaps in the quality of hotel services. *International Journal of Hospitality Management, 6*(2), 83–88.

Lovelock, C. H. (1985). Developing and managing the customer-service function in the service sector. In J. A. Czepiel, M. R. Solomon, C. f. Suprenant, & E. G. Gutman (Eds.), *The service encounter: Managing employee customer interaction in service business* (pp. 265–280). Massachusetts: Lexington Books.

Mak, B., Tsang, N., & Cheung, I. (1999). Taiwanese tourists' shopping preferences. *Journal of Vacation Marketing, 5*(2), 190–198.

Oh, H., & Parks, S. (1997). Customer satisfaction and service quality: A critical review of the literature and research implications for the hospitality industry. *Hospitality Research Journal, 20*(3), 35–62.

Oliver, R. L. (1980). A cognitive model of the antecedents and consequences of satisfaction decisions. *Journal of Marketing Research, 17*, 460–469.

Peterson, R. A., & Wilson, W. R. (1992). Measuring customer satisfaction: Fact and artifact. *Journal of the Academy of Marketing Science, 20*(1), 61–71.

Pizam, A., & Ellis, T. (1999). Customer satisfaction and its measurement in hospitality enterprises. *International Journal of Contemporary Hospitality Management, 11*(7), 1–18.

Pizam, A., & Milman, A. (1993). Predicting satisfaction among first time visitors to a destination by using the expectancy disconfirmation theory. *International Journal of Hospitality Management, 12*, 197–209.

Qu, H., & Li, I. (1997). The characteristics and satisfaction of Mainland Chinese visitors to Hong Kong. *Journal of Travel Research, 35*(4), 37–41.

Summers, N. (2001). Foreword of Hong Kong Hotel Industry 2001. *Hong Kong Hotel Industry 2001.* Hong Kong: Hong Kong Tourism Board, p. 5.

The Sun (2001). Cheating co-operation between Mainland and Hong Kong travel agencies. *The Sun*, 21 July, p. A2.

Name Index